Treat this book with care and respect.

*It should become part of your personal
and professional library. It will
serve you well at any number
of points during your
professional career.*

TENTH EDITION ● UCC
COMPREHENSIVE VOLUME

RONALD A. ANDERSON
Professor of Law and Government,
      Drexel University
Member of the Pennsylvania and Philadelphia Bars

Coauthor of **Business Law Principles and Cases**
Author of **Anderson on the Uniform Commercial Code**
      Government and Business
      Social Forces and the Law
      Anderson's Pennsylvania Civil Practice
      Purdon's Pennsylvania Forms
      Couch's Cyclopedia of Insurance Law
      Wharton's Criminal Law and Procedure
      Insurer's Tort Law
      Hotelman's Basic Law
Consulting Editor of the **Pennsylvania Law Encyclopedia**

WALTER A. KUMPF
Editor in Chief, Emeritus, South-Western Publishing Co.

Coauthor of **Business Law Principles and Cases**

Published by

L62   **SOUTH-WESTERN PUBLISHING CO.**

CINCINNATI   WEST CHICAGO, ILL.   DALLAS   PELHAM MANOR, N.Y.
PALO ALTO, CALIF.   BRIGHTON, ENGLAND

Business Law

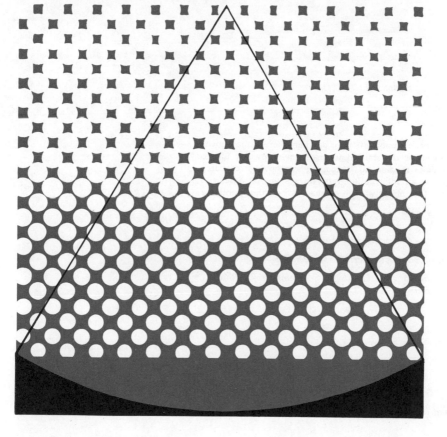

Standard Book Number: 0-538-12620-5

Library of Congress Catalog Card Number: 75-28605

4 5 6 K 0 9 8 7

Printed in the United States of America

PREFACE

Our twentieth century world is changing rapidly. The many changes in the law of business, together with the long-honored basic rules, are presented in this Tenth Edition of BUSINESS LAW, both as new chapters and as new and expanded topics within chapters on traditional subjects.

CONSUMER PROTECTION

The interests of the consumer are being increasingly recognized by federal and state legislation and by administrative regulation. The importance of this area of the law is recognized by Chapter 8, Consumer Protection, which embraces important provisions of the Uniform Consumer Credit Code and the federal Consumer Credit Protection Act. Corrective advertising, seals of approval, home solicitation sales, referral sales, credit cards, balloon payments, preservation of consumer defenses, credit collection and billing methods, protection of credit standing, mutual funds, and consumer remedies are some of the topics in this new chapter.

The following topics are examples of those pertaining to consumer protection which are incorporated in other chapters: unordered goods, disclosure in a separate statement for an installment loan, fine print in contracts, domination by seller, unequal bargaining power, credit insurance, unconscionable and oppressive contracts, consumer protection rescission, and waiver of defenses in secured credit sales.

ENVIRONMENTAL LAW

Society increasingly recognizes the social importance of the conservation of natural resources and of the protection of our physical environment. Man's desire to obtain an unpolluted environment is becoming crystallized into a right, as set forth in Chapter 7, Environmental Law and Community Planning.

ADMINISTRATIVE AGENCIES

The importance of administrative agencies, particularly those on the federal level, continues to grow. The special character of these agencies is recognized in Chapter 6. Consideration is given to the administrator's power, the pattern of administrative procedure, and the finality of administrative determination.

FRANCHISES

Numerous questions raised by the recent tremendous growth of franchising operations necessitate an understanding of the basic principles of the law involved. These are considered in Chapter 47.

COMPUTERS AND OTHER NEW TOPICS

The impact of data processing, computers, and retrieval systems is recognized in such topics as defamation by computer, computer programs as property, and computers and corporate management.

Antidiscrimination legislation affects several areas of business law, as reflected by topics dealing with businesses serving the public (restaurants, common carriers of passengers, and hotels and motels), employment, deeds. leases, and insurance.

Numerous other topics include: transfer of title in self-service stores, condominiums, and no-fault insurance.

UCC AND UCCC

The rapid growth in the number of court decisions under the Uniform Commercial Code since the publication of the Ninth Edition has necessitated an expanded presentation of the law in such areas as sales, commercial paper, and secured transactions. More evident in the opinions too is the influence of the UCC on contracts in general. An appendix includes the Official Text of the Uniform Commercial Code.

The Uniform Consumer Credit Code has been adopted in several states. Regardless of the number of additional states that adopt the UCCC, this uniform act is having a definite influence on state legislation concerning consumer credit practices. Chapter 14, Legality and Public Policy, and Chapter 8, Consumer Protection, incorporate provisions of the UCCC.

SOCIAL FORCES

The unique treatment of social forces in the prior editions is continued in this Tenth Edition. In Chapter 2, Law As an Expression of Social Forces, the specific objectives of the law are discussed against the background of the general objective of creating, maintaining, and restoring order, stability, and justice. The student also learns to think of the law as an evolutionary process and as a synthesis of prior law.

AUTHORITATIVE

Reference is made by the footnotes to uniform statutes, model acts, and restatements of the law as well as to recent cases. In addition to the UCC and UCCC, the uniform statutes and model acts cited pertain to arbitration, anatomical gifts, gifts to minors, fraudulent conveyances, vendor and purchaser risks, disposition of unclaimed property, partnerships, limited partnerships, and business corporations.

The material in this edition has been made up-to-date through an examination of professional publications in the field, new federal legislation, administrative agency regulations, and every reported decision of the federal courts, the state supreme courts, and the intermediate state courts.

This updating process has been conducted continuously since 1950. This background of a quarter century brings to BUSINESS LAW not only an accuracy of content but also a sense of direction and a sense of significance which is particularly important for the undergraduate student.

STUDENT SUPPLEMENT

An optional Student Supplement includes for each chapter a study guide consisting of objective-type questions, and several case problems for which the student is required to state in his own words the principle or rule of law that applies. A number of instructors report improved results through the use of this supplement. A tested procedure is that of making the use of the supplement optional with students. A student's manual of answers to the study-guide questions only is available, and copies are free in the quantity needed.

SUPPLEMENTARY CASE PROBLEMS AND TESTS

Supplementary problems with answers, which are included in the instructor's manual, may be reproduced for use as reviews or examinations. For testing purposes, printed objective tests are available from the nearest office of the publisher without charge. The instructor may wish to use selected supplementary case problems with the objective tests.

R. A. A.
W. A. K.

CONTENTS

xi

LEGAL RIGHTS AND THE AGENCIES FOR THEIR ENFORCEMENT

Law has developed because men and society have wanted relationships between men, and between men and government, to conform to certain standards. Each person has desired to know what conduct he could reasonably expect from others as well as what conduct others could reasonably expect from him so that he could make decisions intelligently in terms of his legal rights and obligations. The rules or laws adopted for this purpose have expressed the social, economic, and moral standards and aspirations of society.

A. NATURE OF LEGAL RIGHTS AND THE LAW

Law consists of the entire body of principles that govern conduct and the observance of which can be enforced in courts. If there were no man-made law, no doubt many persons would be guided by principles of moral or natural law. Most people would act in accordance with the dictates of conscience, the precepts of right living that are a part of religion, and the ethical concepts that are generally accepted in the community. Those who would choose to act otherwise, however, would constitute a serious problem for society. Man-made law is necessary, therefore, to provide not only rules of conduct but also the machinery and procedures for enforcing right conduct, for punishing wrongful acts, and for settling disputes that arise even when both parties are motivated by good intentions.

§ 1:1. **LEGAL RIGHTS.** What are legal rights? And who has them? In answering these questions, we tend to make the mistake of thinking of the present as being characteristic of what was and what will be. But consider the evolution of the concept of the "rights of man" and the right of privacy.

(a) **The "Rights of Man" concept.** Our belief in the American way of life and in the concepts on which our society or government is based should not obscure the fact that at one time there was no American way of life and that the concept of man possessing rights recognized by government was the fruit of more than a revolution—that concept was a product of creation. While many religious leaders, philosophers, and poets spoke of the rights of man and of the dignity of man, rulers laughed at such pretensions and held man tightly in a society based on status. A nobleman had the rights of a nobleman of his degree. A warrior had the rights of a warrior. A slave had very few rights at all. In each case, the law saw only status; rights attached not to a man but to his status.

In the course of time, serfdom displaced slavery in much of the Western world. Eventually feudalism disappeared and, with the end of the Thirty Years War, the modern nation-state began to emerge. Surely one might say that, in such a "new order," man had legal rights. No, not as a man but only as a subject. Even when the English colonists settled in America, they brought with them not the rights of men but the rights of British subjects. Even when the colonies were within one year of war, the Second Continental Congress presented to King George III the Olive Branch Petition which beseeched the king to recognize the colonists' rights as Englishmen. For almost a year the destiny of the colonies hung in the balance with the colonists unable to decide between remaining loyal to the Crown, seeking to obtain recognition of their rights as Englishmen (a "status" recognition), or doing something else.

Finally, the ill-advised policies of George III and the eloquence of Thomas Paine's Common Sense tipped the scales and the colonies spoke on July 4, 1776, not in the terms of the rights of English subjects but in terms of the rights of man existing independently of any government. Had the American Revolution been lost, the Declaration of Independence would have gone rattling down the corridors of time with many other failures. But the American Revolution was won, and the new government that was established was based upon "man" as the building block rather than upon "subjects." Rights of man replaced the concept of rights of subjects. With this transition, the obligations of a king to his faithful subjects were replaced by the rights of man existing without regard to will or authority of any kind. Since then, America has been going through additional stages of determining what is embraced by the concept of "rights of man."

(b) **The right of privacy.** Today everyone recognizes that there is a right of privacy. Before 1890, however, this right did not exist in American law. Certainly the men who wrote the Declaration of Independence and the Bill of Rights Amendments to the Constitution were conscious of rights. How can we explain that the law did not recognize a right of privacy until a full century later?

The answer is that at a particular time people worry about the problems which face them. Note the extent of the fears and concern of the framers of the Bill of Rights Amendments to the Constitution. The Fourth Amendment states, "The right of the people to be secure in their persons, houses, papers, and effects, against unreasonable searches and seizures, shall not be violated, and no Warrants shall issue, but upon probable cause, supported by Oath or affirmation, and particularly describing the place to be searched, and the persons or things to be seized." The man of 1790 was afraid of a recurrence of the days of George III.

The framers of the Fourth Amendment declared what we today would regard as a segment of privacy—protection from police invasion of privacy.

The man of 1790 just was not concerned with invasion of privacy by a private person. While a snooping person could be prosecuted to some extent under a Peeping Tom Statute, this was a criminal liability. The victim could not sue for damages for the invasion of his privacy.

If we are honest with history, all that we can say is that modern man thinks highly of his privacy and wants it to be protected. And, knowing that the law is responsive to the wishes of society, we can also say that the right is protected by government. But note that we should go no further than to say that it is a right which society wishes to protect at the present time. If circumstances arise in our national life of such a nature that privacy will hamper or endanger national defense, we can expect that the "right" of privacy will be limited or modified. We should therefore approach problems relating to rights with an open mind, realizing that there are only such legal rights as we the people, through our legal system, choose to recognize.

§ 1:2. **WHAT IS THE LAW?** The expression, "a law," is ordinarily used in connection with a statute enacted by a state legislature or the Congress of the United States, such as an act by the federal Congress to extend the benefits of old-age insurance. All of the principles that make up law, however, are not laws adopted by legislative bodies.

Constitutional law includes the constitutions in force in the particular area or territory. In each state, two constitutions are in force, the state constitution and the national constitution.

Statutory law includes statutes adopted by the lawmakers. Each state has its own legislature and the United States has the Congress, both of which enact laws. In addition, every city, county, or other subdivision has some power to adopt ordinances which, within their sphere of operation, have the same binding effect as legislative acts.

Of great importance are the *administrative regulations*, such as rules of the Securities and Exchange Commission and the National Labor Relations Board. The regulations promulgated by national and state administrative agencies generally have the force of statute and are therefore part of "the law."

Law also includes principles that are expressed for the first time in court decisions. This is *case law*. For example, when a court must decide a new question or problem, its decision becomes a *precedent* and stands as the law for that particular problem in the future. This rule that a court decision becomes a precedent to be followed in similar cases is the *doctrine of stare decisis*.

Law also includes treaties made by the United States, and proclamations and orders by the President of the United States or by other public officials.

§ 1:3. **UNIFORM STATE LAWS.** To secure uniformity as far as possible, the National Conference of Commissioners on Uniform State Laws, composed of representatives from all the states, has drafted statutes on various business subjects for adoption by the states. The most outstanding of such laws is the Uniform Commercial Code (UCC).[1] The Code regulates the fields of sales of goods; commercial paper, such as checks; secured transactions in personal property; and particular aspects of banking, letters of credit, warehouse receipts, bills of lading, and investment securities.

National uniformity has also been brought about in some areas of consumer protection by the adoption of the federal Consumer Credit Protection Act (CCPA), Title I of which is popularly known as the Truth in Lending Act.[2] A Uniform Consumer Credit Code (UCCC) has been proposed and is now before the states for adoption. To the extent that it is adopted, it will complement the Uniform Commercial Code.[3]

§ 1:4. CLASSIFICATIONS OF LAW. Law is classified in many ways. For example, *substantive law*, which defines the substance of legal rights and liabilities, is contrasted with *procedural law*, which specifies the procedure that must be followed in enforcing those rights and liabilities. The following additional classifications will prove useful:

(a) **Law and equity.** Law is frequently classified as being "law" or "equity." During the early centuries following the Norman Conquest, it was common for subjects of the English Crown to present to the King petitions requesting particular favors or relief that could not be obtained in the ordinary courts of law. The extraordinary or special relief granted by the chancellor, to whom the King referred such matters, was of such a nature as was dictated by principles of justice and equity. This body of principles was called *equity*. While originally applied by separate courts, today the same court usually administers both "law" and "equity."

(b) **Classification based upon historical sources.** Law is sometimes classified in terms of its source as the *civil law*, which comes from the Roman civil law, and the *common law*, which is based upon the English common law or the common law that has developed in the United States.

The *law merchant*, which was recognized by early English merchants, has been absorbed to a large extent by the common law. During the centuries that the common law was developing in England, merchants of different nations, trading in all parts of the world, developed their own sets of rules to govern their business transactions. Much of our modern business law relating to commercial paper, insurance, credit transactions, and partnerships originally developed in the law merchant.

B. AGENCIES FOR ENFORCEMENT OF LEGAL RIGHTS

Legal rights are meaningless unless they can be enforced. Agencies for law enforcement may be classified as private or public.

---

[1] The Code has been adopted in every state except Louisiana. It has also been adopted in the Virgin Islands and for the District of Columbia. In 1972, a group of amendments to the Code was recommended. These have been adopted in Arkansas, California, Illinois, Iowa, Nebraska, Nevada, North Dakota, Oregon, Texas, Virginia, West Virginia, and Wisconsin. The changes made by the 1972 amendments to the UCC are confined mainly to Article 9 on secured transactions. Louisiana, the exception has adopted Articles 1, 3, 4, and 5 of the Code.

[2] 15 United States Code § 1601 et seq., and 18 USC § 891 et seq.

[3] As of January, 1975, the Uniform Consumer Credit Code has been adopted in ten states: Colorado, Idaho, Indiana, Iowa, Kansas, Maine, Oklahoma, Utah, Wisconsin, and Wyoming.

§ **1:5. PRIVATE AGENCIES.** Because of the rising costs, delays, and complexities of litigation, businessmen often seek to determine disputes out of court.

(a) Arbitration. By the use of *arbitration* a dispute is brought before one or more arbitrators who make a decision which the parties have agreed to accept as final. This procedure first reached an extensive use in the field of commercial contracts. Parties to a contract which is to be in effect for some time may specify in the contract that any dispute shall be submitted to arbitrators to be selected by the parties. Arbitration today is encouraged as a means of avoiding expensive litigation and easing the workload of courts. Arbitration is now favored by law where once it was viewed with hostility. Arbitration enables the parties to present the facts before trained experts because the arbitrators are familiar with the practices that form the background of the dispute.

A Uniform Arbitration Act has been adopted in a number of states.[4] Under this Act and similar statutes, the parties to a contract may agree in advance that all disputes arising thereunder will be submitted to arbitration. In some instances the contract will name the arbitrators for the duration of the contract. Frequently the parties provide their own remedy against failure to abide by the award of the arbitrators. The parties may execute a mutual indemnity bond by which each agrees to indemnify the other for any loss caused by his failure to carry out the arbitration award.

The growth of arbitration has been greatly aided by the American Arbitration Association not only in the development of standards, procedures, and forms for arbitration, but also by the creation of panels of qualified arbitrators from which the parties to a contract may select those who will settle their dispute.

(b) Reference to third person. An out-of-court determination of disputes under construction contracts is often made under a term of the contract that any dispute shall be referred to the architect in charge of the construction and that his decision shall be final.

Increasingly, other types of transactions provide for a third person or a committee to decide rights of persons. Thus, employees and an employer may have agreed as a term of the employment contract that claims of employees under retirement and pension plans shall be decided by a designated board or committee. The seller and buyer may have selected a third person to determine the price to be paid for goods. Ordinarily the parties agree that the decision of such a third person or board shall be final and that no appeal or review may be had in any court. In most cases, the referral situation involves the determination of a particular fact in contrast to arbitration which seeks to end a dispute.

§ **1:6. COURTS.** A *court* is a tribunal established by government to hear and decide matters properly brought before it, giving redress to the injured or

---

[4] The 1955 version of the Uniform Arbitration Act has been adopted in Alaska, Arizona, Arkansas, Delaware, Illinois, Indiana, Kansas, Maine, Maryland, Massachusetts, Michigan, Minnesota, Nevada, New Mexico, North Carolina, South Dakota, Texas, and Wyoming. The earlier 1925 version of the Act is in force in Pennsylvania, Utah, and Wisconsin.

enforcing punishment against wrongdoers, and to prevent wrongs. A *court of record* is one whose proceedings are preserved in an official record. A *court not of record* has limited judicial powers; its proceedings are not recorded, at least not officially.

Each court is empowered to decide certain types or classes of cases. This power is called *jurisdiction*. A court may have original or appellate jurisdiction, or both. A court with *original jurisdiction* has the authority to hear a controversy when it is first brought into court. A court having *appellate jurisdiction*, on the other hand, has authority to review the judgment of an inferior court.

The jurisdiction of a court may be general as distinguished from limited or special. A court having *general jurisdiction* has power to hear and decide all controversies involving legal rights and duties. A court of *limited* or special *jurisdiction* has authority to hear and decide only those cases that fall within a particular class, such as cases in which the amounts involved are below a specified sum.

Courts are frequently classified in terms of the nature of their jurisdiction. A *criminal court* is one that is established for the trial of crimes, which are regarded as offenses against the public. A *civil court*, on the other hand, is authorized to hear and decide issues involving private rights and duties and also noncriminal public matters. In like manner, courts are classified into equity courts, juvenile courts, probate courts, and courts of domestic relations upon the basis of their limited jurisdiction.

Each court has inherent power to establish rules necessary to preserve order in the court or to transact the business of the court. An infraction of these rules or the disobedience to any other lawful order, as well as a willful act contrary to the dignity of the court or tending to pervert or obstruct justice, may be punished as *contempt of court*.

QUESTIONS AND CASE PROBLEMS

1. (a) What is law?   (b) Why has law developed?
   (c) What is the difference between law and "a law"?
2. Statutory law, which is law enacted by a legislative body (Congress, state legislature, city council), is probably the type of law best known by most people. Identify and explain each of the other types of law.
3. What does each of the following abbreviations stand for?
   (a) UCC   (b) UCCC   (c) CCPA
4. A state statute provides that no person shall be allowed to work in specified occupations for more than eight hours a day. Is this a substantive or procedural law?
5. Are legal rights static? Support your answer by tracing the evolution of the concept of the rights of man.
6. (a) What is the procedure for settling a dispute by arbitration?
   (b) What is the advantage of this procedure?

LAW AS AN EXPRESSION OF SOCIAL FORCES

The purpose of law is to provide order, stability, and justice. Thus viewed, the law consists of relatively fixed rules which regulate conduct according to the morality of the community. Proper conduct, as determined by the community, is allowed or required; improper conduct is prohibited. Law, then, is a social institution. It is not an end unto itself but is an instrument for attaining social justice.

§ 2:1. LAW AS SOCIAL JUSTICE. Many factors and institutions contribute to molding the concepts of justice. Home and school training, religion, enlightened self-interest, social and business groups, and the various media of modern communication and entertainment, all play a part. For example, various organizations such as chambers of commerce, better business bureaus, informal groups of businessmen, trade groups, and conferences have emphasized what is ethical in business by stressing fair competition and service to the community. In turn, these organizations and groups have helped to bring about the adoption of statutes that modify the law to reflect the changed business ethics.

It would be a mistake, however, to assume that justice is a universal value which means the same to all people in all ages. Individual concepts of justice vary in terms of personality, training, and individual social and economic position. Justice has different meanings to the employer and the employee, to the millionaire and the pauper, to the industrial worker and the farmer, to the retired person and the young married adult, to the progressive and the conservative, or to the professor and the student. For this reason, special interest groups attempt to modify the law so that it will be more favorable to the members of those groups. Absolute justice is unattainable by human beings, but that is no reason why society should ever relent in its efforts to attain as high a level of substantial justice as is humanly possible.

§ 2:2. SPECIFIC OBJECTIVES OF THE LAW. The objectives of the Constitution of the United States are included in its preamble. Important statutes frequently include a statement of their objectives. In many instances, however, the objective of the law is not stated or it is expressed in very general terms. Whether stated or not, each law has an objective; and it is helpful in understanding the purpose of the law to know the objectives of the law.

In the following enumeration the more important specific objectives of the law are discussed against the background of our understanding of the general objective of creating and providing order, stability, and justice.[1]

1. Protection of the state. A number of laws are designed to protect the existing governments, both state and national. Laws condemning treason, sedition, and subversive practices are examples of society taking measures to preserve governmental systems. Less dramatic are the laws that impose taxes to provide for the support of those governments.

2. Personal protection. At an early date, laws developed to protect the individual from being injured or killed. The field of criminal law is devoted to a large extent to the protection of the person. In addition, under civil law a suit can be brought to recover damages for the harm done by criminal acts. For example, a grossly negligent driver of an automobile who injures a pedestrian is subject to a penalty imposed by the state in the form of imprisonment or a fine, or both. The driver is also liable to the injured person for the payment of damages, which may include not only medical and hospital costs but also loss of time from work and mental anguish. Over a period of time the protection of personal rights has broadened to protect reputation and privacy and to protect contracts and business relations from malicious interference by outsiders.

It is a federal offense knowingly to injure, intimidate, or interfere with anyone exercising a basic civil right (such as voting), taking part in any federal government program, or receiving federal assistance. Interference with attendance in a public school or college, with participation in any state or local governmental program, with service as a juror in a state court, or with the use of any public facility (common carrier, hotel, or restaurant) is likewise prohibited when based on race, color, religion, or national origin discrimination.[2]

Protection of the person is expanding to protect the "economic man." Laws prohibiting discrimination in employment, in furnishing hotel accommodations and transportation, and in commercial transactions and the sale of property represent an extension of the concept of protecting the person. When membership in a professional association, a labor union, or a trade or business group has economic importance to its members, an applicant cannot be arbitrarily excluded from the membership, nor may a member be expelled without notice of the charge against him and an opportunity to be heard.[3]

3. Protection of public health, safety, and morals. The law seeks to protect the public health, safety, and morals in many ways. Laws relating to

---

[1] For a fuller treatment of the social forces, see Ronald A. Anderson, *Social Forces and the Law* (Cincinnati: South-Western Publishing Co., 1969).

[2] Civil Obedience Act of 1968, PL 90-284, 19 United States Code § 245.

[3] Silver v New York Stock Exchange, 373 US 341; Cunningham v Burbank Board of Realtors, 262 CalApp2d 211, 68 CalRptr 653.

quarantine, food inspection, and compulsory vaccination are designed to protect the public health. Laws regulating highway speeds and laws requiring fire escapes or guard devices around moving parts of factory machinery are for the safety of the public. Laws prohibiting the sale of liquor to minors and those prohibiting obscenity protect the morals of the public.

4. Property protection. Just as laws have developed to protect the individual's physical well-being, laws also have developed to protect one's property from damage, destruction, and other harmful acts. If a thief steals an automobile, he is liable civilly to the owner of the automobile for its value and is criminally responsible to the state.

5. Title protection. Because of the importance of ownership of property, one of the objectives of the law has been to protect the title of an owner to his property so that he remains the owner until it is clearly proved that he had transferred the title to someone else. Thus, if property is stolen, the true owner may recover it from the thief. He may even recover his property from a person who purchased it in good faith from the thief.

6. Freedom of personal action. In the Anglo-American stream of history, man's desires for freedom from political domination gave rise to the American Revolution, and the desire for freedom from economic domination gave rise to the free enterprise philosophy. Today we find freedom as the dominant element in the constitutional provisions for the protection of freedom of religion, press, and speech, and also in such laws as those against trusts or business combinations in restraint of trade by others.

This right of freedom of personal action, however, cannot be exercised by one person in such a way that it interferes to an unreasonable extent with the rights of others. Freedom of speech, for example, does not mean freedom to speak or write a malicious, false statement about another person's character. In effect, this means that one person's freedom of speech must be balanced with another person's right to be free from defamation of character or reputation.

7. Freedom of use of property. Closely related to the objective of protection of freedom of action is that of protecting the freedom of the use of property. This freedom is achieved by prohibiting, restraining, or penalizing acts of others that would hamper the reasonable use of property by its owner.

FACTS: The Great Atlantic & Pacific Tea Co. owned a building several hundred feet away from one of the boundaries of the grounds for the New York World's Fair of 1964. On the top of the building, approximately 110 feet above the ground, was a red neon A & P sign approximately 250 feet long with letters 10 feet high. The World's Fair placed artificial trees and shrubbery along the boundary line to hide the electric sign, which the Fair claimed was generally unesthetic and interfered with a fountain and electric light display of the Fair. A & P sued to enjoin the Fair from hiding its sign in this manner.

DECISION: Injunction refused. The fact that an occupier's use of his land causes harm to the owner of neighboring land is not controlling. Here the use by the Fair of its land was a reasonable use to protect its exhibits from outside interference. The fact that it was advantageous to A & P that the Fair make no use of its land did not justify the conclusion that the use which the Fair made was unreasonable and subject to injunction as a nuisance. [Great A & P Tea Co. v New York World's Fair, 42 Misc2d 855, 249 NYS2d 256].

Absolute freedom of this kind would permit an owner to make any use he chose of his property—even in a way that would harm others, to sell it at any price he desired, or to make any disposition of it that he wished. Such freedom is not recognized today, for everywhere we find some limitation of the right of the owner of property to do as he pleases with it.

The law prohibits an owner from using his property in such a way as to injure another or another's property. Further, zoning laws may limit the use of his land. Building restrictions in a deed may restrict the type of building that the owner may construct on his land. Fire laws and building codes may specify details of construction of his building. Labor laws may require that he equip a business building with safety devices. Likewise, an antipollution law restricts the freedom of the owner of property to use it in any way that he desires.

8. Enforcement of intent. The law usually seeks to enforce the intent of the contracting parties. This objective is closely related to the concept that the law seeks to protect the individual's freedom of action. For example, if a person provides by his will for the distribution of his property when he dies, the law will generally allow the property to pass to the persons intended by the deceased owner. The law will likewise seek to carry out the intention of the parties to a business transaction. To illustrate, if you and an electrician agree that he shall rewire your house for $200, the law will ordinarily enforce that contract because that is what was intended by both parties.

The extent to which the intent of one person or of several persons will be carried out has certain limitations. Sometimes the intent is not effective unless it is manifested by a particular written formality. For example, a deceased person may have intended that his friend should receive his house, but in most states that intent must be shown by a written will signed by the deceased owner. Likewise, in some cases the intent of the parties may not be carried out because the law regards the intent as illegal.

9. Protection from exploitation, fraud, and oppression. Many rules of law have developed in the courts and many statutes have been enacted to protect certain groups or individuals from exploitation or oppression by others. Thus, the law developed that a minor (a person under legal age) could set aside his contract, subject to certain exceptions, in order to give the minor an opportunity to avoid a bad bargain.

Persons who buy food that is packed in tin cans are given certain rights against the seller and the manufacturer. Since they cannot see the contents, buyers of such products need special protection against unscrupulous canners. The consumer is also protected by laws against adulteration and poisons in foods, drugs, and household products because he would ordinarily be unable to take care of himself. Laws prohibiting unfair competition and discrimination, both economic and social, are also designed to protect from oppression.

For the purpose of brevity, "oppression" is used here to include not only conscious wrongdoing by another but also cases where the consequences of another's act causes the victim extreme or oppressive hardship.

10. Furtherance of trade. Society may seek to further trade in a variety of ways, as by establishing a currency as a medium of payment; by recognizing and giving legal effect to installment sales; by adopting special rules for checks, notes, and similar instruments so that they can be widely used as credit devices and substitutes for money; or by enacting laws to mitigate the harmful effects of alternating periods of depression and inflation.

Laws that have been considered in connection with other objectives may also serve to further trade. For example, laws protecting against unfair competition have the objective of furtherance of trade, as well as the objective of protecting certain classes from exploitation by others.

11. Creditor protection. Society seeks to protect the rights of creditors and to protect them from dishonest or fraudulent acts of debtors. Initially creditors are protected by the law which declares that contracts are binding and which provides the machinery for the enforcement of contracts, and by the provision of the federal Constitution that prohibits states from impairing the obligation of contracts. Further, creditors may compel a debtor to come into bankruptcy in order to settle his debts as far as his property permits. If the debtor has concealed his property or transferred it to a friend in order to hide it from his creditors, the law permits the creditors to claim the property for the payment of the debts due them.

12. Debtor rehabilitation. Society has come to regard it as unsound that debtors should be ruined forever by the burden of their debts. The passing centuries have seen the debtor's prison abolished. Bankruptcy laws have been adopted to provide the debtor with a means of settling his debts as best he can and then starting upon a new economic life. In times of widespread depression the same objective has been served by special laws that prohibit the foreclosure of mortgages and regulate the amount of the judgments that can be entered against mortgage debtors.

13. Stability. Stability is particularly important in all business transactions. When you buy a house, for example, you not only want to know the exact meaning of the transaction under today's law but you also hope that the transaction will have the same meaning in the future. When the businessman invests money, he desires the law to remain the same as it was when he acted.

Because of the objective of stability, the courts will ordinarily follow former decisions unless there is some valid reason to depart from them.

When no former case directly bears on the point involved, the desire for stability will influence the courts to reach a decision that is a logical extension of some former decision or which follows a former decision by analogy rather than to strike off on a fresh path and to reach a decision unrelated to the past.

14. Flexibility. If stability were an absolute objective of the law, the cause of justice would often be thwarted. The reason that originally gave rise to a rule of law may have ceased to exist.[4] The rule then appears unjust because it reflects a concept of justice that is outmoded or obsolete. For example, capital punishment, which one age believed just, has been condemned by another age as unjust. We must not lose sight of the fact that the rule of law under question was created to further the sense of social justice existing at that time; but our concepts of justice may change.

The law itself may be flexible in that it makes provision for changes in rules to meet situations that cannot be anticipated or for which an explicit set of rules cannot be developed satisfactorily in advance. Our constitutions state the procedures for their amendment. Such changes in constitutional law are purposely made difficult in order to serve the objective of stability, but they are possible when the need for change is generally recognized by the people of the state or nation.

Changes by legislative action in federal and state statutes and local ordinances are relatively easier to make. Furthermore, some statutes recognize the impossibility of laying down in advance a hard and fast rule that will do justice in all cases. The typical modern statute, particularly in the field of regulation of business, will therefore contain "escape clauses" by which a person can escape from the operation of the statute under certain circumstances. Thus, a rent control law may impose a rent ceiling—that is, a maximum above which landlords cannot charge; but it may also authorize a greater charge when special circumstances make it just to allow such exception, as when the landlord has made expensive repairs to the property or when his taxes have increased materially.

The rule of law may be stated in terms of what a reasonable or prudent person would do. Thus, whether you are negligent in driving your automobile is determined in court by whether you exercised the same degree of care that a prudent person would have exercised driving your car under the circumstances in question. This is a vague and variable standard as to how you must drive your car, but it is the only standard that is practical. The alternative would be a detailed motor code specifying how you should drive your car under every situation that might arise, a code that obviously could not foresee every possibility and which certainly would be too long for any driver to know in every detail by memory.

---

[4] "It is revolting to have no better reason for a rule of law than that it was laid down in the time of Henry IV. It is still more revolting if the grounds upon which it was laid down have vanished long since, and the rule simply persists from blind imitation of the past." Holmes, Collected Papers 187 (1920).

"The law must be stable, but it must not stand still." Roscoe Pound, *Introduction to the Philosophy of Law* (Connecticut: Yale University Press, 1922).

15. Practical expediency. Frequently the law is influenced by what is practical or expedient in the situation. In some of these situations, the law will strive to make its rules fit the business practices of society. For example, a signature is frequently regarded by the law as including a stamping, printing, or typewriting of a name, in recognition of the business practice of "signing" letters and other instruments by mechanical means. A requirement of a handwritten signature would impose a burden on business that would not be practically expedient.

§ 2:3. **CONFLICTING OBJECTIVES.** As we have seen, the specific objectives of the law sometimes conflict with each other. When this is true, the problem is one of social policy, which in turn means a weighing of social, economic, and moral forces to determine which objective should be furthered. Thus, we find a conflict at times between the objective of the state seeking protection from the conduct of individuals or groups and the objective of freedom of action by those individuals and groups.

Thus, while protection of the freedom of the individual urges the utmost freedom of religious belief, society will impose limitations on religious freedom where it believes such freedom will cause harm to the public welfare. Thus, state laws requiring vaccination against smallpox were enforced against the contention that this violated religious principles. Similarly, parents failing to provide medical care for a sick child will be held guilty of manslaughter if the child dies, even though the parents sincerely believed as a matter of religious principle that medical care was improper. In contrast, when the harm contemplated is not direct or acute, religious freedom will prevail, so that a compulsory child education law will not be enforced against Amish parents who as a matter of religion are opposed to state education.[5]

As another example, the objective of protecting title may conflict with the objective of furthering trade. Consider again the example of the stolen property that was sold by the thief to one who purchased it for value and in good faith, without reason to know that the goods had been stolen. If we are to further the objective of protecting the title to the property, we will conclude that the owner can recover the property from the innocent purchaser. This rule, however, will discourage trade, for people will be less willing to buy goods if they run the risk that the goods were stolen and may have to be surrendered. If we instead think only of taking steps to encourage buying and selling, we will hold that the buyer takes a good title because he acted in good faith and paid value. If we do this, we then destroy the title of the original owner and obviously abandon our objective of protecting title to property. As a general rule, society has followed the objective of protecting title. In some instances, however, the objective of furthering trade is adopted by statute and the buyer is given good title, as in certain cases of commercial paper (notes, drafts, and checks) or of the purchaser from a regular dealer in other people's goods.

---

[5] Wisconsin v Yoder, 406 US 205 (high school student).

FACTS: The City of Columbia, South Carolina, provided for the fluoridation of the city water supply. Hall claimed that this deprived him of his constitutional right to drink unfluoridated water since there was no other water supply. He further attacked the validity of the plan on the ground that dental cavities are not contagious, and therefore a public health problem did not exist.

DECISION: Judgment for the City. The interest of the public in advancing general health through a program of teeth improvement is superior to the right of the individual to refrain from participating in the program because he does not believe in it. Furthermore health improvement is not limited to protection from contagion but extends to anything that improves the individual health of each member of the public. [Hall v Bates, Mayor of Columbia, 247 SC 511, 148 SE2d 345].

§ 2:4. **LAW AS AN EVOLUTIONARY PROCESS.** Law changes as society changes. Let us consider an example of this type of change. When the economy was patterned on a local community unit in which everyone knew each other and each other's product, the concept of "let the buyer beware" expressed a proper basis on which to conduct business. Much of the early law of the sales of goods was predicated on this philosophy. In today's economy, however, with its emphasis on interstate, national, and even international activities, the buyer has little or no direct contact with the manufacturer or seller, and the packaging of articles makes their presale examination impossible. Under the circumstances, the consumer must rely on the integrity of others to an increasing degree. Gradually practices that were tolerated and even approved in an earlier era have been condemned, and the law has changed to protect the buyer by warranties when his own caution can no longer protect him.

Moreover, new principles of law are being developed to meet the new situations that have arisen. Every new invention and every new business practice introduces a number of situations for which there is no satisfactory rule of law. For example, how could there have been a law governing the liability of a food canner to the consumer before canning was invented? How could there have been a law relating to stocks and bonds before those instruments came into existence? How could there have been a law with respect to the liability of radio and television broadcasters before such methods of communication were developed? This pattern of change will continue as long as man strives for better ways to achieve his desires.

§ 2:5. **LAW AS A SYNTHESIS.** Law as a synthesis may be illustrated by the law as it relates to contracts for the sale of a house. Originally such a contract could be oral—that is, merely spoken words with nothing in writing to prove that there was such a contract. Of course, there was the practical question of proof—that is, whether the jury would believe that there was such a contract—but no rule said that the contract must be in writing. This situation made it possible for a witness in court to swear falsely that Jones had agreed to sell his house for a specified sum. Even though Jones had not made such an agreement, the jury might believe the false witness and Jones would have to give up his house on terms to which he had not agreed. To help prevent such a miscarriage of justice, a statute was passed in England in 1677 declaring that contracts for the sale of houses had to be evidenced by a writing.

This law ended the evil of persons lying that there was an oral agreement for the sale of a house, but was justice finally achieved? Not always, for cases arose in which Jones did in fact make an oral agreement to sell his land to Smith. Smith would take possession of the land and would make valuable improvements at great expense and effort, and then Jones would have Smith thrown off the land. Smith would defend on the ground that Jones had orally agreed to sell the land to him. Jones would then say, "Where is the writing that the statute requires?" To this, Smith could only reply that there was no writing. No writing meant no enforceable legal agreement; and therefore Smith lost the land, leaving Jones with the land and all the improvements that Smith had made. That certainly was not just. What then?

Gradually the law courts developed the rule that in spite of the fact that the statute required a writing, the courts would enforce an oral contract for the sale of land when the buyer had gone into possession and made valuable improvements of such a nature that it would be difficult to determine what amount of money would be required to make up the loss if he were to be put off the land.

Thus, the law passed through three stages: (a) The original concept that all land contracts could be oral. Because the perjury evil arose under this rule of law, society swung to (b) the opposite rule that no such contract could be oral. This rule gave rise to the hardship case of the honest buyer under an oral contract who made extensive improvements. The law then swung, not back to the original rule, but to (c) a middle position, combining both (a) and (b), that is, combining the element of the written requirement as to the ordinary transaction but allowing oral contracts in the special cases to prevent hardship.

This example is also interesting because it shows the way in which the courts "amend" the law by decision. The flat requirement of the statute was "eroded" by decisions and by exceptions created by the courts in the interest of furthering justice.

§ 2:6. PERSPECTIVE. As you study the rules of law in the chapters that follow, consider each rule in relationship to its social, economic, and moral background. Try to determine the particular objective of each important rule. To the extent that you are able to analyze law as the product of man striving for justice in society, you will have a greater insight into the law itself, the world in which you live, the field of business, and the mind of man.

QUESTIONS AND CASE PROBLEMS

1. What is the general purpose of law?

2. Of the specific objectives of the law, which do you consider to be the most important? Why?

3. (a) When specific objectives of the law conflict in a given situation, which objective prevails?

   (b) Are creditor protection and debtor rehabilitation conflicting specific objectives of the law?

4. (a) How can law be dynamic if stability is one of its specific objectives?

   (b) How do some statutes provide for "built-in" flexibility?

5. Sometimes the development of the law seems to follow a zig-zag course. What is the explanation?

6. When O'Brien was prosecuted for burning his draft card, he raised the defense that the right of free speech gave him the privilege to express his disapproval of the draft and of the war in this manner. Was he correct? [United States v O'Brien, 391 US 367]

7. Two high school girls on the Ann Arbor Union High School tennis team wished to enter the interscholastic tennis matches to represent their school. The Michigan High School Athletic Association regulations prohibited competition between boys and girls. The girls brought a suit against the State Board of Education to prevent enforcing this regulation. Was the regulation valid? [Morris v Michigan State Board of Education (CA6 Mich) 472 F2d 1207]

8. Briney owned an unused farmhouse. Annoyed with repeated stealing of personal property from the house, he set up a loaded shotgun so that anyone who entered through the front door would be shot in the legs. There was nothing to indicate the presence of the gun. Katko was a stranger who had been sentenced to 60 days in jail for stealing private property from a building. He was paroled for good behavior. Without any permission from Briney, Katko entered the farmhouse. When he opened the door, the gun went off and he was struck in the legs. He sued Briney for the injuries which he sustained. The jury returned a verdict of $20,000 compensatory damages and $10,000 punitive damages. Briney appealed on the grounds that he was not liable because a property owner can protect his property from being stolen by a trespasser. Was he correct? [Katko v Briney (Iowa) 183 NW2d 657]

CRIMINAL LAW AND BUSINESS

A. GENERAL PRINCIPLES

§ 3:1. CLASSIFICATION OF CRIMES

(a) Source of criminal law. Crimes are classified in terms of their origin as common-law and statutory crimes. Some offenses that are defined by statute are merely declaratory of the common law. Each state has its own criminal law, although a general pattern among the states may be observed.

(b) Seriousness of offense. Crimes are classified in terms of their seriousness as treason, felonies, and misdemeanors. *Treason* is defined by the Constitution of the United States, which states that "Treason against the United States, shall consist only in levying War against them, or in adhering to their Enemies, giving them Aid and Comfort."
Felonies include the other more serious crimes, such as arson, homicide, and robbery, which are punishable by confinement in prison or by death.
Crimes not classified as treason or felonies are *misdemeanors*. Reckless driving, weighing and measuring goods with scales and measuring devices that have not been inspected, and disturbing the peace by illegal picketing are generally classified as misdemeanors. An act may be a felony in one state and a misdemeanor in another.

(c) Nature of crimes. Crimes are also classified in terms of the nature of the misconduct. *Crimes mala in se* include acts that are inherently vicious or, in other words, that are naturally evil as measured by the standards of a civilized community. *Crimes mala prohibita* include those acts that are wrong merely because they are declared wrong by some statute.

§ 3:2. BASIS OF CRIMINAL LIABILITY. A crime generally consists of two elements: (a) an act or omission, and (b) a mental state. In the case of some crimes, such as the illegal operation of a business without a license, it is immaterial whether the act causes harm to others. In other cases the defendant's act must be the sufficiently direct cause of harm to another in order to impose criminal liability, as in the case of unlawful homicide.

Mental state does not require an awareness or knowledge of guilt. In most crimes it is sufficient that the defendant voluntarily did the act that is criminal, regardless of motive or evil intent. In some instances a particular mental state is required, such as the necessity that a homicide be with malice aforethought to constitute murder. In some cases it is the existence of a specific intent that differentiates the crime committed from other offenses, as an assault with intent to kill is distinguished by that intent from an ordinary assault or an assault with intent to rob.

§ 3:3. **PARTIES TO A CRIME.** Two or more parties may directly or indirectly contribute to the commission of a crime. At common law participants in the commission of a felony are sometimes known as *principals* and *accessories*.

(a) **Principals.** Principals may be divided into two classes: (1) *principals in the first degree*, who actually engage in the perpetration of the crime, and (2) *principals in the second degree*, who are actually or constructively present and aid and abet in the commission of the act. For example, a person is a principal in the second degree if he assists by words of encouragement, stands ready to assist or to give information, or keeps watch to prevent surprise or capture.

The distinction as to degree is frequently abolished by statute so that all persons participating in a crime are principals.

(b) **Accessories.** Accessories to a crime are also divided into two classes, accessories before the fact and accessories after the fact. An *accessory before the fact* differs from a principal in the second degree only by reason of his absence from the scene of the act. An *accessory after the fact* is a person who knowingly assists one who has committed a felony. Thus, a person is an accessory after the fact if, after the commission of the crime and with intent to assist a felon, he gives warning to prevent arrest or shelters or aids in an escape from imprisonment.

§ 3:4. **RESPONSIBILITY FOR CRIMINAL ACTS.** In some cases certain classes of persons are not fully responsible for their criminal acts.

(a) **Minors.** Some states have legislation fixing the age of criminal responsibility of minors. At common law, when a child is under the age of seven years, the law presumes him to be incapable of committing a crime; after the age of fourteen he is presumed to have capacity as though he were an adult; and between the ages of seven and fourteen, no presumption of law arises and it must be shown that the minor has such capacity. The existence of capacity cannot be presumed from the mere commission of the act.

(b) **Insane persons.** An insane person is not criminally responsible for his acts. There is a conflict of opinion over what constitutes such insanity as to excuse a person legally from the normal consequence of his acts. All courts, however, agree that intellectual weakness alone is not such insanity.

A test commonly applied is the *right-and-wrong test*. The responsibility of the defendant is determined in terms of his ability to understand the nature of his act and to distinguish right from wrong in relation to it.

Some courts also use the *irresistible-impulse test*, the theory of which is that although the defendant may know right from wrong, if he acts under an uncontrollable impulse because of an unsound state of mind caused by disease of any nature, he has not committed a voluntary act and is not criminally responsible. If the mental instability is not caused by disease, the irresistible-impulse test is not applied.

In many jurisdictions the right-and-wrong test and the irresistible-impulse test have been replaced by the rule stated in the Model Penal Code of the American Law Institute that "A person is not responsible for criminal conduct if at the time of such conduct as a result of mental disease or defect he lacks substantial capacity to appreciate the wrongfulness of his conduct or to conform his conduct to the requirements of the law."

When insanity takes the form of delusions or hallucinations, the defendant is not legally responsible when the imagined facts, if they were true, would justify or excuse the act.

(c) Intoxicated persons. Involuntary intoxication relieves a person from criminal responsibility; voluntary intoxication generally does not. An exception to this rule is made in the case of a crime requiring specific intent when the accused was so intoxicated that he was incapable of forming such intent.

(d) Corporations. The modern tendency is to hold corporations criminally responsible for their acts. A corporation may also be held liable for crimes based upon the failure to act. In some instances, the crime may be defined by statute in such a way that it requires or is interpreted as requiring a living "person" to commit the crime, in which case a corporation cannot be held criminally liable.

Certain crimes, such as perjury, cannot be committed by corporations. It is also usually held that crimes punishable only by imprisonment or corporal punishment cannot be committed by corporations. If the statute imposes a fine in addition to or in lieu of imprisonment or corporal punishment, a corporation may be convicted for the crime. Thus a corporation may be fined for violating the federal antitrust law by conspiring or combining to restrain interstate commerce. A corporation may be fined for committing criminal manslaughter when death has been caused by the corporation's failure to install safety equipment required by statute.

B. SECURITY FROM BUSINESS CRIMES

§ 3:5. LARCENY. *Larceny* is the wrongful or fraudulent taking and carrying away by any person of the personal property of another, with a fraudulent intent to deprive the owner of his property. The place from which the property is taken is generally immaterial, although by statute the offense is sometimes subjected to a greater penalty when property is taken from a particular kind of building, such as a warehouse. Shoplifting is a common form of larceny.

At common law a defendant taking property of another with the intent to return it was not guilty of larceny. This has been changed in some states so that a person who "borrows" a car for a joyride is guilty of larceny, theft, or some other statutory offense. Statutes in many states penalize as larceny by trick the use of any device or fraud by which the wrongdoer obtains the possession of, or title to, personal property from the true owner. In some states all forms of larceny and robbery are consolidated in a statutory crime of theft. At common law there was no single offense of theft.

The concept of property which may be the subject of larceny has been expanded. For example, the theft of computer programs constitutes larceny. One half of the states have statutes punishing the theft of trade secrets as larceny.

The fact that the person from whom the thief has taken the personal property is not the owner does not constitute a defense to the prosecution of the thief for larceny.

§ 3:6. ROBBERY. At common law *robbery* was the unlawful taking of personal property of any value from the possession or from the presence of another by means of force or by putting the possessor in fear. It differed from larceny primarily in the necessity of the use of force or fear, so that a pickpocket whose act of stealing was unknown to his victim committed larceny but not robbery.

In most states there are special penalties for various forms of aggravated robbery, such as robbery by use of a deadly weapon.

§ 3:7. BURGLARY. At common law *burglary* was the breaking and entering in the nighttime of the dwelling house of another, with the intent to commit a felony. While one often thinks of a burglary as stealing property, any felony would satisfy the definition. The offense was aimed primarily at protecting the habitation and thus illustrates the social objective of protection of the person, in this case the persons living or dwelling in the building.

Modern statutes have eliminated many of the requirements of the common-law definition so that it is immaterial when or where there is an entry to commit a felony, and the elements of breaking and entering are frequently omitted. Under some statutes the offense is aggravated and the penalty is increased in terms of the place where the offense is committed, such as a bank building, freight car, or warehouse. Related statutory offenses have also been created, such as the crime of possessing burglar's tools.

§ 3:8. ARSON. At common law *arson* was the willful and malicious burning of the dwelling-house of another. As such, it was designed to protect human life, although the defendant was guilty if there was a burning even though no one was actually hurt. In most states, arson is a felony so that if someone is killed in the resulting fire, the offense is murder by application of the felony-murder rule, under which a homicide, however unintended, occurring in the commission of a felony is automatically classified as murder.

In virtually every state a special offense of *burning to defraud insurers* has been created by statute, such burning not constituting arson when the defendant burns his own house to collect on his fire insurance, since the definition of arson required that the dwelling house be that of another person. In many states it is now arson to burn any building owned by another, even though it is not a dwelling.

§ 3:9. **RECEIVING STOLEN GOODS.** The crime of *receiving stolen goods* is the receiving of goods which have been stolen, with knowledge of that fact, and with the intent to deprive the owner of them. It is immaterial that the goods were received from a person who was not the person who stole them, such as another receiver of the goods or an innocent middleman, and it is likewise immaterial that the receiver does not know the identity of the owner or the thief.

FACTS: Scaggs acquired possession of property that was stolen. He did not know this at the time but learned of it later. Upon so learning, he decided to keep the property for himself. He was prosecuted for receiving stolen goods. He raised the defense that at the time he "received" the goods, he did not know that they were stolen and therefore was not guilty of the offense.

DECISION: Scaggs was guilty. The offense of "receiving" is, in effect, a continuing offense including retaining possession of stolen goods. When Scaggs retained possession of the goods after knowing that he would thereby deprive the true owner of his property, he committed the offense of "receiving." [California v Scaggs, 153 CalApp2d 339, 314 P2d 793]

§ 3:10. **EMBEZZLEMENT.** *Embezzlement* is the fraudulent conversion of property or money owned by another by a person to whom it has been entrusted, as in the case of an employee. It is a statutory crime designed to cover the case of unlawful takings that were not larceny because the wrongdoer did not take the property from the possession of another, and which were not robbery because there was neither a taking nor the use of force or fear.

It is immaterial whether the defendant received the money or property from the victim or from a third person. Thus, an agent commits embezzlement when he receives and keeps payments from third persons which he should remit to his principal, even though the agent is entitled to retain part of such payments as his commissions.

Today every jurisdiction has not only a general embezzlement statute but also various statutes applicable to particular situations, such as embezzlement by trustees, employees, and government officials.

Generally the fact that the defendant intends to return the property or money which he embezzles, or does in fact do so, is no defense. However, as a practical matter an embezzler returning what he has taken will ordinarily not be prosecuted because the owner will not desire to testify against him.

§ 3:11. **OBTAINING GOODS BY FALSE PRETENSES.** In almost all of the states, statutes are directed against obtaining money or goods by means of false pretenses. These statutes vary in detail and scope. Sometimes the statutes are directed against particular forms of deception, such as using bad checks.

§ 3:12. FALSE WEIGHTS, MEASURES, AND LABELS. Cheating, defrauding, or misleading the public by the use of false, improper, or inadequate weights, measures, and labels is a crime. Numerous federal and state regulations have been adopted on this subject.

§ 3:13. SWINDLES AND CONFIDENCE GAMES. The act of a person who, intending to cheat and defraud, obtains money or property by trick, deception, fraud, or other device, is an offense known as a *swindle* or *confidence game.* False or bogus checks and spurious coins are frequently employed in swindling operations directed toward the man engaged in business.

§ 3:14. COUNTERFEIT MONEY. It is a federal crime to make, to possess with intent to pass, or to pass counterfeit coins, bank notes, or obligations or other securities of the United States. Legislation has also been enacted against the passing of counterfeit foreign securities or notes of foreign banks.

The various states also have statutes prohibiting the making and passing of counterfeit coins and bank notes. These statutes often provide, as does the federal statute, a punishment for the mutilation of bank notes or the lightening or mutilation of coins.

FACTS: Wolfe gave some counterfeit money to Ballinger, telling her that the bills were counterfeit and that she should go downtown to pass them and that, being New Year's Eve, it was a good time to pass them. Ballinger thereafter spent two of the bills and attempted to destroy the balance. Wolfe was arrested and prosecuted for passing counterfeit obligations of the United States with the intent to defraud. He raised the defense that he could not be guilty because Ballinger had been told that the money was counterfeit.

DECISION: Wolfe was instrumental in putting the counterfeit money in circulation and in its being passed to some persons who would not know its false character. He was guilty, therefore, of passing counterfeit money even though the person to whom he gave it had not been deceived. [United States v Wolfe (CA7 Ill) 307 F2d 798, cert den 372 US 945]

§ 3:15. USE OF MAILS TO DEFRAUD. Congress has made it a crime to use the mails to further any scheme or artifice to defraud. To constitute the offense, there must be (a) a contemplated or organized scheme or artifice to defraud or to obtain money or property by false pretenses, and (b) the mailing or the causing of another to mail a letter, writing, or pamphlet for the purpose of executing or attempting to execute such scheme or artifice. Illustrations of schemes or artifices that come within the statute are false statements to secure credit, circulars announcing false cures for sale, false statements to sell stock in a corporation, and false statements as to the origin of a fire and the value of the destroyed goods for the purpose of securing indemnity from an insurance company. Federal law also makes it a crime to use a telegram to defraud.

§ 3:16. **LOTTERIES.** There are three elements to a lottery: (a) a payment of money or something of value for the opportunity to win (b) a prize (c) by lot or chance. If these elements appear, it is immaterial that the transaction appears to be a legitimate form of business, or advertising, or that the transaction is called by some name other than a lottery.

The sending of a chain letter through the mail is generally a federal offense, both as a mail fraud and as an illegal lottery, when the letter solicits contributions or payments for a fraudulent purpose.

In many states, government lotteries are legal.

§ 3:17. **FORGERY.** *Forgery* consists of the fraudulent making or material altering of an instrument, such as a check, which apparently creates or changes a legal liability of another. The instrument must have some apparent legal efficacy to constitute forgery.[1]

Ordinarily forgery consists of signing another's name with intent to defraud. It may also consist of making an entire instrument or altering an existing one. It may result from signing a fictitious name or the offender's own name with the intent to defraud.

When the nonowner of a credit card signs the owner's name on a credit card invoice, such an act is a forgery. In most states a special statute makes it a crime to fraudulently use a credit card. In such a case, the prosecuting attorney may choose either to prosecute the defendant for violation of the forgery statute or the special credit card statute.

FACTS: Morse was convicted of forging the name "Hillyard Motors" as the drawer of a check. He appealed on the ground that signing such a name had no legal effect and that therefore he was not guilty of forgery.

DECISION: Commercial paper may be signed with a trade name. The check signed by Morse appeared to have been signed in this manner. It therefore apparently had legal efficacy. Whether it did or not was immaterial as long as the signing had been made with intent to defraud. [Washington v Morse, 38 Wash2d 927, 234 P2d 478]

§ 3:18. **CRIMINAL LIBEL.** A person who falsely defames another without legal excuse or justification may be subject to criminal liability as well as civil liability. *Criminal libel* is based upon its tendency to cause a breach of the peace. Under some statutes, however, the offense appears to be based upon the tendency to injure another.

No publication or communication to third persons is required in the case of criminal libel. The offense is committed when the defendant

---

[1] Although the Uniform Commercial Code does not contain any provisions relating to crimes, if the defendant is indicted for forgery of a check, which is a form of commercial paper regulated by the Code, reference will be made to the Code to determine whether the writing in question is a check. Faulkner v Alaska, 445 P2d 815.

communicates the libel directly to the person libeled as well as when he makes it known to third persons.

The truth of the statement is a defense in civil libel. In order to constitute a defense to criminal libel, the prevailing view requires that a proper motive on the part of the accused be shown and proof that the statement is true.

In a number of states, slander generally or particular kinds of slander have been made criminal offenses by statute.

§ 3:19. RIOTS AND CIVIL DISORDERS. Damage to property in the course of a riot or civil disorder is ordinarily a crime to the same extent as though only one wrongdoer were involved. That is, there is larceny, or arson, and so on, depending on the nature of the circumstances, without regard to whether one person or many are involved. In addition, the act of assembling as a riotous mob and engaging in civil disorders is generally some form of crime in itself, without regard to the destruction or theft of property, whether under common-law concepts of disturbing the peace or under modern antiriot statutes.

A state may make it a crime to riot or to incite to riot, although a statute relating to inciting must be carefully drawn to avoid infringing constitutionally protected free speech.

QUESTIONS AND CASE PROBLEMS

1. What is the objective of the rule of law that an irresistible impulse to commit a crime does not excuse criminal liability when the mental instability is not the result of disease?

2. The Fire Prevention Code of the City of Atlanta stated "Any person smoking or attempting to light or smoke a cigarette, cigar, pipe, or tobacco in any form for which lighters, matches, flammable liquids, or chemicals are used, who sets fire to any bedding, furniture, curtains, drapes, house, or household furnishings shall be subject to the penalties [declared thereby]." Was this offense malum in se or malum prohibitum? [Marzetta v Steinman, 117 GaApp 971, 160 SE2d 590]

3. Swanson wanted to procure a loan from the Lincoln Bank. He falsely represented to the bank that he owned 629 head of cattle when in fact he owned only 80. The bank made a loan to him of approximately $3,000 and credited his account with this amount. Before Swanson drew any money from the bank, the bank's agent learned of the falsity of Swanson's representation. Swanson thereafter drew out by check the amount of the loan. Swanson was then prosecuted by the state for obtaining property by false pretenses. He defended on the ground that he had not actually drawn any money from the bank until after the bank, through its agent, knew of the fraud and that since the bank took no steps to prevent the money from going out thereafter, it was in effect the

bank's own negligence that made it sustain loss. Was this a valid defense? [Nebraska v Swanson, 179 Neb 639, 140 NW2d 618]

4. Socony Mobil Oil Co. ran a telephone bingo game series. The gasoline station dealers purchased the bingo cards from Socony and gave them free to anyone requesting them, whether a customer or not. It was not possible to play the game without a card. A cash prize was awarded the winner. The State of Texas brought an injunction action against Socony to stop this on the ground that it was a lottery. Socony raised the defense that since no value or consideration was given by the persons participating in the bingo games, it was not a lottery. Decide. [Texas v Socony Mobil Oil Co. (TexCivApp) 386 SW2d 169]

5. Krehbiel was the manager of a vacuum cleaning company. In order to promote sales, he and the company adopted a plan by which any purchaser of a vacuum cleaner who gave the name of a prospective customer would receive $25 if the named person thereafter purchased a vacuum cleaner. The Attorney General of Oklahoma brought an action against the manager and the company to stop the plan on the ground that it was a lottery under a statute which declared that "Every person who sets up, promotes, or engages in any plan by which goods or anything of value is sold to a person, firm, or corporation for a consideration and upon the further consideration that the purchaser agrees to secure one (1) or more persons to participate in the plan by respectively making a similar purchase or purchases and in turn agreeing to secure one (1) or more persons likewise to join in said plan, each purchaser being given the right to secure money, credits, goods, or something of value, depending upon the number of persons joining in the plan, shall be held to have set up and promoted a lottery." Decide. [Krehbiel v Oklahoma (Okla) 378 P2d 768]

6. Koonce entered a gas station after it was closed for the night. By means of force, he removed the cash box from a soft drink vending machine. He was prosecuted for burglarizing a "warehouse." Was he guilty? [Koonce v Kentucky (Ky) 452 SW2d 822; Shumate v Kentucky (Ky) 433 SW2d 340]

7. Tauscher was prosecuted for embezzlement. It was shown that while claiming to act as agent, he, without authority, had drawn a check on his employer's bank account and kept the proceeds of the check for his own use. Was he guilty of embezzlement? [Oregon v Tauscher, 227 Ore 1, 360 P2d 764]

8. Dumont was prosecuted for obtaining merchandise by using a stolen credit card and signing a sales slip with the name of the card holder. Dumont was prosecuted under a general criminal law statute that classified the offense as a felony. Dumont claimed that this statute had been superseded by a later statute specifically applying to the unlawful use of credit cards, under which the offense was merely a misdemeanor, and that she could not be prosecuted under the earlier forgery statute. Was she correct? [Oregon v Dumont, 3 OreApp 189, 471 P2d 847]

9. Rapp opened a checking account under an assumed name. He then issued worthless checks on that account using the assumed name. He was prosecuted for passing forged instruments. Was he guilty? [Rapp v Florida (FlaApp), 274 So2d 18]

10. A New York statute declares that possession of a firearm is not a felony if it is kept "in a place of business." Santiago drove a taxicab in New York City. The taxicab company assigned the cab to him. He kept his receipts in a cigar box, along with an automatic pistol. He was prosecuted for the illegal possession of firearms. He raised the defense that the pistol was kept "in a place of business." Was this a valid defense? [New York v Santiago, 343 NYS2d 805]

THE LAW OF TORTS AND BUSINESS

A. GENERAL PRINCIPLES

A *tort* is a private injury or wrong arising from a breach of a duty created by law. It is often defined as a wrong independent of contract. Most torts, although not all, involve moral wrongs, but not all moral wrongs are torts.

Tort law includes harm to the person, as well as damage to property caused negligently or intentionally. In some instances, liability is imposed although there is no fault merely because the activity of the wrongdoer is so dangerous that it is deemed proper that he should pay for any harm that has been caused.

§ 4:1. TORT, CRIME, AND BREACH OF CONTRACT.
A crime is a wrong arising from a violation of a public duty, whereas a tort is a wrong arising from a violation of a private duty. An act may be both a crime and a tort as in the case of the theft of an automobile.

Although the state recognizes both crimes and torts as wrongs, it attaches different consequences to them. In the case of a crime, the state brings the action to enforce a prescribed penalty or punishment. On the other hand, when an act or omission is a tort, the state allows an action for redress by the injured party.

The wrongs or injuries caused by a breach of contract arise from the violation of an obligation or duty created by consent of the parties. A tort arises from the violation of an obligation or duty created by law. The same act may be both a breach of contract and a tort. For example, when an agent exchanges property instead of selling it as directed by his principal, he is liable for breach of contract and for the tort of conversion.

§ 4:2. BASIS OF TORT LIABILITY.
The mere fact that a person is hurt or harmed in some way does not mean that he can sue and recover damages from the person causing the harm. There must exist a recognized basis for liability.

(a) Voluntary act. The defendant must be guilty of a voluntary act or omission. Acts that are committed or omitted by one who is confronted with sudden peril or pressing danger not of his own making are considered as having been committed or omitted involuntarily.

(b) Intent. Whether intent to do an unlawful act or intent to cause harm is required as a basis for tort liability depends upon the nature of the act involved. Liability is imposed for some torts even though the person committing the tort acted in complete ignorance of the nature of his act and without any intent to cause harm. Thus, a person going on land that does not belong to him is liable for the tort of trespass unless he has permission.

In the case of other torts, such as assault, slander, malicious prosecution, or interference with contracts, it is necessary for the plaintiff to show that there was an intent on the part of the defendant to cause harm or at least the intent to do an act which a reasonable man would anticipate as likely to cause harm.

(c) Motive. As a general rule, motive is immaterial except as it may be evidence to show the existence of intent. In most instances, any legal right may be exercised even with bad motives, and an act that is unlawful is not made legal by good motives.

(d) Proximate cause. In order to fix legal responsibility upon one as a wrongdoer, it is necessary to show that the injury was the proximate result of his voluntary act. Whether an act is the proximate cause of an injury is usually a question of fact for the jury to determine.

§ 4:3. **LIABILITY-IMPOSING CONDUCT.** In the more elementary forms, intentional harm involves wrongs such as an assault; a battery; intentionally causing mental distress; and intentional wrongs directed against property, such as stealing another's automobile, cutting timber from his land, or setting his house on fire. Note that most of these "elementary" torts are also crimes. Somewhat more complex are the torts of fraud, slander and libel, the invasion of privacy, and the intentional interference with contract rights or business relations of others.

§ 4:4. **ABSOLUTE LIABILITY.** In some areas of the law, liability for harm exists without regard to whether there was any negligence or intention to cause harm. For example, in most states when a contractor blasts with dynamite and debris is hurled onto the land of another, the landowner may recover damages from the contractor even though the contractor had used due care, and therefore was not negligent, and did not intend to cause the landowner any harm by committing an intentional trespass on his land.

By this concept of absolute liability, society is in effect taking a middle position between (a) liability based on moral fault and (b) illegality. That is, society is saying that the activity is so dangerous to the public that liability must be imposed even though no fault is present. Yet society will not go so far as to say that the activity is so dangerous that it must be outlawed. Instead, the compromise is made to allow the activity but make it pay its injured victims regardless of the circumstances under which the injuries were sustained. Statutes are expanding the area of absolute liability.

(a) Industrial activity. There is generally absolute liability for harm growing out of the storage of inflammable gas and explosives in the middle of a populated city; crop dusting, where the chemical used is dangerous to life and the dusting is likely to be spread by the wind; factories emitting dangerous fumes, smoke, and soot in populated areas.

(b) Consumer protection. Pure foods statutes may impose absolute liability upon the seller of foods in favor of the ultimate consumer who is harmed by them. Decisions and statutes have imposed a nearly absolute liability on the manufacturer of goods.

(c) Wild animals. A person keeping a wild animal is absolutely liable for any harm caused by it. This liability is not affected by the fact that the animal was tame and the owner had no reason to foresee that harm would occur or that the plaintiff had exposed himself to danger.

§ 4:5. **NEGLIGENCE.** The widest range of tort liability today arises in the field of *negligence*, which exists whenever the defendant has acted with less care than would be exercised by a reasonable person under the circumstances. More specifically stated, the defendant has failed to exercise that degree of care which a reasonable person would exercise under the circumstances, and such negligence is the proximate cause of harm to a person or property.

(a) The imaginary reasonable person. The reasonable person whose behavior is made the standard is an imaginary person. In a given case which is tried before a jury, the reasonable person becomes the model person as he appears to the composite or combined minds of the jurors.

This reasonable person is not any one of the jurors nor an average of what the jurors would do. The law is not concerned with what the jurors would do in a like situation, for it is possible that they may be more careful or less careful than the abstract reasonable person. Likewise it is not what is done in the community, for the community may live above or below the standard of the reasonable person.

(b) Variable character of the standard. By definition, the standard is a variable standard for it does not tell you specifically in any case what should have been done. This flexibility is confusing to everyone, in the sense that you never know the exact answer in any borderline case until after the lawsuit is over. From the standpoint of society, however, this very flexibility is desirable because it is obviously impossible to foresee every possible variation in the facts that might arise and even more impossible to keep such a code of conduct up-to-date. Imagine how differently the reasonable person must act while driving today's automobile on today's superhighways than when he drove a Model-T more than a half century ago.

Many states have made an exception to the common-law rule by requiring the landowner to anticipate the presence of trespassing children and a few states have extended that duty to adult trespassers.

> **FACTS:** Drew sued Lett for damages arising from the death of Drew's eleven-year-old son. Lett was the owner of an abandoned mine. The entrance was open and unguarded. The child entered the mine and was suffocated by poisonous gases.

DECISIONS: Judgment for Drew. Ordinarily there would be no liability for the injury or death of a trespasser, but most states recognize an exception in favor of children, called the "attractive nuisance" doctrine. Under this theory the owner of property is liable for injury caused to small children who will not realize the danger of harm. The owner must anticipate that children will be children and must take reasonable steps to safeguard them, although he is not required to make his land "accident-proof." [Drew v Lett, 95 IndApp 89, 182 NE 547]

(c) **Degree of care.** The degree of care required of a person is that which an ordinarily prudent man would exercise under similar circumstances. It does not mean such a degree of care as would have prevented the harm from occurring, nor is it enough that it is just as much care as everyone else exercises. Nor is it sufficient that one has exercised the degree of care which is customary for persons in the same kind of work or business, or that one has employed the methods customarily used. If one is engaged in services requiring skill, the care, of course, must measure up to a higher standard. The degree of care exercised must be commensurate with the danger that would probably result if such care were lacking. In all cases it is the diligence, care, and skill that can be reasonably expected under the circumstances. Whether one has exercised that degree of care which is required under the circumstances is a question that is determined by the jury.

(d) **Contributory negligence.** Generally, one cannot recover for injuries caused by another's negligence if his own negligence has contributed to the injury. The plaintiff's negligence, however, must be a proximate cause of the injury; that is, it must contribute to the injury in order to defeat recovery.

In this connection there has developed a doctrine variously called the *doctrine of last clear chance*, the *humanitarian doctrine*, or the *doctrine of discovered peril*. Under this doctrine, although the plaintiff is negligent, the defendant is held liable if he had the last clear chance to avoid the injury. In such a case the theory is that the plaintiff's negligence is not the proximate cause and therefore does not contribute to the injury.

When the plaintiff is guilty of contributory negligence, he is ordinarily denied recovery without regard to whether the defendant was more negligent than he. The common law does not recognize comparative degrees of negligence, nor does it try to apportion the injury to the two parties in terms of the degree of their respective fault. As an exception to these principles, a number of states provide that the plaintiff's negligence does not bar his recovery but merely reduces the amount which he recovers in proportion to the degree or extent of his own negligence.

(e) **Proof of negligence.** The plaintiff ordinarily has the burden of proving that the defendant did not exercise reasonable care. In some instances, however, it is sufficient for the plaintiff to prove that the injury was caused by some thing that was within the control of the defendant. If injury ordinarily results from such an object only when there is negligence, the proof of these facts is prima facie proof that the defendant was negligent. This is expressed by the maxim *res ipsa loquitur* (the occurrence or thing speaks for itself). The burden of proving that the plaintiff was contributorily negligent is upon the defendant.

> **FACTS:** Deveny, who was visiting her aunt, went into the cellar to light the hot water heater. The control unit, which was factory sealed, exploded and injured her. She then sued the manufacturer of the hot water heater and its supplier that manufactured the control unit. The defendants raised the defense that no negligence was shown.

> **DECISION:** A boiler unit does not ordinarily explode unless someone has been negligent. As the exploding control unit was factory sealed, any negligence necessarily occurred in the course of its manufacture. The principle of res ipsa loquitur therefore applied even though at the time harm was sustained, the defendants no longer had possession of the unit. [Deveny v Rheem Mfg Co. (CA2 Vt) 319 F2d 124]

(f) Violation of statute. By the general rule, if harm is sustained while the defendant is violating a statute, the defendant is deemed negligent and is liable for the harm. Many courts are narrowing this concept so that the defendant is liable only if the statute is intended to protect against the kind of harm which was sustained due to violation of the statute. Courts which make this distinction will ignore the fact that the defendant was driving his automobile without proper tags in violation of the Automobile Registration Law, as that has no bearing on whether the defendant was driving with due care or was negligent. Similarly, an employer is not liable for injuries sustained by a minor employee merely because the employment was in violation of the age limitation of the child labor law.[1]

§ **4:6. DIVISION OF LIABILITY.** In some instances, when two or more defendants have caused harm to the plaintiff or his property, it is difficult or impossible to determine just what damage was done by each of such wrongdoers or tort-feasors. For example, automobile No. 1 strikes automobile No. 2, which is then struck by automobile No. 3. Ordinarily, it is impossible to determine how much of the damage to automobile No. 2 was caused by each of the other cars. Similarly, a tract of farm land down the river may be harmed because two or more factories have dumped industrial wastes into the river. It is not possible to determine how much damage each of the factories has caused the farm land.

By the older view, a plaintiff was denied the right to recover from any of the wrongdoers in these situations. The courts followed the theory that a plaintiff is not entitled to recover from a defendant unless the plaintiff can prove what harm was caused by that defendant. The modern trend of the cases is to hold that all of the defendants are jointly and severally liable for the total harm sustained by the plaintiff.

---

[1] Sloan v Coit International, Inc. (FlaApp) 278 So2d 326.

FACTS: Maddux was injured when the car in which she was riding was hit by a skidding truck driven by Donaldson, and then by the car following the truck. Maddux sued Donaldson for injuries caused by both collisions. Donaldson claimed that he could be sued only for those injuries which Maddux could show were caused by him and not for the total amount of damages. Because Maddux could not show which injuries were caused by Donaldson, the trial court dismissed the action. Maddux appealed.

DECISION: The lower court was reversed. When independently acting tort-feasors successively cause harm to the plaintiff and it is not possible to determine what harm was done by each tort-feasor, all are jointly and severally liable for the total harm caused the plaintiff. While it is unfair that any one defendant should be required to pay for more damage than he actually caused, it is an even greater injustice to refuse to allow the admittedly harmed plaintiff to recover because he cannot show just what harm was caused by each tort-feasor. The rule that each tort-feasor is jointly and severally liable for the total harm is more in harmony with the twentieth century problems created by chain collisions on super highways which give rise to situations in which plaintiffs cannot determine just what specific damage was caused by each of the colliding automobiles. [Maddux v Donaldson, 362 Mich 425, 108 NW2d 33]

§ 4:7. WHO MAY SUE. In some torts, the wrongdoer's act gives not only the immediate victim the right to sue but also persons standing in certain relationships to the victim. Thus, under certain circumstances a husband can sue for an injury to his wife, or a parent can sue for an injury to the child. In a wrongful death action the surviving group (typically the spouse, child, and parents of the person who has been killed) have a right to sue the wrongdoer for such death.

§ 4:8. IMMUNITY FROM LIABILITY

(a) Governments. Governments are generally immune from tort liability. This rule has been eroded by decision and in some instances by statutes, such as the Federal Tort Claims Act, which, subject to certain exceptions, permits the recovery of damages for property, personal injury, or death action claims arising from the negligent act or omission of any employee of the United States under such circumstances that the United States, "if a private person, would be liable to the claimant in accordance with the law of the place where the act or omission occurred." A fast-growing number of states have abolished governmental immunity.[2]

(b) Minors. All persons are not equally liable for torts. A minor of tender years, generally under 7, cannot be guilty of negligence or contributory negligence. Between the ages of 7 and 14, a minor is presumed to have capacity to commit a tort, although the contrary may be shown. Above 14 years, no distinction is made in terms of age. A minor who drives a motorcycle or an automobile on the public highway must observe the same standard of care as an adult.

---

[2] Ayala v Philadelphia Board of Education 453 Pa 584, 305 A2d 877.

In many states, statutes impose liability upon parents for property damage caused by the child, up to a stated maximum without regard to whether the parent was at fault or negligent in any way.

(c) Family relationships. At common law no suit could be brought by a husband against his wife and vice versa. By statute this immunity has been abolished as to torts involving property. The immunity continues in most states with respect to personal torts, whether intentional or negligent, although some two fifths of the states now allow personal tort actions between spouses. The trend of judicial decisions rejects the argument that the allowance of such suits would open the door to fraud and collusion between spouses when one of them is insured. A similar immunity exists between parent and child in most states with respect to personal tort claims.

(d) Charities. Charities were once exempt from tort law. For example, a hospital could not be held liable for the negligent harm to a patient caused by its staff or employees. Within the last three decades this immunity has been rejected in nearly two thirds of the states. It is quite likely that in the coming years it will be repudiated generally.

B. SECURITY FROM BUSINESS TORTS

§ 4:9. INTENTIONAL CAUSING OF MENTAL DISTRESS. When the defendant commits an act which by itself is a tort, there is ordinarily recovery for the mental distress which he causes thereby. With the turn of the century, and particularly in the last quarter century, recovery has been allowed in a number of cases in which no ordinary or traditional form of tort was committed and the common element in these cases was that the defendant had willfully subjected the plaintiff to unnecessary emotional disturbance. This result was reached when the common carrier or the hotel insulted a patron; a collection agency used unreasonable means of collection designed to harass the debtor; an outrageous practical joke was played upon the plaintiff, or his personal or physical condition was purposely exploited by such joke; the corpse of a close relative was concealed, mistreated, or interference made with the burial; or the defendant engaged in a steady campaign to intimidate a critic of the defendant's product, including illegal electronic eavesdropping.[3]

Statements made to humiliate the plaintiff because of his race, creed, or national origin will impose liability for the emotional distress caused thereby and for any physical illness which results therefrom. Generally the theory on which recovery is allowed in these cases is clouded by efforts to bring the case within the standard patterns of liability. Occasionally a court frankly recognizes that it is imposing liability merely because mental distress was intentionally caused.

---

[3] Nader v General Motors Corp. 25 NY2d 560, 255 NE2d 765.

§ 4:10. **FALSE IMPRISONMENT.** False imprisonment is the intentional, unprivileged detaining of a person without his consent. It may take the extreme form of kidnapping. At the other extreme, a shopper who is detained in the store manager's office and questioned as to shoplifting is the victim of false imprisonment where there is no reasonable ground for believing that the shopper was a thief. False imprisonment also includes detention under an official arrest when there is no legal justification for that arrest.

(a) Detention. Any detention at any place by any means for any duration of time is sufficient. Stone walls are not required to make a false imprisonment. If a bank robber holds a bank teller at gun point for the purpose of preventing him from attacking the other robbers or from escaping, there is a detention.

(b) Consent and privilege. By definition, no false imprisonment occurs when the person detained consents thereto. For example, when a merchant without any justification detains a person on the suspicion of shoplifting, such detention is not a false imprisonment if the victim consents to it without any protest. If the merchant has reasonable ground for believing that the victim had been guilty of shoplifting, the action of the merchant is not false imprisonment even though the victim is detained under protest and does not consent thereto. Statutes in some states give merchants a privilege to detain persons reasonably suspected of shoplifting. This privilege protects the merchant not only with respect to detention within the store for questioning but also protects the merchant when the shopper is turned over to the police under a formal arrest.

§ 4:11. **FRAUD.** A person is entitled to be protected from fraud and is entitled to recover damages for the harm caused by fraud.

FACTS: Waters advertised that he possessed expertise in tax matters. Relying on such advertising, Midwest Supply had Waters prepare its federal income tax return. Waters assigned the preparation of the return to a new employee who was not qualified, and the tax return was defective. Midwest was required to pay additional taxes and sued Waters for damages. The jury returned a verdict in favor of Midwest for extra damages of $100,000 to punish Waters. Judgment was entered on this verdict and Waters appealed.

DECISION: Judgment affirmed. The defendant had misrepresented to the public that tax returns prepared by it were prepared by experts. The new employee preparing the Midwest returns was not qualified. He was a former construction worker and did not have any special training in tax return preparation. The claim of Waters that expert service was provided his clients was fraudulent. The damages were therefore properly awarded. [Midwest Supply, Inc. v Waters 89 Nev 210, 510 P2d 876]

§ 4:12. DEFAMATION. SLANDER. Reputation is injured by *defamation,* which is a publication tending to cause one to lose the esteem of the community. *Slander* is a form of actionable defamation consisting of the publication or communication to another of false spoken words or gestures. Liability for slander is imposed to provide security of reputation.

   (a) Damages. Whether the plaintiff must actually prove that he was injured by the slander depends upon the nature of the defamatory matter. Words that charge another with the commission of a crime involving moral turpitude and infamous punishment; that impute a disease at the present time that will exclude one from society; or that have a tendency to injure one in his business, profession, or occupation are regarded by the law as *actionable per se* because from common experience it is known that damages occur as a natural sequence of the communication of such words. If defamatory matter is actionable per se, the plaintiff is not required to prove actual damage sustained in consequence of the slander. Otherwise he must do so and, if he cannot prove injury, he is not entitled to recover damages.

   (b) Privilege. Under certain circumstances no liability arises when false statements are published and cause damages. An *absolute privilege* exists in the case of public officers who, in the performance of their duties, should have no fear of possible liability for damages.
   Other circumstances may afford a *qualified* or *conditional privilege.* A communication made in good faith upon a subject in which the party communicating has an interest, or in reference to which he has a right, is privileged if made to a person having a corresponding interest or right, although it contains matter which, without this privilege would be slanderous. Thus, a person, in protecting his interests, may in good faith charge another with the theft of his watch. A mercantile agency's credit report is privileged when made to an interested subscriber in good faith in the regular course of its business. In some states a manager or other person in charge of a store has a qualified privilege; that is, he is not liable in damages for making an accusation of shoplifting if he acted in a reasonable manner in seeking to ascertain the facts. If he did not act in a reasonable manner or acted with malice, he is liable for damages to the person unjustly accused. When a client falsely tells his attorney that a customer owes him money, such statement is not slander even though it is wrong.

   FACTS: The defendant wrote to the county department of health a letter in which she sharply criticized the plaintiff's performance of her duties as a registered nurse employed by the department. The defendant did not make her complaint known in any way to other persons. The nurse sued the defendant for defamation and claimed that the letter was malicious.

   DECISION: As a citizen, the defendant had a right to complain to the government about the official conduct of one of its employees. This gave the defendant a qualified privilege to make statements that would otherwise be defamatory. While such privilege would have been destroyed if the defendant had acted maliciously, there was nothing to show that there was any malice. The fact that the complaint was not spread among other persons but was made only to the nurse's superior indicated that the defendant had acted in good faith and, in the absence of proof to the contrary, was therefore entitled to protection under the privilege. [Nuyen v Slater, 372 Mich 654, 127 NW2d 369]

(c) Malice. It is frequently said that there must be "malice" in order to constitute slander. This is not, however, malice in fact, but merely malice in law, which exists when the speaker is not privileged to make his defamatory statements.

§ 4:13. **DEFAMATION. LIBEL.** Another wrong against the security of business relations takes the form of written defamation. This is known as *libel*. Although usually in writing, it may be in print, picture, or in any other permanent, visual form. For example, to construct a gallows in front of another's residence is libelous.

The elements necessary to maintain an action for libel are the same as for slander. In the case of libel, however, it is not necessary, as a general rule, to allege and prove damages because damages will be presumed. In other words, all forms of libel are actionable per se.

§ 4:14. **DEFAMATION BY COMPUTER.** A person's credit standing or reputation may be damaged because a computer contains erroneous information relating to him. When the computer is part of a data bank system and the erroneous information is supplied to third persons, that could be more than merely annoying and could be damaging. Will the data bank operator or service company be held liable to the person so harmed? There does not appear to be any reported decision on this point, but it is believed that if the operator or the company has exercised reasonable care to prevent errors and to correct errors, there will not be any liability on either the actual programmer-employee operating the equipment or the management providing the computer-service. Conversely, if negligence or an intent to harm is shown, existing principles of law would sustain the liability of the persons involved for what might be given a distinctive name of *defamation by computer*. It might be that liability could be avoided by supplying the person to whom the information relates with a copy of any printout of information which the data bank supplies to third persons, as this would tend to show good faith on the part of the management of the data bank operation and a reasonable effort to keep the information accurate.

Liability for defamation by computer may arise under the federal Fair Credit Reporting Act of 1970 when the person affected is a consumer. The federal Credit Card Act of 1970 further protects from defamation by computer. These acts, which are not limited to situations involving computers, are discussed in Chapter 8 on consumer protection.

§ **4:15. DISPARAGEMENT OF GOODS AND SLANDER OF TITLE.** In the transaction of business one is entitled to be free from interference by means of malicious false claims or statements made by others in respect to the quality or the title of his property. Actual damages must be proved by the plaintiff to have proximately resulted from the false communication by the defendant to a third person. The plaintiff must show that in consequence thereof the third person has refrained from dealing with the plaintiff.

§ **4:16. INFRINGEMENT OF TRADEMARKS.** A *trademark* is a word, name, device, symbol, or any combination of these, used by a manufacturer or seller to distinguish his goods from those of other persons. When the trademark of a particular person is used or substantially copied by another, it is said that the trademark is infringed. The owner of the trademark may sue for damages and enjoin its wrongful use.

§ **4:17. INFRINGEMENT OF PATENTS.** A grant of a *patent* entitles the patentee to prevent others for a period of 17 years from making, using, or selling the particular inventions. Anyone so doing without the patentee's permission is guilty of a patent infringement.

An infringement exists, even though all the parts or features of an invention are not copied, if there is a substantial identity of means, operation, and result between the original and new devices. In the case of a process, however, all successive steps or their equivalent must be copied. In the case of a combination of ingredients, the use of the same ingredients with others constitutes an infringement, except when effecting a compound essentially different in nature.

§ **4:18. INFRINGEMENT OF COPYRIGHTS.** A wrong similar to the infringement of a patent is the infringement of a copyright. A *copyright* is the right given by statute to prevent others for a limited time from printing, copying, or publishing a production resulting from intellectual labor. The right exists for a period of 28 years and can be renewed for another period of 28 years.

Infringement of copyright in general consists of copying the form of expression of ideas or conceptions. There is no copyright in the idea or conception itself, but only in the particular way in which it is expressed. In order to constitute an infringement, the production need not be reproduced entirely nor be exactly the same as the original. Reproduction of a substantial part of the original, although paraphrased or otherwise altered, constitutes an infringement; but appropriation of only a word or single line does not.

One guilty of infringement of copyright is liable to the owner for damages and profits, or only damages, which are to be determined by the court. The owner is also entitled to an injunction to restrain further infringement.

§ 4:19. **UNFAIR COMPETITION.** Unfair competition is unlawful and the person injured thereby may sue for damages or for an injunction to stop the practice, or he may report the matter to a trade commission or other agency.

It is unfair competition to imitate signs, store fronts, advertisements, and packaging of goods of a competitor. Thus, when one adopts a box of distinctive size, shape, and color in which to market candy, and a competitor copies the same style, form, and dress of the package, the latter may be enjoined from so doing and in some cases may be liable for damages.

Every similarity to a competitor, however, is not necessarily unfair competition. For example, the term "downtown" is merely descriptive, so the Downtown Motel cannot obtain an injunction against the use of the name Downtown Motor Inn, because a name that is merely descriptive cannot be exclusively appropriated or adopted. As an exception, if the descriptive word has been used by a given business for such a long time as to be identified with the business in the public mind, a competitor cannot use that name.

The goodwill that is related to a trade name is an important business asset; and there is a judicial trend in favor of protecting a trade name from a competitor's use of a similar name, not only when such use is intentionally deceptive but also when it is merely confusing to the public.

FACTS: Anheuser-Busch holds a trademark registry for the names of Budweiser and Bud as applied to beer which it manufactured and sold under the slogan, "Where there's life . . . there's Bud." It spent millions of dollars advertising with this slogan. Chemical Corporation of American manufactured a combined floor wax and insecticide which it marketed under the slogan of "Where there's life . . . there's bugs." In addition, there was a similarity between the pattern, background, and stage settings of the television commercials employed by both companies. Anheuser-Busch sued for an injunction to prevent the use of such a slogan. The defendant objected on the ground that the parties were not in competing businesses.

DECISION: It was improper practice for the defendant to imitate the advertising of another enterprise and thus get a "free ride" on the advertising image created by the other enterprise at great expense. It was immaterial that the other enterprise was not a direct competitor of the defendant. [Chemical Corp. v Anheuser-Busch (CA5 Fla) 306 F2d 433, cert den 372 US 965]

Historically the law was only concerned with protecting competitors from unfair competition by their rivals. Under consumer protection statutes most states now give protection to the consumer who is harmed by the unfair competitive practices.

§ 4:20. **COMBINATIONS TO DIVERT TRADE.** Business relations may be disturbed by a combination to keep third persons from dealing with another who is the object of attack. Such a combination, resulting in injury, constitutes an actionable wrong known as *conspiracy* if the object is unlawful, or if a lawful object is procured by unlawful means.

If the object of a combination is to further a lawful interest of the association, no actionable wrong exists so long as lawful means are employed. For example, when employees are united in a strike, they may peacefully persuade others to withhold their patronage from the employer. On the other hand, all combinations to drive or keep away customers or prospective employees by violence, force, threats, or intimidation are actionable wrongs. To illustrate, a combination is usually treated as an unlawful conspiracy for which damages may be recovered when the customers are threatened and for this reason withdraw their patronage.

Labor laws prohibit some combinations as unfair labor practices, while other combinations to divert trade are condemned as illegal trusts.

§ 4:21. WRONGFUL INTERFERENCE WITH BUSINESS RELATIONS.
One of the fundamental rights of an individual is to earn his living by selling his labor or by engaging in trade or business. A wrongful interference with this liberty is a tort for which damages may be recovered and which, in some cases, may be restrained by an injunction.

The right to conduct one's business is, nevertheless, subject to the rights of others. Hence, the injuries suffered by one in business through legitimate competition give no right of redress. It has been considered wrongful interference, however, if one destroys the business of another for a malicious purpose, even though legal means are used.

§ 4:22. INTERFERENCE WITH CONTRACT.
The tort law relating to interference with contracts and other economic relationships has increased greatly in recent years as a result of the law's seeking to impose upon the marketplace higher ethical standards to prevent the oppression of victims of improper practices. In general terms, when the defendant interferes with and brings about the breach of contract between a third person and the plaintiff, the circumstances may be such that the plaintiff has an action in tort against the defendant for interfering with his contractual relations. Likewise, the plaintiff may have such a claim for the defendant's interfering with performance by the plaintiff of his contract.

The mere fact that the defendant's voluntary conduct has the effect of interfering with the plaintiff's contract does not establish that the defendant is liable to the plaintiff. For example, when the defendant is acting for what the law regards as his own legitimate economic end, the fact that there results a breach of contract between a third person and the plaintiff does not impose liability on the defendant.

(a) Contracts terminable at will. The fact that a contract is terminable at will does not deprive it of the right to protection from interference.

(b) Prospective contracts. In addition to protecting existing contracts from intentional interference, tort liability is imposed for acts intentionally committed to prevent the making of a contract.

To illustrate, an action may be brought for slander of title when the malicious false statements of the defendant as to the plaintiff's ownership of property scares a buyer away and prevents the plaintiff from making a sale.

(c) Requirement of malice. There is no liability for interference with contractual relations unless such interference is malicious. The term "malicious" is misleading because it may mean either (1) acting with actual malice, that is, the desire to harm for the sheer sake of causing harm, or (2) the infliction of harm only as a matter of competition in order to advance the actor's personal interest.

§ 4:23. **VIOLENCE.** Statutes in many states impose upon counties and cities liability for harm caused by rioting mobs. Some statutes extend only to property damage, but others impose liability for personal injuries or death. The statute may define the term "mob" although ordinarily it does not do so. A police officer who kills or injures someone in the performance of his duties is not a "mob" within the meaning of the statutes here considered. Some statutes are so drafted that liability is imposed only when the mob shows or evidences an intent to punish or exercise "correctional power" over its victim.

The term "property" in a mob violence statute generally applies only to tangible property and does not authorize recovery for loss of profits or goodwill resulting from business interruption. Under a statute or ordinance which refers to liability for property "injured or destroyed," it is generally sufficient to show that the property was stolen or looted, although there is some authority to the contrary. The fact that the government was unable to prevent the harm or damage is no defense to liability under such statutes.

§ 4:24. **TRESPASS TO THE PERSON.** *Trespass to the person* consists of any contact with the victim's person to which he has not consented. It thus includes what is technically described as a battery. It likewise includes an assault in which the victim apprehends the commission of a battery, but he is in fact not touched, and includes false imprisonment. There is liability also for intentionally causing mental stress that results in physical harm to or illness of the victim.

As an aspect of the freedom of the person from unreasonable interference, the law has come to recognize and give constitutional protection to a *right of privacy*. This right is most commonly invaded in one of the following ways: (a) invasion of physical privacy, as by planting a microphone in a person's home; (b) giving unnecessary publicity to personal matters of the plaintiff's life, such as his financial status or his past career; (c) false public association of the plaintiff with some product or principle, such as indicating that he endorses a product or is in favor of a particular law, when such is not the fact; or (d) commercially exploiting the plaintiff's name or picture, as using them in advertising without his permission.

§ 4:25. TRESPASS TO LAND. A *trespass to land* consists of any unpermitted entry below, on, across, or above land. This rule is modified to permit the proper flight of aircraft above the land so long as it does not interfere with a proper use of the land.

§ 4:26. TRESPASS TO PERSONAL PROPERTY. An illegal invasion of property rights with respect to property other than land constitutes a *trespass to personal property* when done negligently or intentionally. When done in good faith and without negligence, there is no liability, in contrast with the case of trespass to land where good faith is not a defense.

Negligent damage to personal property, as in the case of negligent collision of automobiles, imposes liability for harm done. Intentional damage to personal property will impose liability for the damage done and also may justify exemplary or punitive damages.

Conversion occurs when personal property is taken by the wrongdoer and kept from its true owner or prior possessor. Thus a bank clerk commits conversion when he takes money from the bank. Conversion is thus seen to be the civil side of the crimes relating to stealing. The good faith of the converter, however, is not a defense, and an innocent buyer of stolen goods is liable for damages for converting them.

QUESTIONS AND CASE PROBLEMS

1. What is the objective of each of the following rules of law?
   (a) In some areas of law, liability for harm exists without regard to whether there was any negligence or intention to cause harm.
   (b) Geographical and descriptive names cannot ordinarily be adopted as trademarks.

   Note: As you study the various rules of law that follow, consider each rule in relationship to its social, economic, and moral background. Try to determine the particular objective(s) of each important rule. To the extent that you are able to analyze law as the product of man striving for justice in society, you will have a greater insight into the law itself, the world in which you live, the field of business, and the mind of man.

2. Burdett repaired a neon sign on the restaurant of Cinquanta. They disagreed whether Cinquanta or his insurance company should pay for the work. Burdett and some friends went to the restaurant and ordered an expensive meal for which they refused to pay. A heated argument followed in which Burdett stated to Cinquanta. "I don't like doing business with crooks. You're a deadbeat. You've owed me $155 for three or four months. You're crooks." Cinquanta sued Burdett for slander but did not show in what way he had been damaged by these remarks. Burdett claimed that he was not liable for slander in the absence of proof of any damages as his remarks were not slanderous per se. Decide. [Cinquanta v Burdett, 154 Colo 37, 388 P2d 779]

3. The Attorney General of the State of Washington informed the news media that a proceeding had been started by him against a dealer because of alleged violations of the State Consumer Protection Act. The dealer sued the State claiming that this was libelous. Decide. [See Gold Seal Chinchillas, Inc. v Washington, 69 Wash2d 828, 420 P2d 698]

4. Henry Niederman was walking on a center city pavement with his small son. An automobile driven by Brodsky went out of control, ran up on the sidewalk, and struck a fire hydrant, a litter pole and basket, a newstand, and Niederman's son. The car did not touch Niederman, but the shock and fright caused damage to his heart. He sued Brodsky for the harm that he sustained as the result of Brodsky's negligence. Brodsky defended on the ground that he was not liable because he had not touched Niederman. Was this a valid defense? [Niederman v Brodsky, 436 Pa 401, 261 A2d 84]

5. Catalano ran a gasoline service station which was licensed by the State of New York to conduct inspections of motor vehicles. Capital Cities Broadcasting Corporation prepared and televised a "news special" on the subject of the difficulty of obtaining an automobile inspection. It sent an on-the-spot interviewer and photographer to Catalano's station. Catalano, believing that the interviewer was a customer, told her that he could not inspect her automobile because the space in the station was filled with cars being repaired but that, as soon as one of the car stalls was empty, he would take the interviewer's car. This discussion was recorded by the interviewer by means of a concealed tape recorder; but before it was televised, it was edited by eliminating the explanation given by Catalano and thus merely broadcasted his flat refusal to inspect the car. Catalano claimed that this caused him a loss of business and sued Capital for damages. Was it liable? [Catalano v Capital Cities Broadcasting Corp. 313 NYS2d 52]

6. Giles, a guest at a Pick Hotel, wanted to remove his briefcase from the righthand side of the front seat of his auto. To support himself while so doing, he placed his left hand on the center door pillar of the right-hand side of the car. The hotel bellboy closed the rear door of the car without noticing Giles' hand. One of Giles' fingers was smashed by the closing of the door and thereafter had to be amputated. Giles sued the Pick Hotel Corp. Was he entitled to recover? [Giles v Pick Hotels Corp. (CA6 Mich) 232 F2d 887]

7. A statute required that air vent shafts on hotel roofs have parapets at least 30 inches high. Edgar Hotel had parapets only 27 inches high. Nunneley was visiting a registered guest at the Edgar Hotel. She placed a mattress on top of a parapet. When she sat on the mattress, the parapet collapsed and she fell into

the air shaft and was injured. She sued the hotel, claiming that its breach of the statute as to the height of the parapets constituted negligence. Decide [Nunneley v Edgar Hotel, 36 Cal2d 493, 225 P2d 497]

8. Carrigan, a district manager of Simplex Time Recorder Company, was investigating complaints of mismanagement of the Jackson office of the company. He called at the home of Hooks, the secretary of that office. She expressed the opinion that part of the trouble was caused by stealing of parts and equipment by McCall, another employee. McCall was later discharged and sued Hooks for slander. Was she liable? [Hooks v McCall (Miss) 272 So2d 925]

9. Morris insured his automobile with the South Texas Lloyds. He drove it to a local grocery store and parked on the grocery store lot, leaving the keys in the ignition. While he was in the store, Jones drove the car away without permission and wrecked it. Lloyds paid the loss to Morris and then sued Jones to recover the money which it had paid Morris. Jones denied liability on the grounds that (1) a statute prohibited leaving ignition keys in an unattended vehicle parked on a street, and (2) Morris had been negligent in leaving his keys in the car on the parking lot. Were these defenses valid? [South Texas Lloyds v Jones (LaApp) 273 So2d 853]

10. A, B, and C owned land. They did some construction work on their land which prevented the free flow of surface water and caused a flooding of land owned by D. D sued A for the damage caused his land by the flooding. A claimed that D could not hold him liable for any damage since D could not prove how much of the damage had been caused by A and how much by B and C, and that in any event, A could not be liable for more than one third of the total damage sustained by D. Decide. [See Thorson v Minot (ND) 153 NW2d 764]

11. Miller fell in a Woolworth store. The store employees testified that the place where Miller fell had been swept clean shortly before by using a push broom made of an oil-treated cloth. A third person who happened to be in the store, as well as the employees, testified that there was nothing slippery on the floor. Was Miller entitled to recover from Woolworth? [Miller v F. W. Woolworth Co. 238 Ark 709, 384 SW2d 947]

GOVERNMENT REGULATION

§ 5:1. POWER TO REGULATE. The states, by virtue of their police power, may regulate business in all of its aspects so long as they do not impose an unreasonable burden on interstate commerce or any activity of the federal government. The federal government may impose any regulation upon any phase of business that is required by "the economic needs of the nation."

For the most part, there are no significant constitutional limitations on the power of government, state or federal, to regulate business. As long as the regulation applies uniformly to all members within the same class, it is likely that it will be held valid.

§ 5:2. REGULATION OF PRODUCTION, DISTRIBUTION, AND FINANCING. In order to protect the public from harm, government may establish health and purity standards for food, drugs, and cosmetics, and protect consumers from false advertising and labeling. Without regard to the nature of the product, government may regulate business with respect to what materials may be used, the quantity of a product that may be produced or grown, and the price at which the finished product is to be sold. Government may also engage in competition with private enterprises or own and operate an industry.

Under its commerce power the federal government may regulate all methods of interstate transportation and communication, and a like power is exercised by each state over its intrastate traffic. The financing of business is directly affected by the national government in creating a national currency and in maintaining a federal reserve bank system. State and other national laws may also affect financing by regulating the contracts and documents used in financing, such as bills of lading and commercial paper.

§ 5:3. REGULATION OF COMPETITION. The federal government, and the states in varying degrees, prohibit unfair methods of competition. Frequently, a commission is established to determine, subject to review by the courts, whether a given practice comes within the general class of unfair methods of competition. In other instances the statute specifically defines the practice that is condemned.

The Congress has declared "unlawful" all "unfair methods of competition" and has created a Federal Trade Commission to administer the law.

In the current decade a shift of emphasis is taking place in appraising methods of doing business. Instead of harm to competitors being the sole consideration, the effect upon the consumer is being given increasing recognition. Many practices that were condemned earlier only because they would harm a competitor by diverting customers from him are now condemned because such practices prevent the customer from obtaining his money's worth.

The FTC has also condemned the practice of using harassing tactics, such as coercion by refusing to sell, boycotting, discrimination, disparagement of a competitor or his products, enforcing payment wrongfully, cutting off or restricting the market, securing and using confidential information, spying on competitors, and inducing breach of customer contracts. Another form of unfair competition that has been condemned is misrepresentation by appropriating business or corporate names, simulating trade or corporate names, appropriating trademarks, simulating the appearance of a competitor's goods, simulating a competitor's advertising, using deceptive brands or labels, and using false and misleading advertising.

§ 5:4. REGULATION OF PRICES.

Governments, both national and state, may regulate prices. This may be done directly by the lawmaker, that is, the Congress or the state legislature, or it may be delegated to an administrative office or agency.

The federal Clayton Act of 1914, applicable to interstate and foreign commerce, prohibits price discrimination between different buyers of commodities "where the effect of such discrimination may be substantially to lessen competition or tend to create a monopoly in any line of commerce."

FACTS: Moore ran a bakery in Santa Rosa, New Mexico. His business was wholly intrastate. Mead's Fine Bread Co., his competitor, engaged in an interstate business. Mead cut the price of bread in half in Santa Rosa but made no price cut in any other place in New Mexico or any other state. As a result of this price cutting, Moore was driven out of business. Moore then sued Mead for damages for violation of the Clayton and Robinson-Patman Acts. Mead claimed that the price cutting was purely intrastate and therefore did not constitute a violation of the federal statutes.

DECISION: Judgment for Moore. The price cutting was a violation of the federal statutes because the company cutting the price did so as part of its business in interstate commerce. The fact that the victim of such price cutting was an intrastate enterprise was not material. A contrary interpretation of the statutes would permit large interstate enterprises to destroy small local enterprises by local price cutting. [Moore v Mead's Fine Bread Co., 348 US 115]

The federal law prohibits the furnishing of advertising or other services that, when rendered to one purchaser but not another, will have the effect of granting the former a price discrimination or lower rate. It is made illegal for a seller to accept any fee or commission in connection with the sale except for services actually rendered and unless his services are equally available to all on the same terms. The act makes either the giving or the receiving of any illegal price discrimination a criminal offense.

§ 5:5. PREVENTION OF MONOPOLIES AND COMBINATIONS. To
protect the public from monopolies and combinations in restraint of trade, almost all of the states have enacted antitrust statutes.

The federal antitrust act, known as the Sherman Act,[1] is applicable to both sellers and buyers. It provides that [§ 1] "Every contract, combination in the form of a trust or otherwise, or conspiracy, in restraint of trade or commerce among the several states, or with foreign nations, is declared to be illegal. [§ 2] Every person who shall monopolize, or attempt to monopolize, or combine or conspire with any other person or persons to monopolize any part of the trade or commerce among the several states, or with foreign nations, shall be deemed guilty of a misdemeanor."[2]

FACTS: Three California suger refiners agreed among themselves to pay California suger-beet farmers a uniform price for their crops. The refined suger would be sold by the refiners in interstate markets. Mandeville Island Farms, a sugar-beet farmer, sued American Crystal Sugar Co., one of the refiners, for treble damages under the Sherman Act. The defendant claimed that the Act was not applicable because the conduct of the refiners had not taken place in interstate commerce.

DECISION: The combination of refiners was a conspiracy in interstate commerce. While their acts were committed locally, the consequences of those acts would be seen in the prices charged in distant markets in other states. This made their acts "in interstate commerce." [Mandeville Island Farms v American Crystal Sugar Co. 334 US 219]

The punishment fixed for the violation of either of the Sherman Act provisions stated above is a fine not exceeding $50,000, or imprisonment not exceeding one year, or both. In addition to this criminal penalty, the law provides for an injunction to stop the unlawful practices and permits the victim of such practices to sue the wrongdoers and recover from them three times the damages that he has sustained.

(a) **The rule of reason.** The general approach of the Supreme Court of the United States to the trust problem has been that an agreement is not automatically or per se to be condemned as a restraint of interstate commerce merely because it creates a power or a potential to monopolize interstate commerce. It is only when the restraint actually imposed is unreasonable that the practice is unlawful.

---

[1] This Act has been amended by the Clayton Act, the Federal Trade Commission Act, the Shipping Act, and other legislation.
[2] 15 United States Code, Ch. 1, §§ 1 and 2.

Under Section 2 of the Sherman Act one man or corporation may violate the law if he or it monopolizes or attempts to monopolize interstate commerce. To some extent the question of bigness, at least when it results from merger, has been met by Congress by amending Section 7 of the Clayton Act to provide that a merger of corporations doing interstate business shall be illegal when the effect of the acquisition by one corporation of all or any part of the assets of the other "may be substantially to lessen competition, or to tend to create a monopoly."[3]

(b) Price-fixing. *Horizontal price-fixing*, that is, agreements between persons performing similar economic functions, such as agreements between manufacturers or between distributors, is illegal under the federal law without regard to whether the price so fixed is reasonable or fair. *Vertical resale price agreements*, that is, agreements made between a manufacturer and his distributor or distributors, a distributor and his dealer or dealers, and so on, are generally valid.[4]

Price-fixing agreements otherwise invalid are not made valid by the fact that they may have been intended to protect, or that they do have the effect of protecting, consumers. Thus, the federal antitrust law is violated by an agreement of manufacturers that they will not raise the price above a specified maximum, and also by an agreement made by a hospital subscription plan and druggists that the latter would sell drugs to participating hospitals at fixed prices.

(c) Stock and director control. The federal Clayton Act prohibits the purchase by a corporation of the stock of another corporation engaged in interstate or foreign commerce when the effect is to lessen competition substantially, or when it restrains commerce or tends to create a monopoly.

FACTS: From 1917 to 1919, Du Pont acquired a 23 percent stock interest in General Motors. During the following years, General Motors brought substantial quantities of automotive finishes and fabrics from Du Pont. In 1949, the United States claimed the effect of the stock acquisition had been to lessen competition in interstate commerce on the theory that the sales to General Motors had not been the result of successful competition but were the result of the stock ownership, and therefore such stock ownership violated the Clayton Act. The United States brought an action against Du Pont, General Motors, and others.

DECISION: The ownership of the General Motors stock by the Du Pont company was a violation of the Clayton Act since such stock ownership tended to lessen competition by making it less likely that General Motors would purchase its supplies from an outside supplier. It was immaterial that no unfair advantage had been taken of this power by supplying inferior products. [United States v E. I. du Pont de Nemours & Company, 353 US 586]

---

[3] 15 USC § 18.

[4] The validity of the contract is distinct from the question of whether third persons are bound thereby. State courts disagree as to whether nonsigners are bound by such contracts.

The Clayton Act does not prohibit the holding of stock in competing corporations by the same person. Although it prohibits the director of one corporation from being a director of another competing corporation engaged in commerce if either corporation has assets in excess of $1 million, this prohibition is not effective in checking the monopoly potential of interlocking private shareholding.

(d) Tie-in sales and exclusive dealer agreements. The federal Clayton Act of 1914, applicable to interstate and foreign commerce, prohibits the *tie-in sale* or *tie-in lease* by which the person buying or renting goods agrees that with such goods he will only use other material sold or leased by the other party. The Act also prohibits *exclusive dealer agreements* by which a dealer agrees not to handle a competitor's articles. These tie-in and exclusive dealer arrangements are not absolutely prohibited, but only when their effect "may be substantially to lessen competition or tend to create a monopoly in any line of commerce." By virtue of this qualification, a provision that a person leasing machinery shall use only the materials furnished by the lessor is a lawful restriction if the nature of the materials and the machine are such that the machine will not operate properly with the materials produced or offered by any other person. When the materials furnished by any other competitor would be equally satisfactory, however, the agreement is illegal. Thus, an agreement that the lessee of office machinery should use only the paper sold by the lessor for that type of office machine was illegal when it was shown that any other seller could supply paper of suitable quality.

The restriction on the tie-in and exclusive dealer agreements is limited by the right of a seller to state the terms on which he will deal in bona fide transactions not in restraint of trade. There has also been a judicial trend to approve such agreements when the seller does not hold a dominant position in the market.

(e) Refusal to deal. A combination of manufacturers, distributors, and retailers, acting in concert to deprive a single merchant of goods which he needs to compete effectively, is a group boycott in violation of the Sherman Antitrust Act.

(f) Exceptions to the antitrust law. By statute or decision, associations of exporters, marine insurance associations, farmers' and dairymen's cooperatives, and labor unions are exempt from the Sherman Antitrust Act with respect to agreements between their members. Under certain circumstances a minimum resale price maintenance agreement is also exempt. Congress has also authorized freight pooling and revenue division agreements between railroad carriers, provided the approval of the Interstate Commerce Commission (ICC) is obtained.

Price discrimination is expressly permitted when it can be justified on the basis of: (1) difference in grade, quality, or quantity involved; (2) the cost of the transportation involved in making the sale; or (3) when the sale is made at the lower price in good faith in order to meet competition.

The Robinson-Patman Act of 1936 permits price differentials based on differences in methods or quantities. Price differentials are also permitted because of the deterioration of goods or when the seller in good faith is making a close-out sale of a particular line of goods. The Robinson-Patman Act reaffirms the right of a seller to select his customers and to refuse to deal with anyone he chooses so long as he acts in good faith and not for the purpose of restraining trade.

By virtue of statutory exemptions, traffic and trust agreements otherwise prohibited by the antitrust law may be made by ocean carriers, and interstate carriers and telegraph companies may consolidate upon obtaining the approval of the government commission having jurisdiction over them. The Newspaper Preservation Act of 1970 grants an antitrust exemption to operating agreements entered into by newspapers to prevent financial collapse.

§ 5:6. REGULATION OF EMPLOYMENT. Basically the parties are free to make an employment contract on any terms they wish, but by statute employment is subject to certain limitations. Thus, persons under a certain age cannot be employed at certain kinds of labor. Statutes commonly specify minimum wages and maximum hours which the employer must observe. A state may also require employers to pay employees' wages for the time that they are away from work for the purpose of voting.

(a) Fair Labor Standards Act. By this statute, which is popularly known as the Wage and Hour Act, Congress provides that, subject to certain exceptions, persons working in interstate commerce or in an industry producing goods for interstate commerce must be paid not less than $2.10 an hour; and they cannot be employed for more than 40 hours a week unless they are paid time and a half for overtime. The Act prohibits the employment of children under the age of 14 years. It permits the employment of children between the ages of 14 and 16 years in all industries, except mining and manufacturing, under certain prescribed conditions. This Act has been followed by a number of states in regulating those phases of industry not within the reach of the federal statute.

(b) Hours of Service Act. Congress provides in this Act that an employee engaged in moving trains must be given a specified number of off hours after having worked a specified number of hours. For every 14-hour tour of continuous duty, he must be given 12 consecutive off hours. Employees whose duties are to receive and transmit orders by telephone or telegraph for moving trains can be employed up to 12 hours in any 24 when one work shift is employed. If there are two shifts, the maximum is 9 hours. In case of an emergency, the work hours may be extended.

(c) Public Contracts Act. Whenever a contract to manufacture or furnish materials, supplies, and equipment for the United States exceeds $10,000 in amount, the Walsh-Healey Act requires that the contract specify that the contractor shall pay minimum wages and overtime pay, shall not employ child labor, and shall observe standards set by the Act or by the Secretary of Labor of the United States.

(d) Public Works Contracts Act. When a building is constructed or repaired for the United States for more than $2,000, the Davis-Bacon Act requires that the contractor agree to pay his laborers and mechanics not less than the prevailing rate of wages as determined by the Department of Labor. It is made a federal crime for an employer, or an employee with power to hire and fire, to require any employee on public works construction to return or "kickback" to him any part of the employee's wages.

(e) Fair Employment Practices Acts. With some exceptions, employers of 15 or more persons are forbidden to discriminate as to compensation and other privileges, and conditions of employment against any person because of race, religious creed, color, sex, or national origin, or because of age.[5]

FACTS: Griggs and other Negro workers were employed in the labor department of Duke Power Co. They sought promotion to higher paying departments of their employer but could not obtain promotion because the employer had established promotion standards of (1) high school education, and (2) satisfactory scores on two professionally prepared aptitude tests. The tests were not designed to measure ability to perform the work in the particular department to which they sought promotion. Griggs and other employees brought a class action under Title VII of the federal Civil Rights Act of 1964, claiming the promotion criteria discriminated against them because of race. The Court of Appeals held that there was no prohibited discrimination even though white workers apparently obtained better scores in the tests because of having obtained a better public school education. Griggs appealed to the Supreme Court.

DECISION: The tests were in violation of the federal law because they did not test for a skill or ability related to the desired work and had the effect of freezing the Negro worker in the labor department. [Griggs v Duke Power Co. 401 US 424]

The federal law does not require that every employee be treated the same as every other. It does not prohibit the testing or screening of applicants or employees for the purpose of determining whether a person is qualified to be hired, or promoted, or given a wage increase, or given special training. The Civil Rights Act has no effect upon the employer's right to establish compensation scales, providing for bonus pay and incentive pay, or paying different rates in different geographic areas. The employer may also recognize seniority status, whether voluntarily or as part of a collective bargaining agreement.

An employer cannot discriminate on the basis of sex. An employer may not hire on the basis of a stereotype pattern of what is woman's work and what is man's work. Women, therefore, cannot be excluded from working as bartenders and men cannot be excluded from working as airline cabin attendants. Indirect discrimination against sex is also prohibited, as when

---

[5] Federal Civil Rights Act of 1964, Title VII, as amended by the Equal Employment Opportunities Act of 1972. In some states and cities, statutes and ordinances make similar provision. The Federal Anti-Age Discrimination Act prohibits such discrimination only as to persons between 40 and 65 years of age.

the employer establishes height and weight specifications for job applicants but such requirements have no bearing on the performance of the work and their effect is to exclude women from the job.

The equality of the sexes is literally applied so that a law is unconstitutional when it gives to women a protection or an advantage which it does not give to men performing the same work. Likewise, it is a discriminatory labor practice to allow women overtime pay which is denied men, to allow women seniority rights which are not available to men on the same terms, to prohibit women from working at jobs which involve the lifting of heavy weights, and to prohibit long hair for male employees without imposing the same restriction on female employees. A standardized "compulsory pregnancy leave" regulation for public school teachers is unconstitutional because no consideration is given the fitness of the individual teacher to continue teaching and there is no proof that pregnant teachers as a class are necessarily and universally unfit to teach.[6]

> **FACTS:** Ohio statutes required employers to furnish seats and lunchroom facilities for female employees, limited the hours that women could be employed, and prohibited the employment of women in certain specified occupations or at work requiring the frequent or repeated lifting of weights over 25 pounds. The statutes were challenged as invalid on the ground that they violated the federal Civil Rights Act of 1964 because they did not treat male and female employees alike.

> **DECISION:** The statutes were unconstitutional. The concept of equal rights prevents a legislature from treating female employees differently than male employees in the absence of actual proof that there is a factual basis for the classification distinct from discriminating only because the employees were female. [Jones Metal Products Co. v Walker, 29 Ohio 173, 281 NE2d 1, reversing 25 OhioApp2d 141, 267 NE2d 814]

The federal Civil Rights Act expressly declares that an employer is not required to readjust the "balance" of his payroll in order to include any particular percentage of each race, creed, and sex as his employees. When he hires new employees, the only obligation upon him is to refrain from discriminating as to each applicant.

§ 5:7. **LABOR REPRESENTATION.** Statutes generally declare the right of employees to form unions and require employers to deal with the union as the bargaining representative of their employees.

(a) Machinery to enforce collective bargaining. To protect the rights of workers to unionize and bargain collectively, the federal government created the National Labor Relations Board (NLRB). The NLRB determines the proper collective bargaining unit and eliminates unfair practices by which the employer and the unions might interfere with employees' rights.

(b) Selection of bargaining representative. Generally there is an election by secret ballot to select the bargaining representative of the employees within a particular collective bargaining unit.

---

[6] Cleveland Board of Education v La Fleur, 414 US 632.

(c) Equal representation of all employees. Any union selected by the majority of the workers within the unit is the exclusive representative of all the employees in the unit for the purpose of bargaining with respect to wages, hours of employment, or other conditions of employment. Whether or not all the workers are members of the representative union is immaterial for, in any case, this union is the exclusive representative of every employee. It is unlawful for an employee, either a member or a nonmember of the union, to attempt to make a contract directly with the employer. Except as to grievances, every worker must act through the representative union with respect to his contract of employment. At the same time the union is required to represent all workers fairly, nonmembers as well as members. It is unlawful for the union, in bargaining with the employer, to discriminate in any way against any of the employees. The union cannot use its position as representative of all workers to further its interests as a union.

§ 5:8. **UNFAIR LABOR PRACTICES.** The labor laws prohibit certain practices as unfair and authorize an agency, such as the NLRB, to conduct proceedings to stop such practices.

(a) Unfair employer practices. The federal law declares that it is an unfair labor practice for an employer to interfere with unionization, to discriminate against any employee because of his union activities, or to refuse to bargain collectively.

(b) Unfair union practices. The federal law declares it to be an unfair labor practice for a union to interfere with employees in forming their unions or in refraining from joining a union; to cause an employer to discriminate against an employee because he belongs to another union or no union; to refuse to bargain collectively; and under certain circumstances to stop work or refuse to work on materials or to persuade others to stop work.

(c) Procedure for enforcement. Under the National Labor Relations Act, the NLRB issues a complaint whenever it is claimed that an unfair labor practice has been committed. The complaint informs the party of the charges made against him and notifies him to appear at a hearing. At the hearing the General Counsel of the board acts as a combination of prosecuting attorney and referee, charged with the duty of presenting the case on behalf of the complainant and of seeing that the hearing is properly conducted. After the hearing, the board makes findings of fact and conclusions of law and either dismisses the complaint or enters an order against the party to stop the unfair labor practices "and to take such affirmative action including reinstatement of employees with or without back pay, as will effectuate the policy of the Act. . . ."

§ 5:9. **UNION ORGANIZATION AND MANAGEMENT.** In order to insure the honest and democratic administration of unions, Congress adopted the Labor-Management Reporting and Disclosure Act of 1959 to regulate unions operating in or affecting interstate commerce.

The Act protects the rights of union members within their unions by guaranteeing equality, the right to vote on specified matters, and the right to information on union matters and contracts. It also protects members from interference with the enjoyment of these rights.

§ **5:10. SOCIAL SECURITY.** The federal Social Security Act establishes a single federal program of aid to the needy aged, the blind, and the disabled. This is called the Supplemental Security Income Program (SSI). Payments are administered directly by the Department of Health, Education, and Welfare.[7]

The states also have plans of assistance for the unemployed, aged, and disabled. The federal law encourages the making of payments under state programs in addition to those received under the federal program. Such additional programs are called State Supplemental Payments (SSP). State plans typically establish an administrative board or agency with which claims for assistance are filed by persons coming within the category to be benefited by the statute. If the board approves a claim, assistance is given to the applicant in the amount specified by the statute for the number of weeks or other period of time designated by the statute.

Federal law allows a state which elects to supplement the SSI payments with an SSP program to choose whether it will retain control over the administration of such supplements or delegate that responsibility to HEW.

Unemployment compensation laws generally deny the payment of benefits when the employee was discharged for good cause, when he abandoned work without cause, failed or refused to seek or accept an offer of suitable employment, or when the unemployment was the result of a labor dispute.

QUESTIONS AND CASE PROBLEMS

1. What is the objective of each of the following rules of law?
    (a) Horizontal price-fixing is illegal under the federal law without regard to whether the price fixed is fair and reasonable.
    (b) Farmers' and dairymen's cooperatives are exempt by statute from the operation of the Sherman Antitrust Act.
2. The Delco Cleaners and Dyers did business in Delaware County. The name Delco was a contraction of the name of the county. A suit was brought to enjoin the use of the name "Delco" by another local concern calling itself the "Delco Valet Service." Decide. [Berberian v Ferm, 166 PaSuper 108, 70 A2d 394]

---

[7] California League of Senior Citizens, Inc. v Brian, 35 CalApp3d 443, 110 CalRptr 809. This system of centralized and unified federal administration replaces the prior Social Security system under which the federal government made grants to states which administered aid under four different programs.

3. The Winsted Hosiery Co. labeled mixed woolen articles as "natural wool," "Australian wool," and other similar terms that did not indicate the mixed nature of the article. The Federal Trade Commission ordered the company to stop the practice of using a "wool" label to describe a mixed article, on the ground that it was an unfair trade practice. The company defended on the ground that all other manufacturers understood that the label was not to be taken as true and that the competitors of the company were not deceived. Was this a valid defense? [Federal Trade Commission v Winsted Hosiery Company, 258 US 483]

4. A manufacturer, The White Motor Co., gave each of its dealers an exclusive right to sell its product within a specified territory. The United States claimed that this was an illegal restraint of trade. White replied that the division of territory between its dealers was a marketing necessity because each dealer had to be protected within his territory against the competition of the other White dealers so that he would be free to concentrate on competing with the dealers of other companies. Was the White dealership plan a restraint of trade? [The White Motor Co. v United States, 372 US 253]

5. The El Paso Natural Gas Company acquired the stock and assets of the Pacific Northwest Pipe Line Company. El Paso, although not a California enterprise, supplied over half of the natural gas used in California; all the other natural gas was supplied by California sources. No gas was sold in California by Pacific Northwest, although it was a strong experienced company within the Northwest area and had attempted several times to enter the California market. United States claimed that the acquisition of Pacific by El Paso constituted a violation of § 7 of the Clayton Act, as amended, because the effect would be to remove competition between the two companies within California. The defense was raised that (a) California was not a "section" of the country within the Clayton Act, and (b) the sale of natural gas was not a line of commerce, and (c) the acquisition did not lessen competition when there had not been any prior sales by Pacific within the area. Decide. [United States v El Paso Natural Gas Co. 376 US 651]

6. Kinney Shoe Company and the Brown Shoe Company proposed to merge by giving the Kinney shareholders shares of the Brown Shoe Company stock in exchange for their shares. By dollar value, Brown was the third largest seller of shoes in the United States and fourth largest manufacturer. Kinney was the eighth largest seller and owned and operated the largest independent chain of family shoe stores in the nation. It was claimed that the merger would not lessen competition as Kinney manufactured less than ½ percent of shoes in the United States and Brown produced about 4 percent. Decide. [Brown Shoe Company v United States, 370 US 294]

7. The Nevada Fair Trade Act validated contracts to maintain minimum resale prices and declared that other persons "whether [or] not a party to such contract" were bound thereby. The Bulova Watch Company brought an action against Zale-Las Vegas, Inc., a jewelry store, for selling below the price established by a fair trade agreement between Bulova and the Ginsburg Jewelry Company. Zale-Las Vegas defended on the ground that it was not a party to that contract and that the statute binding it by that contract was unconstitutional. Decide. [Zale-Las Vegas, Inc. v Bulova Watch Co. 80 Nev 483, 396 P2d 683]

8. Sun Oil sells gasoline retail in its own gas stations, as well as selling gas to independently owned gas stations. In selling to one independent, it gave that independent a price cut to enable it to meet the competition of other independent gas stations. The Federal Trade Commission claimed this was an unlawful price discrimination. Sun Oil defended on the ground that the price cut was made as authorized by the statute "in good faith to meet an equally low price of a competitor." Was this defense valid? [Federal Trade Commission v Sun Oil Co. 371 US 505]

9. A New Jersey statute provides that no rebates, allowances, concessions, or benefits shall be given, directly or indirectly, so as to permit any person to obtain motor fuel from a retail dealer below the posted price or at a net price lower than the posted price applicable at the time of the sale. An action was brought by Fried, a retail gasoline dealer, to prevent the enforcement of the statute. He claimed that it was invalid because it was discriminatory in that it related only to the sale of gasoline and that it denied due process by regulating the price. Was the law constitutional? [Fried v Kervick, 34 NJ 68, 167 A2d 380]

10. A Nevada statute required that at all gas stations a sign should be displayed on each pump setting forth the price of the gasoline and certain other information as to taxes and brand. The sign was to be not less than 7 inches high and 8 inches wide nor larger than 12 inches by 12 inches. The statute prohibited any other signs showing prices on the premises. The Redman Petroleum Corporation maintained proper signs on its pumps but also had large signs near the side of the road. There was no claim that any fraud or price-cutting was involved. The signs by the road stated information that conformed to the information of the signs on the pumps. Redman claimed that a substantial sum of money had been invested in these signs by the side of the road and that they had been used for over ten years. Redman claimed that the statute was unconstitutional. Was Redman correct? [Nevada v Redman Petroleum Corp. 77 Nev 163, 360 P2d 842]

11. Collier sued Roth for damages for violating a state Unfair Milk Sales Practices Act. He claimed that he was entitled to recover treble damages. The statute declared that "Any person who is injured in business or property by reason of another person's violation of any provision [of the statute] may intervene in the suit for injunction . . . against the other person or he may bring a separate action and recover three times the actual damages sustained as a result of the violation, together with the cost of the suit, or he may sue to enjoin the violation. . . ." Was he entitled to treble damages? [Collier v Roth (MoApp) 468 SW2d 57]

ADMINISTRATIVE AGENCIES

§ 6:1. UNIQUENESS OF ADMINISTRATIVE AGENCIES. The structure of government common in the states and the national government is a division into three branches—executive, legislative, and judicial—with the lawmaker selected by popular vote and with the judicial branch acting as the superguardian to prevent either the executive or the legislative branch from exceeding the proper spheres of their respective powers. In contrast, members of administrative agencies are ordinarily appointed (in the case of federal agencies, by the President of the United States with the consent of two thirds of Congress), and the major agencies combine legislative, executive, and judicial powers in that they make the rules, police the community to see that the rules are obeyed, and sit in judgment to determine whether there have been violations of their rules.

Although an appeal to the courts may be taken from the action of an administrative agency, the agency is for practical purposes not subject to control by the courts. The subject matter involved is ordinarily so technical and the agency is clothed with such discretion that courts will not reverse agency action unless it can be disapproved as arbitrary and capricious. Very few agency decisions are reversed on this ground. Administrative action is not held to be arbitrary or capricious merely because the judge would have decided the matter otherwise, because the administrative action is new or strange to the law, or because the administrative action causes someone to lose money.

§ 6:2. THE ADMINISTRATOR'S POWERS

(a) Legislative powers. The modern administrator has the power to make the laws that regulate the segment of life or industry entrusted to his care.

FACTS: The Congress made it a federal crime to transport fish in interstate commerce from a state if such transportation was "contrary to the law of the state." Howard transported fish from Florida. No Florida statute made it unlawful, but such transportation violated a rule of the Florida Game and Fresh Water Fish Commission. Howard was convicted for violating the federal statute. She claimed that she had not violated the statute because no Florida "law" prohibited such transportation.

DECISION: The reference in the federal statute to state "law" was not limited to such laws as had been adopted by the state legislatures. The order of a state administrative agency is the law of the state. Howard had violated the Florida law and therefore came within the federal statute. [United States v Howard, 352 US 212]

There once was a great reluctance to accept the fact that the administrator made law, because of our constitutional doctrine that only the lawmaker, the Congress or the state legislature, can make laws. It therefore seemed an improper transfer or delegation of power for the lawmaker to set up a separate body or agency and give to it the power to make the laws.

The same forces that led society initially to create the administrator caused society to clothe the administrator with the power to make the laws. Practical expediency gradually prevailed in favor of the conclusion that if we want the administrator to do a job, we must grant the power sufficiently extensive to do so; and we must take the practical approach and ignore the theoretical objection that when we authorize an administrator to do the job, we are in fact telling him to make the law which governs the area that he regulates.

In the early days of administrative regulation, the legislative character of the administrative rules was not clearly perceived, largely because the administrator's sphere of power was so narrow that he was, in effect, merely a thermostat. That is, the lawmaker told him when to do what, and all that the administrator did was to act in the manner in which he had been programmed. For example, the cattle inspector was told to take certain steps when he determined that the cattle had hoof-and-mouth disease. Here it was clear that the lawmaker had set the standard, and the administrator merely "swung into action" when the specified fact situation existed.

The next step in the growth of the administrative power was to authorize the cattle inspector to act when he found that cattle had a contagious disease, leaving it to him to formulate a rule or guide as to what diseases were contagious. Here again, the discretionary and legislative aspect of the administrator's conduct was obscured by the belief that the field of science would define "contagious," leaving no area of discretionary decision to the administrator.

Today's health commission will be authorized to make such rules and regulations for the protection or improvement of the common health as it deems desirable. In this respect, it is making the "health law" by its rules. In regulating various economic aspects of national life, the administrator is truly the lawmaker.

Gradually, the courts have come to recognize, or at least to tolerate, the entrusting of a certain job to an agency without doing more than stating to the agency the policy that the administrator should seek to advance, or the goal or objective that he should seek to attain.

FACTS: The practice developed for owners of trucks who drove their loaded trucks from one point to another to hire themselves and their trucks out to a common carrier so that the return trip would not be made with empty trucks. The Interstate Commerce Commission concluded that these one-trip rentals made it possible for the carriers to operate in part without satisfying the requirements otherwise applicable to them. In order to stop this, the Commission adopted a set of rules which provided that trucks could not be rented by a carrier for less than 30 days. A number of suits were brought to prevent the enforcement of these rules on the ground that they were not authorized by the Interstate Commerce Act and their enforcement would cause financial loss and hardship.

DECISION: The one-trip rental regulations were authorized. The fact that Congress had not expressly authorized the Commission to adopt such regulations did not mean that the Commission did not have the power to do so. The Commission had the responsibility of making regulations to promote the transportation system of the country, and, if it deemed that the one-trip rental regulation was desirable to achieve this goal, the Commission could impose such regulation. As the Commission had the power to act, it was immaterial what the economic consequences would be. These would not be considered by the court as the court did not have the responsibility or power to consider the economic wisdom or effect of administrative regulations. [American Trucking Associations v United States, 344 US 298]

Thus, it has been sufficient for a legislature to authorize an administrator to grant licenses "as public interest, convenience, or necessity requires;" "to prohibit unfair methods of competition;" to regulate prices so that they "in [the administrator's] judgment will be generally fair and equitable;" to prevent "profiteering;" "to prevent the existence of intercorporate holdings, which unduly or unnecessarily complicate the structure [or] unfairly or inequitably distribute voting power among security holders;" and to renegotiate government contracts to prevent "excessive profits."

The authority of an administrator is not limited to the technology existing when the administrator was created. To the contrary, the sphere in which the administrator may act expands with new scientific developments. So it has been held that although community cable television (CATV) was developed after the Federal Communication Commission was created by the Federal Communications Act of 1934, the Commission can regulate CATV. This power to regulate includes both the mechanical aspects of broadcasting and reception and also the content of the broadcast. Thus the commission may require such systems to originate local programs (cablecasting) in order to serve the local communities, in addition to their activity of transmitting programs from a distance.[1]

---

[1] United States v Midwest Video Corp. 406 US 649 (sustaining a Commission regulation which provided that "no CATV system having 3,500 or more subscribers shall carry the signal of any television broadcast station unless the system also operates to a significant extent as a local outlet by cablecasting and has available facilities for local production and presentation of programs other than automated services.").

(b) Executive powers. The modern administrator has executive power to investigate and to require persons to appear as witnesses, and to produce papers for any reason coming within his sphere of operation. Thus, the administrator may investigate in order to police the area subject to his control to see if there is any violation of the law or of its rules generally, to determine whether there is a need for the adoption of additional rules, to ascertain the facts with respect to a particular suspected or alleged violation, and to determine whether its decisions are being obeyed.

The Federal Antitrust Civil Process Act of 1962 is an outstanding example of the extent to which administrative investigation is authorized. The Act provides that upon written demand to a corporation, association, or partnership, the production of documents can be compelled to provide the Department of Justice with information to determine whether there is sufficient ground to bring a civil antitrust suit against the enterprise so directed. Similar power to require the production of papers is possessed by the Federal Trade Commission, the Federal Maritime Commission, the National Science Foundation, the Treasury Department, the Department of Agriculture, the Department of the Army, the Department of Labor, and the Veterans Administration.

The power to investigate is a continuing power, with the result that the administrative agency can, in effect, put the party on probation and require periodic reports to show whether the party has complied with the law.[2]

(c) Judicial powers. The modern administrator may be given power to sit as a court and to determine whether there have been any violations of the law or of its regulations. Thus, the National Labor Relations Board determines whether there has been a prohibited unfair labor practice, the Federal Trade Commission will act as a court to determine whether there is unfair competition, and so on.

When the administrator sits as a judge as to the violation of a regulation that it has made, there is also the element that the "judge" is not impartial because it is trying the accused for violating "its" law rather than "the" law. There is also the objection that the administrator is determining important rights but does so without a jury, which seems inconsistent with the long-established emphasis of our history upon the sanctity of trial by jury. In spite of these objections to the administrator's exercise of judicial power, such exercise is now firmly established.

Accepting as a fact that the administrator can make judicial determinations, the question arises as to whether he must proceed exactly as a court, following all of the procedure of a court.

Cutting across these procedures are the practical devices of informal settlement and consent decrees. In many instances, the alleged wrongdoer will be willing to change his practices or his conduct upon being informally notified that a complaint has been made against him. It is therefore sound public relations, as well as expeditious handling of the matter, for the administrator to inform the alleged wrongdoer of the charge made against

---

[2] United States v Morton Salt Co. 338 US 632.

him prior to the filing of any formal complaint in order to give him the opportunity to settle the matter voluntarily. A matter that has already gone into the formal hearing stage may also be terminated by agreement, and a stipulation or consent degree may be filed setting forth the terms of the agreement.

A further modification of this general pattern is made in the case of the Interstate Commerce Commission. Complaints received by the Commission are referred to the Bureau of Informal Cases, which endeavors to secure an amicable adjustment with the carrier. If this cannot be done, the complainant is notified that it will be necessary to file a formal complaint. At this stage of the proceedings, the parties can expedite the matter by agreeing that the case may be heard on the pleadings alone. In this case, the complainant files a pleading or memorandum to which the defendant files an answering memorandum, the plaintiff then filing a reply or rebuttal memorandum. If the parties do not agree to this procedure, a hearing is held after the pleadings have been filed.

§ 6:3. PATTERN OF ADMINISTRATIVE PROCEDURE. At the beginning of the era of modern regulation of business, the administrator was, to a large extent, a minor executive or police officer charged with the responsibility of enforcing the laws applicable to limited fact situations. The health officer empowered to condemn and destroy diseased cattle was typical. In view of the need for prompt action and because of the relative simplicity of the fact determination to be made, it was customary for him to exercise summary powers; that is, upon finding cattle which he believed diseased, he would have them killed immediately without delaying to find their true owner or without holding a formal hearing to determine whether they were in fact diseased.

Today, the exercise of summary powers is the exceptional case. Now it is permitted mainly in connection with the fraudulent use of the mails or the sending of such improper matter as lottery tickets or obscene matter through the mails, the enforcement of navigation regulations and tax laws, and the exercise of the police power in order to protect the public health and safety. As the regulation of business assumes the aspect of economic rather than health or safety regulation, the need for immediate action by the administrator diminishes, if not disappears, when the administrator acts to determine whether particular conduct comes within the scope of a regulation or whether there has been a violation thereof. Accordingly, concepts of due process generally require that some notice be given those who will be adversely affected and that some form of hearing be held at which they may present their case. As a practical matter, also, the more complicated the nature of the determinations to be made, the longer the period of investigation and deliberation required.

(a) **Preliminary steps.** It is commonly provided that either a private individual aggrieved by the conduct of another or the administrator on his own motion may present a complaint. This complaint is served on the alleged wrongdoer, and he is given opportunity to file an answer. There may be other phases of pleading between the parties and the administrator, but eventually the matter comes before the administrator to be heard. After a hearing, the administrator makes a decision and enters an order either dismissing the complaint or directing the adverse party to do or not to do certain acts. This order is generally not self-executing and, in order to enforce it, provision is generally made for an application by the administrator to a court. Sometimes the converse is provided, so that the order of the administrator becomes binding upon the adverse party unless he appeals to a court within a stated period for a review of the order.

The complaint filing and prehearing stage of the procedure may be more detailed. In many of the modern administrative statutes, provision is made for an examination of the informal complaint by some branch of the administrator to determine whether it presents a case coming within the scope of the administrator's authority. It is also commonly provided that an investigation be made by the administrator to determine whether the facts are such to warrant a hearing of the complaint. If it is decided that the complaint is within the jurisdiction of the administrator and that the facts appear to justify it, a formal complaint is issued and served on the adverse party, and an answer is filed by him as above stated.

With the rising complexity of the subjects regulated by administrative agencies, the trend is increasingly in the direction of greater preliminary examination upon the basis of an informal complaint.

(b) The administrative hearing. In order to satisfy the requirements of due process, it is generally necessary for the administrator to give notice and to hold a hearing. A significant difference between the administrator's hearing and a court hearing is that there is no right of trial by jury before an administrator. For example, a workmen's compensation board may pass on a claim without any jury. The absence of a jury does not constitute a denial of due process. The theory is that a new right unknown to the common law has been created, and the right to a jury trial exists only where it was recognized at the common law.

The law could have taken the position that whenever a person is brought before any tribunal, he is entitled to have the facts determined by a jury. But the law "froze" the right to trial by jury as it existed in pre-Revolutionary days. Consequently, if there was no right of jury trial in 1775, there is no right of trial by jury today. Since the wide array of government regulation of business today was unknown in 1775, we have the consequence that a great area of twentieth century economic life is determined without a jury. If I wish to sue you for $100, you would be entitled to a trial by jury; but if I am complaining before an administrator you are not entitled to a jury trial, even though his determination or regulation may cost you a million dollars. The inconsistency in the net result in these two situations is not regarded as legally important.

Another significant difference between an administrative hearing and a judicial hearing is that the administrator may be authorized to make a determination first and then hold a hearing afterwards to verify his result, as contrasted with a court which must have the trial before it makes a judgment. This has important practical consequences in that when the objecting party seeks a hearing after the administrator has acted, he has the burden of proof and the cost of going forward. In consequence of this, the result is that fewer persons go to the trouble of seeking such a hearing. This, in turn, reduces the amount of hearing and litigation in which the administrator becomes involved, with the resultant economy of money and personnel from the government's standpoint.

In some instances the administrator may even establish standards that have the effect of barring a hearing unless there is compliance with such standards. This is an illustration both of the "lawmaking" power, that is, determining who shall be entitled to a hearing, as well as the extent to which a person is entitled to a "court-form" hearing.

When it is sought to obtain an exception from an administrative regulation, the moving party has the burden of proof.

(c) Constitutional limitations on investigation. For the most part the constitutional guarantee against unreasonable search and seizure does not afford much protection against the investigation of an administrator, since that guarantee does not apply in the absence of an actual seizure. That is, a subpoena to testify or to produce records cannot be opposed on the ground that it is a search and seizure, as the constitutional protection is limited to cases of actual search and seizure rather than the obtaining of information by compulsion.

The protection afforded by the guarantee against self-incrimination is likewise narrow, for it cannot be invoked (1) as to records which by law must be kept by the person subject to investigation; (2) as to corporate records even though the officer or employee of the corporation in producing them may be producing evidence that would incriminate him; and (3) the protection of the Constitution may be denied when a sufficient immunity from future prosecution is given to the person who is compelled to present evidence that incriminates him.

FACTS: Shapiro was a wholesaler of fruit and produce. The Price Administrator acting under the federal Emergency Price Control Act subpoenaed him to produce his business records. Under protest of constitutional privilege, he furnished the records. He was later prosecuted for making illegal tie-in sales contrary to the Emergency Price Control Regulations. The evidence on which the prosecution was based was obtained from information found in the records that he had been required to produce before the administrator. He claimed that he was entitled to immunity from prosecution for any matter arising out of those records.

DECISION: Judgment against Shapiro. The records which he kept as his sales could be used as evidence against him. He could not claim an immunity on the theory that this would make him incriminate himself. The constitutional guaranty against self-incrimination was not applicable because the records which the administrator required to be maintained were to be deemed "public records," and records which are public records are open to inspection by anyone and such inspection cannot be refused on the ground of self-incrimination. [Shapiro v United States, 335 US 1]

§ 6:4. **FINALITY OF ADMINISTRATIVE DETERMINATION.** Basic to the Anglo-American legal theory is that no one, not even a branch of the government, is above the law. Thus, the growth of powers of the administrative agency was frequently accepted or tolerated on the theory that the administrative agency could not go too far because the courts would review the administrative action. The typical modern statute provides that an appeal may be taken from the administrative action by any person in interest or any person aggrieved. When the question decided by the administrator was a question of law, the court on appeal will reverse the administrator if the court disagrees with him. But if the controversy turns on a question of facts, a court will generally accept the conclusion of the administrator as final. The net result is that the determination by the administrative agency will, in most cases, be final.

FACTS: The National Labor Relations Board may order the reinstatement of an improperly discharged employee and direct that the employer pay him the "back pay" that he lost during the period of his wrongful discharge. The benefits obtained under another statute, the Social Security Act, are affected by the amount of wages received by an employee. The question arose whether the back pay awarded by the National Labor Relations Board to Nierotko, a reinstated employee, should be regarded as "wages" for the purpose of the Social Security Act and whether the employee should be regarded as having been employed during the period from the date of his wrongful discharge until his reinstatement under the order of the Board. The Social Security Administration held that the back pay did not constitute wages because the sum was not compensation for productive labor.

DECISION: Judgment for Nierotko. The Social Security Act defines wages as "remuneration for employment." The back pay was awarded to Nierotko because of his status as employee and was therefore remuneration for employment. The decision of the Administration to the contrary was therefore improper and was reversed. [Social Security Board v Nierotko, 327 US 358]

(a) **Factors limiting court review.** There are two procedural reasons why administrative appeals are frequently lost: (1) absence of standing to appeal, and (2) failure to exhaust the administrative remedy.

Illustrative of the former, the party that appeals (the appellant) may lose because the regulatory statute does not indicate that he may sue. As an example of the latter, if the appellant has not allowed the proceeding before the administrator to take its full course, generally he cannot take an appeal.

(b) **Discretion of the administrator.** The greatest limitation upon court review of the administrative action is the rule that a matter involving discretion will not be reversed in the absence of an error of law, or a clear abuse, or the arbitrary or capricious exercise of discretion.

FACTS: Moog Industries was ordered by the Federal Trade Commission to stop certain pricing practices. It raised the objection that its competitors were also guilty of the same practices and that Moog would be ruined if it were required to stop the practices without the FTC's requiring competitors to stop such practices.

DECISION: Judgment against Moog. The administrator has the discretion of determining where and how to begin solving a problem. The fact that the administrator does not act as to everyone at the same time does not constitute a defense to an enterprise which is subjected to an otherwise valid regulation. [Moog Industries v Federal Trade Commission, 355 US 411]

The courts reason that since the administrator was appointed because of his expert ability, it would be absurd for the court that is manifestly unqualified technically to make a decision in the matter to step in and determine whether the administrator made the proper choice. As has been said by the Supreme Court with reference to the Securities Exchange Commission: "The very breadth of the statutory language precludes a reversal of the Commission's judgment save where it has plainly abused its discretion in these matters. . . .

". . . The Commission's conclusion here rests squarely in that area where administrative judgments are entitled to the greatest amount of weight by appellate courts. It is the product of administrative experience, appreciation of the complexities of the problem, realization of the statutory policies, and responsible treatment of the uncontested facts. It is the type of judgment which administrative agencies are best equipped to make and which justifies the use of the administrative process. . . . Whether we agree or disagree with the result reached, it is an allowable judgment which we cannot disturb."[3]

And with reference to the Federal Communications Commission, the court has declared that ". . . it is the Commission, not the courts, which must be satisfied that the public interest will be served by renewing the license. And the fact that we might not have made the same determination on the same facts does not warrant a substitution of judicial for administrative discretion since Congress has confided the problem to the latter."[4]

The frequent reference of the courts to what would be done if action of the administrator was found to be "arbitrary or capricious" is somewhat misleading because it suggests that there is a wide area in which the court does actively review the administrative action. As a practical matter, the action of the administrator is rarely found to be arbitrary or capricious. As long as the administrator has apparently conducted himself properly, the fact that the court disagrees with his conclusion does not make that conclusion arbitrary or capricious. The fact that the administrative decision will cause a person to lose money is not proof that the action of the administrator was arbitrary. The judicial attitude is that for protection from laws and regulations which are unwise, improvident, or out of harmony with a particular school of thought, the people must resort to the ballot box and not to the court.

---

[3] Securities and Exchange Commission v Chenery Corporation, 332 US 194, 209.
[4] Federal Communications Commission v WOKO, 329 US 223, 229.

Thus, it is sufficient that the administrator had a reasonable basis for his action and a court will not attempt a "second guess" as to "complex criteria" with which an administrative agency is "intimately familiar."

In order to give the individual a direct pathway to his government, the office of Ombudsman for Business has been created within the Department of Commerce. This official is patterned after the Swedish Ombudsman and the British Parliamentary Commission for Administration. He has authority to receive grievances and complaints and to initiate appropriate action.

QUESTIONS AND CASE PROBLEMS

1. Woodham held a license as insurance agent. He was notified to appear in person or by counsel at a hearing to be held by Williams, the State Insurance Commissioner, for the purpose of determining whether Williams should revoke Woodham's license because of improper practices as agent. Woodham appeared at the hearing and testified in his own behalf. He did not make any objection that what he was asked would incriminate him. Williams revoked Woodham's license. Woodham appealed and claimed, among other grounds, that the proceeding before Williams was invalid because Woodham had not been warned that what he would say could be used against him. Were the proceedings valid? [Woodham v Williams (FlaApp) 207 So2d 320]

2. The New York City charter authorizes the New York City Board of Health to adopt a health code and declares that it "shall have the force and effect of law." The Board adopted a Code in 1964 that provided for the fluoridation of the public water supply. A suit was brought to enjoin the carrying out of this program on the ground that it was unconstitutional and that money could not be spent to carry out such a program in the absence of a statute authorizing such expenditure. It was also claimed that the fluoridation program was unconstitutional because there were other means of reducing tooth decay; fluoridation was discriminatory in that it benefited only children; it unlawfully imposed medication on the children without their consent; and fluoridation "is or may be" dangerous to health. Was the Code provision valid? [Paduano v City of New York, 257 NYS2d 531]

3. A federal statute provides that when a contract between the government and a contractor provides for the determination of a dispute by a federal department head or agency, the decision "shall be final and conclusive unless the same is fraudulent or capricious or arbitrary or so grossly erroneous as necessarily to imply bad faith, or is not supported by substantial evidence." Bianchi contracted with the government to build a water tunnel. The contract contained a standard provision for additional compensation in the event of "changed conditions." The contractor claimed that conditions discovered after the work was begun constituted "changed conditions" and claimed additional compensation. In accord with a provision of the contract, he submitted this claim first to the contracting officer and then to the Board of Claims and Appeals of the Corps of

Engineers. Both rejected his claim. Six years thereafter Bianchi sued in the Court of Claims claiming that he was entitled to additional compensation and that he was not bound by the decision of the contracting officer and of the Board of Claims because their decisions were "capricious or arbitrary or so grossly erroneous as necessarily to imply bad faith, or were not supported by substantial evidence." In this proceeding, a substantial amount of new evidence was heard and a decision made in favor of the contractor. The United States appealed. Decide. [United States v Bianchi, 373 US 709]

4. Ordinarily the testimony of a witness at a trial in one case is not admissible as evidence in the trial of a different case involving different parties. W, a workman, was injured and filed a workmen's compensation claim. He testified before the compensation board with respect to his injuries. He thereafter died and his widow began a new proceeding before the board to recover damages for his death under the workmen's compensation statute. At the trial of this second case, brought by the widow, the testimony of the deceased husband in the first case was offered in evidence. Should it have been admitted? [See Welch v Essex County, 6 NJS 422, 68 A2d 787]

5. The state insurance commissioner was authorized to regulate "advertising" by insurance companies. A bill was introduced in the state legislature affecting insurance companies. One of the companies circulated printed matter in opposition to the proposed law. The state insurance commissioner began to investigate this printed matter. The insurance company claimed that he did not have jurisdiction. Decide. [See Ex parte Allstate Insurance Co. 248 SC 550, 151 SE2d 849]

6. The Pennsylvania Air Pollution Commission prohibited the emitting of smoke any darker than Number 2 on the Ringelmann Smoke Chart. The Bortz Coal Company operated a battery of 70 coke ovens built in 1898. Complaint was made that these emitted smoke-carrying particulate matter in excess of the maximum permitted under the standard established by the Air Pollution Commission. An engineer acting for the Commission looked at the smoke coming from the ovens and on the basis of textbook information calculated that each oven was emitting 45 pounds of particulate matter per hour and that this violated the standard set by the Commission. Bortz was ordered to stop this pollution. It appealed from the action of the Commission. Decide. [Bortz Coal Co. v Air Pollution Commission, 2 Pa Commonwealth Court 441, 279 A2d 388]

ENVIRONMENTAL LAW AND COMMUNITY PLANNING

A. PREVENTION OF POLLUTION

§ 7:1. FEDERAL ENVIRONMENTAL PROTECTION. A number of federal statutes provide for research into the effect of the environment upon man and the economy. Congress has adopted the National Environmental Policy Act (NEPA) of 1969[1] and the Water and Environmental Quality Improvement Act of 1970.[2] Congress has also provided for the study of health hazards caused by pollution,[3] and for informing the public of the significance of the environment and the problems involved.[4]

§ 7:2. ENVIRONMENTAL IMPACT STATEMENTS. Environmental protection legislation typically requires that any activity which might have a significant effect upon the environment be supported by an environmental impact statement. Whenever any bill is proposed in Congress and whenever any federal action significantly affecting the quality of the human environment is undertaken, a statement must be prepared as to the environmental impact of the action.[5]

FACTS: Morton, the U.S. Secretary of the Interior, announced that the United States proposed to sell certain offshore oil drilling rights. The Director of the Bureau of Land Management prepared an environmental impact statement. An injunction against the proposed governmental action was obtained by the Natural Resources Defense Council which claimed that the environmental impact statement was not adequate. The Government moved to dismiss the injunction. The statement was claimed to be inadequate because it did not discuss alternatives to the

---

[1] PL 91-190, 83 Stat 852, 42 United States Code § 4321 et seq. Among other things, this Act creates a Council on Environment Quality as part of the executive branch of the national government.
[2] PL 91-224, 84 Stat 91.
[3] Heart Disease, Cancer, Stroke, and Kidney Disease Amendments of 1970, PL 91-515, 84 Stat 1297, § 501.
[4] Environmental Education Act, PL 91-516, 84 Stat 1312.
[5] Pl 9-190, 83 Stat 853, § 102; 42 USC § 4332.

proposed sale plan and the environmental effect of such alternatives. This it did not do because the Secretary of the Interior declared that the alternatives involved complex factors, including national security, which were outside the scope of his authority.

DECISION: The environmental impact statement was inadequate because it did not discuss the alternatives and their environmental effect. The object of the statement was to gather into one place all the data necessary to make a decision in terms of effect upon the environment. Whether the person or official making the statement would himself have authority to carry out each alternative considered is not material. The statement should still serve as a source of information for other appropriate branches of government which would have authority to carry out the alternatives. Likewise, the fact that legislation must be adopted to carry out an alternative does not justify ignoring an alternative as the statement also serves as a guide to Congress. [Natural Resources Defense Council, Inc. v Morton (CA DistCol) 458 F2d 827]

§ 7:3. **AIR POLLUTION.** The federal Clean Air Act[6] (as amended and supplemented by the Air Quality Act of 1967[7]), the Clean Air Amendments of 1970,[8] and the National Motor Vehicles Emissions Standards Act[9] provide for establishing standards to reduce pollution from automobiles and require the industry to produce "a substantially pollution-free" automobile.

§ 7:4. **NOISE POLLUTION.** The term "noise pollution" refers to the imposition upon the air of excessive noise. The prior law had developed some protection for a landowner from noise damage. By this law the use of a sound truck or loudspeaker for advertising purposes can be restrained when its noise unreasonably interferes with the use of the neighboring land. Excessive noise from a drive-in theater may be enjoined.[10] When the flight of planes from an airport creates such an unreasonable noise and vibration as to interfere greatly with the use and enjoyment of neighboring land, the landowner may be entitled to an injunction to stop the use of the airport or to change the particular flight pattern. In any case, damages may be recovered for the loss of value of the neighboring land. Such deprivation of value is also generally considered a taking of property so as to require compensation to be made under eminent domain.[11]

The Noise Control Acts of 1970 and 1972 declare a federal policy to promote for all Americans an environment free from noise that jeopardizes their health and welfare.[12] The administrator of EPA[13] is given authority to establish noise emission standards for equipment, motors, and engines. Similar standards may be set for airplanes, railroads, and motor carriers in

---

[6] 42 USC § 1857 et seq.

[7] PL 90-148, 81 Stat 485.

[8] PL 91-604, 84 Stat 1676.

[9] 42 USC § 1857f-1 et seq.

[10] Guarina v Bogart, 407 Pa 307, 180 A2d 557.

[11] Griggs v Allegheny County, 369 US 84.

[12] PL 91-604, 84 Stat 1676; PL 92-574, 86 Stat 1234, 42 USC § 4901.

[13] The Environmental Protection Agency is a federal agency established under the Reorganization Plan No. 3 of 1970.

cooperation with the Secretary of Transportation, the Federal Aviation Administration, and other appropriate agencies.

The states regulate the noise created by automobiles, motorcycles, and other motor vehicles. When local noise pollution control laws conflict with the federal regulations on the same subject or impose an unreasonable restriction on interstate commerce, the local control is invalid.

A state may not prohibit the local landing of commercial supersonic transport aircraft, because this would interfere with federal control of interstate commerce.[14]

§ 7:5. **WATER POLLUTION.** The discharge of refuse into navigable water is prohibited by the River and Harbors Appropriation Act of 1899,[15] and the Federal Water Pollution Control Act amendments of 1972.[16] The federal law prohibiting dumping of waste in navigable waters is violated even though it is not shown that navigation was affected thereby.[17] The federal statutes have been supplemented by federal administrative regulations establishing standards for water quality and guidelines for the design, operation, and maintenance of water waste treatment facilities.

§ 7:6. **WASTE DISPOSAL.** Waste disposal is to a large degree an aspect of water pollution because of the extent to which waste is dumped into rivers and lakes. It is also an aspect of air pollution through the burning of waste accumulated in open dumping. Various federal statutes seek solutions for the problems involved: the Solid Waste Disposal Act,[18] the Resource Recovery Act of 1970, and Materials Policy Act of 1970.[19]

The Marine Protection, Research, and Sanctuaries Act of 1972 prohibits ocean-dumping of any waste or matter which contains active chemical, biologic, or radioactive agents. The Act also prohibits transporting such materials from the United States for the purpose of dumping in the ocean. The Secretary of Commerce, after consultation with specified agencies, may designate particular areas of the ocean as sanctuaries and then seek to obtain international treaties protecting such areas.[20]

State laws seek to reduce the problem of waste disposal by requiring recycling or reuse of various products.

FACTS: The State of Oregon adopted a law, commonly called the "bottle bill," which prohibited the use of nonreturnable containers for beverages and required returnable glass bottles. The American Can Company brought an action against the Oregon Liquor Control Board and sought to have the statute declared unconstitutional. From a decision sustaining the law, American Can appealed. American Can claimed that the shipping cost of returning empty bottles placed foreign sellers at a disadvantage in selling in the Oregon market.

---

[14] Opinion of the Justices 359 Mass 778, 271 NE2d 354.
[15] 33 USC § 407.
[16] 33 USC § 1251 et seq.
[17] United States v United States Steel Corp. (CA7 Ind) 482 F2d 439.
[18] 42 USC § 3251 et seq.
[19] PL 91-512, 84 Stat 1227.
[20] PL 92-532, 86 Stat 1052.

DECISION: The law was valid. While it would cause loss to some sellers, the legislature had concluded that this loss was outweighed by the greater benefit to the public in reducing litter and thereby reducing the public money spent for waste disposal, and in protecting people and animals from being hurt by discarded can pulls, and by advancing the esthetic interest of the state. The fact that loss was caused the foreign sellers did not invalidate the law because "with every change of circumstance in the market place, there are gainers and there are losers." [American Can Co. v Oregon Liquor Control Commission (OreApp) 517 P2d 691]

§ 7:7. REGULATION BY ADMINISTRATIVE AGENCIES.

For the most part the law against pollution is a matter of the adoption and enforcement of regulations by administrative agencies, such as the federal EPA. Administrative agency control is likely to increase in the future because of the technical nature of the problems involved, and because of the interrelationship of pollution problems and nonpollution problems. It is also likely that there will be increasing cooperative effort made by both government and industry to achieve desired goals.

§ 7:8. LITIGATION.

The right to bring a private lawsuit to recover damages or to obtain an injunction against pollution will continue. The prior law will probably be changed by giving an individual the right to bring an antipollution suit even though he cannot show that he sustained any harm different than that sustained by any other member of the general public. For example, the Clean Air Amendments Act of 1972,[21] the Water Pollution Prevention and Control Act of 1972,[22] and the Noise Control Act[23] authorize a private suit by "any person" in a federal district court to stop a violation of the air, water, and noise pollution standards. "The courts have been increasingly willing to recognize the right of organizations to sue on behalf of their members. . . . Some courts have held that organizations have standing to represent their members' interest even without any organization interest being involved."[24]

A private person does not always have the right to sue for violation of an environmental protection control. In some instances the right to sue is restricted to a particular government agency. For example, the right to sue for a violation of the Federal Water Pollution Act is vested exclusively in the administrator of the Environmental Protection Agency. A private citizen or property owner cannot bring suit against an alleged polluter for violating this Act, as distinct from proving that the conduct of the defendant constituted a nuisance affecting the plaintiff.[25] Likewise, an action brought for a violation of the Marine Protection, Research, and Sanctuaries Act of 1972 is brought by the Attorney General of the United States on his own initiative or at the request of the Secretary of Commerce.[26]

---

[21] PL 91-604, 84 Stat 1676, § 304.
[22] PL 92-500, 86 Stat 888 § 505, 33 USC § 1365.
[23] PL 92-574, 86 Stat 1243, 42 USC § 4911.
[24] Undergraduate Student Association v Peltason, (DC ND Ill) 359 FSupp 320.
[25] Higginbotham v Barrett (CA5 Ga) 473 F2d 745.
[26] PL 92-532, 86 Stat 1052, § 303 (d).

It is reasonable to expect that courts will not take an active part in the solution of pollution problems. It is likely that they will defer to the decisions on these technical problems made or to be made by the appropriate administrative agency.[27] As evidence of judicial reluctance to become involved in pollution problems, the United States Supreme Court has refused to exercise the jurisdiction given it by the Constitution to hear an original action brought by a state against nonresidents to stop pollution, on the ground that no federal question was involved and that its entertaining of the suit was undesirable because of the scientific questions involved in determining whether there was pollution, that any legal questions involved were "bottomed on state law," and that administrative agencies and commissions, both state and international, were already devoting attention to the particular pollution problem.[28]

Courts will be particularly likely to avoid pollution litigation when the matter before them is merely a small segment of the total pollution problem involved so that the exercise of jurisdiction by a court would hamper or disrupt the work of administrative agencies and study groups.

§ 7:9. CRIMINAL LIABILITY. In many states, criminal proceedings to impose a fine are provided to punish violation of the environmental protection regulations. Antipollution statutes may make it a crime to cause improper pollution. Under such statutes, it is no defense that the defendant did not intend to violate the law or was not negligent.

The fact that the defendant operated his business in the customary way and did not produce any greater amount of pollution than other similar enterprises is not a defense to a prosecution for polluting the environment.

B. COMMUNITY PLANNING

§ 7:10. RESTRICTIVE COVENANTS IN PRIVATE CONTRACTS. In the case of private planning, a real estate developer will take an undeveloped tract or area of land, map out on paper an "ideal" community, and then construct the buildings shown on the plan. These he will then sell to private purchasers. The deeds by which he transfers title will contain *restrictive covenants* that obligate the buyers to observe certain limitations as to the use of their property, the nature of buildings that will be maintained or constructed on the land, and so on.

> FACTS: McCord owned two houses in a real estate development. His deed specified that the property "shall be used only as a residence property" and that "only a dwelling house, and for not more than two families, shall be built" on the land. Eight or more college students lived in McCord's houses. They were unrelated, and their homes were in different places. Pichel owned a neighboring house. He sued for an injunction to stop the occupancy by the students.

---

[27] Boomer v Atlantic Cement Co. 26 NY2d 219, 309 NYS2d 312, 257 NE2d 870.

[28] Ohio v Wyandotte Chemicals Corp. 401 US 493 (Ohio sought to enjoin Canadian, Michigan, and Delaware corporations from dumping mercury into tributaries of Lake Erie, which allegedly polluted that lake which was used by parts of Ohio as a water supply).

DECISION: Judgment for Pichel. The restrictive covenant in McCord's deed limited the nature of the use of the land as well as the kind of buildings that could be erected on the land. The covenant therefore required use of the land by "families." As the unrelated students did not constitute a family, their occupancy was a breach of the restrictive covenant and would be stopped by injunction. [McCord v Pichel, 35 AppDiv2d 879, 315 NYS2d 717]

Frequently a buyer will purchase a lot in an undeveloped tract in the expectation that the seller is going to develop the area in a particular way. Such expectations do not bind the seller and he may change his plans unless the carrying out of those plans was made an express part of the contract with the buyer.

§ 7:11. PUBLIC ZONING. Public community planning is generally synonymous with zoning. By *zoning*, a city adopts an ordinance imposing restrictions upon the use of the land. The object of zoning is to insure an orderly physical development of the regulated area. In effect, zoning is the same as the restrictive covenants with the difference as to the source of their authority.

Zoning is always based upon a legislative enactment. In most cases this is an ordinance of a local political subdivision, such as a municipality or a county ordinance, as distinguished from a statute adopted by a state legislature or the United States Congress.[29] A local zoning ordinance may be supplemented or reinforced by a general state statute, such as a statute that makes it a crime to violate a local zoning ordinance.

Zoning is to be distinguished from building regulations, although the distinction between the two is not always apparent. For example, a requirement that there be at least four feet of clear space between a building wall and a boundary line is regarded as a zoning requirement, whereas a law requiring that the walls of the building be built of fireproof material is regarded as a building regulation. Both of these requirements, however, have the common element of concern for others. The property owner must maintain a four-foot setback for the benefit of the community—the passage of light and air is facilitated; in case of fire there is less likelihood of fire spreading if buildings are separated by a substantial space; in case of police or fire emergency it will be possible to cut across the lot instead of going around the block; and the building will probably be aesthetically more attractive if set off by space. The building regulation that seeks to protect from fire is likewise community-oriented in that the neighborhood is less likely to be destroyed by fire if each building is in itself not of a flammable construction.

(a) **Validity of zoning.** In terms of social forces, zoning represents the subordination of the landowner's right to use his property as he chooses to the interests of the community at large. Zoning is held constitutional as an

---

[29] In some states, the legislative enactment of a local political subdivision is called a "resolution."

exercise of the police power as long as the zoning regulation bears a reasonable relation to health, morals, safety, or general welfare.

FACTS: The City of Colby prohibited placing a mobile home within the city limits except in a mobile home park or community. Hurtt owned a mobile home. He requested permission from the city to place his home on a tract of land in the city owned by his father. Permission was refused because of the ordinance. In spite of this refusal, Hurtt placed his home on his father's land. He was then prosecuted and convicted in the police court for violating the ordinance. He claimed that the zoning ordinance was unconstitutional because it prevented the owner of land from using the land as he desired.

DECISION: The regulation was valid. Mobile homes present peculiar health problems. Also if scattered through a city, they may stunt its growth as a residential community. In order to protect the public from these evils, the local community could exercise its police power and restrict the location of mobile homes. The fact that this caused loss to some property owners did not invalidate the regulation as a taking of property without due process. [City of Colby v Hurtt, 212 Kan 113, 509 P2d 1142]

A zoning ordinance may constitutionally exclude gas stations from downtown shopping areas. Zoning laws may seek to limit population density by limiting the number of dwelling units which may be included in a high-rise apartment by fixing a ratio of surrounding land to units.

The fact that the use authorized by zoning is not the most profitable to the owner does not affect the validity of the zoning. That is, the fact that a landowner could make more money if his land were zoned to permit a business use does not render unconstitutional a zoning ordinance which restricts the land to a noncommercial use.

The refusal of a building permit because of a zoning law is not in itself a denial of equal protection.

A landowner does not have a vested right in the continuance of the zoning ordinance in force when he purchased his land. Consequently, an owner cannot complain when a subsequent amendment of the zoning ordinance imposes additional restrictions on the future use of his land.

Just as restrictive covenants in a deed may become unenforceable because of a change in the nature of the area, a zoning classification may become invalid for the same reason.

(b) Nonconforming use. When the use to which the land is already being put when the zoning ordinance goes into effect is in conflict with the zoning ordinance, such use is described as a *nonconforming use.* For example, when a zoning ordinance was adopted which required a setback of 25 feet from the boundary line, an already existing building that was only set back 10 feet was a nonconforming use.

The nonconforming use represents one of the major problems involved in zoning. A nonconforming use has a constitutionally protected right to continue. That is, a business or activity which is in itself lawful cannot be wiped out by a zoning ordinance even though it is in conflict with the zoning pattern. Thus, a grocery store already in existence cannot be ordered away when the area is zoned as residential. The hope of the zoners is that the nonconforming use will disappear. This tends to be a very slow process because the effect of the zoning restriction is to give the nonconforming use a monopoly advantage, and its economic life tends to be extended thereby.

If the nonconforming use is discontinued, it cannot be resumed. The right to make a nonconforming use may thus be lost by abandonment; as when the owner of a garage stops using it for a garage and uses it for storing goods, a return to the use of the property as a garage will be barred by abandonment. Zoning ordinances commonly provide that when a nonconforming use is discontinued for a period of time, such as one year, such discontinuance is evidence of an intention to abandon or is in itself sufficient to terminate the right to resume the nonconforming use.

(c) **Variance.** The administrative agency charged with the enforcement of the zoning ordinance may generally grant a *variance*. This permits the owner of the land to use it in a specified manner inconsistent with the zoning ordinance. When a departure from the zoning plan is authorized for a general area, it is called *rezoning*.

> FACTS: Stokes owned a house in the City of Jacksonville in a section which was zoned for one-family residences. He and other property owners wished to change the zoning to commercial. The city refused to rezone the area. When the property owners had purchased their homes, a two-lane highway ran through the area. This had been increased to six lanes and the increased noise and fumes from the heavy automobile traffic made the area no longer fit for residential purposes. Gas stations were located on three of the four corners of the nearby intersection and the area contained a number of automobile dealers, a Super Burger restaurant, a fish market, and a cocktail lounge.

> DECISION: Rezoning ordered. The area was so definitely nonresidential that it was unreasonable to insist that it be used for residential purposes. To impose such a limitation on the landowner in effect took his property from him. [Stokes v Jacksonville (FlaApp) 276 So2d 200]

The agency will ordinarily be reluctant to permit a variance when neighboring property owners object because, to the extent that variation is permitted, the basic plan of the zoning ordinance is defeated. Likewise, the allowance of an individual variation may result in such inequality as to be condemned by the courts as *spot zoning*. In addition, there is the consideration of practical expediency that if variances are readily granted, every property owner will request a variance and thus flood the agency with such requests.

§ 7:12. **FEDERAL LEGISLATION.** Federal legislation in the area of community planning is largely directed toward research and financial aid to cities and housing projects. A series of national housing acts of 1948, 1954, 1956, and 1961 has been followed by the Demonstration Cities and

Metropolitan Development Act of 1966[30] and the Housing and Urban Development Act of 1970.[31]

The executive branch of the national government has been expanded by the creation of a Department of Housing and Urban Development (HUD).

The Coastal Zone Management Act of 1972 [32] provides financial assistance to states in protecting coastal zones from overpopulation and to preserve and protect the natural resources of the coast. The Rural Development Act of 1972 [33] amends a number of earlier laws relating to farming and makes additional provision for protection from fire and flood and for the furthering of research for education with the objective of raising the standards of rural life and thereby discouraging the steady population shifts from farm to city.

§ 7:13. EMINENT DOMAIN. *Eminent domain* is the power of government to take private property for a public purpose. The power of eminent domain plays an important role in community planning because it is the means by which the land required for housing, redevelopment, and other projects may be acquired. Eminent domain has not become important in the area of environmental law, although it is always present as a possible alternative on the theory that a government-owned plant would be more concerned with protection of the environment.

When property is taken by government by eminent domain, it must be taken for a public purpose. The taking of property for a private purpose is void as a deprivation of property without due process of law.

Whether the purpose of the taking is public is a question for the courts to determine. The courts are not bound by the declaration in a statute that a particular purpose shall be deemed a public purpose when in fact it is a private purpose. As a practical matter, however, a declaration by the lawmaker, particularly by Congress, that a taking is a public purpose will generally be given great respect by the courts.[34] With the widening of the concept of "public purpose," the possibility of a conflict between the lawmaker and the courts as to whether a particular taking is for a public purpose becomes increasingly unlikely.

QUESTIONS
AND CASE
PROBLEMS

1. "Smoke, fumes, and noise from public utilities and power plants are not to be condemned as nuisances merely because some harm is sustained from their activity by a particular plaintiff." Objective(s)?

---

[30] 42 USC § 1416 et seq.
[31] PL 91-609, 84 Stat 1770.
[32] PL 92-419, 86 Stat.
[33] PL 92-583, 86 Stat 1280, 16 USC § 1451 et seq.
[34] United States v Welch, 327 US 546.

2. A zoning ordinance of the City of Dallas, Texas prohibited the use of property in a residential district for gasoline filling stations. Lombardo brought an action against the City to test the validity of the ordinance. He contended that the ordinance violated the rights of the owners of property in such districts. Do you agree with this contention? [Lombardo v City of Dallas, 124 Tex 1, 73 SW2d 475]

3. Causby owned a chicken farm. The United States Air Force maintained an air base nearby. The flight of heavy bombers and fighter planes frightened the Causbys and the chickens. Although flying at proper altitude, the planes would appear to be so close as to barely miss striking the trees on the farm. The lights of the planes lit up the farm at night. The noise and the lights so disturbed the chickens that Causby abandoned the chicken business. He claimed compensation from the United States. Decide. [United States v Causby, 328 US 256]

4. The Urban Redevelopment Law of Oregon authorized the condemning of blighted urban areas and the acquisition of the property by the Housing Authority by eminent domain. Such part of the land condemned as was not needed by the Authority could be resold to private persons. Foeller and others owned well-maintained buildings within the Vaughn Street area that was condemned under this statute by the Portland Housing Authority as "physically substandard and economically deteriorated." The plaintiffs brought an action to have the statute declared unconstitutional. Decide. [Foeller v Housing Authority of Portland, 198 Ore 205, 256 P2d 752]

5. An action was brought to determine whether a condominium building could be constructed on a particular tract of land. The deed to the land permitted only single-family dwellings and prohibited apartment houses and further declared that the property could only be used by white persons. Did these restrictions bar a condominium building? [See Callahan v Weiland, 291 Ala 183, 279 So2d 451]

6. In the course of generating electricity in its atomic-energy-powered plant, the Jersey Central Power & Light Company took cold water from a river to cool its condensers. This raised the temperature of the water, which was then discharged into a nearby creek. On January 28, 1972, the river water temperature was under 40°F and the creek temperature was over 50°F. The electric company shut down its generators on that date; consequently, the river water was not heated by the condensers. When the cold water was dumped into the warm creek, the temperature change killed fish in the creek. The State of New Jersey sued the electric company to recover a statutory penalty for violating the prohibition against placing "any hazardous, deleterious, destructive, or poisonous substance" in waters of the state. The electric company claimed that the water which it discharged did not come within the statute. Was the electric company liable for the penalty? [New Jersey v Jersey Central Power & Light Co. 125 NJ Super 97, 308 A2d 671, affirmed NJ Super, 336 A2d 750]

CONSUMER PROTECTION

8

§ 8:1. **WHO IS A CONSUMER?** Many persons are given the protection of a consumer.[1] For example, one does not usually think of a borrower or an investor as a "consumer." The pedestrian run over when your car goes out of control is not ordinarily regarded as a consumer. There is in all these situations, however, a common denominator of protecting someone from a hazard from which he cannot by his own action protect himself.

Product safety is discussed in Chapter 26, and pollution in Chapter 7. This chapter deals with protection of the person as a consumer, a borrower, and an investor.

§ 8:2. **ADVERTISING.** Statutes commonly prohibit fraudulent advertising, but most advertising regulations are entrusted to an administrative agency, such as the Federal Trade Commission (FTC), which is authorized to issue orders to stop false, misleading advertising.[2]

(a) **Deception.** Under the Federal Trade Commission Act, deception in advertising, rather than fraud, is the significant element. This is a shift of social point of view. That is, instead of basing the law in terms of fault of the actor (Did he with evil intent make a false statement?), the law is concerned

---

[1] The National Consumer Act (NCA) defines *consumer* as "a person other than an organization who seeks or acquires business equipment for use in his business, or real or personal property, services, money, or credit for personal, family, household or agricultural purposes." NCA § 1.301(8). This definition includes a small business sole proprietor and thus goes beyond the ordinary image of a consumer.

Consumer protection is not limited to the protection of persons of limited education or economic means. This is clearly seen in Weisz v Parke-Bernet Galleries, Inc. (NYCivCt) 67 Misc2d 1077, 325 NYS2d 576. There it was held that the seller art gallery was liable for breach of warranty where paintings sold by it proved to be forgeries and the fact that there had been an announcement that the sale was subject to the conditions in the catalog, one of which was a warranty disclaimer, did not bind a person not having actual knowledge of the provision.

Additional protection for consumers who are servicepersons is provided by the Soldiers' and Sailors' Civil Relief Act, 50 United States Code App §§ 501-548.

[2] 15 USC §§ 45, 52.

with the problem of the buyer who is likely to be misled by statements made without regard to whether the defendant had any evil intent.

> FACTS: The Colgate-Palmolive Co. ran a television commercial to show that its shaving cream "Rapid Shave" could soften even the toughness of sandpaper. The commercial showed what was described as the sandpaper test. Actually what was used was a sheet of plexiglas on which sand had been sprinkled. The FTC claimed that this was a deceptive practice. The advertiser contended that actual sandpaper would merely look like ordinary colored paper and that plexiglas had been used to give the viewer an accurate visual representation of the test. Could the FTC prohibit the use of this commercial?
>
> DECISION: Yes. The commercial made the television viewer believe that he was seeing with his own eyes an actual test, and this would tend to persuade him more than it would if he knew that he was seeing merely an imitation of a test. To that extent, the use of the mockup without disclosing its true character was deceptive, and it therefore could be prohibited by the FTC. [Federal Trade Commission v Colgate-Palmolive Co. 380 US 374]

The good faith of an advertiser or the absence of intent to deceive is immaterial as the purpose of false advertising legislation is to protect the consumer rather than to punish the advertiser. The sale of an automobile with its odometer set back to show about one half of its actual mileage is a violation of a consumer protection statute even though the salesperson acting for the seller did not know that this had been done.

It is improper to advertise that one brand of sugar has a superior nutritional value over competing brands when in fact all refined sugars are essentially identical in composition and food value; or to advertise in such a way as to convey the impression that the advertised sugar was adopted by a national athletic league as the "official sugar" because of superior quality and nutritional value, when the choice was based solely on its lower cost.

The FTC requires that an advertiser maintain a file containing the data claimed to support an advertising statement as to the safety, performance, efficacy, quality, or comparative price of an advertised product. The FTC can require the advertiser to produce this material. If it is in the interest of the consumer, the Commission can make this information public, except to the extent that it contains trade secrets or matter which is privileged.

(b) Corrective advertising. When an enterprise has made false and deceptive statements in its advertising, the Federal Trade Commission may require that a new advertisement be made in which the former statements are contradicted and the truth stated. For example, a manufacturer of sugar who advertised that his brand of sugar would give "strength, energy, and stamina to everyone" was required to advertise that "actually [the sugar] is not a specific or unique source of strength, energy, and stamina. No sugar is because what you need is a balanced diet and plenty of rest and exercise."[3]

---

[3] FTC Docket 8887.

Corrective advertising required by the Federal Trade Commission is also called *retractive advertising.*

§ 8:3. **SEALS OF APPROVAL.** Many commodities are sold or advertised with a sticker or tag stating that the article has been approved or is guaranteed by some association or organization. Ordinarily, when a product is thus sold, it will in fact have been approved by some testing laboratory and will probably have proven adequate to meet ordinary consumer needs. A seller who sells with a seal of approval of a third person makes, in effect, a guarantee that the product has been so approved, so that he is liable for breach of an express warranty if the product was in fact not approved. In addition, the seller would ordinarily be liable for fraud if the statement were not true.

In some instances, such as in the case of approval by the *Good Housekeeping* and *Parents'* magazines, the magazine promises to refund the purchase price or to replace the purchased article should it prove defective (within 30 days after purchase in the case of *Parents' Magazine*).

The *Good Housekeeping* testing is limited to those products which are advertised in the magazine, and testing is conducted primarily to determine that the advertising statements are true. The testing by the *Parents' Magazine* is to determine whether the products that are advertised in the magazine "are suitable for families with children."

§ 8:4. **LABELS AND PACKAGING.** Closely related to the regulation of advertising is the regulation of labels and marking of products. Various federal statutes are designed to give the consumer accurate information about the product, while others require warnings as to dangers of use or misuse. State consumer protection may prohibit the use of such terms as "jumbo," "giant," "full," which tend to exaggerate and mislead.

Federal statutes that protect the consumer from being misled by labels or by packaging methods include the Fair Packaging and Labeling Act; the Fur Products Labeling Act, the Wool Products Labeling Act; the federal Cigarette Labeling and Advertising Act; the Food, Drug, and Cosmetic Act; the Wholesome Meat Act; the Wholesome Poultry Products Act; and the Flammable Fabrics Act. The last three statutes seek to protect the consumer from personal harm as well as economic loss.

The Fair Packaging and Labeling Act applies generally to consumer goods and requires that a product bear a label stating (a) the identity of the product; (b) the name and place of business of the manufacturer, packer, or distributor; (c) the net quantity of the contents; and (d) the net quantity of a serving when the number of servings is stated. The Act gives to the FTC and the Department of Health, Education, and Welfare (HEW) authority to add additional requirements with respect to (a) the use of terms describing packages, such as "large"; (b) the use of "cents-off" or "savings" claims; (c) requiring the disclosure of information as to ingredients in the case of nonfoods;[4] and (d) preventing the deceptive partial filling of packages. The

---

[4] Such disclosure is required with respect to foods by the Food, Drug, and Cosmetic Act.

disclosure of the name and address of the manufacturer, packer, or distributor of the product is initially important to the consumer who may be purchasing in reliance upon the fact that the product came from a particular source. In the event that the consumer has a product liability claim, this information as to the source is important so that the consumer knows against whom suit can be brought other than his own seller.

§ 8:5. SELLING METHODS. Consumer protection statutes prohibit the use of improper and deceptive selling methods.[5]

> FACTS: The Attorney General of Colorado brought an action against Gym of America to enjoin it from certain selling practices which he claimed were prohibited by the Colorado Consumer Protection Act. Gym of America claimed that the statute was unconstitutional because the terms of the statute such as "advertise," "bait-and-switch," "disparagement," and "tie-in sales" were too vague and that the state lacked power to regulate the practices in question.
>
> DECISION: The statute was constitutional. The terms were sufficiently definite to identify the conduct which was outlawed. The legislature could properly prohibit such practices in order to further the protection of the public. [Colorado v Gym of America, Inc. 177 Colo 97, 493 P2d 660]

(a) Disclosure of transaction terms. The federal law requires the disclosure of all interest charges for loans, points paid for granting the loan, and similar charges. These must be set forth as an annual percentage rate so that the borrower can see just how much the loan costs him during a year.[6] If lenders advertise, certain information must be set forth in the ad.

If sellers advertise their willingness to sell on credit, they cannot state merely the monthly installment that will be due. They must give the consumer additional information: (1) the total cash price; (2) the amount of the down payment required; (3) the number, amounts, and due dates of payments; and (4) the annual percentage rate of the credit charges.[7]

In various ways consumer protection statutes seek to protect the consumer from surprise or unbargained-for terms and from unwanted contracts.[8]

---

[5] The Uniform Consumer Sales Practices Act has been adopted in Kansas, Ohio, and Utah; a Uniform Deceptive Trade Practices Act (1966 revision) has been adopted in Colorado, Georgia, Hawaii, Minnesota, Nebraska, New Mexico, and Ohio; the 1964 version of the Uniform Deceptive Trade Practices Act was adopted in Connecticut, Delaware, Idaho, Illinois, and Oklahoma; and a Uniform Land Sales Practice Act has been adopted in Alaska, Connecticut, Florida, Hawaii, Kansas, Montana, South Carolina, and Utah.

[6] Consumer Credit Protection Act (CCPA), 15 USC §§ 1605, 1606, 1636; Regulation Z adopted by the Federal Reserve Board of Governors, § 226.5. "The avowed purpose of the Consumer Protection Act was to 'assure a meaningful disclosure of credit terms so that the consumer will be able to compare more readily the various credit terms available to him and avoid the uninformed use of credit.' The Act is remedial in nature, designed to remedy what Congressional hearings revealed to be unscrupulous and predatory creditor practices throughout the nation." N. C. Freed Co. Inc. v Board of Governors of Federal Reserve System (CA2 NY) 473 F2d 1210.

[7] Regulation Z § 1210.

[8] Uniform Commercial Code § 2-316 is in effect a forerunner of such antisurprise protection in requiring that a disclaimer of certain warranties be conspicuous.

The federal Real Estate Settlement Procedures Act of 1974 protects consumers purchasing homes by requiring disclosure of charges, prohibiting kickbacks and splitting of fees except for services actually rendered, and limiting the amount that a borrower must pay into a special or escrow fund for taxes and insurance.[9] The Motor Vehicle Information and Cost Savings Act requires the disclosure to the buyer of various elements in the cost of an automobile. The Act prohibits selling an automobile without informing the buyer that the odometer has been reset below the true mileage. A buyer who is caused loss by odometer fraud may recover from the seller three times his actual loss or $1,500, whichever is greater.[10]

Whenever a sale or contract provides for payment in four or more installments it is subject to the Truth in Lending Act. This is so even though no service or finance charge is added because of the installment pattern of paying.

FACTS: Acting under the Truth in Lending Act, the Federal Reserve Board adopted a Regulation Z. Among other things, this Regulation declared that whenever a consumer paid the price for goods purchased on credit in more than four installments, the person dealing with him was subject to the Truth in Lending Act. The Family Publications Service sold a magazine to Leila Mourning but failed to disclose the information required by the Act although payment was to be made by her in 30 monthly installments. Family Publications claimed that the four-month rule of Regulation Z was invalid and that the Federal Truth in Lending Act could not apply to it because it did not make any extra charge for the making of installment payments.

DECISION: The Regulation applied to the sale and was valid in so doing. Such application of the Regulation was necessary to prevent evasion of the statute's disclosure provisions. If not so applied, a seller could conceal the items of which disclosure was required by increasing his price and then permitting the buyer to pay in installments on a price to which apparently no "charges" were added. [Mourning v Family Publication Service, Inc. 411 US 356]

When consumer credit is advertised as repayable in more than four installments and no financing charge is expressly imposed, the advertisement must "clearly and conspicuously" state that "the cost of credit is included in the price quoted for the goods and services.[11]

In order to be sure that disclosures required by the federal law are in fact noticed by the consumer, special provision is made for the case when the terms of the transaction are printed on both the front and the back of a sheet or contract. In such case, (1) both sides of the sheet must carry the warning: "NOTICE: See other side for important information," and (2) the page must be signed at the end of the second side. Conversely, the requirements of the federal law are not satisfied when there is no warning of "see other side"

---

[9] PL 93-533, 88 Stat 724.
[10] PL 92-513, 86 Stat 947, §§ 403, 409, 15 1901 et seq.
[11] PL 93-495 88 Stat 1500, Title IV.

and when the parties sign the contract on the face or first side of the paper only.[12]

In some states, transactions are subject to a state law rather than to the federal Truth in Lending Act. Under Regulation Z, the Federal Reserve Board may grant a state an exemption from the federal law when the state law imposes requirements similar to the federal law and makes adequate provision for enforcement.

(b) Home solicitation sales. A number of statutes are aimed at the evils involved in home solicitation sales. The typical remedy is to give the buyer a chance to think things over and then decide that he does not want his purchase after all. A Trade Regulation of the FTC gives a consumer three days to set aside a home transaction for goods or services of $25 or more and requires the seller to give the consumer a contract stating his right to rescind.[13] This is a reasonably good remedy for the consumer against the "hit-and-run" salesman, provided the consumer knows that he has the remedy available and has not paid in full. In some instances the home solicitation salesman brings the store to the home where the buyer cannot afford to pay cash in a store and lacks the credit standing to deal with a store on a credit basis. In such cases, the consumer either does not want to or cannot "afford" to set aside his contract of purchase. Consequently, if there is any evil or hardship in the transaction, some other remedy must be found.

When a consumer-purchaser of goods or services avoids a home solicitation contract as authorized by the UCCC, the seller may retain from any down payment a cancellation fee of 5 percent of the cash price.[14] In contrast, when a debtor rescinds a transaction under the federal Truth in Lending Act, "he is not liable for any finance or other charge, and any security interest given by [him] becomes void upon such a rescission. Within 10 days after receipt of notice of rescission, the creditor shall return to the [consumer] any money or property given as earnest money, down payment, or otherwise. . . ."[15]

(c) Referral sales. The technique of giving the buyer a price reduction for customers referred by him to the seller is theoretically lawful. In effect, it is merely paying the buyer a "commission" for the promotion by him of other sales. In actual practice, however, the referral sales technique is often accompanied by fraud or by exorbitant pricing, so that consumer protection laws variously condemn referral selling.

Illustrative of the fraud aspect, the credit-seller may falsely represent to the buyer that the product will not cost him anything because of the referral system when the seller in fact knows that this is unlikely to happen. The

---

[12] McDonald v Savoy (TexCivApp) 501 SW2d 400.
[13] Donnelly v Mustang Pools, Inc. 374 NYS2d 967.
[14] Uniform Consumer Credit Code § 2.504. In states where the UCCC is in force, this 5 percent provision would displace the provision of the UCC stated in the text (see § 27:22), where the buyer is a "consumer" within the scope of the UCCC.
[15] CCPA § 125(b), 15 USC § 1635(b).

referral system of selling has been condemned as "unconscionable" under the UCC,[16] and is expressly prohibited by the UCCC.[17]

In some states a sale of goods on the referral plan of giving the buyer a price reduction for every prospective buyer referred to the seller constitutes the sale of a security within the local blue-sky law; and when the seller is not licensed to sell securities, the sale is void. In some states, it is condemned as an unfair trade practice or lottery. In other jurisdictions, referral selling is held not a lottery on the theory that the buyer must use skill and judgment in preparing referral lists, and therefore the matter is not solely dependent on chance and is not a lottery.

§ 8:6. CREDIT CARDS. Today's credit card may cover travel and entertainment, as in the case of the cards issued by American Express, or a particular group of commodities, as in the case of a gasoline credit card; or it may be a general-purpose card, covering the purchase of any kind of goods or services. In the case of credit cards issued by banks, the bank may also assure the person cashing a check for the holder that the check will be honored for an amount not exceeding some specified amount, such as $100.

The unsolicited distribution of credit cards to persons who have not applied for them is prohibited.

A card holder is not liable for the unauthorized use of his credit card for more than $50. In order to impose liability up to that amount, the issuer of the card must show that (a) the credit card is an accepted card,[18] (b) the issuer has given the holder adequate notice that he may be held liable in such case, (c) the issuer has furnished the holder with a self-addressed, prestamped notification to be mailed by the card holder in the event of the loss or theft of the credit card, (d) the issuer has provided a method by which the user of the card can be identified as the person authorized to use it,[19] and (e) the unauthorized use occurs before the card holder has notified the issuer that an unauthorized use of the card has occurred or may occur as a result of loss, theft, or otherwise. Even though the federal statute permits the imposition of liability up to $50 for the unauthorized use of a credit card when these conditions have been satisfied, courts may refuse to allow the issuer to recover when the person dealing with the unauthorized possessor of the card was negligent in assuming that the possessor was the lawful holder and in failing to take steps to identify such possessor.

The issuer of a credit card cannot avoid the $50 limitation by suing the owner of the lost card on the theory that the owner had been negligent in the care of the card, which led to its being lost and which in turn made possible its unauthorized use.[20]

---

[16] New York v I.T.M. 52 Misc2d 39, 275 NYS2d 303.

[17] UCCC § 2.411.

[18] A credit card is "accepted" when "the card holder has requested and received or has signed or has used, or authorized another to use [it], for the purpose of obtaining money, property, labor, or services on credit." CCPA § 103(1).

[19] Regulation Z of the Board of Governors of the Federal Reserve § 226.13(d), as amended, provides that the identification may be by "signature, photograph, or fingerprint on the credit card or by electronic or mechanical confirmation."

[20] Lechmere Tire & Supply v Burwick, 360 Mass 718, 277 NE2d 503.

§ 8:7. CONTRACT TERMS. Consumer protection legislation does not ordinarily affect the right of the parties to make a contract on such terms as they choose. It is customary, however, to prohibit the use of certain clauses which, it is believed, bear too harshly on the debtor or which have too great a potential for exploitive abuse by a creditor. For example, the UCCC prohibits provisions authorizing the confessing of judgment against the debtor.[21]

The federal Warranty Disclosure Act of 1974 establishes disclosure standards for consumer goods warranties in order to make them understood by the consumer.[22]

Methods of computing charges and billing methods are frequently regulated. This is done to prevent the creditor from adding back into the contract an element or a charge that could not have been included in the original contract or from enforcing a contract which was different from that bargained for by the consumer.

(a) Unconscionability. To some extent, consumer protection has been provided under the UCC by those courts which hold that the "unconscionability" provision protects from "excessive" or "exorbitant" prices when goods are sold on credit, and that this provision invalidates a clause requiring that a buyer bring any lawsuit against the seller in a state which bears no reasonable relationship to the transaction or to the parties.

> **FACTS:** Romain sold "educational materials" on a house-to-house sales basis, catering to minority groups and persons of limited education and economic means. The materials were sold at a price approximately two and a half times the reasonable market value of the materials if they were fit for their intended purpose, but there was evidence that much of it was practically worthless. Kugler, the Attorney General, brought an action on behalf of all customers of Romain to declare their contracts invalid.
>
> **DECISION:** Judgment for Kugler. Under the circumstances, the price was unconscionable under UCC § 2-302. Unconscionability is to be equated with fraud when there is an exploitation of persons of limited income and education by selling them goods of little or no value at high prices. [Kugler v Romain, 58 NJ 522, 279 A2d 640]

(b) Assignment of wages. State statutes variously restrict or prohibit the assignment of wages for the payment of debt. The UCCC prohibits the consumer from making an absolute assignment of wages as payment, or as security for the payment, of the amount due by him under a sale, lease, or loan agreement. He may, however, make an agreement for the deduction of installment payments from his salary as long as he has the power to revoke the agreement when he chooses.[23]

(c) Form of contract. Consumer protection laws commonly regulate the form of the contract, requiring that certain items be specifically listed, that payments under the contract be itemized and indicate the allocation to

---

[21] UCCC §§ 2.415, 3.407.
[22] PL 93-637 88 Stat 2183.
[23] UCCC §§ 2.410, 3.403. As to the garnishment of wages, see § 43.20.

principal, interest, insurance, and so on. Generally certain portions of the contract or all of the contract must be printed in type of a certain size and a copy of the contract must be furnished the buyer. Such statutory requirements are more demanding than the statute of frauds section of the UCC. It is frequently provided that the copy furnished the consumer must be completely filled in. Back-page disclaimers are void if the front page of the contract does not call attention to the presence of such terms.[24]

(d) **Limitation of credit.** Various laws may limit the ability to borrow money or purchase on credit. In some states it is prohibited to make "open end" loan mortgages by which the mortgage secures a specified debt and such additional loans as may thereafter be made. Some statutes prohibit liquor distillers from selling to retailers on credit in order to avoid the economic control of the retailers by the distillers.[25]

In some states consumer protection is afforded by placing a time limit on smaller loans.[26]

§ 8:8. **PAYMENTS.** Under the UCCC, when a consumer sale or lease is made, the consumer may pay only by check or cash. The consumer cannot be required to sign a promissory note.

(a) **Progressive application of payments.** Consumer legislation may provide that when a consumer makes a payment on an open charge account, the payment must be applied to pay the oldest items. The result is that, should there be a default at a later date, any right of repossession of the creditor is limited to the later unpaid items. This outlaws a contract provision by which, upon the default of the buyer at a later date, the seller could assert the right to repossess all purchases that had been made at any prior time. Such a provision is outlawed by the UCCC[27] and may be unconscionable under the UCC.[28]

(b) **Balloon payments.** Installment contracts sometimes provide for a payment, usually the final payment, which may be substantially larger than the usual or average installment under the contract. Sometimes the purpose of requiring such a payment is to impose on the debtor a greater obligation than he can perform, with the result that the debtor is almost certain to go into default and entitle the creditor to repossess the collateral. The UCCC seeks to outlaw this practice by providing that whenever a payment balloons out to more than double the average of earlier scheduled payments, the debtor has a right to refinance that payment on terms no less

---

[24] The same conclusion is reached under the UCC on the ground that such a back page disclaimer of a warranty is not "conspicuous," and therefore does not satisfy the requirements of UCC §§ 2-316(2), 1-201(10). Hunt v Perkins Machine Co. 352 Mass 535, 226 NE2d 228. A front page disclaimer is also invalid if not conspicuous. Woodruff v Clark County Farm Bureau Coooperative Association (Ind) 286 NE2d 188.

[25] Re Parkway Distributing Co. 204 Pa Super 514, 206 A2d 660.

[26] Abrams v Commercial Credit Plan, Inc. 120 GaApp 520, 197 SE2d 384.

[27] UCCC § 2.409(1).

[28] Williams v Walker-Thomas Furniture Co. (CA Dist Col) 350 F2d 445.

favorable to him than those of the original transaction. That is, the creditor must extend further credit rather than claim that the debt is in default.[29]

Regulation Z of the Federal Reserve Board, adopted under the CCPA, provides that "if any payment is more than twice the amount of an otherwise regularly scheduled equal payment, the creditor shall identify the amount of such payment by the term 'balloon payment' and shall state the conditions, if any, under which that payment may be refinanced if not paid when due."[30]

(c) Acceleration of payment. The ability of a creditor to accelerate payment of the balance due upon default has worked great hardship where the default was trivial in nature or where in fact there was no default. Although the right to accelerate payments upon default is permitted under both the UCC and the UCCC, the former seeks to impose some limitation on the power to accelerate by providing that a power of the creditor to accelerate "at will" or "when he deems himself insecure" must be exercised in good faith,[31] and the UCCC requires the refund of unearned credit charges when the due date has been accelerated.[32]

Some debtor protection laws require that the debtor be in default for a minimum period of time or with respect to a minimum number of installment payments before the balance of the debt can be accelerated.

§ 8:9. PRESERVATION OF CONSUMER DEFENSES. Consumer protection legislation generally prohibits the consumer from waiving the benefit of any provision of a statute designed for his protection. If he does so, the waiver is void but the transaction otherwise binds the consumer. Some courts hold a waiver of defense is invalid on the ground that it violates public policy.

(a) Waiver of exemptions and defenses against assignee. Statutes commonly prohibit a buyer from agreeing that he will not assert against the seller's assignee any defense which he could have asserted against the seller.[33] Some statutes take a modified position and permit barring the buyer if, when notified of the assignment, he fails to inform the assignee of his defense against the seller.

> **FACTS:** Donnelly purchased a television set on credit from D.W.N. Advertising, Inc. He also contracted for service on the set. D.W.N. assigned the sales contract to the Fairfield Credit Corporation. D.W.N. went out of existence and the service contract was never performed. Fairfield sued Donnelly for the balance due on the purchase price. Donnelly raised the defense that the service contract had never been performed. Fairfield claimed that this defense could not be asserted against it because the sales contract contained a waiver of defenses.

---

[29] UCCC §§ 2.405, 3.402.

[30] Regulation § 226.8(b)(3).

[31] UCC § 1-208.

[32] UCCC § 2.210(8). "If the maturity is accelerated for any reason and judgment is obtained, the buyer is entitled to the same rebate as if payment had been made on the date judgment is entered."

[33] John Deere Industrial Equipment Co. v Delphia, 266 Ore 116, 511 P2d 386 (refusing to apply the statute to the purchase of heavy farm equipment).

DECISION: The assignee was subject to the defenses which the obligor-consumer could have asserted against the assignor-seller. The waiver of defenses would not be given effect as it was contrary to public policy to permit an assignee to recover from a consumer when the assignor would not be able to do so. Donnelly therefore could assert his defenses against Fairfield Credit Corporation. [Fairfield Credit Corp. v Donnelly, 158 Conn 543, 264 A2d 547]

(b) Assertion of defenses against holder of commercial paper. Consumer protection statutes often permit the buyer to assert the defense of failure of consideration as against the seller's transferee of the commercial paper signed by the buyer to finance the sale, even though by ordinary rules of law, such transferee would be a holder in due course against whom such defense could not be asserted. In some states this result is achieved expressly by preserving the defenses of the buyer. In other states the statutes go further and declare that "consumer paper" is not negotiable.

The UCCC contains alternative provisions as to the effect of a consumer's defense against a transferee of commercial paper. By Alternative A, the transferee is subject to all defenses of the consumer under a consumer sale or lease,[34] which in effect destroys the concept of holder in due course as to the paper involved in such transactions. It is immaterial whether the consumer has purported to waive his defenses as against the transferee.

Under Alternative B, a provision waiving defenses against the assignee is given effect by application of the principle of estoppel. That is, if the assignee of the seller or lessor gives the consumer written notice of the assignment but the consumer does not give the assignee written notice of the facts giving rise to his claim or defense within three months after such notice, the assignee is not subject to such claims or defenses.

Neither alternative applies when the sale or lease is primarily for an agricultural purpose.

§ 8:10. CREDIT, COLLECTION, AND BILLING METHODS. Consumer protection statutes sometimes provide for the licensing of persons selling on credit; selling particular kinds of goods, such as automobiles, or home improvements and services; or lending money. When such licensing is required, procedures are established for suspending or revoking the license of a licensee who seriously violates the statute.

The federal Fair Credit Billing Act is aimed at preventing improper billing practices.[36]

The federal Equal Credit Opportunity Act prohibits discriminating against an applicant for credit on the basis of sex or marital status.[37]

(a) Collection methods. In 1930, the FTC began to take steps to prevent scare tactics in debt collection. In 1965, it promulgated, and in 1968

---

[34] Note that this includes "services" as well as "goods." UCCC § 2.105(3), (5).
[35] § 2.404.
[36] PL 93-495, 88 Stat 1500, Title III.
[37] PL 93-495, 88 Stat 1500, Title VII.

amended, "Guides Against Deceptive Debt Collection." Bar associations have adopted similar guidelines.

Unreasonable methods of debt collection are often expressly prohibited by statute or are held by courts to constitute an unreasonable invasion of privacy. Statutes generally prohibit sending bills in such form that they give the impression that a lawsuit has been initiated against the consumer and that the bill is legal process or a warrant issued by the court.[38] The CCPA prohibits the use of extortionate methods of loan collection. A creditor may be prohibited from informing the employer of the debtor that the latter owes him money.

(b) Small claims procedures. In a number of states small claims courts are created or compulsory arbitration is provided to reduce the cost and the delay of enforcing small claims.

Some procedures are designed so that a party may proceed without any attorney if he so desires.[39]

FACTS: The Consumer Protection Law of 1969 for the City of New York created the office of Commissioner of Consumer Affairs and authorized him to adopt regulations outlawing "unconscionable trade practices." He adopted a regulation by which a creditor, or an agency on his behalf, was prohibited from informing a debtor's employer that money was owed by the employee unless a judgment had been obtained by the creditor. This regulation was adopted in the belief that there had been widespread harassment of employees by notifying their employers, with the result that employees frequently paid nonmeritorious claims for fear of losing their jobs. The Commercial Lawyers Conference brought an action against Grant, the Commissioner of Consumer Affairs, to enjoin enforcement of the regulation on the ground that it interfered with a creditor's freedom of speech.

DECISION: The regulation was constitutional even though it interfered with freedom of speech. Such freedom is not without some limitation, and this limitation was reasonable in order to protect debtors from harassment. [Commercial Lawyers Conference v Grant, 318 NYS2d 966]

(c) Repossession and deficiency liability. The UCCC provides that in the case of a consumer credit sale under $1,000, the seller must choose between repossessing the goods upon a default in the payment of installments and suing the buyer for the balance of the purchase price due. That is, the seller cannot repossess the goods because of a default of the buyer, resell the goods, and then hold the buyer liable for any deficiency that remains because the proceeds from the resale cannot pay the balance due. If the

---

[38] Florida Stat §§ 817.561, 817.751.

[39] Brooks v Small Claims Court, 8 CalApp3d 661, 105 CalRptr 785, 504 P2d 1249. The court commented on the fact that small claims were predominantly asserted by merchants against individual defendants with the consequence that the statutory prohibition against representation by lawyers worked to the disadvantage of the individual debtors because the institutional plaintiffs' representative, although not an attorney, would acquire skill through repetition.

contract price is over $1,000, the UCCC does not prevent the seller from repossessing and reselling the goods and then obtaining a deficiency judgment.[40]

§ 8:11. PROTECTION OF CREDIT STANDING AND REPUTATION. In many instances one party to a transaction wishes to know certain things about the other party. This situation arises when a person purchases on credit or applies for a loan, a job, or a policy of insurance. Between two and three thousand private credit bureaus gather such information on borrowers, buyers, and applicants for sale to interested persons.

The Fair Credit Reporting Act (FCRA) of 1970[41] seeks to afford protection from various abuses that may arise. FCRA applies only to consumer credit, which is defined as credit for "personal, family, and household" use, and does not apply to business or commercial transactions.

(a) **Privacy.** A report on a person based on personal investigation and interviews, called an *investigative consumer report*, may not be made without informing the person investigated and advising him of his right to discover the results of the investigation.[42] Bureaus are not permitted to disclose information to persons not having a legitimate use for it. It is a federal crime to obtain or to furnish a bureau report for an improper purpose.

On request, a bureau must tell a consumer the names and addresses of persons to whom it has made a credit report during the previous six months. It must also tell him when requested which employers were given such a report during the previous two years.

(b) **Protection from false information.** Much of the information obtained by bureaus is based on statements made by persons, such as neighbors, when interviewed by the bureau's investigator. Sometimes the statements are incorrect. Quite often they would constitute hearsay evidence and would not be admissible in a legal proceeding. Nevertheless, they will go on the records of the bureau without further verification and will be furnished to a client of the bureau who will tend to regard them as accurate and true.

A person has a limited right to request an agency to disclose to him the information that it has in its files. In general he may learn the nature and substance of the information possessed by the bureau. The right to know does not extend to medical information. It is not required that the bureau identify the persons giving its information to its investigators. The bureau is not required to give the applicant a copy of, nor to permit him to see, its file.

(1) Correction of Error. When a person claims that the information of the bureau is erroneous, the bureau must take steps within a reasonable time to determine the accuracy of the disputed item. It is not required to do so, however, if the bureau has reasonable grounds for believing that the

---

[40] UCCC § 5.103.
[41] PL 91-508, 15 USC § 1681 et seq. adding Title VI to the Consumer Credit Protection Act.
[42] CCPA § 606, 15 USC § 1681(d).

objection is frivolous and irrelevant. If it determines that the information is erroneous, it must give notice of the correction to anyone to whom it had sent a credit report in the preceding six months or for employment in the preceding two years. If the bureau and the applicant do not reach an agreement as to the disputed item, the applicant may give the bureau a written statement of his version of the matter. The bureau must supply a copy of this statement when it furnishes any subsequent report, and on request must send copies of the statement to persons to whom it has already sent a report within the time limitations stated above.

In some instances a stubborn insistence of management on the accuracy of its computers and its clerks has been held to constitute a denial of due process, where such attitude made it impossible for a customer to make any fair presentation of his story before gas or electric services were discontinued.[43]

(2) Elimination of Stale Items. Adverse information obtained by investigation cannot be given to a client after 3 months unless verified to determine that it is still valid. Most legal proceedings cannot be reported by a bureau after 7 years. A bankruptcy proceeding cannot be reported after 14 years.[44] Information based on a public record must be up-to-date, or the applicant must be notified that information based on the public record is being furnished. This is designed to eliminate the danger that the bureau will not have been aware of the latest developments in the matter. In many instances cases are settled out of court without any formal notation being made thereof on the court record, with the consequence that if the bureau or anyone else relied only on the court record, there would appear to be an outstanding claim or unpaid judgment in existence.

(3) Inadequacy of Prior Law. In some instances the person harmed by false information could sue the informant for damages for the tort of interference with economic relations or defamation. Ordinarily the injured party cannot recover under either theory because as a practical matter he will not be able to prove that the defendant acted with malice, and in the absence of malice the informant is protected from liability by a qualified privilege.

FACTS: Bartels applied to the Northwestern Mutual Life Insurance Company and to the Surety Life Insurance Company for life insurance. These companies requested information on Bartels from the Retail Credit Company, a mercantile reporting agency. The report falsely indicated that Bartels was an excessive drinker. Because of this, he was refused life insurance and the Farmers Insurance Group canceled his automobile insurance. Bartels sued the Retail Credit Company for damages for defamation. Retail Credit Company defended on the ground that it was privileged to supply the information and therefore was not liable because of its falsity.

---

[43] Turner v Rochester Gas and Electric Corp. 345 NYS2d 421.
[44] These time limitations do not apply to an application for a loan or for life insurance of $50,000 or more or for employment at a salary of $20,000 a year or more.

DECISION: Retail Credit Company had a privilege which protected it from liability. This privilege, however, was not an absolute but only a qualified privilege and was therefore lost if the Retail Credit Company had not exercised reasonable care in obtaining its information. [Bartels v Retail Credit Co. 185 Neb 304, 175 NW2d 292]

§ 8:12. **EXPANSION OF CONSUMER PROTECTION.** Various state laws aimed at preventing fraudulent sales of corporate securities, commonly called blue-sky laws, have been adopted. It was not until the 1930's, however, that federal legislation was adopted. These statutes are discussed in Chapter 51 on corporate stock.

(a) **Mutual funds.** Because it is extremely difficult for the small investor to learn all the facts material to the value of a given security, mutual funds have proved very popular in the last two decades. The individual investor will purchase shares in the mutual fund, and the fund in turn will make investments in the securities of various enterprises. The great advantage to the individual is that the problem of investment guidance is passed from his shoulders to those of the investment counselors of the fund. Another advantage to the small investor is that mutual funds will accept for investment sums of money that are relatively small and which ordinarily could not be invested directly in stocks and bonds.

By the Investment Company Act Amendments of 1970,[45] restrictions are imposed by the federal government to prevent mutual funds from overcharging investors for the services they render. If a fund pays an excessive amount to its investment counselor, the dissatisfied investor in the fund or the Securities Exchange Commission may sue the counselor to recover the improper excess portion of the fee.

(b) **Real estate development sales.** Anyone promoting the sale of a real estate development which is divided into fifty or more parcels of less than five acres each must file with the Secretary of Housing and Urban Development a *development statement* setting forth significant details of the development specified by the federal Land Sales Act.[46]

When anyone buys or rents one of the parcels in the subdivision, a *property report* must be given to him. This is a condensed version of the development statement filed with the Secretary of HUD. This report must be given to the prospective customer more than 48 hours before he signs the contract to buy or lease.

If the development statement is not filed with the Secretary, the sale or renting of the real estate development may not be promoted through the channels of interstate commerce nor by use of the mail.

If the property report is given to the prospective buyer or tenant less than 48 hours before he signs a contract to buy or lease, or after he has signed, he has 48 hours in which to avoid his contract. If he never receives the property report, he may avoid the contract and there is no statutory limitation on the time in which he must act.

---

[45] PL 91-547, 84 Stat 1413.
[46] PL 90-448, 82 Stat 590, 15 USC § 1701 et seq.

(c) **Insurance.** The states have made extensive regulation of insurance companies by establishing standards for their financial structure as by regulating the reserves which must be maintained in order to assure policyholders that there will be sufficient funds with which to pay policy claims. In the case of a foreign insurance company doing business within a state, the company is commonly required to deposit a substantial sum with a local state official to hold available for the payment of policies issued to persons living within the state.

Statutes often seek to protect the policyholder or applicant from misconduct of insurance agents and brokers. Apart from requiring their licensing, statutes may make certain conduct illegal. For example, it is commonly a crime, called *twisting,* for an insurance salesman to induce a policyholder to cancel his existing policy and change to another company when the policyholder is not benefited from the change and the objective of the salesman is merely to obtain the commissions that the second company will pay him for selling its policy. In some states payments to an insurance broker are declared to be as effective as though made to the insurance company,[47] even though the broker is not the agent of the insurer; thus protecting the customer from the failure of the broker, whether accidental or intentional, to send the money to the insurance company.

(d) **Service contracts.** The UCCC treats a consumer service contract the same as a consumer sale of goods if payment is made in installments or a credit charge is made and the amount financed does not exceed $25,000.[48] It defines "services" broadly as embracing work, specified privileges, and insurance provided by a noninsurer. The inclusion of "privileges" makes the UCCC apply to contracts calling for payment on the installment plan or including a financing charge for transportation, hotel and restaurant accommodations, education, entertainment, recreation, physical culture, hospital accommodations, funerals, and similar accommodations.

Some states have adopted statutes requiring that any present payments for future funeral services or goods must be deposited in a bank account or similar depository to be held for the benefit of the customer. A contract which does not provide for such deposit is void as being against public policy.

The mere extension of credit to the consumer of services does not bring the transaction under the UCCC. That is, the fact that a doctor does not require immediate payment from his patient does not make it a transaction within the UCCC.[49]

Closely related to the exploitation of consumers by charging excessive prices is the practice of charging for unperformed services. To some extent, such practice is condemned.

---

[47] Zak v Fidelity-Phenix Insurance Co. 58 IllApp2d 341, 208 NE2d 29.

[48] UCCC § 2.104(1). Credit card transactions are exempted unless the person selling the services and the consumer expressly agree that the transaction is subject to the UCCC. § 2.104(2)(a).

[49] Official Comment to § 2.105(3).

FACTS: The Hotel Waldorf-Astoria in New York added a 2 percent charge to the bill of every guest. The charge was described as "sundries," but no further explanation or itemization was made. The hotel claimed that this charge was justified as covering messenger services, but only 77 percent of the guests used such service. The attorney general brought an action to enjoin the making of the charge for sundries and to refund the money which the guests had paid for such item.

DECISION: Judgment against the hotel. The charge for unperformed and unexplained services was a fraud upon the guests and was therefore a violation of the consumer protection statute. [New York v Hotel Waldorf-Astoria, 323 NYS2d 917]

§ 8:13. CONSUMER REMEDIES. The theoretical right of the consumer to sue or to assert a defense is often of little practical value to the consumer because of the small size of the amount involved and the high cost of litigation. Consumer protection legislation provides special remedies.

(a) Government agency action. The UCCC provides for an administrator who will in a sense police business practices to insure comformity with the law.[50] This is not regarded by some as an improvement and has been criticized on the ground of the danger that the administrator may be creditor-oriented, and the debtor might as a consequence be deprived of protection in many cases when it is a question of policy or discretion as to what action, if any, should be taken by the administrator.[51]

(b) Action by attorney general. A number of states provide that the state attorney general may bring an action on behalf of a particular group of consumers to obtain cancellation of their contracts and restitution of whatever they had paid. Many states permit the attorney general to bring an action to enjoin violating the consumer protection statute.

Consumer protection statutes commonly give the Attorney General the authority to seek a voluntary discontinuance of improper practices. If this fails, he is authorized to obtain an injunction from a court.

(c) Action by consumer. Some consumer protection statutes provide that a consumer who is harmed by a violation of the statutes may sue the wrongdoing enterprise to recover a specified penalty or that he may bring an action on behalf of consumers. Consumer protection statutes are often designed to rely on private litigation as an aid to enforcement of the statutory provisions. The Consumer Protection Safety Act of 1972 authorizes "any interested person" to bring a civil action to enforce a consumer product safety rule and certain orders of the Food, Drug, and Consumer Protection Agency (FDCPA).[52] But in some cases the individual consumer cannot bring any action, and enforcement of the law is entrusted exclusively to an administrative agency.

---

[50] UCCC § 6.103-6.116.

[51] Furthermore, this opens the door to all the other problems involved in the regulation of business by administrative agencies.

[52] PL 92-573, 86 Stat 1207, § 23.

§ 8:14. CIVIL AND CRIMINAL PENALTIES. The seller or lender engaging in improper consumer practices may be subject to civil penalties and criminal punishment. In some instances the laws in question are the general laws applicable to improper conduct, while in other cases the laws are specifically aimed at the particular consumer practices.

Illustrative of the applicability of the general law, a contractor who falsely stated to a homeowner that certain repairs needed on the roof of her home cost, with labor and materials, $650 when in fact it was only $200, was guilty of the crime of obtaining money by false pretenses. Under the Truth in Lending Act each periodic statement which violates the disclosure requirements subjects the creditor to a separate claim for damages, as against the contention that there could only be one recovery per customer.

Consumer protection statutes of the disclosure type generally provide that the creditor cannot enforce the obligation of the debtor if the specified information is not set forth in the contract, without regard to whether the statute expressly declares that a nonconforming contract shall be invalid or nonenforceable.

QUESTIONS AND CASE PROBLEMS

1. What is the objective of each of the following rules of law:
   (a) Back-page disclaimers are void if the front page of the contract does not call attention to the presence of such terms.
   (b) A consumer's waiver of a statute designed for his protection is void, but the transaction otherwise binds the consumer.

2. Greif obtained credit cards from Socony Mobil Oil Co. for himself and his wife. The card specified, "This card is valid unless expired or revoked. Named holder's approval of all purchases is presumed unless written notice of loss or theft is received." Later Greif returned his card to the company, stating that he was canceling it, but that he could not return the card in his wife's possession because they had separated. Subsequently Socony sued Greif for purchases made by the wife on the credit card in her possession. He defended on the ground that he had canceled the credit card contract. Decide. [Socony Mobil Oil Co. v Greif, 10 AppDiv2d 119, 197 NYS2d 522]

3. Wilke was contemplating retiring. In response to an advertisement, he purchased from Coinway 30 coin-operated testing machines. He purchased these because Coinway's representative stated that, by placing these machines at different public places, Wilke could obtain supplemental income. This statement was made by the representative although he had no experience as to the cost of servicing such machines or their income-producing potential. The operational costs of the machines by Wilke exceeded the income. Wilke sued Coinway to rescind the contract for fraud. Coinway defended on the ground that the statements made were merely matters of opinion and did not constitute fraud. Was Wilke entitled to rescission? [Wilke v Coinway, Inc. 257 CalApp2d 126, 64 CalRptr 845]

4. Clairol is a manufacturer of hair dyes. In order to save packaging costs and for advertising purposes, it sold to jobbers for resale to beauty parlors and beauty schools bottles of dyes in cartons containing six bottles marked "Professional Use Only." Cody's Cosmetics, a discount retailer, procured and broke the six-packs and sold the bottles individually to the general public. Clairol's products would deteriorate with time when exposed to light. Cody's displayed the individual bottles in open bins exposed to bright store lighting and sold some bottles after the product life date placed on the bottles by Clairol had expired. Clairol sought to enjoin as unfair competition the sale of its hair dyes by Cody's in the manner above described. Was it entitled to an injunction? [Clairol v Cody's Cosmetics, 353 Mass 385, 231 NE2d 912]

5. Jordan purchased a stereo from Montgomery Ward & Co. on credit in reliance on the statement in the seller's catalog that the purchase could be charged and no payment would be required until several months later. It was not disclosed that the credit charge was computed by the seller from the date of purchase and not from the later date when payment was due. Jordan claimed that this violated the federal Truth in Lending Act, which requires a disclosure of financing terms in advertising and further provides that "any creditor who fails in connection with any consumer credit transaction to disclose to any person any information required under this Act to be disclosed to that person is liable to that person in an amount equal to . . . twice the amount of the finance charges . . . except that liability under this paragraph shall not be less than $100 nor greater than $1,000." The seller contended that Jordan could not bring suit. Decide. [Jordan v Montgomery Ward & Co. (CA8 Ill) 442 F2d 78]

6. A New York statute authorized a buyer to cancel a home-solicited sale by giving written notice within three days. Becerra went to the office of Nu Dimensions Figure Salons and signed a contract to take a course of 190 weight-reducing sessions. The contract declared that "buyer specifically acknowledges and understands that the sum promised to be paid herein shall be paid whether or not buyer avails herself of the sessions purchased." When Becerra got home she decided that she did not want the course and notified Nu Dimensions that she canceled her contract. Was she entitled to do so? [Nu Dimensions Figure Salons v Becerra (NY Civil Court) 340 NYS2d 268]

7. Cheney purchased an automobile on credit from Zimmerman Ford. The seller required a cosigner and Cheney gave the dealer a written contract bearing the signature of his aunt, Winnie Ambrose. When Cheney did not pay, the seller claimed that Winnie's signature was a forgery. Winnie signed a second contract to take the place of this first contract. When sued on the second contract, she claimed that it was not binding because the Illinois statute governing installment sales declared "no retail installment contract shall be enforceable by the seller when it contains blank spaces to be filled in after it has been signed by the buyer." She claimed that when the replacement contract was signed, there were blank spaces. Was this a defense? [Zimmerman Ford, Inc v Cheney, 132 IllApp3d 871, 271 NE2d 682]

NATURE AND CLASSES OF CONTRACTS

§ 9:1. INTRODUCTION. Practically every personal business activity involves a contract—an enrollment in college, the purchase of a color TV on the installment plan, the rental of an apartment. Similarly, in each transaction relating to the acquisition of raw materials, their manufacture, and the distribution of the finished products by businesses, a contract that defines the relationship and the rights and obligations of the parties is involved.

Essential to free enterprise in our economic system is the protection of rights created by contracts. Each party to a contract is legally obligated to observe the terms of the agreement, and government generally cannot impair those obligations.

§ 9:2. DEFINITION OF CONTRACT. A contract is a binding agreement.[1] By one definition "a *contract* is a promise or a set of promises for the breach of which the law gives a remedy, or the performance of which the law in some way recognizes as a duty."[2] Contracts arise out of agreements; hence, a contract is often defined as "an agreement creating an obligation."[3]

Generally a contract is an exchange of promises or assents by two or more persons, resulting in an obligation to do or to refrain from doing a particular act, which obligation is recognized or enforced by law. A contract may also be formed when a promise is made by one person in exchange for the act of the refraining from the doing of an act by another.

The substance of the definition of a contract is that by mutual agreement or assent the parties create legally enforceable duties or obligations that had not existed before. If a party to a contract does not discharge his obligation, the usual legal remedy is the awarding of damages to the other party through court action.

---

[1] The Uniform Commercial Code defines "contract" to mean "the total legal obligation which results from the parties' agreement as affected by [the Code] and any other applicable rules of law," UCC § 1-201(11).

[2] Restatement, Contracts, § 1; Mag Construction Co. v McLean County (ND) 181 NW2d 718.

[3] H. Liebes & Co. v Klengenberg (CA9 Cal) 23 F2d 611.

§ **9:3. ESSENTIAL ELEMENTS OF A CONTRACT.** The requirements of a contract are: (1) an agreement, (2) between competent parties, (3) based upon the genuine assent of the parties, (4) supported by consideration, (5) made for a lawful objective, and (6) in the form required by law, if any. These elements will be considered in the chapters that follow.

§ **9:4. SUBJECT MATTER OF CONTRACTS.** The subject matter of a contract may relate to the performance of personal services, such as contracts of employment to work on an assembly line in a factory, to work as a secretary in an office, to sing on television, or to build a house. The contract may provide for the transfer of the ownership of property, such as a house (real property) or an automobile (personal property), from one person to another. A contract may also call for a combination of these things. For example, a builder may contract to supply materials and do the work involved in installing the materials, or a person may contract to build a house and then transfer the house and the land to the buyer.

§ **9:5. PARTIES TO A CONTRACT.** A person who makes a promise is the *promisor*, and the person to whom the promise is made is called the *promisee*. If the promise is binding, it imposes upon the promisor a duty or obligation and he may be called the *obligor*. The promisee who can claim the benefit of the obligation is also called the *obligee*. The parties to a contract are said to stand in privity with each other, and the relationship between them is termed *privity of contract*.

In written contracts, parties may be referred to as "party of the first part" and "party of the second part." Frequently, however, they are given special names that serve better to identify each party. For example, the parties to a contract by which one person agrees that another may occupy his house upon the payment of money are called landlord and tenant, or lessor and lessee, and the contract between them is known as a lease. Other parties have their distinctive names, such as vendor and vendee, for the parties of a sales contract; shipper and carrier, for the parties to a transportation contract; insurer and insured, for the parties of an insurance policy.

A party to a contract may be an individual, a partnership, a corporation, or a government. A person may act for himself, or he may act on behalf of another. There may be one or more persons on each side of the contract. In some cases there are three-sided contracts, as in the case of a credit card, in which there are the company issuing the card, the holder of the card, and the business furnishing goods and services in reliance on the credit card.

In addition to the original parties to the contract, other persons may have rights or duties with respect to it. For example, one party may to some extent assign his rights under the contract to a third person. Again, the contract may have been made for the benefit of a third person, as in a life insurance contract, and the third party (the beneficiary) is permitted to enforce the contract.

§ **9:6. HOW A CONTRACT ARISES.** A contract is based upon an agreement. An agreement arises when one person, the *offeror*, makes an offer and the

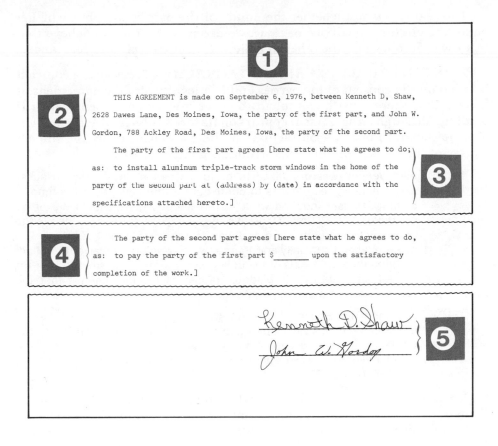

THIS AGREEMENT is made on September 6, 1976, between Kenneth D, Shaw, 2628 Dawes Lane, Des Moines, Iowa, the party of the first part, and John W. Gordon, 788 Ackley Road, Des Moines, Iowa, the party of the second part.

The party of the first part agrees [here state what he agrees to do; as: to install aluminum triple-track storm windows in the home of the party of the second part at (address) by (date) in accordance with the specifications attached hereto.]

The party of the second part agrees [here state what he agrees to do, as: to pay the party of the first part $_____ upon the satisfactory completion of the work.]

CONTRACT

Note that this contract includes the important items of information: (1) the date, (2) the name and address of each party, (3) the promise or consideration of the seller, (4) the promise or consideration of the buyer, and (5) the signatures of the two parties.

person to whom the offer is made, the *offeree*, accepts. There must be both an offer and an acceptance. If either is lacking, there is no contract.[4]

An offeror may make an offer to a particular person because he wants only that person to do what he has in mind. On the other hand, he may make the offer to the public at large because he does not care by whom something is done so long as it is done. The latter case arises, for example, when a reward is offered to the public for the return of lost property.

It is frequently said that a meeting of the minds is essential to an agreement or a contract. Modern courts do not stress the meeting of the minds, however, because in some situations the law finds an agreement even though the minds of the parties have not in fact met.

---

[4] Milanko v Jensen, 404 Ill 261, 88 NE2d 857.

The real test is not whether the minds of the parties met, but whether under the circumstances one party was reasonably entitled to believe that there was an offer and the other to believe that there was an acceptance.

§ 9:7. INTENT TO MAKE A BINDING AGREEMENT. Because a contract is based on the consent of the parties and is a legally binding agreement, it follows that there must be an intent to enter into an agreement which is binding. Although an agreement appears on its face to be a final agreement, it may be shown to be "noncontractual" by its own terms or by the subject matter of the agreement and the surrounding circumstances.

FACTS: A movement was organized to build a Charles City College. Hauser and others signed pledges to contribute to the college. At the time of signing, Hauser inquired what would happen if he should die or be unable to pay. The representative of the college stated that the pledge would not then be binding and was merely a statement of intent. The college failed financially and Pappas was appointed receiver to collect and liquidate the assets of the college corporation. He sued Hauser for the amount due on his pledge. Hauser raised the defense that the pledge was not a binding contract.

DECISION: Judgment for Hauser. From the statements of the representative of the college, it was clear that the pledge had not been intended by the parties as a binding agreement. It was therefore not a contract and could not be enforced against Hauser. [Pappas v Hauser, 293 Iowa 102, 197 NW2d 607]

When the elements of a contract exist there is a binding contract, even though there is no express statement that the parties are making a contract, that a promise is made, or that something is consideration for a promise. Consequently, when the subcontractors on a construction job were threatening to quit work because they were afraid the contractor would not pay them, the owner became bound by a contract to pay them when he told the subcontractors, "Don't do that. I'll see that you get your money," and "Don't worry about it"; as against the contention that there was no contract because the owner had not stated that he promised to pay the subcontractors.

§ 9:8. WORKING ARRANGEMENTS. Working arrangements between parties are sometimes not regarded as "contracts" because it was in fact not the intention of the parties to be so bound thereby that suit could be brought for nonperformance. For example, when a city had agreed to provide firefighting protection for an area adjoining the city in order to protect the city from the hazard of the spread of an outlying fire, there was no contract, even though persons in the outlying area made money donations or payments in exchange for such fire protection.

When a working arrangement is part of a clearly contractual relationship, the transaction remains a binding contract because the purpose of the working arrangement is merely to provide flexibility to a contract. Consequently, a contract by which a bank agrees to accept the assignment of such contracts from a dealer as the bank shall deem "acceptable" remains a contract, even though theoretically the bank could refuse to find any contract acceptable. Likewise, a contract to pay commissions to a sales agent on a specified sliding scale on orders under one-quarter million dollars and to pay on larger orders such compensation as shall be agreed to remains a binding contract obligating the employer to pay the agent reasonable compensation for orders over one-quarter million dollars, as against the contention that there was no contract because the parties might never agree to the compensation to be paid on the large orders.

§ 9:9. **STATISTICAL PROJECTIONS.** Many transactions contemplate future events or benefits. For example, a person may obtain a life insurance policy which pays a certain amount of income per month when he retires; or he might deposit money in a bank and receive a certificate of deposit on which he will receive interest; or he might take a particular job because of the pension plan benefits offered by that employer. In the course of negotiation or discussion leading up to a contract, one party to a transaction may show the other party various charts, tables, and statistical projections into the future to show the actual dollar value of the particular transaction to the other party. It is a question of intent to what extent such matter is merely illustrative and to what extent it is part of the contract. If it is merely illustrative and there is no element of fraudulent deception, there is no liability when the subsequent facts are different than had been projected or estimated. If it is part of the contract, then if there is a difference between the projection and the subsequent reality, there is breach of contract and liability will be imposed accordingly.

§ 9:10. **ENCLOSED PRINTED MATTER.** Frequently a contract is mailed or delivered by one party to the other in an envelope which contains additional printed matter. Similarly, when goods are purchased, the buyer often receives with the goods a manufacturer's manual and various pamphlets. What effect do all these papers have upon the contract?

(a) **Incorporation of other statement.** The contract itself may furnish the answer. Sometimes the contract will expressly refer to and incorporate into the contract the terms of the other writing or printed statement. For example, a warehouse contract may expressly state that it covers the "goods" of the customer, but instead of listing the goods, the contract will continue by following the words "goods of the customer" with the words "as set forth in Schedule A which is delivered to the buyer with this contract." Frequently such a schedule will be stapled or otherwise attached to the contract itself. Or the contract may say that the customer will be charged at the rates set forth in the approved tariff schedule posted on the premises of the warehouse, and may continue with the words, "a copy of which is attached hereto and made part of this contract."

(b) **Exclusion of other statement.** As the opposite of incorporation, the contract may declare that there is nothing outside of the contract. This means that either there never was anything else or that any prior agreement was merely a preliminary step which is finally canceled out or erased and the contract in its final form is stated in the writing. For example, the seller of goods may state in his contract that no statements as to the goods had been made to the buyer and that the written contract contains all of the terms of the sale.

In a strict sense an exclusion clause is unnecessary because if there is a written contract, it will ordinarily be regarded as the entire contract and anything outside of that contract will be ignored. As a practical matter, however, the exclusion clause has value in that some situations arise when it is not quite clear whether the writing is the entire contract or whether the situation is to be treated as though the writing had expressly stated that the earlier terms were incorporated into the contract. In order to avoid uncertainty and make clear the intent of the parties, a provision stating that the writing is the total and exclusive contract has practical value.

(c) Reduction of contract terms. The effect of accompanying or subsequently delivered printed matter may be to reduce the terms of the written contract. That is, one party may have had a better bargain under the original contract. In this case the accompanying matter will generally be ignored if it is not shown that the party who would be harmed has agreed that it be part of the contract.

> **FACTS:** The School District mailed a teaching contract to Adamick. In the same envelope there was a copy of the school calendar. Adamick and other teachers later brought an action against the school to prevent it from holding classes on three dates specified in the calendar as holidays. The District defended on the ground that the calendar could be changed by the District.

> **DECISION:** The contract did not make any specific reference to the school calendar which had been mailed in the same envelope. The school calendar was therefore not part of the contract and there was no contract obligation on the school district to treat as holidays any days which had been so specified in the calendar. [Adamick v Ferguson-Florissant School District (MoApp) 483 SW2d 629]

If a contract has already been made and the accompanying matter seeks to reduce the rights of one party, as when the manufacturer's manual reduces the rights which the buyer would otherwise have, such reducing writing has no effect. A contract once made cannot be changed by unilateral action; that is, by the action of one party or one side to the contract.

§ 9:11. FORMAL AND SIMPLE CONTRACTS. Contracts are classified in terms of their forms as (a) contracts under seal, (b) contracts of record, and (c) simple contracts. The first two classes are formal contracts.

(a) Contracts under seal. A *contract under seal* is executed by affixing a seal or by making an impression upon the paper or upon some tenacious substance, such as wax, attached to the instrument. Although at common law an impression was necessary, the courts now treat various signs or marks to be the equivalent of a seal. To illustrate, most states hold that there is a seal if a person's signature or a corporation's name is followed by a scroll or scrawl, the word "seal," or the letters "L.S."

A contract under seal is binding at common law solely because of its formality. In some states this has been changed by statute. The Uniform Commercial Code abolishes the law of seals for the sale of goods. In some states the law of seals has been abolished generally without regard to the nature of the transaction involved.

(b) Contracts of record. One form of *contract of record* arises when one acknowledges before a proper court that he is obligated to pay a certain sum unless a specified thing is done or not done. For example, a party who has been arrested may be released on his promise to appear in court and may bind himself to pay a certain sum in the event that he fails to do so. An obligation of this kind is known as a *recognizance*.

(c) Simple contracts. All contracts other than contracts of record and contracts under seal are called *simple contracts* or informal contracts, without regard to whether they are oral or written.

§ 9:12. EXPRESS AND IMPLIED CONTRACTS. Simple contracts may be classified in terms of the way in which they are created as express contracts or implied contracts.

(a) Express contracts. An *express contract* is one in which the parties have made oral or written declarations of their intentions and of the terms of the transaction.

(b) Implied contracts. An *implied contract* (or, as sometimes stated, a contract implied in fact) is one in which the evidence of the agreement is not shown by words, written or spoken, but by the acts and conduct of the parties.[5] Such a contract arises, for example, when one person, without being requested to do so, renders services under circumstances indicating that he expects to be paid for them, and the other person, knowing such circumstances, accepts the benefit of those services.

FACTS: Glenn owned and operated the Seminole Bus Company. The First National Bank held a chattel mortgage on the buses. Stoberl ran a gas and service station. Glenn and Stoberl made an agreement that, if Glenn would buy all his gas and have all his repairs made at Stoberl's, he could park his buses at Stoberl's without charge. Because of illness, Glenn stopped running the bus business. Sometime thereafter, the bank sued Stoberl for the buses. He defended on the ground that he was holding the buses for storage charges under agreement for storage with the bank. The bank replied that there was no contract for storage.

---

[5] Capital Warehouse Co. v McGill-Warner Farnham Co. 276 Minn 108, 148 NW2d 31. Contracts of this nature may be more accurately described as contracts "expressed" by conduct, as distinguished from contracts expressed in words. It is more common, however, to refer to these contracts as implied.

DECISION: The land occupied by the buses had commercial value. When the land was used for the bank's benefit and at its request, an implied contract arose that the bank would pay the reasonable storage charge for the use of that land. As the bank was not buying any gas or service from Stoberl, there would be no reasonable ground for finding that the parties intended that the storage should be provided free to the bank. [First National Bank v Stoberl, 132 IllApp2d 322, 270 NE2d 493]

An implied contract cannot arise when there is an existing express contract on the same subject. Likewise, no contract is implied when the relationship of the parties is such that by a reasonable interpretation the performance of services or the supplying of goods was intended as a gift.

In terms of effect, there is no difference between an implied contract and an express contract. The difference relates solely to the manner of proving the contract.

FACTS: Prior to the death of Emma Center, her nephew's wife, Clara Stewart, rendered various household services to Emma. All of the parties lived in the same house as a family group. During most of the time in question, Clara had a full-time job. After Emma's death, Clara sued Emma's estate for the value of her household services.

DECISION: Judgment for the estate. When a member of a family group renders ordinary household services, it is presumed that they are rendered gratuitously unless the claimant can prove that there was an express contract to pay for them or that the services were extraordinary in character. In the absence of such proof, no contract is implied and no recovery is allowed. [Stewart v Brandenburg (Ky) 383 SW2d 1122]

When a plumber, in repairing a sewer pipe for a homeowner, found other pipes in need of replacement and so informed the homeowner and proceeded to replace such pipes with her knowledge and without any objection, a contract was implied from the conduct of the parties to pay for such additional work.

FACTS: Hix was employed as a teacher by the Tuloso-Midway Independent School District. He began to work in 1962 under a contract which was renewed each year for another year. In 1968, the contract was not renewed and he brought suit against the District on the theory that there was an obligation to renew his contract in the absence of any ground for discharge.

DECISION: Judgment for School District. When a contract is to run for a fixed period of time, it ceases to exist upon the expiration of that term. The fact that, in prior years, the parties had repeatedly renewed the contract when it expired does not give rise to an implied contract that they should continue to do so. [Hix v Tuloso-Midway Independent School District (TexCivApp) 489 SW2d 706]

§ 9:13. VALID AND VOIDABLE CONTRACTS AND VOID AGREEMENTS. Another classification of contracts is in terms of their enforceability or validity.

(a) Valid contracts. A *valid contract* is an agreement that is binding and enforceable.

(b) Voidable contracts. A *voidable contract* is an agreement that is otherwise binding and enforceable but, because of the circumstances surrounding its execution or the capacity of one of the parties, it may be rejected at the option of one of the parties. For example, one who has been forced to sign an agreement against his will may in some instances avoid liability on the contract.

(c) Void Agreements. A *void agreement* is without legal effect. Thus, an agreement that contemplates the performance of an act prohibited by law is usually incapable of enforcement; hence it is void. Likewise, it cannot be made binding by later approval or ratification.[6]

§ 9:14. EXECUTED AND EXECUTORY CONTRACTS.
Contracts may be classified, in terms of the extent to which they have been performed, as executed contracts and executory contracts.

(a) Executed contracts. An *executed contract* is one that has been completely performed. In other words, an executed contract is one under which nothing remains to be done by either party. A contract may be executed at once, as in the case of a cash sale; or it may be executed or performed in the future.

(b) Executory contracts. In an *executory contract*, something remains to be done. For example, if a utility company agrees to furnish electricity to another party for a specified period of time at a stipulated price, the contract is executory. If the entire price is paid in advance, the contract is still deemed executory; although, strictly speaking, it is executed on one side and executory on the other.

Whether a contract is executory determines in some cases whether it can be set aside by a minor or a trustee in bankruptcy of a party. In some cases, if it is executed, it cannot be set aside; if it is executory, it can.

§ 9:15. BILATERAL AND UNILATERAL CONTRACTS.
In making an offer the offeror is in effect extending a promise to do something, such as to pay a sum of money, if the offeree will do what the offeror requests. If the offeror extends a promise and asks for a promise in return and if the offeree accepts the offer by making the promise, the contract is called a *bilateral contract* because one promise is given in exchange for another. Thus, each party is bound by the obligation to perform his promise.

In contrast, the offeror may agree to obligate himself only when something is done by the offeree. Since only one party is obligated to perform after the contract has been made, this kind of contract is called a *unilateral contract*. This is illustrated by the case of the reward for the return of lost property because the offeror does not wish to have promises by members of the public that they will try to return the lost property. The offeror wants the property, and he promises to pay anyone who returns the property.

---

[6] See § 15:1. Although the distinction between a void agreement and a voidable contract is clear in principle, there is frequently confusion because some courts regard a given transaction as void while others regard it as merely voidable.

FACTS: The Weil Furniture Co. stated in a local newspaper advertisement that each person who sent in an accurate estimate of the number of dots in the ad would receive a credit certificate which could be applied on the purchase of a certain make of television set. Schreiner mailed his estimate and was notified that he had won one of the certificates. The certificate he received stated that it could be used only in the purchase of certain models. The newspaper ad had not contained this restriction. Schreiner objected to this restriction.

DECISION: Judgment for Schreiner. The ad constituted an offer which was accepted when Schreiner mailed in an estimate that was a "winner." This unilateral contract was based upon the terms of the ad. The limitation found in the certificate was not binding on Schreiner since it was not a term of the contract between the parties. [Schreiner v Weil Furniture Co. (La) 68 So2d 149]

§ 9:16. QUASI CONTRACTS. Under certain circumstances the law imposes an obligation to pay for a benefit received as though a contract had actually been made. This will be done in a limited number of situations in order to attain an equitable or just result. For example, when a homeowner permits repairs to be made on his home with the knowledge that they are being made by a stranger who would expect to be paid for such repairs, there is a quasi-contractual duty to pay for the reasonable value of the improvements in order to avoid the homeowner's unjust enrichment at the expense of the repairman. In order to distinguish this type of obligation from a true contract which is based upon the agreement of the parties, the obligation is called a *quasi contract*.

FACTS: Dozier and his wife, daughter, and grandson lived in the house Dozier owned. At the request of the daughter and grandson, Paschall made some improvements to the house. Dozier did not authorize these, but he knew that the improvements were being made and did not object to them. Paschall sued Dozier for the reasonable value of the improvements. Dozier defended on the ground that he had not made any contract for such improvements.

DECISION: Judgment for Paschall. When a homeowner permits repairs to be made to his home with knowledge that they are being made by a stranger who would expect to be paid for such repairs, there is a quasi contractual duty to pay for the reasonable value of the improvements to avoid the homeowner's unjust enrichment at the expense of the repairman. [Paschall's v Dozier, 219 Tenn 45, 407 SW2d 150]

While the objective of the quasi contract is to do justice, one must not jump to the conclusion that a quasi contract will arise every time there is an injustice. The mere fact that someone has benefited someone else and has not been paid will not necessarily give rise to a quasi contract.

Likewise, no quasi contractual obligation arises when the plaintiff merely confers upon the defendant a benefit to which the defendant was already entitled.

The fact that performance of the contract proves more difficult or more expensive than had been expected does not entitle a party to extra compensation when there was no misrepresentation as to the conditions that would be encountered or the events that would occur and particularly when the party complaining is experienced with the particular type of contract and the problems which are likely to be encountered. That is, the contractor is not entitled to a quasi contractual recovery for the extra expense on the theory that he had conferred a greater benefit than had been contemplated.

QUESTIONS AND CASE PROBLEMS

1. State the specific objective(s) of the law (from the list in Chapter 2, pages 8-13) illustrated by the following quotation: "A person shall not be allowed to enrich himself unjustly at "the expense of another."

2. Lombard insured his car under a theft policy that required the insurer to repair damages to the car when stolen or to pay the money equivalent of the damages. Lombard's car was stolen, and he and the insurance adjuster agreed as to what repairs should be made. The adjuster then took the car to General Auto Service, Inc. to make the repairs. When the insurance company was unable to pay for the repairs, General Auto Service sued Lombard because he had received the benefit of the contract. Was he liable for the repair bill? [General Auto Service, Inc. v Lombard (La) 151 So2d 536]

3. Tetrauld made a written agreement to sell his land to Bauer. Tetrauld died. Bauer claimed that after agreement for the sale of the land had been made, they had orally agreed that Tetrauld would give the land to Bauer for his past services instead of selling it to him. Monroe, who was administering the estate of Tetrauld, objected to changing the written contract. A Montana statute provided that a "contract in writing may be altered by a contract in writing or by an executed oral agreement, and not otherwise." Was the oral agreement barred by this statute? [Bauer v Monroe, 117 Mont 306, 158 P2d 485]

4. Mrs. Herbert, the owner of an orchard, and Cantor, to whom she had leased the orchard, desired to borrow money so that a crop could be grown by the tenant. Part of the money required by them was loaned by the Pinnacle Packing Co. and the Medford National Bank. The loan agreement stated that the lenders would "furnish" the money and that when the crops were sold, there would be deducted a sufficient amount "to repay the advances made by [the lenders] before any payments would be made to the borrowers." There was no express provision in the agreement that the borrowers would repay the money. No oral agreement to repay was made by either borrower. Pinnacle Packing Co. then sued Herbert to recover the amount of the money advanced. She defended on the ground that she had not expressly agreed to repay the money borrowed. Decide. [Pinnacle Packing Co. v Herbert, 157 Ore 96, 70 P2d 31]

5. McNulty signed a contract with the Medical Service of District of Columbia, Inc. The contract, which was on a printed form prepared by the corporation, concluded with the clause: "In witness whereof, the party of the first part has caused its corporate seal to be hereunto affixed and these presents to be signed by its duly authorized officers and the party of the second part has hereunto set his hand and seal the day and year first above written." The contract had been sent to McNulty, who signed and sealed it, and then returned it to the corporation. The latter signed but did not seal it, and then sent an executed copy of the contract to the plaintiff without referring to the lack of a seal. When McNulty sued on the contract, the corporation claimed that it was an unsealed contract because it had not been sealed by both parties. Was it correct? [McNulty v Medical Service of District of Columbia (MCApp DistCol) 176 A2d 783]

6. Martha Parker reared Louis Twiford as a foster son from the time he was 6 or 7 years of age. He lived with her until he was 27 years of age when he married and moved into another house. During the next few years Martha was very ill, and Louis took care of her. She died; and Louis made a claim against Waterfield, her executor, for the reasonable value of the services he had rendered. Was he entitled to recover? [Twiford v Waterfield, 240 NC 582, 83 SE2d 548]

7. A state statute required the County Board of Commissioners to advertise their proceedings in a newspaper. The *Greensburg Times* published the notices for the commissioners. The commissioners later refused to pay the newspaper on the ground that they had not executed a written contract with the newspaper on behalf of the county. Decide. [Board of Commissioners v Greensburg Times, 215 Ind 471, 19 NE2d 459]

8. A rented a building from B under a long-term lease. A contracted with C for the installation of an air-conditioning unit in such a way that it could not be removed. B had no knowledge of the installation. When A did not pay for the work, C sued B on the ground that C had improved B's property and that B would be unjustly enriched if not required to pay for the benefit he received. Was C entitled to recover the reasonable value of the installation from B? [See Kemp v Majestic Amusement Co. 427 Pa 429, 234 A2d 846]

9. William was a certified public accountant. He did all the accounting work for his wife, Frances. William and Frances were divorced but remained friendly. William continued to perform the accounting services as before and also for North Star Motors, a business operated by the brother of Frances. When Frances sued William on a promissory note, he counterclaimed for compensation for his accounting services rendered to his ex-wife and her brother on the theory that an implied contract arose to pay him for such services. Was he entitled to recover on the counterclaim? [Ryan v Ryan (DelSuper) 298 A2d 343]

10. A sued B. A claimed that because of certain conduct B was under a quasi contractual liability to pay A a sum of money spent by A in performing certain work. B claimed that he could not be liable because he had never made any agreement with A to do the work nor to pay him any sum of money. Was this a valid defense? [See Minnesota Avenue, Inc. v Automatic Packages, Inc. 211 Kan 461, 507 P2d 268]

11. A made a contract to construct a house for B. Subsequently, B sued A for breach of contract. A raised the defense that the contract was not binding because it was not sealed. Is this a valid defense? [See Cooper v G.E. Construction Co. 116 GaApp 690, 158 SE2d 305]

THE AGREEMENT

An *offer* expresses the willingness of the offeror to enter into a contractual agreement regarding a particular subject. It is a promise which is conditional upon an act, a forbearance, or a return promise that is given in exchange for the promise or its performance.

A. REQUIREMENTS OF AN OFFER

§ 10:1. **CONTRACTUAL INTENTION.** To constitute an offer, the offeror must intend to create a legal obligation or must appear to intend to do so. When there is neither such intention nor the appearance of such intention, it makes no difference whether the offeree takes any action concerning the offer. The following are examples of a lack of contractual intention on the part of the offeror.

(a) **Social invitations.** Ordinary invitations to social affairs are not "offers" in the eyes of the law. The acceptance of a social invitation, such as an invitation to go to dinner, does not give rise to a legally binding agreement or contract.

(b) **Offers made in jest or excitement.** If an offer is made in obvious jest, the offeree cannot accept it and then sue the offeror for breach of the agreement. Here the offeree, as a reasonable person, should realize that no contract is intended and therefore no contract arises even though the offeror speaks words which, if seriously spoken, could be accepted and result in a contract. Likewise, an extravagant offer of a reward made in the heat of excitement cannot be acted upon as a valid offer.

It is not always obvious or apparent to the offeree when the offer is made in jest or when excited. If it is reasonable under the circumstances for the offeree to believe that the offer was made seriously, a contract is formed by the offeree's acceptance.

FACTS: Zehmer discussed selling a farm to Lucy. After some discussion of a
first draft of a contract, Zehmer and his wife signed a paper stating:

"We hereby agree to sell to W. O. Lucy the Ferguson Farm complete for $50,000.00, title satisfactory to buyer." Lucy agreed to purchase the farm on these terms. Thereafter the Zehmers refused to transfer title to Lucy and claimed that they had made the contract for sale as a joke. Lucy brought an action to enforce the contract.

DECISION: Judgment for Lucy. It would appear from the circumstances that Zehmer was serious but, even if he were joking, it was apparent that Lucy had believed that Zehmer was serious and Lucy, as a reasonable person, was entitled to do so under the circumstances. Hence, there was a binding contract. [Lucy v Zehmer, 196 Va 493, 84 SE2d 516]

(c) Invitations to negotiate. The first statement made by one of two persons is not necessarily an offer. In many instances there may be preliminary discussion or an *invitation* by one party to the other *to negotiate* or talk business.

Ordinarily, when a seller sends out circulars or catalogs listing prices, he is not regarded as making an offer to sell at those prices but as merely indicating that he is willing to consider an offer made by a buyer on those terms. The reason for this rule is in part the practical consideration that since a seller does not have an unlimited supply of any commodity, he cannot possibly intend to make a contract with everyone who sees his circular. The same principle is applied to merchandise that is displayed with price tags in stores or store windows and to most advertisements. A "for sale" advertisement in a newspaper is merely an invitation to negotiate and is not an offer which can be accepted, even though the seller has only one of the particular item advertised.

FACTS: Lee Calan Imports directed the Chicago-Sun Times to run an ad in its newspaper for the sale of one 1964 Volvo Station Wagon for $1,795. The newspaper mistakenly stated the price as $1,095. O'Brien agreed to purchase the car at that price. Lee Calan refused to sell the car. O'Brien sued Lee Calan for breach of contract. Thereafter O'Brien died, and the executor of his estate, O'Keefe, continued the action.

DECISION: Judgment for Lee Calan. The ad was merely an invitation to negotiate, not an offer that could be accepted by a customer. Hence, when O'Brien stated that he would buy the car, there was no contract but merely an offer which Lee Calan had not accepted. [O'Keefe v Lee Calan Imports, Inc. 128 IllApp2d 410, 262 NE2d 758]

The circumstances may be such, however, that even a newspaper advertisement constitutes an offer. Thus, the seller made an offer when he advertised specific items that would be sold at a clearance sale at the prices listed and added the words "first come, first served."[1]

Quotations of prices, even when sent on request, are likewise not offers in the absence of previous dealings between the parties or the existence of a trade custom which would give the recipient of the quotation reason to believe that an offer was being made to him. Whether a price quotation is to be treated as an offer or merely an invitation to negotiate is a question of fact as to the intent of the party making such quotations. Although sellers

---

[1] Lefkowitz v Great Minneapolis Surplus Store, Inc. 251 Minn 188, 86 NW2d 689.

are not bound by quotations and price tags, they will as a matter of goodwill ordinarily make every effort to deliver the merchandise at those prices.[2]

In some instances, it is apparent that an invitation to negotiate and not an offer has been made. When construction work is done for the national government, for a state government, or for a political subdivision, statutes require that a printed statement of the work to be done be published and circulated. Contractors are invited to submit bids on the work, and the statute generally requires that the bid of the lowest responsible bidder be accepted. Such an invitation for bids is clearly an invitation to negotiate, both from its nature and from the fact that it does not specify the price to be paid for the work. The bid of each contractor is an offer, and there is no contract until the government accepts one of these bids. This procedure of advertising for bids is also commonly employed by private persons when a large construction project is involved.

In some cases the fact that material terms are missing serves to indicate that the parties were merely negotiating and that an oral contract had not been made. When a letter or printed promotional matter of a party leaves many significant details to be worked out later, the letter or printed matter is merely an invitation to negotiate and is not an offer which may be accepted and a contract thereby formed.

(d) Statement of intention. In some instances a person may make a statement of his intention but not intend to be bound by a contract. For example, when a lease does not expressly allow the tenant to terminate the lease because of a job transfer, the landlord might state that should the tenant be required to leave for that reason, the landlord would try to find a new tenant to take over the lease. This declaration of intention does not give rise to a binding contract, and the landlord cannot be held liable for a breach of contract should the landlord fail to obtain a new tenant or should he not even attempt to do so.

(e) Agreements to make a contract at a future date. No contract arises when the parties merely agree that at a future date they shall consider making a contract or shall make a contract on terms to be agreed upon at that time. In such a case, neither party is under any obligation until the future contract is made. Thus, a promise to pay a bonus or compensation to be decided upon after three months is not binding.

(f) Sham transactions. Sometimes what appears to be a contract is entered into for the purpose of deceiving a third person or a government examiner. For example, when a bank does not hold sufficient assets to meet the deposit reserve ratio established by the Federal Reserve Bank, a friend of the bank may sign a promissory note payable to the bank so that the bank would appear to hold more assets than it actually does. Such a sham transaction cannot be enforced between the parties. That is, the bank cannot enforce the note against the maker because the bank knew that it was never intended to be a binding transaction.

---

[2] Meridian Star v Kay, 207 Miss 78, 41 So2d 746. Statutes prohibiting false or misleading advertising may also require adherence to advertised prices.

§ **10:2. DEFINITE OFFER.** An offer, and the resulting contract, must be definite and certain. If an offer is indefinite or vague or if an essential provision is lacking, no contract arises from an attempt to accept it.[3] The reason is that the courts cannot tell what the parties are to do. Thus, an offer to conduct a business for such time as should be profitable is too vague to be a valid offer. The "acceptance" of such an offer would not result in a contract that could be enforced. A promise to give an injured employee "suitable" employment that he was "able to do" is too vague to be a binding contract.

> **FACTS:** Bonnevier, an employee of the Dairy Cooperative Association, lived in his own home near the employer's plant. The employer wished to expand the plant and decided to purchase Bonnevier's house. Bonnevier was not then working because of an injury. He claimed that an agreement was made to sell the house to the Association in return for which he would be paid $12,000 and would be given "suitable" employment that he "was able to do." The Association did not thereafter employ Bonnevier, who then sued the Association for breach of contract.

> **DECISION:** Judgment for the Association. Any agreement as to employment was too vague to be a binding contract because it could not be determined what kind of employment was intended nor what was suitable. [Bonnevier v Dairy Cooperative Association, 227 Ore 123, 361 P2d 262]

The offer and contract may be made definite by reference to another writing, as when the parties agreed that the written lease which was to be executed by them should be the standard form of lease with which both were familiar.

A *divisible contract* consists of two or more parts and calls for corresponding performances of each part by the parties. If part of a divisible contract provides for the execution of a future agreement pertaining to certain matters and that part by itself is too vague to be binding, such a provision does not alter the enforceability of other parts of the same contract that are otherwise binding.

> **FACTS:** Fincher was employed by Belk-Sawyer Co. as fashion coordinator for the latter's retail stores. The contract of employment also provided for additional services of Fincher to be thereafter agreed upon in connection with beauty consultation and shopping services to be established at the stores. After Fincher had been employed as fashion coordinator for several months, Belk-Sawyer Co. refused to be bound by the contract on the ground that it was indefinite.

> **DECISION:** Judgment for Fincher. The contract was sufficiently definite as to the present employment, and the intention of the parties to have a present contract on that subject was not to be defeated because they recognized that an additional agreement might be made by them as to other work. [Fincher v Belk-Sawyer Co (FlaApp) 127 So2d 130]

---

[3] Williamson v Miller, 231 NC 722, 58 SE2d 743; Wm. Muirhead Construction Co. v Housing Authority of Durham, 1 NCApp 181, 160 SE2d 542.

Although an offer must be definite and certain, not all of its terms need be expressed. Some of the terms may be implied. For example, an offer "to pay $50 for a watch" does not state the terms of payment. A court would consider that cash payment was to be made upon delivery of the watch. The offer and contract may also be made definite by reference to another writing, or by referring to the prior dealings of the parties and to trade practices.

§ 10:3. EXCEPTIONS TO DEFINITENESS. As exceptions to the requirement of definiteness, the law has come to recognize certain situations where the practical necessity of doing business makes it desirable to have a "contract," yet the situation is such that it is either impossible or undesirable to adopt definite terms in advance. Thus, the law recognizes binding contracts in the following situations, although at the time that the contract is made there is some element which is not definite:

(a) Cost-plus contracts. Cost-plus contracts are valid as against the contention that the amount to be paid is not definite when the contract is made. Such contracts protect the contractor by enabling him to enter into a contract without setting up extraordinary reserves against cost contingencies that may arise.

(b) Requirements and output contracts. Contracts by which a supplier agrees in advance to sell its entire future output to a particular buyer or by which a buyer agrees to buy all of its needs or requirements from a particular supplier are valid, as discussed in § 23:4(d), even though at the time of contracting the amount of goods to be covered by the contract is not known.

A contract by which the buyer agrees to purchase its fuel oil requirements for its electricity generating system from the seller is binding, even though the buyer was free to purchase natural gas which could be used as well as oil in the buyer's system; this is so as against the contention that the contract was not binding and was illusory because there was no obligation on the part of the buyer to purchase any quantity from the seller.

(c) Services as needed. An enterprise may desire to be assured that the services of a given person, customarily a professional or a specialist, will be available when needed. It is thus becoming valid to make a contract with the professional to supply such services as in the professional's opinion will be required, although this is indefinite and would appear to give such person the choice of doing nothing if the person so chooses.[4]

(d) Indefinite duration contracts. Contracts with no specific time limit are valid. The law meets the objection that there is a lack of definiteness by interpreting the contract as being subject to termination at the election of

---

[4] Under such contracts the duty to act in good faith supplies the protection found in most contracts in the "usual rules as to certainty and definiteness." McNussen v Graybeal, 141 Mont 571, 405 P2d 447.

either party. This type of contract is used most commonly in employment and in sales transactions.

(e) Open-term sales contracts. Contracts for the sale of goods are valid even though the price or some other term remains open and must be determined at a future date. This is discussed further in § 23:4(c).

(f) Current market price. An agreement is not too indefinite to enforce because it does not state the exact price to be paid but specifies that the price shall be that prevailing on a recognized market or exchange. Thus, a provision in a lease is sufficiently definite to be binding when it specifies that if the lease were renewed, the rental should be that of similar properties at the time of renewal.

(g) Standard form contracts. In some instances, what would appear to be too vague to be a binding agreement is given the effect of a contract because it is clear that the parties had a particular standard or printed form in mind so that the terms of that standard form fill out the agreement of the parties. Thus, an agreement to lease real estate is binding when the agreement of the parties specified that a particular standard form of lease was to be used.[5] Likewise, an agreement to insure property does not fail to be binding because the terms are not stated, because the law will regard the parties as having intended that the standard form of insurance contract used by the insurance company should govern.

(h) First refusal contract. The owner of property may agree to give to the other contracting party a first right to buy the property by matching any serious offer made by a third person. A contract conferring such a *preemptive right* or right of first refusal is binding (against the contention that it is not definite because it does not specify the terms of the subsequent sale), for the parties recognize that the offer made by a third person will supply those details.

(i) Joint venture participation. When two or more persons or enterprises pool resources in order to obtain a government contract, agreements as to the manner of dividing the work or profits between them may be enforced even though they are dependent upon future negotiation.[6] In effect, the law is influenced by the practical consideration that from the nature of the activity it would be impossible or impractical to make the agreements between the parties more specific until the government contract was awarded.

§ 10:4. COMMUNICATION OF OFFER TO THE OFFEREE. The offer must be communicated directly to the offeree by the offeror. Until the offer is made known to the offeree, the offeree does not know that there is something which can be accepted. Sometimes, particularly in the case of unilateral contracts, the offeree performs the act called for by the offeror without knowing of the offer's existence. Thus, without knowing that a

---

[5] Emerman v Baldwin, 186 PaSuper 561, 142 A2d 440.
[6] Air Technology Corp. v General Electric Co. 347 Mass 613, 199 NE2d 538.

reward is offered for the arrest of a particular criminal, a person may arrest the criminal. In most states, if that person learns thereafter that a reward had been offered for the arrest, the reward cannot be recovered.[7]

B. TERMINATION OF OFFER

An offer gives the offeree power to bind the offeror by contract. This power does not last forever, and the law specifies that under certain circumstances the power shall be terminated.

§ 10:5. EFFECT AND METHODS. Once the offer is terminated, the offeree cannot revive it. If an attempt to accept the offer is made after it has been terminated, this act is meaningless, unless the original offeror is willing to regard the "late acceptance" as a new offer which the offeror then accepts.

Offers may be terminated in any one of the following ways: (1) revocation of the offer by the offeror, (2) counteroffer by offeree, (3) rejection of offer by offeree, (4) lapse of time, (5) death or disability of either party, and (6) subsequent illegality.

§ 10:6. REVOCATION OF THE OFFER BY THE OFFEROR. Ordinarily the offeror can revoke the offer before it is accepted. If this is done, the offeree cannot create a contract by accepting the revoked offer. Thus, the bidder at an auction sale may withdraw (revoke) his bid (offer) before it is accepted. The auctioneer cannot thereafter accept that bid.

An ordinary offer may be revoked at any time before it is accepted, even though the offeror had expressly promised that the offer would be good for a stated period which had not yet expired, or even though the offeror had expressly promised the offeree that the offer would not be revoked before a specified later date.

(a) What constitutes a revocation. No particular form of words is required to constitute a revocation. Any words indicating the offeror's termination of the offer is sufficient. A notice sent to the offeree that the property which is the subject of the offer has been sold to a third person is a revocation of the offer. An order for goods by a customer, which is an offer to purchase at certain prices, is revoked by a notice to the seller of the cancellation of the order, provided such notice is communicated before the order is accepted.

(b) Communication of revocation. A revocation of an offer is ordinarily effective only when it is made known to the offeree. Until it is communicated to the offeree, directly or indirectly, the offeree has reason to believe that there is still an offer which may be accepted; and the offeree may rely on this belief.

---

[7] With respect to the offeror, it should not make any difference as a practical matter whether the services were rendered with or without knowledge of the existence of the offer. Only a small number of states have adopted this view, however.

Except in a few states, a letter or telegram revoking an offer made to a particular offeree is not effective until received by the offeree.[8] It is not a revocation at the time it is written by the offeror nor even when it is mailed or dispatched. A written revocation is effective, however, when it is delivered to the offeree's agent, or to the offeree's residence or place of business, under such circumstances that the offeree would be reasonably expected to be aware of its receipt.

It is ordinarily held that there is a sufficient "communication" of the revocation when the offeree learns indirectly of the offeror's intent to revoke. This is particularly true when the seller-offeror, after making a written offer to sell land to the offeree, sells the land to a third person, and the offeree, who indirectly learns of such sale, necessarily realizes that the seller cannot perform his offer and therefore must be deemed to have revoked it.

If the offeree accepts an offer before it is effectively revoked, a valid contract is created. Thus, there may be a contract when the offeree mails or telegraphs his acceptance without knowing that a letter of revocation has been mailed to him.

When an offer is made to the public it may usually be revoked in the same manner in which it was made. For example, an offer of a reward that is made to the general public by an advertisement in a newspaper may be revoked in the same manner. A member of the public cannot recover the amount of the reward by thereafter performing the act for which the reward was originally offered. This exception is made to the rule requiring communication of revocation because it would be impossible for the offeror to communicate the fact that the offer was revoked to every member of the general public who knows of the offer. The public revocation of the public offer is effective even though it is not seen by the person attempting to accept the original offer.

(c) **Option contracts.** An *option contract* is a binding promise to keep an offer open for a stated period of time or until a specified date. The offeror cannot revoke the offer if the offeror has received consideration, that is, has been paid, for the promise to keep the offer open. If the owner of a house gives a prospective purchaser a 60-day written option to purchase the property at $25,000 and the customer pays the owner a sum of money, such as $500, the owner cannot revoke the offer within the 60-day period. Even though the owner expressly tells the purchaser within that time that the option contract is revoked, the purchaser may exercise the option; that is, the purchaser may accept the offer.

Under an option contract there is no obligation on the offeree to exercise the option. If the option is exercised, the money paid to obtain the option is ordinarily, but not necessarily, applied as a down payment. If the option is not exercised, the offeror keeps the money paid by the offeree.

An option exists only when the option holder has the right to determine whether performance called for by the option is required. If the agreement

---

[8] Hogan v Aluminum Lock Shingle Corp. 214 Ore 218, 329 P2d 271.

states that the "option" may be exercised only with the consent of the other party, it is not an option even though so called by the agreement.

If a promise is described by the parties as an "option" but no consideration is given, the promise is subject to revocation as though it were not described as an "option." In those jurisdictions in which the seal retains its common-law force, however, the option contract is binding on the offeror if it is set forth in a sealed writing, even though the offeror does not receive any payment for his agreement.

Frequently an option contract is combined with a lease of real estate or personal property. Thus, a tenant may rent a building for a number of years by an agreement which gives him the option of purchasing the building for a specified amount at the end of the lease.

An option is to be distinguished from a preemptive right or first refusal contract by which a person is given the right to buy if the owner chooses to sell, but the holder of such right cannot require the owner to sell, as would be the case in an option contract.

An *option*, when supported by consideration, is a contract to keep an offer open for a specified period of time.[9] Generally the consideration given for an option is the payment of a sum of money. In the case of employee stock options, the consideration is the agreement of the employee to work for the employer corporation for a certain period of time.

(d) Firm offers. As another exception to the rule that an offer can be revoked at any time before acceptance, statutes in some states provide that an offeror cannot revoke an offer prior to its expiration when he has made a *firm offer*, that is, an offer which states that it is to be irrevocable for a stated period. This doctrine of firm offers applies to a merchant's written offer to buy or sell goods, but with a maximum of three months on its duration.[10]

> **FACTS:** Gordon, a contractor, requested bids on structural steel from various suppliers. Coronis submitted an offer by letter. He later withdrew the offer. Gordon sued Coronis for breach of contract on the ground that he could not revoke his offer.

> **DECISION:** Judgment for Coronis. The mere making of an offer without an express declaration therein which "gives assurance that it will be held open" does not constitute a firm offer but is merely an ordinary offer which can be revoked at any time. [Coronis Associates v Gordon Construction Co. 90 NJSuper 69, 216 A2d 246]

(e) Detrimental reliance. There is growing authority that when the offeree relies on the offer, the offeror is obligated to keep the offer open for a reasonable time after such action has been taken by the offeree.

(f) Revocation of offer of unilateral contract. Since the offer of a unilateral contract can be accepted only by performing the act called for, it

---

[9] Steel v Eagle, 207 Kan 146, 483 P2d 1063.
[10] Uniform Commercial Code § 2-205.

theoretically follows that there is no acceptance until that act is fully performed by the offeree and that the offeror is free to revoke his offer even though the offeree has partly performed and has expended time and money. To avoid this hardship, a number of courts hold that after the offeree has done some substantial act toward acceptance, the offeror cannot revoke the offer until after the lapse of a reasonable time in which the offeree could have completed performance. Some courts hold that the offeror of a unilateral contract cannot revoke the offer once the offeree begins to perform the called-for act.[11]

§ 10:7. COUNTEROFFER BY OFFEREE. Ordinarily if *A* makes an offer, such as to sell a used automobile for $1,000, and *B* makes an offer to buy at $750, the original offer is terminated. *B* is in effect saying, "I refuse your original offer, but in its place I make a different offer." Such an offer by the offeree is known as a *counteroffer*. In substance, the counteroffer presupposes a rejection of the original offer. In some instances, however, circumstances may show that both parties knew and intended that the offeree's response was not to be regarded as a definite rejection of the original offer but merely as further discussion or as a request for further information.

FACTS: Feaheny offered to sell Quinn her house. She made an offer to sell on an installment payment basis, but also asked Quinn to make a cash offer. Quinn made a cash offer which Feaheny rejected. Quinn then accepted the installment payment basis. Feaheny refused to perform the contract, and Quinn sued her.

DECISION: Judgment for Quinn. Under the circumstances the making of the cash offer was not a counteroffer which rejected the installment plan offer that the seller had made. When the purchaser accepted that offer after his cash proposal was rejected, a contract was created because the offer was still in existence and could be accepted. [Quinn v Feaheny, 252 Mich 526, 233 NW 403]

Counteroffers are not limited to offers that directly contradict the original offers. Any departure from, or addition to, the original offer is a counteroffer even though the original offer was silent as to the point changed or added by the counteroffer. For example, when the offeree stated that the offer had been accepted and added that time was of the essence, the "acceptance" was a counteroffer when the original offer had been silent on that point. Likewise, when a financer made an offer to a business enterprise to obtain a bank loan for the enterprise in "a local bank," the enterprise rejected the offer when it specified that, instead of "a local bank," the transaction should utilize the Bank of Tacoma.[12]

A counteroffer is by definition an offer and, if the original offeror (who is now the offeree) accepts it, a binding contract results.

---

[11] Sylvestre v Minnesota, 298 Minn 142, 214 NW2d 658.
[12] H. M. Johnson v Star Iron and Steel Co. 9 Wash App 202, 511 P2d 1370.

§ 10:8. REJECTION OF OFFER BY OFFEREE. If the offeree rejects the offer and communicates this rejection to the offeror, the offer is terminated, even though the period for which the offeror agreed to keep the offer open has not expired. It may be that the offeror is willing to renew the offer; but unless he does so, there is no offer for the offeree to accept.

The fact that the offeree replies to the offeror without accepting the offer does not constitute a rejection when it is apparent that the failure to accept at that time was not intended as a rejection. For example, when the seller on receiving an order from a customer sent a reply that a "formal confirmation" of the order would be sent as soon as the seller received confirmation from his source of supply that the goods were available, the reply of the seller was not a rejection of the offer made by the customer.

§ 10:9. LAPSE OF TIME. When the offer states that it is open until a particular date, the offer terminates on that date if it has not been accepted. This is particularly so where the offeror declares that the offer shall be void after the expiration of the specified time. Such limitations are strictly construed. For example, it has been held that the buyer's attempt to exercise an option one day late had no effect.[13]

If the offer does not specify a time, it will terminate after the lapse of a reasonable time. What constitutes a "reasonable" time is to be determined by what a reasonable person in the position of the offeree would believe was satisfactory to the offeror. Conversely, it does not mean a time which is desired by the offeree.

A reasonable time depends upon the circumstances of each case; that is, upon the nature of the subject matter, the nature of the market in which it is sold, the time of the year, and other factors of supply and demand. If the commodity is perishable in nature or fluctuates greatly in value, the reasonable time will be much shorter than if the commodity or subject matter is a staple article. An offer to sell a harvested crop of tomatoes would expire within a very short time. When a seller purports to accept an offer after it has lapsed by the expiration of time, the seller's acceptance is merely a counteroffer and does not create a contract unless that offer is accepted by the buyer.

FACTS: Boguszewski made a written offer to purchase a tract of land owned by a corporation, 22 West Main Street, Inc. The offer, made on February 21, stated that the closing or settlement date on which the deed should be delivered was on or before March 22. On March 26, the seller crossed out the closing date, changed it to April 10, and signed the offer indicating its acceptance. Boguszewski denied that he was bound by a contract.

DECISION: Boguszewski was not bound. Since no time was stated for acceptance of his offer, the seller had a reasonable time in which to accept; but it

---

[13] Watts v Teagle, 124 GaApp 726, 185 SE2d 803, (buyer was given an option on February 19. He attempted to exercise it on August 19. The option stated that it expired 180 days from its date when it would "become void and of no force and effect.")

was clear that acceptance of the offer would necessarily occur before the closing date. Hence a delay until after the offered closing date of March 22 was unreasonable. The seller's "acceptance" thereafter was merely a counteroffer and did not create a contract unless that offer was accepted by the buyer. Since it had not been accepted by Boguszewski, he was not bound by the contract. [22 West Main Street, Inc. v Boguszewski, 34 AppDiv2d 358, 311 NYS2d 565]

An option must be exercised within the time specified, whether or not it expressly declares that time is of the essence. If no time is specified, it must be exercised within a reasonable time.

An option can only be exercised by doing that which is specified in the option contract by the specified date. If the option contract requires payment or a tender of payment by a specified date, the option cannot be exercised by giving notice of intent to exercise before that date but actually not making tender of payment until three days after the date.

§ 10:10. **DEATH OR DISABILITY OF EITHER PARTY.** If either the offeror or the offeree dies or becomes insane before the offer is accepted, it is automatically terminated.

§ 10:11. **SUBSEQUENT ILLEGALITY.** If the performance of the contract becomes illegal after the offer is made, the offer is terminated. Thus, if an offer is made to sell alcoholic liquors but a law prohibiting such sales is enacted before the offer is accepted, the offer is terminated.

C. ACCEPTANCE OF OFFER

Once the offeror expresses or appears to express his willingness to enter into a contractual agreement with the offeree, the latter is in a position to accept the offer.

§ 10:12. **PRIVILEGE OF OFFEREE.** Ordinarily the offeree may refuse to accept an offer. Certain partial exceptions exist.

(a) **Public utilities and places of public accommodation.** These are under a duty to serve any fit person. Consequently, when a fit person offers to register at a hotel, that is, offers to hire a room, the hotel has the obligation to accept his offer and enter into a contract for the renting of the room. This is a partial exception to the general rule because there is not an absolute duty to accept on the part of the hotel unless the person is fit and the hotel has space available.

(b) **Antidiscrimination.** When offers are solicited from members of the general public, an offer may generally not be rejected because of the race, nationality, religion, or color of the offeror. If the solicitor of the offer is willing to enter into a contract to rent, sell, or employ, as the case may be, antidiscrimination laws compel him to accept an offer from any otherwise fit person.

§ 10:13. NATURE OF THE ACCEPTANCE. An *acceptance* is the assent of the offeree to the terms of the offer. No particular form of words or mode of expression is required, but there must be a clear expression that the offeree agrees to be bound by the terms of the offer. In the absence of a contrary requirement in the offer, an acceptance may be indicated by an informal "O.K.," by a mere affirmative nod of the head, or, in the case of an offer of a unilateral contract, by performing the act called for.

While the acceptance of an offer may be shown by conduct, it must be very clear that the offeree intended to accept the offer. To illustrate the strictness that is often applied, a contractor requested a bid from a subcontractor. The subcontractor made a bid. The contractor then made a bid to the owner on the basis of the subcontractor's bid and also told the subcontractor to proceed with preliminary planning. It was held that this conduct did not constitute an acceptance of the subcontractor's bid, with the result that the subcontractor could revoke the bid.[14]

(a) Unqualified acceptance. The acceptance must be absolute and unconditional. It must accept just what is offered. If the offeree changes any term of the offer or adds any new term, he does not accept the offer because he does not agree with what was offered.

Where the offeree does not accept the offer exactly as made, the addition of any qualification to the acceptance constitutes a counteroffer and no contract arises unless such counteroffer is accepted by the offeror.

An acceptance that states what is implied by law, however, does not add a new term within this rule. Thus, a provision in an acceptance that payment must be made in cash will usually not be deemed to introduce a new term since a cash payment is implied by law in the absence of a contrary provision. Likewise, an acceptance otherwise unconditional is not impaired by the fact that an additional matter is requested as a favor rather than being made a condition or term of the acceptance. Accordingly, there is an effective acceptance when the buyer, upon accepting, simply requests additional time in which to complete the transaction.

(b) Clerical matters. A provision in an acceptance relating to routine or mechanical details of the execution of a written contract will usually not impair the effect of the acceptance. An acceptance by a buyer of an offer to sell real estate is effective even though it contains a request that the title be conveyed to a third person.

FACTS: Britt owned real estate which he listed for sale with Carver, a broker. Carver obtained a buyer and notified Britt of the buyer's offer. Britt sent Carver the following telegram: "Your telegram relative sale my property is accepted subject to details to be worked out by you and my attorney. . . ." Thereafter Britt sold and deeded the property to Vallejo, another buyer, for a greater price. Carver sued Britt for his commissions on the theory that he had obtained a buyer and that Britt had entered into a binding contract to sell to that buyer.

---

[14] K. L. House Construction Co. Inc. v Watson, 84 NMex 783, 508 P2d 592.

DECISION: Judgment for Carver. The "additional terms" merely recognized that there would be certain routine details, the disposition of which was necessarily part of the transaction. Reference to them merely expressed what was necessarily implied in the offer and did not amount to adding "new terms" to the acceptance. The acceptance was therefore effective, and there was a binding contract. [Carver v Britt, 241 NC 538, 85 SE2d 888]

§ 10:14. WHO MAY ACCEPT. An offer may be accepted only by the person to whom it is directed. If anyone else attempts to accept it, no agreement or contract with that person arises.

FACTS: Shuford offered to sell a specified machine to the State Machinery Co. The Nutmeg State Machinery Corp. heard of the offer and notified Shuford that it accepted. When Shuford did not deliver the machine, the Nutmeg Corp. sued him for breach of contract. Could the Nutmeg Corp. recover?

DECISION: No. Nutmeg did not have a contract with Shuford since Shuford had made the offer to State Machinery. Only the person to whom an offer is made can accept an offer. No contract arises when a third person accepts the offer. [Nutmeg State Machinery Corp. v Shuford, 129 Conn 659, 30 A2d 911]

If the offer is directed not to a specified individual but to a particular class, it may be accepted by anyone within that class. If the offer is made to the public at large, it may be accepted by any member of the public at large who has knowledge of the existence of the offer.

§ 10:15. MANNER OF ACCEPTANCE. The acceptance must conform to any conditions expressed in the offer concerning the manner of acceptance. When the offeror specifies that there must be a written acceptance, no contract arises when the offeree makes an oral acceptance.[15] If the offeror calls for an acceptance by a specified date, a late acceptance has no effect. When an acceptance is required by return mail, it is usually held that the letter of acceptance must be mailed the same day that the offer was received by the offeree. If the offer specifies that the acceptance be made by the performance of an act by the offeree, he cannot accept by making a promise to do the act but must actually perform it.

Ordinarily, if the offeree departs from the terms of the offer, there is no acceptance. As a qualification to this strict rule, when the offeror actually receives notice of the acceptance from the offeree, there is an acceptance even though the communication had not been made in the manner specified by the offeror.[16]

---

[15] Town of Lindsay v Cooke County Electrical Cooperative Ass'n (Tex) 502 SW2d 117.
[16] University Realty & Development Co. v Omid-Graf, Inc. 19 ArizApp 488, 508 P2d 747 (lease provided for notice by registered mail of the tenant's exercise of option to renew the lease. It was held that there was a sufficient acceptance of the option offer when the tenant delivered the notice by hand instead of registered mail.)

Some courts avoid the strict rule by holding that the directions of the offeror were not conditions but merely indicated an acceptable alternative. Frequently, the offer will be made by sending a form of contract and requesting the offeree to sign the contract if the offeree agrees or accepts the offer. This does not make signing the contract the exclusive method of accepting. Consequently, there was an acceptance, although the contract was not signed, when the offeree wrote to the offeror that the offer was accepted, enclosed a check in payment in full, and recited that the contract which was to be signed could not be found.[17]

Unless the offer is clear that a specified manner of acceptance is exclusive, a manner of acceptance indicated by the offeror will be interpreted as merely a suggestion and the offeree's entering upon the performance of the contract will be an acceptance when the offeror has knowledge that the offeree is doing so.

An order or offer to buy goods for prompt or current shipment may be accepted by the seller either by promptly making the shipment or promising to do so.[18] When shipment of goods is claimed to constitute an acceptance of the buyer's order, the seller must notify the buyer of such acceptance within a reasonable time.[19]

When a person accepts services offered by another and it reasonably appears that he expects to receive compensation, the acceptance of the services without any protest constitutes an acceptance of the offer and a contract exists for the payment for such services.

(a) Silence as acceptance. In most cases the silence of the offeree and his failure to act cannot be regarded as an acceptance. Ordinarily the offeror is not permitted to frame his offer in such a way as to make the silence and inaction of the offeree operate as an acceptance.

In the case of prior dealings between the parties, as in a record or book club, the offeree may have a duty to reject an offer expressly, and the offeree's silence may be regarded as an acceptance.

FACTS: Everlith obtained a one-year liability policy of insurance from the insurance company's agent, Phelan. Prior to the expiration of the year, Phelan sent Everlith a renewal policy covering the next year, together with a bill for the renewal premium. The bill stated that the policy should be returned promptly if the renewal was not desired. Everlith did not return the policy or take any other action relating to the insurance. Phelan sued for the renewal premium.

DECISION: The silence of Everlith did not constitute an acceptance since there was not a sufficient prior course of conduct between the parties which would lead a reasonable person to believe that the silence indicated an acceptance. The single transaction that had occurred in the past did not establish a course of conduct. [Phelan v Everlith, 22 ConnSupp 377, 173 A2d 601]

---

[17] McAfee v Brewer, 214 Va 579, 203 SE2d 129.
[18] UCC § 2-206(1)(b).
[19] § 2-206(2).

In transactions relating to the sale of goods, silence is in some instances treated as an acceptance when the parties are both merchants.[20]

(b) Unordered goods and tickets. When a seller writes to a person with whom the seller has not had any prior dealings that, unless notified to the contrary, he will send specified merchandise to be paid for at specified prices, or sends the merchandise directly to that person, there is no acceptance if the offeree ignores the offer and does nothing. The silence of the person receiving the letter or the merchandise is not intended by that person as an acceptance, and the sender as a reasonable person should recognize that none was intended.

This rule applies to all kinds of goods, books, magazines, and tickets sent to a person through the mail when they have not been ordered and are not used. The fact that the items are not returned does not mean that they have been accepted; that is, the offeree is neither required to pay for nor return the goods or other items. A practical solution to the problem is for the recipient of the unordered goods to write "Return to Sender" on the unopened package and put the package back into the mail without any additional postage.

The Postal Reorganization Act of 1970 provides that the person who receives unordered mailed merchandise has the right "to retain, use, discard, or dispose of it in any manner he sees fit without any obligation whatsoever to the sender."[21] It provides further that any unordered merchandise that is mailed must have attached to it a clear and conspicuous statement of the recipient's rights to treat the goods in this manner.

The mailing of unordered merchandise, other than a free sample conspicuously marked as such, or of a bill for its payment, constitutes an unfair method of competition and an unfair trade practice. The distribution of unsolicited goods as part of a scheme to use the mail to defraud violates federal statutes. The payment of money orders made payable to a sender of unsolicited goods may be forbidden.

(c) Insurer's delay in acting on application. The delay of an insurance company in acting upon an application for insurance generally does not constitute an acceptance. A few courts have held that an acceptance may be implied from the company's failure to reject the application promptly, that there is accordingly a binding contract and the application cannot be rejected. This is particularly true when the applicant has paid the first premium and the insurer fails to return it. Some decisions attain the same practical result by holding the insurer liable for tort if, through its unjustified delay in rejecting the application, the applicant remains unprotected by insurance and then, in the interval, suffers loss that would have been covered by the insurance if it had been issued.

§ 10:16. COMMUNICATION OF ACCEPTANCE. If the offeree accepts the offer, must the offeror be notified? The answer depends upon the nature of

---

[20] See § 23:4(b)(2).
[21] Federal Postal Reorganization Act § 3009.

the offer. When communication is required, the acceptance must be communicated directly to the offeror or the offeror's agent. A statement made to a third person is not effective as an acceptance of the offer.

(a) Communication of acceptance in a bilateral contract. If the offer pertains to a bilateral contract, an acceptance is not effective unless communicated to the offeror.

(b) Communication of acceptance in a unilateral contract. If the offeror makes an offer of a unilateral contract, communication of acceptance is ordinarily not required. In such a case, the offeror calls for a completed or accomplished act. If that act is performed by the offeror with knowledge of the offer, the offer is accepted without any further action by way of notifying the offeree. As a practical matter, there will eventually be some notice to the offeror because the offeree who has performed the act will ask the offeror to carry out his promise.

> **FACTS:** Mrs. Hodgkin told her daughter and son-in-law, Brackenbury, that if they would leave their home in Missouri and come to Maine to care for her, they could have the use of her house during her life and that she would will it to them. The daughter and son-in-law moved to Maine and began taking care of the mother. Family quarrels arose, and the mother ordered them out of the house. They brought an action to determine their rights. Mrs. Hodgkin defended on the ground that the plaintiffs had not notified her that they would accept her offer.

> **DECISION:** Judgment for daughter and son-in-law. The contract offered by the mother was a unilateral contract. She called for the moving to Maine of the plaintiffs and their taking care of her. This they did and, by so doing, they accepted the offer of the mother. The fact that they did not notify the mother of their acceptance of the offer or did not make a counterpromise to her was immaterial since neither is required in the case of a unilateral contract. [Brackenbury v Hodgkin, 116 Maine 399, 102 A 106]

(c) Communication of acceptance in a guaranty contract. The general rule that notification of acceptance is not necessary in cases of an offer requesting the performance of an act is not applied in many states when the offer calls for the extension of credit to a buyer in return for which the offeror promises to pay the debt if it is not paid. To illustrate, an uncle may write to a local merchant that if the merchant allows his nephew to purchase goods on credit, the uncle will pay the bill if the nephew does not. The uncle makes an offer of a unilateral contract because he has not asked for a promise by the merchant to extend credit but for the act of extending credit. If the merchant extends the credit, he is doing the act which the uncle calls for by his offer. If the general rule governing acceptance applied, the performance of this act would be a complete acceptance and would create a contract. In the guaranty case, however, another requirement is added, namely, that within a reasonable time after extending credit, the merchant must notify the uncle.

(d) Communication of the exercise of an option. Since an option obligates the offeror to hold an offer open and to refrain from revoking it, the same principles which govern the communication of the acceptance of an offer generally apply to the exercise of an option. This means that there must be a clear and unequivocal expression of the intention of exercising the option. Conduct that is ambiguous or which is as consistent with nonexercise of the option as it is with its exercise is not sufficient.

§ 10:17. **ACCEPTANCE BY MAIL OR TELEGRAPH.** When the offeree conveys his acceptance by mail or telegraph, questions may arise as to the right to use such means of communication and as to the time when the acceptance is effective.

(a) Right to use mail or telegraph. Express directions of the offeror, prior dealings between the parties, or custom of the trade may make it clear that only one method of acceptance is proper. For example, in negotiations with respect to property of rapidly fluctuating value, such as wheat or corporation stocks, an acceptance sent by mail may be too slow. When there is no indication that mail or telegraph is not a proper method, an acceptance may be made by either of those instrumentalities without regard to the manner in which the offer was made. The trend of the modern decisions supports the following provision of the Uniform Commercial Code relating to sales of personal property: "Unless otherwise unambiguously indicated by the language or circumstances, an offer to make a [sales] contract shall be construed as inviting acceptance in any manner and by any medium reasonable in the circumstances."

(b) When acceptance by mail or telegraph is effective. If the offeror specifies that an acceptance shall not be effective until received by him, the law will respect the offeror's wish. If there is no such provision and if acceptance by letter is proper, a mailed acceptance takes effect when the acceptance is properly mailed.

FACTS: The Thoelkes owned land. The Morrisons mailed an offer to the Thoelkes to buy their land. The Thoelkes agreed to this offer and mailed back a contract signed by them. While this letter was in transit, the Thoelkes notified the Morrisons that their acceptance was revoked. Were the Thoelkes bound by a contract?

DECISION: Yes. The acceptance was effective when mailed, and the subsequent revocation of the acceptance had no effect. [Morrison v Thoelke (FlaApp) 155 So2d 889]

The letter must be properly addressed to the offeror, and any other precaution that is ordinarily observed to insure safe transmission must be taken. If it is not mailed in this manner, the acceptance does not take effect when mailed, but only when received by the offeror.

The rule that a properly mailed acceptance takes effect at the time it is mailed is applied strictly. The rule applies even though the acceptance letter never reaches the offeror.

An acceptance sent by telegraph takes effect at the time that the message is handed to the clerk at the telegraph office, unless the offeror specifies otherwise or unless custom or prior dealings indicate that acceptance by telegraph is improper.

(c) **Proof of acceptance by mail or telegraph.** How can the time of mailing be established, or even the fact of mailing in the case of a destroyed or lost letter? A similar problem arises in the case of a telegraphed acceptance. In either case the problem is not one of law but one of fact, that is, a question of proving the case to the jury. The offeror may testify in court that he never received an acceptance, or he may claim that the acceptance was sent after the offer had been revoked. The offeree or his stenographer may then testify that the letter was mailed at a particular time and place. The offeree's case will be strengthened if he can produce postal receipts for the mailing and delivery of a letter sent to the offeror, although these of course do not establish the contents of the letter. Ultimately the case goes to the jury, or to the judge if a jury trial has been waived, to determine whether the acceptance was made at a certain time and place.

(d) **Payment and notice by mail distinguished from acceptance.** The preceding principles relate to the acceptance of an offer. When a contract exists and the question is whether a notice has been given or a payment has been made under the contract, those principles do not necessarily apply. Thus the mailing of a check is not the payment of a debt as of the time and place of mailing.

Contracts, however, will often extend the "mailed acceptance" rule to payment and giving notice. Thus insurance contracts commonly provide that the mailing of a premium is a sufficient "payment" of the premium to prevent the policy from lapsing for nonpayment of the premium. Likewise, an insurance policy provision requiring that notice of loss be given to the insurer is generally satisfied by a mailing of the notice without actual proof that the notice was received.

§ 10:18. ACCEPTANCE BY TELEPHONE. Ordinarily acceptance of an offer may be made by telephone unless the circumstances are such that by the intent of the parties or the law of the state no acceptance can be made or contract arise in the absence of a writing.

§ 10:19. AUCTION SALES. At an auction sale the statements made by the auctioneer to draw forth bids are merely invitations to negotiate. Each bid is an offer, which is not accepted until the auctioneer indicates that a particular offer or bid is accepted. Usually this is done by the fall of the auctioneer's hammer, indicating that the highest bid made has been accepted.[22] As a bid is merely an offer, the bidder may withdraw his bid at any time before it is accepted by the auctioneer.

Ordinarily the auctioneer may withdraw any article or all of the property from the sale if he is not satisfied with the amounts of the bids that are being made. Once he has accepted a bid, however, he cannot cancel the

---

[22] "Where a bid is made while the auctioneer's hammer is falling in acceptance of a prior bid, the auctioneer may in his discretion reopen the bidding or declare the goods sold under the bid on which the hammer is falling." UCC § 2-328(2).

sale. In addition, if it had been announced that the sale was to be made "without reserve," the goods must be sold to the person making the highest bid regardless of how low that may be.

QUESTIONS AND CASE PROBLEMS

1. What objective of the law is illustrated by each of the following quotations?
   (a) "Economic life would be most uncertain . . . if we did not have the assurance that contracts once made would be binding."
   (b) An offer is terminated by the lapse of a reasonable time when no time has been stated.

2. The Willis Music Co. advertised a television set at $22.50 in the Sunday newspaper. Ehrlich ordered a set, but the company refused to deliver it on the ground that the price in the newspaper ad was a mistake. Ehrlich sued the company. Was it liable? Reason? [Ehrlich v Willis Music Co. 93 OhioApp 246, 113 NE2d 252]

3. Laseter was employed by Pet Dairy Products Co. When he was injured at work, Pet promised to continue to employ him and to give him light work. Pet later discharged him, and he sued Pet for breach of contract. Was he entitled to recover? [Laseter v Pet Dairy Products Co. (CA4 SC) 246 F2d 747]

4. Owen wrote to Tunison asking if Tunison would sell his store for $6,000. Tunison replied, "It would not be possible for me to sell unless I received $16,000 cash." Owen replied, "Accept your offer." Tunison denied that there was a contract. Decide. [Owen v Tunison, 131 Maine 42, 158 A 926]

5. Ranch owned land. Bentzen and Ranch entered into an "agreement for warranty deed" which provided for the sale of the property to Bentzen, with the purchase price to be paid $1,000 down and the balance "payable by future agreement on or before" a specified date. Thereafter Bentzen sued Ranch for breach of contract and to enforce the contract. Decide. [Bentzen v Ranch, 78 Wyo 158, 320 P2d 440]

6. A buyer sent an offer in the form of a written contract signed by him to the seller on January 15. The seller signed the contract and delivered it to his attorney on January 17. On January 17 the buyer mailed a letter to the seller revoking his offer. The seller received this letter on January 19 but the seller's lawyer sent the signed contract to the buyer on January 22. The buyer refused to perform the contract and the seller sued for damages for its breach. Was the buyer liable? [See Kendel v Pontious (FlaApp) 244 So2d 543]

7. The Canonie Construction Company sent Dayhuff a signed paper reading: "Field Purchase Order CANONIE CONSTRUCTION COMPANY . . . To Jack R. Dayhuff . . . Haul sand [for a highway construction project] as required. Approximately 35,000 to 50,000 cubic yards 0.95 per ton scaled." Thereafter Canonie gave the hauling work to the Gibson Coal Company. Dayhuff sued

Canonie on the grounds that the purchase order form gave him the right to do all the hauling for the specified construction job. Was he correct? [Dayhuff v Canonie Construction Co. (IndApp) 283 NE2d 425]

8. The United Steelworkers, a labor union, and O'Neal Steel, Inc., an employer, were negotiating a collective bargaining labor contract. As they neared agreement, the employer submitted to the union a final written contract. The union representative signed the contract contingent upon the omission of paragraph 18 relating to strikes. Was the employer bound by the contract? [United Steelworkers v O'Neal Steel, Inc. (DC ND Ala) 321 FSupp 235]

9. The Great A. & P. Tea Co. rented a store from Geary. On February 25 the company wrote Geary offering to execute a lease for an additional year, commencing on May 1. At 10:30 a.m. on March 7, Geary wrote a letter containing a lease for the additional year and accepting the offer. On the same day at 1:30 p.m. the company mailed Geary a letter stating that it withdrew the offer to execute the new lease. Each party received the other's letter the following day. Was there an effective acceptance of the offer to make a lease? [Geary v Great A. & P. Tea Co. 366 Ill 625, 10 NE2d 350]

10. A sent B a letter stating "You have a 30-day option in which to purchase my car for $2,000." Twenty-five days later, B tendered $2,000 to A and informed him that he exercised the option. A claimed that he could not exercise the option because the option was not binding as A had not received anything for it. Was A correct? [See Mobile Oil Corp. v Wroten (Del) 303 A2d 698]

11. The owner of a business made an offer to sell an interest in the business for a specified price. The buyer wrote back agreeing to the terms of the offer and stating that payment would be made in 30 days after the transaction was completed. Was the owner bound by a contract with the buyer? [See Sossamon v Littlejohn, 241 SC 478, 129 SE2d 124]

12. A owned land. He signed a contract agreeing to sell the land reserving the right to take the hay from the land until the following October. He gave the contract form to B, a broker. C, a prospective buyer, agreed to buy the land and signed the contract but crossed out the provision as to the hay crop. Was there a binding contract between A and C? [See Koller v Flerchinger, 73 Wash2d 857, 441 P2d 126]

13. A manufactured electric meters and voltage regulators. B sent an order to A for such equipment but specified that B's representative inspect the meters at A's plant. A agreed to sell the equipment to B but objected to plant inspection and sent additional orders which he accepted although there had not been any plant inspection. A sued B for the purchase price. Can B raise the defense that there was no contract because the parties never agreed as to plant inspection? [See Midwest Engineering & Construction Co. v Electric Regulator Corp. (Okla) 435 P2d 89]

CONTRACTUAL CAPACITY

§ 11:1. INTRODUCTION. All persons do not have the same legal capacity to make a contract. Every party to a contract is presumed to have contractual capacity until the contrary is shown.[1] The fact that a person does not understand a contract does not mean that he lacks contractual capacity.

§ 11:2. MINORS. At common law any person, male or female, under twenty-one years of age was a *minor* (or an infant). At common law, minority ended the day before the 21st birthday. The "day before the birthday" rule is still followed, but the 21 years has been reduced to 18 years in two-thirds of the states and to 19 in a few. Some states provide for the termination of minority upon marriage and some specify that the minority of girls shall terminate sooner than that of boys.[2]

§ 11:3. MINOR'S RIGHT TO AVOID CONTRACTS. With exceptions that will be noted later, a contract made by a minor is voidable[3] at his election.[4] If the minor desires, he may perform his voidable contracts. The adult party to the contract, however, cannot avoid the contract on the ground that the minor could do so if he wished. Until the minor avoids the contract, the adult party is bound by it.

  (a) Minor's misrepresentation of age. Statutes in some states prevent a minor from avoiding a contract if the minor has fraudulently misrepresented

---

  [1] Kruse v Coos Head Timber Co. 248 Ore 294, 432 P2d 1009.

  [2] A statute may constitutionally provide for the termination of minority at an earlier age for girls than for boys, as against the contention that such a distinction constitutes a discrimination because of sex and denies equal protection. Stanton v Stanton 30, Utah2d 315, 517 P2d 1010. Contra: Bassett v Bassett (OklaApp) 521 P2d 434.

  [3] In some jurisdictions the appointment of an agent or an attorney by a minor is void rather than voidable. There is no reason why this exception should be made, and there is a tendency to eliminate it.

  [4] If the minor dies, the personal representative of his estate may avoid a contract which the minor could have avoided.

the minor's age. In the absence of such a statute, however, fraud generally does not affect the right to avoid the contract when sued for its breach, although there is some authority that in such case the minor must pay for any damage to, or determination of, the property he received under the contract.

In any case the other party to the contract may avoid it because of the minor's fraud.

(b) Time for avoidance. A minor's contract, whether executed or not, ordinarily can be disaffirmed or avoided by the minor at any time during minority or for a reasonable time after becoming of age. What is reasonable time is a question of fact to be determined in the light of all the surrounding circumstances.

> **FACTS:** Paolino executed a promissory note to pay the Mechanics Finance Co. $960.92. The note was to be paid in weekly installments. Paolino was 3 months under the age of majority. Installments due on the note were not paid, and the finance company sued Paolino. He was then 3 months over majority. Paolino raised the defense that he was a minor when he signed the note.

> **DECISION:** Judgment for Paolino. A delay of 3 months in avoiding the note was not unreasonable, and it therefore did not bar the defense of minority. It was sufficient that the minor first raised it when sued on the note. [Mechanics Finance Co. v Paolino, 29 NJSuper 449, 102 A2d 784]

After the expiration of a reasonable time following the attainment of majority, the minor ratifies (approves) the contract by a failure to avoid the contract within that time; but in some states an express affirmance is necessary to make a wholly executory contract binding.

In some states, statutes declare that a minor's debt is not binding unless there is some act of ratification after attaining majority. This reverses the pattern of the common law under which the burden would be on the minor to disaffirm the obligation.

As an exception to the right to disaffirm a contract during minority, a minor cannot fully avoid a conveyance for transfer of land until majority is attained.

§ 11:4. WHAT CONSTITUTES AVOIDANCE.

Avoidance or disaffirmance of a contract by a minor may be any expression of an intention to repudiate the contract. If the minor does an act inconsistent with the continuing validity of of the contract, that is deemed a disaffirmance. Thus, when a minor conveyed property to A and later, on reaching majority, made a conveyance of the same property to B, the second conveyance was deemed an avoidance of the first.

There is a conflict of authority as to whether a minor must disaffirm an executory contract on attaining majority. If the contract has been executed by the other contracting party, as by delivering property to the minor, the retention of such property by the minor after the minor attains majority will generally be regarded as a ratification or affirmance of the contract by the minor even though the contract is executory as to performance of the minor's obligation.

§ 11:5. RESTITUTION BY MINOR UPON AVOIDANCE.

When a minor avoids a contract, must the minor return what was received? What happens if what was received has been spent, used, damaged, or destroyed? When the minor has possession or control of the consideration received, or any part of it, the minor must return it or offer to do so before he can require the other party to undo the contract and set things back to their original position, or as it is called, to restore the *status quo ante*.

When a minor disaffirms his contract, he must avoid all of it. He cannot keep part of the contract and reject the balance. Although the minor must make this restitution if he can, the right to disaffirm his contract is not affected by the fact that he no longer has the money or property to return, or that the property has been damaged. In those states which follow the general rule, the minor can thus refuse to pay for what he has received or he can get back what he has paid or given, even though he himself does not have anything to return or returns the property in a damaged condition. There is, however, a trend which would limit this rule.

§ 11:6. RECOVERY OF PROPERTY BY MINOR UPON AVOIDANCE.

When the minor avoids his contract, the other contracting party must return all the money or property of the minor that he has received, or the money equivalent of property which he cannot return. A minor who avoids his sale or trade of personal property cannot recover that property, however, from a third person to whom the other party to the contract has transferred it.[5]

§ 11:7. RATIFICATION.

A minor's voidable contract becomes binding upon him when he ratifies or approves it. Of necessity, the minor can only ratify a contract when he is no longer a minor. He must have attained his majority or his "ratification" would itself be regarded as voidable in order to protect the minor. In contrast, a minor can usually avoid a contract at any time during minority.

Ratification may consist of any expression that indicates an intention to be bound by the contract.

FACTS: While a minor, Lange executed a mortgage. After she was twenty-one she stated to the attorney for the holder of the mortgage that she recognized that she would have to pay interest on the mortgage. Later, suit was brought against Lange on the mortgage by the holder of the mortgage, Ruehle. Lange claimed that the mortgage was invalid because it had been executed by her while she was a minor.

DECISION: Judgment for Ruehle. Lange, in admitting liability to the attorney for the holder of the mortgage after Lange attained majority, waived the right to avoid the contract that she had made while she was a minor. She had ratified the contract. [Ruehle v Lange, 223 Mich 690, 194 NW 492]

---

[5] Uniform Commercial Code § 2-403 (1).

In some states a written ratification or declaration of intention is required. An acknowledgment by the minor that a contract had been made during his minority, without any indication of an intention to be bound thereby, is not a ratification.

The making of payments after attaining majority may constitute a ratification. Many courts, however, refuse to recognize payment as ratification in the absence of further evidence of an intent to ratify, an express statement of ratification, or an appreciation by the minor that such payment might constitute a ratification.[6]

§ **11:8. CONTRACTS FOR NECESSARIES.** A minor is liable for the reasonable value of necessaries that are supplied to him by another person at the minor's request. This duty of the minor is called a quasi contractual liability.[7] It is a duty which the law imposes upon the minor rather than one which he has created by his contract.

Originally necessaries were limited to those things absolutely necessary for the sustenance and shelter of the minor. Thus limited, the term would extend only to the most simple foods, clothing, and lodging. In the course of time, the rule was relaxed to extend generally to things relating to the health, education, and comfort of the minor. Thus, the rental of a house used by a married minor, his wife, and child, is a necessary. And services reasonably necessary to obtaining employment by a minor, such as assistance from an employment agency, have been held to be necessaries.

FACTS: Bobby Rogers, 19, married, quit school and looked for work. He agreed with the Gastonia Personnel Corporation, an employment agency, that if he obtained employment through it, he would pay a stated commission. Rogers obtained work through the agency but refused to pay the agreed commission of $295, for which he denied liability on the ground of minority.

DECISION: Rogers must pay the reasonable value of the agency's services. The services of an employment agency should be deemed a "necessary" on the theory that they enable a minor "to earn the money required to pay the necessities of life for himself and those who are legally dependent upon him." [Gastonia Personnel Corporation v Rogers, 276 NC 279, 172 SE2d 19]

The rule has also been relaxed to hold that whether an item is a necessary in a particular case depends upon the financial and social status, or station in life, of the minor. The rule as such does not treat all minors equally. To illustrate, college education may be regarded as necessary for one minor but not for another, depending upon their respective stations in life.

Property other than food or clothing acquired by a minor is generally not regarded as a necessary. Although this rule is obviously sound in the case of jewelry and property used for pleasure, the same view is held even though

---

[6] Bronx Savings Bank v Conduff, 78 NMex 216, 430 P2d 374.
[7] See § 9:16 as to quasi contractual liability generally.

the minor is self-supporting and uses the property in connection with his work, as tools of his trade, or an automobile which he must have to go to and from work. The more recent decisions, however, hold that property used by the minor for his support is a necessary. Thus, it has been held that a tractor and farm equipment were necessaries for a married minor who supported his family by farming.[8]

> **FACTS:** Bethea, aged 20, purchased an automobile on credit. When sued by Bancredit, Inc. for the purchase price, he raised the defense that he was not liable because he was a minor when he made the contract. Bancredit claimed that the minor was bound by his contract because he used the auto for transportation to and from his place of business.

> **DECISION:** The minor was required to pay the reasonable value of the automobile since it was a necessary in the circumstances of the minor's needs and the twentieth century patterns of life and work. [Bancredit, Inc. v Bethea, 65 NJSuper 538, 168 A2d 250]

It is likely that necessaries will in time come to mean merely what is important by contemporary standards. Thus, a court in considering the right of a secured creditor to obtain an injunction against disposition of the collateral noted the fact that the "great majority of items repossessed at residential locations are appliances, such as television sets, refrigerators, stoves and sewing machines, and furniture of all kinds." The court then referred to these as "items which under modern living standards are somewhat akin to necessities of life."[9]

§ 11:9. CONTRACTS THAT MINORS CANNOT AVOID.
Statutes in many states deprive a minor of the right to avoid an education loan, a contract for medical care, a contract made while running his own business, a contract approved by a court, a contract made in performance of a legal duty, or relating to bank accounts, insurance policies, or corporate stock. In most states, the contract of a veteran, although a minor, is binding, particularly those for the purchase of a home.

> **FACTS:** Stuhl was 20 years of age. He gave checks to Eastern Airlines. These checks were not honored by the bank. Eastern Airlines sued him on the checks. At that time, a minor attained majority at 21. In his answer, which Stuhl filed in the lawsuit five months after he became 21, he disaffirmed the contract for which the checks had been given. Eastern Airlines claimed that he could not avoid liability in this way.

> **DECISION:** Judgment for Eastern Airlines. Stuhl was a mature person and had engaged in business. No advantage had been taken of him and he would not be allowed a "free ride" by being permitted to avoid his contract. [Eastern Airlines, Inc. v Stuhl (NY CivCt) 318 NYS2d 996]

§ 11:10. LIABILITY OF PARENT FOR MINOR'S CONTRACT.
Ordinarily a parent is not liable on a contract executed by a minor child. The parent

---

[8] Williams v Buckler (Ky) 264 SW2d 279.
[9] Chrysler Credit Corp. v Waegele, 29 CalApp3d 681, 105 CalRptr 914.

may be liable, however, if the child is acting as the agent of the parent in executing the contract.[10] If the parent has neglected the child, the parent is liable to a third person for the reasonable value of necessaries supplied by that person to the child.[11] If a parent joins in a contract with a minor, as when the parent acts as a cosigner, the parent is liable on his own undertaking and remains bound by his contract even though the minor avoids the contract as to himself.

If the minor on disaffirming a contract for the sale of goods returns them to the seller in their original condition and the seller then discharges the minor from his contract and from the installment note which he signed, the parent of the minor and any other person who signed is likewise discharged.[12]

§ 11:11. INSANE PERSONS. If a party to an agreement is insane, he lacks capacity and his contract is either voidable or void. In order to constitute insanity within the meaning of this rule, the party must be so deranged mentally that he does not know that he is making a contract or that he does not understand the consequences of what he is doing. If he lacks such understanding, the cause of his mental condition is immaterial. It may be idiocy, senile dementia, lunacy, imbecility, or such excessive use of alcoholic beverages or narcotics as to cause mental impairment.

If at the time the party makes the contract he understands the nature of his action and its consequences, it is immaterial that he has certain delusions or insane intervals, or that he is eccentric. As long as the contract is made in a lucid interval and is not affected by any delusions, it is valid.

(a) Effect of insanity. If a party to a contract is insane, he may generally avoid his contracts in the same manner as a minor.[13] Upon the removal of the disability, that is, upon his becoming sane, he may either ratify or disaffirm the contract. If a proper court has appointed a guardian for the insane person, a contract made before his appointment may be ratified or disaffirmed by the guardian. If the insane person dies, his personal representative or heirs may also affirm or disaffirm his contract.

> **FACTS:** Chiara in Texas purchased furniture from Ellard. He sold some to a third person and moved the balance of it to New York. Chiara, who was of unsound mind, later brought an action to set aside the purchase from Ellard. The latter claimed that Chiara must first return all of the property.
>
> **DECISION:** Judgment for Chiara. As to the property resold by him, he was only required to return so much of the proceeds of the sale as he still held. As to the furniture that he still owned, he was required to account for it. This would not require the actual return of the property as it did not have any unique value and its return from New York would be expensive. It was sufficient that he pay the seller the value of the property that he had moved to New York as of the date of the sale. [Ellard v Chiara (TexCivApp) 252 SW2d 991]

---

[10] See § 41:5.
[11] See § 41:11.
[12] Allen v Small, 129 Vt 77, 271 A2d 840.
[13] Davis v Colorado Kenworth Corp. 156 Colo 98, 396 P2d 958.

As in the case of minors, the other party to the contract has no right to disaffirm the contract merely because the insane party has the right to do so.

§ 11:12. INTOXICATED PERSONS. The capacity of a party to contract and the validity of his contract are not affected by the fact that he was drunk at the time of making the contract so long as he knew that he was making a contract. The fact that the contract was foolish and that he would not have made it had he been sober does not make the contract voidable unless it can be shown that the other party purposely caused the person to become drunk in order to induce him to enter into the contract.

If the degree of intoxication is such that the person does not know at the time that he is making a contract, the contract is voidable. The situation is the same as though he were so insane at the time that he did not know what he was doing. Upon becoming sober, the person may avoid or rescind the contract if he so desires. An unreasonable delay in taking steps to set aside a known contract entered into while intoxicated, however, may bar the intoxicated person from asserting this right.

§ 11:13. CONVICTS. The capacity to contract of a person convicted of a major criminal offense (a felony or treason) varies from state to state. In some states he may make a valid transfer of his property. In others, he is under either partial or total disability. When there is a disability, it generally exists only during the period of imprisonment.[14]

§ 11:14. ALIENS. An *alien* is a national or subject of a foreign country. Originally aliens were subject to many disabilities. These have been removed in most instances by treaty between the United States and the foreign country, under which each nation agrees to give certain rights to the citizens of the other. Generally an alien's right to make a contract is recognized.[15]

If this country is at war with a nation of which an alien is a subject, he is termed an *enemy alien* without regard to whether he assists his country in the prosecution of the war. An enemy alien is denied the right to make new contracts or to sue on existing ones; but if he is sued, he may defend the action. Contracts made by him, even though made before the war began, will at least be suspended during the war. In some instances, if the contract calls for continuing services or performance, the war terminates the contract.

§ 11:15. MARRIED WOMEN. At common law a married woman could not make a binding contract. Her agreements were void, rather than voidable,

---

[14] "Civil death" statutes depriving prisoners of their civil rights have been adopted in one-fourth of the states. Some courts hold these statutes to be unconstitutional. Delmore v Pierce Freightlines Co. (DC D Ore) 353 FSupp 258.

[15] A state cannot restrict or prohibit the employment of aliens in private or public employment. Truax v Raich, 239 US 33; Purdy & Fitzpatrick v California, 79 CalRptr 77, 456 P2d 645.

even when she lived apart from her husband. Consequently, she could not ratify an agreement after the removal of the disability by the death of her husband.

The common-law disability of a married woman has almost been abolished by statute in practically all the states.[16] There are still a few restrictions in some jurisdictions, mainly in instances where the wife might be unduly influenced by the husband. It is probable that these will disappear in the near future.

QUESTIONS AND CASE PROBLEMS

1. (a) What is the objective of the rule of law that when a minor avoids a contract, he usually cannot recover his property if the other party has transferred it to a third person who did not know of the minority and purchased the property for value?

   (b) How is the evolutionary nature of the law illustrated by the changes in the definition of a minor's necessaries?

2. Saccavino made a contract with Carl Gambardella, then 15 years of age, and Carl's parents, that he would train Carl to be a horse rider and that he would receive in return a share of Carl's earnings from exhibitions and racing. When Saccavino sued on the contract years later, Carl claimed that it was void. Was he correct? [Saccavino v Gambardella, 22 ConnSupp 168, 164 A2d 304]

3. Martinson executed a note payable to Matz. At the time Martinson was drunk. The next day he was told that he had signed the note. Five years later, Martinson's wife told Matz's attorney that Martinson would not pay the note as he was drunk at the time he executed the note. Matz brought suit on the note two years after that. Could he recover? [Matz v Martinson, 127 Minn 262, 149 NW 370]

4. South Dakota, as in many other states, establishes a lesser degree of duty owed by the driver of an automobile to a nonpaying guest passenger than to a paying passenger. Bruce Boyd was a passenger in an automobile driven by Roger Alguire, aged 18. Bruce paid 50 cents toward gasoline expenses at Roger's insistence. There was an accident in which Roger was killed and Bruce was injured. Bruce sued Roger's estate. Floyd, the administrator of Roger's estate, claimed that since Roger was a minor, if there was a contract between Roger and Bruce for the latter to "pay" for his transportation, it was not binding. Bruce, therefore, was merely a guest, in which case a lower duty was owed to him and Bruce would not be able to recover on the facts of the case. Was Bruce a fare-paying passenger or a guest? [Boyd v Alguire, 82 SD 684, 153 NW2d 192]

---

[16] United States v Yazell, 382 US 341.

5. On February 28, 1958, Alice Sosik signed a note promising to make certain payments to Conlon. She later sued to have the note set aside on the ground that she lacked mental capacity. A letter from a physician was presented which stated that he had examined her on July 3, 1959, and that she "is suffering from a chronic mental illness and is totally incapable of managing her affairs." Was she entitled to set the note aside? [Sosik v Conlon, 91 RI 439, 164 A2d 696]

6. A minor girl had a guardian who had been appointed for her estate. She was about to be married and applied to the court for permission to use $3,000 of her estate for the wedding reception for some 100 guests and $1,000 more for furniture. Her estate consisted of money paid to her guardian from an action to recover damages for her father's death. Was she entitled to make such expenditures? [In re Anonymous, 44 Misc2d 1082, 252 NYS2d 946]

7. Mary McCoy, a married woman, sold land that she owned to Niblick. Her husband did not sign the contract. Niblick moved onto the property before a deed was delivered and made improvements. Later Mary sought to set the contract aside. A Pennsylvania statute provided that a married woman had the same right as an unmarried woman to sell or dispose of her property but that she could not execute a deed to the property without having her husband sign the deed. Who was entitled to the property? [McCoy v Niblick, 221 Pa 123, 70 A 577]

8. *A*, who appeared to be an adult, purchased an automobile from *B*. He later informed *B* that he was a minor and avoided the contract. *A* gave as his explanation that there were certain defects in the car. *B* claimed that these defects were trivial. Assuming that the defects were trivial, could *A* avoid the contract? [See Rose v Sheehan Buick (FlaApp) 204 So2d 903]

9. In 1936 Palmer was adjudicated incompetent. In 1942 he was adjudicated competent. In 1952 he purchased policies of fire insurance from the Lititz Mutual Insurance Co. The property insured was destroyed by fire. The company refused to pay the policies on the ground that Palmer was insane when he applied for and obtained the insurance. Was this a valid defense? [Palmer v Lititz Mutual Insurance Co. (DC WD SC) 113 FSupp 857]

10. Gary Muniz, a minor, purchased a dune buggy from Jones. When Gary's father learned of the purchase, he ordered Gary to take the dune buggy back to Jones or dispose of it. While taking the buggy back to Jones, Gary was involved in an accident. The father's insurer denied liability on the basis that Gary was not the owner of the dune buggy at the time of the collision because he had avoided the contract. Was the insurer correct? [St. Paul Fire & Marine Insurance Co. v Muniz, 19 ArizApp 5, 504 P2d 546]

GENUINENESS
OF ASSENT

§ 12:1. INTRODUCTION. An agreement is the result of an offer and an acceptance by competent parties. The enforceability of a contract based upon an agreement may be affected, however, because a mistake was made by either or both of the parties or because the assent of one of the parties was obtained through fraud, undue influence, or duress.

The law does not treat all mistakes the same. Some have no effect whatever; others make the agreement voidable or unenforceable. Mistakes may be unilateral or mutual (bilateral).

§ 12:2. UNILATERAL MISTAKE. Ordinarily a unilateral mistake regarding a fact does not affect the contract unless the agreement states that it shall be void if the fact is not as believed, or unless the mistake is known to or should be recognized by the other party.

A unilateral mistake of law or as to expectations does not have any effect upon the contract. The courts refuse to recognize ignorance of the law as an excuse. If they did, the unscrupulous could avoid their contracts at will by saying that they did not understand the law.

Contrary to the rule that a unilateral mistake has no effect, an exception is made in the case of government construction work. Here a contractor who makes a unilateral mistake in the computation of his bid may retract his bid even though it has been accepted.

If one party knows that the other party has made a mistake, the mistaken party is entitled to rescind the contract. In determining whether the offeree knew that the offeror was making a mistake, it is significant that the mistaken offer was not substantially different from the price ordinarily charged or from offers made by other bona fide bidders.

(a) Negligent mistake as to nature of paper. When a party makes a negligent mistake as to the nature of a paper, he is bound according to its terms. For example, when the printed form for applying for a loan to a corporation contained a guaranty by the president of the corporation of the corporate debt, the president signing the application without reading it was bound by this guaranty, even though he did not know it was in the application and the application was headed merely "application for credit." A unilateral mistake as to the provision of a contract, for example, is ordinarily not an excuse from liability of the party who signed the contract without reading it or who only "half read" it before signing.[1]

(b) Mistakes as to releases. An insurance claimant is bound by the release given by her to the insurance company when at most there was a unilateral mistake on her part as to its meaning resulting from her own carelessness in reading the release.

When a release is given and accepted in good faith, it is initially immaterial that the releasor or both of the parties were mistaken as to the seriousness or possible future consequences of a known injury or condition. If the release covers all claims "known and unknown," the courts following the common-law view hold the releasor is bound even though there were other injuries of which the releasor was unaware because the effects of the unknown injuries had not yet appeared.

(c) Identity of other party. When the parties deal face to face, a contract is not affected by the fact that one party may be mistaken as to the identity of the other. When the mistake as to the identity of a party is induced by trick or deception of that party, however, the contract is voidable and may be set aside by the deceived party.

§ **12:3. MUTUAL MISTAKE.** When both parties make the same mistake of fact, the agreement is void. When the mutual or bilateral mistake is one of law, the contract generally is binding. Thus, the fact that both parties to a lease mistakenly believed that the leased premises could be used for boarding animals does not give the tenant a right to rescind the lease for mutual mistake of law, the theory being that in the eyes of the law the parties knew what the zoning regulations allowed. A few courts have refused to follow this rule, and in several states statutes provide that a mutual mistake of law shall have the same vitiating effect as a mutual mistake of fact. A bilateral mistake with respect to expectations ordinarily has no effect on the contract unless the realization of those expectations is made a condition of the contract.

(a) Possibility of performance. An agreement is void if there is a mutual mistake as to the possibility of performing the agreement.

(b) Identity of subject matter. An agreement is void if there is a mutual mistake as to the identity of the subject matter of the contract.

FACTS: Ouachita Air Conditioning Company was a dealer in Amana equipment. Pierce's home was equipped with York air conditioning equipment. Pierce needed a new condenser for the system. Pierce contacted the York distributor from whom he had purchased the original equipment and inquired for their repairman, Mr. Walters. Pierce

---

[1] Dunlap v Warmack-Fitts Steel Co. (CA8 Ark) 370 F2d 876.

was informed that Walters had left and was running the Ouachita Air Conditioning Company. Pierce ordered a new condenser from Ouachita. He apparently believed that he was ordering a new York condenser. The Ouachita representative apparently thought that Pierce was ordering an Amana condenser to replace the old condenser. Pierce did not pay for the Amana condenser and Ouachita sued him for the purchase price. He raised the defense that he was not liable as there was no contract due to a mutual mistake of fact.

DECISION: The misunderstanding as to the brand of condenser was a material mistake of fact and prevented the formation of a contract. Because of this mistake, the parties in fact had not agreed on the subject matter of the transaction. [Ouachita Air Conditioning, Inc. v Pierce (LaApp) 270 So2d 595]

(c) Collateral matters. When a mutual mistake occurs as to a collateral matter, it has no effect on the contract thereafter executed. For example, where the plaintiff asks the fire insurer to issue a policy to protect her if there were no existing policy which protected her, and both she and the insurance company wrongly believed that there was no other policy, the policy which was issued to her was not void because of the mutual mistake that there was no other policy. The mistake was as to a collateral matter; there was no concealment, as the insured had given the insurer all the information which she possessed and the insurer then concluded that the applicant was not already covered; and the circumstances made it clear that the policy had not been issued on the express condition that it was binding only if there were no other policy protecting the applicant.

§ **12:4. MISREPRESENTATION.** Suppose that one party to a contract makes a statement of fact which is false but that he does so innocently without intending to deceive the other party. Can the other party set aside the contract on the ground that he was misled by the statement? It is often held he cannot. In certain instances, however, the law protects the deceived person by permitting him to avoid the contract.

Equity will permit the rescission of the contract when the innocent misstatement of a material fact induces another to make the contract. If the deceived person is a defendant in an action at law, it is generally held that he cannot use as a defense the fact of innocent deception by the plaintiff. There is a tendency, however, for the law courts to adopt the rule of equity. For example, it may be possible for an insurance company to avoid its policy because of an innocent misstatement of a material fact by the applicant. Contracts between persons standing in confidential relationships, such as guardian and ward or parent and child, can be set aside for the same reason.

When a person gives an expert opinion for the purpose of guiding a third person in a business transaction, in which both the expert and the third person are financially interested, there is an ordinary tort duty upon the expert to exercise due care in making his statements. Consequently, when he negligently, although innocently, misrepresents the facts, he is liable to the third person.

FACTS: Maxey purchased a house from Quintana. Dailey was the real estate agent. Dailey innocently but wrongly stated that the property was subject to a VA mortgage. Actually it was subject to an FHA mortgage. The interest payments under a FHA mortgage were greater than under a VA mortgage. Maxey was required to pay the greater amount of interest. He did so and then sued Quintana to recover the difference between the interest payments under the two kinds of mortgages. Quintana defended on the ground that the misrepresentation had not been intentionally made and that therefore damages could not be recovered.

DECISION: Judgment for Maxey. The misrepresentation caused Maxey loss for which he could recover damages. Quintana was liable for the loss which his negligence had caused. It was no defense that Quintana had not been guilty of fraud in making the misstatement nor that Maxey had been negligent in not reading the papers to determine the actual facts. [Maxey v Quintana, 84 NMex 38, 499 P2d 356]

§ 12:5. CONCEALMENT. Generally one party cannot set aside a contract because the other party failed to volunteer information which the complaining party would desire to know. Ordinarily a failure to inform the other party of something which he would like to know is not fraudulent. For example, where a seller and a buyer entered into a settlement agreement of their differences, it was not fraudulent for the seller to fail to inform the buyer that the seller would not do any further business with the buyer, the buyer believing that their business relationship would continue if the dispute were put out of the way by the settlement agreement. If A does not ask B any questions, B is not under any duty to make a full statement of material facts.

There is developing in the law a duty on the seller to inform the buyer of some particular fact of which the buyer is not likely to have knowledge and because of its unusual character would not be likely to inquire of the seller. For example, the owner of a house must inform the prospective buyer that several years before there had been a severe fire in the house, even though the house at the time of sale was structurally sound and had been repaired shortly after the fire so that no signs of fire damage were visible. The failure to disclose such information was held to constitute fraud entitling the buyer to recover damages from the seller.

By this trend the seller of property must disclose to the buyer any defect of which he has knowledge when the circumstances are such that it is not reasonable to expect the buyer to learn the true condition for himself. Silence of the seller in such a case is held to be fraudulent concealment. This rule has been the law in Louisiana for many years in consequence of its civil law background. Under the Louisiana statute "the seller, who knows the vice of the thing he sells and omits to declare it" is liable to the buyer for the refund of the purchase price, damages, and a reasonable attorney's fee. Under this rule it has been held where a house was subject to flooding from a neighboring river, the seller was required to volunteer that fact to his buyer and where there was no such disclosure, the buyer could cancel the contract and obtain the recovery authorized by the statute.

Similarly, in transactions between banks there seems to be a growing concept of a duty to disclose information which one bank should foresee would be desired by another bank even though the latter had not specifically requested the information.[2]

Likewise, an owner is liable if he does not inform a contractor of subsoil difficulties known to the owner which the contractor will encounter in the performance of a contract. The fact that the owner includes in the contract a provision requiring the contractor to make an examination of the "site of the work" does not alter the obligation of the owner to inform the contractor of nonapparent subsoil conditions.

> **FACTS:** The City of Salinas entered into a contract with Souza & McCue Construction Co. to construct a sewer. The city officials knew that unusual subsoil conditions, including extensive quicksands, existed, which would make performance of the contract unusually difficult; but it did not make that information known when it advertised for bids. The advertisement for bids directed bidders to "examine carefully the site of the work" and declared that the submission of a bid would constitute "evidence that the bidder has made such examination." Souza & McCue was awarded the contract, but because of the subsoil conditions it could not complete the contract on time and was sued by Salinas for breach of contract. Souza & McCue counterclaimed on the basis that the City had not revealed its information of the subsoil conditions and was liable for the loss caused thereby.

> **DECISION:** Judgment for contractor. An owner is liable if he does not inform the contractor of unusual difficulties known to the owner which the contractor will encounter in the performance of a contract. As the City knew that the contractor would base its bid on the incomplete information, the City had misled the contractor by such concealment and was liable to the contractor for the loss caused thereby. The provision as to the examination of "site of the work" did not alter this conclusion since there was nothing in that provision which would call to the contractor's attention the conditions that would be encountered nor which disclaimed liability for concealed subsoil conditions. [City of Salinas v Souza & McCue Construction Co. 66 CalApp2d 217, 57 CalReptr 337, 424 P2d 921]

(a) Confidential relationship. If *A* and *C* stand in a confidential relationship, such as that of attorney and client, *A* has a duty to reveal anything that is material to *C's* interests, and his silence is given the same effect as though he had knowingly made a false statement that there was no material fact to be told *C*. In such a case *C* can avoid the contract.

(b) Fine print. An intent to conceal may be present when a printed contract or document contains certain clauses in such fine print that it is reasonable to believe that the other contracting party will never take the time nor be able to read such provisions.

In some instances the legislature has outlawed certain fine-print contracts. Statutes commonly declare that insurance policies may not be printed in type of smaller size than designated by statute. Consumer protection statutes designed to protect the credit buyer frequently require

---

[2] Lehigh Valley Trust Co. v Central National Bank (CA5 Fla) 409 F2d 989.

that particular clauses be set in large type. When a merchant selling goods under a written contract disclaims the obligation that goods be fit for their normal use, the Uniform Commercial Code requires the waiver to be set forth in "conspicuous" writing [3] which is defined as requiring "a term or clause . . . [to be] so written that a reasonable person against whom it is to operate ought to have noticed it. A printed heading in capitals . . . is conspicuous. Language in the body of a form is 'conspicuous' if it is in larger or other contrasting type or color. . . ."[4]

There is a growing trend to treat a fine-print clause as not binding upon the party who would be harmed thereby, without considering whether fraud was involved. This may be justified legalistically on the basis that the person prejudiced by the clause did not know of its existence and could not reasonably be expected to have known of its existence, and therefore the fine-print clause was not one of the terms agreed to by the parties. Moreover, the supplier of the form containing the fine-print clause shall have realized that the victim of the clause would not know nor have reason to know of its existence. As a practical matter, the conclusion is justified by the consideration that the fine-print clause ordinarily appears in a standard printed form of contract prepared by the enterprise and offered to one who has an inferior bargaining position, such as a consumer, and is offered on a "take-it-or-leave-it" basis.

Where air carriers seek to limit liability, such limitations have been held not effective when obscurely set forth in fine print.

Although the Uniform Commercial Code does not establish any general rule governing all fine-print situations, it is likely that the Code concept of "conspicuous" will be applied by courts increasingly in the future, so that no provision in a contract will be deemed a part of the bargain unless the provision is conspicuous or otherwise called to the attention of the other contracting party. Thus, it will be held that a provision which is in fine print, is under a misleading title or heading, or is buried in many unrelated provisions, was not agreed to by the parties and is not binding upon the party who did not know of its existence.

(c) **Active concealment.** Concealment may be more than the passive failure to volunteer information. It may consist of a positive act of hiding information from the other party by physical concealment, or it may consist of furnishing the wrong information. Such conduct is generally classified and treated as fraud.

§ **12:6. FRAUD.** *Fraud* is the making of a false statement of fact with knowledge of its falsity or with reckless indifference as to its truth, with the intent that the listener rely thereon, and the listener does so rely and is harmed thereby.

Conduct that is unethical does not constitute fraud.

---

[3] Uniform Commercial Code § 2-316(2).
[4] UCC § 1-201(10).

FACTS: On December 1, 1964, Neely, a senior in college, made a contract to play the following year for the Houston Oilers professional football team. It was agreed orally that the making of this contract would be kept secret so that Neely would appear to be eligible for a postseason college game. Neely then received a better offer from the Dallas Cowboys, and after college, he went to play for them. Houston sought an injunction against Neely. Neely claimed that the contract with Houston could not be enforced by Houston because of its fraud in stating that the contract would be binding on January 2, 1965, and then filing of the contract with the League Commissioner before that time in violation of the agreement to keep the execution of the contract secret so as to make him appear eligible for the postseason college football game.

DECISION: Judgment in favor of Houston Oilers. Neely had not been deceived and knew that the secrecy was designed to conceal his ineligibility. Although the conduct of the Oilers might be unethical, it was not fraudulent. The Oilers had not deceived Neely as to the nature and effect of their agreement, and there was no duty to make public the fact that they had made any particular contract. [Houston Oilers v Neely (CA 10 Okla) 361 F2d 36]

When one party to the contract is guilty of fraud, the contract is voidable as against the wrondoer and may be set aside by the injured party.

For convenience this discussion refers to fraudulent statements, but any kind of communication may be involved. The misrepresentation may also be made by conduct as well as by words.

(a) Misstatement of fact. A misstatement of a past or present fact is an essential element of fraud. A statement that a painting is the work of Rembrandt when the speaker knows that it is the work of an art student in a neighboring school is such a misstatement.

An intentional misrepresentation of the nature of the transaction between the parties is fraudulent. A person is guilty of fraud when he falsely makes another believe that the contract to be signed is not a contract but is a receipt or a petition.

(b) Mental state. The speaker must intend to deceive. This means that he must either know or believe what he is saying is false and must intend to mislead, or that he is recklessly indifferent as to whether what he says is true or not. The deceiver must intend that the injured party rely upon the statement and be deceived.

(1) Misrepresentation of Intention. A misrepresentation of intention can constitute fraud when a promise is made by a person who does not intend to keep it. To illustrate, a customer purchases goods from a merchant on credit and agrees to pay for them in 60 days. If the customer does not intend to pay for the goods and does not do so, the customer is guilty of fraud in misrepresenting of intention. Similarly, a misrepresentation by a real estate developer that houses would be constructed in accordance with FHA

standards and specifications constitutes fraud when the developer did not actually intend that the houses would be so constructed.[5]

(2) Misstatement of Opinion or Value. Ordinarily a misstatement of opinion or value is not regarded as fraudulent on the theory that the person hearing the statement recognizes or should recognize that it is merely the speaker's personal view and not a statement of fact.

A promotional or sales talk statement as to future events is not fraud. Thus, a statement by a motion picture distributor to a theater owner that a given picture "should be a 'blockbuster'" does not constitute fraud.[6]

(3) Misstatement of Law. A misstatement of law is treated in the same manner as a misstatement of opinion or value. Ordinarily the listener is regarded as having an opportunity of knowing what the law is, an opportunity equal to that of his speaker, so that he is not entitled to rely on what the speaker tells him. When the speaker has expert knowledge of the law or represents that he has such knowledge, however, his misstatement can be the basis of fraud.

(c) Investigation before relying on statement. If the injured person has available the ready means of determining the truth, as by looking at something in front of him, he cannot rely on the false statement. The fact that he relies on the other person or that he is too busy to examine or read a document before signing it does not protect him. He takes the risk that a paper will state what he thinks it does when he signs it without reading it. When a illiterate person or one physically unable to read signs a paper without having it explained or read to him, he is ordinarily bound by its contents. As a limitation on this rule, however, some courts hold that the negligence of the injured party is not a bar to a claim for damages when the wrongdoer takes active steps to conceal the truth, as by substituting one paper for another and falsely informing the injured party as to the nature of the paper.

However, it has been held that when the seller of a house, in reply to the questions of the buyer, knowingly makes false statements that the house has been repaired and does not leak, the buyer may recover damages for fraud as against the contention that the buyer was barred because he had not investigated the truth of the seller's statement.

If an examination by the injured person does not reveal the defect, or if the injured person cannot be expected to understand what he sees because of its technical nature, or if a simple examination is not available, the injured person may rely on the statements of the other party and raise the issue of fraud when he learns that they are false. A misrepresentation made to prevent further inquiry also constitutes fraud.

(d) Use of assumed name. The use of an assumed name is not necessarily fraudulent or unlawful. It is such only when the impostor assumes the name

---

[5] Brennaman v Andes & Roberts Brothers Construction Co. (MoApp) 506 SW2d 462.

[6] Twentieth Century Fox Distributing Corp. v Lakeside Theatres, Inc. (LaApp) 267 So2d 225.

of another person or makes up a name for the purpose of concealing his identity from persons to whom he owes money or a duty, or to avoid arrest, or for the purpose of deceiving the person with whom he is dealing, or of imitating the name of a competitor.

In the absence of any intent to evade or deceive by the use of the assumed name, it is lawful for a person to go by any name he chooses, although other persons may refuse to deal with him unless he uses his actual name. If a person makes a contract in an assumed or fictitious name or in a trade name, he will be bound by his contract because that name was in fact intended to identify him.[7]

FACTS: Euge opened a checking account under the assumed name of Horn with the Manchester Bank. He drew a check for an amount greater than his account and was prosecuted for the crime of issuing a bogus check. The prosecution claimed that the check was drawn by a fictitious person on a fictitious account.

DECISION: Euge was not guilty since there was an actual account although under the fictitious name he had assumed. The contract with the bank was lawful, and the bank would have been protected had it honored Euge's checks in the assumed name that he used. The account was an existing account under a fictitious name, but this did not constitute the crime charged. [State v Euge (Mo) 400 SW2d 119]

(1) Change of Name. In most states a person may obtain a decree of court officially changing his name upon filing a petition with the court, setting forth the reason for the desired change and satisfactory proof that there is no fraudulent or criminal purpose in effecting the change. In addition, a person's name may be changed as an incident to being adopted; and a woman's name may be changed by divorce.

(2) Fictitious Name Registration. If a person or a group of persons, other than a corporation, does business under a fictitious name, a statement must generally be filed in a specified government office setting forth the names and addresses of the persons actually owning or operating the business, together with the name, address, and nature of the business. Violation prevents the enterprise from bringing suit on a business contract so long as the name is not registered. No violation generally exists, however, when the other contracting party knows the identity of the persons doing business under the unregistered fictitious name.

§ 12:7. UNDUE INFLUENCE. An aged parent may entrust all his business affairs to his son; an invalid may rely on his nurse; a client may follow implicitly whatever his attorney recommends. The relationship may be such that for practical purposes the one person is helpless in the hands of the other. In such cases, it is apparent that the parent, the invalid, or the client is not in fact exercising his free will in making a contract suggested by the son, nurse, or attorney, but is merely following the will of the other

---

[7] Weikert v Logue, 121 GaApp 171, 173 SE2d 268.

person. Such relationships are called *confidential relationships*. Because of the great possibility that the person dominating the other will take advantage of him, the law presumes that the dominating person exerts *undue influence* upon the other person whenever the dominating person obtains any benefit from a contract made by the dominated person. The contract is then voidable and may be set aside by the other person unless the dominating person can prove that no advantage was taken by him.

The class of confidential relationships is not well-defined. It includes the relationships of parent and child, guardian and ward, physician and patient, attorney and client, and any other relationship of trust and confidence in which one party exercises a control or influence over another.

In some states, however, the mere fact that there is a close blood relationship, such as parent and child, does not constitute a confidential fiduciary relationship.[8]

> **FACTS:** Studley and Bentson made a contract by which the latter agreed to transfer to the former certain property in consideration of the promise of Studley to provide a home and take care of Bentson for life. The contract was prepared by a third person, and its effect was explained to Bentson by the president of the bank where he deposited his money. Bentson died, and the administratrix of his estate sued to set aside the contract, claiming undue influence.
>
> **DECISION:** Judgment for Studley. The fact that Studley and Bentson had been friends and that the latter had confidence in the former did not make the relationship a confidential relationship so as to cast on Studley the burden of sustaining the validity of the contract. [Johnson v Studley, 80 CalApp 538, 252 P 638]

Whether undue influence exists is a difficult question for the court (ordinarily the jury) to determine. The law does not regard every "influence" as undue. Thus, a nagging wife may drive a man to make a contract, but that is not ordinarily regarded as undue influence. Persuasion and argument are not in themselves undue influence.

An essential element of undue influence is that the person making the contract does not exercise his own free will in so doing. In the absence of a recognized type of confidential relationship, such as that between parent and child, the courts are likely to take the attitude that the person who claims to have been dominated was merely persuaded and consequently there was no undue influence.

(a) Domination by seller. In some instances the domination of the market or of the buyer by a particular seller may make the agreement with a buyer illegal as a violation of the federal antitrust law.

(b) Unequal bargaining power. Sometimes the party with the weaker bargaining power has no practical choice although, as far as the rule of law is concerned, his contract is binding as the voluntary act of a free adult person.

---

[8] Nelson's Estate, 132 IllApp2d 740, 270 NE2d 65.

Underlying the traditional concept of the law of contracts is the belief that a person can go elsewhere to contract and therefore when he makes a given contract, his contract is necessarily voluntary. But "going elsewhere" may be meaningless when better terms cannot be obtained elsewhere because the entire industry does business on the basis of the terms in question, or when the particular person cannot obtain better terms elsewhere because of his inferior economic standing or bargaining position.

FACTS: Henningsen purchased a new Plymouth auto from Bloomfield Motors. He did not read the fine print in the contract, and its terms were not called to his attention. Ten days later the car, while being driven by his wife, went out of control, apparently because of some defect in the steering mechanism, and she was injured in the resulting crash. Suit was brought by Henningsen and his wife against Bloomfield Motors and Chrysler Corporation, the manufacturer of the automobile. The defense was raised that the standard warranty on the back of the contract prevented suit for the wife's injuries. The contract contained a provision that the buyer had read and agreed to the terms on the back. A condition on the back of the contract stated that the only warranty, express or implied, made by the dealer or manufacturer was that the manufacturer would replace defective parts within 90 days or until the automobile had been driven 4,000 miles. This form of warranty was used by all members of the Automobile Manufacturers Association and was consequently used in the sale of virtually all American-made cars. Did this warranty provision bar liability on the ground that the automobile was not fit for normal use?

DECISION: No. The clause was not binding because "under modern marketing conditions, when a manufacturer puts a new automobile in the stream of trade and promotes its purchase by the public, an implied warranty that it is reasonably suitable for use as such accompanies it into the hands of the ultimate purchaser," and any contract term that would exclude this warranty is void as contrary to public policy. Such a limitation is not binding because the parties to the contract for the purchase of an automobile are not on an equal footing as to bargaining power. The prospective buyer would be confronted with the same warranty limitation regardless of where he sought to purchase and was thus in a "take-it-or-leave-it" position, with the seller taking advantage of the "economic necessities" of the buyer. [Henningsen v Bloomfield Motors, 32 NJ 358, 161 A2d 69]

When the condition of relative immobility of either party exists, the tendency is to find that that party might be oppressed or exploited and the social forces which oppose such a result come into play.

In some instances the bargaining scales are sought to be balanced by rules of construction. Thus, an insurance contract is strictly construed against the insurer because it is regarded as a standardized "contract of adhesion" prepared by the insurer to which the insured must adhere if he wants to obtain any insurance.

In some areas statutes have been adopted to create equality of bargaining power, such as the Uniform Commercial Code's provision that establishes higher standards for merchants as compared with casual sellers, and the rights given to labor by the labor-management relations statutes. To these may be added the statute permitting exporters to combine for the purpose of the exporting trade so that they can meet the competition of foreign dealers, such privilege creating an exception to the federal antitrust law under which such combinations in foreign commerce would be prohibited.

§ 12:8. DURESS. A person can show *duress* if a threat of violence or other harm deprives that person of that person's free will. The threat may be directed against a third person who is a near relative of the intimidated person making the contract. Thus, a threat to injure one's parent, child, husband, wife, brother, aunt, grandchild, or son-in-law may be duress.

Generally a threat of economic loss, such as a threat to prevent a contractor from securing further credit necessary to obtain building materials, is not regarded as duress.

FACTS: Loral was awarded a $6 million contract by the United States Navy for the production of radar sets. To perform this contract, Loral required 40 precision-gear component parts. Loral advertised for bids on these parts and let a subcontract to Austin to supply 23 gear parts. In the following year Loral was awarded a second Navy contract. Austin declared that it would not make further deliveries under its subcontract unless Loral agreed to a price increase, both as to parts already delivered and parts to be delivered and also unless Loral gave Austin a subcontract under the second Navy contract for all 40 component gear parts. Loral did not want to increase the prices under the original contract and wished to let subcontracts for parts under the second Navy contract on the basis of individual subcontracts for each part with the lowest bidder thereon. Loral communicated with 10 manufacturers of precision gears but could find none that could supply gears in time to perform its contract with the Navy. Loral then agreed to the price increase in connection with the first Navy contract and awarded Austin the subcontract for all 40 parts under the second Navy contract. After performance of the contracts was completed, Austin sued Loral for the balance due under the contracts. Loral sued Austin to recover the amount of the price increase on the theory that such increase had been agreed to under economic duress.

DECISION: Judgment for Loral. The circumstances showed that Loral could not have obtained the goods from other sources and was therefore exposed to the peril of a costly default under the first contract unless Loral agreed to Austin's terms. Loral had communicated with the 10 manufacturers that it knew were competent to do the precision work required under the Navy contract. Loral was not required to take a chance with any unknown manufacturer. The contract modification which Austin obtained by its economic duress could be avoided by Loral and Loral could recover any money which it had lost as the result thereof. [Austin Instrument, Inc. v Loral Corp. 29 NY2d 124, 324 NYS2d 22, 272 NE2d 533]

§ 12:9. REMEDIES. Mistake, fraud, undue influence, and duress may make the agreement voidable or, in some instances, void. The following remedies are then available.

(a) Rescission. If the contract is voidable, it can be rescinded or set aside by the party who has been injured or of whom advantage has been taken. If not avoided, however, the contract is valid and binding. In no case can the other party, the wrongdoer, set aside the contract. If the agreement is void, neither party can enforce it and no act of avoidance is required by either party to set the contract aside.

> **FACTS:** Thompson bought an automobile on credit from Central Motor Co. The contract required him to pay 35 monthly installments of $125 and a final installment of $5,265. The sales manager fraudulently assured Thompson that when the last payment was due it could be refinanced by signing another note for that amount at 8 percent interest. Thompson agreed to make the purchase and signed the contract and a note in reliance on the assurance that he could refinance the final payment. Thereafter Central Motor refused to finance the final payment unless Thompson promised to pay 12 percent interest. He refused to do so, and returned the car. Central sold the car and then sued Thompson for the balance remaining due.

> **DECISION:** Judgment for Thompson. The misrepresentation of the sales manager constituted fraud which permitted Thompson as the victim of the fraud to avoid the contract and the note. [Central Motor Co. v Thompson (TexCivApp) 465 SW2d 405]

When a contract is voidable, the right to rescind the contract is lost by any conduct that is inconsistent with an intention to avoid it. For example, when a party realizes that there has been a mistake but continues with the performance of the contract, the right to avoid the contract because of the mistake is lost.[9] Likewise, it is generally held that a contract, although procured by duress, may be ratified by the victim of the duress as by his adhering to the terms of the contract or making claims to benefits arising therefrom. The right to rescind the contract is lost if the injured party, with full knowledge of the facts, affirms the transaction, or when, with such knowledge, the injured party fails to object to the guilty party within a reasonable time. In determining whether a reasonable time has expired, the court considers whether the delay benefited the injured party, whether a late avoidance of the contract would cause unreasonable harm to the guilty person, and whether avoidance would harm intervening rights of third persons acquired after the original transaction.

When the contract has resulted in the transfer of property from the guilty person to the victim, the latter also loses the right to rescind if, with knowledge of the true situation, the victim retains and uses the property, sells it to another, or uses it after the guilty person refuses to take it back.

(b) Damages. If the other party was guilty of a wrong, such as fraud, as distinguished from making an innocent mistake, the injured party may sue

---

[9] Dayton v Gibbons & Reed Co. 12 Utah2d 296, 365 P2d 801.

him for damages caused by such a wrong. In the case of the sale of goods, the aggrieved party may both rescind and recover damages;[10] but in other contracts, he must choose one. Thus, a buyer rescinding a contract for the sale of a house because of fraud cannot also recover damages for the fraud.

(c) Reformation of contract by court. When the result of a mutual mistake is that a writing does not correctly state the agreement made by the parties, either party can have the court reform the contract to express the intended meaning. Under modern procedures a person may generally sue on the contract as though it had been reformed and recover if he establishes that he is entitled to reformation of the contract and that there has been a breach of the contract as reformed. Thus, instead of first suing to reform an insurance policy and then bringing a second suit on the policy as reformed, most jurisdictions permit the plaintiff to bring one action in which he may prove his case as to reformation and also his case as to the breach of the contract as reformed.

QUESTIONS
AND CASE
PROBLEMS

1. What is the objective of each of the following rules of law?
   (a) One party generally cannot set aside a contract because the other party failed to volunteer information which the complaining party would desire to know.
   (b) In certain close relationships that are regarded as confidential, it is presumed that a contract which benefits the dominating person was obtained by undue influence, and he has the burden of proving the contrary.
2. Tucker purchased an automobile from Central Motors, relying on the representation that it was the latest model available. The sale was completed on February 9. On February 10, Tucker learned that the representation that the automobile was the latest model was false. He continued to drive the car; and after having driven it in excess of 1,000 miles, he demanded on April 7 that the purchase be set aside for fraud. Decide. [Tucker v Central Motors, 220 La 510, 57 So2d 40]

---

[10] UCC § 2-721. See also § 2-720, providing that, unless a contrary intent clearly appears, an expression of "rescission" of a sale contract will not be treated as a renunciation or discharge of a claim in damages for a prior breach.

3. Roberts, an educated person, purchased real estate from Morrison. Roberts merely "half-read" the contract which she signed. As a result, she did not notice the provision in the contract with respect to interest on the unpaid portion of the purchase price. She refused to pay the interest specified in the contract. Morrison sued her. Could he recover? [Morrison v Roberts, 195 Ga 45, 23 SE2d 164]

4. Jacobs purchased an automobile from Lowell Perkins Agency. She traded in her old car. For some reason she incorrectly believed that she would not be required to pay any sales tax on the purchase of the new car. Lowell asked her to pay $86 to $87 for the tax in addition to the purchase price. She refused to do so and sued to recover her traded-in car. Decide. [Lowell Perkins Agency, Inc. v Jacobs, 250 Ark 952, 469 SW2d 89]

5. A corporation had forfeited its charter and plans were under way to sell its business to a buyer. A was a major shareholder of the corporation and was concerned because he had become liable on leases of equipment used by the corporation and hoped that the leases could be transferred to the new business, which would then assume payment of the rentals. B held a judgment against the corporation and was about to use legal process to enforce the judgment against the equipment which had been leased to and was used by the corporation. A promised B that A would pay the judgment to B if B would drop the execution against the leased equipment and the corporate assets. A did not keep his promise. B sued A who raised the defense that he had made the promise because of economic duress and therefore was not liable. Was he correct? [See Blumenthal v Heron, 261 Md 234, 274 A2d 636]

6. The highway department of the state of Washington advertised for bids for the construction of a section of highway. J. J. Welcome & Sons Construction Company submitted a bid. Thereafter Welcome sent the highway commission a telegram stating that item (1) in the bid was changed from $210,000 to $295,000. Western Union made a mistake and the telegram as delivered to the highway commission made it a change from $210,000 to $285,000. Welcome was the lowest responsible bidder and its bid was accepted by the highway commission at a total figure of $6,560,049.65. The next lowest bidder was approximately one-quarter million dollars higher. Welcome learned that its bid was accepted and that the correction telegram was erroneous. Welcome requested that the contract be increased by $10,000 to rectify the mistake made by Western Union and pointed out that this would not injure the state nor any other bidder because the next lowest bidder was still so much more than Welcome's bid. Was Welcome entitled to reformation to correct the mistake? [J. J. Welcome & Sons Construction Co. v Washington, 6 WashApp2d 985, 497 P2d 953]

7. DeMeo rented a building from Horn. DeMeo was represented by an attorney who prepared the lease. The terms of the lease showed that DeMeo intended to make a particular use of the building which would require alterations necessitating a building permit. Horn knew that the building permit could not be obtained because the building was located in an urban renewal area and was to be demolished but said nothing to DeMeo. The lease recited that "the agreement was entered into after full investigation, neither party relying upon any statement or representation not embodied in this agreement made by the other." When DeMeo learned that he could not obtain the building permit he sued Horn for (1)

rescission of the contract, (2) recovery of the down payment made on the lease, and (3) damages for fraud. What, if any, relief is DeMeo entitled to? [DeMeo v Horn, 70 Misc2d 339, 334 NYS2d 22]

8. A claimed that he was entitled to payment of a specified sum under a contract which he had with B. B denied this liability. A threatened to sue B if he would not agree to pay the claimed amount. B promised to pay the claimed amount. He failed to keep his promise and A sued B on this later promise for the claimed amount. B defended on the ground that the promise was not binding because it was obtained by duress. Was this defense valid? [See Eggleston v Humble Pipe Line Co. (TexCivApp) 482 SW2d 909]

9. A claimed that B owed him money. A was under the impression that B did not have much money. On the basis of this impression, A made a settlement agreement with B for a nominal amount. When A later learned that B was in fact reasonably wealthy, A sought to set the agreement aside. Was he entitled to do so? [See Myers v Bernard, 38 AppDiv2d 619, 326 NYS2d 279]

10. A dealer induced a distributor to sell to him on credit by telling the distributor that the dealer expected to inherit money which he would invest in the business. The dealer did not inherit any money. The distributor claimed that the dealer had been guilty of fraud. Was this correct? [See United Fire and Casualty Co. v Nissan Motor Corp. 164 Colo 62, 433 P2d 769]

11. The State of North Dakota, through the Bank of North Dakota, sold county industrial development revenue bonds to the State Security Bank. Thereafter Security State Bank sued to set aside the contract on the ground that it was prohibited by statute from purchasing such bonds in excess of 5 percent of its capital, and the contract to purchase the bonds represented more than 5 percent. Was it entitled to set aside the contract? [Security State Bank v North Dakota (ND) 181 NW2d 225]

CONSIDERATION

§ 13.1. DEFINITION OF CONSIDERATION. To constitute a contract, the agreement must meet requirements in addition to genuine mutual assent by competent parties. Ordinarily one of these requirements is consideration, but the exceptions to this requirement are increasing.

Consideration is what a promisor demands and receives as the price for his promise. A promise usually is binding upon a person only when he has received consideration.[1] It must be something to which the promisor is not otherwise entitled, and it must be what the promisor specifies as the price for his promise.

The fact that the promisor incidentally obtains a benefit does not make the benefit consideration for his promise when he had not bargained specifically for that benefit.

Although some cases define consideration in terms of benefit to the promisor or detriment to the promisee, it is immaterial whether benefit or detriment is present. The essential element is that the act or thing which is done or promised has been specified by the promisor as the price to be paid in order to obtain his promise.

FACTS: Kemp leased a gas filling station from Baehr. Kemp, who was heavily indebted to the Penn-O-Tex Oil Corporation, transferred to it his right to receive payments on all claims. When Baehr complained that the rent was not paid, he was assured by the corporation that the rent would be paid to him. Baehr did not sue Kemp for the overdue rent but later sued the corporation. The defense was raised that there was no consideration for the promise of the corporation.

DECISION: The promise of the corporation was not binding because there was no consideration for it. While the concept of consideration developed as the way of determining which agreements were serious and intended by the parties to be binding, the converse does not follow that every serious agreement is binding. It is necessary in every case to find that

---

[1] Hanson v Central Show Printing Co. 256 Iowa 1221, 130 NW2d 654.

the promisee gave the promisor that which the promisor required as the price of his promise. Although Baehr's not suing Kemp could have been specified by the corporation as the price of its promise to pay Kemp's obligation, it had not done so and hence there was no consideration. [Baehr v Penn-O-Tex Oil Corporation, 258 Minn 533, 104 NW2d 661]

In view of the fact that consideration is the price paid for the promise, it is unimportant who pays that price as long as it has been agreed that it should be paid in that way. For example, consideration may be the extending of credit to a third person, as extending credit to the corporation of which the promisor is a shareholder or to a husband in return for the promise of his wife to pay the debt.[2]

A promise to make a gift, or a promise to do or not to do something without receiving consideration, is unenforceable; but an executed gift or a performance without consideration cannot be rescinded for lack of consideration.

If the contract is bilateral, each party to the contract is a promisor and must receive consideration to make his promise binding. A unilateral contract has only one promisor, and the performance of the act which he called for is the consideration for his promise.

Consideration is sometimes qualified or described as "valuable consideration." This is done to distinguish it from the so-called "good consideration," that is, the love and affection existing between near relatives. In most states good consideration is not consideration at all but is merely a matter of inducement in the making of the promise. Moral obligation is likewise not consideration.

§ 13:2. BINDING CHARACTER OF PROMISE.

To constitute consideration, the promise must be binding, that is, it must impose a liability or create a duty. Suppose that a coal company promises to sell to a factory all the coal which it orders at a specified price, and that the factory agrees to pay that price for any coal which it orders from the coal company. The promise of the factory is not consideration because it does not obligate the factory to buy any coal from the coal company.

If, however, the factory promises to purchase all the coal it requires for a specified period and the coal dealer agrees to supply it at a specified price per ton, there is a valid contract according to most courts. It is true that it cannot be known beforehand how much coal will be ordered. The factory may have a strike or a fire and not operate at all during the year, and therefore require no coal. Moreover, the factory might convert to oil. In spite of these possibilities, such a contract is usually regarded as valid.

Although a contract must impose a binding obligation, it may authorize one or either party to terminate or cancel the agreement under certain circumstances or upon giving notice to the other party. The fact that the contract may be terminated in this manner does not make the contract any less binding prior to such termination.

---

[2] State Bank of Arthur v Sentel, 10 IllApp3d 86, 293 NE2d 4444.

In some instances where it is manifest that a particular act is impossible to perform, a promise to do that act is not consideration. If there is a possibility that the performance can be made, the consideration is valid.

§ **13:3. PROMISE TO PERFORM EXISTING OBLIGATIONS.** Ordinarily, a promise to do, or the performance of, what one is already under legal obligation to do is not consideration. It is immaterial whether the legal obligation is based upon contract, upon the duties pertaining to an office held by the promisor, or upon statute or general principles of law.

> **FACTS:** An insurance company offered a reward for the arrest and conviction of a thief who robbed insured premises. The reward was claimed by Davis. He was a salaried, full-time "crime detector" employed by the county and assigned to the office of the prosecuting attorney. Other persons claiming the reward contended that Davis was not eligible to receive the reward.

> **DECISION:** Judgment against Davis. As it was the duty of Davis to give the prosecuting attorney any information that he acquired with respect to the commission of crimes, it was contrary to public policy to permit him to accept a reward offered for doing the work which it was his duty to perform. [Davis v Mathews (CA4 WVa) 361 F2d 899]

Similarly, a promise to refrain from doing what one has no legal right to do is not consideration.

(a) Completion of contract. When a contractor refuses to complete a building unless the owner promises a payment or bonus in addition to the sum specified in the original contract, and the owner promises to make that payment, the question arises whether the owner's promise is binding. Most courts hold that the second promise of the owner is without consideration. A few courts hold that the promise is binding on the theory that the first contract was mutually rescinded and that a second contract, including the promise to pay the bonus, was agreed upon. Some courts hold the promise enforceable on the theory that the contractor has given up the right to elect to perform, or to abandon the contract and pay damages.

The courts holding that there is no consideration for the second promise make an exception when there are extraordinary circumstances caused by unforeseeable difficulties or mistakes and when the additional amount demanded by the contractor is reasonable for the extra work done by him. They do so usually upon the theory that the first contract was discharged because of an implied condition that the facts would be or would continue to be as supposed by the parties and that the completion of the contract was the consideration for the new promise. Generally, however, unanticipated difficulty or expense, such as a strike or price increase, does not affect the liabilities of the parties.

If the promise of the contractor is to do something that is neither expressly nor impliedly a part of the first contract, then the promise of the other party is binding. For example, if a bonus of $1,000 is promised in return for the promise of a contractor to complete the building at a date earlier than that specified in the original agreement, the promise to pay the bonus is binding.

(b) Compromise and release of claims. The rule that doing or promising to do what one is bound to do is not consideration applies to a part payment made in satisfaction of an admitted debt. For example, if one person owes another $100, the promise of the latter to take $50 in full payment is not binding upon him and will not prevent him from demanding the remainder later because the partial payment by the debtor is not consideration.

This rule has been severely criticized because it seems unfair. In some instances it has been changed by statute or by court decision. Some courts treat the transaction as a binding gift of the remainder on the part of the creditor. Other courts seize the slightest opportunity to find some new consideration.

If the debtor pays before the debt is due, there is, of course, consideration since on the day when payment was made, the creditor was not entitled to demand any payment. Likewise, if the creditor accepts some article, even of slight value, in addition to the part payment, the agreement is held to be binding.

> **FACTS:** Post owed the bank $9,922.20. The bank agreed to reduce the claim to $8,000 if Post would give the bank a mortgage for that amount. The mortgage was given. The bank subsequently sued Post for $9,922.20.
>
> **DECISION:** Judgment for the bank for only $8,000. The giving of security for an unsecured debt or the changing of security can be consideration when called for by the creditor as the price for his promise to reduce this claim. [Post v First National Bank, 138 Ill 559, 28 NE 978]

If there is a bona fide dispute as to the amount owed or as to whether any amount is owed, a payment by the debtor of less than the amount claimed by the creditor is consideration for the latter's agreement to release or settle the claim. It is generally regarded as sufficient if the claimant believes in his claim. Conversely, if the claimant knows that his claim does not have any merit and he is merely pressing it in order to force the other party to make some payment to buy peace from the annoyance of a lawsuit, the settlement agreement based on the part payment is not binding.

When parties to a contract in a good-faith effort to meet the business realities of a situation agree to a reduction of contract terms, there is some authority that the promise of the one party to accept the lesser performance by the other is binding even though technically the promise to render the lesser performance is not consideration because the obligor was already obligated to render the greater performance. Thus a landlord's promise to reduce the rent was binding when the tenant could not pay the original rent and the landlord preferred to have the building occupied even though receiving a smaller rental. When the contract is for the sale of goods, any modification made by the parties to the contract is binding without regard to the existence of consideration for the modification.

(c) Part-payment checks. The acceptance and cashing of a check for part of a debt releases the entire debt when the check bears a notation that it is intended as final or full payment and the total amount due is disputed or unliquidated.[3] It probably has this same effect even though the debt is not disputed or unliquidated.[4]

In some jurisdictions this principle is applied without regard to the form of payment, it being required only that the part payment was in fact received and accepted as discharging the obligation.[5] The California Civil Code, Sec. 1541, provides: "An obligation is extinguished by a release therefrom given to the debtor by the creditor, upon a new consideration, or in writing, with or without new consideration." If the notation that the acceptance of the check constitutes final payment is in print which the court regards as too small, it may not be binding in the absence of evidence that the notation was actually seen by the creditor receiving the check.[6]

(d) Composition of creditors. In a *composition of creditors*, the various creditors of one debtor mutually agree to accept a fractional part of their claims in full satisfaction thereof. Such agreements are binding and are supported by consideration. When creditors agree to extend the due date on their debts, the promise of each creditor to forbear is likewise consideration for the promise of the other creditors to forbear.

§ 13:4. PRESENT VERSUS PAST CONSIDERATION. Since consideration is what the promisor states must be received for his promise, it must be given after the promisor states what he demands. Past consideration is not valid. When one person performs some service for another without the latter's knowledge or without an understanding that compensation is to be paid, a promise made later to pay for such services is not supported by consideration and is unenforceable. A promise by an employee to refrain from competing with the employee's employer must be supported by consideration when the employment relationship already exists and the employee was not subject to any such restriction under that contract.

FACTS: Warner & Co. procured a purchaser for the property of Brua and submitted to Brua sales papers to be signed. The papers contained a promise to pay Warner & Co. commissions for finding a purchaser. Brua signed the paper but later refused to pay Warner & Co. Thereafter Warner & Co. brought a suit to recover the commissions from Brua, who contended that there was no consideration for his promise.

DECISION: There was no consideration for the owner's promise to pay the broker since the broker's services which the owner promised to compensate had been performed and were therefore past consideration. A promise given because of past consideration is not binding. [Warner & Co. v Brua, 33 OhioApp 84, 168 NE 571]

(a) Moral obligation. Some courts hold that when benefits are obtained by fraud or under circumstances that create a moral obligation, a promise to compensate by the person benefited is supported by consideration. When one promises to pay a debt that was unenforceable because of minority, or

[3] Miller v Montgomery, 77 NMex 766, 427 P2d 275.

[4] Uniform Commercial Code § 3-408. Official Comment, point 2. See also § 1-107, generally, and § 2-209(1) as to the sale of goods.

[5] Rivers v Cole Corp. 209 Ga 406, 73 SE2d 196 (local statutes).

[6] Kibler v Frank L. Garrett & Sons, Inc. 73 Wash2d 523, 439 P2d 416.

that is barred by the statute of limitations, or that has been discharged in bankruptcy, the promise is binding. There must be clear proof, however, that such promise was in fact made.

The better theory is that the new promise is a waiver of the bar or defense to the action and that no consideration is necessary.

To constitute a promise to pay a debt discharged by bankruptcy, the promise must be clear and must reasonably identify the discharged debt. Thus, a promise "to pay debts" does not revive a debt barred by a bankruptcy discharge where it was not clear whether this meant such debts as would be incurred after the bankruptcy discharge or embraced the earlier debts which had been discharged.

(b) **Complex transactions.** In applying the rule that past consideration is not consideration, care must be taken to distinguish between the situation in which the consideration is in fact past and the situation in which the earlier consideration and the subsequent promises were all part of one complex transaction. For example, when an assignment is made and thereafter a third person guarantees the payment of the assigned claim, the earlier transaction may or may not be consideration which will make binding the promise of the guarantor. If the original assignment and the subsequent guarantee are merely parts of a "single transaction" and were all in the contemplation of the parties when the assignment was agreed to, then the prior assignment is consideration for the subsequent guarantee.

In contrast, if the guarantee was not contemplated at the time the assignment was made but was merely an afterthought or later development, the earlier assignment would not serve as consideration for the guarantor's promise. Consequently, if there is no new consideration for that promise, it is not binding on the guarantor.

§ 13:5. **FORBEARANCE AS CONSIDERATION.** In most cases consideration consists of the performance of an act or the making of a promise to act. But consideration may also consist of *forbearance*, which is refraining from doing an act, or a promise of forbearance. In other words, the promisor may desire to buy the inaction of the other party or his promise not to act.

The waiving or giving up of any right, legal or equitable, can be consideration for the promise of another. Thus, the relinquishment of a right in property, of a right to sue for damages, or of a homestead right will support a promise given in return for it.

When the creditor agrees to extend the time for paying his debt in return for the debtor's promise of a higher return of interest, the agreement to extend is consideration for the promise to pay the higher rate of interest.[7]

When a supplier has the right to terminate the contract with the dealer selling its products, the promise of the supplier to refrain from revoking the contract with the dealer is consideration for the dealer's agreement to

---

[7] Bloch v Fedak, 210 Kan 63, 499 P2d 1052.

reduce the commissions taken by him on the resale of the supplier's products.[8]

The right that is surrendered in return for a promise may be a right against a third person or his property, as well as one against the promisor or his property.

As under the rule governing compromises, forbearance to assert a claim is consideration when the claim has been asserted in good faith, even though it is without merit. In the absence of such a belief, forbearance with respect to a worthless claim is not consideration.

When a father gave the owner of a bulldozer a promissory note to cover the damages done to the bulldozer by his son, the owner's giving up his claim against the father in return for the note constituted consideration for the note even though the owner did not establish that his claim against the father was valid.

Forbearance is not consideration unless it is the price for the promise. The mere fact that some act is done, as the giving of a promissory note, and thereafter the creditor does nothing, does not establish that the forbearance was the price for the making of the promissory note. At the same time such an intent may be inferred from the circumstances and it is not necessary that there be an express declaration or a statement that a promise is made in consideration of the forbearance of the creditor.

§ 13:6. ADEQUACY OF CONSIDERATION.

Ordinarily the courts do not consider the adequacy of the consideration given for a promise. In the absence of fraud or other misconduct, the courts usually will not interfere to make sure that each side is getting a fair return.[9]

The fact that the consideration supplied by one party is slight when compared with the burden undertaken by the other party is immaterial, as it is a matter for the parties to decide when they make their contract whether each is getting an adequate return.

FACTS: Upon the death of their mother, the children of James Smith gave their interest in the mother's estate to their father in consideration of his payment of $1 to each and of his promise to leave them the property on his death. The father died without leaving them the property. The children sued their father's second wife to obtain the property in accordance with the agreement.

DECISION: Judgment for children. The promises between the father and the children created a binding contract, as against the objection that the contract was not binding because the children got so little from the father, since all they received was the $1 and the chance that when the father died, there would be something in his estate which could be left to them. This argument was rejected because the law will not consider the adequacy of consideration when there is no element of fraud. [Smith v Smith, 340 Ill 34, 172 NE 32]

---

[8] Mattlage Sales, Inc. v Howard Johnson's Wholesale Division, Inc. 39 AppDiv2d 958, 333 NYS2d 491.

[9] Cook v American States Insurance Co. 150 IndApp 88, 275 NE2d 832.

(a) Wisdom of contract. As a corollary of the concept that the court will not consider the adequacy of consideration, the ordinary rule is that the validity of a contract does not depend upon whether it is a wise or sensible contract. As long as the parties have capacity and there has been genuine assent to the terms of the contract, the court is not concerned with the actual terms of the contract.

(b) Failure of expectations. The fact that what the party obtains in return for his promise is not as advantageous to him as he had expected does not mean that there is an absence or a failure of consideration. Consequently, when an investor obtained the shares of stock which he sought, the contract was fully performed and the fact that the stock proved worthless did not constitute a failure of consideration.

> FACTS: Largosa was promoting the organization of a new corporation, the Direct Selling Corporation of Hawaii. Molina paid $2,000 for 40 shares. The corporation was formed but proved a financial failure. Molina sued to get his money back.

> DECISION: Molina was not entitled to the money. The fact that the business venture was a failure did not mean that Molina did not obtain what he had bargained for, namely, 40 shares. Hence there was no failure of consideration. [Molina v Largosa (Hawaii) 465 P2d 293]

The fact that a club member does not make use of his club privileges does not constitute a lack of consideration for the promise to become a member and to pay for the membership.[10]

§ 13:7. EXCEPTIONS TO ADEQUACY OF CONSIDERATION RULE.

The courts make some exceptions to the rule that the law will not weigh the consideration.

(a) Unconscionability. An excessively hard bargain obtained by a seller of goods at the expense of a small buyer with weak purchasing power has been held to constitute unconscionability,[11] although such a conclusion is merely another way of stating that the consideration received by the buyer was not adequate.

(b) Statutory exception. In a few states, statutes require that the consideration be adequate, or fair or reasonable, in order to make a contract binding.

Adequacy of the consideration may be questioned in computing tax liability. For example, when it is claimed that the taxable balance of a decedent's estate should be reduced by the amount owed a given creditor, such debt may be deducted only to the extent that the decedent had received an equivalent value from the creditor. Thus, if the decedent owed the creditor $1,000 for property that was worth $200, only the sum of $200 could be deducted in computing the value of the estate. This determination

---

[10] Sorensen Health Studio v McCoy, 261 Iowa 891, 156 NW2d 341.

[11] Toker v Westerman, 113 NJSuper 452, 274 A2d 78. See also American Home Improvement, Inc. v MacIver, 105 NH 435, 201 A2d 886.

for tax purposes, however, does not affect the validity of the creditor's contract.

(c) Evidence of fraud. The smallness of the consideration may be evidence of fraud.[12] Suppose that R sells a $15,000 house to E for $500. It might be a perfectly innocent transaction in which R virtually makes a gift in return for the nominal payment. Since R, as the owner of his house, could give it away, nothing prevents his "selling" it at such a low figure. The transaction, however, may be of a different nature. It may be that E has defrauded R into believing that the property is worthless, and R therefore sells it for $500. Or there may be collusion between R and E to transfer the property in order to hide it from creditors of R. The smallness of the consideration does not mean that the transaction is necessarily made in bad faith or a fraudulent purpose; but if other evidence indicates fraud, the smallness of the consideration corroborates that evidence.

(d) Exchange of different quantities of identical units. A promise to pay a particular amount of money or to deliver a particular quantity of goods in exchange for a promise to pay or deliver a greater amount or quantity of the same kind of money or goods at the same time and place is not adequate consideration. If I promise to pay you $50 in exchange for your promise to pay me $100 under such circumstances, my promise is not regarded as adequate consideration for your promise, and your promise therefore is not binding upon you.

(e) Equitable relief. When a plaintiff seeks equitable relief, such as the specific performance of a contract, the courts will generally refuse to assist the plaintiff unless he has given valuable or substantial consideration for his rights.

§ 13:8. EXCEPTIONS TO REQUIREMENTS OF CONSIDERATION.

(a) Voluntary subscriptions. When charitable enterprises are financed by voluntary subscriptions of a number of persons, the promise of each one is generally enforceable. For example, when a number of people make pledges or subscriptions for the construction of a church, for a charitable institution, or for a college, the subscriptions are binding.

The theories for sustaining such promises vary. One view is that the promise of each subscriber is consideration for the promises of the others. This view is not sound because the promises are not given in exchange for each other. Another view is that the liability of the promisor rests upon a promissory estoppel because obligations have been incurred in reliance upon the promise. Still another view treats such a subscription as an offer of a unilateral contract which is accepted by creating liabilities or making expenditures. Under this theory the promise would be revocable until some act is performed. It is also held by some courts that the acceptance of a subscription carries an implied promise creating an obligation to perform in accordance with the offer.

---

[12] Woods v Griffin, 204 Ark 514, 163 SW2d 322.

The real answer to the question of whether consideration is present is that in these cases consideration is lacking according to the technical standards applied in ordinary contract cases. Nevertheless, the courts enforce such promises as a matter of public policy.

(b) Commercial paper. The fact that there was no consideration for commercial paper, such as a check or promissory note, or that the consideration was illegal or had failed, may be raised against an ordinary holder of the paper. Such defenses may not be raised against persons acquiring the paper in the course of ordinary business transactions. The result is that the commercial paper may be enforceable even though no consideration was given.

(c) Sealed instruments. At common law, consideration was not necessary to support a promise under seal. In a state which gives the seal its original common-law effect, the gratuitous promise or a promise to make a gift is enforceable when it is set forth in a sealed instrument.

In some states a promise under seal must be supported by consideration, just as though it did not have a seal. Other states take a middle position and hold that the presence of a seal is prima facie proof that there is consideration to support the promise. This means that if nothing more than the existence of the sealed promise is shown, it is deemed supported by consideration. The party making the promise, however, may prove that there was no consideration. If he does, the promise is not binding upon him.

Even in those states in which the contract under seal is binding, the courts of equity will refuse to grant special relief, such as specifically enforcing the contract, if there is not a fair or reasonable consideration for the promise.

(d) Debts of record. No consideration is necessary to support obligations of record, such as a court judgment. These obligations are enforceable as a matter of public policy.

(e) State statutes. Under statutes in some states no consideration is necessary in order to make certain written promises binding. The Model Written Obligations Act, which has been adopted only in Pennsylvania, provides that no release (or promise) made and signed by the person releasing (or promising) shall be "invalid or unenforceable for lack of consideration, if the writing also contains an additional express statement, in any form of language, that the signer intends to be legally bound" by his promise.

(f) Uniform Commercial Code. Consideration is not required for (1) a merchant's written firm offer as to goods, stated as irrevocable; (2) a written discharge of a claim for an alleged breach of a commercial contract; or (3) an agreement to modify a contract for the sale of goods.[13]

---

[13] UCC § 2-209(1).

(g) Promissory estoppel. Some courts enforce promises that are not supported by a consideration upon the *doctrine of promissory estoppel.* By this doctrine, if a person makes a promise to another and that other person acts upon that promise, the promisor is barred from setting up the absence of consideration in order to avoid his promise. The enforcement of the promise, even though there is no consideration, is deemed proper when the promisor should reasonably expect to induce and does induce action or forbearance of a definite and substantial character on the part of the promisee and when "injustice can be avoided only by enforcement of the promise." The doctrine of promissory estoppel, although conflicting with the basic requirement of consideration, is being given wider recognition as a means of attaining justice.

> **FACTS:** Hoffman wanted to acquire a franchise as a Red Owl grocery store, Red Owl being a corporation that maintained a system of chain stores. The agent of Red Owl informed Hoffman and his wife that if they would sell their bakery in Wautoma, acquire a certain tract of land in Chilton, another city, and put up a specified amount of money, they would be given a franchise as desired. Hoffman sold his business, acquired the land in Chilton, but was never granted a franchise. He and his wife sued Red Owl, which raised the defense that there had only been an assurance that Hoffman would receive a franchise but no promise supported by consideration and therefore no binding contract to give him a franchise.

> **DECISION:** Judgment for the Hoffmans. Injustice would result under the circumstances of the case if the Hoffmans were not granted relief because of the failure of Red Owl to keep the promise made by its authorized agent. The plaintiffs had acted in reliance on such promise and would be harmed substantially if the promise were not held binding. [Hoffman v Red Owl Stores, Inc. 26 Wis2d 683, 133 NW2d 267]

Promissory estoppel differs from consideration in that the reliance of the promisee is not the bargained for response sought by the promisor. To be consideration, it would be necessary that the promisor had specified or requested reliance as the price of his making his promise.

The doctrine of promissory estoppel is not applied when no promise is made and one party merely takes a chance on future developments. Nor does it apply when it is made clear that certain conditions must be met before any obligation will arise and the claimant fails to meet those conditions, such as making payment in advance. Likewise, since promissory estoppel is based on the ground that there has been reliance on a promise, there must be a communication of the promise to the promisee, in the same sense that an offer must be communicated to an offeree.[14]

Promissory estoppel is also applied by some courts to require an offeror to hold an offer open for a reasonable time even though there is no consideration to do so and although the firm offer concept is not applicable.

---

[14] Hilton v Alexander & Baldwin, 66 Wash2d 30, 400 P2d 772.

Thus, when a subcontractor makes a bid to a general contractor and recognizes that the general contractor will rely thereon in making his bid for the construction job, in some states the subcontractor is barred from revoking his offer until a reasonable time has elapsed in which the contractor may accept the offer of the subcontractor.

§ 13:9. LEGALITY OF CONSIDERATION. The law will not permit persons to make contracts that violate the law. Accordingly, a promise to do something which the law prohibits or a promise to refrain from doing something which the law requires is not valid consideration and the contract is illegal. This subject is further discussed in Chapter 14.

§ 13:10. FAILURE OF CONSIDERATION. When a promise is given as consideration, the question arises as to whether the promisor will perform his promise. If he does not perform his promise, the law describes the default as a "failure of consideration." This is a misnomer since the failure of the promisor is one of performance, not of consideration.

> FACTS: Alexander Proudfoot Company was in the business of devising efficiency systems for industry. It undertook to devise such a system for the Sanitary Linen Service Company. The system failed to effect the promised savings and Sanitary sued Alexander to get back the money which it had paid.

> DECISION: Judgment for Sanitary Linen Service. The promised service had not been rendered. There was accordingly a failure of consideration and Sanitary was entitled to recover what it had paid for that which it did not receive. [Sanitary Linen Service Co. v Alexander Proudfoot Co. (CA5 Fla) 435 F2d 292]

The fact that a contract is under seal does not prevent proof that the consideration for the contract had failed. This does not contradict or impeach the writing but merely proves that the writing has never been performed.

The fact that performance of the contract by the other party does not have the results that one hoped for does not mean that there is a failure of consideration. For example, when one buys a store building in a real estate development, he obviously does so in the expectation that he will obtain a large volume of trade by virtue of his location. It may be that this will not occur because of the continuing of earlier purchasing patterns of the public. While the buyer of the store building is disappointed, there has not been any failure of consideration with respect to the contract by which he agreed to purchase the store building from its owner.

> FACTS: The Association of Army and Navy Stores gave a price discount to customer members of the Association. The Association agreed to list Young's store as a member store, and Young agreed to pay the Association a percentage of the sales made at its store to Association customer members plus a fixed monthly charge of $2.50. No new customers purchased at Young's store. He refused to pay the

Association the monthly charge on the ground that the consideration for the contract had failed. The Association sued Young.

DECISION: Judgment against Young. There was no failure of consideration. Young obtained exactly what the other contracting party agreed to provide. Young did not obtain the economic benefit from that performance which he hoped to obtain. While there was a failure of Young's expectations, there was no failure of consideration and Young remained bound by his contract. [Association of Army and Navy Stores v Young, 296 Ky 61, 176 SW2d 136]

QUESTIONS AND CASE PROBLEMS

1. What is the objective of each of the following rules of law?
   (a) An executed gift or a performance that has been rendered without consideration cannot be rescinded for lack of consideration.
   (b) In the absence of fraud, the adequacy of consideration is usually immaterial.
2. Husted made a down payment on a contract to purchase most of the assets of a corporation. He was not able to complete the purchase and forfeited the down payment. Fuller, who in effect owned, controlled, and was the corporation, stated that he felt an obligation to Husted to see that he got his down payment back and promised that he would give him a promissory note covering the amount of the down payment. He failed to do so. Husted sued Fuller for breach of his promise to deliver such a note. Fuller claimed that his promise was not binding on him. Decide. [Husted v Fuller (CA7 Ill) 361 F2d 187]
3. Irene Dewein studied nursing. She did not enter that profession, however, but went to live with and take care of her parents. This she did for 27 years, during which time the father was invalided until his death in 1948. In 1957 the mother died after being frequently bedridden for a period of 2 years. In October, 1956, Irene's brother Edward had said to her, "Sis, I am so grateful you are taking care of mother, and I am certainly going to see you are taken care of for life. You deserve it. Don't worry about the future. I am going to see you are taken care of." The brother died in 1959 without having made any provision in his will for Irene. She sued his estate for the value of her services for 27 years. Decide. [Dewein v Dewein's Executors, 30 IllApp2d 446, 174 NE2d 875]
4. When Helen Suske sued John Straka on a promissory note that he had given her, he raised the defense that his note was a gift and that he had not received any consideration for it. She claimed that at the time John was obligated to her in several ways and that such obligations constituted consideration. It was claimed that he had promised to marry the plaintiff, that he owed the plaintiff for room rent and money loaned to him, and that he had caused her some inconvenience. Was the note binding? [Suske v Straka, 229 Minn 408, 39 NW2d 745]

5. *A* owed money to a bank. *A* had a bank account in the bank, and under the loan agreement the bank could repay itself the amount of the loan from the bank deposit. When *A* died, his widow was made his executrix. She signed a note individually, as executrix, promising to pay the bank the amount of *A*'s debt from his bank account. When the bank sued her on her note, she raised the defense that there was no consideration for it. Was this a valid defense? [See Jeter v Citizens National Bank (TexCivApp) 419 SW2d 916]

6. A prospective buyer of a house told the real estate broker to hire a contractor to inspect the building for termites. A contractor agreed to do so for $35, but he made a negligent inspection and failed to detect the presence of termites. The buyer sued the contractor for the loss caused by the contractor's negligence. The contractor defended on the ground that he had not charged much for the job. Was this a valid defense? [See Mayes v Emery, 3 WashApp2d 315, 475 P2d 124]

7. Sears, Roebuck & Co. promised to give Forrer "permanent employment." Forrer sold his farm at a loss in order to take the job. Shortly after commencing work, he was discharged by Sears which claimed that the contract could be terminated at will. Forrer claimed that promissory estoppel prevented Sears from terminating the contract. Was he correct? [Forrer v Sears, Roebuck & Co. 36 Wis2d 388, 153 NW2d 587]

8. Fedun rented a building to Gomer who did business under the name of Mike's Cafe. Later, Gomer was about to sell out the business to Brown and requested Fedun to release him from his liability under the lease. Fedun agreed to do so. Brown sold out shortly thereafter. The balance of the rent due by Gomer was not paid, and Fedun sued Mike's Cafe on the rent claim. Could he collect after having released Gomer? [Fedun v Mike's Cafe, 204 PaSuper 356, 204 A2d 776]

9. Steve Clark was a member of the Marine Corps. He held a World Service Life Insurance policy. It did not contain any war risk or aviation exclusion clauses. Brumell, an agent of the Prudential Insurance Company, persuaded him to drop this policy on the promise that he would obtain a similar policy from the Prudential Company which likewise would not have any war risk or aviation clauses. The policy which Prudential issued did contain such clauses and thereafter Steve was killed in Vietnam when his helicopter crashed and burned. The Prudential Insurance Company paid his parents as beneficiaries of the policy but then demanded the return of the money on the basis that payment had been made by mistake. They refused to return the money. Were they entitled to retain it? [Prudential Insurance Co. v Clark (CA5 Fla) 456 F2d 932]

10. Allen owned land which was being developed. Her brother, Norburn, wrote to the vice-president of Investment Properties of Asheville, Inc., stating that "this is to certify that I will stand personally liable" for the land preparation expenses. When Investment Properties sued him on this guaranty, he raised the defense that he did not receive any consideration for his promise and therefore it was not binding. Was this a valid defense? [Investment Properties of Asheville, Inc. v Norburn, 281 NC 300, 188 SE2d 342]

11. Youngman went to work for the Nevada Irrigation District. The superintendent promised him that he would receive a specified pay increase in April of each year. When he did not receive the increase, he sued the District. He claimed that he had relied on the promise that he would receive such increase and that accordingly the promise was binding. Was he correct? [Youngman v Nevada Irrigation District 70 Cal3d 240, 74 CalRptr 398, 449 P2d 462]

LEGALITY AND PUBLIC POLICY

A. GENERAL PRINCIPLES

§ 14:1. DEFINITION. An agreement is illegal when either its formation or performance is a crime or a tort, or is opposed to public policy. Ordinarily an illegal agreement is void.

(a) **Effect of illegality.** When an agreement is illegal, the parties are usually regarded as not entitled to the aid of the courts. If the illegal agreement has not been performed, neither party can sue the other to obtain performance or damages. If the agreement has been performed, neither party can sue the other for damages or to set it aside.

(b) **Exceptions.** The following are exceptions to the general rule that the court will not aid a party to an unlawful agreement:

(1) When the law which the agreement violates is intended for the protection of one of the parties, that party may seek relief. For example, when, in order to protect the public, the law forbids the issuance of securities or notes by certain classes or corporations, a person who has purchased them may recover his money.

(2) When the parties are not equally guilty or, as it is said, are not *in pari delicto*, the one less guilty is granted relief when public interest is advanced by so doing. For example, when a statute is adopted to protect one of the parties to a transaction, as a usury law adopted to protect borrowers, the person to be protected will not be deemed to be *in pari delicto* with the wrongdoer when he enters into a transaction which is prohibited by the statute.

(3) An exception may also exist when the illegality is collateral or incidental, as when one of the parties has not obtained a government permit or license necessary to performance of the contract.

(4) When one person has entrusted another with money or property to be used for an illegal purpose, the first person usually may change his mind

and recover the money or property provided it has not been spent for the illegal purpose. Thus, money entrusted to an agent for use as a bribe of a third person may be recovered from the agent before it is so used.

As an extension of this rule, if bets were held by a stakeholder and either of the bettors repudiates the bet, the stakeholder must return his bet to him and would be liable if he paid that money to the other bettor. When the act of betting is itself made a crime, some states deny the debtor the right to recover his bet from the stakeholder.[1]

§ 14:2. **PARTIAL ILLEGALITY.** An agreement may involve the performance of several promises, some of which are illegal and some legal. The legal parts of the agreement may be enforced, provided that they can be separated from the parts which are illegal. The same rule applies when the consideration is illegal in part. The rule is not applied, however, to situations in which the illegal act or consideration is said to taint and strike down the entire agreement.

When there is an indivisible promise to perform several acts, some of which are illegal, the agreement is void. Also when there is a single promise to do a legal act, supported by several considerations, some of which are illegal, the agreement cannot be enforced.

If a contract is susceptible of two interpretations, one legal and the other illegal, the court will assume that the legal meaning was intended unless the contrary is clearly, indicated.

§ 14:3. **CRIMES AND CIVIL WRONGS.** An agreement is illegal and therefore void when it calls for the commission of any act that constitutes a crime. To illustrate, one cannot enforce an agreement by which the other party is to commit an assault, to steal property, to burn a house, to print a libelous article, or to kill a person.

An agreement that calls for the commission of a civil wrong is also illegal and void. Examples are agreements to damage the goods of another, to slander a third person, to defraud another, or to infringe another's patent, trademark, or copyright.

§ 14:4. **GOOD FAITH AND FAIRNESS.** In addition to the limiting factors of illegality and being contrary to public policy, the law is evolving toward requiring that contracts be neither unfair nor manifest bad faith. Affirmatively stated, it is now required that contracts be fair and be made in good faith. The law is becoming increasingly concerned with whether *A* has utilized a superior bargaining power or superior knowledge to obtain better terms from *B* than *A* would otherwise have obtained.

---

[1] Some courts require that a person repudiating his bet do so before the event which was the subject of the bet has occurred. Other courts permit the recovery of the bet from the stakeholder as long as demand is made prior to payment of the money to the other bettor, even though the event which was the subject of the bet has occurred.

In the case of goods, the seller must act in good faith, which is defined as to merchant sellers as "honesty in fact and the observance of reasonable commercial standards of fair dealing in the trade."[2]

§ 14:5. UNCONSCIONABLE AND OPPRESSIVE CONTRACTS.

Ordinarily a court will not consider whether a contract is fair or unfair, wise or foolish, or operates unequally between the parties.[3] However, in a number of instances the law holds that contracts or contract clauses will not be enforced because they are too harsh or oppressive to one of the two parties. This principle is most commonly applied to invalidate a clause providing for the payment by one party of a large penalty upon breaking the contract or a provision declaring that a party shall not be liable for the consequences of his negligence. This principle is extended in connection with the sale of goods to provide that "if the court . . . finds the contract or any clause of the contract to have been unconscionable at the time it was made, the court may refuse to enforce the contract, or it may enforce the remainder of the contract without the unconscionable clause, or it may so limit the application of any unconscionable clause as to avoid any unconscionable result."[4] A provision which gives what the court believes is too much of an advantage over a buyer is likely to be held void as unconscionable.

FACTS: Fontaine bought an automobile on the installment plan. The dealer assigned his contract to Industrial National Bank. Fontaine was late in making several installment payments but the installments were accepted when paid. He did not make the November payment on time and the bank thereupon declared the entire balance due and repossessed the automobile. The bank relied on the provision of the sales contract that if the buyer "shall default in the payment of any installment . . . all installments remaining unpaid shall, at the election of Seller, and without notice to Buyer, become immediately due and payable. The payment and acceptance of any sum on account shall not be considered a waiver of such right of election." Fontaine claimed that this provision was invalid.

---

[2] See Uniform Commercial Code § 2-103(1)(b) as to good faith. Higher standards are also imposed on merchant-sellers by other provisions of UCC. See § 2-314, as to warranties; § 2-603, as to duties with respect to rightfully rejected goods; and § 2-509(3), as to the transfer of risk of loss. While the provisions of the Code above noted do not apply to contracts generally, there is a growing trend of courts to extend Article 2 of the Code, which relates only to the sale of goods, to contract situations generally, on the theory that it represents the latest restatement of the law of contracts made by expert scholars and the legislators of the land.

[3] Oklahoma ex rel. Derryberry v Kerr-McGee Corp. (Okla) 516 P2d 813.

[4] UCC § 2-302(1). The Code as adopted in California and North Carolina omits the unconscionability section. In Lazan v Huntington Town House, Inc. 69 Misc2d 1017, 332 NYS2d 270 (1969), affirmed 69 Misc2d 1019, 330 NYS2d 751, the court held that the plaintiff who had rented a hall in a building was entitled to recover his deposit where timely notice of cancellation was given and there was no evidence that the defendant would suffer any damages from the cancellation. "The court finds that the agreement itself is reasonable and fair, but the court finds, that the enforcement of the agreement is unreasonable and even unconscionable so as to bring it within the purview of § 2-302 of the UCC."

DECISION: Judgment for Fontaine. The provision was unconscionable because it would permit the creditor to repossess the automobile at any time without notice because of a default which had been committed years before and even after the late payment had been accepted. [Fontaine v Industrial National Bank, 111 RI 6, 298 A2d 521]

In order to bring the unconscionability provision into operation, it is not necessary to prove that fraud was practiced. When there is a grossly disproportionate bargaining power between the parties so that the weaker or inexperienced party "cannot afford to risk confrontation" with the stronger party but "just signs on the dotted line," courts will hold that "grossly unfair" terms obtained by the stronger party are void as contrary to public policy.

Under the UCCC a particular clause or an entire agreement relating to a consumer credit sale, a consumer lease, or a consumer loan is void when such provision or agreement is unconscionable.[5] If the debtor waives any of his rights under the UCCC in making a settlement agreement with the seller or lender, such waiver is likewise subject to the power of the court as to unconscionability.[6]

§ 14:6. SOCIAL CONSEQUENCES OF CONTRACTS.

The social consequences of a contract are an important element today in determining its validity and the power of government to regulate it. These social consequences of a contract are related to the concept of unconscionability, although the latter concept would seem to be concerned with the effect of the contract as between the parties, whereas social consequences have a broader concern for the effect of the particular contract and other similar contracts upon society in general.

(a) The private contract in society. The law of contracts, originally oriented to private relations between private individuals, is moving from the field of bilateral private law to multiparty societal considerations. The concept that no man is an island unto himself is recognized by the Supreme Court in holding that private contracts lose their private and "do-not-touch" character when they become such a common part of our way of life that society deems it necessary to regulate them.

The same view that private matters become a public concern underlies the regulation of membership in and expulsion from professional societies and labor unions. The theory is that the position they occupy in today's economic pattern takes them out of the category of fraternal or social organizations, which must be left to themselves and, to the contrary, clothes them with such a character as justifies their regulation. The same concept underlies the requirement that procedures established by trade organizations and associations be fair.

The significance of the socioeconomic setting of the contract is seen in the minimum wage law decisions. The Supreme Court at first held such

---

[5] Uniform Consumer Credit Code § 5.108.
[6] UCCC § 1.107.

laws unconstitutional as an improper interference with the rights of two adult contracting parties. Thereafter it changed its point of view to sustain such laws because of the consequences of substandard wages upon the welfare of the individual, society, and the nation.

This reevaluation of old standards is part of the general move to make modern law more "just." Difficulties arise, however, when each court considers itself free to decide as it chooses.

(b) The n factor. With the expansion of the concepts of "against public policy" and "unconscionability" on the one hand, and government regulation of business on the other, the importance of a given contract to society becomes increasingly significant in determining the validity of the contract as between the parties. Less and less are courts considering a contract as only a legal relationship between A and B. More and more, the modern court is influenced in its decision by the recognition of the fact that the contract before the court is not one in a million but is one *of* a million. That is, n, or the number of times this particular contract is likely to arise, is considered by the modern court.

For example, J makes a contract with K that is of the same nature as one that M makes with N. Also, the insurance policy that the insurer J makes with N, and so on. A like similarity or industry-wide pattern is seen in the case of the bank loan made by bank O to borrower P, by bank Q to borrower R, and so on.

The appreciation that a particular contract is merely one of many has not only influenced the courts in the interpretation of such contracts but has also been held to justify regulation of the contract by government. The view has been adopted that "when a widely diffused public interest has become enmeshed in a network of multitudinous private arrangements, the authority of the state 'to safeguard the vital interests of its people' . . . is not to be gainsaid by abstracting one such agreement from its public context and treating it as though it were an isolated private contract constitutionally immune from impairment."[7]

§ 14:7. ILLEGALITY IN PERFORMING CONTRACT. When a contract is otherwise legal, the fact that one of the parties in performing his part of the contract commits illegal acts not contemplated by the other party does not ordinarily prevent the wrongdoer from recovering on the contract. In some instances, however, the wrong may be regarded as so serious that the wrongdoer is punished by denying him the right to recover on the agreement which he has performed.

FACTS: Commonwealth Pictures Corp. agreed to pay McConnell $10,000 and a specified commission if he could persuade Universal Pictures Company to give Commonwealth the distribution rights to its pictures. Without the knowledge of either Universal or Commonwealth, McConnell obtained the distribution rights by paying an agent of Universal the $10,000 Commonwealth paid McConnell. McConnell thereafter sued Commonwealth for the agreed commission.

---

[7] East New York Savings Bank v Hahn, 326 US 230, 232.

DECISION: Judgment for Commonwealth. The act of the plaintiff in bribing the agent of Universal was against public policy. To allow the plaintiff to recover would be to reward him for his act of corruption. Public policy would not permit this and recovery was therefore denied even though the contract on which the plaintiff sued was itself legal. [McConnell v Commonwealth Picture Corp. 7 NYS2d 465, 166 NE2d 482, 199 NYS2d 483]

B. AGREEMENTS AFFECTING PUBLIC WELFARE

§ **14:8. AGREEMENTS INJURING PUBLIC SERVICE.** An agreement that tends to interfere with the proper performance of the duties of a public officer—whether legislative, administrative, or judicial—is contrary to public policy and void. Thus, an agreement to procure the award of a public contract by corrupt means is not enforceable. Other examples are agreements to sell public offices, to procure pardons by corrupt means, or to pay a public officer more or less than legal fees or salary.

One of the most common agreements within this class is the *illegal lobbying agreement.* This term is used to describe an agreement to use unlawful means to procure or prevent the adoption of legislation by a lawmaking body, such as Congress or a state legislature. Such agreements are clearly contrary to the public interest since they interfere with the workings of the democratic process. They are accordingly illegal and void.

Some courts hold illegal all agreements to influence legislation, regardless of the means contemplated or employed. Other courts adopt the better rule that such agreements are valid in the absence of the use of improper influence or the contemplation of using such influence.

§ **14:9. AGREEMENTS INVOLVING CONFLICTS OF INTERESTS.** Various statutes prohibit government officials from being personally interested, directly or indirectly, in any transaction entered into by such officials on behalf of the government.

§ **14:10. AGREEMENTS OBSTRUCTING LEGAL PROCESSES.** Any agreement intended to obstruct or pervert legal processes is contrary to public interest and therefore void. Agreements that promise to pay money in return for the abandonment of the prosecution of a criminal case, for the suppression of evidence in any legal proceeding, for initiating litigation, or for the perpetration of any fraud upon the court are therefore void.

An agreement to pay an ordinary witness more than the regular witness fee allowed by law or a promise to pay him a greater amount if the promisor wins the lawsuit is void. The danger here is that the witness will lie in order to help his party win the case.

Contracts providing for the arbitration of disputes are generally recognized as valid by modern decisions and statutes. Earlier cases held such agreements void as interfering with the jurisdiction of the courts.

(a) **Selection of the court.** Contracts representing a substantial obligation will generally contain a provision for dispute settlement and tribunal selection. Sometimes it will be specified that any dispute shall be referred to arbitrators. In some instances it will be specified that any lawsuit must be brought in the courts of a particular state. Such provision will ordinarily be held valid as an aspect of the parties' freedom of contract to agree on such terms as they choose.

(b) **Unconscionability and public policy.** When the obvious purpose of the tribunal designation provision is to erect a hurdle against being sued, the provision will be held void when the parties are not in an equal bargaining position. Thus, it has been held that where the contract of the seller of prefabricated homes specified that any suit brought against the seller by a buyer must be brought in a third state which had no relationship to either the consumer buyer, the seller, or to the performance of the contract, the provision was void as unconscionable because it was clearly aimed at discouraging litigation by the consumer purchaser.

Ordinarily a suit on a contract may be brought in any jurisdiction in which service can be effected. When one of the contracting parties does business in many states, he may include in his contracts a provision that suit may only be brought against him in a court of his home state. When a statute in another state expressly requires that the plaintiff sue in that state, rather than the defendant's home state, it will be held that the statutory provision for suit in the other state establishes a public policy which invalidates a contract provision requiring that suit be brought in a different state. When a sale of goods is involved, a provision limiting suit to a state which has no relation to either the plaintiff or the defendant is void as unconscionable because it is obviously an attempt to erect a barrier against the bringing of a suit.[8]

§ 14:11. **SUNDAY LAWS.** Under the English common law, an agreement or contract could be executed on any day of the week. Today, however, most states have statutes that prohibit to some extent the making or performance of contracts on Sunday. The terms of the statutes vary greatly from state to state. The statutes may expressly declare agreements void if they are made on Sunday or if they call for performance on Sunday, or they may prohibit the sale of merchandise on Sunday.[9] They may prohibit only "servile" or manual labor, prohibit "worldly employment," or prohibit labor or business or one's "ordinary calling." Under a provision of the last type, one could legally enter into an agreement or do work outside of his regular calling.

(a) **Works of charity and necessity.** Sunday laws expressly provide that they do not apply to works of charity or necessity. *Works of charity* include those acts that are involved in religious worship or in aiding persons in

---

[8] UCC § 2-302.

[9] McGowan v Maryland, 366 US 420; Braunfeld v Brown, 366 US 599.

distress. In general a *work of necessity* is an act which must be done at the time in order to be effective in saving life, health, or property.

The "necessity" exception to Sunday laws is generally liberally interpreted so as to permit sales where a contrary conclusion would cause serious economic loss or inconvenience. Thus, it has been held that the necessity exception permitted an auto parts dealer to sell a water pump to a motorist traveling through the state when his water pump broke down.

Some courts hold that having a car washed on Sunday at a commercial carwash is a work of necessity because the motor vehicle code requires that certain parts of the car, as the windshield, be kept clean. Other courts hold that this does not make carwashing on Sunday a work of necessity.

FACTS: Seuss operated an automatic car wash in New Rochelle, New York. The state law prohibited Sunday work except "works of necessity." Seuss was prosecuted for operating the car wash on Sunday. He claimed it was a work of necessity since the State Motor Vehicle Code required drivers to keep their lights, windshields, and license tags clean. Was the car wash a work of necessity?

DECISION: No. Although it was required that certain parts of the car be kept clean, there was no necessity for doing the cleaning on Sunday. Hence it was not a work of necessity within the meaning of the exception to the Sunday law. [New York v Seuss (City Court) 313 NYS2d 552]

When an offer is made on Sunday but the acceptance is not made until the next day, the agreement is valid because in law it is made on the weekday when it is accepted. When a preliminary oral agreement is made on Sunday but the parties intend that a formal written contract be prepared by their attorneys during the week, the contract so prepared is not a Sunday contract.[10] If a contract is made on Sunday, some courts hold that it can be ratified on another day. Other courts, however hold the contrary on the ground that the contract was illegal when made, and therefore is void and cannot be ratified.

(b) Sunday as termination date. When the last day on which payment may be made is a Sunday, it is commonly provided by statute that it may be made on the following business day. In the absence of statute, however, the time is not extended because the last day falls on a Sunday.

§ 14:12. ILLEGAL DISCRIMINATION CONTRACTS. A contract that a property owner will not sell his property to a member of a particular race cannot be enforced because it violates the Fourteenth Amendment of the federal Constitution.[11] Hotels and restaurants may not deal with their customers on terms that discriminate because of race, religion, color, national origin, or sex.[12]

---

[10] Wasserman v Roach, 336 Mass 564, 146 NE2d 909.
[11] Shelley v Kraemer, 334 US 1.
[12] Federal Civil Rights Act of 1964, 42 United States Code § 2000a et seq.; Katzenbach v McClung, 379 US 294; Heart of Atlanta Motel v United States, 379 US 241.

C. GAMBLING CONTRACTS

§ 14:13. WAGERS AND LOTTERIES. Largely as a result of the adoption of antigambling statutes, wagers or bets are generally illegal. Private lotteries involving the three elements of prize, chance, and consideration, or similar affairs of chance, also are generally held illegal. Raffles are usually regarded as lotteries. Sales promotion schemes calling for the distribution of property according to chance among the purchasers of goods are held illegal as lotteries, without regard to whether the scheme is given the name of a guessing contest, raffle, or gift.

> FACTS: The Seattle Times ran a football forecasting contest called "Guest-Guesser." The Chief of Police claimed this was illegal as a lottery. The Times brought a declaratory judgment action to determine the legality of the contest.

> DECISION: The contest was a lottery because winning the prize was fundamentally a matter of chance. [Seattle Times Co. v Tielsch, 80 WashApp2d 502, 495 P2d 1366]

Giveaway plans and games are lawful as long as it is not necessary to buy anything or to give anything of value in order to participate.[13] If participation is "free," the element of consideration is lacking and there is no lottery.

In many states public lotteries (lotteries run by a state government) have been legalized by statute.

§ 14:14. TRANSACTIONS IN FUTURES. A person may contract to deliver goods not owned at the time the agreement is made. The fact that the seller does not have the goods at the time the contract is made does not affect the legality of the transaction.

D. REGULATION OF BUSINESS

§ 14:15. INTRODUCTION. Local, state, and national laws regulate a wide variety of business activities and practices. A person violating such regulations may under some statutes be subject to a fine or criminal prosecution or under others to an order to cease and desist by an administrative agency or commission.

Whether an agreement made in connection with business conducted in violation of the law is binding or void depends upon how strongly opposed the public policy is to the prohibited act. Some courts take the view that the agreement is not void unless the statute expressly so specifies. In some instances, as in the case of the failure to register a fictitious name under which the business is done, the statute expressly preserves the validity of the contract by permitting the violator to sue on a contract made while illegally conducting business after his name is registered as required by the statute.

---

[13] Federal Communications Commission v American Broadcasting Co. 347 US 284.

§ 14:16. **STATUTORY REGULATION OF CONTRACTS.** In order to establish uniformity or to protect one of the parties to a contract, statutes frequently provide that contracts of a given class must follow a statutory model or must contain specified provisions. For example, statutes commonly specify that particular clauses must be included in insurance policies in order to protect the persons insured and their beneficiaries. Others require that contracts executed in connection with credit buying and loans contain particular provisions designed to protect the debtor.

Consumer protection legislation gives the consumer the right to rescind the contract in certain situations. Installment sales, and home improvement contracts commonly require that an installment sale contract must specify the cash price, the down payment, the trade-in value, if any, the cash balance, the insurance costs, the interest and finance charges.

When the statute imposes a fine or imprisonment for violation, the court should not hold that the contract is void since that would increase the penalty which the legislature had imposed. If a statute prohibits the making of certain kinds of contracts or imposes limitations on the contracts that can be made, the attorney general or other government official may generally be able to obtain an injunction or court order to stop the parties from entering into a prohibited kind of contract.

§ 14:17. **LICENSED CALLINGS OR DEALINGS.** Statutes frequently require that a person obtain a license, certificate, or diploma before one can practice certain professions, such as law or medicine, or carry on a particular business or trade, such as that of a real-estate broker, peddler, stockbroker, hotelkeeper, or pawnbroker. If the requirement is imposed to protect the public from unqualified persons, an agreement to engage in such a profession or business without having obtained the necessary license or certificate is void. Thus, an agreement with an unlicensed physician for services cannot be enforced by him.

On the other hand, a license may be imposed solely as a revenue measure by requiring the payment of a fee for the license. In that event an agreement made in violation of the statute by one not licensed is generally held valid. The contract may also sometimes be held valid when it is shown that no harm has resulted from the failure to obtain a permit to do the work contemplated by the particular contract.

FACTS: The Ilice Construction Co. made masonry alterations to a building occupied by Caravello as a tenant and owned by Rose. A city ordinance required that anyone making such alterations must first obtain a building license. Ilice had not obtained a license. Caravello and Rose refused to pay Ilice for the work. Ilice joined in an action brought by Meissner, another contractor, to enforce a mechanic's lien against the property. No claim was made that the work as done by Ilice did not satisfy the requirements of the building code, and Ilice obtained a permit for the work after the action had been brought on the mechanic's lien.

DECISION: Judgment for Ilice. While the law required a permit and imposed penalties for failing to have a permit, the law did not specifically state that a contract made without a permit could not be enforced. As the

> permit law was primarily concerned with the construction of proper buildings, the statutory objective of requiring a permit was satisfied when a building that was constructed was in fact proper. The fact that the building was proper was shown by the issuance of the permit after it was constructed. [Meissner v Caravello, 4 IllApp2d 428, 124 NE2d 615]

It is likewise frequently held that the absence of a license cannot be raised as to transactions between persons who should all be licensed, such as dealers, when the purpose of the license requirement is not to protect such persons as against each other but to protect the public generally against such persons.

§ 14:18. FRAUDULENT SALES. Statutes commonly regulate the sale of certain commodities. Scales and measures of grocers and other vendors must be checked periodically, and they must be approved and sealed by the proper official. Certain articles must be inspected before they are sold. Others must be labeled in a particular way to show their contents and to warn the public of the presence of any dangerous or poisonous substance. Since these laws are generally designed for the protection of the public, transactions in violation of such laws are void.

When the aim of the law is to raise revenue by requiring the payment of a fee, the violation merely makes the wrongdoer liable for the penalty imposed by the law but does not make the transaction void.

§ 14:19. ADMINISTRATIVE AGENCIES. Large areas of the American economy are governed by federal administrative agencies created to carry out the general policies specified by Congress. A contract must be in harmony with public policy not only as declared by Congress and the courts but also as applied by the appropriate administrative agency. For example, a particular contract to market goods might not be prohibited by any statute or court decision but may still be condemned by the Federal Trade Commission as an unfair method of competition. When the proper commission has made its determination, a contract not in harmony therewith, such as a contract of a carrier charging a higher or a lower rate than that approved by the Interstate Commerce Commission, is illegal.

E. CONTRACTS IN RESTRAINT OF TRADE

Agreements in restraint of trade constitute a particular segment of agreements which are contrary to public policy. To some extent these agreements are expressly condemned by statute, in which case this kind of agreement is not binding because it is illegal.

§ 14:20. EFFECT OF AGREEMENT. An agreement that unreasonably restrains trade is illegal and void on the ground that it is contrary to public policy. Such agreements take many forms, such as a combination to create a monopoly or to obtain a corner on the market, or an association of merchants to increase prices. In addition to the illegality of the agreement based on general principles of law, statutes frequently declare monopolies illegal and subject the parties to such agreements to various civil and criminal penalties.[14] In some instances, however, the law expressly authorizes combined action.

§ **14:21. AGREEMENTS NOT TO COMPETE.** When a going business is sold, it is commonly stated in the contract that the seller shall not go into the same or a similar business again within a certain geographical area, or for a certain period of time, or both. In early times, such agreements were held void since they deprived the public of the service of the person who agreed not to compete, impaired the latter's means of earning a livelihood, reduced competition, and exposed the public to monopoly. To the modern courts, the question is whether under the circumstances the restriction imposed upon one party is reasonable to protect the other party. If the restriction is reasonable, it is valid.

> **FACTS:** Pierce worked for the Mutual Loan Co. in Sioux City, Iowa, checking up on delinquent borrowers. By the written contract of employment, he agreed not to enter the employ of any competing small loan business in the same town while employed or for one year thereafter. Upon the termination of his employment with Mutual, he went to work for a competing personal loan company. Mutual sought an injunction to prevent him from continuing in such employment.
>
> **DECISION:** Judgment for Pierce. Mutual could not be harmed by Pierce's working for a competitor since Pierce did not possess any secret knowledge gained from Mutual that gave rise to any right of Mutual to keep such knowledge from reaching a competitor. Moreover it was unlikely that Pierce would have made customer friends while working for Mutual who would follow him to his new employer. A restriction on future employment is not valid when it imposes a restraint greater than is needed to protect the employer. As the restriction did not serve to protect Mutual, it was invalid as to Pierce. [Mutual Loan Co. v Pierce, 245 Iowa 1051, 65NW2d 405]

Restrictions to prevent competition by an employee are held valid when reasonable and necessary to protect the interest of the employer. For example, a provision that a doctor employed by a medical clinic would not practice medicine for one year within a 50-mile radius of the city in which the clinic was located is reasonable and will be enforced.

While the validity of an employee's restrictive covenant is generally determined in terms of whether its restraint is greater than is required for the reasonable protection of the employer, some courts use a broader test of whether the contract is fair to the employer, the employee, and the public.[15]

---

[14] Sherman Antitrust Act. 15 USC §§ 1-7; Clayton Act, 15 USC §§ 12-27; Federal Trade Commission Act, 15 USC §§ 41 to 58.

[15] E. P. I. of Cleveland v Basler, 12 Ohio App2d 16, 230 NE2d 552 (holding that a covenant not to compete within a 200-mile radius of a city was unreasonable and not binding when the employer generally did business only within a 60-mile radius and did not operate regularly in 91 percent of the territory within the 200-mile radius).

In the absence of the sale of a business or the making of an employment contract, an agreement not to compete is void as a restraint of trade and a violation of the antitrust law.

When a restriction on competition as agreed to by the parties is held invalid because its scope as to time or geographical area is too great, there is a conflict of authority as to the action to be taken by the court. Some courts apply the "blue pencil" rule and trim the covenant down to a scope which they deem reasonable and require the parties to abide by that revision. Other courts hold that this is rewriting the contract for the parties, which courts ordinarily cannot do, and refuse to revise the covenant, holding that the covenant is totally void and that the contract is to be applied as though it did not contain any restrictive covenant.

§ 14:22. **RESALE PRICE MAINTENANCE AGREEMENTS.** Under antitrust legislation, an agreement between a manufacturer and distributor or between a distributor and dealer that the latter should not resell below a specified minimum price was void.[16] Congress and many of the states have adopted statutes, called *fair trade acts*, which change this rule and sustain the validity of such agreements when they relate to trademark or brand-name articles.[17]

The federal statute and many state laws apply not only to those who are parties to the price maintenance agreement but also to anyone having knowledge of the agreement who thereafter in the course of regular business resells the article under its trade name or mark.[18]

There is a conflict of authority as to whether the giving of trading stamps is a violation of a fair trade act.

§ 14:23. **SELLING BELOW COST.** A majority of the states have adopted statutes prohibiting selling "below cost" if the purpose is to harm competition. Such laws have generally been held constitutional, as against the contention that "below cost" is too vague.

---

[16] Miles Medical Co. v Park, 220 US 373.

[17] The state acts apply only to intrastate sales. The federal statute applies to interstate sales and permits resale price maintenance agreements when such agreements are lawful in the state in which the goods are to be resold or into which they are to be sent.

[18] Miller-Tydings Act, 50 Stat 693, 15 USC § 1; McGuire Act, 66 Stat 632, 15 USC § 45.

Statutes governing price maintenance agreements commonly provide that the parties to such contracts may recover damages from third persons who sell the article below the agreement price or may obtain an injunction to compel the observance of that price. Approximately one third of the states hold that such laws are valid and bind both the parties to such agreements and nonsigners; that is, persons who did not join in the agreements but had knowledge thereof. Olin Mathieson Chemical Corp. v Ontario Store, 9 Ohio2d 67, 223 NE2d 592. In contrast, slightly more than one third of the states hold that the agreements bind only the parties to them and cannot constitutionally bind nonsigners even though so provided by statute. Olin Mathieson Chemical Corp. v Francis, 134 Colo 160, 301 P2d 139; Shakespeare Co. v Lippman's Tool Shop Sporting Goods Co. 334 Mich 109, 54 NW2d 268. In approximately one third of the states resale price maintenance agreements are invalid and bind no one.

F. USURY

§ 14:24. DEFINITION. A person is guilty of *usury* when he lends money that is to be repaid unconditionally and he specifies a rate of interest which is greater than that allowed by statute. It is immaterial that the defendant did not intend to violate the usury law, as merely the intent to require a payment which the law prohibits is sufficient.[19] In determining whether a transaction is usurious, the court will look through the form of the transaction to determine whether there is in fact a loan on which excessive interest is charged.

(a) **Maximum contract rate.** Most states prohibit by statute the taking of more than a stated annual rate of interest. These statutes provide a *maximum contract rate* of interest—commonly 8 or 10 percent— which is the highest annual rate that can be exacted or demanded under the law of a given state. It is usually recoverable only when there is an agreement in writing to pay that amount. A federal statute limits interest charges to servicemen to 6 percent a year on obligations incurred before entering the service.[20]

(b) **Legal rate.** All states provide for a legal rate of interest. When there is an agreement for interest to be paid but no rate is specified or when the law implies a duty to pay interest, as on judgments, the *legal rate* is applied. In most states the legal rate of interest is 6 percent per year.

(c) **National banks.** The fact that the lender is a national bank does not exempt it from state usury laws. For example, a national bank in Alabama was subject to the usury laws of Alabama and the provisions of the Alabama Small Loan Act which prohibits compound interest. Consequently, there was a prohibited compounding of interest when the national bank in connection with its credit cards charged interest on interest and the bank therefore forfeited the right to any interest as specified by the Alabama law.

§ 14:25. SPECIAL SITUATIONS. The deduction by the lender of all of the interest in advance as a discount [21] from the nominal amount of the loan does not constitute usury even though the amount of interest collected represents a rate of interest in excess of that permitted by law. However, a loan transaction is usurious although proper on its face when in fact the borrower does not receive the full amount of the loan and the interest rate would be usurious if the loan had been made for the amount actually received by the debtor. Usury statutes are not violated by contracts that provide for the payment of the annual interest charge at the maximum rate in several installments, such as quarterly or monthly.

---

[19] Freeze v Lemon (Iowa) 210 NW2d 576.

[20] Soldiers and Sailors' Civil Relief Act, § 206, 50 App USC § 526.

[21] The term "discount" refers to the deduction of interest in advance so that the amount received by the borrower is the face of the loan less the amount of the interest or discount.

Usually state statutes permit small loan associations, pawnbrokers, and similar licensed moneylenders to charge a higher rate of interest than is permissible in ordinary business transactions. The reason is that a much greater risk is involved.

A borrower is commonly required to pay some penalty, such as an additional month's interest, when he pays a debt before maturity. Such a payment is generally regarded as not usurious.

When the lender is entitled to repayment of principal and the maximum rate of interest, the transaction is made usurious if in addition he is to receive a percentage of any profit that may be made by the borrower.

(a) Service charges. Service charges and placement fees are ordinarily added to the express interest in order to determine whether a loan is usurious.

The addition of a recording charge of one or a few dollars does not make the transaction usurious where the amount so charged was the amount specified by statute.

(b) Late charges and budget account charges. Courts differ as to the effect of a late payment charge. Some hold that the character of a loan must be determined when the loan is initially made. The fact that at a later date a late payment charge is added does not change the character of the transaction at the time that it was made. These courts hold that the late payment charge is to be ignored in determining the total amount of interest charged. In other states late charges are regarded as interest on the theory that they are payments due because money was not repaid, with the consequence that unless a late charge satisfies the usury law requirement, the lender is subject to the usury statute penalties.[22]

When a seller budgets the purchase and adds a charge to the unpaid balance due by the customer, some courts hold that such charge is subject to the usury law.

FACTS: J. C. Penney Co. permitted its customers to buy on credit by opening charge accounts. It charged each customer a 1½ percent monthly charge on any balance remaining unpaid after 30 days. A state statute limited the annual interest on loans to a maximum of 12 percent. Penney claimed that the statute was not applicable to the monthly charges on the theory that its charges related to time sales.

DECISION: The statute was applicable. The charge was not a time-price differential. It was an amount added to the customer's debt, which was owed to Penney when the customer failed to pay the debt within 30 days. Such a charge was subject to the usury law. [Wisconsin v J. C. Penney Co. 48 Wis2d 125, 179 NW2d 641]

Other courts hold that the charge is not subject to the usury law because it is merely a variation of the time-price differential. These courts also hold that it is immaterial whether the charge account pattern is an in-house

---

[22] Thrift Funds of Baton Rouge, Inc. v Jones (La) 274 So2d 150.

program conducted by the seller for his own customers only, or whether there is a central financing agency which handles accounts for a number of participating merchants.[23]

The "previous balance" method of determining finance charges is proper without regard to whether the unpaid balance on which the finance charge is imposed is the balance at the beginning or the end of the period or is an average daily balance.

(c) Points. In times of relative scarcity of money, it is common for lenders to make a charge for the making of a loan. This is commonly called giving or paying "points" to the lender. It is a fee or charge of one or more percentages of the principal amount of the loan. It is collected by the lender at the time the loan is made and is in the nature of a bonus, premium, or service charge for effecting the loan. Points are distinct from interest, but both must be added together to determine whether the loan is usurious. In computing this total, the points are to be prorated over the years in the life of the loan. Were this not done, the loan would often be usurious as to the first year.

(d) Credit insurance. The lender, in addition to charging the maximum interest rate, may require the borrower to buy life insurance payable to the lender for the amount of the loan. If the lender in some manner retains or receives part of the premiums paid for the insurance, with the result that the interest on the loan plus the share of the premiums total more than the maximum interest which could be charged, the transaction is usurious.

Consumer protection statutes in some states prohibit the lender or seller from requiring that the debtor obtain insurance through the lender or seller, or prohibit the lender or seller from receiving directly or indirectly for his own use any part of a payment made by the debtor for insurance premiums.

The Uniform Consumer Credit Code permits the making of such tied-in sales of insurance as long as the premiums charged do not exceed those permitted by the appropriate state commissioner of insurance or as long as the amount is not so great as to be deemed unconscionable.[24]

§ 14.26. **EFFECT OF USURY.** The effect of an agreement that violates the usury laws differs in the various states. In some states the entire amount of interest is forfeited. In other states the recovery of only the excess is denied. In still others, the agreement is held to be void.[25] If the interest has been paid, the states differ as to whether the borrower recovers merely the amount of the interest paid or two or three times that amount as a penalty.

In some states a lender who charges more than twice the lawful rate of interest forfeits both interest and principal.

In some states a special consumer protection statute governs the effect of usury in an installment contract. In contrast with the penalty ordinarily

---

[23] Kass v Central Charge Service, Inc. (DistColApp) 304 A2d 632.
[24] UCCC §§ 4.106, 5.108, 4.111.
[25] Curtis v Securities Acceptance Corp. 166 Neb 815, 91 NW2d 19.

imposed by the usury statutes of permitting the debtor to recover interest or double or treble the amount of interest, some consumer protection statutes declare the original transaction void and permit the debtor to recover both principal and interest which have been paid and bar the creditor from recovering any of the unpaid debt. Under such a statute, it has been held that where the creditor loaned money to the debtor and paid a gas station for gas purchased by the debtor on credit, the transaction for the repayment of the cash and the gas bills was usurious when the debtor agreed to pay $6 for every $5, the debtor agreeing to pay in installments, which brought him within the scope of the Installment Repayment Small Loan and Consumer Act.[26].

§ **14:27. CREDIT SALE PRICE**. Usury statutes generally do not apply to sales made on credit, such as installment sales, whether of goods or real estate. This rule is based on the narrow definition of usury as the charging of more than the lawful rate of interest on a loan. According to the law, when goods are sold on credit or on the installment plan, the seller does not lend money to the buyer but agrees that he is to be paid by the buyer later or at stated times rather than at the time of sale. Since no loan is made, the usury law does not apply and the seller is free to sell for cash at one price and on time at a different price that is much higher and which would be usurious if the usury law applied. Similarly, when a person buys a house on time, the transaction is not usurious simply because the price is greater than the seller would have demanded for a cash sale and the difference is more than the maximum interest that could have been charged on the cash price.

> **FACTS:** Grannas and his partner purchased heavy equipment from Aggregates Equipment on credit, agreeing to pay in 36 monthly installments including a "credit service charge" of $11,713.44. Aggregates assigned the contract and security agreement to a finance company, Equipment Finance, which later sued Grannas and his partner when they stopped paying the installments. Grannas and his partner raised the defense that the credit service charge was usurious because the cash price of the equipment was $65,075.28.
>
> **DECISION:** Judgment for finance company. The usury statute applied only to a loan. No loan is involved when the seller agrees to accept payment in installments. The fact that an assignment was made to a finance company did not alter the basic nature of the transaction nor require the court to conclude that the transaction was a sham transaction to disguise a loan. These principles were established before and have not been changed by the Uniform Commercial Code. In addition, both parties to the contract were businessmen who must be regarded as knowing what they were doing. The plaintiff was therefore entitled to enforce the contract. [Equipment Finance, Inc. v Grannas, 207 PaSuper 363, 218 A2d 81]

A few states hold that the time-price differential is subject to the usury law or have amended their usury laws or have adopted statutes to regulate

---

[26] Smashed Ice v Lee, 86 SD 658, 200 NW2d 236.

the differential between cash and time prices that may be charged by the seller. Such statutes, however, are sometimes limited to sales by retailers to consumers or apply only to sales under a stated dollar maximum. In any case, the price differential credit sale is held to be a usurious transaction when it is in fact a loan of money that is disguised as a sale for the purpose of avoiding the usury law.

Many states have adoped retail installment sales laws which apply whenever the sale price is to be paid in installments and the seller retains a security interest in the goods. These laws frequently fix a maximum for the time-price differential,[27] thereby remedying the situation created by the fact that the price differential is not subject to the usury laws.

When the credit seller informs the buyer that the purchase will be financed by a particular bank and the original credit sale contract requires the buyer to pay the credit balance directly to the bank, the transaction is not a sale on credit under which the time-price differential is not subject to the usury law. It is instead a loan by the bank to the buyer even though the transaction is not in the form of a sale and the claim of the bank against the buyer for the unpaid balance is subject to the usury law.

§ 14:28. CORPORATIONS AND USURY. In many states corporations are prohibited from raising the defense of usury. A loan is not regarded as usurious even though it is made to a corporation which is organized for the purpose of borrowing the money when the lender refuses to make the loan to an individual and suggests that he form a corporation so that higher interest may be charged than would be lawful on a loan to a natural person.

QUESTIONS AND CASE PROBLEMS

1. The Rhode Island Grocers Association held an annual exhibition. As an added feature to attract public interest, arrangements were made with the Transocean Air Lines for a drawing of a door prize for a free round trip to Hawaii for two. Any spectator attending the exhibition could participate in the drawing by filling out a card with his name and address. Was this a lottery? [Finch v Rhode Island Grocers Association, 93 RI 323, 175 A2d 177]

2. Costello held a license as a professional engineer in New York, Maryland, Illinois, and New Mexico, but he was not licensed in New Jersey. He did consulting engineering work for a New Jersey licensed architect in designing a city swimming pool. When Costello was not paid in full for his services, he sued

---

[27] See, for example, Singer Co. v Gardner, 121 NJ Super 261, 296 A2d 562 (imposing a 10 percent limitation).

the architect, who claimed that Costello was not allowed to recover because he did not have a license in New Jersey to render the services for which he claimed compensation. Was he entitled to recover? [Costello v Schmidlin, (CA3 NJ) 404 F2d 87]

3. Las Vegas Hacienda, Inc., advertised that it would pay $5,000 to anyone shooting a hole in one on its golf course. Gibson, who paid the fee of 50 cents, made a hole in one. The golf course corporation refused to pay the $5,000. When Gibson sued for breach of contract, it raised the defense that the contract was an illegal gambling contract and could not be enforced even though gambling as such was legalized in the state. Decide. [Las Vegas Hacienda, Inc. v Gibson, 77 Nev 25, 359 P2d 85]

4. Colonial Stores was looking for someone to build a store in the city and lease it to Colonial. McArver and Gerukos agreed between themselves that they would obtain options to buy some land for a store site and resell the options to a third person who would build a store and lease it to Colonial. All of this was successfully done, but Gerukos kept all of the profits from the transaction. When McArver sued him for his share of the profits, Gerukos raised the defense that McArver could not recover because a statute required that all real estate brokers and salesmen be licensed and McArver did not have such a real estate license. Was this defense valid? [McArver v Gerukos, 265 NC 413, 144 SE2d 277]

5. Burgess, a salesman for Bowyer, failed to turn over to Bowyer an indefinite amount of money collected by him. In order to avoid a criminal prosecution of Burgess by Bowyer, Burgess and his brother-in-law entered into a contract with the employer by which they agreed to pay Bowyer $5,000 if full restitution was not made. No restitution was made, and Bowyer sued Burgess and his brother-in-law on the contract for $5,000. Was he entitled to recover? [Bowyer v Burgess, 54 Cal2d 97, 4 CalRptr 521, 351 P2d 793]

6. Ellis borrowed money from Small and executed a series of six promissory notes payable with the maximum rate of interest. The notes contained an acceleration clause by virtue of which, upon the borrower's default, the lender could declare the entire balance of the debt to be due, together with the contract rate of interest. By virtue of such acceleration, the creditor would be receiving more than the maximum rate since the borrower would have had the money for the shorter period only and not for the original period for which he bargained. Were the notes usurious? [Small v Ellis, 90 Ariz 194, 367 P2d 234]

7 A Virginia statute required builders and persons doing construction work to obtain a license and imposed a fine for failing to do so. F. S. Bowen Electric Co. installed equipment in a building being constructed by Foley. Bowen had not obtained a license. When Foley did not pay Bowen, the latter sued Foley for the money due. Could he recover? [F. S. Bowen Electric Co. v Foley, 194 Va 92, 72 SE2d 388]

8. James owned property in Virginia Beach. He wanted to sell it for $29,000. Kidd wanted to buy the property but could not obtain financing. Finally Brothers agreed to buy the property from James for $28,000 and to resell it to Kidd for $29,000. No cash was paid on the resale to Kidd and Kidd gave Brothers a promissory note for $29,000, payable in 120 monthly installments. In computing the payment schedule, interest at 8 percent per annum was added to the purchase price. The legal rate of interest under the Virginia Usury Statute was 6 percent. Kidd claimed that the usury statute was violated by the resale transaction. Was he correct? [Kidd v Brothers, 212 Va 197, 183 SE2d 140]

9. Smith was employed as a salesman for Borden, Inc., which sold food products in 63 counties in Arkansas, 2 counties in Missouri, 2 counties in Oklahoma, and 1 county in Texas. The contract with Smith prohibited him from competing with Borden after leaving its employ. Smith left Borden and went to work for a competitor, Lady Baltimore Foods. Working for this second employer, Smith sold in three counties of Arkansas. He sold in two of these counties while he worked for Borden. Borden brought an injunction action against Smith and Lady Baltimore to enforce the anticompetitive covenant in Smith's former contract. Was Borden entitled to the injunction? [Borden, Inc. v Smith, 252 Ark 295, 478 SW2d 744]

10. A borrower borrowed money and executed a promissory note for the loan. The note called for the payment of interest at a usurious rate. Under the local law, this made the note void. The lender sued on the note. When the borrower raised the defense that the note was void because of usury, the creditor asserted that he was only claiming the amount of interest which could be lawfully claimed and that therefore the usury aspect was eliminated and he could recover on the note. Was he correct? [Yakutsk v Alfine, 43 AppDiv2d 552, 346 NYS2d 718]

11. A was employed by B. A embezzled money from B. When his crime was discovered, he promised B that he would repay the money which he had taken. He did not do so. B sued A for breach of his promise. Can B recover? [See Gallaher Drug Co. v Robinson, 13 OhioMisc 216, 232 NE2d 668]

12. A supermarket was prosecuted for selling merchandise on Sunday in violation of a Sunday-closing law. It claimed that it was only guilty of one offense as it had been doing business on only one Sunday. The prosecutor claimed that it had committed a separate violation of the statute for each item sold on that Sunday. Decide. [Vermont v Giant of St. Albans, Inc., 128 Vt 539, 268 A2d 739]

13. B purchased a ticket for an automobile lottery and gave the ticket to A intending to make a gift thereof to A. This ticket won and the lottery delivered the car to B. B refused to give the car to A and when sued by A, B raised the defense that a lottery was illegal and was a felony. Is this defense valid? [See Hardy v St. Matthews Community Center (KyApp) 240 SW2d 95]

FORM OF CONTRACT

§ 15:1. ORAL CONTRACTS ARE GENERALLY VALID. Generally a contract is valid whether it is written or oral. By statute, however, some contracts must be evidenced by a writing. Such statutes are designed to prevent the use of the courts for the purpose of enforcing certain oral agreements or alleged oral agreements. They do not apply when an oral agreement has been voluntarily performed by both parties.

Apart from statute, the parties may agree that their oral agreement is not to be binding until a formal written contract is executed, or the circumstances of the transaction may show that such was their intention. Conversely, they may agree that their oral contract is binding even though a written contract is to be executed later.

Similarly, the failure to sign and return a written contract does not establish that there is no contract as there may have been an earlier oral contract. If one of the parties, with the knowledge or approval of the other contracting party, undertakes performance of the contract before it is reduced to writing, it is generally held that the parties intended to be bound from the moment the oral contract was made.

In order for the prior oral agreement to be a binding contract, it must satisfy the requirement of definiteness. If it does not, that not only means that there is no binding oral contract, but it also lends support to the view that the oral negotiations were not intended to be a contract and that there should not be any contract until a definite written contract has been signed.

§ 15:2. CONTRACTS THAT MUST BE EVIDENCED BY A WRITING. Ordinarily a contract, whether oral or not, is binding if the existence and terms of the contract can be established to the satisfaction of the trier of fact, ordinarily the jury. In some instances a statute, commonly called a *statute of frauds*,[1] requires that certain kinds of contracts be evidenced by a writing or they cannot be enforced. This means that either (a) the contract itself must be in writing and signed by both parties, or (b) there be a sufficient written memorandum of the oral contract signed by the person being sued for breach of contract.

Ordinarily an offer may be written, oral, or expressed by conduct. Even when the contract must be evidenced by a writing under the statute of frauds, the offer which leads up to the contract may be oral. As an exception, statutes regulating the letting of government contracts may require that bids by contractors, the offers, be written and signed.

(a) An agreement that cannot be performed within one year after the contract is made. A writing is required when the contract by its terms cannot be performed within one year after the date of the agreement.

FACTS: In February or March, Corning Glass Works orally agreed to retain Hanan as a management consultant from May 1 of that year to April 30 of the next year for a total fee of $25,000. Was this agreement binding?

DECISION: No. Since it was not to be performed within one year from the making of the oral agreement, it was not enforceable because of the statute of frauds. [Hanan v Corning Glass Works, 63 Misc2d 863, 314 NYS2d 804]

The year runs from the time of the making of the oral contract rather than from the date when performance is to begin. In computing the year, the day on which the contract was made is excluded. The year begins with the following day and ends at the close of the first anniversary of the day on which the agreement was made.

The statute of frauds does not apply if it is possible under the terms of the agreement to perform the contract within one year. Thus, a writing is not required when no time for performance is specified and the performance will not necessarily take more than a year. In this case it would be possible to perform the contract within a year, and the statute is inapplicable without regard to the time when performance is begun or completed. A promise to do an act upon or until the death of a person does not require a

---

[1] The name is derived from the original English Statute of Frauds and Perjuries, which was adopted in 1677 and became the pattern for similar legislation in America. The seventeenth section of that statute governed the sale of goods, and its modern counterpart is § 2-201 of the Uniform Commercial Code, discussed in Chapter 23. The fourth section of the English statute provided the pattern for American legislation with respect to contracts other than for the sale of goods described in this section of the chapter. The English statute was repealed in 1954, except as to land sale and guaranty contracts. The American statutes remain in force, but the liberalization by Uniform Commercial Code § 2-201 of the pre-Code requirements with respect to contracts for the sale of goods may be regarded as a step in the direction of the abandonment of the statute of frauds concept.

When the English Statute of Frauds was adopted, the parties to a lawsuit were not permitted to testify on their own behalf, with the result that a litigant had difficulty in disproving perjured testimony of third persons offered as evidence on behalf of the adverse party. The Statute of Frauds was repealed in England partly because it was felt that it permitted the assertion of a "technical" defense as a means of avoiding just obligations and partly on the ground that with parties in interest now having the right to testify there is no longer the need for a writing to protect the parties from perjured testimony of third persons. Azevedo v Minister, 86 Nev 576, 471 P2d 661.

writing, even though that event may not occur until more than a year from the time the agreement is made.

When the contract calls not for a single act, but for continuing services to run indefinitely into the future, the statute of frauds is applicable. For example, a business contract to pay an agent a commission for new customers procured by the agent for as long as such customers continue to purchase contemplates acts that may performed beyond the statutory year, and a writing is therefore required. An oral promise to pay a bonus of a specified percentage of the employer's gross annual sales does not come within the statute nor require a writing, even though the amount of the bonus cannot be determined until after the year has expired.

In most states a writing is not required if the contract may or must be fully performed within a year by one of the contracting parties. By this view, a loan made today to be repaid in three years does not come within the statute because the performance of the lender necessarily takes place within the year. In a minority of states, the statute is applicable as long as performance by one of the parties may be made after the period of a year.

When the work contemplated by the oral contract has been performed, the employer cannot avoid liability under the contract because it was oral. Thus, an employee who has worked until the age of 65 under an oral contract of employment is entitled to recover the retirement benefits specified by the oral contract as against the contention that the contract was not binding because it did not satisfy the requirements of the statute of frauds.

If a contract of indefinite duration is terminable by either party at will, the statute of frauds is not applicable since the contract may be terminated within a year.

A writing claimed to satisfy the statute of frauds as to a contract which cannot be performed within one year must set forth all the material terms of the contract. Consequently, a letter is not sufficient as a writing for an oral contract of employment for more than one year when the letter does not make any statement as to salary.[2]

(b) An agreement to sell or a sale of any interest in real property. All contracts to sell and sales of land, buildings, or interests in land, such as mortgages which are treated as such an interest, must be evidenced by a writing.

A contract for the sale of sand, coal, or oil without any specification as to its location, such as "ten tons of grade A sand," is merely a contract to sell personal property and not the sale of an interest in land. Such a contract must satisfy the requirements of the Uniform Commercial Code as to a sale of goods.

(1) Collateral Contracts. The statute applies only to the agreement between the owner and purchaser, or between their agents. It does not apply to other or collateral agreements, such as those which the purchaser may make in order to raise the money to pay for the property, or to

---

[2] Olympic Junior, Inc. v David Crystal, Inc. (CA3 NJ) 463 F2d 1141.

agreements to pay for an examination or search of the title of the property. Similarly, a partnership agreement to deal in real estate is generally not required for that reason to be in writing. The statute ordinarily does not apply to a contract between a real estate agent and one of the parties to the sales contract employing him.

Likewise, a promise by a broker to pay a sum of money to the owner of land if he will sell it to a prospective buyer is not within the statute of frauds.

The statute of frauds does not require that a collateral contract, such as an agreement to make certain repairs, be evidenced by a writing.

(c) A promise to answer for the debt or default of another. When A promises C to pay B's debt to C if B does not do so, A is promising to answer for the debt of another. Such a promise must usually be evidenced by a writing to be enforceable. Thus, the oral promise of the president of a corporation to pay the debts owed by the corporation to its creditors if they will not sue the corporation does not bind the president, even though he is a major shareholder of the corporation and would be indirectly benefited by the forbearance of the creditors.[3]

If the promise is made directly to the debtor that the promisor will pay the creditor of the debtor what is owed him, the statute of frauds is not applicable. In contrast, if the promisor makes the promise to the creditor, it comes within the category of a promise made for the benefit of another and must therefore be evidenced by a writing which satisfies the statute of frauds.

(1) Primary Purpose Exception. The fact that a particular promise is made to the creditor and is a promise to answer for the debt of another does not mean that the statute of frauds will necessarily bar enforcement if the promise is oral. If that promise was made primarily for the benefit of the promisor, rather than for the benefit of the debtor, an exception to the statute of frauds is recognized and the promise is not affected by the statute of frauds. It may be enforced even though it is oral.

FACTS: Boeing Airplane Co. contracted with Pittsburgh-Des Moines Steel Co. for the latter to construct a supersonic wind tunnel. R. H. Freitag Mfg. Co. sold material to York-Gillespie Co., which subcontracted to do part of the work. In order to persuade Freitag to keep supplying materials on credit, Boeing and the principal contractor both assured Freitag that he would be paid. When Freitag was not paid by the subcontractor, Freitag sued Boeing and the contractor. They defended on the ground that the assurances given Freitag were not written.

DECISION: Judgment for Freitag. The promises to pay the bills of the subtractor were made by the defendants primarily for their benefit in order to keep the work progressing so that they, in turn, would not be held liable for failure to complete. Hence, the case came within the primary benefit exception to the written guaranty provision of the statute of frauds. [R. H. Freitag Mfg. Co. v Boeing Airplane Co. 55 Wash2d 334, 347 P2d 1074]

---

[3] Mid-Atlantic Appliances v Morgan, 194 Va 324, 73 SE2d 385.

No writing is required when the debt incurred is the debt of the person promising to pay, even though a third person designated by the promisor benefits thereby.

A question of interpretation may arise as to whether the words of one person, written or not, constitute a promise to answer for or to guarantee the debt of another. Where the treasurer of a corporation wrote a letter to a wholesaler in which he said that he personally guaranteed the corporation and then later claimed that this was merely a recommendation and not a guaranty of payment of the corporation's debts, the terms of the entire letter must be examined in order to determine whether the officer had guaranteed payment of the debts.

(d) A promise by the executor or administrator of a decedent's estate to pay a claim against the estate from his personal funds. The personal representative (executor or administrator) has the duty of winding up the affairs of a deceased person, paying the debts from the proceeds of the estate and distributing any balance remaining. The executor or administrator is not personally liable for the claims against the estate of the decedent. If the personal representative promises to pay the decedent's debts from his own money, however, the promise cannot be enforced unless it is evidenced by a writing that complies with the terms of the statute.

If the personal representative makes a contract on behalf of the estate in the course of administering the estate, a writing is not required since the representative is then contracting on behalf of the estate and not on his own behalf. Thus, if he employs an attorney to settle the estate or makes a burial contract with an undertaker, no writing is required.

(e) A promise made in consideration of marriage. If a person makes a promise to pay a sum of money or to give property to another in consideration of marriage or a promise to marry, the agreement must be evidenced by a writing.[4] This provision of the statute of frauds is not applicable to ordinary mutual promises to marry, and it is not affected by the statutes in some states that prohibit the bringing of any action for breach of promise of marriage.

(f) A sale of goods. When the contract price for goods is $500 or more, the contract must ordinarily be evidenced by a writing. See Chapter 23.

(g) Miscellaneous statutes of frauds. In a number of states, special statutes require other agreements to be in writing or evidenced by a writing. Thus, a statute may provide that an agreement to name a person as beneficiary in an insurance policy must be evidenced by a writing.

The Uniform Commercial Code contains three statutes of frauds relating to sales of personal property: (1) goods; (2) securities, such as stocks and bonds; and (3) personal property other than goods and securities.

In some states contracts with brokers relating to the sale of land are also subject to the statute of frauds.[5]

---

[4] Koch v Koch, 95 NJSuper 546, 232 A2d 157; Miller v Greene (Fla) 104 So2d 457.
[5] Osborne v Huntington Beach Union High School District, 5 CalApp3d 510, 85 CalRptr 793.

§ **15:3. NOTE OR MEMORANDUM.** The statute of frauds requires a writing for those contracts which come within its scope. This writing may be a note or memorandum, as distinguished from a contract. It may be in any form because its only purpose is to serve as evidence of the contract. The statutory requirement is, of course, satisfied if there is a complete written contract signed by both parties.

(a) **Contents.** Except in the case of a sale of goods, the note or memorandum must contain all the material terms of the contract so that the court can determine just what was agreed. Thus, it is insufficient if the contract is partly oral and partly written. An ordinary check is not a sufficient memorandum when it bears the notation "payment land" but contains no other details, or lacks any material term. The subject matter must be identified either within the writing itself or in other writings to which it refers. A writing is not sufficient that does not identify the land which is the subject of the contract. Thus, a writing which does not contain any description of the land does not satisfy the statute of frauds.

In some states a description of real estate by street number, city or county, and state, is not sufficient; the writing must show the lot and block numbers of the property as well as name the city or county and the state. When the writing does not contain a description which satisfies the statute of frauds, the land may not be identified by parol evidence.

In some states an exception is made to the general rule and it is not necessary that the writing set forth the consideration or terms of payment. It is not necessary that the writing specifically state a term that would be implied, as that the price therein is to be paid in "cash."

The note or memorandum may consist of one writing or instrument or of separate papers, such as letters or telegrams, or of a combination of such papers.

Separate writings cannot be considered together unless they are linked, either by express reference in each writing to the other or by the fact that each writing clearly deals with the same subject matter. Conversely, when the papers go no further than to show that they deal with similar subject matters, the papers cannot be integrated. For example, a signed memorandum relating to the sale of unidentified land and an unsigned deed could not be deemed one writing for the purpose of the statute of frauds because at most each only showed that it related to a real estate transaction and did not show that they both related to the same transaction and neither writing referred to the other.[6]

It is not necessary that the writing be addressed to the other contracting party or to any person, nor is it necessary that the writing be made with the intent to create a writing to satisfy the statute of frauds. When a corporation made an oral contract of employment with an employee, the minutes of the corporation reciting the adoption of the resolution to employ the employee (which minutes were signed by the president of the corporation) together with the salary check paid the employee constituted a sufficient writing to satisfy the statute of frauds.

---

[6] Young v McQuerrey (Hawaii) 508 P2d 1051.

The memorandum may be made at the time of the original transaction or at a later date. It must, however, ordinarily exist at the time a court action is brought upon the agreement.

(b) Signing. The note or memorandum must be signed by the party sought to be charged or his agent. A letter from an employer setting forth the details of an oral contract of employment satisfies the statute of frauds in a suit brought by the employee against the employer, as the writing was signed by the party "sought to be charged." If the employer had sued the employee in such case, the employer's letter would not satisfy the statute of frauds as it would not be signed by the employee.

It should be noted that a contrary rule exists in some states in regard to contracts for the sale of land. Either because of special language in the statute, or because of the rather extraordinary view that "the party to be charged" necessarily means the vendor, these courts hold not only that the vendor must sign the writing regardless of who the defendant is in the suit, but also that the vendor's signature is sufficient to bind the vendee.

Some states require that the authorization of an agent to execute a contract coming within the statute of frauds must also be in writing. In the case of an auction, it is the usual practice for the auctioneer to be the agent of both parties for the purpose of signing the memorandum. If the seller himself acts as auctioneer, however, he cannot sign as agent for the buyer. An exception is made in some situations when the contract is between merchants and involves the sale of goods.

The fact that an officer or employee is acting on behalf of a corporation does not remove the transaction from the statute of frauds. Consequently, when the statute of frauds requires written authorization for an agent, the corporate officer or employee must have such authorization or the writing which he signs on behalf of the corporation does not satisfy the statute of frauds.

The signature may be made at any place on the writing, although in some states it is expressly required that the signature appear at the end of the writing. The signature may be an ordinary one or any symbol that is adopted by the party as his signature. It may consist of initials, figures, or a mark. When a signature consists of a mark made by a person who is illiterate or physically incapacitated, it is commonly required that the name of the person be placed upon the writing by someone else, who may be required to sign the instrument as a witness. A person signing a trade or an assumed name is liable to the same extent as though he signed in his own name. In the absence of a local statute that provides otherwise, the signature may be made by pencil, as well as by pen, or by typewriter, by print, or by stamp.

> FACTS: A real estate owner received an offer from a buyer. The owner sent a telegram accepting the offer. The acceptance message and the owner's name were typewritten by the telegraph company in the buyer's city and the message delivered to the buyer. When the buyer sued the owner for breach of contract, the owner claimed that there was no signed writing as required by the statute of frauds.

DECISION: The telegraph message received by the buyer with the name placed thereon by the telegraph company was a signed writing for the purpose of the statute of frauds. [Yaggy v B.V.D Co. 7 NCApp 590, 173 SE2d 496]

§ 15:4. EFFECT OF NONCOMPLIANCE. The majority of states hold that a contract which does not comply with the statute of frauds is voidable. A small minority of states hold that such an agreement is void. Under either view, if an action is brought to enforce the contract, the defendant can raise the objection that it is not evidenced by a writing. No one other than the defendant, or his successor in interest, however, can make the objection. Thus, an insurance company cannot refuse to pay on its policy on the ground that the insured did not have any insurable interest in the insured property because he did not have a writing relating to the property that satisfied the statute of frauds.

(a) Part performance. In some cases, when a writing is not made as required by the statute, the courts will nevertheless enforce the agreement if there has been a sufficient part performance to make it clear that a contract existed. In other instances the court will not enforce the contract but will permit a party to recover the fair value of work and improvements that he has made in reliance upon the contract. This situation arises when a tenant improves the land while in possession under an oral lease which cannot be enforced because of the statute of frauds. The situation also arises when a buyer of land under an oral agreement enters into possession of the land. If the purchaser has made valuable improvements to the land, the courts will commonly enforce the oral agreement.

In order for part performance to take an oral contract out of the statute of frauds, the performance must be such as is clearly referable to the terms of the contract. Where this is not so, conduct claimed to be part performance does not establish the oral contract. For example, where the plaintiff claimed that in return for managing and working the defendant's sugar beet operations on certain land for three years he would have the privilege of conducting a cattle feeding operation thereon, the fact that the plaintiff gave up his job and moved his family to the defendant's land and spent much time and effort to learn about the defendant's business did not constitute part performance which would remove the oral cattle feeding agreement from the statute of frauds.

Ordinarily the performance of personal services does not constitute such part performance as will take the case out of the statute of frauds, except in extraordinary cases when the value of the services cannot be measured by money.[7] In any case, evidence as to part performance must be clear and convincing.

(b) Promissory estoppel. When the facts show that the buyer has relied on the oral contract to such an extent that the doctrine of promissory estoppel would be applicable, the promisor will not be permitted to raise the defense of the statute of frauds.

(c) Recovery of value conferred. In most instances a person who is prevented from enforcing a contract because of the statute of frauds is

---

[7] Crosby v Strahan's Estate, 78 Wyo 302, 324 P2d 492.

nevertheless entitled to recover from the other party the value of any services or property furnished or money given under the contract. Recovery is based not upon the terms of the contract but upon the quasi contractual obligation of the other party to restore to the plaintiff what he has received in order to prevent his unjust enrichment at the plaintiff's expense.

There is, however, a division of authority as to whether a real estate broker may recover for the value of his services in procuring a buyer under an oral brokerage agreement in states which require that such agreements be in writing. Recovery is commonly denied on the theory that the real estate broker can be expected to know that his contracts must be in writing and that, as he makes such contracts constantly, it is unlikely that a broker would not appreciate his legal position when he acts under an oral contract. In substance it is held that protecting the public at large from unethical brokers making false claims under alleged oral contracts outweighs the necessity for protecting the occasional broker from oppression at the hands of an unethical customer refusing to recognize an oral contract.

The performance of services for which one is periodically paid is generally regarded as not taking out of the statute an oral contract that cannot be performed in one year. Such performance and payment do not indicate anything more than an agreement to render the services that were rendered and to compensate for them. Furthermore, the person performing the services is in fact paid for what he has done, and therefore he does not sustain any unusual hardship if the alleged oral contract is not enforced.[8]

§ 15:5. PAROL EVIDENCE RULE. Can a written contract be contradicted by the testimony of witnesses? The general rule is that spoken words, that is, *parol evidence*, will not be allowed to modify or contradict the terms of a written contract which is complete on its face unless there is clear proof that because of fraud, accident, or mistake the writing is not in fact the contract or the complete or true contract. This is called the *parol evidence rule*. It refers to words spoken before or at the time the contract was made.

To illustrate, assume that L, the landlord who is the owner of several new stores in the same vicinity, discusses leasing one of them to T (tenant). L considers giving T the exclusive rights to sell soft drinks and stipulating in the leases with the tenants of the other stores that they cannot do so. L and T then execute a detailed written lease for the store. The lease makes no provision with respect to an exclusive right of T to sell soft drinks. Thereafter L leases the other stores to A, B and C without restricting them as to the sale of soft drinks, which they then begin to sell, causing T to lose money. T sues L, claiming that the latter has broken his contract by which T was to have an exclusive right to sell soft drinks. L defends on the ground that there was no prior oral understanding to that effect. Will the court permit T to prove that there was such an oral agreement?

On the facts as stated, if nothing more is shown, the court will not permit such parol evidence to be presented. The operation of this principle can be understood more easily if the actual courtroom procedure is followed. When

---

[8] Rowland v Ewell (Fla) 174 So2d 78.

T sues L, his first step will be to prove that there is a contract between them. Accordingly, T will offer in evidence the written lease between T and L. T will then take the witness stand and begin to testify about an oral agreement giving him an exclusive right. At that point L's attorney will object to the admission of the oral testimony by T because it would modify the terms of the written lease. The court will then examine the lease to see if it appears to be complete; and if the court decides that it is, the court will refuse to allow T to offer evidence of an oral agreement. The only evidence before the court then will be the written lease. T will lose because nothing is in the written lease about an exclusive right to sell soft drinks.

If a written contract appears to be complete, the parol evidence rule prohibits its alteration not only by oral testimony but also by proof of other writings or memorandums made before or at the time the written contract was executed. An exception is made when the written contract refers to and identifies other writings or memorandums and states that they are to be regarded as part of the written contract. In such a case, it is said that the other writings are integrated or incorporated by reference.

(a) **Reason for the parol evidence rule.** The parol evidence rule is based on the theory that either (1) there never was an oral agreement or (2) if there was, the parties purposely abandoned it when they executed their written contract. Some courts enforce the parol evidence rule strictly in order to give stability to commercial transactions.

> FACTS: Evans made a written contract to buy property from Borkowski. Under the sales contract, the buyer was to make payment in certain installments prior to the delivery of the deed. When the buyer could not make payments on time, the parties entered into a new written agreement, the buyer persuading the seller to do so by orally promising him that he would pay interest on late payments. He was late in making the payments and paid the interest under protest. The buyer later sued the seller to recover the interest payments.
>
> DECISION: Judgment for buyer. The seller was not entitled to interest payments based on the oral agreement because the parol evidence rule prohibited proof that there was such an oral agreement. The second written contract which provided for the payment of the installments said nothing about paying interest on them. The alleged oral agreement as to interest therefore contradicted the second written contract and proof thereof was barred by the parol evidence rule in order to give stability to written contracts. [Evans v Borkowski (Fla) 139 So2d 472]

(b) **Conflict between oral and written contracts.** Initially, when there is a conflict between the prior oral contract and the later written contract, the variation is to be regarded as (1) a mistake, which can be corrected by reformation, or (2) an additional term in the written contract, which is not binding because it was not part of the agreement. Illustrative of the latter, when a customer and a warehouse made a storage contract over the telephone and nothing was said as to the warehouse's limitation of liability, a limitation-of-liability clause appearing in the printed contract mailed to the customer was not binding upon him.

In view of the fact that a reasonable man in the twentieth century should anticipate that the formal contract will contain many provisions not mentioned in the brief oral negotiating, as in the case of a life insurance contract, courts are very likely to find that any additional term in the formal written contract has either been authorized because anticipated or has been accepted or ratified because the person receiving the printed form has not repudiated the contract or objected to the term in particular or has performed or accepted performance under the contract. To prevent a loss of rights, it is therefore important to read a formal contract thoroughly and to make prompt objection to any departure from or addition to the original oral contract if such variation is not acceptable.

(c) Liberalization of parol evidence rule. The strictness of the parol evidence rule has been relaxed in a number of jurisdictions. A trend is beginning to appear which permits parol evidence as to the intention of the parties when the claimed intention is plausible from the face of the contract even though there is no ambiguity. There is likewise authority that parol evidence is admissible as to matters occurring before the execution of the contract in order to give a better understanding of what the parties meant by their written contract.[9]

§ 15:6. WHEN THE PAROL EVIDENCE RULE DOES NOT APPLY. The parol evidence rule may not apply in certain cases, which are discussed in the following paragraphs.

(a) Incomplete contract. The parol evidence rule necessarily requires that the written contract sum up or integrate the entire contract. If the written contract is on its face, or is admittedly, not a complete summation, the parties naturally did not intend to abandon the points upon which they had agreed but which were not noted in the contract; and parol evidence is admissible to show the actual agreement of the parties.

FACTS: Reynolds, an architect, made a contract with Long to design a building. Reynolds was to be paid a percentage of costs. The written contract between the parties did not state any maximum cost for the building. Reynolds sued Long for a percentage of the actual cost of the building. Long claimed that a maximum cost had been agreed upon and that the architect's percentage could not exceed the percentage of the maximum amount. Was parol evidence admissible to show the existence of a maximum limitation?

---

[9] Hohenstein v S.M.H. Trading Corp. (CA5 Ga) 382 F2d 530. This is also the view followed by UCC § 2-202(a) which permits terms in a contract for the sale of goods to be "explained or supplemented by a course of dealing or usage of trade . . . or by course of performance." Such evidence is admissible not because there is an ambiguity but "in order that the true understanding of the parties as to the agreement may be reached." Official Code Comment to § 2-202.

It has also been held that UCC § 1-205 permits proof of trade usage and course of performance with respect to non-Code contracts even though there is no ambiguity. Chase Manhattan Bank v First Marion Bank (CA5 Fla) 437 F2d 1040.

DECISION: Since the contract with the architect stated nothing as to cost of the building, it was obviously not complete and the parol evidence was admissible to show the maximum cost agreed upon. [Reynolds v Long, 115 GaApp 182, 154 SE2d 299]

A contract may appear on its face to be complete and yet not include everything the parties agreed upon. It must be remembered that there is no absolute standard by which to determine when a contract is complete. All that the court can do is to consider whether all essential terms of the contract are present, that is, whether the contract is sufficiently definite to be enforceable, and whether it contains all provisions which would ordinarily be included in a contract of that nature.

The fact that a contract is silent as to a particular matter does not mean that it is incomplete, for the law may attach a particular legal result (called *implying a term*) when the contract is silent. In such a case, parol evidence which is inconsistent with the term that would be implied cannot be shown. For example, when the contract is silent as to the time of payment, the obligation of making payment concurrently with performance by the other party is implied, and parol evidence is not admissible to show that there was an oral agreement to make payment at a different time.

(b) Ambiguity. If a written contract is not clear in all its provisions, parol evidence may generally be admitted to clarify the meaning. This is particularly true when the contract contains contradictory measurements or descriptions, or when it employs symbols or abbreviations that have no general meaning known to the court. Parol evidence may also be admitted to show that a word used in a contract has a special trade meaning or a meaning in the particular locality that differs from the common meaning of that word.

The fact that the parties disagree as to the meaning of the contract does not mean that it is ambiguous. Some courts have departed from requiring strict ambiguity and permit parol evidence whenever it is not unreasonably inconsistent with the writing. This is done to throw further light on the intent of the parties and in effect permits parol evidence of anything which is plausible.

FACTS: Delta Dynamics developed a trigger lock as a safety device on firearms. It gave Arioto and his partners, doing business as Pixey Distributing Co., the right to distribute the lock for five years; and Pixey agreed to sell a specified number of such locks in each year. The agreement stated: "Should Pixey fail to distribute in any one year the minimum number of devices to be distributed, . . .this agreement shall be subject to termination by Delta on thirty days' notice." The contract also provided that "in the event of breach of this agreement by either party, the party prevailing in any action for damages or enforcement of the terms of this agreement shall be entitled to reasonable attorneys' fees." Pixey failed to order the contract minimum in the first year. Delta sued Arioto and his partners for breach of contract.

The defendants claimed that suit could not be brought for damages for not ordering the quota on the theory that the only remedy for such breach was that Delta could terminate the contract. At the trial Pixey offered testimony to show that the parties had understood that the termination provision was intended as the sole remedy. Counsel for the defendants called one of the partners and asked, "During the negotiations that culminated in the execution of this contract between your company and Delta Dynamics, was there any conversation or discussion as to what would happen as far as Pixey Distributing Co. is concerned if they failed to meet the minimum quota set up in the contract?" Counsel for Delta objected to this question on the ground that it called for the admission of parol evidence. Counsel for the defendants stated that the contract was ambiguous and that the purpose of the testimony was to show the intention of the parties.

DECISION: The evidence was admissible. It was reasonably possible to interpret the termination provision as the exclusive remedy of Delta for a failure to maintain the sales quota or as merely a provision which terminated the contract as to the future but which did not discharge liability for any past breach. It was therefore proper to admit parol evidence to show what the parties intended even though the terms of the written contract were not in themselves ambiguous. [Delta Dynamics v Arioto, 69 Cal2d 525, 72 CalRptr 785, 446 P2d 785]

(c) **Fraud, accident, or mistake.** A contract apparently complete on its face may have omitted a provision which should have been included.

(d) **Conduct of parties.** The parol evidence rule does not prevent either party from showing by parol evidence that he was fraudulently induced to execute the contract or that the other party to the contract had not performed his obligation.

Likewise, when suit is brought to recover damages for misrepresentation as to what was covered by the plant's insurance policy, parol evidence is admissible to show what statements were made. This does not contradict the terms of the contract, which would be prohibited by the parol evidence rule, but merely shows that the defendant said that the contract was something which it was not.

(e) **Existence or modification of contract.** The parol evidence rule prohibits only the contradiction of a complete written contract. It does not prohibit proof that an obligation under the contract never existed or that the contract was thereafter modified or terminated. Thus, parol evidence may be admitted to show that a construction contract was not to be binding unless and until the contractor procured a 100 percent construction loan.[10]

Written contracts commonly declare that contracts can only be modified by a writing. In the case of construction contracts, it will ordinarily be stated that no payment will be made for extra work unless there is a written order from the owner or architect calling for such extra work. If the parties proceed in disregard of such a clause requiring a writing, it may be shown by parol evidence that they have done so and the contract will be modified accordingly.

---

[10] Sheldon Builders v Trojan Towers, 225 CalApp2d 781, 63 CalRptr 425.

FACTS: McCarthy, as owner, made a contract with Harrington to build a home. The contract stated that no charges could be made for work in addition to that called for by the contract unless there was a written order for such extra work specifying the charges to be made. During the course of construction, McCarthy orally requested Harrington to make certain additions to the work. This was done without any written order being executed. When the work was finished, McCarthy refused to pay for the extra work on the ground that there were no written orders for such work.

DECISION: Judgment for Harrington. Although the contract required written orders for extra work, the subsequent conduct of the parties with respect to the extra work that was done constituted a modification of the original contract. The fact that the original contract contained a requirement of written work modifications did not prevent proof that the parties had proceeded in disregard of such requirement, and thereby modified the original contract with respect to the work done. [Harrington v McCarthy, 91 Idaho 307, 420 P2d 790]

(1) Nonbinding Character of Formal Contract. Persons may sign documents which look like binding contracts but parol evidence is admitted by the court to show that the parties never really intended to be bound by a contract. Frequently, there is present an element of high pressure selling in which one party is reluctant to sign but only does so when assured that the paper is not a binding contract. When the court holds that parol evidence is admissible to show this and then holds that the paper that looks like a contract is not binding, it is in substance providing a form of consumer protection.

(2) Modification of Contract. To return to the illustration of the store lease by *L* to *T* and the alleged oral agreement of an exclusive right to sell soft drinks, three situations may arise. It may be claimed that the oral agreement was made (a) before the execution of the final written lease; (b) at the same time as the execution of the written lease; or (c) subsequent to the execution of the written lease. The parol evidence rule only prohibits the proof of the oral agreement under (a) and (b). It is not applicable to (c), for it can be shown that subsequent to the execution of the contract the parties modified the contract, even though the original contract was in writing and the subsequent modification was oral. Clear proof of the later agreement is required.

When it is claimed that a contract is modified by a later agreement, consideration must support the modifying agreement except in the case of a contract for the sale of goods.[11] In any case, if the parties have performed the part of the contract that is modified, it is immaterial that there was no consideration for the agreement for such modification.

(f) Collateral contract. The parol evidence rule only applies with respect to the written contract of the parties. If they have made two contracts, one

---

[11] UCC § 2-209 (1).

written and the other oral, the parol evidence rule does not bar proof of the oral contract. Difficulty arises in determining whether in fact there are two separate contracts or whether there was merely one contract which was written and the oral agreement is asserted in violation of the parol evidence rule in the effort to contradict or bypass the written contract.

FACTS: Rhodes had an automobile collision and liability policy which was issued by the Southern Guaranty Insurance Company. By an amendment to the policy, an exclusion was made so that it did not apply to any automobile driven by the insured's son, James L. Rhodes. In 1968, the father purchased a 1968 Pontiac for James and sought to obtain liability insurance for him and the new car. The father discussed such insurance with the agent for Southern Guaranty. Thereafter the Southern Guaranty policy was amended to provide liability and collision coverage for the 1968 Pontiac but no change was made to the clause excluding James and the father remained the named insured in the policy. James was in a collision while driving that Pontiac and sued Southern Guaranty. It raised the defense that the policy expressly excluded liability as to James. He replied that he was not suing on the written policy but on a separate and distinct oral contract of insurance which provided liability coverage for him. The insurer asserted that the parol evidence rule prevented proof of any such oral contract because in fact there was no separate contract to cover the son by insurance and the son by suing on an alleged oral contract was merely trying to contradict the exclusion in the written policy, which the parol evidence rule prevented.

DECISION: The parol evidence was not admissible. The collateral contract exception to the parol evidence rule was not applicable because none of the criteria of a collateral contract was satisfied. In order for that exception to apply, it is necessary that (1) the alleged oral contract be collateral in form; (2) it must not contradict the written contract; and (3) its subject matter must be such that one would not ordinarily expect it to be covered by the written contract. The oral contract alleged by Rhodes satisfied none of these elements: (1) it was not collateral, as it in effect was a modification of the written contract and there was no separate consideration for the oral contract, but only the premium paid for the written contract; (2) the oral contract contradicted the written contract by showing that the coverage of the written contract was not as stated in the writing; and (3) the subject of the oral agreement was such that it would ordinarily be included in the written contract. [Southern Guaranty Insurance Co. v Rhodes, 46 AlaApp 454, 243 So2d 717]

QUESTIONS
AND CASE
PROBLEMS

1. State the specific objective(s) of the following rule of law: "Parol evidence is not admissible for the purpose of modifying a written contract when that evidence relates to an agreement made before or at the time that the written contract was executed."

2. Davis went to work for Monorail, Inc. At the time his employment was discussed, Wenner-Gren promised Davis that if Monorail did not pay his salary to him, Wenner-Gren would see that Alwac International, Inc., a corporation which Wenner-Gren controlled, would pay the salary. After 2½ years of employment, Monorail stopped paying his salary, whereupon Davis sued Alwac and Wenner-Gren. Wenner-Gren raised the defense that it was not liable because of the statute of frauds. Was it correct? [Davis v Alwac International, Inc. (TexCivApp) 369 SW2d 797]

3. Aratari obtained a franchise from the Chrysler Corp. to engage in business as an automobile dealer in Rochester, New York. A written franchise contract was executed between the parties identifying the location of the dealer in the city. Aratari later claimed that when the franchise agreement was being negotiated, it had been agreed that Chrysler Corp. would move him to a better location in the city. Was Chrysler liable for damages for having failed to keep this promise? [Aratari v Chrysler Corp. 35 AppDiv2d 1077, 316 NYS2d 680]

4. Williams promised to give her cousin, Robinson, her home in her will if he would leave his home and take care of her for the balance of her life. He did so but Williams did not give the property to him by her will. He sued for breach of the oral contract to give him the property. Did the statute of frauds bar his claim? [Williams v Robinson, 251 Ark 1002, 476 SW2d 1]

5. Burgess signed a paper which stated that Eastern Michigan University had a 60-day option to purchase Burgess' home. The writing acknowledged receipt of "one dollar" and "other valuable consideration." Thereafter, Burgess revoked the option. The University claimed that the option could not be revoked because of the recital of consideration. It further claimed that the revocation was not effective under the statute of frauds because it was orally made. It was admitted that in fact Burgess had not received a dollar nor any valuable consideration as recited. Was Burgess bound by a contract? [Board of Control of Eastern Michigan University v Burgess, 45 MichApp 183, 206 NW2d 256]

6. Lawrence loaned money to Moore. He died without repaying the loan. Lawrence claimed that when he mentioned the matter to Moore's widow, she promised to pay the debt. She did not do so and Lawrence sued her on her promise. Does she have any defense? [Moore v Lawrence, 252 Ark 759, 480 SW2d 941]

7. Toups owed money to Ace Ready-Mix Concrete. Toups agreed to haul sand and gravel for Ace, who agreed to reduce the debt owed it by a third person by the amount it owed Toups. Thereafter, Toups claimed payment for the work which he performed in hauling sand and gravel. Ace defended on the ground that it had already credited the amount due Toups against the debt of the third person as agreed to by him. Toups claimed this oral agreement was not binding because it was an oral promise to answer for the debt of a third person and was therefore condemned by the statute of frauds. Was he correct? [Toups v Ace Ready-Mix Concrete, Inc. (LaApp) 267 So2d 255]

INTERPRETATION OF CONTRACTS

A. RULES OF CONSTRUCTION AND INTERPRETATION

§ 16:1. INTENTION. A contract is to be enforced according to its terms. The court must examine the contract to determine and give effect to what the parties intended, provided their objective is lawful.[1] It is the intention of the parties as expressed in the contract that must prevail.

> **FACTS:** Keyworth was employed by Industrial Sales Co. In the course of employment, he was injured by Israelson. Industrial Sales made a contract with Keyworth to pay him $100 per week until he was able to return to normal work but specified that such payments would be paid back to Industrial Sales from any recovery that Keyworth would obtain in a lawsuit against Israelson, with payments to be made to Industrial Sales upon the "successful conclusion of the case." Keyworth obtained a recovery in the action against Israelson of $16,600 but refused to make any payment to Industrial Sales because he believed there was not a "successful conclusion of the case." Industrial Sales sued Keyworth.
>
> **DECISION:** Judgment for Industrial Sales Co. The fair meaning of the language was that winning the lawsuit was a "successful conclusion of the case." The fact that one of the parties may have a particular belief or intent that it meant winning a particular minimum amount would not be allowed to change the intent of the parties as expressed by the words of the contract. [Keyworth v Industrial Sales Co. 241 Md 453, 217 A2d 253]

A secret intention of one party that is not expressed in the contract has no effect.[2] A party to a contract will ordinarily not be allowed to state what was secretly meant by the words used, for the test is what a reasonable person would have believed was intended by those words. For example,

---
[1] Stevens v Fanning, 59 IllApp2d 285, 207 NE2d 136.
[2] Leitner v Breen, 51 NJSuper 31, 143 A3d 256.

when a person guaranteed payment, it could not be shown that he had secretly intended not to do so.

A court should not remake a contract for the parties under the guise of interpreting it. Therefore, if the contract is so vague or indefinite that the intended performance cannot be determined, the contract cannot be enforced.

No particular form of words is required and any words manifesting the intent of the parties are sufficient. In the absence of proof that a word has a peculiar meaning or that it was employed by the parties with a particular meaning, a common word is given its ordinary meaning.[3]

A word will not be given its literal meaning when it is clear that the parties did not intend such a meaning. For example, "and" may be substituted for "or," "may" for "shall," and "void" for "voidable," and vice versa, when it is clear that the parties so intended.

Rules of grammatical construction and punctuation may be employed to throw light on the intention of the parties, but they are ignored when they clearly conflict with the intention of the parties.

§ 16:2. **WHOLE CONTRACT.** The provisions of a contract must be construed as a whole.[4] This rule is followed even when the contract is partly written and partly oral, but this principle does not apply when an oral agreement must be excluded according to the parol evidence rule. Every word of a contract is to be given effect if reasonably possible.

The objective of viewing the contract in its entirety is not only to make every term of the contract effective but also to understand the objective of the parties in light of the particular transaction involved.

FACTS: Avis Rent-A-Car System gave Southwestern Automotive Leasing Corporation (SALCO) a car and truck rental franchise for three Louisiana cities in 1961. The licensing agreement gave each party the right to terminate with or without cause for a certain period of time and further provided that "five years from the date Licensee first became an Avis System Licensee, . . .Licensor may terminate . . . only with cause. . . ." SALCO was not successful and by common consent its franchise rights were transferred in 1964 to Gulf Shores Leasing Corp. In 1968, Avis notified Gulf that it was terminating the license held by Gulf without cause. Gulf claimed that Avis could only terminate for cause because five years had run from the date of the original franchise agreement and brought suit to prevent termination.

DECISION: Gulf could not add on the term of the prior licensee and therefore Gulf's license could be terminated without cause. The five-year period was a probationary or trial period and each licensee was required to stand on its own merits and to show five years of satisfactory work. The years of a former licensor could not be counted, particularly when, as in the case of SALCO, the prior years were not satisfactory. [Gulf Shores Leasing Corp. v Avis Rent-A-Car System, Inc. (CA5 La) 441 F2d 1385]

---

[3] Reno Club v Young Investment Co. 64 Nev 312, 182 P2d 1011.
[4] Archibald v Midwest Paper Stock Co. (Iowa) 176 NW2d 761.

(a) **Divisible contract.** When a contract contains a number of provisions or performances to be rendered, the question arises as to whether the parties intended merely a group of separate contracts or whether it was to be a "package deal" so that complete performance of every provision of the contract was essential.[5]

(b) **What constitutes the whole contract.** The question may arise whether separate papers or particular parts of a paper constitute part of the whole contract. The inclusion of other papers in the contract was discussed in § 9:9.

Terms in a printed letterhead or billhead or on the reverse side of the printed contract form are not part of a contract written thereon unless a reasonable person would regard such terms as part of the contract. An employer's manual that is shown after the signing of an employment contract is not part of that contract.[6] Similarly, provisions in a manufacturer's instruction manual, or in invoices, or on labels that are never seen or called to the attention of a buyer until after a contract of sale has been made are not part of the contract and do not bind the buyer.

§ 16:3. CONDITIONS. In most bilateral contracts the performance of each party is dependent upon the performance by the other party and each party is bound to render his performance.

(a) **Conditions precedent.** A condition or obligation-triggering event may be described as a *condition precedent* because it precedes the existence of the obligation.

A contract between a contractor and a government may contain a condition precedent that the contract shall not be binding unless the proper fiscal officer of the government indorses on the contract a certification that sufficient money is held to make the payments required by the contract.

(b) **Conditions subsequent.** The parties may specify that the contract shall terminate when a particular event occurs or does not occur. Such a provision is a *condition subsequent*. If government approval is required, the parties may specify that the contract shall not bind them if the government approval cannot be obtained.[7]

A contract for the purchase of land may contain a condition subsequent which cancels the contract if the buyer is not able to obtain a zoning permit to use a building for a particular purpose. When the satisfaction of a condition is dependent on acts to be performed by one of the contracting parties, he must act within the time specified, if any, or within a reasonable time if none is specified. For example, in the zoning permission situation the buyer must make application for the zoning permission within a reasonable time after the contract is made.

---

[5] John v United Advertising, Inc. 165 Colo 193, 439 P2d 53.

[6] Scottsdale School District v Clark 20 ArizApp 321, 512 P2d 853.

[7] Security National Life Insurance Co. v Pre-Need Camelback Plan, Inc. 19 ArizApp 580, 509 P2d 652.

§ 16:4. CONTRADICTORY TERMS. When a contract is partly printed or typewritten and partly written and the written part conflicts with the printed or typewritten part, the written part prevails. When there is a conflict between a printed part and a typewritten part, the latter prevails. When there is a conflict between an amount or quantity expressed both in words and figures, as on a check, the amount or quantity expressed in words prevails.

> **FACTS:** Integrated, Inc., entered into a contract with the State of California to construct a building. It then subcontracted the electrical work to Alec Fergusson Electrical Contractors. The subcontract was a printed form with blanks filled in by typewriting. The printed payment clause required Integrated to pay Fergusson on the 15th day of the month following the submission of invoices by Fergusson. The typewritten part of the contract required Integrated to pay Fergusson "immediately following payment" (by the State) to the general contractor.

> **DECISION:** The typed and printed payment clauses were inconsistent. Therefore, the typewritten clause prevailed. The word "immediately" used therein did not require actual "immediate" action, however, but was satisfied by payment within a reasonable time, having regard to the nature of the circumstances of the case, which necessarily included sufficient time in which to process the payment received from the State before making payment therefrom to the subcontractor. [Integrated, Inc. v Alec Fergusson Electrical Contractors, 250 CalApp2d 287, 58 CalReptr 503]

When it is possible to give a contract two interpretations and one is lawful and the other unlawful, it is assumed that the lawful interpretation was intended by the parties. Similarly, an interpretation that is fair is preferred over one that will work an unjust hardship or cause one of the parties to forfeit valuable rights.

(a) Strict construction against drafting party. An ambiguous contract is interpreted more strictly against the party who drafted it. Thus, printed forms of a contract, such as insurance policies, which are supplied by one party to the transaction, are interpreted against him and in favor of the other party when two interpretations are reasonably possible. If the contract of insurance is clear and unambiguous, however, it will ordinarily be enforced according to its terms, particularly when the insured is a large corporation acting with competent legal advice.[8]

(b) Knowledge of complaining party. The rule that an ambiguity in a contract is interpreted against the person who prepared the contract is not applied when the other party knew what the preparing party intended.

§ 16:5. IMPLIED TERMS. Although a contract should be explicit and provide for all reasonably foreseeable events, it is not necessary that every provision be set forth. In some cases a term may be implied in the absence of an express statement to the contrary.

---

[8] Eastcoast Equipment Co. v Maryland Casualty Co. 207 PaSuper 383, 218 A2d 91.

FACTS: Standard Oil Co. made a nonexclusive jobbing or wholesale dealership contract with Perkins, which limited him to selling Standard's products and required Perkins to maintain certain minimum prices. Standard Oil had the right to approve or disapprove of Perkins' customers. In order to be able to perform under his contract, Perkins had to make a substantial money investment, and his only income was from the commissions on the sales of Standard's products. Standard Oil made some sales directly to Perkins' customers. When Perkins protested, Standard Oil pointed out that the contract did not contain any provision making his rights exclusive. Perkins sued Standard Oil to compel it to stop dealing with his customers.

DECISION: Judgment for Perkins. In view of the expenditure required of Perkins in order to operate his business and to perform his part of the contract and of his dependence upon his customers, the interpretation should be made that Standard Oil would not solicit customers of Perkins, even though the contract did not give him an exclusive dealership within the given geographic area. [Perkins v Standard Oil Co. 235 Ore 7, 383 P2d 107]

An obligation to pay a specified sum of money is implied to mean payment in legal tender. Likewise, in a contract to perform work there is an implied promise to use such skill as is necessary for the proper performance of the work. In a "cost-plus" contract there is an implied undertaking that the costs will be reasonable and proper. When a note representing a loan is extended by agreement, an implied promise to pay interest during the extension period arises when nothing about interest is stated by the parties. When payment is made "as a deposit on account," it is implied that if the payment is not used for the purpose designated, the payment will be returned to the person who made the deposit. When the contract for work to be done does not specify the exact amount to be paid for the work, the law will imply an obligation to pay the reasonable value for such work.[9]

A local custom or trade practice, such as that of allowing 30 days' credit to buyers, may form part of the contract when it is clear that the parties intended to be governed by this custom or trade practice or when a reasonable person would believe that they had so intended.

When a written contract does not specify the time for performance, a reasonable time is implied and parol evidence is not admissible to establish a different time for performance.

A term will not be implied in a contract when the court concludes that the silence of the contract on the particular point was intentional.

§ 16:6. CONDUCT AND CUSTOM. The conduct of the parties in carrying out the terms of a contract may be considered in determining just what they meant by the contract. When performance has been repeatedly tendered and accepted without protest, neither party will be permitted to claim that the contract was too indefinite to be binding. For example, when a travel agent made a contract with a hotel to arrange for "junkets" to the hotel, any

---

[9] New Mexico v Fireman's Fund Indemnity Co. 67 NMex 360, 355 P2d 291.

claim that it was not certain just what was intended must be ignored when some 80 junkets had already been arranged and paid for by the hotel at the contract price without any dispute as to whether the contract obligation was satisfied.[10]

The conduct of parties is admissible to show the meaning of the contract as viewed in the way the parties perform thereunder. Moreover, when the conduct of the parties is inconsistent with the original written contract, proof of such conduct may justify concluding that the parties had orally modified the original agreement.

§ 16:7. AVOIDANCE OF HARDSHIP. When there is ambiguity as to the meaning of a contract, a court will avoid the interpretation that gives one contracting party an unreasonable advantage over the other or which causes a forfeiture of a party's interest. When there is an inequality of bargaining power between the contracting parties, courts will sometimes classify the contract as a *contract of adhesion* in that it was offered on a "take-it-or-leave-it" basis by the stronger party, and the court will interpret the contract as providing what appeared reasonable from the standpoint of the weaker bargaining party.

In some instances, if hardship cannot be avoided in this manner, the court may hold that the contract or a particular provision is not binding because it is unconscionable or contrary to public policy. The extent to which this protection is available is uncertain, and as a general rule a party is bound by his contract even though it proves to be a bad bargain.

§ 16:8. THE ABSENT TERM. What is the effect of the absence of a provision on a particular matter? It must first be determined whether the silence of the contract is intentional or is an accidental omission. Sometimes it will be obvious that the silence was not accidental. For example, a contract to deliver 10 tons of coal on the first Monday of January, February, and March, would obviously be interpreted as meaning just that and it would not be said that the contract was incomplete or ambiguous because it did not say anything about other months. Here the intent of the parties is clear even though it did not say "January, February, and March only" or "January, February, and March and no other months."

Assume, however, that a coal delivery contract purports to sell 50 tons of coal and then states that 10 tons shall be delivered on the first Monday of January, February, and March. Here it is clear that there are 20 more tons to be delivered but the contract says nothing as to that. In this case, the silence of the contract is not an intentional exclusion but is a defect in the contract.

When it is concluded that the omission of a term is a defect, what is the legal result? Generally the result will be one of the following.

(a) **Implied terms.** In some omission cases the law will imply a term to fill up the omission as discussed in § 16:5.

---

[10] Casino Operations, Inc v Graham, 86 Nev 764, 476 P2d 953; see Uniform Commercial Code § 2-208(1) as to course of performance in the interpretation of contracts for the sale of goods and UCC § 1-105 as to both Code and non-Code transactions.

(b) Parol evidence. The omission may be regarded as making the contract ambiguous and justifying the admission of parol evidence to determine what was actually intended. If the parol evidence shows the parties have in fact agreed on the matter not covered by the written contract, the obligation of the parties will be interpreted as a blend or composite of the written contract and the oral terms.

(c) No contract. If a term is omitted from the contract and the omission is not cured by either the implication of a term under (a) or by the introduction of parol evidence under (b), the court may conclude that there is no contract. In some cases the statute of frauds may compel the conclusion that there is no contract when a term is omitted. If the written contract is for the sale of land, the statute of frauds would bar enforcing the contract because the writing does not state the material terms of the contract when nothing more is stated in the contract to identify what land.

(d) Strict enforcement of contract. If the omitted matter does not relate to the primary obligation or heart of the contract, it is likely that the omission has no effect on the contract and instead of concluding that there is no contract under (c), the contract will be enforced to its exact letter. For example, if a contract requires a contractor to build a building by August 1, and says nothing about an extension of time in the event of destruction by accidental fire, the contractor is not given any extra time nor any extra compensation when the construction is so destroyed. That is, the contract called for a completed building by August 1 and that is what the contractor must produce or he has broken his contract. Many modern contracts will meet this particular situation by requiring the contractor to maintain fire insurance on the construction and by allowing him an extension of time if there is fire damage for which he is not at fault. If, however, the contract is silent as to such matters, the contractor must perform according to the letter of the contract.

B. CONFLICT OF LAWS

Since we have 50 state court systems and the federal court system, questions sometimes arise as to what law will be applied by a court. *Conflict of laws* is that branch of law which determines which body of law shall apply.

§ **16:9. STATE COURTS.** It is important to distinguish between the state in which the parties are domiciled or have their permanent home, the state in which the contract is made, and the state in which the contract is to be performed. The state in which the contract is made is determined by finding the state in which the last act essential to the formation of the contract was performed. Thus, when an acceptance is mailed in one state to an offeror in another state, the state of formation of the contract is the state in which the acceptance is mailed if the acceptance becomes effective at that time.

If acceptance by telephone is otherwise proper, the acceptance takes effect at the place where the acceptance is spoken into the phone. Thus, an employment contract is made in the state in which the applicant telephoned his acceptance, and consequently, that state has jurisdiction over his claim to workmen's compensation even though injuries were sustained in another state.

If an action on a contract made in one state is brought in a court of another state, an initial question is whether that court will lend its aid to the enforcement of a foreign (out-of-state) contract. Ordinarily suit may be brought on a foreign contract. But, if there is a strong contrary local policy, recovery may be denied even though the contract was valid in the state where it was made.

The capacity of a natural person to make a contract is governed by the place of contracting; a corporation's capacity to do so is determined by the law of the state of incorporation. The law of the state where the contract is made determines whether it is valid in substance and satisfies requirements as to form. Matters relating to the performance of the contract, excuse or liability for nonperformance, and the measure of damages for nonperformance are generally governed by the law of the state where the contract is to be performed.

Ordinarily the enforceability of a contract, as distinguished from its general validity, is governed by the law of the state where it is made. At times the courts of one jurisdiction refuse to enforce foreign contracts because, although lawful by the law of the jurisdiction where the contract was made or was to be performed, there is a dominant local public policy which bars enforcing the foreign claim or a claim based on a foreign transaction. The fact that a contract requires or contemplates the performance of an act in another state which would be illegal if performed in the state where the contract was made does not make the contract illegal in the absence of a dominant, local policy opposed to such a contract.

> **FACTS:** Camero and Castilleja lived in Texas where lotteries are illegal. They pooled some funds and agreed that Castilleja would go to Mexico to buy national lottery tickets and that they would divide any winnings. A ticket thus purchased by Castilleja was a winning ticket, but he refused to divide the winnings. When Camero sued him in Texas, Castilleja claimed that the contract could not be enforced because it was illegal.

> **DECISION:** The contract contemplating the purchase of lottery tickets in Mexico, where such purchase was legal, was a lawful contract. The fact that lottery tickets could not be lawfully purchased in Texas did not affect the contract of the parties to divide the winnings. The public policy of Texas against lotteries is not so dominant that enforcement of that contract right should be denied. [Castilleja v Camero (Tex) 414 SW2d 424]

When a lawsuit is brought on a contract, the *law of the forum*, that is, of the court in which the action is brought, determines the procedure and the rules of evidence.[11]

---

[11] In contract actions it is generally held that whether a claim is barred by the statute of limitations is determined by the law of the forum. There is a division of authority as to whether a statute of frauds relates to the substance of the contract, the law of the place of making then governing, or whether it is a question of procedure, the law of the forum then governing.

Whether there is any right that can be assigned is determined by the law of the state which determines whether the contract is substantively valid. The formal validity of the assignment is determined by the law of the state in which the assignment is made.

(a) Center of gravity. There is a growing acceptance of the rule that, in place of the rigid or mechanical standards described above, a contract should be governed by the law of the state that has the most significant contracts with the transaction, to which state the contract may be said to gravitate.

(b) Specification by the parties. It is common for the more important contracts to specify that they shall be governed by the law of a particular state. When this is done, it is generally held that if the contract is lawful in the designated state, it will be enforced in another state and interpreted according to the law of the designated state, even though a contrary result would be reached if governed by the law of the state in which the suit is brought. Whenever a transaction is governed by the Uniform Commercial Code, the parties may agree that their rights and duties shall be governed by the law of any state or nation which "bears a reasonable relation" to the transaction.[12]

§ 16:10. FEDERAL COURTS.

When the parties to a contract reside in different states and an action is brought on the contract in a federal court because of their different citizenship, the federal court must apply the same rules of conflict of laws that would be applied by the courts of the state in which the federal court is sitting.[13] Thus, a federal court in Chicago deciding a case involving parties from Indiana and Wisconsin must apply the same rules of conflict of laws as would be applied by the courts of Illinois. The state law must be followed by the federal court in such a case whether or not the federal court agrees with the state law.

§ 16:11. JOINT, SEVERAL, AND JOINT AND SEVERAL CONTRACTS.

When two or more persons are on either side of a contract, an additional question of interpretation may arise, as it may be necessary to determine whether the contract is (a) joint, (b) several, or (c) joint and several.

(a) Joint contracts. A *joint contract* is one in which two or more persons jointly promise to perform an obligation. If A, B, and C sign a contract stating "we jointly promise" to do a particular act, the obligation is the joint obligation of A, B, and C. In the absence of an express intent to the contrary, a promise by two or more persons is generally presumed to be joint and not several.

Each of two or more joint promisors is liable for the entire obligation, but an action must be brought against all who are living and within the jurisdiction of the court. If one of the promisors dies, the surviving

---

[12] UCC § 1-105(1).
[13] Erie R.R. Co. v Tompkins, 304 US 64.

promisors remain bound to perform the contract unless it was personal in character and required the joint action of all the obligors for its performance. If the deceased obligor had received a benefit from the contract, a court of equity will also hold his estate liable for the performance of the contract.

Generally the release by the promisee of one or more of the joint obligors releases all.

(b) Several contracts. *Several contracts* arise when two or more persons separately agree to perform the same obligation even though the separate agreements are set forth in the same instrument.

If *A*, *B*, and *C* sign a contract stating "we severally promise" or "each of us promises" to do a particular act or to pay a specified sum of money, the three signers are severally bound to perform or to pay; that is, each signer is individually bound.

In many jurisdictions persons liable on related causes of action can be sued at one time. Since the liability of each obligor to a several contract is by definition separate or distinct, the release of one or more of the obligors by the promisee does not release the others.

(c) Joint and several contracts. A *joint and several contract* is one in which two or more persons are bound both jointly and severally. If *A*, *B*, and *C* sign a contract stating "we, and each of us, promise" (or "I promise") to pay a specified sum of money, they are jointly and severally bound. The obligee may treat the claim either as a joint claim or as a group of separate claims. He may bring a suit against all at the same time or against one at a time. The plaintiff may also sue any number of the severally liable parties instead of suing them either singly or all at one time.

QUESTIONS AND CASE PROBLEMS

1. Fincher was employed by Belk-Sawyer Co. as fashion coordinator for the latter's retail stores. The contract of employment specified her duties as fashion coordinator and also provided for additional services of Fincher to be thereafter agreed upon in connection with beauty consultation and shopping services to be established at the stores. After Fincher had been employed as fashion coordinator for several months, Belk-Sawyer Co. refused to be bound by the contract on the ground that it was too indefinite. Was it bound? [Fincher v Belk-Sawyer Co. (FlaApp) 127 So2d 130]

2. Avril, a Pennsylvania corporation, agreed to sell certain cleaning products to Center Chemical Co. at a discount of 45 percent for 20 years and gave Center the exclusive right to sell such products in Florida. Four years later, Center stopped purchasing from Avril, which then sued it for breach of contract. Did the law of

Pennsylvania or the Florida law determine the damages which could be recovered? [Center Chemical Co. v Avril (CA5 Fla) 392 F2d 289]

3. *A* and *B* signed a printed form of agreement by which it appeared that *A* promised to sell and *B* promised to buy certain land. On the blank lines of the printed form, there was a typewritten provision that *B* had an option to purchase the land. Could *A* sue *B* for breach of contract if *B* did not buy the land? [See Welk v Fainbarg, 255 CalApp2d 269, 63 CalRptr 127]

4. Holland, doing business as the American Homes Co., sold Sandi Brown a set of kitchenware on the installment plan. When she stated that she did not have the money to make the monthly payments, it was agreed that Holland would put it on the layaway plan for her. Thereafter Holland and American Homes Co. sued her for the purchase price. She claimed that she had not become the owner of the kitchenware by the transaction which, if true, meant that she could not be sued for the purchase price. She offered witnesses who testified that a layaway plan did not make the goods become the property of the customer but merely put them away where they would not be sold to other customers and that the goods did not become the property of a buyer until the buyer claimed and made payment for the goods within a specified time. Holland objected to the admission of this evidence. Decide. [Holland v Brown, 15 Utah2d 422, 394 P2d 77]

5. McGill and his grandson, Malo, made an agreement by which the former would live with the latter and receive support and maintenance in return for deeding to the grandson the house of the former. After a number of years, the grandfather left the house because of the threats and physical violence of the grandson. There was no complaint of lack of support and maintenance. Had the grandson broken the contract? [McGill v Malo, 23 ConnSupp 447, 184 A2d 517]

6. All the shareholders of Continental Title Company signed an agreement giving the Stewart Title Company the option to purchase "all" of their shares for a quarter million dollars. The option contract specified that notice of its exercise was to be given to the chairman of the board of the Continental Title Company. The Stewart Title Company notified one of the shareholders, Herbert, that it exercised the option to purchase his 350 shares, paying for them the prorated portion of a quarter million dollars. Herbert refused to sell. A lawsuit was brought against him and evidence was offered that the executives of Stewart understood that they were obtaining an option to purchase the stock of the Continental shareholders one by one. There was no evidence that this belief was communicated to anyone else. Was Herbert required to sell his shares to Stewart? [Stewart Title Company v Herbert, 6 CalApp3d 957, 85 CalRptr 654]

7. Axford rented land from Shellhart. The lease gave the lessee the option to purchase the leased property "any time during the term of this lease or its extension for the sum of $12,000. This option may be exercised at any time prior to December 1, 1969, by giving the Lessors at least 30 days notice in writing of Lessee's intention to so exercise said option." Could the lessee exercise the option by giving notice without paying the purchase price at the same time? [Shellhart v Axford (Wyo) 485 P2d 1031]

8. Physicians Mutual Insurance Company issued a policy covering the life of Ruby Brown. The policy declared that it did not cover any death resulting from "mental disorder, alcoholism, or drug addiction." Ruby was killed when she fell while intoxicated. The insurance company refused to pay because of the quoted provision. Her executor, Savage, sued the insurance company. Did it have a defense? [Physicians Mutual Insurance Co. v Savage (IndApp) 296 NE2d 165]

9. Carolina Plywood Distributors was a corporation. It purchased building materials from Clear Fir Sales Company. The president of Carolina wrote a letter

to Clear Fir which in part stated, "Please accept this letter as my personal guarantee for the purchases of Carolina Plywood Distributors through December 31, 1970. If we are continuing to do business at that time, we will be glad to renew this guarantee." The debt of Carolina was not paid and Clear Fir sued Carolina and its president. Clear Fir claimed that the quoted letter guaranteed the debt of the corporation. The president defended on the ground that Clear Fir had never accepted his offer of guaranty and therefore he was not bound. Was this defense valid? [Clear Fir Sales Co. v Carolina Plywood Distributors, Inc. 13 NCApp 429, 185 SE2d 737]

10. Ern-Roc Homes, a builder, guaranteed that its homes would have no seepage of water into the basement "through the foundation walls." Water entered the basement of the home purchased by Gomes by passing through a door installed in the basement wall, level with the ground in back of the house. The water caused extensive damage in the house. Gomes sued Ern-Roc Homes claiming that there was a breach of the builder's guaranty. Was Gomes correct? [Gomes v Ern-Roc Homes, Inc. (NYCivCt) 72 Misc2d 410, 339 NYS2d 401]

11. Stribling made a contract to sell land to Ailion. The contract stated that "seller reserves the right to run a credit investigation on purchaser and if in seller's opinion purchaser's credit is not sufficient, then the terms of this contract are null and void. Seller has until December 8, 1966, to complete said credit investigation." Stribling did not make any credit investigation but on December 2, 1966, sold the land to Pierce who had knowledge of Ailion's contract. Ailion sued Stribling and Pierce to enforce his contract. He claimed that since no credit investigation had been made by Stribling, the provision relating thereto was not operative. Decide. [Stribling v Ailion, 223 Ga 662, 157 SE2d 427]

12. A contemplated purchasing a house. He gave B, a real estate broker, a deposit for which the broker executed a "deposit receipt" which acknowledged that the broker had received the deposit on account of the purchase. The sale was not completed by the owner through the broker and A requested the return of the deposit. B refused to return the deposit on the ground that it was not stated that the deposit would be returned to the buyer. Was he correct? [See Wilcox v Atkins (FlaApp) 213 So2d 879]

THIRD PERSONS AND CONTRACTS

A. THIRD PARTY BENEFICIARY CONTRACTS

§ **17:1. DEFINITION.** Ordinarily *A* and *B* will make a contract that concerns only them. They, however, may make a contract by which *B* promises *A* that *B* will make a payment of money to *C*. If *B* fails to perform his promise, *C*, who is not the original promisee, may enforce it against *B*, the promisor. Such an agreement is a *third-party beneficiary contract*.

> **FACTS:** The local labor union made a collective bargaining agreement with the Powder Power Tool Corp. governing the rates of pay for the latter's employees. Springer, an employee, brought a suit on behalf of certain employees of the corporation who had not received the full pay under the agreement. It was claimed by the corporation that Springer could not bring this action for breach of contract since he was not a party to it.

> **DECISION:** Judgment for Springer. Although Springer was not a party to the contract, the contract had been made for the benefit of persons of the class to which he belonged. Accordingly he could sue upon the contract for its breach. [Springer v Powder Power Tool Corp. 220 Ore 102, 348 P2d 1112]

When a contract expressly states that it can only be enforced by the parties thereto, no third person can claim any right thereon as a third-party beneficiary.[1]

A life insurance contract is a third-party beneficiary contract, since the insurance company promises the insured to make payment to the beneficiary.

(a) Termination of contract. If the third-party beneficiary has accepted the contract or changed his position in reliance on it, the original parties generally cannot thereafter rescind the contract so as to release the obligation to the third party beneficiary. The contract, however, may

---
[1] Bewley Furniture Co., Inc. v Maryland Casualty Co. (La) 285 So2d 216.

expressly reserve the power of the original parties to make such modification or rescission,[2] or the third party may consent to such a change.

§ 17:2. INCIDENTAL BENEFICIARY DISTINGUISHED.

Not everyone who benefits from the performance of a contract between other persons is entitled to sue as a third party. If a city makes a contract with a contractor to pave certain streets, property owners living along those streets will naturally receive a benefit from the performance. This fact, however, does not confer upon them the status of third-party beneficiaries. Accordingly, the property owners cannot sue the contractor if he fails to perform. The courts reason that such beneficiaries are only incidentally benefited. The city contracted for the streets to further the public interest, not primarily to benefit individual property owners. Likewise, when a private employer makes a contract with the United States government to employ and train disadvantaged, unemployed persons, such persons are merely incidental beneficiaries of the contract and therefore cannot sue the employer for damages when he breaks his contract with the government.[3]

> **FACTS:** Murray owned a building. He contracted with the McDonald Construction company to make an addition to the building. Queen Anne News, Inc. was to be a tenant in the new addition. The contract required completion of the work within 75 days. It took 239 days to complete. Murray and Queen Anne News sued McDonald for the damages caused by the delay.

> **DECISION:** Queen Anne News was not entitled to recover damages for the delay. As a tenant, it was merely an incidental beneficiary of the contract. Only Murray as the obligee could sue for the breach. [McDonald Construction Co. v Murray, 5 WashApp 68, 485 P2d 626]

§ 17:3. LIMITATIONS ON THIRD-PARTY BENEFICIARY.

While the third-party beneficiary rule gives the third person the right to enforce the contract, it obviously gives him no greater rights than the contract provides. Otherwise stated, the third-party beneficiary must take the contract as he finds it. If there is a limitation or restriction, he cannot ignore it but is bound thereby.

B. ASSIGNMENTS

§ 17:4. DEFINITION.

An *assignment* is a transfer of rights. The party making the assignment is the *assignor*, and the person to whom the assignment is made is the *assignee*. An assignee of a contract may generally sue in his own name as though he were a party to the original contract.

---

[2] A common form of reservation is the life insurance policy provision by which the insured reserves the right to change the beneficiary. § 142 of the 1967 tentative draft Restatement of Contracts 2d provides that the promisor and promisee may modify their contract and affect the right of the third-party beneficiary thereby unless the agreement expressly prohibits this or the third-party beneficiary has changed his position in reliance on the promise or has manifested assent to it.

[3] Martinez v Socoma Companies, Inc. 11 Cal3d 394, 113 CalRptr 585, 521 P2d 841.

§ 17:5. **FORM OF ASSIGNMENT.** Generally an assignment may be expressed in any form. Any words, whether written or spoken, that show an intention to transfer or assign will be given the effect of an assignment. Statutes, however, may require that certain kinds of assignments be in writing or be executed in a particular form. This requirement is common in respect to statutes limiting the assignment of claims to wages.

§ 17:6. **ASSIGNMENT OF RIGHTS TO MONEY.** A person entitled to receive money, such as payment for the price of goods or for work done under a contract, may generally assign that right to another person. A claim or cause of action against another person may be assigned. A contractor entitled to receive payment from the owner can assign that right to the bank as security for a loan, or he can assign it to anyone else.

(a) **Nonexisting contracts.** If the contract is not in existence at the time the assignment is made, the attempt to assign money due on the contract in the future does not have the effect of a legal assignment. If the assignment has been supported by consideration, however, a court of equity will compel the assignor to make a transfer when the money is due.

(b) **Restrictions upon assignment.** A contract provision prohibiting an assignment may be in either of two forms: (1) a condition that if the contract is assigned, the contract shall be void; or (2) a personal agreement by a party that he will not assign the contract. In a given case it is essential to determine which form of clause is in the contract. If it is the condition form, the making of a prohibited assignment makes the contract void and the assignee acquires no interest. If it is the personal agreement or covenant form, the assignment is effective and the assignee acquires the assignor's interest.

There is a division of authority as to the effect of a prohibition in a contract against its assignment. In some jurisdictions, if a right to money is otherwise assignable, the right to transfer cannot be restricted by the parties to the contract. Such a restriction is regarded in those states as contrary to public policy because it places a limitation on the assignor's right of property. In other states such a prohibition is recognized as valid on the theory that the parties to the original contract may include such a provision if they choose to do so. In any event, a prohibition against assignment must be clearly expressed and any uncertainty is resolved in favor of assignability.

FACTS: The Caristo Construction Corp. executed a contract with New York City for the construction of school buildings. It then made a subcontract with the Kroo Painting Co. to do the painting work. The contract with Kroo specified that any assignment of any money due or to become due under the contract was void unless made with the written consent of Caristo. Without obtaining such consent, Kroo assigned its claim to money due under the contract to Allhusen, who then sued Caristo to collect the money.

DECISION: The express condition that the rights arising under the contract should not be assignable is to be given effect, because that was the intention of the parties in making the contract. The court recognized that there was a conflict of authority with some courts which hold that a nonassignment clause is not binding as contrary to public policy. [Allhusen v Caristo Construction Corp. 303 NY 446, 103 NE2d 891]

The nominal or formal assignment that is made when one party to a contract becomes incorporated is ignored for the purpose of determining whether there has been a violation of a prohibition against assignments.[4]

Rights under contracts for the sale of goods may be assigned, "unless otherwise agreed," except when the assignment would materially change the performance of the other party. Unless the circumstances indicate the contrary, a prohibition of the assignment of "the contract" is to be construed only as prohibiting a delegation of the obligation to perform.[5]

Statutes may prohibit the assignment of rights to money. Contractors who build public works are frequently prohibited from assigning money due or money that will become due under the contract. In some states wage earners are prohibited from assigning their future wages, or the law limits the percentage of their wages that can be assigned. In some instances an assignment of wages is lawful, but the assignment must be a separate instrument. The purpose of such a provision is to protect employees from signing printed forms containing "hidden" wage assignment clauses.

§ 17:7. **ASSIGNMENT OF RIGHTS TO A PERFORMANCE.** When the right of the obligee under the contract is to receive a performance by the other party, he may assign his right, provided the performance required of the other party will not be materially altered or varied by such assignment.

FACTS: Oklahoma City made a contract with Hurst, operating under the name of Earth Products Co., giving him the right to remove sand from city property for five years. The contract provided that the city would measure the amount of sand removed and specify the price to be paid per cubic foot, and imposed certain limitations as to location of excavations, depth, and slopes. Hurst assigned the contract to Sand Products, Inc. Oklahoma City claimed that this assignment was a breach of the contract.

DECISION: The assignment of the contract was not a breach. The contract was of such a nature that it was proper to assign it. By its terms, no special reliance was placed on Hurst, and the limitations as to excavations and slopes could be observed by Sand Products or anyone else and did not involve any special skill. The contract was therefore assignable by Hurst, and the act of assigning did not constitute a breach. [Earth Products Co. v Oklahoma City (Okla) 441 P2d 399]

In contrast, if a transfer of a right to a performance would materially affect or alter a duty or the rights of the obligor, an assignment of rights to the performance is not permitted.

---

[4] Ruberoid Co. v Glassman Construction Co. Inc. 248 Md 97, 234 A2d 875.
[5] Uniform Commercial Code § 2-210(2), (3).

When an obligee is entitled to assign his right, he may do so by his unilateral act. There is no requirement that the obligor consent or agree. Likewise, the act of assigning does not constitute a breach of the contract, unless the contract specifically declares so.

(a) Assignment increasing burden of performance. When the assigning of a right would increase the burden of the obligor in performing, the assignment is ordinarily not permitted. To illustrate, if the assignor has the right to buy a certain quantity of a stated article and to take such property from the seller's warehouse, this right to purchase can be assigned. If, however, the sales contract stipulated that the seller should deliver to the buyer's premises and the assignee lived or had his place of business a substantial distance from the assignor's place of business, the assignment would not be given effect. In this case, the seller would be required to give a performance different from that which he contracted to make.

(b) Personal satisfaction. A similar problem arises when the goods to be furnished must be satisfactory to the personal judgment of the buyer. Since the seller only contracted that his performance would stand or fall according to the buyer's judgment, the buyer may not substitute the judgment of his assignee.

(c) Personal services. An employer cannot assign to another the employer's right to have an employee work for him. The relationship of employer and employee is so personal that the right cannot be assigned. The performance contracted for by the employee was to work for a particular employer at a particular place and at a particular job. To permit an assignee to claim the employee's services would be to change that contract.

§ 17:8. **DELEGATION OF DUTIES.** A *delegation of duties* is a transfer of duties by a party to a contract to another person who is to perform them in his stead. Under certain circumstances a contracting party may obtain someone else to do the work for him. When the performance is standardized and nonpersonal so that it is not material who performs, the law will permit the delegation of the performance of the contract. In such cases, however, the contracting party remains liable for the default of the person doing the work just as though the contracting party himself had performed or attempted to perform the job.

If the performance by the promisor requires his personal skill or is a performance in which his credit standing or the other party's confidence in his ability was material in selecting him, delegation of performance is prohibited.

FACTS: The Industrial Construction Co. wanted to raise money to construct a canning factory in Wisconsin. Various persons promised to subscribe the needed amount which they agreed to pay when the construction was completed. The construction company assigned its rights under the agreement to Johnson, who then built the cannery. Vickers, one of the subscribers, refused to pay the amount he had subscribed on the ground that the contract could not be assigned.

DECISION: Judgment for Vickers. Since the construction of the canning factory called for the skill and experience of the builder and reliance upon him by the subscribers, the performance of the contract was a personal matter which could not be delegated by the builder without the consent of the subscribers. As Vickers had not consented to such assignment, Johnson had no rights by virtue of the attempted assignment and could not sue for the subscription. [Johnson v Vickers, 139 Wis 145, 120 NW 837]

(a) **Intention to delegate duties.** A question of interpretation arises as to whether an assignment of "the contract" is only an assignment of the rights of the assignor or is both an assignment of those rights and a delegation of his duties. The trend of authority is to regard such a general assignment as both a transfer of rights and a delegation of duties.

FACTS: Smith, who owned the Avalon Apartments, sold individual apartments under contracts that required each purchaser to pay $15 a month extra for hot and cold water, heat, refrigeration, taxes, and fire insurance. Smith assigned his interest in the apartment house and under the various contracts to Roberts. When Roberts failed to pay the taxes on the building, Radley and other tenants sued Roberts to compel her to do so.

DECISION: Judgment against Roberts. In the absence of a contrary indication, it is presumed that an "assignment" of a contract delegates the performance of the duties as well as transfers the rights. Here there was no indication that a "package" transfer was not intended, and the assignee was therefore obligated to perform in accordance with the contract terms. [Radley v Smith, 6 Utah2d 314, 313 P2d 465]

With respect to contracts for the sale of goods, "An assignment of 'the contract' or of 'all my rights under the contract' or an assignment in similar general terms is an assignment of rights and, unless the language or the circumstances (as in an assignment for security) indicate the contrary, it is a delegation of performance of the duties of the assignor and its acceptance by the assignee constitutes a promise by him to perform the duties. This promise is enforceable by either the assignor or the other party to the original contract."[6]

(b) **Novation.** One who is entitled to receive performance under a contract may agree to release the person who is bound to perform and to permit another person to take his place. When this occurs, it is not a question of merely assigning the liability under the contract but is really one of abandoning the old contract and substituting in its place a new contract. This change of contract is called a *novation*.

(c) **Continuing liability of assignor.** In the absence of a contrary agreement, such as a novation, an assignor continues to be bound by his obligations under the original contract. Thus, the fact that a buyer assigns

---

[6] UCC § 2-210(4).

his rights to goods under a contract does not terminate his liability to make payment to the seller.

§ 17:9. DEFENSES AND SETOFFS. The assignee's rights rise no higher than those of the assignor. If the obligor (the other party to the original contract) could successfully defend against a suit brought by the assignor, he will also prevail against the assignee.

The assigning of a right does not free it from any defense or setoff to which the right would be subject if it were still held by the assignor.

FACTS: McCaslin did plastering work in Nitzberg's home. He did not have a license to do the plastering work, and by statute he was barred from suing for the contract price for such work. McCaslin assigned his claim against Nitzberg to Walker, who then sued Nitzberg for the amount due for McCaslin's work.

DECISION: Judgment for Nitzberg. By virtue of the statute, McCaslin's lack of a license was a defense to recovery on the contract from Nitzberg. Walker, as assignee of McCaslin, had no greater right to sue than McCaslin. [Walker v Nitzberg, 13 CalApp3d 359, 91 CalRptr 526]

The fact that the assignee has given value for the assignment does not give the assignee any immunity from defenses which the other party, the obligor, could have asserted against the assignor. The assignee acquired his rights subject to any limitations thereon.

§ 17:10. NOTICE OF ASSIGNMENT. An assignment, if otherwise valid, takes effect the moment it is made. It is not necessary that the assignee or the assignor give notice to the other party to the contract that the assignment has been made. It is highly desirable, however, that the other party be notified as soon as possible after the making of the assignment.

(a) Defenses and setoffs. Notice of an assignment prevents the obligor from asserting against the assignee any defense or setoff arising after such notice with respect to a matter not related to the assigned claim.

(1) Post-notice Matters. If the matter relates to the assigned claim, the fact of notice does not affect the right of the obligor to assert against the assignee any defense or setoff that would have been available were he sued by the assignor.

For example, O owns two lots of ground, No. 1 and No. 2. O makes two separate contracts with C, a paving contractor, to pave these two lots. C assigns to A his right to be paid for lot No. 1 before he has performed that contract, and A notifies O of the assignment. After making the assignment, C paves both lots but does a poor job on each. When A sues O for the contract price for lot No. 1, O claims a setoff for the damages suffered by him because of the poor work on lots No. 1 and No. 2. The poor work defense with respect to lot No. 1 is obviously related to the claim for the contract price for paving lot No. 1. That defense or setoff may therefore be asserted by O against A, without regard to when the paving was done or when notice of the assignment was given to *O*.

In contrast, the claim of *O* for damages because of the poor work done on lot No. 2 is not related to the claim that was assigned to *A*. Consequently, the giving of notice of the assignment to *O* cut off the right of *O* to assert against *A* any claim which would thereafter arise with respect to an unrelated matter. Since *O* knew of the assignment of the lot No. 1 contract claim before there was any breach as to lot No. 2, *O* cannot assert his defense with respect to lot No. 2 against *A*.[7]

(2) Prenotice Matters. The only way in which the assignee can be protected from defenses and setoffs arising before notice of assignment has been given is to ask the obligor whether there is any defense or setoff or counterclaim against the assignor. If the obligor states that there is none or makes a declaration of no setoff, he is estopped (barred) from contradicting that statement and is not permitted to prove a defense, setoff, or counterclaim based on facts existing prior to the time of the statement to the assignee.

(b) Discharge. Until the obligor knows that there has been an assignment, he is legally entitled to pay to or perform for the assignor just as though there were no assignment. Such payment or performance is a complete discharge of his obligation under the contract; but in such a case the assignee could proceed against the assignor to require him to account for what he had received. If the assignee has given the obligor notice of the assignment, however, the obligor cannot discharge his obligation to the assignee by making a payment to or a performance for the asignor.

If the debtor, knowing of the assignment, pays the assignor, the assignee may sue either the assignor or the debtor. The payment by the latter with knowledge of the existence of the assignment does not discharge his debt, and the assignor is deemed to have received payment from the debtor on behalf of the assignee.

The notice here considered must relate to the particular claim against the defendant. Thus, knowledge that a business enterprise was obtaining refinancing on the basis of its accounts receivable was not a notice to the debtor of one of the accounts that that account had been assigned to the lending agency.

(c) Priority. If a person assigns the same right to two different assignees, the question arises as to which assignee has obtained the right. By the American rule, the assignee taking the first assignment prevails over the subsequent assignees.

§ 17:11. WARRANTIES OF ASSIGNOR. When the assignment is made for a consideration, the assignor is regarded as impliedly warranting that the right he assigns is valid, that he is the owner of the claim which he assigns,

---

[7] UCC § 9-318(1); Dickerson v Federal Deposit Insurance Corp. (FlaApp) 244 So2d 748.

and that he will not interfere with the assignee's enforcement of the obligation. He does not warrant that the other party will pay or perform as required.

QUESTIONS AND CASE PROBLEMS

1. Rexroad contracted with the City of Assaria to improve certain streets within the city. The contract specified that "the contractor shall be liable for all damages to buildings . . . located outside the construction limits (and shall) make amicable settlement of such damage claims. . . ." Anderson, whose house was damaged by the construction work, sued Rexroad for the damages. The latter defended on the ground that Anderson did not have any agreement with him and had not given him any consideration. Decide. [Anderson v Rexroad, 175 Kan 676, 266 P2d 320]

2. McGilco, a building contractor, applied to the Great Southern Savings & Loan Ass'n for a loan to pay for the paving work in the Park Crest Village Development. This paving was done by Stephens. Great Southern agreed to lend the money to McGilco but failed to do so. McGilco did not pay Stephens. Stephens then sued Great Southern for the breach of its contract to lend money to McGilco. Was Stephens entitled to recover in this action? [Stephens v Great Southern Savings & Loan Ass'n (MoApp) 421 SW2d 332]

3. The City of Moab owed Holder for construction work. Holder assigned his claim against the City to Cooper. Cooper gave the City notice that the claim had been assigned to him and demanded payment. The City refused to pay Cooper but paid Holder instead. Cooper sued Holder for such payment. Was Cooper entitled to recover? [Cooper v Holder, 21 Utah2d 40, 440 P2d 15]

4. Enos had a policy of insurance with the Franklin Casualty Insurance Company providing for the payment of all reasonable hospitalization expenses up to $500 for each person injured while a passenger in, or upon entering or leaving, the insured's automobile. Wagner, a guest in the automobile, was injured in a highway accident. She was treated by Dr. Jones, who then sued the insurer to obtain payment. Decide. [Franklin Casualty Insurance Company v Jones (Okla) 362 P2d 964]

5. The City of New Rochelle Humane Society made a contract with the City of New Rochelle to capture and impound all dogs running at large. Spiegler, a minor, was bitten by some dogs while in the school yard. She sued the School District of New Rochelle and the Humane Society. With respect to the Humane Society, she claimed that she was a third party beneficiary of the contract that the Society had made with the City and could therefore sue it for its failure to capture the dogs by which she had been bitten. Was she entitled to recover? [Spiegler v School District, 39 Misc2d 946, 242 NYS2d 430]

6. Ewin Engineering Corporation owed money to Girod. The latter borrowed money from the Deposit Guaranty Bank & Trust Co. and assigned to it as security for the loan the claim he held against Ewin. The bank immediately notified Ewin of the assignment. Thereafter Ewin paid Girod the balance due him. Ewin then

notified the bank that it had paid Girod in full and that it refused to recognize the assignment. The bank sued Ewin. Could it recover? [Ewin Engineering Corp. v Deposit Guaranty Bank & Trust Co. 216 Miss 410, 62 So2d 572]

7. A buyer purchased goods on credit from a seller. Unknown to the buyer, the seller assigned to a finance company his right to the purchase price. Thereafter, the buyer, without knowledge of the assignment, returned the goods to the seller who accepted them and canceled the buyer's debt. The finance company sued the buyer for the purchase price which had been assigned to it and claimed that it was not bound by the act of the seller. Was he entitled to recover the purchase price from the buyer? [See Peoples Finance & Thrift Co. v Landes, 28 Utah2d 392, 503 P2d 444]

8. Tennefos Construction Company did highway construction work for the North Dakota Highway Department. Alexander supplied them with fill for the construction. Alexander owed money to Rheault who supplied him with oil and fuel. Rheault would not supply Alexander further unless payment of his debts was guaranteed. It was finally agreed that when Tennefos paid for the fill, the checks would be made payable to the order of Rheault and Alexander. Was there an assignment to Rheault? [Rheault v Tennefos Construction Co. (ND) 189 NW2d 626]

9. Hardin County entered into a contract with Pettigrew & Finney Contracting Co. to install air conditioning in a building owned by the county. The contractor, with the New Amsterdam Casualty Co., executed a performance bond and a labor and material bond naming the county as obligee. By the labor and material bond, the contractor and its surety promised to pay for all labor and materials used in performing the contract. The contractor then subcontracted all nonelectrical work in the project to T. O. Morris. Morris obtained equipment and materials from Air Temperature, Inc. The latter was not paid and it brought suit against Morris, the contractor, and the surety. Neither the contractor nor the surety had any direct dealings with Air Temperature. At the time when Air Temperature furnished the goods to Morris, Air Temperature did not know that the contractor and the surety had executed bonds and Air Temperature had not acted in reliance on the existence of any bonds. Were the contractor and the surety liable to Air Temperature? [Air Temperature Inc. v Morris, 63 TennApp 90, 469 SW2d 495]

10. A purchased B's business. A orally agreed to pay the business debts of B. C had sold goods to B for B's store but had not been paid. C sued A. A raised the defense that he was not liable because there was no writing for his promise to pay B's debt and the statute of frauds made an oral promise to pay the debt of another unenforceable. Was this a valid defense? [See Campbell v Hickory Farms of Ohio, 258 SC 563, 190 SE2d 26]

DISCHARGE
OF CONTRACTS

§ 18:1. **INTRODUCTION.** A contract is usually discharged by the performance of the terms of the agreement, but termination may also occur by later agreement, impossibility of performance, operation of law, or acceptance of breach.

In most cases the parties perform their promises and the contract is discharged by performance of its terms. If a dispute arises as to whether there has been performance, the party claiming that he has performed has the burden of proving that fact.

§ 18:2. DISCHARGE BY PERFORMANCE.

(a) Payment. When payment is required by the contract, performance consists of the payment of money or, if accepted by the other party, the delivery of property or the rendering of services.

Payment by commercial paper, such as a check, is ordinarily a conditional payment. A check merely suspends the debt until it is presented for payment. If payment is then made, the debt is discharged; if not paid, suit may be brought on either the debt or the check.[1]

(1) Application of Payments. If a debtor owes more than one debt to the creditor and pays him money, a question may arise as to which debt has been paid. If the debtor specifies the debt to which his payment is to be applied and the creditor accepts the money, the creditor is bound to apply the money as specified. Thus, if the debtor specifies that a payment is made for a current purchase, the creditor may not apply the payment to an older balance.

If the debtor does not specify the application to be made, the creditor may apply the payment to any one or more of the debts in such manner as he chooses. As between secured and unsecured claims, the creditor is free to apply the payment to the unsecured claim. The creditor, however, must apply the payment to a debt that is due as contrasted with one which is not

---

[1] Uniform Commercial Code § 3-802(1)(b).

yet due. He cannot apply a payment to a claim that is illegal or invalid; but he may apply the payment to a claim which cannot be enforced because it is barred by the statute of limitations and, according to some authority, to a claim that cannot be enforced for want of a writing required by the statute of frauds.

If neither the debtor nor the creditor has made any application of the payment, application will be made by the court. There is a division of authority, however, whether the court is to make such application as will be more favorable to the creditor or the debtor. The courts tend to favor the latter view when the rights of third persons are involved, such as the rights of those furnishing the money for the payment. In some instances the court will apply the payment to the oldest outstanding debt.

(b) Time of Performance. When the date or period of time for performance is stipulated, performance should be made on that date or in that time period.

> FACTS: The Tinchers signed a contract to sell land to Creasy. The contract specified that the sales transaction was to be completed in 90 days. At the end of the 90 days, Creasy requested an extension of time. The Tinchers refused to grant an extension and stated that the contract was terminated. Creasy sued the Tinchers to compel specific performance of the agreement.

> DECISION: Judgment for Tinchers. The provision for completion of the contract in 90 days made time of the essence and therefore Creasy was not entitled to an extension. His failure to act within the specified time discharged the contract duty of the Tinchers. [Creasy v Tincher 154 WVa 18, 173 SE2d 332]

Performance may usually be made later than the contract date, however, unless the nature or terms of the contract indicate clearly that time of performance is vital, as in the case of contracts for the purchase or sale of property of a fluctuating value.[2] When time is vital, it is said to be "of the essence."

Ordinarily, time is not of the essence. Performance within a reasonable time is sufficient, and if no time is specified, an obligation to perform within a reasonable time will be implied.[3]

In the case of the sale of property, time will not be regarded as of the essence when there has not been any appreciable change in the market value or condition of the property and when the person who delayed does not appear to have done so for the purpose of speculating on a change in market value.

> FACTS: The Federal Sign Co. installed an outdoor tower and sign for Fort Worth Motors under a contract that included five years' maintenance. It also specified that the sign company would repair the sign, if possible,

---

[2] Mercury Gas & Oil Corp. v Rincon Oil & Gas Corp. 79 NMex 537, 445 P2d 958.
[3] Time can be made of the essence by imposing a time limitation on performance.

within 24 normal working hours after notice of any damage to the sign. The sign was blown down in a windstorm. The sign company knew of this the same day but failed to repair the sign. Fort Worth Motors sued the sign company for damages three months later. Two months thereafter, while the suit was pending, the sign company stated that it would replace the sign.

DECISION: Judgment for Fort Worth Motors. The obligation to repair the sign within 24 normal working hours, if possible, after notice of damage made time of the essence. Since there was nothing to show that impossibility excused performance, the company had broken its contract by failing to make timely performance. [Federal Sign Co. v Fort Worth Motors (TexCivApp) 314 SW2d 878]

In some contracts the time of performance is conditional, that is, it depends upon the happening of a particular event, the failure of a certain event to happen, or the existence of a certain fact. If the condition is not fulfilled, the promisor has no obligation to perform. To illustrate, a fire insurance policy does not impose any duty for performance on the insurance company until there is a loss within the coverage of the contract. Thus, there may be no performance by the company during the life of the contract.

Statutes may provide that a contract shall not be forfeited because of a provision making time of the essence when the complaining party is not harmed by the delay and has been fully compensated.

(c) **Tender of performance.** An offer to perform is known as a *tender*. If performance requires the doing of an act, a tender that is refused will discharge the party offering to perform. If performance requires the payment of a debt, however, a tender that is refused does not discharge the obligation. But it stops the running of interest charges and prevents the collection of court costs if the party is sued, providing the tender is kept open and the money is produced in court.

A *valid tender of payment* consists of an unconditional offer of the exact amount due on the date when due or an amount from which the creditor may take what is due without the necessity of making change. It is unnecessary for the debtor to produce the money, however, if the creditor informs him in advance that he will not accept it. The debtor must offer *legal tender* or, in other words, such form of money as the law recognizes as lawful money and declares to be legal tender for the payment of debts. The offer of a check is not a valid tender of payment since a check is not legal tender. A tender of part of the debt is not a valid tender.

A tender of less than the total amount due has no legal effect unless the creditor accepts it. In addition to the amount owed, the debtor must tender all accrued interest and any costs to which the creditor is entitled. If the debtor tenders less than the amount due, the creditor may refuse the offer without affecting his rights in any way. If he accepts it, the question then arises whether it is accepted as a payment on account or in full payment of the balance due.

§ 18:3. ADEQUACY OF PERFORMANCE.

(a) **Substantial performance.** If the plaintiff in good faith substantially performed the contract, he can sue the other party for payment. He then recovers the contract price subject to a counterclaim for the damages caused the other party by the plaintiff's failure to perform to the letter of the contract.

This *rule of substantial performance* applies only when the departures from the contract or the defects are not made willfully.[4] If the contractor makes a substantial willful departure from the contract, he is in default and cannot recover from the other party to the contract.

FACTS: Deck, who had a well 650 feet deep, made a contract with Hammer to drill another well for water to the depth of 1,000 feet. He drilled to the depth of 701 feet and then stopped because of unexpected rock formation. Hammer claimed that he was entitled to be paid under his contract.

DECISION: Hammer was not entitled to payment. He had not performed as required by the contract, and what he had done could not be regarded as substantial performance of his contract obligation. [Deck v Hammer, 7 ArizApp 466, 440 P2d 1006]

In the case of large construction contracts when the total value of the partial performance is large compared to the damages sustained through incomplete or imperfect performance, the courts tend to ignore whether or not the breach was intentional on the part of the contractor.

(b) **Satisfaction of promisee or third person.** When the agreement requires that the promisor perform an act to the satisfaction, taste, or judgment of the other party on the contract, the courts are divided as to whether the promisor must so perform as to satisfy the promisee or whether it is sufficient that he perform in a way that would satisfy a reasonable person under the circumstances. When personal taste is an important element, the courts generally hold that the performance is not sufficient unless the promisee is actually satisfied, although in some instances it is insisted that the dissatisfaction be shown to be in good faith and not merely to avoid paying for the work that has been done.[5] The personal satisfaction of the promisee is generally required under this rule when one promises to make clothes or to paint a portrait to the satisfaction of the other party.

There is a similar division of authority when the subject matter involves the fitness or mechanical utility of the property. With respect to things mechanical and to routine performances, however, the courts are more likely to hold that the promisor has satisfactorily performed if a reasonable person should be satisfied with what was done.

---

[4] Lautenbach v Meredith, 240 Iowa 166, 35 SW2d 335.

[5] Commercial Mortgage & Finance Corp. v Greenwich Savings Bank, 112 GaApp 388, 145 SE2d 249; American Oil Co. v Carey (DC ED Mich) 246 FSupp 773.

FACTS: Johnson was operating a school bus for School District #12 under a two-year written contract which specified that Johnson "is to have option for next 3 years if a bus is run and his service has been satisfactory." At the end of the two-year period Johnson notified the School District that he had elected to exercise the option, but the School District refused to renew the contract. Johnson sued the School District for breach of the option provision. It raised the defense that it was not satisfied with his services and therefore there was no option to renew.

DECISION: This was not a defense. When a contract requires "satisfactory" performance, it merely requires performance satisfactory to a reasonable man unless it is clear from the terms or circumstances that "personal" satisfaction is required. Here it should be the "reasonable-person" test since there was no evidence to the contrary. [Johnson v School District #12, 210 Ore 585, 312 P2d 591]

When a building contract requires the contractor to perform the contract to the "satisfaction" of the owner, the owner generally is required to pay if a reasonable person would be satisfied with the work of the contractor.

Similarly, when a building owner makes a contract for painting and paperhanging, and the contract specifies that "work will be completed in the best workmanship manner by union skillful craftsmen," the work is properly performed when it conforms to the standards specified and the owner cannot avoid liability on the ground that he in fact was not satisfied with the work.

When performance is to be approved by a third person, the tendency is to apply the reasonable-person test of satisfaction, especially when the third person has wrongfully withheld his approval or has become incapacitated.

When work is to be done subject to the approval of an architect, engineer, or other expert, ordinarily his determination is final and binding upon the parties in the absence of fraud.

§ 18:4. GUARANTEE OF PERFORMANCE. It is common for an obligor to guarantee his performance. Thus, a builder may guarantee for one year that the workmanship will be satisfactory.

The guarantee may be made by a third person. Thus, the surety company may guarantee to the owner that a contractor will perform his contract. In such case, it is clear that the obligation of the surety is in addition to the liability of the contractor and does not take the place of such liability.

§ 18:5. CONSUMER PROTECTION RESCISSION. Contrary to the basic principle of contract law that a contract between competent persons is a binding obligation, consumer protection legislation is introducing into the law a new concept of giving the consumer a chance to think things over and to rescind the contract. Thus the federal Consumer Credit Protection Act

(CCPA) gives a debtor the right to rescind a credit transaction within three days when the transaction would impose a lien upon his home.[6]

The same concept of rescission to protect the consumer is found in the provision of the Uniform Consumer Credit Code, which gives a customer three days in which to avoid any contract for goods or services made in his home by the personal solicitation of the seller or the seller's agent.[7] The seller must inform the buyer of his right to cancel; and if he fails to do so, the right of the buyer to cancel continues and is not terminated by the expiration of the three days.[8]

Under the UCCC the debtor may ordinarily rescind a home solicitation sale of goods or services. Some local statutes, however, are limited to particular transactions.

§ 18:6. DISCHARGE BY AGREEMENT. A contract may be terminated by the operation of one of its provisions or by a subsequent agreement.

(a) Provision of original contract. The contract may provide that it shall terminate upon the happening of a certain event, such as the destruction of a particular building, or upon the existence of a certain fact, even though the intended performance by one party or both parties has not been completed. Notice to terminate must be clear and definite.

When a contract provides for a continuing performance but does not specify how long it shall continue, it is terminable at the will of either party, with the same consequence as though it had expressly authorized termination upon notice.

FACTS: Youngstown Sheet & Tube Co. made a contract to employ Pearson. After continuing to work for 28 years, at which time Pearson could not obtain other employment, he was discharged by Youngstown. He claimed that the contract entitled him to permanent employment.

DECISION: The contract for indefinite employment was terminable at will, even though it had continued for a long time and even though termination would be prejudicial to Pearson. [Pearson v Youngstown Sheet & Tube Co. (CA7 Ind) 332 F2d 439]

(b) Rescission by agreement. The parties to a contract may agree to undo the contract and place each one in his original position by returning any property or money that had been delivered or paid. It is said that they agree to rescind the contract or that there is a *mutual rescission*. Ordinarily no formality is required for rescission; and an oral rescission, or conduct

---

[6] Consumer Credit Protection Act § 125; 15 United States Code § 1635(a), (e), although it would appear that this section has been to a large extent canceled by the regulation of the Federal Reserve Board permitting the debtor to waive his right of rescission. Regulation Z, § 226.9(e), 12 CFR 226. Likewise the statute does not permit a home buyer to avoid a lien created in the financing of his purchase. If the creditor does not inform the debtor of his right to rescind at the time of the transaction or make the other disclosures required by federal law, the time within which the debtor may rescind is extended until such disclosures are made. § 226.9(a).

[7] Uniform Consumer Credit Code § 2.502. The seller may retain a cancellation fee of 5 percent of the cash price but not exceeding the amount of the cash down payment. § 2.504.

[8] UCCC § 2.503.

evidencing such an intent, may terminate a written contract. An oral rescission is not effective, however, in the case of a sale of an interest in land; for, in such a case, the purpose of the rescission is to retransfer the interest in land. Accordingly, the retransfer or rescission must satisfy the same formalities of the statute of frauds as are applied to the original transfer.

A mutual rescission works a final discharge of the contract in the absence of an express provision in the rescission agreement providing for the later revival of the original contract. Consequently, when there is a mutual rescission of a sales contract following a fire which destroyed the seller's factory, the contract is not revived by the subsequent rebuilding of the factory.[9] If an agreement is voidable because of the fraud of one of the parties, the aggrieved or complaining party may obtain a decree from the court rescinding the contract. This is distinct, however, from rescission based on the agreement of the parties.

(c) **Waiver.** A term of a contractual obligation is discharged by *waiver* when one party fails to demand performance by the other party or to object when the other party fails to perform according to the terms of the contract. Unlike rescission, a waiver does not return the parties to their original positions; it leaves the parties where they are at the time.

(d) **Substitution.** The parties may decide that their contract is not the one they want. They may then replace it with another contract. If they do so, the original contract is discharged by substitution.

It is not necessary that the parties expressly state that they are making a substitution. Whenever they make a new contract that is clearly inconsistent with a former contract, the court will assume that the earlier contract has been superseded by the later. Since the new contract must in itself be a binding agreement, it must be supported by consideration. The agreement modifying the original contract may be expressed by words or by conduct, but in any event, it is essential that an agreement to modify be found.

(e) **Novation.** In a novation, as explained in Chapter 17, the original contract may be discharged by the new contract. When a party's liability under a contract is discharged by a novation, he cannot thereafter sue to enforce a contract or to recover damages for its breach.

(f) **Accord and satisfaction.** In lieu of the performance of an obligation specified by a contract, the parties may agree to a different performance. Such an agreement is called an *accord*. When the accord is performed or executed, there is an *accord and satisfaction*, which discharges the original obligation. An accord is not binding until the satisfaction is made. Either party may therefore revoke an accord agreeing upon the payment to be made before it has been made.

(g) **Release.** A person who has a contract claim or any other kind of claim against another may agree to give up or release his claim against the other.

---

[9] Goddard v Ishikawajima-Harima Heavy Industries Co. 27 Misc2d 863, 287 NYS2d 901.

This may be done by delivering a writing which states that the claim is released. At common law, this writing destroyed or extinguished the releasor's claim, with the consequence that a release of one obligor would also discharge a joint obligor. To avoid this result, a releasor will today often execute a written promise not to sue the adverse party. Such a *covenant not to sue* is binding and bars suit against the adverse party but does not bar the one who makes the covenant from suing other persons.

Ordinarily there will be a preliminary agreement to deliver a written release or covenant not to sue for which payment will be made. Generally the preliminary agreement is not a binding contract because it is contemplated that the obligee shall not be bound until he has delivered the writing and has been paid.

§ 18:7. DISCHARGE BY IMPOSSIBILITY.

Impossibility of performance refers to external or extrinsic conditions as contrasted with the obligor's personal inability to perform. Thus, the fact that a debtor cannot pay his debt because he does not have the money does not present a case of impossibility.

Likewise, riots, shortages of materials, and similar factors usually do not excuse the promisor from performing his contract. The fact that the seller who sold property not owned by him has not been able to purchase it from its owner does not excuse him from his obligation to his buyer. The fact that it will prove more costly to perform the contract than originally contemplated, or that the obligor has voluntarily gone out of business, does not constitute impossibility which excuses performance. No distinction is made in this connection between acts of nature, man, or governments.

FACTS: The Transatlantic Financing Corp. made a contract with the United States to haul a cargo of wheat from the United States to a safe port in Iran. The normal route lay through the Suez Canal. As the result of the nationalization of the Canal by Egypt and the subsequent international crisis which developed, the Canal was closed and it was necessary for Transatlantic to go around Africa to get to the destination. It then sued for additional compensation because of the longer route on the theory that it had been discharged from its obligation to carry to Iran for the amount named in the contract because of "impossibility."

DECISION: Judgment for United States. Although impossibility does not mean literally impossible, it may be apparent from the contract that the risk of performance becoming commercially impracticable was assumed by one of the parties, in which case such impracticality is necessarily not a defense which that party may raise. As no route was specified and everyone was aware of the problems of international shipping, the unqualified contract to deliver the cargo at a specified point must be interpreted as indicating that the carrier assumed the risk that the shorter route through the Suez Canal might not be available; the carrier thus assumed the risk of "impossibility." [Transatlantic Financing Corp. v United States (CA DistCol) 363 F2d 312]

Frequently this problem is met by a provision of the contract that expressly excuses a contractor or provides for extra compensation in the event of certain unforeseen or changed conditions. A party seeking to excuse himself by, or to claim the benefit of, such a clause has the burden of establishing the facts that justify its application.

Interference with the performance of a contract by fire does not excuse performance. Consequently, when a contractor is constructing a building and it is destroyed by fire, he must rebuild the building at his own expense or the expense of his insurer. The fire does not excuse him from performing his contract. The inability to obtain a government license or approval is not an "impossibility" which discharges the contract when the necessity of obtaining such license or approval was foreseeable.[10]

When the condition or event that is claimed to have made performance impossible is the result of foreseeable wartime conditions, a party is not excused because of the occurrence of such condition or event. By failing to have made express provision therefor in the contract, he must be regarded as having assumed that risk.

(a) Destruction of particular subject matter. When the parties contract expressly for or with reference to a particular subject matter, the contract is discharged if the subject matter is destroyed through no fault of either party. When a contract calls for the sale of a wheat crop growing on a specific parcel of land, the contract is discharged if that crop is destroyed by blight.

On the other hand, if there is merely a contract to sell a given quantity of a specified grade of wheat, the seller is not discharged because his wheat crop is destroyed by blight. The seller makes an absolute undertaking.

(b) Change of law. A contract is discharged when its performance is made illegal by a subsequent change in the law of the state or country in which the contract is to be performed. Thus, a contract to construct a nonfireproof building at a particular place is discharged by the adoption of a zoning law prohibiting such a building within that area. Mere inconvenience or temporary delay caused by the new law, however, does not excuse performance.

(c) Death or disability. When the contract obligates a party to perform an act that requires personal skill or which contemplates a personal relationship with the obligee or some other person, the death or disability of the obligor, obligee, or other person (as the case may be) discharges the contract, as when a newspaper cartoonist dies before the expiration of his contract. If the act called for by the contract can be performed by others or by the promisor's personal representative, however, this rule does not apply.

The death of the person to whom personal services are to be rendered also terminates the contract when the death of that person makes impossible the rendition of the services contemplated. Thus, a contract to employ a person as the musical director for a singer terminates when the singer dies.

---

[10] Nebaco, Inc. v Riverview Realty Co. 87 Nev 55, 482 P2d 305.

When the contract calls for the payment of money, the death of either party does not affect the obligation. If the obligor dies, the obligation is a liability of his estate. If the obligee dies, the right to collect the debt is an asset of his estate. The parties to a contract may agree, however, that the death of either the obligee [11] or the obligor shall terminate the debt. In the latter case, the creditor can obtain insurance on the life of the debtor so that while he loses the debt upon the debtor's death, he is paid by the proceeds of the insurance on the debtor's life.

(d) Act of other party. There is in every contract "an implied covenant of good faith and fair dealing" in consequence of which a promisee is under an obligation to do nothing that would interfere with performance by the promisor. When the promisee prevents performance or otherwise makes performance impossible, the promisor is discharged from his contract. Thus, a subcontractor is discharged from his obligation when he is unable to do the work because the principal contractor refuses to deliver to him the material, equipment, or money as required by the subcontract. When the default of the other party consists of failing to supply goods or services, the duty may rest upon the party claiming a discharge of the contract to show that he could not have obtained substitute goods or services elsewhere, either because they were not reasonably available or were not acceptable under the terms of the contract.

When the conduct of the other contracting party does not make performance impossible but merely causes delay or renders performance more expensive, the contract is not discharged; but the injured party is entitled to damages for the loss that he incurs.

Acts of third parties do not constitute an excuse for failing to perform a contract.

FACTS: La Gasse Pool Construction Company made a contract with the City of Fort Lauderdale to renovate and resurface a swimming pool. When the work was almost completely performed, vandals damaged the pool. The contractor did the work over again and billed the City for the additional work. The City refused to pay for such additional work. The contractor sued the City.

DECISION: Judgment for the City. The contractor was bound to complete the performance that he had contracted to render. While the acts of the vandals made this more expensive, it did not excuse the contractor nor entitle him to any additional compensation. [La Gasse Pool Construction Co. v Fort Lauderdale (FlaApp) 288 So2d 273]

A promisor is not excused from his contract when it is his own act which has made performance impossible. Consequently, when a data service contracted with a bank to keypunch all its daily operations and to process the cards, the bank was not excused from its obligation under the contract by the fact that it converted to magnetic tapes and installed its own computers. Accordingly the bank could not ignore its contract. It could

---

[11] Woods v McQueen, 195 Kan 380, 404 P2d 955.

only terminate the contract with the data service by giving the notice required by the contract.

§ **18:8. ECONOMIC FRUSTRATION.** In order to protect from the hardship imposed by the strict principles relating to impossibility, some courts excuse performance on the ground of *economic frustration* as distinguished from impossibility.

The effect of the economic frustration concept is to substitute "impracticability" for "impossibility," and to regard performance as impracticable, and therefore excused, when it can only be done at an excessive and unreasonable cost. When property is leased in order to use the building for a particular purpose, some courts hold that the lease is discharged when the building burns down, on the theory that the purpose of the lease has been frustrated.[12] The doctrine of frustration will not be applied to protect a party who has taken a calculated risk and lost.

> **FACTS:** McCants and others wished to form a federal savings and loan association. They rented office space from the North American Capital Corporation by a lease which specified that the premises could only be used as an office for the proposed federal savings and loan association. In order to operate such an enterprise, approval was required by the Federal Home Loan Bank Board. The Board refused to give permission to McCants. The rent was not paid to North American. It sued for the rent. McCants raised the defense that he and others were released from liability for the rent because of the refusal of the government agency caused a frustration of the purpose of the lease.
>
> **DECISION:** The defense of frustration of commercial purpose requires (1) a total or near total destruction of the purpose of the contract by (2) a cause arising outside of the contemplation of the parties at the time of contracting. The refusal of the government agency to approve the location was not wholly outside of the contemplation of the parties and therefore the tenant did not satisfy the second of the two conditions and could not raise the defense of commercial frustration. [North American Capital Corp. v McCants (Tenn) 510 SW2d 901]

§ **18:9. TEMPORARY IMPOSSIBILITY.** Ordinarily a temporary impossibility has either no effect on the obligation to perform of the party who is affected thereby, or at most suspends his duty to perform so that the obligation to perform is revived upon the termination of the impossibility. If, however, performance at that later date would impose a substantially greater burden upon the obligor, some courts excuse him from performing at that time.

(a) Weather. Acts of God, such as tornadoes, lightning, and sudden floods, usually do not terminate a contract even though they make performance difficult or impossible. Thus, weather conditions constitute a

---

[12] Jones v Fuller-Garvey Corp. (Alaska) 386 P2d 838. In some jurisdictions, this result is reached by statute authorizing the termination of the lease in such a case. At common law the destruction of the building did not discharge the obligation of the tenant.

risk that is assumed by a contracting party in the absence of a contrary agreement. Consequently, extra expense sustained by a contractor because of weather conditions is a risk which the contractor assumes in the absence of an express provision that he is entitled to additional compensation in such case.

Modern contracts commonly contain a "weather" clause, which either expressly grants an extension for delays caused by weather conditions or expressly denies the right to any extension of time or additional compensation because of weather condition difficulties. Some courts hold that abnormal weather conditions excuse what would otherwise be a breach of contract. Thus, nondelivery of equipment has been excused when the early melting of a frozen river made it impossible to deliver.

§ 18:10. DISCHARGE BY OPERATION OF LAW.
In certain situations the law provides for the discharge of a contract, such as when the contract has been altered, has been destroyed by the obligee, is subject to bankruptcy proceedings, or exceeds the statutes of limitations.

(a) Alteration. A written contract, whether under seal or not, may be discharged by alteration.[13] To have this effect, (1) it must be a *material alteration*, that is, it must change the nature of the obligation; (2) it must be made by a party to the contract, because alterations made by a stranger have no effect; (3) it must be made intentionally, and not through accident or mistake; and (4) it must be made without the consent of the other party to the contract. For example, when one party to an advertising contract, without the consent of the other party, added "at a monthly payment basis," thus making the rate of payment higher, the advertiser was discharged from any duty under the contract.

There is no discharge of the contract by alteration when the term added is one which the law would imply, for in such a case the change is not material.

(b) Destruction of the contract. The physical destruction of a written contract may be a discharge of the contract. When the person entitled to performance under a sealed instrument destroys the writing with the intent to terminate the liability of the obligor, the latter's liability is discharged. In any case, the physical destruction of the writing may be evidence of an intention to discharge the obligation by mutual agreement.

FACTS: J. A. Reed and his wife, Bertha, signed a contract the day before they were married. Several months after their marriage, Reed, with the participation of Bertha and without any objection from her, destroyed the contract by burning it in a stove. After his death, Bertha claimed the contract was still in force.

DECISION: The contract had been discharged by the physical destruction of the contract with the mutual consent of the parties. [In re Reed's Estate (Mo) 414 SW2d 283]

---

[13] The definition and effect of alteration in the case of commercial paper has been modified by UCC § 3-407.

(c) Merger. In some instances contract rights are merged into or absorbed by a greater right. When an action is brought upon a contract and a judgment is obtained by the plaintiff against the defendant, the contract claim is merged into the judgment.

(d) Bankruptcy. Most debtors may voluntarily enter into a federal court of bankruptcy or be compelled to do so by creditors. The trustee in bankruptcy then takes possession of the debtor's property and distributes it as far as it will go among his creditors. After this is done, the court grants the debtor a discharge in bankruptcy if it concludes that he had acted honestly and had not attempted to defraud his creditors.

Even though all creditors have not been paid in full, the discharge in bankruptcy is a bar to the subsequent enforcement of their ordinary contract claims against the debtor. The cause of action or contract claim is not destroyed, but the bankruptcy discharge bars a proceeding to enforce it. Since the obligation is not extinguished, the debtor may waive the defense of discharge in bankruptcy by promising later to pay the debt. Such a waiver is governed by state law. In a few states waiver must be in writing.

(e) Statutes of limitations. Statutes provide that after a certain number of years have passed a contract claim is barred. Technically, this is merely a bar of the remedy and does not destroy the right or cause of action. A few states hold that the statute bars the right as well as the remedy and that there is accordingly no contract after the lapse of the statutory period.

The time limitations provided by the state statutes of limitations vary widely. The period usually differs with the type of contract—ranging from a relatively short period for open accounts (ordinary customers' charge accounts), usually 3 to 5 years; to a somewhat longer period for written contracts, usually 5 to 10 years; to a maximum period for judgments for record, usually 10 to 20 years. In the case of a contract for a sale of goods, the time period is 4 years.[14]

The statute of limitations begins to run the moment that the cause of action of the plaintiff arises, that is, when he is first entitled to bring suit. When the party entitled to sue is under a disability, such as insanity, at the time the cause of action arises, the period of the statute does not begin to run until the disability is removed. When a condition or act prevents the period of the statute of limitations from running, it is said to *toll the running of the statute.*

Statutes of limitations do not run against governments because it is contrary to public policy that the rights of society generally, as represented by the government, should be prejudiced by the failure of the proper governmental officials to take the necessary action to enforce the claims of the government.

The defense of a statute of limitations may be waived by the debtor. The waiver must ordinarily be an express promise to pay or such an acknowledgment of the existence of the debt that the law can imply from the acknowledgment a promise to pay the debt. In some states the promise

---

[14] UCC § 2-725(1).

or acknowledgment must be in writing. Part payment of the principal or interest is also regarded as a waiver of the bar of the statute and revives the debt.

Some contracts, particularly insurance contracts, contain a time limitation within which suit may be brought. This is, in effect, a private statute of limitations created by agreement of the parties. When a party fails to give notice within the time specified by the contract, he is barred from suing thereon and his noncompliance is not excused by the fact that he wrongly believed that he did not have any claim about which to give notice.

FACTS: The State Bank of Viroqua obtained a banker's blanket bond from the Capitol Indemnity Corporation to protect it from loss by forgery. The bond required that the bank give the insurer notice of any loss at "the earliest practicable moment." DeLap borrowed money from the bank by means of paper on which he forged the name of Mellem. This was learned in October, 1969. In October, 1970, an agent of Capitol was discussing the bond with the bank. The bank then realized for the first time that the bond covered the DeLap forgery loss. Fifteen days later the bank notified Capitol of that claim. Capitol denied liability because of the delay. The bank sued Capitol.

DECISION: The bank was barred as it had not given notice at the earliest practicable moment after it knew that a loss had been sustained. The failure of the bank to realize sooner that it had a claim under the contract did not excuse it from complying therewith. [State Bank of Viroqua v Capitol Indemnity Corp. 61Wis2d 699, 214 NW2d 42]

§ 18:11. DISCHARGE BY ACCEPTANCE OF BREACH. There is a *breach of contract* whenever one party or both parties fail to perform the contract. A contract is discharged by breach if, when one party breaks the contract, the other party accepts the contract as ended. When a breach occurs, however, the injured party is not required to treat the contract as discharged. Since the contract bound the defaulting party to perform, the injured party may insist on the observance of the contract and resort to legal remedies. When the aggrieved party chooses to treat the other party's breach as terminating the contract, he must give unequivocal notice to the other party that he no longer considers the contract to be in effect.

A breach of a part of a divisible contract is not a breach of the entire contract.

A breach does not result in the discharge of a contract if the term broken is not sufficiently important. A term of a contract that does not go to the root of the contract is a *subsidiary term*. When there is a failure to perform such a term, the agreement is not terminated, but the defaulting party may be liable for damages for its breach.

In addition to the effect of a breach as such, the occurrence of a breach also excuses the injured party from his performance if it is conditioned or dependent upon the defaulter's performance of his obligation.

(a) **Renunciation.** When a party to a contract declares in advance of the time for performance that he will not perform, the other party may (1) ignore this declaration and insist on performance in accordance with the terms of the contract, (2) accept this declaration as an *anticipatory breach* and sue the promisor for damages, or (3) accept the declaration as a breach of the contract and rescind the contract. It is for the injured party to determine what he wishes to do when the other party has made a renunciation.

To constitute a renunciation there must be a clear, absolute, unequivocal refusal to perform the contract according to its terms.[15]

(b) Incapacitating self. Another form of anticipatory breach occurs when the promisor makes it impossible for himself to perform his obligation. Under such circumstances, the promisee is entitled to treat the contract as discharged. For example, when one party who is bound by the terms of the contract to turn over specific bonds, stocks, or notes to another party transfers them to a third party instead, the promisee may elect to treat the contract as discharged; or he may hold the promisor accountable for nonperformance when the time for performance arrives. The same is true when one agrees to sell specific goods to another person and then sells them to a third person in violation of his original contract.

QUESTIONS AND CASE PROBLEMS

1. What is the objective of each of the following rules of law?
   (a) When a construction contract is substantially performed in good faith, the contractor may recover the contract price less damages caused the other party by shortcomings in his performance.
   (b) Impossibility of performance that arises subsequent to the making of the contract ordinarily does not excuse the promisor from his obligations.
2. Coastal Water Co. gave a promissory note to Davis Meter and Supply Co. for $17,662.61. Thereafter Coastal made payments of $4,500 to Davis Meter. Nothing was said as to what accounts were to be credited with these payments. Davis applied some of the money to two items on Coastal's account, leaving a credit balance of $3,023.55. Davis then sued Coastal for $17,662.61 on the note that had become due but was not paid. Coastal claimed that the amount of the note should be reduced by $3,023.55. Davis said that it was holding this as a reserve against future purchases to be made by Coastal. Was it entitled to do so? [Davis Meter and Supply Co. v Coastal Water Co. (DC D SC) 266 FSupp 887]
3. Brown loaned money to Halvorson, a relative, with the understanding that if Brown should die before the money was repaid, the loan was canceled. The loan was not paid by the time Brown died and Fabre, the executor of the estate of Brown, sued Halvorson for the amount of the debt. Was he entitled to recover? [Fabre v Halvorson, 250 Ore 238, 441 P2d 640]

---

[15] Golf Cars, Inc. v Mid-Pacific Country Club (Hawaii) 493 P2d 1338.

4. A contractor was engaged in open-air sandblasting. The sand caused damage to machinery on neighboring land. A court injunction was obtained against the contractor, requiring him to take precautions to prevent such damage. He claimed that it was impossible for him to perform his contract for sandblasting and that he was discharged from his obligation. Was he correct? [Savage v Kiewit, 249 Ore 147, 432 P2d 519]

5. A leased a trailer park to B. At the time, sewage was disposed of by a septic tank system which was not connected with the public sewage system. B knew this and the lease declared that B had examined the premises and that A made no representation or guarantee as to the condition of the premises. Some time thereafter, the septic tank system stopped working properly and the county public health department notified B that he was required to connect the sewage system with the public sewage system or else close the trailer park. B did not want to pay the additional cost involved in connecting with the public system. B claimed that he was released from the lease and was entitled to a refund of the deposit which he had made. Was he correct? [See Glenn R. Sewell Sheet Metal v Loverde, 70 Cal2d 666, 75 CalRptr 889, 451 P2d 721]

6. Maze purchased 50 shares of stock in the Union Savings Bank, but he did not pay the full purchase price. Maze was later discharged in bankruptcy. Thereafter he was sued for the balance of the purchase price due. Decide. [Burke v Maze, 10 CalApp 206, 101 P438]

7. Warren and Geraldine Bates, husband and wife, were about to be divorced. They made a written agreement that Warren would pay Geraldine $50 a month until their younger child attained the age of 18 years and that in consideration thereof Geraldine released Warren from all property claims. The agreement did not say that it was binding upon Warren's estate. Upon his death it was claimed by his second wife that the obligation to make the monthly payments terminated with his death. Decide. [Hutchings v Bates (TexCivApp) 393 SW2d 338]

8. Banks Construction Co. made a contract with the United States for construction work in connection with an air force base. Because of abnormally large rainfall, the job site was flooded and the contractor was put to extra expense. Banks then sued the United States for the extra cost that it had thus incurred. United States claimed that Banks was bound by the original contract terms. Decide. [Banks Construction Co. v United States (Ct Claims) 364 F2d 357]

9. Fettig purchased a farm combine from Hansen. Hansen later did truck repair work for Fettig. Hansen was not paid for the combine or the repair work. Fettig received checks from the Federal Farmers Home Administration. These checks were indorsed and sent to Hansen bearing the notation that they were to be used to pay the repair bills. The notation had not been made by Fettig. Hansen applied the checks to the payment of the oldest item, which was the combine, although that bill was barred by the statute of limitations. Hansen then sued Fettig for the repair bill. Fettig claimed that the checks should have been applied to the repair bill. Was he correct? [Hansen v Fettig (ND) 179 NW2d 739]

BREACH OF CONTRACT AND REMEDIES

A. REMEDIES FOR BREACH OF CONTRACT

§ 19.1. INTRODUCTION. The injured party is always entitled to bring an action for damages. In some instances he may bring a suit in equity to obtain specific performance.

§ 19:2. DAMAGES. Whenever a breach of contract occurs, the injured party is entitled to bring an action for damages to recover such sum of money as will place him in the same position as he would have been in if the contract had been performed. If the defendant has been negligent in performing the contract, the plaintiff may sue for the damages caused by the negligence. Thus, a person contracting to drill a well for drinking water can be sued for the damages caused by his negligently drilling the well so as to cause the water to become contaminated.

   (a) Mitigation of damages. The injured party is under a duty to *mitigate the damages* if reasonably possible. That is, he must not permit the damages to increase if he can prevent them from doing so by reasonable efforts. He may thus be required to stop performance on his part of the contract when he knows that the other party is in default.

   In the case of the breach of an employment contract by an employer, the employee is required to seek other similar employment and the wages earned or which could have been earned from the other similar employment must be deducted from the damages claimed.

   If there is nothing which the injured party can reasonably do to reduce damages, there is by definition no duty to mitigate damages. For example, when a leasing company broke its contract to supply a specified computer and auxiliary equipment by delivering a less desirable computer and the specified computer and equipment could not be obtained elsewhere by the customer, the customer was entitled to recover full damages.[1]

---

[1] I.O.A. Leasing Corp. v Merle Thomas Corp. 260 Md 243, 272 A2d 1.

(b) Measure of damages. When the injured party does not sustain an actual loss from the breach of the contract, he is entitled to a judgment of a small sum, such as one dollar, known as *nominal damages*. If the plaintiff has sustained actual loss, he is entitled to a sum of money that will, so far as possible, compensate him for that loss; such damages are termed *compensatory damages*.

Ordinarily only compensatory damages are recoverable for breach of contract. This is so even though the breach was intentional. The fact that damages cannot be established with mathematical certainty is not a bar to their recovery. All that is required is reasonable certainty and the trier of fact is given a large degree of discretion in determining the damages.

When the contract is to purchase property, the damages are generally the difference between the contract price and the market price. The theory is that if the market price is greater, the buyer has sustained the loss of the indicated price differential because he must purchase in the general market instead of obtaining the property from the defendant. When the contract is to sell property, the loss incurred on its resale represents basically the damages for the breach.

When a party breaks his contract, he is liable for damages for the injury which was reasonably foreseeable as resulting from a breach of the contract. That is, the wrongdoer is liable for those *consequential damages* which were within the contemplation of the parties at the time of contracting. Thus, an electrical power company, which interrupted service without warning for six hours during a summer heat wave, is liable to food stores for spoiling of perishable food items.[2]

In business activities and construction contracts, the damages for the contractor are initially the loss of profits; while to the other contracting party, the damages sustained upon breach by the contractor are primarily any extra cost in having someone else render the performance.[3]

When a contractor delays in completing the performance of a contract, the injured party may generally recover the cost of renting other premises or goods. For example, when a contractor is late in completing the construction of a potato cellar, the injured person is entitled to recover the fair rental value of another cellar for the period of the delay, together with the cost of transporting the potatoes to the alternate place of storage.

Damages may not be recovered for loss caused by remote injuries unless the plaintiff, at the time the contract was executed, had informed the defendant of the existence of facts that would have given the defendant reason to foresee that his breach of the contract would cause such loss. What constitutes remote loss for which there can be no recovery depends largely upon the facts of each case. Recovery is likewise not allowed as to losses that are not clearly related to the defendant's breach.

---

[2] National Food Stores, Inc. v Union Electric Co. (MoApp) 494 SW2d 379.
[3] Crowe v Holloway Development Corp. 114 GaApp 856, 152 SE2d 913.

FACTS: Crommelin was a candidate in a primary election seeking ultimate election to the United States Congress. He made a contract for televising two political speeches with the Montgomery Independent Telecasters. The television company refused to allow him to make the scheduled telecasts. He lost the primary election and then sued for breach of contract, claiming damages consisting of the money that he had spent for campaign expenses and the salary which he would have received as a congressman.

DECISION: Judgment for Montgomery Independent Telecasters. Whether a person would win a primary and thereafter win the election was too speculative to conclude that the plaintiff had been deprived of the political office by the defendant's breach of contract. Therefore the defendant could not be held responsible for "causing" the plaintiff's harm, and the plaintiff could not recover the damages claimed from the telecaster. [Crommelin v Montgomery Independent Telecasters, 280 Ala 391, 194 So2d 548]

As a general rule, damages that are in excess of actual loss for the purpose of punishing or making an example of the defendant cannot be recovered in actions for breach of contract; such damages are known as *punitive damages* (or exemplary damages). In some consumer situations, the right is given to recover punitive damages in order to discourage the defendant from breaking his contract with others.

The plaintiff must establish that the defendant's breach of contract was the cause of the loss which he sustained. Ordinarily damages representing annoyance or mental anguish may not be recovered for breach of contract.

(c) Present and future damages. The damages recoverable on a breach of a contract may also be analyzed in terms of whether the plaintiff has already maintained the loss in question or will do so in the future. If the plaintiff was required to buy or rent elsewhere, he is ordinarily entitled to recover the cost thereof as an element of damages. When damages relate to future loss, the plaintiff is entitled to recover if he can establish the amount of such future loss, such as the loss of future profits, with reasonable certainty.[4] Mathematical precision is not required; but if the plaintiff cannot establish future loss items with reasonable certainty, they cannot be recovered.

(d) Interest. The right to interest has been considered in Chapter 14 as a term of a contract. Distinct from such interest, the law allows the recovery of interest as an element of damages. Generally interest runs from the date when an obligation is due if the amount at the time is liquidated, meaning definite and specific. If the amount due the plaintiff is not liquidated, interest runs only from the date that judgment is entered in his favor.

§ 19:3. LIQUIDATED DAMAGES. The parties may stipulate in their contract that a certain amount shall be paid in case of default. This amount is known as *liquidated damages*. Such a provision will be enforced if the

---

[4] Schafer v Sunset Packing Co. 256 Ore 539, 474 P2d 529.

amount specified is not excessive and if the contract is of such a nature that it would be difficult to determine the actual damages.[5] For example, it is ordinarily very difficult, if not impossible, to determine what loss the owner of a building under construction suffers when the contractor is late in completing the building. It is therefore customary to include a liquidated damages clause in a building contract, specifying that the contractor is required to pay a stated sum for each day of delay. When a liquidated damages clause is held valid, the injured party cannot collect more than the amount specified by the clause; and the defaulting party is bound to pay that much damages once the fact is established that he is in default and has no excuse for his default.

> **FACTS:** The Oregon Highway Commission made a contract with the DeLong Corporation for the construction of the major components of a bridge across the Columbia River. The contract specified that $2,000 would be paid for each day's delay. DeLong abandoned the contract. The Highway Commission then had a second contractor finish the work which was finished 476 days after the original completion date. The State then sued DeLong for damages for breach of the contract and for $2,000 for each day's delay. The State claimed that, because of the delay, it lost approximately $1.4 million in bridge tolls, ferry operations, and a state bridge subsidy.

> **DECISION:** Judgment for Oregon for liquidated damages at the rate of $2,000 × 476 days of delay. The actual damages sustained by Oregon could not be determined, but the amount stipulated appeared reasonable in the light of the various losses caused the State by the contractor's delay. Therefore the provision for liquidated damages was binding upon the contractor and entitled the State to recover according to the terms of such provision. [Oregon v DeLong Corp., 9 OreApp 550, 495 P2d 1215]

If the liquidated damages clause calls for the payment of a sum which is clearly unreasonably large and unrelated to the possible actual damages that might be sustained, the clause will be held void as a *penalty*.

Whether damages can be readily determined within the meaning of the above rule is to be determined as of the time the parties make their contract, rather than at the later date when the damages have been sustained.

§ 19:4. LIMITATION OF LIABILITY.

A party to a contract generally may include a provision that he shall not be liable for its breach generally, or for a breach that is due to a particular cause. Common illustrations of such clauses are the seller's statement that he is not liable beyond the refund of the purchase price or the replacement of defective parts, or a construction contract provision that the contractor shall not be liable for delays caused by conduct of third persons. Generally such provisions are valid.

There is a growing trend, however, to limit such *exculpatory* provisions or to hold them invalid when it is felt that because of the unequal bargaining power of the contracting parties, the surrender of a right to damages for breach by the other is oppressive or unconscionable. When the provision is

---

[5] Massey v Love (Okla) 478 P2d 948; Uniform Commercial Code § 2-718(1); Mellor v Budget Advisors (CA7 Ill) 415 F2d 1218 (recognizing the Code provision in a nonsales transaction).

expanded so as to free the contracting party from liability for his own negligence, the provision is sometimes held void as contrary to public policy. This is particularly likely to be the result when the party in question is a public utility, which is under the duty to render the performance or to provide the service in question in a nonnegligent way.

The fact that a limitation of liability limits or destroys the liability of one party for his nonperformance does not mean that there is no binding contract between the parties (as against the contention that if one party may break the contract without being liable in damages, he in fact is not bound by any contract and hence the other party should not be bound either). Thus, there is a binding contract between the supplier of natural gas and its customer even though the supplier declares that while it would make "reasonable provision to insure a continuous supply," it does not insure a continuous supply of gas, will not be responsible for interruptions beyond its control, and "assumes no obligation whatever regarding the quantity and quality of gas delivered . . . or the continuity of service."[6]

§ 19:5. RESCISSION UPON BREACH. The injured party may also have the right to treat the contract as discharged. When one party commits a material breach of contract the other party may rescind the contract because of such breach, although in some situations the right to rescind may be governed or controlled by civil service statutes or similar regulations or by an obligation to submit the matter to arbitration or to a grievance procedure.

FACTS: Pennel was a first-grade teacher in the Pond Elementary School. She signed a contract to teach the fourth grade for one year. She claimed that she had been coerced into signing the contract and when the school term began, she did not come to school but claimed to be ill. The school superintendent decided that she was not ill and discharged her. She brought an action to compel her reinstatement. The lower court refused to order Pennel's reinstatement on the basis that her conduct justified the school board in terminating her contract of employment in accordance with general principles of contract law.

DECISION: Judgment reversed. In terminating a teacher's employment, it was necessary that the school board comply with the provisions of the State Education Code. Whether the action was justified by general principles of contract law was therefore immaterial. [Pennel v Pond Union School District, 29 CalApp2d 832, 105 CalRptr 817]

If the injured party exercises the right to rescind after he has performed or paid money due under the contract, he may recover the value of the

---

[6] Texas Gas Utilities Co. v Barrett (Tex) 460 SW2d 409. It would appear that the same consideration of practical expediency that has led the law to sustain output and requirements contract and to trust to the good faith needs of businessmen for the definition of contract obligations, rather than insisting upon precise contract terms, is tending to favor limitation of liability clauses even though, if given literal effect, they would seem to permit a party to ignore his contract without any legal consequence. This is subject to the qualifications or exceptions noted in the first paragraph of this subsection, in order to protect a person in an inferior bargaining position.

performance rendered or the money paid. He sues, not on the express contract, but on a quasi contract which the law implies in order to compel the wrongdoer to pay for what he has received and to keep him from profiting by his own wrong.

The rescinding party must restore the other party to his original position as far as circumstances will permit, and he must rescind the entire contract. If he cannot make restoration because of his own acts, he cannot rescind the contract. Thus, a buyer who has placed a mortgage on property purchased by him cannot rescind the sales contract because he cannot return the property the way he received it.

The party who takes the initiative in rescinding the contract acts at his risk that he has proper cause to do so. If he does not have proper cause he is guilty of a breach of the contract.

§ 19:6. **SPECIFIC PERFORMANCE.** Under special circumstances the injured party may seek the equitable remedy of *specific performance* to compel the other party to carry out the terms of his contract. The granting of this relief is discretionary with the court and will be refused (a) when the contract is not definite; (b) when there is an adequate legal remedy; (c) when it works an undue hardship or an injustice on the defaulting party or the consideration is inadequate; (d) when the agreement is illegal, fraudulent, or unconscionable; or (e) when the court is unable to supervise the performance of such acts, as when services of a technical or complicated nature, such as the construction of a building, are to be rendered. The right to specific performance is also lost by unreasonable delay in bringing suit.

As a general rule, contracts for the purchase of land will be specifically enforced. Each parcel of land is unique and the payment of money damages would only enable the injured person to purchase a similar parcel of land but not the particular land specified in the contract. The sale of a business and the franchise held by the business from a third company will be enforced specifically.[7]

Specific performance of a contract to sell personal property generally cannot be obtained. Money damages are deemed adequate on the basis that the plaintiff can purchase identical goods. Specific performance will be granted, however, when the personal property has a unique value to the plaintiff or when the circumstances are such that identical articles cannot be obtained in the market. Thus, specific performance of a contract is granted to sell articles of an unusual age, beauty, unique history, or other distinction, as in the case of heirlooms, original paintings, old editions of books, or relics. Specific performance is also allowed a buyer in the case of a contract to sell shares of stock essential for control of a close corporation,[8] having no fixed or market value, and not being quoted in the commercial reports or sold on a stock exchange.

Ordinarily contracts for the performance of personal services will not be specifically ordered, both because of the difficulty of supervision by the

---

[7] DeBauge Bros., Inc. v Whitsitt, 212 Kan 758, 512 P2d 487.

[8] In a close corporation the stock is owned by a few individuals, and there is no opportunity for the general public to purchase shares.

courts and because of the restriction of the Thirteenth Amendment of the Federal Constitution prohibiting involuntary servitude except as criminal punishment. In some instances, a court will issue a negative injunction which prohibits the defendant from rendering a similar service for anyone else. This may indirectly have the effect of compelling the defendant to work for the plaintiff.

§ **19:7. WAIVER OF BREACH.** The fact that one party has broken a contract does not necessarily mean that there will be a lawsuit or a forfeiture of the contract. For practical business reasons, one party may be willing to ignore or waive the breach. When it is established that there has been a waiver of a breach, the party waiving the breach cannot take any action on the theory that the contract was broken. The waiver in effect erases the past breach and the contract continues as though the breach had not existed.

> **FACTS:** Puga assigned a contract in order to transfer his interest in a cable television enterprise to a corporation to be formed with the Harrisons if, among other things, he was paid $20,000 by June 20, 1967. Partial payments were made of $5,000 on March 27, and $2,500 on July 30, 1967. On December 13, 1967, Puga notified Harrison that the agreement was terminated because the Harrisons had failed to pay the money by the day specified. The Harrisons sued Puga for breach of contract.

> **DECISION:** Judgment for the Harrisons. By accepting the late payments, Puga had waived the time provision of the contract and could not thereafter claim that the Harrisons were in default because they had not paid on time. Puga had not at any time notified the Harrisons that he would insist on compliance with the time of payment provision and there was no clause in the contract which declared that time was of the essence or that there would be forfeiture if payment was not made on time. [Harrison v Puga, 4 WashApp 52, 480 P2d 247]

(a) **Scope of waiver.** The waiver of a breach of contract only extends to the matter waived. It does not show any intent to ignore other provisions of the contract. For example, when a contractor is late in completing the construction of a building but the owner waives his objection to the lateness and permits the contractor to continue and finish the construction, such waiver as to time does not waive the obligation of the contractor to complete the building according to the plans and specifications. Only the time of performance requirement has been waived.

(b) **Reservation of right.** It may be that the party waiving the breach is willing to accept the defective performance or breach but he does not wish to surrender any claim for damages for the breach. For example, the buyer of coal may need a shipment of coal so badly that he is forced to accept it although it is defective, yet at the same time he does not wish to give up his right to claim damages from the seller because the shipment was defective. In such a case, the aggrieved party should accept the tendered performance with a reservation of rights. In the above illustration the buyer would in effect state that he had accepted the coal but reserved his right to damages for nonconformity to the contract.[9] Frequently the buyer will express the same thought by stating that he accepts the coal without prejudice to his right to damages for nonconformity or that he accepts under protest.

The acceptance under reservation described above may be oral. It is preferable for practical reasons that it be in writing. In many cases the practical procedure is to make the declaration orally as soon as possible and then send a confirming letter. When the matter is sufficiently important, it is also desirable to have the wrongdoer countersign or make a written acknowledgement of the reservation letter.

(c) Waiver of breach as modification of contract. When the contract calls for a continuing performance, such as making delivery of goods or the payment of an installment on the first of each month, the acceptance of a later delivery or a late payment may have more significance than merely waiving a claim for damages because of the lateness. If there are repeated breaches and repeated waivers, the circumstances may show that the parties had modified their original contract. For example, the contract calling for performance on the first of the month may have been modified to permit performance in the first week of the month. When there is a modification of the contract, neither party can go back to the original contract without the consent of the other.

(d) Antimodification clause. Modern contracts commonly specify that the terms of a contract shall not be deemed modified by waiver as to any breaches. This means that the original contract remains as agreed to and either party may therefore return to and insist upon compliance with the original contract. In order to do this, notice must be given to the other party that in the future the terms of the contract will be insisted upon. For example, where the insurance company followed the pattern of accepting the late payment of insurance premiums, it could not declare a policy lapsed for failure to pay the premiums within the required time without first notifying the insured that it was going to insist on compliance with the terms of the policy contract.

§ 19:8. REFORMATION OF CONTRACT. When a written contract does not correctly state what has been agreed to and its correction cannot be obtained by voluntary cooperation, a court will order the correction of the contract when it is clear that a reforming or *reformation* of the contract should be made. In some instances reforming the contract is the first step in showing that the contract which was actually made has been broken by the defendant. For example, assume that A owns two houses at 510 and 512 N. Main Street. Assume that he obtains a fire insurance policy on 510 but by mistake the policy refers to 512. Thereafter 510 is destroyed by fire and the insurance company refuses to pay the loss on the theory that it did not insure 510 but insured 512. At this point A would ask the court (a) to reform the insurance contract to show that there was in fact insurance on 510, and

---

[9] UCC § 1-207.

(b) to award damages to *A* because of the insurer's breach of its contract as to 510.

B. TORT LIABILITY TO THIRD PERSONS FOR BREACH

When a party to a contract fails to perform his obligation, a third person may be harmed. If the third person cannot bring suit as a third party beneficiary, he might seek to recover damages on a theory of tort liability.

§ 19:9. TORT LIABILITY TO THIRD PERSON FOR NONPERFOR-MANCE. By the general rule, a total failure to perform a contract does not confer upon a third person a right to sue for tort.[10]

(a) Discharge of obligee's duty. An exception is made to the general rule when the obligee, that is, the other party to the contract who will receive the benefit of performance, owes a duty to the third person or the general public, and the performance by the contractor will discharge that duty. Here the breach of the duty by the contractor gives rise to a tort liability in favor of the injured third person against the contractor. To illustrate, the operator of an office building owes the duty to third persons of maintaining its elevators in the safe operating condition. In order to discharge this duty, the building management may make a contract with an elevator maintenance contractor. If the latter fails to perform its contract and a third person is injured because of the defective condition of an elevator, the third person may sue the elevator maintenance contractor for the damages sustained.

> **FACTS:** The U.S.F. & G. Co. issued policies of fire and public liability insurance to the Roosevelt Hotel and agreed to make periodic inspections of the premises for fire hazards and conditions dangerous to guests. Marie Hill and her husband were guests at the hotel. The insurer negligently failed to find a hazard which resulted in a fire that injured Marie Hill and killed her husband. She sued the insurer for damages for her injuries and for the wrongful death of her husband.
>
> **DECISION:** U.S.F. & G. Co. was liable to Hill for the harm she sustained and for the wrongful death of her husband. Even though the only contract of the insurer was with the hotel, tort liability arises in favor of guests of the hotel since the insurer should have foreseen that negligence in performing its inspection contract with the hotel would expose the guests to serious danger. [Hill v U.S.F. & G. Co. (CA5 Fla) 428 F2d 112]

(b) Partial performance. Confusion exists in the law as to the classification to be made of conduct involved when the contracting party has entered upon the performance of the contract but omits some act or measure in consequence of which harm is sustained by a third person. The problem is the same as that involved in determining whether the negligent actor who omits a particular precaution has "acted" negligently or has been

---

[10] Resort to tort liability is unnecessary if the aggrieved person is entitled to recover as a third party beneficiary of the contract.

guilty of a negligent "omission." In many of the older cases, the courts disposed of the matter by stating that no tort arose when a third person was injured by the breach of a contract between other persons.

§ 19:10. TORT LIABILITY TO THIRD PERSON FOR IMPROPER PERFORMANCE.

When one person contracts to perform a service for another person and his defective or improper performance causes harm to a third person, such third person may sue the contractor. This is at least true when the performance of the contract would discharge an obligation or duty which is owed to the injured plaintiff by the person dealing with the contractor. By the older rule of contract law, only the person who had contracted for the services could sue when the services were improperly performed.

FACTS: The More-Way Development Company contracted with Link to construct a building. DeQuardo, Robinson, Crouch & Associates, Inc., were the architects who designed the building. After the building was constructed, A.E. Investment Corporation rented a part of the building. Because of the negligence of the architects, the building settled. The Investment Corporation was forced to leave the building because of this condition. It then sued the architects for the economic loss sustained thereby. The architects asserted that they did not owe the plaintiff any duty because the plaintiff had not made any contract with them.

DECISION: Judgment for A. E. Investment Corp. The defendant had been negligent in failing to take into account the condition of the subsoil. As the architects knew that the building was being built for the purpose of renting, it was foreseeable that tenants of the building, such as the plaintiff, would sustain harm in consequence of any negligence of the defendant. It was therefore no defense, when such harm was sustained, that the person injured did not have any contract with the defendant. [A.E. Investment Corp. v Link Builders, Inc., 62 Wis2d 79, 214 NW2d 764]

When the contractor fails to perform properly his contract for repairs or alterations, there is a conflict of authority as to whether he is liable to a third person who is injured as the result thereof. For example, suppose that an automobile repairman negligently repairs the brakes of an automobile with the result that it does not stop in time when driven by the owner and runs into a pedestrian. Can the pedestrian sue the repairman for tort damages?

By the older view, the injured plaintiff was automatically barred because he was not a party to the contract with the repairman. The modern view, however, emphasizes the fact that the person who makes a poor repair of the brakes is launching a dangerous instrumentality on the highway just as much as the manufacturer who manufactures an automobile with defective brakes. Both should recognize that their negligence will expose persons on the highway to an unreasonable risk of foreseeable harm. The modern view accordingly holds the negligent repairman liable to the injured third person.

modern view

A party to a contract is, of course, directly liable to a third person injured by his negligence in the course of performing the contract. For example, when a contractor used a heavy pile driver close to very old neighboring buildings without taking various precautions to protect them from vibration damage, the contractor was liable to the owners of such houses for the vibration damages caused by his negligence.[11]

QUESTIONS AND CASE PROBLEMS

1. What is the objective of each of the following rules of law?
   (a) A party injured by a breach of contract is under a duty to mitigate the damages as far as is reasonably possible.
   (b) Specific performance of certain contracts is granted as an equitable remedy.
2. Kuznicki made a contract for the installation of a fire detection system by Security Safety Corp. for $498. The contract was made one night and canceled at 9:00 a.m. the next morning. Security then claimed one third of the purchase price from Kuznicki by virtue of a provision in the contract that "in the event of cancellation of this agreement . . . the owner agrees to pay 33⅓ percent of the contract price, as liquidated damages." Was Security Safety entitled to recover the amount claimed? [Security Safety Corp. v Kuznicki, 350 Mass 157, 213 NE2d 866]
3. Scheppel, a furniture dealer, received a telephone order on March 9 for furniture subject to the condition that it be delivered to the customer's home by March 23. Scheppel telephoned the factory, which gave the ordered furniture to a motor carrier, Arkansas-Best Freight System, with directions to use Cline Motor Freight for the last leg of the shipment. A different carrier was used, and for some unknown reason the furniture was not delivered in time and the customer canceled his order. Scheppel then sued Arkansas-Best for loss of the profit on the canceled sale to his customer. Decide. [Scheppel v Arkansas-Best Freight System, 117 IllApp2d 60, 254 NE2d 280]
4. Brewer, who operated a lounge, contracted to give Roberts the right to place amusement machines therein. When Brewer sought to exclude the machines, Roberts sued for specific performance, which Brewer opposed on the ground that specific performance would require the court to supervise the lounge to see that the machines were allowed in it. Decide. [Roberts v Brewer (Tex CivApp) 371 SW2d 424]
5. Avril agreed to sell certain cleaning products to Center Chemical Co. at a 45 percent discount for 20 years and gave Center an exclusive franchise to sell such products in Florida. If Center did not make specified monthly minimum purchases, Avril could restrict or terminate Center's exclusive rights. The contract provided for periodic readjustment of prices to meet market conditions. Four years later Center stopped purchasing from Avril, which then sued for breach of contract, claiming that it was entitled to recover for the loss of profits

---

[11] Dussell v Kaufman Construction Co. 398 Pa 369, 157 A2d 740.

which it would have received in the remaining 16 years of the contract. It offered evidence of what the sales and profits had been the first 4 years. Was it entitled to recover profits for the remaining 16 years? [Center Chemical Co. v Avril (CA5 Fla) 392 F2d 289]

6. Melodee Lane Lingerie Co. was a tenant in a building that was protected against fire by a sprinkler and alarm system maintained by the American District Telegraph Co. Because of the latter's fault, the controls on the system were defective and allowed the discharge of water into the building which damaged Melodee's property. When Melodee sued A.D.T., it raised the defense that its service contract limited its liability to 10 percent of the annual service charge made to the customer. Was this limitation valid? [Melodee Lane Lingerie Co. v American District Telegraph Co. 18 NY2d 57, 271 NYS2d 937, 218 NE2d 661]

7. A, who had contracted to build a house for B, departed from the specifications at a number of points. It would cost approximately $1,000 to put the house in the condition called for by the contract. B sued A for $5,000 for breach of contract and emotional disturbance caused by the breach. Decide. [See Jankowski v Mazzotta, 7 MichApp 483, 152 NW2d 40]

8. Dankowski contracted with Cremona to perform construction work on a house for $5,060 and to make a down payment of $2,500. When the work was about 80 percent completed, Dankowski refused to permit Cremona to do any further work because the work done was defective. Cremona brought suit for breach of contract. It was found that the defects in the work could be remedied at a cost of $500 and that Cremona had spent $4,167.26 in performance of the contract. He was awarded damages of $4,167.26 less the $500 necessary for repairs and less the down payment of $2,500, making damages of $1,167.26. The owner appealed. Decide. [Dankowski v Cremona (TexCivApp) 352 SW2d 334]

9. Contrary to its subscription contract, the Sourthern Bell Telephone & Telegraph Co. failed to list the trade name of Scheinuk The Florist, Inc. in the white pages of the phone directory and only listed it in the yellow pages. In order to offset this omission, Scheinuk spent $508 in advertising. He sued the telephone company for damages of $25,147.53, which he asserted was the loss sustained in the 13-month period before the new directory was published. He showed that he was the second largest florist in New Orleans with a mailing list of 20,000 customers, doing approximately 95 percent of his business over the phone. Scheinuk showed that his loss of gross profits during the 13-month period was $2,912.81. He claimed that since florists in the city had a general increase of business of 11.4 percent, the amount of $16,726.72 was the gross profit on the income from sales he would have received if he had been properly listed and thus able to increase at the same rate. He also estimated that he would lose $5,000 in the future as the result of the past omission. The trial judge, hearing the case without a jury, allowed Scheinuk damages of $2,008. To what amount was he entitled? [Scheinuk The Florist, Inc. v Southern Bell Tel. & Tel. Co. (LaApp) 128 So2d 683]

10. A contract for the sale of real estate declared that, if the seller was not able to deliver a good title to the property, the buyer's deposit would be returned to him and the contract would be ended. The seller refused to go through with the contract, the buyer's deposit was returned to him, and the buyer then sued the seller for damages. The seller raised the defense that refunding of the deposit was the exclusive remedy of the buyer. Was the seller correct? [See Ocean Air Tradeways, Inc. v Arkay Realty Corp. (CA9 Cal) 480 F2d 1112]

20 PERSONAL PROPERTY

A. GENERAL PRINCIPLES

§ 20.1. BASIC PROPERTY CONCEPTS. *Property* means the rights and interests which one has in anything subject to ownership, whether that thing be movable or immovable, tangible or intangible, visible or invisible. As a legal concept, "property" refers to rights. In common usage, it refers to the thing or object that is subject to the rights.[1] A right in a thing is property, without regard to whether such right is absolute or conditional, perfect or imperfect, legal or equitable.

§ 20:2. PERSONAL PROPERTY. *Personal property* consists of (a) things which are tangible and movable, such as furniture and books, and (b) claims and debts, which are called *choses in action*. Common forms of choses in action are insurance policies, stock certificates, bills of lading, and evidences of indebtedness, such as notes.

Personal property can be defined indirectly as including all property that is neither real property nor a lease of real property. *Real property* means all rights and interests of indefinite duration in land and things closely pertaining to land, such as trees and buildings.

(a) Expanding concept of personal property. New types of personal property have developed. Thus, gas and water are generally regarded by courts as "property" for the purpose of criminally prosecuting persons who tap water mains and gas pipes and thus obtain water and gas without paying.

The modern techniques of sound and image recording have led to the necessity of giving protection against copying and competition. Federal and state statutes provide for the copyright protection of musical compositions and create new crimes of record and tape piracy.[2]

The theft of papers on which computer programs are written is larceny or "theft of property" under a statute which defines "property" as including "all writings, of every description, provided such property possesses any

---

[1] Virginia Marine Resources Commission v Forbes, 214 Va 109, 197 SE2d 195.
[2] PL 92-140, 85 Stat 391, 17 United States Code §§ 1, 5, 20, 101; Pennsylvania, Act of January 10, 1972, PL 872, 18 PS § 1878.1.

ascertainable value," even though the exact value of such programs cannot be determined.

§ **20:3. LIMITATIONS ON OWNERSHIP.** When one has all possible existing rights in and over a thing, he is said to have *absolute ownership*. The term "absolute," however, is somewhat misleading, for one's rights in respect to the use, enjoyment, and disposal of a thing are subject to certain restrictions, such as the following:

(a) **Rights of government.** All property is subject to the *power to tax*. By another power, called the *police power*, the government can adopt reasonable rules and regulations in respect to the use and enjoyment of property for the protection of the safety, health, morals, and general welfare of the community. This police power is in substance the power to govern for the common good. Zoning laws that restrict the use of property within specified areas may be adopted under this power.

Private property is also subject to the right of the government to take it for public purposes. This right of *eminent domain* may also be exercised by certain corporations, such as railroads and public utilities. Constitutional provisions require that fair compensation be paid the owner when property is taken by eminent domain. Such provisions do not apply when there is merely a loss of value caused by the use of the police power.

(b) **Rights of creditors.** Property is subject to the rights of one's creditors. It may be taken by judical proceedings to satisfy just claims against the owner or his estate. A person cannot dispose of his property in any way so as to defeat the rights of his creditors.

(c) **Rights of others.** The law restricts the use and enjoyment of property in that the owner is not allowed to use it in a way that will unreasonably injure other members of society.

What is a reasonable or unreasonable use of property by the owner depends upon the circumstances in a particular situation.

§ **20:4. LIABILITY FOR USE OF PERSONAL PROPERTY.** Ordinarily an owner is not liable for harm sustained by someone else merely because the owner's personal property was involved. Thus, the owner of an automobile generally is not liable to a third person who is run into by a thief driving the automobile. This conclusion is reached even though the owner did not take every possible precaution against theft. For example, a transportation firm which left the ignition keys in its airport limousine was not liable when a boy of 14 years of age attempted to steal the car and, in so doing, ran into and injured another person. The transportation company had no reason to foresee that the limousine would be stolen or that the thief would then drive in such a way as to cause harm.[3]

---

[3] Canavin v Wilmington Transportation Co. 208 PaSuper 506, 223 A2d 902. Statutes frequently make it a crime to leave an automobile with keys in the ignition. When such a statute is violated, some courts hold that the person leaving the keys is liable for the damages sustained by the third person with whom the fleeing thief has a collision.

B. ACQUIRING TITLE TO PERSONAL PROPERTY

§ 20:5. INTRODUCTION. Title to personal property may be acquired in different ways. In this chapter the following methods will be discussed: copyrights, patents, and trademarks; accession; confusion; gifts; lost property; transfer by nonowner; occupation; escheat; and judgments.

§ 20:6. COPYRIGHTS, PATENTS, AND TRADEMARKS. Under its constitutional authority, Congress has adopted copyright and patent right laws to further the arts and sciences by granting artists and inventors exclusive rights in the product of their mental labors.

(a) Common-law copyright. At common law an author or compiler of data who did not make his work public had a right that no one could use his work without his permission. This is called a common-law copyright. It is closely related to the concept of privacy as is seen from the fact that the common-law copyright is destroyed when a publication is made. Publication does not mean printing, but means any communication to others under such circumstances as to justify the belief that it was made known with the intent that it be common property. Thus, anyone is free to copy material not covered by a copyright when its creator had distributed it publicly.[4]

A person having a conversation with someone has the right to repeat that conversation in a book, as against the contention of the other party, or someone on his behalf, that the conversation is subject to a common-law copyright which prevents literary use being made of the conversation without the consent of both parties.[5]

(b) Statutory copyright. Federal statutes authorize a copyright that is not destroyed by publication. Under the federal statutes a *copyright* is a grant to an author giving him the exclusive right to possess, make, publish, and sell copies of his intellectual productions, or to authorize others to do so, for a period of 28 years, with the privilege of a renewal and an extension for an additional term of 28 years. A copyright may be secured for lists of addresses, books, maps, musical compositions, motion pictures, and similar productions, provided the work is an original expression of an idea.

Works of domestic origin exported to foreign countries that have ratified the Universal Copyright Convention may use the internationally accepted copyright symbol © in place of or in addition to the word "Copyright" or its abbreviation. Note the form of the copyright notice on the back of the title page of this book.

There is no right in an idea that is voluntarily communicated. Thus, if *A* discloses to *B* an idea that *A* has for a play or a sales promotion program, *A*

---

[4] Columbia Broadcasting System, Inc. v DeCosta (CA1 RI) 377 F2d 315 (creator of "Have Gun Will Travel" had made public distribution of cards bearing the uncopyrighted phrase and therefore could not recover damages for misappropriation of the phrase by the television network program).

[5] Hemingway's Estate v Random House, 53 Misc2d 462, 279 NYS2d 51.

is not entitled to payment from *B* when *B* uses that idea unless there is a contract between the parties that *B* should make such payment.

A copyright does not protect ideas but only the manner of expressing ideas.[6]

(c) **Right of privacy.** To some extent a right of privacy may afford protection against exploitation similar to that of the common-law copyright. When a person is a public figure, however, his public life is generally not protected by either a common-law copyright or a right of privacy. When a person dies, his family may not object to publicity or artistic works relating to the dead person. The theory of the law is that only the dead person could have objected to the invasion of his privacy, and that ordinarily those who survive him cannot claim that their privacy is being invaded by the publicity given to the person who had died. Consent to publicity removes any restriction based on a common-law copyright or a right of privacy.

(d) **Patents.** A *patent* is a grant to one who has given physical expression to an idea, giving him the exclusive right to make, use, and sell, and to authorize others to make, use, and sell the invention for a period of 17 years. A patent is not renewable. The invention must be a new and useful art, machine, or composition of matter not previously known and used.

The law of patents is evolving to provide protection for computer programs. Initially, such patents were denied on the theory that a program merely respresented "thinking." The commercial necessity of protecting programs has led to the adoption of the view that a program may be patented when something more than mere thinking is shown. This is not a satisfactory rule of law, and corrective legislation is now pending in Congress. A patent cannot be obtained for a computer program for programming any type of general purpose digital computer to convert binary-coded-decimal numerals into pure binary numerals, as such a conversion method is not a "process" within the patent law but is merely an idea and can be performed with other existing equipment or without any equipment.[7]

If a thing is not patented or if the patent has expired, anyone may make, use, or sell it without the permission of or any payment to the original designer or creator.

(e) **Trademarks.** A trademark is "any word, name, symbol, or device or combination thereof adopted and used by a manufacturer or merchant to identify his goods to distinguish them from those manufactured or sold by others."[8]

By federal statute, a trademark can be registered by its owner or user. This entitles him to the exclusive use of the trademark for 20 years. A person using a trademark without the permission of the registered owner may be sued by the owner for damages.[9]

---

[6] M.M. Business Forms Corp. v Uarco, Inc. (CA6 Ohio) 472 F2d 1137.
[7] Gottschalk v Benson, 409 US 63.
[8] 15 USC § 1127.
[9] 15 USC § 1125(a).

In order to be registered, a trademark must be distinctive. Ordinarily a name or symbol which is merely descriptive of the article or the name of a city or a geographic area cannot be registered as a trademark. An exception to this statement is made when the particular words have been used for so long that to the public at large they now identify the particular product and its origin. When the descriptive or geographic terms have acquired such a *secondary* meaning, they may be registered as a trademark.

> **FACTS:** Atomic Oil Company sold an oil product for automobiles under the name of SAVMOTOR. It registered the name under the federal Lanham Trademark Act of 1964. Bardahl Oil Company sold an oil additive under the name of SAVOIL. Atomic Oil sued Bardahl for an injunction and damages, claiming that the name SAVOIL infringed the registration of SAVMOTOR. Bardahl defended on the ground that the registration of SAVMOTOR under the Act was improper and that the public did not associate that name with Atomic Oil.

> **DECISION:** Atomic Oil was not entitled to an injunction. The name of its product was merely descriptive of its qualities and there was no evidence that it had acquired a secondary meaning so that it was associated in the mind of the public with the Atomic Oil Company. [Bardahl Oil Co. v Atomic Oil Co. (CA10 Okla) 351 F2d 148]

§ 20:7. ACCESSION. Property may be acquired by *accession*, that is, by means of an addition to or an increase of the thing that is owned, as in the case of produce of land or the young of animals. As a general rule, repairs and additions become a part of the article that is repaired or modified. Likewise, when materials are furnished to another to be manufactured into an article, title to the finished article is in the owner of the materials. If the manufacturer, however, adds a large proportion of other materials, title will then usually vest in him.

A more difficult problem arises when a change in property is made against the wishes or at least without the consent of the owner. In such a case, the gaining of property by accession depends upon whether the act was done intentionally and willfully, or unintentionally and innocently.

To illustrate, when a stolen car is retaken on behalf of the owner, the car owner is entitled to keep a new engine which had been put into the car by a good faith purchaser, on the basis that the engine had become part of the car by accession.

In other instances the courts determine whether title has passed by accession on the basis of whether or not the labor and materials of the trespasser have changed the property into a different specie. Another rule frequently used is that title does not change by accession even though the former value of the goods has been changed, so long as there is no loss of identity. Under this rule the owner of the original material may follow it and seize it in its new shape or form, regardless of the alteration which it has undergone, so long as he can prove the identity of the original material. The factor that influences the courts in applying one or the other rule is the desire to attain as fair a result as possible under the circumstances.

These rules merely relate to the right of the original owner to obtain the return of the property taken from him. They do not relate to his right to sue the person taking the property. Under other rules of property and tort law, the person taking the owner's property from him, however innocently, is liable for money damages representing the value of the property. If the taking is not innocently done, punitive damages may also be recovered by the owner.

§ **20:8. CONFUSION.** Title to personal property may be acquired when the property of two persons becomes intermingled under such circumstances that one owner forfeits his right in his goods. Under this *doctrine of confusion of goods*, if a person willfully and wrongfully mixes his own goods with those of another so as to render them indistinguishable, he loses his part of the property and the innocent party acquires title to the total mass.

The doctrine of confusion does not apply (a) when the mixture is by consent of the parties; (b) when the mixture is made without fraudulent intent, as by accident or mistake; or (c) when the goods that have been mixed are of equal kind and grade, as in the case of oil, tea, and wheat. In these cases each owner is entitled to his proportionate share of the mixture.

§ **20:9. GIFTS.** Title to personal property may be transferred by the voluntary act of the owner without receiving anything in exchange, that is, by *gift*. The person making the gift, the *donor*, may do so because of things which the recipient of the gift, the *donee*, has done in the past or which he is expected to do in the future, but such matters of inducement are not deemed consideration so as to alter the "free" character of the gift. A donor may make a gift of a fractional interest in property.

(a) Inter vivos gifts. The ordinary gift that is made between two living persons is an *inter vivos gift*. For practical purposes the rule is that the gift takes effect upon the donor's expressing an intention to transfer title and making delivery, subject to the right of the donee to divest himself of title by disclaiming the gift within a reasonable time after learning that it has been made. Since there is no consideration for a gift, an intended donee cannot sue for breach of contract, and the courts will not compel the donor to complete the gift.

The fact that the donee is willing to return the gift if needed by the donor does not destroy the effect of a gift, where such return would be at the option of the donee and the donor did not have any right to compel the return.

(1) Intent. The intent "to make" a gift requires an intent to transfer title at that time. In contrast, an intent to confer a benefit at a future date is not a sufficient intent to create any right in the intended donee. The absence of an intent to make a gift may be shown to contradict what otherwise would appear to be a gift. Thus, it may be shown that the owner of shares of stock retained such control over the stock that there was no gift even though the shares were registered in the name of the owner's wife and she received and kept the dividends on the stock, the owner proving that the transfer was made

to the wife for convenience and that he did not intend that she should receive more than the dividends.

A gift may be made by delivering a deed or an assignment to the donee. Thus, *A* may give his television set to *B* by delivering to *A* a signed and sealed writing which declares that *A* gives the set to *B*. This sealed writing is called a deed and would be used when the subject of the gift is a thing. If the subject of a gift is a claim, an assignment would be used. For example, if *C* was owed $100 by *D*, *C* could make a gift of that money to *E* by giving him a writing saying that he assigned to *E* his claim against *D*. The fact that a deed is used instead of an assignment, or vice versa, is unimportant as the courts will carry out the intent of making a gift regardless of what the document is called.

(2) Delivery. The delivery of a gift may be a *symbolic delivery*, as by the delivery of means of control of property, such as keys to a lock or ignition keys to an automobile, or by the delivery of papers that are essential to or closely associated with ownership of the property, such as documents of title or ship's papers. The delivery of a symbol is effective as a gift if the intent to make a gift is established; this is in contrast to merely giving the recipient of the token temporary access to property, as for example, until the deliveror comes back from the hospital.

A gift may be made by depositing money in the bank account of an intended donee. If the account is a joint account in the names of two persons, a deposit of money in the account by one person may or may not be a gift to the other. Parol evidence is generally admissible to show whether there was an intention to make a gift.

When a savings account passbook is essential to the withdrawal of money from a savings account, parents do not make a gift to a minor child when they open a savings account in his name but keep possession of the passbook.

FACTS: The parents of Benny Ruffalo, who had opened a savings account in his name when he was a small child, made periodic deposits in the account. The parents retained possession of the passbook with the exception of six instances when withdrawals were made from the account by the son. In each of those instances, the passbook was handed to him by his mother with instructions to withdraw a particular amount and to return the passbook. The passbook was in each case returned immediately after making the specified withdrawal. The bank regulations required the presentation of the passbook for every withdrawal or deposit. Benny was killed in military service 21 years after the account was opened. The balance in the account was then approximately $4,000 which was claimed by his parents and by the administrator of his estate for Benny's widow.

DECISION: Judgment for the parents. There was no gift of the bank account to the son. The restrictions imposed on the son in each instance when he had been given the savings passbook showed that there never was a delivery to him of the passbook as a symbol of the savings account. The parents were therefore still the owners of the money in the savings account since no effective gift had been made. [Ruffalo v Savage, 252 Wis 175, 31 NW2d 175]

The essential element of delivery is the relinquishment of control over the property. If the owner retains control, there is no delivery. Hence, the fact that property is placed in a jointly-owned safe deposit box does not make the sharer of the box a co-owner of the property. Consequently, upon the death of the person depositing the property, the other party does not become the owner merely because the box was rented by them as "joint tenants with the right of survivorship." This term is narrowly construed to relate only to the use of the box and not to the ownership of its contents.

(3) Donor's Death. If the donor dies before doing what is needed to make an effective gift, the gift fails. An agent or the executor or administrator of the donor cannot thereafter perform the missing step on behalf of the donor. For example, in a state where a transfer of title to a motor vehicle could not be made without a transfer of the title certificate, that transfer must be made while the donor is living and cannot be made after his death by his executor.[10]

(b) Gifts causa mortis. A *gift causa mortis* is made when the donor, contemplating his imminent and impending death, delivers personal property to the donee with the intent that the donee shall own it if the donor dies. This is a conditional gift, and the donor is entitled to take the property back (1) if he does not die; (2) if he revokes it before he dies; (3) if the donee dies before the donor does.

(c) Uniform Gifts to Minors Act. Most states have adopted the Uniform Gifts to Minors Act,[11] which provides an additional method for making gifts to minors of money and of registered and unregistered securities. Under the Act a gift of money may be made by an adult to a minor by depositing it with a broker of a bank in an account in the name of the donor or another adult or a bank with trust powers "as custodian for [name of minor] under the [name of state] Uniform Gifts to Minors Act." If the gift is a registered security, the donor registers the security in a similar manner. If the security is unregistered, it must be delivered by the donor to another adult or a trust company accompanied by a written statement signed by the donor and the custodian acknowledges receipt of the security.[12]

Under the Uniform Act the custodian is in effect a guardian of the property for the minor, but he may use it more freely and is not subject to the many restrictions applicable to a true guardian. When property is held by a custodian for the benefit of a minor under the Uniform Gifts to Minors Act, the custodian has discretionary power to use the property for the "support, maintenance, education, and benefit" of the minor but the custodian may not use the custodial property for his personal benefit. The gift is final and irrevocable for tax and all other purposes upon complying

---

[10] Estes v Gibson (Ky) 257 SW2d 604.
[11] The Uniform Gifts to Minors Act (UGMA) was originally proposed in 1956. It was revised in 1965 and again in 1966. One of these versions, often with minor variations, has been adopted in every state except Georgia and Louisiana. It has been adopted for the Virgin Islands and the District of Columbia.
[12] UGMA § 2.

with the procedure of the Act. The property can be transferred by the custodian to a third person free from the possibility that a minor donee might avoid the transfer.

(d) Conditional gifts. A gift may be made on condition, such as "This car is yours when you graduate" or "This car is yours unless you drop out of school." The former gift is subject to a *condition precedent*, and the latter to a *condition subsequent*. That is, the condition to the first gift must be satisfied before any gift or transfer of title takes place, while the satisfaction of the second condition operates to destroy or divest a transfer of title that had taken place. Ordinarily, no condition is recognized unless it is expressly stated; but some courts regard an engagement ring as a conditional gift, particularly if the girl is the one who breaks or causes the breaking of the engagement.[13] Other gifts made by the man or by friends in contemplation of marriage are not regarded as conditional.

(e) Anatomical gifts. The Uniform Anatomical Gift Act [14] permits anyone 18 years or older to make a gift of his body or any part or organ to take effect upon his death. The gift may be made to a school, a hospital, an organ bank, or a named patient. Such a gift may also be made, subject to certain restrictions by the spouse, adult child, parent, adult brother or sister, or guardian of a deceased person.[15] Independently of the Act, a living person may make a gift, while living, of part of his body, as in the case of a blood transfusion or a kidney transplant.

§ 20:10. LOST PROPERTY. Personal property is *lost* when the owner does not know where it is located but intends to retain title or ownership to it. The person finding lost property does not acquire title but only possession. Ordinarily the finder of lost property is required to surrender the property to the true owner when the latter establishes his ownership. Meanwhile the finder is entitled to retain his possession as against everyone else.

Without a contract with the owner or a statute so providing, the finder of lost property is not entitled to a reward or to compensation for his services.

(a) Finding in public place. If the lost property is found in a public place, such as a hotel, under such circumstances that to a reasonable man it would appear that the property had been intentionally placed there by the owner and that he is likely to recall where he left it and to return for it, the finder is not entitled to possession of the property but must give it to the proprietor or manager of the public place to keep it for the owner.[16] This exception does not apply if it appears that the property was not intentionally placed where it was found, because in such case it is not likely that the owner will recall having left it there.

---

[13] Goldstein v Rosenthal (NYCivCt) 56 Misc2d 311, 288 NYS2d 503.

[14] This Act has been adopted in every state except Massachusetts. It has been adopted for the District of Columbia. California and Louisiana have local statutes substantially similar to the Uniform Act.

[15] Uniform Anatomical Gift Act (UAGA) §§ 2, 3.

[16] Jackson v Steinberg, 186 Ore 129, 200 P2d 376.

(b) Statutory change. In some states, statutes have been adopted permitting the finder to sell the property or claim it as his own if the owner does not appear within a stated period of time. In such a case the finder is required to give notice, as by newspaper publication, in order to attempt to reach the owner.

§ 20:11. **TRANSFER BY NONOWNER.** Ordinarily a sale or other transfer by one who does not own the property will pass no title. No title is acquired by theft. The thief acquires possession only; and if he makes a sale or gift of the property to a third person, the latter accordingly only acquires the possession of the property. The true owner may reclaim the property from the thief or from his transferee, or he may sue them for the conversion of his property and recover the value of the stolen property.

In some states this rule is fortified by statutes which declare that the title to an automobile cannot be transferred, even by the actual owner, without a delivery of a properly indorsed title certificate. The states that follow the common law do not make the holding of a title certificate essential to the ownership of an automobile, although as a matter of police regulation the owner must obtain such a certificate.

As an exception to the rule that a nonowner cannot transfer title, an agent, who does not own the property but who is authorized to sell it, may transfer the title of his principal. Likewise, certain relationships create a power to sell and transfer title, such as pledge or an entrustment. An owner of property may also be barred or estopped from claiming that he is still the owner when he had done such acts as deceive an innocent buyer into believing that someone else was the owner or had authority to sell.

§ 20:12. **OCCUPATION OF PERSONAL PROPERTY.** Title to personal property may be acquired under certain circumstances by *occupation*, that is, by taking and holding possession of the property.

(a) Wild animals. Wild animals, living in a state of nature, are not owned by any individual. Title to them is held by the state, as sovereign, in a trustee-like capacity for the public. In the absence of restrictions imposed by game laws, the person who acquires dominion or control over a wild animal becomes its owner. What constitutes sufficient dominion or control varies with the nature of the animal and all the surrounding circumstances. If the animal is killed, tied, imprisoned, or otherwise prevented from going at its will, the hunter exercises sufficient dominion or control over the animal and becomes the owner.

If the wild animal, subsequent to its capture, should escape and return to its natural state, it resumes the status of a wild animal. The first captor thereby loses his title, and a new hunter can acquire title to the animal by capture.

As a qualification to the ordinary rule, the exception developed that if the animal is killed or captured on the land of another while the hunter is guilty of trespassing, that is, if he is upon the land without the permission of the owner, the animal, when killed or captured, does not belong to the hunter but to the landowner.

(1) Game Laws. Generally state game laws narrow the common-law rights by establishing closed seasons during which the hunter is not permitted to capture the game. A federal statute similarly protects migratory birds which fly across national boundaries. Violation of these statutes is punishable by fine or imprisonment or both.

(2) Pollution Damage to Wild Animals. When a business enterprise pollutes the environment and such pollution causes the death of wildlife, some courts allow the state to bring a suit against the polluter to recover damages for destruction of the wildlife. Other courts deny recovery by the state.

> **FACTS:** In the process of manufacturing cheese, the Dickinson Cheese Company discharged whey into the Heart River in North Dakota. This violated the North Dakota Antipollution Act. It caused the death of some 36,000 pounds of fish. North Dakota sued Dickinson for the damage.

> **DECISION:** Judgment for Dickinson Cheese Company. Although the state as sovereign had the power to regulate the taking of game and wildlife, the state was not the owner thereof and therefore could not recover damages for the destruction of the fish. The state antipollution law did not change that conclusion but merely gave the right to impose additional regulations for the protection of wildlife. [North Dakota v Dickinson Cheese Company, Inc. (ND) 200 NW2d 59]

(b) Abandoned personal property. Personal property is deemed abandoned when the owner relinquishes possession of it with the intention to disclaim title to it. Yesterday's newspaper which is thrown out in the trash is abandoned personal property. Title to abandoned property may be acquired by the first person who obtains possession and control. A person becomes the owner the moment he takes possession of the abandoned personal property.

When the owner of property flees in the face of an approaching peril, the fact that he leaves property without taking it does not constitute an abandonment of the property, as an abandonment occurs only when the leaving of the property is a truly voluntary act of the owner.

> **FACTS:** Menzel fled from Europe upon the approach of enemy armies in World War II, leaving in his apartment certain paintings that were seized by the enemy. After World War II, the paintings were discovered in an art gallery owned by List. Menzel sued List for the paintings. List defended on the ground that Menzel had abandoned the paintings; and therefore title had passed to the person taking possession of them and from such possessor had been transferred lawfully to List.

> **DECISION:** Judgment for Menzel. There is an abandonment, so as to permit the first occupant to acquire title, only when the act of abandoning is voluntary. When property is left in order to escape from a danger, there is not a voluntary act of abandoning the property and the ownership of the original owner is not lost or affected. [Menzel v List, 49 Misc2d 300, 267 NYS2d 804]

§ 20:13. ESCHEAT. Difficult questions arise in connection with unclaimed property. In the case of personal property, the practical answer is that the property will probably disappear after a period of time, or it may be sold for unpaid charges, as by a carrier, hotel, or warehouse. A growing problem arises with respect to unclaimed corporate dividends, bank deposits, insurance payments, and refunds. Most states have a statute providing for the *escheat* of such unclaimed property to the state government. A number of states have adopted the Uniform Disposition of Unclaimed Property Act.[17]

§ 20:14. JUDGMENTS. The entry of a judgment ordinarily has no effect upon the title to personal property owned by the judgment debtor. Exceptions arise when (a) the purpose of entering the judgment is to determine title to the property as against the whole world, or (b) the action is brought to recover the value of converted personal property. In the latter case the payment of the judgment entered against the converter for the value of the goods transfers title to him as though there had been a voluntary sale.[18]

C. MULTIPLE OWNERSHIP OF PERSONAL PROPERTY

§ 20:15. INTRODUCTION. All interests in a particular object of property may be held in *severalty*, that is, by one person alone. Ownership in severalty also exists when title is held in the form of "*A or B*," as the use of the word "or" is inconsistent with co-ownership.

Several persons may have concurrent interests in the same property, and the relative interests of co-owners as between themselves may differ. For example, when the owner of a bank account causes the bank to add the name of another person to the account so that either may draw checks on the account, both the original and the new owner are co-owners of the account as far as the bank is concerned. As between themselves, however, they may in fact be co-owners or the one whose name is added may merely be an agent for the other. In the latter case, while the agent has the right to withdraw money, he cannot keep the money for himself.

§ 20:16. TENANCY IN COMMON. A *tenancy in common* is a form of ownership by two or more persons. The interest of a tenant in common may be transferred or inherited, in which case the taker becomes a tenant in common with the others. This tenancy is terminated only when there is a partition, giving each a specific portion, or when one person acquires all of the interests of the co-owners.

---

[17] The 1954 version of the Act was adopted in Arizona, California, Florida, Idaho, Illinois, Montana, New Mexico, Oregon, Utah, Virginia, Washington, and West Virginia. A revision of the Act was made in 1966, and this revised form has been adopted in Alabama, Georgia, Indiana, Iowa, Minnesota, Montana, New Mexico, Oklahoma, Rhode Island, South Carolina, South Dakota, and Wisconsin.

[18] Some courts hold that title passes to the converter upon the mere entry of a judgment against him although it has not yet been paid. In contrast, others hold that title passes only upon payment of the judgment of the plaintiff.

§ **20:17. JOINT TENANCY.** A *joint tenancy* is another form of ownership by two or more persons. A joint tenant may transfer his interest to a third party, but this destroys the joint tenancy. In such a case the remaining joint tenant becomes a tenant in common with the third person who has acquired the interest of the other joint tenant.

Upon the death of a joint tenant, the remaining tenants take the share of the deceased, and finally the last surviving joint tenant takes the property as a holder in severalty.

> **FACTS:** Eva opened a joint account in her name and the name of her daughter, Alice. Later Alice withdrew all the money from the account. The next day Eva died. Eva's husband claimed that the money withdrawn by Alice was an asset of Eva's estate.

> **DECISION:** The money that was withdrawn by Alice belonged to her by survivorship. As there was no evidence of an agency, the money was owned by her and Eva. When Alice withdrew all the money on deposit, it was still owned by her and Eva as joint tenants. When Eva died, Alice became the sole owner by survivorship and therefore the withdrawn money was not part of Eva's estate. [In re Filfiley's Will, 63 Misc2d 1052, 313 NYS2d 793]

When the surviving joint tenant receives the share of the predeceasing joint tenant by virtue of survivorship, the survivor does not "inherit" from the joint tenant and therefore is not subject to any estate or inheritance tax in states that follow the common law.[19] In some states, however, statutes have been adopted that subject the surviving tenant to the same tax as though he had inherited the fractional share of the predeceasing tenant.

(a) Statutory change. Statutes in many states have modified the common law by adding a formal requirement to the creation of a joint tenancy with survivorship. At common law such an estate would be created by a transfer of property to "*A* and *B* as joint tenants." Under these statutes it is necessary to add the words "with right of survivorship," or similar words, if it is desired to create a right of survivorship. If there is no right of survivorship, the transfer does not create a joint tenancy. Thus, a certificate of deposit issued only in the name of "*A* or *B*" does not create a joint tenancy because it does not refer to a survivor.[20]

Joint tenancy statutes permit the owner of property to transfer it directly to himself and another to obtain the advantage of survivorship without the necessity of an intermediate transfer to a strawman.

Courts do not favor joint tenancy and will construe a transfer of property to several persons to be a tenancy in common whenever possible. Statutes in many states have abolished or modified joint tenancy, especially as to supervisorship.

(b) Bank accounts. The deposit of money in a joint account constitutes a gift of a joint ownership interest in the deposit of money when that is the

---

[19] Calvert v Wallrath (Tex) 457 SW2d 376.
[20] Dalton v Eyestone, 240 Ark 1032, 403 SW2d 730.

intent of the depositor. The mere fact that money is deposited in a joint account does not in itself establish that there was such a gift, particularly where the evidence indicates that the deposits were made in the joint account "solely for the convenience of enabling either of the parties to draw therefrom for family purposes." When the joint account is merely an agency device, the account agent is not entitled to use any part of the deposit as his own money.

FACTS: Jean Weaver opened a bank account in her name and later added the name of her daughter, Mary Lock. When Jean died, the court administering Jean's estate treated the account balance as part of Jean's estate. Mary claimed the balance. The evidence showed that Mary's name had been added to Jean's account so that she could handle the money if Jean was not able to do so.

DECISION: Judgment for Jean's estate. There was no evidence that Jean intended to make a gift of any part of the account to Mary when she added Mary's name to the account. The evidence showed that Mary's only interest was as an agent for Jean. The full ownership of the account therefore remained in Jean and at her death passed to her estate. [Weaver's Estate v Lock, 75 IllApp2d 227, 220 NE2d 321]

In many states, the common law as to joint tenants has been abolished with respect to joint bank accounts and these are merely governed by the agreement between the parties.[21]

§ 20:18. TENANCY BY ENTIRETY. At common law a *tenancy by entirety* (or tenancy by the entireties) was created when property was transferred to husband and wife in such a manner that it would create a joint tenancy if transferred to other persons, not husband and wife.[22] It differs from joint tenancy, however, in that the right of survivorship cannot be extinguished and one tenant alone cannot convey his interest to a third person, although in some jurisdictions he may transfer his right to share the possession and the profits. This form of property holding is popular in common-law jurisdictions because creditors of one of the spouses cannot reach the property while both are living. Only a creditor of both the husband and the wife under the same obligation can obtain execution against the property. Moreover, the tenancy by entirety is in effect a substitute for a will since the surviving spouse acquires the complete property interest upon the death of the other. There may be other reasons, however, why each spouse should make a will.

Generally a tenancy by the entirety is created by the mere fact that property is transferred to two persons who are husband and wife, even though it is not expressly stated that such a tenancy is thereby created, unless, of course, it is expressly stated that a different tenancy is created. This type of tenancy may also be created by either husband or wife. Thus, when a husband opens a bank account in the name of himself and his wife, or the survivor of them, and either the husband or wife may make

---

[21] Owen v Owen, 29 Utah2d 194, 507 P2d 368.
[22] Hoffman v Nerwell, 249 Ky 270, 60 SW2d 607.

withdrawals, a tenancy by the entirety is created as to any money that is deposited in the account, even though all deposists are made by the husband.

If the grantees are not lawfully married to each other, a tenancy by the entireties does not arise. However, the fact that a tenancy by the entireties was intended is often held a sufficient indication that there was to be survivorship, with the result that on the death of one spouse the share of the dying spouse passes to the other by survivorship.

FACTS: Alejo Lopez was married to Soledad. While still married to her, he "married" Helen in 1946. In 1947 and 1952, two parcels of real estate were conveyed to Alejo and Helen, "his wife," "as tenants by the entireties." Soledad divorced Alejo in 1954, and a week later Alejo remarried Helen. Alejo was killed in an accident. Helen claimed both tracts of land by survivorship.

DECISION: Helen was the sole owner. While she and Alejo were not tenants by the entireties because they were not married when they took title, the use of the term "tenants by the entireties" showed an intent to create an estate which would have the characteristic of survivorship. That intention would be given effect by construing the ownership as a joint tenancy. [Lopez v Lopez, 250 Md 491, 243 A2d 588]

In many states the granting of an absolute divorce converts a tenancy by the entireties into a tenancy in common.

§ 20:19. **COMMUNITY PROPERTY.** In some states property acquired during the period of marriage is the *community property* of the husband and wife. Some statutes provide for the right of survivorship; others provide that half of the property of the deceased husband or wife shall go to the heirs, or permit such half to be disposed of by will. It is commonly provided that property acquired by either spouse during the marriage is prima facie community property, even though title is taken in the spouse's individual name, unless it can be shown that it was obtained with property possessed by that spouse prior to the marriage.

QUESTIONS AND CASE PROBLEMS

1. Carol and Robert, both over 21, became engaged. Robert gave Carol an engagement ring. He was killed in an automobile crash before they were married. His estate demanded that Carol return the ring. Was she entitled to keep it? [Cohen v Bayside Federal Savings and Loan Ass'n, 62 Misc2d 738, 309 NYS2d 980]

2. Adele Barret purchased corporate stock jointly in her name and the name of her niece, Mary Oliver, with the right of survivorship. When Adele died, the persons

who received her estate claimed that the taxes on the estate should be paid proportionately by Mary since she was benefiting from the death of Adele. Decide. [Barret's Estate (FlaApp) 137 So2d 587]

3. Hughes and Kay were not married, but property was deeded to them as "husband and wife." Subsequently they brought an action to determine their rights in the property. What type of tenancy was created by the deed? [Hughes v Kay, 194 Ore 519, 242 P2d 788]

4. The owner of an investment account certificate issued by a savings and loan association directed the association to name him and the church of which he was a member "as joint tenants with right of survivorship." When the owner opened the account he had signed a signature card. The association did not require a new signature card after being told to add the church as co-owner, and no representative of the church ever signed any card or other document. Interest payments on the certificate were made to the original owner until his death and the church never knew of the transaction until the original owner died. The executor of the original owner then brought action against the church to determine ownership of the certificate. Was the church the owner? [Wantuck v United States Savings and Loan Association (Mo) 461 SW2d 692]

5. Brogden acquired a biblical manuscript in 1945. In 1952 he told his sister Lucy that he wanted Texas A. & M. College to have this manuscript. He dictated a note so stating and placed it with the manuscript. He made some effort to have an officer of the college come for the manuscript. In 1956 he delivered the manuscript to his sister, stating that he was afraid that someone would steal it. Later in the year he told a third person that he was going to give the manuscript to the college. In 1957 he was declared incompetent. In 1959 the sister delivered the manuscript to the college. In April, 1960, Brogden died, and his heirs, Bailey and others, sued Harrington and other officers of the college to have the title to the manuscript determined. Decide [Harrington v Bailey (TexCivApp) 351 SW2d 946]

6. Lyons and his wife had a savings account in a bank in the names of "E. L. Lyons or Mrs. E. L. Lyons." Both husband and wife signed a signature card agreeing to the rules and regulations of the bank. Did this create a tenancy by the entireties? [Lyons' Estate (Fla) 90 So2d 39]

7. In 1922 John Vlcek and Julia were married in Europe. He came alone to the United States and lived with Matilda. In 1948 property was purchased by them and the deed made the transfer to "John and Matilda Vlcek." John died in 1958. The two women and their children claimed the property. Who was entitled to the property? [Vlcek v Vlcek, 42 AppDiv2d 308, 346 NYS2d 893]

8. Henry Larson delivered a check to his son, Clifford, for $8,500. The check bore the notation "As Loan." Some time later the son asked the father what he should do about the loan. Henry wrote Clifford a note in broken English saying "Keep it No Return." Henry died and the canceled check with the notation "As Loan" was found among his papers. Harry's administratrix sued Clifford for repayment of the loan. Did he have any defense? [Larson's Estate, 71 Wash2d 349, 428 P2d 558]

9. Land was conveyed to Mattie Moring and Richard Roundtree as joint tenants with the right of survivorship. Mattie mortgaged the land to D.A.D., Inc., without the consent or knowledge of Richard. D.A.D. brought a foreclosure action on the mortgage, Mattie died. Was D.A.D. entitled to enforce the mortgage (a) as to all of the land, (b) as to Mattie's one-half interest, (c) as to none of the land? [D.A.D., Inc. v Moring (FlaApp) 218 So2d 451]

BAILMENTS

A. GENERAL PRINCIPLES

§ 21:1. DEFINITION. A *bailment* is the legal relation that arises whenever one person delivers possession of personal property to another person under an agreement, express or implied, by which the latter is under a duty to return the identical property to the former or to deliver it or dispose of it as agreed. The person who turns over the possession of the property is the *bailor*. The person to whom he gives the possession is the *bailee*.

Many instances arise in which the owner of personal property entrusts it to another. A person checks a coat at a restaurant or loans a car to a friend, delivers a watch to a jeweler for repairs, takes furniture to a warehouse for storage, or delivers goods to an airline for shipment. The delivery of property under such circumstances is a bailment.

§ 21:2. ELEMENTS OF BAILMENT. Because of the complex nature of a bailment, it is often necessary to break it down into specific elements in order to obtain a clear understanding of each element.

(a) Agreement. The bailment is based upon an agreement. Technically the bailment is the act of delivering the property to the bailee and the relationship existing thereafter. The agreement that precedes this delivery is an agreement to make a bailment rather than the actual bailment. Generally this agreement will contain all the elements of a contract so that the bailment transaction in fact consists of (1) a contract to bail and (2) the actual bailing of the property. Ordinarily there is no requirement that the contract of bailment be in writing.

The statute of frauds does not apply to a bailment agreement. If there is a written agreement, the parol evidence rule is applicable to the agreement if it is complete. If the written agreement is not complete, the missing terms may be proven by parol evidence.[1]

---

[1] In some states, however, a writing or recording of the bailment agreement may be necessary to protect the interest of the bailor.

(b) Personal property. The subject of a bailment may be any personal property of which possession may be given. Real property cannot be bailed.

(c) Bailor's interest. The bailor is usually the owner of the property, but ownership by the bailor is not required. It is sufficient that the bailor have physical possession. Thus, an employee may be a bailor in leaving his employer's truck at a garage. Whether possession is lawful or not is immaterial. A thief, for example, may be a bailor.

(d) Bailee's interest. Title to the property does not pass to the bailee, and he cannot sell the property to a third person unless the bailee is also an agent to make such a sale. If the bailee attempts to do so, his act only transfers possession and the owner may recover the property from the third person.

The bailor may cause third persons to believe that the bailee is the owner of the bailed property. If he does so, he may be estopped to deny that the bailee is the owner as against persons who have relied on the bailor's representations. As a further exception, if the bailee is a dealer in goods of the kind entrusted to him by the bailor, a sale by the bailee to a buyer in the ordinary course of business will pass the bailor's title to the buyer.

(e) Delivery and acceptance. The bailment arises when, pursuant to the agreement of the parties, the property is delivered to the bailee and accepted by the bailee as subject to the bailment agreement.

FACTS: Theobald went to the beauty parlor operated by Satterthwaite. When it was her turn, she left her coat on a hook on the wall and went into the back room for her treatment. There was no one in the outer room when she left. Nothing had been stolen from the outer room in its 20 years of operation. When Theobald returned to the outer room, her coat was not there. She sued Satterthwaite claiming that the latter was liable as a negligent bailee.

DECISION: Judgment for Satterthwaite. She was not a bailee, and therefore she was not liable as a negligent bailee. A bailment cannot arise unless the personal property is delivered into the possession of the bailee. The fact that it was left on the premises did not give rise to a bailment. [Theobald v Satterthwaite, 30 Wash2d 92, 190 P2d 714]

Likewise, no bailment arises when an employee leaves tools on a workbench overnight, particularly when the employee had been informed by the employer that the latter would not be responsible for any loss of tools.

Delivery may be actual, as when the bailor physically hands a book to the bailee, or it may be a *constructive delivery*, as when the bailor points out a package to the bailee who then takes possession of it.

(f) Return of specific property. A bailment places a duty upon the bailee to return the specific property that was bailed or to deliver or dispose of it in the manner directed by the bailor. If a person has an option of paying money or of returning property other than that which was delivered to him, there is generally no bailment. Thus, when a farmer delivers wheat to a grain elevator that gives him a receipt and promises to return either the wheat or a certain amount of money upon presentation of the receipt, the relationship is not a bailment.[2] The importance of this distinction lies in the fact that when the relationship is not a bailment but some other relationship, such as a sale, the risk of loss will ordinarily be on the warehouse if the property is damaged or destroyed; whereas, if it is a bailment, the bailor would ordinarily bear the loss.

(1) Bailment of Fungible Goods. In the case of the bailment of *fungible goods*, such as grain and oil, where any one unit or quantity is exactly the same as any other unit or quantity, the law treats the transaction as a bailment when there is an obligation to return only an equal quantity of goods of the same description as the goods originally delivered. Thus, an agreement by a grain elevator receiving 1,000 bushels of Grade A wheat from a farmer to return to him on demand 1,000 bushels of Grade A wheat gives rise to a bailment even though there is no agreement that the identical wheat delivered by the farmer is to be returned to him.

An "identical return" bailment might be made in some cases, as when a farmer has developed some experimental seed which he desires to be returned to him. Ordinarily, however, the grain that a farmer delivers to the elevator will be a recognized commercial variety so that the elevator is likely to have, or is likely to receive thereafter, identically similar gain from other farmers. In that case, the warehouse will not ordinarily undertake to return to any one customer the identical grain delivered by that customer to the elevator but merely an equivalent quantity of grain.

(2) Option to Purchase. In an option to purchase, the transaction is a bailment, with the rights and liabilities of the parties being determined on that basis, until the bailee exercises the option. Theoretically this is inconsistent with the definition of bailment because it contradicts the obligation of the bailee to return the identical property.

The bailment with an option to purchase may sometimes be used in connection with credit sales, in which case the "rental" payments by the bailee (who is actually the buyer) will be calculated in terms of the amount due on the balance of the purchase price; and upon exercising the option to purchase, the bailee-buyer will be required to pay any unpaid balance of the purchase price.

§ 21:3. CLASSIFICATIONS OF BAILMENTS.

Bailments are classified as ordinary and extraordinary. *Extraordinary bailments* are those in which the bailee is under unusual duties and liabilities by law, as in the case of bailments in which a motel or a common carrier is the bailee. *Ordinary bailments* include all other bailments.

Bailments may or may not provide for compensation to the bailee. Upon that basis they may be classified as *contract bailments* and *gratuitous*

---

[2] In some states, however, statutes declare that the relationship between the farmer and the grain elevator is a bailment and not a sale. United States v Haddix & Sons, Inc. (CA6 Mich) 415 F2d 584.

bailments. If a minor rightfully cancels a purchase and offers to return the goods to the seller but the latter wrongly refuses to accept the goods, the minor, while still in possession of the goods, is a gratuitous bailee.

The fact that no charge is made by the bailor does not necessarily make the transaction a gratuitous bailment. If the bailment is made to further a business interest of the bailor, as when something is loaned "free" to a customer, the bailment is not gratuitous.[3]

Bailments may also be classified as for the (a) sole benefit of the bailor, as when a farmer gratuitously transports another's produce to the city; (b) sole benefit of the bailee, as when a person borrows the automobile of a friend; or (c) benefit of both parties (mutual-benefit bailment), as when one rents a power tool. A mutual-benefit bailment also arises when a prospective buyer of an automobile leaves his present car with the dealer so that the latter may test and make an appraisal of it for a contemplated trade-in.[4]

§ 21:4. CONSTRUCTIVE BAILMENTS. When one person comes into possession of personal property of another without the owner's consent, the law treats the possessor as though he were a bailee. Sometimes this relationship is called a *constructive bailment*. It is thus held that a person who finds lost property must treat that property as if he were a bailee.

When a city impounds an automobile, a bailment arises as to the vehicle and its contents.[5] A police officer taking possession of stolen goods is deemed a bailee for the true owner. A seller who has not yet delivered the goods to his buyer is treated as the bailee of the goods if title has passed to the buyer. Similarly, a buyer who is in possession of goods, the title to which has not passed to him, is a bailee.

> **FACTS:** Armored Car Service made daily trips to carry cash to be deposited in the accounts of its customers in local banks. A money bag that should have been deposited in the Curtiss National Bank in the account of Dade County Board of Public Instruction was by mistake delivered to the First National Bank and then apparently disappeared without any trace of what happened. Armored Car Service sued First National Bank, claiming that the bank had been negligent in the handling of the misdelivered money bag and that it was under the duty to exercise reasonable care.
>
> **DECISION:** Judgment for Armored Car Service. When the money bag was left without any prior agreement, the First National Bank became a constructive bailee under a gratuitous bailment. As such, the bank was obligated to exercise reasonable care under the circumstances and the fact that it had not kept any record of the money bag was prima facie proof that it had been negligent. [Armored Car Service, Inc. v First National Bank (FlaApp) 144 So2d 431]

§ 21:5. RENTING OF SPACE DISTINGUISHED. The renting of space in a locker or building does not give rise to a bailment by the placing of goods by

---

[3] Coe Oil Service, Inc. v Hair (La) 283 So2d 734.
[4] Sampson v Birkeland, 63 IllApp2d 178, 211 NE2d 139.
[5] St. Paul v Myles, 298 Minn 298, 218 NW2d 697.

the renter in the space when under the rental agreement he has the exclusive right to use the space. In such a case, putting property into the space does not constitute a delivery of the goods into the possession of the owner of the space. On this basis, there is no bailment in a self-service parking lot when the car owner parks his car, retains the key, and his only contact with any parking lot employee is upon making payment when leaving the lot. In such situations the car owner merely rents the space for parking.

The practical consequence of this conclusion is that if the car is damaged or if it disappears, the car owner cannot recover damages from the parking lot management unless the owner can show some fault on the part of the parking lot. If the transaction were a bailment, the owner of the car would establish a prima facie right to recover by proving the fact of the bailment and that there was a loss.

If the parking lot is a locked enclosure with a guard to whom the patron must surrender a parking ticket received on entering the lot and pay any parking fee that is not yet paid, a modern trend regards the transaction as a bailment. The theoretical objection to this view is that the lot does not have full dominion and control over the car since it cannot move the car because the patron has retained possession of the keys. At the same time, since it has the power to exclude others from the car, it is "realistic" to treat the parking lot as a bailee and hold it to a bailee's standard of care.

§ **21:6. BAILMENT OF CONTENTS OF CONTAINER.** It is a question of the intention of the parties, as that appears to a reasonable person, whether the bailing of a container also constitutes a bailment of articles contained in it; that is, whether a bailment of a truck is a bailment of articles in the truck, whether a bailment of a coat is a bailment of articles in the pockets of the coat, and so on. When the contained articles are of a class that is reasonably or normally to be found in the container, they are regarded as bailed in the absence of an express disclaimer. If the articles are not of such a nature and their presence in the container is unknown to the bailee, there is no bailment of such articles. Consequently, although the circumstances were such that the parking of a car constituted a bailment, there was no bailment of valuable drawings and sporting equipment that were on the back seat but which were not visible from the outside of the car.[6] When a car is bailed with the trunk locked, there is ordinarily a bailment of whatever is locked in the trunk.

> **FACTS:** Gilchrist took an automobile to a dealer, Winmar J. Ford, Inc., to have the tires rotated. Gilchrist was a refrigerator mechanic and had a special set of tools in the trunk of the car. He did not inform Ford that the tools were in the car. The car was stolen and Gilchrist was paid by his insurance company for the value of the tools. Ford defended on the ground that it was not liable for the value of the tools and that it had never been informed of their value and therefore was not alerted to take special precautions.

---

[6] Cerreta v Kinney Corp. 50 NJSuper 514, 142 A2d 917.

DECISION: Judgment for Gilchrist, There was a bailment of the contents of the trunk when the car was bailed. Ford was therefore liable for the value of the tools which were stolen. [Gilchrist v Winmar J. Ford, Inc. 355 NYS2d 261]

B. DUTIES AND LIABILITIES

§ 21:7. DUTIES AND LIABILITIES OF THE BAILEE.

(a) **Performance.** If the bailment is based upon a contract, the bailee must perform his part of the contract and is liable to the bailor for any loss arising out of his failure to do so. If the bailment is for repair, the bailee is under the duty to make the repairs properly. The fact that the bailee uses due care does not excuse him from failing to perform according to his contract.

FACTS: Welge owned a sofa and chair which Baena Brothers agreed to reupholster and to reduce the size of the arms. The work was not done according to the agreement, and the furniture when finished had no value to Welge and was not accepted by him. Baena then sued him for the contract price. Welge counterclaimed for the value of the furniture.

DECISION: Judgment for Welge on the counterclaim. When Baena Brothers made a contract with respect to the furniture, they were required to perform that contract according to ordinary principles of contract law. The concept of due care, which would protect them if the goods were damaged by a third person, act of God, or accident, does not apply when the question is whether the bailee has performed his contract. As there was a failure to perform their contract, Baena Brothers were liable for damages for such breach. [Baena Brothers v Welge, 3 ConnCir 67, 207 A2d 749]

A repairman to whom property, such as an automobile, is entrusted is both a bailee and a contracting party. Consequently, in addition to his obligation to care for the property as a bailee, he must perform his duties as a contracting party. When he undertakes to repair, some courts find an implied warranty that the repair will be effective. Should the repairman fail to repair properly, the bailor who uses the property with knowledge that it had not been effectively repaired, will be barred from claiming for damages sustained through injury arising from such use. For example, when the bailor was aware of the fact that the automobile repairman had failed to repair the brakes, the bailor would be barred by his contributory negligence from recovering damages from the repairman for an injury sustained when the automobile could not be stopped because of the defective brakes and struck a utility pole.[7]

(b) **Care of the property.** The bailee is under a duty to care for the property entrusted to him. If the property is damaged or destroyed, the bailee is liable for the loss (1) if the harm was caused in whole or in part by the bailee's failure to use reasonable care under the circumstances, or (2) if the harm was sustained during unauthorized use of the property by the

---

[7] Bereman v Burdolski, 204 Kan 162, 460 P2d 567.

bailee. Otherwise the bailor bears the loss. Thus, if the bailee was exercising due care and was making an authorized use of the property, the bailor must bear the loss of or damage to the property caused by an act of a third person, whether willful or negligent, by an accident or occurrence for which no one is at fault, or by an act of God. In this connection the term, *act of God*, means a natural phenomenon that it is not reasonably foreseeable, such as a sudden flood or lightning.

FACTS: Sky Aviation Corporation rented an airplane to Colt. In flying to his destination, Colt did not make use of weather reports. When he arrived at the destination, there were high winds. He landed, instead of turning back to his point of origin where there were no high winds. In landing, he did not make use of a ground crew man who sought to hold down a wing of the plane while he was taxiing to the tie-down area. The wind flipped the plane over. Sky Aviation sued Colt for the damage to the plane. He defended on the ground that it was an act of God.

DECISION: Judgment for Sky Aviation. The damage to the plane was not the result of an act of God but of Colt's negligence in attempting to land in the high winds instead of returning to a safe base, in ignoring weather reports in flight, and in failing to use the assistance of the ground crew man. Likewise there was no proof that the winds were so unusual as to constitute an act of God. Colt was therefore a negligent bailee and was liable to the bailor for the damage to the bailed property. [Sky Aviation Corp. v Colt (Wyo) 475 P2d 301]

Some courts hold that in the automobile parking lot situation the operator of the lot has the duty to exercise ordinary care for the protection of the automobile regardless of whether the relationship is a bailment or some other relationship, such as a leasing of space or the granting of a license to use the parking lot.[8]

(1) *Standard of Care.* The standard for ordinary bailments is reasonable care under the circumstances, that is, the degree of care which a reasonable person would exercise in the situation in order to prevent the realization of reasonably foreseeable harm. The significant factors in determining what constitutes reasonable care in a bailment are the time and place of making the bailment, the facilities for taking care of the bailed property, the nature of the bailed property, the bailee's knowledge of its nature, and the extent of the bailee's skill and experience in taking care of goods of that kind.

The bailee is not an insurer of the safety of the property, even though he assures the bailor that he will take good care of the property; and he is not liable when there is no proof of his negligence as a cause of the harm nor of his unauthorized use of the property.

(2) *Contract Modification of Liability.* A bailee's liability may be expanded by contract. A provision that he assumes absolute liability for the property is binding, but there is a difference of opinion as to whether a

---

[8] In some states, statutes expressly prohibit certain kinds of paid bailees from limiting their liability. Universal Cigar Corp. v The Hertz Corp. 55 Misc2d 84, 284 NYS2d 337.

stipulation to return the property "in good condition" or "in as good condition as received" has the effect of imposing such absolute liability. An ordinary bailee may limit his liability, except for his willful conduct, by agreement or contract; but modern cases hold that a specialized commercial bailee, such as an auto parking garage, cannot limit its liability for either its willful or negligent conduct.

By definition a limitation of liability must be a term of the bailment contract before any question arises as to whether it is binding. Thus, a limitation contained in a receipt mailed by a bailee after receiving a coat for storage is not effective to alter the terms of the bailment as originally made.

(3) Insurance. In the absence of a statute or contract provision, a bailee is not under any duty to insure for the benefit of the bailor the property entrusted to his care.

FACTS: Brown left his automobile at the Five Points Parking Center. A sign at the entrance read, "Insured Garage." The battery was stolen from Brown's car. Parking Center did not carry any insurance against theft. Brown sued Parking Center, claiming that it had breached its contract duty to insure.

DECISION: Judgment for Parking Center. There was no agreement by Parking Center to insure against theft. The sign "Insured Garage" did not impose any contract duty because it was too vague in that it did not specify any kind of insurance. For the same reason, Parking Center was not liable for fraud, as against the contention that it had deceived Brown into believing that his automobile would be insured against theft while parked. [Brown v Five Points Parking Center, 121 GaApp 819, 175 SE2d 901]

(c) Unauthorized use. The bailee is liable for conversion, just as though he stole the property, if he uses the property without authority or uses it in any manner to which the bailor had not agreed. Ordinarily he will be required to pay compensatory damages, although punitive damages may be inflicted when the improper use was deliberate and the bailee was recklessly indifferent to the effect of his use upon the property.

(d) Return of property. The bailee is under a duty to return the identical property which is the subject of the bailment or to deliver it as directed. The redelivery to the bailor or delivery to a third person must be made in accordance with the terms of the contract as to time, place, and manner. When the agreement between the parties does not control these matters, the customs of the community govern.

Special statutes may protect the lessor of personal property, as by making it a special criminal offense for the lessee to convert rented property. The statute may create a presumption or inference to aid in the prosecution of the wrongdoer, similar to the presumption created in the case of a bad-check law. For example, a statute may declare that it is prima facie evidence of intent to defraud for a person renting property to sign the rental agreement or lease with a name other than his own or to fail to return the property to its owner within 10 days after being personally served with a written demand for it. In some states it is a crime to abandon or conceal rented goods, such as an automobile.

The bailee is excused from delivery when the goods are lost, stolen, or destroyed without his fault. If his fault or neglect has caused or contributed to the loss, however, he is liable. To illustrate, certain goods are destroyed by a flood while in the possession of the bailee. If the bailee could have protected the goods from the flood by taking reasonable precautions, the bailee is liable. The bailee is excused from the duty to return the goods when they have been taken from him under process of law.

(1) Bailee's Lien. By common law or statute, a bailee is given a *lien* or the right to retain possession of the bailed property until the bailee has been paid for any charges for storage or repairs. If the bailee has a lien on the property he is entitled to keep possession of the property until he has been paid the claim on which the lien is based.

A bailee who is authorized by statute to sell the bailed property to enforce his charge or claim against the bailor must give such notice as is required by statute. If he sells the property without giving the required notice, he is liable for conversion of the property.[9]

(2) Constitutionality of Bailee's Lien. There is authority, however, that the repairman's lien statute is unconstitutional in allowing the lienor to sell the property to enforce the lien upon giving notice and advertising the sale.

For example, a garageman's sale to enforce a lien is unconstitutional when the statute under which he acts permits the sale of an automobile for storage and repair charges without prior notice and hearing as to the existence of the amount alleged to be due.[10]

§ 21:8. BURDEN OF PROOF. When the bailor sues the bailee for damages to the bailed property, as distinguished from a suit for breach of contract, the bailor has the burden of proving that the bailee was at fault and that such fault was the proximate cause of the loss. A prima facie right of the bailor to recover is established, however, by proof that the property was delivered by the bailor to the bailee and thereafter could not be returned or was returned in a damaged condition.

FACTS: Axelrod took home draperies to Wardrobe Cleaners to be dry cleaned. The head of the drapery department examined the draperies to determine if they were strong enough to be cleaned. He accepted the drapes from Axelrod. The colors of the drapes were ruined in the process of dry cleaning and Axelrod sued Wardrobe cleaners for the damages. The head of the drapery department of Wardrobe Cleaners testified that, because of new imported dyes, it could not be determined whether colors would stand cleaning without pretesting, and that Wardrobe was not equipped to chemically test fabrics for color fastness.

---

[9] Lewis v Ehrlich, 14 OklaApp 529, 513 P2d 153.
[10] Hernandez v European Auto Collision, Inc. (CA2 NY) 487 F2d 378.

DECISION: Judgment for Axelrod. A bailment was created when the draperies were given to Wardrobe. As soon as it was shown that damage had occurred to them while in the possession of Wardrobe, a prima facie case of negligence was established and the burden was then on Wardrobe to go forward with evidence that it had acted with due care. The evidence showed that it had not so acted because it proceeded to clean the drapes, although it knew there was a danger and that it was not equipped to pretest for that danger. Wardrobe was negligent in that it should have refused to accept the draperies or should have subjected them to the necessary tests. [Axelrod v Wardrobe Cleaners, Inc. (LaApp) 289 So2d 847]

If the loss was caused by fire or theft, the bailee need show only the cause of the loss; and the bailor does not recover from the bailee unless the bailor is able to prove affirmatively that the bailee was negligent and that such negligence contributed to or caused the loss.[11]

§ 21:9. RIGHTS OF THE BAILOR. The typical commercial bailment is a mutual benefit bailment. Under such a bailment, the bailor has the right to compensation, commonly called rent, for the use of the bailed property. If the bailor is obligated to render a service to the bailee, his failure to do so will ordinarily bar the bailor from recovering compensation from the bailee.

FACTS: Bryant rented a typewriter from Royal McBee Co. The lease stated that Royal would keep the typewriter in good working condition. The typewriter did not work, and Royal was not able to put it in working condition. Royal sued for the rental payment.

DECISION: Bryant was not liable because the maintenance of the typewriter in good condition was a condition precedent to Bryant's duty to pay. As Royal had not satisfied this condition, Bryant never became liable to pay. [Royal McBee Corp. v Bryant (DistColApp) 217 A2d 603]

(a) Rights against the bailee. The bailor may sue the bailee for breach of contract if the goods are not redelivered to the bailor or delivered to a third person as specified by the bailment agreement. He may also maintain actions for negligence, willful destruction, and unlawful retention or conversion of the goods. Actions for unlawful retention or conversion can be brought only after the bailor is entitled to possession.

When the bailee obtains possession of the goods by fraudulently inducing the bailor to make the bailment, the bailee is guilty of conversion. For example, when a television serviceman fraudulently told a customer that he wanted to take the set from the customer's home to the shop of the repairman's employer in order to show the employer how badly prior

---

[11] This is the majority view. The minority courts are influenced by the consideration that fire or theft loss may often be the result of the bailee's negligence and that in any case the bailee has the means of protecting the property and superior means of knowing just what happened. By these courts the bailees should be required to prove freedom from negligence as well as the fact that the loss was caused by fire or theft. Threlkeld v Breaux Ballard, 296 Ky 344, 177 SW2d 157.

repairs had been made by another employee of the employer, but the actual purpose was to obtain and keep possession of the set until the customer paid improper service charges, the conduct of the repairman constituted a conversion and the customer may recover from the employer the value of the set and may also recover punitive damages of three times the value of the set.

The fact that the bailment contract stipulates that the bailee shall return the goods in good condition, reasonable wear and tear excepted, is generally regarded as not changing the rules as to incidence of loss. Thus, the bailor, as in the ordinary case, bears the risk of loss from fire of unknown origin; and the bailee is not made an insurer against fire by the inclusion of such terms in the bailment contract.

(b) Rights against third persons. The bailor may sue third persons damaging or taking the bailed property from the bailee's possession, even though the bailment is for a fixed period that has not expired. In such a case the bailor is said to recover damages for injury to his *reversionary interest*, that is, the right which he has to regain the property upon the expiration of the period of the bailment.

§ 21:10. DUTIES AND LIABILITIES OF BAILOR.

(a) Condition of the property. In a mutual-benefit bailment for hire, the bailor is under a duty to furnish goods reasonably fit for the purpose contemplated by the parties. If the bailee is injured or if his property is damaged because of the defective condition of the bailed property, the bailor may be liable. If the bailment is for the sole benefit of the bailee, the bailor is under a duty to inform the bailee of known defects. If the bailee is harmed by a defect that was known by the bailor, the bailor is liable for damages. If the bailor receives a benefit from the bailment, he must not only inform the bailee of known defects, but he must also make a reasonable investigation to discover defects. The bailor is liable for the harm resulting from defects which would have been disclosed had he made such an examination, in addition to those which were known to him from an unknown defect.

If the defect would not have been revealed by a reasonable examination, the bailor, regardless of the classification of the bailment, is not liable for harm which results.

In any case the bailee, if he knows of the defective condition of the bailed property, is barred by his contributory negligence or assumption of risk if, in spite of that knowledge, he makes use of the property and sustains injury because of its condition.

(1) Harm to Bailee's Employee. When harm is caused a bailee's employee because of the negligence of the bailor, the latter is liable to the employee of the bailee, even though the employee did not have any direct dealings or contractual relationship with the bailor.

(2) Bailor's Implied Warranty. In many cases the duty of the bailor is described as an implied warranty that the goods will be reasonably fit for their intended use. Apart from an implied warranty, the bailor may expressly warrant the condition of the property, in which event he will be liable for the breach of the warranty to the same extent as though he had made a sale rather than a bailment of the property.

With the modern rise of car and equipment renting, there is beginning to appear a new trend in cases that extends to the bailee and third persons the benefit of an implied warranty by the bailor that the article is fit for its intended use and will remain so, as distinguished from merely that it was reasonably fit, or that it was fit at the beginning of the bailment, or that the property was free from defects known to the bailor or which reasonable investigation would disclose.

> **FACTS:** Contract Packers rented a truck from Hertz Truck Leasing. Packers' employee, Cintrone, was injured while riding in the truck, being driven by his helper, when the brakes of the truck did not function properly and the truck crashed. Cintrone sued Hertz.
>
> **DECISION:** Judgment for Cintrone. As Hertz was in the business of renting trucks, it should have foreseen that persons renting would rely on it to have the trucks in safe condition and would not be making the inspection and repair that an owner could be expected to make of his own car. Hence, there was an implied warranty or guaranty by Hertz that the truck was fit for normal use. That warranty continued for the duration of the truck rental, and the right to sue for its breach ran in favor of third persons, such as employees of the customer of Hertz, and conversely was not limited to suit by the customer. [Cintrone v Hertz Truck Leasing & Rental Service, 45 NJ 434, 212 A2d 769]

The significance of analysis on the basis of warranty lies in the fact that warranty liability may exist even though the bailor was not negligent.[12]

When a used car is loaned to a prospective buyer to "test drive," there is no implied warranty that it is fit for use although the dealer as bailor will be liable for negligence if he failed to exercise reasonable care to discover any defect in the car, or failed to disclose to the buyer any defect of which he had knowledge. When the bailee has reason to know that the bailor has purchased, rather than manufactured, the equipment he is renting to the bailee and that the bailor has no special knowledge with respect to the equipment, a warranty of fitness for purpose may be disclaimed by the bailment agreement.[13]

---

[12] United Airlines, Inc. v Johnson Equipment Co. (FlaApp) 227 So2d 528 (sustaining right of plaintiff to a new trial on the warranty theory, although the first trial on the theory of negligence had ended with a verdict in favor of the defendant, that is, with the conclusion that the defendant was not negligent. The commercial lessor may also be liable on the strict tort theory). See § 26:3(2) and § 26:18.

[13] Northwest Collectors, Inc. v Gerritsen, 74 Wash2d 690, 446 P2d 197. (The lessee selected the supplier, and the particular goods were then purchased from that supplier by the bailor under an agreement that the bailor would rent the goods to the bailee.) Note that if the bailment is actually a plan of selling on installment payments to the bailee, a disclaimer of warranties must satisfy the requirements of a disclaimer provision in a sales contract under Article 2 of the Uniform Commercial Code.

(b) Repair of the property. Under a rental contract the bailor has no duty to make repairs that are ordinary and incidental to the use of the goods bailed. The bailee must bear the expense of such repairs, in the absence of a contrary contract provision. If, however, the repairs required are of an unusual nature or if the bailment is for a short period of time, the bailor is required to make the repairs unless they were caused by the negligence or fault of the bailee.

§ **21:11. LIABILITY TO THIRD PERSONS.** When the bailee injures a third person with the bailed property, as when a bailee runs into a third person while he is driving a rented automobile, the bailee is liable to the third person to the same extent as though the bailee were the owner of the property. When the bailee repairs bailed property, he is liable to third persons who are injured in consequence of the negligent way in which he has made the repair. Conversely, the bailee is not liable to a third person who is injured by a thief who steals the bailed property from the bailee even though the theft was possible because the bailee was negligent. The bailor is ordinarily not liable to a third person.

In states which follow the common law, a person lending an automobile to another is not liable to a third person injured by such other person when the lender did not know or have reason to know that such other person was not a fit driver.

FACTS: Joan took driving lessons at the A-North Shore Driving School. Later the school loaned her an automobile and took her for her state driving test. Crowley was the state examiner. Joan drove into a signal box on the side of the road. Crowley was seriously injured. He sued the driving school.

DECISION: Judgment for the driving school. There was no evidence that it knew or should have known that Joan was unfit or incompetent and therefore the school was not liable for her conduct while driving the loaned automobile. [Crowley v A-North Shore Driving School, 19 IllApp3d 1035, 313 NE2d 200]

The bailor is liable, however, to the injured third person: (a) if the bailor has entrusted a dangerous instrumentality to one whom he knew was ignorant of its dangerous character; (b) if the bailor has entrusted an instrumentality, such as an automobile, to one whom he knows to be so incompetent or reckless that injury of third persons is a foreseeable consequence; (c) if the bailor has entrusted property with a defect that causes harm to the third person when the circumstances are such that the bailor would be liable to the bailee if the latter were injured by the defect; or (d) if the bailee is using the bailed article, such as driving an automobile, as the bailor's employee and in the course of his employment.

FACTS: Anders was interested in purchasing a used car from Glover Motors. He was trying out one of the cars when, in consequence of a defect in the brakes, he collided with the car driven by Wilcox. The latter sued Glover Motors, claiming that there was liability because Glover Motors knew or should have known that the brakes were defective.

DECISION: As the motor vehicle law imposes upon every owner the duty of exercising due care in maintaining the brakes of his automobile in good condition, Glover, as bailor, would be liable to Wilcox for violation of that duty. It was for the jury to determine whether Glover knew or had reason to know that the brakes were defective when it entrusted the car into the possession of Anders. [Wilcox v Glover Motors, 269 NC 473, 153 SE2d 76]

(a) Statutory change. A number of states have enacted statutes by which a person granting permission to another to use his automobile automatically becomes liable for any negligent harm caused by the person to whom he has entrusted the automobile. That is, permissive use imposes liability on the owner or provider for the permittee's negligence. In some states the statute is limited to cases where the permittee is under a specified age, such as 16 years. Under some statutes the owner is only liable with respect to harm sustained while the permittee is using the automobile for the purpose for which permission was granted. The fact that a lessee under a long-term lease may be embraced within the term of "owner" for the purpose of a motor vehicle statute does not affect the tort liability of the true owner if such liability otherwise exists.

(b) Family-purpose doctrine. Under what is called the *family-purpose doctrine,* some courts hold that when the bailor supplies a car for the use of his family, or members thereof, he is liable for the harm caused by a member of the family while negligently driving the car. Other jurisdictions reject this doctrine and refuse to impose liability on the bailor of the automobile unless there is an agency relationship between him and the driver.

QUESTIONS AND CASE PROBLEMS

1. Harris, who owned a commercial fishing boat, contracted with Deveau to install radar equipment in the boat. Deveau temporarily loaned Harris some radar equipment, and Harris put out to sea on a fishing trip. When he returned, the borrowed radar equipment was found ruined by salt water. Deveau sued Harris for the damage to the equipment. Apparently the sea water had entered when heavy seas broke a window. Was Harris liable for the damage? [Harris v Deveau (Alaska) 385 P2d 283]

2. The Hawkeye Specialty Co. had a contract to supply the United States with bolts that were heat chemically treated to protect against corrosion. Hawkeye sent a quantity of untreated bolts to Bendix Corporation under a contract by which Bendix was to treat the bolts as required by Hawkeye's contract with the United States. What was the relationship between Hawkeye and Bendix with respect to

the bolts thus delivered? [Hawkeye Specialty Co. v Bendix Corporation (Iowa) 160 NW2d 341]

3. Lewis put a paper bag containing $3,000 in cash in a railroad station coin-operated locker. After the period of the coin rental expired, a locker company employee opened the locker, removed the money, and because of the amount, surrendered it to the police authorities, as was required by the local law. When Lewis demanded the return of the money from Aderholdt, the police property clerk, the latter required Lewis to prove his ownership to the funds because there were circumstances leading to the belief that the money had been stolen by Lewis. He sued the police property clerk and the locker company. Was the locker company liable for breach of duty as a bailee? [Lewis v Aderholdt, (CA DistColApp) 203 A2d 919]

4. Taylor parked his automobile in a garage operated by the Philadelphia Parking Authority and paid a regular monthly charge therefor. There was a written agreement between them which provided: "The Authority shall have the right to move the applicant's automobile to such location as it may deem necessary in order to facilitate the most effective use of the parking space on the roof. Ignition keys must be left in the automobile at all times." It was thereafter agreed between the parties that Taylor could retain the ignition key at all times and lock the auto in order to protect the valuable merchandise which he carried in his car. Taylor brought the car into the garage, locked it. and left with the keys. The car was missing when he returned. He sued the Parking Authority on the theory that it had breached a duty as bailee. The Authority claimed that it was not a bailee. Was the Authority correct? [Taylor v Philadelphia Parking Authority, 398 Pa 9, 156 A2d 525]

5. King owned a credit card issued by the Air Travel Company. It was lost or stolen and King reported it. Thereafter Jackson presented the credit card to the Hertz Corporation office at the Newark, New Jersey, airport. By impersonating King and forging his name, Jackson rented a car from Hertz. Jackson failed to return the car and sometime thereafter had a collision with Zuppa. Zuppa sued Hertz under a statute which had the effect of imposing liability on Hertz for harm to third persons by any bailee of a Hertz automobile. Was Jackson a bailee? [Zuppa v Hertz Corp. 111 NJSuper 419, 268 A2d 364]

6. Morse, who owned a diamond ring, valued at $2,000, took the ring to Homer's, Inc., to sell for him. Homer placed the ring in the window display of his store. There was no guard or grating across the opening of the window inside his store. There was a partitioned door that was left unlocked. On two former occasions Homer's store had been robbed. Several weeks after Morse left his ring, armed men robbed the store and took several rings from the store window, including Morse's ring. He sued Homer, who defended on the ground that he was not liable for the criminal acts of others. Decide. [Morse v Homer's, Inc. 295 Mass 606, 4 NE2d 625]

7. Nutrodynamics delivered a quantity of loose pills that it manufactured to Ivers-Lee for the latter to place them in foil packages and then in shipping containers suitable for delivery to customers of Nutrodynamics. Approximately 193 cartons of packaged pills were finished and in Ivers-Lee's possession when Beck brought a suit against Nutrodynamics and directed the sheriff to attach the pills in the possession of Ivers-Lee. Ivers-Lee had not been paid for its work in packaging. It claimed the right to keep the goods until paid but nevertheless surrendered them to the sheriff. Was it entitled to any claim on the goods in the hands of the sheriff? [Beck v Nutrodynamics, Inc., 77 NJSuper 448, 186 A2d 715]

8. O'Donnell was driving his father's automobile when he had a collision with a car driven by Collins and a car driven by Ebel. In the resulting lawsuit, O'Donnell asserted against Collins a claim for the total amount of the damage to his father's car. Collins claimed that O'Donnell could not recover for the damage since it was not his car. Decide. [Ebel v Collins and O'Donnell, 47 IllApp2d 327, 198 NE2d 552]

9. Osell, who held a private pilot's license, rented an airplane from Hall. While attempting to land the plane, he flew through a cloud formation, although he could have avoided doing so. In turning out of the clouds, he struck a hillside and wrecked the plane. Flying through clouds under these circumstances was a violation of the federal civil air regulations. Hall sued Osell for the destruction of the plane. Decide. [Hall v Osell, 102 CalApp2d 849, 228 P2d 293]

10. The State of New York loaned a sand loading machine to the Village of Catskill without charge. Hood was employed by the Village and, while using the loader as part of his work, was injured because the drive chain, which was worn and out of alignment, caught his leg. He sued the State of New York for the damages he sustained. The State produced evidence that the machine had been serviced shortly before the accident and that it was then in good working order. Was Hood entitled to recover? [Hood v New York (NY Ct Cl) 48 Misc2d 43, 264 NYS2d 134]

11. Virginia McGimsey loaned her auto to Terry to whom she was then engaged and did later marry. At the time of lending the car, Terry was 18, had recently been discharged from the Army, and Virginia knew that he did not have a driver's license. Some time thereafter, Terry became intoxicated and while driving Virginia's car, ran into Edgar Dukes. Dukes sued Terry and Virginia. Was he entitled to recover from Virginia? [Dukes v McGimsey (TennApp) 500 SW2d 448]

12. Rhodes parked his car on the self-service park-and-lock lot of Pioneer Parking Lot, Inc. The car was later stolen from the lot by an unknown thief. Rhodes sued the parking lot on the theory that it had breached its duty as a bailee. The parking lot defended on the ground that it was not a bailee. Was it a bailee? [Rhodes v Pioneer Parking Lot, Inc. (Tenn) 501 SW2d 569]

SPECIAL BAILMENTS AND DOCUMENTS OF TITLE

A special bailment relation, rather than an ordinary bailment, arises when goods are stored in a warehouse, or delivered to a merchant to sell for the owner, or delivered to a carrier to be transported. In some instances a hotelkeeper may have a bailee's liability. Some of these special bailees issue a document of title, such as a warehouse receipt or bill of lading, on receiving goods from the bailor.

A. WAREHOUSEMEN

§ 22:1. DEFINITION. A person engaged in the business of storing the goods of others for compensation is a *warehouseman*. A *public warehouseman* holds himself out generally to serve the public without discrimination.

An enterprise which stores boats outdoors on land is a "warehouseman" since it is "engaged in the business of storing goods for hire," as against the contention that the storage was out-of-doors and not in a warehouse or similar structure.

§ 22:2. RIGHTS AND DUTIES OF WAREHOUSEMEN. The common-law rights and duties of a warehouseman, in the absence of modification by statute, are in the main the same as those of a bailee in an ordinary mutual-benefit bailment.[1]

FACTS: Brace and his brother delivered cabbage to the Salem Cold Storage Company for refrigerated storage. The cabbage was later returned to them in a damaged condition. They sued Salem on the ground that through its negligence it had failed to keep the cabbage at a proper temperature. The evidence was conflicting as to what had been done. The jury returned a verdict in favor of the plaintiffs, but the trial judge

---

[1] Uniform Commercial Code § 7-204; Belland v American Auto Insurance Co. (DistColApp) 101 A2d 517. The UCC does not change the prior rule by which when loss by fire is shown, the burden is upon the warehouseman to disprove negligence. Canty v Wyatt Storage Corp. 208 Va 161, 156 SE2d 582.

set the verdict aside on the ground that the negligence of the warehouseman had not been established and that therefore the verdict in favor of the plaintiffs was not proper. The plaintiffs appealed from this action.

DECISION: Judgment for plaintiffs. The warehouse was subject to the duties of a bailee for hire. The plaintiffs had the burden of proving that Salem was negligent but a prima facie case of negligence was established when the goods were returned to the customer in a damaged condition. The burden was then on Salem to show that it had exercised reasonable care. Proof of such care would excuse it from liability as it was not an insurer against loss. In view of the circumstance that the evidence was conflicting, it was necessary for a jury to determine whether Salem had acted in a nonnegligent manner. It was therefore improper for the trial judge to have set the verdict of the jury aside and the verdict in favor of the plaintiffs was therefore reinstated. [Brace v Salem Cold Storage, Inc. 146 WVa 180, 118 SE2d 799]

(a) **Statutory regulation.** Most states have passed warehouse acts defining the rights and duties of the warehouseman and imposing regulations as to charges and liens, bonds for the protection of patrons, and maintenance of storage facilities in a suitable and safe condition, inspections, and general methods of transacting business.

(b) **Warehouseman's lien.** The public warehouseman has a lien against the goods for reasonable charges.[2] It is a *specific lien* in that it attaches only to the property with respect to which the charges arose and cannot be asserted against other property of the same owner in the possession of the warehouseman. The warehouseman, however, may make a lien carry over to other goods by noting on the receipt for one lot of goods that a lien is also claimed thereon for charges as to other goods.[3] The warehouseman's lien for storage charges may be enforced by sale after due notice has been given to all persons who claim any interest in the property stored.

FACTS: Flores stored his furniture with Didear Van & Storage Company. The storage charges were not kept up to date and a notice dated April 15 was sent to Flores stating that the goods would be sold for nonpayment of storage charges if the charges were not paid on or before April 24. Didear sold the furniture. Flores thereafter sued Didear for conversion.

DECISION: Judgment for Flores. Uniform Commercial Code § 7-210(2)(c) requires that the warehouseman give notice to the customer specifying a final payment date which must be "not less than ten days after receipt of the notification." A warehouseman must comply strictly with the procedure for enforcing his lien and when he does not give the notice that is required by the Code, his subsequent foreclosure sale of the stored goods is a conversion; the customer may recover the value of the goods and interest thereon from the date of sale. [Flores v Didear Van & Storage Co. (TexCivApp) 489 SW2d 406]

---

[2] UCC § 7-209(1).
[3] § 7-209(1).

When a person is not a warehouseman, he may not assert a warehouseman's lien.

§ 22:3. **WAREHOUSE RECEIPTS.** A *warehouse receipt* is a written acknowledgment by a warehouseman that certain property has been received for storage from a named person. It also sets forth the terms of the contract for storage. The warehouse receipt is a document of title because the person lawfully holding the receipt is entitled to the goods or property represented by the receipt. Certain details describing the transaction must be included, but beyond this no particular form for a warehouse receipt is required.

§ 22:4. **RIGHTS OF HOLDERS OF WAREHOUSE RECEIPTS.** A warehouse receipt in which it is stated that the goods received will be delivered to the depositor, or to any other specified person, is a *nonnegotiable warehouse receipt*; but a receipt in which it is stated that the goods received will be delivered to a bearer, or to the order of any person named in such receipt, is a *negotiable warehouse receipt*.[4]

The transfer of negotiable warehouse receipts is made by delivery or by indorsement and delivery. It is the duty of the warehouseman to deliver the goods to the holder of a negotiable receipt and to cancel such receipt before making delivery of the goods. The surrender of a nonnegotiable receipt is not required.

If the person who deposited the goods with the warehouse did not own the goods or did not have the power to transfer title to them, the holder of the warehouse receipt is subject to the title of the true owner.[5] Accordingly, when goods are stolen and delivered to a warehouse and a receipt is issued for them, the owner prevails over the holder of the receipt.[6]

The transferee of a warehouse receipt is given the protection of certain warranties from his immediate transferor; namely, that the instrument is genuine, that its transfer is rightful and effective, and that the transferor has no knowledge of any facts that impair the validity or worth of the receipt.[7]

§ 22:5. **FIELD WAREHOUSING.** Ordinarily, stored goods are placed in a warehouse belonging to the warehouseman. The owner of goods, such as a manufacturer, may keep the goods in his own storage room or building. When the warehouse company takes exclusive control of the property, it may issue a warehouse receipt for the goods even though they are still on the premises of the owner. Such a transaction has the same legal effect with respect to other persons and purchasers of the warehouse receipt as though the property were in the warehouse of the warehouseman. This practice is

---

[4] § 7-104.

[5] § 7-503(1).

[6] § 7-503(1).

[7] § 7-507. These warranties are in addition to any that may arise between the parties by virtue of the fact that the transferor is selling the goods represented by the receipt to the transferee. See Chapter 26 as to sellers' warranties.

called *field warehousing* since the goods are not taken to the warehouse but remain "in the field."

The purpose is to create warehouse receipts which the owner of the goods is able to pledge as security for loans. The owner could, of course, have done this by actually placing the goods in a warehouse, but this would have involved the expense of transportation and storage.

§ 22:6. **LIMITATION OF LIABILITY OF WAREHOUSEMEN.** A warehouseman may limit liability by a provision in the warehouse receipt specifying the maximum amount for which he will be liable. This privilege is subject to two qualifications: (a) the customer must be given the choice of storing the goods without such limitation if he pays a higher storage rate, and (b) the limitation must be stated as to each item or unit of weight. A limitation is in proper form when it states that the maximum liability for a piano is $1,000 or that the maximum liability per bushel of wheat is a stated amount. Conversely, there cannot be a blanket limitation of liability, such as "maximum liability $50," when the receipt covers two or more items.

General contract law determines whether a limitation clause is a part of the contract between the warehouseman and his customer. A warehouse receipt is not part of the contract of deposit when it is delivered to the customer a substantial period of time after the goods have been left for storage.

FACTS: Olson stored a Persian rug with Security Van Lines. Nothing was said to her as to liability for moth damage. Ten days thereafter Security Van Lines sent her a warehouse receipt for the rug. The receipt contained a provision stating that the warehouseman was not liable for moth damage. While in the possession of Security, the rug was damaged greatly by moths. Olson sued Security for the value of the rug. It raised the defense that it was not liable because of the warehouse receipt provision.

DECISION: Judgment for Olson. The contract of storage had been made when Olson left her rug with Security. The warehouse receipt which was sent to her ten days later was not part of that contract. Therefore the clause of the receipt which excluded liability for moth damage was not binding upon Olson and therefore was not a defense to her claim against Security Van Lines. [Olson v Security Van Lines, Inc. (LaApp) 297 So2d 674]

B. FACTORS

§ 22:7. **DEFINITION.** A *factor* is a special type of bailee who sells goods consigned to him as though he were the owner of the goods. The device of entrusting a person with the possession of property for the purpose of sale is commonly called *selling on consignment*. The owner who seeks or consigns the goods for sale is the *consignor*. The person or agent to whom they are consigned is the *consignee*; he may also be known as a commission merchant. His compensation is known as a *commission* or *factorage*. The property remains the property of the owner, and the consignee acts as his agent to pass title to the buyer.[8]

Factoring as defined above has to a large degree been displaced, except with respect to the sale of livestock, by other methods of doing business. Today one is more likely to find the seller selling the goods on credit to a middleman with the latter having the right to return goods not sold, the seller then assigning his account receivable. Or the seller may store the goods in a warehouse or place them on board a carrier and then effect a sale by delivering the warehouse receipts or bills of lading rather than by sending the goods to a factor.

§ 22:8. EFFECT OF FACTOR TRANSACTION. Since a factor is by definition authorized by the consignor to sell the goods entrusted to him, such a sale will pass the title of the consignor to the purchaser. Before the factor makes the sale, the goods belong to the consignor; but in some instances creditors of the factor may ignore the consignor and treat the goods as though they belonged to the consignee.[9] If the consignor is not the owner, as when a thief delivers stolen goods to the factor, a sale by the factor is an unlawful conversion. It is constitutional, however, to provide that the factor who sells in good faith in ignorance of the rights of other persons in the goods he sells is protected from liability and cannot be treated as a converter of the goods,[10] as would be the case in the absence of such a statutory immunity.[11]

C. COMMON CARRIERS

§ 22:9. DEFINITION. A *carrier* of goods is one who undertakes the transportation of goods, regardless of the method of transportation or the distance covered. The *consignor* or shipper is the person who delivers goods to the carrier for shipment. The *consignee* is the person to whom the goods are shipped and to whom the carrier should deliver the goods.

A carrier may be classified as (a) a *common carrier*, which holds itself out as willing to furnish transportation for compensation without discrimination to all members of the public who apply, assuming that the goods to be carried are proper and that facilities of the carrier are available; (b) a *contract carrier*, which transports goods under individual contracts; or (c) a *private carrier*, such as a truck fleet owned and operated by an industrial firm. The common carrier law applies to the first, the bailment law to the second, and the law of employment to the third.

> FACTS: The J. C. Trucking Co., Inc., was engaged under contracts to transport dress material from New York City to dressmaking establishments in New Haven, Hartford, and Bridgeport, Connecticut, and then to transport the finished dresses back to New York City. Dresses that were being carried to Ace-High Dresses, Inc., were stolen from the trucking company. Ace-High Dresses sued the trucking company and claimed that the latter was liable for the loss as a common carrier.

---

[8] If the factor guarantees payment to the consignor, he is called a *del credere factor*.
[9] UCC § 2-326.
[10] Montana Meat Co. v Missoula Livestock Auction Co. 125 Mont 66, 230 P2d 955.
[11] Sig Ellington & Co. v De Vries (CA8 Minn) 199 F2d 677.

DECISION: The trucking company was not liable for the loss as a common carrier since it did not hold itself out to carry for the general public. It was a contract carrier, because it would transport goods only if it had a preexisting contract with a shipper to do so. [Ace-High Dresses v J. C. Trucking Co. 122 Conn 578, 191 A 536]

Common carriers are bailees with respect to the property which they carry as freight. They typically issue documents of title or bills of lading for such property.

§ 22:10. FREIGHT FORWARDERS. A *freight forwarder* accepts freight from shippers, ordinarily in less-than-carload lots, combines such freight into carloads, and delivers them as carloads to a carrier for shipment to a particular point where the carload lots are separated and the items carried to their respective destinations. A freight forwarder does not own or operate any of the transportation facilities. Freight forwarders in some jurisdictions are subject to the same government regulations as common carriers.

§ 22:11. BILLS OF LADING. When the carrier accepts goods for shipment or forwarding, it ordinarily issues to the shipper a *bill of lading* [12] in the case of land or marine transportation or an *airbill* [13] for air transportation. This instrument, which is a document of title, is both a receipt for the goods and a contract stating the terms of carriage. Title to the goods may be transferred by a transfer of the bill of lading made with that intention.

With respect to intrastate shipments, bills of lading are governed by the Uniform Commercial Code.[14] Interstate transportation is regulated by the federal Bills of Lading Act.[15]

A bill of lading is a *negotiable bill of lading* when by its terms the goods are to be delivered to bearer or to the order of a named person.[16] Any other bill of lading, such as one that consigns the goods to a specified person, is a nonnegotiable or *straight bill of lading*.

(a) Contents of bill of lading. The form of the bill of lading is regulated in varying degrees by administrative agencies.[17]

As against a bona fide transferee of the bill of lading, a carrier is bound by the recitals in the bill as to the contents, quantity, or weight of goods.[18] This means that the carrier must produce the goods which are described, even though they had not existed, or pay damages for failing to do so. This

---

[12] In order to avoid the delay of waiting for a bill of lading mailed to the destination point from the point where the goods were received by the carrier, UCC § 7-305(1) authorizes the carrier at the request of the consignor to provide for the issuance of the bill at the destination rather than the receipt point.
[13] UCC § 1-201(6).
[14] Article 7.
[15] Title 49, United States Code § 81 et seq.
[16] UCC § 7-104(1)(a).
[17] The UCC contains no provision regulating the form of the bill of lading.
[18] UCC § 7-301(1).

rule is not applied if facts appear on the face of the bill that should keep the transferee from relying on the recital.

(b) Negotiability. The person to whom a bill of lading has been negotiated acquires the direct obligation of the carrier to hold possession of the goods for him according to the terms of the bill of lading as fully as if the carrier had contracted with him, and ordinarily he acquires the title to the bill and the goods it represents. The rights of the holder of a negotiable bill are not affected by the fact (1) that the former owner of the bill had been deprived of it by misrepresentation, fraud, accident, mistake, duress, undue influence, loss, theft, or conversion; or (2) that the goods had already been surrendered by the carrier or had been stopped in transit.[19]

The rights of the holder of a bill of lading are subject to the title of a true owner of the goods who did not authorize the delivery of the goods to the carrier. For example, when a thief delivers the goods to the carrier and then negotiates the bill of lading, the title of the owner of the goods prevails over the claim of the holder of the bill.[20]

(c) Warranties. The transferee for value of either a negotiable or nonnegotiable bill of lading acquires from his transferor, in the absence of any contrary provision, the benefit of implied warranties (1) that the bill of lading is genuine, (2) that its transfer is rightful and is effective to transfer the goods represented thereby, and (3) that the transferor has no knowledge of facts that would impair the validity or worth of the bill of lading.[21]

§ 22:12. RIGHTS OF COMMON CARRIER. A common carrier of goods has the right to make reasonable and necessary rules for the conduct of its business. It has the right to charge such rates for its services as yield it a fair return on the property devoted to the business of transportation, but the exact rates charged are regulated by the Interstate Commerce Commission in the case of interstate carriers and by state commissions in the case of intrastate carriers. As an incident of the right to charge for its services, a carrier may charge *demurrage:* a charge for the detention of its cars or equipment for an unreasonable length of time by either the consignor or consignee.

As security for unpaid transportation and service charges, a common carrier has a lien on goods that it transports. The carrier's lien also secures demurrage charges, the costs of preservation of the goods, and the costs of sale to enforce the lien.[22] The lien of a carrier is a specific lien. It attaches only to goods shipped under the particular contract, but includes all of the shipment even though it is sent in installments. Thus, when part of the shipment is delivered to the consignee, the lien attaches to the portion remaining in possession of the carrier.

---

[19] § 7-502(2).
[20] § 7-503(1).
[21] UCC § 7-507; Federal Bill of Lading Act (FBLA), 49 USC §§ 114, 116. When the transfer of the bill of lading is part of a transaction by which the transferor sells the goods represented thereby to the transferee, there will also arise the warranties that are found in other sales of goods.
[22] UCC § 7-307(1); FBLA, 49 USC § 105.

§ 22:13. DUTIES OF COMMON CARRIER. A common carrier is generally required (a) to receive and carry proper and lawful goods of all persons who offer them for shipment; (b) to furnish facilities that are adequate for the transportation of freight in the usual course of business, and to furnish proper storage facilities for goods awaiting shipment or awaiting delivery after shipment; (c) to follow the directions given by the shipper; (d) to load and unload goods delivered to it for shipment (in less-than-carload lots in the case of railroads), but the shipper or consignee may assume this duty by contract or custom; (e) to deliver the goods to the consignee or his authorized agent, except when custom or special arrangement relieves the carrier of this duty.

Goods must be delivered at the usual place for delivery at the specified destination. When goods are shipped under a negotiable bill of lading, the carrier must not deliver the goods without obtaining possession of the bill properly indorsed. When goods are shipped under a straight bill of lading, the carrier is justified in delivering to the consignee, unless notified by the shipper to deliver to someone else. If the carrier delivers the goods to the wrong person, it is liable for breach of contract and for the tort of conversion.

§ 22:14. LIABILITIES OF COMMON CARRIER. When goods are delivered to a common carrier for immediate shipment and while they are in transit, the carrier is absolutely liable for any loss or damage to the goods unless it can prove that it was due solely to one or more of the following excepted causes: (a) act of God, or a natural phenomenon that is not reasonably foreseeable; (b) act of public enemy, such as the military forces of an opposing government, as distinguished from ordinary robbers; (c) act of public authority, such as a health officer removing goods from a truck; (d) act of the shipper, such as fraudulent labeling or defective packing; or (e) inherent nature of the goods, such as those naturally tending to spoil or deteriorate.

Unusually heavy rains do not constitute an act of God even though flood conditions are created thereby, for the reason that rains and even heavy rains are not unexpectable. Consequently, a common carrier is liable for loss caused by delay resulting from such flood conditions.

When a carrier claims the benefit of an excepted cause, it must show that the excepted cause was the sole cause of the harm.

FACTS: The Ozark White Lime Co. shipped lime from Arkansas by the St. Louis-San Francisco Railway. The shipment was stopped at McBride, Oklahoma, by a landslide which blocked the tracks. The car containing the shipment was placed on a spur line several feet lower than the main tracks. The lime was then destroyed by flood waters from the Grand River. The lime company sued the railroad for the loss. The lime company showed that the railroad had an engine available to take cars from the spur track up to higher ground and that it had taken other cars beyond the reach of the flood waters. No reason was shown for the failure to remove the car with the plaintiff's shipment.

DECISION: Judgment for the lime company. If the carrier relies on an act of God to excuse it from its liability as an insurer, it must show that the act of God was the sole cause of the damage. Here the carrier was negligent in failing to move the shipment to higher ground, which it could have done. [St. Louis-San Francisco Railway Co. v Ozark White Lime Co. 177 Ark 1018, 9 SW2d 17]

(a) Carrier's liability for delay. A carrier is liable for losses caused by its failure to deliver goods within a reasonable time. Thus, the carrier is liable for losses arising from a fall in price or a deterioration of the goods caused by its unreasonable delay. The carrier, however, is not liable for every delay. Risks of ordinary delays incidental to the business of transporting goods are assumed by the shipper.

(b) Liability of initial and connecting carriers. When goods are carried over the lines of several carriers, the initial and the final carrier, as well as the carrier on whose line the loss is sustained, may be liable to the shipper or the owner of the goods; but only one payment may be obtained.

(c) Limiting liability. In the absence of a constitutional or statutory prohibition, a carrier generally has the right to limit its liability by contract. A clause limiting the liability of the carrier is not enforceable unless consideration is given for it, usually in the form of a reduced rate, and provided further that the shipper is allowed to ship without limitation of liability if he chooses to pay the higher or ordinary rate.[23]

A carrier may by contract relieve itself from liability for losses not arising out of its own negligence. A carrier accepting freight for shipment outside the state cannot require the shipper to agree that it will not be liable for losses occurring on the line of a connecting carrier.

A common carrier may make an agreement with the shipper as to the value of the property. If the amount is reasonable, such an agreement will usually bind the shipper whether or not the loss was due to the carrier's fault.

Limitation of liability is governed by the Carriage of Goods by Sea Act in the case of water carriers, and by the Warsaw Convention in the case of international air transportation. By the Warsaw Convention, liability is limited to a stated amount. Its provisions apply both to regular commercial flights and to charter flights. Under the latter, transportation details are arranged by an association which charters a flight with the airline and then makes individual arrangements with association members for such flights, with the airline delivering individual tickets to each passenger. When the airline is also the actual operator of the plane, there is no practical difference between a voyage charter flight and an ordinary scheduled commercial flight.

(d) Notice of claim. The bill of lading and applicable government regulations may require that a carrier be given notice of any claim for

---

[23] UCC § 7-309(2).

damages or loss of goods within a specified time, generally not less than nine months. A provision in the tariff limiting the time for such notice is not binding on a consignee who has not received a copy of the bill of lading.

> **FACTS:** Irwin sold to Wells & Coverly merchandise that was shipped to the buyer by Red Star Express, a motor carrier. The goods never arrived. Red Star notified Irwin that the goods were lost. Wells & Coverly sued Red Star, which raised the defense that it had not been given notice of the loss within nine months as required by the tariff or regulations on file with the appropriate governmental agency and as required by the bill of lading that Red Star had issued on receiving the goods. Wells & Coverly proved that they had never received a copy of the bill of lading and had no prior knowledge of the time limitation.

> **DECISION:** The time limitation was not binding on Wells & Coverly. The fact that it was included in the government-approved tariff did not make it binding as to a consignee who had no knowledge of the limitation. While the limitation had been stated in the bill of lading, Wells & Coverly had never received a copy of the bill of lading. The provision of the bill of lading did not serve to give notice to them of the time limitation and was not binding upon them. Moreover, as Red Star knew the goods were lost, it could have easily notified the consignee and informed it of the time for filing a claim. [Wells & Coverly v Red Star Express, 62 Misc2d 269, 306 NYS2d 710]

(e) Liability for baggage. A common carrier of passengers is required to receive a reasonable amount of baggage. Its liability in this respect is the same as the liability of a carrier of goods. If the passenger retains custody of his baggage, the carrier is liable only for lack of reasonable care or willful misconduct on the part of its agents and employees. Limitations on baggage liability are commonly authorized by law and are binding upon passengers even though unknown to them.

D. HOTELKEEPERS

A hotelkeeper has a bailee's liability with respect to property specifically entrusted to his care. With respect to property in the possession of the guest, the hotelkeeper has supervisory liability.

§ 22:15. DEFINITIONS.

(a) Hotelkeeper. The term *hotelkeeper* is used by the law to refer to an operator of a hotel, or tourist home, or to anyone else who is regularly engaged in the business of offering living accommodations to all transient persons.[24] In the early law he was called an innkeeper or a tavernkeeper.

(b) Guest. The essential element in the definition of *guest* is that he is a transient. He need not be a traveler or come from a distance. A person living

---

[24] A person furnishing the services of a hotelkeeper has the status of such even though the word "hotel" is not used in the business name. Lackman v Department of Labor and Industries 78 Wash2d 212, 471 P2d 82.

within a short distance of a hotel who engages a room at the hotel and remains there overnight is a guest.

§ 22:16. GUEST RELATIONSHIP DURATION. The relationship of guest and hotelkeeper does not begin until a person is received as a guest by the hotelkeeper. The relationship terminates when the guest leaves or when he ceases to be a transient, as when he arranges for a more or less permanent residence at the hotel. The transition from the status of guest to the status of boarder or lodger must be clearly indicated. It is not established by the mere fact that one remains at the hotel for a long period, even though it runs into months.

A person who enters a hotel at the invitation of a guest or attends a dance or a banquet given at the hotel is not a guest. Similarly, the guest of a registered occupant of a motel room who shares the room with the occupant without the knowledge or consent of the management is not a guest of the motel, since there is no relationship between that person and the motel.

§ 22:17. DISCRIMINATION. Since a hotel is by definition an enterprise holding itself out to serve the public, it follows that members of the public, otherwise fit, must be accepted as guests. If the hotel refuses accommodations for an improper reason, it is liable for damages, including exemplary damages. A guest has been held entitled to recover punitive damages when improperly ejected under circumstances indicating an intentional and willful disregard of the guest's rights.

A hotel may also be liable under a civil rights or similar statutory provision, and it may also be guilty of a crime. By virtue of the federal Civil Rights Act of 1964, neither a hotel nor its concessionaire can discriminate against patrons or segregate them on the basis of race, color, religion, or national origin. The federal Act is limited to discrimination for the stated reasons and does not in any way interfere with the right of the hotel to exclude those who are unfit persons to admit because they are drunk or criminally violent, nor persons who are not dressed in the manner required by reasonable hotel regulations applied to all persons. When there has been improper discrimination or segregation or it is reasonably believed that such acts may occur, the federal Act authorizes the institution of proceedings in the federal courts for an order to stop such prohibited practices.

§ 22:18. LIABILITY OF HOTELKEEPER. In the absence of a valid limitation, the hotelkeeper is generally an insurer of the safety of goods of a guest.[25] As exceptions, the hotelkeeper is not liable for loss caused by an act of God, a public enemy, act of public authority, the inherent nature of the property, or the fault of the guest.

In most states, statutes limit or provide a method of limiting the liability of a hotelkeeper. The statutes may limit the extent of liability, reduce the

---

[25] Zurich Fire Insurance Co. v Weil (Ky) 259 SW2d 54.

liability of the hotelkeeper to that of an ordinary bailee, or permit him to limit his liability by contract or by posting a notice of the limitation. Some statutes relieve the hotelkeeper from liability when directions for depositing valuables with the hotelkeeper are posted on the doors of the rooms occupied and the guest fails to comply with the directions. When a statute permits a hotel receiving valuables for deposit in its safe deposit box to limit its liability to the amount specified in the agreement signed by the guest, such limitation binds the guest even though the loss was caused by negligence on the part of the hotel.[26]

Even when there is no limitation on the liability of a hotel, it is not liable for more than the value of the guest's property and is not liable for consequential harm that may flow from the loss of the property.

> **FACTS:** Morse, a jewelry salesman, was a guest in the Piedmont Hotel. He entrusted a sample case to a bellboy of the hotel to place on the airport bus of an independent taxicab company. At some point between the hotel and the airport the sample case disappeared. The guest's employer was paid for the loss by his insurer, but the insurer then canceled the policy as to Morse and Morse was fired by the employer. No other insurance company would cover him as a jewelry salesman with the result that he was unable to get another job as such, although he had been a jewelry salesman for 40 years. This shock induced a heart attack that confined him at home for several months. Morse then sued the hotel for the earnings that he had lost, claiming $100,000; and damages for pain and suffering, claiming $25,000.

> **DECISION:** Judgment for the hotel. While the hotel was liable for the loss of the guest's property, this did not make it liable for every consequence that flowed therefrom. Consequently, there was no liability for the items of damage claimed by Morse as these were indirect damages which would not be anticipated as the probable and natural consequences of the loss of property. Accordingly no recovery could be allowed. [Morse v Piedmont Hotel Co. 110 GaApp 509, 139 SE2d 133]

When the guest has checked his coat in the hotel checkroom, it is no defense to the hotel that the checkroom was operated by a concessionaire when there was nothing to call that fact to the attention of the guest.[27]

§ 22:19. LIEN OF HOTELKEEPER. The hotelkeeper is given a lien on the baggage of his guests for the agreed charges or, if no express agreement was made, the reasonable value of the accommodations furnished. Statutes permit the hotelkeeper to enforce his lien by selling the goods at public sale.[28] The lien of the hotelkeeper is terminated by (a) the guest's payment of

---

[26] Kalpakian v Oklahoma Sheraton Corp. (CA10 Okla) 398 F2d 243.

[27] Aldrich v Waldorf Astoria Hotel (NY CivCt) 343 NYS2d 830.

[28] There is authority that the hotelkeeper's lien may not be exercised unless the guest is given an impartial hearing and that it is unconstitutional as a denial of due process to permit the hotelkeeper to hold or sell the guest's property without such a hearing. Klim v Jones (DC ND Cal) 315 FSupp 109. A hotel cannot seize the goods of a guest under a statutory lien law without first affording the guest a hearing as to his liability, and the failure to do so deprives the guest of the due process guaranteed by the federal Constitution. New York v Skinner, 33 NYS2d 23, 300 NE2d 716.

the hotel's charges, (b) any conversion of the guest's goods by the hotelkeeper, and (c) surrender of the goods to the guest. In the last situation an exception is made when the goods are given to the guest for temporary use.

§ 22:20. **BOARDERS OR LODGERS.** To those persons who are permanent boarders or lodgers, rather than transient guests, the hotelkeeper owes only the duty of an ordinary bailee of their personal property under a mutual-benefit bailment.

A hotelkeeper has no common-law right of lien on property of his boarders or lodgers, as distinguished from his guests, in the absence of an express agreement between the parties. In a number of states, however, legislation giving a lien to a boardinghouse or a lodginghouse keeper has been enacted.

QUESTIONS AND CASE PROBLEMS

1. Johnston, a guest in a hotel operated by the Mobile Hotel Co., entrusted his property to the hotel. During the night the property was stolen from the hotel in spite of the careful protection given the property by the hotel. Johnston sued the hotel, which claimed it was not liable because the robbers were public enemies and that fact excused the hotel. Was this defense valid? [Johnston v Mobile Hotel Co. 27 AlaApp 145, 167 So 595 cert den 232 Ala 175, 167 So 596]

2. Norvell took certain trunks containing samples to the St. George Hotel. The hotelkeepers knew that the sample trunks belonged to J. R. Torrey & Co. The trunks were retained to secure payment of Norvell's unpaid board bill under an alleged statutory right. The statute gave any hotelkeeper a "specific lien upon all property or baggage deposited with them for the amount of the charges against them or their owners if guests at such hotel." J. R. Torrey & Co. brought an action against the owners of the hotel to recover for a wrongful detention of the trunks. Was it entitled to judgment? [Torrey v McClellan, 17 TexCivApp 371, 43 SW 64]

3. Evers owned and operated a warehouse. De Cecchis phoned and inquired as to the rates and then brought furniture in for storage. Nothing was said at any time about any limitation of liability of Evers as a warehouseman. A warehouse receipt was mailed to De Cecchis several days later. The receipt contained a clause that limited liability to $50 per package stored. Was the limitation of liability binding on De Cecchis? [De Cecchis v Evers, 54 Del 99, 174 A2d 463]

4. Dovax Fabrics, Inc. had been shipping goods by a common carrier, G & A Delivery Corp., for over a year, during which all of G & A's bills to Dovax bore the notation, "Liability limited to $50 unless greater value is declared and paid for. . . ." Dovax gave G & A three lots of goods, having a total value of $1,799.95. A truck containing all three was stolen that night, without negligence on the part of G & A. Should Dovax recover from G & A (a) $1,799.95, (b) $150 for the three shipments, or (c) nothing? [Dovax Fabrics, Inc. v G & A Delivery Corp. (NYCivCt) 4 UCCRS 492]

5. McCarley sued the Foster-Milburn Co., a medical manufacturing company. He claimed that there was jurisdiction to bring the lawsuit because Foster was doing business within the state through an agent, Obergfel. Foster supplied Obergfel with a product called *Westsal*, made by a subsidiary of Foster. Obergfel was to sell this product directly to doctors. He also sold products produced by other medical manufacturers. Obergfel solicited orders from doctors, sold in his own name, incurred all expenses, made all collections, and after deducting his commissions, remitted the balance to Foster. Foster shipped the Westsal to Obergfel, who warehoused it and then reshipped it to the purchasers. If Obergfel was not an agent of Foster, the suit was not properly brought. Was Obergfel the agent of Foster? [McCarley v Foster-Milburn Co., (DC WD NY) 93 FSupp 421]

6. Vanguard Transfer Co. ran a moving and storage business. It obtained an insurance policy from the St. Paul Fire & Marine Insurance Co. covering goods which it had "accepted at the warehouse for storage." Dahl rented a room in Vanguard's building. Both Dahl and Vanguard had keys to the room. Dahl was charged a flat monthly rental for the room and could keep any property there which he desired. Vanguard did not make any record of the goods which Dahl brought to the warehouse. There was a fire in the warehouse and Dahl's property was destroyed. He sued the insurance company. Was it liable? [Dahl v St. Paul & Marine Insurance Co., 36 Wis2d 420, 153 NW2d 624]

7. David Crystal sent merchandise by Ehrlich-Newmark Trucking Co. The truck with Crystal's shipment of goods was hijacked in New York City. Crystal sued Ehrlich-Newmark for the loss. It defended on the ground that it was not liable because the loss had been caused by a public enemy. Was this defense valid? [David Crystal, Inc. v Ehrlich-Newmark Trucking Co., Inc. (NYCivCt) 314 NYS2d 559]

8. The patron of a motel opened the bedroom window at night and went to sleep. During the night a prowler pried open the screen, entered the room, and stole property of the guest. The patron sued the motel. The motel raised the contentions that it was not responsible for property in the possession of the guest and that the guest had been contributorily negligent in opening the window. Under what circumstances could the patron recover damages? [Buck v Hankin, 217 PaSuper 262, 269 A2d 344]

9. The Utah Public Service Commission granted a contract carrier permit to the Salt Lake Transportation Company to transport passengers between the Salt Lake airport for four principal airlines and the three leading hotels in the city. The Realty Purchasing Company and various hotels and taxicab companies objected to the granting of the permit on the ground that the company performed a taxicab service and was therefore a common carrier. Decide. [Realty Purchasing Co. v Public Service Commission, 9 Utah2d 375, 345 P2d 606]

10. Wells Fargo wished to operate an armored car service in Nebraska and applied to the State Railway Commission for permission to solicit business from all persons desiring to ship cash, letters, books, and data processing materials. The Commission granted it a license as a contract carrier. Was it a contract carrier? [Wells Fargo Armored Service Corp. v Bankers Dispatch Corp. 186 Neb 263, 182 NW2d 648]

11. The Whitney National Bank obtained a banker's blanket bond from Transamerica Insurance Company to protect it from loss from having extended credit on "counterfeit" instruments. The bank loaned money to Allied Crude

Vegetable Oil Refining Corp. on the strength of warehouse receipts issued by companies which were owned by the American Express Company. Each of the receipts stated that a specified large quantity of crude soy bean oil was stored and held by the issuing warehouse. Allied failed to repay the loan. It was then discovered that the warehouse did not have the quantity of oil specified in the receipts. This had occurred because of the fraud of Allied and the cooperation or mistakes of warehouse employees. The bank sought to recover its loss by suing on the blanket bond on the theory that the warehouse receipts were "counterfeit." Was it correct? [Whitney National Bank v Transamerica Insurance Co. (CA3 NJ) 476 F2d 632]

12. The Birmingham Television Corporation stored some equipment with Harris Warehouse Company. A water main in the city burst. The warehouse was flooded. The television corporation sued the water works and the warehouse. The warehouse raised the defense that the action had not been commenced within nine months after notice was given of the damage, as was expressly required by the terms of the warehouse receipt. The television corporation claimed that the provision was not binding because it was on the back of the receipt. Summary judgment was entered in favor of the warehouse. The television corporation appealed. Decide. [Birmingham Television Corp. v Water Works, 292 Ala 147, 290 So2d 636]

13. Motor Freight Lines delivered a shipment of frozen waffles to the Liberty Ice & Cold Storage Co. to hold for a few days awaiting reshipment. The only space available for storage was a compartment already partly filled with frozen lobsters and fish. Motor Freight was not informed of this fact nor of the danger that the waffle cartons would pick up the smell of seafood. The cartons of the waffles became so contaminated that it was necessary to repack them. Motor Freight sued Liberty for this expense. Was it liable? [Motor Freight Lines v Liberty Ice & Cold Storage Co. (LaApp) 85 So2d 708]

23 NATURE AND FORM OF SALES

A. NATURE AND LEGALITY

§ 23:1. DEFINITION. A *sale of goods* is a present transfer of title to movable personal property in consideration of a payment of money, an exchange of other property, or the performance of services. The consideration in a sale, regardless of its nature, is known as the *price*; it need not be money. The parties to a sale are the person who owns the goods and the person to whom the title is transferred. The transferor is the seller or vendor, and the transferee is the buyer or vendee. If the price is payable wholly or partly in goods, each party is a seller insofar as the goods he is to transfer are concerned.

A transaction may be held a sale although the parties have not so regarded it. For example, when a "subcontractor" was obligated to deliver ready mix concrete to the "general contractor" by pouring the concrete into forms at the construction site, the relationship between the parties was actually that of seller and buyer.[1]

When a free item is given with the purchase of other goods, it is the purchasing of the other goods which is the price for the "free" goods and hence the transaction as to the free goods is a sale.

§ 23:2. SALE DISTINGUISHED. A sale is an actual present transfer of title. If there is a transfer of a lesser interest than ownership or title, the transaction is not a sale.

(a) Bailment. A bailment is not a sale because only possession is transferred to the bailee. The bailor remains the owner.

Since a bailment is distinct from a sale, the common practice of leasing equipment and automobiles on a long-term basis would have the effect of making bailment law applicable to many transactions that would otherwise be governed by the law of sales. There is a trend in a law, however, to hold

---

[1] Wilson v Daniel International Corp., 260 SC 548, 197 SE2d 686.

the bailor to the same responsibilities as a seller. Likewise, statutes applicable to "owners" may define that term to include lessees under long-term leases.[2]

(b) Gift. There can be no sale without consideration, or a price. A gift is a gratuitous transfer of the title of property.

(c) Contract to sell. When the parties intend that title to goods will pass at a future time and they make a contract providing for that event, a *contract to sell* is created.[3]

(d) Option to purchase. A sale, a present transfer of title, differs from an *option to purchase*. The latter is neither a transfer of title nor a contract to transfer title but a power to require a sale to be made at a future time.

(e) Conditional sale. A *conditional sale* customarily refers to a "condition precedent" transaction by which title does not vest in the purchaser until he has paid in full for the property purchased. This was formerly a common type of sale used when personal property was purchased on credit and payment was to be made in installments. This transaction is now classified as a secured transaction under Article 9 of the UCC.

(f) Furnishing of labor or services. A contract for personal services is to be distinguished from a sale of goods even when some transfer of personal property is involved in the performing of the services. For example, the contract of a repairman is a contract for services even though in making the repairs he may supply parts necessary to perform his task. The supplying of such parts is not regarded as a sale because it is merely incidental to the primary contract of making repairs, as contrasted with the purchase of goods, such as a television set, with the incidental service of installation.

Similarly, when a surgical pin is inserted in the bone as part of hospitalization, the transaction as to the pin cannot be isolated and treated as a sale but is merely part of a broad contract for services. And an agreement by an artist to make a painting on a television program and donate the painting as part of a charitable drive is an agreement to render services and not a contract for sale of goods.

FACTS: Lovett, a patient in the hospital of Emory University, was given a blood transfusion for which a separate charge was made on his hospital bill. He contracted serum hepatitis from the transfusion and died. Suit was brought against the hospital on the ground that there was a breach of implied warranty of fitness of the blood.

DECISION: Judgment for the University. The furnishing of blood as part of a blood transfusion is a service and not a sale, and therefore no implied warranty of fitness arises. The fact that a separate charge was made for the blood did not give the blood the character of goods, because the transfusion was still the rendering of a service. [Lovett v Emory University, 116 GaApp 277, 156 SE2d 923]

---

[2] The New York Vehicle and Traffic Law defines "owner" to include a lessee renting an automobile for more than 30 days. Aetna Casualty & Surety Co. v World Wide Rent-A-Car, Inc. 28 AppDiv2d 286, 284 NYS2d 807.

[3] Uniform Commercial Code § 2-106(1).

In four fifths of the states, statutes limit the liability of hospitals and blood banks for harm resulting from transfusions to cases in which negligence of the defendant is shown.

When there is a contract only to install and maintain a burglar alarm system but there is no sale of the equipment to the customer, the Code does not apply.[4]

(g) Crimes. The word "sale" is often broadly defined by criminal law to include "negotiation" and "solicitation" and other transactions not involving a transfer of title. The Uniform Narcotic Drug Act defines "sale" to include "barter, exchange, or gift, or offer thereof, and each such transaction made by any person, whether as principal, proprietor, agent, servant, or employee."[5]

§ **23:3. SUBJECT MATTER OF SALES.** The subject matter of a sale is anything that is movable when it is identified as the subject of the transaction.[6] The subject matter may not be (a) investment securities, such as stocks and bonds, the sale of which is regulated by Article 8 of the UCC; (b) choses in action, such as insurance policies and promissory notes, since they are assigned or negotiated rather than sold, or which, because of their personal nature, are not transferable in any case; or (c) real estate, such as a house, factory, or farm.

(a) Nature of goods. Most goods are tangible and solid, such as an automobile or a chair. But goods may also be fluid, as oil or gasoline. Goods may also be intangible, as natural gas and electricity.

FACTS: Wabash County REMC supplied electricity. It supplied current of 135 volts which caused damage to the household appliances of Helvey. These appliances were rated to use only 110 volts. Helvey sued Wabash County REMC more than four years after the harm was sustained. Wabash County REMC raised the defense that the suit was barred by the four-year statute of limitations applied by the Uniform Commercial Code to causes of action arising from sales. Helvey claimed that this statute was not applicable because it applied only to "goods" and the defendant was a supplier of "electricity."

DECISION: Electricity constituted "goods" within the meaning of the Uniform Commercial Code as electricity is movable and is subject to ownership. The contract was therefore governed by the four-year statute of limitations. [Helvey v Wabash County REMC (IndApp) 278 NE2d 608.]

The UCC does not apply to the sale of a business.

(b) Nonexistent and future goods. Generally a person cannot make a present sale of nonexistent or future goods or goods that he does not own.

---

[4] Feary v Aaron Burglar Alarm, Inc. 32 CalApp3d 553, 108 CalRptr 242.

[5] Kansas v Woods 214 Kan 739, 522 P2d 967.

[6] UCC § 2-105(1). It may also include things which are attached to the land, such as those consisting of (a) timber or minerals or buildings or materials forming part of buildings if they are to be removed or severed by the seller, (b) other things attached to land to be removed by either party. § 2-107.

He can make a contract to sell such goods at a future date; but since he does not have the title, he cannot transfer that title now. For example, an agreement made today that all fish caught on a fishing trip tomorrow shall belong to a particular person does not make him the owner of those fish today.

When the parties purport to effect a present sale of future goods, the agreement operates only as a contract to sell the goods.[7] Thus a farmer purporting to transfer the title today to the future crop would be held subject to a duty to transfer title to the crop when it came into existence. If he did not keep the promise, he could be sued for breach of contract; but the contract would not operate to vest the title in the buyer automatically.

§ 23:4. LAW OF CONTRACTS APPLICABLE. A sale is a voluntary transaction between two persons. Accordingly, most of the principles that apply to contractual agreements in general are equally applicable to a sale. Modern marketing practices, however, have modified the strict principles of contract law, and this approach to the problem is carried into the UCC. Thus, a sales contract can be made in any manner; and it is sufficient that the parties by their conduct recognize the existence of a contract, even though it cannot be determined when the contract was made, and generally even though one or more terms are left open.[8]

In some instances the UCC treats all buyers and sellers alike. In others, it treats merchants differently than it does the occasional or casual buyer or seller; in this way the UCC recognizes that the merchant is experienced in his field and has a specialized knowledge of the relevant commercial practices.[9]

(a) Offer. Contract law as to offers is applicable to sales except that an offer by a merchant cannot be revoked, even though there is no consideration to keep the offer open, if the offer expresses an intention that it will not be revoked, is made in writing, and is signed by the merchant.[10] The expressed period of irrevocability, however, cannot exceed three months. If nothing is said as to the duration of the offer, this irrevocability continues only for a reasonable time.

(b) Acceptance. The UCC redeclares the general principle of contract law that an offer to buy or sell goods may be accepted in any manner and by any medium which is reasonable under the circumstances, unless a specific manner or medium is clearly indicated by the terms of the offer or the circumstances of the case.[11]

(1) Acceptance by Shipment. Unless otherwise clearly indicated, an order or other offer to buy goods that are to be sent out promptly or

---

[7] § 2-105(2).
[8] § 2-204. This provision of the UCC is limited by requiring that there be "a reasonably certain basis for giving an appropriate remedy."
[9] § 2-104(1).
[10] § 2-205.
[11] § 2-206(1)(a).

currently can be accepted by the seller either by actually shipping the goods, as though a unilateral contract offer had been made; or by promptly promising to make shipment, as though a bilateral contract, that is, an exchange of promises, had been offered. If acceptance is made by shipping the goods, the seller must notify the buyer within a reasonable time that the offer has been accepted in this manner.[12]

(2) *Additional Terms in Acceptance.* Unless it is expressly specified that an offer to buy or sell goods must be accepted just as made, the offeree may accept a contract but at the same time propose an additional term. This new term, however, does not become binding unless the offeror thereafter consents to it. Consequently, when the buyer sends an order which the seller acknowledges on his own printed form, any additional material term in the seller's printed form that is not in the buyer's order form or which is not implied by custom or prior dealings is merely regarded as an additional term that may or may not be accepted by the buyer. That is, the order is deemed "accepted" in spite of the addition of this new material term, but the new term does not become part of the contract until it in turn is accepted by the buyer.

The acceptance by the buyer may be found either in his express statement, orally or in writing, that he accepts the additional term, or it may be deduced from his conduct, as when he accepts the goods with knowledge that the additional term has been made.

FACTS: Universal Oil Products discussed the sale of an incinerator to S. C. M. Corporation. Universal sent a written offer. S. C. M. sent back a purchase order form that purported to order on the terms of the offer but which also stated that any dispute arising under the contract was to be determined by arbitration. On receipt of the purchase order, Universal shipped the incinerator to S. C. M. Some time thereafter, the incinerator exploded and a dispute arose as to the cause of the explosion. S. C. M. claimed that Universal was required to submit this dispute to arbitration.

DECISION: S. C. M. was correct. The arbitration provision was an additional term in the "acceptance" by S. C. M. and was therefore a counteroffered term. This counteroffer was accepted by Universal when it shipped the incinerator to the buyer. [Universal Oil Products Co. v S. C. M. Corporation (DC Conn) 313 FSupp 905]

When the form used by the seller to acknowledge the buyer's order contains a provision limiting the seller's liability but such provision was not in the buyer's order form and the buyer never expressly agreed to the limitation in the seller's form, the limitation provision is not part of the contract between the parties and does not bind the buyer.[13]

In a transaction between merchants, the additional term becomes part of the contract if that term does not materially alter the offer and no objection is made to it.[14] If such an additional term in the seller's form of

---

[12] § 2-206(2).
[13] Air Products and Chemicals, Inc. v Fairbanks Morse, Inc. 58 Wis2d 193, 206 NW2d 414.
[14] UCC § 2-207; Application of Doughboy Industries, Inc. 17 AppDiv2d 216, 233 NYS2d 488.

acknowledgment operates solely to his advantage, however, it is a material term which must be accepted by the buyer to be effective.

(c) Determination of price. The price for the goods may be expressly fixed by the contract, or the parties may merely indicate the manner of determining price at a later time.[15] A sales contract is binding even though it calls for a specified price "plus extras" but does not define the extras, which it leaves for future agreement.

When persons experienced in a particular industry make a contract without specifying the price to be paid, the price will be determined by the manner which is customary in the industry.

> FACTS: California Lettuce Growers contracted to grow and deliver to Union Sugar Co. the crop of sugar beets from 239 acres in a certain year. No price was specified, but Growers knew that it was the custom to make agreements to pay at a later date on the basis of the sugar content of the beets supplied and of the selling price of sugar for the current year. Growers later claimed that the contract was void because the price was not specified in the contract.

> DECISION: Judgment for Union. Since the parties contracted with the knowledge of the custom as to the method of price determination, the price was to be determined in that manner and the contract was not void because no price was specified in the contract. [California Lettuce Growers v Union Sugar Co. 45 Cal2d 474, 289 P2d 785]

Ordinarily, if nothing is said as to price, the buyer is required to pay the reasonable value of the goods. The reasonable price is generally the market price, but not necessarily, as when the market price is under the control of the seller.

In recent years there has been an increase in use of the "cost plus" formula for determining price. Under this form of agreement the buyer pays the seller a sum equal to the cost to the seller of obtaining the goods plus a specified percentage of that cost.

The contract may expressly provide that one of the parties may determine the price, in which case he must act in good faith in so doing.[16] Likewise, the contract may specify that the price shall be determined by some standard or by a third person. If for any reason other than the fault of one of the parties the price cannot be fixed in the manner specified, the buyer is required to pay the reasonable value for the goods unless it is clear that the parties intended that if the price were not determined in the manner specified, there would be no contract. In the latter case the buyer must return the goods and the seller refund any payment made on account. If the buyer is unable to return such goods, he must pay their reasonable value at the time of delivery.

(d) Output and requirement contracts. Somewhat related to the open-term concept concerning price is that involved in the output and require-

---

[15] UCC § 2-305.

[16] Good faith requires that the party in fact act honestly and, in the case of a merchant, also requires that he follow reasonable commercial standards of fair dealing which are recognized in the trade. UCC §§ 1-201(19), 2-103(b).

ment contracts in which the quantity which is to be sold or purchased is not a specific quantity but is such amount as the seller should produce or the buyer should require. Although this introduces an element of uncertainty, such sales contracts are valid. To prevent oppression, they are subject to two limitations: (1) the parties must act in good faith; and (2) the quantity offered or demanded must not be unreasonably disproportionate to prior output or requirements or to a stated estimate.[17]

FACTS: Romine, a contractor, had a construction contract with the government. Savannah Steel Co. contracted to supply Romine with the steel required for the construction. Because of an error in the government specifications, the amount of steel actually needed was less than one tenth of the amount of the estimate on which Romine and Savannah had relied. Savannah sued Romine for breach of the requirements contract. It was shown that the contractor had agreed to pay $2,725 for "all" the steel required for construction and that this computation had been made on the basis that 15.5 tons were required. Because of the government's error, less than 1.5 tons were required.

DECISION: Savannah was not entitled to recover the full contract price. The supply contract was a requirements contract and by UCC § 2-306, it was not binding if the actual requirements were unreasonably disproportionate to the estimated requirements. This had occurred since the actual requirements were less than one tenth of the estimated amount. The contractor was therefore not required to pay the contract price. Instead the price would be recomputed by dividing the contract price by 15.5 tons to obtain a price per ton and then multiply that by the number of tons actually required. [Romine, Inc. v Savannah Steel Co. 117 GaApp 353, 160 SE2d 659]

When the sales contract is a continuing contract, as one calling for periodic delivery of fuel, but no time is set for the life of the contract, the contract runs for a reasonable time but may be terminated on notice by either party.[18]

(e) Seals. A seal on a contract or on an offer of sale has no effect. Thus, in determining whether there is consideration or if the statute of limitations is applicable, the fact that there is a seal on the contract is ignored.[19]

(f) Usage of trade and course of dealing. Established usages or customs of trade and prior courses of conduct or dealings between the parties are to be considered in connection with any sales transaction. In the absence of an express term excluding or "overruling" the prior pattern of dealings between the parties and the usages of the trade, it is to be concluded that the parties contracted on the basis of the continuation of those patterns of doing business. More specifically, the patterns of doing business as shown by the prior dealings of the parties and usages of the trade enter into and form part

---

[17] § 2-306(1).

[18] UCC § 2-309(2); Sinkoff Beverage Co. v Schlitz Brewing Co. 51 Misc2d 446, 273 NYS2d 364.

[19] UCC § 2-203.

of their contract and may be looked to in order to find what was intended by the express provisions and to supply otherwise missing terms.

FACTS: Boone Livestock Co. was in the business of buying and selling cattle. It purchased cattle and resold them, specifying to its customers that the cattle weighed certain amounts. In fact, these amounts were the weights at which the cattle had been purchased by Boone from its suppliers increased by arbitrary amounts. It was claimed that these weights were false because they were not the weights at which Boone had purchased the cattle. Boone defended on the ground that no statement had been made by it that the weights recited were the weights at which it had purchased the cattle and that consequently it had not made a false statement. It was shown that it was customary for middlemen buying and reselling cattle to resell them at the weight at which they had been purchased.

DECISION: By virtue of UCC § 1-105, the usage of the trade entered into the contract so that a statement of the cattle weight without any qualifying statement amounted to a statement that that was the weight at which Boone had purchased the cattle. In order to have made the statement of weight truthful, it would have been necessary for Boone to expressly state that the specified weights were not the purchase weights. As no such express statement was made, the recital of the weights gave a false impression to persons in the business and was therefore false. [In re Boone Livestock Co. (US Dept. of Agriculture) 27 AD 475, 5 UCCRS 498]

(g) **Implied conditions.** The field of implied conditions under contract law is broadened to permit the release of a party from obligation under a sales contract when performance has been made commercially impracticable, as distinguished from impossible: (1) by the occurrence of a contingency, the nonoccurrence of which was a basic assumption on which the contract was made; or (2) by compliance in good faith with any applicable domestic or foreign governmental regulation or order, whether or not it is later held valid by the courts.[20] "A severe shortage of raw materials or of supplies due to a contingency such as war, embargo, local crop failure, unforeseen shutdown of major sources of supply, or the like, which either causes a marked increase in cost or altogether prevents the seller from securing supplies necessary to his performance, is within the contemplation" of this provision of the UCC.[21]

(h) **Modification of contract.** A departure is made from the general principles of contract law in that an agreement to modify the contract for the sale of goods is binding even though the modification is not supported by consideration.[22]

---

[20] UCC § 2-615(a). If under the circumstances indicated in the text the seller is totally disabled from performing, he is discharged from his contract. If he is able to produce some goods, he must allocate them among customers, but any customer may reject the contract and such fractional offer. § 2-615(b), § 2-616.

[21] § 2-615, Official Comment, point 4.

[22] § 2-209(1).

(i) Parol evidence rule. The parol evidence rule applies to the sale of goods with the slight modification that a writing is not presumed or assumed to represent the entire contract of the parties unless the court specifically decides that it does. If the court so decides, parol evidence is admissible to show what the parties meant by their words but cannot add additional terms to the writing. If the court decides that the writing was not intended to represent the entire contract, the writing may be supplemented by parol proof of additional terms so long as such terms are not inconsistent with the original written terms.[23]

A sales contract, although written, may be modified by an oral agreement except to the extent that a writing is required by the statute of frauds. Even when the sales contract specifies that there cannot be an oral modification, the conduct of the parties may be such that there is a waiver of such prohibition and an oral modification is then binding.

(j) Fraud and other defenses. The defenses that may be raised in a suit on a sales contract are in general the same as on any other contract. When one party is defrauded, he may cancel the transaction and recover what he has paid or the goods that he has delivered, together with damages for any loss which he has sustained. If title was obtained by the buyer by means of his fraud, the title is voidable by an innocent seller while the goods are still owned by the buyer and the sale may be set aside.

If the sales contract or any clause in it was unconscionable when made, a court may refuse to enforce it, as discussed in Chapter 14.

§ 23:5. ILLEGAL SALES. Certain conditions must exist for a sale to be considered illegal.

(a) Illegality at common law. At common law a sale is illegal if the subject matter is itself wrong. The transaction may also be illegal even though the subject matter of the sale may be unobjectionable in itself, as when the agreement provides that the goods that are sold shall be employed for some unlawful purpose or when the seller assists in the unlawful act. To illustrate, when the seller falsely brands goods, representing them to be imported, to assist the buyer in perpetrating a fraud, the sale is illegal. The mere fact, however, that the seller has knowledge of the buyer's unlawful purpose does not, under the general rule, make the sale illegal unless the purpose is the commission of a serious crime.

(b) Illegality under statutes. Practically every state has legislation prohibiting certain sales when they are not conducted according to the requirements of the statutes. Thus, a statute may require that a particular class of goods, such as meat, be inspected before a legal sale can be made. In addition to statutes which invalidate the sale, a number of statutes make it a criminal act or impose a penalty for making a sale under certain circumstances. Statutes commonly regulate sales by establishing standards as to grading, size, weight, and measure, and by prohibiting adulteration.

---

[23] UCC § 2-202; Hunt Foods and Industries v Doliner, 49 Misc2d 246, 267 NYS2d 364.

In addition to the restrictive state statutes, federal legislation regulates the sale of goods in interstate commerce. The federal Food, Drug, and Cosmetic Act, for example, prohibits the interstate shipment of misbranded or adulterated foods, drugs, cosmetics, and therapeutic devices. A product which does not carry adequate use instructions and warnings is deemed "misbranded" for the purpose of the statutes. Other statutes, such as those designed to regulate competition, further protect the consumer.

FACTS: Sullivan, a druggist, received from a manufacturer in another state a properly labeled container of sulfa tablets. He placed some of these tablets in small pill boxes for resale to the public. These boxes were labeled only "Sulfathiazole." Sullivan was prosecuted for violating the federal law prohibiting the sale of misbranded drugs.

DECISION: Sullivan was convicted. The boxes did not carry adequate instructions to the buyers regarding the use of the tablets which, if not taken according to directions, could be harmful. Sullivan therefore violated the federal law. The fact that the tablets had left the channels of interstate commerce did not prevent the federal law from applying since Congress could and had intended "to safeguard the consumer by applying the Act to articles from the moment of their introduction into interstate commerce all the way to the moment of their delivery to the ultimate consumer." [United States v Sullivan, 332 US 689]

States may prohibit the making of sales on Sunday either generally or as to particular commodities or classes of stores. Such laws do not violate any guarantee of religious freedom nor deprive persons of the equal protection of the laws. In some instances, however, a Sunday closing law may be unconstitutional because it is too vague.

Statutes may regulate the sale of "secondhand" goods. Such a statute does not apply to a casual seller, but only applies to one whose regular business consists of selling goods of the kind covered by the statute.[24]

(c) **Effect of illegal sale.** An illegal sale or contract to sell cannot be enforced. This rule is based on public policy. As a general rule, courts will not aid either party in recovering money or property transferred pursuant to an illegal agreement. Relief is sometimes given, however, to an innocent party to an unlawful agreement. For example, if one party is the victim of a fraudulent transaction, he may recover what he has transferred to the other party even though the agreements between them arose out of some illegal scheme.

When a sale is made illegal by statute, a seller who violates the law may be held liable for the damage caused.

FACTS: The State of Minnesota prohibited the sale of glue to minors in order to protect them from the brain-damaging consequences of glue sniffing. In violation of this statute, Warren sold glue to Ricken, a minor. Zerby, Ricken's minor friend, sniffed the glue and was killed by the fumes. Suit was brought against Warren, who raised the defenses of contributory negligence and assumption of risk.

[24] Michigan v E.L. Rice & Co. 33 MichApp2d 699, 190 NW2d 309.

DECISION: The statutory prohibition was intended to protect minors. Its violation therefore imposed an absolute liability on the violator. Contributory negligence and assumption of risk could not be raised as defenses to this liability. [Zerby v Warren, 297 Minn 134, 210 NW2d 58]

§ 23:6. BULK TRANSFER. Whenever a merchant is about to transfer a major part of his materials, supplies, merchandise, or other inventory, not in the ordinary course of business, advance notice of the transfer must be given to his creditors in accordance with Article 6 of the Uniform Commercial Code. The essential characteristic of businesses subject to Article 6 is that they sell from inventory or a stock of goods, as contrasted with businesses which render services. If the required notice is not given, the creditors may reach the sold property in the hands of the transferee and also in the hands of any subsequent transferee who knew that there had not been compliance with the UCC or who did not pay value.[25] This is designed to protect creditors of a merchant from the danger that he may sell all of his inventory, pocket the money, and then disappear, leaving them unpaid. The protection given to creditors by the bulk transfer legislation is in addition to the protection which they have against their debtor for fraudulent transfers or conveyances, and the remedies that can be employed in bankruptcy proceedings.

Ordinarily, the transferee who receives the goods does not become liable for the debts of his transferor merely because the requirements of Article 6 have not been satisfied. If the transferee has mixed the transferred goods with his own goods so that it is not possible to identify the transferred goods, the transferee is personally liable for debts of the transferor.

FACTS: Costello owned an automobile accessory and appliance business. He purchased goods for his inventory from J & R Motor Supply Corporation. The goods were not paid for at the time when Costello sold his business to Cornelius. Cornelius mixed the Costello inventory with his own so that the two could not be identified. J & R and another creditor claimed that Cornelius was liable for the amount of the bills owed by Costello because the sale of the business had been made without complying with Article 6 of the Uniform Commercial Code.

DECISION: Cornelius was personally liable. Ordinarily, noncompliance with the bulk transfer article only makes the transferred goods subject to the claims of the transferor's creditors and does not impose personal liability on the transferee. When, however, the transferee mingles his own goods with the transferred goods so that it cannot be determined what goods were the "transferred bulk," the transferee becomes personally liable for the claims of the creditors of the transferor. [Cornelius v J & R Motor Supply Corp. (Ky) 468 SW2d 781]

The fact that there has been noncompliance with Article 6 of the UCC regulating bulk transfers, however, does not affect the validity of a bulk sale of goods as between the immediate parties to the transfer since Article 6 is operative only with respect to the rights of creditors of the seller.

---

[25] UCC § 6-101 et seq.

B. FORMALITY OF THE SALES CONTRACT

In order to afford protection from false claims, certain sales of goods must be evidenced by a writing.

§ 23:7. AMOUNT. The statute of frauds provision of the Uniform Commercial Code applies whenever the sales price is $500 or more.[26] If the total contract price equals or exceeds this amount, the law applies even though the contract covers several articles, the individual amounts of which are less than $500, provided the parties intended to make a single contract rather than a series of separate or divisible contracts. In the latter case, if each contract is for less than $500, no writing is required.

§ 23:8. NATURE OF THE WRITING REQUIRED. To be effective, the writing evidencing the sales contract must meet certain requirements.

(a) Terms. The writing need only give assurance that there was a transaction. Specifically it need only indicate that a sale or contract to sell has been made and state the quantity of goods involved. Any other missing terms may be shown by parol evidence in the event of a dispute.[27]

(b) Signature. The writing must be signed by the person who is being sued or his authorized agent. The signature must be placed on the writing with the intention of authenticating the writing. It may consist of initials or be printed, stamped, or typewritten as long as made with the necessary intent.

When the transaction is between merchants, an exception is made to the requirement of signing. The failure of a merchant to repudiate a confirming letter sent him by another merchant binds him just as though he had signed the letter or other writing.[28] This ends the evil of a one-sided writing under which the sender of the letter was bound, but the receiver could safely ignore the transaction or could hold the sender as he chose.

The provision as to merchants makes it necessary for a merchant buyer or merchant seller to watch his mail and to act promptly if he is not to be bound by a contract for sale with respect to which he has signed no writing. It deprives the party who fails to reject the confirmation of the defense of the statute of frauds.

(c) Time of execution. The required writing may be made at any time at or after the making of the sale. It may even be made after the contract has been broken or a suit brought on it, since the essential element is the existence of written proof of the transaction when the trial is held. Accordingly, when the buyer writes in reply to the seller, after a 45-day delay, and merely criticizes the quality of some of the goods, the conduct of the buyer is a confirmation.

---

[26] § 2-201.
[27] § 2-201(1).
[28] § 2-201(2). The confirming letter must be sent within a reasonable time after the transaction, and the receiving merchant must give written notice of his objection thereto within ten days after receiving the confirming letter.

(d) Particular writings. The writing may be a single writing, or it may be several writings considered as a group. Formal contracts, bills of sale, letters, and telegrams are common forms of writings that satisfy the requirement. Purchase orders, cash register receipts, sales tickets, invoices, and similar papers generally do not satisfy the requirements as to a signature, and sometimes they do not specify any quantity or commodity.

In most cases, the writing which will satisfy the statute of frauds will be either (1) a complete written contract signed by both parties, or (2) a memorandum signed by the party who is being sued. There is no requirement that the writing must be a contract signed by both parties.

§ 23:9. EFFECT OF NONCOMPLIANCE. A sales agreement that does not comply with the statute of frauds is not enforceable. However, the contract itself is not unlawful and may be voluntarily performed by the parties.[29]

> **FACTS:** Crown Central Petroleum Corporation, a refiner, orally agreed to supply Davis, an independent dealer, with 1.2 million gallons of gas a month. Because of the oil shortage, Crown refused to deliver the gas as promised. Davis sued Crown.
>
> **DECISION:** Judgment for Crown. The contract was for the sale of goods in excess of $500. The oral contract was not enforceable because of the statute of frauds. [Davis v Crown Central Petroleum Corp. (CA4 NC) 483 F2d 1014]

When the question is whether there has been a sale or a bailment, the fact that there is a writing under the statute of frauds is evidence indicating that the transaction was a sale. Conversely, the fact that an automobile dealer did not execute either a bill of sale or a memorandum satisfying the requirement of a writing was evidence which confirmed the contention of the car owner that he had not sold his automobile to the dealer but had entrusted it to him for resale. The result was that the dealer was the owner's agent or bailee, and the dealer was therefore guilty of embezzlement when he did not account to the owner for the proceeds from the resale of the car.

§ 23:10. WHEN PROOF OF ORAL CONTRACT IS PERMITTED. The absence of a writing does not always bar proof of a sales contract.

(a) Receipt and acceptance. An oral sales contract may be enforced if it can be shown that the goods were delivered by the seller and were received and accepted by the buyer. Consequently, when the buyer purchases and receives goods on credit, the seller may sue for the purchase price even though the total is $500 and there is no writing, for the reason that the receipt and acceptance of the goods by the buyer took the contract out of the statute of frauds. Both a receipt and an acceptance by the buyer must be shown. If only part of the goods have been received and accepted, the contract may be enforced only insofar as it relates to those goods received and accepted.[30]

---

[29] UCC § 2-201(1).
[30] § 2-201(3)(c).

The buyer's receipt of the goods may be symbolic, as in the case of the seller's transfer of a covering bill of lading to the buyer.

When the goods are delivered at the buyer's direction to a third person who accepts the goods, the oral contract of the buyer is taken out of the statute of frauds. Consequently, a buying broker's oral contract is taken out of the statute when, following his instructions, the goods are delivered to the broker's customer and are then accepted by the customer.

(b) Payment. An oral contract may be enforced if the buyer has made full payment. In the case of part payment for divisible units of goods, a contract may be enforced only with respect to goods for which payment has been made and accepted.[31] When the goods are not divisible, as in the case of an automobile, the part payment takes the entire contract out of the statute of frauds.

> **FACTS:** Smigel orally agreed to sell his automobile to Lockwood for $11,400. Lockwood made a down payment of $100. Thereafter Smigel sold the car to another buyer. Lockwood sued Smigel for breach of contract. Smigel claimed that the oral contract for the sale of the car was not binding because a part payment only took the transaction out of the statute of frauds with respect to goods for which payment had been made.
>
> **DECISION:** Judgment for Lockwood. The rule asserted by the seller applies when the goods are divisible. When the goods are not divisible, as in the case of one automobile, the part payment takes the entire contract out of the statute of frauds. [Lockwood v Smigel, 18 CalApp3d 800, 96 CalReptr 289]

There is some uncertainty under this rule as to the effectiveness of "payment" by check or a promissory note executed by the buyer. Under the law of commercial paper a check or note is conditional payment when delivered, and it does not become absolute until the instrument is paid. The earlier decisions held that the delivery of a negotiable instrument was not such a payment as would make the oral contract enforceable unless it was agreed at that time that the instrument was to be accepted as absolute, and not conditional, payment. A modern contrary view, which is influenced by the fact that business persons ordinarily regard the delivery of a check or note as "payment," holds that the delivery of such an instrument is sufficient to make the oral contract enforceable.[32]

When the buyer has negotiated or assigned to the seller a commercial paper that was executed by a third person and the seller has accepted the instrument, a payment has been made within the meaning of the statute of frauds.

---

[31] § 2-201(3)(c).

[32] Cohn v Fisher, 118 NYSuper 286, 287 A2d 222. The Restatement of Contracts, § 205, adopts this view. It would appear that the draftsmen of the UCC are also in favor of this view, for the comment to § 2-201 states that "part payment may be made by money or check, accepted by the seller."

(c) Nonresellable goods. No writing is required when the goods are specifically made for the buyer and are of such an unusual nature that they are not suitable for sale in the ordinary course of the seller's business. For example, when 14 steel doors were tailor-made by the seller for the buyer's building and were not suitable for sale to anyone else in the ordinary course of the seller's business, and could only be sold as scrap, the oral contract of sale was enforceable.

In order for the nonresellable goods exception to apply, however, the seller must have made a substantial beginning in manufacturing the goods or, if he is a middleman, in procuring them, before receiving notice of a repudiation by the buyer.[33]

> FACTS: The LTV Aerospace Corporation manufactured all-terrain vehicles for use in Southeast Asia. LTV made an oral contract with Bateman under which he would supply the packing cases needed for their overseas shipment. Bateman made substantial beginnings in the production of packing cases following LTV's specifications. LTV thereafter stopped production of its vehicles and refused to take delivery of the cases. When sued by Bateman for breach of contract, LTV raised the defense that the contract could not be enforced because there was no writing which satisfied the statute of frauds.

> DECISION: Judgment for Bateman. The packing cases could not be resold by Bateman in the ordinary course of his business. The contract therefore came within the exception made by UCC § 2-201(c)(1). Bateman had made a substantial beginning in the production of the cases and could therefore enforce the oral contract. [LTV Areospace Corp. v Bateman (TexCivApp) 492 SW2d 703]

(d) Judicial admission. No writing is required when the person alleged to have made the contract voluntarily admits in the course of legal proceedings that he has done so.

§ 23:11. NON-CODE LOCAL REQUIREMENTS. In addition to the UCC requirement as to a writing, other statutes may impose requirements. For example, consumer protection legislation commonly requires the execution of a detailed contract and the giving of a copy thereof to the consumer. The result is that even though the Code requirements have been satisfied, the buyer may still be able to avoid the transaction for noncompliance with some other statutory requirement.

§ 23:12. BILL OF SALE. Regardless of the requirement of the statute of frauds, the parties may wish to execute a writing as evidence or proof of the sale. Through custom this writing has become known as a *bill of sale*; but it is neither a bill nor a contract. It is merely a receipt or writing signed by the seller in which he recites that he has transferred the title of the described property to the buyer.

In many states provision is made for the public recording of bills of sale when goods are left in the seller's possession. In the case of the sale of

---

[33] UCC § 2-201(3)(a).

certain types of property, a bill of sale may be required in order to show that the purchaser is the lawful owner. Thus, some states require the production of a bill of sale before the title to an automobile will be registered in the name of the purchaser.

QUESTIONS AND CASE PROBLEMS

1. Suburban Gas Heat of Kennewick sold propane gas for domestic consumption. As the result of its negligence in supplying propane gas mixed with water, there was an explosion which caused damage to Kasey. When Kasey sued to enforce the liability of Suburban Gas Heat as a seller, Suburban raised the defense that it was engaged in furnishing a public service and not in the sale of personal property within the meaning of the Uniform Sales Act. Was Suburban correct? [Kasey v Suburban Gas Heat of Kennewick, Inc., 60 Wash2d 468, 374 P2d 549]

2. Crocker printed and distributed Christmas cards. At certain intervals such cards which could not be sold would be destroyed. Crocker's employees took a large quantity of Christmas cards for that purpose to McFaddin who ran a dump and salvage operation. Persons bringing material to McFaddin would pay one fee for material that could be salvaged by him and a higher fee if instructions were given to destroy the material. When Crocker's employees took the Christmas cards to McFaddin, nothing was said as to the disposition to be made of them and only a salvage fee was paid. Later, Crocker learned that McFaddin had resold the cards. He sued McFaddin, claiming that McFaddin could not make such a sale because the transaction between Crocker and McFaddin was a bailment. McFaddin defended on the ground that the transaction was a sale, an abandonment, or a gift, and that in any instance McFaddin could sell the property and otherwise treat it as his own. Decide. [H. S. Crocker Co. v McFaddin, 148 CalApp2d 639, 307 P2d 429]

3. Berger did business under the name of Warren Freezer Food Co. A consumer named Vernon made a contract for the purchase of a large quantity of freezer items, under which it was agreed that Warren Freezer would keep Vernon's food in its freezer, Vernon would take a portion of the order each week and would make a weekly installment payment, which would be applied to the note that Vernon had signed for the total bill. When Vernon would call for a part of the order of food, each item was individually wrapped in plain paper. When Vernon requested delivery, the individual packages were put into cardboard boxes on the exterior of which was a statement of the gross and net weight of the total contents and the defendant's name and place of business. Berger was prosecuted for violating the Michigan statute against "misbranding," which statute declared that an article was misbranded "if in package form" and the package did not show the true net weight. Was Berger guilty of violating this statute? [Michigan v Berger, 7 MichApp 695, 153 NW2d 161]

4. The Tober Foreign Motors, Inc., sold an airplane to Skinner on installments. Later it was agreed that the monthly installments should be reduced in half. Thereafter Tober claimed that the reduction agreement was not binding because it was not supported by consideration. Was this claim correct? [Skinner v Tober Foreign Motors, Inc., 345 Mass 429, 187 NE2d 669]

5. Members of the Colonial Club purchased beer from outside the state and ordered it sent to the Colonial Club. The club then kept it in the club refrigerator and served the beer to its respective owners upon demand. The club received no compensation or profit from the transaction. The club was indicted for selling liquor unlawfully. Decide. [North Carolina v Colonial Club, 154 NC 177, 69 SE 771]

6. A customer purchased furniture from a dealer. The furniture selected by the customer was not in stock, and the dealer loaned the customer some furniture to use until the selected furniture was delivered. An item of the loaned furniture collapsed and injured the customer. The customer sued the dealer three years and four months later. The dealer defended on the ground that the non-Code two-year statute of limitations had expired. The customer claimed that there was a sale and that accordingly suit could be brought within the four-year period authorized by the UCC § 2-725. Decide. [See Garfield v Furniture Fair-Hanover, 113 NJSuper 509, 274 A2d 325]

7. Gallick sold sugar to Castiglione with knowledge that the latter intended to use it in the illegal manufacture of liquor. The buyer did not pay the purchase price. Gallick then sued him for the purchase price. Castiglione defended on the ground that the contract was illegal. Decide. [Gallick v Castiglione, 2 CalApp2d 716, 38 P2d 858]

8. Fallis farmed about 550 acres. He made an oral contract to sell and deliver to Grains 5,000 bushels of soybeans at $2.54 per bushel. Shortly thereafter, Grains sent Fallis a written contract signed by Grains. Fallis did not sign the contract and did not return it. When he failed to deliver the soybeans under the contract, he was sued for the breach thereof by Grains. He raised the defense of the statute of frauds. Grains claimed that the statute of frauds was not applicable because Fallis had not rejected the written contract that had been sent to him. Decide. [Grains v Fallis, 239 Ark 962, 395 SW2d 555]

9. Distribu-Dor orally agreed to sell wall mirrors to Karadanis for use in the Tahoe Inn, which was being built by the buyer. The mirrors were cut to size. When suit was brought for the purchase price, Karadanis raised the defense that there was no required writing. Was this defense valid? [Distribu-Dor, Inc. v Karadanis, 11 CalApp3d 463, 90 CalRptr 231]

RISK AND
PROPERTY RIGHTS

§ 24:1. TYPES OF PROBLEMS. In most sales transactions the buyer receives the proper goods, makes payment, and the transaction is thus completed; however, several types of problems may arise—(a) problems pertaining to damage to goods, (b) those resulting from creditors' claims, and (c) problems relating to insurance. These problems usually can be avoided if the parties make express provisions concerning them in their sales contract. When the parties have not specified by their contract what results they desire, however, the rules stated in this chapter are applied by the law.

(a) Damage to goods. If the goods are damaged or totally destroyed without any fault of either the buyer or the seller, must the seller bear the loss and supply new goods to the buyer; or is it the buyer's loss, so that he must pay the seller the price even though he now has no goods or has only damaged goods?[1] The fact that there may be insurance does not diminish the importance of this question, for the answer to it determines whose insurer is liable and the extent of that insurer's liability.

(b) Creditors' claims. Creditors of a delinquent seller may seize the goods as belonging to the seller, or the buyer's creditors may seize them on the theory that they belong to the buyer. In such cases the question arises whether the creditors are correct as to who owns the goods. The question of ownership is also important in connection with the consequence of a resale by the buyer, or the liability for or the computation of certain kinds of taxes, and the liability under certain registration and criminal law statutes.[2]

(c) Insurance. Until the buyer has received the goods and the seller has been paid, both the seller and buyer have an economic interest in the sales

---

[1] Uniform Commercial Code § 2-509.
[2] UCC § 2-401.

transaction.[3] The question arises as to whether either or both have enough interest to entitle them to insure the property involved, that is, whether they have an insurable interest.[4]

§ 24:2. NATURE OF THE TRANSACTION. The answer to be given to each of the questions noted in the preceding section depends upon the nature of the transaction between the seller and the buyer. Sales transactions may be classified according to (a) the nature of the goods and (b) the terms of the transaction.

(a) Nature of goods. The goods may be (1) existing and identified goods or (2) future goods.

(1) Existing and Identified Goods. Existing goods are physically in existence and owned by the seller. When particular goods have been selected by either the buyer or seller, or both of them, as being the goods called for by the sales contract, the goods are described as identified goods. If the goods are existing and identified, it is immaterial whether the seller must do some act or must complete the manufacture of the goods before they satisfy the terms of the contract.

(2) Future Goods. If the goods are not both existing and identified at the time of the sales transaction, they are future goods. Thus, goods are future goods when they are not yet owned by the seller, when they are not yet in existence, or when they have not been identified.

(b) Terms of the transaction. Ordinarily, the seller is only required to make shipment, and the seller's part is performed when he hands over the goods to a carrier for shipment to the buyer. The terms of the contract, however, may obligate the seller to deliver the goods at a particular place, for example, to make delivery at destination. The seller's part of the contract then is not completed until the goods are brought to the destination point and there tendered to the buyer. If the transaction calls for sending the goods to the buyer, it is ordinarily required that the seller deliver the goods to a carrier under a proper contract for shipment to the buyer. Actual physical delivery at destination is only required when the contract expressly states so.

Instead of calling for the actual delivery of goods, the transaction may relate to a transfer of the document of title representing the goods. For example, the goods may be stored in a warehouse, the seller and the buyer having no intention of moving the goods, but intending that there should be a sale and a delivery of the warehouse receipt that stands for the goods.

---

[3] See UCC § 2-501(1)(a), and note also that the seller may have a security interest by virtue of the nature of the shipment or the agreement of the parties. The buyer also acquires a special property right in the goods that entitles him to reclaim the goods on the seller's insolvency if payment of all or part of the purchase price has been made in advance. § 2-502.

[4] To insure property, a person must have such a right or interest in the property that its damage or destruction would cause him financial loss. When he would be so affected, he is said to have an insurable interest in the property. The ownership of personal property for the purpose of insurance is determined by the law of sales. Motors Insurance Corp. v Safeco Insurance Co. (Ky) 412 SW2d 584.

Here the obligation of the seller is to produce the proper paper as distinguished from the goods themselves. The same is true when the goods are represented by any other document of title, such as a bill of lading issued by a carrier.

As a third type of situation, the goods may be stored with, or held by, a third person who has not issued any document of title for the goods, but the seller and buyer intend that the goods shall remain in that bailee's hands, the transaction being completed without any delivery of the goods themselves or of any document of title.

§ 24:3. RISK, RIGHTS, AND INSURABLE INTEREST IN PARTICULAR TRANSACTIONS. The various kinds of goods and terms may be combined in a number of ways. Only the six more common types of transactions will be considered in relationship to the time when risk, rights, and insurable interest are acquired by the buyer. The first three types pertain to existing and identified goods; the last three, to future goods.

Keep in mind that the following rules of law apply only in the absence of a contrary agreement by the parties concerning these matters.

Title to the goods cannot pass to the buyer before the parties so intend.

FACTS: Hargo Woolen Mills manufactured woolen cloth. In doing this, use was made of card waste. This was supplied to Hargo by a waste dealer, the Shabry Trading Co. Shabry delivered 24 bales of waste to Hargo which Hargo did not wish to use as it had an adequate supply. To save storage and transportation costs, it was agreed to leave the bales in the possession of Hargo and that, if Hargo should use any of them, Hargo would notify Shabry and make payment for such bales. Hargo owed money to Meinhard-Commercial Corporation. It began a court procedure by which a receiver was appointed to take over possession of the assets of Hargo. The receiver seized the 24 bales of waste which had been delivered to Hargo by Shabry. Shabry claimed these bales.

DECISION: Judgment for Shabry. The receiver was entitled to the bales only if title had passed from Shabry to Hargo but as Hargo had not indicated its intent to use the 24 bales in question, no title had yet passed to Hargo. The receiver was therefore not entitled to the bales. [Meinhard-Commercial Corp. v Hargo Woolen Mills, 112 NH 500, 300 A2d 321]

(a) Existing goods identified at time of contracting.

(1) No Documents of Title. If the seller is a merchant, the risk of loss passes to the buyer when he receives the goods from the merchant; if a nonmerchant seller, the risk passes when the seller makes the goods available to the buyer. Thus, the risk of loss remains longer on the merchant seller, a distinction which is made on the ground that the merchant seller, being in the business, can more readily protect himself against such continued risk.

The title to existing goods identified at the time of contracting, when no document of title (such as a warehouse receipt or a bill of lading) is involved, passes to the buyer at the time and place of contracting.

Risk and Property Rights in Sales Contracts

Nature of Goods	Terms of Transaction	Transfer of Risk of Loss to Buyer	Transfer of Title to Buyer	Acquisition of Insurable Interest by Buyer *
Existing Goods Identified at Time of Contracting	1. Without document of title	Buyer's receipt of goods from merchant seller; tender of delivery by nonmerchant seller § 2-509(3)	Time and place of contracting § 2-401(3)(b)	Time and place of contracting § 2-501(1)(a)
	2. Delivery of document of title only	Buyer's receipt of negotiable document of title § 2-509(2)(a)	Time and place of delivery of documents by seller § 2-401(3)(a)	Time and place of contracting § 2-501(1)(a)
	3. Goods held by bailee, without document of title	Time of bailee's acknowledgment of buyer's right to possession § 2-509(2)(b)	Time and place of contracting § 2-401(3)(b)	Time and place of contracting § 2-501(1)(a)
Future Goods	4. Marking for buyer	No transfer	No transfer	At time of marking § 2-501(1)(b)
	5. Contract for shipment to buyer	Delivery of goods to carrier § 2-509(1)(a)	Time and place of delivery of goods to carrier § 2-401(2)(a)	Time and place of delivery to carrier or of marking for buyer § 2-501(1)(b)
	6. Contract for delivery at destination	Tender of goods at destination § 2-509(1)(b)	Tender of goods at destination § 2-401(2)(b)	Time and place of delivery to carrier or of marking for buyer § 2-501(1)(b)

* The seller retains an insurable interest in the goods as long as he has a security interest in them. When the buyer acquires an insurable interest, he also acquires a special property in the goods, less than title, which entitles him to certain remedies against the seller.

When it is agreed that the buyer will not take the goods until the seller has given the buyer instructions as to use, the risk of loss remains upon the seller until the obligation has been performed.

> **FACTS:** Ellis purchased a helicopter from Bell Aerospace Corp. It was agreed that Ellis would not take the craft until he had completed flight instruction and that meanwhile the craft would be stored with Spink. Thereafter, while a Bell employee was flying the craft and giving Ellis a flight lesson, the craft crashed. Ellis claimed that the risk of loss was on Bell.

> **DECISION:** Judgment for Ellis. Bell was a merchant-seller, and therefore risk of loss did not pass until there was an actual physical delivery to Ellis. Neither the fact of storing the craft with Spink with the consent of Ellis nor his presence in the craft while controlled by the Bell employee-teacher constituted delivery of the craft to Ellis. [Ellis v Bell Aerospace (DC D Ore) 315 FSupp. 221]

When testing or operating of installed goods is part of the seller's obligation, the risk of loss will generally remain on the seller until such obligation has been performed.

When the buyer becomes the owner of the goods, he has an insurable interest in them. Conversely, the seller no longer has an insurable interest unless he has reserved a security interest to protect his right to payment.

The operation of the rule that title is transferred at the time of the transaction applies even though a local statute requires the registration of the transfer of title. Thus, the transfer of title of an automobile is complete as between the parties, in the absence of a contrary intention, when the agreement is made to sell or transfer the title to a specific car, even though the delivery of a title certificate as required by law has not been made. For example, when the parties intend a sale of an automobile and unconditional possession of it is given to the buyer, the buyer becomes the owner and the car is no longer "owned" or "held for sale" by the seller within the meaning of his insurance policy, even though the title certificate has not been executed. In some states, however, it is expressly declared by statute that no title is transferred in the absence of a delivery of the certificate of title.

The fact that "title" has not been transferred to a motor vehicle because of a statute making the issuance of a title certificate essential for that purpose does not affect the transfer of the risk of loss as between the seller and buyer. Likewise, the fact that the buyer pays with a check that is subsequently dishonored does not affect the transfer of title for him.

(2) Goods Represented by Negotiable Document of Title. Here the buyer has an insurable interest in the goods at the time and place of contracting; but he does not ordinarily become subject to the risk of loss nor acquire the title until he receives delivery of the document.[5]

---

[5] Express provision is made for the case of a nonnegotiable document and other factual variations. UCC § 2-509(2)(c), § 2-503(4). When delivery of a document is to be made, the seller may send the document through customary banking channels as well as make a tender in person or by an agent. § 2-503(5)(b). Even though the form of the document of title is such that title is retained by the seller for security purposes, the risk of loss nevertheless passes to the buyer.

(3) Goods Held by Bailee, Without Document of Title. Here the goods owned by the seller are held by a warehouseman, garageman, repairman, or other bailee, but there is no document of title and the sales contract does not call for a physical delivery of the goods—the parties intending that the goods should remain where they are. In such a case the answers to the various problems are the same as in situation (1), § 24:3(a), except that the risk of loss does not pass to the buyer, but remains with the seller, until the bailee acknowledges that he is holding the goods in question for the buyer.

(b) Future Goods.

(1) Marking for Buyer. If the buyer sends an order for goods to be manufactured by the seller or to be filled by him from inventory or by purchases from third persons, one step in the process of filling the order is the seller's act of marking, tagging, labeling, or in some way doing an act for the benefit of his shipping department or for himself to indicate that certain goods are the ones to be sent or delivered to the buyer under the order. This act of unilateral identification of the goods is enough to give the buyer a property interest in the goods and gives him the right to insure them.[6] Neither risk of loss nor title passes to the buyer at that time, however, but remains with the seller who, as the continuing owner, also has an insurable interest in the goods. Thus, neither title nor risk of loss passes to the buyer until some other event, such as a shipment or delivery, occurs.

The parties may by their agreement delay the transfer of title until a later date, as by specifying that title shall not pass until payment is made or until the goods arrive at their destination. This retention of title by the seller is for the purpose of security only and the buyer nevertheless acquires an insurable interest upon identification.

(2) Contract for Shipment to Buyer. In this situation the buyer has placed an order for future goods to be shipped to him, and the contract is performed by the seller when he delivers the goods to a carrier for shipment to the buyer. Under such a contract the risk of loss and title pass to the buyer when the goods are delivered to the carrier, that is, at the time and place of shipment. After that happens, the seller has no insurable interest unless he has reserved a security interest in the goods.[7]

FACTS: Brown was a local distributor for the Storz Brewing Co. Under the distribution contract, sales were made at prices set by the company "all f.o.b. Storz Brewing Company's plant, from which shipment is made. . . . Distributor agrees . . . to pay all freight and transportation charges from Storz Brewing Company's place of business or to the delivery point designated by the distributor and all delivery expenses." Brown wrote the company to deliver a quantity of beer to a trucker by the name of Steinhaus as soon as the latter would accept the goods. The company delivered the goods to Steinhaus. Snow delayed the transportation and caused the beer to freeze. Brown rejected the beer and was sued by the company for the purchase price.

---

[6] UCC § 2-501(1)(b). Special provision is made as to crops and unborn animals. § 2-501(1)(c).

[7] The reservation of a security interest by the seller does not affect the transfer of the risk to the buyer.

DECISION: Judgment for the company. As the contract called for shipment of f.o.b. the seller's plant, the risk of loss passed to the buyer at that time and place. The fact that the goods were damaged thereafter did not affect the buyer's duty to pay for the goods. [Storz Brewing Co. v Brown, 154 Neb 204, 47 NW2d 407]

The fact that a shipment of goods is represented by a bill of lading or an airbill issued by the carrier, and that in order to complete the transaction it will be necessary to transfer that bill to the buyer, does not affect these rules or bring the transaction within situation 2 of § 24:3(a).

A provision for the inspection or testing of the goods by the buyer or by a third person at the buyer's place of business, at a building site, or at a place where the goods are to be installed may have the effect of delaying the transfer of the risk of loss to the buyer until the time when the goods are inspected or tested and approved as conforming.

(3) Contract for Delivery at Destination. When the contract requires the seller to make delivery of future goods at a particular destination point, the buyer acquires a property right and an insurable interest in the goods at the time and place they are marked or shipped; but the risk of loss and the title do not pass until the carrier tenders or makes the goods available at the destination point. The seller retains an insurable interest until that time; and if he has a security interest in the goods, he continues to retain that interest until the purchase price has been paid.

§ 24:4. SELF-SERVICE STORES. In the case of goods sold in a self-service store, the reasonable interpretation of the agreement of the parties is that the store by its act of putting the goods on display on the shelves makes an offer to sell such goods for cash and confers upon a prospective customer a license to carry the goods to the cashier in order to make payment, thus effecting the transfer of title or sale. On this rationale, no warranty liability of the store arises prior to the buyer's payment.[8] Another contrary rule has been recognized by which "a contract to sell" is formed when the customer "accepts" the "seller's offer" by taking the item from the shelf. By this view, there is a contract but no transfer of title.

§ 24:5. AUTOMOBILES. In general, preexisting motor vehicle registration statutes have not been expressly affected by the adoption of the UCC.

In some states the proper execution or indorsement and delivery of a title certificate is an essential element to the transfer of title to a motor vehicle;[9] while in other states, following the common-law view or influence, such a document is merely evidence of a transfer of title but is not an essential element of effecting transfer. In the latter states, a transfer of title may occur when the parties agree that the automobile "belongs" to the

---

[8] A contrary view is beginning to be recognized by which the sale occurs when the buyer takes the item from the shelf. The fact that the buyer can return the item to the shelf is regarded under this view as being a "return" by the buyer who thereby transfers back to the seller the title which had already passed to the buyer when he selected the item.

[9] Bonnell v Mahaffey (MoApp) 493 SW2d 688.

other party even though nothing has been done with respect to the title certificate.[10] In such a state, when the purchased automobile has been delivered to the buyer on a cash and trade-in sale, the ownership passes to the buyer for the purpose of his insurance contract at the time of delivery even though the title papers are to be executed and the cash balance paid on the following day. In most states the pre-Code motor vehicle statute remains in force to determine the location of "ownership" for the purpose of imposing tort liability or determining the coverage of liability insurance.

§ 24:6. **DAMAGE OR DESTRUCTION OF GOODS.** In the absence of a contrary agreement,[11] damage to or the destruction of the goods affects the transaction as follows:

(a) Damage to identified goods before risk of loss passes. When goods that were identified at the time the contract was made are damaged or destroyed without the fault of either party before the risk of loss has passed, the contract is avoided if the loss is total. If the loss is partial or if the goods have so deteriorated that they do not conform to the contract, the buyer has the option, after inspection of the goods, (1) to treat the contract as avoided, or (2) to accept the goods subject to an allowance or deduction from the contract price. In either case the buyer cannot assert any claim against the seller for breach of contract.[12]

When the buyer makes an effective rejection of nonconforming goods and the goods are then stolen before the seller has come for them, the buyer is not liable for the value of the stolen goods, unless the seller can establish that the buyer was negligent in caring for the goods after their rejection.

> FACTS: Shook ordered three reels of burial cable from Graybar Company for use in construction work. By mistake, two of the three reels which were sent were aerial cable, although each carton was marked "burial cable." Shook accepted the one reel of proper cable and rejected the nonconforming reels. Because of their size, they were left on the ground at the construction site and Graybar was notified of the rejection. Graybar did not collect the cable. Shook attempted to return the cable but could not do so because there was a strike of truck drivers. About four months later, the two reels of cable were stolen by unidentified persons. Graybar sued Shook for the purchase price.
>
> DECISION: Judgment for Shook. He was justified in rejecting the two reels of cable as they did not conform to the contract. After notifying Graybar of the rejection, the only duty of Shook was to exercise reasonable care of the goods while waiting for Graybar to take them away. In view of the size of the reels and the nature of the enterprise, it was not unreasonable to leave the reels on the ground at the construction site. As Graybar has not shown that Shook had been negligent in caring for the rejected goods, the risk of loss remained on Graybar and Shook was not liable for the purchase price. [Graybar Electric Co. v Shook, 283 NC 213, 195 SE2d 514]

---

[10] UCC § 2-401; Metropolitan Auto Sales Corp v Koheski, 252 Md 145, 249 A2d 141.
[11] UCC § 2-303.
[12] § 2-613.

A provision in a credit sale agreement that the buyer will at all times keep the goods fully insured against loss is not a "contrary agreement" within the UCC so as to shift the loss to the buyer at an earlier time.

(b) Damage to identified goods after risk of loss passes. If partial damage or total destruction occurs after the risk of loss has passed, it is the buyer's loss. It may be, however, that the buyer will be able to recover the amount of the damages from the person in possession of the goods or from a third person causing the loss.

(c) Damage to unidentified goods. So long as the goods are unidentified, no risk of loss has passed to the buyer. If any goods are damaged or destroyed during this period, the loss is the seller's. The buyer is still entitled to receive the goods for which he contracted. If the seller fails to deliver the goods, he is liable to the purchaser for the breach of his contract. The only exception arises when the parties have expressly provided in the contract that destruction of the seller's supply shall be deemed a release of the seller's liability or when it is clear that the parties contracted for the purchase and sale of part of the seller's supply to the exclusion of any other possible source of such goods.

(d) Reservation of title or possession. When the seller reserves title or possession solely as security to make certain that he will be paid, the risk of loss is borne by the buyer if the circumstances are such that he would bear the loss in the absence of such reservation.

§ 24:7. SALES ON APPROVAL AND WITH RIGHT TO RETURN. A sales transaction may give the buyer the privilege of returning the goods. In a *sale on approval*, the sale is not complete until the buyer approves. A *sale or return* is a completed sale with the right of the buyer to return the goods and thereby set aside the sale. The agreement of the parties determines whether the sale is on approval or with return; but if they have failed to indicate their intention, it is a sale on approval if the goods are purchased for use, that is, by a consumer, and a sale or return if purchased for resale, that is, by a merchant.[13]

(a) Sale on approval. In the absence of a contrary agreement, title and risk of loss remain with the seller under a sale on approval. Use of the goods by the buyer consistent with the purpose of trial is not an election or approval by him. There is an approval, however, if he acts in a manner that is not consistent with a reasonable trial, or if he fails to express his choice within the time specified or within a reasonable time if no time is specified. If the goods are returned, the seller bears the risk and the expense involved.[14] Since the buyer is not the "owner" of the goods while they are on approval, his creditors cannot reach them.[15]

---

[13] § 2-326(1). An "or return" provision is treated as a sales contract for the purpose of applying the statute of frauds, and cannot be established by parol evidence when it would contradict a sales contract indicating an absolute sale. § 2-326(4).

[14] § 2-327(1).

[15] § 2-326(2).

(b) Sale or return. In a sale or return, title and risk of loss pass to the buyer as in the case of an ordinary or absolute sale. In the absence of a contrary agreement, the buyer under a sale or return may return all of the goods or commercial unit thereof. A *commercial unit* is any article, group of articles, or quantity which commercially is regarded as a separate unit or item, such as a particular machine, a suite of furniture, or a carload lot.[16] The goods must be substantially in their original condition, and the option to return must be exercised within the time specified by the contract or within a reasonable time if none is specified. The return under such a contract is at the buyer's risk and expense.[17] As long as the goods are in the buyer's possession under a sale or return contract, his creditors may treat the goods as belonging to him.[18]

The delivery of goods to an agent for sale is not a sale and return. Therefore, when the owner of an automobile leaves it with a dealer to obtain an offer of purchase which the owner would then be required to approve in order to effect the sale, there is no "sale or return" and creditors of the dealer have no claim against the automobile.

(c) Consignment sale. A consignment or a sale on consignment is merely an authorization or agency to sell. It is not a sale on approval or a sale with right to return. Since the relationship is an agency, the consignor, in the absence of some contrary contract restriction, may revoke the agency at will and take possession of his property by any lawful means. If such repossession of the goods constitutes a breach of his contract with the consignee, the consignor is liable to the consignee for damages.

Whether goods are sent to a person as buyer or on consignment to sell for the seller is a question of the intention of the parties. In some instances the creditors of the consignee may treat the goods held by the consignee on consignment as though they belonged to him, thereby ignoring and destroying the consignor's ownership.

§ 24:8. SALE OF FUNGIBLE GOODS. *Fungible goods* are of a homogeneous nature that may be sold by weight or measure. They are goods of which any unit is from its nature or by commercial usage treated as the equivalent of any other unit.[19] Wheat, oil, coal, and similar bulk commodities are fungible goods since, given a mass of the same grade or uniformity, any one bushel or other unit of the mass will be exactly the same as any other bushel or similar unit.

Title to an undivided share or quantity of an identified mass of fungible goods may pass to the buyer at the time of the transaction, making the buyer an owner in common with the seller.[20] For example, when a person sells to another 600 bushels of wheat from his bin which contains 1,000 bushels, title to 600 bushels passes to the buyer at the time of the transaction, giving him a 6/10ths undivided interest in the mass as an owner

---

[16] § 2-105(6).
[17] § 2-327(2).
[18] § 2-326(2); Guardian Discount Co. v Settles, 114 GaApp 418, 151 SE2d 530.
[19] UCC § 1-201(17).
[20] § 2-105(4).

in common. The courts in some states, however, have held that the title does not pass until a separation of the purchased share has been made.

§24:9. **SALE OF UNDIVIDED SHARES.** The problem of the passage of title to a part of a larger mass of fungible goods is distinct from the problem of the passage of title when the sale is made of a fractional interest without any intention to make a later separation. In the former case the buyer is to become the exclusive owner of a separated portion. In the latter case he is to become a co-owner of the entire mass. Thus, there may be a sale of a part interest in a radio, an automobile, or a flock of sheep.[21]

§ 24:10. **AUCTION SALES.** When goods are sold at an auction in separate lots, each lot is a separate transaction, and title to each passes independently of the other lots.[22] Title to each lot passes when the auctioneer announces by the fall of the hammer or in any other customary manner that the auction is completed as to that lot.[23]

§ 24:11. **RESERVATION OF A SECURITY INTEREST.** The seller may fear that the buyer will not pay for the goods. The seller could protect himself by insisting that the buyer pay cash immediately. This may not be practical for geographic or business reasons. The seller may then give credit but protect himself by retaining a security interest in the goods.

(a) **Bill of lading.** The seller may retain varying degrees of control over the goods by the method of shipment. Thus, the seller may ship the goods to himself in the buyer's city, receiving from the carrier the bill of lading for the goods.[24] In such a case the buyer cannot obtain the goods from the carrier since the shipment is not directed to him, in the case of a straight bill of lading, or because he does not hold the bill of lading, if it is a negotiable or order bill. The seller's agent in the buyer's city can arrange for or obtain payment from the buyer and then give him the documents necessary to obtain the goods from the carrier.

If the goods are sent by carrier under a negotiable bill of lading to the order of the buyer or his agent, the seller may also retain the right of possession of the goods by keeping possession of the bill of lading until he receives or is assured of payment.[25]

(b) **C.O.D. shipment.** In the absence of an extension of credit, a seller has the right to keep the goods until paid, but he loses this right if he delivers possession of the goods to anyone for the buyer. However, when the goods are delivered to a carrier, the seller may preserve his right to possession by making the shipment C.O.D., or by the addition of any other terms indicating an intention that the carrier should not surrender the goods to the buyer until the buyer has made payment. Such a provision has no effect

---

[21] § 2-403(1).
[22] § 2-328(1).
[23] § 2-328(2).
[24] § 2-505.
[25] § 2-505(1)(a).

other than to keep the buyer from obtaining possession until he has made payment. The C.O.D. provision does not affect the problem of determining whether title or risk of loss has passed.

Under a C.O.D. shipment, the carrier acts as an agent for the shipper. If the carrier accepts a check from the consignee and the check is not honored by the bank on which it is drawn, the carrier is liable to the shipper for the amount thereof.[26]

§ 24:12. EFFECT OF SALE ON TITLE.

As a general rule, a person can sell only such interest or title in goods as he possesses. If the property is subject to a bailment, a sale by the bailor is subject to the bailment. Similarly, the bailee can only transfer his right under the bailment, assuming that the bailment agreement permits his right to be assigned or transferred. The fact that the bailee is in possession does not give him the right to transfer the bailor's title.

Similarly, a thief or finder generally cannot transfer the title to property since he can only pass that which he has, namely the possession but not the title. In fact, the purchaser from the thief not only fails to obtain title but also becomes liable to the owner as a converter of the property even though he made the purchase in good faith.

A thief cannot pass good title to a stolen automobile. The owner may recover the automobile from the subpurchaser although the latter buys in good faith and pays value. The fact that the negligence or the act of the owner contributed to or facilitated the theft does not stop the true owner from asserting his title. Thus the owner of a stolen automobile remains its owner even though he had signed a title certificate in blank and left it in the glove compartment, and left the keys near the car, apparently with the intent that should he die, his son would be able to take the car readily.[27]

The buyer of stolen goods must surrender them to the true owner even though he had acted in good faith.

> **FACTS:** Owen told Snyder that he wished to buy Snyder's auto. He drove the car for about ten minutes, returned to Snyder, stated that he wanted to take the auto to show to his wife, and then left with the auto but never returned. Later Owen sold the auto in another state to Pearson and gave him a bill of sale. Pearson showed the bill of sale to Lincoln, falsely told him the certificate of title for the auto was held by a bank as security for the financing of the auto, and then sold the auto to Lincoln. Snyder sued Lincoln to recover the automobile.
>
> **DECISION:** Judgment for Snyder. Owen had been guilty of larceny in obtaining the automobile, and no title had passed to him. The automobile could therefore be recovered even though the ultimate purchaser gave value and acted in good faith. [Snyder v Lincoln, 150 Neb 581, 35 NW2d 483]

There are certain instances, however, when either because of the conduct of the owner or the desire of society to protect the bona fide

---

[26] National Van Lines, Inc. v Rich Plan Corp. (CA5 Tex) 385 F2d 800.
[27] Stohr v Randle, 81 Wash2d 881, 505 P2d 1281.

purchaser for value, the law permits a greater title to be transferred than the seller possessed.

(a) Sale by entrustee. If the owner entrusts his goods to a merchant who deals in goods of that kind, the latter has the power to transfer the entruster's title to anyone who buys from him in the ordinary course of business.

It is immaterial why the goods were entrusted to the merchant. Hence, the leaving of a watch for repair with a jeweler who sells new and secondhand watches would give the jeweler the power to pass the title to a buyer in the ordinary course of business.[28] Goods in inventory have a degree of "negotiability" so that the ordinary buyer, whether a consumer or another merchant, buys the goods free of the ownership interest of the person entrusting the goods to the seller.[29] The entrustee is, of course, liable to the owner for damages caused by the entrustee's sale of the goods and is guilty of some form of statutory offense of embezzlement.

If the entrustee is not a merchant, such as a prospective customer trying out an automobile, there is no transfer of title to the buyer of the car from the entrustee. Likewise, there is no transfer of title when a mere bailee, who is not a seller of goods of that kind, sells the property of a customer.

(b) Consignment Sale. A manufacturer or distributor may send goods to a dealer for sale to the public with the understanding that the manufacturer or distributor is to remain the owner, and the dealer in effect is to act as his agent. When the dealer maintains a place of business at which he deals in goods of the kind in question under a name other than that of the consigning manufacturer or distributor, the creditors of the dealer may reach the goods as though they were owned by him.[30]

(c) Estoppel. The owner of property may estop himself from asserting that he is the owner and denying the right of another person to sell the property. A person may purchase something and have the bill of sale made out in the name of a friend to whom he then gives possession of the product and the bill of sale. He might do so in order to deceive his own creditors or to keep other persons from knowing that he made the purchase. If the friend should sell the product to a bona fide purchaser who relies on the bill of sale as showing that the friend was the owner, the true owner is estopped or barred from denying the friend's apparent ownership and his right to sell.

(d) Powers. In certain circumstances, persons in possession of someone else's property may sell the property. This arises in the case of pledgees, lienholders, and some finders who, by statute, may have authority to sell the property to enforce their claim or when the owner cannot be found.

(e) Negotiable documents of title. By statute, certain documents of title, such as bills of lading and warehouse receipts, have been clothed with a

---

[28] UCC § 2-403(2), (3). There is authority that, for this section to apply, the merchant status of the entrustee must be known both to the entruster and the purchaser. Atlas Auto Rental Corp. v Weisber, 54 Misc2d 168, 281 NYS2d 400.

[29] UCC § 2-403(1); Mattek v Malofsky, 42 Wis2d 16, 165 NW2d 406.

[30] UCC § 2-326(3). The manufacturer or dealer may protect himself from this under Article 9 of the Code or by complying with any local statute that protects him in such case.

degree of negotiability when executed in proper form.[31] By virtue of such provisions, the holder of a negotiable document of title directing delivery of the goods to him or his order, or to bearer, may transfer to a purchaser for value acting in good faith such title as was possessed by the person leaving the property with the issuer of the document. In such cases, it is immaterial that the holder had not acquired the document in a lawful manner.

(f) Recording and filing statutes. In order to protect subsequent purchasers and creditors, statutes may require that certain transactions be recorded or filed and may provide that if that is not done, the transaction has no effect against a purchaser who thereafter buys the goods in good faith from the person who appears to be the owner or against the execution creditors of such an apparent owner. Thus, if a seller retains a security interest in the goods sold to the buyer but fails to file a financing statement in the required manner, the purchaser appears to be the owner of the goods free from any security interest and subsequent bona fide purchasers or creditors of the buyer can acquire title from him free of the seller's security interest.

(g) Voidable title. If the buyer has a voidable title, as when he obtained the goods by fraud, the seller can rescind the sale while the buyer is still the owner. If, however, the buyer resells the property to a bona fide purchaser before the seller has rescinded the transaction, the subsequent purchaser acquires valid title.[32] It is immaterial whether the buyer having the voidable title had obtained title by fraud as to his identity, or by larceny by trick, or that he had paid for the goods with a bad check, or that the transaction was a cash sale and the purchase price had not been paid.[33]

(h) Goods retained by seller. When the seller after making the sale is permitted to retain possession of the goods, he has the power to transfer the title to a buyer in the ordinary course of business. Such permitted retention is an entrusting within the sale by entrustee rule described in § 24:12(a). The purpose is to protect the second purchaser, on the ground that he had the right to rely on the apparent ownership of his seller.

(i) Protection of seller. As will be discussed in connection with the remedies of the parties, a seller who is lawfully in possession of property that he has sold may resell it to a second purchaser if the first purchaser is in default in the payment of the purchase price. Here the object of the statute is not to protect the second purchaser but to enable the seller to remedy the situation created by the first purchaser's default.

(j) Protection of creditors of seller. The continued possession of goods by the seller after their sale is generally deemed evidence that the sale was a fraud upon creditors, that is, that the sale was not a bona fide actual transfer of title but was merely a device to place the title out of the reach of the creditors of the seller. When the sale is fraudulent by local law, creditors

---

[31] § 7-502(2).
[32] § 2-403(1).
[33] § 2-403(1)(a) to (d).

of the seller may treat the sale as void and may have the property put up for sale on execution as though the property still belonged to the seller. The retention of possession by a merchant seller is declared not fraudulent, however, when made in good faith in the current course of business and when it does not exceed a period of time which is commercially reasonable.[34] For example, the fact that the merchant retains possession until transportation of the goods is arranged is not fraudulent as to creditors.

QUESTIONS AND CASE PROBLEMS

1. A buyer purchased furniture on credit and made a number of payments thereafter. When he stopped making payments, the seller claimed the right to repossess the furniture on the theory that it had been sold on approval and that the buyer had never manifested his approval. Was the seller correct? [See Gantman v Paul, 203 PaSuper 158, 199 A2d 519]

2. B purchased nationally advertised camping equipment from S for $1,000 and paid S with a bad check. B immediately resold the goods to C for $200. C had asked B if he had a bill of sale or a receipt for the goods. B had stated that he did not. S sued C to recover the goods. Decide. [See Hollis v Chamberlin, 243 Ark 201, 419 SW2d 116]

3. B purchased a used automobile from A with a bad check. B then took the automobile to an auction in which the automobile was sold to C, who had no knowledge of the prior history of the automobile. When B's check was dishonored, A brought suit against C to reclaim the automobile. Was he entitled to do so? [See Greater Louisville Auto Auction, Inc. v Ogle Buick, Inc. (Ky) 387 SW2d 17]

4. Eastern Supply Co. purchased lawn mowers from the Turf Man Sales Corp. The purchase order stated on its face "Ship direct to 30th & Harcum Way, Pitts., Pa." Turf Man delivered the goods to Helm's Express, Inc. for shipment and delivery to Eastern at the address in question. Did title pass on delivery of the goods to Helm or upon their arrival at the specified address? [In re Eastern Supply Co. (Pa) 21 D&C2d, 107 PittsLegJ 451]

5. Di Lorenzo had possession of certain goods that belonged to Wolf, a dealer in household furniture. The goods were destroyed by fire. Not knowing of this, Di Lorenzo agreed to buy the goods from Wolf. The dealer brought an action against Di Lorenzo to recover the purchase price of the goods. Decide. [Wolf v Di Lorenzo, 22 Misc 323, 49 NYS 191]

6. Lieber had possession of military souvenirs that he had obtained while on active duty in the Armed Forces of the United States in World War II. Many years later his chauffeur stole the souvenirs and sold them to a dealer, Mohawk Arms, which purchased in good faith. Lieber located the souvenirs and sued Mohawk Arms. Did it have a defense? [Lieber v Mohawk Arms, Inc., 64 Misc2d 206, 314 NYS2d 510]

---

[34] § 2-402(2).

7. Burke fraudulently induced Cavanaugh Bros. to sell him a horse. Three months later Burke sold the horse to Porell, a bona fide purchaser. Cavanaugh sued Porell to obtain the horse on the theory that because of Burke's fraud he never obtained title and Cavanaugh Bros. still owned the horse. Decide. [Porell v Cavanaugh Bros. 69 NH 364, 41 A 860]

8. Atlas Auto Rental Corp., which rented automobiles to the public, would sell its used cars from time to time. It permitted Schwartzman, a prospective buyer, to test drive a two-year-old station wagon. Before Schwartzman left with the car, he gave Atlas a check which was later returned by the drawee bank marked "No funds." Schwartzman and the car disappeared. Schwartzman apparently sold the car to Weisberg, a licensed automobile wrecker and junk dealer for $300. Weisberg did not obtain a bill of sale or a title certificate from Schwartzman. Weisberg resold the automobile on the same day for $1,200. Atlas sued Weisberg for converting the automobile. Weisberg raised the defense that he was protected by the UCC. Was he correct? [Atlas Auto Rental Corp. v Weisberg (NYCivCt) 54 Misc2d 168, 281 NYS2d 400]

9. Coburn bought cattle from Regan and paid for them with a check at the time of sale. The parties agreed that Regan would hold the cattle for a few days. The day before Coburn was to take the cattle, Regan sold them to Drown who gave him a check at that time. After Regan took the check but before Drown had taken possession of the cattle, Regan told Drown that Coburn had purchased the cattle. Drown took the cattle. Coburn sued Drown for their value. Decide. [Coburn v Drown, 114 Vt 158, 40 A2d 528]

10. The Auburn Motor Co. sold five automobiles to Levasseur of Rhode Island to be shipped C.O.D. via the Adams Express Co. from Indiana to Providence, Rhode Island. While the goods were in transit, Levasseur borrowed money from the New England Auto Insurance Co. to pay for the cars and executed a mortgage on the cars to secure payment of the loan. On the day the cars were received, Lavasseur transferred one of them to the Whitten Motor Vehicle Co. The Whitten company sold the car to Andrews. In an action brought by the New England Auto Investment Co. against Andrews, the defendant alleged that the mortgage was invalid and contended that the Auburn Motor Co. had retained title and right of possession. Do you agree with these contentions? [New England Auto Investment Co. v Andrews, 47 RI 299, 132 A 883]

11. Wilke purchased a generator from Cummins Diesel Engines, subject to field tests after delivery and installation at a job site where Wilke was engaged in construction work as a subcontractor on certain facilities. Cummins delivered the generator in August, long before needed. The next spring, in hooking it up, Wilke found it severly damaged from water frozen in its cooling system. He notified Cummins, who removed and repaired it and billed Wilke for the repairs. Was Wilke liable for the repairs? [Wilke v Cummins Diesel Engines, 252 Md 611, 250 A2d 886]

12. Smith operated a marina and sold and repaired boats. Gallagher rented a stall at the marina at which he kept his vessel, the River Queen. Without any authorization, Smith sold the vessel to Courtesy Ford. Gallagher sued Courtesy Ford for the vessel. Courtesy Ford claimed that the sale by Smith had passed title to it by virtue of UCC § 2-403. Was it correct? [Gallagher v Unenrolled Motor Vessel River Queen (CA5 Tex) 475 F2d 117]

25 OBLIGATIONS AND PERFORMANCE

§ 25:1. BASIC OBLIGATIONS. Each party to a sales contract is bound to perform according to its terms. Each is likewise under the duty to exercise good faith in its performance and to do nothing that would impair the expectation of the other party that the contract will be duly performed.

(a) Good faith. "Every contract or duty . . . imposes an obligation of good faith in its performance or enforcement."[1] The UCC defines good faith as meaning "honesty in fact in the conduct or transaction concerned."[2] In the case of the merchant seller or buyer of goods, the Code carries the concept of good faith further and imposes the additional requirement that the merchant seller or buyer observe "reasonable commercial standards of fair dealing in the trade."[3]

FACTS: Umlas made a contract to buy a new automobile from Acey Oldsmobile. He was allowed to keep his old car until the new car was delivered. The sales contract gave him a trade-in on the old car of $650, but specified that it could be reappraised when it was actually brought in to the dealer. When Umlas brought the trade-in to the dealer, an employee of Acey took it for a test drive and told Acey that it was worth from $300 to $400. Acey stated to Umlas that the trade-in would be appraised at $50. Umlas refused to buy from Acey and purchased from another dealer who appraised the trade-in at $400. Umlas sued Acey for breach of contract. Acey defended on the ground that its conduct was authorized by the reappraisal clause.

DECISION: Judgment for Umlas. While the contract reserved the right to reappraise the trade-in, this required a good faith reappraisal. From the fact that the reappraised figure was substantially below the value stated by the employee making the test drive, it was clear that the reappraisal had not been made in good faith and it was therefore not binding on the buyer; and the seller remained bound by the original contract and the original appraisal of the trade-in. [Umlas v Acey Oldsmobile, Inc. (NYCivCt) 310 NYS2d 147]

---

[1] Uniform Commercial Code § 1-203.
[2] UCC § 1-201(19).
[3] § 2-103(1)(b).

§ 25:2. CONDITIONS PRECEDENT TO PERFORMANCE. In the case of a cash sale not requiring the physical moving of the goods, the duties of the seller and buyer are concurrent. Each one has the right to demand that the other perform at the same time. That is, as the seller hands over the goods, the buyer theoretically must hand over the purchase money. If either party refuses to act, the other party has the right to withhold his performance.[4] In the case of a shipment contract, there is a time interval between the performances of the parties: the seller will have performed his part of the contract by delivering the goods to the carrier, but the buyer's obligation will not arise until he has received and accepted the goods.

The duty of a party to a sales contract to perform his part of the contract may be subject to a *condition precedent*, that is, by the terms of the contract he is not required to perform until some event occurs or until some act is performed. Quite commonly the condition precedent is performance by the other party. Thus, a contract may provide that the seller shall deliver merchandise but that the buyer must first pay for it in full. Under this contract the duty of the seller to deliver the merchandise is subject to the condition precedent of payment in full by the buyer. If the buyer never performs his part of the contract, the duty of the seller under that contract never arises.

If there is a promise that the condition precedent shall happen or be performed, the promisee may treat nonperformance as a breach of contract and claim damages of the other party for failing to bring about the fulfillment of the condition.

§ 25:3. SELLER'S DUTY TO DELIVER. It is the seller's duty to make "delivery," which does not refer to a physical delivery but merely means that the seller must permit the transfer of possession of the goods to the buyer. That is, the seller makes the goods available to the buyer. The delivery must be made in accordance with the terms of the sale or contract to sell.

(a) Place, time, and manner of delivery. The terms of the contract determine whether the seller is to send the goods or the buyer is to call for them, or whether the goods must be transported by the seller to the buyer, or whether the transaction is to be completed by the delivery of documents without the movement of the goods. In the absence of a provision in the contract or a contrary course of performance or usage of trade, the place of delivery is the seller's place of business, if he has one; otherwise, it is the seller's residence. If, however, the subject matter of the contract consists of identified goods that are known by the parties to be in some other place, that place is the place of delivery. Documents of title may be delivered through customary banking channels.[5]

When a method of transportation called for by the contract becomes unavailable or commercially impracticable, the seller must make delivery

---

[4] §§ 2-507, 2-511.
[5] § 2-308.

by means of a commercially reasonable substitute if available and the buyer must accept such substitute.[6] This provision is applicable when a shipping strike makes impossible the use of the specified means of transportation.

(b) Quantity delivered. The buyer has the right to insist that all the goods be delivered at one time. If the seller delivers a smaller quantity than that stipulated in the contract, the buyer may refuse to accept the goods. In the case of a divisible contract, if the buyer accepts or retains part of the goods with knowledge of the seller's intention to deliver no more, the buyer must pay the proportionate price representing the items or units which he has received; if the contract is not divisible, he must pay the full contract price. If the goods are used or disposed of by the buyer before he learns of the seller's intention, the buyer is only required to pay the fair value of the goods he has received.

(1) Delivery in Installments. The buyer is under no obligation or duty to accept delivery of goods by installments unless the contract contemplates such deliveries [7] or unless the circumstances are such as to give rise to the right to make delivery in lots.[8]

If payment is to be made for each installment, the delivery of each installment and the payment for each installment are conditions precedent to the respective duties of the buyer to accept and of the seller to deliver subsequent installments.

(c) Delivery to carrier. When the seller is required to or may send the goods to the buyer but the contract does not require him to make a delivery at a particular destination, the seller, in the absence of a contrary agreement, must put the goods in the possession of a proper carrier and make such contract for their transportation as is reasonable in view of the nature of the goods and other circumstances of the case. For example, if the goods require refrigeration and the risk of loss passes to the buyer on delivery to the carrier, the seller must contract with the carrier to provide the necessary refrigeration.

(d) Delivery at destination. If the contract requires the seller to make delivery at a destination point, the seller must make a proper tender of the goods at that point. If any documents that are necessary to obtain possession of the goods are issued by a carrier, the seller must also tender such documents.[9]

(e) Cure of defective tender. The seller or vendor has the right to *cure*, or remedy, a defective tender by making a second tender or delivery after the first has been properly rejected by the buyer because it did not conform to the contract. If the time for making delivery under the contract has not

---

[6] § 2-514(1).

[7] § 2-307.

[8] § 2-307. This situation would arise whenever it is physically impossible because of the buyer's limited facilities or commercially impractical for any reason for the seller to make complete delivery.

[9] UCC § 2-503(3).

expired, the seller need only give the buyer seasonable (timely) notice of his intention to make a proper delivery within the time allowed by the contract, and he may then do so. If the time for making the delivery has expired, the seller is given an additional reasonable time in which to make a substitute conforming tender if he so notifies the buyer and if he had acted reasonably in making the original tender, believing that it would be acceptable.[10]

§ 25:4. BUYER'S DUTY TO ACCEPT GOODS. It is the duty of the buyer to accept the delivery of proper goods.

(a) **Right to examine goods.** Unless otherwise agreed, the buyer, when tender of the goods is made, has the right before payment for or acceptance of the goods to inspect them at any reasonable place or time and in any reasonable manner to determine whether they meet the requirements of the contract.[11] A C.O.D. term, however, bars inspection before payment unless there is an agreement to the contrary.

(b) **What constitutes acceptance of goods.** Acceptance ordinarily is an express statement by the buyer that he accepts or approves the goods. It may also consist of conduct which expresses such an intent, such as the failure to object within a reasonable period of time or the use of the goods in such a way as would be inconsistent with a rejection of them by the buyer.[12] A buyer accepts the goods when he makes continued use and does not attempt to return the goods until after 14 months.

A buyer, of course, accepts the goods when he modifies them, because such action is inconsistent with the continued ownership of the goods by the seller. Consequently, when the purchaser of a truck installed a hoist and dump bed on it, such action was inconsistent with ownership by the seller, and the buyer therefore became liable for the contract price of the truck.[13]

FACTS: Crawford, who was constructing a building for the United States Navy, purchased fuel equipment from Fram Corp. and installed the equipment in the building. Fram sued for the purchase price. Crawford claimed that he had not accepted the equipment.

DECISION: Judgment for Fram. Crawford's act of installing the equipment in the building was an act inconsistent with the seller's ownership and was therefore an acceptance of the goods. Having accepted the goods, Crawford was required to pay for the goods unless he could establish that he had given proper notice of a defect which would entitle him to counterclaim for damages, or had made a proper revocation of acceptance which would avoid liability for the contract price. [United States for the use of Fram Corp. v Crawford (CA5 Ga) 443 F2d 611]

Likewise there is an acceptance of goods by a dealer when he puts a tag on them showing his inventory serial number.[14]

---

[10] § 2-508.
[11] § 2-513(1).
[12] § 2-606(1).
[13] Park County Implement Co. v Craig (Wyo) 397 P2d 800.
[14] Chrysler Corp. v Adamatic, Inc. 59 Wis 29 219, 208 NW2d 97.

(c) Effect of acceptance on breach. Acceptance of the goods by the buyer does not discharge the seller from liability in damages or other legal remedy for breach of any promise or warranty in the contract to sell or the sale. But the seller is not liable if, after acceptance of the goods, the buyer fails to give notice of the breach of any promise or warranty within a reasonable time after the buyer knows or ought to know of the breach.[15]

§ 25:5. BUYER'S DUTY TO PAY. The buyer is under a duty to pay for the goods at the contract rate for any goods accepted.[16] In the absence of a contrary provision, payment must be made in cash and must be made concurrently with receipt of the goods; and, conversely, payment cannot be required before that time.[17]

A buyer is not required to pay for partial or installment deliveries unless the contract so requires.

> **FACTS:** Cameras for Industry made a contract to purchase component parts from Precision Components Corp. for use in the manufacture of security camera systems. When full deliveries were not made under the purchase orders, Cameras brought suit against Precision. Precision claimed that Cameras had broken the contract because it had not paid for the items which had already been delivered.

> **DECISION:** Cameras had not broken its contract by failing to pay for the partial delivery which had been made. A buyer is only obligated to pay for goods after all the goods under the contract have been delivered unless the contract itself expressly requires that payments be made as installments are delivered. This was not specified by the contract with Precision and therefore Cameras had not breached the contract. [Cameras for Industry v I.D. Precision Components Corp. 49 Misc2d 1044, 268 NYS2d 860]

If delivery by lots is proper and the price can be apportioned, however, the buyer must pay for each lot as delivered.[18]

The parties may agree to a sale on credit. This may be done for each sale individually or for sales generally, as in the case of a charge account in a department store. When a sale is made on credit, the parties may include special provisions to protect the seller.

Tender or offer of the purchase price has the same effect as actual payment in imposing upon the seller the duty to make delivery. If the seller fails to make delivery when a proper tender of payment is made, he is in default under the contract.

It must also be remembered that if the seller is in default, the buyer may cancel the contract.

---

[15] UCC § 2-607(2), (3). This section rejects the view that acceptance of the goods is a waiver of any claim for damages.

[16] §§ 2-301, 2-607(1).

[17] § 2-310(a). If delivery under the contract is to be made by a delivery of document of title, payment is due at the time and place at which the buyer is to receive the document regardless of where the goods are to be received. § 2-310(c).

[18] § 2-307.

(a) Payment with commercial paper. The seller may accept a commercial paper, such as a check, in payment of the purchase price. This form of payment, unless the parties expressly agree otherwise, is merely a conditional payment, that is, conditional upon the instrument's being honored and paid. If the instrument is not paid, it ceases to be payment of the purchase price and the seller is then an unpaid seller.[19] Refusal of payments by check does not affect the rights of the parties under the sales contract as long as the seller gives the buyer a reasonable time in which to procure the legal tender with which to make payment.

(b) Escrow payment. When money is deposited with a bank or other third person under an agreement, it is commonly called an escrow deposit and the fund so deposited must be maintained as a separate or distinct fund. The escrow payment provides a form of security. This technique can be employed where one party is unwilling to act until the other party pays while the payor is unwilling to pay until the other party acts. For example, the goods which the seller is selling to the buyer may be in the warehouse of a supplier in a distant city. If the buyer would pay the seller in advance, the buyer would then be taking a number of risks which he might not wish to assume. The same would be true if the seller would obtain and deliver the goods before he was paid. In such a case the parties could agree that the buyer would deposit the purchase price in an escrow account in a bank, with instructions to the bank to pay the money to the seller when proper papers were submitted by the seller to the bank showing that the goods had been sent to the buyer, or to return the money to the buyer if the seller had not performed within a specified time.

§ 25:6. DUTIES UNDER PARTICULAR TERMS. A sale may be as simple as a face-to-face exchange of money and goods, but it frequently involves a more complicated pattern, with some element of transportation, generally by a common carrier. This, in turn, generally results in the addition of certain special terms to the sales transaction.

(a) F.O.B. The term f.o.b. or "free on board," may be used with reference to the seller's city, or the buyer's city, or an intermediate city, as in the case of a transshipment. It may also be used with reference to a named carrier, such as f.o.b. a specified vessel, car, or other vehicle. In general, an f.o.b. term is to be construed as requiring delivery to be made at the f.o.b. point, as contrasted with merely a shipment to that point,[20] and as imposing upon the seller the risk and expense involved in getting the goods to the designated place or on board the specified carrier.[21]

FACTS: Custom Built Homes purchased unassembled prefabricated houses from Page-Hill in Minnesota to be delivered by the seller "f.o.b. building site . . . Kansas." The seller brought the houses to the building site by

---

[19] § 2-511.

[20] See § 25:3(c). When a port is selected as the f.o.b. point for an imported article, the price is frequently described as the price p.o.e. or "port of entry."

[21] UCC § 2-319(1).

tractor-trailer, where he would unhitch the trailer and unload the shipment. Kansas taxed Custom Built on the sale.

DECISION: Judgment for Tax Commission. Under the terms of the contract the seller was required to deliver the goods to the buyer at the building site in Kansas without charge for transportation to that point. As no contrary intention appeared from the contract, the title to the goods passed at the building site. The sale therefore took place in Kansas and was subject to tax there. [Custom Built Homes Co. v Kansas State Commission of Revenue, 184 Kan 31, 334 P2d 808]

(b) C.I.F. The term c.i.f. indicates that the payment by the buyer is a lump sum covering the cost (selling price) of the goods, insurance on them, and freight to the specified destination of the goods. The c.i.f. term imposes upon the seller the obligation of putting the goods in the possession of a proper carrier, of loading and paying for the freight, of procuring the proper insurance, of preparing an invoice of the goods and any other document needed for shipment, and of forwarding all documents to the buyer with commercial promptness.[22]

Under a c.i.f. contract the buyer bears the risk of loss after the goods have been delivered to the carrier.[23] The buyer must pay for the goods when proper documents representing them are tendered to him, which in turn means that he is not entitled to inspect the goods before paying for them, unless the contract expressly provides for payment on or after the arrival of the goods.[24]

(c) Ex-ship. If the contract provides for delivery ex-ship, the seller bears the risk of loss until the goods have left the ship's tackle or have otherwise been properly unloaded. The seller must discharge all liens arising from the transportation of the goods and must furnish the buyer with such documents or instructions as enable the buyer to obtain the goods from the carrier.[25]

(d) No arrival, no sale. When goods are sent under such a term, the seller bears the risk of loss during transportation; but if the goods do not arrive, he is not responsible to the buyer for in such case there is no sale. The buyer is protected in that he is only required to pay for the goods if they arrive.

The "no arrival, no sale" contract requires the seller to ship proper conforming goods and to tender them on their arrival if they do arrive. He must, of course, refrain from interfering with the arrival of the goods.[26]

---

[22] § 2-320(1), (2). The term c. & f. or c.f. imposes the same obligations and risks as a c.i.f. term with the exception of the obligation as to insurance. Under a c.f. contract, the seller completes his performance by delivery of the goods to the carrier and by proper payment of the freight charges on the shipment, whereupon title and risk of loss pass to the buyer.

[23] UCC § 2-320(2)(c). The c.i.f. and c.f. contracts may be modified to place the risk of deterioration during shipment on the seller by specifying that the price shall be based on the arrival or "out turn" quality, or by having the seller warrant the condition or quality of the goods on their arrival. § 2-321(2).

[24] § 2-320(4), 2-321(2).

[25] § 2-322(2).

[26] § 2-324(a).

§ 25:7. ADEQUATE ASSURANCE OF PERFORMANCE.

Whenever a party to the sales transaction has reason to believe that the other party may not perform his part of the contract, he may make a written demand upon the other party for adequate assurance that he will in fact perform his contract. For example, when goods are to be delivered at a future date or in installments over a period of time, the buyer may become fearful that the seller will not be able to make the future deliveries required. The buyer may in such case require assurance from the seller that the contract will be performed.[27]

(a) **Form of assurance.** The person upon whom demand for assurance is made must give "such assurance of due performance as is adequate under the circumstances of the particular case."[28] The exact form of assurance is not specified. If the party on whom demand is made has an established reputation, his reaffirmation of his contract obligation and a statement that he will perform may be sufficient to assure a reasonable man that it will be performed. In contrast, the person's reputation or economic position at the time may be such that there is no assurance that there will be a proper performance in the absence of a guarantee by a third person or the furnishing of security by way of a pledge or other device to protect the demanding party against default.[29]

(b) **Failure to give assurance.** The party on whom demand is made may state he will not perform; that is, he repudiates the contract. In contrast with a flat repudiation, the party upon whom demand is made may fail to reply or may give only a feeble answer that is not sufficient to assure a reasonable person that performance will be made. The failure to provide adequate assurance within 30 days after receiving the demand, or a lesser time when 30 days would be unreasonable, constitutes a repudiation of the contract.[30]

QUESTIONS AND CASE PROBLEMS

1. A computer manufacturer promoted the sale of a digital computer as a "revolutionary breakthrough." It made a contract to deliver one of these computers to a buyer. It failed to deliver the computer and explained that its failure was caused by unanticipated technological difficulties. Was this an excuse for nonperformance by the seller? [See United States v Wegematic Corp. (CA2 NY) 360 F2d 674]

---

[27] § 2-609(1). Between merchants the reasonableness of the grounds for insecurity is determined according to commercial standards. § 2-609(2).

[28] § 2-609(4).

[29] Between merchants the adequacy of any assurance is determined according to commercial standards. UCC § 2-609(2).

[30] § 2-609(4). This enables the adverse party to take steps at an earlier date to protect himself against the default of the other party, as by making substitute contracts to replace the repudiated contracts.

2. International Minerals and Metals Corporation contracted to sell Weinstein scrap metal to be delivered within 30 days. Later the seller informed the buyer that it could not make delivery within that time. The buyer agreed to an extension of time, but no limiting date was set. Within what time must the seller perform? [International Minerals and Metals Corp. v Weinstein, 236 NC 558, 73 SE2d 472]

3. Fleet purchased an ice cream freezer and compressor unit from Lang. Thereafter Fleet disconnected the compressor and used it to operate an air conditioner. When sued for the purchase price of the freezer and compressor unit, Fleet claimed that he had not accepted the goods. Was he correct? [Lang v Fleet, 193 PaSuper 365, 165 A2d 258]

4. George A. Ohl & Co. made a contract "to sell to A. J. Ellis a No. 5 press . . . for the sum of $680." The press was known by both parties to be stored in the factory of another company. The agreement contained no stipulation as to the place of delivery, and there was no usage of the trade governing the question. In an action brought by Gruen, assignee of Ellis, against the Ohl company, the place of delivery was a point of contention. Decide. [Gruen v George A. Ohl & Co. 81 NJL 626, 80 A 547]

5. Price agreed to purchase two barge-loads of coal from Brown. The coal was delivered on barges of the buyer on the Green River at or near Mining City, Kentucky, in accordance with the agreement. The buyer, after being given an opportunity to inspect the coal, hooked onto the barges and transported them up the river to Bowling Green, several miles away. During subsequent litigation the buyer contended that he had not accepted the coal. Do you agree? [Brown v Price, 207 Ky 8, 268 SW 590]

6. The Spaulding & Kimball Co. ordered from the Aetna Chemical Co. 75 cartons of window washers. The buyer received them and sold about a third to its customers. The buyer later refused to pay for them, claiming that the quality was poor. The seller sued for the price, claiming that the goods had been accepted. Decide. [Aetna Chemical Co. v Spaulding & Kimball Co. 98 Vt 51, 126 A 582]

7. The Tri-Bullion Smelting & Development Co. agreed to sell, and Jacobsen to buy, the seller's output of zinc concentrates for a two-year period. A year and a half later, the Tri-Bullion Co. closed its mine and notified Jacobsen that it would make no further deliveries. Jacobsen refused to pay for the last shipment. Jacobsen sued the Tri-Bullion Co. The defendant contended that the plaintiff had breached the contract by failure to pay for the goods delivered. Do you agree? [Tri-Bullion Smelting & Development Co. v Jacobsen, 147 CCA 454, 233 F 646]

8. The seller sold goods to a township. Under the state law governing townships, it was not possible for the township to make immediate payment of any bill presented to it. To the contrary, it was necessary that a bill be presented to the township auditor and approved by him before payment could be made. The seller claimed that the township was obligated to pay for the goods upon delivery. Decide. [J. C. Georg Service Corp. v Summit, 28 AppDiv2d 578, 279 NYS2d 674]

WARRANTIES AND OTHER PRODUCT LIABILITIES

A. GENERAL PRINCIPLES

§ 26:1. INTRODUCTION. When a product is defective, harm may be caused to (1) person, (2) property, or (3) commercial or economic interests. Under (1) the buyer of the product may be injured when the truck he has purchased goes out of control and plunges down the side of a hill. Third persons may also be injured, such as other passengers in the car, bystanders, or the driver of another car. The defective car may also cause injury to a total stranger who seeks to rescue one of the victims. Property damage under (2) is sustained when the buyer's truck is damaged when it plunges down the slope. The car of the other driver may be damaged or a building into which the runaway truck careens may be damaged. Commercial and economic interests of the buyer (3) are affected by the fact that the truck is defective. Even if no physical harm is sustained, the fact remains that the truck is not as valuable as it would have been, and the buyer who has paid for the truck on the basis of the value it should have had has been deprived of some of his money to the extent that he is not getting what he bargained for. If the buyer is required to rent a truck from someone else or loses his opportunity to haul freight for compensation, the fact that the truck was defective causes him economic or commercial loss.

When there is a loss as above described, product liability may often arise on the basis of any of six theories of product liability: negligence, fraud, strict tort, express guarantee, express warranty, and implied warranty. Statutes may create product liability.

(a) Consumer protection. The Consumer Product Safety Act of 1972 [1] created an independent federal agency with broad power to establish safety regulations for all food, drugs, and common household products. The purpose of this agency, the Food, Drug, and Consumer Protection Agency (FDCPA), is to protect the consumer from physical injury, adulteration, misbranding, and illegal distribution of products.

---

[1] PL 92-573, 86 Stat 1207, 15 United States Code § 2051 et seq.

(b) Employee protection. The federal Occupational Safety and Health Act [2] authorizes the Secretary of Labor to establish job safety standards and creates an agency under him known as the Occupational Safety and Health Administration (OSHA).

§ 26:2. WHO MAY SUE AND BE SUED.

(a) The plaintiff. The law is moving to the conclusion that anyone harmed because of an "improper" product may sue whoever is in any way responsible. Only a half century ago, the circle of liability was narrowly drawn so that only a buyer could sue his seller or only a person negligently making a product could be sued for the tort damage thereby caused. Thus, a suit for a breach of warranty could only be brought by a plaintiff against a person with whom he was in privity; that is, the other party to the sales contract by which the plaintiff purchased the article. If the plaintiff was not a party to the contract with the defendant, he could not sue for breach of warranty. When suit was brought for negligence, the remote plaintiff who had been injured by the product was likewise barred from suing the seller or the manufacturer of the product. This rule has generally been abolished. The modern rule is that whenever the manufacturer, as a reasonable person, should foresee that if he is negligent, a particular class of persons will be injured by his product, the manufacturer is liable to an injured member of that class without regard to whether such plaintiff purchased from him or from anyone, as in the case of a person injured by something which was given to him or to a bystander.

The UCC expressly abolishes the requirement of privity to a limited extent by permitting a suit for breach of warranty to be brought against the seller by members of the buyer's family, his household, and his guests, with respect to personal injury sustained by them.[3]

> **FACTS:** Knorr purchased from Ivarson a dining room table for his house. Knorr rented his house with furnishings to Barry. The table top fell down and injured Barry's wife. Barry sued Ivarson for breach of warranty of fitness.
>
> **DECISION:** Judgment for Ivarson. The lack of privity between Barry and Ivarson barred the suit. A buyer's tenant is not permitted to collect damages when the buyer is not in the business of leasing and the seller does not have any reason to know that there would be such a lease. Under such circumstances, use of the table by Barry was not foreseeable by the seller. Barry therefore did not satisfy the foreseeability aspect of UCC § 2-318, even if that section were extended to tenants of the buyer. [Barry v Ivarson, Inc. (FlaApp) 249 So2d 44]

(1) Subpurchasers. When privity is not required for suit, subpurchasers, that is, customers of the buyer, may sue the original seller from whom their seller purchased his goods. Thus, the purchaser of a can of soup from the corner grocery store can sue the distributor from whom the

---

[2] 29 USC § 651 et seq.
[3] Uniform Commercial Code § 2-318.

store purchased the can. When privity is required, the customer can only sue the store from which he made the purchase.

With the rise of modern mass marketing it became apparent that the contemplated user of goods, the consumer, constituted a broader class than the actual buyers and that a concept, namely privity, which would only protect buyers and not consumers did not satisfy the needs of the modern situation.

(2) Employees. Most states permit employees to sue a remote party, as a manufacturer of the product or machine purchased by the employer of the injured employee.

(3) Bystanders. Historically a bystander, that is, a third person who was not a buyer from the defendant nor a subpurchaser from anyone, could not recover from a defendant in a product liability suit. This limitation has been abandoned when the buyer is able to establish the negligence of the defendant.

In some states the courts have ignored privity of contract when the injured person was a member of the public or a stranger at large, by adopting a doctrine of strict tort liability which makes a manufacturer liable to one who is harmed or sustains property loss because of a defect in the product when such defect makes use of the product dangerous to the user or to persons or property in the vicinity. Thus, a strict tort liability action may be brought by the driver or passenger of a second car when it has a collision with a first car because of a defect in the steering mechanism [4] or brakes of the first car; or there is a collision because of a defective drive shaft in the first car; or the bystander was injured by a runaway vehicle which started by itself because of an accelerator or transmission defect or a short circuit. A bystander may sue the manufacturer of a defective shotgun shell which bursts the gun barrel and the manufacturer of a defective beer keg which exploded; and a neighbor may sue the manufacturer of a propane gas tank which exploded. There is also a trend to allow recovery by the "stranger" for breach of warranty.

FACTS: Rooney was a city sewer engineer. While at work, he was overcome by sewer gas and died when his gas mask failed to function. The mask was made by the Mine Safety Appliance Company. Guarino and other construction workers attempted to rescue Rooney and were killed by the gas. A suit was brought for the death of Guarino and the others on the theory that Mine Safety was liable because it had broken the implied warranty of fitness for the normal or intended purpose of the goods.

DECISION: Judgment for Guarino's estate. When the breach of warranty exposes a person to danger from which a third person seeks to rescue him, the warrantor is liable for the harm sustained by such third person in making or attempting the rescue. The rescue death of Guarino and the others was part of the harm caused by Mine Safety's breach of warranty. [Guarino v Mine Safety Appliance Co. 25 NY2d 460, 306 NYS2d 942, 255 NE2d 173]

---

[4] Codling v Paglia, 32 NY2d 330, 345 NYS2d 461, 298 NE2d 622.

There is a growing trend to eliminate the requirement of privity when the plaintiff suing the manufacturer is a third person injured by the defective product—such as a bystander, pedestrian, or garage mechanic.

(b) The defendant.

(1) Seller. A person selling goods may be sued by his buyer on any theory of liability applicable to the facts. It is immaterial whether the seller sells at wholesale or retail. It is important, however, whether the seller deals in goods of the kind in question. If he does, he is classified as a "merchant" and is held to a higher degree of responsibility for the product than one who is merely making a casual sale.

When privity is required, the seller is subject to product liability suit only by his buyer.

(2) Manufacturer. There is little difference today between the product liability of a manufacturer and a seller. This logically follows from the fact that the manufacturer is also a seller in that he sells his manufactured goods to a distributor, wholesaler, or other outlet, and is thus the first seller of the finished product.

(3) Manufacturer of Component Part. Many items of goods in today's market place are not made entirely by one manufacturer. Thus, the harm may be caused in a given case by a defect in a component part of the finished product. The fact that the part of the total product containing the defective part which caused the plaintiff's harm was made by another manufacturer is not a defense to a defendant who is sued for breach of warranty or for strict tort liability. If the purchase of the component part was made from a reputable supplier and there was no prior history of complaints or defects with respect to that part, such circumstances would show the absence of negligence or of fraud on the part of the defendant when product liability is asserted on such grounds.   *EXCEPTIONS*

The buyer of an automobile may sue the component part manufacturer for negligence and breach of warranty.

(c) Advertising.

In many instances recovery by the buyer against the remote manufacturer or seller is based on the fact that the defendant had advertised directly to the public and therefore made a warranty to the purchasing consumer of the truth of his advertising. Thus, the purchaser of an automobile can sue the remote manufacturer when the purchaser has relied on mass media advertising that the car was trouble free, economical, and built with high quality workmanship.

FACTS: Hamon purchased Lestoil, a household detergent, from Digliani. She was severely burned by it and sued the seller and its manufacturers, the Lestoil Corporation and the Adell Chemical Company. The manufacturers had extensively promoted the product by television, radio, and newspapers, stating that it could be used safely for household and cleaning tasks and that it was "the all-purpose detergent—for all household cleaning and laundering." The manufacturers defended on the ground that Hamon had not purchased the bottle of Lestoil from them.

DECISION: Judgment for Hamon against the manufacturers. In view of their direct appeal to the public to purchase, the manufacturers could not avoid warranty liability when members of the public did as was desired by the manufacturer and purchased the product from local stores. Such purchase was the very act which the manufacturer sought to induce and they would not be permitted to deny warranty liability to the customer of the local store on the ground that privity was lacking. [Hamon v Digliani, 148 Conn 170, 174 A2d 294]

Although advertising by the manufacturer to the consumer is often a reason for not requiring privity when the consumer sues the manufacturer, the absence of advertising by the manufacturer does not bar such action by the buyer.[5]

(d) Direct sales contact. In many instances recovery is allowed by a buyer against a remote manufacturer because there have been direct dealings between them which justify regarding the buyer and the manufacturer as being in privity, as against the contention that the buyer was only in privity with the local dealer from whom he bought the product. For example, where the manufacturer enters into direct negotiations with the ultimate buyer in any phase of the manufacturing or financing of the transaction, the sale will probably be treated as though it were made directly by the manufacturer to the ultimate purchaser even though, for the purpose of record keeping, the transaction is treated as a sale by the manufacturer to a dealer and by that dealer to the ultimate purchaser. Thus, when the dealer arranges a meeting between the representative of the manufacturer and the customer, and the customer makes the purchase price check payable directly to the manufacturer, and the manufacturer sends the goods directly to the customer, the manufacturer is in effect the seller and no question of privity is involved.[6] Likewise, recovery may be allowed when the consumer mails to the manufacturer a warranty registration card which the manufacturer had packed with the manufactured article.

CARS ?

B. EXPRESS WARRANTIES

A warranty may be express or implied. Both have the same legal effect and operate as though the seller had made an express guarantee. An express guarantee is governed by general principles of contract law.

§ 26:3. DEFINITION. An *express warranty* is a part of the basis for the sale; that is, the buyer has purchased the goods on the reasonable assumption that they were as stated by the seller. Thus, a statement by the seller with respect to the quality, capacity, or other characteristic of the goods is an express warranty. To illustrate, the seller may say: "This cloth is all wool," "This paint is for household woodwork," or "This engine can produce 50 horsepower." The good faith of a warranty defendant is immaterial.

---

[5] Lonzrick v Republic Steel Corp. 6 Ohio2d 227, 35 OO2d 404, 218 NE2d 185.
[6] Marion Power Shovel v Huntsman, 246 Ark 149, 437 SW2d 784.

§ 26:4. FORM OF EXPRESS WARRANTY. No particular form of words is necessary to constitute an express warranty. A seller need not state that he makes a warranty nor in fact even intends to make a warranty.[7] It is sufficient that the seller assert a fact that becomes a part or term of the bargain or transaction between the parties.

It is not necessary that the seller make an express statement, for the express warranty may be found in his conduct. Accordingly, if the buyer asks for a can of outside house paint and the seller hands him a can of paint, the seller's conduct expresses a warranty that the can contains outside house paint.

The seller's statement may be written or printed, as well as oral. The words on the label of a can and in a newspaper ad for "boned chicken" constitute an express warranty that the can contains chicken that is free of bones.

A seller is not bound by the express warranty of the manufacturer unless he has in some manner obligated himself to be bound thereby.

> **FACTS:** Farrior purchased a Ford automobile from Courtesy Ford Sales, Inc. She received a copy of the manufacturer's warranty. When the car proved defective she brought suit against Courtesy Ford and the Ford Motor Company claiming that they were jointly liable for the breach of the manufacturer's warranty.
>
> **DECISION:** Courtesy Ford was not liable on the manufacturer's warranty. There was no proof that it had become a party to that warranty nor that it had adopted it as its own. Consequently, Courtesy Ford was not liable on the express warranty of the manufacturer. [Courtesy Ford Sales, Inc. v Farrior (AlaCivApp) 298 So2d 26]

The illustrations in a seller's catalog are descriptions of the goods and therefore an express warranty arises that the goods will conform to a catalog illustration.[8]

§ 26:5. TIME OF MAKING EXPRESS WARRANTY. It is immaterial whether the express warranty is made at the time of or after the sale. No separate consideration is required for the warranty when it is part of a sale. If a warranty is made after the sale, no consideration is required since it is regarded as a modification of the sales contract.[9]

§ 26:6. SELLER'S OPINION OR STATEMENT OF VALUE. "An affirmation merely of the value of goods or a statement purporting to be merely the seller's opinion or commendation of the goods does not create a warranty."[10] A purchaser, as a reasonable person, should not believe such statements implicitly, and therefore he cannot hold the seller to them should they prove false. Thus, "sales talk" by a seller that "this is the best piece of cloth in the market" or that glassware "is as good as anyone else's" is merely an opinion which the buyer cannot ordinarily treat as a warranty.

---

[7] UCC § 2-313(2).
[8] Rinkmasters v Utica (Utica City Ct) 348 NYS2d 940.
[9] UCC § 2-313. Official Comment, point 7.
[10] § 2-313(2).

It is probable, however, that the UCC will permit an exception to be made, as under the prior law, when the circumstances are such that a reasonable person would rely on such a statement. If the buyer has reason to believe that the seller is possessed of expert knowledge of the conditions of the market and the buyer requests his opinion as an expert, the buyer would be entitled to accept as a fact the seller's statement as to whether a given article was the best obtainable. The statement could be reasonably regarded as forming part of the basis of the bargain. Thus, a statement by a florist that bulbs are of first-grade quality may be a warranty.[11]

C. IMPLIED WARRANTIES

Whenever a sale of goods is made, certain warranties are implied unless they are expressly excluded. The scope of these warranties may differ in terms of whether the seller is a merchant or a casual seller.

§ 26:7. DEFINITION. An *implied warranty* is one that was not made by the seller but which is implied by the law. In certain instances the law implies or reads a warranty into a sale although the seller did not make it. That is, the implied warranty arises automatically from the fact that a sale has been made; as compared with express warranties, which arise because they form part of the basis on which the sale has been made.

The fact that express warranties are made does not exclude implied warranties; and when both express and implied warranties exist, they should be construed as consistent with each other and as cumulative if such construction is reasonable. In case it is unreasonable to construe them as consistent and cumulative, an express warranty prevails over an implied warranty as to the same subject matter, except in the case of an implied warranty of fitness for a particular purpose. When there is an express warranty as to a particular matter, it is unnecessary to find an implied warranty relating thereto.

§ 26:8. WARRANTIES OF ALL SELLERS. A distinction is made between a merchant seller and the casual seller. There is a greater range of warranties in the case of the merchant seller.

(a) Warranty of title. Every seller, by the mere act of selling, makes a warranty that his title is good and that the transfer is rightful.[12]

FACTS: American Container Corp. purchased a semitrailer from Hanley Trucking Corp. The semitrailer was seized and impounded by the New Jersey police on the ground that it was stolen, and American was notified that it had 90 days in which to prove its ownership. Within 2 weeks, American notified Hanley of the above facts and declared that it canceled the contract for breach of warranty. American sued Hanley for breach of warranty damages.

---

[11] Diepeveen v Vogt, 27 NJSuper 254, 99 A2d 329.
[12] UCC § 2-312(1)(a). A warranty of title, as well as a warranty of freedom from encumbrances, which arises when a sale is made, is not classified as an implied warranty by the UCC even though it is in the nature of an implied warranty.

DECISION: Judgment for American. The seizure of the semitrailer by the police cast such a shadow on American's title that regardless of what the outcome would be of a lawsuit to determine ownership, the police seizure was a violation of the seller's implied warranty of title. [American Container Corp. v Hanley Trucking Corp. 111 NJSuper 322, 268 A2d 313]

A warranty of title may be specifically excluded, or the circumstances may be such as to prevent the warranty from arising. The latter situation is found when the buyer has reason to know that the seller does not claim to hold the title or that he is claiming to sell only such right or title as he or a third person may have. For example, no warranty of title arises when the seller makes the sale in a representative capacity, such as a sheriff, an auctioneer, or an administrator of a decedent's estate. Likewise, no warranty arises when the seller makes the sale as a pledgee or mortgagee.

(b) **Warranty against encumbrances.** Every seller by the mere act of selling makes a warranty that the goods shall be delivered free from any security interest or any other lien or encumbrance of which the buyer at the time of the sales transaction had no knowledge.[13] Thus, there is a breach of warranty if the automobile sold to the buyer is delivered subject to an outstanding encumbrance that had been placed on it by the original owner and which was unknown to the buyer at the time of the sale.

This warranty refers to the goods only at the time they are delivered to the buyer and is not concerned with an encumbrance which existed before or at the time the sale was made. For example, a seller may not have paid in full for the goods which he is reselling and the original supplier may have a lien on the goods. The seller may resell the goods while that lien is still on them, and his only duty is to pay off the lien before he delivers the goods to the buyer.

(c) **Warranty of conformity to description, sample, or model.** When the contract is based in part on the understanding that the seller will supply goods according to a particular description or that the goods will be the same as the sample or a model, the seller is bound by an express warranty that the goods shall conform to the description, sample, or model.[14] Ordinarily a *sample* is a portion of a whole mass that is the subject of the transaction, while a *model* is a replica of the article in question. The mere fact that a sample is exhibited in the course of negotiations does not make the sale a sale by sample, as there must be an intent manifested that the sample be part of the basis of contracting.

(d) **Warranty of fitness for a particular purpose.** If the buyer intends to use the goods for a particular or unusual purpose, as contrasted with the ordinary use for which they are customarily sold, the seller makes an implied warranty that the goods will be fit for the purpose when the buyer relies on the seller's skill or judgment to select or furnish suitable goods,

---

[13] Fields v Sugar, 251 Ark 1062, 476 SW2d 814.
[14] UCC § 2-313(1)(b), (c).

and when the seller at the time of contracting knows or has reason to know the buyer's particular purpose and his reliance on the seller's judgment.[15] For example, where a farmer relied on the sales representative in purchasing feed for his cattle, a particular purpose warranty arose. Where a government representative inquired of the seller whether the seller had a tape suitable for use on the government's NCR 304 computer system, there arose an implied warranty, unless otherwise excluded, that the tape furnished by the seller was fit for that purpose.

When the buyer does not purchase in reliance on the seller's recommendation, no warranty of fitness for a particular purpose arises.

> **FACTS:** The United Geological Survey made a contract with Layne-Atlantic Company to construct an underground well. It contemplated that a particular pipe, "Koppers Fiberglass Casting," would be used. Koppers recommended that the pipe be .5-inch thick. In order to reduce the cost of construction, UGS specified pipe .3-inch thick. The pipe collapsed. Koppers sued Layne for the purchase price. Layne raised the defense that there was a breach of warranty of fitness for a particular purpose.

> **DECISION:** Judgment for Koppers. There was no evidence that Layne had relied on the skill and judgment of Koppers in making the purchase. The thickness purchased had been the decision of UGS. The mere fact that the pipe had collapsed did not show that it was not fit. [Layne-Atlantic Co. v Koppers Co., Inc. 214 Va 467, 201 SE2d 609]

§ 26:9. ADDITIONAL IMPLIED WARRANTIES OF MERCHANT SELLER.

(a) Warranty against infringement. Unless otherwise agreed every seller who is a merchant regularly dealing in goods of the kind which he has sold warrants that the goods shall be delivered free of the rightful claim of any third person by way of patent or trademark infringement or the like.

(b) Warranty of merchantability or fitness for normal use. A merchant seller who makes a sale of goods in which he customarily deals[16] makes an implied warranty of merchantability. The warranty is in fact a group of warranties, the most important of which is that the goods are fit for the ordinary purposes for which they are sold. Consequently, when the seller of ice-making and beverage-vending machines is a merchant of such machines, an implied warranty of fitness for use arises. Also included are implied warranties as to the general or average quality of the goods, and their packaging and labeling.[17]

---

[15] UCC § 2-315. This warranty applies to every seller, but as a matter of fact it will probably always be a merchant seller who has such skill and judgment so that the Code provision would be applicable. In contrast, when a seller of coal has had no experience in the selection of coal for the manufacture of coke, no implied warranty of fitness for that purpose arises. Sylvia Coal Co. v Mercury Coal & Coke Co. 151 WVa 818, 156 SE2d 1.

[16] This includes the seller of food or drink to be consumed on the premises or to be taken out. UCC § 2-314(1).

[17] § 2-314(2). Other implied warranties on the part of a merchant may also arise from a course of dealing or usage of trade. § 2-314(3).

The implied warranty of merchantability relates to the condition of the goods at the time the seller is to perform under the contract. Once the risk of loss has passed to the buyer, there is no warranty as to the continuing merchantability of the goods unless such subsequent deterioration or condition is proof that the goods were in fact not merchantable when the seller made delivery.

(1) Absence of Negligence Immaterial. A seller is not protected from warranty liability by the fact that he took every possible step to make the product safe. Similarly, it is no defense that the defendant could not have known of or discovered the dangerous character of the product, for warranty liability is not merely an assurance that the defendant has exercised due care but is an undertaking or guarantee that the product is fit for use.

(2) Second Collision Injury. When an automobile is in a collision, there is frequently a secondary consequence as when the driver is thrown forward and strikes the steering wheel. This consequential effect is sometimes called a *second collision.* In some cases, the harm caused by the second collision is increased because of the design of the automobile. Can product liability be based on this design?

Courts have been reluctant to recognize as a "defect" a design detail which magnifies or enhances the consequence of the collision because such second collision cause was not a cause of the original occurrence. When the harm-causing condition is obvious, it is likely that courts will refuse to allow the recovery of damages for second collision harm. For example, the fact that a steering wheel is not padded does not impose liability on the manufacturer even though the driver is seriously injured when the impact of a collision throws him forward and his face hits the uncovered steering wheel.

In contrast, when the defect is not obvious, the courts will tend to impose second collision damage liability. For example, when in addition to striking the steering wheel, the horn cap flew off and exposed sharp metal prongs on which the driver was severely cut, the manufacturer has been held liable for the injury so inflicted. Likewise, the manufacturer has been held liable when the gas tank of the car was so weakly attached to the car that it sheared off when there was a low-speed rear-end collision and threw gasoline into the car, causing the death by fire of its occupants. These cases follow the view that a manufacturer is under duty to so design an automobile that it will not be unreasonably dangerous when involved in a collision.[18]

FACTS: Thiel bought a Mercury automobile manufactured by Ford. He was driving and Evancho was in the rear seat as a passenger. Thiel collided with another automobile which was negligently parked. The impact threw Evancho forward. His body struck the front seat. This impact caused the front seat to move forward and expose the rails of the tracks

---

[18] Volkswagen of America, Inc. v Young (Md) 321 A2d 737.

on which it ran. There were sharp jagged edges on the rails and Evancho fell and hit those edges and was cut so severely that he died. Suit was brought by his wife against the driver and Ford.

DECISION: Judgment against Ford. The design of the seat track was the cause of the death of the passenger. Therefore, the manufacturer could be held liable for negligence or breach of implied warranty of fitness for normal use for the harm caused by the defective product. The fact that the collision had not been caused by the defect did not shield the manufacturer from liability. [Evancho v Thiel (FlaApp) 297 So2d 40]

In other states, recovery is not allowed on the basis of a defect aggravating the effect of a collision or accident on the ground that such defect was not a cause of the accident.

§ 26:10. WARRANTIES IN PARTICULAR SALES. Particular types of sales may involve special considerations.

(a) Sale of food or drink. The sale of food or drink, whether to be consumed on or off the seller's premises, is a sale and, when made by a merchant, carries the implied warranty that the food is fit for its ordinary purpose, that is, human consumption.[19]

The UCC does not end the conflict between courts applying the foreign-natural test and those applying the reasonable-expectation test. The significance of the two is that in the first test a buyer cannot recover as a matter of law when he is injured by a "natural" substance in the food, such as a cherry pit in a cherry pie; whereas under the reasonable-expectation test, it is necessary to make a determination of fact, ordinarily by the jury, to determine whether the buyer could reasonably expect the object in the food. It is, of course, necessary to distinguish the foregoing situations from those in which the preparation of the food contemplates the continued presence of some element that is not removed, such as prune stones in cooked prunes. The reasonable-expectation test is to be applied in determining whether a restaurant is liable to a patron who broke a tooth on an olive pit.

FACTS: Webster ordered a bowl of fish chowder in the Blue Ship Tea Room. She was injured by a fish bone in the chowder. She sued the Tea Room for breach of warranty. It was shown that when chowder is made, the entire unboned fish is cooked.

DECISION: As the soup was typically made with whole fish, it was apparent that the presence of fish bones in the soup should be foreseen by a reasonable person. Thus, there was no breach of warranty of merchantability. [Webster v Blue Ship Tea Room, 347 Mass 421, 198 NE2d 309]

The buyer of food that is unwholesome, as in the case of a customer purchasing a spoiled sandwich at a lunch counter, may recover either on strict tort or breach of warranty theory.

---

[19] UCC § 2-314(1), (2)(c).

Warranty liability extends to any harm resulting from the nonconformity of the goods and is not limited to personal injuries. For example, the economic loss sustained when seeds for plants fail to grow and mature properly may be recovered in a suit for breach of the implied warranty of fitness.

(b) Sale of article under patent or trade name. The sale of a patented or trade-name article is treated with respect to warranties in the same way as any other sale. If the seller is a merchant selling goods of the kind in question, the ordinary merchant's warranty of merchantability arises even though the parties have described the goods by a patent number or trade name. The fact that the sale is made on the basis of the patent or trade name does not bar the existence of a warranty of fitness for a particular purpose when the circumstances giving rise to such a warranty otherwise exist.

FACTS: Sperry Rand Corp. agreed to convert the record-keeping system of Industrial Supply Corp. so that it could be maintained by a computer and to sell a computer and nine other items necessary for such a record-keeping system. The computer and the equipment were ordered by identified trade name and number. When the system did not work, Industrial Supply sued Sperry Rand for breach of implied warranty of fitness. Sperry Rand raised the defense that the equipment had been ordered by trade name and number.

DECISION: The fact that the equipment was ordered by trade name and number did not show that the buyer was purchasing at its risk. The circumstances showed the sale was made in reliance on the seller's skill and with appreciation of the buyer's problems, and the sale of the particular equipment to the buyer was made as constituting the equipment needed by it. Under such circumstances, a warranty of the fitness of the equipment for such purpose was implied. [Sperry Rand Corp. v Industrial Supply Corp. (CA5 Fla) 337 F2d 363]

(c) Sale on buyer's specifications. When the buyer furnishes the seller with exact specifications for the preparation or manufacture of such goods, the same warranties arise as in the case of any other sale of such goods by the particular seller. No warranty of fitness for a particular purpose can arise, however, since it is clear that the buyer is purchasing on the basis of his own decision and is not relying on the seller's skill and judgment.

In sales made upon the buyer's specifications, no warranty against infringement is impliedly made by the merchant seller; and conversely, the buyer in substance makes a warranty to protect the seller from liability should the seller be held liable for patent violation by following the specifications of the buyer.[20]

(d) Sale of secondhand or used goods. No warranty arises as to fitness of used property for ordinary use when the sale is made by a casual seller. If made by a merchant seller, such a warranty may sometimes be implied. Prior to the UCC a number of states followed the rule that no warranty arose in connection with used or secondhand goods, particularly automobiles and

---

[20] § 2-312(3).

machinery; whereas some courts found a warranty of fitness for ordinary use in the sale of secondhand goods, particularly airplanes and heavy farm equipment. It is likely that this conflict will continue under the UCC.[21]

(e) Goods for animals. There is a trend to hold that goods intended for animals are covered by the same warranties that cover goods intended for human consumption. Thus, it has been held that an implied warranty arises that animal vaccines are fit for their intended use.

D. DISCLAIMER OF WARRANTIES

§ 26:11. VALIDITY OF DISCLAIMER. Warranties may be disclaimed by agreement of the parties,[22] subject to the limitation that such a provision must not be unconscionable.[23]

If a warranty of fitness [24] is excluded or if it is modified in writing, it must be conspicuous in order to make certain that the buyer will be aware of its presence. If the implied warranty of merchantability is excluded, the exclusion clause must expressly mention the word "merchantability" and it must be conspicuous.

A disclaimer provision is made conspicuous by printing it under a conspicuous heading, but in such case the heading must indicate that there is an exclusion or modification of warranties. Conversely, a heading cannot be relied upon to make such a provision "conspicuous" when the heading is misleading and wrongfully gives the impression that there is a warranty, as a heading stating "Vehicle Warranty," when in fact the provision that follows contains a limitation of warranties. And a disclaimer that is hidden in a mass of printed material handed to the buyer is not conspicuous and is not effective to exclude warranties.

An exclusion of warranties made in the manner specified by the Code is not unconscionable.[25] But there is also authority that when the breach of warranty was the result of negligence of the seller, the disclaimer of warranty liability and a limitation of remedies to refunding of purchase price is not binding because such a limitation is "unreasonable, unconscionable, and against sound public policy."[26] In some states, warranty disclaimers are invalid as contrary to public policy or because prohibited by consumer protection laws.

---

[21] See UCC § 2-314, Official Comment, point 3.

[22] The term *disclaimer* refers to the consensual agreement of the parties which constitutes an express term of their contract. *Exclusion of warranties* may refer to any conduct which excludes warranties, and embraces not only disclaimers but also exclusion by examination and by custom or course of doing. *Modification of warranties* is often misused to refer to a partial disclaimer.

[23] UCC §§ 2-316(1), 2-302(1). A distinction must be made between holding that the circumstances do not give rise to a warranty, thus precluding warranty liability, and holding that the warranty which would otherwise arise was excluded or surrendered by the contract of the parties.

[24] By the letter of the Code, the text statement is applicable to any warranty of fitness, see UCC § 2-316(2), although by the Official Comment to § 2-316, point 4, it would appear to be only the warranty of fitness for a particular purpose.

[25] Avery v Aladdin Products Division, National Service Industries, Inc. 128 GaApp 266, 196 SE2d 357.

[26] Kohlenberger, Inc. v Tyson's Foods, Inc. (Ark) 510 SW2d 555.

A disclaimer of warranty made orally may be ignored where the seller has given the impression that it is not serious.

§ 26:12. PARTICULAR PROVISIONS.

Such a statement as "there are no warranties which extend beyond the description on the face hereof" excludes all implied warranties of fitness.[27] Implied warranties are excluded by the statement of "as is," "with all faults," or other language which in normal common speech calls attention to the warranty exclusion and makes it clear that there is no implied warranty.[28]

In order for a disclaimer of warranties to be a binding part of an oral sales contract, the disclaimer must be called to the attention of the buyer.

These provisions as to exclusions of warranties apply to leases of personal property that in substance are sales.

§ 26:13. EXCLUSION OF WARRANTIES BY EXAMINATION OF GOODS.

There is no implied warranty with respect to defects in goods that an examination should have revealed when the buyer before making the final contract has examined the goods, or model or sample, or has refused to make such examination.[29]

The examination of the goods by the buyer does not exclude the existence of an express warranty unless it can be concluded that the buyer thereby learned of the falsity of the statement claimed to be a warranty, with the consequence that such statement did not in fact form part of the bargain.

§ 26:14. POST-SALE DISCLAIMER.

Frequently the statement excluding or modifying warranties appears for the first time in a written contract sent to confirm or memorialize the oral contract made earlier; or it appears in an invoice, a bill, or an instruction manual delivered to the buyer at or after the time that he receives the goods. Such post-sale disclaimers have no effect on warranties that arose at the time of the sale. Likewise, an oral express warranty made by the salesperson is not excluded by a disclaimer of oral warranties made on the back of the credit sale printed form which was not called to the buyer's attention.

An exclusion of warranties in a manufacturer's manual given to the buyer after the sale is not binding on a buyer because it is not a term of the sales contract.

> **FACTS:** Cooper Paintings ordered a specified kind of liquid roofing material. When it was delivered to Cooper, there were statements on the printed label that the manufacturer did not make any warranties as to the goods. Were such statements effective to exclude the implied warranty that the roofing material was fit for use as roofing material?

---

[27] UCC § 2-316(2).
[28] § 2-316(3)(a).
[29] § 2-316(3)(b).

DECISION: No. A disclaimer of warranties made after the sale is not effective. The label on the goods was not seen by the buyer until the goods were received, and therefore the statement on the label could not have been a term of the contract. [Cooper Paintings & Coatings, Inc. v SCM Corp. 62 TennApp 13, 457 SW2d 864]

If the buyer would assent to the post-sale disclaimer, however, it would be effective as a modification of the sales contract.

§ **26:15. NEGLIGENCE.** Another basis for recovering damages from the seller is his negligence. Independently of the UCC, a person injured through the use or condition of personal property may be entitled to sue the manufacturer for the damages which he sustains, on the theory that the defendant was negligent in the preparation or manufacture of the article, or in the preparation of instructions as to proper use or warning as to dangers. In this respect, a manufacturer is responsible for having the knowledge of an expert in his line of production and must therefore take reasonable steps to guard against the dangers that would be apparent to an expert.

There is no duty on the seller to test a product which he purchases from a reputable manufacturer if he has no reason to believe that there may be a defect. Statutes, however, sometimes impose upon dealers, as in the case of automobiles, the duty to make tests.

§ **26:16. FRAUD.** The UCC expressly preserves the pre-Code law as to fraud, with the consequence that a person defrauded by false statements made by the seller or the manufacturer with knowledge that such statements were false, or with reckless indifference as to their truth, will generally be able to recover damages for the harm sustained because of such misrepresentation.

§ **26:17. STRICT TORT LIABILITY.** Another and separate basis for recovering damages is the theory of strict tort liability. Independently of the UCC, a manufacturer or distributor of a defective product is liable to a person who is injured by the product when such injury is foreseeable, without regard to whether the person injured is a purchaser, a consumer, or a third person such as a bystander or a pedestrian. This concept is not one of the absolute liability; that is, it must first be shown that there was a defect in the product. It is like warranty liability in that the defendant is liable from the fact that his defective product caused harm, that it is no defense that no negligence is shown, or that the defect was in a component part purchased from another manufacturer.[30]

---

[30] The concept of strict tort liability was judicially declared in Greenman v Yuba Power Products, 59 Cal2d 57, 27 CalRptr 697, 377 P2d 897. This concept was also declared by and is often identified as Restatement of Torts 2d § 402A. In some jurisdictions the term "products liability" is used to refer to the strict tort theory of liability. Willeford v Mayrath, 7 IllApp3d 357, 287 NE2d 502.

"The doctrine of strict liability is hardly more than what exists under implied warranty when stripped of the contract doctrines of privity, disclaimer, requirements of notice of defect, and limitations through inconsistencies with express warranties." Shepard v Alexian Brothers Hospital, Inc. 33 CalApp3d 606, 109 CalRptr 132.

A plaintiff does not set forth a claim for strict tort liability when he merely avers that the defendant represented that his product "offered unprecedented safety" as such a statement was merely sales talk or opinion which could not be used as the basis for a strict tort liability claim.

E. PARTICULAR PROBLEMS OF PRODUCT LIABILITY

§ 26:18. CUMULATIVE LIABILITIES. The theories of product liability are not mutually exclusive. Thus, a given set of facts may give rise to two or more theories of liability. For example, where a rock-crushing machine was dangerous to workers because an unguarded rotating axle projected from the machine, it was held that there was (a) liability for breach of the express warranty that the machine was safe, (b) liability for breach of the implied warranty of fitness for the particular purpose of crushing rock, and (c) liability for strict tort.

In many instances it will not make any difference to anyone whether there is only one basis of product liability or several. In some instances it may be important. For example, a warranty liability is barred if injury is sustained in the fifth year after the delivery of the goods for the reason that the statute of limitations as to warranty claims runs from the date of delivery of the goods and not from the later date when injury is sustained. In contrast, the statute of limitations applicable to strict tort generally runs from the date of the injury so that an injured plaintiff probably would have two years after the date of his injury in which to sue. Thus, the plaintiff injured in the fifth year could bring suit for strict tort in the sixth and seventh years although he would be barred from suing on either an express or an implied warranty. In such a situation it is obviously highly important to the plaintiff that he has the right to recover in strict tort.

It is to be remembered that any seller or manufacturer, by the express terms of his contract, may assume a liability broader than would arise without such an express undertaking.

FACTS: Spiegel purchased a jar of skin cream from Saks 34th Street. It had been manufactured by the National Toilet Co. The carton and the jar stated that it was chemically pure and absolutely safe. When Spiegel used the cream, it caused a severe skin rash. She sued Saks and National.

DECISION: Judgment for Spiegel. The statements on the carton and the jar constituted an express warranty binding both the seller and the manufacturer. The statement that it was safe was an absolute undertaking that it was safe for everyone; as distinguished from merely an implied warranty of reasonable fitness, which would be subject to an exception of a particular allergy of a plaintiff. [Spiegel v Saks 34th Street, 43 Misc2d 1065, 252 NYS2d 852]

§ 26:19. NATURE OF THE TRANSACTION. Warranty liability arises only when there has been a sale or a commercial leasing of goods. Fraud liability and negligence liability may arise without regard to the nature of the transaction involving the plaintiff or the defendant.

The strict tort liability concept may be applied whenever there is any transfer of possession of goods, whether the transaction is a sale, a free distribution of samples, or a commercial leasing of goods.

Neither the strict tort liability concept nor the UCC warranties apply to transactions that are regarded as the sale of services, although a modern trend appears to extend the sale-of-goods concepts to service transactions. Likewise, consumer protection laws frequently treat contracts for services the same as contracts for the sale of goods. If one views the situation from the standpoint of the buyer, many of the reasons which give rise to the modern law of product liability also urge the extension of those concepts to service contracts. It is probable that this will occur in time. Contracts to render computer services have in several instances been interpreted as sales contracts.

An intermediate step in the direction of eliminating the distinction between services and goods insofar as warranties are concerned has been taken by holding that the sale of electricity was a service but that it was nevertheless subject to warranties.[31] When the transaction is a service contract or a hybrid of a supplying of materials and the rendition of services, liability must rest either upon breach of contract, fraud, or negligence and ordinarily neither warranty nor strict tort liability can arise. Thus, the concept of strict tort liability does not extend to services, such as the professional services rendered by an optometrist in fitting contact lenses, and this conclusion is not altered by the fact that the business is conducted on a large-scale advertising basis with standardized techniques. Likewise, it is generally held that neither a sales warranty nor strict tort liability arises in connection with materials or equipment used in connection with medical care or treatment.

§ 26:20. IMPROPER PRODUCT.

(a) **Defect.** The mere fact that harm is sustained by using the defendant's product does not impose liability under any theory. There must be some defect in the product which was caused or not removed by the defendant. If the product is defective when it leaves the control of the defendant, this element of product liability is satisfied.

There is conflict of authority as to whether the strict tort liability defect must be such as to make the product "dangerously defective" to the consumer or whether it is sufficient that the product was in fact defective and that the defect caused harm.[32]

(b) **Design.** Is a product defective because it could have been designed better? At present neither negligence nor warranty liability can be based on the fact that the product could have been designed so that it would have been safer, whether this would have prevented the occurrence of any harm

---

[31] Buckeye Union Fire Insurance Co. v Detroit Edison Co. 38 MichApp 325, 196 NW2d 316. Some courts have taken the longer step and hold that the sale of electricity is a sale of goods. See § 24:2.

[32] Cronin v J. B. E. Olson Corp. 8 Cal3d 121, 104 CalRptr 433, 501 P2d 1153; Glass v Ford Motor Co. 123 NJSuper 599, 304 A2d 562.

or would have reduced the extent of injury when harm occurred. At present the law does not require that a product be "accident-proof" or "other-party proof." A manufacturer or seller is not liable merely because his product could have been constructed in a way that would have made its use less dangerous or which would have protected the user from the mistakes of other persons, such as other drivers. Thus, the fact that an automobile would be less subject to crushing the driver when involved in a collision if steel side rails were welded to the automobile frame does not in itself impose liability on the manufacturer for failing to use such a design. Administrative regulations have imposed higher standards of safety.

The Motor Vehicle Information and Cost Savings Act of 1972 [33] is designed to reduce the high cost of collisions by producing automobiles that can withstand the impact of collision more readily. The Act authorizes the Secretary of Transportation to establish loss reduction standards.

(c) Malfunction. The fact that the product doesn't work or does not work properly may constitute a breach of an implied warranty of fitness for ordinary use or for a particular purpose or an express warranty as to performance.

A malfunction of the product is not sufficient to impose liability for negligence or strict tort. However, when the product is destroyed so that it is impossible to make a post-accident examination to determine whether there was a defect, there is an increasing tendency of the courts to find that malfunction before or at the time of the accident is sufficient evidence of a defect or that the mere fact of malfunctioning was a sufficient basis for a recovery, although the plaintiff could not prove that there was a defect. For example, when the evidence establishes a malfunctioning of the steering wheel of an automobile which caused the automobile to cross into the other lane and strike the oncoming plaintiff, it will generally be held that the "defect" element is satisfied when the lane-crossing car is destroyed by a fire following the collision or is so badly damaged that an examination of the steering mechanism is useless. In many instances it is sufficient to establish that the malfunctioning of the product was the cause of the harm, without specifically establishing why the product malfunctioned.

> **FACTS:** Bombardi purchased a television set from Pochel's Appliance and TV Company. For no apparent reason, the set caught on fire and set fire to other furniture and the building in which Bombardi had placed the set. The set was destroyed in the fire. Bombardi sued the dealer and the manufacturer. The defense was raised that Bombardi did not show that part of the set was defective.
>
> **DECISION:** Although a plaintiff must show that the product was defective, circumstantial evidence is sufficient and a plaintiff is not barred from recovering because he cannot designate the exact part of the product which was defective. This is particularly so when a product has been destroyed from the very malfunctioning which is indicative of a defect. [Bombardi v Pochel's Appliance and TV Co. 9 WashApp 797, 515 P2d 540]

---

[33] PL 92-513, 86 Stat 947.

(d) Foreseeable misuse. A product is "defective" for the purpose of the product liability principles when it is not safe to use in either the way the product was intended to be used or when misused for a purpose not intended by the defendant but which was reasonably foreseeable by him.

§ 26:21 INSTRUCTIONS AND WARNINGS.

When the proper manner of use is part of the common knowledge of man and the dangers are obvious, there is ordinarily no duty to furnish instructions as to use or to furnish with warnings as to any dangers. If the product is not a common object, instructions may be essential to enable the user to know how to use it. In such case the product alone without the necessary instructions would not satisfy the warranty of fitness for normal use embraced within the warranty of merchantability nor the warranty of fitness for a particular purpose. Furthermore, if use of the product without instructions would expose the user or bystanders to an unreasonable risk of harm, the absence of instructions would make the product defective so as to impose liability for negligence or strict tort upon the defendant.

Various state and federal statutes regulate the subject of instructions and warnings as to certain kinds of products, such as drugs, explosives, and inflammable products. If a defendant fails to furnish the proper instructions and warnings, he may be liable for violation of such a statute as well as subject to product liability for the harm caused. If a seller knows that a buyer is purchasing for resale and the product is not "packaged" in the manner required by law for a lawful resale, the seller would be guilty of a breach of the implied warranty of merchantability.[34]

§ 26.22. DISCLAIMER OF LIABILITY.

A party may disclaim warranty liability under a sale or commercial leasing if the requirements of the UCC § 2-316 are satisfied. As an exception to this statement, a few states hold that such a disclaimer is contrary to public policy and may not be given effect when there is a substantial inequality in the bargaining power of the seller and the buyer.[35]

In any case, a disclaimer included in a contract by the defendant will be strictly interpreted against the defendant and not given wider application than is required by its terms. For example, when a sales contract disclaims the seller's liability for breach of warranty, it will not have any effect on

---

[34] Frequently the reselling buyer will require a seller to make an express warranty as to compliance of the product with government regulations, so that any violation of the government regulation constitutes a breach of the express warranty. The breach of the government standard is often sufficient to establish negligence liability of the defendant and to establish the defective character of the product both for negligence and strict tort liability.

[35] Henningsen v Bloomfield Motors, 32 NJ 358, 161 A2d 69. When warranty liability is disclaimed as between the parties, the seller will ordinarily be free of warranty liability to a third person, such as a subpurchaser of a bystander.

When the defendant is negligent, a disclaimer of liability will often be held invalid as contrary to public policy, particularly when the sale relates to consumer goods which the buyer is purchasing for consumer use as contrasted with a merchant purchasing for resale. When the defendant would otherwise be liable for strict tort, a disclaimer of liability made by the buyer does not bind the buyer nor any third person injured by the product.

product liability based on theories other than warranty. That is, a disclaimer of warranty liability does not disclaim product liability based on fraud, negligence, or strict tort.

(a) Limitation of remedy. A manufacturer or seller will often seek to avoid the question of the validity of a disclaimer of warranties by limiting the buyer's remedies rather than purporting to disclaim all warranty liability. This is commonly done by declaring that the warranty liability shall be limited to refunding the cost of the product or replacing the defective parts. In terms of dollars recovered by the injured plaintiff, there is no great difference between declaring that the plaintiff shall not recover anything or that he shall recover only a few dollars. For example, consider situations in which a defective electric fan causes a fire that burns down a house, or a boiler safety valve fails to function and a destructive explosion occurs.

(b) Unconscionability. When personal injury is sustained in consequence of the breach of a warranty, the UCC declares that a limitation on the remedy is prima facie unconscionable.[36] This means that the "refund or replace" provision has no effect as against a plaintiff who is personally injured unless the defendant can show that in fact the limitation was not unconscionable. As a practical matter, a defendant will never be able to do this in the ordinary consumer situation so that for all practical purposes the UCC can be regarded as declaring such a provision void when a person sustains personal injury.

§ 26:23. CAUSE OF HARM. The harm sustained by the product liability plaintiff must have been "caused" by the defendant. Here the concepts are the same as in the case of "proximate" in tort liability, without regard to whether suit is brought for negligence or on the theory of strict tort liability or breach of warranty.

§ 26:24. EXISTENCE OF MIDDLEMAN. In many product liability situations the product is distributed or resold by a middleman as a dealer. The question then arises whether a defendant manufacturer is shielded from liability to the ultimate purchaser or a third person if it is the act or omission of the middleman which made the product defective.

If the act of the middleman makes the product defective, the manufacturer is not liable when there is no reason to foresee such negligence. To illustrate, if the mechanic of the car dealer tightens the steering mechanism of an automobile but does so in an improper way which causes a cable to snap and this thereafter makes the car go out of control, the manufacturer is not liable for this intervening act.

If the manufacturer expects or depends upon the middleman to make the product safe for use, there is no negligence liability when the middleman fails to make the car safe if the manufacturer had no reason to foresee that

---

[36] UCC § 2-719(3).

there would be such a failure. Consequently, negligence liability of the manufacturer or supplier to the ultimate customer does not arise when the manufacturer or supplier believes or has reason to believe that an intermediate distributor or processor is to complete processing or is to take further steps that will remove an otherwise foreseeable danger.

When the circumstances are such that a manufacturer would be liable in strict tort to a person injured because of a defect, however, the duty to take steps to avoid the harm is absolute, and liability cannot be avoided by delegating the function of checking or repairing to a distributor or dealer. More specifically, when there is a defect in an automobile for which the manufacturer would be liable on the strict tort theory, he cannot avoid liability to the injured customer by shifting to the local distributor or dealer the function of making the final inspection and repairs to new cars.

§ 26:25. ACCIDENT AND MISCONDUCT OF PLAINTIFF. Ordinarily no product liability arises when the harm is the result of accident. Thus, a seller or manufacturer is not liable for negligence or for breach of warranty of fitness when the harm is caused not by a defect in the goods but by an accident or the conduct of the buyer. Consequently, there is no liability based on negligence or breach of warranty when the buyer of a rotary power lawnmower is injured by the mower when he slipped on grass and his foot slid under the protective guard which he had raised from 3 to 3¼ inches above the ground.

The defendant is generally not liable on any theory of product liability when the harm was caused by the plaintiff's misuse of the product or his voluntary use of the product with knowledge that it was defective.

FACTS: Erdman purchased a television set from Johnson Brothers. Repeated repairs were made on the set. On one occasion the set turned itself on automatically. On several occasions, smoke and sparks were seen coming out of the set. On one evening when the set was used for several hours, smoke and sparks were observed. The set was turned off at 1:30 a.m. but was not unplugged. A half hour later the house was on fire, apparently having been started by a fire in the television set. Erdman claimed that the seller was liable for the damage to the house.

DECISION: A seller is liable for damages that are the proximate result of the defect which constitutes a breach of warranty. The conduct of the buyer in using the television set in spite of sparks and smoke, and in failing to remove the plug, constituted such conduct on his part, however, as barred recovery for the consequences of the defective condition of the set. [Erdman v Johnson Brothers Radio and Television Co. 260 Md 190, 271 A2d 744]

§ 26:26. NOTICE OF DEFECT.

(a) Breach of warranty. When a buyer seeks to recover from his seller for breach of warranty, he must establish that he gave the seller notice of the defect within a reasonable time after he discovered or should have discovered the defect.[37]

---

[37] § 2-607(3).

If the warranty suit by the plaintiff is not brought against his immediate seller, this notice requirement is not applicable.

(b) Tort liabilities. When the product liability plaintiff sues for fraud, negligence, or strict tort, there is no requirement that notice was given to the defendant of the existence of the defect.

Ordinarily the facts are such that the strict tort liability plaintiff is generally a subpurchaser or a third person so that he could not have given notice of any defect prior to his injury. For example, the buyer of an automobile could be required to give notice to the seller that the brakes of the car were defective; but it is obvious that a bystander who is run over when the brakes fail to hold would not know in advance of being run over that there was any defect, or the identity of the car which would run over him, or the identity of the manufacturer who should be notified, and so on.

QUESTIONS AND CASE PROBLEMS

1. An automobile manufacturer was sued for negligence in the construction of the automobile which injured the plaintiff. The manufacturer raised the defense that it had sold the automobile "as is." Was this a good defense? [See Fleming v Stoddard Wendle Motor Co. 70 Wash2d 465, 423 P2d 926]

2. Epstein went to the beauty parlor operated by Giannattasio. The hair coloring used by the beauty shop operator caused harm to Epstein. She brought suit claiming that there was a breach of the implied warranty of fitness for the intended purpose. Was she correct? [Epstein v Giannattasio, 25 ConnSupp 109, 197 A2d 342]

3. Frank purchased a used automobile from the McCafferty Ford Co. The person who sold the auto to McCafferty was not the owner, and the true owner successfully reclaimed it from Frank. Frank then sued McCafferty although McCafferty had said nothing about the title to the automobile. Was McCafferty liable to Frank? [Frank v McCafferty Ford Co. 192 Pa Super 435, 161 A2d 896]

4. Wetzel was a dealer. He purchased a poultry feed additive called Gro-factor Poultry Supplement from Bingman Laboratories. The public did not buy the supplement. When Bingman sued Wetzel for the purchase price, he claimed that there was a breach of warranty of merchantability because the goods did not sell. Was he correct? [Wetzel v Bingman Laboratories, Inc. 39 AlaApp 506, 104 So2d 452]

5. Scanlon was a factory employee. At lunch he purchased from a cart vendor, Food Crafts, a hard roll sandwhich. It was later shown that the roll was stale and unfit for human consumption. Because of the hardness of the roll, Scanlon broke a tooth. He then sued Food Crafts for the dental bill. Food Crafts denied liability and claimed that the plaintiff's tooth had broken because it was weak. Decide. [Scanlon v Food Crafts, Inc. 2 ConnCir 3, 193 A2d 610]

6. Queen ordered goods by sample from Loomis Bros. Corporation, a dealer in that kind of goods. The goods that were delivered conformed to the sample but were not fit for the normal intended use. Loomis claimed that it had fully performed its

contract since it was only required to deliver goods that conformed to the sample. Was it correct? [Loomis Bros. Corp. v Queen (Pa) 17 D&C 2d 482, 46 Del County 79]

7. Filler was a member of the high school baseball team. The coach had purchased sunglasses manufactured by Rayex Corp. for use by the team members. The glasses were advertised and the package described them as "professional" glasses for baseball as "sports-world's finest sunglasses" and that they gave "instant eye protection." Unknown to everyone, the glasses were very thin, with the lens ranging from 1.2 to 1.5 millimeters. Because of this thinness, the glasses, when struck by a baseball, shattered into fine splinters and injured Filler's right eye. He sued Rayex Corp., claiming that there was a breach of implied warranty of fitness for a particular purpose. Rayex denied liability and raised the defense of lack of privity. Decide. [Filler v Rayex Corp. (CA7 Ind) 435 F2d 336]

8. The Yamaha Motor Co. sold a motorcycle to a dealer, Harley Davidson of Essex, New Jersey. The motorcycle was partly assembled, and Yamaha depended upon Harley Davidson to assemble it and make it ready to use. Sabloff purchased a motorcycle made by Yamaha from Harley Davidson. He was injured while riding when the front wheel locked for no apparent reason. He sued Yamaha. It raised the defense that Sabloff had been harmed because Harley Davidson had not assembled the motor cycle in a proper manner. Decide. [Sabloff v Yamaha Motor Co. 113 NJSuper 270, 273 A2d 606]

9. Bennet was a passenger in a taxi in Kentucky. When she reached her destination, the driver shot her with a pistol which he had purchased through the mail from a New York dealer. She sued the taxi company and the dealer. She asserted that the dealer was liable for (1) negligence and (2) strict tort. Was the dealer liable? [Bennet v Cincinnati Checker Cab. Co., Inc. (DC ED Ky) 353 FSupp 1206]

10. Eli Lilly manufactured a weed killer called Treflan. Casey purchased some Treflan from a local dealer. It did not kill the weeds. Casey sued Lilly for the damage to his crops resulting from the weeds. Was he entitled to recover? [Eli Lilly & Co. v Casey (TexCivApp) 472 SW2d 598]

REMEDIES FOR BREACH OF SALES CONTRACT

A. STATUTE OF LIMITATIONS

§ 27:1. CODE CLAIM. An action for a breach of a sales contract must be commenced within four years after the cause of action arises, regardless of when the aggrieved party learned that he had a cause of action.[1] In the case of a warranty, the breach occurs when tender of delivery is made to the buyer even though no defect then appears and no harm is sustained until a later date. No distinction is made as to the nature of the harm sustained. That is, a claim for personal injury or for property damage resulting from a breach of a sales contract is governed by the four-year statute of limitations.

(a) Future performance warranty. When a warranty relates to performance that is to begin in the future, the statute of limitations does not begin to run at the time of the sale but only when the time for the performance would begin. The result is that when a heating system was installed in midsummer under a warranty that it would heat to a certain degree in subzero weather, the cause of action for the breach of warranty did not arise until subzero weather existed. Hence, the statute of limitations did not begin to run in the summer when the heater was sold or installed but later in the winter when the heating system was found to be inadequate.

(b) Notice of defect. In addition to bringing suit within four years under the UCC statute of limitations, the plaintiff who sues the person from whom he purchased the goods for damages claimed because of a breach of the sales contract must have given the seller notice of such breach within a reasonable time after he (the plaintiff) discovered or should have discovered it.[2]

§ 27:2. NON-CODE CLAIMS. When the plaintiff sues on a non-Code theory, even though it relates to goods, the UCC statute of limitations does not apply. Thus, when the plaintiff sues a remote manufacturer on the basis of strict tort liability, the action is subject to the general tort statute of limitations and not the UCC four-year statute.

---

[1] Uniform Commercial Code § 2-725(1), (2).
[2] UCC § 2-607(3)(a).

B. REMEDIES OF THE SELLER

§ 27:3. SELLER'S LIEN. In the absence of an agreement for the extension of credit to the purchaser, the seller has a lien on the goods, that is, the right to retain possession of the goods until he is paid for them. Even when the goods are sold on credit, the seller has a lien on the goods if the buyer becomes insolvent or if the credit period expires while the goods are in the seller's possession.

The seller's lien may be lost by (a) waiver, as by a later extension of credit, (b) delivery of the goods to a carrier or other bailee, without a reservation of title or possession, for the purpose of delivery to the buyer, (c) acquisition of the property by the buyer or his agent by lawful means, or (d) payment or tender of the price by the buyer.

> FACTS: McAuliffe & Burke Co. sold plumbing fixtures to Levine but refused to deliver them unless immediate payment was made in cash. The buyer gave the sellers a worthless check which he assured the sellers was "good as gold." On the basis of this statement, the sellers surrendered the goods to the buyer. Thereafter a creditor of Levine brought an action against him, and the sheriff, Gallagher, seized the goods thus delivered to Levine. The sellers, learning that the check was worthless, claimed that they were entitled to a lien on the goods and sued Gallagher for their return.

> DECISION: Judgment for the sellers. The lien of the seller is not lost when possession is unlawfully obtained. Here possession had been obtained by the fraudulent representation that the check was "as good as gold," and the sellers could therefore recover the property. [McAuliffe & Burke Co. v Gallagher, 258 Mass 215, 154 NE 755]

§ 27:4. COMPLETION OR SALVAGE OF REPUDIATED CONTRACT. It may be that the buyer repudiates or otherwise breaches the contract while the seller has some or all of the goods in his possession in either a finished and ready-to-deliver stage or in a partially manufactured stage. If the seller has in his possession goods that satisfy or conform to the contract with the buyer, he may identify those goods to the contract which the buyer has broken. This will enable the seller to sue the buyer for the purchase price and to make a resale of the goods, holding the buyer responsible for any loss thereon.

If the goods intended for the buyer are in an unfinished state, the seller must exercise reasonable commercial judgment to determine whether (a) to sell them for scrap or salvage or (b) to complete their manufacture, then identify them to the buyer's contract, and resell them. In any case the buyer is liable for the loss sustained by the seller if the latter has acted properly.

> FACTS: The Detroit Power Screwdriver Company made a contract to manufacture a very complicated stud-driving machine for Ladney. The machine was to be made to Ladney's specifications and was not like the machines made by Detroit. When the manufacturing of the machine was nearly completed, Ladney notified Detroit that he would not take the machine. Detroit stopped production and sued Ladney.

.DECISION: Detroit was entitled to recover damages because Ladney had repudiated the contract. The amount of the damages depended upon whether the machine was regarded as a "specialty item" or an item which could be normally resold in the seller's business. If it was a specialty item, the plaintiff was entitled to recover lost profits. If it was not a specialty item, the plaintiff could only recover the difference between the market price and the contract price. [Detroit Power Screwdriver Co. v Ladney, 25 MichApp 478, 181 NW2d 848 (ordering a new trial to determine character of goods)]

§ 27:5. STOPPING DELIVERY BY CARRIER OR OTHER BAILEE. The goods may be in transit on their way to the buyer. They also may be in the .hands of a noncarrier bailee who is to surrender them to the buyer. The seller may stop delivery of the goods to the buyer, without regard to the quantity involved, if the buyer is insolvent. In addition, the seller may stop delivery if the quantity involved is a carload, truckload, or planeload, or more, whenever the buyer has repudiated the contract or failed to make a payment due before delivery or if for any reason the seller would have the right to retain or reclaim the goods.[3]

After the seller regains possession of the goods by stopping delivery, he is in the same legal position as though he had not placed them on the carrier or delivered them to the bailee and may assert against them a seller's lien. When the seller reserves title or the right to possession, the seller need not invoke the right to stop delivery since he can withhold the property from the buyer by virtue of such reservation.

(a) Exercise of the right. The seller exercises the right to stop delivery by notifying the carrier or bailee that the goods are to be returned to or held for him. If the seller gives the carrier or bailee proper notice in sufficient time so that through the exercise of due diligence it can stop delivery, the carrier or bailee must obey the seller's order. Any additional cost involved must be borne by the seller. If the carrier or bailee fails to act, it is liable to the seller for any loss he sustains.

After proper notice has been given to it, the carrier or bailee must follow the instructions of the seller as to the disposal of the goods. When a negotiable document of title for the goods is in circulation, however, the carrier or bailee is not obliged to deliver the goods until the document is surrendered. The holder of such a document may defeat the seller's right of stopping delivery.

(b) Termination of right to stop delivery. The seller's right to stop delivery is terminated or lost, even though a proper notification is given, when (1) the goods have been delivered to the buyer, (2) the carrier acknowledges the right of the buyer by reshipping at his direction or by agreeing to hold for him as a warehouseman, (3) the bailee in possession acknowledges that he holds the goods for the buyer, or (4) a negotiable document of title covering the goods has been negotiated to the buyer.

---

[3] § 2-705(1).

§ 27:6. RECLAMATION OF GOODS RECEIVED BY INSOLVENT BUYER.

The buyer may have obtained goods from the seller on credit when, unknown to the seller, the buyer was insolvent. If the buyer made a false written statement to the seller that he was solvent and received the goods within three months after that time, the seller may at any time demand and reclaim the goods sold to the buyer on credit. If the buyer never made a false written statement of solvency, or if he made it more than three months before he received the goods, the seller, in order to reclaim the goods, must demand the return of the goods within ten days after they are received by the buyer.

§ 27:7. RESALE BY SELLER.

When the buyer has broken the contract by wrongfully rejecting the goods, wrongfully revoking his acceptance, failing to pay, or repudiating the contract, the seller may resell the goods or the balance of them remaining in his possession, or the goods over which he has reacquired possession as by stopping delivery. After the resale, the seller is not liable to the original buyer upon the contract or for any profit obtained by him on the resale. On the other hand, if the proceeds are less than the contract price, the seller may recover the loss from the original buyer.[4]

Reasonable notice must be given to the original buyer of the intention to make a private sale. Such notice must be given him of a public sale unless the goods are perishable in character or threaten to decline speedily in value. Notice of a public sale must also be given to the general public in such manner as is commercially reasonable under the circumstances.

§ 27:8. CANCELLATION BY SELLER.

When the buyer wrongfully rejects the goods, wrongfully revokes an acceptance of the goods, repudiates the contract, or fails to make a payment due on or before delivery, the seller may cancel the contract. Such action puts an end to the contract, discharging all obligations on both sides that are still unperformed, but the seller retains any remedy with respect to the breach by the buyer.[5] Cancellation necessarily revests the seller with title to the goods.

A seller should not jump to the conclusion that he is free to cancel the contract because the buyer has breached the contract. It is only when such breach substantially impairs the value of the contract to the seller that he is entitled to cancel. If the seller cancels without justification, he is himself in breach of the contract and can be held liable for damages. Consequently, when the buyer's breach did not justify cancellation by the seller, the seller who proceeded to cancel could be held liable to the buyer for damages for nondelivery of the goods.[6]

§ 27:9. SELLER'S ACTION FOR DAMAGES.

If the buyer wrongfully refuses to accept the goods or if he repudiates the contract, the seller may sue him for the damages that the seller sustains. In the ordinary case, the

---

[4] § 2-706(1), (6).

[5] § 2-106(4).

[6] Gulf Chemical and Metallurgical Corp. v Sylvan Chemical Corp. 122 NJSuper 499, 300 A2d 878.

amount of damages is to be measured by the difference between the market price at the time and place of the tender of the goods and the contract price.[7]

If this measure of damages does not place the seller in the position in which he would have been placed by the buyer's performance, recovery may be permitted of lost profits, together with an allowance for overhead. The seller may in any case recover as incidental damages any commercially reasonable charges, expenses, or commissions incurred in enforcing his remedy, such as those sustained in stopping delivery; in the transportation, care, and custody of the goods after the buyer's breach; and in the return or resale of the goods.[8] Such incidental damages are recovered in addition to any other damages that may be recovered by the seller.

When a tailor's customer stopped payment on his check and the tailor, who had already cut cloth for the customer's suit, stopped further work on the suit, he was entitled to recover only the damages that he had sustained; that is, his costs and lost profits, but he was not entitled to recover the full contract price of a finished suit.

§ 27:10. SELLER'S ACTION FOR THE PURCHASE PRICE. The seller may bring an action to recover the purchase price, together with incidental damages as described in connection with the action for damages, if (a) the goods have been accepted and there has not been any rightful revocation of acceptance; (b) conforming goods were damaged or destroyed after the risk of loss passed to the buyer; or (c) the seller has identified proper goods to the contract but after the buyer's breach has been or will be unable to resell them at a reasonable price.[9] In consequence of these limitations, the right to sue for the contract price, as distinguished from a suit for damages for breach, is a remedy that is not ordinarily available to the seller.

§ 27:11. REPOSSESSION OF GOODS BY SELLER. The fact that the seller has not been paid does not give him any right to take back or repossess the goods. In modern commercial practice, however, when goods are sold on credit, a provision will ordinarily be included in the contract expressly giving the seller the right to repossess the goods if the buyer defaults in payment,[10] but the mere fact that a sale is made on credit or is an installment sale does not confer any right of repossession.

C. REMEDIES OF THE BUYER

§ 27:12. REJECTION OF IMPROPER DELIVERY. If the goods or the tender made by the seller do not conform to the contract in any respect, the buyer may reject the goods.

---

[7] UCC § 2-708(1); Iverson v Schnack, 263 Wis 266, 57 NW2d 400.
[8] UCC § 2-710.
[9] § 2-709(1).
[10] In addition, a security agreement will ordinarily be executed by the buyer, thus giving rise to a secured transaction.

FACTS: Smith bought a new automobile from Zabriskie Chevrolet. It was represented that the car was a brand-new one that would operate perfectly. Smith's wife drove it from the showroom to their home. Within seven-tenths of a mile, the transmission ceased to function properly and the car would only drive with the transmission set at "low low." Because of this defect, Smith stopped payment on the check which he had given for the purchase price. Zabriskie sued Smith for the purchase price. Smith asserted that there had been a breach of warranty because of which he revoked acceptance of the automobile and canceled the purchase. Zabriskie claimed that the acceptance of the automobile could not be revoked.

DECISION: Judgment for Smith. There had not been any acceptance of the automobile. The mere fact of driving it home was not an acceptance because the buyer did not yet have a reasonable opportunity to examine the goods. His wife's driving home was such an examination. Within a few minutes and a short distance away after the driving home had begun, the defect became apparent, and the buyer had then rejected the automobile as nonconforming. Not having yet accepted the goods, the buyer could reject them as nonconforming. [Zabriskie Chevrolet v Smith, 99 NJSuper 441, 248 A2d 195]

The buyer has the choice (a) of rejecting the entire quantity tendered, (b) of accepting the entire tender, or (c) of accepting any one or more commercial units and rejecting the rest.[11] Delivery of the goods to a carrier is not an "acceptance" of the goods by the buyer. The rejection must be made within a reasonable time after the delivery or tender, and the buyer must notify the seller of his action.[12] A two-month delay bars rejection when several times during this interval the buyer visited the building in which the purchased goods were kept and took away with him several small articles.

After rejecting the goods, the buyer may not exercise any right of ownership as to the goods but must hold them awaiting instructions from the seller.

§ 27:13. REVOCATION OF ACCEPTANCE. The buyer may revoke his acceptance of the goods when they do not conform to the contract to such an extent that the defect substantially impairs their value to him, provided (a) he accepted the goods without knowledge of the nonconformity, because it could not be reasonably discovered or because the seller had assured him that the goods were conforming; or (b) he accepted the goods with knowledge of the nonconformity but reasonably believed that the defect would be cured by the seller.[13] The buyer may not revoke his acceptance merely because the goods do not conform to the contract unless such nonconformity substantially impairs their value to him. Revocation of acceptance may be made not only with respect to the entire quantity of goods but also with respect to any lot or commercial unit that is

[11] UCC § 2-601.
[12] § 2-602(1). The failure to specify the particular ground for rejection may bar the buyer from proving it in a subsequent action. § 2-605. As to the right of the seller to cure the default, see § 2-508.
[13] § 2-608(1).

nonconforming. A buyer who revokes his acceptance stands in the same position as though he had rejected the goods when they had been originally tendered.

(a) Notice of revocation. The acceptance of goods cannot be revoked unless the buyer gives the seller a notice of revocation. This notice must be given within a reasonable time after the buyer discovers that the goods do not conform or after he should have discovered it.

A revocation of acceptance is effective when the buyer notifies the seller. It is not necessary that the buyer make an actual return of the goods in order to make his revocation effective.

(b) Time for revocation. A buyer is not required to notify the seller of his intention to revoke his acceptance until the buyer is reasonably certain that the nonconformity of the goods substantially impairs the value of the goods. Thus, the mere fact that the buyer suspects that the goods do not conform and that such nonconformity substantially impairs the value of the contract does not in itself require that he immediately give notice.

A seller has a reasonable time to attempt to correct defects in the goods, and a buyer is not barred from revoking his acceptance of the goods because he has delayed until the attempts of the seller to correct the defects proved unsuccessful.

§ 27:14. POSSESSION OF GOODS ON SELLER'S INSOLVENCY. The
buyer may have paid in advance for the goods that are still in the seller's possession. Assuming that the seller then becomes insolvent, can the buyer claim the goods from the possession of the seller or is he limited to making a general claim for the refund of the amount paid for them? If the goods have been identified to the contract by either or both the buyer and seller, and the seller becomes insolvent within ten days after payment of the first installment of the price, the buyer is entitled to recover the goods. The buyer who makes a partial payment has a similar right of reclamation if the seller becomes insolvent within ten days after the first payment is made, but he must pay the balance due.[14]

§ 27:15. BUYER'S ACTION FOR DAMAGES FOR NONDELIVERY. If the
seller fails to deliver as required by the contract or repudiates the contract, or if the buyer properly rejects tendered goods or revokes his acceptance as to such goods, the buyer is entitled to sue the seller for damages for breach of contract. The buyer is entitled to recover the difference between the market price at the time the buyer learned of the breach and the contract price.[15]

---

[14] § 2-502.
[15] § 2-713(1). In the case of anticipatory breach, as when the seller states in advance of the delivery date that he will not perform, the buyer has the option of waiting until the performance date or of treating such repudiation as a breach fixing damages as of that time, unless the buyer effects cover. § 2-610.

Within a reasonable time after the seller's breach, the buyer may *cover*, that is, procure the same or similar goods elsewhere. If the buyer acts in good faith, the measure of damages for the seller's nondelivery or repudiation is then the difference between the cost of cover and the contract price.[16]

The buyer is not under any duty to cover as far as direct damages are concerned, but he may not recover for consequential damages that could have been avoided by reasonably effecting cover.[17] For example, when a trucker cannot haul freight for his customers because the truck purchased from the seller is defective, he may recover damages equal to the difference between the value of the truck as it was and as it should have been. If the buyer does not cover by purchasing or renting a truck from another source, he is barred from recovering the lost profits that he could have obtained had he been able to use the original truck in hauling freight for his customers.

In any case, the buyer is entitled to recover incidental damages, but he must give the seller credit for expenses saved as a result of the seller's breach.

§ 27:16. ACTION FOR BREACH OF WARRANTY.

(a) **Notice of breach.** If the buyer has accepted goods that do not conform to the contract or as to which there is a breach of warranty, he must notify the seller of the breach within a reasonable time after he discovers or should have discovered the breach. Otherwise he is not entitled to complain.[18] If the buyer has given the necessary notice of breach, he may recover damages measured by the loss resulting in the normal course of events from the breach.

FACTS: Klein sold water softening equipment. His local agent, Schuster, sold a unit to Kopet. After two weeks the unit showed defects about which Kopet complained to Schuster. After about six months of Schuster's attempting to fix the machine, Kopet notified Klein of the defect. Attempts were made by Klein's repairman to fix the unit. After six more months of attempting to repair the unit, an attorney acting for Kopet wrote Klein that the unit was not operating properly and should be replaced or the purchase price refunded. Klein refused to do either on the ground that Kopet had not given notice within a reasonable time.

DECISION: Judgment for Kopet. Notice had been given within a reasonable time, although the demand for replacement or refund was not made directly to the defendant and not until a year later. The continuing demands upon the defendant's local agent and the attempts, first of the agent, and then of the defendant's repairman, to repair the unit, showed that the letter to the defendant was not the first "notice" the defendant had of the defect. [Kopet v Klein, 275 Minn 525, 148 NW2d 385]

(b) **Measure of damages.** If suit is brought for breach of warranty, the measure of damages is the difference between the value of the goods as they

---

[16] § 2-712(2).
[17] § 2-712(3).
[18] San Antonio v Warwick Ginger Ale Co. 104 RI 700, 248 A2d 778.

were when accepted and the value that they would have had if they had been as warranted.

The buyer may only recover the difference between the contract price and the actual value of the goods.

The buyer may recover as damages for breach of warranty the loss directly and naturally resulting from that breach. In other words, he may recover for the loss proximately resulting from the failure to deliver the goods as warranted.[19]

Whenever the buyer is entitled to recover damages from the seller, he may deduct the amount of them from any balance remaining due on the purchase price provided he notifies the seller that he intends to do so.[20] When the buyer who has accepted the goods is sued for the contract price, he may counterclaim damages for breach of warranty even though the time for revoking the acceptance or rejecting the goods has passed.[21]

(c) Notice of third-party action against buyer. The buyer may be sued in consequence of the seller's breach of warranty, as when the buyer's customers sue him because of the condition of the goods which he has resold to them. In such a case it is optional with the buyer whether or not he gives the seller notice of the action against him and requests the seller to defend the action.[22]

The buyer may also be sued by a third person because of patent infringement. In this case he must give notice of the action to the seller. Moreover, the seller can demand that the buyer turn over the defense of that action to him.[23] When the seller is given notice of a suit against the buyer but fails to defend the buyer, the seller cannot dispute the facts shown in that action when he in turn is sued by the buyer.

§ 27:17. CANCELLATION BY BUYER. The buyer may cancel or rescind the contract if the seller fails to deliver the goods or if he repudiates the contract, or if the buyer has rightfully rejected tendered goods or revoked his acceptance of the goods. When the buyer cancels, he is entitled to recover as much of the purchase price as he has paid, including the value of property given as a trade-in as part of the purchase price. The fact that the buyer cancels the contract does not destroy his cause of action against the seller for breach of contract. The buyer may therefore recover from the seller not only any payment made on the purchase price[24] but, in addition, damages for the breach of the contract. The damages represent the difference between the contract price and the cost of cover if the buyer has purchased other goods.[25]

---

[19] W & W Livestock Enterprises v Dennler (Iowa) 179 NW2d 484.
[20] UCC § 2-717.
[21] Marbelite Co. v Philadelphia, 208 PaSuper 256, 222 A2d 443.
[22] UCC § 2-607(5)(a).
[23] § 2-607(3)(b), (5)(b).
[24] Lanners v Whitney, 247 Ore 223, 428 P2d 398.
[25] UCC § 2-712(1), (2). In any case, the buyer is entitled to recover incidental damages.

FACTS: Barke was a widow who was not employed. She traded in the house trailer that she used as her home for a new trailer, which was sold to her by Grand Mobile Homes Sales. Because of various defects, she later sued Grand Mobile to rescind the sale. Grand Mobile raised the defense that she could not bring the action without first returning or offering to return the trailer to Grand Mobile.

DECISION: A tender was unnecessary. When a buyer is not claiming to have made a rescission, thereafter suing for a price refund and damages, but is instead bringing an action to have the court set aside the transaction, the buyer is not barred by the fact that the goods had not been returned or tendered to the seller but may await the entry of a court decree directing such return. This rule is followed when it would work a great hardship on the buyer to make an earlier tender. In the present case, a surrender of the trailer prior to the bringing of the action would have made the plaintiff homeless for a number of months. [Barke v Grand Mobile Homes Sales, 6 MichApp 386, 149 NW2d 236]

The right of the buyer to cancel or rescind the sales contract may be lost by a delay in exercising that right. A buyer loses the right when he refuses to permit the seller to attempt to make normal adjustments to remedy the defect.

A buyer cannot cancel when with full knowledge of defects in the goods he makes partial payments and performs acts of dominion inconsistent with any intent to cancel.

FACTS: Barnes purchased a used car on credit from Chester Burnham Chevrolet. He made some payments and a dispute then arose over the making of repairs. The seller refused to provide free repairs. Nine months later, Barnes returned the car to Chester. When Chester sued Barnes for the purchase price, Barnes raised the defense that he had rescinded or canceled the sale.

DECISION: There was no cancellation. Barnes could not prove a cancellation by showing that he had returned the car. Cancellation was barred by his long delay and the return could not constitute a cancellation because there was no manifestation of any attempt to cancel the contract. [Barnes v Chester Burnham Chevrolet (Miss) 217 So2d 630]

The mere fact that a written sales contract was not filled in before signing does not entitle a buyer who has received delivery of the goods to cancel the contract,[26] although consumer protection legislation may sometimes prohibit the signing of a sales contract in blank and give the buyer the right to cancel the sale when he has done so.

The fact that the buyer cancels the sale does not destroy his liability on commercial paper which he had already given the seller when such paper is held by a holder in due course or a person having the rights of such a holder.

§ 27:18. BUYER'S RESALE OF GOODS. When the buyer has possession of the goods that he has rightfully rejected or as to which he has revoked his

---

[26] Woods v Van Wallis Trailer Sales Co. 77 NMex 121, 419 P2d 964.

acceptance, he is treated the same as a seller in possession of goods after the default of a buyer. That is, he has a security interest in the goods for his claim against the other party and may resell the goods as though he were a seller. From the proceeds of the sale he is entitled to deduct for himself any payments made on the price and any expenses reasonably incurred in the inspection, receipt, transportation, care and custody, and resale of the goods.[27]

§ 27:19. ACTION FOR CONVERSION OR RECOVERY OF GOODS. When, as a result of the sales agreement, ownership passes to the buyer and the seller wrongfully refuses or neglects to deliver the goods, the buyer may maintain any action allowed by law to the owner of goods wrongfully converted or withheld.

The obligation of the seller to deliver proper goods may be enforced by an order for specific performance when the goods are "unique or in other proper circumstances."[28]

The fact that the contract price is unusually low does not establish that the goods are unique so as to entitle the buyer to specific performance. If the buyer is required to pay more for the goods elsewhere, he will be adequately compensated by recovering the difference between the contract and such price when he claims damages from the seller.[29]

§ 27:20. REMEDIES FOR FRAUD OF SELLER. Independently of the preceding remedies, the buyer has the right to sue the seller for damages for the latter's fraud or to cancel the transaction on that ground. As these remedies for fraud exist independently of the provisions of the UCC, the buyer may assert such remedies even when he is barred by the UCC from exercising any remedy for a breach of warranty.

The general principles of agency law remain in force under the UCC and a seller will be held liable for the fraud of his agent in effecting a sale.

Suit for fraud is generally not a satisfactory solution for the consumer because of the difficulty of proving the existence of fraud. Likewise, some courts require him to show fraud by clear and convincing proof; and it is not sufficient to prove the existence of fraud by a mere preponderance of evidence, although that ordinarily is a sufficient degree of proof in civil litigation.

FACTS: The Peerless Corporation sold 50 appliances to a dealer, the Hammond Appliance Co. The seller then assigned its contract to Walter E. Heller & Co. When Heller sued Hammond for the purchase price, the latter showed that following the purchase, the seller and it had agreed that the goods were defective and had mutually rescinded the contract. In spite of this, the seller never came to pick up the goods although Hammond repeatedly requested it to do so. After about a year, Hammond began repairing the appliances and finally sold 27 of the 50,

---

[27] UCC § 2-715(1).
[28] § 2-716(1).
[29] Hilmor Sales Co. v Helen Neushaefer (NY) 6 UCCRS 325.

still having possession of the remaining 23 at the time of the trial. At the trial, in addition to denying liability, Hammond made a counterclaim for the cost of repairing the appliances, the cost of their storage while waiting for the seller to retake them, and the cost of moving the appliances from one store to another in the effort to sell them.

DECISION: Judgment for Hammond Appliance. It was entitled to cancel the contract for nonconformity. Moreover, when the seller failed to reclaim the properly rejected goods, the buyer was entitled to sell them after the lapse of a reasonable time and to hold the proceeds of the sale for the account of the seller. The buyer was entitled to reimbursement for incidental expenses which he had incurred in caring for the goods and in making the sale. [Walter E. Heller & Co. v Hammond Appliance Co. 29 NJ 589, 151 A2d 537]

D. CONTRACT PROVISIONS ON REMEDIES

§ 27:21. **LIMITATION OF DAMAGES.** The parties may in their sales contract specify that in the event of breach by either party the damages are to be limited to a certain amount. If this amount is unreasonably large, it is void as a penalty. If the amount is reasonable, the injured party is limited to recovering that amount. Whether the limitation is reasonable is determined in the light of the actual harm that would be caused by breach, the difficulty of proving the amount of such loss, and the inconvenience and impracticality of suing for damages or enforcing other remedies for breach.[30]

§ 27:22. **DOWN PAYMENTS AND DEPOSITS.** The buyer may have made a deposit with the seller or an initial or down payment at the time of making the contract. If the contract contains a valid liquidation-of-damages provision and the buyer defaults, the seller must return any part of the down payment or deposit in excess of the amount specified by the liquidated damages clause. In the absence of such a clause, and in the absence of proof of greater damages sustained by him, the seller's damages are computed as 20 percent of the purchase price or $500, whichever is the smaller. The extent to which the down payment exceeds such amount must be returned to the buyer.

The rule just stated applies to payments made by the buyer in goods as well as in cash as, for example, by making a trade-in. Such goods given in payment are assigned a dollar value for the purpose of determining the payment made by the buyer. If the goods have been resold, their value is the proceeds of the resale; if not, it is the reasonable value of such goods.

§ 27:23. **LIMITATION OF REMEDIES.** The parties may validly limit the remedies. Thus, a seller may specify that the only remedy of the buyer for breach of warranty shall be the repair or replacement of the goods, or that the buyer shall be limited to returning the goods and obtaining a refund of the purchase price. How much further the restrictions may go is not clear, but the limitation is not binding if it is unreasonable or unconscionable.

---

[30] UCC § 2-718(1).

FACTS: Dow Corning contracted to purchase an airplane from Capitol Aviation with delivery to be made in August, 1965. Both parties knew that the plane was being developed experimentally by Aero-Commander, Inc., and Capitol contracted to purchase the plane from Aero. Delivery of the plane was not made to Dow; and when Dow sued Capitol for breach of contract, Capitol sued Aero for breach of its contract with Aero. Aero defended on the ground that this latter contract limited its liability for nondelivery to a return of any payment made by Capitol on the purchase price. Capitol claimed that such limitation was void under the Code.

DECISION: The limitation was binding in view of the unknown experimental character of producing the goods and the fact that the contract was between parties with equal experience and bargaining power. [Dow Corning Corp. v Capitol Aviation, Inc. (CA7 Ill) 411 F2d 622]

The limitation of consequential damages for personal injuries caused by defective goods is prima facie unconscionable, and therefore prima facie not binding, when the goods are sold for consumption by the buyer.[31] Thus, the warranty-defendant cannot rely on a limitation of liability provision in such a case unless the defendant meets the burden of showing that the limitation of liability is commercially reasonable and fair rather than oppressive and surprising. That is, the warranty-defendant cannot defend by the limitation provision against a claim for personal injuries unless he can prove that the limitation is not unconscionable. Moreover, when the seller would be liable to his buyer for a breach of warranty, the seller cannot exclude liability for personal injuries to members of the buyer's family, his household, or his guests.[32] When the seller knows that the failure of the product, such as a harvester, to perform will cause serious economic loss, a limitation of damages for breach to the return of the purchase price is void as unconscionable.[33]

The provision limiting the seller's obligation to the repair of the goods or the replacement of defective parts fails of its essential purpose and is not binding when the seller is unable or refuses to make the goods function properly within a reasonable time; because the buyer is entitled to goods which will be fit to the extent required by the particular warranties which have been made expressly or which are implied.[34]

§ 27:24. WAIVER OF DEFENSES.

A buyer may be barred from objecting to a breach of the contract by the seller because the buyer has waived his right to do so.

(a) Express waiver. When sales are made on credit, the seller will ordinarily plan to assign the sales contract to a bank or other financer and thereby convert into immediate cash his customer's obligation to pay in

---

[31] § 2-719(3).

[32] § 2-318.

[33] Steele v Case Co. 197 Kan 554, 419 P2d 902 (pre-Code but citing UCC § 2-719(3) "as evidencing a trend of modern thought").

[34] Kohlenberger, Inc. v Tyson's Foods, Inc. (Ark) 510 SW2d 555.

the future. To make the transaction more attractive to banks and financers, the credit seller will generally include in the sales contract with each buyer a *waiver of defense* clause. By this clause the buyer agrees that he will not assert against the seller's assignee any defense which he has against the seller. For example, if the television set does not work properly, the buyer agrees that he will only complain to the seller. He will not complain to the seller's assignee but will continue to pay the assignee just as though everything were satisfactory.

(b) Implied waiver. When the buyer executes a promissory note as part of the credit transaction described above, he automatically waives with respect to the seller's assignee any defense which he could not raise against a holder in due course of the note. This will be considered in greater detail in the chapters on commercial paper. What it means in the ordinary situation is that when the buyer signs a promissory note for the balance due he cannot assert against the finance company or the bank the defense that he never got the goods called for by the contract, that the goods were defective and did not work, or that he had entered into the contract because of fraudulent misstatements of the seller.

(c) Validity. Consumer protection statutes commonly nullify the waiver of defenses by providing that the buyer may assert against the seller's transferee any defense which he might have against the seller. Under some statutes the buyer must give notice of his defense within a specified number of days after being notified of the assignment. Some courts extend consumer protection beyond the scope of the statute by ignoring a time limitation on the giving of notice of defenses.[35]

QUESTIONS AND CASE PROBLEMS

1. *B* purchased a television set from *S*. There was something wrong with the color, and *S*'s serviceman was not able to correct the defect in *B*'s home. The serviceman told *B* that the defect could be corrected if he took the set to his shop. *B* refused to allow this and declared that he canceled the sale. Was he entitled to do so? [See Wilson v Scampoli (DistColApp) 228 A2d 848]
2. After a sales contract was made, the seller's factory was destroyed by fire. The seller and the buyer then agreed to cancel the contract. Thereafter the seller's factory was rebuilt, and the buyer demanded that the seller perform the contract. Was the seller required to do so? [See Goddard v Ishikawajima-Harima Heavy Industries Co. 29 AppDiv2d 754, 287 NYS2d 901]

---

[35] Star Credit Corp. v Molina, 59 Misc2d 290, 298 NYS2d 570.

3. A seller sold goods to a buyer on credit. The buyer did not pay for the goods. The seller claimed that the title to the goods revested in him because of the buyer's default. Was he correct? [See Jordan v Butler, 182 Neb 626, 156 NW2d 778]

4. Carta bought from Barker, a dealer, a bicycle that was manufactured by the Union Cycle Co. He took it home for his minor daughter. Sandra, a guest at the Carta home, was injured while using the bicycle. Suit was brought against the town of Cheshire, claiming that it had defectively maintained the road, and against the manufacturer, claiming that the bicycle was defectively constructed. The manufacturer, Union Cycle, defended on the ground that Sandra had not given it notice of the defect in the bicycle as required by UCC § 2-607. Decide. [Tomczuk v Town of Cheshire, 26 ConnSupp 219, 217 A2d 71]

5. Wolosin purchased a vegetable and dairy refrigerator case from the Evans Manufacturing Corp. Evans sued Wolosin for the purchase price. Wolosin raised as a defense a claim for damages for breach of warranty. The sales contract provided that Evans would replace defective parts free of charge for one year and that "this warranty is in lieu of any and all other warranties stated or inferred, and of all other obligations on the part of the manufacturer, which neither assumes nor authorizes anyone to assume for it any other obligations or liability in connection with the sale of its products." Evans claimed that it was only liable for replacement of parts. Wolosin claimed that the quoted clause was not sufficiently specific to satisfy the requirement of UCC § 2-719. Decide. [Evans Mfg. Corp. v Wolosin (Pa) 47 Luzerne County Leg Reg 238]

6. The buyer of a truck noticed on the first day he drove it that the speed control was defective and that the truck used excessive oil. He continued to use the truck and made several payments. Five months later he demanded that the seller take the truck back. Decide. [See Hudspeth Motors, Inc. v Wilkinson, 238 Ark 410, 382 SW2d 191; Marbelite Co. v Philadelphia, 208 PaSuper 256, 222 A2d 443]

7. The buyer of goods at an auction sale did not pay for and take the goods. The auctioneer sued the buyer for the amount of the buyer's bid. Was the buyer liable for that amount? [See French v Sotheby & Co. (Okla) 470 P2d 318]

8. McInnis purchased a tractor and scraper as new equipment of current model from the Western Tractor & Equipment Co. The written contract stated that the seller disclaimed all warranties and that no warranties existed except as were stated in the contract. Actually, the equipment was not the current model but that of the prior year. Likewise, the equipment was not new but had been used for 68 hours as a demonstrator model and then the hour meter had been reset to zero. The buyer sued the seller for damages. The latter defended on the ground that all liability for warranties had been disclaimed. Was this defense valid? [McInnis v Western Tractor & Equipment Co. 63 Wash2d 652, 388 P2d 562]

9. Skopes Rubber Corp. purchased skin-diving suits from the United States Rubber Co. The sale was made on the basis of a sample on which the vinyl coating on the suits had been hand applied and was smooth. The suits that were delivered were wrinkled because the vinyl had been machine applied. In use, the suits split at the wrinkle lines. Skopes returned the first installment of the suits because of this defect. He then sued United States Rubber Co. for breach of warranty. It raised the defense that by returning the first installment, Skopes had rescinded the contract and could not thereafter sue for damages. Was this correct? [Skopes Rubber Corp. v United States Rubber Co. (CA1 Mass) 299 F2d 584]

NATURE, KINDS, AND PARTIES

§ 28:1. DEFINITION. *Commercial paper* includes written promises (such as promissory notes) or orders (such as checks or drafts) to pay money that may be transferred by the process of negotiation. Much of the importance of commercial paper lies in the fact that it is more readily transferred than ordinary contract rights and that the transferee of commercial paper may acquire greater rights than would an ordinary assignee. A person who acquires a commercial paper may therefore be subject to less risk.

§ 28:2. FUNCTIONS OF COMMERCIAL PAPER. Commercial paper often serves as a substitute for money.

FACTS: Stainton bid at a public auction of public lands conducted by Ocean City, New Jersey. Kensil, the second highest bidder, brought suit against Ocean City and Stainton to set aside the sale on the ground that Stainton did not comply with the statute which required that a deposit of 20 percent of the bid be "paid" by the successful bidder. He based his claim on the fact that Stainton delivered to Ocean City an uncertified check drawn on an account which was insufficient to meet the check at that moment, although the check was thereafter honored by the drawee bank.

DECISION: Judgment against Kensil. Although he was technically correct that the delivery of the check did not constitute the making of payment at the time that the check was delivered, the check was in fact paid. The city, as the other contracting party, had not objected to the payment by check; and the public had not been harmed by the payment by check. [Kensil v Ocean City, 89 NJSuper 342, 215 A2d 43]

When a person pays a debt by check, he is using a commercial paper. He might have paid in cash, but for convenience and possibly for safety, he used commercial paper. Such payment is usually conditional upon the instrument being paid.[1]

---

[1] Uniform Commercial Code § 3-802(1); Makel Textiles v Dolly Originals (NY) 4 UCCRS 95.

Commercial paper may create credit. If a debtor gives his creditor a promissory note by which he agrees to pay him in 60 days, that is the same as an agreement that the creditor will not attempt to collect the claim until 60 days later.

§ 28:3. KINDS OF COMMERCIAL PAPER. Commercial paper falls into four categories: (a) promissory notes, (b) drafts or bills of exchange, (c) checks, and (d) certificates of deposit.

(a) **Promissory notes.** A *negotiable promissory note* is an unconditional promise in writing made by one person to another, signed by the maker, engaging to pay on demand or at a definite time a sum certain in money to order or to bearer.[2]

If the promissory note is payable "on demand," that is, immediately, it may be used as a substitute for money. If it is not payable until a future time, the payee in effect extends credit to the maker of the note for the period of time until payment is due.

$ *200 00*	Albany, New York *July 6,* 19 *76*
One year	after date *I* promise to pay to
the order of *Ronald Adams* PAYEE	
Two hundred	Dollars
Payable at *First Union Bank*	
with interest at *6* %.	
No. *21* Due *July 6, 1977*	*John Clark*

Promissory Note

Parties: maker (buyer, borrower, or debtor)—John Clark;
payee (seller, lender, or creditor)—Ronald Adams.

(b) **Drafts.** A *negotiable draft* or *bill of exchange* is an unconditional order in writing addressed by one person to another, signed by the person giving it, requiring the person to whom it is addressed to pay on demand or at a definite time a sum certain in money to order or to bearer.[3] In effect, it is an order by one person upon a second person to pay a sum of money. The person who gives the order is called the *drawer* and is said to draw the bill. The person on whom the order to pay is drawn is the *drawee*. The person to whom payment is to be made is the payee. The drawer may designate himself as the payee.

The drawee who is ordered to pay the money is not bound to do so unless he accepts the order. After he accepts, he may be identified as the *acceptor*.

[2] UCC § 3-104(1).
[3] § 3-104(1).

```
$ 400.00                        Des Moines, Iowa  September 8,    19 76
Thirty days after date                                           ____ PAY TO THE
ORDER OF  Freedom National Bank                                  _____
Four hundred                                                     ____ DOLLARS
VALUE RECEIVED AND CHARGE TO ACCOUNT OF
TO  Harold Monroe
No. 12      Iowa City, Iowa       Jean Jefferson
```

Draft (Bill of Exchange)

Drawer (seller or creditor)—Jefferson; drawee (buyer or debtor)—Monroe;
payee (seller's or creditor's bank)—Freedom National Bank.

From the practice of "accepting" a bill of exchange, the term "trade acceptance" is sometimes applied to these instruments.

(1) Sight and Time Drafts. A *sight draft* is one that is payable on sight or when the holder presents it to the drawee for payment. A *time draft* is payable at a stated time after sight, such as "30 days after sight" or "30 days after acceptance," or at a stated time after a certain date, such as "30 days after date" (of instrument).

(2) Domestic and International Bills. If a draft is drawn and payable in the same state, or is drawn in one state and payable in another, it is a *domestic bill*. If it appears on the face of the instrument that it was drawn in one nation but is payable in another, it is an *international bill of exchange* or a foreign draft.

(3) Trade Acceptances. A time draft may be sent by a seller of goods to the buyer, as drawee, with the understanding that the buyer will accept the draft, thereby assuming primary liability for its payment. This type of paper is a *trade acceptance*.

(c) Checks. A *check* is a draft drawn on a bank payable on demand.[4] It is an order by a depositor (the drawer) upon his bank (the drawee) to pay a sum of money to the order of another person (the payee). A check is always drawn upon a bank as drawee and is always payable upon demand.

(1) Cashier's Checks. A *cashier's check* is drawn by a bank upon itself, ordering itself to pay the stated sum of money to the depositor or to the person designated by him. The depositor requests his bank to issue a cashier's check for a given amount, which amount either the depositor pays the bank or the bank charges against the depositor's account. The depositor then forwards the cashier's check, instead of his own, to the seller or creditor.

---

[4] § 3-104(2)(b).

(2) Bank Drafts. A *bank draft* is in effect a check drawn by one bank upon another bank in which the first bank has money on deposit, in the same way that a depositor draws a check upon his own bank. It is commonly used for the same purpose as a cashier's check.

(d) Certificates of deposit. A *certificate of deposit* is an instrument issued by a bank that acknowledges the deposit of a specific sum of money and promises to pay the holder of the certificate that amount, usually with interest, when the certificate is surrendered.[5]

§ 28:4. PARTIES TO COMMERCIAL PAPER. A note has two original parties—the maker and the payee; and a draft or a check has three original parties—the drawer, the drawee, and the payee. In addition to these original parties, a commercial paper may have one or more of the parties described under (d) through (i) of this section.

(a) Maker. The *maker* is the person who writes out and creates a promissory note. If the paper is not a promissory note, this person has a different name, as the drawer of a check. It is essential to bear in mind the distinction between a maker and a drawer for the reason that the liability of the maker is primary while that of a drawer is secondary.

(b) Drawer. The *drawer* is the person who writes out and creates a draft. This includes bills of exchange, trade acceptances, and checks. The liability of a drawer is secondary.

(c) Payee. The *payee* is the person named on the face of the paper to receive payment. In "pay to the order of John Jones," the named person, John Jones, is the payee.

A payee has no rights in the paper until it is delivered to him. He is not liable on the paper in any way until he transfers the paper or receives payment.

(d) Indorser.[6] A person who owns a commercial paper may transfer it to another person by signing his name on the back of the instrument and delivering it to the other person. When he does so, he is an *indorser*. Thus, if a check is made payable to the order of *P* to pay a bill owed to him, *P* may indorse it to *E* to pay a debt that *P* owes *E*. In such a case *P*, who is the payee of the check since it was originally made payable to him, is now also an indorser.

(e) Indorsee. The person to whom an indorsement is made is called an *indorsee*. He in turn may indorse the instrument; in that case he is also an indorser.

(f) Bearer. The person in physical possession of a commercial paper which is payable to bearer is called a *bearer*.

---

[5] A certificate of deposit "is an acknowledgement by a bank of receipt of money with an engagement to repay it," as distinguished from a note, which "is a promise other than a certificate of deposit." UCC § 3-104(2)(c), (d).

[6] The form *endorse* is commonly used in business. The form *indorse* is used in the UCC.

(g) Holder. A *holder* is a person in possession of a commercial paper which is payable at that time either to him, as payee or indorsee, or to bearer. A holder may be (1) a holder for value or (2) a holder in due course.

(1) Holder for Value. Ordinarily a commercial paper is given to a person in the course of business in return for or in payment for something. If the holder gives consideration for the instrument or takes it in payment of a debt, he is a *holder for value.* Thus, if an employee is paid wages by check, he is a holder for value of the check since he received it in payment of wages earned and due. If he indorses the check to his landlord to pay the rent, the landlord becomes the holder for value.

A person may receive a commercial paper without giving anything for it. Thus, when an aunt gives her niece a check for $100 as a birthday present, the niece becomes the owner or holder, but she has not given anything for the check and she is not a holder for value.

(2) Holder in Due Course. A person who becomes a holder of the paper under certain circumstances is given a favored standing and is immune from certain defenses. He is termed a *holder in due course.* A person becoming the holder of an instrument at any time after it was once held by a holder in due course is described as a *holder through a holder in due course.* He is ordinarily given the same special rights as a holder in due course.

(h) Accommodation party. A person who becomes a party to a commercial paper in order to add the strength of his name to the paper for the benefit of another party thereto is called an *accommmodation party.*

FACTS: DeGroot borrowed money from the Bucks County Bank & Trust Company. The loan was used to pay the debt of her friend, DiMiglio. DeGroot signed a promissory note for the amount of the loan. When sued on the note, DeGroot claimed that she was an accommodation maker.

DECISION: She was not an accommodation maker. Even though DiMiglio was benefited by the transaction, DiMiglio was not a party to the paper. DeGroot was therefore liable as an ordinary maker and not as an accommodation party. [Bucks County Bank & Trust Co. v DeGroot 226 PaSuper 419, 313 A2d 357]

Parol evidence is admissible to determine whether a party is an accommodation party, the manner of signing not being controlling.[7]

An accommodation party is liable for payment of the paper regardless of whether he signs the paper merely as a friend or because he is paid for doing so.[8] When the paper is taken for value before it is due, the accommodation party is liable in the capacity in which he signed, even though the holder knows of his accommodation character.

The accommodation party is not liable to the party accommodated.[9] If the accommodation party is required to pay the instrument, he may recover the amount of the payment from the person accommodated.

---

[7] White v Household Finance Corp. (IndApp) 302 NE2d 828.
[8] UCC § 3-415(1).
[9] § 3-415(5). United Refrigerator Co. v Applebaum, 410 Pa 210, 189 A2d 253.

(i) Guarantor. A *guarantor* is a person who signs a commercial paper and adds a statement that he will pay the instrument under certain circumstances. Ordinarily this is done by merely adding "payment guaranteed" or "collection guaranteed" to the signature of the guarantor on the paper.

The addition of "payment guaranteed" or similar words means that the guarantor will pay the instrument when due even though the holder of the paper has not sought payment from any other party. "Collection guaranteed" or similar words means that the guarantor will not pay the paper until after the holder has sought to collect payment from the maker or acceptor and has been unable to do so. In such a case the holder must first obtain a judgment against the maker or acceptor, which judgment remains unpaid because the sheriff cannot find sufficient property of the debtor in question to pay it, or the debtor must be insolvent.[10]

When a guarantor makes a guarantee of payment, he is liable upon his guarantee and it is immaterial that payment was not demanded from the primary debtor nor that the debtor had sufficient assets to pay the paper.

> **FACTS:** Ruth Laudati obtained a student loan from Brown University and signed a promissory note for the repayment of the loan. Her mother, Josephine, guaranteed payment of the note. When the note was not paid, Brown University sued Josephine. She raised the defense that Brown had not sued Ruth.
>
> **DECISION:** A guarantor of payment may be sued upon default on the paper and the holder is not required to proceed against any other party before suing the guarantor. [Brown University v Laudati (RI) 320 A2d 609]

If the meaning of the guaranty is not clear, it is construed as a guaranty of payment. For example, when an indorser adds a statement that the paper is "guaranteed" or adds the word "guarantor" after his signature without specifying whether it is payment or collection which is guaranteed, the indorser is deemed to be a guarantor of payment, with the consequence that the holder of the paper may proceed directly against such guarantor without first proceeding against any other party on the paper.

The liability of a guarantor is as extensive as that of the original debtor.

§ **28:5. LIABILITY OF PARTIES.** A person who by the terms of the instrument is absolutely required to pay is primarily liable. For a note, the maker is primarily liable; for a draft, the acceptor (the drawee who has accepted) is primarily liable. A guarantor of payment is primarily liable in any case. Other parties are either secondarily or conditionally liable, as in the case of an indorser, or they are not liable in any capacity. A person who transfers the paper but does not sign it is not liable for its payment.[11]

---

[10] UCC § 3-416(1)(2). The guaranty written on the commercial paper is binding without regard to the requirements of a local statute of frauds. § 3-416(6).

[11] § 3-401(1). Such a person, however, may be bound by certain warranties that bind any person who transfers commercial paper.

Each party liable on commercial paper may be sued individually by the holder. Modern procedure generally permits the plaintiff-holder to join as many persons as he chooses who are liable as defendants in one action on the paper. A defendant who is sued cannot object that the plaintiff has omitted other parties who could also have been sued.

FACTS: Pardi drew a check to the order of Schnell who indorsed it to Shotts. Thereafter Pardi stopped payment on the check because Schnell had broken his contract with Pardi. Shotts sued Pardi. Pardi raised the defense that Schnell should be joined in the action as a codefendant.

DECISION: Joinder was not required. The liability of a drawer is separate from that of a payee who becomes an indorser. The holder may therefore sue the drawer without joining the payee-indorser as a codefendant. [Shotts v Pardi (TexCivApp) 483 SW2d 879]

QUESTIONS AND CASE PROBLEMS

1. Cortner and Wood, in payment for certain sheep, executed and delivered an instrument whereby they promised to pay $2,000 to the order of W. C. Thomas. Thomas signed his name on the back and delivered the note to Fox, at the latter's bank in Lewisburg, Tennessee. Who of the foregoing parties, if any, are properly described as (a) payee, (b) maker, (c) drawer, (d) indorser, (e) acceptor, (f) drawee, and (g) indorsee? [See Fox v Cortner, 145 Tenn 482, 239 SW 1069]

2. Kay was the holder of a note. Sadler indorsed the note and added "Guarantor" after his name. When Kay demanded payment, Sadler claimed that he was not required to pay until Kay had first obtained a judgment against the primary party. Was he correct? [Sadler v Kay, 120 GaApp 758, 172 SE2d 202]

3. Herbert Simms owed money to Personal Finance, Inc., on a note signed only by him. Personal Finance brought a lawsuit against both Herbert and Katie, his wife. What liability, if any, did she have on the note? [Personal Finance, Inc. v Simms (LaApp) 123 So2d 646]

4. Herdlicka and Thieda executed a promissory note as makers. The latter was, in fact, an accommodation party. Subsequently Kratovil, the holder of the note, agreed with Herdlicka to extend the time for paying the note and to reduce the monthly payments that were to be made. When the note was not paid in full, Kratovil sued Thieda who claimed that he was released by the fact that the obligation of Herdlicka had been changed by the extension of time, which was made without Thieda's consent. Decide. [Kratovil v Thieda, 62 IllApp2d 234, 210 NE2d 819]

5. B wished to pay a bill that he owed to C but did not have sufficient money in his bank. He drew a postdated check on his bank account and gave it to A. A then

gave *B* a check drawn on *A*'s bank account for the amount of *B*'s check. When *A* was sued on his check by *C*, *A* claimed that he was an accommodation party. Was he correct? [See Midtown Commercial Corp. v Kelner, 29 AppDiv2d 349, 288 NYS2d 122]

6. McCornick & Co. brought suit against the Gem State Oil Co. on an instrument that bore the following notation in the margin:

> The obligation of the acceptor of this bill arises out of the purchase of goods from the drawer. Upon the acceptor hereof suspending payment, giving a chattel mortgage, suffering a fire loss, [or] disposing of his business, . . . this [instrument], at the option of the holder, shall immediately become due and payable.

What kind of an instrument was this? [McCornick & Co. v Gem State Oil & Products Co. 38 Idaho 470, 222 P 286]

7. Fowler, Allen, and Flanagan signed a promissory note as makers. When Majors sued them on the note, Flanagan claimed that he had signed for the accommodation of the other parties and therefore was only liable as a surety (undertaking to become primarily liable for the obligation), and that his liability was therefore not determined under the law governing negotiable instruments. Was he correct? [Flanagan v Majors, 85 GaApp 31, 67 SE2d 786]

8. The Collins Wholesale Drug Company owed money to Warner-Lambert Pharmaceutical Company. Collins executed 13 promissory notes to cover 13 installments of the debt. The notes provided that upon default in any installment, the holder could accelerate the balance which was due. The notes also promised to pay the holder's attorneys' fees. Sylk indorsed all of these notes and added a guaranty of payment to the indorsement. Collins failed to pay one of the notes when due. Warner-Lambert accelerated the entire unpaid balance and sued Sylk for this amount together with attorneys' fees. Sylk raised the defense that he was not liable for attorneys' fees and that the notes could not be accelerated as to him. Was this defense valid? [Warner-Lambert Pharmaceutical Co. v Sylk (CA3 Pa) 471 F2d 1137]

NEGOTIABILITY

§ 29:1. REQUIREMENTS OF NEGOTIABILITY. In order to be negotiable, an instrument must be (a) in writing and (b) signed by the maker or drawer; it must contain (c) a promise or order (d) of an unconditional character (e) to pay in money (f) a sum certain; (g) it must be payable on demand or at a definite time; and (h) it must be payable to order or bearer.[1] (i) If one of the parties is a drawee, he must be identified with reasonable certainty.

In addition to these formal requirements, the instrument usually must be delivered or issued by the maker or drawer to the payee or the latter's agent with the intent that it be effective and create a legal obligation.

If an instrument is not negotiable, the rights of the parties are governed by the general body of contract law.[2]

(a) Writing. A commercial paper must be in writing. Writing includes handwriting, typing, printing, and any other method of setting words down. The use of a pencil is not wise because such writing is not as durable as ink and the instrument may be more easily altered. A commercial paper may be partly printed and partly typewritten with a handwritten signature.

(1) Parol Evidence. As the commercial paper is in writing, the parol evidence rule applies. This rule prohibits modifying the instrument by proving the existence of a conflicting oral agreement alleged to have been made before or at the time of the execution of the commercial paper.

(b) Signature. The instrument must be signed by the maker or drawer. His signature usually appears at the lower right-hand corner of the face of the instrument, but it is immaterial where the signature is placed. If the signature is placed on the instrument in such a manner that it does not in itself clearly indicate that the signer was the maker, drawer, or acceptor, however, the signer is held to be only an indorser.

---

[1] Uniform Commercial Code § 3-104(1).

[2] Business Aircraft Corp. v Electronic Communications (TexCivApp) 391 SW2d 70. Note however, that if the nonnegotiability results from the fact that the instrument is not payable to order or bearer, it is governed by Article 3 of the Code with the limitation that there cannot be a holder in due course of such paper. UCC § 3-805.

The signature itself may consist of the full name or of any symbol adopted for that purpose. It may consist of initials, figures, or a mark.[3] A person signing a trade or an assumed name is liable to the same extent as though he signed his own name.[4]

In the absence of a local statute that provides otherwise, the signature may be made by pencil, by typewriter, by print, or by stamp, as well as by pen.

(1) Agent. A signature may be made for a person by his authorized agent.[5] No particular form of authorization to an agent to execute or sign a commercial paper is required.

An agent signing should indicate that he acts in a representative capacity, and he should disclose his principal. When he does both, the agent is not liable if he has acted within the scope of his authority.[6] The representative capacity of an officer of an organization is sufficiently shown when he signs his name and the title of his office either before or after the organization name.[7]

(2) Nondisclosure of Agency. If a person who signs a commercial paper in a representative capacity, such as an officer or other agent of a corporation, executes the instrument in such a way as to make it appear that it is his own act, he is personally bound with respect to subsequent holders, regardless of whether he intended it to be his own act or an act in his representative capacity.

FACTS: Nichols was the president of Mr. Carl's Fashions, Inc. The corporation did business under the name of the Fashion Beauty Salon. Nichols executed a promissory note which appeared to be signed by the Fashion Beauty Salon and by Nichols. There was nothing on the note to indicate that he signed in a representative capacity. When Seale sued Nichols on the note, the latter raised the defense that he had signed as president of the corporation.

DECISION: Judgment against Nichols. The paper did not disclose that he had signed in a representative capacity. Seale was not the original payee of the paper and therefore Nichols could not show by parol evidence that he had in fact acted in a representative capacity. The fact that he may have had the subjective intent of acting on behalf of the corporation was immaterial if that intent was not disclosed. Nichols was therefore personally bound by the paper. [Seale v Nichols (Tex) 505 SW2d 251]

As to subsequent holders, parol evidence is not admissible to show that it was not intended that the representative or agent be bound or to show

---

[3] When a signature consists of a mark made by a person who is illiterate or physically incapacitated, it is commonly required that the name of the person be placed upon the instrument by someone else, who may be required to sign the instrument as a witness. Any form of signature is sufficient in consequence of the definition of "signed" as including any symbol executed or adopted by a party with the present intention to authenticate a writing. UCC § 1-201(39).

[4] § 3-401(2).

[5] § 3-403(1).

[6] § 3-403; Childs v Hampton, 80 GaApp 748, 57 SE2d 291.

[7] UCC § 3-403(3).

that it was intended to bind the undisclosed principal. Such evidence is admissible, however, against the person with whom the officer or agent had dealt.

When the representative is personally bound because he fails to disclose his representative capacity, he is jointly and severally liable with the principal. For example, when the name of the corporation appears as maker with the name of its treasurer signed immediately below but without any notation indicating a representative capacity, the treasurer is jointly and severally liable with the corporation.

(3) Partial Disclosure of Agency. The instrument may read or the agent may sign in a way that either identifies his principal or discloses the agent's representative capacity; but both are not done. In such a case, the agent is personally liable on the instrument to third persons acquiring the instrument; but if sued by the person with whom he dealt, he may prove that it was intended that the principal should be bound.[8]

(c) Promise or order to pay. A promissory note must contain a promise to pay money.[9] No particular form of promise is required; the intention as gathered from the face of the instrument controls. If the maker uses such phrases as "I certify to pay" or "the maker obliges himself to pay," a promise is implied; but a mere acknowledgment of a debt, such as a writing stating "I.O.U.," is not a commercial paper.

A draft or check must contain an order or command to pay money.[10] As in the case of a promise in a note, no particular form of order or command is required.

(d) Unconditional. The promise or order to pay must be unconditional. For example, when an instrument makes the duty to pay dependent upon the completion of the construction of a building or upon its placement in a particular location, the promise is conditional and the instrument is nonnegotiable. A promise to pay "when able" is generally interpreted as being conditional.[11]

The use of a term of politeness, such as "please," before an otherwise unconditional order to pay does not destroy the effect of the order within the meaning of the requirements for negotiability. But if the effect of the provision is only to seek payment of money or to request it if certain facts are true, the "order" to pay is conditional and the instrument is nonnegotiable.

An order for the payment of money out of a particular fund, such as ten dollars from next week's salary, is conditional.[12] If, however, the instrument is based upon the general credit of the drawer and the reference to a particular fund is merely to indicate a source of reimbursement for the

---

[8] § 3-403(2)(b).
[9] § 3-104(1)(b).
[10] § 3-104(1)(b).
[11] A minority of states regard such a promise as requiring payment within a reasonable time and as therefore being an absolute promise. Mock v First Baptist Church, 252 Ky 243, 67 SW2d 9.
[12] UCC § 3-105(2)(b).

drawee, such as "charge my expense account," the order is considered to be absolute.[13]

> **FACTS:** Wilkes, the agent of the Cow Creek Sheep Co., drew a company check on the First National Bank payable to Brown. On the check was the notation "For Wilkes." Before Brown cashed the check, the company told the bank not to pay the check. When the bank refused to make payment, Brown sued the company. The company defended on the ground that there was no consideration for the promise and that consideration was necessary because the check was nonnegotiable since it did not contain an unconditional order to pay.

> **DECISION:** Judgment for Brown. Paper is not made nonnegotiable because it contains a recital of the purpose for which it is drawn or the account to be charged with its payment. [Brown v Cow Creek Sheep Co. 21 Wyo 1, 126 P 886]

A promise or order that is otherwise unconditional is not made conditional by the fact that it "is limited to payment out of a particular fund or the proceeds of a particular source, if the instrument is issued by a government or governmental agency or unit; or is limited to payment out of the entire assets of a partnership, unincorporated association, trust, or estate by or on behalf of which the instrument is issued."[14]

(e) Payment in money. A commercial paper must call for payment in *money*, that is, any circulating medium of exchange which is legal tender at the place of payment. It is immaterial, as far as negotiability is concerned, whether it calls for payment in a particular kind of current money. If the order or promise is not for money, the instrument is not negotiable. For example, an instrument which requires the holder to take stock or goods in lieu of money is nonnegotiable.

An instrument is also nonnegotiable when the promise or order to pay money is coupled with an agreement by the maker or drawee to do something else, unless that agreement will make it easier for the holder of the instrument to collect the money due on the instrument. A provision of the latter type does not impair negotiability because the effect of its inclusion is to make the paper more attractive to a purchaser and thus it encourages the exchange or transfer of the commercial paper.

(f) Sum certain. The instrument must not only call for payment in money but also for a sum certain. Unless the instrument is definite on its face as to how much is to be paid, there is no way of determining how much the instrument is worth.

The fact that the instrument may require certain payments in addition to the amount specified as due does not make the instrument nonnegotiable when such additional amounts come within any of the following categories:

(1) Interest. A provision for the payment of interest does not affect the certainty of the sum, even though the interest rate increases upon default in

---

[13] § 3-105(1)(f).
[14] § 3-105(1)(g), (h).

payment.[15] In contrast, a note payable "with interest at bank rates" is not for a sum certain because bank rates of interest are not constant, and a paper calling for payment of bank rate interest is therefore not negotiable.

(2) Installments. A provision for payment in installments does not affect certainty. Nor is certainty affected when the installment provision is coupled with a provision for acceleration of the date of payment for the total amount upon default in any payment.

(3) Exchange. A provision for the addition of exchange charges does not affect the certainty of the sum payable since its object is in effect to preserve the constancy of the value involved. In this connection, the fact that the money due on the instrument is stated in a foreign currency does not make the instrument nonnegotiable.[16]

(4) Collection Costs and Attorney's Fees. The certainty of the sum is not affected by a provision adding collection costs and attorney's fees to the amount due, although general principles of law may place a limit upon the amount that can be recovered for such items.

(5) Discount and Addition. The certainty of the sum and the negotiability of the instrument are not affected by a provision that allows a discount if earlier payment is made or which increases the amount due if late payment is made.[17]

(g) Time of payment. A commercial paper must be payable on demand or at a definite time. If it is payable "when convenient," the instrument is nonnegotiable because the day of payment may never arrive. An instrument payable only upon the happening of a particular event that may never happen is not negotiable. For example, a provision to pay when a person marries is not payable at a definite time since that particular event may never occur. It is immaterial whether the contingency in fact has happened, because from an examination of the instrument alone it still appears to be subject to a condition that may never happen.

(1) Demand. An instrument is payable on demand when it is expressly specified to be payable "on demand," or at sight or upon presentation, that is, whenever the holder tenders the instrument to the party required to pay and demands payment; or when no time for payment is specified.[18] To illustrate the last point, when a note is completely executed except that the time for payment and the lines indicating payment by installments are left blank, the full amount of the note is payable on demand, as opposed to the contention that no amount is payable.

(2) Definite Time. The time of payment is definite if it can be determined from the face of the instrument. An instrument satisfies this requirement when it is payable (a) on or before a stated date, (b) at a fixed

---

[15] § 3-106(1)(b).
[16] § 3-107(2).
[17] § 3-106(1)(c).
[18] § 3-108.

period after a stated date, (c) at a fixed period after sight, (d) at a definite time subject to any acceleration, (e) at a definite time subject to extension at the option of the holder, (f) at a definite time subject to extension to a further definite date at the option of the maker or acceptor, or (g) at a definite time subject to an extension to a further definite date automatically upon or after the occurrence of a specified act or event.[19]

> **FACTS:** Ferri made a note payable to the order of Sylvia "within 10 years after date." Within less than that time Sylvia sued for the money due, claiming that the note was uncertain and therefore parol evidence could be admitted to show that it had been agreed that she could have the money any time she needed it.

> **DECISION:** Judgment for Ferri. A commercial paper payable "within" a stated period does not mature until the time fixed arrives, which in this instance was 10 years after the date of the note. Since the time for payment was certain and complete on the face of the instrument, parol evidence could not be admitted to show that there was a different oral agreement, regarding the date of maturity. [Ferri v Sylvia, 100 RI 270, 214 A2d 470]

An instrument payable in relation to an event which though certain to happen will happen on an uncertain date, such as a specified time after death, is not negotiable.[20]

(h) Order or bearer. A commercial paper must be payable to order or bearer. This requirement is met by such expressions as "Pay to the order of John Jones," "Pay to John Jones or order," "Pay to bearer," and "Pay to John Jones or bearer."[21] The use of the phrase "to the order of John Jones" or "to John Jones or order" is important in showing that the person executing the instrument is indicating that he does not intend to restrict payment of the instrument to John Jones and that he does not object to paying anyone to whom John Jones orders the paper to be paid. Similarly, if the person executing the instrument originally states that it will be paid "to bearer" or "to John Jones or bearer," he is not restricting the payment of the instrument to the original payee. If the instrument is payable "to John Jones," however, the instrument is not negotiable.

> **FACTS:** Nation-Wide Check Corp. sold money orders through local agents. A customer would purchase a money order by paying an agent the amount of the desired money order plus a fee. The customer would then sign his name on the money order as the remitter or sender and would fill in the name of the person who was to receive the money following the printed words "Payable to." In a lawsuit between Nation-Wide and Banks, a payee on some of these orders, the question was raised whether these money orders were negotiable.

---

[19] § 3-109(1).

[20] § 3-109(2).

[21] It is not necessary that the instrument actually use the word "order" or "bearer." Any other words indicating the same intention are sufficient. It has been held that the words "pay to holder" could be used in place of "bearer" without affecting the negotiability of the instrument. UCC §§ 3-110, 3-111.

DECISION: The money orders were not negotiable because they were payable to a specified or named payee and not to the order of a named payee or bearer. [Nation-Wide Check Corp. v Banks (DistColApp) 260 A2d 367]

(1) Order Paper. An instrument is *payable to order* when by its terms it is payable to the order or assignee of any person specified therein with reasonable certainty (Pay to the order of H. F. Rousch), or to a person so described or his order (Pay to H. F. Rousch or his order).[22]

(2) Bearer Paper. An instrument is *payable to bearer* when by its terms it is payable (a) to bearer or the order of bearer, (b) to a specified person or bearer, or (c) to "cash," or "the order of cash," or any other designation that does not purport to identify a person.[23]

An instrument payable to order and indorsed in blank becomes payable to bearer and may be negotiated by transfer of possession until specially indorsed.[24]

(i) Drawee. In the case of a draft or check, the drawee must be named or described in the instrument with reasonable certainty.[25] This requirement, which is based upon practical expediency, is designed to enable the holder of the instrument to know to whom he must go for payment.

When there are two or more drawees, they may be either joint drawees (*A* and *B*) or alternative drawees (*A* or *B*).[26]

§ 29:2. EFFECT OF PROVISIONS FOR ADDITIONAL POWERS OR BENEFITS.
Certain provisions in an instrument that give the holder certain additional powers and benefits may or may not affect negotiability.[27]

(a) Collateral. The inclusion of a power to sell collateral security, such as corporate stocks and bonds, upon default does not impair negotiability. An instrument secured by collateral contains as absolute a promise or order as an unsecured instrument. Negotiability is not affected by a promise or power to maintain or protect collateral or to give additional collateral,[28] or to make the entire debt due, if the additional collateral is not supplied.

(b) Acceleration. A power to accelerate the due date of an instrument upon a default in the payment of interest or of any installment of the principal, or upon the failure to maintain or provide collateral does not affect the negotiability of an instrument. However, a power to accelerate "at will" or when a person "deems himself insecure" must be exercised in good faith.[29]

---

[22] An instrument is also payable to order when it is conspicuously designated on its face as "exchange" or the like, and names a payee. UCC § 3-110(1).

[23] § 3-111.

[24] § 3-204(2).

[25] § 3-102(1)(b).

[26] § 3-102(1)(b). The instrument is nonnegotiable if there are successive drawees. *Successive drawees* exist when, if one drawee fails to pay, the holder is required to go to the next drawee for payment rather than proceed at once against secondary parties.

[27] UCC § 3-112.

[28] § 3-112(1)(c).

[29] § 1-208.

FACTS: Bellino was a maker of a promissory note payable in installments. The note contained the provision that upon default in the payment of any installment, the holder had the option of declaring the entire balance "due and payable on demand." The note was negotiated to Cassiani who sued Bellino for the full debt when there was a default on an installment. Bellino raised the defense that no notice of acceleration had been given to her prior to the suit.

DECISION: Judgment for Cassiani. An acceleration clause is valid and there is no requirement of notifying the party liable since he, having signed the note, knows the presence of such a clause and the accelerating fact, his default. [Cassiani v Bellino, 338 Mass 765, 157 NE2d 409]

(c) Confession of judgment. Negotiability is not affected by a provision authorizing the entry of a judgment by confession upon a default. If the holder of the instrument is authorized to confess judgment at any time, whether before maturity or not, however, the instrument is generally nonnegotiable.

(d) Waiver of statutory benefit. State statutes commonly provide that when a person is sued for a debt, a certain amount or kind of his property is exempt from the claim. If the party who executes a commercial paper promises to waive his rights under such a statute in order that it will be a little easier to collect the amount due, negotiability is ordinarily not affected. A waiver of this kind is void in some states, however.

(e) Requirement of another act. A provision authorizing the holder to require an act other than the payment of money, such as the delivery of goods, makes the instrument nonnegotiable.[30]

§ 29:3. ADDITIONAL DOCUMENTS. The fact that a separate document is executed that gives the creditor additional protection, as by a mortgage on real estate or the right to repossess goods sold to the maker of the instrument, does not impair the negotiability of the commercial paper.

§ 29:4. IMMATERIAL PROVISIONS. The addition or omission of certain other provisions has no effect upon the negotiability of a commercial paper that is otherwise negotiable.

A commercial paper is not affected by the omission of the date. In such case it is regarded as carrying the date of the day on which it was executed and delivered to the payee. If the date is essential to the operation of the instrument, as when the instrument is payable a stated number of days or months "after date," any holder who knows the true date may insert that date.

When a commercial paper is dated, the date is deemed prima facie to be the true date, whether the date was originally inserted or was thereafter added.[31] A commercial paper may be antedated or postdated, provided that

---

[30] § 3-104(1)(b).
[31] § 3-114(3). If the wrong date is inserted, the true date can be proved unless the holder is a holder in due course or a holder through a holder in due course, in which case the date, even though wrong, cannot be contradicted.

is not done to defraud anyone. The holder acquires title as of the date of delivery without regard to whether this is the date stated in the instrument.

It is immaterial so far as negotiability is concerned (a) whether an instrument bears a seal; (b) whether it fails to state that value has been given; or (c) whether it recites the giving of value without stating its nature or amount, although local law may require such a recital.

Negotiability is not affected by a provision that by indorsing or cashing the instrument, the person receiving it takes it in full settlement of a specified claim or of all claims against the drawer.[32]

QUESTIONS AND CASE PROBLEMS

1. *A* borrowed $1,000 from *B* and gave *B* a promissory note which required *A* to repay the amount in monthly installments of $100. The note further provided that upon any default by *A*, *B* could accelerate the unpaid balance of the note which would thereupon become due. After *A* had paid two monthly installments, he missed the third installment. *B* sued *A* for the balance due on the note. *A* raised the defense that *B* had not notified him that he accelerated the debt, and therefore *B* could only recover $100. Was *A* correct? [See Smith v Davis (TexCivApp) 453 SW2d 340]

2. A contractor signed a note promising to pay to the order of the holder $10,000 payable from "jobs now under construction." Was the note negotiable? [See Webb & Sons, Inc. v Hamilton, 30 AppDiv2d 597, 290 NYS2d 122]

3. James G. Dornan was the treasurer and vice-president of Chet B. Earle, Inc. On behalf of the corporation he executed a promissory note that was signed in the following manner:

$$\left(\begin{array}{c} \text{Corporate} \\ \text{Seal} \end{array} \right) \qquad \begin{array}{ll} \text{Chet B. Earle, Inc.} & \text{(Seal)} \\ \text{James G. Dornan} & \text{(Seal)} \end{array}$$

The holder of the note, an indorsee, sued Dornan on the ground that he was personally liable as a comaker. He defended on the ground that he was merely an agent for the corporation and was not personally liable. Was this defense valid? [Bell v Dornan, 203 PaSuper 562, 201 A2d 324]

4. Snowden signed a note as maker for $10,000 and delivered it to the Franklin National Bank, directing the bank to loan $10,000 to a corporation, which was then done by the bank. When the bank sued Snowden on the note, he objected on the ground that he had signed the note to accommodate the corporation which had received the loan and that the bank had assured him that since the corporation had adequate collateral for the loan of $10,000, the bank would never look to Snowden for payment of his note. Was Snowden liable? [Snowden v Franklin National Bank (CA5 Tex) 338 F2d 995]

5. Mar obtained a cashier's check from the Washington Mutual Savings Bank. Apparently the check was lost by Mar. It was claimed that the check was not

---

[32] UCC § 3-112(1)(f).

negotiable because it had been lost before it had been negotiated. Was this correct? [Mar v Washington Mutual Savings Bank, 64 Wash2d 793, 394 P2d 367]

6. Cortis made a contract for storm windows and gave the seller a promissory note in payment. The note promised to pay $3,400 in installments as set forth in the schedule of payments stated in the note. The schedule of payments, however, was left blank. Was the note void? [Liberty Aluminum Products Co. v Cortis (Pa) 14 D&C 2d 624, 38 Wash County 223]

7. Mr. and Mrs. Gulas took care of Dulak. When the latter desired to draw checks, Mr. Gulas would prepare the checks and Dulak would sign them. Six days before Dulak died, he told Mr. and Mrs. Gulas that he was obligated to their two sons for $3,000 each, requested his checkbook, and directed Gulas to prepare a check for each son for $3,000. Dulak then signed each check, and the two checks were torn from the checkbook but were not separated from each other. The checks were replaced in the checkbook, which was then put in the dresser drawer in Dulak's room where it was usually kept. After his death, Mrs. Gulas showed the checkbook and the checks to the executors under Dulak's will, and they kept possession of the checks. The two sons then sued to enforce the payment of the checks. Decide. [Dulak's Will, 209 NYS2d 928]

8. The Buffingtons borrowed $14,000 from Bradley to purchase lumber and to run a lumber mill. They executed a promissory note which promised to pay the stated sum and then stated "the makers of this note are to pay 2% of Gross Sales to the holder of this note each 30 days. . . . The makers of this note do not have the privilege of assigning this note, and any time a sale is made of either the mill or the standing timber to anyone else, this note becomes immediately due and payable." Suit was brought on the note by Bradley. Was the note negotiable? [Bradley v Buffington (MoApp) 500 SW2d 314]

9. The East Penn Broadcasting Company borrowed money from the Hershey National Bank. A promissory note representing the loan was executed "payable to the Hershey National Bank." The note authorized the confession of judgment at any time. Frank was a comaker on the note. When the loan was not repaid on time, the bank sued Frank. He raised certain defenses under the Uniform Commercial Code. The bank claimed that the Uniform Commercial Code was not applicable. Was the bank correct? [Frank v Hershey National Bank, 269 MdApp 138, 306 A2d 207]

10. A signed a note in which he promised to pay to the order of B the sum of $3,000 with interest payable every two weeks. When B sued A, A claimed that the note was demand paper and was therefore due on the date it was executed and that the suit was barred by the statute of limitations which had expired if the paper was due as claimed by A. B claimed that the note was not demand paper because a time for payment was specified in that interest payments were to be made every two weeks. Was this demand paper? [See Davis v Dennis (TexCivApp) 448 SW2d 495]

30

TRANSFER OF COMMERCIAL PAPER

A. INDORSEMENTS

§ 30:1. INTRODUCTION. Some commercial paper may be transferred without an indorsement. An indorsement is required in other cases. If the transfer is made in the manner required by the Uniform Commercial Code, the transfer is called a negotiation and the transferee becomes a holder. If there is no negotiation, the transferee is merely an assignee.

The person to whom an instrument is payable either on its face or by indorsement or the person in possession of bearer paper may indorse it for the purpose of negotiating it by merely signing his name on it, or he may add certain words or statements as part of his indorsement. By definition, an indorsement is properly written on the back of the instrument.

An indorsement must be written on the commercial paper itself, or, if necessary, on a paper attached to it called an *allonge*.[1] If there is no space on the paper, the indorsement may be written on another piece of paper provided it is so firmly attached to the commercial paper that it becomes part of it. A signature on a separate paper which is stapled, pinned, or clipped to the commercial paper is not effective as an indorsement.

§ 30:2 KINDS OF INDORSEMENTS.

(a) Blank indorsement. When the indorser signs only his name, the indorsement is called a *blank indorsement* since it does not indicate the person to whom the instrument is to be paid, that is, the indorsee. A person who is in possession of paper on which the last indorsement is blank is the holder and may sue thereon without proving ownership of the paper.

FACTS: Schroeder, the payee of a note, indorsed the instrument in blank and delivered it to Enyart, Van Camp and Feil, Inc. That corporation changed its name and then merged with the First Securities Co. The cashier of the Enyart company delivered its securities, including the Schroeder note, to the office of the new company. When this company sued Schroeder, he claimed that there was no proof that it was the owner of the note.

---

[1] Uniform Commercial Code § 3-202(2).

DECISION: Judgment for First Securities Co. The instrument was bearer paper because the last indorsement was blank. As such, it was negotiated by the physical transfer of the instrument. [First Securities Co. v Schroeder, 351 IllApp 173, 114 NE2d 426]

The holder of an instrument on which the last indorsement is blank may protect himself by writing above the signature of the blank indorser a statement that the instrument is made payable to him.[2] This is called "completing" the indorsement or "converting" the blank indorsement to a special indorsement by specifying the identify of the indorsee.

Negotiation by a blank indorsement does three things: (1) it passes the ownership of the instrument; (2) it makes certain warranties; and (3) it imposes upon the indorser a secondary liability to pay the amount of the instrument if the maker or drawee fails to do so and certain conditions are then satisfied by the holder.

(b) Special indorsement. A *special indorsement* consists of the signature of the indorser and words specifying the person to whom the indorser makes the instrument payable, that is, the indorsee. Common forms of this type of indorsement are "Pay to the order of Robert Hicks, E. S. Flynn" and "Pay to Robert Hicks or order, E. S. Flynn." It is not necessary that the indorsement contain the words "order" or "bearer." Thus, a commercial paper indorsed in the form "Pay to Robert Hicks, E. S. Flynn" continues to be negotiable and may be negotiated further. In contrast, an instrument which on its face reads "Pay to E. S. Flynn" is not negotiable.

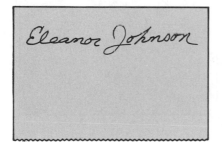

Blank Indorsement

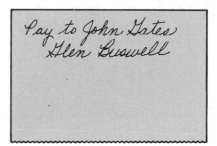

Special Indorsement

When the last indorsement on the instrument is special, both an indorsement and a delivery by or on behalf of the last indorsee is required for further negotiation.[3]

As in the case of the blank indorsement, a special indorsement transfers title to the instrument and results in the making of certain warranties and in imposing a secondary liability upon the indorser to pay the amount of the instrument under certain conditions.

---

[2] UCC § 3-204(3).
[3] § 3-204(1).

(c) Qualified indorsement. A *qualified indorsement* is one that qualifies the effect of a blank or a special indorsement by disclaiming or destroying the liability of the indorser to answer for the default of the maker or drawee. This may be done by including the words "without recourse" in the body of the indorsement, or by using any other words that indicate an intention to destroy the indorser's secondary liability for the default of the maker or drawee.[4]

The qualification of an indorsement does not affect the passage of title or the negotiable character of the paper. It merely limits the indorser's liability to the extent of the qualification. Consequently, where an automobile dealer was payee and indorsed his customer's note without recourse, the note was not an obligation of the dealer; and therefore when it was dishonored, the person who guaranteed that the dealer would pay "his obligation" was not liable on the guaranty.

This form of indorsement is most commonly used when the qualified indorser is admittedly a person who has no personal interest in the transaction, as in the case of an attorney or an agent who is merely indorsing to his client or principal a check made payable to him by a third person. Here the transferee recognizes that the transferor is not a party to the transaction and therefore is not in a position where he should be asked to vouch for the payment of the paper.

Qualified Indorsement   Restrictive Indorsement

(d) Restrictive indorsements. A *restrictive indorsement* specifies the purpose of the indorsement or the use to be made of the paper.

(1) Indorsement for Deposit. This indorsement indicates an intent that the instrument be deposited, such as "For deposit only," "For deposit only to the account of John Sacuto" and "Pay to the Springfield National Bank for deposit only."[5]

---

[4] § 3-414(1).
[5] § 3-205(c).

(2) Indorsement for Collection. This indorsement indicates an intention that the instrument be received by the indorsee, usually for the purpose of effecting the collection of the instrument. "For collection only" or "Pay to any bank or banker"[6] are examples of this type of indorsement.

(3) Indorsement Prohibiting Further Negotiation. The indorsement, "Pay to Harold Singer only," indicates an intent that no further negotiation should occur and is therefore restrictive.[7]

(4) Agency or Trust Indorsement. An indorsement that makes the indorsee the agent of the indorser, such as "Pay to (indorsee, agent) on account of (indorser, principal)," or which makes the indorsee the owner subject to a trust for another person, such as "Pay to (indorsee, mother) to hold for use of (third person, son)," are restrictive indorsements in that they state that the indorsement is for the benefit of the indorser or another person.[8]

(5) Condition as a Part of the Indorsement. An indorsement which indicates that it is to become effective only upon the satisfaction of a particular condition, such as "Pay to Calvin Nash upon completion of Contract #83," is a restrictive indorsement.[9]

(6) Effect of Restrictive Indorsement. A restrictive indorsement does not have the effect of prohibiting further negotiation even though it expressly attempts to do so.[10] In all cases the transferee may therefore be a holder, just as is true under a nonrestrictive indorsement. A bank may ignore and is not affected by the restrictive indorsement of any person except the holder transferring the instrument to the bank or the person presenting it to the bank for payment. However, a *depositary bank*, that is, the one in which the customer deposits the item, and persons not in the bank collection process must recognize the restrictive indorsement to the extent of applying any value given in a manner consistent with the indorsement.[11]

(7) Qualified Indorsement Distinguished. An indorsement "without recourse" is a qualified but not a restrictive indorsement.

§ 30:3. IRREGULAR KINDS OF INDORSEMENTS. The indorser may make an indorsement that does not fall into any of the standard categories

---

[6] § 3-205(c).

[7] § 3-205(b).

[8] § 3-205(d).

[9] § 3-205(a).

[10] § 3-206(1). As to effect of the indorsement, "Pay any bank" or "For deposit," see § 4-201(2).

[11] § 3-206(2). Additional limitations are imposed in the case of collection and conditional indorsements. § 3-206(3), and trust indorsements, § 3-206(4).

of indorsements. For example, he may write, "I hereby assign all my right, title, and interest in the within-note," and then sign his name. The signature in such a case is effective as an indorsement in spite of the added words, on the theory that the indorser actually intended to indorse and was merely attempting to make certain that he transferred his interest.[12]

§ 30:4. CORRECTION OF NAME BY INDORSEMENT.

Sometimes the name of the payee or indorsee of a commercial paper is improperly spelled. Thus, H. A. Price may receive a paycheck which improperly is payable to the order of "H. O. Price." If this was a clerical error and the check was intended for H. A. Price, the employee may ask his employer to write a new check payable to him in his proper name.

The payee or indorsee whose name is misspelled may indorse the wrong name, his correct name, or both. A person giving or paying value for the instrument may require both.[13]

This correction of name by indorsement may only be used when it was intended that the instrument should be payable to the person making the corrective indorsement. If there were in fact two employees, one named H. A. Price and the other H. O. Price, it would be illegal as a forgery for one to take the check intended for the other and by indorsing it obtain for himself the benefit of proceeds of the check.

§ 30:5. BANK INDORSEMENTS.

In order to simplify the transfer of commercial paper from one bank to another in the process of collecting items, "any agreed method which identifies the transferor bank is sufficient for the item's further transfer to another bank."[14] Thus, a bank may indorse with its Federal Reserve System number instead of using its name.

Likewise, when a customer has deposited an instrument with a bank but has failed to indorse it, the bank may make an indorsement for him unless the instrument expressly requires the payee's personal indorsement. Furthermore the mere stamping or marking on the item of any notation showing that it was deposited by the customer or credited to his account is as effective as an indorsement by the customer would have been.[15]

B. NEGOTIATION

§ 30:6. DEFINITION.

Negotiation is the transferring of commercial paper in such a way as to make the transferee the holder of the paper.

§ 30:7. METHODS OF NEGOTIATION.

(a) **Negotiation of order paper.** An instrument payable to order may be negotiated only by the indorsement of the person to whom it is payable at

---

[12] § 3-202(4).
[13] § 3-203.
[14] § 4-206.
[15] § 4-205(1).

the time and delivery by him or with his authorization. The indorsement must be placed on the instrument by the person to whom it is then payable.

(1) Multiple Payees and Indorsers. Ordinarily one person is named as payee by the instrument, but two or more payees may be named. In that case, the instrument may specify that it is payable to any one or more of them or that it is payable to all jointly. If nothing is specified, the instrument is payable to all of the payees and they are *joint payees.* For example, if the instrument is made payable "to the order of A and B," the two persons named are joint payees.

The importance of this kind of designation is that it requires the indorsement of both *A* and *B* to negotiate the instrument further. This protects *A* against the action of *B*, and vice versa. Each knows that the other cannot secretly negotiate the instrument and pocket the proceeds. This rule does not apply, however, when the payees are partners or when one person is authorized to act for all and he indorses for all.

> FACTS: The Feldman Construction Company made a contract with Interstate Steel Corporation for construction work. General Pipe & Supply furnished building materials to Interstate. Feldman drew a check on its bank, the Union Bank, payable to the order of "Interstate Steel Corp. General Pipe & Supply." Interstate indorsed the check and Union Bank then paid the check. Feldman sued Union Bank for the amount of the check because it had not been properly indorsed. Union Bank claimed that the check was payable in the alternative and therefore the indorsement of one of the payees was sufficient.
>
> DECISION: Judgment for Feldman. The absence of "and" or "or" is not controlling in determining whether payees are joint or several. By UCC § 3-116(b), a paper payable to two or more persons is jointly payable if not stated in the alternative. As there was no statement that the paper was payable in the alternative, It was payable jointly. Thus the indorsement of both payees was required to negotiate the paper and the bank had improperly made payment on the indorsement of only one payee. The bank was therefore liable to its customer, Feldman, for having disobeyed the order of his check. [Feldman Construction Co. v Union Bank, 28 CalApp3d 731, 104 CalRptr 912]

Joint payees or joint indorsees who indorse are deemed to indorse jointly and severally. If the instrument is payable to *alternate payees* or if it has been negotiated to alternate indorsees, as *A* or *B*, it may be indorsed and delivered by either of them.

The UCC declares only the rights of joint payees with respect to the paper. Non-Code principles will determine the rights of the joint payees as between themselves. Thus, a check payable to husband and wife is initially "their" property but when it is a check for a refund of income taxes for a year in which the husband alone produced the income on which the tax had been paid, the husband is entitled to the proceeds of the check to the exclusion of the wife.

(2) Agent or Officer as Payee. The instrument may be made payable to the order of an officeholder. For example, a check may read, "Pay to the

order of the Receiver of Taxes." Such a check may be received and negotiated by the person who at the time is the Receiver of Taxes. This is a matter of convenience since the person writing the instrument is not required to find out the name of the Receiver of Taxes at that time.

If the instrument is drawn in favor of a person as "Cashier" or some other fiscal officer of a bank or corporation, it is prima facie payable to the bank or corporation of which he is such an officer, and may be negotiated by the indorsement of either the bank or corporation, or of the named officer. If drawn in favor of an agent, it may similarly be negotiated by the agent or his principal.[16]

(3) Partial Negotiation. A negotiation of part of the amount cannot be made.[17] The entire instrument must be negotiated to one person or to the same persons. If the instrument has been partly paid, however, the unpaid balance may be transferred by indorsement. This is proper since the entire amount then due, although it is only a portion of the original amount due, is being transferred.

(4) Missing Indorsement. Although order paper cannot be negotiated without indorsement, it can be assigned to another without indorsement. In such a case, the transferee has the same rights as the transferor; and if the transferee gave value for the paper, he also has the right to require that the transferor indorse the instrument unqualifiedly to him and thereby effect the negotiation of the instrument.

(b) Negotiation of bearer paper. Any commercial paper payable to bearer may be negotiated by merely transferring possession, that is, by handing it over to another person.[18]

FACTS: Higgins, who owed a bill to the Westerly Hospital, gave it an installment note for the amount of the debt. The note required him to make 18 monthly installments. The hospital negotiated the note to the Industrial National Bank by an indorsement which consisted of the name of the hospital and a guarantee by the hospital that payment of the note would be made by the maker. Higgins made three payments on the note and then stopped, whereupon the bank wrote on the back of the note an indorsement to the hospital and delivered the note to the hospital. The hospital sued Higgins on the note. He raised the defense that the hospital could not sue because it was not the holder, contending that the indorsement by the bank was not effective on the theory that the person who wrote the indorsement on behalf of the bank did not have authority to make such indorsement.

DECISION: Judgment for the hospital. If the indorsement on behalf of the bank was authorized, the hospital was the holder and entitled to sue. If that indorsement was not authorized, the effect would be the same as though the indorsement was not on the paper. In that case, the last

---

[16] § 3-117.

[17] § 3-202(3). The partial negotiation is not a nullity but is given the effect of a partial assignment.

[18] UCC § 3-202(1).

effective indorsement on the paper was the signature of the hospital. This was a blank indorsement. As the last effective indorsement was blank, the paper was bearer paper and could be negotiated by mere physical transfer without any indorsement. When the bank returned the paper to the hospital, there was consequently a transfer of possession and a negotiation of the bearer paper, and the hospital was therefore the holder and was entitled to sue Higgins on the note. The indorsement which had been made on behalf of the bank was unnecessary to effect a negotiation and consequently it was immaterial whether that indorsement was effective. [Westerly Hospital v Higgins, 106 RI 155, 256 A2d 506]

The paper may be negotiated by a mere transfer of possession not only when the instrument expressly states that it is payable to bearer, but also when the law interprets it as being payable to bearer, as in the case of a check payable to the order of "Cash."

Although bearer paper may be negotiated by such transfer, the one to whom it is delivered may insist that the bearer indorse the paper so as to impose upon him the liability of an indorser. This situation most commonly arises when a check payable to "Cash" is presented to a bank for payment.

(c) **Time for determining character of paper.** The character of the paper is determined as of the time when the negotiation is about to take place, without regard to what it was originally or at any intermediate time. Accordingly, when the last indorsement is special, the paper is order paper without regard to whether it was bearer paper originally or at any intermediate time, and the holder cannot ignore or strike out intervening indorsements, or otherwise treat it as bearer paper because it had once been bearer paper.

(d) **Government checks.** The regulations of the United States Treasury govern the payment and indorsement of government checks. These regulations require a party presenting a Treasury check to the government to guarantee that all prior indorsements on the check are genuine, and grant the Treasurer the right to demand a refund if that guarantee is breached. Consequently, a bank presenting a government check to the government for payment is liable to the government when it is established that the payee was dead and his signature had been forged, as against the contention that UCC § 3-406 should apply and estop the United States because of its negligence in issuing a check to a deceased payee.[19]

§ 30:8. **FORGED AND UNAUTHORIZED INDORSEMENTS.** A forged or unauthorized indorsement is by definition no indorsement of the person by whom it appears to have been made and, accordingly, the possessor of the paper is not the holder when the indorsement of that person was necessary for effective negotiation of the paper to the possessor.

If payment of commercial paper is made to one claiming under or through a forged indorsement, the payor is ordinarily liable to the person

---

[19] United States v City National Bank & Trust Co. (CA8 Mo) 491 F2d 851.

who was the rightful owner of the paper, unless such person is estopped or barred by his negligence or other conduct from asserting any claim against the payor.

FACTS: The Gasts owned a building which they contracted to sell to the Hannas. The building was insured against fire with the American Casualty Co. Thereafter, when the house was damaged by fire, a settlement was reached with the insurance company through Sidney Rosenbaum, a public fire adjuster. In order to make payment for the loss, the insurance company drew a draft on itself payable to the Hannas, the Gasts, and to Sidney Rosenbaum. Apparently the Hannas indorsed the draft, forged the names of the other payees as indorsers, cashed the draft by presenting it to the American Casualty Co., and disappeared. Thereafter, the Gasts sued the American Casualty Co.

DECISION: Judgment for the Gasts. The payment of the draft by the defendant was a conversion of the paper with respect to the Gasts regardless of whether the defendant had exercised due care. Paper is converted when it is paid on a forged indorsement; and when payment is made by the drawee in such case, the drawee is liable for the face amount of the paper to the person whose name was forged. [Gast v American Casualty Co. 99 NJSuper 538, 240 A2d 682.]

§ 30:9. THE IMPOSTOR RULE.

The "forgery" of the payee's name in an indorsement is as effective as if the payee had made or authorized the "signature" when the case comes within one of the three impostor situations: (a) an impostor has induced the maker or drawer to issue the instrument to him or a confederate in the name of the payee; (b) the person signing as, or on behalf of, the drawer intends that the named payee shall have no interest in the paper; or (c) an agent or employee of the drawer has given the drawer the name used as the payee intending that the latter should not have any interest in the paper.

The first situation is present when a person impersonates the holder of a savings account and, by presenting a forged withdrawal slip to the savings bank, gets the bank to issue a check payable to the bank's customer but which it hands to the impersonator in the belief that he is the customer. The second situation arises when the owner of a checking account, who wishes to conceal the true purpose of his taking money from the bank, makes out a check purportedly in payment of a debt which in fact does not exist.

The last situation is illustrated by the case of the employee who fraudulently causes his employer to sign a check made to a customer or other person, whether existing or not, but the employee does not intend to send it to that person but rather intends to forge the latter's indorsement, to cash the check, and to keep the money for himself.

The impostor rule applies when the person whose name is forged is a copayee of the paper as well as when he is the sole payee.

The impostor rule does not apply when there is a "valid" check to an actual creditor for a correct amount owed by the drawer and someone thereafter forges the payee's name, even though the forger is an employee of the drawer.

FACTS: The Snug Harbor Realty Co. had a checking account in the First National Bank. When construction work was obtained by Snug Harbor, its superintendent, Magee, would examine the bills submitted for labor and materials. He would instruct the bookkeeper as to what bills were approved, and checks were then prepared by the bookkeeper in accordance with such instructions. After the checks were signed by the proper official of Snug Harbor, they were picked up by Magee for delivery. Instead of delivering certain checks, he forged the signatures of the respective payees as indorsers and cashed the checks. The drawee bank then debited the Snug Harbor account with the amount of these checks. Snug Harbor claimed this was improper and sued the bank for the amount of such checks. Was Snug Harbor entitled to recover such amount?

DECISION: Yes. This was not an impostor situation. The impostor rule does not apply when there is a "valid" check to an actual creditor for a correct amount and someone thereafter forges the payee's name, even though the forger is an employee of the drawer. Consequently, there had been no effective negotiation of the check and the payment to its possessor was improper. The amount of such payment should not have been deducted from the checking account of Snug Harbor. [Snug Harbor Realty Co. v First National Bank, 105 NJSuper 572, 253 A2d 581, affirmed 54 NJ 95, 253 A2d 545]

Even when the impostor's indorsement is effective, he is subject to civil or criminal liability for making such an indorsement.[20]

§ 30:10. **EFFECT OF INCAPACITY OR MISCONDUCT ON NEGOTIATION.** A negotiation is effective even though (1) it is made by a minor or any other person lacking capacity; (2) it is an act beyond the powers of a corporation; (3) it is obtained by fraud, duress, or mistake of any kind; (4) or the negotiation is part of an illegal transaction or was made in breach of duty. Under general principles of law apart from the UCC, the transferor in such cases may be able to set aside the negotiation or to obtain some other form of legal relief. If, however, the instrument has in the meantime been acquired by a holder in due course, the negotiation can no longer be set aside.[21]

§ 30:11. **LOST PAPER.** The effect of losing commercial paper depends upon who is suing or demanding payment from whom and whether the paper was order paper or bearer paper when it was lost. If the paper is order paper, the finder does not become the holder because the paper, by definition, is not indorsed and delivered by the person to whom it was then payable. The former holder who lost it is still the rightful owner of the paper, although technically he is not the holder because he is not in possession of the paper.

---

[20] UCC § 3-405.
[21] § 3-207.

If the lost paper is a promissory note, it is less likely that the maker will oblige by executing a new promissory note. In any event, the owner of the lost paper may bring suit on it against any party liable thereon. There is, of course, the practical difficulty of proving just what the lost paper provided and explaining the loss of the paper. The court may also require that the plaintiff suing on the lost instrument furnish the defendant with security to indemnify the defendant against loss by reason of any claim on the lost instrument.[22]

If the paper is in bearer form when it is lost, the finder becomes the holder of the paper, since he is in possession of bearer paper and, as holder, is entitled to enforce payment.

C. ASSIGNMENT OF COMMERCIAL PAPER

§ 30:12. **TRANSFER BY ASSIGNMENT.** In addition to transfer by negotiation, a commercial paper may be transferred by assignment.

§ 30:13. **ASSIGNMENT BY ACT OF THE PARTIES.** Commercial paper may be assigned in the same manner as any other contract right by the express act of the holder. A commercial paper is also regarded as assigned when a person whose indorsement is required on the instrument transfers it without indorsing it.

> FACTS: Jerry Waters and his wife Patsy entered into a property settlement agreement as part of a divorce proceeding. By the agreement, it was agreed that a demand note which had been signed by Jerry payable to the order of Jim Still, who was Patsy's father, should be "transferred to Patsy . . . in the future." Jim delivered the note to Patsy without any indorsement or writing. Jim thereafter died. Patsy sued Jerry on the note to her. [Waters v Waters (TexCivApp) 498 SW2d 236.]
>
> DECISION: Judgment for Patsy. Order paper may be transferred by delivery without indorsement and the transferee has the ownership and the transferor's right to sue, even though the transferee is not a holder because he does not have the transferor's indorsement. The delivery of the note to Patsy pursuant to the settlement agreement transferred the note to her and she was entitled to sue thereon. [Waters v Waters (TexCivApp) 498 SW2d 236.]

When a necessary indorsement is missing, the transferee has only the rights of an assignee. If the transferee acquires the paper for value, he is entitled, however, to require that the transferor indorse the instrument.[23] If the indorsement is obtained, then the transferee is deemed a holder but only as of the time when the indorsement is made.

---

[22] § 3-804.

[23] § 3-201(3). The indorsement can only be required if the transferee gave value for the paper.

§ 30:14. **ASSIGNMENT BY OPERATION OF LAW.** An assignment by operation of law occurs when by virtue of the law the title of one person is vested in another. If the holder of a commercial paper becomes a bankrupt or dies, the title to the instrument vests automatically in the trustee in bankruptcy or in the personal representative of the estate.

D. WARRANTIES OF TRANSFEROR

§ 30:15. **INTRODUCTION.** The transferor of commercial paper may make an express guarantee. Whether he does so or not, certain warranties are implied. The transferor, by the act of making the transfer, warrants the existence of certain facts. The warranties of the transferor are not always the same but vary according to the nature of the indorsement he makes or whether he transfers the instrument without indorsement. A distinction is made between warranties arising in connection with acceptance or payment and those arising in connection with transfer. In the case of transfer by indorsement, the warranty may run to a subsequent holder; in the case of transfer by delivery only, to the immediate transferee.

§ 30:16. **WARRANTIES OF UNQUALIFIED INDORSER.** When the holder of a commercial paper negotiates it by an unqualified indorsement, and receives consideration, the transferor warrants that:

(1) He has a good title, which includes the genuineness of all indorsements necessary to his title to the instrument, or that he is authorized to act for one who has such good title.[24]

(2) His act of transferring the instrument is rightful, independent of the question of his title or authority to act.[25]

(3) The signatures on the instrument are genuine or executed by authorized agents.[26]

(4) The instrument has not been materially altered.[27]

(5) He has no knowledge of the existence or commencement of any insolvency proceeding against the maker or acceptor of the instrument, or against the drawer of an unaccepted draft or bill of exchange.[28]

(6) No defense of any party is good as against him.[29]

These warranties made by the unqualified indorser pass to his transferee and to any subsequent holder who acquires the instrument in good faith.[30]

When the holder presents a check to the drawee bank for payment, his indorsement of the check does not give rise to any warranty that the account of the drawer in the drawee bank is sufficient to cover the check.

---

[24] UCC § 3-417(2)(a).
[25] § 3-417(2)(a).
[26] § 3-417(2)(b).
[27] § 3-417(2)(c).
[28] § 3-417(2)(e).
[29] § 3-417(2)(d).
[30] § 3-417(2).

When an item has been paid to the possessor on the basis of a forged indorsement, a collecting bank which sustains loss by being required to pay the true owner of the paper or prior collecting bank may recover its loss from its customer because of the customer's warranty of the genuineness of prior signatures when the customer deposited the item with the collecting bank. This right of recovery may be enforced in an ordinary lawsuit or by charging back the account of the customer or of a collecting bank to which the proceeds of the item had been paid. When the bank claiming the right of recovery or charge-back has delayed unreasonably under the circumstances, its right to recover or charge-back is barred by such delay if the other party has sustained loss because of the delay.

> **FACTS:** Hanover Insurance Company drew a draft payable to Geraldine Stallings and Winter Park Federal Savings & Loan Association. The draft, bearing the forged indorsement of Winter Park, was deposited by Stallings with First Federal Savings & Loan Association. First Federal then sent it to Branch Banking and Trust Company which sent it to Chase Manhattan Bank which presented the draft to and was paid by Hanover. When the forgery was discovered, Hanover paid Winter Park the amount of the draft and that amount was then charged back against Chase which charged it back against Branch Banking which charged it against First Federal. This was done approximately 27 months after the draft had originally been paid by Hanover. Meanwhile Stallings had already withdrawn from her First Federal account all of the proceeds of the draft. First Federal sued Branch Banking for the amount of the draft.

> **DECISION:** Judgment for First Federal. A bank paying on a forged indorsement may recover the payment from the person to whom it made the payment provided that it acts within a reasonable time under the circumstances and before an innocent recipient of the money would sustain loss by such a recovery. The charge-back had been made 27 months after the payment on the forged indorsement and First Federal would be subjected to loss if such charge-back were allowed because its customer had in the meantime withdrawn all of the proceeds of the draft. The right to charge-back against First Federal had therefore been lost by delay. [The Federal Savings & Loan Association v Branch Banking and Trust Company (NC) 191 SE2d 683]

§ 30:16. WARRANTIES OF OTHER PARTIES.

(a) **Qualified indorser.** The qualified indorser makes the same warranties as an unqualified indorser except the warranty as to "no defenses" (6) is limited to a warranty that the indorser does not have knowledge of any defense, rather than that no such defense exists.[31] The warranties of a qualified indorser run to the same persons as those of an unqualified indorser.

---

[31] § 3-417(3). The qualified indorsement does not exclude other warranties unless it is specified to be "without warranties."

FACTS: Brown executed and delivered a promissory note to E. E. Cressler, who negotiated the note to C. W. Cressler by indorsement without recourse. When C. W. Cressler sued to enforce the note, Brown claimed that there was a lack of consideration. E. E. Cressler knew that consideration was lacking, but he claimed that this did not impose liability on him because he had indorsed the note without recourse.

DECISION: Judgment against E. E. Cressler. The indorsement "without recourse" only freed him from liability for the face of the paper. It did not free him from liability based on warranties arising from indorsement without any limitation on warranties. As an element of his warranty liability, he warranted that he had no knowledge of any defense which would be good against him, which warranty was broken because he knew that there was the defense of lack of consideration. [Cressler v Brown, 79 Okla 170, 192 P 417]

(b) Transferor by delivery. The warranties made by one who transfers a commercial paper by delivery are the same as those made by an unqualified indorser except that they run only to the immediate transferee and then only if he has given consideration for the transfer.[32] Subsequent holders cannot enforce such warranties against this prior transferor by delivery regardless of the status or character of such holders.

(c) Selling agent or broker. A selling agent or broker who discloses the fact that he is acting as such warrants only his good faith and authority to act. One who does not disclose such capacity is subject to the warranties of an ordinary transferor who transfers in the manner employed by him.[33]

QUESTIONS AND CASE PROBLEMS

1. A check given in settlement of a lawsuit was drawn to the order of "*A*, attorney for *B*." Could *A* indorse the check? [See Maber, Inc. v Factor Cab Corp. 19 AppDiv2d 500, 244 NYS2d 768]
2. Kavlick hired Rothman to do construction work and paid him by a note. Rothman indorsed the note "without recourse" to the Eastern Acceptance Corp. The corporation sued Kavlick on the note. He defended on the ground that the consideration for the note had failed and that this defense was available against the corporation because it could not be a holder in due course on account of the form of the indorsement. Decide. [Eastern Acceptance Corp. v Kavlick, 10 NJSuper 253, 77 A2d 49]
3. Searcy executed and delivered a promissory note payable to the order of the Bank of Ensley. A later holder, the First National Bank of Birmingham, sued Searcy on the note. A dispute arose as to whether the First National Bank was

---

[32] UCC § 3-417(2).
[33] § 3-417(4).

the holder of the instrument on January 10, before the closing of the Ensley Bank on January 11. The First National Bank proved that on January 10 the note was indorsed to it by the Ensley Bank. Did this prove that the First National Bank was the holder on January 10? [First National Bank of Birmingham v Searcy, 31 AlaApp 553, 19 So2d 559]

4. Benton, as agent for Savidge, received an insurance settlement check from the Metropolitan Life Insurance Co. He indorsed it "For deposit" and deposited it in the Bryn Mawr Trust Company in the account of Savidge. What was the nature and effect of this indorsement? [Savidge v Metropolitan Life Insurance Co. 380 Pa 205, 110 A2d 730]

5. Humphrey drew a check for $100. It was stolen and the payee's name forged as an indorser. The check was then negotiated to Miller who had no knowledge of these facts. Miller indorsed the check to the Citizens Bank. Payment of the check was voided on the ground of the forgery. The Citizens Bank then sued Miller as indorser. Decide. [Citizens Bank of Hattiesburg v Miller, 194 Miss 557, 11 So2d 457]

6. Commercial Credit Corporation drew a check payable to the order of Rauch Motor Company. Rauch indorsed the check in blank and deposited it in its account in University National Bank. University transmitted the check to the drawee bank which returned it because payment had been stopped by Commercial Credit Corporation. University Bank and Lamson entered into an agreement which stated that the bank "hereby" negotiated the check to Lamson. This agreement was stapled to the check and the papers were delivered to Lamson. Was he the holder of the check? [Lamson v Commercial Credit Corp, 33 ColoApp 343, 521 P2d 785]

7. C, an employee of A, prepared a check drawn on Bank E and made payable to B, a nonexistent person. C had A sign the check. C then indorsed the name of B and deposited the check in Bank D. Bank D then indorsed the check and sent it to Bank E for payment. In a subsequent lawsuit, Bank E claimed that Bank D was liable on the warranty that it had title to the check, and that this warranty had been broken because there was not a chain of genuine indorsements. Was Bank D liable for breach of warranty because of the forged name of B? [See Aetna Life & Casualty Co. v Hampton State Bank (TexCivApp) 497 SW2d 80]

8. A check was drawn by Calumet and Hecla, Inc. on the State National Bank payable to Sumco Engineering and Madison Construction and Supply Company. Madison presented the check to the drawee bank for payment. The bank paid Madison the full amount of the check although it had not been indorsed by Sumco. Suit was then brought against the drawee bank by Sumco. Was the drawee liable? [State National Bank v Sumco Engineering, 36 AlaApp 244, 240 So2d 266]

9. Edmund Jezemski and Paula Jezemski were husband and wife but were separated. Paula and another man who impersonated Edmund borrowed money. The loan check drawn by the Philadelphia Title Insurance Company was payable to the order of Edmund Jezemski and Paula Jezemski. The check was then indorsed by Paula and Edmund's signature was forged. The check was paid by the Fidelity-Philadelphia Trust Company on which it was drawn. When the forgery was discovered, the Philadelphia Title Insurance Company claimed that the Fidelity-Philadelphia Trust Company was liable for the amount of the check because the latter company had made payment on a forged indorsement. Was Fidelity-Philadelphia liable? [Philadelphia Title Insurance Co. v Fidelity-Philadelphia Trust Co. 419 Pa 78, 212 A2d 222]

PAYMENT AND ACCEPTANCE OF PAPER

A. PRESENTMENT OF NOTES FOR PAYMENT

§ 31:1. INTRODUCTION.   promissory note is a two-party commercial paper, which means that originally only the maker and payee are involved. The maker is liable for payment on the due date specified in the note or on demand if the note is a demand instrument. If the maker dishonors the note when it is presented to him for payment, the indorsers, if there are any, may become liable for payment of the paper.

This chapter considers the rules of law that must be followed in order to enforce the liability of a party to a note. It must be remembered that even though these rules have been satisfied, a plaintiff will lose in a given case if he is not the holder as discussed in Chapter 28 or if the defendant has a defense that may be asserted against the plaintiff as discussed in Chapter 33.

The procedures for presenting a promissory note for payment and for giving notice of dishonor, which are explained in this chapter, apply also to other types of commercial paper, that is, drafts and checks.

§ 31:2. LIABILITY OF MAKER. The liability of a maker of a promissory note is primary. This means that payment may be demanded of him and that he may be sued by the holder as soon as the debt is due, but not before that time. The maker is under the duty to pay the note at the time and at the place named, if any place is specified by the note, unless he can set up a defense that is valid against the holder.

FACTS: Burke executed a promissory note. He later informed Bertolet, the holder of the note, that he would not make payment on the note when it became due. Bertolet immediately sued Burke. The defendant moved for summary judgment.

DECISION: Judgment for Burke. The doctrine of anticipatory repudiation does not apply to commercial paper. Consequently, when paper is due on a specific date, it does not become due at an earlier date merely because the obligor declares that he will default on the day when the paper is due. [Bertolet v Burke (DC Virgin Islands) 295 FSupp 1176]

By the very act of signing the promissory note, the maker deprives himself of two possible defenses. He admits (1) the existence of the payee named in the instrument and (2) the payee's capacity at that time to indorse the paper.[1] Thus, even though the payee of a note is a minor or a bankrupt, the maker cannot deny the validity of the title of a subsequent holder of the instrument on the ground that the payee lacked capacity to transfer title.

When a note is issued in payment of a debt, the original obligation is suspended until the instrument is due or until presentment for payment in the case of demand paper. If the note is dishonored by nonpayment, the holder may sue either on the note or on the underlying obligation.[2]

§ 31:3. NEED FOR PRESENTMENT FOR PAYMENT. The holder of a promissory note need not present the instrument to the maker for payment in order to hold the latter liable on the note. If the note is payable at a definite time, the maker is under a duty to pay the holder the amount due on the instrument as soon as that date is reached. The liability of the maker continues until barred by the statute of limitations.

If the note is demand paper, no special demand for payment is required. The holder may even begin a lawsuit against the maker without first making a demand for payment since the act of bringing suit is regarded as the making of a demand. If the note is payable at a definite time, the holder may bring suit on or after the due date without making a prior demand upon the maker.

An unqualified indorser is secondarily liable for the payment of the instrument, which means that he must pay the amount of the instrument to the holder under certain circumstances. Generally this duty arises only if (1) the instrument was presented for payment to the primary party on the due date or at maturity, (2) the primary party defaulted by failing to pay the amount of the instrument to the holder, and (3) the secondary party in question was given proper notice of the primary party's default.

A qualified indorser or a former holder of bearer paper who negotiates the instrument without indorsing it is not liable for payment. However, such parties, as well as an unqualified indorser, who does have a secondary liability, may be liable for a breach of warranty.

§ 31:4. PRESENTMENT FOR PAYMENT. When presentment for payment of notes and other commercial paper is required, the following rules apply:

(a) Person making presentment. Presentment for payment must be made by the holder of the paper or by one authorized to act and receive payment for him.

(b) Manner of presentment. Demand for payment in any manner is sufficient. The party to whom the demand is made may require, however, that greater formality be observed, such as by requiring (1) reasonable

---

[1] Uniform Commercial Code § 3-413(3).
[2] UCC § 3-802(1)(b).

identification of the person making presentment and evidence of his authority if he acts for another; (2) production of the instrument for payment at a place specified in it or, if there be none, at any place reasonable under the circumstances; and (3) a signed receipt on the instrument for any partial or full payment and its surrender upon full payment. If the party presenting the instrument does not comply with such requests at the time of making presentment, he is allowed a reasonable time within which to do so; but if he does not so comply, the presentment has no effect.[3]

The presentment must make a clear demand for payment and a mere inquiry as to whether payment would be made in the future is not sufficient.

> **FACTS:** Mason wished to purchase a tract of land from Kohlhepp's estate. He made out a check payable to the order of Holt, as executor under the will of Kohlhepp. Holt's secretary was taking the check to deposit in Holt's bank when she was met by the attorney of one of the heirs of the estate who suggested that they go to the bank on which the check was drawn and inquire whether the check would be paid when presented for collection. This was done. Thereafter, a dispute arose as to whether the check had been presented for payment.

> **DECISION:** There was no presentment for payment. There had been only an inquiry as to whether payment would be made in the future. [Kohlhepp's Estate v Mason, 25 Utah2d 155, 478 P2d 339]

In addition to a presentment for payment made directly between the parties, presentment may be made by sending the paper through the mail to the debtor, or by sending it through a clearinghouse.[4] A collecting bank may also make presentment for payment by sending merely a notice to the nonbank party to whom the demand for payment is made.[5] If the party so notified fails to act within a specified time, his inaction is treated as a dishonor of the note.[6]

(c) On whom presentment is made. Presentment for payment must be made to the party primarily liable, that is, the maker of the promissory note, or to a person who has authority to make or refuse payment on his behalf.[7]

(d) Place of making presentment. Presentment for payment is properly made at the place that is specified in the instrument. When a place of payment is not specified, presentment of the instrument is to be made at the place of business or the residence of the person from whom payment is to be demanded.[8]

---

[3] § 3-505.
[4] § 3-504(2)(a), (b).
[5] § 4-210(1). This provision is not applicable if the paper is payable by, through, or at a bank.
[6] UCC § 4-210(2).
[7] § 3-504(3).
[8] § 3-504(2)(c).

§ 31:5. TIME OF MAKING PRESENTMENT. A note payable at a stated date must be presented for payment on that date. If the time for paying the balance due on the note has been accelerated, presentment must be made within a reasonable time after the default in a scheduled payment of principal or interest. For the purpose of determining the secondary liability of any party, presentment for payment must be made within a reasonable time after such person became liable on the instrument.

Presentment must be made at a reasonable time, and if made at a bank, must be made during its banking day.

(a) Computation of time. In determining the date of maturity of an instrument, the starting day is excluded and the day of payment is included. Thus, an instrument dated July 3 (which leaves 28 days in July) and payable 30 days from date is due on August 2.

(b) Instrument due on legal or business holiday. When the presentment of the paper is due on a day that is not a full business day, presentment is due on the following full business day. This rule is applied when the due day is not a full business day either because it is a legal holiday or merely because the bank or other person required to make payment on the instrument, as a matter of its business practice, is closed all day or for a half day.

This rule is also applied when the due date is a business holiday for either party, that is, if either the person required to present the instrument or the person who is required to pay upon presentment is not open for a full business day on the due date, the date for presentment is extended to the first day that is a full business day for both of them.[9]

(c) Excuse for delay in making presentment. Failure to present an instrument for payment at the proper time will be excused when the delay is caused by circumstances beyond the control of the holder. It must not, however, be caused by his misconduct, negligence, or fault. Mere inconvenience, such as that arising from inclement weather, is not a valid excuse for delay. When the circumstances that excuse the delay are removed, presentment must be made within a reasonable time.[10]

(d) Effect of delay. An unexcused delay in any necessary presentment for payment discharges an indorser's liability for payment of the paper. If the note is *domiciled*, that is, payable at a bank, the delay may also operate to discharge the maker. The UCC provides as to such paper that "any . . . maker of a note payable at a bank who because the . . . payor bank becomes insolvent during the delay is deprived of funds maintained with the . . . payor bank to cover the instrument may discharge his liability by written assignment to the holder of his rights against the . . . payor bank in respect of such funds, but such . . . maker is not otherwise discharged."

---

[9] § 3-503(3).

[10] § 3-511(1). Delay is also excused when the holder does not know that the instrument is due, UCC § 3-511(1), as could occur if the due date had been accelerated by a prior holder.

§ 31:6. WHEN PRESENTMENT FOR PAYMENT IS EXCUSED OR UNNECESSARY.

(a) Waiver. Presentment for payment is not required if it has been waived by an express or implied agreement of the secondary party in question. A waiver of presentment is binding upon all parties if it appears on the face of the original note. If the waiver is part of an indorsement, however, it binds only that indorser.

(b) Inability. Presentment for payment is not required if it cannot be made in spite of the exercise of due diligence, as when presentment is attempted at the place where payment is to be made but neither the person who is to make payment nor anyone authorized to act for him can be found at that place.[11]

FACTS: Samuel and Annie Jacobson executed a promissory note payable to Frank and Angelo Sarandrea. The payees indorsed the note to Cuddy. The makers of the note had moved, leaving no address, and presentment for payment was therefore not made. Notice of dishonor, however, was given to the indorsers. When Cuddy sued the Sarandreas, the defense was raised that Cuddy was not excused from making presentment on the Jacobsons and that the holder was negligent because he failed to ask the payee for the address of the makers.

DECISION: The defendants were liable. There is no duty to ask the payee where the primary parties live. [Cuddy v Sarandrea, 52 RI 465, 161 A 297]

(c) Death or insolvency. Presentment for payment is not required if the maker of the note has died or if he has gone into insolvency proceedings after he had issued the note.

(d) Refusal to pay. The holder is not required to make presentment upon the maker if he has already refused to pay the note for no reason, or for any reason other than an objection that proper presentment was not made.

(e) Belief or conduct of secondary party. The secondary party cannot demand that presentment be made if he has no reason to expect that the instrument will be paid and no right to require that payment be made.[12]

§ 31:7. DISHONOR OF NOTE.
If the maker fails or refuses to pay the note when it is properly presented to him, he has dishonored the instrument by nonpayment. The fact that the maker does not make immediate payment of the note when it is presented to him may not dishonor the note. He has the right to withhold making payment until he has made a reasonable examination to determine that the note is properly payable to the holder. He cannot, however, delay payment beyond the close of business on the day of presentment.[13]

---

[11] UCC §§ 3-504(2), 3-511(2)(c).
[12] § 3-511(2)(b).
[13] § 3-506(2).

§ 31:8. NOTICE OF DISHONOR. If commercial paper is dishonored by nonpayment, any secondary party who is not given proper notice thereof is released from liability, unless the giving of notice is excused.[14] It is only necessary that a party be given notice once because a notice operates for the benefit of all parties who have rights against the party notified.

(a) Who may give notice. The notice of dishonor is ordinarily given by the holder who has been refused payment or by his agent. If the agent made the presentment for payment, he of course may give notice of the dishonor to his principal who in turn may give it to the secondary party in question. When any person who is liable on the paper receives notice of its dishonor, he may in turn give notice to other secondary parties.

(b) Person notified. The notice of dishonor may be given to any party who is liable on the instrument. Notice to one partner is notice to all, even though the firm has been dissolved. When the party to be notified is dead or incompetent, notice may be sent to his last-known address or be given to his personal representative.

(c) Form of notice. Notice may be given in any reasonable manner. It may be oral or written, and it may be sent by mail. It may have any terms as long as it identifies the instrument and states that it has been dishonored. A misdescription that does not mislead the party notified does not nullify or vitiate the notice. Notice may be effected by sending the instrument itself, with a stamp, ticket, or writing attached thereto, stating that payment has been refused or by sending a notice of debit with respect to the paper.[15]

(d) Place of notice. The UCC does not specify a place to which notice is to be given, but it provides that notice generally shall be deemed given whenever such steps have been taken as may be reasonably required to inform the other person, whether or not he actually comes to know of it. Furthermore, a person is deemed to receive notice or notification whenever the matter comes to his attention, or when the notice is delivered at the place of business through which the contract was made or at any other place held out by him as the place for the receipt of such communications.[16]

> **FACTS:** The Century L. & W. Co. gave a note to Merrill, who indorsed it to another person who indorsed it to the Bank of America National T. & S. Association. When Century defaulted in payment of the note, the bank notified both indorsers. The notice sent to Merrill did not reach him because it was sent to an old address shown in the bank's files. The bank used the current city directory to obtain the address of the other indorser, who received the notice sent him. Merrill defended on the ground that he had not been notified.

---

[14] § 3-501(2)(a). In the case of a "domiciled" note payable at a bank, the maker must be given notice that the note was not paid when presented at the bank and, if notice is not so given, the maker is released to the same extent already noted in connection with the effect of failure to present at the bank. UCC § 3-501(2)(b).

[15] § 3-508(3).

[16] § 1-201(26).

DECISION: Judgment for Merrill. The holder had not used due diligence in giving Merrill notice, as established by the fact that the holder had not made use of the same current directory which it used with respect to the other indorser. Merrill was therefore not liable upon his indorsement. [Bank of America National T. & S. Association v Century L. & W. Co. 19 CalApp2d 197, 65 P2d 110]

(e) **Time of notice.** Notice must be given before midnight of the third business day after dishonor. If the notice is given following the receipt of notice of dishonor from another party, it must be given before midnight of the third business day after receiving such notice. When required of a bank, notice of dishonor must be given before midnight of the banking day following the banking day on which the note is dishonored or the bank receives notice of such dishonor.[17] A written notice of dishonor is effective when sent. Hence, a notice sent by mail is sufficient even though it is never received, provided it was properly addressed, bore the necessary postage, and was properly mailed.[18]

FACTS: Browne made a promissory note which was indorsed by Siegel. On the default of Browne, the holder of the note, Durkin, gave notice to Siegel by certified mail, return receipt requested. The notice was returned unopened and undelivered, marked, "Refused," and with the blank form of post office receipt unsigned. When sued later, Siegel defended on the ground that he had not been given proper notice, that ordinary first-class mail could have been forwarded, and that he had been in Canada at the time the notice was sent.

DECISION: Judgment for Durkin. Since only the "giving" of notice is required, a proper mailing is sufficient. A mailing is proper when the correct addresses of the addressee and the sender are on the envelope, and the proper postage is attached. The fact that certified mail is used does not impair the sufficiency of the notice for such mail is safer, even though it is not forwarded to a new address. [Durkin v Siegel, 340 Mass 445, 165 NE2d 81]

If notice is not given within the required time and the delay in or absence of notice is not excused, the person entitled to notice cannot be held liable for the payment of the paper.

§ 31:9. **EXCUSE FOR DELAY OR ABSENCE OF NOTICE OF DISHONOR.** Delay in giving notice of dishonor is excused under the same circumstances as delay in making presentment for payment.[19]

The absence of any notice of dishonor is excused for three of the reasons considered as excusing the absence of presentment; namely (1) waiver, (2) inability to give notice in spite of due diligence, and (3) the fact that the party not notified did not have any reason to believe that the instrument would be paid nor any right to require payment.[20] When an indorser has

---

[17] §§ 3-508(2), 4-105(1)(h).
[18] § 3-504(4).
[19] § 3-511.
[20] § 3-511(2).

such knowledge or so participates in the affairs of the primary party that the indorser knows the commercial paper will not be honored by the primary party, it is not required that the holder go through the useless gesture of making a presentment and of notifying the secondary party in order to hold him liable.

Delay by a bank in returning a dishonored item is excused by equipment failure.

> **FACTS:** Port City State Bank received two checks for collection. It sent them to American National Bank, the drawee bank. The drawee bank returned the checks as dishonored for insufficient funds after the midnight deadline. Port City sued American National, basing liability on the late return. American National raised the defense that its computer had broken down.

> **DECISION:** Judgment for American National. While a bank must ordinarily return a dishonored item before its midnight deadline, delay in so doing is excused when caused by the breakdown of the bank's computer system and there is no evidence of any failure to exercise due diligence. [Port City State Bank v American National Bank (CA10 Okla) 486 F2d 196]

The requirements as to notice of dishonor are not applicable in determining the rights of co-obligors as between themselves. For example, when two indorsers are jointly liable and one pays the full amount, he is entitled to recover one half of such payment by way of contribution from his coindorser without regard to whether the holder had given the coindorser proper notice of dishonor.

§ **31:10. PROOF OF DISHONOR.** Since the liability of the secondary party depends upon whether certain steps were taken within the proper time, it is important for the holder to be able to prove that he has complied with the requirements of the law. In order to aid him in proving such essential facts, certain documents and records are considered evidence of dishonor and of any notice recited therein. The trier of fact must accept such evidence in the absence of proof to the contrary.[21] These documents and records include (1) protests, (2) bank stamps and memorandums, and (3) bank records.

(a) **Protests.** A *protest* is a memorandum or certificate executed by a notary public, or certain other public officers, upon information satisfactory to him, which sets forth that the particular identified instrument has been dishonored. It may also recite that notice of dishonor was given to all parties or to specified parties.

(b) **Bank stamps and memorandums.** If the stamp put on the paper by a bank or the memorandum attached to the note by the bank is consistent with or suggests a dishonor, it is evidence of that fact. For example, a notation "Not sufficient funds" or "Payment stopped" indicates a dishonor or nonpayment of the instrument and therefore comes within this rule. On

---

[21] §§ 3-510, 1-201(31).

the other hand, a notation of "Indorsement missing" is not consistent with dishonor and is therefore not admissible as evidence of a dishonor.

(c) Bank records. Bank records kept in the usual course of business are admissible as evidence of dishonor even though it cannot be shown who made the entry in the books.

B. PRESENTMENT OF DRAFTS

§ 31:11. INTRODUCTION. This part considers the rules of law that must be followed in order to enforce the liability of a party to a draft. It must be remembered that even though these rules have been satisfied, a plaintiff will lose in a given case if he is not the holder as discussed in Chapter 28 or if the defendant has a defense which may be asserted against the plaintiff as discussed in Chapter 33.

A note must be presented for payment in order to hold secondary parties liable; under certain circumstances a draft must be presented for acceptance as well as for payment to accomplish that purpose.

If the drawer names himself as drawee, the paper is effective as a promissory note.[22] In such a case, the drawer is the primary party and procedures peculiar to drafts, such as presentment for acceptance, are eliminated.

§ 31:12. LIABILITY OF DRAWEE.

(a) Before acceptance. An *acceptance* is the written assent of the drawee to the order of the drawer. Before a drawee accepts a draft, he is not liable for its payment. In the absence of a prior contract to accept the draft, the drawee is not under any duty to do so. His act of refusing to accept the draft does not give the holder any right to sue him on the paper, even though he may thereby break a contract with the drawer or some other party that he would accept the bill. Neither does the draft operate as an assignment of any money, even though the drawee has in his possession funds of the drawer.[23]

(b) After acceptance. When the drawee accepts a draft, he is an acceptor and becomes primarily liable for its payment. By the acceptance he also admits (1) the existence of the payee and (2) the payee's capacity at the time to indorse the draft.[24]

If the drawee pays the instrument to a person who claims it through a forged indorsement, the drawee must bear the loss of such payment.

§ 31:13. LIABILITY OF DRAWER. The drawer has a secondary liability. By executing the draft, he undertakes to pay the amount of the draft to the holder if, when the instrument is presented to the drawee for acceptance or payment, it is dishonored and proper proceedings are taken by the holder.

---

[22] § 3-118(a).
[23] § 3-409(1); Aiken Bag Corp. v McLeod, 89 GaApp 737, 81 SE2d 215.
[24] UCC § 3-413(3).

FACTS: Gill sold his airplane to Hobson for $8,000. The purchase price was paid by delivering to Gill a draft drawn by Yoes on the Phoenix Savings & Loan Co. to the order of Gill. Yoes had no money in the savings and loan association but had applied to it for a loan. The loan application was rejected; and when the draft was presented on the association, it refused to pay it. Gill then sued Yoes on the draft. Yoes raised the defense that she had nothing to do with the purchase of the airplane and that she did not need one.

DECISION: Judgment for Gill. Since Yoes had signed the draft as a drawer, she became secondarily liable as a drawer without regard to whether she had any interest in any transaction in which the draft was used as payment. [Gill v Yoes (Okla) 360 P2d 506]

The drawer, however, may insert in the draft a provision to exclude or limit his own liability as by adding "without recourse" above his signature.

The drawer admits two things by the act of drawing the draft. He admits (1) the existence of the payee, and (2) the payee's capacity at the time to transfer the instrument. The effect of these statutory admissions is the same as in the case of the maker of a promissory note or the acceptor of a draft.[25]

When the drawer executes and delivers to the payee a draft in payment of a debt, the original obligation is suspended until the draft is due, or until presentment for payment if it is demand paper. If the paper is dishonored, the holder may sue either on the paper or on the underlying obligation.[26]

§ 31:14. LIABILITY OF INDORSER.

The liability of an unqualified indorser of a draft is broader than that of an unqualified indorser of a promissory note. Any unqualified indorser is under a secondary liability for the nonpayment of the instrument when due. In addition, the unqualified indorser of a draft is under a secondary liability for the refusal of the drawee to accept the instrument when it is thereafter presented to him for acceptance.

In order to charge the unqualified indorser of the draft for either nonacceptance or nonpayment, it is necessary to prove that a presentment to the drawee had been properly made and due notice given to the indorser of the drawee's failure to accept or pay.

§ 31:15. NECESSITY OF PRESENTMENT FOR ACCEPTANCE.

The best way for the holder to find out whether the drawee will pay a time draft when it becomes due is to present it to the drawee for acceptance. If the drawee is not willing to pay the instrument according to its terms, he will reject it, dishonor it by nonacceptance. If he is willing to pay it when it becomes due, he will accept it.[27]

Any draft may be presented to the drawee for acceptance. A presentment for acceptance must be made if (1) it is necessary in order to fix the date of

---

[25] § 3-413(3).
[26] § 3-802(1)(b). Special provisions apply when a bank is the drawer. UCC § 3-802(1)(a).
[27] § 3-410(1).

maturity of the draft, such as when the instrument is payable a specified number of days after sight; (2) the draft expressly states that it must be presented for acceptance; or (3) the draft is made payable elsewhere than at the residence or place of business of the drawee.[28]

§ 31:16. MANNER OF PRESENTING FOR ACCEPTANCE.

Presentment of a draft for acceptance is made in the same manner as the presentment of a note for payment,[29] with the obvious difference that the presentment is made upon the drawee rather than upon the maker.

(a) **Time for presentment for acceptance.** Unless a different time is specified in the draft, presentment for acceptance must be made on or before the date on which the instrument is payable by its express provisions. If it is payable after sight, it must be presented for acceptance or negotiated within a reasonable time after its date or issue, whichever is later. With respect to the liability of any secondary party on any other form of instrument, presentment for acceptance must be made within a reasonable time after that party became liable for it.[30]

The time for presentment of a draft for acceptance with respect to the hour and day or the effect of holidays is the same as in the case of presentment of a note for payment.

(b) **Delay or absence of presentment for acceptance.** Delay in a necessary presentment of a draft for acceptance and the failure to make any presentment are excused under the same circumstances as in the case of the presentment of a note for payment.

An unexcused delay in making any necessary presentment for acceptance discharges an indorser's liability for payment of the paper. If the draft is domiciled, that is, payable at a bank, the drawer or acceptor is discharged under the circumstances that discharge the maker of a note for dishonor by nonpayment.[31]

(c) **Time allowed for acceptance.** It is not necessary that the drawee accept or dishonor the draft immediately upon its presentment to him. In order to afford him an opportunity of determining from his records whether he should accept, he may postpone making a decision, without thereby dishonoring the draft, until the close of the next business day following the presentment of the draft. Likewise, the holder may allow the postponement of acceptance for an additional business day when he acts in good faith in the hope that he will be able to obtain an acceptance. If the holder agrees to such additional postponement, the liability of the secondary parties is not affected and the draft is not thereby dishonored.[32]

---

[28] § 3-501(1)(a).
[29] § 3-504.
[30] § 3-503(1)(a), (b), (e).
[31] § 3-502(1)(b). See § 31:5(4).
[32] UCC § 3-506(1). The time allowed the drawee to determine whether to accept is distinct from any right of representment after dishonor when authorized by the paper. UCC § 3-507(4).

§ 31:17. KINDS OF ACCEPTANCES.

(a) **General acceptance.** A *general acceptance* (or simply an "acceptance") is one in which the acceptor agrees without qualification to pay according to the order of the drawer.

(b) **Draft-varying acceptance.** A *draft-varying acceptance* is one in which the acceptor agrees to pay but not exactly in conformity with the order of the draft. An acceptance varies the draft when it changes the time or place of payment, when it agrees to pay only a part of the amount of the draft, or when it sets up a condition that must be satisfied before the acceptance is effective.

An acceptance to pay at a particular bank or place in the United States is a general acceptance, unless the draft expressly states that it is to be paid there only and not elsewhere. In the latter case the acceptance varies the draft.[33]

If the holder does not wish to take the varying acceptance, he may reject it and treat the draft as dishonored by nonacceptance. After giving due notice, he can proceed at once against secondary parties.

If the holder assents to the draft-varying acceptance, however, he in effect consents to the execution of a new instrument; and each drawer and indorser is released from liability unless he affirmatively assents to such acceptance. The fact that a secondary party fails to object is not sufficient to prevent his release from liability.

§ 31:18. FORM OF ACCEPTANCE.

§ 31:18. FORM OF ACCEPTANCE. An acceptance is the drawee's notation on the draft itself that he will make payment as directed thereby. It may be merely his signature, but customarily it will be the word, "Accepted," and his signature, and generally the date. In any case, however, the acceptance must be written on the draft itself.[34] Usually it is written across the face of the instrument.

FACTS: Temple was the drawee of a draft of which Lawless was payee. When the draft was presented to Temple for acceptance, he merely wrote his name on its face. Later, when he was sued by Lawless, he denied that he had accepted the draft.

DECISION: Judgment for Lawless. A drawee is charged as an acceptor when he merely writes his name on the draft, although it is customary to add the word, "Accepted." When a blank acceptance is made, any holder can write "Accepted" above the signature of the acceptor. [Lawless v Temple, 254 Mass 395, 150 NE 176]

An acceptance cannot be oral, nor can it be contained in some other writing. Thus, a bank is not bound by its oral promise to pay a draft drawn upon it. The fact that the drawee is not liable on the draft because he has not accepted it does not necessarily prevent his being liable because of other obligations or principles of law.

---

[33] § 3-412(2).
[34] § 3-410(1).

FACTS: Schenk's Motor Sales had a checking account in the Home Savings Bank. The balance in the account was $3,080.56. Schenk drew a check for $9,700 payable to the order of the General Finance Corporation. The bank certified the check when General Finance Corporation orally promised to accept a draft drawn on General by Schenk that had just been deposited in Schenk's account. The certified check was paid by the bank, but General refused to pay the draft on the ground that its oral acceptance was not binding. The bank sued General for the amount of the certified check.

DECISION: Judgment for the bank for $6,619.44. General Finance was not liable on the paper because an oral acceptance is not binding. However, General Finance obtained a certified check for $9,700. This was $6,619.44 more than Schenk could have paid General without the bank's certification, as the Schenk bank account was only $3,080.56. In order to prevent the unjust enrichment of General Finance, it must repay the bank the excess of $6,619.44. [Home Savings Bank v General Finance Corp. 10 Wis2d 417, 103 NW2d 117]

There can be no acceptance by misconduct. The refusal to return the draft or its destruction by the drawee does not constitute an "acceptance." If the drawee retains the draft and refuses to return it, he is guilty of conversion.[35] The measure of damages is the face amount of the instrument.

§ 31:19. DISHONOR BY NONACCEPTANCE.
When a draft that is presented for acceptance is not accepted within the allowed time, the person presenting it must treat the draft as dishonored by nonacceptance.[36] If he fails to do so, the secondary parties are released from liability.

When a draft is dishonored by nonacceptance, the holder must give the same notice of dishonor as in the case of dishonor of paper by nonpayment. If the draft on its face appears to be drawn or payable outside of the United States, its territories, and the District of Columbia, it is also necessary to protest the dishonor in order to charge the drawer and the indorsers.

§ 31:20. PRESENTMENT OF DRAFT FOR PAYMENT.
The requirements and limitations upon the necessity of presentment of a draft for payment are the same as in the case of a promissory note, with the circumstances excusing delays or failure to make presentment of a note likewise excusing delay or failure to make presentment of a draft for payment. The failure to present for payment is likewise excused with respect to a party who has countermanded payment of the draft.

Furthermore, when a draft has been dishonored by nonacceptance, a later presentment for payment is excused unless the instrument has since been accepted.[37]

The provisions governing notice of dishonor of a draft by nonpayment are the same as those for a note.[38]

---

[35] § 3-419(1)(a).
[36] § 3-507(1)(a).
[37] § 3-511(4).
[38] §§ 3-501(2), 3-508. See § 31:8.

§ 31:21. PROTEST OF DISHONOR. A protest of dishonor of a draft by nonacceptance or nonpayment is not necessary unless the draft appears on its face to be drawn or payable outside of the United States, its territories, or the District of Columbia. The holder, however, may protest the dishonor of any instrument. Delay in protesting dishonor or the absence of a protest are excused under the same circumstances that apply in the case of a note dishonored by nonpayment.

(a) **Waiver of protest.** A *waiver of protest* is effective to excuse the absence of an otherwise required protest. Protest is commonly waived, particularly in the case of out-of-town instruments, because protest does involve an additional cost and some inconvience. Frequently, therefore, the instrument will contain a clause stating that protest is waived, or it may be stamped with the words, "Protest waived" or "No Protest." A waiver of protest is a waiver of the requirement of presentment and notice of dishonor as well as of the protest itself even though protest is not required.

When words of guaranty, such as "payment guaranteed" or "collection guaranteed," are used, presentment, notice of dishonor, and protest are not necessary to charge the person using such language.[39]

QUESTIONS AND CASE PROBLEMS

1. Four promissory notes were executed by Continental Diamond Mines, Inc. payable to the order of M. Kopp. The notes were thereafter indorsed to M. Kopp, Inc. and then to Rafkin. Rafkin was the holder on the due date. Was it necessary for him to make a presentment of the notes to Continental Diamond Mines in order to hold it liable on the notes? [Rafkin v Continental Diamond Mines, Inc. 33 Misc2d 156, 228 NYS2d 317]

2. A indorsed a promissory note on the back. At the top of the back, above all indorsements, there were printed the words "Notice of protest waived." The note was not paid when due. The holder sent A notice that the note was not paid, but A did not receive the notice because it was sent to a former address at which he no longer lived. A denied liability because he had not been properly notified. Decide. [See Lizza Asphalt Construction Co. v Greenvale Construction Co. (NY) 4 UCCRS 954]

3. Dubinsky borrowed money from the Columbian National Life Insurance Co. He sold his house to Cohen who promised to pay this debt to the insurance company and gave it a promissory note. Later Dubinsky gave the company a renewal note. In a suit upon the renewal note Dubinsky claimed that he was an accommodation maker. Decide. [Columbian National Life Insurance Co. v Dubinsky, 349 Mo 299, 160 SW2d 727]

---

[39] UCC § 3-416(5).

4. Womack executed two drafts drawn on Durrett through the Abilene State Bank. When the drafts were not paid, Womack recovered judgment on the drafts against Durrett. He also sued the bank to which the drafts had been given for collection, contending that the bank had orally agreed to pay the drafts. Was the bank liable? [Womack v Durrett (TexCivApp) 24 SW2d 463]

5. The X Bank sold money orders in which it was the drawer and by which it ordered itself to pay the amount of the money order through the Z Bank to the person designated by the purchaser of the money order. (a) Assuming that the instruments were negotiable, what kind of commercial paper were the money orders? (b) Was the X Bank or the Z Bank the drawee? [See Comet Check Cashing Service v Hanover Insurance Group (NY CivCt) 5 UCCRS 852]

6. The Perfection Curing Co. gave the First National Bank of Winnfield a sight draft drawn by it on the Citizens Bank of Campti. The First National Bank sent the sight draft to the Citizens' Bank for acceptance and payment. The Citizens' Bank received the draft on September 28. On October 11 the Citizens' Bank returned the draft to the First National Bank without either accepting or rejecting the draft. The First National Bank sued the Citizens' Bank on the draft. Can it recover? [First National Bank of Winnfield v Citizens' Bank of Campti, 163 La 919, 113 So 147]

7. Lowe & Myers were contractors doing construction work for the Druid Realty Co. In order to pay for their materials they drew a draft on the realty company directing it to pay $2,000 to the order of the Crane Co. The realty company, through its president, wrote on the instrument that it accepted the instrument and agreed to pay it within 30 days after the completion of the work, provided Crane Company continued to furnish materials to Lowe & Myers. What was the effect of the action by the realty company? [Crane Co. v Druid Realty Co. 137 Md 324, 112 A 621]

8. Fuller Brothers, as the holder, brought an action against Bovay, as indorser. It was shown that the notice of default of the primary party was given to Bovay by a letter addressed "Jonesboro Rice Mill Co., Jonesboro, Ark., Attention Mr. Bovay." Was this a proper notice? [Bovay v Fuller (CA8 Ark) 63 F2d 280]

9. Drummond executed a draft on the Webb Packing Co. to pay for cattle purchased from Hales. The Webb Packing Co. refused to accept or pay the draft. Hales gave proper notice to Drummond and then sued him on the draft. Drummond raised the defense that he had been acting merely as the agent of the Webb Packing Co. and that it was understood with Hales that Drummond should not be personally liable on the instrument. Was this a good defense? [Drummond v Hales (CA10 Okla) 191 F2d 972]

CHECKS AND BANK COLLECTIONS

§ 32:1. NATURE OF A CHECK. A check is a particular kind of draft. The following features of a check distinguish it from other drafts or bills of exchange:[1]

(1) The drawee of a check is always a bank.

(2) As a practical matter, the check is drawn on the assumption that the bank has on deposit in the drawer's account an amount sufficient to pay the check. In the case of a draft, there is no assumption that the drawee has any of the drawer's money with which to pay the instrument. Actually, the rights of the parties are not affected by the fact that the depositor does not have funds on deposit with the bank sufficient to pay the check.

If a draft is dishonored, the drawer is civilly liable; but if a check is drawn with intent to defraud the person to whom it is delivered, the drawer is also subject to criminal prosecution in most states under what are known as *bad check laws*. Most states provide that if the check is not made good within a stated period, such as 10 days, it will be presumed that the check was originally issued with the intent to defraud.

(3) A check is demand paper. A draft may be payable either on demand or at a future date. The standard form of check does not specify when it is payable, and it is therefore automatically payable on demand. This eliminates the need for an acceptance since the holder of the check will merely present it for payment.

One exception arises when a check is postdated, that is, when the check shows a date later than the actual date of execution and delivery. Here the check is not payable until the date arrives. This, in effect, changes the check to time paper without expressly stating so.

---

[1] Checks are governed by both Article 3 of the Uniform Commercial Code relating to commercial paper and Article 4 governing bank deposits and collections.

FACTS: Kelinson was president of the Barkel Meat Packing Co., a wholesale meat packer. On February 2, a shipment of meat was delivered to the company. Kelinson gave the driver a check in payment for the full amount but dated it February 4. Approximately thirty checks given in payment of prior shipments had also been postdated. All prior checks had been paid, but the check of February 2 was not paid. Kelinson was prosecuted for the offenses of passing a worthless check and of obtaining money by false pretenses.

DECISION: Kelinson was not guilty as charged. The fact that the check was post-dated was a warning that there was not then sufficient funds on deposit to pay the check. Consequently, it was not a bad check but rather a draft that would be due on the date of the check. Likewise, there was no false representation. [Pennsylvania v Kelinson, 199 PaSuper 135, 184 A2d 374]

The delivery of a check is not regarded as an assignment of the money on deposit. It therefore does not automatically transfer the rights of the depositor against his bank to the holder of the check, and there is no duty on the part of the drawee bank to pay the holder the amount of the check.[2]

§ **32:2. LIABILITY OF DRAWER.** If the check is presented for payment and paid, no liability of the drawer arises. If the bank refuses to make payment, the drawer is then subject to a liability similar to that in the case of the nonpayment of an ordinary draft. If proper notice of dishonor is not given the drawer of the check, he may be discharged from liability to the same extent as a drawer of an ordinary draft.

§ **32:3. DUTIES OF DRAWEE BANK.** It is necessary to distinguish between the status of the drawer with respect to his check and his relationship with his bank on the contract of deposit.

(a) Privacy. The bank owes the depositor the duty of maintaining secrecy concerning information which the bank acquires in connection with the depositor-bank relationship.

FACTS: Peterson, a depositor in the First National Bank, sued the bank for disclosing to his employer without Peterson's consent details relating to Peterson's checking account with the bank and his financial condition.

DECISION: Judgment for Peterson. As an implied incident of the contract between a bank and its customers, the bank has the duty to refrain from disclosing to third persons any information relating to its customer's account. [Peterson v Idaho First National Bank, 83 Idaho 578, 367 P2d 284]

(b) Payment. The bank is under a general contractual duty to its depositor to pay on demand all of his checks to the extent of the funds

---

[2] UCC § 3-409(1).

deposited to his credit. When the bank breaches this contract, it is liable to the drawer for damages. In the case of a draft, there is ordinarily no duty on the drawee to accept it, or to make payment if he has not accepted it.

(c) Stale checks. A bank acting in good faith may pay a check presented more than six months after its date (commonly known as a *stale check*); but, unless the check is certified, it is not required to do so.[3] The fact that a bank may refuse to pay a check which is more than six months old does not mean that it must pay a check which is less than six months old or that it is not required to exercise reasonable care in making payment of any check.

§ 32:4. STOPPING PAYMENT. The drawer has the power of stopping payment of a check. After the check is issued, he can notify the drawee bank not to pay it when it is presented for payment. This is a useful device when a check is lost or mislaid. A duplicate check can be written and, to make sure that the payee does not receive payment twice or that an improper person does not receive payment on the first check, payment on the first check can be stopped. Likewise, if payment is made by check and then the payee defaults on his contract so that the drawer would have a claim against him, payment on the check can be stopped, assuming that the payee has not cashed it.

The *stop-payment order* may be either oral or written. If oral, however, it is only binding on the bank for 14 calendar days unless confirmed in writing within that time. A written order is not effective after 6 months unless renewed in writing.

If the bank makes payment of a check after it has been properly notified to stop payment, it is liable to the depositor for the loss he sustains, in the absence of a valid limitation of the bank's liability. The burden of establishing the loss resulting in such case rests upon the depositor.[4] Thus, the bank does not become automatically liable for the amount of the check paid in violation of the stop-payment order. The bank is only liable to the extent that it is shown that the payment has caused loss to the depositor through the making of a payment on a claim which the depositor was not legally obligated to pay.

FACTS: Tusso sent a check for $600 drawn on the Security National Bank payable to the order of the Adamson Construction Company. He then realized that he had already paid Adamson. At 9:00 a.m. the next morning, he notified the bank to stop payment. Later that morning, the check was brought to the bank, and, at 10:40 a.m., the bank certified the check and charged it to Tusso's account. Tusso sued the bank to recover the amount so charged. The bank claimed that he was required to prove that the bank had been negligent.

DECISION: The depositor was not required to prove that the bank had been negligent in making payment over the stop-payment order. The bank was liable because it had violated the order; the absence of negligence was not a defense. [Tusso v Security National Bank, 349 NYS2d 914]

---

[3] § 4-404.
[4] § 4-403(3).

The act of stopping payment may in some cases make the depositor liable to the holder of the instrument. If the depositor has no proper ground for stopping payment, he is liable to the payee to whom he has delivered the check. In any case, he is liable for stopping payment with respect to any holder in due course or other party having the rights of a holder in due course, unless he stops payment for a reason that may be asserted against such holder as a defense. The fact that the bank refuses to make payment because of the drawer's instruction does not make the case any different from any other instance in which the drawee refuses to pay.

When the depositor does not give the bank the stop-payment notice in person but makes use of a means of communication such as the telegraph, he cannot hold the bank liable if the notice is delayed in reaching the bank which makes payment before receiving the notice. If negligence on the part of the telegraph company can be established, however, the depositor can sue that company.

It is to the advantage of the seller to require either a certified check of the buyer or a cashier's check from the buyer's bank payable to the order of the seller, for with respect to either check neither the buyer nor the buyer's bank can stop payment to the seller.

§ 32:5. TIME OF PRESENTMENT OF CHECK FOR PAYMENT. In order
to charge a secondary party to demand paper, presentment for payment must generally be made upon the primary party to the instrument within a reasonable time after that secondary party signs it. Reasonable time is determined by the nature of the instrument, by commercial usage, and by the facts of the particular case.[5]

Failure to make such timely presentment discharges all prior indorsers of the instrument. It also discharges the drawer, if the draft is payable at a bank, to the extent that he has lost, through the bank's failure, money which he had on deposit at the bank to meet the payment of the instrument.[6]

As a modification to the foregoing principles, the UCC establishes two presumptions as to what is a reasonable time in which to present a check for payment.[7] If the check is not certified and is both drawn and payable within the United States, it is presumed as to the drawer that 30 days after the date of the check or the date of its issuance, whichever is later, is the reasonable period in which to make presentment for payment. In the case of an indorser, it is presumed to be 7 days after his indorsement.[8]

(a) Bank's liability to drawer of check. The contract between the drawer-depositor and the drawee-bank obligates the latter to pay in accordance with the orders of its depositor as long as there is sufficient money on deposit to make such payment. If the bank improperly refuses to

---

[5] § 3-503(1)(e), (2).
[6] § 3-502(1).
[7] A presumption means that the trier of fact is bound by the presumption in the absence of evidence that supports a contrary conclusion. UCC § 1-201(31).
[8] § 3-503(2).

make payment, it is liable to the drawer for damages which he sustains in consequence of such dishonor.

FACTS: Allison obtained cashier's checks from the First National Bank which he sent to a bank in Mexico. First National notified the Mexican bank that the cashier's checks would not be paid and that it had requested the return of the checks for cancellation. First National refused to honor the cashier's checks when presented thereafter for payment. Because of this, assets of Allison were seized by legal process in order to satisfy his debt to the Mexican bank, his reputation was damaged, and he was threatened with criminal prosecution. He sued First National for damages for wrongful dishonor. The bank denied liability for the harm which followed the dishonor of the checks.

DECISION: Judgment for Allison. The dishonor of the checks was wrongful and he was therefore entitled to recover damages for the consequence of such dishonor, including damages for the seizure of his assets, the threat of criminal prosecution, and the harm to his reputation. [Allison v First National Bank 85 NMex 283, 511 P2d 769]

(b) Bank's liability to holder. If the check has not been certified, the holder has no claim against the bank for the dishonor of the check, regardless of the fact that the bank had acted in breach of its contract with its depositor. If the bank had certified the check, it is liable to the holder when it dishonors the check as the certification imposes upon the bank a primary liability to pay the face amount of the check.

Regardless of whether the holder has any right against the bank, he may proceed against the secondary parties, the drawer, and any unqualified indorsers.

§ 32:6. DISHONOR OF CHECK. When a check is dishonored by nonpayment, the holder must follow the same procedure of notice to each of the secondary parties as in the case of a draft or bill of exchange if he wishes to hold them liable for payment. As in the case of any drawer of a draft or bill of exchange who countermands payment, notice of dishonor need not be given to the drawer who has stopped payment on a check. Notice is also excused under any circumstances that would excuse notice in the case of a promissory note. For example, no notice need be given a drawer or an indorser who knows that sufficient funds to cover the check are not on deposit, since such party has no reason to expect that the check will be paid by the bank.[9]

A check that is dishonored by nonpayment may be presented to the drawee bank at a later time in the hope that by the later date there will be sufficient funds in the account of the drawer so that the drawee bank will be able to make payment. Although there is this right to make a subsequent presentation for payment, it is essential that notice be given secondary parties after the dishonor of the instrument upon the first presentation. If they are not duly notified at that time, they are discharged and no new

---

[9] § 3-511(2)(b).

rights can be acquired against them by making a subsequent presentment and then notifying the secondary parties of the second dishonor.

When a check is sent in the course of the collection process to the bank on which it is drawn, that bank must either pay or promptly return the check as unpaid, or send notice of its dishonor, as by returning the check unpaid for "insufficient funds." If the drawee bank does not act before the midnight of the business day on which it received the check, it automatically becomes liable for the face of the instrument.[10] Oral notice of dishonor is sufficient.

§ 32:7. SETOFF OF BANK LOAN AGAINST DEPOSIT. When a depositor borrows money from his bank, the loan agreement generally specifies that the bank may deduct the amount due on the loan from the customer's deposit account. The loan agreement may specify that the bank may make such a setoff even though the loan is not due. In effect, this is a form of acceleration of the loan or of acceleration when the holder deems himself insecure. In the absence of an express provision permitting the bank to set off a loan before it is due, however, no such right exists.

§ 32:8. LIABILITY OF BANK FOR IMPROPER PAYMENT OF CHECK. A bank that honors a check after the depositor has stopped payment is liable to the depositor for the loss he sustains. In addition, the bank is generally liable if it makes payment under the following circumstances:

(a) Payment on forged signature of drawer. The bank is liable to the depositor (drawer) if it pays a check on which his signature has been forged since a forgery ordinarily has no effect as a signature.[11] A *forgery* of the signature occurs when the name of the depositor has been signed by another person without authority to do so and with the intent to defraud by making it appear that the check was signed by the depositor.[12] The burden of knowing the signatures of all its depositors is thus placed on the bank. Accordingly, upon opening an account in a bank, the depositor is required to sign a card in the way in which he will sign his checks. This signature card remains on file in the bank and is used to make a comparison to determine whether checks presented to the bank for payment have been signed by the depositor.

Although the bank has no right to pay a check on which the drawer's signature is forged, the drawer may be barred from objecting that his signature was a forgery. If the drawer's negligence contributed substantially to the forging of his signature, he cannot assert that it was forged when the drawee bank makes payment of the check while acting in good faith and conforming to reasonable commercial standards.[13] For example, if the

---

[10] §§ 4-302, 4-104(1)(h); Rock Island Auction Sales v Empire Packing, 32 Ill2d 269, 204 NE2d 721.

[11] § 3-404(1).

[12] A forgery as thus defined is to be distinguished from a changing of the instrument as originally executed, which constitutes an alteration when done by a party to the instrument and a spoliation when done by a stranger to the instrument.

[13] UCC § 3-404(1), 4-406.

drawer signs his checks with a mechanical writer, he must exercise reasonable care to prevent unauthorized persons from making use of it to forge or "sign" his name with such device. If the depositor's negligence enables a third person to make such improper use of it, the depositor is barred from objecting to the payment of the check by the bank.

When a check is presented to the drawee bank for payment, it alone is responsible for determining whether the signature of the drawer, its customer, is a forgery. Prior indorsers do not warrant that the signature of the drawer is genuine; and, if the bank pays money or gives a cashier's check in payment of the depositor's check, it cannot thereafter recover the money paid or defend against payment on the cashier's check on the ground that the drawer's signature had been forged.

(b) Payment on forged indorsement. A bank that pays a check on a forged indorsement may be liable for conversion.[14] The true owner of an instrument collected on a forged indorsement may recover in a direct suit against a collecting bank even though the bank had acted in good faith and with the highest degree of care and even though it had remitted the amount of the instrument to a prior party.[15]

FACTS: Jett wrote a check for $12,000 as a loan payable to the order of a newly formed corporation, National Giant Portable Fun Slide, Inc. The three officers and sole shareholders of the corporation took the check to another bank, Lewis State Bank, to open a corporate account. The check was indorsed "for deposit only to the account of within named payee." In spite of this, the Lewis Bank was directed to credit only $7,000 to the account of the corporation and to pay $5,000 cash to one of the three officers. National Giant went out of business and Jett sued Lewis Bank for diverting $5,000 from the corporation account.

DECISION: Judgment for Lewis State Bank. That bank was not the drawee bank but it was a collecting bank. The drawer of a check cannot hold a collecting bank liable for taking a check on which a necessary indorsement is missing. This follows from the fact that the check is not the property of the drawer and the collecting bank does not owe any contractual duty to the drawer, as does the drawee bank. In the absence of any duty owed by the collecting bank to the drawer, it follows that the collecting bank is not liable to the drawer. [Jett v Lewis State Bank (FlaApp) 277 So2d 37]

A bank that has dealt with an instrument or the proceeds of it for an indorsee who was not the true owner is only partly liable to the true owner if the bank had acted in good faith and in accordance with the reasonable commercial standards applicable to a bank. In the latter case, the liability of the bank is limited to surrendering the instrument or the proceeds of it to the true owner if the bank still has either in its possession.[16]

---

[14] § 3-419(1)(c).
[15] Cooper v Union Bank, 9 Cal3d 123, 107 CalRptr 1, 507 P2d 609.
[16] UCC § 3-419(3).

The failure to make an inquiry may constitute a failure to act in accordance with reasonable commercial standards, as where the employee's bank was charged with notice of a breach of fiduciary duty from the fact that a check payable to the order of the employer was indorsed by the employee and deposited in the employee's personal bank account but the employee's bank made no inquiry, the court holding that as a matter of law the failure to make inquiry under these circumstances constituted a failure to act in accordance with reasonable commercial standards.

When a drawee bank pays a check to a collecting bank on the basis of a forged indorsement of the payee's name and is held liable therefor, the drawee bank may recover for its loss from the collecting bank which obtained payment of the check.

(c) Payment on missing indorsement. A drawee bank is liable for the loss when it pays a check that lacks an essential indorsement. In such a case, the instrument has not been properly presented; and by definition the person presenting the check for payment is not the holder of the instrument and is not entitled to demand or receive payment. It is a defense to the bank, however, that although the person to whom payment was made was not the holder of the instrument, he was in fact the person whom the drawer or the last holder of the check intended should be paid.

When a person deposits a check in his bank but neglects to indorse it, the bank may make an indorsement for him unless the check contains a statement that it must be signed personally by that person. Even if the bank does not indorse, there is an effective negotiation from the customer to his bank when the check is stamped by the bank to indicate that it was deposited by the customer or was credited to his account.[17]

(d) Alteration of check. If the face of the check has been altered so that the amount to be paid has been increased, the bank is liable to the drawer for the amount of the increase when it makes payment for the greater amount. The bank has the opportunity of examining the check when it is presented for payment and, if it fails to detect the alteration, it is responsible for the loss.

The drawer may be barred from claiming that there was an alteration by virtue of his conduct with respect to writing the check or his conduct after receiving the canceled check from the bank. As to the former, he is barred if in writing the check he was negligent and that negligence substantially contributed to the making of the material alteration and the bank honored the check in good faith and observed reasonable commercial standards in so doing.[18] For example, the drawer is barred when he leaves blank spaces on his check so that it is readily possible to change "four" to "four hundred," and the drawee bank pays out the latter sum without any cause to know of the alteration. The careful person will therefore write figures and words close together and run a line through or cross out any blank spaces.

---

[17] § 4-205(1).
[18] § 3-406.

(e) Payment after depositor's death. The effectiveness of a check ordinarily ceases with the death of a drawer. The death of the drawer, however, does not revoke the agency of the bank until it has knowledge of the death and has had reasonable opportunity to act. Even with such knowledge, the bank may continue for 10 days to pay or certify checks drawn by the drawer unless ordered to stop payment by a person claiming an interest in the account.[19]

FACTS: Schenk, who had a checking account in the Bridgehampton Bank, obtained several loans from the bank and signed a number of notes representing the loans. On March 6, he wrote and issued checks drawn on his account to make part payments of these loans. On March 7, Schenk was killed in an automobile accident. On March 8, the bank entered Schenk's checks on its records to show the payments made by them. Other creditors of Schenk thereafter objected on the ground that since he was dead at that time, the bank could not apply the checks to his loans.

DECISION: Judgment for the bank. The bank could honor checks of Schenk for 10 days after his death in the absence of a proper stop order. No stop order had been received by the bank within that time. The bank could therefore make the bookkeeping entries the day after Schenk's death to give effect to Schenk's intention of making payments on his loans. [In re Schenk's Estate (NY Surrogate) 313 NYS2d 277]

§ 32:9. CERTIFIED CHECKS. The drawee bank may certify a check drawn on it, which has the same legal consequence as the acceptance of a draft. The effect of the certification is to set aside in a special account maintained by the bank as much of the depositor's account as is needed to pay the amount of the certified check. With respect to the holder of the check, the certification is an undertaking by the bank that when the check is presented for payment, it will make payment according to the terms of the check without regard to the standing of the depositor's account at that time.

A check may be certified by a bank upon the request of the drawer or the holder. In the latter case all prior indorsers and the drawer are automatically released from liability.[20] Since the holder could have received payment, as the bank was willing to certify the check, and since the holder did not take the payment but chose to take the certification, the prior secondary parties are released from liability. When the certification is obtained by the drawer, there is no release of the secondary parties.

While, as a practical matter, the certification of a check by a bank makes it "as good as money," it must be remembered that the check is still a check, and that even a certified check is not money.

§ 32:10. AGENCY STATUS OF COLLECTING BANK. When a person deposits a commercial paper in a bank, he is ordinarily making it his agent to collect or obtain the payment of the paper. Unless the contrary intent

---

[19] § 4-405.
[20] § 3-411(1).

clearly appears, a bank receiving an item is deemed to take it as agent for the depositor rather than as becoming the purchaser of the paper from him. This presumption is not affected by the form of the indorsement nor by the absence of any indorsement. The bank is also regarded as being merely an agent even though the depositor has the right to make immediate withdrawals against the deposited item.[21] In consequence of the agency status, the depositor remains the owner of the item and is therefore subject to the risks of ownership involved in its collection, in the absence of fault on the part of any collecting bank.[22]

When a bank cashes a check deposited by its customer or cashes the customer's check drawn on the strength of a deposited check, it is a holder of the customer's check and may sue the parties thereon, even though as between the customer and the bank the latter is an agent for collection and has the right to charge back the amount of the deposited check if it cannot be collected. When the bank receives final settlement for an item taken for collection, the agency status ends and the bank is merely a debtor of its customer just as though the customer had made an ordinary cash deposit in the bank.[23]

§ 32:11. LIABILITY OF BANK FOR IMPROPER COLLECTION OF CHECK.

Although a bank acts as agent for its customer in obtaining payment of a check deposited with it by its customer, it may be liable to a third person when the act of its customer is unauthorized or unlawful with respect to the third person.

> FACTS: Arthur Odgers died. His widow, Elizabeth Odgers, thereafter Salsman by remarriage, retained Breslow as the attorney for her husband's estate. She received a check payable to her order drawn on the First National City Bank, which Breslow told her should be deposited in her husband's "estate." She signed an indorsement "Pay to the order of Estate of Arthur J. Odgers." Breslow then deposited this check in his "trustee" account in the National Community Bank. National Community collected the amount of the check from the drawee, the First National Bank. Thereafter the widow, as administratrix of the estate of Arthur J. Odgers, sued the Community Bank for collecting this check and crediting Breslow's trustee account with the proceeds.

> DECISION: The Community Bank was liable to the estate of Arthur J. Odgers. The widow had indorsed the check to the order of that estate. By collecting the check without an indorsement on behalf of that estate, and by depositing the proceeds of the estate's check in the account of another person, the bank had converted property which belonged to the estate. The bank was therefore liable for conversion of such property. [Salsman v National Community Bank, 102 NJSuper 482, 246 A2d 162 affirmed 105 NJSuper 164, 251 A2d 460]

---

[21] § 4-201(1).
[22] § 4-202.
[23] Cooper v Union Bank, 9 Cal3d 123, 107 CalRptr 1, 507 P2d 609; UCC Official Code Comment to § 4-213, point 9.

QUESTIONS AND CASE PROBLEMS

1. *A* drew a check payable to the order of *B*. The bank on which it was drawn refused to pay the check. *B* sued *A* for the amount of the check. *A* raised the defense that *B* had not shown that he sustained any damages by reason of the refusal of the bank to pay. Was this defense valid? [See Duncan v Baskin, 8 MichApp 509, 154 NW2d 617]

2. Berg, who had a checking account in the Central National Bank, drew a check on that bank payable to the order of Anschutz. Colucci obtained the check from Berg by fraudulent misrepresentation and forged the name of Anschutz as an indorsement. The check was subsequently negotiated several times and then presented by a subsequent holder to the Central National Bank for payment. The bank, without knowing that the payee's indorsement was a forgery, paid the amount of the check to the apparent holder. Thereafter Anschutz sued the bank for the amount of the check. Was the bank liable? [Anschutz v Central National Bank, 173 Neb 60, 112 NW2d 545]

3. Stone & Webster drew a check on the First National Bank of Boston payable to the order of Westinghouse in payment of a debt. Before the check could be mailed to Westinghouse, an employee of Stone & Webster forged the indorsement of Westinghouse and cashed the check at the First National Bank & Trust Company of Greenfield. The Greenfield bank then presented the check for payment to the drawee bank, the First National Bank of Boston. The latter paid the Greenfield bank the amount of the check and then debited the account of Stone & Webster with the amount of the check. Stone & Webster then sued the Greenfield bank for the amount of the check. Was the plaintiff entitled to recover? [Stone & Webster Engineering Co. v First National Bank of Greenfield, 345 Mass 1, 184 NE2d 358]

4. Silver, an attorney, had an account labeled "special account" in the Commonwealth Trust Co. Part of the fund on deposit was money belonging to his client, Goldstein. Silver drew a check on this account for his own use. Goldstein sued the bank, claiming that it had no right to honor the check because the bank should have known that the account included the money of third persons and that the attorney was making improper use of the money. Decide. [Goldstein v Commonwealth Trust Co. 19 NJSuper 39, 87 A2d 555]

5. The Virginia Salvage Co. drew a check on the National Mechanics Bank and had the bank certify the check. The check was indorsed by the payee, and a subsequent holder, Schmelz National Bank, demanded payment of the check from the National Mechanics Bank. The latter defended on the ground that the salvage company by that time owed the bank more than the amount of the certified check. Was this a valid defense? [National Mechanics Bank v Schmelz National Bank, 136 Va 33, 116 SE 380]

6. Bogash drew a check on the National Safety Bank and Trust Co. payable to the order of the Fiss Corp. At the request of the corporation, the bank certified the check. The bank later refused to make payment on the check because there was a dispute between Bogash and the corporation as to the amount due the corporation. The corporation sued the bank on the check. Decide. [Fiss Corp. v National Safety Bank and Trust Co. 191 Misc 397, 77 NYS2d 293]

7. Moats, acting with intent to defraud, forged the drawer's name on a check which did not state any amount or name any payee. Was he guilty of forgery? [Illinois v Moats, 8 IllApp3d 944, 291 NE2d 285]

8. A depositor drew a check and delivered it to the payee. Fourteen months later the check was presented to the drawee bank for payment. The bank did not have any knowledge that anything was wrong and paid the check. The depositor then sued the person receiving the money and the bank. The depositor claimed that the bank could not pay a stale check without asking the depositor whether payment should be made. Was the depositor correct? [See Advanced Alloys, Inc. v Sergeant Steel Corp., 340 NYS2d 266]

9. Steinbaum executed and delivered a check payable to the order of the White Way Motors, the name under which DiFranco was doing business. Before the check was paid, Steinbaum stopped payment on the check. DiFranco sued Steinbaum on the check. Decide. [DiFranco v Steinbaum (MoApp) 177 SW2d 697]

10. Cicci drew a check on his bank, Lincoln National Bank and Trust Co., payable to the order of Santo. He thereafter notified the bank to stop payment. The bank ignored the stop-payment order and made payment of the check. Cicci then sued Lincoln National Bank for the amount of the check. The bank raised the defense that Cicci had not shown that he was damaged by the payment of the check. Was this defense valid? [Cicci v Lincoln National Bank and Trust Co. 46 Misc2d 465, 260 NYS2d 100]

RIGHTS
OF HOLDERS
AND DEFENSES

A. SPECIAL HOLDERS

§ 33:1. FAVORED AND ORDINARY HOLDERS. The law gives certain holders of commercial paper a preferred standing by protecting them from the operation of certain defenses in lawsuits to collect payment. If the holder is not one of these favored holders, he has only the same standing as an ordinary assignee and is subject to all defenses to which an ordinary assignee would be subject.[1]

When the defendant does not have a defense that can be raised against anyone, it is immaterial that the holder is merely an ordinary holder and not a holder in due course.[2]

A holder, whether favored or not, or an assignee, is the only person who has the right to demand payment or to sue on the instrument.[3] Whether he recovers depends upon whether the person sued is liable to him and whether any defense may be asserted against the holder.

Ordinarily a holder may sue any one or more prior parties on the paper without regard to the order in which such persons may be liable to each other or to the order in which they became parties.

The holder or assignee is the only one who may grant a discharge of or cancel the liability of another party on the instrument.

§ 33:2. HOLDER IN DUE COURSE. In order to have the preferred status of a holder in due course, a person must first be a holder. This means that he must be in possession of bearer paper, or in possession of order paper made or issued to him or properly indorsed to him.

(a) Necessary elements. In addition to being a holder, the holder in due course must meet certain conditions that pertain to (1) value, (2) good faith,

---

[1] See § 17:10.
[2] Blake v Coates, 292 Ala 351, 294 So2d 433.
[3] Uniform Commercial Code § 3-301.

(3) ignorance of paper overdue or dishonored, and (4) ignorance of defenses and adverse claims.[4]

(1) Value. Since the law of commercial paper is fundamentally a merchant's or businessperson's law, it favors only the holders who have given value for the paper. For example, since a legatee under a will does not give value, a person receiving bonds as a legacy is not a holder in due course. The courts do not measure or appraise the value given.

A person has taken an instrument for value (1) when he has performed the act for which the instrument was given, such as delivering the goods for which the check is sent in payment; (2) when he has acquired a security interest in the paper, such as when it has been pledged with him as security for another obligation; or (3) when he has taken the instrument in payment or as security for a debt.[5]

A promise not yet performed, although sufficient as consideration for a contract, ordinarily does not constitute value to satisfy this requirement for a holder in due course.

> **FACTS:** Southern New England Distributing Corporation, which held two notes of Supreme Radio, indorsed them to Korzenik, an attorney, and his partner "as a retainer for services to be performed." When Korzenik sued Supreme Radio on the notes, it raised the defense of fraud in the procurement. Korzenik claimed that he was a holder in due course. From a decision against him, Korzenik appealed.

> **DECISION:** Korzenik was not a holder in due course because he had not acquired the notes by giving value. He had received the notes as consideration for services to be rendered by him thereafter. Although the promise to perform later services was consideration, it did not constitute value because the promise had not yet been performed. [Korzenik v Supreme Radio, 437 Mass 309, 197 NE2d 702]

(2) Good Faith. The element of good faith requires that the taker of commercial paper has acted honestly in the acquisition of the instrument. Bad faith may sometimes be indicated by the small value given. This does not mean that the transferee must give full value, but that a gross inadequacy of consideration may be evidence of bad faith. Bad faith is established by proof that the transferee had knowledge of such facts as rendered it improper for him to acquire the instrument under the circumstances.

If the transferee takes the instrument in good faith, it is immaterial whether his transferor acted in good faith. The fact that the transferee is negligent and fails to conform to industry standards or to its own house rules does not establish that the transferee did not act in good faith, as good faith requires only that the transferee acted with honesty.

---

[4] UCC § 3-302(1).
[5] § 3-303. It is also provided that there is a taking for value when another commercial paper is given in exchange or when the taker makes an irrevocable commitment to a third person as by providing a letter of credit, UCC § 3-303(c).

FACTS: The Angelinis made a contract for substantial home repairs with Lustro Aluminum Products and signed a promissory note for the contract price. The contract specified that payments were not due until 60 days after completion of the work. Ten days later, Lustro transferred the note and the contract to General Investment Corp. General knew from prior dealing with Lustro that the 60-day provision was typical of Lustro's contracts. Lustro's indorsement on the note warranted that the work had been completed. The work in fact was never completed, and the Angelinis raised this defense when sued on the note by General. General, claiming that it was a holder in due course, contended that its failure to have inquired of the Angelinis whether the work was completed was immaterial.

DECISION: The failure to inquire of the Angelinis constituted bad faith under the circumstances, for it justified the conclusion that General was willfully seeking to avoid learning the facts that an inquiry would have disclosed. Since General knew that payment was not due until 60 days after completion and that the work was substantial, it was bad faith for it to accept the contractor's warranty that the work had been completed when it could have readily obtained a completion certificate from the Angelinis if the work had in fact been completed. [General Investment Corp. v Di Angelini, 58 NJ 396, 278 A2d 193]

(3) Ignorance of Paper Overdue or Dishonored. Commercial paper may be negotiated even though (1) it has been dishonored, whether by nonacceptance or nonpayment; or (2) the paper is overdue, whether because of lapse of time or the acceleration of the due date; or (3) demand paper has been outstanding more than a reasonable time. In other words, ownership may still be transferred. Nevertheless, the fact that the paper is circulating at a late date or after it has been dishonored is a suspicious circumstance that is deemed to put the person acquiring the paper on notice that there is some adverse claim or defense. A person who acquires title to the paper under such circumstances therefore cannot be a holder in due course.

(4) Ignorance of Defenses and Adverse Claims. Prior parties on the paper may have defenses which they could raise if sued by the person with whom they had dealt. For example, the drawer of a check, if sued by the payee of the check, might have the defense that the merchandise delivered by the payee was defective. In addition to defenses, third persons, whether prior parties or not, may be able to assert that the instrument belongs to them and not to the holder or to his transferor. A person cannot be a holder in due course if he acquires the commercial paper with notice or knowledge that any party might have a defense or that there is any adverse claim to the ownership of the instrument. Thus, he cannot be a holder in due course when he has knowledge of a failure of consideration in an earlier transaction involving the instrument.

The fact that the payee, subsequent to the paying of value, learns of a defense does not operate retroactively to destroy his character as a holder in due course. When the transferee makes payment for the transfer of the paper in installments and learns of a defense after he has paid in part, he can be a holder in due course as to the payments made before, but not as to payments made after, learning of the existence of the defense. Knowledge acquired by the taker after acquiring the paper has no effect on his status as a holder in due course.

> **FACTS:** Statham drew a check. The payee indorsed it to the Kemp Motor Sales. Statham then stopped payment on the check on the ground that there was a failure of consideration for the check. Kemp sued Statham on the check. When Statham raised the defense of failure of consideration, Kemp replied that it was a holder in due course. Statham claimed that Kemp could not recover because it learned of his defense before it deposited the check in its bank account.
>
> **DECISION:** Kemp was a holder in due course. The knowledge acquired by it after acquiring the check had no effect on its status. The fact that it learned of the defense before it deposited the check in its account or did anything to collect the check was immaterial. [Kemp Motor Sales v Statham, 120 GaApp 515, 171 SE2d 389]

Knowledge of certain facts constitutes notice to the person acquiring a commercial paper that there is a defense or an adverse claim. The holder or purchaser of the paper is deemed to have notice of a claim or defense (1) if the instrument is so incomplete, bears such visible evidence of forgery or alteration, or is otherwise so irregular as to call into question its validity, terms, or ownership, or to create an ambiguity as to the party who is required to pay; or (2) if the purchaser has notice that the obligation of any party is voidable in whole or in part, or that all parties to the paper have been discharged. For example, if the subsequent holder knows that a note given for home improvement work in fact covers both the improvements and a loan and that the transaction is usurious because excessive costs were charged to conceal the usurious interest, the subsequent holder is not a holder in due course. The purchaser has notice of a claim of ownership of another person to the instrument if he has knowledge that a fiduciary has negotiated the paper in breach of his trust.[6]

In general, a holder is deemed to have notice when he has knowledge of facts which would put a reasonable man upon inquiry, that is, which would make him curious to investigate further, which investigation, if made, would reveal the existence of the defenses.

> **FACTS:** Auman was employed by the Richardson Company. She purchased an automobile on credit and the claim for the unpaid balance was held by the First National Bank. Auman gave the bank a check to pay the balance. The check was drawn by the Richardson Company and made payable to the First National Bank. The bank received the check for this purpose and released the security interest in the car which the bank held to secure payment of the unpaid balance. Auman told the bank that her employer had given her the check as compensation. This was not true and Auman had apparently misled her employer into signing the check. The Richardson Company sued the First National Bank on the theory that the bank knew or should have known of the misconduct of Auman and was guilty of conversion in applying the company's check to the discharge of Auman's personal debt.

---

[6] § 3-304(2).

DECISION: Judgment for the bank. The fact that the bank was put on notice that its customer, Auman, held a position of trust as an employee of the Richardson Company did not affect the status of the bank as a holder in due course. The Code expressly states that notice of the fiduciary character of a depositor does not in itself constitute notice of a defense or claim. The court rejected the contention that the defendant had acted in bad faith on the theory that it had been negligent, for the reason that "good faith" required only a mental state or belief and is not affected by whether the person was negligent in so believing. [Richardson Co. v First National Bank in Dallas (TexCivApp) 504 SW2d 812]

The fact that a holder knows that the payee had a fluctuating financial record does not prevent his becoming a holder in due course. The fact that the payee negotiates a large volume of commercial paper, such as the notes received in the course of the week, does not put the indorsee on notice of any defect or defense.

The fact that there is a standing business relationship between the seller and his assignee, and that to facilitate such relationship the assignee supplied printed forms bearing its name, does not bar the assignee from being a holder in due course.[7]

The duty of inquiry is greater when consumer transactions are involved and the payee has followed a known general pattern of exploitation and deception. "Where lenders facilitate consumer credit financing they must be held to a high standard of inquiry to make certain their services are not being misused by unscrupulous merchandisers." Thus, it has been held that the transferee of commercial paper of a home improvement company did not take in good faith and was not a holder in due course when the transferee knew that the improvement company was taking advantage of persons of limited economic means and education and that the company did not make any inquiries as to defenses even though it took a substantial quantity of paper from the improvement company and knew that the broker who dealt with the public was in fact acting for the improvement company although he pretended to act for the individual home owners.

(b) Who may be a holder in due course. Any person may be a holder in due course. This includes the payee of the instrument provided he satisfies the necessary elements. Ordinarily the payee deals directly with the drawer and therefore would have knowledge of any defense that the latter might raise. But the payee becomes a holder in due course when he acts through an intermediary so that in fact he did not deal with the drawer but acquired the paper from the intermediary, even though the paper was made payable to his order. The net result is the same as though the drawer has made the check payable to the intermediary who in turn indorsed it to the payee.

FACTS: Shulman purchased equipment from Sayve on conditional (installment) sale. The contract specified that the seller could transfer the contract to James Talcott, Inc. The contract was thereafter assigned and the

---

[7] Talcott v Shulman, 82 NJSuper 438, 198 A2d 98.

buyer's note indorsed to Talcott. The latter was an industrial finance company, which had executed a blanket discounting agreement with Sayve and had supplied it with printed forms bearing Talcott's name. In a suit between the parties, Shulman claimed that the finance company was not a holder in due course because of the blanket discounting agreement and the supplying of forms bearing Talcott's name.

DECISION: Judgment against the buyer. The fact that there was a standing business relationship between the parties and that, to facilitate such relationship, the finance company had supplied printed forms bearing its name did not show it was not a holder in due course. [Talcott v Shulman, 82 NJSuper 438, 198 A2d 98]

Certain types of purchases of commercial paper do not make the purchaser a holder in due course although he otherwise satisfies all the elements here considered. Such sales are not of an ordinary commercial nature, and therefore the buyer need not be given the protection afforded a holder in due course. Thus, a person is not a holder in due course when he acquires the paper by means of a judicial sale, a sale of the assets of an estate, or a bulk sale not in the regular course of business of the transferor.[8]

The seller of goods on credit frequently assigns the sales contract and his buyer's promissory note to the manufacturer who made the goods, or to a finance company or a bank. In such a case, the assignee of the seller will be a holder in due course of the buyer's commercial paper if the paper is properly negotiated and the transferee satisfies all the elements of being a holder in due course. When there is no evidence of any defense, it is immaterial whether the plaintiff is only a holder or is a holder in due course. The transferee, however, may take such an active part in the sale to the seller's customer or may be so related to the seller that it is proper to conclude that the transferee was in fact a party to the original transaction and had notice or knowledge of any defense of the buyer against the seller, which conclusion automatically bars holding that the transferee is a holder in due course.

In what may be regarded a form of "participant liability," many cases hold that it may be shown that there was such a close working arrangement between the seller and the finance company that the transfer of the buyer's note to the finance company was merely a device to bar defenses. In these circumstances, it can be concluded that the finance company is not a holder in due course.[9]

(c) Proof of status as holder in due course. The status of the holder does not become important until a person sued by the holder raises a defense that can be asserted against an ordinary holder but not against a holder in due course or a holder through a holder in due course. Initially the plaintiff in the action is entitled to recover as soon as the commercial paper is put in evidence and the signatures on it are admitted to be genuine. If the genuine character of any signature is specifically denied, the burden is then on the

---

[8] UCC § 3-302(3).
[9] Avco Security Corp. v Post, 42 AppDiv2d 395, 348 NYS2d 409.

plaintiff to prove that the signature is genuine.[10] Once the signatures are admitted or established, the plaintiff-holder is entitled to recover unless the defendant establishes a defense. In the latter situation, the plaintiff has the burden of establishing that he is a holder in due course, or a holder through a holder in due course, in order to avoid such defense.[11]

§ 33:3. HOLDER THROUGH A HOLDER IN DUE COURSE. Those persons who become holders of the instrument after a holder in due course are given the same protection as the holder in due course provided they are not parties to fraud or illegality that would affect the instrument.

This means that if an instrument is indorsed from A to B to C to D and that if B is a holder in due course, both C and D will enjoy the same rights as B. If C received the instrument as a gift or with knowledge of failure of consideration or other defense, or if D took the instrument after maturity, they could not themselves be holders in due course. Nevertheless, they are given the same protection as a holder in due course because they took the instrument through such a holder, namely, B. It is not only C, the person taking directly from B, but also D, who takes indirectly through B, who is given this extra protection.

B. DEFENSES

§ 33:4. CLASSIFICATION OF DEFENSES. The importance of being a holder in due course or a holder through a holder in due course is that those holders are not subject to certain defenses when they demand payment or bring suit upon a commercial paper. These may be described as *limited defenses*. Another class of defenses, *universal defenses*, may be asserted against any holder without regard to whether he is an assignee, an ordinary holder, a holder in due course, or holder through a holder in due course. A holder who is neither a holder in due course nor a holder through a holder in due course is subject to every defense just as though the instrument were not negotiable.

The defenses that cannot be raised against a holder in due course as to an original commercial paper are likewise barred with respect to any instrument which is executed to renew or extend the original instrument.

§ 33:5. DEFENSES AVAILABLE AGAINST AN ASSIGNEE. An assignee of commercial paper is subject to all the defenses to which an assignee of an ordinary contract right is subject. It is immaterial whether the assignment is by voluntary act of a former holder of the paper or whether the assignment occurs by operation of law.

---

[10] UCC § 3-307(1). The plaintiff is aided by a presumption that the signature is genuine or authorized except where the action is to enforce the obligation of a signer who has died or become incompetent. § 3-307(1)(b). Carr Estate, 436 Pa 47, 258 A2d 628.

[11] UCC § 3-307(3). If the defense is one that may be asserted against any holder, it is immaterial whether the plaintiff is a holder in due course.

§ 33:6. DEFENSES AVAILABLE AGAINST AN ORDINARY HOLDER.

When suit is brought by the original payee, he is subject to every defense that the defendant may possess, unless he qualifies as a holder in due course. An ordinary holder is also subject to any defense of the defendant.

The fact that a person cannot recover on a commercial paper does not necessarily mean that he is not entitled to recover in another action or against another party. He may be able to recover on a contract that was part of the transaction in which the instrument was given. It is also possible that he may be able to hold a party to the instrument liable for breach of an implied warranty or to recover from a person expressly guaranteeing payment of the instrument.

§ 33:7. LIMITED DEFENSES—NOT AVAILABLE AGAINST A HOLDER IN DUE COURSE.

Neither a holder in due course nor one having the rights of such a holder is subject to any of the following defenses.[12] They are limited defenses. These defenses are barred with respect to any instrument that is executed to renew or extend the original instrument.

(a) Ordinary contract defenses. In general terms the defenses that could be raised against a suit on an ordinary contract cannot be raised against the holder in due course. He is not subject to defenses based on defects in the underlying contract. Accordingly, the defendant cannot assert against the holder in due course the defense of lack, failure,[13] or illegality of consideration with respect to the transaction between the defendant and the person with whom he dealt.

FACTS: At various times Woodward purchased goods from the Moody Manufacturing Company. In 1968 he made a purchase and arranged for its payment by accepting a trade acceptance drawn on him. He accepted it although the amount was blank because it had not yet been determined what goods he would be purchasing from Moody. An amount was later filled in and thereafter Moody assigned the acceptance to Illinois Valley Acceptance Corp. Illinois sued Woodward on the trade acceptance. He raised the defenses that there had been fraud, that he had never received the goods, and that the trade acceptance had been accepted with the amount in blank. Illinois Valley showed that it paid Moody 85 percent of the face of the paper and held the remaining 15 percent as a reserve against nonpayment of the acceptance and of other paper purchased by it from Moody. It was also shown that the purchase of paper by Illinois Valley from Moody was a continuing business relationship.

DECISION: The defenses could not be raised against Illinois Valley Acceptance since it proved itself to be a holder in due course as it had taken the acceptance for value and in good faith without notice of any defense. The fact that Illinois paid 85 percent of the face and held the balance of 15 percent in reserve and that this was a continuing pattern of doing business showed that the action was in good faith and for value. Illinois

---

[12] UCC § 3-305.
[13] Federal Factors, Inc. v Wellbanks, 241 Ark 44, 406 SW2d 712.

Valley had therefore met the burden of proving that it was a holder in due course, which burden fell upon it when evidence was presented of Woodward's defense. [Illlinois Valley Acceptance Corp. v Woodward (IndApp) 304 NE2d 859]

(b) Incapacity of defendant. The incapacity of the defendant may not be raised against a holder in due course unless by general principles of law that incapacity, such as insanity of a person for whom a guardian has been appointed by a court, makes the instrument a nullity.[14]

(c) Fraud in the inducement. When a person knows that he is executing a commercial paper and knows its essential terms but is persuaded or induced to execute it because of false statements or representations, he cannot defend against a holder in due course or a holder through a holder in due course on the ground of such fraud. As an illustration, *M* is persuaded to purchase an automobile because of *P*'s statement concerning its condition. *M* gives *P* a note, which is negotiated until it reaches *H*, who is a holder in due course. *M* meanwhile learns that the car is not as represented and that *P*'s statements were fraudulent. When *H* demands payment of the note, *M* cannot refuse to pay him on the ground of *P*'s fraud. He must pay the instrument and then recover his loss from *P*.

Likewise, the buyer of goods which in fact are stolen cannot claim as against a subsequent holder in due course of the check which he gave in payment for goods that had been defrauded in the sale as such fraud was merely fraud as to the inducement and therefore could not be raised against a holder in due course.

> **FACTS:** Holler sold stolen goods to the Star Provision Co. which paid by check, believing that Holler was the owner. The check was subsequently negotiated to Sears, Roebuck & Co., which was a holder in due course. When Sears sued Star for nonpayment of the check, Star raised the defense that the goods had been stolen.

> **DECISION:** Judgment for Sears. The fact that the goods were stolen constituted fraud in the inducement and therefore could not be raised against Sears, a holder in due course. [Star Provision Co. v Sears, Roebuck & Co. 93 GaApp 799, 92 SE2d 835]

(d) Prior payment or cancellation. When a commercial paper is paid before maturity, the person making the payment should demand the surrender of the instrument. If he fails to obtain the instrument, it is possible for the holder to continue to negotiate it. Another person may thus become the holder of the instrument. When the new holder demands payment of the instrument, the defense cannot be raised that payment had been made to a former holder, if the new holder is a holder in due course. The fact that the person making the payment obtained a receipt from the former holder does not affect the application of this principle.

When the holder and the party primarily liable have agreed to cancel the instrument but the face of the instrument does not show any sign of cancellation, the defense of cancellation cannot be asserted against the

---

[14] UCC § 3-305(2)(b).

holder in due course. Similarly, an order to stop payment of a check cannot be raised as a defense by the drawer of a check against a holder in due course.

(1) *Overpayment.* The fact that the maker or the drawer of the paper has overpaid the payee is a simple contract defense. Thus, it may not be asserted against a holder in due course but may be asserted against anyone who does not have the rights of a holder in due course. To illustrate the latter, an employer is required by law to deduct from the pay of his employees a specified percentage which is remitted by the employer to the federal government as an advance payment on the federal income tax of the employees. If the employer by mistake makes out a note or check for the gross amount of an employee's wages, the employer may assert the federal tax as a setoff when sued by the employee for the face of the paper. That is, the employee cannot recover the full face of the paper but only the net amount which he should have received after the federal taxes were deducted from that gross amount.[15]

(e) Nondelivery of an instrument. A person may make out a commercial paper or indorse an existing instrument and leave it on his desk for future delivery. At that moment the instrument or the indorsement is not effective because there has been no delivery.

Assume that through the negligence of an employee or through the theft of the instrument, it comes into the hands of another person. If the instrument is in such form that it can be negotiated, as when it is payable to bearer, a subsequent receiver of the instrument may be a holder in due course or a holder through a holder in due course. As against him, the person who made out the instrument or indorsed it cannot defend on the ground that he did not deliver it.

(f) Conditional or specified purpose delivery. As against a favored holder, a person who would be liable on the instrument cannot show that the instrument which is absolute on its face was in fact delivered subject to a condition that had not been performed, or that it was delivered for a particular purpose but was not so used. Assume A makes out a check to the order of B and hands it to C with the understanding that C shall not deliver the check to B until B delivers certain merchandise. If C should deliver the check to B before the condition is satisfied and B then negotiates the check, a holder in due course or a holder through a holder in due course may enforce the instrument.

(g) Duress consisting of threats. The defense that a person signed or executed a commercial paper under threats of harm or violence may not be raised as a defense against a holder in due course when the effect of such duress is merely to make the contract voidable at the election of the victim of the duress. Such duress is not present when the maker of the note had business experience, dealt at arm's length with the party alleged to have been guilty of duress, acted with the advice of counsel, and delayed a month before signing the note.

---

[15] Lukens v Goit (Wyo) 430 P2d 607.

(h) Unauthorized completion. If a maker or drawer signs a commercial paper and leaves blank the name of the payee, or the amount, or any other term, and then hands the instrument to another to be completed, the defense of an improper completion cannot be raised when payment is demanded or suit brought by a subsequent holder in due course or a holder through a holder in due course. That is, he may enforce the instrument as completed.[16]

This situation arises when an employer gives a signed blank check to an employee with instructions to make certain purchases and to fill in the name of the seller and the amount when these are determined. If the employee fills in the name of a friend and a large amount and then the employee and the friend negotiate the instrument, the employer cannot defend against a subsequent holder in due course or a holder through a holder in due course on the ground that the completion had been without the authority of the employer.

In any case, the defendant has the burden of providing that the commercial paper was completed in an unauthorized manner.[17]

(i) Theft. As a matter of definition, a holder in due course will not have acquired the paper through theft and any defense of theft therefore must relate to the conduct of a prior party. Assuming that the theft of the paper does not result in a defect in the chain of necessary indorsements, the defense that the instrument had been stolen cannot be asserted against a holder in due course.[18]

§ 33:8. UNIVERSAL DEFENSES—AVAILABLE AGAINST ALL HOLDERS.

Certain defenses are regarded as so basic that the social interest in preserving them outweighs the social interest of giving commercial paper the free-passing qualities of money. Accordingly, such defenses are given universal effect and may be raised against all holders, whether ordinary holders, holders in due course, or holders through a holder in due course. Such defenses are therefore appropriately called universal defenses.

(a) Fraud as to the nature or essential terms of the paper. If a person signs a commercial paper because he has been fraudulently deceived as to its nature or essential terms, he has a defense available against all holders. This is the situation when an experienced business person induces an illiterate person to sign a note by falsely representing that it is a contract for repairs. This defense, however, cannot be raised when it is the negligence of the defending party that prevented him from learning the true nature and terms of the instrument.

(b) Forgery or lack of authority. The defense that a signature was forged or signed without authority may be raised against any holder unless the person whose name was signed has ratified it or is estopped by conduct or negligence from denying it.[19]

---

[16] UCC § 3-407(3).

[17] Charter Finance Co. v Henderson (IllApp3d) 305 NE2d 338.

[18] UCC § 3-305(1).

[19] § 3-404(1); Cohen v Lincoln Savings Bank, 275 NY 399, 10 NE2d 475.

The fact that the drawer may have been lax and unbusinesslike in issuing the check to a named payee does not constitute negligence which under UCC § 3-406 bars the assertion that the signature of the payee was a forgery.

(c) Duress depriving control. When a person executes or indorses a commercial paper in response to a force of such a nature that under general principles of law there is duress which makes the transaction a nullity, rather than merely voidable, such duress may be raised as a defense against any holder.

(d) Incapacity. The fact that the defendant is a minor, who under general principles of contract law may avoid his obligation, is a matter that may be raised against any kind of holder. Other kinds of incapacity may only be raised as a defense if the effect of the incapacity is to make the instrument a nullity.

(e) Illegality. If the law declares that an instrument is void when executed in connection with certain conduct, such as gambling or usury, that defense may be raised against any holder. Similarly, when contracts of a corporate seller are a nullity because its charter has been forfeited for nonpayment of taxes, a promissory note given to it by a buyer is void and that defense may be raised as against a holder in due course. If the law merely makes the transaction illegal but does not make the instrument void, the defense cannot be asserted against a holder in due course or a holder through a holder in due course.[20]

FACTS: The United States mailed a tax refund to a taxpayer. Another person who had the same name as the taxpayer obtained possession of the check, indorsed it with his name, and cashed it at the Fulton National Bank. The bank collected the amount of the check from the United States Treasury. The United States then sued the bank for the return of this payment.

DECISION: Judgment for the United States. Although the person who indorsed the check used his own name, which also happened to be the name of the payee, the indorsement was forged or made without authority because it had not been made or authorized by the person whom the drawer intended to designate as the payee. Accordingly, the Fulton National Bank never became the holder of the check and had no right to receive or retain the payment which it had received. [Fulton National Bank v United States (CA5 Ga) 197 F2d 763]

(f) Alteration. The fact that an instrument has been altered may be raised against any holder. Unlike other defenses, however, it is only a partial defense as against a holder in due course. That is, the latter holder may enforce the instrument according to its original terms prior to its alteration.[21] Moreover, if the person sued by the holder in due course has

---

[20] UCC § 3-305(2)(b).
[21] § 3-407(3).

substantially contributed by his negligence to making the alteration possible, that defendant is precluded from asserting the defense of alteration.

An alteration does not have any effect unless it is both material and fraudulently made. An alteration is material when it changes the contract of any party in any way, as by changing the date, place of payment, rate of interest, or any other term. It also includes any modification that changes the number or the relationship of the parties to the paper, by adding new terms, or by cutting off a part of the paper itself.[22]

FACTS: A promissory note was made and delivered to Du Pont, who indorsed it to the First National Bank. Baumer, the receiver of the bank, demanded payment from the maker of the note. When this payment was refused by the maker, due notice of this fact was given Du Pont and suit was later brought against him as indorser. Du Pont showed that, without his consent and at the request of the receiver of the bank, the maker had added a seal after the maker's name, subsequent to the making of his indorsement.

DECISION: Judgment for Du Pont. The addition of a seal had materially changed the obligation by extending the time under the statute of limitations in which suit could be brought from 6 years to 20 years. As a material change, its effect was to avoid the instrument except with respect to those authorizing or assenting to the alteration and to persons who became parties to the papers subsequent to the alteration. [Baumer v Du Pont, 338 Pa 193, 12 A2d 566]

An alteration must be made to the instrument itself. An oral or a collateral written agreement between the holder and one of the parties that modifies the obligation of the party is not an "alteration" within the sense just discussed, even though the obligation of the party is changed or altered thereby.

By definition, an alteration is a change made by a party to the instrument. A change of the instrument made by a stranger has no effect, and recovery on the instrument is the same as though the change had not been made, provided it can be proved what the instrument had been in its original form.

§ 33:9. ADVERSE CLAIMS TO THE PAPER. Distinct from a defense which a defendant may raise against a plaintiff as a reason why he should not be required to pay the instrument is a claim of a third person that he, and not the possessor of the paper, is the owner of the paper. Assume that a check was made to the order of *A*; that thereafter blank indorsements are made by *B, C* and *D*; and that *E* in possession of the check appears to be the holder. *B* might then claim and show, if such be the case, that he indorsed the check because he was fraudulently deceived by *C*; that he avoids his indorsement because of such fraud; and that accordingly the check still belongs to him. *B* in such case is making an adverse claim to the instrument.

---

[22] § 3-407(1).

A holder in due course holds commercial paper free and clear from all adverse claims of any other person to the paper, including both equitable and legal interests of third persons, and the right of a former holder to rescind his negotiation.[23] In contrast, such adverse claims may be asserted against a holder who is not a holder in due course, which means that the adverse claimant may bring such action against the holder since the law generally provides for the recovery of property by the owner from anyone else.

Ordinarily a defendant when sued by a holder cannot raise against the holder the defense that the holder's ownership is subject to an adverse claim. This may be done only when the adverse claimant has also become a party to the action or is defending the action on behalf of the defendant.[24] Otherwise, it would be unfair to the adverse claimant to pass upon the merits of his claim in his absence, as well as being undesirable in opening the door to perjury by giving any defendant the opportunity of beclouding the issues by raising a false claim that a third person has an adverse interest.

§ 33:10. CONSUMER PROTECTION. Consumer protection legislation frequently provides that when the debtor executes a commercial paper which is negotiated thereafter by the creditor, the transferee cannot be a holder in due course. This protects the debtor by permitting him to raise against the transferee, such as the seller's finance company, the same defenses that the debtor could raise against his creditor, the seller.[25]

QUESTIONS AND CASE PROBLEMS

1. *H* was the holder of a promissory note. When he sued *M*, the maker of the note, *M* raised as a defense the objection that *H* was not a holder in due course. Can *H* recover? [See Brock v Adams, 79 NMex 17, 439 P2d 234]

---

[23] §§ 3-305(1), 3-207(2).

[24] § 3-306(d).

[25] Randolph National Bank v Vail, 131 Vt 390, 308 A2d 588. The Uniform Consumer Credit Code proposes two alternative rules: one which would abolish the holder in due course protection of the creditor's transferee in practically all cases; the other which would preserve it to the extent of barring the consumer from asserting against a good faith assignee not related to the assignor a defense which he failed to raise within three months after being notified of the assignment. UCCC § 2.404. The Federal Trade Commission is studying the formulation of a regulation on the preservation of buyers' claims and defenses in consumer installment sales.

2. *D* drew a check to the order of *P*. It was later claimed that *P* was not a holder in due course because the check was postdated and because *P* knew that *D* was having financial difficulties and that the particular checking account on which this check was drawn had been frequently overdrawn. Do these circumstances prevent *P* from being a holder in due course? [See Citizens Bank, Booneville v National Bank of Commerce, (CA10 Okla) 334 F2d 257; Franklin National Bank v Sidney Gotowner (NY SupCt) 4 UCCRS 953]

3. Henry executed and delivered a check to Jesse Farly in payment of an automobile. On the face of the check was written "Car to be free and clear of liens." The check was indorsed and delivered by Farley to the Zachry Company. When the latter sued Henry, Henry raised the defense of fraud in the inducement and failure of consideration, and claimed that Zachry was not a holder in due course because the words "Car to be free and clear of liens" gave notice of defenses. Was Henry correct? [C. D. Henry v A. L. Zachry Co. 93 GaApp 536, 92 SE2d 225]

4. Vanella sold his automobile to Blackburn Motors by falsely representing that there were no liens on the car. Blackburn paid Vanella with a check that was cashed by the Marine Midland Trust Co. When Blackburn learned of Vanella's fraud, it stopped payment on the check. Midland then sued Blackburn to enforce its secondary liability as drawer. Blackburn raised the defense of Vanella's fraud. Was this defense available to it? [Marine Midland Trust Co. v Blackburn, 50 Misc2d 954, 271 NYS2d 388]

5. Wolsky executed a promissory note payable to the order of Green. Green indorsed it "Pay to the order of M. E. Grasswick, (signed) Albert E. Green" and delivered it to Grasswick. Grasswick then indorsed and delivered it to McGuckin, a holder in due course. When the note was not paid, McGuckin sued Wolsky and the indorsers. Green claimed that the negotiation by him to Grasswick was agreed between them to be without recourse. Was this a valid defense? [McGuckin v Wolsky, 78 ND 921, 53 NW2d 852]

6. Ten negotiable notes were negotiated to the First National Bank, which paid for them with a draft on another bank. The First National Bank then learned that the notes had been procured by fraud. Thereafter the bank on which the draft of the First National Bank had been drawn made payment. When the bank sued the maker, Motors Acceptance Corp., the latter claimed that the bank was not a holder in due course because it had not "paid" for the notes before it learned of the defense. Decide. [First National Bank of Waukesha v Motors Acceptance Corp., 15 Wis2d 44, 112 NW2d 381]

7. Rocchio executed and delivered a note payable to the order of Berta. When Berta sued Rocchio on the note, the latter offered parol evidence to show that the note had been given as payment for a business and its inventory and that less inventory had been delivered than had been agreed upon. Berta claimed that the obligation of the instrument could not be modified by parol evidence. Was he correct? [Berta v Rocchio, 149 Colo 325, 369 P2d 51]

8. *A* and *B* were negotiating for the sale of land. *A* paid *B* in advance with a postdated check. When *A* and *B* could not agree on a final contract, *A* stopped payment of the check. Was *B* a holder in due course? [See Briand v Wild, 110 NH 373, 268 A2d 896]

9. In an action on a promissory note it was claimed that there had been a material change of the note. Was this a sufficient defense? [See Mandel v Sedrish (NY) 3 UCCRS 526]

DISCHARGE OF COMMERCIAL PAPER

A. DISCHARGE OF INDIVIDUAL PARTIES

A party to a commercial paper who would otherwise be liable on it may be discharged either individually or by some act that has discharged all parties to the paper at one time. The nature of the transaction or occurrence determines which takes place.

§ 34:1. MANNER OF DISCHARGE. A party is discharged from liability to any other party (a) with whom he enters into an agreement for his discharge, or (b) with whom he enters into a transaction which under the law of contracts is effective to discharge liability on an ordinary contract for the payment of money.[1] Accordingly, there may be a discharge by accord and satisfaction, a novation, a covenant not to sue, rescission, or the substitution of another instrument. The liability may also be barred by operation of law as in the case of a discharge in bankruptcy, the operation of the statute of limitations, or by the merger of liability into a judgment in favor of the holder when an action has been brought on the instrument.

§ 34:2. DISCHARGE BY PAYMENT. The obligation of a particular party on commercial paper is discharged when he pays the amount of the instrument to the holder or to his authorized agent. Payment to anyone else, even though in physical possession of the instrument, is not effective.

FACTS: Gorman executed and delivered a promissory note to the First National Bank. After several payments, the note was stolen from the bank. Subsequently, Gorman paid the remainder to one representing himself to be Richardson, who previously had been connected with the payee bank. In an action brought by the bank to collect the remainder of the note from Gorman, the latter pleaded payment and produced the note marked paid by the impostor.

---

[1] Uniform Commercial Code § 3-601(2).

DECISION: Judgment for First National Bank. Payment of commercial paper is not a discharge when made to a person who is not the holder. This conclusion is not altered by the fact that the person receiving payment of order paper had possession of the paper at the time. [First National Bank v Gorman, 45 Wyo 519, 21 P2d 549]

If the holder consents, payment may be made by a third person, even a total stranger to the paper; and surrender of the paper to such a person gives him the rights of a transferee of the instrument.[2]

By definition, a commercial paper provides for the payment of a sum of money. Any party liable on the instrument and the holder thereof may, however, agree that the transfer or delivery of other kinds of property shall operate as payment. Sometimes a new instrument may be executed or delivered to the holder of the original instrument. In the absence of proof of an agreement to the contrary, a delivery of a subsequent instrument, without the destruction or other act to discharge the first, is regarded as merely the giving of additional security for the payment of the original instrument but not as being a payment or discharge of the first.

FACTS: John Fladeland borrowed money from the Farmers Union Oil Co. He and his brother, Terrance, signed a note representing the loan. When the note was due, John signed and gave Farmers a renewal note. Thereafter Terrance claimed that he was discharged from his liability on the original note because he had not signed the renewal note.

DECISION: Terrance was liable. The delivery of a renewal note does not discharge the liability of any party to the original note in the absence of an express agreement that it should have that effect. [Farmers Union Oil Co. v Fladeland, 287 Minn 315, 178 NW2d 254]

(a) Knowledge of adverse claim to the paper. When the payment of the amount of the paper is made to the holder, the party making payment may know that some other person claims an interest in or ownership of the paper. The knowledge that there is an adverse claimant does not prevent making a payment to the holder, and such payment is still a discharge of the obligation of the party making payment. Specifically, an adverse claim may thus be disregarded unless (1) the adverse claimant furnishes the payor with indemnity to protect him in the event that he, the payor, does not pay but then the adverse claim proves to be worthless or (2) the adverse claimant obtains a court injunction against making payment.[3]

The purpose of this provision is to give commercial paper greater acceptance since the person writing such paper knows that he will be able to discharge the instrument by making payment in the ordinary case to the holder without the risk of deciding whether an adverse claim is valid.

(b) Satisfaction. The principles governing payment apply to a satisfaction entered into with the holder of the instrument.[4] Instead of

---

[2] UCC § 3-603.

[3] § 3-603(1). Certain exceptions are made to this rule when payment is made in bad faith on a stolen instrument or when the instrument is restrictively indorsed.

[4] UCC § 3-601(1).

paying the holder in full in money, a payment of less than all is accepted as full payment, or some service is rendered or property is given by the party discharged.

(c) Tender of payment. A party who is liable may offer to the holder the full payment when or after the instrument is due. If the holder refuses such payment, the party making the tender of payment is not discharged from his liability for the amount then due; but the holder cannot hold him liable for any interest that accrues after that date. Likewise, in the event that the holder sues the person making the tender, the holder cannot recover legal costs from him nor attorney's fees.

If the holder refuses a proper tender, his refusal may discharge third persons even though it does not affect the liability of the person making the tender. Specifically, any party to the paper who would have a right, if he made payment, to recover that amount from the person making the tender is discharged if the tender is not accepted.[5] For example, if the paper is negotiated through the unqualified indorsers, *A*, *B*, and *C*, to the holder *D*, and if *B* or *C* is required to pay *D*, the party making such payment would have the right to sue *A*, the prior indorser, to recover from him the amount paid the holder *D*. In such a case, if *A* makes a proper tender of payment which *D* refuses, *B* and *C* are discharged from any liability to *D*.

(d) Payment by secondary party. When a party secondarily liable pays, such payment does not discharge the paper or prior parties but merely transfers the rights of the holder to the party making the payment. This is so even though there is no assignment or transfer of the paper from the paid holder to the secondary party.

> **FACTS:** Howard, who purchased farm equipment on credit from K & S International, signed a promissory note for the balance of the purchase price. K & S transferred the note to a Jonesboro bank. When Howard stopped making payments, K & S paid the bank the balance due on the note. The bank marked the note paid. K & S then sued Howard for the amount they had paid the bank. Howard claimed that he was discharged because the note had been marked paid and K & S could not sue because the note had not been reassigned to them.

> **DECISION:** Judgment for K & S. When a secondary party pays the paper, the primary party is not discharged even though the holder of the paper marks the paper as "paid." By virtue of the payments, the secondary party becomes the holder of the paper and is entitled to enforce payment by the primary party even though there is no assignment or transfer of the paper from the paid holder to the secondary party. [K & S International, Inc. v Howard, 249 Ark 901, 462 SW2d 458]

§ 34:3. CANCELLATION. The holder of an instrument, with or without consideration, may discharge the liability of a particular party by cancellation by a notation on the paper which makes that intent apparent, or by destroying, mutilating, or striking out the party's signature on the

---

[5] § 3-604(2).

paper. Even though this cancels an indorsement necessary to the chain of title of the holder, his title to the paper is not affected, since the paper had been properly negotiated.

A cancellation is not effective if it is made by a person who is not the holder or who is not acting by his authority or if the physical destruction of the instrument is made by accident or mistake. The party who claims that an apparent cancellation should not take effect has the burden of proof.

§ 34:4. RENUNCIATION. The holder of an instrument, with or without consideration, may discharge the liability of a particular party by renunciation. This is effected either (1) by surrendering the instrument to the party to be discharged, or (2) by executing a signed written renunciation which is then delivered to the party to be discharged.[6] If the holder surrenders the instrument in effecting the renunciation, he ceases to be the holder and thereafter cannot hold any party liable on the paper, although such other parties are not themselves discharged with respect to the person to whom the paper was surrendered or any other subsequent holder thereof. There is no renunciation when the written renunciation is not delivered but is retained by the holder.

> **FACTS:** Cotton was the maker of a note held by Jones. After the death of Jones, his executor, Greene, found a letter written by Jones in his safe deposit box which stated that if Cotton's note was not paid at the time of Jones' death, it should be marked paid and returned to Cotton. Cotton brought an action against Green for a declaratory judgment that he was not liable on the note.

> **DECISION:** Cotton remained liable on the note. There was no renunciation because the writing had not been delivered but had been retained by the holder, Jones. Delivery was required to make the renunciation effective. [Greene v Cotton (Ky) 457 SW2d 493]

By definition, a renunciation can only be made by the person who is the owner of the paper, or his authorized agent. When not so made, the renunciation has no effect and the person making the renunciation may be liable for the tort of conversion of the paper to any person whose joinder in the renunciation was required. For example, one payee who surrenders the paper without the indorsement of the other copayee and a bank accepting the surrender without the missing indorsement are liable to such other copayee for conversion.

> **FACTS:** As part of a sales transaction, Riley Management obtained a cashier's check payable to the order of it and Gillespie, the other party to the transaction. The transaction was abandoned and William Riley, the president of the corporation, took the cashier's check to the National City Bank, indorsed it "not used for purpose issued" and surrendered it in return for two other checks payable to the order of Riley Management. Gillespie then sued Riley Management and the bank for conversion of the cashier's check.

---

[6] § 3-605(1).

DECISION: Judgment for Gillespie. As copayee, he was a co-owner of the cashier's check. This interest was destroyed by Riley and the bank when Riley surrendered the check and the bank received it without Gillespie's indorsement. This destruction of his interest was a conversion of Gillespie's property for which the copayee and the bank were both liable to him. [Gillespie v Riley Management Corp. 13 IllApp3d 988, 301 NE2d 506]

§ 34:5. IMPAIRMENT OF RIGHT OF RECOURSE.

In most instances there is at least one party to commercial paper who, if required to pay, will have a right of recourse, or a right to obtain indemnity, from some other party. For example, in the least complicated situation the payee of a note has indorsed it without qualification to the present holder. If the holder obtains payment from the indorsing payee, the latter has a right of recourse against the maker of the note. If the holder, without the indorser's consent, discharges the liability of the maker, extends the time for payment, or agrees not to sue him, the indorser is also discharged unless he consented thereto, on the theory that his right of recourse has been impaired.[7]

§ 34:6. IMPAIRMENT OF COLLATERAL.

When commercial paper is executed, the maker may give the holder property, such as stocks or bonds, to hold as security for the payment of the instrument. Likewise, any other party liable on the instrument may give collateral as security to the holder for the same purpose. This collateral security benefits all parties who might be liable on the paper because to the extent that payment is obtained from the security, they are not required to make payment. Conversely, if the collateral security is impaired or harmed in any way that reduces its value, the parties who are liable are harmed since the possibility that they will be required to pay increases. Accordingly, a particular party is discharged if the holder unjustifiably impairs collateral security provided by that party or by any person against whom such party has a right of recourse.[8]

FACTS: Paul McAtee signed a promissory note, which was secured by a mortgage executed by McAtee Builders, Inc. Christensen became the holder of Paul's note. Without his consent, Christensen released the mortgage given by the corporation. When Christensen sued Paul, the latter claimed that he was released by the discharge of the mortgage.

DECISION: Paul was not released. The discharge of the mortgage impaired collateral, but impairment of collateral discharges commercial paper only to the extent that it reduces the security for the paper. The burden was on Paul to show the actual value of the lost collateral. If he showed such

---

[7] § 3-606(1)(a). Note that this is similar to the situation where a holder refuses to accept a proper tender of payment from the maker in which case an indorser is discharged. The operation of this rule is avoided, and the other party not released, if the holder executes a reservation of his right against the other party at the time when he discharges the party subject to the latter's right of recourse. UCC § 3-606(2).

[8] § 3-606(1)(b).

value, his liability would be reduced by that amount. Since Paul did not show any value for the lost collateral, no reduction could be made. He therefore remained liable for the full amount of his note. [Christensen v McAtee, 256 Ore 233, 473 P2d 659]

(a) Reservation of rights. When a creditor releases a debtor, such release may constitute an impairment of collateral. The creditor may prevent his release from discharging another party by making an express reservation of his right to proceed against such other party.

FACTS: Kohntopp and Turner signed a promissory note as makers. Hallowell held the note. In consideration of a payment of $2,500 to him made by Kohntopp, Hallowell executed an agreement not "to execute" against Kohntopp. This agreement expressly reserved Hallowell's rights against Turner. Turner did not know of the existence of this agreement and thus did not consent to it. Later Hallowell sued Turner on the note. The defense was raised that the agreement not to execute against Kohntopp operated as a discharge of Turner. From a judgment for Turner, an appeal was taken by Hallowell.

DECISION: Judgment for Hallowell. An agreement not to sue a party impairs the security of any other party who upon paying the paper would have the right to sue the released party. As an exception to this, there is no release of the third party when the person releasing expressly reserves the right to proceed against the third party. Hallowell's release of Kohntopp did not release Turner because Hallowell expressly reserved his rights against Turner. The fact that Turner did not know of the releasing agreement nor of the reservation of rights against him had no effect. His consent to the reservation was not required. [Hallowell v Turner, 95 Idaho 392, 509 P2d 1313]

§ 34:7. REACQUISITION OF PAPER BY INTERMEDIATE PARTY.

Commercial paper is sometimes reacquired by a party who had been an earlier holder. This occurs most commonly when that earlier party pays the then existing holder the amount due, thereby in effect purchasing the paper from that holder. When this occurs, the prior party may cancel all indorsements subsequent to his and then reissue or future negotiate the paper. Then the intervening indorsers subsequent to him whose indorsements have been canceled are discharged as to the reacquirer and all subsequent holders.[9]

§ 34:8. ALTERATION.

When an instrument is materially and fraudulently altered by the holder, any party whose obligation on the paper is changed thereby is discharged, unless he had assented to the alteration or is barred by his conduct from asserting that he is discharged. The effect of the discharge by alteration is limited, however; for, if the altered instrument is held by a holder in due course, he may enforce it according to its original terms.[10]

---

[9] § 3-208.
[10] UCC § 3-407. See § 35:8(f).

A notice by a lending bank to the borrower that the bank has increased the rate of interest on his loan does not constitute an "alteration" of the note which the borrower had executed when he obtained the loan, since there is no changing of the terms of the note itself and since the intent of the bank in giving such notice is not "fraudulent."

§ 34:9. DISCHARGE FOR MISCELLANEOUS CAUSES. In addition to the discharge of a party as discussed in the preceding sections, the conduct of certain parties with respect to the commercial paper or the enforcement of rights thereunder may release some of the parties to the paper. This occurs (a) when a check has been certified on the application of the holder; (b) when the holder accepts an acceptance that varies the terms of the draft; and (c) when a presentment, notice of dishonor, or protest, when required, is delayed beyond the time permitted or is absent and such delay or absence is not excused.

In addition, federal or local statutes may provide for the discharge of a party by bankruptcy proceedings or by local laws declaring certain obligations not enforceable because they violate particular statutes.

B. DISCHARGE OF ALL PARTIES

§ 34:10. DISCHARGE OF PARTY PRIMARILY LIABLE. The primary party on an instrument, that is, the maker of a note or the acceptor of a draft,[11] has no right of recourse against any party on the paper. Conversely, every other party who may be held liable on the paper has a right of recourse against persons primarily liable. If the holder discharges in any way a party who is primarily liable, all parties to the instrument are discharged, since the discharge of the primary party discharges the persons who had a right of recourse against him.[12]

§ 34:11. PRIMARY PARTY'S REACQUISITION OF PAPER. When a party primarily liable on the paper reacquires it in his own right at any time, whether before or after it is due, the instrument is then held by one who has no right to sue any other party on the paper. Such reacquisition therefore discharges the liability of all intervening parties to the instrument. Moreover, as reacquisition requires a lawful transfer, it necessarily involves the negotiation or surrender by the person who was then the holder of the right against that party and no party thereafter remains liable on the paper. The reacquisition by the party who has no right of action or recourse against anyone else on the paper therefore discharges the liability of all parties on it.[13]

---

[11] An accommodated payee is in effect also a primary party since the accommodating party, if required to pay an indorsee, has a right of recourse against such payee.

[12] UCC § 3-601(3). In some instances this rule is modified by § 3-606.

[13] § 3-208.

C. EFFECT OF DISCHARGE ON HOLDER IN DUE COURSE

An ordinary holder or an assignee of paper is subject to any discharge. A holder in due course may or may not be subject to a prior discharge.

§ 34:12. **DISCHARGE OF INDIVIDUAL PARTY.** The fact that a party has been discharged of liability, and even that a new holder of the paper knows of it, does not prevent the new holder from being a holder in due course as to any party remaining liable on the paper.[14] If the holder in due course does not have notice or knowledge of a discharge of a party obtained before he acquired the paper, he is not bound by the discharge and may enforce the obligation of the discharged party as though he had never been discharged.[15] In order to protect himself, a party securing his own discharge should have a notation of it made on the paper so that any subsequent holder would necessarily have notice of that fact.

§ 34:13. **DISCHARGE OF ALL PARTIES.** The fact that the liabilities of all parties to a commercial paper have been discharged does not destroy the negotiable character nor the existence of the commercial paper. If it should thereafter be negotiated to a person who qualifies as a holder in due course, the latter may enforce the liability of any party on the paper, although otherwise discharged, of whose discharge the holder in due course had no notice or knowledge.

**QUESTIONS
AND CASE
PROBLEMS**

1. *H* was the holder of a note on which *M* was the maker. *H* owed money to *C* and indorsed *M*'s note to *C* in payment of his debt. Thereafter *M* failed to pay his note to *C*. When *C* demanded that *H* pay his original debt to *C*, *H* raised the defense that *C* had taken *M*'s note in payment of that debt so that it no longer existed. Decide. [See Central Stone Co. v John Ruggiero, Inc. 49 Misc2d 622, 268 NYS2d 172]

2. *H* was the holder of a promissory note made by *M*. The note was payable in 12 months. After preliminary discussion between the parties in the eleventh month with respect to refinancing, *H* telephoned *M* that he "canceled" the note. The next day, *H* changed his mind and negotiated the note to *C* who satisfied the requirements of being a holder in due course. When *C* demanded payment of *M*, *M* asserted that he was not liable because he had been discharged when *H* canceled the note. Was he correct? [See Citizens Fidelity Bank & Trust Co. v Stark (Ky) 431 SW2d 722; Bihlmire v Hahn (DC Wis) 43 FRD 503]

---

[14] § 3-305(2)(e).

[15] § 3-602. As an exception to this rule, the holder in due course is bound by a prior discharge in insolvency proceedings, such as bankruptcy, whether he had notice thereof or not. UCC § 3-305(2)(d).

3. The Citizens State Bank issued a cashier's check payable to the order of Donovan. He indorsed it to Denny, who did business as the Houston Aircraft Co., and included in the indorsement a recital that it was "in full [payment of] any and all claims of any character whatever." Denny crossed out this quoted phrase and wrote Donovan and the bank that he had done so. The Houston Aircraft Co. sued the Citizens National Bank on the check. Was the bank liable? [Houston Aircraft Co. v Citizens State Bank (TexCivApp) 184 SW2d 335]

4. Satek authorized his agent to execute a mortgage with Fortuna as mortgagor. Fortuna executed a note secured by the mortgage. Later Fortuna made a part payment on the note to the agent. This payment was made before maturity, and the agent at the time did not have possession of the note. Satek later sued to foreclose the mortgage. The court refused to allow Fortuna credit for the payment made to the agent. Why? [Satek v Fortuna, 324 IllApp 523, 58 NE2d 464]

5. Burg executed and delivered a promissory note for $1,060 payable to Liesemer. When the note was due, Burg paid $893 and demanded credit for the remainder of the amount due because of the boarding expense incurred by Liesemer's daughter. Liesemer gave Burg the note so that he could compute the amount due. Burg refused to give credit for Liesemer's claim and kept the note. When Liesemer brought an action to recover the remainder of the note, it appeared that Burg had written across the face of the note, "Paid February 9th." It was contended that the note had been discharged by cancellation. Do you agree? [Liesemer v Burg, 106 Mich 124, 63 NW 999]

6. C. Neal executed and delivered a promissory note payable to the order of A. Neal, who indorsed the instrument to his wife, Mary Neal, a holder in due course. Before maturity, the maker paid the amount of the note to the payee. After maturity, Mary, who had divorced A. Neal and resumed her maiden name of Fogarty, brought an action against C. Neal to recover on the note. Neal contended that the note had been discharged by payment. Do you agree with this contention? [Fogarty v Neal, 201 Ky 85, 255 SW 1049]

7. Twombly, who owned negotiable bonds of the Muskogee Electric Traction Co., was advised by her financial agent, the State Street Trust Co., that the bonds had no value. Acting on this belief, Twombly burned the bonds. Some years later it was found that the bonds had some value, and the trust company, on behalf of Twombly, demanded payment on the bonds. Was it entitled to payment? [State Street Trust Co. v Muskogee Electric Traction Co. (CA10 Okla) 204 F2d 920]

8. As part of a business plan, Schwald executed and delivered a note to Montgomery. The parties then made a new business arrangement, and Montgomery intentionally tore up the note and threw it into the wastebasket. It was subsequently contended that this note had been canceled. Do you agree? [Montgomery v Schwald, 117 MoApp 75, 166 SW 831]

SECURED CONSUMER
CREDIT SALES

A. GENERAL PRINCIPLES

§ 35:1. NATURE OF A SECURED CREDIT SALE. Various devices have been developed to provide the credit seller of goods with protection beyond his right to sue the buyer for the purchase price. Today such devices, and others discussed in Chapter 36, are known as *secured transactions* and are governed by Article 9 of the UCC.[1]

A *secured credit sale* is a sale in which the possession and the risk of loss pass to the buyer but the seller retains a security interest in the goods until he has been paid in full. In some instances the seller retains the title until paid, but this is not essential. The seller's security interest entitles him to repossess the goods when the buyer fails to make payment as required or when he commits a breach of the purchase contract in any other way. This right is in addition to the right to sue for the purchase price.

Forerunners of this credit device include: (1) a *conditional sale*, where the seller retained title until the condition of payment in full had been satisfied; (2) a *bailment lease*, under which transaction the buyer rented the property and, after the payment of sufficient rentals to equal the purchase price, could elect to take title to the property; and (3) a *chattel mortgage*, by which the buyer, upon taking title from the seller, in turn gave the seller a mortgage on the property for the amount of the unpaid balance of the purchase price. The laws pertaining to these three types of transactions have been replaced by the secured transaction provisions of the UCC.[2]

---

[1] This book is based on the 1962 version of the Uniform Commercial Code which is set forth in the Code Appendix. In 1972, amendments to the 1962 version were approved by the UCC sponsors and, thus far, have been adopted in Arkansas, California, Illinois, Iowa, Nebraska, Nevada, North Dakota, Oregon, Texas, Virginia, West Virginia, and Wisconsin. The changes made by the 1972 amendments to the UCC are confined mainly to Article 9 on secured transactions. Some of the changes made thereto are indicated in the footnotes.

[2] The UCC, however, has not abolished these transactions nor made them illegal. The parties may still enter into a conditional sale, bailment lease, or chattel mortgage; but if they do, the transaction must satisfy the requirements of the secured transaction under the Code. Thus, the UCC establishes certain minimum requirements applicable to all types of security devices employed by the credit seller. An instrument that is called a "chattel mortgage" will be interpreted as a "security agreement." Strevell-Patterson Finance Co. v May, 77 NMex 331, 422 P2d 366.

The Uniform Commercial Code is not designed solely to aid sellers. The provisions of Article 9 increase the protection given the buyers over that available to them under the former law. Special consumer protection statutes designed to protect buyers, in addition to the UCC, may also be in force within a given state.[3]

§ 35:2. CREATION OF SECURITY INTEREST. A security interest for the protection of the seller of goods to a buyer arises or *attaches* as soon as the seller and buyer agree that the buyer shall have property rights in particular goods and that the seller shall have a security interest in them.[4] It is immaterial whether or not the sales agreement provides for the seller's retaining title until the buyer has paid for the goods in full, as the location of title to the property involved, called *collateral*, is immaterial.[5]

(a) Security agreement. The agreement of the seller and buyer that the seller shall have a security interest in the goods must be evidenced by a written *security agreement* which is signed by the buyer and which describes the collateral.[6] This description need only reasonably identify the collateral. It is not necessary that the goods be described specifically, as by serial number or by manufacturer's model.[7] A description is sufficient when it would enable a third person aided by inquiries made to others to determine what goods were involved.[8]

The description in the security agreement must be sufficiently broad to include all property which the parties intended to include. The creditor does not have any security interest in property which is not included in the description of the collateral in the security agreement. This concept applies to all collateral, whether consumer goods, farm products, inventory, or equipment.

FACTS: Jones & Laughlin Supply held a security interest in certain drilling equipment of the Lucky Drilling Company. The property of that company was sold at a sheriff's sale and purchased by Dugan Production Corporation and McDonald. Jones & Laughlin claimed that the property they purchased was subject to its security interest. The security agreement did not include the items in question but a filed, unsigned financing statement and oral testimony showed that the disputed items were to have been subject to the security interest. Jones & Laughlin brought an action to recover the disputed items.

DECISION: Judgment against Jones & Laughlin. A security agreement does not create a security interest in any property which is not described therein. The unsigned financing statement and the oral testimony could not enlarge the scope of collateral covered by the agreement. [Jones & Laughlin Supply v Dugan Corp., 85 NMex 51, 508 P2d 1348]

---

[3] Such laws continue in effect under UCC §§ 9-201, 9-203(2) and supplement its provisions.

[4] UCC § 9-204(1).

[5] § 9-202.

[6] § 9-203(1)(b).

[7] § 9-110.

[8] The term "accounts receivable" is sufficient to cover future accounts receivable since the quoted words adequately put third persons on notice as to the interest of the creditor in accounts receivable: In re Platt (DC ED Pa) 257 FSupp 478.

Whether the agreement between the parties is a security agreement depends upon its construction or interpretation. Hence, a buyer cannot claim that an outright sale was made to him when the contract is conspicuously entitled as a "conditional sales contract" and states that the sale is made "subject to the terms and conditions set forth below and upon the reverse side hereof," when the conditional sale provisions were specified on the reverse side but the buyer apparently neglected to read the reverse side. The fact that a financing statement has been filed does not eliminate the requirement of a security agreement.

(b) Future transactions. The security agreement may contemplate future action by extending to goods not in existence that are to be acquired and delivered to the buyer at a future date. In general the security interest does not attach to future goods until the buyer has rights in such goods.[9]

(c) Perfection. When a security interest in property is superior to other interests and claims to the property, it is said to be *perfected* or superior.

§ 35:3. CONSUMER GOODS. *Consumer goods* are those which are used or bought for use primarily for personal, family, or household purposes.[10] It is the intended use, rather than the nature of the article which determines its character. For example, goods purchased by a buyer for resale to ultimate consumers are not consumer goods in the hands of such middleman but constitute a part of his inventory.

A mobile home in the possession of the person making use thereof is a consumer good. An automobile is a consumer good when purchased by the buyer to go to and from work. Equipment used in business is not a consumer good. Hence, a tractor purchased by a construction contractor is not a consumer good, but equipment. Likewise, a musical instrument used by a nightclub entertainer is equipment.

In this chapter, secured credit sales relating to consumer goods are considered. In Chapter 36, attention will be given to secured credit sales of inventory and equipment, and to secured loan transactions.

In many states security interests in automobiles in the hands of the ultimate consumer are governed by special installment sale or consumer protection statutes. As to automobiles which constitute a dealer's inventory, security interests are governed by Article 9 of the Uniform Commercial Code.

B. RIGHTS OF PARTIES INDEPENDENT OF DEFAULT

§ 35:4. RIGHTS OF THE SELLER OF CONSUMER GOODS INDEPENDENT OF DEFAULT. The seller stands in a dual position of being both a seller, having rights under Article 2 of the UCC governing sales,

---

[9] UCC § 9-204(1)(2).
[10] § 9-109(1).

and a secured creditor, having rights under Article 9 of the UCC regulating secured transactions.[11]

The seller may transfer or assign his interest under the sales contract and under the security agreement to a third person, and the assignee acquires all the rights and interest of the seller. The rights of the assignee may rise higher than those of the seller to the extent that there is a defense or claim valid against the seller which is not effective against the assignee because the buyer has waived such a right as against an assignee.

The secured credit seller of consumer goods has rights that are effective not only against the buyer but also against purchasers of the property from the buyer as soon as the security agreement is executed with respect to goods in which the buyer has acquired an interest. From that moment on, the seller's interest is generally effective against third persons [12] and is described as a *perfected security interest*. Whether a security interest is perfected is immaterial, however, when the question is the effect of the security agreement as between the creditor and the debtor.

(a) Filing not required. In an ordinary sale of consumer goods under a secured transaction, no filing in any government office is required in order to perfect the secured seller's interest. Such a seller is protected against purchasers from the creditors of the buyer who may acquire the property thereafter.[13]

As an exception to the rule that the seller of such goods has a perfected security interest as soon as the agreement is executed and the buyer has an interest in the property, the seller's security interest is not perfected, and filing is required to perfect it, if the goods purchased are to be attached to buildings or land as a fixture, or if they consist of farm equipment sold for a purchase price of over $2,500. A security interest in a motor vehicle required to be licensed is not perfected unless the vehicle is licensed with a notation of the security interest made in the title certificate, if such is required by law, or if not so required, unless there is a filing under the UCC.[14]

(b) Interstate security interests. The UCC regulates not only transactions within the state but also the effect to be given security interests in property brought into the state from another state. If the interest of the secured party was perfected in the other state, his interest will be regarded as perfected by the state into which the property is brought. Within the second state, however, it is necessary to file within four months in order to keep the security interest continuously perfected.

---

[11] § 9-113. No civil liability rests upon the seller for harm sustained by third persons as a result of acts or omissions of the debtor or in consequence of the existence of the secured transaction. UCC § 9-317.

[12] § 9-201.

[13] § 9-302(1)(d). The UCC makes detailed provisions as to the priority of conflicting security interests with respect to fixtures, accessions, and commingled and processed goods. UCC § 9-313 et seq. A good faith subpurchaser will, in some cases, be protected from the security interest, See § 35:7.

[14] UCC § 9-302(1)(c), (d), (3), (4).

FACTS: On July 7, Mulry sold a Ford Thunderbird to Greene in Rhode Island by a conditional sales contract. The contract was never recorded or filed since this was not required in Rhode Island to perfect the interest of Mulry. Unknown to Mulry, Greene took the automobile to Pennsylvania and sold it to Miracle Mile Motors on July 11. The latter obtained a Pennsylvania title certificate to the automobile which stated that it was the owner but bore a notation indicating that the automobile had been brought in from outside of the state. On July 25, Miracle Mile resold the automobile in Pennsylvania to A. C. Lohman, Inc., a New York automobile dealer, who brought the automobile back to New York and sold it in the following May to Churchill Motors, expressly warranting the title. On October 10, Mulry took the automobile from the parking lot of Churchill because he had never been paid by Greene. Churchill then sued Lohman for breach of the warranty of title.

DECISION: Judgment for Churchill. When collateral subject to a perfected interest is moved to another state, it remains subject to such security interest for a 4-month period. A purchaser during that time takes the goods subject to the perfected security interest. Even though the perfected interest loses its perfection by failure to refile before the end of the 4-month period, the party who purchased before the end of the period remains subordinated to the security interest; but a good-faith purchaser who would purchase after the expiration of the 4-month period and the loss of perfection would not be subject to the then unperfected security interest. [Churchill Motors, Inc. v A. C. Lohman, Inc. 16 AppDiv2d 560, 229 NYS2d 570]

If the secured party's interest in the goods was unperfected when they were brought into the second state, that interest may be perfected therein, in which case the perfection of the security interest dates from such perfection in the second state.[15]

If title to the property, such as an automobile, is represented by a title certificate, the law of the state which issued the certificate determines whether an interest is perfected. Accordingly, if the law of the certificate-issuing state requires that a security interest be noted on the title certificate in order to be binding, that requirement is the exclusive means of perfecting the interest of the secured creditor.[16]

(c) Repair and storage lien. In most states, persons making repairs to or storing property have a right to assert a lien against the property for the amount of their charges. A question of priority arises when the customer bringing the goods for repair or storage is not the absolute owner and there is an outstanding security interest in the goods. In such a case, the lien for repairs or storage charges prevails over the outstanding security interest.[17]

---

[15] § 9-103(3).

[16] § 9-103(4). This provision does not apply to an automobile which was purchased originally in a state that did not provide for the notation of a security interest on the certificate of title, although it was thereafter brought into a state which had such a notation requirement. First National Bank v Stamper, 93 NJSuper 150, 225 A2d 162.

[17] UCC § 9-310.

The contrary result is reached, however, when the lien for repairs or storage is based on a statute which expressly states that the lien shall be subordinate or inferior to the interest of the secured creditor.

§ 35:5. RIGHTS OF THE BUYER OF CONSUMER GOODS INDEPENDENT OF DEFAULT.

The buyer in a secured transaction, like the seller, has a double status under the UCC. By virtue of Article 2 he has certain rights because he is a buyer, and by virtue of Article 9 he has certain rights because he is a debtor in a secured transaction.

(a) **Rights as a buyer.** The secured credit sale of consumer goods remains fundamentally a sale that is governed by Article 2, and therefore the debtor-buyer has the same rights as an ordinary buyer under that article.[18]

FACTS: Stuski purchased 123 beverage pourers from L. & N. Sales Co., which was the sales outlet for the manufacturer. He signed (1) a purchase contract on September 28, which did not exclude or limit any warranties of the seller; (2) an express written warranty of merchantability given on September 28, which stated that it was in place of any other warranty, express or implied, and all other liabilities or obligations of the seller; and (3) a purchase money security agreement, in the nature of a conditional sales contract executed on October 5, to secure the purchase price due the seller, the latter reciting that no warranties, guarantees, or representations of any kind were made. The buyer thereafter refused to make payments because the pourers did not work and sought to cancel the purchase. Was Stuski entitled to do so?

DECISION: Yes. The defects in the goods constituted a breach of warranty of merchantability because the goods were not fit for their ordinary use. Stuski, as a buyer of goods, had the right to cancel for breach of warranty even though a security agreement was executed after the sale and the agreement purported to exclude all warranties [L. & N. Sales. Co. v Stuski, 188 PaSuper 117, 146 A2d 254]

The buyer has certain rights of ownership in the collateral. It is not material whether technically he is the owner of the title. Whatever interest he owns he may transfer voluntarily, and his creditors may reach it by the process of law as fully as though there were no security agreement. Such third persons generally cannot acquire any greater rights than the buyer, and therefore they hold the property subject to the security interest of the seller.

It is common practice for credit sellers to seek to protect themselves by prohibiting the buyer from reselling the property. Such a provision has no effect and does not prevent an effective resale, even though the security agreement in addition to prohibiting such resale also expressly makes it a default or breach of the contract to make a resale.[19]

---

[18] § 9-206(2).
[19] § 9-311.

(b) Rights as a debtor. The secured transaction buyer is a debtor to the extent that there is a balance due on the purchase price. In order for the buyer to know just how much he owes and to check with his own records what the seller claims to be due, the buyer has the right to compel the seller to state what balance is owed and also to specify in which collateral the seller claims a security interest. This is done by the buyer's sending the seller a statement of the amount which he believes to be due, or a statement of the collateral which he believes to be subject to the security agreement, with the request that the seller approve or correct the statement. The seller must so indicate; and if he has assigned the contract and the security interest to a third person, he must furnish the buyer with the name and address of such successor in interest.[20]

(c) Waiver of defenses. It is common practice for finance companies that have a standing agreement to purchase sales contracts from a credit seller to provide him with forms to be signed by the buyer. These forms generally specify that the buyer waives, as against the assignee of the sales contract and security agreement, any right that he would have against the seller. In addition to an express agreement waiving his defenses, a buyer who, as part of the purchase transaction, signs both a commercial paper and a security agreement is deemed as a matter of law to waive such defenses, even though nothing is said as to any waiver.

Both express and implied waivers are valid and bind the buyer if the assignee takes his assignment for value, in good faith, and without notice or knowledge of any claim or defense of the buyer.[21] Consequently, when a construction contractor purchases a tractor on credit under a security agreement which states that he will not assert against an assignee of the seller any claim available to the contractor against the seller, such statement is binding and bars proof by the buyer when sued by the assignee that the tractor was older and of less value than represented by the seller.

The validity of any waiver of defense is subject to two limitations: (1) those defenses which could be raised against the holder in due course of commercial paper cannot be waived; (2) the waiver is not effective if a statute or decision establishes a different rule for buyers of consumer goods.[22]

A provision in a purchase money contract that the buyer will not assert any defense against the assignee of the seller and will hold only the seller responsible for the performance of the contract is not unconscionable.[23]

§ 35:6. DEFINED DEFAULT. A *default* by the debtor is merely his failure to pay the money as due. In order to provide greater protection to the creditor, the modern financing agreement will expand the definition of default to include matters which are not directly related to nonpayment. Thus, it will be specified that if the debtor moves away without notifying the creditor, such conduct is a default. This is merely a shorthand way of saying that

---

[20] § 9-208.
[21] § 9-206(1), (2).
[22] UCC § 9-206(1). See § 29:24.
[23] Westinghouse Credit Corp. v Chapman, 129 GaApp 830, 201 SE2d 686.

although moving away is not a default, the creditor shall be entitled to exercise the same remedies when the debtor moves away as though he had defaulted in payment of the debt. When a security agreement states that the debtor's bankruptcy shall constitute a default, such bankruptcy is given the effect of a default within the meaning of Uniform Commercial Code § 9-504(1), so that upon the debtor's bankruptcy the creditor may exercise the rights which the UCC states may be exercised upon default.

§ 35:7. PROTECTION OF SUBPURCHASER. When the seller of consumer goods sells on credit, his security interest in the goods is perfected even though the buyer is given possession of the goods and the seller does not file a financing statement. When no financing statement is filed, however, a resale by the consumer to another consumer will destroy the seller's security interest in the goods if the second buyer does not have knowledge of the security interest of the original seller and buys for his own personal, family, or household use.[24]

> **FACTS:** Balon and Gibert each purchased a Cadillac for personal use from Saia, a private owner. Saia had purchased the cars from the Cadillac Automobile Company of Boston. Cadillac Automobile held security interests in the cars sold to Saia but had failed to file under the Code. Balon and Gibert purchased the cars from Saia for their personal use. Cadillac Automobile repossessed the cars. Balon and Gibert sued Cadillac Automobile, claiming that the latter's security interests had been destroyed by the resale to them.

> **DECISION:** Judgment for Balon and Gibert. When they purchased the cars in good faith from a consumer for their own personal use, Balon and Gibert acquired their cars free of the unperfected security interest of Cadillac Automobile. [Balon v Cadillac Automobile Co. 113 NH 108, 303 A2d 194]

In order for sale to destroy a security interest, it is necessary that the security interest had been created by the seller who has sold the goods to the consumer who resold them to another consumer. The security interest is not destroyed if it was created by a former seller or owner.

When the consumer sells the collateral to a dealer as a trade-in on a new purchase from the dealer, the latter is not a consumer purchasing for a consumer use and therefore takes subject to the original creditor's security interest in the goods.[25]

C. RIGHTS OF PARTIES AFTER DEFAULT

§ 35:8. SECURED SELLER'S REPOSSESSION AND RESALE OF COLLATERAL. Upon the buyer's default, the secured party is entitled to

---

[24] UCC § 9-307(2). The same provision applies to farm equipment other than fixtures having an original purchase price not in excess of $2,500 when the purchase by the subpurchaser is for his own farming operations.

[25] Bennett v W. T. Grant Company (CA4 Va) 481 F2d 664.

take the collateral or purchased property from the buyer. If he can do so without causing a breach of the peace, the seller may repossess the property without legal proceedings.

When the credit seller repossesses in a peaceful, open manner, he does not commit larceny or any other crime.[26] In any case he may use legal proceedings if he desires.[27]

The seller who has repossessed the goods may resell them at a private or public sale at any time and place and on any terms. He must, however, act in good faith in a manner that is commercially reasonable.[28] The seller must give the buyer reasonable advance notice of a resale unless the goods are perishable, or unless they threaten to decline speedily in value, or unless they are a type customarily sold on a recognized market.[29] The seller's resale destroys all interest of the buyer in the goods.

If the secured creditor is the highest bidder or the only bidder at a public sale, the creditor may purchase the collateral even though such a sale is conducted in the creditor's office.

(a) Compulsory resale. If the buyer has paid 60 percent or more of the cash price of the consumer goods, the seller must resell them within 90 days after repossession, unless the buyer, after default, has signed a written statement surrendering the right to require the resale. If the seller does not resell within the time specified, the buyer may sue him for conversion of the collateral or proceed under the UCC provision applicable to failure to comply with the UCC.[30]

(b) Notice. Ordinarily notice must be given of the sale of collateral. The UCC does not specify the form of notice, and any form of notice that is reasonable is sufficient. A letter to the debtor can satisfy this requirement. If a public sale is made, the notice must give the time and place of the sale. If a private sale is made, it is sufficient to give reasonable notice of the time after which the private sale will be made. No notice is required when the collateral is perishable or is threatening to decline rapidly in value or is sold on a recognized market or exchange.[31] Notice must be given of the resale of an automobile that is collateral because there is no "recognized market" for the sale of used cars.

When notice is given to the public, it should be sufficiently explicit to enable a third person to form a basis for evaluating the collateral so that he can determine whether he wishes to bid at the sale. A warning that if payments are not made, the collateral will be put up for public sale is not a sufficient notice of the sale to satisfy the requirement of the UCC, because there is no notice of the time and place of the sale. Likewise, a declaration by the creditor after repossession that the collateral will be sold to the highest bidder is not sufficient notice of sale when there is no statement as to the time or place of the sale.

---

[26] White v Alabama (AlaCrimApp) 288 So2d 175.
[27] UCC § 9-503.
[28] § 9-504(1)(3).
[29] § 9-504(3).
[30] § 9-507(1).
[31] § 9-504(3).

(c) **Redemption of collateral.** If the buyer acts in time, he may redeem or obtain the return to him of the goods by tendering to the secured party the amount that is owed him, including expenses and any legal costs that have been incurred. The right to redeem is destroyed if the seller has made a resale or entered into a binding contract for resale.[32]

(d) **Manner of resale.** Upon the debtor's default, the creditor may sell the collateral at public or private sale or he may lease it to a third person, as long as he acts in a manner that is commercially reasonable.[33] The UCC does not require any particular kind of sale but only that the disposition be "commercially reasonable." The fact that higher offers are received after the making of a contract for resale of the collateral does not show that the contract was not "commercially reasonable."

(e) **Accounting after resale.** When the secured party makes a resale of the goods, the proceeds of the sale are applied in the following order to pay (1) reasonable costs of repossession, storage, and resale of the goods; (2) the balance due, including interest and any proper additions such as attorney's fees; and (3) subsequent security interests in the property that are discharged by the sale.[34]

If any balance remains after the payment of these claims, the buyer is entitled to the surplus. Conversely, if the net proceeds of sale are insufficient to pay the costs and the debt due the seller, the buyer is liable to him for such deficiency unless it has been otherwise agreed by the parties.[35]

In computing a deficiency judgment, a trade-in must be taken at its actual value and not at the amount allowed by the seller for the trade-in.[36]

(f) **Priority as to other creditors.** When a creditor holds a perfected security interest, he is entitled to exercise his rights with respect to the collateral as against (1) a creditor having an unperfected security interest, (2) a general creditor having no security interest, and (3) the debtor's trustee in bankruptcy. If the collateral is claimed by another creditor having a perfected security interest in the same collateral and both creditors have perfected by filing, the one first filing prevails over the other creditor.[37]

§ 35:9. SECURED SELLER'S RETENTION OF COLLATERAL TO DISCHARGE OBLIGATION.

If a compulsory disposition of the collateral is not required, the secured party may propose in writing that he keep the collateral in payment of the debt. If the buyer does not object to this proposal, the secured party may do so and the secured obligation is automatically discharged. If written objection to the retention of the collateral by the secured party is made within 30 days, he must then proceed to dispose of it by resale or other reasonable manner.[38]

---

[32] § 9-506.
[33] § 9-504(1).
[34] § 9-504(1).
[35] § 9-504(2).
[36] Webster v General Motors Acceptance Corp. 267 Ore 304, 516 P2d 1275.
[37] UCC § 9-312(5)(a). Other provisions regulate priorities in other circumstances.
[38] UCC § 9-505(2).

§ 35:10. BUYER'S REMEDIES FOR VIOLATION OF UCC BY SECURED PARTY.

The UCC authorizes both injunctive and money-damage relief against the secured party who violates the provisions of the UCC applicable upon default. The remedies provided by the UCC are not exclusive, and the buyer may also invoke any remedies authorized by any other statute applicable to the particular transaction.

When the sales contract is not executed in the manner required by a statute relating to installment sales, the contract is generally voidable at the election of the buyer and the seller is subject to some form of penalty, such as a criminal fine or loss of financing charges.

Local statutes, such as motor vehicle retail installment sales acts, may impose notice requirements upon a creditor repossessing collateral and subject him to a penalty for failing to give the required notice.

FACTS: Shaw purchased an automobile from Countrywide Motors on credit. The seller financed the purchase. Countrywide then sold the buyer's contract to Alliance Discount Corp. When the installments on the purchase price were not paid, Alliance repossessed the automobile and sold it at a private sale for a very nominal amount. No notice was given to Shaw of any of the proceedings. He petitioned for leave to show the true value of the automobile so that the balance owed on the purchase price could be reduced by the fair value of the automobile. The pre-Code state Motor Vehicle Sales Finance Act required that this be done and declared that the resale price was not conclusive as to its reasonable value. The UCC does not contain such a provision.

DECISION: The value of the sold collateral had to be determined in the manner specified by the Motor Vehicle Sales Finance Act. That statute was not displaced by the UCC, and the remedies afforded by that statute were not abolished nor the debtor limited to those specified by the UCC. [Alliance Discount Corp. v Shaw, 195 PaSuper 601, 171 A2d 548]

The buyer is entitled to recover the damages caused him by the secured party's failure to comply with the UCC. In the absence of proof of a greater amount of damages, the buyer is entitled to recover not less than the credit service charge together with 10 percent of the principal amount of the debt or the time price differential plus 10 percent of the cash price.[39]

If a resale has not yet been made nor a binding contract therefore entered into, the buyer may obtain a court order or injunction requiring the seller to comply with the UCC provisions.

If the creditor repossesses the collateral when the debtor is not in default or takes other property in which he has no security interest, the creditor commits a conversion. The debtor may recover damages from the creditor for the conversion representing the value of his interest in the goods. If the creditor has acted recklessly and with willful indifference to the rights of the debtor, the latter may also recover punitive damages.

---

[39] § 9-507(1).

FACTS: Beggs owned a 1958 and a 1959 tractor. Universal C.I.T. Credit Corporation held a security interest in the 1959 tractor. Beggs became delinquent in payment and Universal sent an agent to repossess the tractor which was subject to its security interest. The agent took the 1958 tractor, although Beggs informed the agent that it was the wrong tractor and the agent did nothing to verify the identity of the collateral. The towing company hired by the agent damaged the tractor. Beggs sued Universal for damages for the harm caused the tractor and for punitive damages.

DECISION: Judgment for Beggs for compensatory and punitive damages. The act of the creditor's agent was wrongful and showed a wanton disregard for the rights of Beggs. [Beggs v Universal C.I.T. Credit Corporation (Mo) 409 SW2d 719]

When the creditor makes a sale of the collateral without giving the debtor notice, the creditor deprives the debtor of his opportunity to bid at the sale and to retain the property. Consequently, the creditor will not be allowed to recover from the debtor any loss sustained or expenses incurred at such sale. Thus, the creditor who has not given the debtor sufficient notice of the sale of the collateral is barred from obtaining a deficiency judgment against the debtor when the collateral is resold for less than the amount due the creditor.[40]

FACTS: Turk was president of Bob King, Inc. which sold automobiles. To finance the obtaining of Inventory for Bob King, Turk borrowed money from the St. Petersburg Bank. The loan was represented by a note which was secured by the inventory of Bob King. The bank repossessed the collateral and resold it without giving notice of the sale to Turk. The amount obtained by the sale was substantially less than the balance due on the debt and the bank sued Turk for the deficiency.

DECISION: Judgment for Turk. When the creditor sells the collateral without giving proper notice of the sale to the debtor, the creditor is barred from obtaining any deficiency judgment against the debtor. [Turk v St. Petersburg Bank and Trust Co. (FlaApp) 281 So2d 534]

QUESTIONS AND CASE PROBLEMS

1. Hull-Dobbs sold an automobile to Mallicoat and then assigned the sales contract to the Volunteer Finance & Loan Corp. Later Volunteer repossessed the automobile and sold it. When Volunteer sued Mallicoat for the deficiency between the contract price and the proceeds on resale, Mallicoat raised the

---

[40] Some courts hold that the failure to give notice does not bar the creditor but merely raises a presumption that the collateral was actually of the value of the balance of the debt and that unless the creditor can show otherwise there is no liability for a deficiency judgment. In most cases this presumption has the same effect as a flat prohibition of a deficiency judgment.

defense that he had not been properly notified of the resale. The loan manager of the finance company testified that Mallicoat had been sent a registered letter stating that the car would be sold. He did not state whether the letter merely declared in general terms that the car would be sold or specified a date for its resale. He admitted that the letter never was delivered to Mallicoat and was returned to the finance company "unclaimed." The loan manager also testified that the sale was advertised by posters, but on cross examination he admitted that he was not able to state when or where it was thus advertised. It was shown that Volunteer knew where Mallicoat and his father lived and where Mallicoat was employed. Mallicoat claimed that he had not been properly notified. Volunteer asserted that sufficient notice had been given. Was the notice of the resale sufficient? [Mallicoat v Volunteer Finance & Loan Corp. 57 TennApp 106, 415 SW2d 347]

2. Allen, who operated a trailer park, rented a trailer, which at all times remained in the park, to Cady under a lease which gave Cady the option to purchase the trailer. The lease stated that the cash price of the trailer plus various charges was $5,800, of which the down payment was $1,934, and specified that $17 of each weekly payment of $32 was to be applied to the down payment. The lease was for 24 months so that the total payments, if the trailer was not purchased, would be $3,578, or 62 percent of the price of the trailer. Cady became bankrupt and Cohen, his trustee in bankruptcy, claimed that the interest of Allen in the trailer was void because the transaction was a conditional sale and there had not been any recording of the sales contract. Was Allen's claim to the trailer binding? [Allen v Dohen (CA2 NY) 310 F2d 312]

3. Bailey purchased a freezer-and-food plan from Pen Del Farms on the installment plan. The latter sold its rights under the contract to the Associated Acceptance Corp. and gave it a copy of the original contract. When Associated sued Bailey, he claimed that the transaction was void under the Maryland Retail Installment Sales Act because the copy of the contract that had been given him had not been fully signed on behalf of the seller. Associated replied that the copy which it had received had been fully executed and that it contained the statement of Bailey that "purchaser acknowledges receipt of true, executed copy of this contract at time of execution hereof." Was Bailey's defense valid? [Associated Acceptance Corp. v Bailey, 226 Md 550, 174 A2d 440]

4. Hileman purchased a washer from the Maytag Rice Co. on credit and executed a chattel mortgage. The mortgage gave the seller authority "to make use of such force as may be necessary to enter upon, with or without breaking into any premises, where the [goods] may be found." Maytag assigned the contract and mortgage to the Harter Bank & Trust Company. When Hileman failed to pay the installment due, Harter Bank had its employees remove a screen in Hileman's house and enter through a window for the purpose of removing the mortgaged washer. Hileman sued the Harter Bank for unlawfully trespassing upon his property. Was he entitled to damages? [Hileman v Harter Bank & Trust Co. 174 Ohio 95, 186 NE2d 853]

5. A rented a compressor to B for use in operating pneumatic equipment in construction work. The compressor ordinarily sold at $5,000. The lease ran for one year with monthly rentals of $500, with an option given to B to purchase the compressor at the end of the year for the payment of $1. After the lease had run five months, B went into bankruptcy. A filed a petition in the proceeding to recover the compressor. The trustee in bankruptcy claimed the lease was a secured transaction. Was he correct? [See In re Merkel, Inc. 45 Misc2d 753, 258 NYS2d 118]

6. The National Bank had a perfected security interest in South Dakota in property of Welker. Without the knowledge of the bank, he brought the property to Pennsylvania. A year later he went into bankruptcy and the trustee in bankruptcy claimed the property. The National Bank claimed the property on the ground that it had a security interest. The trustee in bankruptcy asserted that the perfection of such security interest had been lost because there had been no filing in Pennsylvania within four months after the property was brought into Pennsylvania, or at any time thereafter. The National Bank claimed that it was not bound by any requirement of filing in Pennsylvania because it did not know that the goods had been brought to Pennsylvania. Decide [In re Welker (DC WD Pa Ref Bankruptcy) 2 UCCRS 169]

7. Little Brown Jug, Inc., purchased goods from L. & N. Sales Co. Little Brown Jug later claimed that it was not bound by the conditional sales contract because its representative had been too busy to read it and thought that he was merely signing an order form. Was that a valid defense? [L. & N. Sales Co. v Little Brown Jug, Inc. (Pa) 12 D&C 2d 469]

8. Cook sold to Martin a new tractor truck for approximately $13,000 with a down payment of approximately $3,000 and the balance to be paid in 30 monthly installments. The sales agreement provided that upon default in any payment Cook could take "immediate possession of the property . . . without notice or demand. For this purpose vendor may enter upon any premises where the property may be." Martin failed to pay the installments when due, and Cook notified him that the truck would be repossessed. Martin had the tractor truck, attached to a loaded trailer, locked on the premises of a company in Memphis. Martin intended to drive to the West Coast as soon as the trailer was loaded. When Cook located the tractor truck, no one was around. In order to disconnect the trailer from the truck, as Cook had no right to the trailer, Cook removed the wire screen over a ventilator hole by unscrewing it from the outside with his penknife. He next reached through the ventilator with a stick and unlocked the door of the tractor truck. He then disconnected the trailer and had the truck towed away. Martin sued Cook for unlawfully repossessing the truck by committing a breach of the peace. Decide. [Martin v Cook, 237 Miss 267, 114 So2d 669]

9. A held a promissory note on which B was the maker. A recorded the note in the office of the recorder of deeds of the county in which B resided. A claimed that this gave him a security interest under the Uniform Commercial Code in all property of B within the country. Was he correct? [See First State Bank v Raiton (DC Pa) 377 FSupp 859]

10. A buyer purchased an airplane on credit for his personal use. In order to keep up the payments, he rented the airplane to others. The financer claimed that the airplane was "equipment" because it was used primarily for rental and because it was too expensive an item to be classified as "consumer goods." The buyer claimed that the airplane was consumer goods. Was he correct? [See Commercial Credit Equipment Corp. v Carter, 83 Wash2d 136, 516 P2d 767]

OTHER SECURED TRANSACTIONS, SURETYSHIP, AND LETTERS OF CREDIT

A. SECURED CREDIT SALES OF INVENTORY

§ 36:1. NATURE OF TRANSACTION. In contrast with one who buys personal property for his own use, the buyer may be a merchant or dealer who intends to resell the goods. The goods which such a merchant or dealer buys are classified as *inventory*. The financing of the purchase of inventory may involve a third person, rather than the seller, as creditor. For example, a third person, such as a bank or finance company, may loan the dealer the money with which to make the purchase and to pay the seller in full. In such a case the security interest in the goods may be given by the buyer to the third person and not to the seller.[1] Accordingly, the terms "creditor" and "secured party" as used in this chapter may refer to a seller who sells on credit or to a third person who finances the purchase of goods.

In general, the provisions regulating a secured transaction in inventory follow the same pattern as is applicable to the secured credit sale of consumer goods. Variations recognize the differences in the commercial settings of the two transactions.

Initially there must be a security agreement to give rise to the security interest. If perfection of the interest is desired, there must also be a filing of a financing statement or the creditor must hold possession of the collateral.

§ 36:2. USE OF PROPERTY AND EXTENT OF SECURITY INTEREST. A secured transaction relating to inventory will generally give the buyer full freedom to deal with the collateral goods as though he were the absolute owner and the goods were not subject to a security interest. Thus, the parties may agree that the buyer-dealer may mingle the goods with his own existing inventory, resell the goods, take goods back and make exchanges, and so on, without being required to keep any records of just what became

---

[1] Prior to the adoption of the Uniform Commercial Code, security was frequently provided the person financing the purchase of inventory by the device of a trust receipt, under which the purchaser-merchant would declare that he held the inventory in trust for the creditor. This device was regulated by the Uniform Trust Receipts Act (UTRA).

of the goods covered by the security agreement, or to replace the goods sold with other goods, or to account for the proceeds from the resale of the original goods.[2]

(a) After-acquired property. The security agreement may expressly provide that the security interest of the creditor shall bind after-acquired property, that is, other goods, whether inventory or equipment, thereafter acquired by the buyer. The combination of the buyer's freedom to use and dispose of the collateral and the subjecting of after-acquired goods to the interest of the secured creditor permits the latter to have a *floating lien* on a changing or shifting stock of goods of the buyer. Conversely stated, the UCC rejects the common-law concept that the security interest was lost if the collateral was not maintained and accounted for separately and that a floating lien upon the buyer's property was void as a fraud against the latter's creditors.

> FACTS: In 1969, Galleon borrowed money from the Central Bank and Trust Company. As security for the loan, Galleon gave Central a security interest in the equipment and inventory owned or thereafter acquired by Galleon. Central filed a financing statement and perfected this security interest. Thereafter, in 1970, Lewyn sold equipment to Galleon. The equipment was made by Lancaster and the sale was to be made for cash but, through a mistake, the goods were sent by Lancaster directly to Galleon before it paid for the goods. Lewyn then sent Galleon an invoice stating that payment was to be made "net 30 days." Galleon failed to pay the loan to Central Bank and Trust Company which then took possession of the equipment sold by Lewyn, claiming such equipment under the authority of the after-acquired property clause. Lewyn then sued Galleon and Central Bank to obtain possession of the equipment.
>
> DECISION: Judgment for Central Bank. When Galleon obtained rights in the equipment sold by Lewyn, the after-acquired property clause of the security agreement with Central Bank gave that bank a security interest in such equipment, even though the seller was not paid by Galleon. [Galleon Industries, Inc. v Lewyn Machinery Co., Inc. (AlaCivApp) 279 So2d 137]

The security interest in inventory covered as after-acquired property has priority over claims of subsequent creditors and third persons, except buyers in the ordinary course of business and sellers to the debtor holding perfected purchase money security interests in the goods sold the debtor.

(b) Proceeds of resale. The security agreement also may expressly cover proceeds resulting from the resale of the goods.[3] If the financing statement

---

[2] UCC § 9-205. The 1972 amendments to the Code contain a section expressly governing security interests when there has been a consignment of the goods. UCC § 9-114.

[3] UCC § 9-203(1)(b); In re Platt, (DC ED Pa) 257 FSupp 478. Under the 1972 amendment to the UCC, a security agreement automatically covers the proceeds unless the security agreement provides otherwise. UCC § 9-306(2).

Under the 1972 amendment, proceeds of insurance are deemed proceeds of the collateral and are subject to the security interest. UCC § 9-306(1) [1972 amendment].

covers the proceeds, the secured party's security interest, together with any perfection thereof, continues in the proceeds obtained by the buyer on the resale of the goods. If the original financing statement does not cover such proceeds, the perfection of the security interest in the original goods continues for only 10 days unless within that time the secured party perfects his interest in the proceeds by filing or by taking possession of the proceeds.[4]

When the creditor has a security interest in a tractor that is traded in and the financing statement covering his interest also covers "proceeds," the creditor has a security interest in the replacement tractor that the buyer obtains by the new purchase.

The term *proceeds* refers to what is obtained upon a sale or exchange of the collateral. It does not include payments made by way of indemnification by a tort-feasor who damaged the collateral or by an insurance company that made payment under a policy covering the collateral.

§ 36:3. FILING OF FINANCING STATEMENT. Filing is usually required to perfect the creditor's interest in inventory or the proceeds therefrom. An exception is made when a statute requires the security interest to be noted on the title certificate issued for the property.[5] A security interest in a motor vehicle that is inventory is perfected by filing under the Code; but if it is an individual vehicle owned by a private owner, there must be a notation of the interest on the title registration certificate.[6]

An unperfected security interest is likewise valid as against anyone standing in the position of the debtor or whose rights rise no higher than those of the debtor.

(a) Financing statement. The paper that is filed is a financing statement and is distinct from the security agreement which was executed by the parties to give rise to the secured transaction.[7] The *financing statement* must be signed by both the debtor and the secured party, and it must give an address of the secured party from which information concerning the security interest may be obtained and a mailing address of the debtor; and it must contain a statement indicating the types, or describing the items, of collateral.[8]

---

[4] UCC § 9-306(3). Proceeds includes not only money but also checks and other commercial paper, and the account or debt owed by the subpurchaser. § 9-306(1). Under the 1972 amendment to the UCC, a security interest in proceeds is perfected even though the financing statement did not refer to proceeds.

[5] UCC § 9-302(1), (3), (4). Reference must be made to the UCC as adopted in a particular state as to the place of filing, for the UCC as submitted for adoption gave the states the option of providing as to certain kinds of property for a system of state-wide-effective filing with the Secretary of State or of requiring a local county filing. See UCC § 9-401.

[6] Apeco Corp. v Bishop Mobile Homes, Inc. (TexCivApp) 506 SW2d 711.

[7] UCC § 9-402. However, the security agreement may be filed as a financing statement if it contains the required information and is signed by both parties.

[8] UCC § 9-402(1). The financing statement is insufficient when it does not contain the address of the creditor. Strevell-Patterson Finance Co. v May, 77 NMex 331, 422 P2d 366. The financing statement may be signed only by the secured creditor if the collateral is subject to a security interest arising in a foreign state and the creditor makes a filing in the state into which the collateral is thereafter taken. Likewise, a signing by the secured creditor alone is sufficient if the filing is made to perfect a security interest in proceeds.

The UCC adopts the system of "notice filing," which requires a filing only of a simple notice which indicates merely that the secured party who has filed may have a security interest in the collateral described. The criterion for the sufficiency of a financing statement is whether anyone searching the records would be misled by the matter of which complaint is made.

Errors in the financing statement have no effect when not misleading, but they nullify the effect of the filing if they are seriously misleading.

> **FACTS:** Muska borrowed money from the Bank of California. He secured the loan by giving the bank a security interest in equipment and machinery that he had at his place of business. The bank filed a financing statement to perfect this interest. The statement contained all the information required by the Code, except that it failed to state the residence address of the debtor. Muska went bankrupt. The trustee in bankruptcy claimed that the security interest of the bank was not perfected on the theory that the omission of the residence address from the financing statement made it defective.

> **DECISION:** The interest of the bank was perfected because the filing of the financing statement was effective, since the omission of the debtor's residence address was not seriously misleading. As the collateral was equipment and machinery used in the debtor's business and the business address was given, a third person would be put on notice of the security interest of the bank and could easily have made further inquiry even though he did not know where the debtor lived. [Lines v Bank of California (CA9 Cal) 467 F2d 1274]

A description in the financing statement of collateral as "all personal property" is not sufficient and therefore its filing does not perfect the security interest.

§ 36:4. DURATION AND CONTINUATION OF FILING.

If the debt is due within 5 years, the filing of the financing statement is effective for the entire period until the debt matures and for 60 days thereafter. If the debt is not due within 5 years, a filing is effective only for 5 years. At the expiration of the designated period, the perfection of the security interest terminates unless a continuation statement has been filed prior thereto.[9] The *continuation statement* is merely a written declaration by the secured party which identifies the original filing statement by its file number and declares that it is still effective. The filing of the continuation statement continues perfection of the security for a period of 5 years after the last date on which the original filing was effective. The filing of successive continuation statements will continue the perfection indefinitely.[10]

---

[9] UCC § 9-403(2). If the obligation is payable on demand, the filing is effective for 5 years from filing. The 1972 amendment provides for a continuation of perfection for 5 years in all cases, without regard to when the obligation matures, thereby eliminating the extra sixty days allowed by the 1962 UCC when the financing statement showed a maturity of less than 5 years. UCC § 9-403(2) [1972 amendment]

[10] § 9-403(3).

(a) Termination statement. When the buyer has paid the debt in full, he may make a written demand on the secured party, or the latter's assignee if the security interest has been assigned, to send the buyer a *termination statement* that a security interest is no longer claimed under the specified financing statement. The buyer may then present this statement to the filing officer who marks the record "terminated" and returns to the secured party the various papers which had been filed by him.

(b) Assignments. The secured party may have assigned his interest either before the filing of the financing statement or thereafter. If the assignment was made prior to its filing, the financing statement may include a recital of the assignment and state the name and address of the assignee, or a copy of the assignment may be attached thereto. If the assignment is made subsequent to the filing of the financing statement, a separate written statement of assignment may be filed in the same office.[11]

§ 36:5. PROTECTION OF CUSTOMER OF THE BUYER. The customer of
the dealer selling from inventory takes the goods free from the security interest of the dealer's supplier. That is, one who buys in the ordinary course of business items of property taken from the original buyer's inventory is free of the secured party's interest, even though that interest was perfected and even though such ultimate customer knew of the secured party's interest.[12]

The sale to a buyer in ordinary course when not authorized by the secured party does not destroy a security interest, whether perfected or not, which was created by a debtor prior to acquisition of the goods by the buyer's seller.

FACTS: Wasil purchased an automobile on the installment plan from Connelly Pontiac. Connelly assigned the sales contract and the security agreement to General Motors Acceptance Corporation, a finance company. Wasil sold the automobile to Cars Unlimited, Inc. without informing that dealer of the interest of GMAC. Troville purchased the Wasil car from Cars Unlimited for use as a family car. Thereafter GMAC filed a financing statement covering its interest in the Wasil car now owned by Troville. When payments on the Wasil contract stopped, GMAC repossessed the car from Troville. He claimed that it could not do so on the theory that the sale to him had destroyed the security interest of GMAC.

DECISION: Judgment for GMAC. Even though Troville was a buyer in ordinary course, he took subject to the security interest created by the owner who sold the goods to Cars Unlimited. Troville only purchased free of a security interest created by Cars Unlimited. UCC § 9-307(2) did not apply since Troville's seller was not a consumer. GMAC had not authorized the reselling of the collateral. [General Motors Acceptance Corp. v Troville (MassApp) 6 UCCRS 409]

---

[11] § 9-405.
[12] § 9-307(1).

A security interest created by a manufacturer is destroyed by a resale of the goods by the dealer to a buyer on the theory that such sale, which was obviously contemplated by the manufacturer, was authorized, and the destruction of the security interest was likewise authorized.

The buyer of consumer goods or of farm equipment not having an original purchase price in excess of $2,500 is subject to a security interest created by a former owner or his seller if it had been perfected by filing prior to the ultimate sale to the buyer. If it had been perfected without filing, the ultimate buyer is not subject to a security interest created by his seller if he buys without knowledge of its existence, for value, and for his own personal, family, or household purposes, or his own farming operations.[13]

§ 36:6. RIGHTS AND REMEDIES AFTER DEFAULT. The rights and remedies of the secured party and the buyer of inventory after a default on the part of the latter are the same as in the case of a secured credit sale of consumer goods. As a partial modification of that pattern, the creditor taking possession of inventory on the buyer's default is not required to make a sale of the goods but may retain them in full discharge of the debt due, unless an objection is made by the buyer to such retention. In the latter case the creditor must then make a sale.[14]

B. SECURED CREDIT SALES OF EQUIPMENT

§ 36:7. USE OF COLLATERAL. For the purpose of secured transactions, a distinction is made as to the purpose for which the buyer procures the goods. If the ultimate consumer purchases primarily for his personal, family, or household use, the goods are described as *consumer goods*. The consumer's purchase, however, is described as *equipment* if used or purchased for use primarily in a business, in farming, or in a profession, or if the goods do not constitute consumer goods, inventory, or farm products.[15]

§ 36:8. FILING. In general, the equipment secured sale is treated the same as a secured transaction as to inventory, except that the various provisions relating to resale by the buyer and the creditor's rights in proceeds have no practical application because the buyer does not resell the property but makes the purchase with the intention to keep and use or operate it.

Filing is required to perfect a purchase money security interest in equipment, with the exception of farm equipment having a purchase price not in excess of $2,500, and motor vehicles which must be licensed under a specific licensing statute.[16]

---

[13] § 9-307(2).

[14] § 9-505(22). In this situation the secured creditor must give notice not only to his debtor but also to any other party who has an interest in the goods and who has properly filed a financing statement.

[15] UCC § 9-109(2).

[16] § 9-302(1), (c), (3).

If the equipment becomes a fixture, the priority between the creditors holding security interests therein and other creditors is determined by UCC § 9-313. Whether equipment becomes a fixture so as to come within the scope of this section is determined by the local non-Code law governing fixtures.

C. SECURED LOAN TRANSACTIONS

§ 36:9 NATURE OF TRANSACTION. A secured transaction may be employed to protect one who lends on credit apart from a sale, as well as protecting sellers and the persons financing the sale of goods. In the former situation, the secured transaction may be one in which the collateral is delivered to or pledged with the creditor, or it may be one in which the borrower retains possession of the collateral.

§ 36:10. PLEDGE. A *pledge* is a secured transaction in which the lender is given possession of the personal property or collateral in which he has the security interest. More specifically, a pledge is a bailment created as security for the payment of a debt. Under a pledge, specific property is delivered into the possession of a bailee-creditor with the authority, express or implied, that in the event that the debt is not paid, the property may be sold and the proceeds of the sale applied to discharge the debt secured by the pledge. For example, a person borrowing $1,000 may give his creditor property worth $1,000 or more to hold as security. If the borrower repays the loan, the property is returned to him. If he does not repay the debt, the creditor may sell the property and reduce the debt by the amount of the net proceeds. The notice of the sale must be specific enough to identify the nature of the property to be sold so as to alert persons possibly interested in purchasing.

Upon default, the pledgee does not become the owner of the pledge but has merely the right to foreclose upon it or expose it to sale. If the pledgee makes a fictitious sale of the property to himself and then resells the property to a third person at a profit, the pledgor is entitled to damages caused thereby.

In general terms, the rights of the debtor (the *pledgor*) and the creditor (the *pledgee*) under a pledge relationship are the same as the rights of a buyer and seller under a secured credit sale of consumer goods. A distinction arises from the fact that the pledgee is given possession from the commencement of the secured transaction, whereas under a secured credit sale the secured party obtains possession only upon default. After a default occurs, the two transactions may be regarded as the same.

(a) Creation and perfection. The pledge relation arises as soon as it is agreed that the pledgee shall have a security interest in the property which is delivered to him and on the basis thereof he gives value, such as lending money.[17]

---

[17] § 9-204(1).

A contract of pledge provides for (1) possession of the pledged property passing from the pledgor to the pledgee; (2) legal title of the pledged property remaining in the pledgor; (3) the pledgee having a lien on the property for the payment of the debt; (4) the pledgor having a right of redemption of the property.[18]

Perfection arises from the fact that the collateral is in the possession of the creditor and filing is not required.[19]

If the creditor returns the pledged property to the debtor, the pledge is terminated.[20]

(b) Duties of pledgee. Because the secured party or pledgee is in possession of the property or collateral, he must use reasonable care in preserving the property and is liable for damage which results from his failure to do so.[21] The pledgee must keep the collateral separate and identified, although fungible goods of the same kind and quality may be commingled. If money, such as dividends, is received by the pledgee by virtue of his holding the collateral, he must apply such money to the reduction of the debt or send it to the debtor.

Commercial paper may be transferred by way of pledge.[22]

§ 36:11. PAWN. The term *pawn* is often used to indicate a pledge of tangible personal property, rather than documents representing property rights. A person engaged in the business of lending money at interest, in which he requires a pawn as security, is known as a *pawnbroker*. In order to avoid usurious loan practices and trafficking in stolen goods, the business of professional pawnbroking is generally regulated by statute. State and municipal regulations commonly require the licensing of pawnbrokers, and regulate the general conduct of the business and the charges that may be made for loans. In most states pawnbrokers are permitted to charge a higher rate of interest on small loans than would otherwise be legal.

§ 36:12. SECURING OF DEBT WITHOUT CHANGE OF POSSESSION. This situation is illustrated by the owner of a television set who borrows money from the bank and, to protect the latter, gives the bank a security interest in his property. In general terms, the relation between the lender and the borrower is regulated in the same manner as in the case of a secured credit sale of inventory goods. Filing is required whether or not the collateral constitutes consumer goods.[23] When there is a default in the payment of the debt, the lender has the same choice of remedies under such a secured transaction as the secured credit seller of inventory.

---

[18] Barnett v Maida (TexCivApp) 503 SW2d 610.

[19] UCC §§ 9-302(1)(a), 9-305.

[20] Civic Plaza National Bank v University Nursing Home, Inc. (MoApp) 504 SW2d 193.

[21] UCC § 9-207(1), (3). The reasonable expenses of caring for the collateral, including insurance and taxes, are charged to the debtor and are secured by the collateral. UCC § 9-207(2)(a).

[22] Salem Development Co. v Ross, 251 CalApp2d 53, 59 CalRptr 548. The collection rights of the creditor as respects parties on the paper are defined by UCC § 9-502. As the pledge will ordinarily be accompanied by an indorsing of the paper, the creditor will be a holder of the commercial paper and will have the rights of such.

[23] UCC § 9-302(1).

§ 36:13. SECURITY INTEREST IN GOODS BEING MANUFACTURED. A manufacturer may borrow and use as collateral goods that are partly finished or goods not yet manufactured. In such a case, the financing party and the manufacturer execute a security agreement giving the lender a security interest in existing goods and in goods to be manufactured thereafter, and the proceeds of all such goods. In general, this security transaction follows the same pattern as a secured credit sale of inventory.

D. SURETYSHIP AND GUARANTY

§ 36:14. DEFINITION. The relationship by which one person becomes responsible for the debt or undertaking of another person is used most commonly to insure that a debt will be paid or that a contractor will perform the work called for by his contract. A distinction may be made between the two kinds of such agreements. One kind is called a contract or undertaking of *suretyship*, and the third person is called a *surety*. The other kind is called a contract or undertaking of *guaranty*, and the third person is called a *guarantor*. In both cases the person who owes the money or is under the original obligation to pay or perform is called the *principal*, the principal debtor, or debtor, and the person to whom the debt or obligation is owed is known as the *creditor*.[24]

Suretyship and guaranty undertakings have the common feature of a promise to answer for the debt or default of another; but they have a basic difference. The surety is primarily liable for the debt or obligation of the principal; ordinarily the guarantor is only secondarily liable. This means that the moment the principal is in default, the creditor may demand performance or payment of the surety. He generally cannot do so in the case of the guarantor; he must first attempt to collect from the principal. An exception is an "absolute guaranty" which creates the same obligation as a suretyship. A guaranty of payment creates an absolute guaranty.

There is frequently confusion in the use of the terms suretyship and guaranty, and it becomes a question of construction to determine what the parties really intended by their contract. In some states a statute provides that an undertaking to answer for the debt of another is to be interpreted as a suretyship agreement in the absence of an express statement that only a guaranty agreement was intended. In some states the distinction is in effect abolished.

§ 36:15. INDEMNITY CONTRACT. Both suretyship and guaranty differ from an *indemnity contract*, which is an undertaking by one person for a consideration to pay another person a sum of money to indemnify him if he incurs a certain loss. A fire insurance policy is a typical example of an indemnity contract.

---

[24] Unless otherwise stated, "surety" as used in the text includes guarantor as well as surety, and "guaranty" is limited to a conditional guaranty. The word "principal" is also used by the law to identify the person who employs an agent. The "principal" in suretyship must be distinguished from the agent's "principal."

§ **36:16. CREATION OF THE RELATION.** Suretyship and guaranty are ordinarily based upon contract, express or implied. All of the principles applicable to the capacity, formation, validity, and interpretation of contracts are therefore generally applicable to the law of suretyship. The liability of a surety is measured by the terms of his contract or bond, and his obligation is not necessarily as broad as that of his principal.

Generally the ordinary rules of offer and acceptance apply. Notice of the acceptance, however, must sometimes be given by the creditor to the guarantor.

In most states the statute of frauds requires that contracts of guaranty be in writing in order to be enforceable, subject to the exception that no writing is required when the promisor makes the promise primarily for his own benefit.

In the absence of a special statute, no writing is required for contracts of suretyship or indemnity, because they impose primary liability, and not a secondary liability to answer for the debt or default of another. Special statutes or sound business practice, however, commonly require the use of written contracts of both suretyship and indemnity.

When the contract of guaranty is made at the same time as the original transaction, the consideration for the original promise which is covered by the guaranty is also consideration for the promise of the guarantor. When the guaranty contract is entered into subsequent to the original transaction, it is necessary that there be a new consideration for the promise of the guarantor.[25]

§ **36:17. RIGHTS OF SURETY.** The surety has a number of rights to protect him from sustaining loss, to obtain his discharge because of the conduct of others that would be harmful to him, or to recover the money that he had been required to pay because of his contract.

(a) Exoneration. If the surety finds his position threatened with danger, as when the debtor is about to leave the state and take his property with him, the surety may call upon the creditor to take steps to enforce his claim against the debtor while he can still do so. If at that time the creditor could proceed against the debtor and fails to do so, the surety is released or exonerated from liability to the extent that he can show that he has been harmed.

(b) Subrogation. When a surety pays a debt that he is obligated to pay, he automatically acquires the claim and the right of the creditor. This right is known as *subrogation.* That is, once the creditor is paid in full, the surety stands in the same position as the creditor and may sue the debtor, or enforce any security that was available to the creditor, in order to recover the amount that he has paid. The effect is the same as if the creditor, on being paid, made an express assignment of all his rights to the surety.

The right of subrogation, which arises when a surety on a contractor's labor and material bond pays labor and material claimants is not a

---

[25] Union National Bank v Schimke (ND) 210 NW2d 176.

security interest and the surety is therefore entitled to recover the payments made even though no filing was made under the UCC.[26]

(c) Indemnity. A surety who has made payment of a claim for which he was liable as surety is entitled to indemnity from the principal, that is, he is entitled to demand from the principal reimbursement of the amount which he has paid.

(d) Contribution. If there are two or more sureties, each is liable to the creditor for the full amount of the debt, until the creditor has been paid in full. As between themselves, however, each is only liable for a proportionate share of the debt. Accordingly, if a surety has paid more than his share of the debt, he is entitled to demand that his cosureties contribute to him in order to share the burden which, in the absence of a contrary agreement, must be done equally.

§ 36:18. DEFENSES OF THE SURETY. The surety's defenses include not only those that may be raised by a party to any contract but also the special defenses that are peculiar to the suretyship relation.

(a) Ordinary defenses. Since the relationship of suretyship is based upon a contract, the surety may raise any defense that a party to an ordinary contract may raise, such as lack of capacity of parties, absence of consideration, fraud, or mistake.

Fraud and concealment are common defenses. Since the risk of the principal's default is thrown upon the surety, it is unfair for the creditor to conceal from the surety facts that are material to the surety's risk.

Fraud on the part of the principal that is unknown to the creditor and in which he has not taken part does not ordinarily release the surety.

(1) Disclosure. By common law the creditor was not required to volunteer information to the surety and was not required to disclose that the principal was insolvent. There is a growing modern view which requires the creditor to inform the surety of matters material to the risk when the creditor has reason to believe that the surety does not possess such information. Thus, the creditor is under a duty to inform the surety when there is reason to believe that the surety is in effect walking into a trap of which it is not aware. That is, the creditor is required to volunteer information it possesses about the principal when (a) the creditor has reason to believe that those facts materially increase risk beyond that which surety intends to assume; (b) the creditor has reason to believe that the facts are unknown to surety; and (c) the creditor has reasonable opportunity to communicate the facts to the surety.

(b) Suretyship defenses. In addition to the ordinary defenses that can be raised against any contract, the following defenses are peculiar to the suretyship relation:

---

[26] Jacobs v Northeastern Corp. 416 Pa 417, 206 A2d 49.

(1) Invalidity of original obligation.

(2) Discharge of principal by payment or any other means.

(3) Material modification of the original contract to which the surety does not consent, as by a binding extension of time for performance.

FACTS: Tiernan contracted with American Structures to construct a building according to plans and specifications. A bond was obtained from the Equitable Fire & Marine Insurance Co. to protect Tiernan from loss in the event that there was a breach by American Structures. This performance bond specified that no modification could be made to the plans and specifications without the consent of Equitable. Acting without such consent, Tiernan and American Structures agreed to substitute a cheaper air conditioning system for the system specified in the contract. The system proved defective, and Tiernan sued Equitable on the ground that the contract had not been properly performed by American Structures.

DECISION: The surety was not liable to the extent that the modification of the contract had caused Tiernan loss. The surety was only bound for the performance of the contract that existed when it undertook to be liable for the performance of the contract. The court recognized that some states would discharge the surety from all liability because of any modification of the contract, while others would require a material modification. The court adopted a third view of discharging the surety to the extent of loss caused it by the contract modifications. [Equitable Fire & Marine Insurance Co. v Tiernan Building Corp. (Fla) 190 So2d 197]

The compensated surety of a building contractor is not discharged when the owner makes payments to the contractor earlier than called for by the contract, unless it can show that it was prejudiced thereby and then it is only discharged to the extent of such prejudice.

To discharge a surety by the granting of an extension, there must be a binding contract to forebear and the mere fact that the creditor accepts two late payments does not establish that there is such a contract to forebear and hence does not discharge the surety.

(4) Loss of securities that had been given the creditor to hold as additional security for the performance of the original contract, to the extent that such loss is caused by the misconduct or negligence of the creditor.

E. LETTERS OF CREDIT

§ 36:19. INTRODUCTION. A letter of credit is a form of agreement that the issuer of the letter will pay drafts drawn on him by the creditor. It is thus a form of advance arranging of finances in that it is known in advance how much money may be obtained from the issuer of the letter. It is likewise a security device because the creditor knows that the draft which he draws will be accepted or paid by the issuer.

Article 5 of the Uniform Commercial Code establishes certain minimum requirements for letters of credit but for the most part they are governed in international trade by Rules of the International Chamber of Commerce. The use of letters of credit arose in international trade. While this continues to be the primary area of use, there is a growing use of letters in domestic sales and some evidence of the use of a letter of credit in place of a surety bond.[27]

§ 36:20. DEFINITION, PARTIES, AND DURATION.

(a) Definition. A letter of credit is an engagement by its issuer that it will pay or accept drafts drawn on it when the conditions specified in the letter are satisfied. The issuer is usually a bank.

Three contracts are involved in most letter-of-credit transactions: (1) the contract between the issuer and the account party for the issuance of the credit; (2) the letter of credit itself; and (3) the underlying agreement, often a contract of sale, between the beneficiary and the account party. The letter of credit is completely independent from the other two contracts.[28]

(b) Parties. The parties to a letter of credit are (1) the issuer, (2) the customer who makes the arrangements with the issuer, and (3) the beneficiary who will be the drawer of the drafts which will be drawn under the letter of credit. The beneficiary benefits by the existence of the letter of credit because the letter gives greater assurance that the drafts will be paid. There may also be (4) an advising bank.[29] This will occur when the local issuer of the letter of credit requests its correspondent bank where the beneficiary is located to notify or advise the beneficiary that the letter has been issued.

As an illustration of the above definitions, an American merchant may buy goods from a Spanish merchant. There may be a prior course of dealings between the parties so that the seller is willing to accept the buyer's commercial paper as payment or to accept trade acceptances drawn on the buyer. If the foreign seller is not willing to do this, the American buyer, as customer, may go to his bank, the issuer, and obtain a letter of credit naming the Spanish seller as beneficiary. The American bank's correspondent or advising bank in Spain notifies the Spanish seller that this has been done. The Spanish seller will then draw drafts on the American buyer. By the letter of credit, the issuer is required to accept or pay these drafts.

(c) Duration. A letter of credit continues for any time specified in the letter. Generally a maximum amount is stated in the letter so that the letter

---

[27] "Uniform Customs and Practice for Documentary Credits, fixed by the Thirteenth Congress of the Internal Chamber of Commerce (1962 Revision) . . . is the standard reference for banks dealing with letters of credit." Barclays Bank D.C.O. v The Mercantile National Bank (CA5 Ga) 481 F2d 1224.

[28] Barclays Bank D.C.O. v The Mercantile National Bank (CA5 Ga) 481 F2d 1224.

[29] UCC § 5-103(e).

is exhausted or used up when drafts aggregating that maximum amount have been accepted or paid by the issuer. A letter of credit may be used in installments as the beneficiary chooses. A letter of credit cannot be revoked or modified by the issuer or the customer without the consent of the beneficiary unless that right is expressly reserved in the letter.

§ 36:21. FORM. A letter of credit must be in writing and signed by the issuer. Other than this, any form is sufficient. Consideration is not required to establish or to modify a letter of credit.

§ 36:22. DUTY OF ISSUER. The issuer is obligated to honor drafts drawn under the letter of credit if the conditions specified in the letter have been satisfied. Generally this means that the bank must assure itself that all specified papers have been submitted. The issuer has no duty to verify that the papers are properly supported by facts or that the underlying transaction has been performed. It is thus immaterial that the goods sold by the seller in fact do not conform to the contract as long as the seller tenders the documents specified by the letter of credit.

(a) **Liability of issuer for wrongful dishonor.** If the issuer dishonors a draft without justification, it is liable to its customer for breach of contract. The issuer is also liable to the beneficiary,[30] as though the issuer had accepted the draft and then dishonored it.

§ 36:23. LIABILITY OF BENEFICIARY. The beneficiary is a drawer and therefore has a drawer's liability with respect to the paper drawn by him. When he presents the paper for acceptance of payment, the beneficiary-drawer becomes subject to the ordinary warranty liabilities specified by Article 3 of the UCC. In addition, he warrants that all necessary conditions specified in the letter of credit have been satisfied.[31]

QUESTIONS AND CASE PROBLEMS

1. King was the president of Magnolia Swift Homes, Inc., a construction company. The corporation purchased building materials from John A. Denies Sons Co. King personally guaranteed that payment would be made for the purchases of Magnolia. Later Magnolia went through bankruptcy and was discharged. John A. Denies then sued King on his guaranty. King claimed that, since the debt

---

[30] § 5-115(1).
[31] § 5-111(1).

which he guaranteed had been discharged in bankruptcy, there was nothing for which he was liable. Decide. [King v John A. Denies Sons Co. 56 TennApp 39, 404 SW2d 580]

2. A. D. Runnels purchased goods from J. R. Watkins Co. He asked Hinds Runnels to sign a paper. This paper was, in fact, an agreement to guarantee that Hinds would pay for whatever A. D. Runnels would purchase from Watkins. When sued . on this promise by Watkins, Hinds raised the defense that he signed some paper but did not know what he was signing. Was this a valid defense? [J. R. Watkins Co. v A. D. Runnels, 252 Miss 87, 172 So2d 567]

3. Henry Platt, who did business under the name of Platt Fur Co., owed money to The Finance Company of America. The financing statement filed by the latter to protect its interests described the debtor as Platt Fur Co. When Henry Platt went into bankruptcy, it was claimed that this financing statement was not sufficient because it was not in the name of Henry Platt. Decide. [In re Platt (DC ED Pa) 257 FSupp 478]

4. The Minneapolis-Moline Co. gave Shepler a dealer's franchise to sell its farm equipment. Shepler went bankrupt and the equipment that he had on hand, which had come from Minneapolis-Moline, was claimed by the trustee in bankruptcy because Minneapolis-Moline had failed to file to protect its interest in the equipment. The manufacturer claimed that it did not have to file because there is no necessity for filing to perfect "a purchase money security interest in farm equipment." Was this contention valid? [In re Shepler (DC ED Pa) 54 Berks ColLJ 110, 58 LancLRev 43]

5. The Northwest Recapping Inc. negotiated with Industrial Credit Co. to obtain loans on the security of its accounts receivable. In order to persuade Industrial to enter into such an agreement, Dahmes executed a "guarantee" of the repayment of any such loans. The guarantee stated that the liability of Dahmes was "direct and unconditional" and "may be enforced without requiring lender first to resort to any other right, remedy, or security." Under the applicable local statute, the loans made by Industrial were usurious, but under the same law Northwest Recapping could not raise the defense of usury because a statute prohibited corporations from raising such a defense. Later, when Industrial Credit sued Dahmes, he contended that his undertaking under the "guarantee" was his own personal contract so that he, as an individual, could assert the defense of usury. Decide. [Dahmes v Industrial Credit Company, 261 Minn 26, 110 NW2d 484]

6. Are any of the following statements sufficient for a description of the collateral subject to a security interest:

(a) "Passenger and commercial automobiles financed by Girard Trust Corn Exchange Bank?" [Girard Trust Corn Exchange Bank v Warren Lepley Ford, Inc. No. 2 (Pa) 13 D&C2d 119]

(b) "All present and future accounts receivable?" [Industrial Packaging Products Co. v Fort Pitt Packaging International, Inc. 399 Pa 643, 161 A2d 19]

(c) A description of an automobile that does not contain a serial number? [Girard Trust Corn Exchange Bank v Warren Lepley Ford, Inc. No. 2 (Pa) 13 D&C2d 119]

7. Lambert loaned Heaton $25,000 for six months. Heaton gave a promissory note, payable at the end of six months, in the face amount of $30,000, thereby concealing the fact that usurious interest was charged. Under the local statute, the loan contract was, in fact, void, because of the usury. Heaton obtained a bond from the United Bonding Insurance Co., which guaranteed to Lambert that the promissory note would be paid when due. When the note was not paid,

Lambert sued Heaton and the bonding company. The latter raised the defense that its obligation was voided because the usurious character of the transaction had not been disclosed to it. Decide. [Lambert v Heaton (FlaApp) 134 So2d 536]

8. McDivitt purchased two trucks from Harris Ford, Inc., under "bailment leases" which provided for the obtaining of title by McDivitt after the "rentals" paid under the leases reached a specified amount. Harris Ford sold its rights under the sales contract and bailment leases to the Universal C.I.T. Credit Corporation. Thereafter, McDivitt failed to pay the installments when due and was notified that if he did not pay up the back installments by a specified date, action would be taken by the finance company to enforce its rights. Subsequent thereto, but before any such action was taken, McDivitt was fined for having the two trucks drive with excess loads in violation of the Motor Vehicle Code. As the fine was not paid for this offense, the two trucks were put up for sale under the provisions of the local statute. This was proper if McDivitt was the owner of the trucks. The finance company objected that it was the owner and therefore the enforcement proceeding was illegal. Decide. [Commonwealth v Two Ford Trucks, 185 PaSuper 292, 137 A2d 847]

9. Bank *B* loaned money to luncheonette *L*. *B* and *L* executed a security agreement giving *B* a security interest in "all of the contents of the luncheonette including equipment." *B* filed in the proper office a financing statement in which the collateral was described in the same manner as in the security agreement. Thereafter *S* sold *L* a cash register on credit and delivered it on the first of the month. When *L* did not pay the monthly installment on its loan from *B*, *B* took possession of the luncheonette equipment including the cash register. *S* claimed that it was entitled to the cash register. Decide. [See National Cash Register Co. v Firestone & Co. 346 Mass 255, 191 NE2d 47]

10. A debtor and creditor agreed that a third person would act as agent to receive property from the debtor and that if the debtor should default in making payments to the creditor, the agent would deliver the property to the creditor who would then have the rights therein which the Code confers on a secured transaction creditor. When the property was delivered to the agent, was a pledge created? [See In re Dolly Madison Industries, Inc. (DC ED Pa) 351 FSupp 1038]

INSURANCE

§ 37:1. NATURE OF INSURANCE. *Insurance* is a contract by which a promise is made to pay another a sum of money if the latter sustains a specified loss. Insurance is basically a plan of security against risk by charging losses against a fund created by the *premiums* or payments made by many individuals. The promisor is called the *insurer*, sometimes the underwriter. The person to whom the promise is made is the *insured*, the assured, or the policyholder. The promise of the insurer is generally set forth in a contract called a *policy*.

§ 37:2. THE PARTIES. As the result of statutory regulation, virtually all insurance policies are today written by corporations, fraternal or benefit societies, and national or state governments.

The insured must have the capacity to make a contract. If a minor procures insurance, the policy is generally voidable by him.[1]

Insurance contracts are ordinarily made through an agent or a broker. The agent is an agent of the insurance company, generally working exclusively for one company. For the most part, the ordinary rules of agency law determine the effect of his dealings with the applicant for insurance.

An *insurance broker* is ordinarily an independent contractor. He is not employed by any one insurance company. He is the agent for the insured in obtaining insurance for him. In some instances, however, the broker is regarded as the agent of the insurance company when this will permit the conclusion that the insurance company is bound by the act of the broker. Some state statutes treat the broker as an agent of the insurer, declaring in effect that payments made to him are payments to the insurer.

§ 37:3 INSURABLE INTEREST. The insured must have an insurable interest in the subject matter insured. If he does not, he cannot enforce the insurance contract.

---

[1] In an increasing number of states, however, statutes make a minor's contract of insurance binding as though he were an adult. The lowering in most states of the age of majority from 21 to 18 years will in many instances avoid the question of the effect of the minority upon an insurance contract as the person will no longer be deemed a minor.

(a) **Insurable interest in property.** A person has an insurable interest in property whenever he has any right or interest in the property so that its destruction or damage will cause him a direct pecuniary or money loss.

A partner has an insurable interest in property owned by the partnership, as its destruction would cause him an actual and substantial economic loss. This is so even though with respect to "ownership," it is the partnership which owns the property.

It is immaterial whether the insured is the owner of the legal or equitable title, a lienholder, or a person in possession of the property. Thus, a person who is merely a possessor, such as the innocent purchaser of a stolen automobile, has an insurable interest therein. Likewise, a contractor remodeling a building has an insurable interest in the building to the extent of the money that will be paid him under the contract, because he would not be able to receive that money if the building were destroyed by fire.

In the case of property insurance, the insurable interest must exist at the time the loss occurs. Except when expressly required by statute, it is not necessary that the interest exist at the time when the policy or contract of insurance was made.

(b) **Insurable interest in life.** Every person has an insurable interest in his own life and may therefore insure his own life and name anyone he chooses as beneficiary.

FACTS: Wisley obtained a policy of life insurance from the National Reserve Life Insurance Co. In the policy, he named "Sarah A. Wisley, wife" as beneficiary and named his father, Rufus, as beneficiary "should she not live." Two years later, Wisley and his wife were divorced. She then married Mullenax. Upon the death of Wisley, both Sarah and Rufus claimed the proceeds of the policy. Rufus claimed that Sarah did not have an insurable interest.

DECISION: Judgment for Sarah. Whether a person has an insurable interest is a matter to be raised by the insurance company. It cannot be raised by one beneficiary seeking to disqualify another beneficiary. In any event, Sarah was entitled to recover because there was no requirement that she have an insurable interest in the life of Wisley since that policy had been obtained by him. A person can insure his own life in favor of anyone he chooses, and in most states the beneficiary is not required to have an insurable interest in the insured life unless the policy is procured and paid for by the beneficiary. [Mullenax v National Reserve Life Insurance Co. 29 ColoApp 418, 485 P2d 137]

A person has an insurable interest in the life of another if he can expect to receive pecuniary gain from the continued life of the other person and, conversely, would suffer financial loss from the latter's death. Thus, it is held that a creditor has an insurable interest in the life of his debtor since the death of the debtor may mean that the creditor will not be paid the amount owed him. The creditor may take out insurance in excess of the amount of the debt; but if the amount of the insurance is unreasonably greater than the debt, the policy will generally be void.

A partnership has an insurable interest in the life of each of the partners, for the death of any one of them will dissolve the firm and cause some degree of loss to the partnership. A business enterprise has an insurable interest in the life of an executive or a key employee because his death would inflict a financial loss upon the business to the extent that he could not be replaced or could not readily be replaced.

In the case of life insurance the insurable interest must exist at the time the policy is obtained. It is immaterial that the interest no longer exists when the loss is actually sustained. Thus, the fact that the insured husband and wife beneficiary are divorced after the life insurance policy was procured does not affect the validity of the policy.

Whether a person has an insurable interest is a matter to be raised by the insurance company. It cannot be raised by one beneficiary seeking to disqualify another beneficiary.

Where an insurer issues a policy to a beneficiary who has no insurable interest in the insured's life and particularly when it does so without the consent of the insured, it has been held that the insurer is liable for tort damages to the estate of the insured when the beneficiary thereafter kills the insured in order to collect on the insurance.[2]

§ 37:4. THE INSURANCE CONTRACT. The formation of the contract of insurance is governed by the general principles applicable to contracts. Frequently a question arises as to whether advertising material, estimates, and statistical projections constitute a part of the contract.

FACTS: Martell obtained two policies of life insurance from the National Guardian Life Insurance Co. Attached to one of the policies by a paper clip was a specimen value sheet showing that if dividends were left with the company by Martell, the policies would become paid-up endowment policies when he attained the age of 66. When he attained that age, he sued for the combined face value of the two policies, $10,000. National denied that the policies were paid-up endowments, denied that the specimen value sheet was part of its obligation, and offered to pay only the cash surrender value of the policies with dividends and interest. Each policy expressly stated that it and the attached application for insurance constituted the entire contract between the parties. The specimen value sheet was not signed by anyone.

DECISION: Judgment for National. The specimen value sheet attached to one of the policies by a paper clip was not part of that policy nor of the other policy. Mere attachment with a paper clip does not make an attached paper a part of the contract to which it is clipped. There was no provision in the policy which expressly stated that the specimen value sheet was part of the policy and each policy in fact said the contrary when it declared that the policy and the attached application constituted the entire contract. The specimen value sheet could not take effect as a separate contract since it was not signed by or on behalf of the insurance company. [Martell v National Guardian Life Insurance Co. 27 Wis2d 164, 133 NW2d 721]

---

[2] Ramay v Carolina Life Insurance Co. 244 SC 16, 135 SE2d 362.

By statute it is now commonly provided that an insurance policy must be written. In order to avoid deception, many statutes also specify the content of certain policies, in whole or in part, and some even specify the size and style of type to be used in printing them. Provisions in a policy in conflict with a statute are generally void.

In the absence of statute or government regulation, an insurer may enter into a contract of insurance on such terms and upon such examination as it deems fit. An insurer that sold air flight insurance through a vending machine was held not liable to surviving heirs of other passengers killed when the insured caused the plane to crash. The fact that the insurer did not screen persons purchasing flight insurance to determine the existence of any suicide or murder potential did not make the insurer liable for negligence.[3]

(a) **The application as part of the contract.** In many instances the application for insurance is attached to the policy when issued and is made part of the contract of insurance by express stipulation of the policy. When a policy is delivered to an insured, he must examine the policy and the attached application and is bound by any false statement which appears in the application if he retains the policy and attached application without making objection to such statement.

§ 37:5. WHEN THE INSURANCE CONTRACT IS EFFECTIVE.

(a) **Preliminary insurance.** An applicant for insurance may or may not be protected by insurance before a formal written policy is issued to him. Four situations may arise:

(1) When the applicant tells a broker to obtain property or liability insurance, the applicant is merely making the broker his agent. If the broker procures a policy, the customer is insured. If the broker fails to do so, the customer does not have any insurance. But the broker may be personally liable to the customer for the loss.

(2) The person seeking insurance and the insurer or its agent may orally agree that the applicant will be protected by insurance during the interval between the time the application is received and the time when the insurer either rejects the application, or accepts it and issues a policy. This agreement to protect the applicant by insurance during such an interval is binding even though it is oral.[4] Generally, however, when such a preliminary contract is made, the agent will sign a memorandum stating the essential terms of the policy to be executed. This memorandum is a *binder*.[5]

An "oral binder" of insurance is a temporary contract which terminates when the written policy contemplated by it is issued. In some states a maximum duration for an oral contract of insurance is set by statute.

---

[3] Galanis v Mercury International Insurance Underwriters, 247 CalApp2d 690, 55 CalRptr 890.

[4] Overton v Washington National Insurance Co. 106 RI 387, 260 A2d 444.

[5] Altrocchi v Hammond, 17 IllApp2d 192, 149 NE2d 646.

(3) The parties may agree that at a later time a policy will be issued and delivered. In that case the insurance contract is not in effect until the policy is delivered or sent to the applicant. Accordingly, loss sustained after the transaction between the applicant and the insurance agent but before the delivery of the policy is not covered by the policy thereafter delivered.

(4) The parties may agree that a policy of life insurance shall be binding upon the payment of the first premium even though the applicant has not been examined, provided he thereafter passes an examination. Under such an agreement the applicant is ordinarily covered by insurance when he dies before the examination, if it can be shown he would have passed a fair examination.

When the application clearly states that the policy is not in force until the applicant is approved as a risk by an authorized officer of the insurer, coverage is not effective at the time of paying the first premium and submitting the application to the soliciting agent, even though the latter wrongly informs the applicant that he is covered by the policy.

(b) Delivery of policy. Ordinarily delivery of the policy is not essential to the existence of a contract of insurance. Thus, there may be an interim or temporary oral contract or binder of insurance or a contract based upon the acceptance by the insurer of the insured's written application.[6] As an exception, delivery of the policy may be made an express condition to coverage.

(c) Prepayment of premiums. Ordinarily a contract of property insurance exists even though the premium due has not been paid. Thus, it is possible to effect property and liability insurance in most cases by an oral binder or agreement, as by a telephone call. In the case of life insurance policies, it is common to require both delivery of the policy to the insured while in a condition of good health and the prepayment of the first premium on the policy.

(d) When coverage is effective. Distinct from the question of when is there a contract of insurance is the question of when does the coverage of the risk commence under a contract of insurance. Some policies of insurance do not cover the specified risk until after a certain period of time has elapsed after the policy becomes binding. That is, there is a waiting period before the contract of insurance provides protection. In most kinds of insurance, the coverage is immediately effective so that there is no waiting period once the insurer has accepted the application and there is a contract of insurance.

FACTS: Metts filled out a printed application form for polio insurance distributed by the Central Standard Life Insurance Co. He mailed the application to the company on May 15. It was received by the company on May 23. On May 21, Metts' son was stricken with polio, of which the insurer was notified on May 28. The company refused to pay on the ground that it had not accepted the application. Metts sued the insurer. He proved that

---

[6] Krause v Washington National Insurance Co. 225 Ore 446, 468 P2d 513.

the application which he had received from the insurer stated "immediate first day coverage automatically covers the entire family." He claimed that his family was covered by the policy as soon as he signed and mailed the application to the insurer.

DECISION: Judgment for Metts. The words "immediate" and "automatically" on the application indicated that the insurer intended to be bound at once. Even if there were any uncertainty as to the meaning, such ambiguity must be interpreted against the insurer. A person in the position of the insured would reasonably interpret the application as meaning that he was protected from the moment the signed application was mailed to the insurer. [Metts v Central Standard Life Insurance Co. 142 CalApp2d 445, 297 P2d 621.]

(e) Machine-vended insurance. When insurance is sold by a vending machine, as in the case of air flight insurance, it becomes effective when the applicant places the application and the premium in the machine and receives his receipt.

§ **37:6. MODIFICATION OF CONTRACT FORM.** In order to make changes or corrections to the policy, it may not be necessary to issue a new policy. An indorsement on the policy or the execution of a separate *rider* is effective for the purpose of changing the policy.

When a provision of an indorsement conflicts with a provision of the policy the indorsement controls.

§ **37:7. INTERPRETATION OF INSURANCE CONTRACT.** The contract of insurance is interpreted by the same rules that govern the interpretation of ordinary contracts. Words are to be given their ordinary meaning and interpreted in the light of the nature of the coverage intended. Thus, an employee who had been killed was not regarded as "disabled" within the meaning of a group policy covering employees.[7]

The courts are increasingly recognizing the fact that most persons obtaining insurance are not specially trained, and therefore the contract of insurance is to be read as it would be understood by the average man or the average businessman rather than by one with technical knowledge of the law.

If there is an ambiguity in the policy, the provision is interpreted against the insurer.[8] In some instances courts will give a liberal interpretation to the policy terms in order to favor the insured or the beneficiary on the basis that the insured did not in fact have a free choice.

When there is any uncertainty as to whether a contract of insurance exists before the delivery of the written policy, the uncertainty will be determined against the insurer and it will be concluded that the policy was effective immediately. If the insurer claims that a statement in the application form bars this conclusion, it is necessary that the provision would have been so understood by a person of ordinary intelligence and knowledge.

---

[7] Marriot v Pacific National Life Assurance Co. 24 Utah2d 182, 467 P2d 981.

[8] Murray v Western Pacific Insurance Co. 2 WashApp 985, 472 P2d 611. This principle is not applied if the provision in question is in the policy because it is required by statute.

§ 37:8. ANTIDISCRIMINATION. A number of state statutes prohibit insurers from refusing to write or renew policies of insurance because of the age, residence, occupation, national origin, or race of the applicant or insured and prohibit the cancellation of a policy except for nonpayment of premiums or, in the case of automobile insurance, the insured's loss of his motor vehicle license or registration.[9]

Statutes also commonly prohibit insurance companies from making premium discriminations among members of the same risk class and from making rebates or refunds to particular individuals only.

§ 37:9. PREMIUMS. Premiums may be paid by check. If the check is not paid, however, the instrument loses its character as payment.

If the premiums are not paid, the policy will ordinarily lapse because of nonpayment, subject to antilapse statutes or provisions.

(a) Return of premiums. When an insurance policy is canceled according to the terms of the policy before the expiration of the term for which premiums have been paid, the insurer is required to return such part of the premiums as has not been earned.

(b) Nonforfeiture and antilapse provisions. As to the payment of premiums due on life insurance policies subsequent to the first premium, the policies now in general use provide or a statute may specify that the policy shall not automatically lapse upon the date the next premium is due if payment is not then made. By policy provision or statute, the insured is also allowed a *grace period* of 30 to 31 days, in which to make payment of the premium due. When there is a default in the payment of a premium by the insured, the insurer may be required by statute (1) to issue a paid-up policy in a smaller amount, (2) to provide extended insurance for a period of time, or (3) to pay the cash surrender value of the policy.

§ 37:10. EXTENT OF INSURER'S LIABILITY. In the case of life and disability insurance, the insurer is required to pay the amount called for by the contract of insurance. When the policy is one to indemnify against loss, the liability of the insurer is to pay only to the extent that the insured sustains loss, subject to a maximum amount stated in the contract. Thus, a fire insurer is liable for only $1,000, even though it has written a $20,000 policy, when the fire loss sustained by the insured is in fact only $1,000. If the loss were $22,000, the liability of the insurer would be only $20,000.

§ 37:11. CANCELLATION. The contract of insurance may expressly declare that it may or may not be canceled. By statute or policy provision, the insurer is commonly required to give a specific number of days' written notice of a cancellation.

Property and liability policies generally reserve to the insurer the right to cancel the policy upon giving a specified number of days' notice. In some states antidiscrimination statutes restrict the right of insurers to cancel. An

---

[9] Pennsylvania, 40 PS § 1008.1 et seq.

insurance company may not exercise its right to cancel the policy when it does so to punish the insured because he appeared as a witness in a case against it.

Only the insured is entitled to notice of cancellation unless the policy or an indorsement expressly declares otherwise. The mere fact that a creditor is entitled to the proceeds of the insurance policy in the case of loss does not in itself entitle him to notice of cancellation.[10]

§ 37:12. COVERAGE OF POLICY. When an insurance claim is disputed by the insurer, the person bringing suit has the burden of proving that there was a loss, that it occurred while the policy was in force, and that the loss was of a kind which was within the coverage of the policy. The insurer has the burden of proving that there is no coverage because one of the contract exceptions is applicable, or of proving that there is a defense to the claim of liability on the policy.

§ 37:13. NONPOLICY LIABILITY OF INSURER. In certain instances, an insurer will be liable because of the breach of a nonpolicy duty. These situations arise most commonly against a background of automobile liability insurance, although the principles involved are not necessarily so limited.

(a) Mental distress of claimant. When an insurer or its adjuster intentionally subjects a claimant to mental distress, the insurer may be liable for the tort of intentional infliction of mental distress. Threats and harassment employed in the effort to persuade a claimant to accept a settlement may impose such liability. The mere fact that the insurer or its agent has acted in a way which appears unreasonable and unethical, however, does not necessarily impose liability for the mental distress which follows.[11]

(b) Invasion of privacy. When a person makes a claim against an insurance company, he confers a qualified privilege upon the insurer to observe and study his public actions in order to determine the truth of the statement made by the claimant. For example, when a claimant asserts that he has been so injured that he cannot leave his house or work, the insurer may photograph him leaving the house and at work. Such conduct of the insurer does not constitute a violation of the claimant's right of privacy because the activity under surveillance occurs in a public place.

The right of the insurer to observe public activity does not give it a right to make an invasion of privacy which would not be allowed a private person. For example, while the insurer may photograph a claimant working at his regular place of employment, the insurer's investigator cannot secretly enter the claimant's home and photograph him working inside his house.

---

[10] Ford Motor Credit Co. Commonwealth County Mutual Insurance Co. (TexCivApp) 420 SW2d 732.
[11] Cluff v Farmers Insurance Exchange, 10 ArizApp 560, 460 P2d 666.

When proper investigation is made of a claimant's activity, the insurer is not liable because the claimant experienced mental distress when he became aware that he was under surveillance.

FACTS: Forster was involved in an automobile accident. She made a claim against the insurer of the other driver. The insurer, Manchester, had a private detective make an activity check on Forster. This involved following her during the day when she left the house in her automobile, noting where she stopped, and taking some motion pictures of her. Several times, because of traffic conditions, the investigator came sufficiently close to Forster that she became aware that she was being followed. She began to worry about such conduct, became very nervous, had frequent nightmares and hallucinations which required medical treatement. Her attorney asked the insurance company whether it was making a check on Forster. The insurance company denied that it was so doing. When the investigator was asked, he admitted that he was following the plaintiff, but stated it was for a legitimate purpose and that he was privileged against disclosing the identity of his client. Forster then sued him to recover money damages for the invasion of her privacy and the intentional infliction of emotional distress.

DECISION: Judgment for Manchester. When a person makes a claim against an insurance company to recover for physical injuries, it is proper for the insurer to observe the conduct of the claimant in public and no liability arises because such surveillance causes the claimant mental distress when the claimant becomes aware of its existence. [Forster v Manchester, 410 Pa 192, 189 A2d 147]

§ 37:14. **DEFENSES OF THE INSURER.** The insurer may raise any defense that would be valid in an action upon a contract. Some defenses that do not apply to an action on an ordinary contract may also be raised.

QUESTIONS AND CASE PROBLEMS

1. Rebecca Foster obtained a policy of life insurance from the United Insurance Co. insuring the life of Lucille McClurkin and naming herself as beneficiary. Lucille did not live with Rebecca, and Rebecca did not inform Lucille of the existence of the policy. Rebecca paid the premiums on the policy, and on the death of Lucille sued the United Insurance Co. for the amount of the insurance. At the trial, Rebecca testified vaguely that her father had told her that Lucille was her second cousin on his side of the family. Was Rebecca entitled to recover on the policy? [Foster v United Insurance Co. 250 SC 423, 158 SE2d 201]

2. A policy of insurance had the words "double indemnity" across the top imprinted with a rubber stamp. Nothing was said in the policy about double indemnity. When a loss was sustained, the insured claimed that he was entitled

to double indemnity. Was he correct? [See Niewoehner v Western Life Insurance Co. 149 Mont 57, 422 P2d 644]

3. On October 29, Griffin sent an application for life insurance and the first premium to the Insurance Company of North American. In the application, her son, Carlisle Moore, was named as beneficiary. On November 25 of the same year, Griffin died. On November 26, the company rejected the application and notified the broker who took the application, who in turn notified Moore by letter dated November 30. Moore sued the company for breach of contract. Decide. [Moore v Insurance Co. of North American, 49 IllApp2d 287, 200 NE2d 1]

4. Lisle applied for life insurance with the Federal Life & Casualty Co. Both Lisle and his wife made false, fraudulent statements to the insurer in connection with the application. The insurer's physician examined Lisle twice but did not ascertain anything that revealed the falsity of those statements. After the insured's death about a year later, the insurer denied liability on the ground of fraud. Lisle's widow claimed that the insurer could not raise the question of fraud since it had examined the insured before accepting his application. Was the insurer liable? [Federal Life & Casualty Co. v Lisle, 140 Ohio2d 269, 172 NE2d 919]

5. Moore's wife applied for accident insurance on her husband. She paid the premium due. Unknown to her, the application was rejected. However, when she inquired of the agent as to the status of the application, the agent said that he had had no word. When she inquired some time later, the agent said he thought that the policy had come in and, if it had not, she would be notified in a few days. She heard nothing. Two weeks later her husband was killed accidentally. After his death the insurance company informed her that the application had been rejected. She sued the insurance company. Decide. [Moore v Palmetto State Life Insurance Co. 222 SC 492, 73 SE2d 688]

6. Einhorn held warehouse receipts as collateral security for a loan that he had made to the prior holder of the receipts. Einhorn obtained a fire insurance policy from the Firemen's Insurance Co., which insured him against loss of the property by fire to the extent of his interest in the collateral. The property represented by the receipts was destroyed by fire. Einhorn assigned his claim on the policy to Flint Frozen Foods, which then sued the insurer. Was the policy obtained by Einhorn valid? [Flint Frozen Foods v Firemen's Insurance Co. 8 NJ 606, 86 A2d 673]

7. Hicks obtained an automobile collision policy from the Alabama Farm Bureau Mutual Casualty Insurance Co. The policy provided that there was no coverage of loss during the period between the expiration of the term of the policy and the date of the actual payment of a renewal premium. Hicks did not pay the renewal premium until several months after the expiration of the policy. During the noncovered period, he was in a collision. When he paid the renewal premium to the agent-manager at the insurer's local office, he informed him of this collision. He then filed a proof of loss for the damage sustained in the collision. The insurer refused to pay the loss. The insured sued the insurer. Decide. [Alabama Farm Bureau Mutual Casualty Insurance Co. v Hicks, 41 AlaApp 143, 133 So2d 217]

8. John Carroll was killed in a collision with John Mimms. Lorraine Carroll, as administratrix of John Carroll's estate, sued Preferred Risk Insurance Company on the theory that Mimms was an uninsured motorist. Preferred claimed that Mimms had a policy with Adams Mutual Insurance Company. Carroll claimed that the policy of Mimms had been canceled by Adams because of Mimms'

failure to disclose the accident in which Carroll was killed. It was shown that Mimms had applied to Adams for an automobile liability policy stating, what was true at the time, that he had not been involved in any accident within 36 months. He applied for coverage beginning at 12:01 a.m. on June 22. The application was mailed on June 22 and received by Adams Insurance Company on June 25 and approved. Unknown to Adams, on June 22 at 10:00 p.m., Carroll was killed in the collision with Mimms. Was Mimms insured? [Carroll v Preferred Risk Insurance Company, 34 Ill2d 310, 215 NE2d 801]

9. An air conditioning system was defectively installed in that there were unwrapped pipes and the electric motors were not sufficiently powerful to operate the system. Over a period of time, this resulted in damage to the pipes from the accumulation of condensation. It was claimed that this damage was covered by an "accident" policy. Was this correct? [See A. D. Irwin Investments, Inc. v Great American Insurance Co. (ColoApp) 475 P2d 633]

10. Anderson, who is 17 years old insures his house against loss by fire. When the house is destroyed by fire, the insurance company refuses to pay the amount of the loss on the ground that the policy was not binding because of Anderson's minority. Anderson brings an action to recover on the policy. Is he entitled to judgment?

11. Purdy gives the agent of his insurance company a check for the amount of the premium on his life insurance 30 days after the premium was due. Two days later the check is returned to the branch office of the insurance company marked 'N.S.F." (not sufficient funds). A week later Purdy dies. The executor of Purdy's estate brings an action to collect from the company on the policy. Is he entitled to judgment?

KINDS OF INSURANCE

A. FIRE INSURANCE

§ 38:1. NATURE OF CONTRACT.

A *fire insurance policy* is a contract to indemnify the insured for destruction of or damage to property caused by fire. In almost every state the New York standard fire insurance form is the standard policy.

(a) Actual, hostile fire. In order for fire loss to be covered by fire insurance, there must be an actual flame or burning, and the fire must be hostile. The hostile character is easily determined when the fire is caused by accident, such as a short circuit in electric wiring; but it is often difficult to determine when the fire is intentional, as when it is being used for heating or cooking. A *hostile fire* in the latter case is one which to some extent becomes uncontrollable or escapes from the place where it is intended to be. To illustrate, when soot is ignited and causes a fire in the chimney, the fire is hostile. On the other hand, a loss caused by the smoke or heat of a fire in its ordinary container, which has not broken out or become uncontrollable, results from a *friendly fire*.

> **FACTS:** Youse owned a ring that was insured with the Employers Fire Insurance Co. against loss, including "all direct loss or damage by fire." The ring was accidentally thrown by Youse into a trash burner and was damaged when the trash was burned. He sued the insurer.
>
> **DECISION:** Judgment for insurer. A fire policy only covers loss caused by a hostile fire. The fire was not hostile in that it burned in the area in which it was intended to burn. [Youse v Employers Fire Insurance Co. 172 Kan 111, 238 P2d 472]

By indorsement, the coverage may be and frequently is extended to include loss by a friendly fire.

Damage by heat alone is not covered, but damage from heat or smoke caused by a hostile fire is covered.

(b) Immediate or proximate cause. The fire must be the immediate or proximate cause of the loss. In addition to direct destruction or damage by fire, a fire may set in motion a chain of events that damages the property. When there is a reasonable connection between a fire and the ultimate loss sustained, the insurer is liable for the loss.

The New York standard form of fire insurance policy excludes loss or damage caused directly or indirectly by enemy attack by armed forces, invasion, insurrection, rebellion, revolution, civil war, or usurped power, or by order of any civil authority; or by neglect of the insured to use all reasonable means to save and preserve the property at and after a fire or when the property is endangered by fire in neighboring premises; or by theft.

Damage by explosion is also excluded unless fire follows, and then the insurer is liable only for that part of the damage caused by the fire. The standard form of fire insurance policy includes protection from lightning damage even though no fire is caused thereby.

§ 38:2. DETERMINATION OF INSURER'S LIABILITY.

Basically the insurer is liable for the actual amount of the loss sustained. This liability is limited, however, by the maximum amount stated in the policy or the amount of damages sustained by total destruction of the property, whichever is less.

(a) Amount of loss. The amount of the loss, in the absence of statute or agreement to the contrary, is the actual cash value at the time of the loss. If the insurer and the insured cannot agree, policies commonly provide for the determination of the amount of loss by appraisers or arbitrators.[1]

(b) Total loss. A *total loss* does not necessarily mean that the property has been completely destroyed. The loss is regarded as being total if the unconsumed portion is of no value for the purposes for which the property was utilized at the time of the insurance. Consequently, the mere fact that some of the walls and the roof remained after the fire did not prove that the loss was not total.

> **FACTS:** Greene insured her home against fire loss with the Home Insurance Co. A fire destroyed two of the walls and part of the roof, all windows were broken, and there was water and smoke damage throughout the house. Greene claimed that the house was a total loss. The insurance company contended that it was only a partial loss. Greene sued the insurance company.
>
> **DECISION:** Judgment for Greene. Whether there is a reasonably usable or repairable part of the building surviving the fire is a question for the jury. The evidence was sufficient to support the finding of the jury that Greene's home was a "total loss" even though parts of it were still in existence. [Home Insurance Co. v Greene (Miss) 229 So2d 576]

---

[1] Saba v Homeland Insurance Co. 159 Ohio 237, 112 NE2d 1.

(c) **Replacement by insurer.** Frequently the insurer will stipulate in the policy that it has the right to replace or restore the property to its former condition in lieu of paying the insured the cash value of the loss.

(d) **Coinsurance.** A *coinsurance clause* requires the insured to maintain insurance on his property up to a certain amount or a certain percent of the value, generally 80 percent. Under such a provision, if the policyholder insures his property for less than the required amount, the insurer is liable only for his proportionate share of the amount of insurance required to be carried. To illustrate, suppose the owner of a building valued at $40,000 insures it against loss to the extent of $24,000, and the policy contains a coinsurance clause requiring that insurance of 80 percent of the value of the property be carried. In case a $16,000 loss is sustained, the insured would not receive $16,000 from the insurer but only $12,000 because the amount of insurance he carries ($24,000) is only three fourths of the amount required ($32,000, that is, 80 percent of $40,000).

The use of a coinsurance clause is not permitted in all states. In some states it is prohibited or is permitted only with the consent of the insured.

§ 38:3. ASSIGNMENT OF FIRE INSURANCE POLICY.

Fire insurance is a personal contract, and in the absence of statute or contractual authorization it cannot be assigned before a loss is sustained without the consent of the insurer.[2] In addition, it is commonly provided that the policy shall be voided if an assignment to give a purchaser of the property the protection of the policy is attempted. Such a forfeiture clause applies only when the insured attempts to transfer his entire interest in the policy. It does not apply to equitable assignments. To illustrate, if the policy prohibits an assignment before loss, a pledge of the policy as security for a loan by the insured does not constitute a violation of the provision.

§ 38:4. MORTGAGE CLAUSE.

If the insured property is subject to a mortgage, either or both the mortgagor and mortgagee may take out policies of fire insurance to protect their respective interests in the property. Each has an insurable interest therein. In the absence of a contrary stipulation, the policy taken out by either covers only his own interest. That is, the mortgagor's policy protects only the value of his right of redemption or the value of the property in excess of the mortgage, while the policy of the mortgagee covers only the debt. Neither can claim the benefit of insurance money paid to the other.

It is common, however, for the mortgagee to insist as a condition of making the loan that the mortgagor obtain and pay the premiums on a policy covering the full value of the property and providing that in case of loss the insurance money will be paid to the mortgagor and the mortgagee as their respective interests may appear. As the amount of the mortgage debt is reduced, the interest of the mortgagee in the property becomes less and the share of insurance proceeds that he would receive accordingly

---

[2] Shadid v American Druggist Fire Insurance Co. (Okla) 386 P2d 311.

becomes less. Such a mortgage clause has the advantage of protecting both the mortgagor and mortgagee by one policy and of providing a flexible method of insuring each of them.

§ 38:5. **EXTENDED COVERAGE.** The term *extended coverage* generally refers to protection of property against loss from windstorm, hail, explosions other than those within steam boilers on the premises, riot, civil commotion, aircraft damage, vehicle damage, and smoke damage.

(a) **Vandalism.** A special form of extended coverage may be obtained to protect property from vandalism. Generally this protects from damage to property which breaks or defaces. If vandals burn a building, fire insurance would provide coverage. Likewise, if the harm occurs as part of a riot, standard extended coverage would afford protection.

§ 38:6. **OTHER PROVISIONS.** Fire insurance policies commonly prohibit the insured from doing certain acts that will or may increase the hazard or risk involved and provide that the policy is void if the insured commits the prohibited acts.

It is commonly provided that false statements made by the insured when they are known to be false shall avoid the policy. Under such a provision a fraudulent misstatement of the value of the property avoids the policy.

The insured may take out more than one policy on the same property, in the absence of a provision in any of the policies to the contrary; but in the event of loss he cannot recover more than the total loss he sustains. Such a loss is prorated among the insurers.

An insurer is not liable when the damage or destruction of the property is intentionally caused by the insured. The fact that the insured negligently caused a fire is not a defense to the insurer, even when there is a stipulation that the insured shall not change or increase the hazard insured against.

§ 38:7. **CANCELLATION.** It is common to provide by statute or by the terms of the policy that under certain circumstances the policy may be terminated or canceled by the act of one party alone. When this is done, the provisions of the statute and the policy must be strictly followed in order to make the cancellation effective.[3]

The provision governing a cancellation of a policy may be waived. Thus, when a policy requires five days' notice by the insurer but it gives only three days' notice, the insured waives the notice requirement if he surrenders the policy for cancellation without objection.

B. AUTOMOBILE INSURANCE

§ 38:8. **NATURE OF CONTRACT.** In the case of insurance to compensate the driver or owner for his own damages, it is immaterial whether his negligence caused or contributed to the harm which had befallen him. In

---

[3] Mobile Fire & Marine Insurance Co. v Kraft, 36 AlaApp 684, 63 So2d 34.

the case of the insurance that protects him from the claims of others, there is no liability on the insurer in favor of those persons unless he has so acted that he would be liable to them without regard to the insurance. If he were not negligent in the operation of his automobile, he would not be liable, ordinarily, for the harm caused, and a person injured by his auto could not hold his insurance company liable since its liability is no greater than his own.

Associations of insurers, such as the National Bureau of Casualty Underwriters and the National Automobile Underwriters Association, have proposed standard forms of policies that have been approved by their members in virtually all the states.

§ 38.9. FINANCIAL RESPONSIBILITY LAWS. In a few states and under some no-fault insurance statutes, liability insurance must be obtained before a driver's license will be issued. In other states *financial responsibility laws* require that if a driver is involved in an accident, he must furnish proof of financial responsibility. Under some laws this means that the driver must deposit security sufficient to pay any judgment that may be entered against him with respect to that accident. Under other statutes, it is sufficient that the driver produce a liability policy in a specified amount as to future accidents.

The security form of statute may not protect the victim of the first accident. If the driver is unwilling or unable to deposit the required security, he will forfeit his license; but this does not provide any payment to the victim of the first accident. By definition the second type of law does not protect the victim of the first accident. Moreover, the efficiency of financial responsibility laws has been reduced by the decision that the United States Constitution requires that there be a hearing to establish the probable liability of the driver to the victim before his driver's license can be suspended or revoked,[4] as the requirement of such a hearing has the effect of delaying and making cumbersome what was formerly a relatively simple and swift administrative remedy.

§ 38:10. LIABILITY INSURANCE. The owner or operator of a motor vehicle may obtain *liability insurance* to protect himself from claims made by third persons for damage to their property (property damage liability) or person (bodily injury liability) arising from the use or operation of an automobile. When the insurer pays under such a policy, it makes the payment directly to the third person and is liable to pay him for the same items as the insured would be required to pay, but for not more than the maximum stated in the policy.

If the insurer is liable for the damage caused a third person or his property, it is likewise liable for cost of repairs, destruction of property, loss of services, and other damages for which the insured himself would be liable, subject to the policy maximum.

---

[4] Bell v Burson, 402 US 535.

(a) Ownership of automobile. Basically, liability insurance protects the insured with respect to an automobile that he owns. Whether or not he owns the automobile in question is determined by Article 2 of the Uniform Commercial Code, and it is immaterial whether the steps required by the motor vehicle statute have been taken.

(b) Use and operation. The terms "use" and "operation" are very liberally interpreted to include events in which there is some involvement of the automobile, although not for the purpose of transportation. For example, where a supermarket bagboy was loading a customer's car and accidentally shut the door on her hand, the insurer was liable as there had been a "use of the automobile" within the coverage of the policy.

FACTS: Mrs. Coleman had an automobile liability insurance policy that was issued by the Employers' Liability Assurance Corp. When she was leaving the supermarket operated by Wrenn & Outlaw, the bagboy employed by the supermarket accidently closed the door of her car on her hand. Coleman sued Wrenn & Outlaw for the injury caused by its employee, the bagboy. Wrenn notified Employers' Liability to defend this action on the ground that Wrenn came within the policy provision protecting from liability "any person . . . legally responsible for the use" of the insured automobile. The insurer admitted that Wrenn, as the employer of the bagboy, was legally responsible for what had been done but denied that the bagboy had "used" the automobile. Coleman obtained a judgment for damages and costs from Wrenn, who then sued Employers' to recover the amount it was required to pay Coleman. The insurer denied liability on the ground that there had not been any "use of the automobile."

DECISION: Judgment against insurer. The use of an automobile includes loading and unloading as an incident to the transportation contemplated or completed. Therefore the action of the bagboy constituted a use of the automobile; and since Wrenn was responsible for the action of the bagboy, it came within the policy provision protecting from liability any person legally responsible for the use of the car. [Wrenn & Outlaw v Employers' Liability Assurance Corp. 246 SC 97, 142 SE2d 741]

The liability of the insured is not affected by the fact that he is insured. This means that if for any reason his policy does not cover the full loss or if the insurance company is not solvent or in business at that time, he is liable for any amount not paid, assuming that he would be liable in the absence of insurance.

(c) Person operating. Liability policies ordinarily protect the owner of the auto from liability when it is operated by another person with the permission of the insured, as in the case of an employee or agent of the owner.

Liability insurance may also protect an insured individual or his spouse against liability incurred while operating another person's automobile. This is referred to as *D.O.C.* (drive-other-car) *coverage*, or *temporary replacement coverage*.

(1) *Members of Household of Insured.* Automobile liability policies variously extend coverage to members of the insured's household or residence. Such terms are generally liberally construed to reach the conclusion that a given relative is a member of the insured's "household" or "residence."

To illustrate this liberality in interpretation, it has been held that when the insured took title to the automobile and in the following year transferred it to his daughter, aged 20, who took the automobile to another city where she was attending a job training school, the daughter was still a resident of the insured's household, even though her future plans were indefinite and there was no obligation to follow the employment for which she was being trained nor any obligation of the company training her to employ her.

(2) *Other Driver.* The automobile liability policy protects the insured when he is driving. If someone else is driving with the insured's permission, the policy protects both the original insured and such other driver. This *omnibus* or *other-driver clause* is generally liberally interpreted so that permission is often found in acquiescence in the other driver's use or in the insured's failing to object or to prevent such use. In the absence of an express prohibition by the insured against the permittee's lending the car to another, a permission by A given to B to use the car generally includes an implied permission to B to permit C to drive, in which case the liability of the insurer is the same as though A or B were driving.[5]

The buyer of an automobile does not come within the scope of an omnibus clause because his operation of the automobile is not based upon the permission of the seller but upon his ownership of the automobile. To avoid litigation, policies commonly expressly exclude buyers from the scope of the omnibus clause.

FACTS: Erardi was an automobile dealer. He obtained a liability insurance policy from the Aetna Insurance Company. The policy expressly declared that there was no coverage of an automobile "possession of which had been transferred to another by the named insured pursuant to an agreement of sale." Cannatelli purchased an automobile from Erardi and paid for it in cash. Over a month later, Cannatelli was driving the automobile and was involved in a collision in which DeRubbo and others were injured. At the time, the automobile was still registered in the name of Erardi as dealer because he had not given Cannatelli a certificate of title in spite of the latter's repeated demands. DeRubbo and the other persons injured obtained a judgment against Cannatelli and then sued Aetna on the theory that Cannatelli was an additional insured under the omnibus clause of Aetna's policy issued to Erardi. Aetna denied liability because Cannatelli was a buyer to whom possession and title had been transferred.

---

[5] Some courts interpret the omnibus clause more strictly and refuse to recognize a second permittee when the original insured did not expressly authorize such relending or where the use made by the second permittee was not the same use which the insured contemplated would be made by the first permittee. Hanegan v Horace Mann Mutual Insurance Co. 77 Ill2d 142, 221 NE2d 669; St. Paul Insurance Co. v Carlyle (MoApp) 428 SW2d 753.

DECISION: Judgment for Aetna. Cannatelli was not in possession of the automobile by virtue of permission of the insured and therefore was not an additional insured under the omnibus clause. Conversely, he was a person to whom possession and title had been transferred and was therefore expressly excluded by the provision of the policy. [DeRubbo v Aetna Insurance Co. 16 Conn 388, 288 A2d 430]

(d) Exclusions. In liability insurance the insurer may protect itself by excluding damage claims arising out of certain types of causes. Such policies may exclude claims of employees of the owner or claims under the workmen's compensation laws, or liability for claims when the insured admits to the injured third person that the insured is liable and agrees to pay his claim.

In the case of commercial vehicles the insurer may stipulate that it shall only be bound by the policy "provided: (a) the regular and frequent use of the automobile is confined to the area within a fifty mile radius of the limits of the city or town where the automobile is principally garaged . . . , (b) no regular or frequent trips are made by the automobile to any locations beyond such radius."

(e) Notice and cooperation. A liability policy generally provides that the insurer is not liable unless the insured (a) gives the insurer prompt notice of any serious accident or claim or lawsuit brought against him, (b) furnishes the insurance company with all details of the occurrence, and (c) cooperates with the insurer in the preparation of the defense against a lawsuit brought on the policy and participates at the trial. Notice and cooperation under such a policy are conditions precedent to the liability of the insurer.

These requirements are subject to modification in terms of "reasonableness." Thus, the insured is not required to report a trivial accident when there was no reason to believe that the injured person was going to proceed further with the matter. The notice to the insurer need only be given within a reasonable time after the occurrence, and "reasonable" is determined in the light of all the surrounding circumstances.

(f) Duty to defend. A liability insurer has the duty to defend any suit brought against its insured on a claim which, if valid, would come within the policy coverage. That is to say, the liability insurer cannot refuse to defend the insured on the ground that it does not believe the claim of the third person. Consequently, when the third person's complaint against the insured states a claim within the policy coverage, a liability insurer cannot refuse to defend on the ground that its investigation shows that the claim is without merit.

If the insurer wrongly refuses to defend and the third person recovers a judgment against the insured in excess of the policy maximum, the insurer is liable to the insured for the full amount of the judgment. Under statutes in some states, the insurer may also be required to pay the insured the amount of his costs and attorney's fees when the insurer refuses in bad faith to settle or defend the action.[6]

§ **38:11. COLLISION AND UPSET INSURANCE.** Liability insurance does not indemnify the owner for damage to his own automobile. In order to obtain this protection, the owner of the auto must obtain property insurance to cover damage from collision and upset.

The term "collision" is generally liberally interpreted so that there is insurance coverage whenever there is an unintended striking of another object even though the object is not an automobile or is not moving. For example, there is a collision when a wheel comes off of the automobile and the automobile falls to the ground.

FACTS: Ryburn obtained a collision policy from the Washington Fire & Marine Insurance Co. Because of a wet surface on the road, the insured truck careened off the highway and plunged into a ditch filled with water. Ryburn claimed that there was a "collision" with another "object" within the coverage of the policy.

DECISION: Judgment for Ryburn. The body of water was an "object" distinct from the road, and there was a collision with it. Although there is some conflict, the policy is to be interpreted liberally in favor of the insured to afford indemnity in such a case. [Washington Fire & Marine Insurance Co. v Ryburn, 228 Ark 930, 311 SW2d 302]

The phrase "struck by automobile" is likewise liberally interpreted so that there is coverage when the insured ran his motor scooter into an automobile, as against the contention that "struck by automobile" required that the automobile run into the insured.[7]

The term "upset" is generally liberally construed to cover an event which destroys the normal balance of the automobile even though it does not turn over. Thus, it has been held that there is an "upset" when a front wheel of a dump truck slips into a rut and the resulting stress causes the frame and hoist of the truck to twist out of shape.

In the case of an accident, if the driver of the other automobile has liability insurance, the first driver may be able to collect the damages to his automobile from the liability insurer of the other car. It is desirable, however, to have property insurance on his car. The reason is that his own insurer must pay him for damage to his car without regard to whether he was negligent, but the liability insurer of the other driver is not required to pay unless the first driver was not negligent and the other driver was negligent.

(a) Exclusions. Although the insurer against loss from collision will ordinarily pay damages without serious dispute, it is not required to pay

---

[6] Pendlebury v Western Casualty & Surety Co. 89 Idaho 456, 406 P2d 129.
[7] Foundation Reserve Insurance Co. v McCarthy, 77 NMex 118, 419 P2d 963.

in every case. It is commonly provided that the insurer is not liable when the automobile is used by a person who is violating the law. It may also be stipulated that liability is avoided if the auto is subject to a lien or encumbrance that has not been disclosed. It is common to exclude damages, resulting from collision, for the loss of the use of the auto, depreciation, or for loss of personal property in the auto.

(b) Notice and cooperation. As in the case of public liability insurance, the auto owner is under a duty to give notice, to inform, and to cooperate with the insurer. He must also give the insurer an opportunity to examine the automobile to determine the extent of damage before making repairs.

§ 38:12. UNINSURED MOTORISTS. Statutes and liability policies commonly provide for special coverage when the insured sustains loss because of an uninsured motorist. Since the *uninsured motorist coverage* is a liability coverage, there is no liability of the insurer in the absence of establishing that the uninsured motorist was negligent so that he would be held liable in a suit brought against him by the insured. Consequently, collision and accident insurance provide greater protection in that under such coverage the insurer is bound by its contract without regard to whether anyone could be held liable to the insured.

Uninsured motorist coverage generally includes the hit-and-run driver who leaves the scene of the collision before he can be identified. Policies commonly require that the collision be reported to the police or other appropriate authorities within 24 hours and that diligent effort be made to locate the hit-and-run driver. These restrictions are imposed in order to guard against the fraud of reporting the other car as "unknown" when its driver was in fact known, or against the fraud of having a one-car accident and then falsely claiming that the damage was the result of a collision with a hit-and-run driver.

This coverage differs from other insurance that the insured could obtain in that only personal injury claims are covered and generally only up to $10,000. Contact with the uninsured or unidentified vehicle is required, so that there is no uninsured motorist coverage when the insured runs off the road to avoid a collision and sustains injury thereby, or when the insured is injured upon striking oil or a substance dropped from the uninsured vehicle.[8]

§ 38:13. NO-FAULT INSURANCE. A state statute may require that every automobile liability policy provide for *no-fault coverage*. This means that when the insured is injured while using the insured automobile, the insurer will make a payment to him without regard to whether the other driver was legally liable for the harm. In effect, this is insurance for medical expense and loss of wages that runs in favor of the holder of the liability policy and is in addition to or in lieu of the coverage which the policy provides him with respect to his liability to other persons.

---

[8] Wynn v Doe, 255 SC 509, 180 SE2d 95.

The no-fault insurance statutes generally do not provide for payment for pain and suffering.

If another person is harmed, such as a pedestrian, no-fault insurance statutes generally provide for a similar kind of payment to such third person either by his own auto insurer or by that of the car inflicting the injury. There is authority that no-fault insurance is constitutional, as against the contention that it violates the guarantees of equal protection and due process. It has been sustained as a carefully studied plan to provide a new remedy to meet the problems caused by the automobile: rising costs of insurance, over-loading of courts, and delay in making payment to the injured person.[9] In contrast, other cases have held no-fault insurance is unconstitutional.

Disputes under no-fault insurance are sometimes determined by arbitration. In addition, some states require the arbitration of small claims of any nature. The concept of no-fault insurance does not have an exact definition because it is still in an evolutionary stage with no uniform pattern of legislation being followed and with frequent amendments changing the statutory pattern.

§ 38:14. THEFT INSURANCE. The owner of an automobile can secure theft insurance, which will protect him from loss through the theft and from damage to the auto caused by a theft. The standard form of policy covers loss from larceny, robbery, and pilferage as well as theft.

FACTS: The Muttontown Golf & Country Club insured six electric golf carts against "larceny." Without the permission of the club, the carts were taken out of the shed in which they were stored overnight and apparently used to bump into one another. In the morning they were found scattered over the golf course in a badly damaged condition. At the time when the policy was obtained, "larceny" was defined so as to include the unauthorized joyriding use that had been made of the carts. After the policy became effective but before the loss was sustained, the larceny statute was amended so that unauthorized use was no longer "larceny" but was made simply a "misdemeanor." When the club made claim on the insurance policy, the insurer raised the defense that there had not been any "larceny."

DECISION: Judgment for the Country Club. While the unauthorized use that had been made did not constitute larceny when the loss was sustained, it was "larceny" by virtue of the earlier statute at the time when the policy was obtained. "Considerations of equity and fair dealing" require the conclusion that the words in the insurance contract should be interpreted according to their meaning at the time when the contract was made, in the absence of an express provision that the contract should change as the statutory definitions might change. [Muttontown Golf & Country Club, Inc. v Firemen's Insurance Co. (NY CivCt) 320 NYS2d 369]

An automobile theft policy does not ordinarily protect against loss of contents. It is common to exclude liability for equipment or personal

---

[9] Pinnick v Cleary, 271 Mass 592, 271 NE2d 592.

property taken from the auto, but additional insurance protecting from such theft can be secured. It is common also to exclude liability for loss sustained while a passenger auto is used for commercial transportation or is rented to another.

§ 38:15. FIRE, LIGHTNING, AND TRANSPORTATION INSURANCE. In this type of insurance the insurer agrees to pay for any loss arising out of damage to or the destruction of a motor vehicle or its equipment caused by fire originating in any manner, by lightning, or by the stranding, sinking, burning, collision, or derailment of any conveyance in or upon which the automobile or the truck is being transported. This type of policy is commonly combined with a policy against theft and pilferage and is usually subject to the same exclusions.

§ 38:16. COMPREHENSIVE INSURANCE. In many automobile insurance policies, comprehensive material damage coverage, which protects the policyholder against virtually all such risks except collision or upset, replaces fire and theft insurance. The exclusions for this kind of insurance include wear and tear, freezing, mechanical breakdown, and loss of personal effects.

C. LIFE INSURANCE

§ 38:17. KINDS OF LIFE INSURANCE POLICIES. A contract of *life insurance* requires the insurer to pay a stipulated sum of money upon the death of the insured. It is not a contract of indemnity since the insurer does not undertake to indemnify the beneficiary for the financial loss sustained as the result of the death of the insured.

(a) **Ordinary life insurance.** Ordinary life insurance in turn may be subclassified as (1) *straight life insurance*, which requires payments of premiums throughout the life of the insured; (2) *limited payment insurance*, requiring the payment of premiums during a limited period, such as ten, twenty, or thirty years, or until the death of the insured if that should occur before the end of the specified period; (3) *endowment insurance*, under which the insurer undertakes to pay a stipulated sum when the insured reaches a specified age, or upon his death if that occurs; and (d) *term insurance*, under which the insurer undertakes to pay a stipulated sum only in the event of the death of the insured during a specified period, such as one, two, five, or ten years.

Somewhat similar to policies of endowment insurance are *annuity policies* and *retirement income insurance* under which the insured either pays a lump sum to the insurer and thereafter receives fixed annual payments, or pays periodic premiums to the insurer until a certain date and then receives fixed annual payments.

(b) **Group insurance.** *Group life insurance* is insurance of the lives of employees of a particular employer or persons engaged in a particular business or profession. Such policies are usually either term policies or straight life insurance. A medical examination is usually not required.

(c) Industrial insurance. *Industrial insurance* is in substance ordinary life insurance written for a small amount, usually from $100 to $1,000. Premiums are generally paid weekly or monthly and are collected from door to door by the agent of the insured. No physical examination is required for industrial insurance. The industrial policy may be either term, straight life, limited payment, or endowment.

(d) Double indemnity. Many life insurance companies undertake to pay double the amount of the policy, called *double indemnity*, if death is caused by an accident and occurs within ninety days after the accident. A comparatively small, additional premium is charged for this special protection. These policies generally define accidental death as "death resulting from bodily injury effected solely by external, violent, and accidental means, independently and exclusively of all other causes and within ninety days after such injury." In order to avoid the assertion of false claims of accidental death, most policies now require that there be a visible wound on the surface of the body. An exception is made in the case of death by drowning or by asphyxiation.

FACTS: Rollins had a life insurance policy with the Life & Accident Insurance Co. It contained a double indemnity clause for death by accidental means. Rollins was working in the hot sun loading railroad ties on a railroad car when he collapsed and later died from heat exhaustion. The insurance company paid a single indemnity but refused to pay the additional indemnity on the ground that death was not caused by accidental means. The widow, as beneficiary, sued the insurance company.

DECISION: Judgment for the insurance company. If a voluntary act of the insured (loading railroad ties in the hot sun) results in death, the means or cause of the death is not accidental. It is not sufficient that the death is an unforeseen result when the means or cause of the result was not in itself an accident. [Rollins v Life & Accident Insurance Co. 190 Tenn 89, 228 SW2d 70]

Double indemnity clauses generally exempt the insurer from liability for a death occurring while the insured is serving in the armed forces, while engaged in riots or insurrections, or when the insured is over 65 years of age.

(e) Disability insurance. In consideration of the payment of an additional premium, many life insurance companies also provide insurance against total permanent disability of the insured. *Disability* is usually defined in a life insurance policy as any "incapacity resulting from bodily injury or disease to engage in any occupation for remuneration or profit." The policy generally provides that a disability which has continued for a stated minimum period, such as four to six months, will be regarded as a *total permanent disability*.

It has become common for insurers, upon the payment of an additional premium, to include in the policy a clause waiving premiums becoming due during the total or permanent disability of the insured. The effect of such a provision is to prevent the policy from lapsing for nonpayment of premiums during the period of such disability.

(f) Risks not covered. Life insurance policies frequently provide that death shall not be within the protection of the policy or that a double indemnity provision shall not be applicable when death is due to or caused by (1) suicide, (2) narcotics, (3) violation of the law, (4) execution for crime, (5) war activities, or (6) operation of aircraft. For such exclusions to operate, there must be a proximate relationship between the prohibited conduct or condition and the harm sustained in order to relieve the insurer from liability on the policy. It is generally provided by statute or stated by court decision that a beneficiary who has feloniously killed the insured is not entitled to receive the proceeds of the policy.

§ 38:18. THE BENEFICIARY.

The person to whom the proceeds of a life insurance policy are payable upon the death of the insured is called the *beneficiary*. He may be a third person, or the beneficiary may be the estate of the insured. There may be more than one beneficiary.

As a practical matter, it is preferable to provide for the payment of insurance money directly to named beneficiaries rather than to one's estate, even though the same persons would receive the proceeds on the distribution of the estate. When the insurance is paid into the estate, the proceeds will be reduced by the administration charges of the estate, such as the fees of the attorneys of the estate and the commissions of the executor or administrator; and the distribution will be subject to the delay required in the formal administration of an estate.

In addition, since the insurance proceeds that pass through the estate of the insured are subject to his debts, it is possible that the proceeds of the insurance policy will be consumed in whole or in part for the payment of debts and thus not be received by the beneficiary. When the policy is payable directly to a named beneficiary, the proceeds of the policy are generally not subject to the debts of the insured.[10]

The beneficiary named in the policy may be barred from claiming the proceeds of the policy because of a prior settlement agreement, by which it was agreed to do otherwise.

FACTS: Stoddard insured his life with the Beneficial Life Insurance Company. His wife, Phyllis, was named as beneficiary. Thereafter they were divorced. They entered into a property settlement agreement which was approved by the divorce court and made part of the divorce decree. By the settlement agreement, the policy was awarded to Stoddard. No change was ever made to the beneficiary designation and, on Stoddard's death, Phyllis claimed the proceeds of the policy because she was still named as the beneficiary. The administrator of Stoddard's estate also claimed the proceeds. The insurance company admitted liability and paid the proceeds into court.

---

[10] Succession of Onorato, 219 La 1, 51 So2d 804.

DECISION: Judgment for the administrator of the husband's estate. Although the ex-wife was still named as the beneficiary in the policy, she was barred from claiming the proceeds because of the divorce decree approving the property settlement by which the proceeds of insurance were given to the husband. [Beneficiary Life Insurance Co. v Stoddard, 95 Idaho 628, 516 P2d 187]

(a) Primary and contingent beneficiaries. It is desirable to name a primary and a contingent beneficiary. Thus, *A* may make his insurance payable to *B*; but if *B* dies before *A*, the insurance shall be payable to *C*. In such cases *B* is the *primary beneficiary*, and *C* is the *contingent beneficiary* because he takes the proceeds as beneficiary only upon the contingency that *B* dies before *A*.

The designation of the contingent beneficiary should not be made conditional only upon the death of the primary beneficiary before the death of the insured. The change should also be effective in case of the death of the insured and the primary beneficiary in a common disaster or under such circumstances that it cannot be determined who died first. For example, if a man's wife is named as the primary beneficiary and their two children as contingent beneficiaries, the policy should be written so that the proceeds will be payable to the contingent beneficiaries either if the wife dies before the husband does or in the case of the death of husband and wife in a common disaster, such as an automobile accident.

(b) Change of beneficiary. The customary policy provides that the insured reserves the right to change the beneficiary without the latter's consent. When the policy contains such a provision, the beneficiary cannot object to a change that destroys all rights which he had under the policy and which names another as beneficiary in his place.[11]

In the absence of a provision in the policy so authorizing, the beneficiary acquires a vested interest, even though he gave no consideration. The insured, therefore, cannot thereafter change the beneficiary even with the consent of the insurer.

In industrial policies, it is customary for the policy to contain a *facility-of-payment clause* under which the insurer is given the option of selecting from a designated class or group anyone whom the insurer deems equitably entitled to receive payment and to make payment to that person. Such a clause enables the insurer to pay the amount of the insurance proceeds directly to any person who pays the debts of the decedent, such as his funeral bills, rather than to a named beneficiary who had not expended any money on behalf of the decedent.

The insurance policy will ordinarily state that in order to change the beneficiary, the insurer must be so instructed in writing by the insured and the policy must then be endorsed by the company with the change of the beneficiary. These provisions are generally liberally construed. If the insured has notified the insurer but dies before the endorsement of the change is made by the company, the change of beneficiary is effective. If the

---

[11] Reliance Life Insurance Co. v Jaffe, 121 CalApp2d 241, 263 P2d 82.

insured has clearly indicated his intention to change the beneficiary, the consent of the insurer to the change is not required.

§ 38:19. INCONTESTABLE CLAUSE. Statutes commonly require the inclusion of an incontestable clause in life insurance policies. Ordinarily this clause states that after the lapse of two years the policy cannot be contested by the insurance company. The insurer is free to contest the validity of the policy at any time during the contestable period; but once that period has expired, it must pay the stipulated sum upon the death of the insured and cannot claim that in obtaining the policy the insured had been guilty of misrepresentation, fraud, or any other conduct that would exempt it from liability.

The incontestable clause does not bar matters of defense that arise subsequent to the sustaining of loss. The incontestability clause does not bar proof that the loss was sustained by a risk not covered by the policy.

> **FACTS:** George Rogers insured his life with the National Producers Life Insurance Company. Ten years later he committed suicide. The insurance company denied liability because the policy stated that death by suicide was excepted. The beneficiary of the policy claimed that the insurer could not raise this defense because the two years specified by the two-year incontestability clause had expired. She sued the insurance company.
>
> **DECISION:** Judgment for National Producers. The policy did not cover death by suicide. The incontestability clause does not bar proof that the loss was sustained by a risk not covered by the policy. [National Producers Life Insurance Co. v Rogers, 8 ArizApp 53, 442 P2d 876]

Generally the incontestable clause is not applicable to double indemnity or disability provisions of the policy.

§ 38:20. SURRENDER OF POLICY AND ALTERNATIVES. Surrender of a life insurance policy is ordinarily made when a person finds that he cannot afford to pay further premiums on the policy or that he needs the surrender value of the policy in money.

(a) **Cash surrender value.** By modern statute or policy provision, it is commonly provided that if the life insurance policy has been in force a stated number of years, usually two or three, the insured may surrender the policy and the insurer will then make a payment of the cash value of the policy to him. Ordinarily term policies do not have a cash surrender value.

Each year a certain percentage of the premiums is set aside by the insurer to hold as a reserve against the date when payment must be made under the policy. If the policy is surrendered or canceled, the potential liability of the reserve fund is removed and part of the fund can then be released as a payment to the insured. The longer the policy has been in existence, the larger is the cash surrender value.

(b) **Loan on policy.** Sometimes the insured's problem can be solved by borrowing from the insurer. The modern policy contains a definite scale of maximum amounts that can be borrowed depending upon the age of the policy. The insurer is able to make such loans because it has the security of the cash surrender value if the loan is not repaid; or if the insured dies without making repayment, it may deduct the debt from the proceeds payable to the beneficiary.

The loan value of a policy is usually the same amount as the cash surrender value. The policyholder, as a borrower, must pay interest to the insurance company on the loan.

(c) Paid-up policy. Under modern statutes or common forms of policies, if the insured can no longer afford the expense of his insurance, he may request the insurer to issue to him a new policy of paid-up insurance. The insured in effect takes out a new paid-up policy through the transfer of the reserve value of the old policy. In some states, when a policy lapses for nonpayment of premiums, the insurer must automatically issue a paid-up policy on the basis of the reserve value of the lapsed policy.

(d) Extended insurance. Instead of a paid-up policy for a smaller amount, it is generally possible under modern statutes and policies for the insured to obtain term insurance that provides the original amount of protection. This remains effective until the reserve value of the original policy has been consumed.

(e) Reinstatement of lapsed policy. When a premium on a policy is not paid within the required period or within the grace period, the insured generally may reinstate the policy within a reasonable time thereafter as long as he is still an insurable risk and provided he pays all premiums that are in arrears.

§ 38:21. SETTLEMENT OPTIONS. Although an ordinary life insurance policy will provide for the payment of a specified amount upon the death of the insured, the insured generally may designate one or several plans of distribution of this fund. These plans of distribution are called *settlement options*. When the insured has designated a particular option, the beneficiary generally cannot change it after his death. Sometimes the policy reserves to the beneficiary the right to change the settlement option.

In addition to payment of a lump sum in settlement of all claims against the insurer arising under the policy, the standard form of policy provides the following options: (1) retention by the insurer of the proceeds of the policy until the death of the beneficiary, during which period the insurer pays interest to the beneficiary at a specified rate; (2) payment of equal monthly installments for a specified number of years; (3) payment of equal monthly installments for a specified number of years or until the beneficiary dies, whichever period is longer; or (4) payment of equal monthly installments in an amount specified by the beneficiary as long as there is a sufficient principal-and-interest fund from which to make payment.

§ 38:22. RIGHTS OF CREDITORS. If a man takes out insurance on his own life, can his creditors complain? To the extent that he is paying premiums to the insurance company, the amount of his money available to pay creditors is reduced. Can the creditors reach the cash surrender value of the policy or the proceeds upon the insured's death?

If the insured makes the policy payable to his estate, the proceeds become part of the general assets of his estate upon his death and, in the absence of statute, are subject to the claims of his creditors. If the insured is at all times solvent when he pays the premiums, his creditors cannot reach the policy in payment of their claims, and the beneficiary is entitled to the entire proceeds of the policy.

Between these two extremes are a variety of situations. The insured may have been insolvent during part or all of the life of the policy; or the obtaining of the insurance policy or the assignment of it or the changing of the beneficiary may have been done to defraud the creditors.

If the policy is originally payable to the estate of the insured, an assignment by the insured of his interest when made in fraud of creditors will not defeat the rights of his creditors.

If the policy is made payable to a third person as beneficiary but the insured is insolvent, courts differ as to the rights of the insured's creditors.

FACTS: Jones had insured his life, making the policy payable to his estate. When he was insolvent, he changed the beneficiary of the policy to name his sister, Cramer, and his son as beneficiaries. After his death, Davis and Giles, creditors, claimed that the proceeds of the insurance policy should be paid into the decedent's estate on the theory that the change of the beneficiary was a transfer made in fraud of the decedent's creditors.

DECISION: Judgment for creditors in part. The court held that the change had been n.ade in fraud of creditors but that the surrender value of the policies on the date of the change of the beneficiaries was all the creditors were entitled to since that was the only amount over which Jones had control at the time he made the change of beneficiaries. [Davis v Cramer, 133 Ark 224, 202 SW 239]

QUESTIONS AND CASE PROBLEMS

1. A father told his son that the son could have the father's car but that the son must not drive it. The son had a friend drive the car. The friend ran into another car. The insurer denied liability on the ground that the father had not given permission to the friend to drive the car and that therefore the friend was not an "other driver" within the protection of the omnibus clause. Decide. [See Esmond v Liscio, 209 PaSuper 200, 224 A2d 793]

2. Harsha had a policy of automobile liability insurance issued by the Fidelity General Insurance Co. that provided coverage as to personal injuries by an "uninsured motorist" to the extent of $10,000. Harsha's son was injured while a

passenger when Harsha's automobile collided with Leffard's automobile. The insurance policy carried by Leffard had a liability maximum of $10,000, and his insurer paid $9,500 to Harsha on behalf of her son. Harsha, claiming that her son's injuries were $50,000, sued Fidelity on the theory that Leffard was an uninsured motorist with respect to the $40,000 not covered by his policy. Was she correct? [Harsha v Fidelity General Insurance Co. 11 ArizApp 438, 465 P2d 377]

3. The Hess-Mace Trucking Co. was delivering sand to a contractor, A. Teichert & Son. One of the sand trucks got stuck in a soft ramp. A water truck owned by Marlon's Trucking Co. tried to tow the stuck truck. In arranging the tow line, the driver of the sand truck was injured. The insurer of the water truck claimed that the insurer of the sand truck was required to pay for the injury on the theory that the latter's policy covered accidents arising out of the "use" of the sand truck. Decide. [St. Paul Fire & Marine Insurance Co. v Hartford Accident & Indemnity Co. 244 CalApp2d 826, 53 CalRptr 650]

4. Marshall Produce Co. insured its milk and egg processing plant against fire with the St. Paul Fire & Marine Insurance Co. Smoke from a fire near its plant was absorbed by its egg powder. Cans of the powder delivered to the United States Government were rejected as contaminated. Marshall Produce sued the insurance company for a total loss. The insurer contended that there had been no fire involving the insured property and no total loss. Decide. [Marshall Produce Co. v St. Paul Fire & Marine Insurance Co. 256 Minn 404, 98 NW2d 280]

5. A father owned an automobile. He insured it under a policy which also covered temporary substitute and newly-acquired vehicles. Thereafter, when the finance company repossessed the father's car, his son bought a new automobile. Was the son's automobile covered by the father's policy? [See Hays v Robertson, 20 Utah2d 816, 435 P2d 925]

6. The owner of an automobile went to an amusement park. He locked his car with the keys inside. When he went to leave, he requested one of the security guards of the park to break a window of the car. The guard broke a window with his gun, but in so doing, the gun was accidentally discharged and injured one of the persons who had come to the playground with the owner. It was claimed that the injury to the friend was within the coverage of the car owner's policy relating to harm "which arises out of the use" of the car. Was the harm covered? [See Cagle v Playland Amusement, Inc. (LaApp) 202 So2d 396]

7. Sackett insured his automobile with the Farmer's Insurance Exchange against loss by accidental means. A gas station attendant improperly fastened the radiator cap with the result that the water boiled out of the radiator and damaged the engine. The Farmers Insurance Exchange claimed that it was not liable because the harm came within the exception of "mechanical breakdown and failure." Was the insurer correct? [Sackett v Farmers Insurance Exchange, 237 CalApp2d 899, 47 CalRptr 350]

8. The owner of an automobile gave permission to someone else to drive the car. The permittee had insurance with the Government Employees Insurance Co. with a drive-other-car provision. The owner had insurance with the Globe Indemnity Co. with an omnibus clause. The driver had a collision with another person, and the two insurance companies disagreed as to what part of the third person's claim each company should pay. The driver's policy contained an excess insurance clause stating in substance that if the loss arose out of the use by an insured of a nonowned automobile, the policy would be "excess insurance over any other valid and collectible insurance." The owner's policy provided in substance that when the automobile was driven by a permittee, the owner's

insurance would be only "excess" insurance. It further stated in effect that the owner's policy would not apply if the permittee had valid and collectible insurance "either primary or excess." What was the liability of the two insurers? [See Government Employees Insurance Co. v Globe Indemnity Co. (Ky) 415 SW2d 581]

9. Turner had a policy of life insurance issued by the Equitable Life Assurance Society. His wife was the beneficiary. When she died, Turner changed the beneficiary to Olsen. Thereafter he began drinking heavily and was committed two times to institutions for alcoholism. About two years after he was released the second time, he changed the beneficiary of the policy to Hawkins. When Turner died, Olsen sued Hawkins and the insurance company for the proceeds of the policy, claiming that the change of beneficiary was not valid on the theory that Turner lacked capacity to change the beneficiary. In addition to Turner's confinement to institutions for alcoholism, it was shown that on a number of instances he had been arrested for minor offenses committed while intoxicated, and there was evidence that he was childish and forgetful. Was Olsen entitled to the proceeds of the policy? [Olsen v Hawkins, 90 Idaho 28, 408 P2d 462]

10. Walker obtained a policy of life insurance from the National Life and Accident Insurance Company. The policy reserved the right to change the beneficiary. Walker named his wife as beneficiary, and she paid the premiums on the policy. Walker changed the beneficiary designation. Later Walker's wife sued the insurance company and claimed that the insured could not change the beneficiary because she had paid the premiums on the policy. Decide. [National Life and Accident Insurance Co. v Walker (Ky) 246 SW2d 139]

11. Woodard obtained a collision policy from Canal Insurance Co. to cover a Ford automobile. He purchased a new Dodge from Lord and traded in the Ford. Two days after the sale, Woodard was involved in a collision with the Dodge. The policy of insurance had not been changed from the Ford to the Dodge, but Woodard claimed that the Dodge was covered by the provision of the policy which extended to "newly acquired automobiles." Canal Insurance Co. claimed the Dodge did not come within this category because there had not been any transfer of the title certificate, and it was provided by statute that "except . . . as between the parties, a transfer . . . is not effective until" the motor vehicle title certificate had been properly transferred. Was the Dodge a newly acquired automobile? [Canal Insurance Co. v Woodard, 121 GaApp 356, 173 SE2d 727]

BANKRUPTCY

A. GENERAL PRINCIPLES

§ 39:1. NATURE AND THE SCOPE. Our society has provided a system by which the honest debtor can, in substance, pay into court what he has, be relieved of all unpaid debts, and start economic life anew. This is achieved by bankruptcy laws in the case of the federal government and insolvency laws in the case of the states.

Historically these laws were not concerned with benefiting the debtor as much as they were with benefiting creditors. In their origin, bankruptcy laws were designed to enable creditors to compel a fraudulent debtor to bring his property into court and to pay it to his creditors, thus preventing him from concealing his property or from paying it only to some of his creditors. Today bankruptcy and insolvency proceedings partake of both features as can be seen from the fact that such a proceeding may be started by the debtor himself or by his creditors.

State insolvency laws have only a limited sphere of operation today because the federal bankruptcy laws have superseded them to a large degree.

§ 39:2. CLASSIFICATION OF BANKRUPTS.

(a) Voluntary bankrupts. A *voluntary bankrupt* is one who subjects himself to the bankruptcy law. Any person, and in most instances any corporation or an association, may become a voluntary bankrupt. The filing of a voluntary petition automatically operates as an adjudication or determination that the petitioner is bankrupt.

Municipal, railroad, insurance, and banking corporations, and savings and loan associations cannot be voluntary bankrupts.[1]

(b) Involuntary bankrupts. An *involuntary bankrupt* is one who has been subjected to the bankruptcy law upon the petition of his creditors. Under

---

[1] 11 United States Code § 22(a).

the prescribed circumstances, most natural persons, partnerships, and corporations owing debts that amount to the sum of $1,000 or more may be forced by creditors into bankruptcy. Wage earners [2] and farmers; municipal, railroad, insurance, and banking corporations; and building and loan associations cannot be adjudicated involuntary bankrupts.[3]

§ 39:3. INVOLUNTARY PROCEEDINGS.

If there are 12 or more creditors, 3 or more of them must join in the petition. If there are less than 12 creditors, one of them may file the petition.[4]

The petitioning creditor or creditors must have provable claims [5] against the debtor totaling $500 or more. The amount of the claims must be in excess of the value of pledged securities held by the creditors.

> **FACTS:** Okamoto owed money to Hornblower & Weeks-Hemphill, Noyes. Hornblower filed a petition to have Okamoto declared in involuntary bankrupt. Okamoto moved to dismiss the petition on the ground that he had more than 12 creditors and therefore the petition could not be filed by only one. Hornblower replied that the claims of the other creditors were too small to count and therefore, as Okamoto did not have more than 12 creditors, the petition could accordingly be filed by one creditor. The lower court held that every creditor was to be counted and dismissed Hornblower's petition. Hornblower appealed.
>
> **DECISION:** Judgment affirmed. In determining the number of creditors of a debtor every creditor must be counted. The Bankruptcy Act does not make any distinction between creditors in terms of the amount owed. Therefore, creditors cannot be ignored on the ground that they have small claims. [In re Okamoto (CA9 Cal) 491 F2d 496]

The debtor against whom the petition is filed may appear and oppose the petition.[6] If there are more than 11 creditors when less than 3 filed the petition, the creditors who have not joined in the petition are given an opportunity to join. If the statutory number of creditors do not join in the petition, it will be dismissed.[7]

§ 39:4. ACTS OF BANKRUPTCY.

An involuntary petition may not be filed unless the debtor has committed an act of bankruptcy within 4 months prior to the filing of the petition.[8]

A debtor commits an act of bankruptcy under federal statute (1) by concealing, removing, or permitting to be concealed or removed, any part of

---

[2] A "wage earner" for this purpose is defined as an individual who works for wages, salary, or hire, and whose compensation does not exceed $1,500 a year. 11 USC § 1(32).

[3] Special statutory provision is made for the reorganization and liquidation of such corporations because of the nature of the enterprise and in order to protect the public.

[4] 11 USC § 95(b).

[5] See § 39:14. A claim may be unliquidated as to amount, provided that it is not contingent as to liability, although the unliquidated claim may be disqualified if a maximum value cannot be estimated. 11 UCS § 95(b).

[6] § 41(b).

[7] § 95(d).

[8] § 21(b).

his property with intent to hinder, delay, or defraud his creditors, or any of them; (2) by transferring, while insolvent, any portion of his property to one or more of his creditors with intent to prefer such creditor or creditors over his other creditors; (3) by suffering or permitting, while insolvent, any creditor to obtain a lien upon any of his property through legal proceedings and not having vacated or discharged such lien within 30 days from date thereof or at least 5 days before the date that was set for any sale or other disposition of such property; (4) by making a general assignment for the benefit of his creditors; (5) while insolvent, by permitting or being forced to put a receiver or a trustee in charge of his property; or (6) by admitting in writing his inability to pay his debts and his willingness to be adjudged a bankrupt.[9]

§ 39:5. INSOLVENCY. Insolvency is a necessary element of the second, third, and fifth acts of bankruptcy, but not of the others. The bankruptcy act declares that a person is deemed to be *insolvent* under the provisions of the statute "whenever the aggregate of his property, exclusive of any property which he may have conveyed, transferred, concealed, removed, or permitted to be concealed or removed, with intent to defraud, hinder, or delay his creditors, shall not at a fair valuation be sufficient in amount to pay his debts."[10]

A debtor is insolvent under the bankruptcy act when his assets, fairly valued, are not sufficient to pay his debts. This contrasts with the equity concept of insolvency, which is the inability to pay debts as they become due.[11]

§ 39:6. BANKRUPTCY OFFICIALS. The actual bankruptcy·proceeding, apart from that which takes place in court, is under the control of certain officials: (a) the referee, (b) the receiver, and (c) the trustee.

(a) Referee. A *referee* is appointed for a 6-year term to hear the evidence in bankruptcy cases. He acts in the nature of a special bankruptcy court. A referee may impose fines for contempt up to $250.[12]

(b) Receiver. On the petition of creditors who fear that the assets of the debtor will be lost, a *receiver* may be appointed as custodian to preserve the assets [13] and turn them over to the trustee when appointed.

---

[9] The filing of a voluntary petition in bankruptcy is in itself an act of bankruptcy since the debtor admits in writing his inability to pay his debts and his willingness to be adjudged a bankrupt.

[10] 11 USC § 1(19).

[11] Note that under the Uniform Commercial Code both criteria for insolvency are employed. "A person is 'insolvent' who either has ceased to pay his debts in the ordinary course of business or cannot pay his debts as they become due or is insolvent within the meaning of the federal bankruptcy law." UCC § 1-201(23).

[12] 1973 Bankruptcy Rule No. 920(a). He may not impose a punishment of imprisonment. If it appears to the referee that conduct warrants a greater fine or imprisonment, he may certify the matter to the district court.

[13] USC § 11(3).

(c) Trustee. The creditors of the debtor elect, or if they fail to do so, the court appoints, a trustee. The *trustee* has a double role as owner of the property of the debtor and as holder of the rights of a most favored creditor.

§ 39:7. THE BANKRUPTCY TRUSTEE AS SUCCESSOR TO THE DEBTOR.

The trustee in bankruptcy automatically becomes by operation of the law the owner of all property of the bankrupt in excess of such property as the bankrupt is entitled to under local state exemption laws.

As the statutory owner or successor to the bankrupt's property, the trustee has only the status of an assignee. That is, the trustee will not be a holder in due course of paper as to which the bankrupt was merely an ordinary holder.

(a) Payment of bankrupt's outstanding checks. The rule that the title to the property of the bankrupt passes to his trustee in bankruptcy is subject to an exception that a drawee bank in which the bankrupt has a checking account may make payment on a bankrupt's check when it has had no notice or knowledge of his bankruptcy.

FACTS: Marin Seafoods drew a check on the Bank of Marin to pay a bill. Seafoods then went into bankruptcy, was adjudicated bankrupt, and England was elected the trustee in bankruptcy. Thereafter the Bank of Marin paid the holder the amount of the check. England sued the Bank of Marin for making this payment, asserting that the title to Seafoods' bank account passed to him and terminated the right of the bank to honor the check of Seafoods.

DECISION: Judgment for the bank. The principle that title to the debtor's property passes to the trustee in bankruptcy is subject to an equitable exception in the check-paying case. A drawee bank that honors a bankrupt's check in good faith without notice or knowledge of the bankruptcy is not liable to the trustee in bankruptcy for the amount of such payment. [Bank of Marin v England, 385 US 99]

§ 39:8. THE BANKRUPTCY TRUSTEE AS A FAVORED CREDITOR.

The bankruptcy trustee possesses the rights that are possessed by the most favored creditor of the bankrupt. Specifically, this means that the trustee can avoid certain preferences gained by a judgment against the bankrupt or by a transfer of property, of which a recording or registering is required, within 4 months prior to the filing of the petition or after the filing thereof and before adjudication.[14] He is required by the terms of the bankruptcy act to recover for the benefit of the creditors any of the bankrupt's property that has been transferred within 4 months prior to the filing of the petition, with the intent to hinder, delay, or defraud any creditors, or that is in the hands of a person under a transfer that is void by the laws of any state or that was received by such person with knowledge or reason to know that the debtor was insolvent.[15]

---

[14] § 96(b).
[15] §§ 107(d), 110 (e).

§ 39:9. VOIDABLE PREFERENCES. To constitute a voidable preference, with the consequence that it may be avoided by the debtor's trustee in bankruptcy, there must be (1) transfer of property (2) within four months of bankruptcy (3) to or for the benefit of a creditor (4) which enables him to obtain a greater percentage of his debt than other creditors of the same class, and which is made (5) when the debtor is insolvent and (6) the creditor knows or has reason to know that the debtor is insolvent.[16]

§ 39:10. AVOIDANCE OF LIENS. The mere adjudication in bankruptcy does not automatically avoid or vacate a lien created within the 4-month period, and the lien remains in force unless avoided by the trustee as a preferential transfer. If the lien is not avoided in the bankruptcy proceeding and if the trustee in bankruptcy sells the assets of the bankrupt that are subject to a judicial lien, the purchaser from the trustee in bankruptcy, in an action in a state court, may avoid the creditor's lien to the same extent as could the trustee in bankruptcy.

When a creditor has an unperfected security interest in personal property of the bankrupt, such security interest cannot be asserted against the trustee in bankruptcy of the debtor, without regard to whether it would otherwise be preferential within the meaning of the bankruptcy act.[17] If the security interest has been perfected and is not preferential in character, the trustee in bankruptcy and any purchaser of the debtor's assets from the trustee holds such assets subject to the interest of the creditor.[18]

As Article 9 of the UCC has eliminated the significance of title in transactions involving personal property, the determination of whether the creditor prevails over the bankrupt debtor's trustee in bankruptcy is not controlled by the name of the transaction between the creditor and the debtor nor by whether the creditor has or has not reserved title to the collateral. The same conclusion is to be reached when a mortgage of real estate is involved since even in title theory states, the mortgage is merely a lien with respect to third persons even though it purports to transfer title to the mortgagee.

The federal statutes regulate in detail the manner in which claims against the bankrupt are to be determined and his assets distributed in payment of them.

B. AMINISTRATION OF BANKRUPTS' ESTATE

§ 39:11 MEETINGS OF CREDITORS. At various times in the administration of the bankruptcy, a meeting of the creditors is held, such as the initial meeting to appoint a trustee, subsequent meetings to pass on

---

[16] Bankruptcy Act § 60, 11 USC § 96.

[17] UCC § 9-301 (applicable to security interests in personal property).

[18] When a security interest in personal property is involved, perfection is governed by Article 9 of the Uniform Commercial Code. If land is involved, the perfection of a security interest therein, such as a mortgage, is governed by non-Code law of the state where the land is located.

particular matters authorized by the bankruptcy act, and a final meeting when the estate is to be closed.[19]

A majority in number and in the amount of claims of all creditors and who are present and whose claims have been allowed is required for any decision by the creditors. Creditors who have priority or security are not entitled to vote, nor are their claims counted in computing the number of creditors or the amounts of their claims, unless their claims exceed the values of such priorities of security, and then only for such excess.[20]

§ 39:12. INTERROGATION OF PERSONS. Provision is made for the examination of the bankrupt and other persons as to his property and his conduct relating thereto. The wife of the bankrupt may be examined only in respect to business transacted by her or to which she is a party, and to determine whether she has transacted or has been a party to any business of her husband.[21]

§ 39:13. PROOF AND ALLOWANCE OF CLAIMS. Each creditor is required to file a sworn statement setting forth his claim and the basis thereof. These claims are ordinarily passed upon by the referee. The claim is then allowed or disallowed as in any other lawsuit. A claim must ordinarily be disallowed if not presented until more than six months after the first meeting of creditors.[22]

The six-months time limitation on the filing of claims is mandatory and a creditor is not excused from filing within that time by the circumstance that the trustee in bankruptcy in fact knew of the existence of the creditor's claim.

FACTS: The Vega Baja Lumber Yard owed money to the First City National Bank. The bank sued the lumber yard and attached some of its property. Thereafter, bankruptcy proceedings were begun and the lumber yard was adjudicated a bankrupt. The bank filed a claim in bankruptcy. The referee rejected the bank's claim because it had been filed more than six months after the debtor had been adjudicated a bankrupt. The bank claimed that the six-months limitation did not bar it because the trustee knew of its claim.

DECISION: The claim of the bank was barred. The fact that the trustee in bankruptcy knew of the existence of the claim of the bank did not affect the operation of the six-months limitation. [In re Vega Baja Lumber Yard, Inc. (DC D Puerto Rico) 285 FSupp 143]

A creditor who received some preferential payment or transfer of property within four months prior to the filing of the petition in bankruptcy cannot prove his claim unless he surrenders such payment or transfer.[23] If the claim of a creditor is secured, he is also barred from proving his claim except as to that part of his claim in excess of the security.

---

[19] 11 USC § 91(d), (e).
[20] § 92(a), (b).
[21] § 44(a).
[22] § 93(n).
[23] §§ 93(g), 96(b), 107.

§ 39:14. CLAIMS THAT ARE PROVABLE.

§ 39:14. CLAIMS THAT ARE PROVABLE. Not all claims may be proven, that is, be permitted to share in the distribution of the assets of the bankrupt debtor. The claims that may be proved are: (1) a debt evidenced by a judgment or an instrument in writing, absolutely owing at the time of the filing of the petition by or against the bankrupt, whether then payable or not; (2) a debt due as costs against a bankrupt who was, at the time of the filing of the petition, by or against the bankrupt, the plaintiff in an action that would pass to the trustee and that the trustee, upon notice thereof, declines to prosecute; (3) a debt founded upon a claim for costs, incurred in good faith by a creditor before the filing of the petition, in an action to recover a provable debt; (4) a debt based upon an open account, or upon a contract express or implied; (5) a debt based upon a provable debt reduced to judgment after the filing of the petition and before the consideration of the bankrupt's application for a discharge, less costs and interest after the filing of the petition; (6) an award of workmen's compensation; (7) a right to damages for negligence; (8) contingent debts and contingent contractual liabilities; and (9) claims for anticipatory breach of contract.[24]

In respect to an *unliquidated claim* of a creditor, that is, a claim for an uncertain or disputed amount, the bankruptcy act provides that upon application to the court of bankruptcy, such a claim shall be liquidated or estimated in such a manner as the court shall direct. If possible to liquidate or estimate the claim within a reasonable time, the claim may be allowed against the bankrupt's estate.[25]

It is the nature of the claim against the debtor at the time of bankruptcy which is controlling. Consequently, when an agreement is made to settle a claim for embezzlement or conversion and the obligation under the agreement has not been paid at the time of bankruptcy, the liability of the bankrupt is a contract liability on the settlement agreement and the referee may not go back to the underlying tort occurrence so as to bar the discharge of the claim.

§ 39:15. SALE OF BANKRUPT'S ASSETS.

§ 39:15. SALE OF BANKRUPT'S ASSETS. In order to pay the debts of the bankrupt, it is necessary to convert his assets into cash and the trustee is accordingly authorized to sell his property. The sale in general may be made in any manner that is in the best interests of the estate. Such sales are under the supervision of the bankruptcy court.

§ 39:16. DISTRIBUTION OF ESTATE.

§ 39:16. DISTRIBUTION OF ESTATE. After all of the bankrupt's debts are determined, the assets that have been collected by the trustee are distributed first to those creditors with priorities; then to the general creditors without priorities; and, should any balance remain after all creditors have been paid, the balance to the bankrupt. These payments to creditors, called *dividends,* are made in installments.

The bankruptcy act confers a prior right of payment to (a) costs of administration and expenses necessary to preserve the estate, filing fees

---

[24] § 103(a).
[25] §§ 93(d), 103(d).

paid by creditors in involuntary proceedings, expenses of creditors in recovering property transferred or concealed by the bankrupt, and the reasonable expenses of creditors in opposing a composition that is refused or set aside; (b) wages due to workmen, clerks, traveling or city salesmen, or servants, earned within 3 months preceding the petition, but not to exceed $600 to each person; (c) expenses of creditors in opposing an arrangement or a plan for the discharge of a bankrupt, or in convicting a person of violating the bankruptcy law; (d) taxes owed by the bankrupt, except taxes against property over and above the value of the interest of the bankrupt therein; and (e) debts owed persons, including the United States, who by law are entitled to priority.

Payments due by an employer to a trust for employees are not "wages" within the priority provision where payments from the trust were only made upon retirement, disability, or death.

> **FACTS:** An industry-wide collective bargaining contract required employers to make specified contributions to a trust for employees. A & S Electrical Corporation was an employer subject to this contract. It went into bankruptcy. At the time, it had not made all the payments due by it to the employee trust. The Joint Board of the Electrical Industry, as trustee of the funds, asserted that the claim for the contributions was entitled to priority as "wages due workmen." This was opposed by the United States. Priority was denied the claim of the trust and the Joint Board appealed.

> **DECISION:** The priority was given to claims for "wages . . . due to workmen," and the rationale of such priority was that it gave employees a source of money which could tide them over a certain period of unemployment following the bankruptcy of their original employer. This was not the purpose of payments to the welfare trust. Such payments were made to the trustee of the fund to be held until a terminating event, such as retirement, death, or entry into military service, occurred. The payments made from the welfare trust under these terms would not aid the employees in the interim in which they were seeking to obtain new jobs upon the bankruptcy of their former employer. Therefore, the payments due the welfare trust were not "wages" within the priority given by bankruptcy to wage earners' claims. [Joint Industry Board v United States, 391 US 224]

C. STATUS OF BANKRUPT

§ 39:17. RIGHTS AND DUTIES OF BANKRUPT. When a debtor is adjudicated a bankrupt, an important change takes place in his legal status. When he is thereafter granted a discharge, he is released of his ordinary debts. The bankruptcy act confers certain rights upon and imposes certain duties on the bankrupt.[26] If the debtor fails to cooperate or if he deceives the court as by the concealment of property which he hopes to save for himself, the law provides specific penalties, in addition to denying the bankrupt the benefits of the statute.

---

[26] § 25.

(a) Rights. The debtor has the right to object to being declared or adjudicated a bankrupt. If so adjudicated, he may request a discharge in bankruptcy. He is protected generally from arrest on civil process while within the court district on matters relating to the bankruptcy proceeding. The debtor is given an immunity from criminal prosecution based on his testimony at meetings other than at the hearing on his discharge and other than in a prosecution for perjury.

(b) Duties. The debtor is required to file statements showing the property he possesses, any claim to an exemption, and the names of his creditors, with detailed information as to their claims. He must also attend meetings of creditors and hearings before the referee and court, and answer all proper questions relating to his estate. He must examine the proofs of claim filed against him to see if he disputes them, and he must obey orders of the bankruptcy court.

§ 39:18. DISCHARGE IN BANKRUPTCY. The decree terminating the bankruptcy proceeding is generally a discharge or release of the debtor from his debts.

(a) Application for discharge. The adjudication of any individual to be a bankrupt operates automatically as an application for a discharge in bankruptcy. A corporation may file an application for a discharge within six months after it is adjudged to be a bankrupt.[27]

(b) Denial of discharge. The application for discharge will be denied if the bankrupt has: (1) committed certain offenses punishable by imprisonment as provided in the Act; (2) unjustifiably destroyed, mutilated, falsified, concealed, or failed to keep books of account or records from which his financial status and business transactions might be ascertained; (3) obtained money or property on credit for a business by a false representation in writing concerning financial condition; (4) permitted others, within a year previous to the filing of the petition, to remove, transfer, conceal, or destroy any of his property, with the intent to hinder, delay, or defraud creditors, or has been guilty of this himself; (5) been granted a discharge in bankruptcy within 6 years; (6) refused, during the proceedings, to answer any material question approved by the court, or to obey any lawful order of the court; (7) failed to explain satisfactorily the loss of any assets, or the deficiency of his assets to pay his debts; or (8) failed to pay in full the filing fees required by the bankruptcy act.[28]

A discharge in bankruptcy cannot be refused for any ground not stated in the bankruptcy act. Consequently, a discharge cannot be refused because the bankrupt was a gambler.[29]

When the debtor has obtained credit by making a false written statement as to financial condition, the claim of the creditor who extended credit

---

[27] § 32(a).
[28] § 32(c).
[29] In re Zidoff (CA7 Ill) 309 F2d 417.

in reliance on that statement is not affected by the debtor's discharge in bankruptcy if the misstatement was material and was fraudulently made.[30]

When a debtor has obtained an additional loan on the basis of a fraudulent written misrepresentation as to his financial condition, the debtor's subsequent bankruptcy discharge has no effect as to his total indebtedness.[31]

The obtaining of credit by means of a false financial statement is a bar to a discharge only when the bankrupt is engaged in business.[32] If the bankrupt is a nonbusiness debtor, such as an ordinary consumer, the false financial statement does not bar his discharge in bankruptcy but merely prevents the discharge in bankruptcy from barring the claim of the particular creditor who had extended credit.

A false financial statement does not bar a discharge in bankruptcy unless the creditor had relied thereon and had acted reasonably in so doing. If the surrounding circumstances indicated to a reasonable man that the statement may be false and that further inquiry should be made, a creditor who merely relies or claims to rely on the statement without making any further inquiry cannot raise the falsity of the statement as a bar to the debtor's discharge and the debtor will not be denied a discharge merely because he had made the false financial statement.

> **FACTS:** Kentile sold goods over an extended period to Winham. The credit relationship began without Winham's being required to furnish any financial statement. After some time, payments were not made regularly. Kentile requested a financial statement. Winham submitted a statement for the year which had then just ended. Thereafter Kentile requested a second statement. The second statement was false. Kentile continued to extend credit to Winham. Winham was later adjudicated bankrupt. Kentile objected to Winham's discharge in bankruptcy because of the false financial statement.

> **DECISION:** The false financial statement did not bar the granting of a discharge in bankruptcy because the creditor had not relied thereon before extending credit to the bankrupt. [Kentile Floors, Inc. v Winham (CA9 Ariz) 440 F2d 1128]

§ 39:19. EFFECT OF DISCHARGE. A discharge in bankruptcy releases the bankrupt from all his provable debts, except debts that:[33] (a) are due as taxes which became due and owing within the 3 years preceding bankruptcy; (b) are liabilities (1) for obtaining property by false pretenses or false representation, (2) for a loan of property obtained on credit or an extension of credit obtained by a materially false written statement by the debtor as to financial condition, (3) for willful and malicious injuries to the

---

[30] 11 USC § 35(a)(2).
[31] Budget Finance Plan v Haner, 92 Idaho 56, 436 P2d 722.
[32] 11 USC § 32(c)(3).
[33] § 35.

person or the property of another,[34] (4) for alimony for the support of a wife or child, (5) for seduction of an unmarried female, (6) for breach of promise accompanied by seduction, and (7) for criminal conversation; (c) have not been listed by the bankrupt in time to be proved, unless the creditor had notice or actual knowledge of the proceedings; (d) are created by the bankrupt's fraud, embezzlement, misappropriation, or defalcation while acting as an officer or in any fiduciary position; (e) are wages due to workmen, clerks, salesmen, or servants, which have been earned within 3 months preceding the petition; or (f) are due for moneys of an employee received or retained by the bankrupt to secure the faithful performance by such employee of the provisions of the contract of employment.

When a claim is discharged in bankruptcy, it must be ignored for all purposes. For example, when a collision damage judgment entered against the bankrupt is discharged, the judgment ceases to exist, even though in fact it has not been paid.

> **FACTS:** Perez was involved in an automobile collision. Pinkerton, the other driver, was injured; and suit was brought against Perez in a state court for personal property damage. Judgment was entered against Perez. He thereafter went into and was discharged in bankruptcy. The Pinkerton judgment was listed in the bankruptcy proceeding, and Perez was discharged by the bankruptcy court from all debts including the Pinkerton judgment. Campbell, the Superintendent of the state Motor Vehicle Division, acting in accordance with the state financial responsibility law, then suspended the operator's license of Perez and the registration of his automobile because Perez was not insured and the Pinkerton judgment had remained unsatisfied for more than 60 days. The state statute expressly specified that a discharge in bankruptcy of the unsatisfied judgment did not affect the suspension provisions of the statute. Perez claimed that the statute was unconstitutional.

> **DECISION:** The Pinkerton judgment had been discharged in bankruptcy and therefore could not be made the basis of applying a state financial responsibility law. The constitutional principle of the supremacy of federal statutes bars a state from taking any action, even for the purpose of protecting the public from the financial hardship that may result from the use of automobiles by financially irresponsible persons, when such action is inconsistent with the federal banktuptcy statute which is designed to give the debtor "a new opportunity in life . . . unhampered by preexisting debt." [Perez v Campbell, 402 US 637]

The discharge in bankruptcy does not destroy the debts but merely gives the debtor a protection from their enforcement. The order discharging the bankrupt, however, expressly declares that a judgment obtained in any other court upon a discharged claim is "null and void" and enjoins all

---

[34] A judgment based on a claim for willful and wanton negligence is within the bankruptcy exception as to "willful and malicious" claims. Bice v Jones, 45 AlaApp 709, 236 So2d 718. It is generally held that conduct which is "intentional" is "willful and malicious," although a minority of courts require proof of actual willfulness and malice. Robinson v Early, 248 CalApp2d 19, 56 CalRptr 183.

creditors of the bankrupt from bringing suit against him on such obligations.[35]

After a debtor has been discharged in bankruptcy, there are no restraints upon his activities or use of property. If he can obtain necessary capital, he can reengage in any business, including the same business in which he was engaged prior to bankruptcy. The property that he acquires subsequent to his discharge in bankruptcy cannot be reached by prebankruptcy creditors even though their claims had not been paid in full. It is immaterial in what manner the postbankruptcy property is acquired, whether as earnings, gifts, inheritance, or investment gains.

A state cannot in any way penalize a person for going through bankruptcy.

> **FACTS:** A California statute provided that the license of a contractor could be revoked if he failed to pay his debts in full by obtaining a discharge in bankruptcy. Grimes was a licensed contractor. He was adjudicated a bankrupt. Thereafter, the state licensing board revoked his contractor's license. He brought an action against the registrar of the board to compel the reissuance of his license.

> **DECISION:** Judgment for Grimes. The Bankruptcy Act is a federal statute and therefore is the supreme law of the land. Although the state had a legitimate interest in licensing contractors, the state could not impair the supremacy of the federal statute by penalizing a contractor who obtained the benefit of the federal statute. The state law was therefore unconstitutional when it forfeited Grimes' license because he had obtained the benefit of the federal bankruptcy law. [Grimes v Hoschler, 12 Cal3d 305, 115 CalRptr 625, 525 P2d 65]

§ 39:20 LIABILITY OF THIRD PERSONS AND COLLATERAL.

The fact that a debtor obtains a discharge in bankruptcy does not ordinarily bar a claimant or creditor with respect to third persons or collateral. For example, the bankruptcy of the maker of a promissory note does not discharge the liability of an indorser. Similarly, when an automobile public liability insurer is liable directly to the injured third person, that liability is not affected by the fact that the insured driver has been discharged in bankruptcy. Similarly, if a creditor has a valid security interest in collateral that was perfected more than four months before the filing of the bankruptcy petition, the creditor's security interest is not affected by the debtor's discharge in bankruptcy. Likewise, a tax lien on the bankrupt's property is not affected by the debtor's discharge.

D. BANKRUPTCY COMPOSITIONS

§ 39:21 CORPORATE REORGANIZATIONS.

The provisions for corporate reorganizations[36] permit a corporation, an indenture trustee, or 3 or more

---

[35] 11 USC § 32(f)(2).
[36] 11 USCA §§ 501 to 676, inclusive.

creditors of the corporation with certain claims amounting in the aggregate to $5,000 or over, to file a petition for a reorganization. The petition must show among other things that the corporation is insolvent or is unable to pay its debts as they mature and that relief is necessary under the statute. It may also include a proposed scheme of reorganization. The statute directs the court to confirm a plan of reorganization, provided that it is fair and that all payments made or promised are approved as reasonable.[37]

§ 39:22. ARRANGEMENTS. The provisions for arrangements permit any debtor who could become a bankrupt to file a petition for the acceptance of a plan for the settlement, satisfaction, or extension of the time of payment of his unsecured debts. The statute directs the court to confirm the plan if it is satisfied that the plan is fair, equitable, and feasible, that the debtor has done no act which would bar a discharge in bankruptcy, and that the proposal and the acceptance are made in good faith.

§ 39:23. REAL PROPERTY ARRANGEMENTS. The provisions for real property arrangements permit any debtor who could become a bankrupt, except a corporation, to file a petition for the acceptance of a plan for the alteration or the modification of the rights of creditors holding debts secured by real property or a leasehold interest of which the debtor is the legal or equitable owner. The statute stipulates that the court shall confirm a plan that is accepted by the creditors in good faith.

§ 39:24. WAGE EARNER'S PLANS. The provisions for wage earner's plans permit an individual who is insolvent or is unable to pay his debts as they mature and whose principal income is derived from salary, wages, or commissions to file a petition for the acceptance of a composition or an extension of time, or both, in view of future earnings or salary. The statute directs the court to confirm a plan that is proposed and accepted by the creditors in good faith.

QUESTIONS AND CASE PROBLEMS

1. Shelton owed money to Winthrop Sales. Shelton went into bankruptcy and was granted a discharge. Later Winthrop Sales sued Shelton although its claim against him had been discharged in bankruptcy. Shelton did not raise any defense with respect to the bankruptcy discharge. A judgment was entered against him. Shelton, on appeal, claimed that the bankruptcy discharge prevented the suit against him. Decide. [Winthrop Sales Corp. v Shelton (MoApp) 389 SW2d 70]

---

[37] SEC v United States Realty and Improvement Co. 310 US 434.

2. A Utah statute provided for the revocation of an operator's license if he failed to pay a judgment entered against him because of his negligent operation of an automobile. Kesler's license was revoked under this statute. He thereafter went into bankruptcy and the judgment was discharged. He then claimed that his state license should be restored. The Utah Department of Public Safety refused to restore the license because the Utah statute expressly provided that the revocation of the license shall not be affected by a subsequent discharge in bankruptcy. Kesler claimed that the Utah statute was unconstitutional on the theory that it conflicted with the bankruptcy power of the national government. Decide. [Kesler v Department of Public Safety, 369 US 153]

3. Putman, as executrix of the estate of Fred Putman, obtained a judgment for $10,000 against the Ocean Shore Railway Co. for negligently causing the death of Putman. She and two others filed a petition in bankruptcy against Folger, who had a statutory liability for the debts of the railway corporation. In opposing the petition, he contended that the claim of Mrs. Putman was not a provable debt in bankruptcy. Do you agree? [In re Putman (DC ND Cal) 193 F 464]

4. De Shazo owed the Household Finance Corporation $349.02. In order to borrow additional money, he submitted a false statement to Household as to the total amount of his debts. Household, relying on this false statement, loaned him $150.98 more and had him sign one note for $500, representing both the unpaid balance of the old loan and the total amount of the new loan. Thereafter De Shazo was discharged in bankruptcy. What effect did the discharge have on the note held by Household Finance and listed in the bankrupt's schedule of indebtedness? [Household Finance Corp. of Seattle v De Shazo, 57 Wash 771, 359 P2d 1044]

5. An involuntary petition in bankruptcy was filed against a merchant doing business in a building leased from Abbot. On the same day a receiver was appointed, and he took possession of the store and the stock of goods. In an action brought by Abbot upon a claim connected with the possession of the building by the receiver, a question arose as to whether the receiver was vested with title to the bankrupt's assets. What is your opinion? [In re Rubel (DC ED Wis) 166 F 131]

6. At the instigation of Perry, trustee in bankruptcy of Martin, the court directed a referee to decide the validity of claims made by several claimants to a gas and oil leasehold in which the bankrupt had some interest. Chandler and other claimants opposed the proceeding on the ground that the referee did not have power to hear and decide such a question and that it was for a bankruptcy court to decide. Was this contention sound? [Chandler v Perry (CCA5 Tex) 74 F2d 371]

7. Certain creditors filed a petition in bankruptcy against the Percy Ford Co. An adjudication of bankruptcy followed. At the time of the filing of the petition, the National Shawmut Bank held four notes upon which the bankrupt was absolutely liable, but the notes were not then due and payable. The bank contended that the notes constituted provable debts. Do you agree? [In re Percy Ford Co. (DC D Mass) 199 F 334]

AGENCY—
CREATION AND
TERMINATION

A. NATURE OF THE AGENCY RELATIONSHIP

§ 40:1. DEFINITION. One of the most common legal relationships is that of agency. When it exists, one person can act for and can stand in the place of another. *Agency* is a relation based upon an express or implied agreement whereby one person, the *agent*, is authorized to act under the control of and for another, his *principal*, in making contracts with third persons.[1] The acts of the agent obligate the principal to third persons and give the principal rights against the third persons.

Agency is based upon the consent of the parties and, for that reason, it is called a contractual relation. If consideration is present, the relationship is also contractual. The law sometimes imposes an agency relationship.

The term "agency" is frequently used with other meanings. It is sometimes used to denote the fact that one has the right to sell certain products, such as when a dealer is said to possess an automobile agency. In other instances the term is used to mean an exclusive right to sell certain articles within a given territory. In these cases, however, the dealer is not an agent in the sense of representing the manufacturer. The right of the dealer under such arrangements is frequently represented by a franchise which he purchases from the manufacturer or supplier.

§ 40:2. AGENT DISTINGUISHED.

(a) Employees and independent contractors. An agent is distinguished from an ordinary employee, who is not hired to represent the employer in dealings with third persons. It is possible, however, for the same person to be both an agent and an employee. For example, the driver of a milk

---

[1] Restatement, Agency, 2d § 1; Rule v Jones, 256 Wis 102, 40 NW2d 580. When the question is the tax liability of an enterprise (see Boise Cascade Corp. v Washington, 3 WashApp 78, 473 P2d 429), the definition of agency may be different that when the question is contract or tort liability, which are the areas of law considered in this part.

delivery truck is an agent, as well as an employee,[2] in making contracts between the milk company and its customers, but he is only an employee with respect to the work of delivering milk.

An agent or employee differs from an *independent contractor* in that the principal or employer has control and can direct an agent or an employee, but the other party to the contract does not have control over the performance of the work by an independent contractor.

A person who appears to be an independent contractor may in fact be so controlled by the other contracting party that he is regarded as the agent of the latter. For example, when all the management decisions of a franchisee are made by the franchisor, the franchisee is held to be the agent of the franchisor, with the consequence that third persons dealing with the franchisee may assert against the franchisor the typical claims of third persons against a principal, as against the contention that the franchisee was an independent contractor and that it alone was liable for such claims as customers of the franchisee might possess.

The fact that the person contracting with a contractor reserves the right to inspect the work or that the owner's architect has the right to require a redoing of work that does not meet contract specifications does not give such control over the independent contractor as to make him merely an employee. That is, the reservation of power to determine and insure compliance with the terms of the contract does not constitute control of how the work is to be done.[3]

A person may be an independent contractor generally but an agent with respect to a particular transaction. Thus, an "agency" or a "broker" rendering personal services to customers is ordinarily an independent contractor, but he may be the agent of a customer when the rendition of a service involves making a contract on behalf of the customer with a third person.

Likewise, when a group policy of insurance covered the employees of an employer, the employer was the "agent" of the insurer with respect to the handling of applications for group insurance and the sending of premiums, although its ordinary status was that of employer.[4]

The fact that an agreement does or does not call a person an agent or an independent contractor is ignored in determining whether the person is an agent or an independent contractor.[5]

(b) Real estate brokers. In many cases, a real estate broker is merely a middleman who seeks to locate a buyer or seller for his client. In such a case, the broker is not an agent because he does not have authority to make a contract with a third person that will bind his client.

(c) Bailees. When personal property is delivered to another under an agreement that the property will be returned to the deliveror or transferred

---

[2] In business practice, all employed persons, regardless of the nature of the work performed or the services rendered, are considered as employees.
[3] Lipka v United States (CA2 NY) 369 F2d 288.
[4] Weeks v Pilot Life Insurance Co. 256 SC 81, 180 SE2d 875.
[5] Rust Engineering Co. v Alabama (Ala) 234 So2d 695.

to a third person, a bailment arises. The person to whom the property is delivered, the bailee, is not an agent because he has no authority to make any contract on behalf of the bailor.

Situations commonly arise, however, in which the same person is both an agent and a bailee. When a salesman is loaned a company car, he is a bailee with respect to the car; but with respect to making sales contracts, he is an agent.

(d) Required act. The mere fact that one person requires another person to do an act does not make the latter person the agent of the former. For example, when a bank directs a borrower to obtain the signature of another person in order to obtain a bank loan, the borrower is not the agent of the bank in contacting the other person and procuring his signature.[6]

§ 40:3. PURPOSE OF AGENCY. Usually an agency may be created to perform any act which the principal himself could lawfully do. The object of the agency may not be criminal, nor may it be contrary to public policy.

However, some acts must be performed by a person himself and cannot be entrusted or delegated to an agent. Voting, swearing to the truth of documents, testifying in court, and making a will are instances where personal action is required. In the preparation of a document, however, it is proper to employ someone else to prepare the paper which is then signed or sworn to by the employing party. Various forms that are required by statute, such as applications for licenses and tax returns, will in some instances expressly authorize the execution of such forms by an agent as long as the identities of both principal and agent and the latter's representative capacity are clearly shown.

§ 40:4. WHO MAY BE A PRINCIPAL. Any person, if he is competent to act for himself, may act through an agent. An appointment of an agent by a person lacking capacity is generally regarded as void or voidable to the same extent that a contract made by such person would be. Thus, a minor may act through an agent, and a resulting contract will be voidable to the same extent as though made by the minor.

Groups of persons may also appoint agents to act for them.

§ 40:5. WHO MAY BE AN AGENT. Since a contract made by an agent is in law the contract of the principal, it is immaterial whether or not the agent has legal capacity to make a contract for himself. It is permissible to employ as agents aliens, minors, and others who are under a natural or legal disability.

FACTS: An automobile was owned by Peterson. He gave possession of the car to his son, Edward, and Edward's wife, Gloria, but retained the title to the car. Edward's daughter, Christine, was 16 and was driving the car to the city at Gloria's direction in order to buy her younger sister a pair of shoes. Because of Christine's negligent driving, the car struck Johnson who was riding a motorcycle. He sued Christine's mother.

---

[6] First National Bank v Caro Construction Co., Inc. 211 Kan 678, 508 P2d 516.

DECISION: Judgment for Johnson. Christine was acting as agent for her mother who was therefore liable for Christine's negligence. [Johnson v Peterson, 38 CalApp3d 619, 113 CalRptr 445]

While ordinarily an agent is one person acting for another, an agent may be a partnership or a corporation.

§ 40:6. CLASSIFICATION OF AGENTS.

A *general agent* is authorized by the principal to transact all of his affairs in connection with a particular kind of business or trade, or to transact all of his business at a certain place. To illustrate, a person who is appointed as manager by the owner of a store is a general agent.

A *special agent* is authorized by the principal to handle a definite business transaction or to do a specific act. One who is authorized by another to purchase a particular house for him is a special agent.

A *universal agent* is authorized by the principal to do all acts that can be delegated lawfully to representatives. This form of agency arises when a person in the military service gives another person a "blanket" power of attorney to do anything that must be done while he is in the service.

§ 40:7. AGENCY COUPLED WITH AN INTEREST.

An agent has an *interest in the authority* when he has given a consideration or has paid for the right to exercise the authority granted to him. To illustrate, when a lender, in return for making a loan of money, is given, as security, authority to collect rents due to the borrower and to apply those rents to the payment of the debt owed him, the lender becomes the borrower's agent with an interest in the authority given him to collect the rents.[7]

An agent has an *interest in the subject matter* when for a consideration he is given an interest in the property with which he is dealing. Hence, when the agent is authorized to sell certain property of the principal and is given a lien on such property as security for a debt owed to him by the principal, the agent has an interest in the subject matter.

B. CREATING THE AGENCY

§ 40:8. AUTHORIZATION BY APPOINTMENT.

The usual method of creating an agency is by express authorization, that is, a person is appointed to act for and on behalf of another.

In most instances the authorization of the agent may be oral. Some appointments, however, must be made in a particular way. A majority of the states, by statute, require the appointment of an agent to be in writing when the agency is created to acquire or dispose of any interest in land. A written authorization of agency is called a *power of attorney*.

Ordinarily no agency arises from the fact of co-ownership of property or of relationship of the parties. Consequently, when a check was made payable to the order of husband and wife, it was necessary for each to

---

[7] Halloran-Judge Trust Co. v Heath, 70 Utah 124, 258 P 342.

indorse the check because there was no agency by which the husband could indorse the name of his wife and deposit the money in his own account.[8]

§ 40:9. AUTHORIZATION BY CONDUCT.

(a) **Principal's conduct as to agent.** Since agency is created by the consent of the parties, any conduct, including words, that gives the agent reason to believe that the principal consents to his acting as agent is sufficient to create an agency. If one person, knowingly and without objection, permits another to act as his agent, the law will find in his conduct an expression of authorization to the agent, and the principal will not be permitted to deny that the agent was in fact authorized. Thus, if the owner of a hotel allows another person to assume the duties of hotel clerk, that person may infer from the owner's conduct that he has authority to act as the hotel clerk.

(b) **Principal's conduct as to third persons.** The principal may have such dealing with third persons as to cause them to believe that the "agent" has authority. Thus, if the owner of a store places another person in charge, third persons may assume that the person in charge is the agent for the owner in that respect. The "agent" then appears to be authorized and is said to have *apparent authority*, and the principal is estopped or prevented from contradicting the appearance that he has created.

When a franchisor permits the franchisee to do business under the name of a franchisor, the latter is estopped from denying that the franchisee has authority to make customary contracts, such as a contract for advertising, and to bind the franchisor by such contracts.

FACTS: Paul's Opticians did business in Duluth, Minnesota. Paul's obtained a franchise from the Plymouth Optical Co. to do business under that name. Paul's did so for more than three years—advertised under that name, paid bills with checks bearing the name of Plymouth Optical Co., and listed itself in the telephone and city directories by that name. Paul's contracted with the Duluth Herald and News Tribune for advertising, making the contract in the name of Plymouth Optical Co. When the advertising bill was not paid, the Duluth Herald sued Plymouth Optical for payment.

DECISION: Plymouth was liable. Paul's had apparent authority to make the contract in the name of Plymouth Optical Co. After having permitted Paul's to do business in the manner described for three years, Plymouth was estopped to deny that Paul's had authority to make the advertising contract on its behalf. [Duluth Herald and News Tribune v Plymouth Optical Co. 286 Minn 495, 176 NW2d 552]

The term "apparent authority" is used only when there is merely the appearance of authority but no actual authority, and the appearance of authority of the agent must be caused by the acts of the principal. This apparent authority extends to all acts that a person of ordinary prudence, familiar with business usages and the particular business, would be justified in assuming that the agent has authority to perform.

---

[8] Glasser v Columbia Federal Savings and Loan Ass'n (Fla) 197 So2d 6.

The mere placing of property in the possession of another person does not give him either actual or apparent authority to sell the property.[9]

While it is essential to the concept of apparent authority that the third person reasonably believes that the agent has authority, the converse is not to be implied. That is, the mere fact that a third person believes someone has an agent's authority does not give rise to authority or to apparent authority.

Any person may be clothed with apparent authority. Not only an existing employee or agent who exceeds his actual authority but also a third person who is independent of the alleged principal and has no authority at all.

> **FACTS:** The Rockford Carriage House ran a restaurant, and made purchases from the Milwaukee Cheese Company. The Milwaukee salesman would stop in the restaurant and receive orders from its manager or, in his absence, from the chef. Rockford made a contract with Food Service under which Food Service was to manage the restaurant and was to order and pay for what was needed. Milwaukee was not expressly informed that Food Service was to pay for food but one of the Rockford shareholders told a Milwaukee salesman that the restaurant was under new management. Milwaukee delivered goods on credit to Food Service. When payment was not made, Milwaukee sued Rockford for payment. Rockford raised the defense that Food Service was an independent contractor and that Rockford was not liable on contracts which Food Service had made.

> **DECISION:** Judgment for Milwaukee. The statement that the restaurant was "under new management" did not expressly show that there was any change in the relationship between the corporation and the restaurant. Thus, the restaurant was clothed with apparent authority to purchase on the credit of Rockford as had been done in the past. [Milwaukee Cheese Co. v Rockford Carriage House, Inc. (IllApp2d) 271 NE2d 670]

(c) Acquiesence by principal. The conduct of the principal that gives rise to the agent's authority may be acquiescence in or failing to object to acts done by the purported or apparent agent over a period of time. For example, a person collecting payments on a note and remitting the proper amounts to the holder of the note will be regarded as the latter's agent for collection when this conduct has been followed over a period of years without objection.[10]

Where the drawer's employee drew checks to herself for fourteen months which were debited to the drawer's account and no complaint was made by him, this lack of objection was in effect a communication to the bank that the employee had the authority to draw the checks in question.

No question can be raised as to whether a person signing as an agent was authorized to do so when the parties have been following the contract for six years after its signing by the apparent agent.[11]

---

[9] Brunette v Idaho Veneer Co. 86 Idaho 193, 384 P2d 233. Although under Uniform Commercial Code, § 2-403, if the entrustee deals in goods of that kind, he has the power but not the right to transfer title to a person buying in good faith in the ordinary course of business.

[10] Holsclaw v Catalina Savings & Loan Association, 13 ArizApp 362, 476 P2d 883.

[11] Feary v Aaron Burglar Alarm, Inc. 32 CalApp3d 553, 108 CalRptr 242.

§ **40:10. AGENCY BY RATIFICATION.** An agent may attempt on behalf of the principal to do an act which he has not been authorized to do. Or a person who is not the agent of another may attempt to act as his agent. Ordinarily a person can ratify any unauthorized act done on his behalf which he could have authorized. The effect is the same as though he had authorized the act in the first place.

When the principal ratifies the act of an unauthorized person purporting to be his authorized agent, such ratification releases the agent from any liability which he would otherwise have as to third persons because of a breach of an implied warranty of authority and from any liability which he may have as to the principal ratifying his act.

Initially, ratification is a question of intention. Just as in the case of authorization, where there is the question of whether or not the principal authorized the agent, so there is the question of whether or not the principal intended to approve or ratify the action of the agent. Ratification may thus be found in conduct indicating an intention to ratify, such as paying for goods ordered by the agent.[12]

Ratification of an earlier loan transaction is shown when the principal executes a renewal note and papers which make an extension of the earlier loan.

FACTS: Holbrook applied to Doxey-Layton Co. for a 20-year loan. The transaction was handled by Doxey's loan officer, Teerlink. Holbrook signed a note and mortgage papers in blank. Apparently the long-term loan could not be obtained, and Teerlink filled in the papers which Holbrook had signed to show a one-year loan. When the loan was due at the end of the year, Holbrook gave Doxey a renewal note for the amount of the debt. He later gave Doxey three other renewal notes. When Doxey sued on the loan, Holbrook claimed that Teerlink did not have any authority to fill in the blanks to show a one-year loan.

DECISION: Judgment for Doxey. It was immaterial whether Teerlink had been authorized by Holbrook to fill in the blanks to show a one-year loan, because Holbrook's subsequent execution of renewal notes with knowledge that the loan was a short-term loan ratified the act of Teerlink in filling in the papers to show a one-year loan. [Doxey-Layton Co. v Holbrook, 25 Utah2d 194, 479 P2d 348]

If the other requirements of ratification are satisfied, a principal ratifies an agent's acts when, with knowledge of the act, he accepts or retains the benefit of the act, or brings an action to enforce legal rights based upon the act [13] or defends an action by asserting the existence of a right based on the unauthorized transaction, or fails to repudiate the agent's act within a reasonable time. The receipt, acceptance, and deposit of a check by the principal with knowledge that it arises from an unauthorized transaction is a common illustration of ratification of the unauthorized transaction by conduct.

---

[12] Southwestern Portland Cement v Beavers, 82 NMex 218, 478 P2d 546.
[13] Mattila v Olsevick, 228 Ore 606, 365 P2d 1072.

(a) Conditions for ratification. In addition to the intent to ratify, expressed in some instances with certain formality, the following conditions must be satisfied in order that the intention take effect as a ratification:

(1) The agent must have purported to act on behalf of the principal.[14] If the person without authority informed the other person that he was acting as agent for the principal, this requirement is satisfied.

(2) The principal must have been capable of authorizing the act both at the time of the act and at the time when ratified.

(3) A principal must ratify the entire act of the agent.

(4) The principal must ratify the act before the third person withdraws. If the third person brings an action against the agent because of lack of authority to make the contract, the bringing of the action is equivalent to a withdrawal that prevents the principal from thereafter ratifying the contract.

(5) The act to be ratified must generally be legal.

(6) The principal must have full knowledge of all material facts.[15] If the agent conceals a material fact, the ratification of the principal made in ignorance of such fact is not binding. Of course, there can be no ratification when the principal does not know of the making of the contract by his agent. Consequently, when the owner's agent and a contractor made unauthorized major changes to an installation contract without the knowledge of the principal, the fact that the principal had no knowledge of the matter barred any claim that he had ratified the act of his agent.

FACTS: Kirk Reid Co. made a contract to install an air conditioning and heating system in a building owned by Fine. Construction work was under the "general supervision" of Oliver and Smith, architects, and Hart, an independent engineer. The contract of Fine with the architects and engineer expressly stated that they were to supervise construction and could only authorize minor changes in the construction contract. Because of difficulties encountered in the performance of the contract, the architects and engineers agreed with Kirk to certain major changes in the construction plans which increased the cost of performance. When Kirk demanded payment from Fine of this additional amount, Fine refused to pay on the ground that, since no one had authority to modify the original contract, Kirk was not entitled to any additional payment.

DECISION: Fine was not liable for the additional expense. He had not authorized the major contract changes which necessitated the additional expense and since he did not have any knowledge of the changes that had been made, he could not be deemed to have ratified them. [Kirk Reid Co. v Fine, 205 Va 778, 139 SE2d 829]

It is not always necessary, however, to show that the principal had actual knowledge; for knowledge will be imputed to him if he knows of such other facts as would put a prudent man on inquiry, or if that knowledge can

---

[14] State ex rel Olsen v Sundling, 128 Mont 596, 281 P2d 499.
[15] Pacific Trading Co. v Sun Insurance Office, 140 Ore 314, 13 P2d 616.

be inferred from the knowledge of other facts or from a course of business. Knowledge is likewise not an essential factor when the principal has indicated that he does not care to know the details and is willing to be bound by the contract regardless of his lack of knowledge.

(b) **Circumstances not affecting ratification.** Ratification is not affected by the fact (1) that the third person has not agreed again to the transaction after it has been ratified; (2) that the principal first repudiated but then changed his mind and ratified the transaction, provided the third party had not withdrawn prior to the ratification; (3) that the agent would be liable to the third person for breach of the warranty of his authority or misrepresentation if the principal were not bound; (4) that the agent or the third person knew the agent was unauthorized; (5) that the agent died or lost capacity prior to the ratification; or (6) that the principal did not communicate his ratifying intent to the third person.

§ **40:11. AGENCY BY OPERATION OF LAW.** In certain instances the courts, influenced by necessity or social desirability, create or find an agency when there is none. For example, a wife may purchase necessaries and charge them to her husband's account when he does not supply them. Here the social policy is the furtherance of the welfare of the neglected wife. The services of an employment agency rendered to a wife have been held not to constitute necessaries, however, so that the husband cannot be held liable therefor on the theory that his wife was his agent by operation of law.[16]

As another example of agency by operation of law, a minor may purchase necessaries upon the credit of his father when the latter fails to supply them. If the minor is already adequately supplied by the father, the mother cannot make additional purchases or contracts and charge the father, even though this could have been done if the minor had not been already adequately provided for by the father.

FACTS: Watkins was divorced, and custody of his young daughter was granted to him. Watkins sent her to a dentist, Dr. Burrell. On days on which the child was visiting her mother, the mother sent her to another dentist, Dr. Fuller. The latter's bill was not paid, and he assigned it to the Medical & Dental Finance Bureau, which then sued the father for the dentist bill, on the ground that it was a necessary.

DECISION: Judgment for Watkins. The fact that the dentistry work was a necessary did not impose liability on the father unless he had neglected to provide for such work. As he had so provided and the mother had chosen to have a different dentist, the situation was not that of an abandoning father and an agency could not arise by operation of law. [Watkins v Medical & Dental Finance Bureau, 101 Ariz 580, 422 P2d 696]

An emergency power of an agent to act under unusual circumstances not covered by his authority is recognized when the agent is unable to communicate with the principal and failure to act will cause the principal substantial loss.

---

[16] Approved Personnel Service v Dallas (TexCivApp) 358 SW2d 150.

§ 40:12. **PROVING THE AGENCY RELATIONSHIP.** The burden of proving the existence of an agency relationship rests upon the person who seeks to benefit by such proof. The third person who desires to bind the principal because of the act of an alleged agent has the burden of proving that the latter person was in fact the authorized agent of the principal and possessed the authority to do the act in question. For example, when the buyer asserts that there has been a breach of an express warranty made by the seller's agent, the buyer must establish that there was an actual or apparent authority to make the warranty. In the absence of sufficient proof, the jury must find that there is no agency. The authority of the agent may be established by circumstantial evidence.

C. TERMINATION OF AGENCY

§ 40:13. TERMINATION BY ACT OF PARTIES.

(a) **Expiration of agency contract.** The ordinary agency may expire by the terms of the contract creating it. Thus, the contract may provide that it shall last for a stated period, as five years, or until a particular date arrives, or until the happening of a particular event, such as the sale of certain property. In such a case, the agency is automatically terminated when the specified date arrives or the event on which it is to end occurs. When one appoints another to represent him in his business affairs while he is away, the relation ends upon the return of the principal.[17]

When it is provided that the agency shall last for a stated period of time, it terminates upon the expiration of that period without regard to whether the acts contemplated by the creation of the agency have been performed. If no period is stated, the agency continues for a reasonable time, but it may be terminated at the will of either party.

(b) **Agreement.** Since the agency relation is based upon consent, it can be terminated by the consent of the principal and agent.

(c) **Option of a party.** An agency agreement may provide that upon the giving of notice or the payment of a specified sum of money, one party may terminate the relationship.

(d) **Revocation by principal.** The relationship between principal and agent is terminated whenever the principal discharges the agent even though the agency was stated to be "irrevocable."[18] If the agency was not created for a specified time but was to exist only at will, or if the agent has been guilty of misconduct, the principal may discharge the agent without liability of the principal.

Expressions of dissatisfaction with the work of an agent do not constitute a revocation of his authority. The intent to revoke must be clearly and unequivocally expressed.

---

[17] Freed Finance Co. v Preece, 14 Utah2d 409, 385 P2d 156.
[18] Shumaker v Hazen (Okla) 372 P2d 873.

FACTS: Kinmon owned a summer home which he wanted to sell at auction. He employed the J.P. King Auction Company to make the sale. Kinmon complained about the efforts made by King. King sold the property to the highest bidder for $35,000. Kinmon had expected twice that much and refused to convey title to the buyer or to pay commissions to King. King sued Kinmon to collect the commissions. Kinmon raised the defense that he had revoked King's authority to sell the property.

DECISION: Judgment for King. His authority had not been revoked by Kinmon. The mere expression of dissatisfaction with the work of an agent does not constitute a revocation of his authority. The intent to revoke must be clearly and unequivocally expressed. As there was no such clear expression, the authority of the agent continued and he was therefore entitled to compensation for his services. [Kinmon v J.P. King Auction Co., Inc. 290 Ala 323, 276 So2d 569]

Any conduct which manifests an intent to revoke the authority is sufficient, as when the principal takes back from the agent the property which had been entrusted to him for the purpose of the agency or retains another agent to do what the original agent had been authorized to do.

When the agency is based upon a contract to employ the agent for a specified period of time, the principal is liable to the agent for damages if the principal wrongfully discharges the agent. The fact that the principal is liable for damages does not, however, prevent the principal from terminating the agency by discharging the agent. In such a case it is said that the principal has the power to terminate the agency by discharging the agent but he does not have the right to do so.

(e) Renunciation by agent. The agency relationship is terminated if the agent refuses to continue to act as agent, or when he abandons the object of the agency and acts for himself in committing a fraud upon the principal.

If the relationship is an agency at will, the agent has the right as well as the power to renounce or abandon the agency at any time. In addition, he has the right of renunciation of the relationship in any case if the principal is guilty of making wrongful demands upon him or of other misconduct.

If, however, the agency is based upon a contract calling for the continuation of the relationship for a specified or determinable period, that is, until a particular date arrives or a certain event occurs, the agent has no right to abandon or renounce the relationship when the principal is not guilty of wrong.

When the renunciation by the agent is wrongful, the agent is liable to the principal for the damages that the principal sustains.

(f) Rescission. The agency contract may be terminated by rescission to the same extent that any other contract may be so terminated.[19]

§ 40:14. TERMINATION BY OPERATION OF LAW.

(a) Death. The death of either the principal or agent ordinarily terminates the authority of an agent automatically even though the death is

---

[19] Cutcliffe v Chestnut, 122 GaApp 195, 176 SE2d 607.

unknown to the other. Some state statutes provide that the death of the principal is not a revocation until the agent has notice nor as to third persons who deal with the agent in good faith and are ignorant of the death. Generally, however, these statutes are limited to principals who are members of the armed forces.

FACTS: Julius Stalting had a notary public prepare two deeds, but he left blank the name of the person to receive the property. He executed the deeds but did not fill in the blanks and then left the deeds with the notary public. Subsequently Stalting died. After his death the notary public inserted the names of grandchildren of Stalting. The sons of Stalting brought an action to have the two deeds set aside.

DECISION: Judgment for the sons. The notary public, in filling in the deeds was attempting to act as the agent for Stalting. As the latter was dead when the notary public filled in the blanks, the notary public's act was void. The death of Stalting terminated any agency powers that the notary public had. [Stalting v Stalting, 52 SD 318, 217 NW 390]

The fact that a contract of agency is terminated by death does not impose any liability for damages even though the contract has not been completed. In an attorney-client relationship the death of the client does not terminate the agency if the client had expressly agreed that the attorney should conduct the proceeding to its conclusion.[20]

(b) Insanity. The insanity of either the principal or agent ordinarily terminates the agent's authority. If the incapacity of the principal is only temporary, the agent's authority may be merely suspended rather than terminated.

(c) Bankruptcy. Bankruptcy of the principal or agent usually terminates the relationship. It is generally held, however, that the bankruptcy of an agent does not terminate his power to deal with goods of the principal that are in his possession.

Insolvency, as distinguished from a formal adjudication of bankruptcy, usually does not terminate the agency. In most states, accordingly, the authority of an agent is not terminated by the appointment of a receiver for the principal's financial affairs.[21]

(d) Impossibility. The authority of an agent is terminated when it is impossible to perform the agency for any reason, such as the destruction of the subject matter of the agency, the death or loss of capacity of the third person with whom the agent is to contract, or a change in law that makes it impossible to perform the agency lawfully.

(e) War. When the country of the principal and that of the agent are at war, the authority of the agent is usually terminated or at least suspended

---

[20] Jones v Miller (CA3 Pa) 203 F2d 131.
[21] Chilletti v Missouri, Kansas & Texas Railway Co. 102 Kan 297, 171 P 14.

until peace is restored. When the war has the effect of making performance impossible, the agency is, of course, terminated. For example, the authority of an agent who is a nonresident enemy alien to sue is terminated because such an alien is not permitted to sue.

(f) Unusual events or changes of circumstances. The view is also held that the authority of an agent is terminated by the occurrence of an unusual event or a change in value or business conditions of such a nature that the agent should reasonably infer that the principal would not desire the agent to continue to act under the changed circumstances. For example, an agent employed to sell land at a specified price should regard his authority to sell at that price as terminated when the value of the land increases greatly because of the discovery of oil on the land.

§ 40:15. TERMINATION OF AGENCY COUPLED WITH AN INTEREST.

If the agency is coupled with an interest in the authority, the agency cannot be terminated by the act of the principal. The Restatement of the Law of Agency adopts the rule that the principal's death does not terminate such an agency. In some states, however, it is held to be terminated by his death.

An agency coupled with an interest in the authority is not revoked by the death of the agent.

When the agency is coupled with an interest in the subject matter, the principal cannot terminate the agency nor is it terminated or affected by the death of insanity of either the principal or the agent.

§ 40:16. EFFECT OF TERMINATION OF AUTHORITY.

If the agency is revoked by the principal, the authority to act for the principal is not terminated until notice of revocation is given to or received by the agent. As between the principal and agent, the right of the agent to bind his principal to third persons generally ends immediately upon the termination of his authority. Such termination is effective without the giving of notice to third persons.

When the agency is terminated by the act of the principal, notice must be given to third persons. If such notice is not given, the agent may have the power to make contracts that will bind the principal and third persons. This rule is predicated on the theory that a known agent will have the appearance of still being the agent unless notice to the contrary is given to third persons.

FACTS: Record owned a farm that was operated by his agent, Berry, who lived on the farm. The latter hired Wagner to bale the hay in 1953 and told him to bill Record for this work. Wagner did so and was paid by Record. By the summer of 1954, the agency had been terminated by Record but Berry remained in possession as tenant of the farm and nothing appeared changed. In 1954 Berry asked Wagner to bale the hay the same as in the prior year and bill Record for the work. He did so, but Record refused to pay on the ground that Berry was not then his agent. Wagner sued him.

DECISION: Judgment for Wagner. As the agency of Berry had been terminated by the voluntary action of the principal, it was necessary that notice of termination be given to third persons who had dealt with the agent. Since this had not been done, the agent continued to appear to have authority to bind the principal, and he therefore could do so in spite of the actual termination of the authority. [Record v Wagner, 100 NH 419, 128 A2d 921]

When the law requires the giving of notice in order to end the power of the agent to bind the principal, individual notice must be given or mailed to all persons who had prior dealings with the agent or the principal. Notice to the general public can be given by publishing a statement that the agency had been terminated in a newspaper of general circulation in the affected geographical area.

If a notice is actually received, the power of the agent is terminated without regard to whether the method of giving notice had been proper. Conversely, if proper notice is given, it is immaterial that it did not actually come to the attention of the party notified. Thus, a member of the general public cannot claim that the principal is bound to him on the ground that the third person did not see the newspaper notice stating that the agent's authority had been terminated.

QUESTIONS AND CASE PROBLEMS

1. What is the objective of each of the following rules of law?
   (a) The burden of proving the existence of an agency relationship rests upon the person who seeks to benefit by such proof.
   (b) If a principal fails to notify third persons when he terminates the agency, his agent may continue to make contracts that are binding on the principal.
2. A daughter was using the family car to buy sweet corn for the family from a roadside stand. When she collided with another driver, the latter claimed that the former was the father's agent and that the father was liable for her tort. Was she the agent of her father? [See Grimes v Labreck, 108 NH 26, 226 A2d 787]
3. Whitehead had a policy of hospital insurance. The authority of the agent who had "sold" him the policy and to whom Whitehead paid premiums was terminated by the insurance company, but Whitehead was never notified of this fact. He continued to pay premiums to the former agent. When Whitehead told a hospital that he had an insurance policy, the company confirmed this statement and admitted that the policy was in force. Thereafter the insurer refused to pay any hospital bills on the ground that the former agent to whom premium payments were made had no authority to receive the payments. Was the insurer liable? [American Casualty Co. v Whitehead (Miss) 206 So2d 838]

4. Through his agent, Davis, Fieschko executed a written agreement to sell his real estate to Herlich. The agreement had been negotiated by Dykstra as Herlich's agent. The contract for the purchase of the land was signed by Dykstra as the agent for Herlich. Thereafter Herlich sent a check for the down payment to Davis. The check did not contain any reference to the sale or terms of the sale. Herlich did not go through with the sale and, when sued for breach of the contract, he argued that he was not bound by the contract since he had not signed it and Dykstra had not been authorized in writing to sign it. Fieschko claimed that Herlich had ratified the contract when he sent the check for the down payment. Decide. [Fieschko v Herlich, 32 IllApp2d 280, 177 NE2d 376]

5. Coffin had a liability and property damage insurance policy on his automobile issued by the Farm Bureau Mutual Insurance Co. He purchased a new automobile and wanted to transfer the insurance. He phoned the home office of the insurance company, stated his request, and was transferred to two different girls who each stated that she did not have authority to make such a transfer and finally connected him with Pierson. Coffin stated to Pierson that he wanted to transfer his existing insurance and also to add comprehensive and collision coverage. Pierson told him that the new car was insured as requested from that moment on. Coffin had an accident in his car the next day before any change had been made in his policy. He sued the insurance company, which defended on the ground that no change had ever been made and that Pierson was merely a typing supervisor in the auto underwriters' department who had no authority to make any policy change. Was the new car covered by insurance? [Farm Bureau Mutual Insurance Company v Coffin, 136 IndApp 12, 186 NE2d 180]

6. Fishbaugh employed Scheibenberger to run a farm for him. Scheibenberger was authorized to rent the farm, to collect the rent, to superintend and direct repairs, and to allow the tenant to sell corn for the payment of taxes and fencing. The agent leased the farm to Hinsley, who sold certain crops to Spunaugle. Fishbaugh sued Spunaugle for the value of these crops. The decision turned on whether Scheibenberger was a general agent. What is your opinion? [Fishbaugh v Spunaugle, 118 Iowa 337, 92 NW 58]

PRINCIPAL AND AGENT

A. AGENT'S AUTHORITY

§ 41:1. SCOPE OF AGENT'S AUTHORITY.

(a) Express authority. If the principal tells the agent to perform a certain act, the agent has *express authority* to do so. Express authority can be indicated by conduct as well as by words. Accordingly, when the agent informs the principal of his intended plans and the principal makes no objection to them, authorization may be indicated by such silence.

(b) Incidental authority. An agent has implied *incidental authority* to perform any act reasonably necessary to execute the express authority given to him. To illustrate, if the principal authorizes the agent to purchase goods without furnishing funds to the agent to pay for them, the agent has implied incidental authority to purchase the goods on credit.

(c) Customary authority. An agent has implied *customary authority* to do any act which, according to the custom of the community, usually accompanies the transaction for which he is authorized to act as agent. For example, an agent who has express authority to receive payments from third persons has implied authority to issue receipts.[1]

One authorized to act as general manager has the power to make any contract necessary for the usual and ordinary conduct of business.

An agent with express authority to receive checks in payment does not have implied authority to cash them. An employee's authority to indorse checks payable to an employer does not embrace authority to indorse and deposit those checks into the employee's personal bank account. Authorization to a lawyer to settle a client's claim does not authorize the lawyer to indorse the client's name on a check given in settlement of the claim.

An agent does not have incidental or customary power to release or compromise debts owed to his principal or to settle disputed amounts of

---

[1] Degen v Acme Brick Co. 228 Ark 1054, 312 SW2d 194.

debts for smaller sums, even though he is designated as the "field representative" of the principal.

(d) Apparent authority. A person has apparent authority as an agent when the principal by his words or conduct reasonably leads a third party to believe that such a person has that authority.

The mere possession of property of another does not give rise to any apparent authority of the possessor to act with respect to the property.

§ 41:2. EFFECT OF PROPER EXERCISE OF AUTHORITY. When an agent with authority properly makes a contract with a third person that purports to bind the principal, there is by definition a binding contract between the principal and the third person. The agent is not a party to this contract. Consequently, when the owner of goods is the principal, his agent is not liable for breach of warranty with respect to the goods "sold" by the agent because the owner-principal, not the agent, is the seller in the sales transaction.[2]

Furthermore, even though a transaction between the agent and the third person may be formalized by the execution of subsequent documents, such as a written policy of insurance after an oral agreement has been made with the agent, the later writing does not destroy the rights acquired by the principal or the third person under the agent's informal or oral contract; and parol evidence is admissible to determine the actual agreement that had been made with the agent.

§ 41:3. DUTY TO ASCERTAIN EXTENT OF AGENT'S AUTHORITY. A third person who deals with a person claiming to be an agent cannot rely on the statements made by the agent concerning the extent of his authority. If the agent is not authorized to perform the act or is not even the agent of the principal, the transaction between the alleged agent and the third person will have no legal effect between the principal and the third person.

FACTS: The Taylors were depositors of the Equitable Trust Company. In return for their check, Equitable gave them a treasurer's check for $20,000. Thereafter Vittetoe, a loan officer of the bank, received a long-distance telephone call from a person who identified himself as Mr. Taylor and requested that the $20,000 represented by the treasurer's check be transferred to the account of Jody Associates at Irving Trust Company in New York. Vittetoe did not know Mr. Taylor personally and replied that written instructions from Taylor would be required. Some time later, Frank Terranova appeared at the bank and described himself as the Taylors' agent, surrendered the treasurer's check, and requested that the money represented thereby be transferred to the account of Jody Associates in the Irving Trust Company. Terranova surrendered the treasurer's check which was not indorsed. Terranova also presented a letter which he had signed in his own name, addressed to Vittetoe, in which was repeated the request to transfer the $20,000.

---

[2] Gaito v Hoffman, 5 UCCRS 1056.

Equitable made the transfer as requested. Taylor denied that Terranova had the authority to request such transfer and sued Equitable for damages.

DECISION: Judgment against Equitable. It was not protected in dealing with Terranova. The Taylors owned the check and there was no proof that Terranova was their agent to deliver the check on their behalf. Terranova's own statement that he was their agent did not give Equitable the right to accept him as their agent. Equitable had the burden of verifying that he was in fact the agent of the Taylors. The telephone call with a person not known to the Equitable employee was not a sufficient confirming of the existence of the agency as the person so confirming could have been an impostor. [Taylor v Equitable Trust Co. 269 Md 149, 304 A2d 838]

When the third person should realize that the agent is merely a soliciting agent of an insurance company with no greater authority than to obtain an application from third persons and transmit it to the insurance company, the insurer is not bound by an agreement which such agent makes with an applicant by which the applicant had been promised unlimited medical expenses coverage, whereas the policy as delivered contained a maximum limitation on such coverage.

(a) **Authority dependent on an event.** If the authority of an agent is contingent upon the happening of some event, one may not ordinarily rely upon the statement of the agent as to the happening of that event. Thus, when an agent is authorized to sell for his principal a given quantity of oranges only in the event of the arrival of a specified ship, one dealing with the agent should ascertain for himself whether the ship has arrived and should not rely on the agent's statement that it has.

An exception to this rule is made in cases in which the happening of the event is peculiarly within the knowledge of the agent and cannot be ascertained easily, if at all, by the party dealing with the agent. As an illustration, if the agent of a railroad issues a bill of lading for goods without actually receiving the goods, the railroad, as principal, is liable to one who accepts the bill in good faith and for value. This exception [3] is justified because, although the authority of the agent to issue bills of lading is dependent upon receiving the goods, persons taking bills of lading have no way of ascertaining whether the agent did receive the goods.

(b) **Agent's acts adverse to principal.** The third party who deals with an agent is also required to take notice of any acts that are clearly adverse to the interest of the principal. Thus, if the agent is obviously making use of funds of the principal for his own benefit, the person dealing with the agent acts at his peril.

The only certain way that the third person can protect himself is to inquire of the principal whether the agent is in fact the agent of the principal and has the necessary authority. If the principal states that the

---

[3] Uniform Commercial Code § 7-301.

agent has the authority, the principal cannot later deny this authorization unless the subject matter is such that an authorization must be in writing in order to be binding.

(c) Death of third party. The extent of the agent's authority becomes particularly significant when the third person dies after the transaction with the agent but before any action has been taken by the principal. If the agent had authority to contract on behalf of the principal, his agreement with the third person would give rise immediately to the binding contract and the third person's subsequent death would ordinarily not effect that contract. In contrast, if the agent did not have authority to contract but only to transmit an offer from the third person, the death of the third person before the principal had accepted the offer would work a revocation of the offer and the principal could not create a contract by purporting to accept after the death of the third person.

§ 41:4. **LIMITATIONS ON AGENT'S AUTHORITY.** A person who has knowledge of a limitation on the agent's authority cannot disregard that limitation. When the third person knows that the authority of the agent depends upon whether financing has been obtained, the principal is not bound by the act of the agent if the financing was not obtained. If the authority of the agent is based on a writing and the third person knows that there is such a writing, he is charged with knowledge of the limitations contained in it. The third person is likewise charged with such knowledge when the contract submitted to him indicates the existence of a limitation on the agent's authority.

> **FACTS:** Rausch owned the Black Acres Farm. It was subject to a first mortgage. Rausch wanted to refinance the mortgage debt, and sent an agent to the Citizens State Bank with authority to make a new loan and to pledge stock as security for the new loan if a second mortgage was obtained on the farm. This existence of the mortgage was known to the bank. The second mortgage was not obtained but the agent and the bank made a new loan agreement, part of which obligated Rausch to deliver certain shares of stock to the bank as security. The bank sued Rausch and his wife to compel them to deliver the stock to it under the second loan agreement.

> **DECISION:** Judgment for the Rauschs. When the third person knows that the authority of an agent depends upon whether financing has been obtained, the principal of the agent is not bound by the act of the agent if the financing is not obtained. As the bank knew of the condition, it acted with knowledge of the limitation on the authority of the agent and the principal of the agent was therefore not bound. [Citizens State Bank v Rausch, 9 IllApp3d 1004, 293 NE2d 678]

If the agent informs the third person that he lacks authority to do a particular act but that he will endeavor to obtain authorization from his principal, the third person cannot successfully claim that the agent has apparent authority. If the third person enters into a contract on the assumption that the agent will be able to obtain authorization, the third person does so at his risk.

(a) Apparent limitations. In some situations, it will be apparent to the third person that he is dealing with an agent whose authority is limited. When the third person knows that he is dealing with an officer of a private corporation or a representative of a governmental agency, he should recognize that such person will ordinarily not have unlimited authority [4] and that a contract made with him might not be binding unless ratified by his principal.

(b) Secret limitations. If the principal has clothed his agent with authority to perform certain acts but the principal has given him secret instructions that limit his authority, the third person is allowed to take the authority of the agent at its face value and is not bound by the secret limitations of which he has no knowledge.

§ 41:5. DELEGATION OF AUTHORITY BY AGENT. As a general rule, an agent cannot delegate his authority to another. In other words, unless the principal expressly or impliedly consents, an agent cannot appoint *subagents* to carry out his duties. The reason for this rule is that since an agent is usually selected because of some personal qualifications, it would be unfair and possibly injurious to the principal if the authority to act could be shifted by the agent to another. This is particularly true when the agent was originally appointed for the performance of a task requiring discretion or judgment. For example, an agent who is appointed to adjust claims against an insurance company cannot delegate the performance of his duties to another.

> **FACTS:** Bucholtz made reservations through the Sirotkin Travel Agency for a three-day trip to Las Vegas. The reservations were in fact not made by the agency and Bucholtz sued the agency for damages for breach of its contract. The agency raised the defense that the mistake was the fault of another travel agency or "wholesaler" through which the agency made reservations on behalf of its client.
>
> **DECISION:** Judgment for Bucholtz. The travel agency had no authority to delegate its responsibility to another. It was immaterial whether such other was a subagent or an independent contractor. The travel agency was liable to its customer, Bucholtz, for the nonperformance that occurred, without regard as to who was at fault. [Bucholtz v Sirotkin Travel, Ltd. 343 NYS2d 438]

An agent, however, may authorize another to perform his work for him in the following instances:

(a) When the acts to be done involve only mechanical or ministerial duties. Thus, an agent to make application for hail insurance on wheat may delegate to another the clerical act of writing the application. And it may be shown that there is customary authority for a clerk in the office of the insurance agent to sign the agent's name so as to have the effect of a signing

---

[4] Weil and Associates v Urban Renewal Agency, 206 Kan 405, 479 P2d 875.

by the agent and be binding upon the insurance company, the agent's principal.[5]

(b) When a well-known custom justifies such appointment. To illustrate, if one is authorized to buy or sell a grain elevator, he may do so through a broker when that is the customary method.

(c) When the appointment is justified by necessity or sudden emergency and it is impractical to communicate with the principal, and such appointment of a subagent is reasonably necessary for the protection of the interests of the principal entrusted to the agent. For instance, an agent to collect tolls, who is in charge of a bridge, may appoint another to collect tolls in his place when he is required to be on the bridge making repairs.

(d) When it was contemplated by the parties that subagents would be employed. For example, a bank may now generally use subagents to receive payment of notes that have been left for collection since the parties contemplated that this would be done.

B. DUTIES AND LIABILITIES OF PRINCIPAL AND AGENT

§ 41:6. DUTIES AND LIABILITIES OF AGENT TO PRINCIPAL.

(a) **Loyalty.** An agent must be loyal or faithful to his principal. He must not obtain any secret profit or advantage from his relationship. To illustrate, if an agent knows that his employer is negotiating for a lease and secretly obtains the lease for himself, the court will compel the agent to surrender the lease to the principal.

Similarly, if a broker is retained to purchase certain property, the broker cannot purchase the property for himself either in his own name or in the name of his wife. Likewise, an agent cannot purchase property of the principal, which the agent was hired to sell, without the principal's express consent. Similarly, an agent's wife cannot purchase in her own name property of the principal which the agent was hired to sell.

If the agent owns property, he cannot purchase it from himself on behalf of his principal without disclosing to the principal his interest in the transaction. If he fails to disclose his interest, the principal may avoid the transaction even if he was not financially harmed by the agent's conduct. Or the principal can approve the transaction and sue the agent for any profit realized by the agent.

An agent cannot act as agent for both parties to a transaction unless both know of the dual capacity and agree to it. If he does so act without the consent of both parties, the transaction is voidable at the election of any principal who did not know of the agent's double status.

An agent must not accept secret gifts or commissions from third persons in connection with his activities as agent. If he does, the principal may sue him for those gifts or commissions. Such practices are condemned because the judgment of the agent may be influenced by the receipt of gifts or commissions. A principal may also recover from his agent any secret profit

---

[5] United Bonding Insurance Co. v Banco Suizo-Panameno (CA5 Fla) 422 F2d 1142.

that the latter has made in violation of his duty of loyalty to his principal. If an agent makes a false report to the principal in order to conceal the agent's interest, the principal is not only entitled to recover the secret profit made and property acquired by the agent but may also be awarded punitive damages by way of punishing and discouraging such wrongdoing.

> **FACTS:** Kribbs owned real estate that had been rented through his agent, Jackson, at a monthly rental of $275. When this lease terminated, Jackson and a third person, Solomon, made an agreement that if the latter obtained a new tenant for a rental of $500 a month, Jackson would pay Solomon $100 a month. The latter obtained a new tenant who paid a monthly rental of $550. Jackson continued to send Kribbs $275 a month, less his commissions and janitor and utility costs; paid Solomon $100 a month; and kept the balance of the rental for himself. When Kribbs learned of these facts three years later, he sued Jackson for the money he had kept for himself and that which he had paid Solomon.

> **DECISION:** Judgment for Kribbs. An agent must account to his principal for all profits he has secretly made in an agency transaction and for all sums of money he improperly permitted third persons to receive in connection with such transactions. [Kribbs v Jackson, 387 Pa 611, 129 A2d 490]

An agent violates his duty of loyalty when he uses the name of his principal in perpetrating a fraud upon third persons.

An agent is, of course, prohibited from aiding the competitors of his principal or disclosing to them information relating to the business of the principal. It is also a breach of duty for the agent to deceive his principal with false information.

(b) Obedience and performance. An agent is under a duty to obey all lawful instructions given to him. He is required to perform the services specified for the period and in the way specified. If he does not, he is liable to the principal for any harm caused him. For example, if an agent, without authority to do so, releases one who is in debt under circumstances that the release is binding upon the principal, the agent is liable to the principal for the loss.

If an agent is instructed to take cash payments only but accepts a check in payment, he is liable for any loss caused by his act, such as that which arises when the check accepted by him is not collectible because it is forged. Likewise, when an insurance broker undertakes to obtain a policy of insurance for his principal that will provide a specified coverage as to workmen's compensation claims but fails to obtain a policy with the proper coverage, the broker must indemnify the principal for the loss caused by the agent's failure to obtain the proper insurance.

> **FACTS:** Willing ran an insurance agency. He persuaded Pittman to apply for a major medical policy from the Great American Life Insurance Company to cover Pittman's family. The application stated "I understand and agree that no coverage will be in force until the policy is issued, and if issued, that coverage will be in force as of the effective date

shown on the issued policy." Pittman did not see this provision. The application was rejected by the insurance company and the rejection notice sent to Willing. He did not inform Pittman of the rejection. Pittman's son was thereafter injured in an accident. When Pittman presented his medical bills for payment by the insurer, the latter refused to make payment and Pittman then learned that his application had been rejected. He sued Willing and the insurance company.

DECISION: The insurance company was not liable because it had not accepted the application. Willing was liable to Pittman because, in seeking to obtain insurance for Pittman, Willing made himself the agent of Pittman and therefore owed him an agent's duty of care. Hence, he was liable for his negligence in failing to inform Pittman that the application had been rejected, thereby preventing Pittman from obtaining insurance elsewhere. The application provision stating that there was no coverage until the policy was issued protected the insurer but did not affect the obligation of an applicant's agent to exercise reasonable care. [Pittman v Great American Life Insurance Co. (MoApp) 512 SW2d 857]

If the agent violates his instructions, it is immaterial that he acts in good faith or intends to benefit the principal. It is the fact that he violates the instructions and thereby causes his principal a loss which imposes a liability on the agent. In determining whether the agent has obeyed his instructions, they must be interpreted in the way that a reasonable man would interpret them.

(c) **Reasonable care.** It is the duty of an agent to act with the care that a reasonable man would exercise under the circumstances. In addition, if the agent possesses a special skill, as in the case of a broker or an attorney, he must exercise that skill.

(d) **Accounting.** An agent must account to his principal for all property or money belonging to his principal that comes into the agent's possession. The agent should, within a reasonable time, give notice of collections made and render an accurate account of all receipts and expenditures. The agency agreement may state, of course, at what intervals or on what dates accountings are to be made.

An agent should keep his principal's property and money separate and distinct from his own. If an agent mingles his property with the property of his principal so that the two cannot be identified or separated, the principal may claim all of the commingled mass. Furthermore, when funds of the principal and of the agent are mixed, any loss that occurs must be borne by the agent. For example, when the agent deposits the funds of the principal in a bank account in his own name, he is liable for the amount if the bank should fail.

(e) **Information.** It is the duty of an agent to keep the principal informed of all facts pertinent to the agency that may enable the principal to protect his interests.[6] In consequence, a principal's promise to pay a bonus to his agent for information secured by the agent in the performance of his duties

---

[6] Restatement, Agency, 2d § 381; Spritz v Brockton Savings Bank, 305 Mass 170, 25 NE2d 155.

is unenforceable on the ground that the principal was entitled to the information anyway. The promise is therefore not supported by consideration.

If the agent fails to communicate information to his principal which should have been communicated, and the principal sustains loss because of it, the principal may recover the amount of such loss from the agent.

FACTS: Bliesener consulted a real estate agency in Chicago, Baird & Warner, to find a house for him. The agency informed him that it had an exclusive listing for a house owned by Emerson. It was finally decided that Bliesener would rent Emerson's house with an option to purchase it. A mortgage on Emerson's house, which was in default, was known to Baird & Warner, but they did not inform Bliesener. He signed a lease for the house and made a down payment of $3,000 as was required by the contract. Baird & Warner deducted their commissions from the $3,000 and remitted the balance to Emerson. Sometime later, the holder of the mortgage foreclosed on the mortgage. Bliesener sued Baird & Warner for the $3,000.

DECISION: Judgment for Bliesener. Baird & Warner knew that the mortgage was in default. Because of the existence of the defaulted mortgage on the rented premises, the mortgagee could take possession of the property or foreclose the mortgage and thereby prevent Bliesener from holding the property under the lease. The existence of the defaulted mortgage was therefore a material fact and Baird & Warner, as agents for Bliesener, were under the duty to inform him of that fact. As they had not done so, they were liable to him for the loss that he had sustained in consequence of their omission. [Bliesener v Baird & Warner, Inc. 88 IllApp2d 383, 232 NE2d 13]

When the insurer's agent fails to inform the insurer that the insured restaurant had changed its location and that the agent had changed the policy to cover the new location, the agent is liable to the insurer for having failed to inform the insurer of the change of risk and thereby depriving the insurer of the opportunity to appraise the new situation.[7]

§ 41:7. ENFORCEMENT OF LIABILITY OF AGENT.
When the agent's breach of duty causes harm to the principal, the amount of the loss may be deducted from any compensation due the agent or may be recovered from him in an ordinary lawsuit.

When the agent handles money for the principal, the contract of employment may provide that the amount of any shortages in the agent's account may be deducted from the compensation to which the agent would otherwise be entitled.

FACTS: Acme Markets required its supermarket checkout cashiers to pay for any shortages in their cash registers. Male, the Commissioner of the State Department of Labor, claimed that this violated a statute which prohibited employers from making deductions from wages except for specified items, which did not include such shortages.

---

[7] Frangos v USF & G Co. 191 IllApp2d 947, 312 NE2d 688.

DECISION: The deductions were proper. Except in the case of fault of a third person, as a thief or a coemployee, a cash register shortage arises only from the negligence or fault of a cashier. Hence employees are liable to their employer for the amount of such loss under general principles of law. It was not contrary to public policy or the statute to require the employees to make good on the shortages. [Male v Acme Markets, 110 NJSuper 9, 264 A2d 245]

If the agent has made a secret profit, the principal may recover the profit from the agent. In any case, the agent may forfeit his right to all compensation, without regard to whether the principal has been benefited by some of the actions of the agent and without regard to whether the principal has actually been harmed.

§ 41:8. DUTIES AND LIABILITIES OF PRINCIPAL TO AGENT. The principal is under certain duties to the agent. He must perform the contract, compensate the agent for his services, reimburse him for proper expenditures, and indemnify him for loss under certain circumstances.

(a) **Employment according to terms of contract.** When the contract is for a specified time, the principal is under the obligation to permit the agent to act as such for the term of the contract, in the absence of any just cause or contract provision which permits the principal to terminate the agency sooner. If his principal gives the agent an exclusive right to act as such, the principal cannot give anyone else the authority to act as his agent nor may the principal himself do the act to which the exclusive agent's authority relates. If the principal does so, the exclusive agent is entitled to his compensation as though he had performed the act.

(b) **Compensation.** The principal must pay the agent the compensation agreed upon. If the parties have not fixed the amount of the compensation by their agreement but intended that the agent should be paid, the agent may recover the customary compensation for such services. If there is no established compensation, he may recover the reasonable value of his services.

When one requests another to perform services under circumstances that reasonably justify the expectation of being paid, a duty to make payment arises. For example, when one requests a broker or an attorney to act as an agent in his professional capacity, it is implied that compensation is to be paid.

When the agent is employed on the contingency that he is to be compensated only if he obtains or produces a specified result, the agent is not entitled to compensation or reimbursement if he does not achieve the desired result, regardless of how much time or money he has spent in the effort. Likewise, an agent is not entitled to compensation with respect to transactions canceled by third persons as long as the principal was not at fault.

FACTS: Eskin was the sales agent of the Acheson Manufacturing Co. which produced brass products. During World War II, at a time when prices were subject to government control, Eskin obtained large orders.

Because of the wartime conditions, these orders could not be filled at once. By the time they could be filled, government price controls were removed. Acheson then informed the customers that because of its increased costs, it could not supply the purchases at the original price and would charge the prices existing when the goods were shipped. Acheson informed the customers that they could cancel their orders if they wished. Customers whose orders exceeded $1 million canceled. Eskin then sued Acheson for the commissions he would have received on the orders if Acheson had not raised the price and caused their cancellation.

DECISION: Judgment for Acheson. Because of the unusual war conditions which existed, it was within the contemplation of the parties that price controls would ultimately be removed and that, when removed, prices would rise and orders might be canceled. Under such circumstances, the employer was not to be required to pay Eskin commissions on contracts which were canceled by its customers. [Eskin v Acheson Manufacturing Co. (CA3 Pa) 236 F2d 135]

In any case an agent may agree to work without compensation; for it is authorization to act, and not compensation for acting, that is the test of agency.

(1) Advance Payment. When agents are compensated on a basis of a percentage of the sales price of goods they sell or the contracts they make, it is customary to allow them to draw a stated amount weekly or monthly subject to adjustment at the end of some longer accounting period in the event that the commissions actually earned should be greater than the sums paid for the drawing account. If the contract between the principal and the agent does not give the principal the right to recover overpayments, the employer does not have such a right. That is, when an agent is allowed to take advances to be charged against future commissions, the principal cannot recover the excess of the advances over the earned commissions in the absence of an express or implied agreement to that effect.

If it is not clear from the agency contract whether the principal has the right to recoup over-advances, the contract is interpreted strictly against the principal and the right to recoup is denied.

(2) Repeating Transactions. In certain industries third persons make repeated transactions with the principal. In such cases the agent who made the original contract with the third person commonly receives a certain compensation or percentage of commissions on all subsequent renewal or additional contracts. In the insurance business, for example, the insurance agent obtaining the policyholder for the insurer receives a substantial portion of the first year's premium and then receives a smaller percentage of the premiums paid by the policyholder in the following years.

Whether an agent or his estate is entitled to receive compensation on repeating transactions, either after the termination of the agent's employment or after the agent's death, depends upon the terms of the agency contract. Frequently it is provided that the right to receive compensation on repeating transactions terminates upon the termination of the agent's authority or employment by the principal.

A provision that an agent's renewal commissions shall terminate if he accepts employment with another insurance company before the expiration of a specified period after the termination of his employment is valid. There is no vested right to renewal premiums but only such right as the contract of employment confers. Such a limitation is not a restraint on trade since it is not to be regarded as restraining the agent from following his profession, trade, or business.

(3) Post-agency Transactions. An agent is not entitled to compensation in connection with transactions, such as sales or renewals of insurance policies, occurring after the termination of the agency, even though the post-agency transactions are the result of the agent's former activities. Some contracts between a principal and agent expressly give the agent the right to post-termination compensation, however, or they may expressly deny the agent such compensation.

(c) Reimbursement. The principal is under a duty to reimburse the agent for all disbursements made at the request of the principal and for all expenses necessarily incurred in the lawful discharge of the agency for the benefit of the principal. The agent cannot recover, however, for expenses caused by his own misconduct or negligence. By way of illustration, if the agent transfers title to the wrong person, he cannot recover from the principal the amount of expense incurred in correcting the error.

(d) Indemnity. It is the duty of the principal to indemnify the agent for any losses or damages suffered without his fault but occurring on account of the agency.

When the loss sustained is not the result of obedience to the principal's instructions but of the agent's misconduct, or of an obviously illegal act, the principal is not liable for indemnification.

QUESTIONS AND CASE PROBLEMS

1. What is the objective of each of the following rules of law?
   (a) A third person who deals with a person claiming to be an agent cannot rely on the statements made by the latter concerning the extent of his authority.
   (b) If the parties have not fixed the amount of the compensation by their agreement but have intended that the agent should be paid, the agent may recover the customary compensation for his services.
2. Can an attorney delegate his authority to represent his client to another attorney with whom he shares the same suite of offices when he does not have the client's approval to do so? [People v Betillo, 53 Misc2d 540, 279 NYS2d 444]
3. A property owner applied to an insurance agent for insurance on his property. The agent told him that he was protected immediately, and thereafter the policy was issued. The agent backdated the policy to the time of the property owner's

application. Between the time when the property owner had applied for the insurance and was told that he was covered and the subsequent time when the policy was issued, the property was damaged by a cause coming within the scope of the policy. The insurance company paid the property owner's claim on the policy and then sued the agent for indemnity on the ground that he did not have authority to backdate a policy. The agent showed that he had repeatedly made oral contracts of insurance and that the policies were backdated to the date of the oral contracts. Was the agent liable to the insurer for the loss? [See Lewis v Travelers Insurance Co. 51 NJ 244, 239 A2d 4]

4. McKinney requested E. M. Christmas, a real estate broker, to sell McKinney's property. A sale to a purchaser was effected with the contract calling for monthly installment payments by the purchaser, which payments were to be collected by the broker. When the purchaser stopped making the payments, McKinney was not notified of that fact but one of the broker's employees bought out the purchaser's contract. The broker continued making payments to McKinney as though they were being made by the purchaser. Later Christmas, the broker, resold the land to another buyer at a substantial profit. McKinney sued Christmas for this profit. Decide. [McKinney v Christmas, 143 Colo 361, 353 P2d 373]

5. Regional Broadcasters of Michigan, Inc. owned and operated radio station WTRU. Moreschini supplied advertising to station WTRU under a contract made with the station manager. When Moreschini sued Regional Broadcasters, it raised the defense that the manager had been instructed not to make any contracts on behalf of the station. Was Regional bound? [Moreschini v Regional Broadcasters, 373 Mich 496, 129 NW2d 859]

6. An insurance company directed its agent to notify the insured under a particular policy that his policy was canceled. The insurance agent instructed his stenographer to notify the insured. She notified the insured. It was later claimed that this notice was not effective to cancel the policy because it had not been given by the insurer's agent. Decide. [See International Service Insurance Co. v Maryland Casualty Co. (TexCivApp) 421 SW2d 721]

7. Hockett employed Snearly as an agent in connection with the sales made at the Gilette Livestock Exchange operated by Hockett. Snearly was to perform various clerical operations in connection with the agent's work, and to write checks on the account of the principal for the payment of the persons selling their cattle and for the payment of his own salary. By the terms of compensation Snearly was to receive $25 on each sale made at the Exchange up to a certain date and $30 thereafter. According to this rate of compensation, Snearly was entitled to approximately $6,000 for the period in question, but he wrote checks to himself for approximately $27,000. Hockett sued Snearly to recover the excess compensation. Snearly defended on the ground that the additional compensation was taken for extra services rendered by him. The extra work was shown to have a value of approximately $2,000. Snearly also defended on the ground that the principal had waived any right to object to an overpayment by failing to take any action sooner. Decide. [Snearly v Hockett (Wyo) 352 P2d 230]

8. Promoters were planning the formation of a new corporation. They retained an attorney to obtain a charter for the corporation. The attorney made a contract with Erickson, selling him stock of the new corporation. Did the attorney have the authority to make this contract? [Erickson v Civic Plaza National Bank (MoApp) 422 SW2d 373]

9. Hihn and Eastland, doing business in California, were authorized to sell certain land in Texas. They in turn employed Maney, of Texas, to sell the land. He made the sale and then sued them for the commissions due him on the sale. Did Hihn and Eastland have authority to employ Maney to make the sale? [Eastland v Maney, 36 TexCivApp 147, 81 SW 574]

10. Wiles ran a taxi business. Mullinax, an insurance broker, agreed to obtain and keep Wiles continuously covered with workmen's compensation insurance. This was done for a number of years, with Mullinax renewing the policy whenever it expired. The insurance company which had issued the policy to Wiles canceled it, and Mullinax attempted to obtain a policy from other companies. He was unable to do so but did not inform Wiles of his difficulties nor of the fact that Wiles was not covered by insurance. An employee of Wiles was killed, and a workmen's compensation claim for his death was successfully made. Wiles then learned for the first time that there was no insurance to cover this claim. Wiles sued Mullinax for the amount of the workmen's compensation claim. Decide. [Wiles v Mullinax, 267 NC 392, 148 SE2d 229]

11. Wormhoudt Lumber Company employed Cloyd as an agent. Cloyd would act as a go-between to bring owners, contractors, and the lumber company together so that the company could sell lumber for use by the contractors in building for the owners. In order to obtain construction work, some of the contractors entered into a plan by which they split with Cloyd the profit that they made on their contracts and the discounts that they received by making early payment for the lumber. Some time after Cloyd left its employment, the lumber company learned what had been done. It then sued Cloyd to recover from him the secret profit which he had obtained from the contractors. Cloyd raised the defense that the lumber company had not sustained any loss. Was this a valid defense? [Wormhoudt Lumber Co. v Cloyd (Iowa) 219 NW2d 543]

12. Pittman purchased a Ford Galaxie from Perry Ford Co. The car caught on fire because of defective wiring. Pittman sued Ford Motor Co. for breach of warranty. Ford Motor Co. raised the defense that it had excluded liability in the manner authorized by the UCC (§ 2-316). Pittman objected that this section only applied to "sellers," and Perry Ford was the seller. Ford Motor Co. countered that Perry was merely its agent so that Ford Motor Co. was the actual seller of the Ford. Was Ford Motor Co. the seller? [Ford Motor Co. v Pittman (FlaApp) 227 So2d 246]

THIRD PERSONS IN AGENCY

42

A. LIABILITIES OF AGENT TO THIRD PARTY

§ 42:1. AUTHORIZED ACTION OF DISCLOSED AGENT. If an agent makes a contract with a third person on behalf of a disclosed principal and has proper authority to do so and if the contract is executed properly, the agent has no personal liability on the contract. Whether the principal performs the contract or not, the agent cannot be held liable by the third party. Thus, an insurance agency arranging for the insuring of a customer with a named company is not liable on the policy which the company issues to the insured. If the agent lacks authority, however, or if certain other circumstances exist, he may be liable.

§ 42:2. UNAUTHORIZED ACTION. If a person purports to act as an agent for another but lacks authority to do so, the contract that he makes is not binding on the principal. Similarly, when A and B had a joint bank account, with each having authority to withdraw but neither having authority to overdraw the account, the bank could not hold B liable for the amount of A's overdraft.

If the agent's unauthorized act causes loss to the third person, however, the agent is generally responsible for his loss. When he purports to act as agent for the principal, he makes an implied warranty that he has authority to do so.[1] Under this implied warranty it is immaterial that the agent acted in good faith or misunderstood the scope of his authority. The fact that he was not authorized imposes liability upon him, unless the third person knew that the agent exceeded his authority.

An agent with a written authorization may protect himself from liability on the implied warranty of authority by showing the written authorization to the third person and permitting the third person to determine for himself the scope of the agent's authority.

---

[1] Darr Equipment Co. v Owens (TexCivApp) 408 SW2d 566.

§ 42:3. NO PRINCIPAL WITH CAPACITY.

When a person acts as an agent, he impliedly warrants not only that he has a principal but also that his principal has legal capacity. If there is no principal or if the principal lacks legal capacity, the person acting as an agent is liable for any loss to the third person.

The agent can protect himself from liability on the implied warranty of the existence of a principal with capacity by making known to the third person all material, pertinent facts or by obtaining the agreement of the third person that the agent shall not be liable.

§ 42:4. UNDISCLOSED AND PARTIALLY DISCLOSED PRINCIPAL.

An agent becomes liable as a party to the contract, just as though he were acting for himself, when the third person is not told or does not know that the agent is acting for a specific principal, that is, when there is an *undisclosed principal*.[2] The agent is also liable on the contract when the third person is told or knows only that the agent is acting as an agent but the identity of the principal is not known or stated, that is, when the principal is only partially disclosed.

> **FACTS:** Brazilian & Colombian Co. ordered 40 barrels of olives from Mawer-Gulden-Annis, Inc., but did not disclose that it was acting for its principal, Pantry Queen, although this later became known. Mawer billed and later sued Brazilian for the payment of the contract price.

> **DECISION:** Judgment for Mawer. The buyer, Brazilian, was liable on the purchase contract because it did not disclose (1) the fact that it was acting as an agent and (2) the identity of its principal. This conclusion is not altered by the circumstance that after the contract was made, such information was acquired by the third person. [Mawer-Gulden-Annis, Inc. v Brazilian & Colombian Coffee Co. 49 IllApp2d 400, 199 NE2d 222]

When an agent sells goods of his principal without disclosing his principal's identity, the agent is bound by the "seller's" implied warranty of title and is liable to the buyer if the goods were in fact stolen and are taken from the buyer by the police. Likewise, when an auctioneer sells without disclosing the identity of his principal, the auctioneer is bound by an implied warranty of title.

An agent is liable as a party to the contract if the third party does not actually know that he is dealing with an agent and does not know the identity of the principal. The fact that sufficient information is disclosed which would enable the third party to inquire further and ascertain the identity of the principal is generally not sufficient to remove the agent from liability for the contract.

§ 42:5. WRONGFUL RECEIPT OF MONEY.

If an agent obtains a payment of money from the third person by the use of illegal methods, the agent is liable to the third person.

---

[2] Sago v Ashford, 145 Colo 289, 358 P2d 599.

If the third person makes an overpayment to the agent or a payment when none is due, the agent is also usually liable to the third person for the amount of such overpayment or payment. If the agent has acted in good faith and does not know that the payment is improperly made, however, he is liable to the third person only so long as he still has the payment in his possession or control. If in such a case he has remitted the payment to the principal before the time the third person makes a demand upon him for its return, the agent is not liable. In the latter case the third person's right of action, if he has one, is only against the principal. But, payment to the principal does not relieve the agent of liability when the agent knows that the payment was not proper.

§ 42:6. ASSUMPTION OF LIABILITY. An agent may intentionally make himself liable upon the contract with the third person. This situation frequently occurs when the agent is a well-established local brokerage house or other agency and the principal is located out of town and is not known locally.

§ 42:7. EXECUTION OF CONTRACT. A simple contract that would appear to be the contract of the agent only can be shown by oral testimony, if believed, to have been intended as a contract between the principal and the third party. If the intention is established, it will be permitted to contradict the face of the written contract, and the contract as thus modified will be enforced.

To avoid any question of interpretation, James Craig, an agent for B. G. Gray, should execute an instrument by signing either "*B. G. Gray, by James Craig,*" that is, "*Principal, by Agent*" or "*B. G. Gray, per James Craig,*" that is, "*Principal, per Agent.*" Such a signing is in law a signing by *Gray*, and the agent is therefore not a party to the contract. The signing of the principal's name by an authorized agent without indicating the agent's name or identity is likewise in law the signature of the principal.

If the instrument is ambiguous as to whether the agent has signed in a representative or an individual capacity, parol evidence is admissible, as between the original parties to the transaction, to establish the character in which the agent was acting.

If an agent executes a sealed instrument in those states in which a seal retains its common-law force and does so without disclosing his agency or the identity of his principal, he is bound and he cannot show that the parties did not intend this result.[3] Because of the formal character of the writing, the liability of the parties is determined from the face of the instrument alone and it cannot be modified or contradicted by proof of intention or other matters not set forth in the writing.

§ 42:8. FAILURE TO OBTAIN COMMITMENT OF PRINCIPAL. In some situations the agent is in effect a middleman or go-between who has the

---

[3] Tooke v Thom (FlaApp) 281 So2d 34. As to the signing of commercial paper by an agent, see § 29:1(a)(2).

duty to the third person to see to it that the principal is bound to the third person. For example, when an agent of an insurance company who has authority to write policies of insurance tells a policyholder whose fire policy had been canceled that the agent will look into the matter and that the insured should forget about it unless he hears from the agent, the latter is under an obligation to make reasonable efforts to obtain the reinstatement of the policy or to notify the insured that he could not do so. The agent is liable to the insured for the latter's fire loss if the agent does not obtain the reinstatement of the policy and does not so inform the insured.

§ 42:9. **TORTS AND CRIMES.** An agent is liable for harm caused the third person by the agent's fraudulent, malicious, or negligent acts. The fact that he is acting as an agent at the time or that he is acting in good faith under the directions of his principal does not relieve him of liability if his conduct would impose liability upon him were he acting for himself. The fact that he is following instructions does not shield him from liability.

When an agent violates a law or administrative agency regulation relating to business, he is liable to the same extent as though there were no principal. This applies both to direct regulations of business, such as price controls and labor-management relations law, and indirect regulations, such as environmental pollution controls.

An agent is not excused from complying with the law because he is an agent. Consequently, if an agent violates a civil rights act, it is no defense that he was acting in obedience to instructions of his principal.

If an agent commits a traditional crime, such as stealing from the third person or shooting the third person, the agent is liable for his crime without regard to the fact that he was acting as an agent, and without regard to whether he had acted for his own self-interest or had sought to advance the interest of the principal.

B. LIABILITIES OF THIRD PARTY TO AGENT

§ 42:10. **AUTHORIZED ACTION OF DISCLOSED AGENT.** Ordinarily the third party is not liable to the agent for a breach of a contract that the agent has made with the third person on behalf of a disclosed principal. In certain instances, however, the third party may be liable to the agent.

§ 42:11. **UNDISCLOSED AND PARTIALLY DISCLOSED PRINCIPAL.** If the agent executed the contract without informing the third person or without the third party's knowing both of the existence of the agency and the identity of the principal, the agent may sue the third party for breach of contract.

In such instances, if the contract was a simple contract, the principal may also sue the third person even though the third person thought that he was contracting only with the agent. The right of the principal to sue the third person is, of course, superior to the right of the agent to do so. If the contract was a specialty, the undisclosed principal, not appearing on the instrument as a party, could not bring an action to enforce the contract.

FACTS: Weisz purchased a painting at an auction sale in the Parke-Bernet Galleries. It was later shown that the painting was a forgery. When Weisz sued the Galleries for breach of warranty, it raised the defense that it was making the sale for the owner and therefore any warranty suit must be brought against the owner.

DECISION: Judgment for Weisz. As the Galleries was selling for an undisclosed principal, it was personally bound by the sales contract and therefore it was liable for any breach of warranty even though in fact it had been acting as an agent. [Weisz v Parke-Bernet Galleries, Inc. (NY CivCt) 325 NYS2d 576.]

§ **42:12. AGENT INTENDING TO BE BOUND.** If the third person knew that the agent was acting as an agent but nevertheless the parties intended that the agent should be personally bound by the contract, the agent may sue the third person for breach of contract.

§ **42:13. EXECUTION OF CONTRACT.** The principles that determine when an agent is liable to the third person because of the way in which he has executed a written contract apply equally in determining when the third person is liable to the agent because of the way in which the contract is executed. If the agent could be sued by the third person, the third person can be sued by the agent. Thus, if the agent executes a sealed instrument in his own name, he alone can sue the third person on that instrument.

§ **42:14. AGENT AS TRANSFEREE.** The agent may sue the third person for breach of the latter's obligation to the principal when the principal has assigned or otherwise transferred his claim or right to the agent, whether absolutely for the agent's own benefit or for the purpose of collecting the money and remitting it to the principal.

§ **42:15. SPECIAL INTEREST OF AGENT.** If the agent has a special interest in the subject matter of the contract, he may bring an action against the third party upon the latter's default. For example, a commission merchant has a lien on the principal's goods in his possession for his compensation and expenses. Such a merchant, therefore, has an interest that entitles him to sue the buyer for breaking his contract.

§ **42:16. TORTS AND CRIMES.** The third party is liable in tort for fraudulent or other wrongful acts causing injury to the agent. If the third party by slander or other means wrongfully causes the principal to discharge the agent, the latter may recover damages from the third party. The agent may also bring an action in tort against the third person for wrongful injuries to his person or property. If the agent has possession of the principal's property, he may sue any third person whose acts injure that property.

If the third party commits any crime with respect to the agent or property of the agent, the criminal liability of the third party is the same as though no agency were involved.

C. LIABILITIES OF PRINCIPAL TO THIRD PARTY

§ 42:17. **AGENT'S CONTRACTS.** When there is a principal with contractual capacity who had authorized or ratified the agent's action and when the agent properly executed the contract as an agency transaction, a contract exists between the principal and the third person on which each usually can be sued by the other in the event of a breach. At common law, if the contract is under seal, an undisclosed principal cannot sue or be sued. If the contract is a simple contract, the third person may sue the principal whether or not the principal was disclosed. Since the agent acts for the principal, the third person may sue the principal directly even though his existence was not disclosed or was unknown and the third person therefore contracted with the agent alone.[4] If the third person thereafter learns of the existence of the undisclosed principal, the third person may sue the principal.

> FACTS: Fishbaugh, acting as agent for his father, made a contract to sell land belonging to his father to Menveg. Fishbaugh did not disclose his agency. Later the father refused to perform the contract made by the son. Menveg, learning of the father's identity as principal, sued him for specific performance.

> DECISION: Judgment for Menveg. When an agent makes an authorized, simple contract on behalf of an undisclosed principal, the third person may sue the principal when he learns of his existence. [Menveg v Fishbaugh, 123 CalApp 460, 11 P2d 438]

The right to sue the undisclosed principal on a simple contract is subject to two limitations. First, the third person cannot sue the principal if in good faith the principal has settled his account with the agent with respect to the contract. Some states refuse to apply this limitation, however, unless the third person reasonably has led the principal to believe that the account between the agent and the third person had been settled.

As a second limitation, the third person cannot sue the principal if the third person has elected to hold the agent and not the principal. To constitute such an election, the third person, with knowledge of the existence of the principal, must express an intention to hold the agent liable or he must secure a judgment against the agent. In those jurisdictions which permit the third person to join the principal and agent as codefendants, the third party, although he may sue both in one action, must choose at the end of the trial the party from whom to collect, thus discharging the other.

This rule as to election does not apply when the principal is partially disclosed, for in that case the right of the third person is not to be regarded as alternatively against either the agent or the principal but as concurrent—that is, a right against both—and therefore the third person may recover a judgment against either without discharging the other.

---

[4] An undisclosed principal may enforce warranty liability arising under the Uniform Commercial Code when the sales contract was made by his authorized agent. Pendarvis v General Motors Corp. (NY) 6 UCCRS 457.

The principal is not liable upon a contract made by the agent in his individual capacity, even though the agent makes the contract in order to further the business of his principal. Likewise, the undisclosed principal is not liable on commercial paper executed by the agent in the agent's own name.

FACTS: Berth Ness signed a promissory note in his own name payable to the order of Greater Arizona Realty, Inc. Subsequently, Greater Arizona sued Louise Ness and three corporations on the theory that, when Berth Ness signed the note in his own name, he was in fact acting as agent for Louise Ness and the three corporations and therefore they were all liable for the payment of the note.

DECISION: Louise Ness and the corporations were not liable on the note because Berth Ness had signed it in his individual capacity. It was therefore his note and no one else was liable thereon. [Ness v Greater Arizona Realty, Inc. 21 ArizApp 231, 517 P2d 1278]

§ 42:18. PAYMENT TO AGENT.
When the third person makes payment to an authorized agent, such payment is deemed as made to the principal. The result is that the principal must give the third person full credit for such payment, even though in fact the agent never remits or delivers the payment to the principal, if the third person made the payment in good faith and had no reason to know that the agent would be guilty of such misconduct.[5]

§ 42:19. PAYMENT TO UNAUTHORIZED PERSON.
When payment by a debtor is made to a person who is not the agent of the creditor, such payment does not discharge the debt.

The act of paying money to a person to be transmitted by him to a third person does not constitute "payment" to the third person when the one receiving the money is not the agent of the third person.

FACTS: Video Independent Theaters advertised in the newspapers published by the Oklahoma Publishing Company. The publishing company would send periodic statements of the amounts due by Video to the advertising agency of Ken Juergens and Associates. The latter would then add its fee to the amount due the publishing company and bill Video for the aggregate. On receiving payment by Video, Juergens was to deduct its fee and then transmit the balance to the publishing company. Juergens kept the entire amount paid by Video. The publishing company sued Video which claimed that it had paid the bill to Juergens.

DECISION: Judgment for the publishing company. Juergens was not the agent of the publishing company. Therefore the making of payment to Juergens did not constitute "payment" to the publishing company and

---

[5] This general rule of law is restated in some states by § 2 of the Uniform Fiduciaries Act, which is expressly extended by § 1 thereof to agents, partners, and corporate officers. Similar statutory provisions are found in a number of other states.

Video's debt to the publishing company therefore remained unpaid. The pattern of billing followed by the publishing company did not make Juergens its agent and did not estop the publishing company from proving that he was not its agent. [Oklahoma Publishing Co. v Video Independent Theaters, Inc. (Okla) 522 P2d 1029]

§ 42:20. AGENT'S STATEMENTS. A principal is bound by a statement made by his agent while transacting business within the scope of his authority. This means that the principal cannot thereafter contradict the statement of his agent and show that it is not true. Statements or declarations of an agent, in order to bind the principal, must be made at the time of performing the act to which they relate or shortly thereafter.

§ 42:21. AGENT'S KNOWLEDGE. The principal is bound by knowledge or notice of any fact that is acquired by his agent while acting within the scope of his authority.

Conversely, if the subject matter is outside the scope of the agent's authority, the agent is under no duty to inform the principal of knowledge acquired by him. For example, when the agent is authorized and employed only to collect rents, his knowledge of the unsatisfactory condition of the premises is not imputed to the landlord-principal, since the reporting of such information is not part of the agent's collection duties. When a commercial paper is indorsed to the principal and the agent acting for the principal has knowledge of a matter which would be a defense to the paper, such knowledge of the agent is imputed to the principal and bars him from being a holder in due course.[6]

The rule that the agent's knowledge is imputed to the principal is extended in some cases to knowledge gained prior to the creation of the agency relationship. The notice and knowledge in any case must be based on reliable information. Thus, when the agent hears only rumors of acts or facts, the principal is not charged with notice.

(a) Exceptions. When the agent knows that a third person's statements are false, the principal is charged with such knowledge and cannot hold the third person liable for such falsity. In such a case the principal is barred from asserting that he has been deceived as the principal is deemed to possess the agent's knowledge. Thus, when the agent of the transferee of a warehouse receipt knew that the receipt had been issued without the delivery of the goods described therein, the warehouseman was not liable to the transferee for the loss caused by the false bill.

FACTS: Trahan, who was in prison on a narcotics charge, wished to apply for a funeral expense insurance policy. His father communicated with an agent of the First National Life Insurance Co. The father signed the application, and the agent falsely acknowledged on the application that Trahan had signed it in his presence. Trahan was killed in prison. When the Miguez Funeral Home sought payment on the policy, the insurer refused to pay on the ground that it had not been signed by Trahan.

---

[6] America Underwriting Corp. v Rhode Island Hospital Trust Co. 131 RI 161, 303 A2d 121.

DECISION: The insurance agent was the agent of the insurance company. The agent knew the facts, and the insurer was charged with the knowledge of its agent. The insurance company, therefore, was estopped from denying that the application had been signed by Trahan as its agent had stated. [Adam Miguez Funeral Home v First National Life Insurance Co. (LaApp) 234 So2d 496]

The principal is not responsible for the knowledge of his agent, that is, he is not charged with having knowledge of what is known by his agent, under the following circumstances: (1) when the agent is under a duty to another principal to conceal his knowledge; (2) when the agent is acting adversely to his principal's interest; or (3) when the third party acts in collusion with the agent for the purpose of cheating the principal. In such cases, it is not likely that the agent would communicate his knowledge to the principal. The principal is therefore not bound by the knowledge of the agent.

(b) Communication to principal. As a consequence of regarding the principal as possessing the knowledge of his agent, when the law requires that a third person communicate with the principal, that duty may be satisfied by communicating with the agent. Thus, an offeree effectively communicates the acceptance of the offer to the offeror when he makes such communication to the offeror's agent, and an offeror effectively communicates the revocation of his offer to the offeree by communicating the revocation to the offeree's agent.

§ 42:22. AGENT'S TORTS. The principal is liable to third persons for the wrongful acts of his agent committed while acting within the scope of the agent's employment. These acts are usually acts of negligence. By the common-law view, a principal was not liable for the willful torts of his agent. The modern decisions hold that the principal is liable for intentional torts committed for the purpose of furthering the principal's business. Thus, the principal is liable for the fraudulent acts or the misrepresentations of the agent made within the scope of his authority.

To illustrate, when an agent in the routine of his authorized agency issues false stock certificates, the principal is liable. In some states the principal is not liable for his agent's fraud if he did not authorize or know of the fraud of the agent at the time of the agent's fraudulent statement or misrepresentation. When the principal's agent induces the buyer to make a purchase because of the agent's fraudulent misrepresentations, the buyer may cancel the sale.[7]

When the activity of the agent is not directly employment-related, the fact that one of the motives of the agent is to find customers for the principal's product does not in itself bring the agent's activity within the scope of his agency so as to impose vicarious liability upon the principal for the tort of the agent.

When the agent's conduct is outside the scope of his authority, the principal is not liable for the loss caused the third party, even though it was the fact that the agent was the principal's agent which gave him the

---

[7] Morris Chevrolet, Inc. v Pitzer (Okla) 479 P2d 958.

opportunity to meet the third person or to do the act which caused harm to the third person.

> **FACTS:** Gandy became acquainted with Webb who, as an employee of Cole, did various bookkeeping and accounting functions for Gandy's gas station. Webb soon took over the management of the business of Gandy, in the course of which he defrauded Gandy. Gandy sued Cole for the loss caused thereby.

> **DECISION:** Judgment for Cole. The damage to Gandy was caused by Gandy's personal dealing with Webb in his individual capacity and not as agent or employee of Cole. Cole had not made any representation nor in any way gave Webb apparent authority to act for him in defrauding Gandy, and Gandy had not relied on any statement of Cole. He was therefore not liable for the fraud of Webb. [Gandy v Cole 35 MichApp 695, 193 NW2d 58]

In determining whether the principal is liable for the wrongful actions of his agent, it is immaterial that the principal did not personally benefit by those acts.

Ordinarily the principal is liable only for compensatory damages for the tort of the agent. If, however, the agent's act is of so offensive or extreme a character that the agent would be liable for punitive or exemplary damages, some courts hold that such damages may be recovered from the principal. An insurance company that employs an agent to collect premiums is liable for compensatory and punitive damages when the agent, in the effort to collect premiums, threatens the insured with a pistol.

When the tort is committed by a person while driving an automobile, some states expand the liability of the supplier of the automobile so as to impose liability for the act of the driver as though the driver were his agent or employee. This has the same effect as imposing agency liability by operation of law and arises in some states in the case of the license-sponsor rule or the family-purpose doctrine.

(a) License-sponsor rule. In a number of states, when a minor under a specified age applies for an automobile operator's license, his parent or a person standing in the position of his parent, is required to sign his license application as a sponsor. In some states the *license-sponsor rule* makes the sponsor jointly and severally liable with the minor for the latter's negligence in driving, although some statutes relieve the sponsor of liability if either he or the minor has filed proof of financial responsibility.

(b) Family-purpose doctrine. In about half of the states, a person who owns or supplies an automoblie that he permits members of his family to use for their own purposes is vicariously liable for harm caused by the negligent operation of the vehicle by any such member of the family. The *family-purpose doctrine* is repudiated in nearly half of the states as illogical and contrary to the general principles of agency law. Even when recognized, the doctrine is not applicable if the use of the vehicle is not with the permission of the owner or if the use is outside of the scope of that contemplated.

The family-purpose doctrine is not limited to cases involving minors nor to the children of the providing parent. That is, a person may be liable for providing an automobile to an adult; and the person so provided may be any family member, however related to the person providing the car. In some jurisdictions that person may even be one who is not related to the provider, as long as he is a bona fide member of the household of the provider, such as a servant who is provided with or allowed to use the car for his own benefit.

Under the family-purpose doctrine, it is not essential that the provider of the car be the owner of it. The essential element is that he is the one who has control of it and has the power to grant or deny permission to use it so that its use at any particular time is with his permission. Hence, the doctrine, when recognized, is applicable to impose liability upon the father who has control of the use of the car that the child has purchased but which is used by the family only to the extent that the father permits.

(c) Civil rights. When the tortious act of an agent or employee is a violation of civil rights legislation, the principal is liable to the same extent as vicarious liability is imposed for any other tort. The federal civil rights legislation is interpreted as only imposing liability on natural persons so that when a policeman without justification beats a person being questioned at a police station, the city employing the policeman is not vicariously liable under the federal civil rights legislation.

§ 42:23. **AGENT'S CRIMES.** The principal is liable for the crimes of the agent committed at the principal's direction. When not authorized, however, the principal is ordinarily not liable for the crime of his agent merely because it was committed while otherwise acting within the scope of the latter's authority or employment.

Some states impose liability on the principal when the agent has in the course of his employment violated liquor sales laws, pure food laws, and laws regulating prices or prohibiting false weights. Thus, by some courts a principal may be held criminally responsible for the sale by his agent or employee of liquor to a minor in violation of the liquor law, even though the sale was not known to the principal and violated his instructions to his agent.[8]

D. LIABILITIES OF THIRD PARTY TO PRINCIPAL

§ 42:24. **THIRD PERSON'S CONTRACTS.** If the principal is bound by a contract to the third person, the third person is usually bound to the principal. The third person is accordingly liable to the principal on a properly authorized contract that is properly executed as a principal-third party contract. The third person is likewise liable on an unauthorized contract that the principal has ratified. He is also liable to the principal

---

[8] In contrast, note the restatement of the traditional rule by the New York Penal Code, § 20.20(c) imposing corporate liability only as to offenses "engaged in by an agent of the corporation while acting within the scope of his employment and in behalf of the corporation."

even though the principal was not disclosed, except when the agent has made a sealed contract or a commercial paper, such as a check or note, in which case only the parties to the instrument can sue or be sued on it. In the case of a commercial paper, however, the undisclosed principal may sue on the contract out of which the instrument arose.

Although the third person is liable to the principal on the contract made by the agent without disclosing any agency, the third person, when sued by the principal, is entitled to assert against the principal any defense that he could have asserted against the agent.

§ 42:25. **TORTS OF THIRD PERSON.** The third party is liable to the principal for injuries caused by the third party's wrongful acts against the principal's interests or property in the care of the agent. He is also responsible to the principal in some cases for causing the agent to fail in the performance of his agreement. Thus, when an agent is willfully persuaded and induced to leave an employment to which he is bound by contract for a fixed term, the principal may bring an action for damages against the party causing the contract to be violated. So, also, one who colludes with an agent to defraud his principal is liable to the principal for damages.

If the third person dealing with the agent acts in good faith and does not know that the agent is violating his duty to his principal, the third party is not liable to the principal for the agent's misconduct.

FACTS: Dobar was employed by Martin Co. to find suitable laboratories to do testing work for Martin. On behalf of Martin, Dobar made a contract for testing with Commercial Chemists, Inc. Under the plan established by the contract, Dobar would locate independent chemists in the county who could perform the tests and enter into individual testing contracts with the independent chemists; and the latter would send their reports to Commercial. Commercial would review their reports and make a report and send a bill to Martin. Martin would pay Commercial, which would then pay Dobar 80 percent of the payment received from Martin. With this payment, Dobar paid the independent chemists for their services, which was substantially less than the 80 percent that was paid to him by Commercial. Dobar kept this difference for himself. Commercial did not know that Dobar was making a secret profit. It believed that this plan of operation was authorized by Martin and that all of the 80 percent was used for paying the independent chemists. Martin sued Dobar and Commercial for the secret profits made by Dobar.

DECISION: Judgment against Dobar but in favor of the Commercial Chemists. Commercial did not know or have reason to know that it was assisting Dobar in unlawfully making a secret profit since it believed that the plan of operation had been authorized by Martin. It was therefore not liable to Martin for the secret profit made by Dobar. [Martin Co. v Commercial Chemists, Inc. (FlaApp) 213 So2d 477]

In contrast, if an agent sells personal property of the principal to a third person which the agent has no authority to sell, the third person must surrender the property to the principal and pay damages for its conversion, regardless of his good faith or ignorance of the agent's misconduct.

§ 42:26. RESTITUTION OF PROPERTY. When property of the principal has been transferred to a third person by an agent lacking authority to do so, the principal may ordinarily recover the property from the third person.

E. TRANSACTIONS WITH SALESPERSONS

§ 42:27. NON-AGENT. The giving of an order to a salesperson does not give rise to a contract with his employer when the salesperson had authority only to solicit and receive orders from third persons; and the employer of the salesperson is not bound by a contract until the employer accepts the order.

(a) **Reason for limitation on authority of salesperson.** The limitation on the authority of the salesperson is commonly based upon the fact that credit may be involved in the transaction, and the employer of the salesperson does not wish to permit its soliciting agent to make decisions as to the sufficiency of the credit of the buyer but wishes all of these matters to be handled by the credit management department of the home office.

Even when sales are made on a cash basis, the employer of the salesperson may want control of the order so as to avoid the danger of overselling its existing and obtainable inventory. For example, if each salesperson could bind the employer by an absolute obligation to deliver certain items and if all of the salespersons in the aggregate sold more than the seller had in inventory or could obtain at the same price at which the items in stock were purchased, the selling success of the salesperson would be an economic disaster for the employer. The employer would lose money obtaining the goods at higher prices in order to fill the orders or would find that he had lawsuits on his hands by buyers seeking to recover damages for nondelivery of goods.

To avoid these difficulties, it is common to limit the authority of a salesperson to that of merely a soliciting agent accepting and transmitting orders to the employer. To make this clear to buyers, order forms signed by the customer, who is given a copy, generally state that the salesperson's authority is limited in this manner and that there is no "contract" with the employer until the order is approved by the home office.

(b) **Withdrawal of customer.** From the fact that the customer giving a salesperson an order does not ordinarily have a binding contract with the employer of the salesperson until the employer approves the order, it necessarily follows that the customer is not bound by any contract until the employer approves the order. Prior to that time the "buyer" may withdraw from the transaction. Withdrawal under such circumstances is not a breach of contract, for by definition there is no contract to be broken. Likewise, if the buyer had given the salesperson any money deposit, down payment, or part payment on the purchase price, the customer, on withdrawing from the transaction, is entitled to a refund of all of his payment.

(c) **Contrast with true agent.** In contrast with the consequences described when the salesperson is only a soliciting agent, if the person with whom the buyer deals is a true agent of the seller, there is, by definition, a binding contract between the principal and the customer from the moment that the agent agrees with the customer, that is, when he accepts the customer's order. Should the customer seek to withdraw from the contract thereafter, he must base his action on a ground which justifies his unilateral repudiation or rejection of the contract. If he has no such justification, his action of withdrawing is a breach of his contract and he is liable for damages which the seller sustains because of his breach of contract. If the buyer has made any down payment, prepayment, or deposit, the seller may deduct his damages from the amount thereof before refunding any excess to the buyer. When the transaction relates to the sale of goods, the seller is entitled to retain from such advance payment either $500 or 20 percent of the purchase price, whichever is less, unless the seller can show that greater damages were in fact sustained by him.[9]

QUESTIONS AND CASE PROBLEMS

1. A corporation entered into a secured transaction. On its default, the secured creditor proceeded to sell the collateral and gave notice of the sale to the president of the corporation. The corporation claimed that the notice was not sufficient because it was merely given to the president and not to the corporation. Was it correct? [See A. J. Armstrong Co. v. Janburt Embroidery Corp. 97 NJSuper 246, 234 A2d 737]

2. An agent received in the mail stock certificates intended for his principal. The agent forged on the certificates an indorsement from the original owner of the certificates to himself. In a lawsuit by the owner of the certificates against the principal, the owner claimed that the principal knew what the agent had done. Was he correct? [See Hartford Accident & Indemnity Co. v Walston & Co. 21 NY2d 219, 287 NY2d 58, 234 NE2d 230; adhered to 22 NY2d 672, 291 NYS2d 366, 238 NE2d 754]

3. Buchanan was a candidate for a political office. His campaign treasurer made a false report of the expenses of the campaign. A statute required the filing of such reports and made it a criminal offense to make a false report. Buchanan was prosecuted for the false report made by his campaign treasurer. Was he guilty of a statutory criminal offense? [Florida v Buchanan (FlaApp) 189 So2d 270]

4. Arnold Israel, acting as authorized agent for an undisclosed principal, Unified Consultants, made an authorized contract on their behalf with Tabloid Lithographers. Unified did not perform its part of the contract, and Tabloid sued both Israel and Unified. Tabloid obtained a judgment in the action against Unified, whereupon Israel claimed that he was released from any liability. Was this correct? [Tabloid Lithographers v Israel, 87 NJSuper 358, 209 A2d 364]

---

[9] Uniform Commercial Code § 2-718(2)(b). See § 8:6(2) as to rescission based on consumer protection legislation.

5. Sawday, the local salesman and representative of the Sunset Milling and Grain Co., executed a contract with Anderson by the terms of which Sunset was to deliver certain goods. The contract was signed by Sawday as "C. Trevor Sawday, representative of the Sunset Milling and Grain Co." Anderson sued Sunset, which defended on the ground that it was not bound because of the form of execution of the contract. Decide. [Sunset Milling and Grain Co. v Anderson, 39 Cal2d 773, 249 P2d 24]

6. Blanche Trembley stated that she was agent for Trembley, Inc., and in the name of that corporation she made a contract with the Puro Filter Corp. of America. There was no corporation by the name of Trembley, Inc. The Puro Filter Corp. brought an action against Trembley to recover on the contract. Was it entitled to recover? [Puro Filter Corp. v Trembley, 266 AppDiv 750, 41 NYS2d 472]

7. Smith made a contract with Hal Anderson for architectural services. Some payments were made with checks bearing the name Hal Anderson, Inc. Payment was not made in full, and Smith sued Anderson for the balance. He defended on the ground that once Smith had received the corporate checks, Smith was put on notice of the fact that Hal was acting as an agent for an identified principal and thereafter could hold only the principal liable. Was this correct? [Anderson v Smith (TexCivApp) 398 SW2d 635]

8. Weeks was a collection agent for the Life Insurance Co. of Georgia. Clemmons held a policy in the company. When Weeks called for the premium at her home, Clemmons did not have the money. Weeks angrily drew a pistol and pointed it at her saying, "I will shoot." He then walked away, stating that she better have the money the next time he called. Clemmons sued the insurance company for damages. It contended that it was not liable for willful assault by its employee. Was this a valid defense? [Clemmons v Life Insurance Co. 274 NC 416, 163 SE2d 761]

9. Peterson was the agent of Federal Auto Systems. Kost wished to be franchised by Federal and gave Peterson an application for a franchise and a check. It was understood that Peterson would have the check certified and forward it with the application to Federal. It was also agreed that if Federal would not grant the franchise, the check would be returned. Peterson obtained a bank money order for the amount of the check instead of having it certified, and sent the application and the bank money order to Federal. Federal did not grant the franchise to Kost but did not return the money paid by him. Kost sued Peterson for breaking the agreement to return the check. Was he liable? [Kost v Peterson, 292 Minn 46, 193 NW2d 291]

10. Arley wished to insure his property in Nevada against fire. He went to Nelson, an insurance broker, and discussed the matter with Chaney, a solicitor for Nelson. It was agreed that a policy would be obtained from the Union Pacific Insurance Company and Arley was told that he was "covered." The policy was not obtained. Arley's property was destroyed by fire several months later. When he notified Nelson of his loss, the latter then obtained a policy of insurance but the insurance company canceled the policy when it learned that the property had been destroyed before the property was insured. Arley sued Chaney and Nelson. The defense was raised that they could not be liable because they had disclosed the principal and had authority to write contracts binding the principal. Was this defense valid? [Arley v Chaney, 262 Ore 69, 496 P2d 202]

11. Oddo purchased baked goods from Interstate Bakeries for sale in his store. Cooley, the delivery man for Interstate, falsely altered the slips showing the daily deliveries to Oddo. In consequence, Interstate billed Oddo for more than was delivered. Each time after Oddo paid his current bill to Cooley, Cooley would

embezzle the amount by which Oddo had been overcharged. When Oddo learned of the overcharges, he sued Interstate, which claimed that it was not liable because Cooley had embezzled the money. Was this defense valid? [Oddo v Interstate Bakeries, Inc. (CA8 Mo) 271 F2d 417]

12. Graham was a salesperson for Collier County Motors. He was required to work on the premises of the employer for two days out of the week. The balance of the time he was free to go as he pleased in the hope that he would find customers. About 75 percent of his sales were obtained by this off-premises solicitation. The only restriction on such activity was that Graham was required to make a weekly report to Collier on the number of contacts made of potential customers. On a day in which he worked the full day on the premises, Graham left work about 5:00 p.m. and about 11:30 p.m. he drove with a friend to a bowling alley to bowl and to make any possible contacts that might be found. On the way to the bowling alley, Graham ran into and killed Morgan. Suit was brought by Morgan's estate gainst Collier County Motors. Collier raised the defense that it was not vicariously liable for the act of the salesperson because he was not within the scope of his agency at the time he committed the act which had caused the harm. Was this a valid defense? [Morgan v Collier County Motors (Fla) 193 So2d 35]

13. McCluskey supplied meat to a restaurant managed by Sullivan. Sullivan told McCluskey that he was opening a new restaurant to be known as "The Shah." McCluskey sold meat to Sullivan for The Shah. Actually, The Shah was owned and operated by Protective Service, Inc., but this was not known to McCluskey nor told to him until after a substantial bill had accumulated. When McCluskey sued Sullivan, the latter raised the defense that he was not liable because he had been acting on behalf of Protective Service. Was this defense valid? [McCluskey Commissary, Inc. v Sullivan (Idaho) 524 P2d 1063]

14. Cardente engaged in the lumber business. He had a fire insurance policy covering his lumberyard. He moved to a new location and requested the insurer's agent to make an indorsement of the policy to cover the business at its new location. The agent of the insurer agreed to do so. He failed to do so. Thereafter Cardente sustained a fire loss at the new location. He sued the agent for the fire loss. Was the agent liable? [Cardente v Maggiacomo Insurance Agency, 108 RI 171, 272 A2d 155]

43 EMPLOYMENT

A. THE EMPLOYMENT RELATION

§ 43:1. NATURE OF RELATIONSHIP. The relationship of an employer and an employee exists when, pursuant to an express or implied agreement of the parties, one person, the *employee*, undertakes to perform services or to do work under the direction and control of another, the *employer*. In the older cases this was described as the master-servant relationship.

An employee without agency authority is hired only to work under the control of the employer, as contrasted with (a) an agent, who is to make contracts with third persons on behalf of and under control of the principal, by whom he may or may not be employed, and with (b) an independent contractor, who is to perform a contract independent of, or free from, control by the other party.

Working on the premises or under the supervision of another does not always establish that the worker is the employee of such other person.

FACTS: Harris and two other registered barbers operated the Golden Sheer Barber Shop. They supplied all the capital which had been required to open the shop. Some time later Olsen, an apprentice barber, joined them at the Golden Sheer. Each of the four barbers was to pay $35 a week into a common fund which was used to pay the rent, utilities, purchase additional equipment, and make alterations. Periodically an account was given to each of the four as to the payments made from this fund. A state law required that an apprentice barber be under the supervision of a registered barber. Each of the four barbers had his own clientele, set his own prices, purchased his own materials, kept his own receipts, and fixed his own hours of work. The state department of employment determined that Olsen was employed by the three registered barbers and required them to pay an unemployment insurance tax for Olsen. They appealed.

DECISION: Judgment against the state department. The independence of each barber showed that the arrangement was merely a space-sharing plan and not an employment relationship. The fact that the state law required that an apprentice barber be under the supervision of a registered barber did not cause the apprentice to have the status of employee of the registered barber when in fact the employment relationship did not exist. [Golden Sheer Barber Shop v Morgan, 258 Ore 105, 481 P2d 624]

§ 43:2. CREATION OF THE EMPLOYMENT RELATION.

The contract upon which the employment relationship is based is subject to all of the principles applicable to contracts generally. The relation of the employer and employee can be created only by consent of both parties. A person cannot be required to work against his will, nor can he become an employee without the consent of the employer.

The contract of employment may be implied, as when the employer accepts services which, as a reasonable person, he knows are rendered with the expectation of receiving compensation. Thus, when a minor worked with his father under the supervision of the company's agent, the company impliedly assented to the relationship of employer and employee, even though the minor's name was not on the payroll.

As a result of the rise of labor unions, large segments of industrial life are now covered by *union contracts*. This means that the union and the employer agree upon a basic pattern or set of terms of employment. For example, a union contract will state that all workers performing a specified class of work shall receive a certain hourly wage. Once the contract has been made between the employer and the union, the employee has the right to receive the rate of pay specified therein.

(a) **Volunteered services.** In various shopping centers and parking lots, persons perform services for customers of the enterprise, such as loading packages in their cars. These persons are not employees of the enterprise, and tips from customers are the only remuneration they receive. The fact that they perform a service which might be rendered by employees of the enterprise does not make them employees. Likewise, they are not employees of the customer. This is important because it means that when the volunteer is negligent and causes injury to another person, the third person cannot recover damages from the enterprise or the customer. Thus, when a volunteer at a parking lot was negligent in driving the customer's car from the place where it was parked to the exit of the lot and, in so doing, damaged a third person's car, the third person could not hold the customer responsible for the harm caused by the volunteer.

(b) **Borrowed employee.** When the regular employer loans his employee to someone else, the other person is the employer both for the purpose of determining tort liability to a third person because of a wrongful act of the employee, and for the purpose of determining workmen's compensation liability to the employee because of an injury sustained while doing the work of the temporary employer. For example, when a hotel as a favor to one of its guests who operated a nearby restaurant permitted the hotel handyman to do odd jobs at the guest's restaurant, the handyman, while working at the restaurant making minor repairs, was an employee of the guest for the purpose of determining workmen's compensation liability.

(c) Self-service. The fact that customers wait on themselves in a self-service store does not make them employees of the store so as to make the store responsible to a customer injured by falling on debris dropped on the floor by another customer.[1]

§ 43:3. TERMS OF EMPLOYMENT. Basically the parties are free to make an employment contract on any terms they wish. The employment contemplated must, of course, be lawful; and by statute it is subject to certain limitations. Thus, persons under a certain age may not be employed at certain kinds of labor. Statutes commonly specify minimum wages and maximum hours which the employer must observe, and they require employers to provide many safety devices. A state may also require employers to pay employees for the time that they are away from work while voting.

Historically, wages constituted the sole reward of labor. Today in many fields of employment additional benefits are conferred upon the worker, either by virtue of the contract of employment or by federal and state statutory provision.

§ 43:4. DUTIES AND RIGHTS OF THE EMPLOYEE. The duties and rights of an employee are determined primarily by his contract of employment with the employer. The law also implies certain provisions.

(a) Services. The employee is under a duty to perform or hold himself in readiness to perform such services as may be required by the contract of employment. If the employee holds himself in readiness to comply with his employer's directions, he has discharged his obligation and he will not forfeit his right to compensation because the employer has withheld directions and has thus kept him idle.

The employee impliedly agrees to serve his employer honestly and faithfully. He also impliedly agrees to serve him exclusively during his hours of employment. The employee may do other work, however, if the time and nature of the employment are not inconsistent with his duties to the first employer and if the contract of employment with the first employer does not contain any provision against it.

An employee must obey reasonable regulations and requirements adopted by the employer.

FACTS: Santora was employed as a cashier by Martin, who ran a store under the name of Gibson's Discount Center. The store was burglarized over the weekend, and Santora moved some of the boxes that had been moved by the burglar. In order to distinguish Santora's fingerprints from other prints on the boxes, it was arranged that Santora's

---

[1] Cameron v Bohack, 27 AppDiv2d 362, 280 NYS2d 483.

fingerprints would be taken by the police. Through an oversight Santora was not informed of this in advance, and she was somewhat disturbed when a police officer appeared and told her to go with him to the police station to have her fingerprints taken. She objected that there was no need to do so but nevertheless went to the police station, her fingerprints were taken, and she was immediately brought back to the store. Thereafter she became ill because of the incident and sued Martin for damages. Decide.

DECISION: Judgment for Martin. He was not liable because there is an implied term of an employment contract that the employee will obey reasonable regulations and requirements. It was reasonable to require Santora to be fingerprinted in order to eliminate her as a suspect and thus cooperate with the employer in the apprehension of the burglar. [Martin v Santora (Miss) 199 So2d 63]

An employee has no constitutional right to wear his hair as he chooses and he may be discharged for failing to comply with the dress and grooming code of the employer.[2]

The employee impliedly purports that, in performing his duties, he will exercise due care and ordinary diligence in view of the nature of the work. When skill is required, the employee need exercise only ordinary skill, unless the employee had held himself out as possessing a special skill required by the work.

When the employee's misconduct has imposed liability upon the employer, the employee can be required to indemnify the employer for the loss which the employee has caused.

(b) Trade secrets. An employee may be given confidential trade secrets by his employer. He is under a duty not to disclose such knowledge. It is immaterial that the contract of employment did not stipulate against such disclosure. If he violates his obligation, the employer may enjoin the use of such information.

FACTS: Defler was in the business of buying and selling industrial carbons, cokes, charcoal, graphite, and related products. These were by-products, being the residues remaining after the manufacture of other products. The composition and quality of these residues would vary greatly, and Defler kept a detailed file on the exact needs of each of his customers. Defler's business was successful because of his ability to meet the needs of his customers by virtue of this information. Years later, Kleeman was hired as general manager by Defler and given access to all of his customer information. A year later Kleeman hired Schneider as a salesman for Defler. Neither of these two men had any experience with or knowledge of the business prior to their employment by Defler. Some time later, Kleeman and Schneider organized the Carchem Products Corporation to engage in the same business as Defler. They thereafter left the employment of Defler.

---

[2] Keys v Continental Illinois National Bank and Trust Co. (DC ND Ill) 357 FSupp 376. (The court noted that when the employee took the job, he had expressly agreed to comply with all rules and regulations of the employer.)

Carchem was successful because of the use of source and customer information compiled by Defler. Defler sued Kleeman, Schneider, and Carchem to enjoin the use of the information and to obtain an accounting of the profits made by the use of such information.

DECISION: Judgment for Defler. Even though there was no express provision in their contract of employment that the information about sources and customers should not be used competitively, the obligation of loyalty owed by an employee prevented Kleeman and Schneider from making use of that information for their own advantage or that of a corporation organized by them. This information was so vital to the success of Defler that it is deemed confidential, and the law will protect it by enjoining the defendants from making further use of it and by requiring them to account for or to pay to the plaintiff the profits that they had made by the improper use of that information. [Harry R. Defler Corp. v Kleeman, 19 AppDiv2d 396, 243 NYS2d 930]

Former employees who are competing with their former employer may be enjoined by him from utilizing information as to suppliers and customers which they had obtained while employees where such information is of vital importance to the employer's business.

The employee is under no duty to refrain from divulging general information of the particular business in which he is employed. Nor is he under a duty not to divulge the information of the particular business when the relation between employer and employee is not considered confidential. Mere knowledge and skill obtained through experience are not in themselves trade secrets, and employees may use the fruits of their experience in later employment or in working for themselves.

(c) Inventions. In the absence of an express or implied agreement to the contrary, the inventions of an employee belong to him, even though he used the time and property of the employer in their discovery, provided that he was not employed for the express purpose of inventing the things or the process which he discovered. The employer has the burden of proving that he is entitled to the invention or a process discovered by an employee in the course of employment.

FACTS: Bandag, Inc. was in the business of recapping used automobile tires. Morenings was employed as its chief chemist. In the course of his work, he discovered a new process for bonding treads to tires that were being recapped. He was not employed to discover such a process, and no agreement had ever been made with Bandag as to the ownership of any discoveries made by Morenings. Bandag sued Morenings, claiming that, as employer, it was entitled to the ownership of the process which had been developed in the course of Morenings' employment.

DECISION: Judgment for Morenings. The employer has the burden of proving that he is entitled to the invention or process discovered by an employee in the course of employment. As Morenings was not employed for the purpose of discovering the process and as there was no provision in the contract of employment giving the employer the right to such discovery, the employer had no right to it. [Bandag, Inc. v Morenings, 259 Iowa 998, 146 NW2d 916]

If the invention is discovered during working hours and with the employer's materials and equipment, the employer has the right to use the invention without charge in the operation of his business. If the employee has obtained a patent for the invention, he must grant the employer a nonexclusive license to use the invention without the payment of royalty. This *shop right* of the employer does not give him the right to make and sell machines that embody the employee's invention; it only entitles him to use the invention in the operation of his plant.

When the employee is employed in order to secure certain results from experiments to be conducted by him, the inventions belong to the employer on the ground that there is a trust relation or that there is an implied agreement by the employee to make an assignment of the inventions to the employer.[3]

In any case an employee may expressly agree that his inventions made during his employment will be the property of the employer. If such a contract is not clear and specific, the courts are inclined to rule against the employer. The employee may also agree to assign to the employer inventions made after the term of employment.

(d) **Compensation.** The rights of an employee with respect to compensation are governed in general by the same principles that apply to the compensation of an agent.

In the absence of an agreement to the contrary, when an employee is discharged, whether for cause or not, the employer must pay his wages down to the expiration of the last pay period. The express terms of employment or union contracts, or custom, frequently provide for payment of wages for fractional terminal periods, however, and they may even require a severance pay equal to the compensation for a full period of employment. Provisions relating to deferred compensation under a profit-sharing trust for employees are liberally construed in favor of employees.

(e) **Employee's lien or preference.** Most states protect an employee's claim for compensation either by a lien or a preference over other claimants of payment out of the proceeds from the sale of the employer's property. These statutes vary widely in their terms. They are usually called *laborers'* or *mechanics' lien laws*. Sometimes the statutes limit the privilege to the workmen of a particular class, such as plasterers or bricklayers. Compensation for the use of materials or machinery is not protected by such statutes.

§ **43:5. PENSION PLANS.** Many employers have established pension plans to benefit their employees after they retire.

(a) **The Pension Reform Act of 1974.** A federal statute, also known as the Employees Retirement Income Security Act (ERISA),[4] was adopted to provide protection for the pension interests of employees.

---

[3] US v Dubilier Condenser Corp. 289 US 178.
[4] PL 93-406.

(1) Fiduciary Standards and Reporting. Persons administering a pension fund must handle it so as to protect the interest of the employees. The fact that an employer contributed all or part of the money does not entitle him to use the fund as though it were still his own. Persons administering pension plans must make detailed reports to the Secretary of Labor.

(2) Early Vesting. The Reform Act requires the early vesting of rights of an employee.

(3) Pension Portability. The Pension Act permits a system of voluntary participation to provide a limited pension portability so that an employee does not lose his credits for years of service with one employer when he goes to work for another. When applicable, the employee may transfer his interest in his ex-employer's pension trust to an Individual Retirement Account (IRA) which may be retained as an individual account or may be added to the pension plan of his new employer with the latter's consent.

(4) Actuarial Funding. The Reform Act requires that contributions be made by employers to their pension funds on a basis which is actuarially determined so that the pension fund will be sufficiently large to make the payments which will be required of it.

(5) Termination Insurance. The Act establishes an insurance plan to protect employees when the employer goes out of business. To provide this protection, the statute creates a Pension Benefit Guaranty Corporation. In effect, this corporation guarantees that the employee will receive benefits in much the same pattern as the Federal Deposit Insurance Corporation protects bank depositors. The Guaranty Corporation is financed by small payments made by employers for every employee covered by a pension plan.

(6) Secretary of Labor. The Act gives the Secretary of Labor extensive powers in the operation and supervision of the pension plan.

(7) Enforcement. The Act authorizes the Secretary of Labor and employees to bring court actions to compel the observance of the statutory requirements.

(8) Criminal Offenses. The Act makes it a crime to fire, discriminate against, or threaten any employee who exercises any right conferred by the federal statute.

§ **43:6. ATTACHMENT AND GARNISHMENT OF WAGES.** It is generally provided that a creditor may require a third person who owes money to his debtor to pay such amount to the creditor to satisfy the creditor's claim against the debtor. That is, if A has a valid claim for $100 against B, and C owes B $100, A can require C to pay him $100, which thereby satisfies both C's debt to B and B's debt to A. The necessary legal procedure generally requires the third person to pay the money into court or to the sheriff rather than directly to the original creditor. The original creditor may also by this process usually reach tangible property belonging to his debtor which is in the custody or possession of a third person. This procedure is commonly called *attachment* and the third person is called a *garnishee*.

Under the federal Truth in Lending Act (Title I of the Federal Consumer Credit Protection Act) only a certain portion of an employee's pay can be garnisheed. Ordinarily, the amount that may be garnisheed may not exceed (a) 25 percent of the employee's weekly take-home pay or (b) the amount by which the weekly take-home pay exceeds 30 times the federal minimum wage, whichever is less.[5] The federal statutes also prohibits an employer from discharging an employee because his wages have been garnisheed for any one indebtedness.

B. EMPLOYER'S LIABILITY FOR EMPLOYEE'S INJURIES

§ 43:7. COMMON-LAW STATUS OF EMPLOYER. In some employment situations, the common-law principles apply. Under them the employer is not an insurer of the employee's safety.[6] It is necessary, therefore, to consider the duties and defenses of an employer apart from statute.

(a) Duties. The employer is under the common-law duty to furnish an employee with a reasonably safe place in which to work, reasonably safe tools and appliances, and a sufficient number of competent fellow employees for the work involved; and to warn the employee of any unusual dangers peculiar to the employer's business. Statutes also commonly require employers to provide a safe working place or safe working conditions. Under the federal Occupational Safety and Health Act of 1970, the Secretary of the Department of Labor is authorized to set safety standards for places of employment.[7] State laws continue in force as to matters not regulated by the federal statutes.

> **FACTS:** Wallace was a part-time cook employed at the Kentucky Fried Chicken of Lawton. He was told how to heat the cooking grease up to 400°, and was told to throw out any grease which was heated beyond this temperature because such "burned grease" could not be used for cooking. He was told to throw this grease in an uncovered 55-gallon drum in the alley behind the restaurant. A few nights after he began this work, he was dumping burned grease in the drum when it splattered back and severely burned him. Apparently there was water in the drum and Wallace had not been warned that hot grease would splatter back if it hit water. Wallace sued Kentucky Fried Chicken for failing to provide a safe place to work and failing to warn him of the hazards of his employment.

---

[5] Consumer Credit Protection Act § 303. Under the Uniform Consumer Credit Code, where adopted, this second alternative has been increased to 40 times the federal weekly minimum pay. UCCC § 5.105(2)(b). Prejudgment attachment of wages without notice and hearing is invalid. Sniadach v Family Finance Corp. 395 US 337.

[6] Workmen's compensation statutes by their terms generally do not apply to agricultural, domestic, or casual employment. In addition, in some states, the plan of workmen's compensation is optional with the employer or the employee.

[7] PL 91-596; 84 Stat 1590, 29 United States Code §§ 651 et seq. The federal statute also creates a National Institute of Occupational Health and Safety.

DECISION: Judgment for Wallace. The employer was obligated to provide a safe means of disposing of the burned grease and was required to warn Wallace of any hazards involved in so doing. The danger which had harmed Wallace was foreseeable. Consequently, the employer was liable because of his failure to provide a safe means of disposing of the grease and for failing to warn Wallace of the dangers involved in the manner of disposal. [Wallace v Kentucky Fried Chicken of Lawton (OklaApp) 526 P2d 504]

(b) Defenses. At common law the employer is not liable to an injured employee, regardless of the employer's negligence, if the employee was guilty of contributory negligence, or if he was harmed by the act of a fellow employee, or if he was harmed by an ordinary hazard of the work, because he assumed such risks.

§ 43:8. STATUTORY CHANGES. The rising incidence of industrial accidents due to the increasing use of more powerful machinery and the growth of the industrial labor population, led to a demand for statutory modification of common-law rules relating to liability of employers for industrial accidents.

(a) Modification of employer's common-law defenses. One type of change by statute was to modify the defenses which an employer could assert when sued by an employee for damages. Under statutes that apply to common carriers engaged in interstate commerce,[8] the plaintiff must still bring an action in a court and prove the negligence of the employer or of his employees, but the burden of proving his case is made lighter by limitations on the employer's defenses.

Under the Federal Employers' Liability Act, contributory negligence is a defense only in mitigation of damages; assumption of risk is not a defense.

In many states the common-law defenses of employers whose employees are engaged in hazardous types of work have also been modified by statute.

(b) Workmen's compensation. A more sweeping development was made by the adoption of workmen's compensation statutes in every state. With respect to certain industries or businesses, these statutes provide that an employee or certain relatives of a deceased employee are entitled to recover damages for the injury or death of the employee whenever the injury arose within the course of the employee's work from a risk involved in that work. In such a case, compensation is paid without regard to whether the employer or the employee was negligent, although generally no compensation is allowed for a willfully self-inflicted injury or one sustained while intoxicated.

There has been a gradual widening of the workmen's compensation statutes, so that compensation today is generally recoverable for accident-inflicted injuries and occupational diseases. In some states compensation for occupational diseases is limited to those specified in the

---

[8] Federal Employer's Liability Act, 45 USC §§ 1 et seq. and the Federal Safety Appliance Act, 49 USC §§ 1 et seq.

statute by name, such as silicosis, lead poisoning, or injury to health from radioactivity. In other states any disease arising from an occupation is compensable.

Workmen's compensation proceedings are brought before a special administrative agency or workmen's compensation board. In contrast, a common-law action for damages or an action for damages under an employer's liability statute is brought in a court of law.

Workmen's compensation statutes do not bar an employee from suing another employee for the injury caused him. Likewise, an employee may sue the employer when liability is based upon some principle not related to the employment relationship.

> **FACTS:** Ruth Panagos was employed by the North Detroit General Hospital. While eating lunch in the hospital cafeteria, she cut her mouth on a foreign particle contained in a piece of pie that she had purchased in the cafeteria. She sued the hospital for damages. The defendant moved to dismiss the claim on the theory that any claim of the plaintiff could only be asserted as a workmen's compensation claim.

> **DECISION:** Motion to dismiss refused. When an employee is harmed by a product purchased from her employer, liability is determined by the law of product liability and not the law of employment or workmen's compensation. [Panagos v North Detroit General Hospital, 35 MichApp 554, 192 NW2d 542]

C. LIABILITY FOR INJURIES OF THIRD PERSONS

§ 43:9. EMPLOYEE'S LIABILITY TO THIRD PERSONS FOR INJURIES. When an employee causes injury to a third person, a question arises as to whether the employee, the employer, or both, are liable to the third person. Whenever the employee injures another person, either another employee or an outsider, the liability of the employee is determined by the same principles that would apply if the employee were not employed.

§ 43:10. EMPLOYER'S LIABILITY TO THIRD PERSONS FOR INJURIES. An employer is liable to a third person for the harm done him by the act of his employee (1) when the employer expressly directed the act; (2) when the harm was due to the employer's fault in not having competent employees, or in failing to give them proper instructions, or a similar fault; (3) when the act by the employee was within the course of his employment; or (4) when the act was done by the employee without authority but the employer ratified or assented to it.

The third basis upon which the employer is made liable for acts of his employees committed within the scope of his employment [9] is known as the *doctrine of respondeat superior*. If the act by the employee is not within the

---

[9] Restatement, Agency 2d declares acts within the scope of the servant's employment to be acts of the kind that the employee was employed to perform, occurring substantially within the authorized time and space limits; and actuated, at least in part, by a purpose to serve the employer. It also requires for this purpose that if force is intentionally used against another, its use was not unexpectable by the employer, § 228(1).

scope of his employment, the employer is not liable under this doctrine. Consequently, when an employer lends an employee the employer's truck or car for the employee's personal use after working hours, the employer is ordinarily not liable for harm caused by the employee to a third person through the employee's negligent operation of the vehicle.

However, when a working employee stops to inquire whether assistance was required by a driver whose car was apparently stuck in the mud on the highway shoulder, the employee was not thereby removed from the course of his employment.[10] And the fact that the employee is giving a ride to a hitchhiker does not take the employee out of the course of his employment.

> **FACTS:** Moore was an electronics engineer employed by the United States. While traveling under a work assignment from one air base to another, he ran into and injured Romitti, who then sued the United States. The United States raised the defense that Moore was not acting within the course of his employment while driving to the new job assignment.
>
> **DECISION:** Judgment for Romitti. Under the circumstances, the action of Moore in traveling to the base was part of his work and the government was therefore liable on the basis of respondeat superior. [United States v Romitti (CA9 Cal) 363 F2d 662]

(a) **Nature of act.** Historically the act for which liability would be imposed under the doctrine of respondeat superior was a negligent act. While it was necessary that the act be in the course of employment, an act did not cease to be within the course of employment merely because it was not expressly authorized nor even because it was committed in violation of instructions. Ordinarily an employer is not liable for a willful, unprovoked assault committed by an employee upon a third person or customer of the employer, but the employer is sometimes held liable for wanton and malicious conduct of an employee on the theory that it is within the scope of employment when the employee inflicts such harm in the belief that he is furthering the employer's interest.[11]

There is a trend toward widening the employer's liability for the tort of his employee. When the employee is hired to retake property of the principal, as in the case of an employee of a finance company hired to repossess automobiles on which installments have not been paid, the employer is generally liable for the unlawful force used by the employee in retaking the property or in committing an assault upon the buyer. In contrast, the majority of court decisions do not impose liability on an employer for an assault committed by his bill collector upon the debtor.

(b) **Insurance.** The fact that the employer is insured does not affect the employer's liability, as the insurer's liability is the same as the employer's.

(c) **Borrowed employee.** In holding an employer liable for the act of an employee, it is immaterial whether the employee is a permanent employee

---

[10] Jack Cole Company v Hoff (Ky) 274 SW2d 658.

[11] R 2d § 231; Bremen State Bank v Hartford Accident & Indemnity Co. (CA7 Ill) 427 F2d 425. Some courts follow the older rule that the employer is never liable for a willful or malicious act by his employee regardless of its purpose.

or a borrowed or temporary employee. Hence, it is no defense to the liability of a repairman for the negligent repair of automobile brakes that the actual work was done by a borrowed employee.

(d) Employee of United States. The Federal Tort Claims Act declares that the United States shall be liable vicariously whenever a federal employee driving a motor vehicle in the course of his employment causes harm under such circumstances that a private employer would be liable. This statute further provides, and here reverses the ordinary rule, that the employee driver in such case shall not be liable to the injured person.

(e) Employee's automobile. When the employee uses his own automobile, there is authority that the employer is not liable for the negligent driving of the employee unless it is determined that the employer expressly or in fact authorized the employee's use of the automobile; and the mere fact that the employee was doing work for the employer at the time does not impose liability upon the employer. If the employee is involved in a collision or causes negligent harm while driving in his own car to or from work, the employer is ordinarily not liable to the injured person. Likewise, the employer is not liable when harm is caused to a third person while the employee is driving to or from meals or an employees' banquet.

§ 43:11. SUPERVISORY LIABILITY. Historically, an employer was liable for the wrongful act of an employee only when the latter was acting in the course of his employment. Conversely, if the harm was done by the employee after working hours or for his own personal benefit, there was no liability of the employer.

This concept is being eroded by the application of a concept of supervisory liability that, in effect, makes the employer liable simply because it was his employee who did the wrong. Sometimes this conclusion is explained in terms that the employer was in the better position to have avoided the harm through a more careful screening of his employees. This is ordinarily mere lip service to the concept that there must be fault as the basis for liability, because ordinarily it would be impossible for the employer to have screened so carefully and so prophetically as to have avoided the harm that resulted. The *doctrine of supervisory liability* has rather limited application, primarily because it is virtually a form of absolute liability, that is, imposing liability because harm has happened without regard to whether any fault was involved.

In the field of tort law, the concept of supervisory liability is found primarily in the case of hotels. In one case the hotel was liable when a bellboy after his working hours stole the keys to a guest's automobile and removed the automobile from the private parking garage to which another bellboy had taken it.

(a) Employer's liability for assault by third person. Assume that an employee while engaged in the course of his employment is injured by the act of a third person, such as an angry customer, a picket, or a rioter. When the employee sustains injury caused by a third person, the employer is not liable therefor to the employee unless it can be shown that the employer was in some way negligent and that such negligence made it possible for the employee to be harmed.

§ 43:12. OWNER'S LIABILITY FOR INJURIES CAUSED BY INDEPENDENT CONTRACTOR.

If work is done by an independent contractor rather than by an employee, the owner is not liable for harm caused by the contractor to third persons or their property. Likewise, the owner is ordinarily not liable for harm caused third persons by the negligence of the independent contractor's employees. For example, the owner of an automobile leaving it for repairs is not liable to a person injured by the repairman while making a road test of the car, because the repairman is not the employee of the owner, even though the road test had been made at the request of the owner.

There is, however, a trend toward imposing liability on the owner even in such a case when the work undertaken is especially hazardous in nature. That is, the law is taking the position that if the owner wishes to engage in a particular activity, he must be responsible for the harm it causes and cannot insulate himself from such liability by the device of hiring an independent contractor to do the work.

The use of independent contractors will not insulate an owner from liability when he retains control of the work. Consequently, when the owner made "subcontracts" directly with contractors and retained control and supervision of the construction work, he is deemed by law to be in possession; and when an employee of one of the contractors fell because of a defective catwalk, the owner could be held liable and could not rely on the defense that the employee's employer was an independent contractor.

§ 43:13. EMPLOYER'S INDEMNITY AGREEMENT.

When the employer performs extensive or dangerous work on the premises of a customer, the contract between the employer and the customer will commonly contain a clause by which the employer expressly agrees to indemnify the customer for any harm occurring in the performance of the work. For example, a contractor installing heavy equipment in an industrial plant may agree to indemnify the plant for any loss sustained by the plant in the course of the installation. In view of the fact that such agreements are generally made between persons who are "in business" and therefore know the significance of what they are doing, the agreements usually are literally enforced.

Depending upon the financial position of the contractor and the respective bargaining powers of the parties, the contractor may find it necessary to furnish the plant with an indemnity bond issued by an insurance company or to deposit certain assets with a bank to hold as a fund from which to pay the plant for any proper claim.

§ 43:14. ENFORCEMENT OF CLAIM BY THIRD PERSON.

When a third person is injured by an employee, he may have a cause of action or an enforceable claim against both the employee and the employer. In most states and in the federal courts, the injured person may sue either or both in one action. If the injured person sues both, he may obtain judgment against both of them but he can only collect the full amount of the judgment once.

If the employee was at fault and if his wrongful conduct was not in obedience to his employer's directions, the employer may recover indemnity from the employee for the loss that the employer sustained when he was required to make payment to the third person. When an employee acting at the direction of his employer uproots shrubbery on what the employer erroneously believes is the employer's side of the boundary line but which in fact is on the neighboring land, the employee is entitled to be indemnified by his employer to the extent that the employee pays the judgment obtained by the third person.

§ 43:15. NOTICE TO EMPLOYER OF DANGER. In a number of situations one person must give notice or warning of danger to another person and is liable for the harm that befalls the other person because of a failure to give such notice or warning. When the persons who will be exposed to the foreseeable danger are employees of a particular person, notice to the employer is generally sufficient. As a matter of practical expediency, the law assumes that the employer can be more certain of reaching each of his employees than an outsider could, and it further assumes that the employer will relay any warning to his employees in order to protect them. Thus, the manufacturer of a dangerous instrumentality satisfies the requirement of giving warning of its dangerous quality if he informs his purchaser, and an employee of the purchaser cannot bring suit against the manufacturer on the ground that the manufacturer did not give him personal warning. Likewise, when the landowner owes "invitee" protection to employees of an independent contractor working on the premises, the owner discharges his duty to inform the employees of a hidden danger by informing the independent contractor.[12]

In some product liability cases involving powerful equipment, it is held that a warning to the employer is not sufficient, and that the manufacturer must attach a warning tag or sign on the equipment.

D. TERMINATION OF EMPLOYMENT CONTRACT

§ 43:16. INTRODUCTION. A contract of employment may, in general, be terminated in the same manner as contracts of any other kind. If a definite duration is not specified in the contract, it is terminable at will and either party may terminate the contract by giving the other reasonable notice of his intention. Local statutes and union contracts commonly regulate the period of notice which the employer must give to the employee.

The employment contract may stipulate that the employer may terminate the relationship if he is not satisfied with the services of the employee. In such cases the employer is generally considered the sole judge of his reason provided that he acts in good faith.

---

[12] Delhi-Taylor Corp. v Henry (Tex) 416 SW2d 390.

§ 43:17. JUSTIFIABLE DISCHARGE BY EMPLOYER. In the absence of a contract or statutory provision to the contrary, an employer may discharge an employee for any reason or for no reason if the employment is at will. When the employment may not be terminated at will, the employer will be liable for damages if he discharges the employee without justification. The employer is justified in discharging an employee because of the employee's (a) nonperformance of duties, (b) misrepresentation or fraud in obtaining the employment, (c) disobedience to proper directions, (d) disloyalty, (e) wrongful misconduct, (f) incompetency, or (g) disability.

When the employer is a government or a branch of government, such as a public school system, the employer cannot terminate an employment contract without notice and hearing.[13]

§ 43:18. REMEDIES OF EMPLOYEE WRONGFULLY DISCHARGED. An employee who has been wrongfully discharged may bring against the employer an action for (a) wages, (b) breach of contract, or (c) value of services already rendered. In certain instances he may also bring (d) an action that results in performance of the employment contract, or (e) a proceeding under a federal or state labor relations statute.

§ 43:19. JUSTIFIABLE ABANDONMENT BY EMPLOYEE. The employee cannot be compelled to perform his contract of employment. Hence, he can at any time end the relationship by a refusal to perform the services for which he was engaged. If the contract is not terminable at will, his refusal to carry out his part of the contract may or may not make him liable for damages, depending upon the reason for leaving his employment.

The employment relationship may be abandoned by the employee for (a) nonpayment of wages, (b) wrongful assault by the employer, (c) requirement of services not contemplated, (d) employer's refusal to permit employee's performance, and (e) injurious conditions of employment.

§ 43:20. REMEDIES OF THE EMPLOYER FOR WRONGFUL ABANDONMENT. When an employee wrongfully abandons his employment, the employer may bring (a) an action for breach of contract; and in certain circumstances he may also bring (b) an action against a third person maliciously inducing the breach of contract, (c) an action to enjoin the employee from working for another employer, or (d) a proceeding under a federal or state labor relations statute.

---

[13] Gray v Board of Education, 41 AppDiv2d 73, 341 NYS2d 193.

QUESTIONS AND CASE PROBLEMS

1. An employer provided an annual outing for his employees, which was held on a working day. Any employee not attending the outing was required to report to work as usual. An employee was killed on the outing. Was his death covered by workmen's compensation? [See Lybrand, Ross Bros. & Montgomery v Industrial Commission, 36 Ill2d 410, 223 NE2d 150]

2. Faunce was employed by the Boost Co., which manufactured a soft drink. After some years he left its employ and began manufacturing a different soft drink. The company claimed that he was using trade secrets learned while he was in its employ and sought to enjoin him. It was proved that the soft drink made by the defendant was not the same as that made by the plaintiff; that the difference between one soft drink and another was primarily due to the 1 percent of the volume that represented flavoring; and that the drink made by the defendant could be made by anyone in the soft drink business on the basis of general knowledge of the trade. Was Boost entitled to an injunction? [Boost Co. v Faunce, 17 NJSuper 458, 86 A2d 283]

3. Thouron did part-time housework in Acree's home in return for an hourly pay and free transportation to and from her home in Acree's automobile driven by Acree's full-time chauffeur. While she was being driven to Acree's house to work, there was a collision because of the chauffeur's negligence. Thouron sued Acree for damages caused by the negligence of the latter's chauffeur. The workmen's compensation law was not applicable since it excluded domestic employees. The liability of the employer was thus governed by common law. Decide. [Thouron v Acree, 54 Del 117, 174 A2d 702]

4. Complitano was an employee of Steel & Alloy Tank Co. The city in which the plant was located sponsored a softball league. Complitano and other employees of Steel & Alloy formed a team which represented the employer in the league. All games were played after hours and off the premises and were managed and controlled in all respects by the employees. Steel Alloy made a financial contribution to the support of the team but had no other interest in it. Complitano was injured while playing in one of the games and filed a claim for workmen's compensation on the theory that the activity was of mutual benefit to the employer and the claimant. Decide. [Complitano v Steel & Alloy Tank Co. 63 NJSuper 444, 164 A2d 792]

5. Baugh was employed by the Lummus Cotton Gin Co. The contract of employment stated that his employment was "conditional on . . . conduct and service being satisfactory to us, we to be the sole judge. . . ." After some time the company discharged Baugh solely because it could not afford to employ him longer. Baugh sued the company. Was it liable for breach of contract? [Lummus Cotton Gin Co. v Baugh, 29 GaApp 498, 116 SE 51]

6. Buffo was employed by the Baltimore & Ohio Railroad Co. With a number of other workers he was removing old brakes from railroad cars and replacing them with new brakes. In the course of the work, rivet heads and scrap from the brakes accumulated on the tracks under the cars, but these were removed only occasionally when the men had time. Buffo, while holding an air hammer in both arms, was crawling under a car when his foot slipped on scrap on the ground, which caused him to strike and injure his knee. He sued the railroad for damages under the Federal Employers' Liability Act. Decide. [Buffo v Baltimore & Ohio Railroad Co. 364 Pa 437, 72 A2d 593]

7. The Central Lumber Co. furnished material to Schroeder for the construction of certain buildings. It also loaned her $465 to enable her to pay the men working in the construction. A mechanics' lien law gave a lien to persons furnishing materials, machinery, or fixtures for the construction of buildings. Was the company entitled to a lien for the $465? [Central Lumber Co. v Schroeder, 164 La 759, 114 So 644]

8. Laeng applied to the city of Covina for a job as a refuse crew worker. As part of the tryout for the job, he went through an obstacle course to measure his physical agility. He was injured when he fell in the course. He claimed that he was entitled to workmen's compensation. The claim was opposed on the ground that he was not an employee at the time that he was injured. Was he correct? [Laeng v Workmen's Compensation Appeals Board, 6 Cal3d 771, 100 Cal Rptr 377, 494 P2d 1]

9. A Louisiana statute requires that when an employee hired for a fixed term is fired without cause, the employer must pay him the full "salary" for the contract term. Brasher was employed by Chenille, Inc. by the year and fired by it without cause. Had he worked the full year, Chenille would have made a contribution on his behalf to a retirement fund or pension plan. Brasher claimed that such a contribution was part of his "salary" and therefore that the statute required Chenille to make that contribution. Was he correct? [Brasher v Chenille (LaApp) 251 So2d 824]

CREATION AND TERMINATION

A. NATURE AND CREATION

§ 44:1. DEFINITION. Modern partnership law shows traces of Roman law, the law merchant, and the common law of England. A Uniform Partnership Act (UPA) has been adopted in most states.[1] The single proprietorship is the most common form of business organization, but many larger businesses have two or more owners. The partnership is a common type of multiple ownership.

A *partnership* or copartnership is a legal relationship created by the voluntary "association of two or more persons to carry on as co-owners a business for profit."[2] The persons so associated are called *partners*.

While each partner is the agent of the partnership, he is not regarded as an "employee" of the partnership.

FACTS: W. M. Ford and James D. Mitcham were partners engaged in construction. Ford was killed at work. His widow made a claim for workmen's compensation. Mitcham opposed the claim on the ground that Ford was a partner and not an employee.

DECISION: Judgment for Mitcham. While a working partner does work, he is not an employee. The essential element of an employment relationship is the right of the employer to control the employee. Although a partner is required to act in a proper manner, he is not subject to the control of the partnership in the same sense as an employee, and therefore he is not an "employee" of the partnership for the purpose of workmen's compensation. [Ford v Mitcham (AlaCivApp) 298 So2d 34]

§ 44:2. CHARACTERISTICS OF A PARTNERSHIP. A partnership can be described in terms of its characteristics:

---

[1] This Act has been adopted in all states except Georgia, Louisiana, and Mississippi; and it is in force in the District of Columbia, Guam, and the Virgin Islands.

[2] Uniform Partnership Act, § 6(1); Carle v Carle Tool & Engineering Co. 33 NJSuper 469, 110 A2d 568.

(1) A partnership is a voluntary contractual relation; it is not imposed by law. Because of the intimate and confidential nature of the partnership relation, courts do not attempt to thrust a partner upon anyone.

(2) The relation of partnership usually involves contributions by the members of capital, labor, or skill, or a combination of these.

(3) The parties are associated as co-owners and principals to transact the business of the firm.

(4) A partnership is organized for the pecuniary profit of its members. If profit is not its object, the group will commonly be an unincorporated association.

The trend of the law is to treat a partnership as a separate legal person, although historically and technically it is merely a group of individuals with each partner being the owner of a fractional interest in the common enterprise. The Uniform Partnership Act does not make the partnership a separate entity and therefore suit cannot be brought by the firm in its firm name,[3] in the absence of a special statute or procedural rule so providing.

When a bank accepts a partnership as a depositor, the bank must treat the deposit as belonging to the partnership and cannot treat it as property of the individual partners. Some courts also regard a partnership as distinct from the individual partners so that a partnership cannot claim the benefit of a personal immunity possessed by an individual partner.

> **FACTS:** Wosek Delivery Service was a partnership composed of Richard Wosek and his wife, Kathleen. Richard was driving a partnership automobile. Mathews was a passenger in the automobile when it was struck by a train. He sued the partnership for his damages. Mathews and Wosek were acting within the scope of their employment by Love Brothers, Inc. By virtue of the appropriate workmen's compensation act, Richard Wosek as a co-worker of Mathews could not be sued by Mathews. Mathews sued the partnership which raised the defense that as Mathews could not have sued Wosek individually, Mathews could not sue the Wosek partnership.
>
> **DECISION:** Judgment for Mathews. The partnership was distinct from the individual partners so that it could not claim the benefit of a personal immunity possessed by an individual partner. [Mathews v Wosek, 44 MichApp 708, 205 NW2d 813]

Since a partnership is based upon the agreement of the parties, the characteristics and attributes of the partnership relationship are initially a matter of the application of general principles of contract law, upon which the principles of partnership law are superimposed.

§ **44:3. PURPOSES OF A PARTNERSHIP.** A partnership, whether it relates to the conduct of a business or a profession, may be formed for any lawful purpose. A partnership cannot be formed to carry out immoral or illegal acts, or acts that are contrary to public policy. When there is an illegal purpose, the partners cannot sue on the contracts that involve the illegality.

---

[3] Allgeier v Martin and Associates (MoApp) 508 SW2d 524.

Moreover, in such cases the partners cannot seek the aid of courts to settle their affairs among themselves. In addition, if the conduct of the partnership constitutes a crime, all persons involved in the commission of the crime are subject to punishment.

§ 44:4. CLASSIFICATION OF PARTNERSHIPS. Ordinary partnerships are classified as general and special partnerships, and as trading and nontrading partnerships.

(a) General and special partnerships. A *general partnership* is created for the general conduct of a particular kind of business, such as a hardware business or a manufacturing business. A *special partnership* is formed for a single transaction, such as the purchase and resale of a certain building.

(b) Trading and nontrading partnerships. A *trading partnership* is organized for the purpose of buying and selling, such as a firm engaged in the retail grocery business. A *nontrading partnership* is one organized for a purpose other than engaging in commerce, such as the practice of law or medicine.

§ 44:5. FIRM NAME. In the absence of a statutory requirement, a partnership need not have a firm name, although it is customary to have one. The partners may, as a general rule, adopt any firm name they desire. They may use a fictitious name or even the name of a stranger. There are, however, certain limitations upon the adoption of a firm name:

(1) The name cannot be the same as or be deceptively similar to the name of another firm for the purpose of attracting its patrons.

(2) Some states prohibit the use of the words "and company" unless they indicate an additional partner.

(3) Most states require the registration of a fictitious partnership name.

§ 44:6. CLASSIFICATION OF PARTNERS. (a) A *general partner* is one who publicly and actively engages in the transaction of firm business.

(b) A *nominal partner* holds himself out as a partner or permits others to hold him out as such. He is not in fact a partner, but in some instances he may be held liable as a partner.

(c) A *silent partner* is one who, although he may be known to the public as a partner, takes no active part in the business.

(d) A *secret partner* is one who takes an active part in the management of the firm but who is not known to the public as a partner.

(e) A *dormant partner* is one who takes no active part in transacting the business and who remains unknown to the public.

§ 44:7. WHO MAY BE PARTNERS. In the absence of statutory provisions to the contrary, persons who are competent to contract may form a partnership. A minor may become a partner, but he may avoid the contract of partnership and withdraw.

In general, the capacity of an insane person to be a partner is similar to that of a minor, except that an adjudication of insanity usually makes subsequent agreements void rather than merely voidable. An enemy alien may not be a partner, but other aliens may enter into the relationship. A corporation, unless expressly authorized by statute or its certificate of incorporation, may not act as a partner. The modern statutory trend, however, is to permit corporations to become partners.

§ 44:8. CREATION OF PARTNERSHIP. A partnership is a voluntary association and exists because the parties agree to be in partnership. If there is no agreement, there is no partnership. If the parties agree that the legal relationship between them shall be such that they in fact operate a business for profit as co-owners, a partnership is created even though the parties may not have labeled their new relationship a "partnership." The law is concerned with the substance of what is done rather than the name. Conversely, a partnership does not arise if the parties do not agree to the elements of a partnership, even though they call it a partnership. Thus, the fact that an agreement described the signers as constituting a "partnership" did not make them a partnership when in fact they were not operating a business as co-owners for profit.

> FACTS: The maximum contract interest rate in Indiana was 8 percent but this did not apply to corporations, general partnerships, limited partnerships, joint ventures, and trusts. Havens and his wife, who were unable to borrow $100 for less than 9 percent interest, executed an agreement declaring that they were a partnership. Then the partnership borrowed the money and signed a partnership note agreeing to pay 9 percent interest. Woodfill, as holder of the note, sought a declaratory Judgment to determine the validity of the note. Could the Havens raise the defense of usury?

> DECISION: Havens and his wife were in fact not partners since they were not running a business. The mere execution of a partnership agreement did not make them a partnership. Therefore the "partnership" was a sham transaction, and the ordinary usury law would be applied. [Havens v Woodfill, 148 IndApp 366, 266 NE2d 221]

The manner in which an enterprise is described in a tax return or an application for a license is significant in determining whether it is a partnership as against a person making the return or the application. The mere fact that the enterprise is described as a partnership is not controlling or binding, however, as against a person named in the return or the application as a partner if he did not know of its preparation, did not sign it, and did not know what it said. When the parties are in fact employer and employee, there is no partnership even though the employer had filed a partnership form of income tax return.

> FACTS: Chaiken and two others ran a barber shop. The Delaware Employment Security Commission claimed that the other two persons were employees of Chaiken and that Chaiken had failed to pay the unemployment compensation tax assessed against employers. He defended on the ground that he had not "employed" the other two and that all three were partners. The evidence showed that Chaiken owned

the barber shop; he continued to do business in the same trade name as he had before joined by the two alleged partners; and he had a separate contract with each of the two, which contract specified the days for work and the days off. It was also shown that Chaiken had registered the partnership name and the names of the three partners and that federal tax returns used for partnership had been filed.

DECISION: The relationship was merely that of employer and employee. The elements of co-ownership of a business conducted for profit were lacking. The fact that each "partner" had a separate contract instead of there being one partnership agreement, and that such contract specified days of work and days off, confirmed the conclusion that the other two alleged partners were merely employees. The registration and filing of returns as a partnership did not convert a nonpartnership into a partnership. [Chaiken v Employment Security Commission (DelSuper) 274 A2d 707]

§ **44:9. PARTNERSHIP AGREEMENT.** As a general rule, partnership agreements need not be in writing. A partnership agreement must be in writing, however, if it is within the provision of the statute of frauds that a contract which cannot be performed within one year must be in writing. In some situations the agreement may come under the provision of the statute that requires a transfer of interest in land to be in writing. Generally, however, the agreement need not be written solely because the partnership is formed to engage in the business of buying and selling real estate.

Even when unnecessary, it is always desirable to have the partnership agreement in writing to avoid subsequent controversies as to mutual rights and duties. The formal document that is prepared to evidence the contract of the parties is termed a *partnership agreement, articles of partnership,* or *articles of copartnership.*

§ **44:10. DETERMINING EXISTENCE OF PARTNERSHIP.** Whether a partnership exists is basically a matter of proving the intention of the parties.

As in the case of agency, the burden of proving the existence of a partnership is upon the person who claims that one exists. Thus, a son has the burden of proving that he is a partner and not the employee of his father and brother who run a family business.[4]

When the parties have not clearly indicated the nature of their relationship, the law has developed the following guides to aid in determining whether the parties have created a partnership:

(a) Control. The presence or absence of control of a business enterprise is significant in determining whether there is a partnership and whether a particular person is a partner.

(b) Sharing profits and losses. The fact that the parties share profits and losses is strong evidence of a partnership.

---

[4] Falkner v Falkner, 24 MichApp 633, 180 NW2d 491.

(c) **Sharing profits.** An agreement that does not provide for sharing losses but does provide for sharing profits is evidence that the parties are united in partnership, since it is assumed that they will also share losses. The UPA provides that sharing profits is prima facie evidence of a partnership; but a partnership is not to be inferred when profits are received in payment (1) of a debt, (2) of wages, (3) of rent, (4) of an annuity to a deceased partner's widow or representative, (5) of interest, or (6) for the goodwill of the business. The fact that one doctor receives one half of the net income does not establish that he is a partner of another doctor where he was guaranteed a minimum annual amount and federal income tax and social security contributions were deducted, thus indicating that the relationship was employer and employee.[5] If there is no evidence of the reason for receiving the profits, a partnership of the parties involved exists.

(d) **Gross returns.** The sharing of gross returns is of itself very slight, if any, evidence of partnership. To illustrate, in a case in which one party owned a show that was exhibited upon land owned by another under an agreement to divide the gross proceeds, no partnership was proved because there was no co-ownership or community of interest in the business. Similarly, it was not established that there was a partnership when it was shown that a farmer rented his airplane to a pilot to do aerial chemical spraying under an agreement by which the pilot would pay the farmer, as compensation for the use of the plane, a share of the fees which the pilot received.

(e) **Co-ownership.** Neither the co-ownership of property nor the sharing of profits or rents from property which two or more persons own creates a partnership. Thus, the fact that a person acquires a 49 percent interest in a trailer park does not establish that he is a partner.[6] This in itself does not establish that the co-owners are together conducting the trailer park business for profit. Conversely, the mere fact that there is a sharing of the income from property by joint owners does not establish that they are partners.

(f) **Contribution of property.** The fact that all persons have not contributed property to the enterprise does not establish that the enterprise is not a partnership. A partnership may be formed even though some of its members furnish only skill or labor.

(g) **Fixed payment.** When a person who performs continuing service for another person receives a fixed payment for his services, not dependent upon the existence of profits and not affected by losses, he is not a partner.

§ **44:11. PARTNERS AS TO THIRD PERSONS.** In some instances a person who is in fact not a partner or a member of a partnership may be held accountable to third persons as though he were a partner. This liability arises when a person conducts himself in such a manner that third persons are reasonably led to believe that he is a partner and to act in reliance on

---

[5] UPA § 7(4).
[6] Sandberg v Jacobson, 253 CalApp3d 663, 61 CalRptr 436.

that belief to their injury.[7] The person who incurs such a liability is termed a nominal partner, a partner by estoppel, or an ostensible partner.

Partnership liability may arise by estoppel when a person who in fact is not a partner is described as a partner in a document filed with the government, provided the person so described has in some way participated in the filing of the document and the person claiming the benefit of the estoppel had knowledge of that document and relied on the statement. For example, suppose that the partnership of A and B, in registering its fictitious name, names A, B, and C as partners and the registration certificate is signed by all of them. If a creditor who sees this registration statement extends credit to the firm in reliance in part on the fact that C is a partner, C has a partner's liability insofar as that creditor is concerned.

Conversely, no estoppel arises when the creditor does not know of the existence of the registration certificate and consequently does not rely thereon in extending credit to the partnership. Likewise, such liability does not arise when C does not know that he was described as a partner.

(a) Effect of estoppel. The existence of a partnership by estoppel means only that the fact of nonpartnership cannot be raised as a defense against a third person in whose favor the estoppel operates. That is, when creditor C sues A and claims that A is liable for the debt of the partnership because A is a partner, A cannot show that he is not a partner or that there is no partnership. In contrast, this estoppel does not make the apparent partner a member of a partnership when in fact there is no partnership. Consequently, the fact that the third person is protected does not entitle the apparent partner to a share of profits earned by the other persons who appear to be his partners, because the fact remains that the apparent partner and the others are not partners.

> **FACTS:** Kelley and Galloway were accountants doing business as a partnership. Smith was employed by them until he left in 1968. When he left the firm, he claimed that as a partner he was entitled to a 20 percent share of the profits. The partnership denied that he was a partner and claimed that he was merely an employee. Smith showed that the partnership had represented to third persons and government agencies that he was a partner in their firm. Smith sued the partnership.
>
> **DECISION:** Judgment for the partnership. Although Smith could be deemed a partner by estoppel in order to protect third persons, such estoppel would not make Smith a partner when in fact he was not. The concept of partner by estoppel protects the third person by permitting him to hold the partnership liable for the contracts made by the apparent partner but does not permit the apparent partner to share in the profits of the partnership, because the fact remains that the apparent partner and the others were not partners. [Smith v Kelley (KyApp) 465 SW2d 39]

§ 44:12. PARTNERSHIP PROPERTY. In general, partnership property consists of all the property contributed by the partners or acquired for the

---

[7] UPA § 16(1).

firm or with its funds.[8] There is usually no limitation upon the kind and amount of property that a partnership may acquire. The firm may own real as well as personal property, unless it is prohibited from doing so by statute or by the partnership agreement.

The parties may agree that real estate owned by one of the partners should become partnership property. When this intent exists, the particular property constitutes partnership property even though it is still in the name of the original owner.

(a) Title to personal property in firm name. A partnership may hold and transfer the title to personal property in the firm name, whether the name is fictitious or consists of the names of living people. Thus, a partnership may hold a mortgage on personal property in the firm name, such as "Keystone Cleaners."

(b) Title to real property in firm name. A majority of states now permit a partnership to hold or transfer the title to real property in the firm name alone, without regard to whether or not the name is fictitious.[9]

(c) Transferees of firm's real property. In order for a transfer of a firm's real property to be technically correct, (1) it must have been made by a partner or agent with the authority to make the transfer and (2) it must have been made in the name of the holder of the title. When both conditions have been satisfied, the transferee has legal title as against the partnership.

If the transfer was authorized but was not made in the name of the title holder, the transferee acquires equitable title to the property and the right to have a proper instrument of conveyance executed. When the transfer of the partnership property was not authorized, the firm may recover the property from the transferee if he knew that it was firm property or if he did not purchase it for value. When the title to the firm property is recorded but not in the name of the firm, a person who purchases from the record holder in good faith, for value, and without notice or knowledge of the partnership title, may keep the property.

A conveyance by a partner of partnership property, even though without authority, cannot be recovered by the partnership where it has been reconveyed by the grantee to a buyer for value and without notice or knowledge that the partner, in making the conveyance, had exceeded his authority.

(d) Title to partnership property in name of individual partner. Frequently property that in fact is partnership property appears of record as owned by one of the partners. This may arise when the property in question was owned by that individual before the partnership was formed and, while he contributed the property to the partnership when it was organized, he never went through the formality of transferring title to the partnership. The situation may also arise when a member of an existing partnership uses partnership funds to acquire property and, either through

---

[8] UPA § 8; All Florida Sand v Lawler Construction Co. 209 Ga 720, 75 SE2d 559.
[9] UPA § 8(3), (4).

a clerical mistake or in order to deceive his partners, takes title in his own name. In such cases the partner holding the title will be treated as a trustee holding the property for the benefit and use of the partnership, just as though the property were held in the name of the firm.

§ 44:13. TENANCY IN PARTNERSHIP. Partners hold firm property by *tenancy in partnership*.[10] The characteristics of such a tenancy are:

(a) In the absence of contrary agreement, all partners have equal right to use firm property for partnership purposes.

(b) A partner possesses no interest in any specific portion of the partnership property that he can sell, assign, or mortgage. The partner has no right in any specific property that he can transfer to a third person.

(c) In most states the creditors of a partner cannot levy on and sell his interest in specific partnership property.[11]

> **FACTS:** Buckman was owed money by one of the partners of a partnership consisting of Goldblatt and several others. Buckman obtained a judgment against his debtor and then began a foreclosure action against land owned by the partnership in order to sell the interest of his debtor. The partnership opposed this execution.

> **DECISION:** Judgment for partnership. The creditor of an individual partner may sell out that partner's interest in the firm by means of a charging order but the creditor cannot sell a fractional interest of any specific item of property. The Uniform Partnership Act, § 24, expressly prohibits execution against property of the partnership except on a claim against the partnership, and § 27 provides for the entry of a charging order against the interest of the debtor partner by virtue of which the share of any profits that would be paid to the debtor partner is to be paid to a receiver on behalf of the creditor or the court may direct the sale of the interest of the debtor partner in the partnership. [Buckman v Goldblatt, 39 OhioApp2d 1, 314 NE2d 188]

(d) The interest of a deceased partner in specific firm property vests in the surviving partners only for partnership purposes.

(e) A partner's interest in specific property is not subject on his death to any rights of his surviving spouse.

This distinct form of tenure is sometimes confused with joint tenancies and tenancies in common. The ordinary joint tenant has full beneficial ownership upon the death of the cotenant, whereas a surviving partner does not. A cotenant may transfer his interest, putting another in his place, but a partner cannot do so.

B. DISSOLUTION AND TERMINATION

§ 44:14. EFFECT OF DISSOLUTION. Dissolution ends the right of the partnership to exist as a going concern. It is followed by a winding-up

---

[10] UPA § 25(1); Williams v Dovell, 202 Md 646, 96 A2d 484.
[11] UPA § 25(2)(c).

period, upon the conclusion of which the partnership's legal existence is terminated.

Dissolution reduces the authority of the partners. From the moment of dissolution, the partners lose authority to act for the firm, "except so far as may be necessary to wind up partnership affairs or to complete transactions begun but not then finished."[12] The vested rights of the partners are not extinguished by dissolving the firm, and the existing liabilities remain. Thus, when the partnership is dissolved by the death of a partner, the estate of the deceased partner is liable to the same extent as the deceased partner.

§ 44:15. DISSOLUTION BY ACT OF PARTIES.

(a) Agreement. A partnership may be dissolved in accordance with the terms of the original agreement of the parties, as by the expiration of the period for which the relation was to continue or by the performance of the object for which it was organized.[13] The relation may also be dissolved by subsequent agreement, as when the partners agree to dissolve the firm before the lapse of the time specified in the articles of partnership or before the attainment of the object for which the firm was created. The sale or assignment by one partner of his interest to the remaining partners does not in itself dissolve the partnership.

(b) Withdrawal. A partner has the power to withdraw at any time; but if his withdrawal violates his agreement, he becomes liable to his copartners for damages for breach of contract. When the relation is for no definite purpose or time, a partner may withdraw without liability at any time, unless a sudden withdrawal would do irreparable damage to the firm.

(c) Expulsion. A partnership is dissolved by the expulsion of any partner from the business in accordance with such a power conferred by the agreement between the partners.

(d) Alienation of interest. Under the UPA neither a voluntary sale of a partner's interest nor an involuntary sale for the benefit of creditors works a dissolution of the partnership.

§ 44:16. DISSOLUTION BY OPERATION OF LAW.

(a) Death. An ordinary partnership is dissolved immediately upon the death of any partner, even when the agreement provides for the continuance of the business. Thus, when the executor of a deceased partner carries on the business with the remaining partner, there is legally a new firm.

(b) Bankruptcy. Bankruptcy of the firm or of one of the partners causes the dissolution of the firm; insolvency alone does not.

(d) Illegality. A partnership is dissolved "by an event which makes it unlawful for the business of the partnership to be carried on or for the members to carry it on in partnership." To illustrate, when it is made

---

[12] § 33.
[13] § 31(1)(a).

unlawful by statute for judges to engage in the practice of law, a law firm is dissolved when one of its members becomes a judge.

(d) **War.** A firm is ordinarily dissolved when there is war between the governments to which the different partners owe allegiance.

§ 44:17. DISSOLUTION BY DECREE OF COURT.

When a partnership is to continue for a certain time, there are several situations in which one partner is permitted to obtain its dissolution through a decree of court. A court will not order the dissolution for trifling causes or temporary grievances that do not involve a permanent harm or injury to the partnership.

The filing of a complaint seeking a judicial dissolution does not in itself cause a dissolution of the partnership as it is the decree of court which has that effect.[14]

(a) **Insanity.** A partner may obtain a decree of dissolution when his partner has been judicially declared a lunatic or when it is shown that he is of unsound mind.

(b) **Incapacity.** A decree of dissolution will be granted when one partner becomes in any way incapable of performing the terms of the partnership agreement. For example, a serious injury to one partner making it physically impossible for him to do his part is a ground for dissolution.

(c) **Misconduct.** A partner may obtain a decree of dissolution when his partner has been guilty of conduct that substantially tends to affect prejudicially the continuance of the business. The habitual drunkenness of a partner is a sufficient cause for judicial dissolution.

(d) **Impracticability.** A partner may obtain a decree of dissolution when another partner habitually or purposely commits a breach of the partnership contract or so conducts himself in matters relating to the partnership business that it is not reasonably practicable to carry on the business in partnership with him. Dissolution will be granted where dissensions are so serious and persistent as to make continuance impracticable, or where all confidence and cooperation between the parties have been destroyed.

(e) **Lack of success.** A decree of dissolution will be granted when the partnership cannot be continued except at a loss.

(f) **Equitable circumstances.** A decree of dissolution will be granted under any other circumstances that equitably call for a dissolution. A situation of this kind, for example, is present when one partner had been induced by fraud to enter into the partnership.

§ 44:18. NOTICE OF DISSOLUTION.

The rule that dissolution terminates the authority of the partners to act for the firm requires some modification.

---

[14] Cooper v Isaacs (CA DistCol) 448 F2d 1202.

Under some circumstances one partner may continue to possess the power to make a binding contract.

(a) Notice to partners. When the firm is dissolved by an act of a partner, notice must be given to the other partners unless his act clearly shows an intent to withdraw from or to dissolve the firm. If he acts without notice to his partners, he is bound as between them upon contracts created for the firm. The UPA declares that "where the dissolution is caused by the act, death, or bankruptcy of a partner, each partner is liable to his copartners for his share of any liability created by any partner acting for the partnership as if the partnership had not been dissolved unless (1) the dissolution being by act of any partner, the partner acting for the partnership had knowledge of the dissolution, or (2) the dissolution being by the death or bankruptcy of a partner, the partner acting for the partnership had knowledge or notice of the death or bankruptcy."[15]

(b) Notice to third persons. When dissolution is caused by the act of a partner or of the partners, notice must be given to third parties. A notice should expressly state that the partnership has been dissolved. Circumstances from which a termination may be inferred are generally not sufficient notice. Thus, the fact that the partnership checks added "Inc." after the partnership name is not sufficient notice that the partnership does not exist and that the business had been incorporated.

> **FACTS:** Paul Babich ran a business under the name of "House of Paul." The latter became a partnership between Babich, Dyson, and Schnepp but continued under the same name. The partners arranged for printing of advertising material with Philipp Lithographing Co., making contracts on three separate occasions for such printing. During the course of these dealings, the "House of Paul" became a corporation. When the printing bills were not paid in full, Philipp sued the partners as individuals. They claimed they were not liable because the corporation had made the contracts.

> **DECISION:** Whether or not the "House of Paul" was a corporation with respect to a particular contract was not important because no notice had been given of its change from a partnership to a corporation. Having done business with the persons originally as a partnership, the plaintiff could hold the firm and the individual persons liable as partners until notice to the contrary was given to the plaintiff. [Philipp Lithographing Co. v Babich, 27 Wis2d 645, 135 NW2d 343]

Actual notice of dissolution must be given to persons who have dealt with the firm. To persons who know of the relation but have had no dealings with the firm, a publication of the fact is sufficient. Such notice may be by newspaper publication, by posting a placard in a public place, or by any similar method. Failure to give proper notice continues the power of each partner to bind the others in respect to third persons on contracts within the scope of the business.

---

[15] UPA § 34.

When dissolution has been caused by operation of law, notice to third persons is not required. As between the partners, however, the UPA requires knowledge or notice of dissolution by death and bankruptcy. And it has been held that when the third party dealing with the partnership is not informed of the death of a partner, the surviving partners and the firm are bound by a notice sent by the third person to the deceased partner.

§ 44:19. WINDING UP PARTNERSHIP AFFAIRS. In the absence of an express agreement permitting continuation of the business by the surviving partners, they must wind up the business and account for his share to any partner who has withdrawn, been expelled, or has died. If the remaining partners continue the business and use that partner's distributive share in so doing, he is entitled to such share, together with interest or the profit earned thereon.

Although the partners have no authority after dissolution to create new obligations, they retain authority for acts necessary to wind up the business.

FACTS: The Stoddard family, father, mother, and son, were a partnership which published a newspaper, the *Walnut Kernel*. The parents died and the son kept running the paper. King performed accounting services for the paper. When he was not paid, he sued the son and the executors of the estates of the deceased partners, the parents, claiming that his bill was a partnership liability for which each was liable. The executors defended on the ground that the son as surviving partner did not have authority to employ an accountant but was only authorized to wind up the partnership business. To this defense, it was answered that the newspaper was continued in order to preserve its asset value as a going concern so that it could be sold, and that the running of the paper was therefore part of the winding up process, which, if true, would give the surviving partner the authority to employ the accountant.

DECISION: The accountant was not entitled to recover the value of his services because the son had no authority to continue the publishing of the newspaper indefinitely. The operation of the paper by the son was not a winding up of the estate but was merely a continuing of the business as usual. [King v Stoddard, 28 CalApp3d 708, 104 CalRptr 903]

With a few exceptions, all partners have the right to participate in the winding up of the business.[16]

When the firm is dissolved by the death of one partner; the partnership property vests in the surviving partners for the purpose of administration. They must collect and preserve the assets, pay the debts, and with reasonable promptness make an accounting to the representative of the deceased partner's estate. In connection with these duties, the law requires the highest degree of integrity. A partner in performing these acts cannot sell to himself any of the partnership property without the consent of the other partners.

---

[16] § 37.

§ **44:20. DISTRIBUTION OF ASSETS.** Creditors of the firm have first claim on the assets of the partnership. Difficulty arises when there is a contest between the creditors of the firm and the creditors of the individual partners. The general rule is that firm creditors have first claim on assets of the firm, and the individual creditors share in the remaining assets, if there are any.

Conversely, creditors of the individual partners have priority in the distribution of the individual assets; the claims of the firm creditors may be satisfied out of the individual partner's assets only after claims of individual creditors are settled.

After the firm liabilities to nonpartners have been paid, the assets of the partnership are distributed as follows: (1) each partner is entitled to a refund of advances made to or for the firm; (2) contributions to the capital of the firm are then returned; (3) the remaining assets, if any, are divided equally as profits among the partners unless there is some other agreement. If the partnership has sustained a loss, the partners share it equally in the absence of a contrary agreement.

Distribution of partnership assets must be made on the basis of actual value when it is clear that the book values are merely nominal or arbitrary amounts.[17]

A provision in a partnership agreement that on the death of a partner his interest shall pass to the deceased partner's widow is valid and takes effect as against the contention that it is not valid because it does not satisfy the requirements applicable to wills.

§ **44:21. CONTINUATION OF PARTNERSHIP BUSINESS.** As a practical matter, the business of the partnership is commonly continued after dissolution and winding up. In all cases, however, there is a technical dissolution, winding up, and a termination of the life of the original partnership. If the business continues, either with the surviving partners, or with them and additional partners, it is a new partnership. Again, as a practical matter, the liquidation of the old partnership may in effect be merely a matter of bookkeeping entries with all parties in interest recontributing or relending to the new business any payment to which they would be entitled from the liquidation of the original partnership.

If any dispute arises, however, it must be determined on the basis that the original partnership had ceased to exist and that the parties in interest had reached a new partnership agreement. Thus, the executor of a deceased partner has no rights in running or winding up the business in the absence of the consent of the other partners either contained in the original partnership agreement or obtained upon the death of the partner in question. The right of such executor is limited to demanding an accounting from the surviving partners upon the completion of the winding up of the partnership affairs. Consequently, a representative of the individual estate of a deceased partner does not have any right to complete a contract between a third person and the partnership.

---

[17] Mahan v Mahan, 107 Ariz 517, 489 P2d 1197.

QUESTIONS
AND CASE
PROBLEMS

1. Bates and Huffman formed a partnership to run a shoe business. In a lawsuit between the partners, Huffman claimed that the partnership agreement was void because Bates was a minor. Was he correct? [Huffman v Bates (MoApp) 348 SW2d 363]

2. Gordon Elliot was a member of a partnership. He withdrew from the partnership. Subsequently he was divorced from his wife, and the divorce decree awarded his wife his interest in the partnership assets. Did this make her a partner? [Elliot v Elliot, 88 Idaho 81, 396 P2d 719]

3. A suit was brought by the heirs of members of a partnership to determine the right to the proceeds of sale of certain real estate. The real estate had been purchased by the partnership with partnership money and in the partnership name. The real estate was not used in the partnership business but was held only for investment purposes. It was claimed by the heirs that this real estate was not subject to the provisions of the Uniform Partnership Act governing tenancy by partnership because it was not used in the business. Were they correct? [See Brown v Brown, 45 TennApp 78, 320 SW2d 721]

4. The Consolidated Loan Co. was owned and operated by three partners. After the death of two of the partners, the surviving partner, Salabes, made an agreement with the estates of the other two to continue the partnership. Thereafter Salabes brought an action for a decree that she "is now the sole remaining partner in, or the sole proprietress of, Consolidated Loan Company" subject to the interests of the estates of the deceased partners. Was she the sole owner of the enterprise? [Miller v Salabes, 225 Md 53, 169 A2d 671]

5. The Weidlich Sterling Spoon Co., a partnership owned by three brothers, was dissolved. By agreement, one of the brothers was designated as liquidating partner. After he completed liquidation, he filed an account which related only to certain legal charges and expenses that had been incurred. Was this a proper accounting? [Weidlich v Weidlich, 147 Conn 160, 157 A2d 910]

6. Williams owned and operated a bakery business. His two sons were employed in the business and from time to time received a share of the profits as a bonus. The father and one of the sons died. The administrator of the son's estate, the First National Bank, then sued the estate of the father for an accounting, claiming that the father and the two sons were a partnership and that the deceased son's estate was therefore entitled to a one-third share. Decide. [First National Bank v Williams, 142 Ore 648, 20 P2d 222]

7. The National Acceptance Co., a partnership, entered into a contract obligating it to make certain payments to the General Machinery & Supply Co. Later, General Machinery claimed that it was not bound by the contract because some of the partners of National were minors and could avoid their contract. Was this a valid defense for General Machinery? [General Machinery & Supply Co. v National Acceptance Co. (ColoApp) 472 P2d 735]

8. A lease was executed by which L rented a property to I. Thereafter C claimed that L and I were in fact partners and that the agreement between L and I was drawn in the form of a lease so as to shield L from the liability to which he would be subject as a partner. Was such evidence admissible? [See Goodpasture Grain & Milling Co. v Buck, 77 NMex 609, 426 P2d 586]

45 AUTHORITY OF PARTNERS

§ 45.1. AUTHORITY OF MAJORITY OF PARTNERS. When there are more than two partners in a firm, the decision of the majority prevails in matters involving the manner in which the ordinary functions of the business will be conducted. To illustrate, a majority of the partners of a firm decide to increase the firm's advertising and enter into a contract for that purpose. The transaction is valid and binds the firm and all of the partners.

The act of the majority is not binding if it contravenes the partnership agreement. For such matters, unanimous action is required.[1] Thus, the majority of the members cannot change the nature of the business against the protests of the minority.

When there are two or any other even number of partners, there is the possibility of an even division on a matter that requires majority approval. In such a case no action can be taken, and the partnership is deadlocked. When the partners are evenly divided on any question, one partner has no authority to act. If the division is over a basic issue and the partners persist in the deadlock so that it is impossible to continue the business, any one of the partners may petition the court to order the dissolution of the firm.

FACTS: Summers and Dooley formed a partnership to collect trash. Summers became unable to work and he hired a third man to do his work and paid him out of his personal funds. Summers suggested to Dooley that the third man be paid from the partnership funds but Dooley refused to do so. Finally Summers sued Dooley for reimbursement for the money he had spent to pay the third man.

DECISION: Judgment for Dooley. Summers had no authority to employ the third man at the expense of the firm. As the partners were evenly divided on the question of such employment, Summers had no authority to act. [Summers v Dooley, 94 Idaho 87, 481 P2d 318]

§ 45:2. EXPRESS AUTHORITY OF INDIVIDUAL PARTNERS. An individual partner may have express authority to do certain acts, either

---

[1] Uniform Partnership Act, § 18(h).

because the partnership agreement so declares or because a sufficient number of partners have agreed thereto. In addition, he has authority to do those acts which are customary for a member of such a partnership. As in the case of an agent, the acts of a partner in excess of his authority do not ordinarily bind the partnership.

In his relations with third persons, a partner's authority to act for the firm is similar to that of an agent to act for his principal.

§ 45:3. CUSTOMARY AUTHORITY OF INDIVIDUAL PARTNERS.

A partner, by virtue of the fact that he is a comanager of the business, customarily has certain powers necessary and proper to carry out that business. In the absence of express limitation the law will therefore imply that he has such powers. The scope of such powers varies with the nature of the partnership and also with the business customs and usages of the area in which the partnership operates.

The following are the more common of the customary or implied powers of individual partners:

(a) Contracts. A partner may make any contract necessary to the transaction of firm business. He cannot make a contract of guaranty, however, merely to induce a third person to purchase from the partnership.

When a plaintiff sues on a promissory note or other contract executed by a partner who does not possess express authority to enter into such transaction, the plaintiff has the burden of proving that the making of the contract or the giving of commercial paper was "usual" for a business of the character of the partnership.

> FACTS: Gonzalez and Bosquez were partners under the name of International American Advertising Agency. The business of the partnership was selling radio broadcasting time on commission. Representing that he was acting on behalf of the partnership, Bosquez executed a promissory note payable to Burns. Bosquez signed the note in his own name, and in the name of the partnership. Burns sued the partners on the note individually and as partners. The defense was made on behalf of Gonzalez and the partnership that Bosquez lacked authority to execute the promissory note and that there was no evidence that the execution of such a note was the usual way of conducting a partnership engaged in the business of selling broadcasting time.
>
> DECISION: Judgment against Burns. When a plaintiff sues a partnership on a promissory note or other contract executed by a partner who does not have express authority to enter into such transaction, the plaintiff has the burden of proving that the making or the giving of the commercial paper or other contract was "usual" for a business of the character of the partnership. Burns had failed to prove that it was usual. [Burns v Gonzalez (TexCivApp) 439 SW2d 128]

(b) Sales. A partner may sell the firm's goods in the regular course of business and make the usual warranties incidental to such sales. This authority, however, is limited to the goods held for sale by the partnership.

(c) Purchases. A partner may purchase any kind of property within the scope of the business, and for this purpose he may pledge the credit of the firm. This authority is not affected by the fact that he subsequently misuses or keeps the goods.

(d) Loans. A partner in a trading firm may borrow money for partnership purposes. In doing so, he may execute commercial paper in the firm name or give security, such as a mortgage or a pledge of the personal property of the firm. If the third person acts in good faith, the transaction is binding even though the partner misappropriates the money. A partner in a nontrading partnership does not ordinarily possess the power to borrow.

FACTS: Wilcomb, Linder, and Darnutzer were partners engaged in a farming and stock-raising business under the name of Trout Creek Land Co. One of the partners executed and delivered four promissory notes, each signed "Trout Creek Land Co., by A. J. Wilcomb." Reid, as receiver of the Bank of Twin Bridges, Montana, a corporation, brought an action against the members of the partnership to recover on the notes. Wilcomb's partners, as a defense, alleged that he had no authority to bind his partners on a firm note, and that he used the money obtained thereby for his personal speculation.

DECISION: Judgment for Reid, the plaintiff. The partnership was a trading partnership since it was engaged in buying and selling. Every partner of a trading partnership has authority to borrow money and to execute promissory notes on the credit of the firm. Consequently the notes so issued by Wilcomb were binding upon the partnership without regard to the use to which the money procured thereby was put by the borrowing partner. [Reid v Linder, 77 Mont 406, 251 P 157]

(e) Insurance. A partner may insure the firm property, cancel a policy of insurance, or make proof and accept settlement for the loss.

(f) Employment. A partner may engage such employees and agents as are necessary to carry out the purpose of the enterprise.

(g) Claims against firm. A partner has the authority to compromise, adjust, and pay bona fide claims against the partnership. He may pay debts out of firm funds, or he may pay them by transfering firm property. Although he has no power to pay his own debts from firm assets, his creditors are protected if they receive such payments in good faith and without knowledge that they come from firm assets.

(h) Claims of firm. A partner may adjust, receive payment of, and release debts and other claims of the firm. He may take money or commercial paper but, as a rule, cannot accept goods in payment. One who makes a proper payment is protected even though the partner to whom payment is made fails to account to the firm for the payment.

(i) Admissions. A partner may bind the firm by admissions or statements that are adverse to the interests of the partnership if they are made in regard to firm affairs and in the pursuance of firm business.

(j) **Notice.** A partner may receive notice of matters affecting the partnership affairs, and such notice, in the absence of fraud, is binding on the others.[2]

§ 45:4. **LIMITATIONS ON AUTHORITY.** The partners may agree to limit the normal powers of each partner. When a partner, contrary to such an agreement, negotiates a contract for the firm with a third person, the firm is bound if the third person was unaware of the agreement. In such a case, the partner violating the agreement is liable to his partners for any loss caused by the breach of his contract. If the third person knew of the limitation, however, the firm would not be bound.[3]

A third person cannot assume that the partner has all the authority which he purports to have. If there is anything that would put a reasonable person on notice that the partner's customary powers are limited, the third person is bound by the limitation.

The third person must be on the alert for the following situations in particular, as they serve to notify him that the partner with whom he deals either has restricted authority or no authority at all:

(a) **Nature of business.** A third person must take notice of limitations arising out of the nature of the business. A partnership may be organized for a particular kind of business, trade, or profession, and third persons are presumed to know the limitations commonly imposed on partners in such an enterprise. Thus, an act of a partner that would ordinarily bind a commercial firm, such as the issuance of a note, would not bind a partnership engaged in a profession. A partner in a trading partnership has much greater powers than one in a nontrading firm.

(b) **Scope of business.** A third person must recognize and act in accordance with limitations that arise from the scope of the business. A partner cannot bind the firm to a third person in a transaction not within the scope of the firm's business unless he had express authority to do so. Thus, when a partner in a dental firm speculates in land or when a partner in a firm dealing in automobiles buys television sets for resale, the third person, in the absence of estoppel or express authority, cannot hold the other partners liable on such a contract. The scope of the business is a question of fact to be determined by the jury from the circumstances of each case. In general, it means the activities commonly recognized as a part of a given business at a given place and time. The usual scope, however, may be enlarged by agreement or by conduct.

(c) **Termination of partnership.** A third person must watch for the termination of the partnership relation, either when the partnership is terminated under conditions requiring no notice or when notice of the termination has been properly given.

---

[2] UPA § 12.
[3] § 9(4).

(d) Adverse interest. A third person must take notice of an act of a partner that is obviously against the interest of the firm. To illustrate, if a partner issues a promissory note in the firm name and delivers it to his creditor in payment of a personal obligation, the latter acts at his peril because such an act may be a fraud upon the firm.

§ 45:5. **PROHIBITED TRANSACTIONS.** There are certain transactions into which a partner cannot enter on behalf of the partnership unless he is expressly authorized to do so. A third person entering into such a transaction therefore acts at his peril when the partner has not been so authorized. In such a case, the third person should check with the other partners to determine whether the transaction is authorized.

The following are prohibited transactions:

(a) Cessation of business. A partner cannot bind the firm by a contract that would make it impossible for the firm to conduct its usual business.

A partner does not have implied authority to sell the business, goodwill, and assets of a partnership business.

FACTS: William and Charlotte Davis conducted the Davis Nursing Home as a partnership. William made a contract to sell the home and all its assets and goodwill to Feingold. Charlotte refused to recognize the contract. Feingold sued William and Charlotte to obtain a decree of specific performance of the sales contract.

DECISION: Judgment for defendants. The partnership was not bound by the contract made by William as he did not have express authority to make the contract. As the performance or enforcement of the contract would make it impossible for the partnership to continue in business, the making of the contract by one partner without prior partnership authorization was prohibited. [Feingold v Davis, 444 Pa 339, 282 A2d 291]

(b) Suretyship. A partner has no implied authority to bind the firm by contracts of surety, guaranty, or indemnity for purposes other than the firm business.

FACTS: John Farson and his son, John Farson, Jr., were partners engaged in the business of buying and selling bonds and other securities under the name of Farson, Son & Co. A salesman of the firm sold to the First National Bank of Ann Arbor, Michigan, five bonds of the Eden Irrigation and Land Co. As an inducement to buy the bonds, the bank was given a written guaranty of payment of the principal and interest executed in the firm name and delivered by the cashier of the partnership under the authorization of John Farson, Sr. When the principal and interest were not paid, the bank brought an action on the guaranty against John Farson, Jr., the surviving partner, and another. The defendants contended that John Farson, Sr., had no power to bind the firm on a guaranty.

DECISION: Judgment for defendants. The authority to sell does not include the power to make a contract of guaranty. There was no local usage of trade or custom that would regard a partner as impliedly having such a power. Hence, the contract of guaranty was made without actual or apparent authority and did not bind the partnership or any of the partners. [First National Bank v Farson, 226 NY 218, 123 NE 490]

(c) Arbitration. A partner in most states cannot submit controversies of his firm to arbitration. The UPA expressly denies this power "unless authorized by the other partners or unless they have abandoned the business."[4]

(d) Confession of judgment. A partner cannot confess judgment against the firm upon one of its obligations, because all partners should have an opportunity to defend in court. This power is expressly denied by the UPA, except when the other partners consent or when "they have abandoned the business."[5]

(e) Assignment for creditors. A partner cannot ordinarily make a general assignment of firm property for the benefit of creditors. Exceptions are usually made in cases of bona fide acts in an emergency. The exceptions appear to be limited by the UPA, which provides that "unless authorized by the other partners or unless they have abandoned the business, one or more but less than all the partners have no authority to assign the partnership property in trust for creditors or on the assignee's promise to pay the debts of the partnership."[6]

(f) Personal Obligations. A partner cannot discharge his personal obligations or claims of the firm by interchanging them in any way.

(g) Sealed Instruments. Instruments under seal are binding upon the firm when they are made in the usual course of business. In a minority of the states, however, a partner cannot bind his copartners by an instrument under seal.

QUESTIONS AND CASE PROBLEMS

1. O'Bryan, Sullivan, and Davis were partners engaged in operating freight steamers on the Yukon River. Sullivan purchased in the firm name and received from Merrill certain lumber for the construction of firm warehouses at terminal points for the storage of freight. In an action on the contract of sale brought by Merrill against the members of the firm, it was contended that some of the partners had no power to bind the firm on this kind of contract. Do you agree with this contention? [Merrill v O'Bryan, 48 Wash 415, 93 P 917]

---

[4] § 9(3)(e).
[5] § 9(3)(d).
[6] § 9(3)(a).

2. Milton Smith, Maude Smith, and Warren Ten Brook were partners doing business as "Greenwood Sales & Service." Pretending to act on behalf of the partnership, Ten Brook borrowed $6,000 from Holloway, giving her a note that was signed: "Greenwood Sales & Service, by Warren Ten Brook, Partner." In fact, Ten Brook borrowed the $6,000 so that he could make his capital contribution to the partnership. The check so obtained from Holloway was payable to the order of the partnership and was in fact deposited by Ten Brook in the partnership account. When the note was not paid, Holloway sued all of the partners. The other partners claimed that neither the partnership nor they were bound by Ten Brook's unauthorized act committed for his personal gain. Was this defense valid? [Holloway v Smith, 197 Va 334, 88 SE2d 909]

3. Wilke, president of the Commercial Bank of Webster City, Iowa, and Wright entered into a farming and stock-raising partnership. The business was conducted under the name of Wilke and Wright Farm Co. The agreement stipulated that Wilke was "to have control and management of said business." Thereafter, Wright sold some partnership cattle to Gross and Gidley, cattle buyers, who resold the cattle to Simon. In an action brought against Simon to recover the cattle, Wilke alleged that Wright had no authority to sell them. Decide. [Wilke v Simon, 46 SD 422, 193 NW 666]

4. Elrod and Hansford were partners under the name of Walter Elrod & Co. Hansford purchased certain merchandise for the firm on credit from Dawson Blakemore & Co. Before the sale, Elrod had notified Dawson Blakemore & Co. that he would not be bound to pay for any purchase for the firm made on credit by Hansford. Thereafter Dawson Blakemore & Co. brought an action against the members of Walter Elrod & Co. to recover the price of the goods. Elrod contended that he was not bound by the contract made by Hansford. Decide. [Dawson Blakemore & Co. v Elrod, 105 Ky 624, 49 SW 465]

5. Petrikis, Ellis, and others, who were partners, signed an agreement stating: "We, the undersigned, hereby agree to sell our interests in the partnership business. If and when the sale takes place and after all bills are accounted for, the remainder of the money is to be divided according to the share each partner now attains in the said business." Petrikis then began negotiations to sell the business to Hanges and finally made a contract selling the business to him for $17,500. Ellis, one of the partners, refused to accept the terms of the contract. Hanges then notified the partners that he called the deal off, whereupon the partners brought suit against him for breach of contract. Was Hanges liable for breach of contract? [Petrikis v Hanges, 111 CalApp2d 734, P2d 39]

6. Damsker and Carey, partners, entered into a contract with Goldberg for the construction of a building. The construction contract provided that disputes arising thereunder would be submitted to arbitration. A dispute arose relating to extra work, and Damsker gave notice that arbitration was requested on behalf of the partnership. Goldberg opposed the entry of an order to arbitrate on the ground that the application for arbitration was not made by both partners. Decide. [Application of Damsker, 283 AppDiv 719, 127 NYS2d 355]

DUTIES, RIGHTS, REMEDIES, AND LIABILITIES

§ 46:1. DUTIES OF PARTNERS. In many respects the duties and responsibilities of a partner are the same as those of an agent.

(a) Loyalty and good faith. Each partner owes a duty of loyalty to the firm, which requires him to devote himself to the firm's business and bars him from making any secret profit at the expense of the firm, or from using the firm's funds for his personal benefit, or from making a secret gain in connection with business opportunities within the field of the business of the partnership. A partner must always act with strict fidelity to the interests of the firm. He must use his powers and the firm's property for the benefit of the partners and not for his personal gain. His duties to the firm must be observed above the furtherance of his own interests. To illustrate, when one partner in his own name renewed a lease on the premises occupied by the firm, he was compelled to hold the lease for the firm on the ground that his conduct was contrary to the good faith required of partners.

A partner, in the absence of an agreement to the contrary, is required to give his undivided time and energy to the development of the business of the partnership. Even when a partner is not required to give all of his time to the firm's business, he cannot promote a competing business. If he does so, he is liable for damages to the partnership. To illustrate, two persons form a partnership for the purpose of making and selling hats, and one of them, unknown to the other, engages in an individual enterprise of the same nature. The latter, not having given his assent, may compel the former to account for the profits of the competing business.

The obligation of a partner to refrain from competing with the partnership continues after the termination of the partnership if the partnership agreement contains a valid anticompetitive covenant. In the absence of any such restriction, or if the restriction agreed upon is held invalid, a partner is free to compete with the remaining partners, even though they continue the partnership business.

(b) Obedience. Each partner is under an obligation to do all that is required of him by the partnership agreement. Duties and restrictions are frequently imposed upon certain members by the partnership agreement.

In addition, each partner must observe any limitations imposed by a majority of the partners with respect to the ordinary details of the business. If a majority of the partners operating a retail store decide that no sales shall be made on credit, a partner who is placed in charge of the store must observe this limitation. If a third person does not know of this limitation of authority, the managing partner will have the power to make a binding sale on credit to the third person. If the third person does not pay the bill and the firm thereby suffers loss, the partner who violated the "no-credit" limitation is liable to the firm for the loss caused by his disobedience.

(c) Reasonable care. A partner must use reasonable care in the transacting of the business of the firm. He is liable for any loss resulting from his failure to do so. He is not liable, however, for honest mistakes or errors of judgment. Nor is he liable when the complaining partner likewise failed in his duty to do or not to do the same act.

(d) Information. A partner has the duty to inform the partnership of matters relating to the partnership. He must "render on demand true and full information of all things affecting the partnership to any partner or the legal representative of any deceased partner or partner under legal disability."[1]

The obligation to inform embraces matters relating to the liquidation of the partnership or the purchase by one partner of the interest of another.

(e) Accounting. A partner must make and keep, or turn over to the proper person, correct records of all business that he has transacted for the firm. When the partners are equally at fault in not making and keeping proper records, however, none can complain.

One partner may be assigned the task of maintaining the books and accounts of the firm. In such a case he has, of course, the duty to maintain proper records. If it is shown that he has been guilty of improper conduct, he has the burden of proving the accuracy of his records. Any doubt will be resolved against him; that is, if it is not clear whether he has or has not accounted for a particular item, it will be assumed that he has not and he will be liable to the firm for the item.

§ 46:2. **RIGHTS OF PARTNERS AS OWNERS.** Each partner, in the absence of a contrary agreement, has the following rights, which stem from the fact that he is a co-owner of the partnership business:

(a) Management. Each partner has a right to take an equal part in transacting the business of the firm. To illustrate, three persons enter into a partnership. The first contributes $10,000 in cash; the second, property valued at $7,500; and the third, his skill and labor. All possess equal rights to participate in the conduct of the partnership business. It is immaterial that one partner contributed more than another to the firm.

[1] Uniform Partnership Act, § 20.

As an incident of the right to manage the partnership, each partner has the right to possession of the partnership property for the purposes of the partnership.

(b) Inspection of books. All partners are equally entitled to inspect the books of the firm. "The partnership books shall be kept, subject to any agreement between the partners, at the principal place of business of the partnership, and every partner shall at all times have access to and may inspect and copy any of them."[2]

(c) Share of profits. Each partner is entitled to a share of the profits. The partners may provide, if they so wish, that profits shall be shared in unequal proportions. In the absence of such a provision in the partnership agreement, each partner is entitled to an equal share of the profits without regard to the extent of his capital contribution to the partnership or to the extent of his services.

The right to profits is regarded as personal property regardless of the nature of the partnership property. Upon the death of a partner, his right to sue for profits and an accounting passes to his executor or administrator.

(d) Compensation. Although one partner performs more duties or renders more valuable services than the others, he is not entitled to compensation for these extra services in the absence of an agreement to that effect. To illustrate, when one partner becomes seriously ill and the other partners transact all of the firm's business, they are not entitled to compensation for these services, because the sickness of a partner is considered a risk assumed in the relation. No agreement can be implied that the active partner is to be compensated, even though the services rendered by the active partner are such that ordinarily they would be rendered in the expectation of receiving compensation.

FACTS: Conrad and his five daughters formed a partnership to manage certain real estate. A suit was later brought by the five daughters for a partnership accounting and a determination of their rights. Conrad had been the manager of the partnership, and the only partner who took any active part in the conduct of the partnership business. Was he entitled to compensation for his services?

DECISION: No. A partner is not entitled to compensation unless there is an agreement therefor. No agreement could be implied, because the very absence of any agreement to compensate the father who was the only active partner showed that it was intended that he should not be given any compensation. [Conrad v Judson (TexCivApp) 465 SW2d 819]

As an exception, "a surviving partner is entitled to reasonable compensation for his services in winding up the partnership affairs."[3]

(e) Repayment of loans. A partner is entitled to have returned to him any money advanced to or for the firm. These amounts, however, must be

---

[2] UPA § 19.
[3] § 18(f).

separate and distinct from original or additional contributions to the capital of the firm.

(f) Payment of interest. In the absence of an agreement to the contrary, contributions to capital do not draw interest. The theory is that the profits constitute sufficient compensation. A partner may, therefore, receive interest only on the capital contributed by him from the date when repayment should have been made.[4] The partners, of course, may agree to pay interest on the capital contributions.

Advances by a partner in the form of loans are treated just as if they were made by a stranger. The Uniform Partnership Act provides that "a partner, who in aid of the partnership makes any payment or advance beyond the amount of capital which he agrees to contribute, shall be paid interest from the date of the payment or advance."[5]

When one partner embezzles or unlawfully withholds partnership property or money, the other partner may recover interest thereon when he sues for a dissolution of the partnership and the recovery of his proportionate share of the assets embezzled or withheld.

(g) Contribution and indemnity. A partner who pays more than his share of the debts of the firm has a right to contribution from his copartners. Under this principal, if an employee of a partnership negligently injures a third person while acting within the scope of his employment and the injured party collects damages from one partner, the latter may enforce contribution from the copartners.

The UPA states that "the partnership must indemnify every partner in respect of payments made and personal liabilities reasonably incurred by him in the ordinary and proper conduct of its business or for the preservation of its business or property."[6] The partner has no right, however, to indemnity or reimbursement when he (1) acts in bad faith, (2) negligently causes the necessity for payment, or (3) has previously agreed to bear the expense alone.

(h) Distribution of capital. Each partner is entitled to receive a share of the firm property upon dissolution after the payment of all creditors and the repayment of loans made to the firm by partners. Unless otherwise stated in the partnership agreement, each partner is entitled to the return of his capital contribution.

After such distribution is made, each partner is the sole owner of the fractional part distributed to him, rather than a co-owner of all the property as he was during the existence of the partnership.

§ 46:3. REMEDIES OF PARTNERS. The remedies available to the members of a firm are, in some instances, limited because of the peculiar relation of the partners and because of the nature of their claims. In the

---

[4] § 18(d).
[5] § 18(c).
[6] § 18(b).

following discussion the distinction between actions at law and actions in equity is preserved, although in most states and in the federal courts there is today only a civil action.

(a) Actions at law. An action on a partnership claim can only be brought in the partnership name. A partner cannot maintain an action at law against the firm upon a claim against the partnership. A partnership cannot bring an action at law against one of its members on claims that the firm holds against him. In the absence of statute a partnership cannot maintain an action against another firm when they have partners in common.

One partner cannot maintain an action at law against another on claims involving partnership transactions. There are two exceptions to this general rule: (1) when the claim has been distinguished from the firm dealings by agreement; and (2) when the firm accounts have been balanced and show the amount to be due.

Partners may sue each other at law in those cases in which there is no necessity of investigating the partnership accounts. Situations of this kind exist when a partner dissolves the relation in violation of his agreement, when a partner fails to furnish capital or services agreed, or when a partner wrongfully causes injuries to his copartner that in no way involve the partnership.

(b) Actions in equity. The proper tribunal to settle all controversies growing out of partnership transactions is a court of equity. For example, an action by a partner to recover his share of profits should be brought in equity. The powers and the procedure of this court are such as to enable it to settle fully problems that arise in winding up the affairs of the firm.

In many instances an accounting is sought in connection with the dissolution of the firm. The Uniform Partnership Act states that a partner is entitled to an accounting (1) if he is wrongfully excluded from the partnership business or possession of its property by his copartners; (2) if the right exists under the terms of any agreement; (3) if he is a trustee; or (4) if other circumstances render an accounting just and reasonable.[7]

§ 46:4. PARTNER'S LIABILITY AS TO PARTICULAR ACTS. Just as a principal is not liable for every act of his agent, so the partnership and the members of the partnership are not liable for every act of each partner. Just as an agent's act binds the principal only when it is within the agent's scope of authority, real or apparent, so a partner's act binds the firm and other partners only when it is within the scope of the partner's authority, real or apparent.

(a) Contracts. All members of the firm are liable on contracts made by a partner for the partnership and in its name if they were made within the scope of his real or apparent authority. This is true even though the partners may be unknown to the third persons. Thus, a dormant partner, when discovered, is bound with the others.

---

[7] § 22.

When a partner, acting on behalf of the partnership, makes an authorized, simple contract in his own name, the other members of the firm are liable as undisclosed principals.

When a partner with necessary authority executes commercial paper in the name of the firm, each partner is bound thereby, even though he had not individually signed the paper. If a partner signs a commercial paper in his own name, the partnership, as undisclosed principal, cannot sue or be sued thereon.

While partnership law determines the authority of a partner to enter into transactions on behalf of the firm, the Uniform Commercial Code governs how commercial paper is to be executed by a partner.

> **FACTS:** Steitz and Hamrick were partners operating a restaurant, the Desert Inn. On behalf of the partnership, Hamrick borrowed money from McCollum and signed a promissory note which read, "For value received _____promise to pay." The note was signed by Hamrick and under his name he wrote the name, "The Desert Inn," and its address. He also wrote the address a second time on the left corner following the word "address." The note was not paid. McCollum sued Steitz, on the theory that the note was a partnership obligation. Steitz claimed that the note was signed by Hamrick as an individual note and therefore did not bind the partnership, in which case Steitz would not be liable for its payment.
>
> **DECISION:** The signing of his individual name followed by the name of the Desert Inn, together with the fact that an address was put on the note at two places indicated that the signing of the name of Desert Inn, with its accompanying address, was intended as a signing of the partnership name on behalf of the partnership. The note was a partnership liability and Steitz was liable thereon, though he had not signed the note. [McCollum v Steitz, 261 CalApp2d 76, 67 CalRptr 703]

When a borrowing partner gives the lender a promissory note which is his personal obligation, the partnership and the other partners cannot be held liable thereon even though the borrowing partner used the money for the benefit of the partnership.

> **FACTS:** William and Woodson Johnson, partners in a dairy, purchased their feed from Edwards Feed Mill. Woodson made a purchase of feed in his own name and executed a promissory note for its payment in his own name. Edwards sued both partners on the note on the theory that William was also liable since the partnership had received the benefit of the purchase.
>
> **DECISION:** Judgment for William. The note was not a partnership note but a personal obligation of Woodson. It was immaterial whether the other partner had in fact received the benefit of the note. [Edwards Feed Mill v Johnson (TexCivApp) 302 SW2d 151]

The fact that a partner has either express or implied authority to bind the partnership does not in itself establish that a contract made by him is a partnership contract. As in the case of agency situations generally, a contract between the third person and the principal, here the partnership, only arises when that is the intention of the parties. Consequently, where a third person and a partner make a contract intending to bind the partner individually rather than the partnership, no contract liability of the partnership is created. Care must be taken to distinguish this situation from that in which the partnership is not disclosed and in which the third person has the intention of dealing with the partner only, as in such cases the partnership may be bound or have rights under the rules governing undisclosed principals who act through authorized agents.

(b) Torts. All partners are liable for torts, such as fraud, trespass, negligence, and assaults, committed by one partner while transacting firm business.[8] The members of a firm are also liable for breach of trust by a partner in respect to goods or money of a third person held by the firm.

When a partner is guilty of fraud in dealing with a third person, the partnership is liable for the consequences even though the commission of fraud was not within the scope of the partner's authority.

> FACTS: Zemelman and others did business as a partnership under the name of Art Seating Company. The partnership obtained a fire insurance policy from the Boston Insurance Company. There was a fire loss and a claim was filed under a policy. The claim was prepared by one of the partners, Irving Zemelman. The insurance company asserted that false statements were made by Zemelman and consequently the insurer was not liable on the policy because the policy contained an express provision stating that it was void if a false claim was made. The partnership replied that it was not bound by any fraudulent statement of Zemelman, as the making of fraudulent statements was not within the scope of his authority.

> DECISION: Judgment for the insurance company. When a partner is guilty of fraud in dealing with a third person, the partnership is liable for the consequences of the fraud even though the commission of such fraud was not within the scope of the partner's authority. [Zemelman v Boston Insurance Co. 4 CalApp3d 15, 84 CalRptr 206]

When one partner is guilty of misconduct with respect to a third person, the partnership and the other partners may be vicariously liable for such misconduct. The circumstances may be such that the other partners are themselves liable for their own failing to take steps to protect the third person's interest. The partnership is not liable for a tort that has no relation to the partnership business. This is so even though the partnership had been informed of the partner's conduct but had not taken any action thereon.

> FACTS: Kelsey-Seybold Clinic was a medical partnership. One of the doctors alienated the affections of the wife of one of the patients. Maclay, the husband, sued the partnership, claiming that although he had informed one of the other doctors, nothing had been done by the partnership about the matter. Was the partnership liable to the husband for the misconduct of one of the doctors in the partnership?

---

[8] § 13.

DECISION: No. The tort of alienating the affections of the patient's wife was actually and obviously outside the scope of the partnership business, and therefore the partnership had no vicarious liability for the act of the wrongdoing partner. The fact that the partnership had not done anything when informed by the husband did not constitute a ratification by the partnership of the improper conduct so as to make it an action of the partnership. [Kelsey-Seybold Clinic v Maclay (Tex) 466 SW2d 716]

(c) **Crimes.** The partners of a firm and the partnership itself are liable for certain crimes committed by a partner in the course of the business, such as selling goods without obtaining a necessary vendor's license or selling in violation of a statute prohibiting sale. If carrying on the firm business does not necessarily involve the commission of the act constituting a crime, the firm and the partners not participating in the commission of a crime or authorizing its commission generally are not criminally liable. This exception is not recognized in some cases, such as the making of prohibited sales to minors or sales of adulterated products.

As a practical matter, the criminal liability of a partnership is limited to the imposition of a fine because it is not possible to imprison the partnership.

§ **46:5. NATURE OF PARTNER'S LIABILITY.** By virtue of the Uniform Partnership Act, partners are jointly liable on all firm contracts. They are jointly and severally liable for all torts committed by an employee or one of the partners in the scope of the partnership business.

When partners are liable for the wrongful injury caused a third person, the latter may sue all or any number of the members of the firm.

§ **46:6. EXTENT OF PARTNER'S LIABILITY.** Each member of the firm is individually and unlimitedly liable for the debts of the partnership regardless of his investment or his interest in its management. Moreover, the individual property of a partner may be sold in satisfaction of a judgment, even before the firm property has been exhausted.

(a) **Liability for breach of duty.** When a partner violates a duty owed to the partnership, his liability is determined by the general principles of law applicable to such conduct.

When one partner commits a fraud upon his partner, the injured partner may recover with compensatory and exemplary damages from the wrongdoing partner.

FACTS: Arnold and Morgan were partners. They voluntarily dissolved the partnership on the basis of a financial statement prepared by Morgan. In this statement, he knowingly undervalued the assets of the partnership so that Arnold received approximately $13,000 less than he was entitled to. Subsequent to the dissolution, Arnold learned of the deception and sued Morgan for damages. The jury awarded Arnold compensatory damages of approximately $13,000 and exemplary damages for $25,000. Morgan appealed.

DECISION: Judgment affirmed. When one partner commits a fraud upon another partner, the injured partner may recover both compensatory and exemplary damages from the wrongdoing partner. The amount of the exemplary damages recovered was not excessive. [Morgan v Arnold (TexCivApp) 441 SW2d 897]

(b) Liability of new partners. At common law a new partner entering an old firm is liable only for obligations arising thereafter. He may, however, expressly or impliedly assume the existing liabilities. When a new firm takes over the assets of an old firm, there is often an agreement that the new firm will pay existing obligations.

The UPA states that a "person admitted as a partner into an existing partnership is liable for all the obligations of the partnership arising before his admission as though he had been a partner when such obligations were incurred, except that this liability shall be satisfied only out of partnership property.[9] Thus, his liability does not extend to his individual property.

(c) Effect of dissolution on partner's liability. A partner remains liable after dissolution unless the creditors expressly release him or unless the claims against the firm are satisfied. The UPA states the following rules: "(1) The dissolution of the partnership does not of itself discharge the existing liability of any partner. (2) A partner is discharged from any existing liability upon dissolution of the partnership by an agreement to that effect between himself, the partnership creditor, and the person or partnership continuing the business; and such agreement may be inferred from the course of dealing between the creditor having knowledge of the dissolution and the person or partnership continuing the business. (3) Where a person agrees to assume the existing obligations of a dissolved partnership, the partners whose obligations have been assumed shall be discharged from any liability to any creditor of the partnership who, knowing of the agreement, consents to a material alteration in the nature or time of payment of such obligations. (4) The individual property of a deceased partner shall be liable for all obligations of the partnership incurred while he was a partner but subject to the prior payment of his separate debts."

§ 46:7. ENFORCEMENT OF PARTNER'S LIABILITY. The manner in which the civil liability of a partner may be enforced depends upon the form of the lawsuit brought by the creditor. The firm may have been sued in the name of all the individual partners doing business as the partnership, as "Plaintiff v *A*, *B*, and *C*, doing business as the Ajax Warehouse." In such a case, those partners named are bound by the judgment against the firm if they have been properly served in the suit. Partners either not named or not served are generally not bound by the judgment.

When there is a dispute on the point, the question of whether one partner was acting in the scope of the partnership business at a particular time is a question to be submitted to the jury.

---

[9] UPA § 17; also see §§ 41(1) and (7).

FACTS: Phillips and Harris were partners selling automobiles. While driving a partnership car on partnership business, Harris collided with Cook. The Cooks sued Phillips and Harris. The trial judge submitted to the jury whether Harris was in fact operating the automobile in the scope of the partnership business at the time of the collision. The jury found that he was.

DECISION: Judgment for the plaintiffs against both partners. When it is found that one partner was driving an automobile in the partnership business, the partnership and all partners are liable for harm caused by the negligence of the driving partner. [Phillips v Cook, 239 Md 215, 210 A2d 743]

If the judgment binds an individual partner, the creditor may enforce the judgment against that partner before, at the same time, or after he seeks to enforce the judgment against the firm or other partners who are also bound by the judgment. If a partner is not bound by the judgment, the creditor must bring another lawsuit against the partner in which he establishes that the defendant is a partner in the particular partnership and that a judgment was entered against the partnership for a partnership liability. When this is established, a judgment is entered in favor of the creditor against the particular partner. The creditor may then have execution on this judgment against the property of the partner.

§ 46:8. SUIT IN THE FIRM NAME. At common law a partnership could not sue or be sued in the firm name on the theory that there was no legal person by that name. If the partnership was composed of A, B, and C, it was necessary for them to sue or be sued as A, B, and C. If the firm name was "The X Bakery," some states required that they appear in the action as "A, B, and C, trading as The X Bakery." By statute or court rule, this principle of the common law has been abolished in many states, and a partnership may sue or be sued either in the names of the partners or in the firm name.

The identity of the parties in an action is determined by the nature of the obligation on which the action is brought. If the action is brought on a commercial paper held by one partner, the action must be brought in his name, although he could readily change this situation by indorsing the instrument to the firm.

QUESTIONS AND CASE PROBLEMS

1. Delay and Foster entered into a partnership. Thereafter Foster wrongfully dissolved the partnership. Delay brought an action at law against Foster to recover damages arising out of the wrongful dissolution and breach of the partnership agreement. The defendant contended that the plaintiff was not

entitled to bring an action at law but should have brought an action in equity. Do you agree? [Delay v Foster, 34 Idaho 691, 203 P 461]

2. The St. John Transportation Co., a corporation, made a contract with the firm of Bilyeu & Herstel, contractors, by which the latter was to construct a ferryboat. Herstel, a member of the firm of contractors, executed a contract in the firm name with Benbow for certain materials and labor in connection with the construction of the ferryboat. In an action brought by Benbow to enforce a lien against the ferryboat, called The James Johns, it was contended that all members of the firm were bound by the contract made by Herstel. Do you agree? [Benbow v The James Johns, 56 Ore 554, 108 P 634]

3. Kittilsby and Vevelstad were partners doing work on a mining claim known as the Sea Level Claim. Kittilsby did the assessment work for one year and then went to Seattle, upon the promise of Vevelstad, to do the work for the following year. Vevelstad did not do the work, and the claim became open to location. Vevelstad procured Singleton, who was to act for him, to locate and prove a claim covering the same district. After Singleton had conveyed the claim to him for a nominal consideration, Vevelstad sold the claim to the Juneau Sea Level Copper Mines. Thereafter Kittilsby brought an action against Vevelstad to recover half of the proceeds of the sale. Was he entitled to judgment? [Kittilsby v Vevelstad, 103 Wash 126, 173 P 744]

4. Martinoff brought a suit against Triboro Roofing Co. and a partnership named Renray Realty Co. The plaintiff named the partnership in its firm name as a defendant and also each of the seven partners. Service of process was made on only one of the partners, namely David Raynes. What liabilities of the firm and the individual partners could be enforced in this action? [Martinoff v Triboro Roofing Co. 228 NYS2d 139]

5. Henslee and Boyd formed a partnership to operate a sawmill business. As part of the agreement, Henslee agreed to sell timber to the partnership at the prevailing market prices. Boyd later sued Henslee to set aside the agreement on the ground of fraud and breach of partnership duties. One of the objections made by Boyd was that Henslee had refused to sell timber to the partnership as required by the agreement. Henslee replied that he had refused to sell because the partnership could not pay in cash. Boyd then answered that Henslee should not have insisted on a cash sale since that would use up the partnership's ready cash. Was Henslee guilty of a breach of his partnership duty? [Henslee v Boyd, 235 Ark 369, 360 SW2d 505]

6. A partnership agreement specified that the partners who worked as full-time employees "shall draw a salary for their work in such amounts as may be agreed on from time to time by unanimous consent and agreement of all the partners." In a dispute between Horn, one of the partners, and the partnership, it was claimed by Horn that this agreement entitled him to compensation for the life of the partnership, and could not be terminated by a vote of the other partners. Was he correct? [Horn v Builders Supply Co. (TexCivApp) 401 SW2d 143]

SPECIAL VENTURES

A. GENERAL PRINCIPLES

§ 47:1. INTRODUCTION. New forms of business organizations are evolving to meet the modern business and investment needs. No one questions the statement that man's way of life and his pattern of doing business are continually changing. As man undertakes new activities, he is faced with the problem of organization. How should he structure the enterprise? This has both a positive and a negative aspect. As to the positive, it is necessary to employ that form of structure or organization which will permit the doing of the desired work or the attainment of the desired goal in the most efficient manner. As to the negative, how can the enterprise and the participants be protected from the hazards that may arise?

Initially the entrepreneur and society tend to follow existing patterns. This is due in part to the fact that the old familiar patterns and devices have been working reasonably well. It is also due to the inability of man to imagine a new structure. Slowly, however, discontent arises with some aspect of the old patterns and man attempts a slight modification. After a while the modifications become so dominant that it can be recognized that the structure is no longer the old pattern modified but is in effect a new pattern. A number of these variant patterns are considered in this chapter. Some of them are of interest today primarily as a matter of legal and societal history. Others are very much in use.

§ 47:2. PURPOSE OF SPECIAL VENTURE. Today's special venture may be either permanent or temporary. Down to the middle of this century, persons organizing a business generally hoped to stay in that business the rest of their lives or for many years. Today it is common to form temporary ventures.

These are sometimes temporary because the subject matter or life of the contemplated enterprise is not continuing. For example, when several contractors pool their resources for the purpose of constructing a highway, that particular venture is terminated when the highway is completed. Had the contractors so agreed, a permanent continuing relationship could have been formed. Structurally it would probably be a partnership or a corporation. In view of the one-project lifespan of the venture above described, the contractors would probably not adopt a formal organization but would have a loose working arrangement or joint venture.

In many instances the special venture is merely a new way of doing old operations in order to obtain a particular advantage, generally a tax advantage. Thus, we have limited partnerships formed, not for the purpose of investing and obtaining a money return on the limited partner's investment, but for the purpose of obtaining tax shelter benefits for the limited partner. Likewise, a general partnership may be formed not for the purpose of staying in business but for the purpose of effecting a sale of a single proprietorship. Here instead of *A*, a single proprietor, selling his business to *B*, *A* and *B* will form a partnership which will be immediately liquidated with the assets being distributed to *B*. This has the same ownership transferring effect as though the business had been sold by *A* directly to *B* but *A* will have in some instances a better tax position than in a direct sale. Sometimes the owner of property wishes to continue to use it but desires to sell it to obtain certain advantages. In such a case, the owner may sell the property to a buyer who will then lease it back to the seller. When the sales price and lease rentals are properly adjusted, this can result in a tax saving.

In this chapter a number of patterns for special ventures are considered. In addition to these, the enterprise may be based upon an agency, a partnership, or a corporation.

B. FRANCHISES

§ 47:3. **DEFINITION.** The use of franchises has expanded rapidly in recent years as a method of controlling and financing operations by the franchisor and as a method of investment and participation for the franchisee. A *franchise* has been defined by the Federal Trade Commission for the purpose of one of its investigations as "an arrangement in which the owner of a trademark, tradename, or copyright licenses others, under specified conditions or limitations, to use the trademark, tradename, or copyright in purveying goods or services." The franchise has developed in the American economy as a means by which a business can expand through numerous outlets and maintain control of operations, but shift to someone else the burdens and problems of actual operation. To the *franchisee* (the holder of the franchise), the franchise has the attraction of permitting him to operate as a single proprietor or one-man business or a small corporation, yet not stand alone in the economic world because he has the advantage of being associated with the *franchisor* (the grantor of the franchise) or of selling the franchisor's nationally advertised product or service.

§ 47:4. **THE FRANCHISOR AND THE FRANCHISEE.** Theoretically the relationship between the franchisor and the franchisee is an arm's length relationship between two independent contractors, their respective rights being determined by the contract existing between them.

(a) Prices and standards. The franchise device is frequently used as a means of maintaining prices or standards, or both. Depending upon the nature of the business, the franchisor may be content to charge the franchisee according to the franchisor's established price scale or contract and is not concerned with the prices or charges of the franchisee in dealing with its customers. If the franchisor is not content with letting the franchisee fix his own prices, the franchisor might be able to require a price maintenance under fair trade acts [1] or by the device of selling on consignment.[2] If the franchise involves licensing the franchisee to use a trademark or formula of the franchisor, the latter may be able to exercise greater control over the franchisee than otherwise.

Ordinarily there should be no question of the validity of provisions seeking to maintain standards since a franchisor has a legitimate interest in maintaining standards in order to protect his name and reputation.

(b) Purchase of materials and supplies. Ordinarily the franchise carries with it an obligation of the franchisee to deal exclusively with the franchisor and thus provides the franchisor with an outlet for his goods and services. When the franchise relates to a product-selling business, the exclusive dealings provision imposes upon the seller the duty "to use best efforts to supply the goods and [upon] the buyer to use best efforts to promote their sale."[3] Exclusive dealings provisions will in some cases be held invalid, however, under the federal antitrust law. For example, when the franchisee is tied to exclusive purchasing of requirements from the franchisor, there may be a violation of the federal antitrust law.

(c) Payment for franchise. The franchise holder will ordinarily pay a flat initial fee for the privilege of being granted the franchise. Commonly there will be a percentage scale clause so that additional payments are made to the franchisor of a stated percentage of the amount of sales or the volume of business of the franchisee. The franchise agreement may also require the franchisee to pay a percentage of advertising costs of the franchisor.

(d) Penalty powers. Franchise contracts contain various provisions by which the grantor of the franchise can enforce the terms of the franchise contract without going to court. When the terms relate to service operations, such as the operation of a hotel or motel, the franchise contract may provide for inspections by the franchisor and may give him the right, at the franchisee's expense, to place an employee of the franchisor in charge of

---

[1] Since the only persons involved are the franchisor and the franchisee, who are the parties to the price maintenance agreement, no question arises as to nonsigners (see § 5:4) although a fair trade act may be inapplicable because the transaction does not relate to a commodity within the scope of the statutes.

[2] Such agreements may violate the federal antitrust law, however, when placed in an economically coercive setting. See Simpson v Union Oil Co. 377 US 13.

[3] Uniform Commercial Code § 2-306(2).

the franchisee's business in the event that the franchise contract terms are not met. More drastic penalties may be provided in the form of the reservation of the power of the franchisor to suspend or revoke the franchise. Such remedies are commonly employed when the franchise holder does not meet "production" or sales quotas.

When the relationship between the franchisor and a franchisee is designed primarily to effect the sale of products manufactured by the franchisor, the relationship is governed by Article 2 of the Uniform Commercial Code and the fundamental "selling" characteristic of the relationship is not to be obscured by provisions in the contract relating to franchising and services.

In some instances the grantor of the franchise has acted in an arbitrary manner or has made unreasonable demands upon the franchise holder. There is no general rule of law protecting franchise holders, although it is possible that in time the concept of unconscionability will be extended by the courts to monitor or police the terms and operation of a franchise contract. At present, federal legislation is the greatest protection of the franchise holder, the antitrust law protecting him from certain oppressive practices, with the Automobile Dealer's Day in Court Act [4] protecting the holders of automobile dealership franchises.

By federal statute, an automobile dealer holding a franchise from a manufacturer may sue the manufacturer for damages arising from the manufacturer's failure to act in "good faith" in complying with any terms or provisions of franchise, or in terminating, canceling, or not renewing the dealer's franchise.

(e) **Duration.** The franchise may run as long as the parties agree. Generally it will run a short period, such as a year, so that the franchise holder is well aware that if he wants to stay in business under the franchise, he must adhere to the terms of the contract and keep the franchise grantor satisfied. Franchise contracts generally contain an additional provision permitting termination of the franchise upon notice. The fact that the franchise holder has spent much time and money on the assumption that he would continue to have the franchise does not bar the franchisor from terminating the franchise agreement when so authorized by its terms, although some courts will bar a termination without cause until the franchise has run sufficiently long to enable the franchisee to recapture his capital investment.

When a lease and dealership contract are executed by a gasoline company and a gas station operator as parts of the same transaction, the gasoline company can terminate the lease only when it would be allowed to terminate the dealership agreement. Consequently, where by statute it could only terminate the dealership for cause, it could not terminate the lease without cause although the lease expressly gave the right to terminate on 10 days' notice.

---

[4] 15 United States Code § 1222. Several states have similar statutes. As to the meaning of good faith, see § 15:5.

FACTS: Shell Oil Company leased a gas station to Marinello and executed a dealership agreement with him for the operation of the station. The lease gave Shell Oil the right to terminate the lease on 10 days' notice. Some time later, Shell notified Marinello that it was terminating the lease. He objected on the ground that there was no "cause" for termination in that he had properly performed his obligations under the dealership agreement. He claimed that Shell was terminating the lease to retaliate against him for not selling sufficient tires, batteries, and accessories, and for requesting a price reduction in gasoline. Shell claimed that it could terminate the lease without cause. Marinello brought a lawsuit to prevent the termination of his lease.

DECISION: Judgment for Marinello. A statute prohibited termination of dealerships without cause. As the lease and dealership had been executed as parts of the same transaction, the gasoline company could only terminate the lease when it would be allowed to terminate the dealership agreement. Therefore it could not terminate the lease without cause even though the lease expressly gave the right to terminate on 10 days' notice. [Shell Oil Co. v Marinello, 63 NJ 402, 307 A2d 598]

(f) **Statutory regulation.** There are several statutory reform movements, both at the federal and the state levels, to provide general protection for the franchise holder. In one sense, this is merely another effort on the part of society to equalize the bargaining positions of the parties, who in theory are bargaining equals but who in actual practice are not. Viewed in this light, the modern movement for consumer protection and the movement for the protection of franchise holders are closely related.

Protective regulation of franchisees generally relates to problems of fraud in the sale of the franchise and protecting the franchisee from unreasonable demands and termination by the franchisor. The sale of franchises is often fraudulent with the franchisor misrepresenting the "get rich quick" aspects and the scope of the enterprise. Members of the small consumer class are particularly vulnerable to the sales appeal of the franchisor for the franchise is sold as a way to obtain financial independence and to "be your own boss." Too often the franchise operation exists only on paper so that the individual franchise is worth substantially less than the price the franchisee pays for it. In such circumstances the franchisee is in the same unfortunate position as the defrauded buyer of stock of a corporation. Because of this similarity, a number of states have proceeded against the fraudulent vendor of franchises by applying the law regulating the sale of securities. Other courts refuse to hold that the statute governing the sale of securities is applicable to the sale of a franchise.

Franchise promotion plans which pay a franchisee a bonus for each new recruit that he obtains have been condemned in some states as an illegal lottery.

(g) **The foreign franchisor.** One of the big problems facing a franchisee is that the franchisor is often an out-of-state enterprise. This imposes a substantial burden on a franchisee who seeks to bring suit against the franchisor. To facilitate suing the foreigner, most states have in recent years adopted long-arm statutes. Under such a statute, the franchisee may bring suit against the franchisor in the state of the franchisee's residence or place of business. When the franchisor conducted a selling campaign within the forum state and was obligated to render certain services, there is a sufficient contact with the forum to justify the application of the long-arm statute as to local contracts and to permit suit by the forum franchisee against the nonresident franchisor.

§ 47:5. THE FRANCHISOR AND THIRD PERSONS. Generally the franchisor is not liable in any way to a third person dealing with or affected by the franchise holder. This freedom from liability, while at the same time maintaining control over the general pattern of operations, is one of the reasons why franchisors grant franchises. If the negligence of the franchisee causes harm to a third person, the franchisor is not liable because the franchisee is regarded as an independent contractor.

When the franchisee makes a contract with a third person, the franchisor is not liable on the contract since the franchisee is not the agent of the franchisor and does not have authority to bind the franchisor by contract.

(a) **Actual control.** An exception is made to the foregoing rules when the franchisor exercises such actual control over the operations of the franchise holder that the latter is not to be regarded as an independent contractor but rather as an employee or agent of the franchisor. This conclusion is likely to be reached when the franchisee makes contracts in the name of the franchisor, the franchisor controls the hiring and firing of employees of the franchisee, and the franchisor alone can adjust customer complaints. Likewise, when a franchisee is so controlled by a franchisor that it is in fact the alter ego of the franchisor, the franchisor will be liable to a customer of the franchisee where a consumer protection statute seeks to protect consumers from exploitation by being charged for unused instructions, services, or goods.

(b) **Product liability.** When the franchise involves the resale of goods manufactured or obtained by the franchisor and supplied by him to the franchisee, there is the growing likelihood that if the product causes harm to the franchisee's customers, the franchisor will be liable to the customer on theories of warranty [5] or strict tort liability.

Similarly, when a franchisor establishes the standards under which franchisees make products, the franchisor is liable to an injured person as though he were a manufacturer or seller, even though the manufacturing franchisee is an independent contractor.[6]

---

[5] UCC §§ 2-313 and 2-314.

[6] It would be more accurate to describe the franchisee as an independent user, as he does not contract "to do" but basically merely "to use." In many instances the franchisee is under an obligation to maintain a specified quota, in which case he may more properly be called an independent contractor.

§ 47:6. THE FRANCHISEE AND THIRD PERSONS.

When the franchise holder has any contract relationship or contact with a third person, the contract or tort liability of the franchisee is the same as though there were no franchise. For example, if the franchise is to operate a restaurant, the franchise holder is liable to a customer for breach of an implied warranty of the fitness of the food for human consumption to the same extent as though the franchise holder were running his own restaurant under his own name. If the franchise holder negligently causes harm to a third person, as by running over him with a truck used in the enterprise, the conclusion is the same and the tort liability of the franchise holder is determined by the principles which would be applicable if no franchise existed. The franchise holder is liable on the contract that he makes in his own name. The fact that there is a franchise does not add or subtract from the liability which the franchisee would have in the same situation had there been no franchise.

C. SPECIAL VENTURE ORGANIZATIONS

§ 47:7. LIMITED PARTNERSHIP.

When joint or common participation is sought, a special venture organization might be formed instead of a decentralized structure, such as that in a franchise system, or instead of a standard organization, such as a corporation. A common form of modified partnership is the limited partnership. This form of partnership is solely a creature of statute; that is, it cannot be created in the absence of a statute authorizing it. Most of the states have adopted the Uniform Limited Partnership Act (ULPA).[7]

In a *limited partnership* certain members contribute capital without assuming personal liability for firm debts beyond the loss of their investment. These members are known as *special* or *limited partners*. The members who manage the business and assume full personal liability for firm debts are *general partners*. A limited partnership can be formed under the UPLA by "one or more general partners and one or more limited partners."[8]

Unlike a general partnership, this special form can be created only by executing and swearing to a certificate setting forth the essential details of the partnership and the relative rights of the partners. The certificate, when executed, must be recorded in the office of the official in charge of public records, such as the Recorder of Deeds, of the county in which the principal place of business of the partnership is located.

The limited partner contributes cash or property, but not services. With certain exceptions, his name cannot appear in the firm name. His rights are limited to receiving his share of the profits and a return of capital upon dissolution; he cannot exercise any control over the business. If improper use is made of his name, giving the public the impression that he is an active partner, or if he exercises a control over the business, he becomes liable as a

---

[7] This Act has been adopted in all states except Delaware and Louisiana, and is in force in the District of Columbia and the Virgin Islands.

[8] Uniform Limited Partnership Act, § 1.

general partner. In any case, a limited partner cannot withdraw his capital contribution when it is needed to pay creditors.

While a limited partner cannot take part in the actual operation of the partnership without subjecting himself to liability as a general partner, he may give general management advice in seeking to salvage a failing enterprise without thereby losing the benefit of his "limited" status with respect to a general partner. That is, a general partner cannot require the limited partner to share in the losses of the enterprise.

> **FACTS:** Diversified Properties was organized as a limited partnership. Weil was the general partner. He brought an action seeking to hold the limited partners on the theory that they had taken such part in the management of the business that they had become general partners.
>
> **DECISION:** Judgment for the defendants. The remedy of holding a limited partner liable as a general partner was designed to protect creditors of the partnership. A general partner cannot invoke this remedy against a limited partner and his remedy is to dissolve the partnership. [Weil v Diversified Properties (DC DistCol) 319 FSupp 778]

The dissolution and winding up of limited partnerships is governed by the same principles applicable to general partnerships. In many respects the ULPA follows the general pattern of the UPA.

A general partner is not to be deemed the agent of the limited partner so that the conducting of the business by the general partner within the forum state does not constitute the doing of business by the foreign limited partner.

Although the limited partner is in fact making an investment in the enterprise, statutes regulating the making of investments by the purchase of securities do not apply to the formation of a limited partnership.

§ 47:8. **JOINT VENTURE.** A *joint venture*, or joint adventure, is a relationship in which two or more persons combine their labor or property for a single undertaking and share profits and losses equally, or as otherwise agreed. Where several contractors pool all their assets in order to construct one tunnel, their relationship is a joint venture.

> **FACTS:** Three corporations and two individuals pooled their equipment, services, and assets for the performance of a contract to construct a tunnel. When Wheatley brought suit against them, he claimed that they were a joint venture.
>
> **DECISION:** The corporations and individuals had formed a joint venture since they had pooled everything and had limited their associating to the performance of the one tunnel construction contract. [Wheatley v Halvorson, 213 Ore 228, 323 P2d 49]

The statute of frauds does not apply to a joint venture agreement even though the object of the adventure is a real estate operation.

A joint venture is similar in many respects to a partnership, but it differs primarily in that the joint venture relates to the prosecution of a single venture or transaction, although its accomplishment may require several years, while a partnership is generally a continuing business or enterprise. This is not an exact definition because a partnership may be expressly created for a single transaction. Because this distinction is so insubstantial, many courts hold that a joint venture is subject to the same principles of law as partnerships.[9] Thus, the duties owed by the joint venturer to each other are the same as in the case of partnerships, with the result that when the joint venturers agree to acquire and develop a certain tract of land but some of the venturers secretly purchase the land in their own names, the other joint venturers are entitled to damages for this breach of the duty of loyalty.

An agreement for farming operations that provides for sharing expenses and profits, or an agreement to purchase real estate for development and resale, will often be regarded as a joint venture.

It is essential that there be a community of interest or purpose and that each coadventurer have an equal right to control the operations or activities of the undertaking. The actual control of the operations may be entrusted to one of the joint adventurers. Thus, the fact that one joint adventurer is placed in control of the farming and livestock operations of the undertaking and appears to be the owner of the land does not destroy the joint adventure relationship.

As in the case of partnerships, a minor may be a member of a joint venture.

FACTS: The Shafer family ran an ice cream business. Milton, the father, who held a franchise from Mr. Softee, purchased a truck and obtained liability insurance from Mutual Creamery Insurance Co. The policy declared that it did not cover an "employee" of Milton. While the truck was being driven by Gaylord, a hired driver, there was a collision in which Milton's daughter, Patricia, was injured. When claim was made against the insurance company for her injuries, it defended on the ground that it was not liable on the theory that Patricia was an employee of Milton. Patricia and another minor daughter worked in the ice cream business. The family planned that one day Patricia would own the business. From time to time Milton would give the two girls money, but the amount bore no relation to the success of the business and was not shown on the books of the business. No Social Security tax was paid with respect to the daughters, no amount was withheld for federal tax purposes from the payment given to them, and the girls were not covered by state workmen's compensation.

DECISION: Judgment for Patricia. She was not an "employee" of the business. The operation of the business was "a joint enterprise, with the members of the family, including the girls, being copartners, and not one which involved an employment situation." [Mutual Creamery Insurance Co. v Gaylord, 290 Minn 47, 186 NW2d 176]

It is generally essential that the joint venture be for a business or commercial purpose.

The fact that there is a common business objective or goal does not establish that the persons seeking that objective or goal are engaged in a

---

[9] Pedersen v Manitowac Co. 27 NYS2d 412, 306 NYS2d 903, 255 NE2d 146.

joint venture. The relationship may be merely a contract to employ an independent contractor or an employee, or a sales contract. In determining whether a relationship is one of employment or a joint venture, it is often important to determine whether one person carries workmen's compensation insurance with respect to the other, whether social security taxes are paid with respect to him, and whether federal withholding tax deductions are made from the share of profits received by any of the persons. Persons who are joint venturers will ordinarily have unlimited joint and several liability with respect to obligations of the enterprise, without respect to whether they have signed any agreement or commercial paper executed on behalf of the venture.

When the joint venture agreement states the time for which the venture is to last, such specification will be given effect. In the absence of a fixed duration provision, a joint venture is ordinarily terminable at the will of any participant,[10] except that when the joint venture clearly relates to a particular transaction, such as the construction of a particular bridge, the joint venture ordinarily lasts until the particular transaction or project is completed or becomes impossible to complete.

When there is joint activity by an owner and a prospective buyer, such activity may be a joint venture so that the negligence of the one is imputed to the other. For example, where an owner of an airplane and a person who contemplated buying a fractional interest in the plane were taking turns flying the plane, such use of the plane was a joint venture and the negligence of the owner piloting the plane is therefore imputed to the prospective buyer so that when he brought suit against a third person, an electric company maintaining a power line into which the plane crashed, the buyer was barred by the negligence of the owner.

Joint venture is a term which is descriptive of the relationship rather than the structure. For example, there may be a corporation through which the joint venture is conducted, as when A and B, the joint venturers, form a corporation to conduct the venture with each probably owning one half of its stock.

Sight is frequently lost of this distinction between relationship and structure for the reason that many joint ventures have no formal structure and therefore the relationship is the concept which attracts attention.

§ 47:9. MINING PARTNERSHIP. A *mining partnership* is an association formed for the purpose of conducting mining operations. In some states it is declared by statute that a mining partnership exists when two or more persons engage in working a mine claim. Apart from statute, the formation of such a partnership is a matter of intention, as in the case of an ordinary partnership, evidenced by words or conduct of the parties. The intent to create a mining partnership must be shown.

In many respects the mining partnership is governed by the same principles as an ordinary partnership. The authority of a mining partner to bind the mining partnership, however, is more limited than in the case of a

---

[10] Maimon v Telman, 40 Ill2d 535, 240 NE2d 652.

general partnership. Ordinarily that authority is limited to matters that are necessary and proper or usual for the purpose of working the mine. Moreover, the interest of a partner is transferable, and his transferee becomes a partner in the firm in his place without regard to the wishes of the other partners. Similarly, there is no dissolution when the interest of a partner passes to another person by operation of law, or when a partner becomes bankrupt or dies. Profits and losses, unless otherwise stipulated, are shared proportionately according to the contributions made or shares held by each partner.

§ **47:10. SYNDICATE.** A *syndicate* is generally defined as an association of persons formed to conduct a particular business transaction, generally of a financial nature. Thus, a syndicate may be formed by which its members agree to contribute sufficient money to purchase the control of a railroad. One of the common types of this form of business is the *underwriting syndicate*, which is an organization of investment banks for the purpose of marketing large issues of stocks or bonds.

A syndicate may be incorporated, in which case it has the attributes of an ordinary corporation. If it is not incorporated, it is treated in many respects the same as a general partnership, although it is held that, as in the case of the mining partnership, the personal factor or relationship between the partners is not important. When this is so held, it also follows that the interest of each member is freely transferable and that his transferee succeeds to his rights and to membership in the syndicate.

§ **47:11. UNINCORPORATED ASSOCIATION.** An *unincorporated association* is a combination of two or more persons for the furtherance of a common nonprofit purpose. No particular form of organization is required, and any conduct or agreement indicating an attempt to associate or work together for a common purpose is sufficient. Social clubs, fraternal associations, and political parties are common examples of unincorporated associations.

Generally the members of an unincorporated association are not liable for the debts or liabilities of the association by the mere fact that they are members. It is generally required to show that they authorized or ratified the act in question. If either authorization or ratification by a particular member can be shown, he is unlimitedly liable as in the case of a general partner.

Except when otherwise provided by statute, an unincorporated association does not have any legal existence, such as has a corporation, apart from the members who compose it. Thus, an unincorporated association cannot sue or be sued in its own name.[11]

§ **47:12. COOPERATIVE.** A *cooperative* consists of a group of two or more independent persons or enterprises which cooperate with respect to a common objective or function. Thus, farmers may pool their farm products

---

[11] Kansas Private Club Association v Londerholm, 196 Kan 319, 410 P2d 429.

and sell them as a group. Consumers may likewise pool their orders and purchase goods in bulk.

(a) Incorporated cooperative. Statutes commonly provide for the special incorporation of cooperative enterprises. Such statutes often provide that any excess of payments over costs of operation shall be refunded to each participant member in direct proportion to the volume of business which he has done with the cooperative. This contrasts with the payment of a dividend by an ordinary business corporation in which the payment of dividends is proportional to the number of shares held by the shareholder and is unrelated to the extent of his business activities with the enterprise. The fact that a cooperative is incorporated does not convert it into a corporation for all purposes and it retains its fundamental characteristic of an association designed to render services to its members.

FACTS: Lambert was a member of the Fisherman's Dock Cooperative, Inc. The cooperative changed its bylaws to provide that, when a shareholder's membership in the cooperative was terminated, he was to receive what he had paid for his shares rather than the book value of his shares. Lambert's membership was terminated and he claimed that he was entitled to the book value of the shares in spite of the contrary bylaw.

DECISION: Judgment against Lambert. A cooperative is designed to bring its members goods or services without a middleman's profit being added to the cost and therefore a cooperative should be allowed to survive the withdrawal of any participant. By making payment to the withdrawing members, the cooperative should not be placed in a position of financial difficulty. Moreover, the participant did not have a vested right to receive the value specified by the bylaws when he became a member. Thus the book value originally specified could be amended so as to pay the smaller refund of the purchase price. [Lambert v Fisherman's Dock Cooperative, Inc. 115 NJSuper 424, 280 A2d 193]

As the agreement by the members of sellers' cooperatives that all products shall be sold at a common price is an agreement to fix prices, the sellers' cooperative is basically an agreement in restraint of trade. The Capper-Volstead Act of 1922 expressly exempts normal selling activities of farmers' and dairymen's cooperatives from the operation of the federal Sherman Antitrust Act as long as they engage in normal cooperative practices and do not conspire with outsiders to fix prices.

§ 47:13. BUSINESS TRUST. A *business trust, common-law trust,* or *Massachusetts trust* arises when the owners of property transfer the ownership to one or more persons, called *trustees,* to be managed for business purposes by the trustees for the benefit of the original owners. In addition to the transfer of the legal title to the trustee or trustees, *trust certificates* or *trust shares* are issued to the former owners as evidence of their interest, and the profits are divided proportionately among the holders of the certificates.

Like shares in a corporation, shares in a business trust may be transferred. Unlike a corporation, the holders of the shares do not have control of the trustees running the business, as do shareholders of the board of directors of a corporation. Some courts hold that the business trust is merely a trust and the fact that it is designed for business operations, rather than to pay money for the support of certain persons or institutions, does not prevent the ordinary trust relationship law from applying.

> **FACTS:** The Greer Investment Co. transferred money to F. H. Greer and others to hold as trustees under a business trust with the name of The Petroleum Royalties Co. The trust was to continue for 20 years. The trust agreement authorized the trustees to convey the property to new trustees when this was deemed judicious. Toward the end of the 20-year period, the trustees, then Catlett and others, decided to continue the business by conveying the assets to a new business trust, Petroleum Royalties, Limited, and to require the shareholders of the old trust to become shareholders of the new trust. To determine the validity of this plan, Catlett and the other trustees brought an action against Hauser and the other shareholders in the original business trust.

> **DECISION:** Judgment against the trustees. The trust was lawful but, since the trust was to terminate at the end of 20 years, the intention of the persons creating the trust could not be evaded by the device of transferring the trust shares to another trust. [Hauser v Catlett, 197 Okla 668, 173 P2d 728]

Other courts hold that for the purpose of taxation or the regulation of the business, the business trust is to be classified as a corporation.

One of the objectives of the business trust is to achieve a limited liability for the members or holders of trust certificates. In most jurisdictions the certificate holders are not liable for the debts of the business trust if they have relinquished all control over management to the trustees. The same conclusion is reached if a clause in the agreement establishing the trust states that the certificate holders shall not be liable, at least with respect to persons dealing with the trust with knowledge or notice of such a limitation. In order to bring knowledge of such a limitation to third persons, it is common for the stationery of the business trust to state that such a limitation exists.

§ 47:14. **JOINT-STOCK COMPANY.** *Joint-stock companies* are of common-law origin, although in a number of states they are now regulated by statute. This form of association has features resembling both a partnership and a corporation, or a business trust. Like a corporation, the shares of its members are transferable. The contract of the members provides that any member may transfer his share and that the person to whom the share is transferred shall be accepted as a member. The management of the company is generally delegated to designated persons because as a general rule the membership is much larger than that of an ordinary partnership. The business is usually conducted under an impersonal name.

§ 47:15. EXPANSION OF PARTICIPANT LIABILITY. The fact that the relationship between persons is not a partnership, a joint venture, or a similar organization does not necessarily establish that a member of the enterprise is not liable to third persons. There is a judicial trend in favor of imposing liability on persons participating in an enterprise or economic activity when it may be reasonably foreseen that harm may be caused third persons. This concept is distinct from the supervisory and vicarious liability of an employer for the acts of his employee, or the product liability of a manufacturer or seller, but the same underlying force of protecting the third person or the consumer may be seen at work.

For example, under this new view it has been held that a savings and loan association financing a home construction project owed a duty to purchasers of the homes to see that the houses were not defectively constructed; and when cutting corners on construction costs made the homes defective but private buyers could not determine this fact for themselves, the savings and loan association was liable on a negligence basis to the purchasers even though there was no privity of contract between them, and the failure in duty of the governmental building inspectors did not relieve the association of such liability.[12]

As an aspect of particpant liability, the character of one participant may affect the status of another. For example, where a state government and a private enterprise are joint venturers or partners in a profit-making venture, the discriminatory conduct of the private enterprise may be deemed "state action" within the meaning of the constitutional guarantee of equal protection.[13]

QUESTIONS AND CASE PROBLEMS

1. Ettelsohn, Allen, and Levinson formed a limited partnership. The proceedings for the formation of the limited partnership complied with requirements of the statute except that Ettelsohn, the limited partner, contributed goods instead of cash as specified by the statute. In an action brought by Claflin, a creditor of the firm, it was claimed that Ettelsohn was a general partner. Decide. [Claflin v Sattler, 41 Minn 430, 43 NW 382]

---

[12] Connor v Great Western Savings and Loan Ass'n, 69 Cal2d 850, 73 CalRptr 369, 447 P2d 609 (a dissenting opinion was filed on the ground that the financer had no control over the construction work and that any duty owed by the financer was to its shareholders and not to the purchasers of the homes). California Civil Code § 3434 was amended after the Connor decision so as to limit the Connor doctrine by prohibiting liability of a lender to third persons for the negligent construction work of a borrower as long as the lender does not engage in any nonlending activity and is not a party to any misrepresentations. Bradley v Craig, 274 CalApp2d 466, 79 CalRptr 401, refused to apply the Connor concept in an individual construction loan transaction when the lender was deemed to do nothing more than lend money.

[13] Burton v Wilmington Parking Authority, 365 US 715. See also Lucas v Wisconsin Electric Power Company (CA7 Wis) 466 F2d 638 cert den 409 US 1114.

2. Merrilees, Hopkins, Mayer, and Adams formed a limited partnership but did not record their partnership agreement until 49 days after the partnership business began operations. Stowe, a creditor, claimed that a general partnership had been created because of the delay in filing the agreement. Decide. [Stowe v Merrilees, 6 CalApp2d 217, 44 P2d 368]

3. Simpson and Saunders each had a used car dealer's license. They made an agreement to run their businesses independently but to share a lot, the building thereon, the furnishings, and the use of a telephone. Bates sued both Simpson and Saunders claiming that they were joint venturers and therefore both were liable for the fraudulent conduct of Simpson. Was Saunders liable? [Bates v Simpson, 121 Utah 165, 239 P2d 749]

4. In 1955 Booth, an experienced broker and trader in oil properties, and Wilson, who had been a jewelry merchant, made an oral agreement to work together in acquiring and trading in oil, gas and mineral leases as a joint venture. As each lease was dealt in and disposed of, the two would take out whatever profit there was, divide it equally between themselves, and treat that operation as closed. In 1958 Booth and Wilson attempted to arrange a lease transaction with Gilbert but were unable to do so because of defects in the title. Booth then told Gilbert to revoke the contract, that he and Wilson did not have the money to go through with the deal, and that Gilbert should try to make the best deal with anyone else that he could. Thereafter, Wilson and Rector took a lease from Gilbert in their names. Booth then sued Wilson and Rector, claiming that he was entitled to share therein. Was he correct? [Booth v Wilson (TexCivApp) 339 SW2d 388]

5. Brenner was in the scrap iron business. Almost daily Plitt loaned Brenner money with which to purchase scrap iron. The agreement of the parties was that when the scrap was sold, Plitt would be repaid and would receive an additional sum as compensation for making the loan. The loans were to be repaid in any case, without regard to whether Brenner made a profit. A dispute arose as to the relationship between the two men. Plitt claimed that it was a joint venture. Decide. [Brenner v Plitt, 182 Md 348, 34 A2d 853]

48 NATURE AND CLASSES

§ 48:1. DEFINITION OF A CORPORATION. A *corporation* is an entity, an artificial legal being, created by government grant and endowed with certain powers. That is, the corporation exists in the eyes of the law as a person, separate and distinct from the people who own the corporation.

This concept means that property of the corporation is not owned by the persons who own shares in the corporation, but by the corporation. Debts of the corporation are debts of this artificial person and not of the people running the corporation or owning shares of stock in it. The corporation can sue and be sued in its own name with respect to corporate rights and liabilities, but the shareholders cannot sue or be sued as to those rights and liabilities. Furthermore, a parent corporation and its wholly-owned subsidiary corporation are regarded as separate entities.

FACTS: The Branmar Theatre Co., a family corporation, leased a theater from Branmar, Inc. The lease prohibited it from transferring the theater. The holders of the stock of Branmar Theatre Co. sold their stock to the Schwartzes. The lessor (Branmar, Inc.) claimed that this was a violation of the antiassignment provision and threatened to cancel the lease. Branmar Theatre Co. thereafter brought an action for a declaratory judgment to enjoin the cancellation of the lease.

DECISION: Judgment for Branmar Theatre. The clause only bound the corporation. It did not prevent the shareholders from transferring their stock. The separate entity of the corporation would not be ignored so as to bind the shareholders by the antiassignment clause. [Branmar Theatre Co. v Branmar, Inc. (DelCh) 264 A2d 526]

A corporation is formed by obtaining approval of a *certificate of incorporation, articles of incorporation,* or a *charter* from the state or national government.[1] The persons who develop the idea of forming a

---

[1] In speaking of corporate matters, one is likely to become confused by the use of the terms "charter," "articles of incorporation," and "certificate of incorporation." Under the modern statute the word "charter" is generally replaced with "certificate of incorporation." That is, an application is filed for a certificate of incorporation rather than requesting or petitioning the government to grant or issue a charter. The application for a certificate of incorporation is accompanied by the blueprint of the proposed corporation or its articles of incorporation. The approval of the application in effect makes "official the right of the corporation to exist and to follow the pattern or blueprint of the articles of incorporation.

corporation and who induce others to join in the enterprise are called *promoters*. The persons who make the application to the government for the charter are called *incorporators*.

The corporation is one of the most important forms of business organization. To the large-scale enterprise it offers an easier way to finance itself by means of dividing its ownership into many small units that can be sold to a wide economic range of purchasers. In addition to assisting financing operations, the corporate device offers a limited liability to the persons interested in the enterprise and a perpetual succession not affected by the death of any particular owner or by the transfer of his interest. Because of its limited liability, the corporation is also popular with many smaller businesses.

§ 48:2. EVOLUTION OF THE CORPORATION. The business corporation arose in the law to meet the economic needs of the modern world. The law was unwilling to permit single proprietors and partnerships to have the attributes that are today possessed by a business corporation; but since society needed those attributes, it created a new legal person, the corporation, and the law was willing to endow it with the attributes that were denied to individuals or partnerships. Various organizations, such as colonial trading companies, municipal and religious corporations, joint stock companies, and limited partnerships contributed to the development of the modern corporation. The evolutionary process continues because of the growing recognition that some corporations have such a specialized function or nature that they should be treated differently than business corporations generally.

The corporation is formed by obtaining government approval. Originally this was in the form of a charter expressly given to the incorporators—at first, by the British Crown, and then, after the American Revolution, by the governor or legislature of the particular state. While the corporation has an older ancestry, the business corporation of the twentieth century can be said to date from the British companies formed in the sixteenth and seventeenth centuries for the purpose of discovering new territory and trading and governing such territories. The Tudor rulers of England, hard put for cash, in effect farmed out or franchised out to corporations the right to explore and rule the undiscovered world.

By the beginning of the twentieth century, American society responded to the increasing demand for incorporation by applying the assembly-line technique to the granting of corporate charters. Obtaining a charter was made a cut-and-dried procedure similar to obtaining most licenses. The promoters filed an application and paid a fee and, if the application was properly filled out, it would be merely a routine operation to get the charter.

§ 48:3. CLASSIFICATIONS OF CORPORATIONS.

(a) Public, private, and quasi-public corporations. A *public corporation* is one established for governmental purposes and for the administration of public affairs. A city is a public or municipal corporation acting under authority granted it by the state.

A *private corporation* is one established by private interests, whether for charitable and benevolent purposes or for purposes of finance, industry, and commerce. Private corporations are often called "public" in business circles when their stock is sold to the public.

A *quasi-public corporation*, which is also known as a public service corporation or a public utility, is a private corporation furnishing services upon which the public is particularly dependent. Examples of this class of corporations are those operating railroads, canals, and bridges or those supplying gas, electricity, and water. Such corporations are usually given special franchises and powers, such as the power of eminent domain.

(b) Public authorities. In the twentieth century, the public is increasingly demanding that government perform services. Some of these are performed directly by government. Others are performed by separate corporations or *authorities* that are created by government. For example, a city parking facility may be organized as a separate *municipal parking authority*. A public low-cost housing project may be operated as an independent *housing authority*.

The use of these separate corporations has two advantages: (1) control, and (2) financing. Under (1), the authority has the ability to concentrate continuously on one set of problems and to hire personnel who are specialists in the areas involved. Accordingly, there is continuing expert control of the problems in question.

With respect to (2), an authority can raise money by selling bonds, that is, borrowing. Generally, the authority is not subject to any of the limitations to which a government would be subject. Particularly, an authority is not subject to a limitation imposed by a state constitution that the state government shall not incur debt greater than a stated maximum.[2]

(c) Domestic and foreign corporations. If a corporation has been created under the law of a particular state or nation, it is called a *domestic corporation* with respect to that state or nation. Any other corporation going into that state or nation is called a *foreign corporation*. Thus, a corporation holding a Texas charter is a domestic corporation in Texas but a foreign corporation in all other states and nations. This distinction becomes important in considering the extent of control that may be exercised by a government over corporations operating within its territorial boundaries. Whether a corporation is domestic is determined without regard to the residence of its shareholders or incorporators, or the state in which it conducts business. A corporation created under the law of one nation is classified as an *alien corporation* in other nations.

(d) Special service corporations. Corporations formed for transportation, banking, insurance, savings and loan operations, and similar specialized functions are subject to separate codes or statutes with regard to their organization. In addition, federal and state laws and administrative agencies regulate in detail the manner in which their business is conducted.

---

[2] State ex rel Warren v Nusbaum, 59 Wis2d 391, 208 NW2d 780.

(e) Close corporations. There is no requirement that an enterprise must be big before it can incorporate. Many corporations are small firms, which in the last century would have operated as single proprietorships or partnerships but which are today incorporated either to obtain the advantages of limited liability or a tax benefit, or both. Such a corporation may have only a small number of outstanding shares and these are owned by the person who formerly would have been the single proprietor or by him and his family or friends. The stock is closely held by this man or group, from whence comes the name of *close corporation;* it is not traded publicly.

It would be foolish to require a close corporation to follow the same procedure as a large corporation; and statutes adopted within the last decade have in many states liberalized the corporation law when close corporations are involved, such as by permitting their incorporation by a smaller number of persons, allowing them to have a one-man board of directors, and authorizing the skipping of meetings.[3]

A number of states have separate *small* or *close corporation codes.*[4] These commonly require that there be no more than a stated number of shareholders, that the stock not be sold publicly, and that the stock be subject to certain transfer restrictions. When a corporation qualifies under such a statute, it is permitted to have a simpler structure than would be possible for a standard corporation, as by eliminating the board of directors, and to function in a simpler manner, as by conducting business in the manner of a partnership [5] rather than a corporation. In some states the general business corporation code has provisions contemplating the possible concentration of corporate ownership and control in one person.[6]

(f) Professional corporations. In every state a corporation may be organized for the purpose of conducting a profession.

The fact that professional men may form a corporation does not permit a converse conclusion that any corporation may render professional services. To some extent a corporation may supply professional services to its members.[7]

FACTS: The State of Kansas, on the complaint of the attorney general, brought an original action in the Supreme Court of Kansas against the Zale Jewelry Co., a corporation, to order it to stop the practice of optometry and to forfeit its charter for engaging therein. The State claimed that Dr.

---

[3] This distinction between big and little corporations is part of the same current of legal development that in the Uniform Commercial Code has given rise to the distinction between the merchant seller or buyer, on the one hand, and the casual seller or buyer, on the other.

[4] See, for example, 8 Delaware Code Ann §§ 341-356.

[5] North Carolina, Gen Stats §§ 55-73(b).

[6] See, for example, New York Business Corporation Law §§ 401, 404, 615, 702.

[7] A labor union has a constitutional right to employ a lawyer on a salary basis to provide free legal services for union members. United Mine Workers v Illinois State Bar Association, 389 US 217. A union may also recommend to its members individual attorneys for the purpose of suing under the federal Employers' Liability Act and may obtain the commitment of such attorneys that they will not charge more than 25 percent of any recovery. United Transportation Union v State Bar of Michigan, 401 US 576.

Marks, who practiced optometry in one part of the store, and the Douglas Optical Co., which also did business in part of the store, were in fact employees of the Zale Co. which, as their employer, was therefore engaging in optometry. Zale defended on the ground that they were not its employees but tenants to whom Zale had leased space in its store. The leases specified that financial affairs of Marks and Douglas were to be controlled by Zale, and work done on credit was carried on Zale's charge account records; and the area in which Marks and the Douglas Optical Co. operated was marked by a sign "Optical Department."

DECISION: The State was correct. Zale exercised such control over the operations and financial affairs of Marks and Optical as to make them Zale's employees. The fact that the relationship was described as a lease did not bar the court from determining the true character of the relationship. [Kansas v Zale Jewelry Co. 179 Kan 628, 298 P2d 283]

(f) Nonprofit corporations. A *nonprofit corporation* (or an eleemosynary corporation) is one that is organized for charitable or benevolent purposes, such as certain hospitals, homes, and universities.[8] Special procedure for incorporation is sometimes prescribed, with provision being made for a detailed examination and hearing as to the purpose, function, and methods of raising money for the enterprise.

§ 48:4. POWER TO CREATE A CORPORATION. Since by definition a corporation is created by government grant, the right to be a corporation must be obtained from the proper government.

(a) Federal power. The federal government may create corporations whenever appropriate to carry out the powers expressly granted to it.

FACTS: Maryland enacted a law that imposed a tax on bank notes issued by any bank not chartered by the state legislature. McCulloch, the cashier of the Baltimore branch of the federally chartered Bank of the United States, issued bank notes on which this tax had not been paid. Suit was brought by the State of Maryland against McCulloch to recover the statutory penalties imposed for the violation of the law.

DECISION: Congress, as a means of carrying out its express powers, had the implied authority to create a national bank; and such a bank could not be subjected to state taxation. [McCulloch v Maryland, 4 Wheat (US) 316]

(b) State power. Generally a state by virtue of its police power may create any kind of corporation for any purpose. Most states have a *general corporation code* that lists certain requirements, and anyone who satisfies the requirements and files the necessary papers with the government may automatically become a corporation. The American Bar Association has

---

[8] Gilbert v McLeod Infirmary, 219 SC 174, 64 SE2d 524. The Committee on Corporate Laws of the American Bar Association has prepared a Model Non-Profit Corporation Act as a companion to the Model Business Association Act. The Non-Profit Corporation Act has formed the basis for nonprofit corporation statutes in Alabama, Iowa, Nebraska, North Carolina, North Dakota, Ohio, Oregon, Texas, Virginia, Washington, Wisconsin, and the District of Columbia.

proposed a Model Business Corporation Act (ABA MBCA).[9] There is no uniform corporation act.

§ 48:5. REGULATION OF CORPORATIONS.

§ 48:5. REGULATION OF CORPORATIONS. In addition to determining whether a corporate power exists, it is necessary to consider whether there is any government regulation imposed upon the exercise of that power. Both the federal and state governments, by virtue of their power to create corporations, can exercise control over them.

Domestic corporations are regulated by the provisions of the code or general statutes under which they are organized and also by the tax laws and general laws of the state of their origin. A foreign corporation is also subject to regulation and taxation in every state in which it does business, except as later noted. Generally a foreign corporation must register to do business within the state.

(a) Constitutional limitations. In regulating a corporation, state and national governments must observe certain limitations because corporations come within the protection of certain constitutional guarantees.

(1) The Corporation as a Person. The Constitution of the United States prohibits the national government and the state governments from depriving any "person" of life, liberty, or property without due process of law. Many state constitutions contain a similar limitation upon their respective state governments. A corporation is regarded as a "person" within the meaning of such provisions.

The federal Constitution prohibits a state from denying to any "person" within its jurisdiction the equal protection of the laws. No such express limitation is placed upon the federal government, although the due process clause binding the federal government is liberally interpreted so that it prohibits substantial inequality of treatment.

While a corporation is regarded as a "person" with respect to rights and liabilities, a corporation is not regarded as a person within a statute which uses the term to refer to natural persons. Thus, a corporation cannot claim that its lawsuit should be given priority at trial because a state statute grants such a priority to a "person" 65 years old or over.

Similarly, a corporation is not a "person" within the scope of a statute authorizing any "person" to prepare the legal papers for a transaction to which he is a party.[10]

FACTS: A federal statute permits a person to proceed in court without paying costs if he is unable to do so. A corporation, Students Opposing Unfair Practices, Inc. (S.O.U.P.), claimed that it was a "person" within the

---

[9] This Act or its 1969 revision has been adopted, or has influenced local legislation, in a substantial number of states. The American Bar Association Model Act of 1950 was revised as of July 1, 1969. References to the Model Act are to the 1969 revision unless otherwise indicated.

[10] Kentucky State Bar Association v Tussey (Ky) 476 SW2d 177 (holding that the preparation of mortgage papers for use by the bank constituted the unauthorized practice of law, even though the bank made no charge against the borrowers for so doing).

meaning of this statute and that it could therefore proceed without the payment of costs to seek a review of a decision of the Federal Trade Commission.

DECISION: S.O.U.P. was not entitled to proceed as a poor person without paying court costs. The statute was designed to protect indigent natural persons and does not protect a corporation because it lacks assets, particularly when it is composed of many non-indigent persons. [S.O.U.P., Inc. v FTC (CA DistCol) 449 F2d 1142]

(2) The Corporation as a Citizen. For certain purposes, such as determining the right to bring a lawsuit in a federal court, a corporation is today deemed a "citizen" of any state in which it has been incorporated and of the state where it has its principal place of business, without regard to the actual citizenship of the individual persons owning the stock of the corporation. Thus, the corporation incorporated in New York is a New York corporation even though its shareholders are citizens of many other states. Likewise, a Delaware corporation having its principal place of business in New York is deemed a citizen of New York as well as Delaware.[11] An environmental protection law authorizing any "citizen" to bring suit to prevent pollution permits a corporation to bring such a suit.

The federal Constitution prohibits states from abridging "the privileges or immunities of citizens of the United States." A corporation, however, is not regarded as a "citizen" within the clause. Thus, with one exception, a foreign corporation has no constitutional right to do business in another state if that other state wishes to exclude it. For example, Pennsylvania can deny a New York corporation the right to come into Pennsylvania to do business. As a practical matter, most states do not exclude foreign corporations but seize upon this power as justifying special regulation or taxation. On this basis it is commonly provided that a foreign corporation must register or even take out a domestic charter, file copies of its charter, pay certain taxes, or appoint a resident agent before it can do business within the state.

As an exception to the power of a state, a state cannot require a license or registration of a foreign interstate commerce corporation or impose a tax on the right to engage in such a business.

The citizenship of a corporation is ordinarily not affected by the fact that it acquires the stock or assets of another corporation.

(b) Multiple regulation of corporations. Government regulation of corporations becomes complicated when the corporation engages in business in several states, and the problem arises as to what extent it must comply with the regulation of each state. In some cases the interstate character of the corporation business brings it within the scope of the federal interstate commerce power and the corporation must therefore comply with both state and federal regulations.[12] Thus, an interstate dealer in food

---

[11] 28 United States Code § 1332(c).

[12] In case of an inconsistency or conflict, a federal regulation displaces or supersedes a state regulation.

will generally be required to satisfy state laws with respect to his product as well as the federal Food, Drug, and Cosmetic Act.[13]

§ 48:6. **IGNORING THE CORPORATE ENTITY.** Ordinarily each corporation will be regarded and treated as a separate legal person and the law will not look behind the corporation to see who owns or controls the corporation.

FACTS: Harmon owned a food supply business which he sold to the Continental Coffee Company. As part of the transaction, the assets of Harmon's business were transferred to a new corporation, Harmon Foods, Inc., of which all of the stock was owned by Continental. Harmon Foods, Inc. ran the business that Harmon had formerly run as an individual and the only control exercised by Continental was through voting the stock held by it. Hassell was employed by Harmon Foods, Inc. He was discharged and claimed that this was a discriminatory act that violated the Federal Civil Rights Act. Harmon Foods raised the defense that this Act did not apply because it did not employ the minimum number of employees specified by the federal statute. Hassell claimed that Harmon Foods and Continental should be treated as one employer, which would bring his employer over the minimum specified by the statute. Was he correct?

DECISION: No. Harmon Foods, Inc. was not a sham corporation but was an actual good faith operating company. Its separate corporate existence therefore could not be ignored by treating it and Continental as a single employer. Hassell was accordingly employed by the subsidiary which did not come within the federal statute. [Hassell v Harmon Foods, Inc. (DC Tenn) 336 FSupp 432]

The fact that a parent or holding company and a subsidiary company have officers and directors or shareholders in common is not sufficient ground for ignoring the separate corporate entity of each corporation. The fact that two corporations have identical shareholders does not justify a court in regarding the two corporations as being only one.

The fact that there is a close working relationship between two corporations does not in itself constitute any basis for ignoring their separate corporate entities when they in fact are separately run enterprises.

When a sale of goods is made between a corporation and its wholly-owned subsidiary, the separate entities of the two corporations will not be ignored for the purpose of reaching the conclusion that no sales tax is due on the theory that the subsidiary was in fact merely a department of the parent corporation so that the transfer was not a taxable "sale."

In some instances, the corporate entity is ignored, however, and rights and liabilities are determined as though there were no corporation and as though the shareholders were the persons doing the act performed by the corporation, meaning that they do not obtain the various advantages of being a corporation. It is frequently held that the inadequate capitalization

---

[13] 21 USC §§ 301-392.

of a corporation is a strong factor in reaching the conclusion that the corporate entity is to be disregarded.[14]

(a) Prevention of fraud or illegality. When the corporation is formed to perpetrate a fraud or conceal illegality, a court will ordinarily ignore the corporate entity, or as it is figuratively called, "pierce the corporate veil."[15] For example, if enemy aliens are not eligible to purchase or own particular kinds of property, they cannot organize an American corporation and purchase the property in the name of the corporation. In such a case, a court will look behind the corporation to see that the alien enemies are really the persons involved and will not allow them to defeat the law by the device of forming a corporation. Similarly, a buyer under a requirements contract remains liable even though he incorporates the business in order to evade the contract obligation.

When a person engages in business and uses the corporation as a mask by which to hide from a person he is defrauding, the law will ignore the separate corporate entity and will hold such person liable for the acts of the corporation on the theory that it is the *alter ego* of the person.

FACTS: Casanova Guns, Inc. applied for a license under the Federal Gun Control Act. It was denied a license because of its close relationship to Casanova's Inc., which had been convicted of violating the federal law. Casanova Guns brought an action against Connally, as Secretary of the Treasury of the United States, to review the refusal of the application. The evidence indicated that the applicant had been formed to take over the business that Casanova's could no longer operate because of the conviction. The officers and shareholders of both enterprises were almost completely the same, and the building, inventory, and equipment of the new enterprise were acquired from the former.

DECISION: The request for a license was denied. The federal statute expressly authorized refusing a license when the licensee would or could be under the control of a convicted felon. As an additional reason, the corporate entity of the applicant could be ignored to determine that the applicant was in fact the convicted felon who had operated the original business and that the formation of the corporation was merely a device to circumvent the statutory disqualification of the first enterprise. [Casanova Guns, Inc. v Connally (CA7 Wis) 454 F2d 1320]

(b) Functional reality. When a corporation is in effect merely a department of a large enterprise, as when a large manufacturer incorporates its marketing department, it is likely that the separate corporate character of the incorporated department will be ignored.

In some instances a court will hold that there is such an identity between a local subsidiary corporation doing business within the state and the foreign parent corporation that the latter may be regarded as doing

---

[14] Automotriz Del Golfo v Resnick, 47 Cal2d 792, 306 P2d 1.

[15] It is likely that the enforcement of the obligation of good faith imposed by Uniform Commercial Code § 1-203 will result in ignoring a corporate entity in some cases. Thompson v United States (CA8 Tex) 408 F2d 1075.

business within the state. For example, where the question was whether the parent corporation was doing business within the state, it was concluded that since the marketing corporation was admittedly doing business within the state and since it was merely a department or branch of the parent holding corporation, the holding corporation was to be deemed doing business within the state; as opposed to the contention that the corporation doing business within the state was a different legal person distinct from the parent holding corporation.

> **FACTS:** A Dodge truck was manufactured by the Chrysler Corp. and sold by it to its wholly owned subsidiary, Chrysler Motors, which in turn sold it to its wholly owned subsidiary, Dodge Trucks, Inc., a retail truck dealer. The latter changed the front axle and neglected to tighten the steering assembly properly after making the change. The truck was then sold to Clark Motor Co., which sold it to Welborn. Vaughn was injured when the Dodge truck went out of control because of the defect. He sued Chrysler Corp. It defended on the ground that the truck was not defective when it left the factory and that the defect had been generated by the act of an independent corporation in making an alteration which was both unauthorized by and unknown to Chrysler.

> **DECISION:** Judgment for Vaughn. Consumer protection requires that there be liability for defective products and the manufacturer cannot escape this liability on the ground that it had been caused by a particular branch of the complicated corporate structure that the manufacturer had created for the distribution of its products. [Vaughn v Chrysler Corp. (CA10 Okla) 442 F2d 619]

The concept of the unity of a parent corporation and its incorporated subsidiary has been carried even to the extent of holding the subsidiary responsible for the tort of the parent corporation.

(1) Independent Subsidiary Corporation. The close functional relation between a parent corporation and a subsidiary does not require that a court ignore the separate corporate entity of the subsidiary. If the subsidiary is in fact operating independently of the parent, its separate indentity will not be ignored. Thus, a parent corporation will be regarded as distinct from its subsidiary when the parent and the subsidiary are each operated by its own management which makes decisions independently of the other.

(2) Actual Control of Subsidiary Corporation. When a parent corporation exercises actual control over a wholly owned subsidiary, the parent corporation will be held liable for the wrongs that the parent corporation commits under the guise of subsidiary corporation action.

> **FACTS:** Data Probe, Inc. had a contract for computer time with Computech, Inc. The latter was acquired and controlled by International Systems Associates. Data Probe did not get the full computer time because International directed that the time be made available to other customers. International then sold the assets of Computech for $150,000 which was paid to creditors of Computech, leaving only assets of $100. Data Probe claimed that International was liable for the breach of its computer-time contract by Computech. International defended on the ground that Computech was a separate legal entity.

DECISION: Judgment for Data Probe. International had in fact run, dominated, and controlled the business operations of Computech. It therefore would not be permitted to avoid liability for its conduct on the ground that the acts complained of had been committed by a separate corporation. [Data Probe, Inc. v 575 Computer Services, Inc. (formerly Computech, Inc.) (NY CivCt) 340 NYS2d 56]

(c) **Preservation of privilege.** When a parent corporation has a right or a privilege, it is possible that a subsidiary corporation, which is merely a branch of the parent corporation, will be entitled to the privilege of the parent corporation. To illustrate, a number of hospitals cooperated to form a laundry corporation to do the laundry work for the hospitals. The tax assessor claimed that this laundry corporation should pay the same kind of tax as was assessed against commercial laundries generally. The court held that although the laundry was a distinct corporation, it was in effect merely the cooperating hospitals doing their laundry work at a central plant which happened to be organized in the corporate form. Consequently, it was not an ordinary commercial laundry subject to tax but retained the same tax exemption as the hospitals would have if they were doing the laundry work.[16]

(d) **Obtaining of advantages of corporate existence.** The court will not go behind the corporate identity merely because the corporation has been formed to obtain tax savings or to obtain limited liability for its shareholders. Likewise, the corporate entity will not be ignored merely because the corporation does not have sufficient assets to pay the claims against it.

The fact that recognizing the corporate entity has the effect of preventing creditors of the corporation from reaching assets which would otherwise be held by the shareholders, in whose hands they would be subject to the claims of the creditors, is not in itself a ground for refusing to recognize the corporate entity. It is immaterial that one individual is the only shareholder in the corporation.

QUESTIONS AND CASE PROBLEMS

1. Several shareholders of a corporation borrowed money from the bank in which the corporation had its bank account. When the shareholders did not pay the loans back to the bank, the bank deducted the amount of the loans from the bank account of the corporation on the theory that the shareholders had used the money for the benefit of the corporation. Was the bank entitled to make this deduction? [See Potts v First City Bank, 7 CalApp3d 341, 86 CalRptr 552]

---

[16] Children's Hospital Medical Center v Board of Assessors, 353 Mass 35, 227 NE2d 908.

2. An action was brought by Alabama Tank Lines and other carriers against the Martin Truck Line, claiming that the truck line was operating without the necessary certificate of the state Public Service Commission. It was shown that Martin Truck Line had obtained a certificate at a time when all of its stock was owned by Thornbury, Cook, and Edwards. The stock was thereafter sold to Houghland and Page. No approval of the transfer of stock to them was obtained from the Public Service Commission. Was Martin Truck Line entitled to continue to do business under the certificate that had been originally issued? [Martin Truck Line v Alabama Tank Lines, 261 Ala 163, 73 So2d 756]

3. The Meridian Life Insurance Co., an Indiana corporation, obtained permission to transact business in South Dakota. In order to obtain this permission, it agreed that, in any action brought against it in South Dakota on an insurance policy, service of the process in the suit could be made upon the Insurance Commissioner of South Dakota with the same effect as though the corporation were actually served. Thomson was the beneficiary of a policy issued by the company in Texas to a Texas resident. Thomson sued on the policy in South Dakota and made service on the Insurance Commissioner. The company objected that a state could not constitutionally compel a foreign corporation to appoint the Insurance Commissioner as its agent for service with respect to lawsuits brought on foreign causes of action. Was the corporation correct? [Thomson v Meridian Life Insurance Co. 38 SD 570, 162 NW 373]

4. Riesberg was the president and sole shareholder of the Carson Steel Co. His wife, driving an automobile owned by the corporation, collided at a grade crossing with a train of the Pittsburgh & Lake Erie Railroad. Riesberg sued the railroad for damage to the automobile. Was he entitled to recover? [Riesberg v Pittsburgh & Erie RR, 407 Pa 434, 180 A2d 575]

5. North Gate Corporation leased property to National Food Stores. The lease contained a provision that neither the corporation nor its "beneficiaries" would engage in a competing business within a specified radius. Some shareholders of North Gate Corporation engaged in such a business within the prohibited area. National Food Stores claimed that the restriction on "beneficiaries" applied to "shareholders" of North Gate. Were the shareholders bound by the anticompetitive covenant? [North Gate Corporation v National Food Stores, Inc. 30 Wis2d 317, 140 NW2d 744]

6. Erlich and his wife owned all the stock of the West Coast Poultry Co. Erlich claimed that Glasner and others had caused the corporation to be prosecuted for food law violations; that these prosecutions were unsuccessful; that the conduct of the defendants was a violation of the federal Civil Rights Act; that, by interfering with the conduct of the corporation's business, the actions of the defendant in turn were "a direct interference with plaintiff's right to operate his business and earn a livelihood for himself and his family"; and that he accordingly was entitled to recover damages under the federal Civil Rights Act. Was he correct? [Erlich v Glasner (CA9 Cal) 418 F2d 226]

7. The Drackett Co. manufactured a bathroom fixture cleaner named "Vanish." All of the products of this company were sold by its wholly owned subsidiary, "The Drackett Products Co." The subsidiary had no other business, and all of the income of the parent company was obtained from the subsidiary company's sales. Shirley purchased a can of Vanish. When she used it, chemical fumes caused extreme damage to her lungs. She sued Drackett Products Co., claiming that it was negligent. It defended on the ground that it did not make the product, that it was not negligent because it had no reason to foresee that any harm

would result, and that it could not be liable for any fault of the manufacturing corporation. Was this a valid defense? [Shirley v The Drackett Products Co. 26 MichApp 644, 182 NW2d 726]

8. Greenberg organized the PSG Company in order to obtain certain tax advantages. He owned all of the stock of the corporation and was its principal officer. El Salto sued PSG Co. and Greenberg, claiming that the corporation was liable for damages for discriminatory price practices and that Greenberg was also liable for such damages on the theory that PSG was the alter ego of Greenberg. Is Greenberg liable to El Salto on the facts above stated? [El Salto v PSG Co. (CA9 Ore) 444 F2d 477]

9. Robinson was a salesman for the Realty Investment Consultants, Inc. (R.I.C., Inc.). Kramer was president, treasurer, and director of the corporation and owned all of its stock. Robinson contacted Ferrarell in answer to the latter's letter of inquiry in response to a newspaper ad of R.I.C. Robinson executed a contract with Ferrarell on behalf of R.I.C. and signed the contract as agent for that corporation. Subsequently, Ferrarell sued Robinson and Kramer for breach of the contract by R.I.C. Were they liable? [Ferrarell v Robinson, 11 ArizApp 473, 465 P2d 610]

10. A Texas statute prohibits the sale of certain items, including automobiles, on "both the two consecutive days of Saturday and Sunday. . . ." Section 1 declares that "any person" so selling is guilty of a misdemeanor. Section 3 imposes a fine for the first offense and adds imprisonment for subsequent offenses. Section 4 declares that the operation of a business "whether by an individual, partnership, or corporation contrary to the provisions of this Act is declared to be a public nuisance" and may be stopped by injunction. An injunction was sought to stop Ralph Williams Gulfgate Chrysler Plymouth, Inc., a corporation, from conducting sales in violation of the Act. It claimed it could not be regarded as selling in violation of the Act as the Act only applied to natural persons. Was it correct? [Ralph William Gulfgate Chrysler Plymouth, Inc. v Texas (TexCivApp) 466 SW2d 639]

49 CREATION AND TERMINATION

A. CREATION OF THE CORPORATION

§ 49:1. **PROMOTERS.** The promoters are the persons who plan the corporation and sell the idea to others. They may also file the necessary papers with the government to create the corporation. They are independent operators. They are not regarded as agents of the corporation since the corporation is not yet in existence.

A promoter, in the absence of statutory authority, cannot bind the corporation or give it rights by a preincorporation contract even though he purports to act for it. The corporation, upon coming into existence, may become a party to such a contract, however, by assignment or by novation. Moreover, when the corporation knowingly accepts the benefits of the promoter's contract, it becomes liable on that contract.

The promoter is personally liable for all contracts made in behalf of the corporation before its existence unless he is exempted by the terms of the agreement or by the circumstances surrounding it. When a promoter makes a contract on behalf of a corporation to be formed thereafter, he is liable thereon if the corporation is not formed, in the absence of agreement that he should not be so liable.

FACTS: Quaker Hill made a contract for the sale of plants to the "Denver Memorial Nursery, Inc." The contract was signed by Parr as Denver's president. Quaker Hill knew that the corporation was not yet formed and the contract so stated, but Quaker Hill had insisted that the contract be executed in this manner rather than wait until the corporation was organized. The corporation was never formed, and Quaker Hill sued Parr and other promoters of the corporation.

DECISION: Judgment against Quaker Hill. A promoter is ordinarily liable on a contract made on behalf of a corporation not yet formed. This rule does not apply, however, where, as here, the third person knows that the corporation is not in existence and enters into the agreement with the intention that the promoter shall not be liable thereon. [Quaker Hill v Parr, 148 Colo 45, 364 P2d 1056]

A promoter is also liable for all torts that he commits in connection with his activities. Although the corporation is not ordinarily liable for the torts of the promoter, it may become so by its conduct after incorporation. Thus, when a corporation, with actual or implied notice of the fraud of the promoter, assumes responsibility for the promoter's contract, it is liable for the promoter's fraud to induce the other party to enter into the contract.

A promoter stands in a fiduciary relation to the corporation and to stock subcribers. He cannot make secret profits at their expense. Accordingly, if a promoter makes secret profits on a sale of land to a corporation, he must account to the corporation for those profits, that is, he must surrender the profits to it. He may be held guilty of embezzlement if he converts to his own benefit property that should have gone to the corporation.

The corporation is not liable in most states for the expenses and services of the promoter unless it subsequently promises to pay for them or unless its charter or a statute imposes such liability upon it.

§ 49:2. INCORPORATORS. The statutes often require three applicants who possess the capacity to contract. A few states require that the incorporators or a specified percentage of the incorporators be citizens of the state or of the United States.

The requirement that there be three incorporators has frequently, in the case of the small business, merely had the result that the single proprietor obtains the cooperation of two dummy or nominal incorporators. The ABA Model Act therefore takes the direct approach and, in common with many modern statutes, permits the formation of a corporation by one incorporator.[1]

As a result of the historical accident that corporations were formed by natural persons, the rule developed that a corporation could not be an incorporator. In recent decades it has been common for a corporation to be the actual moving party in the organizing of another corporation. The Model Act recognizes this by permitting a domestic or foreign corporation to be an incorporator,[2] and many statutes make a similar provision when the new corporation is a consolidation of existing corporations.

§ 49:3. APPLICATION FOR INCORPORATION. The organizers must apply for a certificate of incorporation and file certain documents, such as the proposed articles of incorporation.

The modern trend of statutes simplifies the mechanics of incorporating by providing that the incorporators send to a designated state official two copies of the articles of incorporation; and provides that when the designated official determines that the articles satisfy the statutory requirements, he indorses "approved" or "filed" or similar words and the date on each copy. The officer then retains one copy for his records and returns the other copy to the corporation.[3]

---

[1] American Bar Association Model Business Corporation Act, § 53.
[2] ABA MBCA § 53.
[3] § 55.

Statutes may require incorporators to give some form of public notice, such as by advertisement in a newspaper, of the intention to form the corporation.

(a) Name of proposed corporation. Subject to certain limitations, the incorporators may select any name.

(b) Object of proposed corporation. A corporation may be formed for any lawful purpose.

When the applicants for a charter satisfy the statutory requirements, they are entitled to a charter and cannot be refused a charter for a ground not stated in the statute.[4]

Some states also require a statement of the means to be used to attain the object of the corporation. This is particularly common in the case of nonprofit or charitable corporations.

(c) Capital stock. The amount of capital stock to be authorized and the number and value of the shares into which it is divided must be specified.

The ABA Model Business Corporation Act requires that the articles of incorporation contain a description of the classes of shares, the number of shares in each class, and the relative rights of each class.[5] Other statutes have similar requirements. A number of states require that the incorporators state that the corporation will not begin to do business until a specified amount has been paid into the corporation,[6] but the trend in corporation legislation is to abandon this requirement.[7]

(d) Place of business. The location of the principal office or place of business of the proposed corporation must be stated.

(e) Duration. The period during which the proposed corporation is to exist must be set forth. In a number of states limitations are imposed upon the number of years a corporation may exist, the maximum ranging from 20 to 100 years. Commonly, provision is made for a renewal of extension of corporate life. Many states permit the incorporators to select perpetual life for the corporation.

(f) Directors and officers. In half of the states the number of directors or the names and addresses of directors for the first year must be stated. Sometimes additional information regarding the directors is required. In some instances the names and addresses of the officers for the first year must also be stated.

---

[4] Gay Activists Alliance v Lomenzo, 31 NY2d 965, 341 NYS2d 108, 293 NE2d 255 (Secretary of State may not refuse charter because the purposes are violative of "public policy" and the corporate name is "not appropriate").

[5] ABA MBCA § 54.

[6] When a corporation begins business without the stated paid-in capital having been paid in, liability may be imposed on shareholders or officers for the corporate debts even though they exceed the amount of capital that should have been paid in. Tri-State Developers, Inc. v Moore (Ky) 343 SW2d 812.

[7] Such a provision was included in the original Model Act, § 48, but has been omitted from the current revision of that Act.

The purpose of requiring the naming of the first board of directors is to provide the corporation with a body to govern or manage the corporation during the interval from the moment that the corporate life begins until the organization meeting of the shareholders is held. In some states that do not require the naming of the first board of directors in this manner, the incorporators have the power of management during this period.

(g) Incorporators. The names and addressess of the incorporators must be given, along with the number of shares subscribed by each. Sometimes the method of payment for those shares must also be stated.

(h) Registered office and agent. The trend of current statutes is to require a corporation to give a specific office address and the name of an agent, which are described as the "registered" office and the "registered" agent.[8] The object of such provisions is to provide information to the world as to where someone can be found, to whom to give notice, or where to effect legal service upon the corporation.[9]

§ 49:4. THE CHARTER. After the application for a certificate of incorporation or a charter is filed, the fee paid, and other conditions precedent fulfilled, usually an administrative official, such as the secretary of state, examines the papers. If the requirements of the law have been met, a certificate of incorporation, license, or charter is issued and recorded or filed, as specified by the terms of the local statute.

Under the Model Business Corporation Act, corporate existence begins upon the issuance of the certificate by the state official.[10] In some states corporate existence does not begin until an organization meeting is held under the charter to put the corporation in operation, and in others, not until a report on the organization meeting is made. The statute may declare that the charter shall be void if the certificate of organization is not properly filed within the prescribed time. In a few states there is an additional requirement of a local recording of the certificate of incorporation.[11]

The charter not only creates the corporation but also confers contractual rights and imposes contractual duties as between the state, the corporation, and the shareholders. In theory it is required that the corporation accept the charter which is given to it; but unless expressly required by statute, it is not necessary for the corporation to inform any state officer that the charter is accepted. The acceptance can be inferred from conduct, such as holding an organization meeting or doing business under the charter.

---

[8] ABA MBCA § 12.

[9] The fact that a corporation does not designate such an agent does not mean that it cannot be sued or given notice. Most statutes provide that in such case the service may be made upon or the notice given to a specified state official, such as the secretary of state. In addition, a plaintiff suing a foreign corporation that has not appointed a person upon whom service can be made may in many instances effect service under a "long-arm" statute when the foreign defendant has engaged in local business or committed a local wrong or breach within the terms of such statute. See Gray v American Radiator & Standard Sanitary Corp. 22 Ill2d 432, 176 NE2d 761.

[10] ABA MBCA § 56.

[11] 8 Delaware Code Ann § 103(c).

Since the charter is regarded as a contract, the corporation is protected from subsequent change or modification by the clause of the federal Constitution that prohibits states from impairing the obligation of contracts. This does not mean that in no case can the rights given by a charter be modified. Under many statutes it is expressly provided that the charter granted by the state is subject to the power reserved by the state to change the charter should it desire to do so. Independently of such a reservation, the rule has developed that permits the state, under the exercise of its police power, to modify existing contracts, including corporate charters, to further the public health, safety, morals, or general welfare.

§ 49:5. PROPER AND DEFECTIVE INCORPORATION. If the legal procedure for incorporation has been followed, the corporation has a perfect legal right to exist. It is then called a *corporation de jure*, meaning that it is a corporation by virtue of law.

In some cases everything is not done exactly as it should be and the question then arises as to the consequence of the defect. This problem becomes less and less important as time goes on because (1) with the great number of corporations being formed, it becomes increasingly clear just what should be done to form a corporation so that the likelihood of the corporation's attorney or anyone else making a mistake is increasingly less; (2) standardized incorporation has eliminated a great deal of uncertainty that existed when each corporation was formed by a separately granted charter; and (3) the probability of a corporation's coming into existence with some defect is less because of the pattern of having a full-time government official examine the application and accompanying papers, thereby assuring that if there is any significant mistake, it will probably be noted by the government expert before the application for the certificate is approved.

Assume, however, that there is still some defect in the corporation which is formed. If the defect is not a material one, the law usually will overlook the defect and hold that the corporation is a corporation de jure.

The **ABA MBCA** abolishes objections to irregularities and defects in incorporating. It provides that the "certificate of incorporation shall be conclusive evidence that all conditions required to be performed by the incorporators have been complied with and that the corporation has been incorporated under this Act."[12] State statutes generally follow this pattern. Such an approach is based upon the practical consideration that when countless people are purchasing shares of stock and entering into business transactions with thousands of corporations, it becomes an absurdity to expect that anyone is going to make the detailed search that would be

---

[12] ABA MBCA § 56. The Model Act expressly excepts "a proceeding to cancel or revoke the certificate of incorporation or for involuntary dissolution of the corporation." The provision would likewise not be operative when the original corporate existence was for a specified number of years which had expired, the corporation then becoming a de facto corporation if it continued to do business without obtaining an extension of its corporate life.

required to determine whether a given corporation is a de jure corporation.[13]

(a) De facto corporation. The defect in the incorporation may be so substantial that the law cannot ignore it and will not accept the corporation as a de jure corporation. Yet there may be sufficient compliance so that the law will recognize that there is a corporation. When this occurs, the association is called a *de facto corporation*. It exists in fact but not by right, and the state may bring proceedings to have the corporate charter revoked because of the defect. If, however, the state does not take proceedings against the defective corporation, the de facto corporation has all the rights and privileges of a regular lawful or de jure corporation, and third persons contracting with it cannot avoid their contracts on the ground that the corporation was merely a de facto corporation. The de facto corporation is, in a sense, like a voidable contract. It can be set aside by the state; but unless the state acts, the corporation is lawful with respect to the entire world.

Although there is conflict among the authorities, most courts hold that a de facto corporation must meet four tests: (1) there must be a valid law under which the corporation could have been properly incorporated; (2) the attempt to organize the corporation must have been made in good faith; (3) the attempt to organize must result in colorable compliance with the requirements of the statute; and (4) there must be a use of the corporate powers.

(b) Partnership v corporation by estoppel. The defect in incorporation may be so great that the law will not accept the corporation even as a de facto corporation, let alone as a de jure corporation. In such a case, in the absence of a statute making the incorporation conclusive, there is no corporation. If the incorporators proceed to run the business in spite of such irregularity, they may be held liable as partners.[14]

The partnership liability rule is sometimes not applied when the third person dealt with the business as though it were a corporation. In such instances, it is stated that the third person is estopped from denying that the "corporation" with which he did business has legal existence. In effect, there is a *corporation by estoppel* with respect to that creditor.

FACTS: Namerdy entered into a contract with Generalcar. In the contract the latter was identified as a Belgian corporation. Later when Generalcar sued Namerdy for breach of the agreement, Namerdy defended by asserting that Generalcar failed to prove that it was a corporation.

---

[13] This trend and the reasons therefor may be compared to those involved in giving rise to the concept of the negotiability of commercial paper. Note the similar protection from defenses given to the person purchasing shares for value and without notice. Uniform Commercial Code § 8-202.

[14] In a minority of states the court will not hold the individuals liable as partners, but will hold liable the person who committed the act on behalf of the business on the theory that he was an agent who acted without authority and is therefore liable for breach of the implied warranties of the existence of a principal possessing capacity and of his proper authorization. Doggrell v Great Southern Box Co. (CA6 Tenn) 206 F2d 671.

DECISION: Namerdy, by entering into a contract that described Generalcar as a Belgian corporation, was estopped from challenging the existence of its corporate character; and it was not necessary for Generalcar to prove that it was a Belgian corporation when it sued on the agreement. [Namerdy v Generalcar (DistColApp) 217 A2d 109]

If the incorporators have failed to obtain a charter and have not done business, neither the corporation by estoppel nor the partnership rule will be applied.

(c) Abandoning incorporation. At times a project to form a corporation is abandoned and the corporation is never formed and never engages in any business. In such a case those persons who had actively participated up to that point are regarded as joint venturers with the result that each has the power of an agent or partner to dispose of property held in the name of the corporation that was never formed.

FACTS: Roland and Evans planned to form a corporation under the name of Central American Steel of Texas, Inc. They opened a bank account in that name in the Republic National Bank. The corporation was never formed and never engaged in any business. Evans withdrew the money from the corporate account. Roland then sued the bank for permitting Evans to withdraw the money.

DECISION: Judgment for the bank. When the corporate project collapsed, Roland and Evans were to be regarded as joint venturers. Each had an agent's power to act with respect to the property held for the never-formed corporation and the other was bound by his acts. As far as the bank was concerned, Evans was the authorized agent of Roland in making the withdrawal. Roland therefore could not sue the bank, and his remedy was to obtain an accounting from Evans. [Roland v Republic National Bank (TexCivApp) 463 SW2d 747]

B. DISSOLUTION OR TERMINATION

§ 49:6. DISSOLUTION BY AGREEMENT.

(a) Expiration of time. If the incorporators have selected a corporate life of a stated number of years, the corporate existence automatically terminates upon the expiration of that period.

(b) Surrender of charter. The shareholders may terminate the corporate existence by surrendering the charter to the government. The surrender is not effective until the state accepts the charter. The state's acceptance of a surrender of the charter ends the corporate existence and generally extinguishes the liability of the corporation for debts.

§ 49:7. INSOLVENCY, BANKRUPTCY, AND REORGANIZATION.

(a) Insolvency. The insolvency of a corporation does not in itself terminate the corporate existence. Statutes in some states, however, provide that when the corporation is insolvent, creditors may commence proceedings to dissolve the corporation. Sometimes the statute merely dissolves the corporation as to creditors. This situation is sometimes called a *de facto dissolution* or *quasi dissolution*.

The appointment of a receiver for the corporation does not in itself dissolve the corporation, although the administration of the property by the receiver may result in the practical termination of the corporation. In some states the appointment of liquidators to wind up an insolvent corporation automatically dissolves the corporation. In the absence of statute, a court cannot appoint a receiver for a solvent corporation and order its dissolution.

(b) Bankruptcy. When a corporation is adjudicated bankrupt, a sale of all its assets will be ordered. This leaves the corporation without any assets with which to do business unless there should be a surplus above the amount required to pay off the debts of the corporation. The bankruptcy proceeding does not, however, terminate the legal existence of the corporation.

(c) Reorganization. When a reorganization of a corporation occurs under the federal bankruptcy laws, the corporate existence is not terminated. If the reorganization is successful, the result is the same as though the corporation merely exchanged obligations and securities. Under state law, however, reorganization proceedings generally result in formation of a new corporation.

§ 49:8. FORFEITURE OF CHARTER. The government that granted the charter may forfeit or revoke the charter for good cause. Sometimes the legislature provides in a general statute that the charter of any corporation shall be automatically forfeited when certain acts are committed or omitted.

Common grounds for forfeiture are fraudulent incorporation; *willful nonuser*, that is, failure to exercise powers; or *misuser*, that is, abuse of corporate powers and franchises. When it is claimed that a corporation has abused its privileges, such acts must be willful, serious, and injurious to the public. The action against the corporation to forfeit its charter must be brought by and in the name of the government, meaning ordinarily an action by the attorney general of the state. Forfeiture of a charter is an extreme penalty. Because of its severity, it is rarely used.

In a number of states when a corporation does not pay its taxes, its power to do business is suspended. Some states impose personal liability upon the officers and directors for such taxes.

FACTS: Morse Bros. Painting and Weatherproofing, a corporation, failed to pay its taxes to the State of California. Because of this, the state suspended its authority to do business. Thereafter its president, J. L. Morse, and its secretary, Doris Morse, borrowed money from the Bank of America. The note was signed: "Morse Bros. Painting and Weatherproofing, a Corporation By/s/J. L. Morse, President, By/s/Doris N. Morse, Secretary." When the loan was made, neither the bank nor the Morses knew that the authority of the corporation had been suspended. The California statute provided that contracts made by the corporation while its powers were suspended were voidable at the election of the other contracting party. The bank sued Doris on the note after the death of her husband.

DECISION: Judgment for Doris. The statute merely suspended the right of the corporation to exercise its powers but did not forfeit or terminate its existence. Contracts made on behalf of the corporation during the suspension period were enforceable against it. The corporation was therefore bound by the note which had been executed by its authorized agents. The suspension statute merely suspended the powers of the corporation and did not impose liability on officers for acting as officers during the suspension. As Doris had acted as an authorized agent for a disclosed principal, she was not liable for payment of the note under agency law. Finally, she had executed the note in the manner required by the Uniform Commercial Code to avoid personal liability when paper is signed in a representative capacity; she had identified her principal, the corporation, and had disclosed that she acted in a representative capacity, as an officer. [Bank of America National Trust and Savings Ass'n v Morse, 265 Ore 72, 508 P2d 194]

§ 49:9. JUDICIAL DISSOLUTION. In some states provision is made for the judicial dissolution of a corporation when its management is deadlocked and the deadlock cannot be broken by the shareholders. In some states a "custodian" may be appointed for a corporation when the shareholders are unable to break a deadlock in the board of directors and irreparable harm is threatened or sustained by the corporation because of the deadlock. A statute authorizing judicial dissolution of a deadlocked corporation does not apply to a corporation in which one group of shareholders owns 51 percent of the corporate stock.[15]

C. CONSOLIDATIONS, MERGERS, AND CONGLOMERATES

§ 49:10. DEFINITIONS.

(a) Consolidation. In a *consolidation* of two or more corporations, the separate corporate existences cease, and a new corporation with the property and assets of the old corporations comes into being.

FACTS: Five corporations consolidated to form Mid-America Dairymen, Inc. Schaffner, the state director of revenue, claimed that the transfer of motor vehicles from the original corporations to Mid-America was a "transfer of ownership" within the statute which required the new owner of a motor vehicle to obtain new license tags and a new certificate of ownership. Mid-America claimed that this was not required when there was a "transfer by operation of law," and therefore did not apply to the transfer of ownership which occurred upon a consolidation of corporations.

---

[15] Hebert v Royal Enterprises of Pensacola, Inc. (FlaApp) 259 So2d 750.

DECISION: Judgment for Schaffner. The consolidation of the corporations transferred the ownership of the motor vehicles from the original
corporations to the consolidated corporation. There was accordingly a
"transfer of ownership" within the motor vehicle statute, and it was
immaterial whether such transfer was a voluntary sale or a transfer by
operation of law. [Mid-America Dairymen, Inc. v Schaffner (Mo) 465
SW2d 465]

When a consolidation is effected, the new corporation ordinarily
succeeds to the rights, powers, and immunities of its component parts.[16]
Limitations, however, may be prescribed by certificate of incorporation,
constitution, or statute. As a general rule, the consolidated corporation is
subject to all the liabilities of the constituent corporations.

(b) Merger. *Merger* differs from consolidation in that, when two
corporations merge, one absorbs the other. One corporation preserves its
original charter and identity and continues to exist, and the other
disappears and its corporate existence terminates.

Simplified merger procedure is authorized in some states under *short
merger statutes* when there is a merger of a parent corporation and its
subsidiary. Under most merger statutes a dissenting shareholder has the
right to require the enterprise to purchase his shares from him.

(1) De Facto Combination. The procedure for merger and
consolidation is specifically and minutely regulated in most jurisdictions. If
two corporations have not complied with the specified procedure, there is
no merger or consolidation. In some instances, however, two corporations
have become so combined in fact that it has been held that there was a de
facto merger.

FACTS: Ballman-Cummings Furniture Company and Fort Smith Chair
Company formed a partnership. Pratt owned shares of stock in
Ballman-Cummings Furniture Company. He claimed that the
partnership was in fact a merger of the two corporations and therefore
he had the statutory right to be paid the value of his shares because he
dissented from such merger.

DECISION: Judgment for Pratt. There was in fact a merger of the two enterprises
even though no formal merger procedure had ever been followed. The
failure to have done so cannot be allowed to deprive dissenting
minority shareholders of their right to have their shares purchased.
Consequently, the dissenting shareholders would be allowed to
demand the purchase of their shares because of the de facto merger
which had occurred. [Pratt v Ballman-Cummings Furniture Co. 254
Ark 570, 495 SW2d 509]

(c) Conglomerate. *Conglomerate* is the term describing the relationship
of a parent corporation to subsidiary corporations engaged in diversified
fields of activity unrelated to the field of activity of the parent corporation.
For example, a wire manufacturing corporation that owns all the stock of a

---

[16] ABA MBCA § 69.

newspaper corporation and of a drug manufacturing corporation would be described as a conglomerate. In contrast, if the wire manufacturing company owned a mill to produce the metal used in making the wire and owned a mine which produced the ore that was used by the mill, the relationship would probably be described as an *integrated industry* rather than as a conglomerate. This is merely a matter of usage, rather than of legal definition. Likewise, when the parent company is not engaged in production or the rendering of services, it is customary to call it a holding company.

Without regard to whether the enterprise is a holding company, or whether the group of businesses constitute a conglomerate or an integrated industry, each part is a distinct corporation to which the ordinary corporation law applies. In some instances additional principles apply because of the nature of the relationship existing between the several corporations involved. In some instances the entity of one of the corporations in the conglomerate group may be ignored.

§ 49:11. LEGALITY. Consolidations, mergers, and asset acquisitions between enterprises are often prohibited by federal antitrust legislation on the ground that the effect is to lessen competition in interstate commerce. A business corporation may not merge with a charitable corporation because this would divert the assets of the respective corporations to purposes not intended by their shareholders.[17]

Conglomerates are lawful; but there is a movement to amend or interpret the antimerger provision, Section 7 of the Clayton Act, so as to subject conglomerates to the same limitations as apply to consolidations and mergers.

§ 49:12. LIABILITY OF ENTERPRISE.

(a) **Liability of successor enterprise.** Generally the enterprise engaging in or continuing the business after a merger or consolidation will be subject to the contract obligations and debts of the original corporations.

The corporation which absorbs another corporation by merger is generally liable for the contracts of the corporation which was absorbed and it is no defense that the third party does not have any contract with the absorbing corporation.

FACTS: Gaswint was employed by an Oregon corporation, Amigo Motor Homes, Inc. The stock of the corporation was acquired by Black Diamond Enterprises, Inc. Some time thereafter Gaswint was discharged. He sued Case, a corporate officer, and the two corporations for damages for breach of contract. Black Diamond asserted that it was not liable to the plaintiff because it had never made any contract with him. A local statute declared that when one corporation took over the business of another, the surviving corporation would be liable for the debts of the original corporation.

---

[17] Stevens Bros. Foundation, Inc. v Commissioner of Internal Revenue (CA8 TaxCt) 324 F2d 633, cert den 376 US 969, reh den 377 US 920.

DECISION: The statute imposing liability on the surviving corporation made Black Diamond liable for any claim for which Amigo would have been liable. This liability was based on statute, and therefore it was immaterial that there was no express agreement by Black Diamond to pay the claims. [Gaswint v Case, 265 Ore 248, 509 P2d 19]

The liability of a successor corporation on a contract of the earlier corporation may arise from conduct showing a novation or agreement that the successor be substituted for the earlier corporation. To illustrate, where there was a supply contract between corporations A and B, and corporation C became the successor to corporation B, and thereafter A and C did business just as though C were B, it will be concluded that there was an agreement and that C should have all the rights and liabilities of B under the original A-B contract.

However, the mere fact that one corporation acquires the business or purchases the assets of another corporation does not make the purchasing corporation liable for the debts of the selling corporation where there is no consolidation or merger of the two corporations, nor an assumption of debts by the purchasing corporation nor any design to defraud the creditors of the selling corporation.

When a business reincorporates in order to cure some technical irregularity in the existing organization but the new corporation runs the original business and takes control of its assets, the new corporation is liable for the debts of the former business even though there is no express assumption of debts.[18]

(b) Liability of component enterprise. An existing business may be acquired by another corporation under a variety of circumstances. How does the acquisition affect the rights and liabilities of the business that is acquired? For example, when corporation A buys out corporation B, what becomes of the rights and liabilities of corporation B?

When there is a formal consolidation or merger, statutes commonly provide expressly for the transfer of rights and liabilities to the surviving corporation or the new corporation. The contract of sale or agreement between corporation A and corporation B will ordinarily expressly assign B's rights to A and contain an assumption by A of the liabilities of B. In accord with general principles of contract law, A can sue an assignee on the assigned rights and third persons can sue on the transferred liabilities on the theory that they are third party beneficiaries of such assumption.

Liability on the part of the acquiring corporation does not, however, follow in all cases.

FACTS: McKee was injured while working with a paper cutting machine which had been manufactured in 1916 by Seybold Machine Co. In 1926 Seybold made a contract to sell its assets to Harris Automatic Press, which agreed to assume certain Seybold liabilities. This contract was assigned to a new corporation, Harris-Seybold-Potter Co., which

---

[18] Portland Section of the Council of Jewish Women v Sisters of Charity of Providence, 266 Ore 448, 513 P2d 1183.

thereafter changed its name to Harris-Seybold Co. McKee sued Harris-Seybold, claiming that it was liable to him because of the harm he sustained in using the cutter which had been made by Seybold Machine Co. The defendant raised the defense that it had not assumed any contingent liability with respect to products manufactured by the Seybold Machine Co. The assets of Seybold Machine Co. had been sold for approximately $2 million cash and a small amount of stock. The new corporation, "Harris-Seybold-Potter," was formed by the buyer to run the business.

DECISION: From the substantial cash payment that was made by the buyer and the fact that the new corporation was organized by the buyer, the transaction with Seybold Machine Co. was merely a purchase of its assets. There was no merger or consolidation, either formally or de facto. Consequently, there was no liability of the defendant corporation for the product liability of the Seybold Machine Co. [McKee v Harris-Seybold Co. 109 NJSuper 555, 264 A2d 98]

QUESTIONS AND CASE PROBLEMS

1. *A* made a contract with *B* on behalf of *X* Corporation. *B* knew that *X* Corporation was not yet formed. Thereafter *X* Corporation was properly organized, but *B* refused to perform its contract on the ground that *X* had not been in existence when the contract was made. Was this a valid defense? [See 330 Michigan Avenue, Inc. v Cambridge Hotel, Inc. (FlaApp) 183 So2d 725]

2. The Maid of the Mist Steamboat Co. was organized for operating sight-seeing steamships on the Niagara River. It had a fifty-year charter which expired in 1942. No one realized that fact until 1947. In that year an application was made under the New York law to renew the charter of the corporation. During the intervening period from 1942 to 1947 the corporation had continued to do business as usual. What kind of corporation was it during that period? [Garzo v Maid of the Mist Steamboat Co. 303 NY 516, 104 NE2d 882]

3. The Vincent Drug Co., a single proprietorship, took steps to incorporate. On January 2, articles of incorporation for Vincent Drug Co., Inc., were filed with the secretary of state, together with the firm's check for filing and license fees. The firm after that date conducted its business as a corporation pursuant to the articles. Although retaining the fees, the state later returned the articles to the firm's counsel because of a failure to include, as required by statute, the street addresses of the firm's incorporators and directors. Corrected articles showing such addresses were filed and recorded in May. Later the state tax commission questioned the firm's franchise tax return recitation that it had commenced business as a corporation as of January, the commission contending that the corporation did not exist before May. Was the commission correct? [Vincent Drug Co., Inc. v Utah State Tax Commission, 17 Utah2d 202, 407 P2d 683]

4. Adams and two other persons were promoters for a new corporation, the Aldrehn Theaters Co. The promoters retained Kridelbaugh to perform legal services in connection with the incorporation of the new business and promised to pay him

$1,500. The corporation was incorporated through Kridelbaugh's services, and the promoters became its only directors. Kridelbaugh attended a meeting of the board of directors at which he was told that he should obtain a permit for the corporation to sell stock because the directors wished to pay him for his prior services. The promoters failed to pay Kridelbaugh, and he sued the corporation. Was the corporation liable? [Kridelbaugh v Aldrehn Theaters Co. 195 Iowa 147, 191 NW 803]

5. Akel and his wife organized and incorporated the Akel Corporation. Prior to the actual incorporation, they obtained from Dooley a lease of property in which the Akel Corporation was named as the tenant. Dooley had no information as to whether the corporation was in existence. The corporation was in fact incorporated prior to the commencement of the lease. Later Dooley sued Akel and his wife for the rent. They claimed that they were not liable as individuals because the corporation was the tenant. Decide. [Akel v Dooley (FlaApp) 185 So2d 491]

6. A labor union made a collective bargaining agreement with Interscience Publishers, Inc. The contract made no provision that it was binding on successors of the contracting parties. Later, for general business reasons and not as an antilabor measure, Interscience merged with and disappeared into another publishing corporation, John Wiley & Sons, Inc. The former's employees, with a few exceptions, worked for Wiley. Thereafter the labor union claimed that Wiley was required to submit to arbitration, in accordance with the terms of the contract with Interscience, certain questions relating to employees who had worked for Interscience but were working for Wiley after the merger. Wiley claimed that it was not bound by the arbitration agreement with Interscience. Decide. [John Wiley & Sons v Livingston, 376 US 543]

7. Corporation A owed money to B. The debt was guaranteed by C. Corporation A merged with Corporation D, with D being the surviving corporation. D failed to pay the debt to B, who then sued C on the guarantee. C denied liability on the ground that he had guaranteed the debt of Corporation A and that as Corporation A was no longer in existence, he, C, was not bound by any guarantee. Was this defense valid? [See Essex International, Inc. v Clamage (CA7 Ill) 440 F2d 547]

8. Sanders owned and operated the 521 Club. He was indebted on a note to a creditor. The 521 Club was owned and operated by Sanders as a single proprietor. A corporation was formed to run the club. Sanders transferred all assets of the club to the corporation and received in exchange all the stock of the corporation and remained its sole owner and operator. The corporation made some payments on Sanders' note and then stopped. It then refused to make further payments on the ground that it had not assumed Sanders' note. Was the corporation liable for the payment of the note? [Hilst v Gaffey (Colo) 501 P2d 131]

CORPORATE POWERS

§ 50:1. NATURE AND LIMITATIONS OF CORPORATE POWERS. Some of the powers possessed by a corporation are the same as those powers held by natural persons, such as the right to own property. Others are distinct powers not possessed by ordinary persons, such as the power to exist perpetually.

All corporations do not have the same powers. For example, those that operate banks, insurance companies, savings and loan associations, and railroads generally have special powers.

Except for limitations in the federal Constitution or the state's own constitution, a state may grant to a corporation any powers that it chooses. In addition, a corporation has certain powers that are incidental to corporate existence. These powers are implied because they are reasonably necessary to carry out and make effective the expressly granted powers. Moreover, in exercising their powers, corporations have a choice of employing any lawful means. The ABA MBCA broadly authorizes a corporation "to have and exercise all powers necessary or convenient to effect its purpose."[1] Many state statutes make a similar "catchall" grant of powers.

If a power is expressly prohibited to a corporation, the corporation cannot exercise that power. In addition, certain other powers cannot be implied and therefore cannot be exercised in the absence of express authorization. It is generally held that there is no implied power to lend credit, to enter a partnership, to consolidate, or to merge.

§ 50:2. PARTICULAR POWERS.

(a) Perpetual succession. One of the distinctive features of a corporation is its perpetual succession or continuous life—the power to continue as a unit forever or for a stated period of time regardless of changes in stock ownership. If no period is fixed for its duration, the corporation will exist

---

[1] American Bar Association Model Business Corporation Act § 53.

indefinitely unless it is legally dissolved. When the period is limited, the corporation may in many states extend the period by meeting additional requirements of the statute. In view of such power of extension, a corporation may make a long-term contract running beyond the termination date of its certificate of incorporation.

(b) **Corporate name.** A corporation must have a name to identify it. As a general rule it may select any name for this purpose. It may not, however, select for its exclusive use a name that all may lawfully use, such as a descriptive name, or one that another firm has the exclusive right to use.

Most statutes require that the corporate name contain some word indicating the corporate character [2] and that it shall not be the same as or deceptively similar to the name of another corporation. Some statutes likewise prohibit the use of a name which is likely to mislead the public. The ABA MBCA states that the corporate name "shall not contain any word or phrase which indicates or implies that it is organized for any purpose other than one or more of the purposes contained in its articles of incorporation."[3] Under such a provision it would be improper to include in the corporate name the word "electronic" or "computerized" when such a word had no relation to the actual work of the corporation and the purpose of including such word in the corporate name was to take advantage of the current popularity of those words and thus attract investors to purchase the corporate stock or customers to deal with the corporation. In some states a name similar to one in use may be rejected even though the similarity is not so extreme as to be deceptive but is merely confusing.[4]

A number of states permit persons planning to form a corporation to reserve the name contemplated by filing an appropriate application with a state official. Such reservation is effective for a period generally ranging from 60 to 120 days.

(c) **Corporate seal.** A corporation may have a distinctive seal. However, a corporation need not use a seal in the transaction of business unless it is required by statute to use a seal or unless a natural person in transacting that business would be required to use a seal.

(d) **Bylaws.** The shareholders of a corporation have inherent power to make bylaws to supplement the charter of the corporation, but the right to do so is commonly expressed by statute.

Bylaws are adopted by the action of the shareholders, but some statutes provide for the adoption of bylaws by the directors unless otherwise provided. Action by the state or an amendment of the corporation charter is

---

[2] ABA MBCA § 8(a) declares that the corporate name must contain the word "corporation," "company," "incorporated," "limited," or an abbreviation of one of such words.

With respect to a professional corporation, there may be some additional requirement that the name indicate the nature of the services rendered in addition to the fact that it is a corporation. For example, it may be necessary to have the name of "Jones Accounting Associates, Inc." rather than merely "Jones Associates, Inc."

[3] ABA MBCA § 8(b).

[4] New York Business Corporation Law § 301(a)(2).

not required to make the bylaws effective. The difference between bylaws and provisions of a charter is a practical consideration. The charter represents provisions that should endure throughout the life of the corporation. The *bylaws* represent provisions for governing the corporation but which might become undesirable in the course of events, and therefore they should not be given the same permanence as the charter. This distinction is not always observed, and there is frequently a tendency to put much detail into the charter. No actual harm is done by so doing, except that it makes the charter unnecessarily long and also makes a change more difficult since state approval is required to amend the charter, while bylaws can be changed by corporate action.

The bylaws are subordinate to the general law of the state, including the statute under which the corporation is formed, as well as to the charter of the corporation. Bylaws that conflict with such superior authority or which are in themselves unreasonable are invalid. Bylaws that are valid are binding upon all shareholders regardless of whether they know of the existence of those bylaws or were among the majority which consented to their adoption. Bylaws are not binding upon third persons, however, unless they have notice or knowledge of them.

Statutes commonly provide for the adoption of emergency bylaws by the board of directors in case of war.[5] A few statutes provide for emergency bylaws in time of civil disorder.[6]

(e) Stock. A corporation may issue stock and certificates representing such stock.[7]

(f) Borrowing money. Corporations have the implied power to borrow money in carrying out their authorized business purposes. For example, a fire insurance company may borrow money to pay losses due on its policies. Statutes commonly prohibit corporations from raising the defense of usury.

(g) Execution of commercial paper. The power to issue or indorse commercial paper, or to accept drafts, is implied when the corporation has the power to borrow money and when such means are appropriate and ordinarily used to further the authorized objectives of the corporation.

Such transactions, however, are unauthorized when they are not related to, or if they are detrimental to, the furtherance of the corporate business. For example, it is beyond the power of a corporation to be an accommodation party on a note give by someone buying its stock.

(h) Bonds. A corporation having the power to borrow money has the implied power to issue various types of bonds.

---

[5] ABA MBCA § 27A [Optional] provides that the board of directors "may adopt emergency bylaws . . . operative during any emergency in the conduct of the business of the corporation resulting from an attack on the United States or any nuclear or atomic disaster. . . ."

[6] The problem faced by the corporation when a civil disorder or other emergency is present would ordinarily be solved by a person or persons, such as the executive committee, taking the initiative and performing such acts as they believed were required by the exigency of the situation. Thereafter, when normal times returned, a meeting of either the directors or the shareholders would be held and a resolution adopted ratifying the action that had been taken.

[7] Statutes in approximately one half of the states authorize a corporation to issue stock rights and warrants. See, for example, 8 Delaware Code § 157.

The bonds issued by a corporation are subject to Article 8 of the Uniform Commercial Code. If the bonds satisfy the requirements of UCC § 3-104, they are governed by Article 3 of the Code on commercial paper as far as negotiation is concerned.

Ordinarily conditions inserted in the corporate bonds for the protection of the bondholders have the effect of making the bonds nonnegotiable and therefore not within the scope of Article 3 of the Uniform Commercial Code, and only Article 8 applies to them.

(i) Transferring property. The corporate property may be leased, assigned for the benefit of creditors, or sold. In many states, however, a solvent corporation may not transfer all of its property except with the consent of all or a substantial majority of its shareholders. In any case, the sale must be for a fair price.

A corporation, having power to incur debts, may mortgage or pledge its property as security for those debts. This rule does not apply to franchises of public service companies, such as street transit systems and gas and electric companies.

(j) Acquisition of property. Although the power to acquire and hold property is usually given in the charter, a corporation always has the implied power to acquire and hold such property as is reasonably necessary for carrying out its express powers. In some states the power of a corporation to hold property is restricted as to the method of acquiring it, or is limited as to the quantity or the value of the property or the period of time for which it may be held. Restrictions on holding real estate are also imposed upon corporations by the constitutions of some states.

> **FACTS:** The State of Oklahoma sued the International Paper Company for the statutory penalty for unlawfully owning rural land in violation of the state constitutional provision that no corporation should own rural land "except such as shall be necessary and proper for carrying on the business for which it was chartered." The paper company claimed that the rural land it owned was being reforested by it. It was shown that the reforested area would not develop a crop of timber for 40 to 70 years.
>
> **DECISION:** Judgment for International Paper Company. The concept of "necessary and proper" does not mean absolutely necessary, and is satisfied if the conduct in question is proper, useful, and conducive to the accomplishment of the corporation's objectives. The acquisition of the rural land which the paper company was reforesting was a reasonable step to insure a continuous supply of wood pulp necessary for making paper. In view of the scarcity of wood and the time required to grow a crop of timber, the acquisition of the timberland by the corporation was reasonable and therefore was not prohibited by the Oklahoma constitution. [Oklahoma v International Paper Co. (Okla) 342 P2d 565]

(1) Investments. Modern corporation codes generally provide that a corporation may acquire the stock of other corporations.

(2) Holding Companies. A corporation owning stock of another corporation may own such a percentage of the stock of the other company

that it controls the latter's operations. In such a case the first company is commonly called a *holding company*. Sometimes a holding company is organized solely for the purpose of controlling other companies called *operating* or *subsidiary companies*.

FACTS: Connecticut General Life Insurance Co. obtained a license to write life insurance policies in New York. It thereafter proposed to acquire 80 percent or more of the common stock of the National Fire Insurance Co. of Hartford, a fire and casualty insurance company licensed to write policies in New York. In a declaratory judgment action, the New York State Superintendent of Insurance claimed that the Connecticut Company was prohibited from writing life policies in New York if it acquired such stock because, through its subsidiary, it would then be writing fire and casualty insurance in New York.

DECISION: Judgment for insurer. An insurance company may own stock of other corporations, even to the point that the other corporation becomes a subsidiary of the insurer corporation, and even though the subsidiary engages in a business prohibited to the insurer. In the absence of fraud or illegality, the separate identity of the subsidiary corporation and of its shareholders, here the parent corporation, prevents the conclusion that the parent corporation is engaging in the business of the subsidiary corporation. [Connecticut General Life Insurance Co. v Superintendent of Insurance, 10 NY2d 42, 176 NE2d 63]

The device of a holding company may be socially desirable or undesirable depending upon the circumstances under which it operates. If it is merely a device to coordinate different phases of an economic activity, the holding company is a proper device. If its object is to eliminate competition between the operating companies whose stock is held, it may be illegal under state or federal antitrust laws. If a holding company that operates in interstate commerce holds stock of electric or gas public utility companies, it may be ordered dissolved when it is found by the Securities and Exchange Commission to serve no economically useful purpose. It is no objection, however, that the subsidiary company engages in a business in which the holding company could not lawfully engage.

The fact that one corporation owns its subsidiary does not give it an unlimited right to control the subsidiary. Some degree of restriction is placed on the parent corporation in requiring "fairness" in its dealings with the subsidiary.

(k) Acquisition of own stock. Generally a corporation may purchase its own stock, if it is solvent at the time and the purchase does not impair capital. Sometimes a more precise standard is specified.[8] The Model Act permits a corporation to acquire its own shares ". . . only to the extent of unreserved and unrestricted earned surplus available therefor. . . ."[9] In a few states corporations are denied implied power to purchase their own

---

[8] A corporation may not purchase its own shares "if . . . the present fair value of the remaining assets . . . would be less than one fourth . . . times the amount of its liabilities to creditors." Arkansas Business Corporation Act § 5; Ark Stat Ann § 64-105.

[9] ABA MBCA § 6.

stock, but they are permitted to receive it as a gift, in payment of a debt, or as security for a debt.

Stock which is reacquired by the corporation that issued it is commonly called *treasury stock*. Ordinarily the treasury stock is regarded as still being issued or outstanding stock.[10] As such, the shares are not subject to the rule that original shares cannot be issued for less than par. They can be sold by the corporation at any price. Under the Model Act, "treasury shares may be disposed of by the corporation for such consideration expressed in dollars as may be fixed from time to time by the board of directors."

Although treasury stock retains the character of outstanding stock, it has an inactive status while it is held by the corporation. Thus, the treasury shares cannot be voted nor can dividends be declared on them.

The reacquisition by a corporation of its shares and the holding of them as treasury shares is to be distinguished from what occurs upon the redemption of shares. When shares are redeemed, they are automatically canceled.

Stock which is surrendered is not deemed outstanding without regard to whether it is retained as treasury shares or is formally canceled.

(l) Business in another state. A corporation has the inherent power and generally is expressly authorized to engage in business in other states. This grant of power by the incorporating state does not exempt the corporation, however, from satisfying the restrictions imposed by the foreign state in which it seeks to do business.

(m) Participation in enterprise. Corporations may generally participate in an enterprise to the same extent as individuals. They may enter into joint ventures. The modern statutory trend is to permit a corporation to be a member of a partnership. A corporation may be a limited partner. The Model Act authorizes a corporation "to be a promoter, partner, member, associate, or manager of any partnership, joint venture, trust or other enterprise."[11]

When the power to be a participant in an enterprise is not expressly granted to a corporation, there is a conflict as to whether it has implied authority to be a participant. When the relationship is of a permanent character or is of such a nature as to subject the corporation to the control of the outside enterprise, it is likely that the courts will refuse to imply a power to be a participant. For example, in the absence of express statutory authorization to be a partner, a corporation cannot be a member of a general partnership. Many modern corporation codes expressly grant this power.

In addition to the question of corporate power to participate in an enterprise, such participation is subject to and may be illegal under the federal antitrust legislation.[12]

---

[10]When a corporation reacquires its own shares, it has the choice of "retiring" them and thus restoring them to the status of authorized but unissued shares or to treat them as still issued and available for transfer. It is the latter which are described as treasury shares.

[11] ABA MBCA § 4(p).

[12] United States v Penn-Olin Chemical Co. 378 US 158.

(n) **Employee benefit and aid.** The ABA MBCA empowers a corporation "to pay pensions and establish pension plans, pension trusts, profit sharing plans, stock bonus plans, stock option plans, and other incentive plans for any or all of its directors, officers, and employees."[13]

Corporations have such power under most state codes either by express provision or by judicial decision. Such power is possessed by a professional corporation, and the existence of such power is a major reason for the forming of a professional corporation. The various employee benefit plans enable either the professional corporation or its members or both to obtain an advantage in the computation of federal income tax liability that would not otherwise be open to them as individuals or as partners.

(o) **Charitable contributions.** The Model Act authorizes a corporation without any limitation "to make donations for the public welfare or for charitable, scientific, or educational purposes." In some states some limitation is imposed upon the amount that can be donated for charitable purposes. The federal income tax law tends to set a limitation on charitable contributions, since corporations ordinarily will not make contributions in an amount greater than may be claimed as a deduction for the purpose of federal income tax computation.

Modern courts are more willing to take for granted that a corporation may spend its money for a charitable purpose, as opposed to the earlier theory that the money of a corporation was a fund to be held in trust for the furtherance of the business purpose for which the corporation was created. This transition in theory has been encouraged by the rise of the concept that business has a responsibility for the general welfare of society and may therefore properly spend corporate money for societal betterment.

(p) **Civic improvement.** The Model Act also authorizes a corporation "to transact any lawful business which the board of directors shall find will be in aid of governmental policy." Under such broad authorization a corporation may aid in a military war, in a war on poverty, and take part in measures to prevent civil strife.

§ **50:3. ULTRA VIRES ACTS.** When a corporation acts in excess of or beyond the scope of the powers granted by its charter and the statute under which it was organized, then the corporation's act is described as *ultra vires*. Such an act is improper because it is a violation of the obligation of the corporation to the state. It is also improper with respect to shareholders and creditors of the corporation because corporate funds have been diverted to unauthorized uses.

As an illustration of the latter point, assume that a corporation is created and authorized to manufacture television sets. Various persons purchase stock in the corporation, lend it money, or sell to it on credit because of their estimate of the worth of the television business in general and of the corporation as a television manufacturing company in particular. Assume

---

[13] ABA MBCA §4(o).

that the corporation has funds that it uses for the ultra vires purpose of lending to persons to buy homes. Many of the shareholders and creditors would probably never have become associated with the corporation if it had been organized for that purpose. The fact that the ultra vires use of the money may be better economically or socially than the authorized use does not alter the fact that the shareholders' and the creditors' money is not used the way they intended.

(a) Ultra vires acts and illegality distinguished. Although it is not lawful for a corporation to perform ultra vires acts, the objection to the commission of such acts is distinct from the objection of illegality. In the case of illegality, the act would be wrong regardless of the nature of the person or the association committing it. The fact that an act is ultra vires merely means that this particular corporation does not have permission from the state to do the act. Thus, it would ordinarily be beyond the powers of a business corporation, and therefore ultra vires, to engage in a charitable enterprise, such as the building of a church or college. But the activity would hardly be termed illegal.

> **FACTS:** The Ladd Estate Company brought suit on a promissory note made up by Wheatley and guaranteed by Westover Tower, Inc. Westover claimed that its guarantee of the note was not binding because Wheatley was a director of the corporation when the guarantee was made and the guarantee was therefore ultra vires and illegal as it violated a statute prohibiting loans to directors.
>
> **DECISION:** Judgment for Ladd. The guaranty of a loan is not a loan. The corporation had not made a loan and the statute against loans did not apply. The corporation was therefore liable on the guaranty. [Ladd Estate Co. v Wheatley, 246 Ore 627, 426 P2d 878]

(b) Effect of ultra vires contracts. There is some conflict in the law as to the effect of an ultra vires act. Under the modern statutory trend, ultra vires cannot be raised to attack the validity of any act, contract, or transfer of property,[14] except as noted under § 50:3(c). This trend is recognized by the Model Act which declares that "no act of a corporation and no conveyance or transfer of real or personal property to or by a corporation shall be invalid by reason of the fact that the corporation was without capacity or power to do such an act or to make or receive such a conveyance or transfer."

In the absence of statute, most courts recognize ultra vires as a defense but refuse to apply it in a particular case if it would be inequitable and work a hardship.

> **FACTS:** Members of the Lurie family controlled and were directors of Allied Yuma Farms, Inc. Chapman, a neighboring farmer, persuaded the Luries to engage in a joint farming venture. Arizona Fertilizer and Chemical Company sold fertilizers to the joint venture. When Arizona

---

[14] ABA MBCA § 7; Inter-Continental Corp. v Moody (TexCivApp) 411 SW2d 578.

Fertilizer was not paid, it sued the Luries. They raised the defense that they were not liable because they had acted for the corporation, Allied Yuma Farms, Inc. The plaintiff replied that the forming of a joint venture was ultra vires and therefore the Luries, as directors of Allied, were personally liable for the contracts made in the course of the ultra vires activity.

DECISION: Judgment for Arizona Fertilizer. The existence of the corporation was not made known until it was raised as a defense to the payment of the plaintiff's claim. The Luries were therefore liable to Arizona Fertilizer. [Lurie v Arizona Fertilizer & Chemical Co. 101 Ariz 482, 421 P2d 330]

The courts also refuse to recognize it as a defense against the holder of a commercial paper on which the corporation, without authority, became an accommodation party. Likewise, a transfer of real or personal property cannot be set aside on the ground that it is ultra vires. Here the object of the law is to preserve the security of titles even though the result is to permit the wrongful act of the corporation to stand.

In most states if the ultra vires contract has been completely performed, neither party can rescind the contract on the ground that it was originally ultra vires. Conversely, if neither party to the ultra vires contract has performed his part, the court will neither enforce the contract nor hold either party liable for a breach of the contract. A person who has benefited by the ultra vires act cannot refuse to pay for the value which he has received on the ground that the transaction was ultra vires.

FACTS: The Bank of Campbellsville was practically owned by the men who were its directors and officers. They personally owed a debt to Marshall, one of their depositors, for money they had borrowed to use as funds of the bank. Marshall overdrew his account in the bank. The directors and officers then agreed with him that they would pay the overdraft for Marshall and that their debt to him would be reduced by the amount of such payment. The bank became insolvent, and Webster was appointed to liquidate the bank. He claimed that the overdraft agreement was ultra vires and Marshall was required to pay back to the bank the amount of the overdraft. Marshall brought an action for a declaratory judgment for the purpose of determining his rights.

DECISION: Judgment for Marshall. The transaction with respect to the overdraft, having been completed, would not be deemed inoperative; and the bank that had benefited by the transaction would be held liable for the value which it had received. [Marshall v Webster, 287 Ky 692, 155 SW2d 13]

(c) **Remedies for ultra vires acts.** In all states (1) a shareholder may obtain an injunction to stop the board of directors or other persons involved from entering into an ultra vires transaction; (2) the corporation, or a shareholder acting on behalf of the corporation, may sue the persons who made or approved the contract in order to recover damages for the loss caused the corporation by the ultra vires act; and (3) an action may be brought by the attorney general of the state to revoke the charter on the ground of its serious or repeated violation.

When an action is brought to enjoin or set aside corporate action on the ground that it is ultra vires, there is no requirement that the plaintiffs show that the corporation or they are in any way harmed, as each shareholder has a right to see that his corporation does not do an act which is not authorized. Similarly, when the attorney general brings an action to forfeit the corporate charter because of ultra vires acts, there is no requirement of proof of damage to the corporation; as a practical matter, a court is more likely to forfeit the charter if harm to the community can be shown.

In contrast, when shareholders bring a derivative action to recover damages on behalf of the corporation for the harm caused by the ultra vires acts, the plaintiffs must necessarily show the extent to which the corporation has been harmed. However, the shareholders are not required to prove what individual harm they have sustained.

QUESTIONS AND CASE PROBLEMS

1. In an action by the Federal Savings State Bank as the holder of a note against Grimes, the maker of the note, the authority of the corporate payee, the Industrial Mutual Life Insurance Co., to accept the note from the maker was questioned. It was argued that the corporate payee possessed the power because there was no statute expressly prohibiting the exercise of that power. Was this argument valid? [Federal Savings State Bank v Grimes, 156 Kan 55, 131 P2d 894]

2. A husband, H, borrowed money from bank B. B promised to insure the loan so that if H died before the debt was repaid, the proceeds of the insurance policy would pay off the debt. B failed to obtain the insurance, and H died owing a balance on the debt. H's widow sued the bank to cancel the balance remaining on the debt on the theory that if B had obtained the insurance as it had promised to do, there would not be any balance. B defended on the ground that it could not have obtained the insurance because it would have been ultra vires for it to have done so. Was this defense valid? [See Robichaud v Athol Credit Union, 352 Mass 351, 225 NE2d 347]

3. The H & R Construction Corporation entered into a contract for construction work, and the Seaboard Surety Co. executed a bond assuring that the contract would be performed. The Seaboard Surety Co. was required to pay damages when the contractor did not perform the contract. It then sued the construction corporation and also the H. C. Nelson Investment Co. to recover the money it had so paid. Its suit against the Nelson Investment Co. was based on the theory that the construction corporation and the investment company were partners. Was there a partnership? [Nelson v Seaboard Surety Co. (CA8 Ill) 262 F2d 189]

4. An employee of the Archer Pancoast Co., a corporation, was killed as the result of falling through a hatchway in a building occupied by the company as a factory. Hoffman, superintendent of the factory, called Noll, an undertaker, and arranged for the funeral. Hoffman agreed to pay Noll $100 for his services. After performing the work, Noll brought an action against the Archer Pancoast Co. to recover the agreed sum. The defendant raised the defense of ultra vires. Decide. [Noll v Archer Pancoast Co. 60 AppDiv 414, 69 NYS 1007]

5. A bylaw of the Coleman Realty Co. provided that the corporation could not sell its stock to a person not a shareholder without first offering to sell it at its book value to the corporation or to the remaining shareholders in proportion to their interests. This bylaw was later repealed at a shareholder's meeting by the vote of Mrs. Ludgate who owned a majority of the stock. Bechtold, a minority shareholder, brought an action to declare that the repeal of the bylaw was invalid and had no effect. Was the repeal of the bylaw effective? [Bechtold v Coleman Realty Co. 367 Pa 208, 79 A2d 661]

6. The Columbia Chemical Co. was incorporated under the laws of New York for the purpose of manufacturing and selling chemicals. Thereafter a group of persons filed incorporation papers in the same state for an organization with the name of Columbian Chemical Co. It was contended that the second company had no right to adopt such a name. Do you agree? [New York v O'Brien, 101 AppDiv 296, 91 NYS 649]

7. The Philadelphia Electric Co. was incorporated "for the purpose of supplying heating, lighting, and power by electricity to the public." The company supplied electricity but in addition began to sell electrical appliances. An action was brought by the attorney general against the corporation to forfeit its charter for engaging in ultra vires acts. Decide. [Commonwealth of Pennsylvania ex rel. Baldrige, Attorney General v Philadelphia Electric Co. 300 Pa 577, 151 A 344]

8. The Central Mutual Auto Insurance Co. was a Michigan corporation. A foreign corporation, the Central Mutual Insurance Co., was granted a license to do business in Michigan. Central Mutual Auto Insurance Co. brought an action to prevent the foreign corporation from doing business within Michigan under that name. Decide. [Central Mutual Auto Insurance Co. v Central Mutual Insurance Co. 275 Mich 554, 267 NW 733]

9. A corporation wished to borrow money. A plan was arranged with the lender by which the corporation would issue a block of stock which the lender would hold as collateral to secure the repayment of the loan. A shareholder objected on the ground that a corporation may only issue its stock to one who will become its owner and that it could only be issued for payment and not as security. Could the corporation issue the stock as proposed? [See Costabile v Essex Linoleum and Carpet Co. 98 NJSuper 224, 236 A2d 625]

CORPORATE STOCK AND SHAREHOLDERS

A. CORPORATE STOCK

§ 51:1. NATURE OF STOCK. The ownership of a fractional part of a corporation is evidenced by the share or stock of the shareholder or stockholder. "Share" and "stock" have the same meaning. Stock is the older term and share is more commonly used in modern statutes.

Membership in a corporation is usually based upon ownership of one or more shares of stock of the corporation. Each share represents a fractional interest in the total property possessed by the corporation. Each share confers the right to receive the dividends, when declared, and the right to participate in a distribution of capital upon the dissolution of the corporation. The shareholder does not own or have an interest in any specific property of the corporation; the corporation is the owner of all of its property.

(a) Capital and capital stock. *Capital* refers to the net assets of the corporation. *Capital stock* refers to the declared money value of the outstanding stock of the corporation.

(b) Valuation of stock. Corporate stock commonly has a specified *par value*. This means that the person subscribing to the stock and acquiring it from the corporation must pay that amount. When stock is issued by the corporation for a price greater than the par value, some statutes provide that only the par value amount is to be treated as stated capital, the excess being allocated to surplus.[1]

Shares may be issued with no par value. In such a case no amount is stated in the certificate, and the amount that the subscriber pays the corporation is determined by the board of directors.

The value found by dividing the value of the corporate assets by the number of shares outstanding is the *book value* of the shares. The *market value* of a share of stock is the price at which it can be voluntarily bought or sold.

---

[1] California Corporations Code, § 1901.

§ **51:2. CERTIFICATE OF STOCK.** The corporation ordinarily issues a *certificate of stock* or share certificate as evidence of the shareholder's ownership of stock. Although the issuance of such certificates is not essential either to the existence of a corporation or to the ownership of its stock, it is an almost universal practice since it is a convenient method of proving ownership and since it makes transfer of ownership easier.

Any form of certificate that identifies the interest owned by a person in the corporation is sufficient.

§ **51:3. KINDS OF STOCK.** The stock of a corporation may be divided into two or more classes.

(a) Preferences. *Common stock* is ordinary stock that has no preferences. Each share usually entitles the holder to one vote and to a share of the profits in the form of dividends, when declared, and to participate in the distribution of capital upon dissolution of the corporation. *Preferred stock* has a priority over common stock. The priority may be with respect to dividends. Preferred stock may also have a priority over common stock in the distribution of capital upon dissolution of the corporation. Preferred stock is ordinarily nonvoting.

(1) Cumulative Preferred Stock. Any form of statement with the right to accumulate will be given effect. It is sufficient that the articles of incorporation manifest an intent that the preferred stock be cumulative, as when it was stated that no dividends could be paid upon the common stock until unpaid dividends for all preceding years had been paid to the preferred shareholders. It was immaterial that the articles did not expressly state that the right to dividends was "cumulative" or that the dividends were not guaranteed.

In the absence of a statement that the right to dividends is noncumulative, it is frequently held that preferred stock has the right to cumulate dividends, particularly with respect to each year in which there were earnings available for dividend declaration.

(2) Participating Preferred Stock. Sometimes the preferred stock is given the right of participation. After the common shares receive dividends or a capital distribution equal to that first received by the preferred stock, both kinds share equally in the balance.

(b) Duration of shares. Ordinarily shares continue to exist for the life of the corporation. Under modern statutes, however, any kind of shares, whether common or preferred, may be made terminable at an earlier date.

(1) Redeemable Shares. *Redeemable shares* are surrendered to the corporation, which pays the shareholder the par value of the shares or such amount as is stated in the redemption agreement. Redeemed shares ordinarily cease to exist after redemption, as distinguished from being owned by the corporation as treasury stock.

(2) Convertible Shares. *Convertible shares* entitle the shareholder to exchange his shares for a different type of share or for bonds of the

corporation. Convertible unsecured bonds that may be converted into stock are more common than shares which may be converted into bonds.

(c) Fractional shares. Modern statutes expressly authorize a corporation to issue fractional shares or to issue script or certificates representing such fractional shares that can be sold or combined for the acquisition of whole shares. In some states the holder of a fractional share is entitled to vote, to receive dividends, and to participate in the distribution of corporate assets upon liquidation.

B. ACQUISITION OF SHARES

§ 51:4. SUBSCRIPTION. A *stock subscription* is a contract or an agreement to buy a specific number and kind of shares of stock when they are issued. As in the case of any other contract, the agreement to subscribe to shares of a corporation is subject to avoidance for fraud.

(a) Formality. By the great weight of authority, a contract to subscribe for shares of a corporation not yet formed or for unissued shares of stock of an existing corporation is not within the statute of frauds and need not be evidenced by a writing. In contrast, a contract for the transfer of existing corporate stock is subject to a statute of frauds provision similar to that applicable in the case of goods, except that the security provision applies without regard to the amount involved. Thus, any contract for the sale of a security must be evidenced by a writing to be enforceable or to be available as a defense.[2] This requirement of a writing extends to contracts relating to rights, such as a contract for the sale of stock purchase warrants.

The writing which is required by the statute of frauds must show that there has been a contract for the sale of a stated quantity of described securities at a defined or stated price.[3] The writing must be signed in the manner required of a writing for the sale of goods.

No writing is required for instructions between a customer and his broker because, although such instructions contemplate the subsequent making of a sale, the giving of the instructions does not constitute a contract of sale.

(b) Subscription before incorporation. In many states a pre-incorporation subscription of shares is regarded as an offer to the corporation. By this view it is necessary for the corporation to accept the subscription offer either expressly or by conduct. A few states hold that such subscriptions automatically become binding contracts when the organization has been completed.

In some states the preincorporation subscription is irrevocable for a stated period.[4] The ABA MBCA provides that "a subscription for shares of a corporation to be organized shall be irrevocable for a period of six months,

---

[2] Uniform Commercial Code § 8-319.
[3] UCC § 8-319(a).
[4] New York Business Corporation Law § 503(a).

unless otherwise provided by the terms of the subscription agreement or unless all of the subscribers consent to the revocation of such subscription."[5] As in the case of any contract, there may be a rescission upon proper grounds.

Generally a subscriber is not entitled to receive his share certificate until he has paid for the shares it represents.

(c) Subscription after incorporation. Subscriptions may be made after incorporation. In that event the transaction is like any other contract with the corporation. The offer of the subscription may come from the subscriber or from the corporation, but in either case there must be an acceptance. Upon acceptance the subscriber immediately becomes a shareholder with all the rights, privileges, and liabilities of a shareholder even though the subscriber has not paid any of the purchase price. The transaction, however, may only be a contract for the future issue of shares rather than a present subscription.

§ 51:5. TRANSFER OF SHARES. In the absence of a valid restriction, a shareholder may transfer his shares to anyone he chooses.

(a) Restrictions on transfer. Restrictions on the transfer of stock are valid provided they are not unreasonable. In order to prevent its stock from going into the hands of strangers, it is lawful for a corporation to require the first right to purchase stock before a shareholder may sell it to an outsider.

FACTS: Davis, an employee of the Household Finance Corp., owned 100 shares of stock in the corporation. Davis transferred his shares to Lawson, and indorsed and delivered his stock certificate to him. The stock certificate set forth the provision of the certificate of incorporation and the bylaws of the corporation that the stock could not be sold without giving the corporation first opportunity to purchase it at its fair value to be determined by appraisal. When Lawson presented the purchased certificate to the corporation for cancellation and the issuance to him of a new certificate, the corporation refused to recognize the transfer. Lawson sued to compel it to do so.

DECISION: Judgment for the corporation. In order to insure that its employees would have the best interests of the corporation at heart, it was proper for the corporation to sell its stock to its employees and to keep the stock from going into the hands of strangers by insisting that it be given the first right to purchase. In order to make such a provision effective, the corporation could refuse to recognize any transfer made in violation of such a restriction. [Lawson v Household Finance Corp. 17 DelCh 1, 147 A 312]

The provision of the ABA Model Business Corporation Act has been followed in many states to authorize "any provision . . . for the regulation of the internal affairs of the corporation, including any provision restricting the transfer of shares."[6] There is, however, some statutory authority for

---

[5] American Bar Association Model Business Corporation Act § 17.
[6] ABA MBCA § 54(h).

declaring void a bylaw restriction on the transfer of shares.[7] A provision giving a corporation the right to purchase a shareholder's shares upon his death is valid.[8]

A restriction upon the right to transfer is not valid as against a purchaser of the certificate unless the restriction is conspicuously noted on the certificate or unless the transferee has actual knowledge of the restriction.[9]

(b) Interest transferred. The transfer of shares may be absolute, that is, it may divest all ownership and make the transferee the full owner, or it may be merely for security, as when stock is pledged to secure the repayment of a loan. Since it is an essential element of a pledge transaction that the pledgee be able to sell the pledged property upon default, the pledge of stock requires the delivery to the pledgee of the stock certificate together with a separate assignment of or an indorsement on the stock certificate in favor of the pledgee or bearer. When this is done, the pledgee will be able to transfer title to the shares in case of default. Directors and officers of a corporation may purchase stock held by shareholders of the corporation.

§ 51:6. MECHANICS OF TRANSFER. The ownership of shares is transferred by the delivery of the certificate of stock indorsed by its owner in blank, or to a specified person; or by the delivery of the certificate by such person accompanied by a separate assignment or power of attorney executed by him.[10] A transfer made in this manner is effective as between the parties even though the corporate charter or bylaws specify that shares cannot be transferred until a transfer is made on the books of the corporation or the records of a corporate transfer agent.

A delivery from the owner of the shares directly to his transferee is not required.

> **FACTS:** LaVern Millin owned 3,700 shares of stock in the Western Printing & Lithographing Co. He went with his son James to the local bank and told the vice president that he wanted the stock transferred to his son. LaVern signed his name on the transfer form on the back of each certificate, the vice president signed each certificate as a guarantor of LaVern's signature, and the certificates were sent to Western with a covering letter requesting that a new certificate be issued in the name of the son James and sent directly to him. Thereafter it was claimed that the transaction had no effect because the share certificates were not delivered by the father to his son.
>
> **DECISION:** The transaction was effective to constitute a delivery of the stock certificates. A delivery to the transferee personally is not required. Under the circumstances it was clear that the delivery was made to the corporation, as agent, to act for the son in issuing him new shares. [Kintzinger v Millin, 254 Iowa 173, 117 NW2d 68]

---

[7] New Hampshire Rev Stats Ann § 296:14.

[8] Allen v Biltmore Tissue Corp. 2 NY2d 534, 161 NYS2d 418, 141 NE2d 812.

[9] UCC § 8-204.

[10] § 8-309. The second alternative of a delivery of an unindorsed certificate is designed to keep the certificate "clean," as when the transfer is for a temporary or special purpose as in the case of a pledge of the certificate as security for a loan.

A physical transfer of the certificate without a necessary indorsement is effective as between the parties because indorsement is only necessary to make a transferee a "bona fide" purchaser as against third parties.

In the absence of a delivery of the certificate or an assignment, there can be no effective transfer of ownership of the shares. Hence, the fact that the decedent indorsed stock certificates in blank did not establish a gift when he died in possession of the certificates apparently without having made any delivery of them.

Conversely, when the alleged donee has possession of shares which were never indorsed by the alleged donor and which are registered on the corporate books in the name of the alleged donor, the alleged donee has the burden of proving the alleged gift by clear and convincing evidence.

In general, the transfer agent stands in the same position as the corporation with respect to its stock and must make a formal transfer whenever the corporation would itself be required to recognize a transfer. When a corporation or its transfer agent wrongfully refuses to register a transfer of shares of stock, the new owner of the shares may bring suit for damages sustained and in some states may sue for the face value of the shares on the theory of conversion.

Possession of the certificate is also essential to an involuntary transfer by execution of judicial process.[11]

§ 51:7. EFFECT OF TRANSFER.

(a) **Validity of transfer.** As a transfer of shares is a transfer of ownership, the transfer must in general satisfy the requirements governing any other transfer of property or agreement to transfer property. As between the parties, a transfer may be set aside for any ground that would warrant similar relief under property law. If the transfer of stock has been obtained by duress, the transferor may obtain a rescission of the transfer.

(b) **Negotiability.** Under the common law the transferee of shares of stock had no greater right than the transferor because the certificate and the shares represented by the certificate were nonnegotiable. By statute the common-law rule has been changed by imparting negotiability to the certificate. Just as various defenses cannot be asserted against the holder in due course of a commercial paper, it is provided that similar defenses cannot be raised against the person acquiring the certificate in good faith and for value. As against such a person, the defenses cannot be raised that his transferor did not own the shares, that he did not have authority to deliver the certificate, or that the transfer was made in violation of a restriction upon transfer not known to such person and not noted conspicuously on the certificate. A former owner cannot object as against a subsequent purchaser for value and in good faith that his transferee obtained the certificate from him by fraud, duress, mistake, or did not give him any consideration.[12] Conversely, if the purchaser of stock knows that

---

[11] UCC § 8-317.
[12] §§ 8-301, 8-311, 8-315.

his vendor holds the title subject to the claims of other persons, such as a divorced wife claiming an interest therein, the purchaser is subject to the rights of such third persons.

This concept of negotiability is also recognized as against corporate lien claims on the stock. Although modern statutes commonly give the corporation a lien upon stock for a debt owed it by the shareholder, the corporation cannot assert a lien against a purchaser of the shares unless the right of the corporation to the lien is noted conspicuously on the certificate.[13]

The fact that corporate stock has the quality of negotiability does not make it commercial paper within Article 3 of the Uniform Commercial Code. Shares of stock are classified under the UCC as investment securities; and Article 8, as supplemented by the continuing non-Code law which has not been displaced,[14] is the source of the law governing the rights of the parties to the transaction involving such securities. Nevertheless, courts may look to Article 3 for guidance when a question regarding an investment security cannot be resolved on the basis of the language in Article 8 alone.

(c) **Secured transaction.** Corporate stock is frequently delivered to a creditor as security for a debt owed by the shareholder. Thus, a debtor borrowing money from a bank may deliver shares of stock to the bank as collateral security for the repayment of the loan, or a broker's customer purchasing stock on margin may leave the stock in the possession of the broker as security for the payment of any balance due. The delivery of the security to the creditor or his retention of possession gives rise to a perfected security interest without any filing by the creditor. In itself the pledge does not make the pledgee of the corporate stock the owner of the stock nor of any of the assets of the corporation.

(d) **Effect of transfer on corporation.** Until there is a transfer on its books, the corporation is entitled to treat as the owner the person whose name is on the books.[15] The corporation may properly refuse to recognize the transferee when the corporation is given notice or has knowledge that the transfer is void or in breach of trust. In such a case the corporation properly refuses to effect a transfer until the rights of the parties have been determined.

The corporation may also refuse to register the transfer of shares when the outstanding certificate is not surrendered to it, in the absence of satisfactory proof that it had been lost, destroyed, or stolen.

§ 51:8. LOST, DESTROYED, AND STOLEN SECURITIES. Although for some purposes the negotiable character of a security makes the paper stand for the security, the loss, destruction, or theft of the paper does not destroy the owner's rights. Subject to certain limitations, he may obtain from the issuer of the security a new paper evidencing his ownership, that is, a new

---

[13] § 8-103.
[14] § 1-103.
[15] § 8-207.

share certificate. Two limitations on this right of replacement are expressly stated in the Uniform Commercial Code, and a third is recognized.

(a) Time. The owner of the security must make the request to the issuer or its transfer agent before the missing security has been acquired by a bona fide purchaser and before the issuer has notice of that fact or has entered on its book a transfer of ownership to such purchaser.[16] Ordinarily this can only occur if the security was in "bearer" form, for otherwise a third person could not qualify as a "purchaser" and the issuer's registration of the transfer to him would in itself be wrongful.

(b) Bond. The applicant for the replacement security must furnish the issuer with "a sufficient indemnity bond"[17] to protect the issuer from loss should it issue a replacement security and a bona fide purchaser thereafter present the original security.

The UCC does not specify the amount and terms of such a bond, but the duty to act in good faith [18] will in turn require that the bond terms be commercially reasonable.

(c) Additional requirements. In addition to the two limitations above noted, the UCC permits the issuer to impose "any other reasonable requirements."[19] Ordinarily this will take the form of an affidavit setting forth the facts with respect to the ownership; to the loss, destruction, or theft of the original security; and to the efforts made to find or recover the lost or stolen security.

§ 51:9. PROTECTION OF THE PUBLIC.

(a) Blue-sky laws. In order to protect the public from the sale of securities of nonexistent or worthless corporations, many states have adopted regulations called *blue-sky laws*. The statutes vary in detail. Some impose a criminal penalty for engaging in fraudulent practices, while others require the licensing of dealers in securities and approval by a government agency before a given security can be sold to the public.[20]

The extensive federal regulation of corporate securities does not displace the operation of state blue-sky laws as to intrastate transactions.[21]

(b) Federal Securities Act. The state blue-sky laws are subject to the very important limitation that they can apply only to intrastate transactions and cannot apply to sales made in interstate commerce. To meet this defect the

---

[16] § 8-405(1), (2),(a).

[17] § 8-405(2)(b).

[18] § 1-203.

[19] § 8-405(2)(c).

[20] Uniformity of blue-sky laws has been achieved in one half of the states through the adoption of the Uniform Securities Act, as amended in 1958. This act has been adopted in Alabama, Alaska, Arkansas, Colorado, Hawaii, Idaho, Indiana, Kansas, Kentucky, Maryland, Massachusetts, Michigan, Missouri, Montana, Nebraska, Nevada, New Jersey, New Mexico, Oklahoma, Oregon, South Carolina, Utah, Virginia, Washington, West Virginia, Wisconsin, Wyoming, and is in force in the District of Columbia and Puerto Rico.

[21] 15 United States Code § 77r.

federal Securities Act of 1933 was adopted. This Act requires the filing of a *registration statement* that gives the public certain information.

The registration statement is filed with the Securities and Exchange Commission (SEC). The objective is to provide the interested investor with a place where he can learn certain facts about the security and the enterprise. There is nothing which constitutes an approval by the government that the investment is sound nor is there any guarantee that the investor will not lose money.

(1) Applicability. The statute applies to the issuing of stocks and bonds and any other form of investment security.

(2) Registration Statement Exemption. The issuing of some securities is exempt from the requirement of a registration statement. Registration is not required for issues of less than $500,000 nor for issues by a government or a nonprofit corporation. The statute does not apply to transactions between private investors nor to private offerings to a limited number of persons who would otherwise have access to the kinds of information set forth in the registration statement.[22]

(3) Liability for Fraud. The federal Act imposes civil liability and criminal penalties for fraudulent statements made in connection with the issuance of securities whether or not exempt from the registration statement requirements. Civil and criminal liability is also imposed for false statements made in the registration statement, and for the omission of material matter therefrom. The same liability applies to fraudulent statements in and omissions from a stock prospectus (selling circular).

Any investor who sustains loss because of the false statements or omissions of the registration statement may sue to recover damages.

A defendant sued for damages may defend on the ground that he had exercised due diligence in determining the facts and that after reasonable investigation did not know nor have reason to believe that any statement in the registration statement was false nor that any material fact had been omitted.[23]

(c) Criminal penalties. The Act declares it unlawful for any issuer, underwriter, or dealer in securities to send either the securities or a prospectus for them in interstate commerce or the mails without having first registered the issue with the Securities and Exchange Commission.

A criminal penalty is imposed for failure to register or for making false statements to the Commission. The Commission may enjoin any practice that violates the act, and persons injured may bring suit for civil damages against the violator.

(d) Federal Securities Exchange Act. In addition to the evils connected with the issuing and floating of securities, a number of evils arose from

---

[22] Securities Act Amendment of 1964, PL 88-467, 78 Stat 565, 15 USC § 781(g)(1)(B).
[23] Securities Act of 1933 § 11.

practices at security exchanges. Dealers in security transactions in the interstate market are now subject to the federal Securities Exchange Act of 1934. Exchanges, brokers, and dealers who deal in the securities traded in interstate commerce or on any national security exchange must register if they have assets of $1 million or more and 500 or more shareholders.

A registrant is required to file periodic reports in order to keep the registration information up-to-date. The federal Securities Exchange Act of 1934 declares it unlawful for any broker, dealer, or exchange, directly or indirectly, to make use of the mails or any means of communication for the purpose of using the facilities of an exchange to effect any transaction in a security, unless such exchange is registered as a national securities exchange with the Securities and Exchange Commission or unless it is exempt from registration.

Various practices that were used in market manipulation are declared unlawful and prohibited by the Act. Wash sales, matched orders, and circulation of false rumors and tips are made unlawful and prohibited. These devices attempt to create the impression of great trading activity in a particular stock, thus tending to increase the price that the public is willing to pay for it.

Other practices that can be used either for a lawful trading or an unlawful manipulating purpose are not prohibited by the Act but are subject to the regulation of the Securities and Exchange Commission so that the Commission may see that they are used for a legitimate purpose. Speculative activity on exchanges is restricted by giving the Board of Governors of the Federal Reserve System power to fix the margin on which trading can be conducted and to restrict the extent to which money can be borrowed to finance stock transactions.

(e) Holding company regulation. Later statutes provide for the registration of interstate electric or gas utility holding companies with the Securities and Exchange Commission and authorize the Federal Power Commission to regulate the rates on interstate shipments of natural gas and electric power. In registering, the holding company must file detailed information concerning its corporate structure and financing.

Authority is given to the Securities and Exchange Commission to order the dissolution of holding companies if they were created merely for the purpose of corporate manipulation. If a holding company does not register as required by law, it is illegal for it to engage in interstate transactions. A holding company that has registered is subject to various restrictions as to financing and security issues, and the commission is given supervisory powers over the company's financial records.

C. RIGHTS OF SHAREHOLDERS

§ 51:10. OWNERSHIP RIGHTS.

(a) Certificate of stock. A shareholder has the right to have issued to him a properly executed certificate as evidence of his ownership of shares.

(b) Transfer of shares. Subject to certain valid restrictions, a shareholder has the right to transfer his shares as he chooses. He may sell the shares at any price or transfer them as a gift.

§ **51:11. RIGHT TO VOTE.** The right to vote means the right to vote at shareholders' meetings for the election of directors and on such other special matters as must be passed upon by the shareholders. As an illustration of the latter, a proposal to change the capital stock structure of the corporation or a proposal to sell all or substantially all of the assets of the corporation must be approved by the shareholders.

A shareholder may vote his shares as he pleases for the protection of his own interests, as against the contention that he owes a duty to the corporation or other shareholders to act in a way which will be for their interest. The fact that a shareholder is also a director of the corporation does not restrict his freedom of voting his shares nor disqualify him from voting on any issue on which other shareholders are entitled to vote.

(a) Who may vote. Ordinarily only those common shareholders in whose names the stock appears on the books of the corporation are entitled to vote. Generally the directors may fix a date for determining the shareholders who may vote.[24]

When a shareholder has pledged his shares as security, he may generally continue to vote the shares and the pledgee is not entitled to vote the shares until a transfer of the shares is made to the pledgee by the corporation.[25]

The requirement that a person be a shareholder of record in order to vote excludes a person not so recorded even though he might be entitled to be registered as the shareholder. Thus, a pledgee may not vote shares that are not registered in his name even though, because of the pledgor's default, the pledgee was entitled to have the shares transferred to his name.

The more recent corporation statutes recognize that there may be a conflict of interest between the holders of the voting stock and the holders of a particular class of stock not entitled to vote. In order to protect the interests of the nonvoting stock, some statutes require that action, such as the amendment of the certificate or articles of incorporation that could affect the nonvoting class, must be voted upon and approved by that class as a class, in addition to being approved by the required majority of the voting shares.[26]

(b) Number of votes. Each shareholder is ordinarily entitled to one vote for each voting share. In some states, however, the number of votes allowed to each shareholder is limited by statute. There is a conflict of authority as to whether a shareholder may vote a fractional share. Whole shares may only be voted as whole shares and cannot be voted as fractional shares and divided between candidates.

---

[24] ABA MBCA § 30.

[25] § 33.

[26] See, for example, ABA MBCA § 60, which confers upon nonvoting shareholders the right to vote as a class on the adoption of 10 specified types of amendments affecting their interest.

In most states cumulative voting in the election of directors may be provided for or automatically exists when the contrary is not stated in the charter or articles of incorporation.[27] In nearly half of the states cumulative voting is mandatory, being imposed by either constitution or statute. A few states prohibit cumulative voting.

Under a *cumulative voting* plan each shareholder has as many votes as the number of shares he owns multiplied by the number of directors to be elected, and he can distribute them as he sees fit.

There is a conflict of authority as to the validity of a provision for the election of the directors by classes, as when directors serve for three years and one third of the directors are elected each year. In some jurisdictions such a provision is held invalid as impairing the right of cumulative voting. In other jurisdictions such a system is valid, and cumulative voting is exercised as to the directors within each class to be elected at each election.

(c) Voting by proxy. A shareholder has the right to authorize another to vote for him. This is known as *voting by proxy*. In the absence of restrictions to the contrary, any person, even one who is not a shareholder, may act as a proxy. Ordinarily authority to act as a proxy may be conferred by an informal written instrument.[28] The corporation law of a particular state may expressly require that a proxy be signed although, in the absence of such a requirement, a stamped facsimile signing has been held sufficient. There is also some statutory recognition of the visual transmission of proxies, as in the case of a "photogram appearing to have been transmitted by a shareholder."[29]

(d) Voting agreements and trusts. Shareholders, as a general rule, are allowed to enter into an agreement by which they concentrate their voting strength for the purpose of controlling the management.

A *voting trust* exists when by agreement a group of shareholders, or all of the shareholders, transfer their shares in trust to one or more persons as trustees who are authorized to vote the stock during the life of the trust agreement. In general, such agreements have been upheld if their object is lawful. In some jurisdictions such trusts cannot run beyond a specified number of years. There are some signs of a relaxation as to this matter. Several states have abandoned any time limitation, several have extended the time limitation, and many states provide for an extension or renewal of the agreement. The trustee of a voting trust occupies a fiduciary position similar to that of an ordinary trustee and must deal with the rights of all shareholders he represents.

§ 51:12. PREEMPTIVE OFFER OF SHARES. If the capital stock of a corporation is increased, each shareholder ordinarily has the preemptive right to subscribe to such percentage of the new shares as his old shares

---

[27] ABA MBCA § 33.

[28] See, for example, the regulations of the Securities and Exchange Commission, Rule X-14A-4. By statute it has been declared in at least one jurisdiction that "a telegram . . . is a sufficient writing." In a few states an oral proxy is valid.

[29] North Carolina Gen Stat § 55-68(a).

bore to the former total of capital stock. This right is given in order to enable each shareholder to maintain his relative interest in the corporation.

The existence of a preemptive right may make impossible the concluding of a transaction in which the corporation is to transfer a block of stock as consideration. Moreover, practical difficulties arise as to how stock should be allocated among shareholders of different classes. For these reasons the trend of corporation statutes has been toward the abolition of the preemptive right and court decisions have made many exceptions to the requirement.[30] Statutes in half the states provide that there is no preemptive right with respect to shares sold to employees of the corporation. In many states the certificate of incorporation may expressly prohibit preemptive rights.

§ 51:13. INSPECTION OF BOOKS. A shareholder has the right to inspect the books of his corporation. The shareholder must ask for the examination in good faith, for proper motives, and at a reasonable time and place.[31] The Model Act authorizes inspection of corporate records "for any proper purpose."[32]

The purpose of inspection must be reasonably related to the shareholder's interest as a shareholder. A shareholder is entitled to inspect the records to determine the financial condition of the corporation, the quality of its management, and any matters relating to his rights or interest in the corporate business, such as the value of his stock; to obtain information needed for a lawsuit against the corporation or its directors or officers; or in order to organize the other shareholders into an "opposition" party to remove the board of directors at the next election.

Inspection has frequently been refused when it was sought merely from idle curiosity or for "speculative purposes." Inspection has sometimes been denied on the ground that it was merely sought to obtain a mailing list of persons who would be solicited to buy products of another enterprise. Inspection has also been refused where the object of the shareholder was to advance his political or social beliefs without regard to the economic welfare of the corporation.

FACTS: Pillsbury was opposed to the war in Vietnam. He learned that Honeywell was manufacturing antipersonnel fragmentation bombs to be used in that war. He purchased 100 shares of stock of Honeywell so that he could inspect its books and ascertain just what was being done. Honeywell refused to permit the inspection of its books. Pillsbury began a lawsuit in the name of the state against Honeywell in order to compel inspection of the corporate books.

---

[30] ABA MBCA § 26. The Model Act in effect takes a neutral position by proposing one section that declares that shareholders have no preemptive right, except as expressly stated in the articles of incorporation; and an alternative provision declaring that they have such right, except to the extent expressly denied by the articles or by the alternative section. In recognition of the necessity that the corporation have a free hand in using a block as payment, even the latter alternative section declares that the preemptive right does not exist as to "any shares sold otherwise than for cash."

[31] Sanders v Pacific Gamble Robinson Co. 250 Minn 265, 84 NW2d 919.

[32] ABA MBCA § 52.

DECISION: Judgment against inspection. Inspection will be refused when it is sought because the shareholder disproves of the ethical assumptions underyling corporate activities. The fact that the plaintiff held such a very small percentage of the shares of stock of the corporation and had purchased them recently for the purpose of giving himself standing as a shareholder also weighed against allowing inspection. [Minnesota ex rel Pillsbury v Honeywell, Inc. 291 Minn 322, 191 NW2d 406]

Many cases deny the right of inspection when it would be harmful to the corporation or is sought only for the purpose of annoying, harassing, or causing vexation, or for the purpose of aiding competitors of the corporation. In contrast, the right of inspection is so broadly recognized in some states that the fact that the shareholder may make an improper use of the information obtained does not bar inspection.

The purpose of the inspecting shareholder may be to learn the names and addresses of other shareholders so that he can buy their stock from them. This is a proper reason for inspection as it enables a shareholder to protect his interest in the corporation by increasing his ownership and voting power.

The ABA MBCA seeks to prevent the abuse of the power to inspect corporate books by limiting the right of inspection to persons who have owned the stock for not less than 6 months or who own not less than 5 percent of all the outstanding shares of the corporation. As a further safeguard, the Model Act requires that the request for inspection be made by "written demand stating the purpose thereof."[33]

Inspection need not be made personally. A shareholder may employ an accountant or an attorney to examine the records for him. The Model Act declares that the shareholder "shall have the right to examine, in person, or by agent or attorney, at any reasonable time or times, for any proper purpose its relevant books and records of account, minutes, and record of shareholders and to make extracts therefrom."

(a) Form of books. There are generally no legal requirements as to the form of corporate books and records. The Model Act recognizes that corporate books and records may be stored in modern data storage systems. "Any books, records, and minutes may be in written form or in any other form capable of being converted into written form within a reasonable time."

(b) Financial statements. In recognition of the widespread practice of corporations preparing formal financial statements, the Model Act requires a corporation to send such a statement to a shareholder upon request. It provides that "upon the written request of any shareholder . . . , the corporation shall mail to such shareholder . . . its most recent financial statements showing in reasonable detail its assets and liabilities, and the results of its operations."[34] A number of states have similar provisions.

---

[33] § 52.
[34] § 52.

§ **51:14. DIVIDENDS.** A shareholder has the right to receive his proportion of dividends as they are declared, subject to the relative rights of other shareholders to preferences, accumulation of dividends, and participation. However, there is no absolute right to receive dividends.

(a) **Funds available for declaration of dividends.** Statutes commonly provide that no dividends may be declared unless there is a "surplus" for their payment. This surplus is generally calculated as the amount of the corporate assets in excess of all outstanding liabilities and outstanding shares of the corporation.

As an exception to these rules, a wasting assets corporation may pay dividends out of current net profits without regard to the preservation of the corporate assets. *Wasting assets corporations* include those enterprises that are designed to exhaust or use up the assets of the corporation (as by extracting oil, coal, iron, and other ores), as compared with a manufacturing plant where the object is to preserve the plant as well as to continue to manufacture. A wasting assets corporation may also be formed for the purpose of buying and liquidating a bankrupt's stock of merchandise.

In some states statutes provide that dividends may be declared from current net profits without regard to the existence of a deficit from former years, or from surplus.

If dividends are about to be declared from an unlawful source, an injunction can be obtained to stop their declaration or payment. If the payment has already been made, the directors responsible for the action may be sued individually and be made to indemnify the corporation for the loss they have caused it by the improper payment if they acted negligently or in bad faith in declaring the dividends.

(b) **Discretion of directors.** Assuming that a fund is available for the declaration of dividends, it is then a matter primarily within the discretion of the board of directors whether a dividend shall be declared. The fact that there is a surplus which could be used for dividends does not determine that they must be declared. This rule is not affected by the nature of the shares. Thus, the fact that the shareholders hold cumulative preferred shares does not give them any right to demand a declaration of dividends or to interfere with an honest exercise of discretion by the directors.

The fact that a wasting assets corporation may declare dividends from current earnings does not require the directors to do so, and they have the same discretionary power with respect to dividend declaration as directors of an ordinary business corporation. A very important factor encouraging the declaration of dividends is the federal penalty surtax to which accumulated earnings of a corporation in excess of $150,000 may be subject.[35]

In general, a court will refuse to substitute its judgment for the judgment of the directors and will interfere only when it is shown that their

---

[35] 26 USC §§ 531-537.

conduct is harmful to the welfare of the corporation or its shareholders. The courts, however, will compel the declaration of a dividend when it is apparent that the directors have amassed a surplus beyond any practical business need.

Once dividends are duly declared, a debtor-creditor relation exists between the corporation and the shareholders as to those dividends. The shareholder may accordingly sue the corporation to recover the amount of his lawfully declared dividends if it fails to pay them.

(c) Form of dividends. Customarily, a dividend is paid in money; but it may be paid in property, such as a product manufactured by the corporation, in shares of other corporations held by the corporation, or in shares of the corporation itself.

(d) Effect of transfer of shares. In determining who is entitled to dividends, it is immaterial when the surplus from which the distribution is made was earned. As between the transferor and the transferee, if the dividend is in cash or property other than the shares of the corporation declaring the dividend, the person who was the owner on the date the dividend was declared is entitled to the dividend. Thus, if a cash dividend is declared before a transfer is made, the transferor is entitled to it. If the transfer was made before the declaration date, the transferee is entitled to it. In applying this rule, it is immaterial when distribution of the dividend is made.

The rule that the date of declaration determines the right to a cash dividend is subject to modification by the corporation. The board of directors in declaring the dividend may state that it will be payable to those who will be the holders of record on a later specified date.

If the dividend consists of shares in the corporation declaring the dividend, ownership is determined by the date of distribution. Whichever party is the owner of the shares when the stock dividend is distributed is entitled to the stock dividend. The reason for this variation from the cash dividend rule lies in the fact that the declaration of a stock dividend has the effect of diluting the existing corporate assets among a larger number of shares. The value of the holding represented by each share is accordingly diminished. Unless the person who owns the stock on the date when distribution is made receives a proportionate share of the stock dividend, the net effect will be to lessen his holding.

The transferor and transferee may enter into any agreement they choose with respect to dividends.

These rules determine the right to dividends as between transferor and transferee. Regardless of what those rights may be, the corporation is generally entitled to continue to recognize the transferor as a shareholder until it has been notified that a transfer has been made and the corporate records are accordingly changed. If the corporation, believing that the transferor is still the owner of the shares, sends him a dividend to which the transferee is entitled, the transferee cannot sue the corporation. In that case, the remedy of the transferee is to sue the transferor for the money or property that the latter has received.

§ 51:15. **CAPITAL DISTRIBUTION.** Upon the dissolution of the corporation, the shareholders are entitled to receive any balance of the corporate assets that remains after the payment of all creditors. Certain classes of stock may have a preference or priority in this distribution.

§ 51:16. **SHAREHOLDERS' ACTIONS.** When the corporation has the right to sue its directors or officers or third persons for damages caused by them to the corporation or for breach of contract, one or more shareholders may bring such action if the corporation refuses to do so. This is a *derivative* (secondary) *action* in that the shareholder enforces only the cause of action of the corporation, and any money recovery is paid into the corporate treasury.

An action cannot be brought by minority shareholders, however, if the action of the corporate directors or officers has been ratified by a majority of the shareholders acting in good faith and if the matter is of such a nature that had such majority originally authorized the acts of the directors or officers, there would not have been any wrong.

Shareholders may also intervene or join in an action brought against the corporation when the corporation refuses to defend the action against it or is not doing so in good faith. Otherwise the shareholders may take no part in an action by or against the corporation.

Shareholders in a deadlocked corporation may bring an action to obtain a dissolution of the corporation.

FACTS: Marvin and Betty Goldstein were shareholders of the Missouri Machinery and Engineering Company. They owned one half of its stock. The other half was owned by James and Eileen Studley. The two families held all the corporate offices. They could not agree on how the corporation should be run. Sales dropped sharply. The shareholders could not agree as to data needed for filing a federal tax return. The Goldsteins brought a derivative action to obtain the appointment of a receiver for the corporation and to liquidate the corporation.

DECISION: Liquidation would be ordered and a receiver appointed to carry out the liquidation. This was necessary because the continued attempt to operate the business was hopeless, sales had dropped to about 4 percent of prior years, and the board of directors and the shareholders were evenly and hopelessly deadlocked. [Goldstein v Studley (MoApp) 452 SW2d 75]

D. LIABILITIES OF SHAREHOLDERS

§ 51:17. **LIMITED LIABILITY.** The liability of a shareholder is generally limited. This means that he is not personally responsible for the debts and liabilities of the corporation. The capital contributed by the shareholders may be exhausted by the claims of creditors, but he has no personal liability for any unpaid balance.

§ 51:18. **EXCEPTIONS TO LIMITED LIABILITY.** Liability may be imposed upon a shareholder as though there were no corporation when either the court ignores the corporate entity because of the particular circumstances of the case, or when the corporation is so defectively organized that it is deemed not to exist.

(a) Wage claims. Statutes sometimes provide that the shareholders shall be unlimitedly liable for the wage claims of corporate employees. This principle has been abandoned in some states in recent years or has been confined to the major shareholders of corporations of which the stock is not sold publicly.

(b) Unpaid subscriptions. Most states prohibit the issuance of par value shares for less than par or except for "money, labor done, or property actually received." Whenever shares issued by a corporation are not fully paid for, the original subscriber receiving the shares or any transferee who does not give value, or who knows that the shares were not fully paid, may be liable for the unpaid balance if the corporation is insolvent and the money is required to pay the debts of creditors.[36]

If the corporation has issued the shares as fully paid, or has given them as a bonus, or has agreed to release the subscriber for the unpaid balance, the corporation cannot recover that balance. The fact that the corporation is thus barred does not prevent the creditors of the corporation from bringing an action to compel payment of the balance. The same rules are applied when stock is issued as fully paid in return for property or services which was overvalued so that the stock is not actually paid for in full. There is a conflict of authority, however, as to whether the shareholder is liable from the mere fact that the property or service he gave for the shares was in fact overvalued by the directors or whether in addition it must be shown that the directors had acted in bad faith in making the erroneous valuation. The trend of modern statutes is to prohibit disputing the valuation placed by the corporation on services or property in the absence of proof of fraud.

If a statute makes void the shares issued for less than par, they may be canceled upon suit of the corporation.

(c) Unauthorized dividends. If dividends are improperly paid out of capital, the shareholders generally are liable to creditors to the extent of such depletion of capital. In some states the liability of the shareholder depends on whether the corporation was insolvent at the time, whether debts were existing at the time, and whether the shareholders had notice of the source of the dividend.

(d) Insider information. A person who has knowledge of inside information about a corporation, such as a discovery which it has made or action with respect to dividends, and who takes advantage of another person who lacks that information, as by inducing him to sell his stock at a low price, is liable for the amount of the damages caused the other party.[37]

---

[36] Under ABA MBCA § 25, the transferee is protected if he acts in good faith without knowledge or notice that the shares were not fully paid.

[37] Securities Act of 1934 § 10(b), Rule 10b-5.

(e) **Short-swing profits.** The Act of 1934 permits a corporation to recover from a major shareholder the profit which he has made on a short-swing sale. Specifically, any security holder who owns and sells more than 10 percent of the securities of the corporation within a six-months' period after he purchases them must pay to the corporation the profit that he made on such a sale. This provision also applies to directors and officers of corporations whose securities are registered, without regard to the percentage of stock owned by such director or officer.

The statute authorizes the recovery of a short-swing profit without regard to whether there is any fraudulent intent or conduct that is improper by general principles of law.[38]

§ 51:19. **THE PROFESSIONAL CORPORATION.** The liability of a shareholder in a professional corporation is limited to the same degree as that of a shareholder in an ordinary business corporation. Several fact situations may arise:

(a) **Act of shareholder in creating liability.** If a shareholder in a professional corporation negligently drives the company car in going to attend a patient, or personally obligates himself on a contract made for the corporation, or is guilty of malpractice, he is liable without limit for the liability that has been created. This is the same rule of law that applies in the case of the ordinary business corporation. Professional corporation statutes generally repeat the rule with respect to malpractice liability by stating that the liability of a shareholder for malpractice is not affected by the fact of incorporation.

(b) **Malpractice liability of an associate.** The liability of a shareholder in a professional corporation for the malpractice of an associate is not clear. If Doctors *A*, *B*, and *C* are a partnership, each is unlimitedly liable for any malpractice liability incurred by the others. Assume that Doctors *A*, *B*, and *C* are a professional corporation, will *A* be liable for the malpractice of *C*? If the orthodox rule applicable to business corporations applies here, the answer is "no liability." The statutory reference to malpractice liability is generally not very clear, and it is possible that a conservative court will interpret the statutory preservation of malpractice liability as preserving the liability of one professional man for the act of his associates when such liability would exist if they were a partnership.

(c) **Ordinary torts.** If an ordinary tort, meaning one not related to malpractice, is committed, each shareholder is protected from liability for the acts of others. For example, assume that in order to aid a patient, a medical corporation sends its secretary after hours with medicine to a patient's home. In the course of the trip the secretary negligently runs over a pedestrian. In such a case both the secretary and the corporation would be liable for the harm caused the pedestrian. Would a shareholder be liable?

It should be concluded that a shareholder would not be liable. Here the ordinary rule of limited liability for a shareholder should apply. Since the

---

[38] Securities Act of 1934, § 16(a), 16(b).

situation described does not involve "malpractice," there is no possibility of concluding that there is a liability of a shareholder under a malpractice exception to the general rule of limited liability. Consequently, in the absence of an express contrary statement in the professional corporation statute, a shareholder in the professional corporation is shielded from liability in the case of ordinary torts of others.

QUESTIONS AND CASE PROBLEMS

1. Graham was a shareholder of Commercial Credit Co. As a result of a stock split, he became entitled to additional shares. A certificate representing these shares was sent by registered mail to his home in Baltimore. At the time he was in California. The envelope containing the share certificate was received and receipted for by one servant in his house and was placed in a basket of mail by another servant, awaiting his return. The stock certificate apparently disappeared thereafter. Graham demanded that the corporation issue a new certificate to him for the missing certificate. When this was refused unless he would furnish indemnity against loss should the original certificate be found, Graham refused to furnish security and brought suit claiming that the shares had never been issued to him on the theory that the domestic servant had no authority to receive the stock certificate and to sign a receipt for it. Was he correct? [Graham v Commercial Credit Co. 41 DelCh 580, 200 A2d 828]

2. Elizabeth Szabo, who owned stock of the American Telephone & Telegraph Co., was told by the company that there had been a three-for-one split of the company's stock effective as of April 24, 1959, and that on May 29, 1959, the company would prepare and mail to her an additional stock certificate representing twice the number of shares already held by her. Upon receiving the notice from the company, Szabo indorsed on her certificate a transfer to herself and her son as joint tenants with the right of survivorship. She delivered the indorsed certificate to the stock transfer agent of the corporation but directed him to hold up the transfer of the stock until the new certificate for the split shares was available. The stock transfer agent was also notified to have the new certificate made out to Szabo and her son as joint tenants with the right of survivorship. Three days before the new certificate for the stock split was issued, Szabo died. Her son claimed the original shares of stock from her estate and the new shares issued on the stock split. Was he entitled to all these shares? [Szabo's Estate, 10 NY2d 123, 217 NY2d 593, 176 NE2d 395]

3. Smallwood made a contract to purchase stock of the Re-Mark Chemical Co. from Moretti. Moretti did not deliver the stock certificate to Smallwood but gave him a written assignment of 5,000 shares and directed the company to issue 5,000 shares to Smallwood. There was a delay in issuing the certificate because of certain stock registration problems. Meanwhile, four dividends were declared on the stock. They were received by Moretti, who paid them to Smallwood, who accepted them without question. Shortly thereafter the Re-Mark Co. went into bankruptcy reorganization, and Smallwood then sought to set aside the

purchase from Moretti. He claimed that the purchase was not effective because no stock certificate had been issued to him and therefore he had not been given the legal title to the stock. Was he entitled to set the sale aside? [Smallwood v Moretti (FlaApp) 128 So2d 628]

4. The Skinner Packing Co., which was incorporated under the laws of Maine, was authorized to do business in Nebraska where it had its principal place of business. The company sent an agent to Excelsior Springs, Missouri, where he made a contract for the sale of 100 shares of stock in the company to Rhines. Within a year thereafter, Rhines concluded that he had been swindled and brought an action against the company to recover the purchase price of the stock. He based his claim upon a violation of the Missouri Blue-Sky Law. The defendant asserted that the transaction was not governed by the Missouri statute. Do you agree? [Rhines v Skinner Packing Co. 108 Neb 105, 187 NW 874]

5. The stock of X Corporation was subject to certain transfer restrictions. When X Corporation was dissolved, A, a shareholder, then sold his stock to B but did not comply with the stock transfer restrictions. It was claimed that B had not acquired any of the rights of A by such transfer. Was this correct? [See Mischer v Burke (TexCivApp) 456 SW2d 550]

6. A dealer sold goods to a corporation. When the corporation failed to pay him, he sued X who owned a block of shares of the corporation and had been active in organizing the corporation. Was X liable? [See Blond Lighting Fixture Supply Co. v Funk (TexCivApp) 392 SW2d 586]

7. Lehman was a shareholder of the National Benefit Insurance Co., which had been incorporated under the laws of Iowa. He brought an action to compel the corporation to permit him to inspect and copy records and documents of the corporation. It was admitted that he had the right to inspect the papers. Did he have a right to make copies of them? [Lehman v National Benefit Insurance Co. 243 Iowa 1348, 53 NW2d 872]

8. Siebrecht organized a corporation called the Siebrecht Realty Co. and then transferred his building to the corporation in exchange for its stock. The corporation rented different parts of the building to different tenants. Elenkrieg, an employee of one of the tenants, fell and was injured because of the defective condition of a stairway. She sued Siebrecht individually on the ground that the corporation had been formed by him for the purpose of securing limited liability. Decide. [Elenkrieg v Siebrecht, 238 NY 254, 144 NE 519]

9. Chandler owned stock in a corporation. The stock was taxed by the town of New Gloucester as property owned by Chandler. Sweetsir, the proper official, sued Chandler for the taxes due. Chandler defended on the ground that the stock should be taxed as evidence of a debt, the same as a bond, and that the tax as assessed was therefore unlawful. Was his contention valid? [Sweetsir v Chandler, 98 Maine 145, 56 A 584]

MANAGEMENT
OF CORPORATIONS

§ 52:1. INTRODUCTION. A corporation is managed, directly or indirectly, by its shareholders, board of directors, and officers.

Since the shareholders elect the directors, they indirectly determine the management policies of the business.[1] Without express authorization by the corporation, however, a shareholder cannot bind it by contract.

§ 52:2. MEETINGS OF SHAREHOLDERS. To have legal effect, action by the shareholders must be taken at a regular or special meeting. The time and place of regular or stated meetings are usually prescribed by the articles of incorporation or bylaws. Notice to shareholders of such meetings is ordinarily not required, but it is usually given as a matter of good business practice. Some statutes require that notice be given of all meetings, and generally notice must be given specifying the subject matter when the meeting is of an unusual character. Unless otherwise prescribed, special meetings are called by the directors. It is sometimes provided that a special meeting may be called by a certain percentage of shareholders.[2] Notice of the day, hour, and the place of a special meeting must be given to all shareholders. The notice must also include a statement of the nature of the business to be transacted. No other business may be transacted at such a meeting.

(a) Quorum. A valid meeting requires the presence of a quorum of the voting shareholders. In order to constitute a quorum, usually a specified number of shareholders or a number authorized to vote a stated proportion of the voting stock must attend.[3] If a quorum is present, a majority of those

---

[1] When the voting stock of a large corporation is widely held by small shareholders scattered over an extensive geographic area, this indirect control is not very effective and management tends to determine the policies of the corporation.

[2] New York Business Corporation Law § 603.

[3] The American Bar Association Model Business Corporation Act provides that unless stated in the articles of incorporation, a majority of the voting shares constitutes a quorum and that, in specifying the quorum in the articles, it cannot be set at less than one third of the shares entitled to vote at the particular meeting. ABA MBCA § 32.

present may act with respect to any matter, unless there is an express requirement of a greater affirmative vote.

When a meeting opens with a quorum, the quorum generally is not thereafter broken if shareholders leave the meeting and those remaining are not sufficient to constitute a quorum. This principle is designed to prevent obstructionist tactics by dissenting shareholders.

(b) No meeting action. A number of statutes provide for corporate action by shareholders without holding a meeting. The ABA MBCA provides that "Any action required by this Act to be taken at a meeting of the shareholders of a corporation, or any action which may be taken at a meeting of the shareholders, may be taken without a meeting if they consent in writing, setting forth the action so taken [and] signed by all of the shareholders entitled to vote with respect to the subject matter thereof."[4] Such provisions give flexibility of operation, which is needed by the small or close corporation.

§ 52:3. DIRECTORS. The management of a corporation is usually entrusted to a board of directors which is elected by the shareholders. Most states now permit the number of directors to be fixed by the bylaws.

Most states specify that the board of directors shall consist of not less than three directors. A few states authorize one or more directors.[5] Professional corporation legislation often authorizes or is interpreted as authorizing a one- or two-man board of directors.

Statutory provisions for the classification of directors are common. The Model Act provides that when the board consists of nine or more members, the directors may be divided "into either two or three classes, each class to be as nearly equal in number as possible."[6]

(a) Qualifications. Eligibility for membership on a board of directors is determined by statute, certificate of incorporation, or bylaw. In the absence of a contrary provision, any person is eligible for membership, including a nonresident, a minor, or even a person who is not a shareholder.

Bylaws commonly require a director to own stock in the corporation, although ordinarily this requirement is not imposed by law. If a director is also a shareholder, he has a dual capacity and has rights both as a director and as a shareholder.

(b) Powers of directors. The board of directors has authority to manage the corporation. The court will not interfere with the board's discretion in the absence of illegal conduct or fraud harming the rights of creditors, shareholders, or the corporation.

The board of directors may enter into any contract or transaction necessary to carry out the business for which the corporation was formed. The board may appoint officers and other agents to act for the company, or it may delegate authority to one or more of its members to do so. For

---

[4] § 145.
[5] Delaware Code Ann § 141(b). See also ABA MBCA § 36.
[6] ABA MBCA § 37.

example, it may appoint several of its own members as an executive committee to act for the board between board meetings.

(c) Conflict of interests. A director is disqualified from taking part in corporate action with respect to a matter in which he has a conflicting interest. Since it cannot be known how the other directors would have voted if they had known of the conflict of interest, the corporation generally may avoid any transaction because of the director's disqualification.

A number of states provide by statute that the conflict of interest of a director does not impair the transaction or contract entered into or authorized by the board of directors if the disqualified director discloses his interest and the contract or transaction is fair and reasonable with respect to the corporation.

§ 52:4. MEETINGS OF DIRECTORS.

Theoretically, action by directors can only be taken at a proper meeting of the board. Bylaws sometimes require the meeting to be held at a particular place. Most states expressly provide that the directors may meet either in or outside of the state of incorporation. Directors who participate without objection in a meeting irregularly held as to place or time other than as specified in the bylaws cannot object later. Generally a director is not allowed to vote by proxy.

Most states permit action to be taken by the board of directors without the holding of an actual meeting.[7] It is commonly provided when such action is taken that it be set forth in writing and signed by all the directors. Moreover, when the directors and shareholders are the same persons, there is no objection to running a corporation in an informal manner. It is not necessary that the board of directors then act by means of a formal meeting.

§ 52:5. LIABILITY OF DIRECTORS.

Directors are fiduciaries entrusted with the management of the corporation. Corporate directors must exercise due care in the management of corporate affairs and are liable for loss sustained by the corporation when their negligence results in the selection of improper employees or officers who embezzle money from the corporation.

Directors must manage the corporation for the good of all shareholders and may not ignore the interest or viewpoint of some of the shareholders merely because they constitute only a minority.

While the fiduciary concept imposes liability upon directors for mismanagement, it also protects them as long as they act in a reasonable manner within the scope of their authority. They are not liable merely because, when viewed from the standpoint of later events, it would have been to the advantage of the corporation to have taken different action than the directors had taken. The Model Act imposes liability upon the directors for the illegal payment of dividends, the illegal purchase by the corporation

---

[7] New Jersey Stat Ann § 14A:6-7(2).

of its own shares, and illegal distributions of the assets of the corporation upon liquidation.[8]

Directors are not liable for losses resulting from their management when they have acted in good faith and with due diligence, and have exercised reasonable care. For willful or negligent acts, however, they are held strictly accountable, and they are bound by all rules that the law imposes on those in a fiduciary position. The exact degree to which a director will be deemed to hold a fiduciary position is not clear, however, and a director is not barred from purchasing for himself a controlling block of shares of the stock of the corporation in which he is director.

Directors of a corporation are not personally liable for wrongs committed by the corporation merely by virtue of the fact that they are directors. It must be shown that they have authorized or ratified the improper conduct or have in some way participated therein.

(a) **Director's liability for conflict of interests.** When a director violates the rule prohibiting conflicting interests, the corporation may recover from him any secret profit that he has made. The ordinary rule of agency law as to loyalty determines his liability. When the corporation has sustained loss because it has taken the action advocated by the disqualified director, it will generally be able to hold him liable for the loss by applying the agency principles of loyalty and duty to inform of matters relevant to the transaction, namely, his interest.

(b) **Action against director.** Actions against directors should be brought by the corporation. If the corporation fails to act, as is the case when the directors alleged to be liable control the corporation, one or more shareholders may bring the action in a representative capacity for the corporation.

(c) **Removal of directors.** Ordinarily directors are removed by the vote of the shareholders. In some states the board of directors may remove a director and elect his successor on the ground that the director removed (1) did not accept office; (2) failed to satisfy the qualifications for office; (3) was continuously absent from the state without a leave of absence granted by the board, generally for a period of six months or more; (4) was adjudicated a bankrupt; (5) was convicted of a felony; (6) was unable to perform his duties as director because of any illness or disability, generally for a period of six months or more; or (7) has been judicially declared of unsound mind.[9]

The Model Act provides for removal of directors "with or without cause" by a majority vote of the shareholders.[10]

---

[8] ABA MBCA § 48. The earlier version of the Model Act also imposed liability upon directors for loans made to officers and directors and for the amount of capital not paid into the corporation if it commenced doing business before it obtained $1,000. These two provisions were deleted from the present version of the Model Act, although they are found in a number of state statutes which have followed the earlier Model Act.

[9] See California Corporations Code § 807, recognizing grounds (a), (b), (e), and (g).

[10] ABA MBCA § 39.

§ 52:6. OFFICERS OF THE CORPORATION. Corporations will generally have a president, at least one vice-president, a secretary, and a treasurer. Corporation codes generally expressly permit the same person to be both secretary and treasurer. In larger corporations there will often be a recording secretary and a corresponding secretary.

Sometimes the officers are elected by the shareholders but usually they are appointed by the board of directors. The Model Act follows the general pattern of providing for the selection of officers by the board of directors.[11] Ordinarily no particular formality need be observed in making such appointments. There are seldom particular qualifications required of officers. Unless prohibited, a director may hold an executive office. The Model Act and state statutes commonly provide that one person may hold two or more corporate offices. In some instances, a limitation is imposed, as by the Model Act, which prohibits the same person from being both president and secretary of the corporation.

§ 52:7. POWERS OF OFFICERS. The officers of a corporation are its agents. Consequently, their powers are controlled by the laws of agency. As in the case of any other agency, the third person has the burden of proving that a particular officer has the authority which he purports to have. Moreover, if the third person knows that a particular act requires the adoption of a resolution by the board of directors, he cannot rely on the apparent authority of the president or other corporate officer to perform the act.

(a) **President.** It is sometimes held that in the absence of some limitation upon his authority, the president of a corporation has, by virtue of his office, authority to act as agent on behalf of the corporation within the scope of the business in which the corporation is empowered to engage. It has been held, however, that the president has such broad powers only when he is the general manager of the corporation, and then such powers stem from the office of general manager and not from that of president. In any event, the president does not have authority by virtue of his office to make a contract which because of its unusual character would require action by the board of directors. The president, therefore, cannot make a contract to fix the compensation to be paid a director of the corporation, to make long-term or unusual contracts of employment, to bind the corporation as a guarantor, to release a claim of the corporation, or to promise that the corporation will later repurchase shares which are issued to a subscriber.

It is ordinarily held that the president of a business corporation is not authorized to execute commercial paper in the name of the corporation merely because he is president, although he may do so if he is authorized by the board of directors to borrow money for the corporation.

(b) **Other officers and employees.** The authority of corporate employees and other officers, such as secretary or treasurer, is generally limited to the

---

[11] § 50.

duties of their offices. Their authority may, however, be extended by the conduct of the corporation, in accordance with the general principles governing apparent authority based on the conduct of the principal. An unauthorized act may, of course, be ratified. The authority of a general manager of the corporation is determined by principles of ordinary agency law.

> **FACTS:** Cote Brothers sold bakery products to the Granite Lake Camp that was run by the Granite Lake Realty Corp. and an allied corporation, Granite Lake Camp Associates, Inc. Both corporations were owned, operated, and managed by the same three individuals who were the shareholders, officers, and directors. Liability of the corporations for the plaintiff's bill was denied on the ground that no officer of the corporations had been authorized to purchase the bakery products.

> **DECISION:** Granite Lake was liable because a corporate officer of a small or close corporation has inherent agency power to do what is usually done in running such a corporation. The purchase which had been made was a normal or usual purchase for a camp. [Cote Brothers, Inc. v Granite Lake Realty Corp. 115 NH 111, 193 A2d 884]

§ 52:8. LIABILITY OF OFFICERS. The relation of the officers to the corporation, like that of the directors, is a fiduciary relationship. For this reason, the officers are liable for secret profits made in connection with or at the expense of the business of the corporation.

As an aspect of the corporate officer's fiduciary position, he must not make any profit that is not disclosed to the corporation. If an officer diverts a corporate opportunity to himself, the corporation may recover from the officer the profit of which the corporation had been deprived. This is an application of the prohibition against secret profits applicable to ordinary agents. Thus, the president of a contracting corporation must account to the corporation for a secret profit which he or a member of his family made on the letting of a subcontract.

> **FACTS:** Redmont was the president of Abbott Thinlite Corporation. He left that corporation and ran the Circle Redmont Corporation in competition with his former employer. In so doing, it was claimed that he diverted five contracts from his former employer. The former employer sued Redmont and Circle Redmont Corporation to recover the profit of which the former employer was deprived. Redmont raised the defense that he had not contacted any of the contractors on the five jobs until after he had left Abbott.

> **DECISION:** Judgment for Abbott. While Redmont did nothing until he left Abbott, the preliminary work to obtain those contracts had been performed on behalf of Abbott while Redmont was still employed by it. If such negotiations on behalf of Abbott had progressed to the point that there was a "tangible expectancy" that Abbott would receive the work under the contracts, it was a breach of fiduciary relationship for Redmont to contact the contractors involved after he had left Abbott's employ and to obtain their orders for his own benefit. [Abbott Redmont Thinlite Corp. v Redmont (CA2 NY) 475 F2d 85]

Officers are also liable for willful or negligent acts that cause a loss to the corporation. On the other hand, they are not liable for mere errors in judgment committed while exercising their discretion, provided they have acted with reasonable prudence and care.

§ 52:9. AGENTS AND EMPLOYEES OF CORPORATION. The authority, rights, and liabilities of an agent of a corporation are governed by the same rules applicable when the principal is a natural person.

The authority of corporate employees is governed by general agency principles. The construction foreman of a construction corporation does not have implied authority to modify the terms of the contract between the corporation and a supplier of building materials.

§ 52:10. INDEMNIFICATION OF OFFICERS, DIRECTORS, EMPLOYEES, AND AGENTS. While performing what they believe to be their duty, officers, directors, employees, and agents of corporations may commit acts for which they are later sued or criminally prosecuted. At common law, the expense or loss involved in defending such actions and prosecutions or in making out-of-court settlements was borne by the individual. He had no right to obtain any money from the corporation to indemnify him for such loss. The trend of modern statutes is to authorize or to require the board of directors to make indemnity in such cases. The Model Act broadly authorizes the corporation to indemnify such a person "if he acted in good faith and in a manner he reasonably believed to be in or not opposed to the best interests of the corporation and, with respect to any criminal action or proceeding, had no reasonable cause to believe his conduct was unlawful. . . ."[12]

In some states statutory provision is made requiring the corporation to indemnify directors and officers for reasonable expenses incurred by them in defending unwarranted suits brought against them by shareholders. Such statutes have been adopted to induce responsible persons to accept positions of corporate responsibility.

§ 52:11. CORPORATE MINUTES. Minutes are ordinarily kept of meetings of the shareholders and of the directors of a corporation. The keeping of accurate minutes is important not only for the purpose of preserving continuity in management policies but also because of the consequence that the action taken may have with respect to the liability of individual persons, with respect to tax liability of individual persons, or with respect to tax liability of the corporation. The minutes are not conclusive, however, and they may be supplemented or contradicted by parol evidence.

§ 52:12. COMPUTERS AND CORPORATE MANAGEMENT. The advent of the age of computers has not changed the basic principles of law determining the liability of management, but it gives rise to new situations

---

[12] § 5(a).

to which the old principles will be applied. Is management liable for failing to use computers? Generally this will not raise a legal question, as the courts will feel that it is a matter for the business judgment of management to determine whether the benefits to be derived offset the costs and any possible hazards. It may well be that in a given case the use of computers would provide better information on which management decisions could be made or provide better inventory and product-quality controls. In such a case, the argument could be made that management was negligent in failing to use computers in much the same way that management would ordinarily be regarded as negligent in using water power instead of electricity to run machinery.

When computers are used, management may be liable for failure to exercise proper care in their use. Thus, management must exercise due care in selecting proper equipment and qualified personnel; in protecting the physical equipment, such as machines, tapes, and cards, from fire, atmospheric, and similar hazards; in maintaining safeguards against error; in protecting from misuse of the computers to defraud or embezzle; and in protecting the interests of the company by procuring proper protection through copyrights and antidisclosure agreements with employees, service companies, and customers.

§ 52:13. **LIABILITY OF MANAGEMENT TO THIRD PERSONS.** Ordinarily the management of a corporation—meaning its directors, officers, and executive employees—is not liable to third persons for the effect upon such third persons of their management or unsound advice. The liability of a director or officer for misconduct ordinarily is a liability that may be enforced only by the corporation or by shareholders bringing a derivative action on behalf of the corporation. Ordinarily a director or officer is not liable to a third person for loss caused by the negligent performance of his duties as director or officer, even though because of such negligence the corporation is in turn liable to the third person to whom the corporation owed the duty to use care or was under a contract obligation to render a particular service.

Officers and managers of a corporation are not liable for the economic consequence of their advice upon third persons, even though they caused the corporation to refuse to deal with or to break its contract with such third persons, as long as the officers and managers had acted in good faith to advance the interests of the corporation. Thus, a person who has a contract with the corporation which is not renewed because of the adverse vote of the directors cannot sue the directors for damages even though they had been "wrong" in their decision as such a matter was merely an error in judgment for which there is no tort liability. This differs from the situation in which a person intentionally or maliciously interferes with a contract or the economic expectations of another person.

As exceptions to the above rule, a director or officer may be directly liable to an injured person when the director or officer commits a tort or directs the commission of a tort upon the third person, as when he takes an active part in causing the corporation to conspire to enter into a monopoly or trust agreement to the detriment of the third person. When a corporate officer, director, or employee is liable to a third person for his misconduct, it is no defense that the corporation may also be liable to the third person.

If a director or an officer makes a contract in his individual capacity, he is personally liable thereon to the other person and is not protected from liability by the fact that his motive was to act on behalf of the corporation. Ordinarily when a contract is made on behalf of the corporation, the officer or director is not personally liable in case of breach of the contract.

§ **52:14. INSIDERS.** A person holding an office or a position within a corporation, whether or not a director or shareholder, may be held accountable for any advantage obtained by him from the use of information known to him by virtue of his position. Thus, if a director sells his stock or buys the stock of a shareholder without disclosing to such person matters materially affecting the value of the stock, which matters are known to the insider, redress may be obtained. If the action of the insider constitutes fraud, the injured person may sue for money damages. Whether or not the elements of fraud are present, an action may be brought by the Securities and Exchange Commission to redress the wrong caused the other party.[13]

In some instances it is unlawful for a shareholder to act without disclosing to the other contracting party information he possesses by virtue of his position within the corporation. For example, it is unlawful for a majority shareholder to purchase the stock of a minority shareholder without disclosing material facts affecting the value of the stock known to the majority shareholder by virtue of his position of power within the corporation and not known to the selling minority shareholder. Similarly, directors selling their stock to outsiders without disclosing the fact that the next earnings statement of the corporation would show a drop in corporate income can be held liable to the corporation for the profit which they make on such a sale.[14]

§ **52:15. CRIMINAL LIABILITY.** Officers and directors, as in the case of agents generally, are personally responsible for any crimes committed by them even when they act in behalf of the corporation. At the local level they may be criminally responsible for violation of ordinances relating to sanitation, safety, and hours of closing. At the state level they may be criminally liable for conducting a business without obtaining necessary licenses or after the corporate certificate of incorporation was forfeited for failing to file reports or pay taxes. At the national level they may be prosecuted for violation of the federal antitrust laws.[15]

A number of states impose criminal liability upon the person, corporate officer, or agent who conducts local business on behalf of a foreign corporation that has not qualified to engage in such business.[16]

---

[13] S.E.C. v Capital Gains Research Bureau, 375 US 180; S.E.C. v Texas Gulf Sulphur Co. (DC SD NY) 258 FSupp 262.

[14] Diamond v Oreamuno, 29 AppDiv2d 285, 287 NYS2d 300.

[15] United States v Wise, 370 US 405.

[16] California Corporation Code § 6803.

§ 52:16. CORPORATE DEBTS AND TAXES. As the corporation is a separate legal person, debts and taxes owed by the corporation are ordinarily the obligations of the corporation only. Consequently, neither directors nor officers are individually liable for the corporate debts or taxes, even though it may have been their acts which gave rise to the debts or their neglect which resulted in the failure to pay the taxes. As an exception to this general principle, statutes in some states impose upon corporate officers liability for taxes, such as sales taxes, owed by the corporation.

In some states civil liability for corporate debts is imposed upon the officers and directors of the corporation when it improperly engages in business.

> **FACTS:** Miller was president and Holcomb was treasurer of Chewning Motors, a Michigan corporation. After 1958 they had nothing to do with the business, no corporate meetings were held, and the corporation did not file the annual reports required by the statute. Chewning Motors owed money to Eberts Cadillac Co. Eberts sued Miller and Holcomb on the basis that a Michigan statute imposed liability on corporate offices in such cases. The statute provided that "any officer . . . of such corporation so in default who [has] neglected or refused to join in making such report . . . shall be liable for all debts of such corporation contracted during the period of such neglect or refusal."
>
> **DECISION:** The officers of the corporation were liable for its debts because the statute declared that they would be so liable when the statutory report was not filed. This liability was imposed in order to insure compliance with the law as to filing and to insure that every officer of a corporation would see that his successor was selected and took office. [Eberts Cadillac Co. v Miller, 10 MichApp 370, 159 NW2d 217]

Some states make the directors and officers personally liable for taxes that the corporation neglected to pay.[17]

§ 52:17. PROTECTION OF SHAREHOLDERS. Various devices and limitations have developed to protect shareholders both from misconduct by management and from the action of the majority of the shareholders. Shareholders may protect themselves by voting for new directors, and also officers if the latter are elected, at the next annual election; or they may take special remedial action at a special meeting of shareholders called for that purpose. Even if the objecting shareholders represent only a minority so that they could not control an election, they may bring a legal action when the management misconduct complained of constitutes a legal wrong.

In some cases dissenting shareholders are permitted to require the corporation to buy out their interests even though no legal wrong has been committed. For example, even though a merger or consolidation is otherwise proper, it is commonly provided that a dissenting shareholder may require the corporation to buy his stock from him. In some instances,

---

[17] West Virginia v Calco Awning and Window Corp. 153 WVa 524, 170 SE2d 362 (corporate officers liable for consumer sales tax).

the dissenting shareholder may even be able to prevent the merger or consolidation on the ground that it violates basic principles of fairness or that it is forbidden by amended Section 7 of the Clayton Act.

§ 52:18. IRREGULAR PROCEDURE. There is a strong judicial tendency to ignore the effect of a procedural error or irregularity when the circumstances are such that it can be concluded that all or substantially all of the shareholders have agreed to or waived any objection to the procedure which was followed. Thus, irregularities with respect to the place and notice of a meeting of the board of directors will be ignored in the case of a closely held corporation when all of the directors attended and participated in the meeting or acquiesced in action taken at such meeting. A third person sued by the corporation cannot challenge the right of the corporation to sue on the ground that corporate procedure requirements have not been observed. Similarly, a third person cannot defend against a claim held by a corporation on the ground that the corporation, if it had been sued by the person from whom it acquired the claim, could have raised the defense of the statute of frauds. Thus, when a right under a contract to purchase land from a third person was assigned to the corporation, the third person could not raise the defense that the assignment did not satisfy the requirements of the statute of frauds.

FACTS: Goldman brought an action to rescind a contract with Coastal Pharmaceutical Company on the ground that the contract had never been authorized or ratified by Coastal. Goldman owned the stock of Ghent Arms Corp., which operated a nursing home. Because of its poor financial condition, Goldman contracted to transfer his stock to Coastal Pharmaceutical Company, which would make the Ghent Arms Corp. a wholly owned subsidiary of Coastal. Thereafter Goldman learned that Coastal was on the verge of bankruptcy and sought to rescind the contract on the ground that the contract had never been expressly authorized nor ratified by Coastal.

DECISION: The contract was binding on Goldman and Coastal. The fact that it had never been formally authorized or ratified by the corporation was immaterial. When the officers made the contract, it was clear they were making a contract which they and the shareholders and Goldman intended should bind Goldman and Coastal. No objection was made at any time by any director or shareholder to the informality. Hence, it must be concluded that the contract was binding upon Coastal and Goldman. [Coastal Pharmaceutical Co. v Goldman, 213 Va 831, 195 SW2d 848]

Likewise, when the corporation has received the benefit of a transaction, it will be estopped from claiming that there was some irregularity in the corporate procedure followed. As in the case of agency generally, a corporation may ratify acts of its officers or directors that were otherwise unauthorized.

QUESTIONS AND CASE PROBLEMS

1. Ponder was the president of the Long Beach Motel Hotel Corporation. He requested a quotation from General Electric on air conditioners for the hotel. He was sent a quotation, on the basis of which he sent in a purchase order on behalf of the corporation. General Electric rejected this order made in the name of the corporation and in effect stated that it would only sell to Ponder personally. A new purchase order was sent to Ponder which showed him individually as the buyer. He signed his name but then added "Pres." When General Electric sued him for the purchase price, he claimed that he had signed on behalf of the corporation and that General Electric knew that it was dealing with the corporation. Was he bound by the contract? [General Electric Co. v Ponder (LaApp) 234 So2d 786]

2. The directors of the American Founders Life Insurance Co. made a contract with the Colorado Management Corp. for certain services. American Founders later sued for the return of the money paid to Colorado on the ground that the contract could be set aside because it had been approved by American Founders at a board of directors' meeting at which only six of the eight directors were present and three of these directors were also directors of Colorado and two of them were also officers of Colorado. The bylaws of American Founders required a majority, which was five, to constitute a quorum for a directors' meeting. Was American Founders entitled to recover? [Colorado Management Corp. v American Founders Life Insurance Co. 145 Colo 413, 359 P2d 665]

3. Heyl and others were directors of Western Inn Corporation. The corporation desired to construct a motel but financial difficulties developed. Outside financing did not prove possible, and finally Heyl and several other directors loaned the money to the corporation. At the time of each loan, all details were made known to, and approved by, the board of directors and the shareholders. As part of the loan agreement with Heyl and the others, a mortgage on the corporation's hotel property was given to them. Thereafter the corporation defaulted on the loan agreement, and Heyl and the other directors who had loaned the corporation the money foreclosed on the mortgage and purchased the hotel property at the foreclosure sale. The Western Inn Corporation sued Heyl and the directors on the theory that they had committed a breach of their fiduciary duty as directors by purchasing the property for themselves at the foreclosure sale and that they therefore held the property as constructive trustees for the corporation. Was the corporation correct? [Western Inn Corp. v Heyl (TexCivApp) 452 SW2d 752]

4. The president of the Atlantic & North Carolina Railroad Co. published in one newspaper a notice of a special meeting of shareholders to be held in New Bern, North Carolina. After the shareholders assembled, they adjourned to meet in Morehead City on the same day. After reassembling, the shareholders voted to authorize a lease of the corporate property to the Howland Improvement Co. Twenty days later the regular annual meeting of the corporation was held. A resolution was then introduced by Foy, at the instance of Hill, instructing the proper officers to bring a suit to set the lease aside. The shareholders' meeting

voted to take no action on this resolution and voted that it be tabled. On behalf of himself and other shareholders, Hill then brought a suit against the railroad company to have the lease annulled. He contended that the lease was not properly authorized because the notice of the meeting had not been given as required by the bylaws and because the meeting had not been held at the place of call. Was the special meeting properly held? [Hill v Atlantic & North Carolina Railroad Co. 143 NC 539, 55 SE 854]

5. Anthony Yee was the president of the Waipahu Auto Exchange, a corporation. As part of his corporate duties, he arranged financing for the company. The Federal Services Finance Corporation drew twelve checks payable to the order of the Waipahu Auto Exchange. These were then indorsed by its president: "Waipahu Auto Exchange, Limited, by Anthony Yee, President," and were cashed at two different banks. The Bishop National Bank of Hawaii, on which the checks were drawn, charged its depositor, Federal Services, with the amount of these checks. Federal Services then sued Bishop National Bank to restore to its account the amount of these twelve checks on the theory that Bishop National Bank had improperly made payment on the checks because Anthony Yee had no authority to cash them. Did Yee have authority to indorse and cash the checks? [Federal Services Finance Corp. v Bishop National Bank of Hawaii (CA9 Hawaii) 190 F2d 442]

6. Sacks claimed that, when he was a salesman for Helene Curtis Industries, its president, Stein, made an oral contract with him to the effect that Sacks was to act as the sales manager of the corporation at a compensation of a straight salary and a percentage of the increased volume of the corporation's sales. The corporation later refused to pay compensation on this basis and asserted that it had never been informed of any such agreement. The corporation denied that the contract had in fact been made and asserted that the president had no authority to make such an agreement. Was the agreement binding on the corporation? [Sacks v Helene Curtis Industries, 340 IllApp 76, 91 NE2d 127]

7. Frushour, a director of Kidd Island Bay Development Corp., undertook to acquire for Kidd two parcels of Day's land which Kidd desired, either by exchanging for the two parcels a tract of land owned by Kidd or by money purchase. Instead, Frushour exchanged the Kidd tract for the two Day parcels to which he took title in his own name, while telling other Kidd directors and officers that Day would not exchange but would only buy the Kidd tract. Accordingly, Kidd deeded the 15-acre tract to Day, and a check came to Kidd from a realty company where Frushour worked. Knutsen, also a Kidd director, upon learning what had transpired, brought a shareholder's derivative action against Frushour to have the Day parcels held in trust for Kidd. Frushour's defense was that a director may engage in personal business activities and that Kidd had not forbidden its directors to engage in outside real estate transactions on their own account. Decide. [Knutsen v Frushour, 92 Idaho 37, 436 P2d 521]

8. Cholfin and his wife were two of the three directors of the Allied Freightways Corporation. Cholfin ran the business, and his wife and the other director took no part in its management. Cholfin unlawfully used $16,587.25 of the corporate funds to pay his own debts and $3,086.39 of the corporate funds to pay those of his wife. Allied Freightways brought suit to recover from the Cholfins the money improperly spent from the corporation. Allied Freightways claimed that each of the defendants was liable for the full amount of all improper expenditures. Was this correct? [Allied Freightways v Cholfin, 325 Mass 630, 91 NE2d 765]

REAL PROPERTY— DEEDS

A. NATURE OF REAL PROPERTY

§ **53:1. DEFINITIONS.** *Real property* includes (a) land, (b) buildings and fixtures and (c) rights in the land of another.

(a) Land. *Land* means more than the surface of the earth. It embraces the soil and all things of a permanent nature affixed to the ground, such as herbs, grass, or trees, and other growing, natural products. The term also includes the waters upon the ground and things that are embedded beneath the surface. For example, coal, oil, and marble embedded beneath the surface form part of the land.

The owner of land is the owner of a fossilized skeleton of a prehistoric animal entombed in his land.[1]

Technically, land is considered as extending downward to the earth's center and upward indefinitely. The Uniform Aeronautics Act states that the owner of land owns the space above, subject to the right of aircraft in flight which does not interfere with the use of the land and is not dangerous to persons or property lawfully on the land.[2]

FACTS: Duncan owned a ranch. Airplanes of the Southwest Weather Research, Inc. flew over the ranch and surrounding area for the purpose of "seeding" clouds, a program that Research claimed prevented hail storms. Research had a contract with a number of farmers for this purpose. Duncan sued to enjoin such flights over his land on the ground that the seeding had dissipated clouds which, if permitted to remain, would have brought rain to his land.

---

[1] Hunterfly Realty Corp. v New York (Ct Claims) 346 NYS2d 455 (skeleton of 10,000-year-old mastodon).
[2] The Uniform Aeronautics Act (UAA) has been adopted in Arizona, Delaware, Georgia, Hawaii, Idaho, Indiana, Maryland, Minnesota, Missouri, Montana, Nevada, New Jersey, North Carolina, North Dakota, Pennsylvania, South Carolina, South Dakota, Tennessee, Utah, Vermont, and Wisconsin, but was withdrawn by the Commissioners on Uniform State Laws in 1943.

DECISION: Judgment for Duncan. As an owner of the land, Duncan had the right to receive rain from the clouds free from any interference with them. The act of Research was therefore a wrong to Duncan as a property owner, and he could prevent the wrongful act. [Southwest Weather Research, Inc. v Duncan (TexCivApp) 319 SW2d 940]

(b) Buildings and fixtures. A *building* includes any structure placed on or beneath the surface of land, without regard to its purpose or use. A *fixture* is personal property that has been attached to the earth or placed in a building in such a way or under such circumstances that it is deemed part of the real property.

(c) Rights in the land of another. These rights include *easements*, such as the right to cross another's land, and *profits*, such as the right to take coal from another's land.

§ 53:2. EASEMENTS. An *easement* is not only a right in the land of another, but it is a right that belongs to the land which is benefited. The benefited land is called the *dominant tenement*, and the subject land is called the *servient tenement*.

An easement is an interest in land and therefore an oral promise to create an easement is not binding because of the statute of frauds.

(a) Creation of easement. An easement may be created by:
(1) Deed.
(2) Implication when one conveys part of his land that has been used as a dominant estate in relation to the part retained. To illustrate, if water or drain pipes run from the part alienated through the part retained, there is an implied right to have such use continued. In order that an easement will be implied in such a case, the use must be apparent, continuous, and reasonably necessary.
(3) Implication when it is necessary to the use of the land alienated. This ordinarily arises when one sells land to which no entry can be made, except over the land retained or over the land of a stranger. The right to use the land retained for the purpose of going to and from the land is known as a *way of necessity*.
(4) Estoppel, as when the grantor states that the plot conveyed is bounded by a street. If, in such a case, the grantor owns the adjoining plot, he cannot deny the public the right to use the area which he has described as a street.
(5) Prescription by adverse use for a prescribed period. A cattleman did not obtain an easement by prescription to drive his cattle across a neighbor's land, where such crossing was not adverse because the cattleman always requested permission from the neighbor before he drove his cattle across the land.

(b) Termination of easement. Once an easement has been granted it cannot be destroyed by the act of the grantor. A "revocation" attempted by him, without the easement owner's consent has no effect.

An easement may be lost by nonuse when there are surrounding circumstances which show an intent to abandon the easement. For example, where a surface transit system had an easement to maintain trolley tracks, it could be found that there was an abandonment of the easement when the tracks were removed and all surface transportation was discontinued. Likewise, where the owner of the easement planted a flower bed on his land across the end of the path of the easement, it was evident that he intended to abandon the easement.

§ **53:3. LIENS.** Real property may be subject to liens that arise by the voluntary act of the owner of the land, such as the lien of a mortgage which is created when the owner voluntarily borrows money and the land is made security for the repayment of the debt. Liens may also arise involuntarily as in the case of tax liens, judgment liens, and mechanics' liens. In the case of taxes and judgments, the liens provide a means for enforcing the obligations of the owner of the land to pay the taxes or the judgment.

Mechanics' liens give persons furnishing labor and materials in the improvement of real estate the right to proceed against the real estate for the collection of the amounts due them. If the owner had dealt directly with such persons, the mechanics' lien is a remedy in addition to the right to enforce the contract of the owner. If the claimant did not have a contract directly with the owner, as in the case of a person furnishing labor or materials to the contractor who dealt with the owner, the claimant has no contract claim against the owner. Mechanics' liens are created by statutes which regulate in detail the kinds of claims for which liens may be imposed and the procedure to be followed.

§ **53:4. DURATION AND EXTENT OF OWNERSHIP.** The interest held by a person in real property may be defined in terms of the period of time for which he will remain the owner. He may have (1) a fee simple estate or (2) a life estate. These estates are termed *freehold estates.* In addition, either of these estates may be subject to a condition or may expire or terminate upon the happening of a specified contingency. Although a person may own property for a specified number of years, this interest is not regarded as a freehold estate, but is a *leasehold estate* and is subject to rules of law different from those applicable to freehold estates.

(a) **Fee simple estate.** An *estate in fee,* a *fee simple* or a *fee simple absolute,* is the largest estate known to our law. The owner of such fee has the absolute and entire property in the land. The important characteristics of this estate are as follows: (1) it is alienable during life; (2) it is alienable by will; (3) it descends to heirs generally if not devised (transferred by will); (4) it is subject to rights of the owner's surviving spouse; and (5) it is liable for debts of the owner before or after death.

Statutes commonly declare that a deed conveying property will be held to convey a fee simple estate if nothing is expressly stated that limits the grantee to a lesser estate.

(b) Life estate. A *life estate* (or life tenancy), as its name indicates, lasts only during the life of a person, ordinarily its owner. Upon his death, no interest remains to pass to his heirs or by his will.

B. FIXTURES

§ 53:5. DEFINITION. A *fixture* is personal property that is attached to the earth or placed in a building in such a way or under such circumstances that it is deemed part of the real property.

A person buys a refrigerator, an air conditioner, or a furnace, or some other item that is used in a building. He then has the item installed. The question whether the item is a fixture and therefore part of the building can arise in a variety of situations. (1) The real estate tax assessor assesses the building and adds in the value of the item on the theory that it is part of the building. (2) The buyer of the item owns the building and then sells the building, and his buyer claims that the item stays with the building. (3) The buyer places a mortgage on the building, and the mortgagee claims that the item is bound by the mortgage. (4) The buyer does not own the building in which he puts the item, and the landlord claims that the item must stay in the building when the tenant leaves. (5) The buyer did not pay in full for the item, and the seller of the item has a security interest that he asserts against the buyer of the item or against the landlord of the building in which the buyer installed the item. The seller of the item may be asserting his claim against the mortgagee of the building or against the buyer of the building.

The determination of the rights of these parties depends upon the common law of fixtures, as occasionally modified by statute.[3]

§ 53:6. TESTS OF A FIXTURE. In the absence of an agreement between the parties, the courts apply three tests to determine whether the personal property has become a fixture:

(a) Annexation. Generally the personal property becomes a fixture if it is so attached to the realty that it cannot be removed without materially damaging the realty or destroying the personal property itself. If the property is so affixed as to lose its specific identity, such as bricks in a wall, it becomes part of the realty. Where railroad tracks are so placed as to be immovable, they are to be deemed fixtures.

(b) Adaptation. Personal property especially adapted or suited to the building may constitute a fixture. By the *institutional* or *industrial plant doctrine*, machinery reasonably necessary for the operation of an industrial plant usually becomes part of the realty when installed, without regard to whether it is physically attached or not. This principle does not apply to office equipment and trucks used in the operation of the enterprise.

---

[3] The Uniform Commercial Code regulates the priority of security interests in fixtures, UCC § 9-313, but does not determine when an item is a fixture.

(c) Intent. The true test is the intention of the person affixing the property at the time it was affixed.

In the absence of direct proof, it is necessary to resort to the nature of the property, the method of its attachment, and all the surrounding circumstances to determine what the intent was.

FACTS: In 1958, a supermarket was constructed and owned by Jacobs Realty Corporation. The market contained five large walk-in coolers or refrigerators. Title to the market was thereafter transferred to the Premonstratensian Fathers and was insured against fire by Badger Mutual Insurance Company. The building was severely damaged by fire and the insurer paid approximately $80,000 for the building damage. The Fathers claimed an additional $20,000 for the destruction of the coolers. The insurer refused to pay this amount and asserted that the coolers were not owned by the Fathers.

DECISION: The coolers were fixtures because it was the intent of the affixer that they be permanently attached to the building. Moreover, there was such physical attachment to the building and such adaptation to use as to lead to the conclusion that the coolers had become fixtures. They were therefore owned by the Fathers as part of the building and were covered by fire insurance on the building. [Premonstratensian Fathers v Badger Mutual Insurance Co. 46 Wis2d 362, 175 NW2d 337]

The fact that machinery installed in a plant would be very difficult and expensive to move and so delicate that the moving would cause damage and unbalancing is significant in reaching the conclusion that the owner of the plant had installed the equipment as a permanent addition and thus had the intent which would make the equipment become fixtures. When the floors in a large apartment house are of concrete which is covered with a thin sheet of plywood to which is stapled wall to wall carpeting, the carpeting constitutes a fixture which cannot be removed from the building as removal would probably destroy the carpeting, it having been cut to size, and the carpeting was necessary to make the building liveable as an apartment.

§ 53:7. MOVABLE MACHINERY AND EQUIPMENT. Machinery and equipment that is movable is ordinarily held not to constitute fixtures, even though, in order to move it, it is necessary to unbolt it from the floor or to disconnect electrical wires or water pipes.

It is ordinarily held that refrigerators and freezers, and gas and electric ranges are not fixtures and do not lose their character as personal property when they are readily removable upon disconnecting pipes or unplugging wires. A portable window air conditioner which rests on a rack which is fixed to the window sill by two screws and is connected directly to the building only by an electric cord plug is not a fixture but remains personal property.

The mere fact that an item may be "unplugged," however, does not establish that it is not a fixture. For example, a computer and its related hardware constituted "fixtures" when there was such a mass of wires and cables under the floor that the installation gave the impression of permanence.

§ 53:8. TRADE FIXTURES. Equipment which is attached to a rented building by a tenant for use by him in his trade or business is ordinarily removable by him when he leaves the premises. Such equipment is commonly called a *trade fixture*. In some states the trade fixture is taxed as real estate, which would be normal if it were a true fixture, but the tax is assessed against the tenant, which would not be the case if it were a true fixture.

C. LIABILITY TO THIRD PERSONS FOR CONDITION OF REAL PROPERTY

§ 53:9. STATUS-OF-PLAINTIFF COMMON-LAW RULE. Under the common law, liability to a person injured on real estate was controlled by his status, that is, whether he was a trespasser, a licensee, or an invitee. A different duty was owed to each of these three categories.

(a) **Trespassers.** As to *trespassers*, the occupier ordinarily owes only the duty of refraining from causing intentional harm once the presence of the trespasser is known; but he is not under any duty to warn of dangers or to make the premises safe to protect the trespasser from harm. The most significant exception to this rule arises in the case of small children who, although trespassers, are generally afforded greater protection through the *attractive nuisance doctrine*. For example, the owner of a private residential swimming pool was liable for the drowning of a 5-year old child when the owner did not maintain adequate fencing around the pool, since the placing of such fencing would not have imposed a great burden upon him.

(b) **Licensees.** As to *licensees*, who are on the premises with the permission of the occupier, the latter owes the duty of warning of nonobvious dangers that are known to the licensor. The licensor, however, is not required to take any steps to learn of the presence of dangers.

(c) **Invitees.** As to *invitees*, whose presence is sought to further the economic interest of the occupier, such as his customers, there is the duty to take reasonable steps to discover any danger and the duty to warn the invitee or to correct the danger. For example, a store must make a reasonable inspection of the premises to determine that there is nothing on the floor that would be dangerous, such as a slippery substance that might cause a patron to fall, and must either correct the condition or appropriately rope off the danger area or give suitable warning. If the occupier of the premises fails to conform to the degree of care described and harm results to an invitee on the premises, the occupier is liable to him for such harm.

In most states the courts have expanded the concept of invitees beyond the category of those persons whose presence will economically benefit the occupier so that it includes members of the public who are invited when it is apparent that such persons cannot be reasonably expected to make an inspection of the premises before making use of them and that they would not be making repairs to correct any dangerous condition. Some courts have also made inroads into the prior law by treating a recurring licensee, such as a mailman, as an invitee.

§ 53:10. NEGLIGENCE RULE. Several courts have begun what will probably become a new trend in ignoring these distinctions and holding the occupier liable according to ordinary negligence standards; that is, when the occupier as a reasonable man should foresee from the circumstances that harm would be caused a third person, the occupier has the duty to take reasonable steps to prevent such harm without regard to whether the potential victim would be traditionally classified as a trespasser, a licensee, or an invitee.[4]

Under this rule, the occupier of a parking lot who knows that people customarily cut across the lot to patronize a neighboring coffee shop is liable to such a pedestrian who is injured by falling down the edge of the parking lot where a retaining wall had fallen away, when such occupier knew or should have known that pedestrians would cross the lot during the night and a reasonably prudent man would foresee that in the dark the condition of the lot made harm to such persons probable or foreseeable.

§ 53:11. INTERMEDIATE RULE. Some courts have taken an intermediate position and have merely abolished the distinction between licensees and invitees so that the occupier owes the same duty of care to all unlawful visitors, and whether one is a licensee or an invitee is merely a circumstance to be considered by the jury in applying the ordinary rule of negligence. On this basis it has been held that a policeman may recover from the occupier of premises when he fell and was injured on accumulated ice on the premises, although he had entered for the purpose of serving a parking violation summons.[5]

In some states the distinction between licensees and invitees has been retained in name but destroyed in fact by requiring a licensor to warn the licensee of dangers of which the licensor knew or in the exercise of reasonable care should have known.

D. CO-OWNERSHIP OF REAL PROPERTY

§ 53:12. MULTIPLE OWNERSHIP. Several persons may have concurrent interests in the same real property. The forms of multiple ownership for real property are the same as those for personal property. These have been discussed in Chapter 20.

When cotenants sell property, they hold the proceeds of sale by the same type of tenancy as they held the original property.

---

[4] Rowland v Christian, 69 Cal2d 108, 70 CalRptr 97, 443 P2d 561.
[5] Mounsey v Ellard (Mass) 297 NE2d 43.

§ 53:13. **CONDOMINIUMS.** A *condominium* is a combination of co-ownership and ownership in severalty. As a factual detail, real estate will be involved. For example, persons owning an office building or an apartment house by condominium are co-owners of the land and of the halls, lobby, elevators, stairways, and exits; yards, gardens, and surrounding land; incinerator, laundry rooms, and other areas used in common; but each person individually owns his own apartment or office in the building.[6]

(a) **Control and expense.** In some states the owners of the various units in the condominium have equal voice in the management and share an equal part of its expenses. In others, control and liability for expenses are shared by a unit owner in the same ratio that the value of his unit bears to the value of the entire condominium project. In all states the unit owners have an equal right to use the common areas.

The owner of each condominium unit makes repairs and improvements at his own expense. Generally he will be prohibited from making any major change which would impair or damage the safety or value of an adjoining unit. Any changes or improvements made to outside walls must ordinarily be consistent with the existing pattern of the building.

(b) **Collection of expenses from unit owner.** When a unit owner fails to pay his share of taxes, operating expenses, and repairs, it is commonly provided that a lien be entered against his unit for the amount which is due by him. If payment is not then made, some condominium statutes authorize the association to shut off the unit's water, gas, electricity, and heat, and eventually to sell the delinquent owner's rights in the unit.

(c) **Tort liability.** Most condominium projects fail to make provision as to the liability of unit owners for a tort occurring in the common areas. A few states expressly provide that when a third person is injured in the common areas, his suit may only be brought against the condominium association and any judgment recovered is a charge against the association to be paid off as a common expense.

When the condominium association is incorporated, the same result should be obtained by applying ordinary principles of corporation law under which liability for torts occurring on the premises of the corporation are not the liability of the individual shareholders.

§ 53:14. **ADVANTAGES OF CONDOMINIUM OWNERSHIP.**

(a) **Freedom from enterprise liability.** The owner of a unit is not liable personally for an enterprise liability nor may his unit be taken from him for such a liability. For example, even though the total enterprise be sold for taxes or to pay a tort judgment in favor of a third person injured on the

---

[6] The great majority of states have adopted statutes authorizing condominium ownership in order to obtain the low cost Federal Housing Administration insurance of condominium mortgages which was authorized by the National Housing Act of 1961 in states in which condominium ownership was recognized. 12 United States Code § 234, PL 87-70, 75 Stat 161.

common premises, each unit owner is still the owner of his unit just as before.

(b) Transferability of unit. The condominium unit is property which the unit owner can transfer as freely as any other kind of property. Generally he must give the other unit owners a first offer to purchase his unit. Otherwise he can sell or transfer as he chooses.

Because of this transferability of the unit, it is easier for the unit owner to raise money by mortgaging his unit than would be the case if the enterprise were run as an apartment house or cooperative and the unit owner would have merely a fractional interest or a leasehold interest to put up as security.

(c) Tax deductions. The owner of a unit in a condominium may write off in his personal income tax return a proportionate share of the operating expenses, insurance, taxes, and losses of the condominium. Over a period of time the unit owner can thus effect a savings in his taxes which in effect will lower the cost to him of the condominium unit. If he merely leased an apartment, he would not obtain this advantage.

(d) Stability of restrictions. If a housing project is organized as a cooperative, it is sometimes uncertain as to whether restrictions voluntarily assumed by the present unit owner or tenants will be binding upon others who acquire the units from them by sale or assignment. In the case of the condominium unit, any restriction which is binding on the original owner will remain binding on any subsequent owner of the unit.

E. TRANSFER OF REAL PROPERTY BY DEED

§ 53:15. DEFINITION. A *deed* is an instrument or writing by which an owner or *grantor* transfers or conveys an interest in land to a new owner called a *grantee* or transferee. In some states that have retained the influence of the common law, the deed must be sealed.

Unlike a contract, no consideration is required to make a deed effective. Real property, as in the case of personal property, may either be sold or given as a gift. Although consideration is not required to make a valid deed or transfer of title by deed, the absence of consideration may be evidence to show that the transfer was made by the owner in fraud of his creditors who may then be able to set aside the transfer. A deed is necessary to transfer title to land, even though it is a gift.

§ 53:16: CLASSIFICATION OF DEEDS. Deeds may be classified in terms of the interest conveyed as (1) a *quitclaim deed*, which transfers merely whatever interest, if any, the grantor may have in the property, without specifying that interest in any way, and (2) a *warranty deed*, which purports to transfer a specified interest and which warrants or guarantees that such interest is transferred.

A deed may also be classified as (a) a common-law deed or (b) a statutory deed. The *common-law deed* is a long form that sets forth the details of the transaction. The *statutory deed* in substance merely recites that a named person is making a certain conveyance to a named grantee. It is generally held that the existence of a statute authorizing a short form of deed does not preclude the use of the common-law form.

§ 53:17. **EXECUTION OF DEEDS.** Ordinarily a deed must be signed, by signature or mark, or sealed by the grantor. In order to have the deed recorded, statutes generally require that two or more witnesses sign the deed and that the grantor then acknowledge his deed before a notary public or other officer. In the interest of legibility, it is frequently required that the signatures of the parties be followed by their printed or typewritten names.

In many states the statute that authorizes a short or simplified form of deed also declares that no seal is required to make effective a writing which purports to convey an interest in land.

A deed must be executed and delivered by a person having capacity. It may be set aside by the grantor on the ground of the fraud of the grantee provided that innocent third persons have not acquired rights in the land.

The deed remains binding as between the grantor and his grantee even though it has not been acknowledged or recorded.

§ 53:18. **DELIVERY OF DEEDS.** A deed has no effect and title does not pass until the deed has been delivered. Delivery is a matter of intent as shown by both words and conduct; no particular form of ceremony is required. The essential intent in delivering a deed is not merely that the grantor intends to hand over physical control and possession of the paper on which the deed is written, but that he intends thereby to divest himself of ownership of the property described in the deed. That is, he must deliver the deed with the intent that it should take effect as a deed and convey an interest in the property.

FACTS: Jennie Shroyer executed a deed transferring her farm to Wayne and Wesley, the sons of her deceased brother. By her will, Jennie left the same farm to Jessie, the widow of her deceased brother. An action was brought after Jennie's death to determine who owned Jennie's farm. The evidence showed that, after Jennie had executed the deed, it was acknowledged before a notary public and shown to Wayne, who looked at it and returned it to Jennie. Thereafter, she remained in possession of the land and acted in all respects as though she still owned it. However, Jennie told other persons that the boys were the owners of the farm and she was merely holding the deed for safekeeping. The unrecorded deed was found among Jennie's papers after her death. An action was brought by Jessie to cancel the deed on the ground that it was not effective because it had never been delivered.

DECISION: The fact that the deed was found among the papers of the grantor at the time of her death and that it had never been recorded raised a presumption that it had never been delivered. This placed upon the grantee in the deed the burden of proving by the preponderance of the evidence that the deed in fact was delivered. This was not done and therefore it must be concluded that the deed had never been delivered. Jennie's conduct was consistent with this conclusion. Her continued use of the farm as her own indicated that it was her intention that the farm should belong to her grantees after her death. The deed was never effective as a deed and the land passed under Jennie's will at her death. [Shroyer v Shroyer (Mo) 425 SW2d 214]

A deed is ordinarily made effective by handing it to the grantee with the intention that he should thenceforth be the owner of the property described in the deed. A delivery may also be made by placing the deed, addressed to the grantee, in the mail or by giving it to a third person with directions to hand it to the grantee. Where the grantor mailed the deed to the grantee, there was a valid delivery by the act of mailing and the grantee's interest was not affected by the fact that the grantor committed suicide later that day and the deed was not received by the grantee until after the grantor's death.

When a deed is delivered to a third person for the purpose of delivery by him to the grantee upon the happening of some event or contingency, the transaction is called a *delivery in escrow*. No title passes until the fulfillment of the condition or the happening of the event or contingency.

An effective delivery of a deed may be made symbolically as by delivering to the grantee the key to a locked box and informing the grantee that the deed to him of the property is in the box.

§ 53:19. ACCEPTANCE OF DEEDS. Generally there must be an acceptance by the grantee. In all cases, however, an acceptance is presumed, but the grantee may disclaim the transfer if he acts within a reasonable time after learning that the transfer has been made.

§ 53:20. CANCELLATION OF DEEDS. A deed, although delivered, acknowledged, and recorded, may be set aside or canceled by the grantor upon proof of such circumstances as would warrant the setting aside of a contract. For example, when a conveyance is made in consideration of a promise to support the grantor, the failure of the grantee to perform will ordinarily justify cancellation of the deed.

§ 53:21. RECORDING OF DEEDS. If the owner of the land desires to do so, he may record his deed in the office of a public official sometimes called a recorder or commissioner of deeds. The recording is not required to make the deed effective to pass title, but it is done so that the public will know that the grantee is the present owner and thereby prevent the former owner from making any other transaction relating to the property. The recording statutes provide that a person purchasing land from the last holder of record will take title free of any unrecorded claim to the land of which the purchaser does not have notice or knowledge.

The fact that a deed is recorded charges everyone with knowledge of its existence even though they in fact do not know of it because they have neglected to examine the record. The recording of a deed, however, is only such notice if the deed was properly executed. Likewise, the grantee of land cannot claim any protection by virtue of the recording of a deed when (a) an adverse claim is made by one whose title is superior to that of the owner of record; (b) the grantee had notice or knowledge of the adverse claim when he acquired title; (c) a person acting under a hostile claim was then in possession of the land; (d) the grantee received the land as a gift; or (e) the transfer to the grantee was fraudulent.

§ 53:22. ADDITIONAL PROTECTION OF BUYERS. Apart from the protection given to buyers and third persons by the recorded title to property, a buyer may generally also protect himself by procuring title insurance or an *abstract of title*, which is a summarized report of the title to the property as shown by the records, together with a report of all judgments, mortgages, and similar claims against the property that have also been recorded.

§ 53:23. DONEES AND PURCHASERS WITH NOTICE. Donees or persons who do not give value and persons who have knowledge or notice of outstanding claims always take title to property subject to any claims, such as unrecorded deeds and equitable or statutory liens on the land.

§ 53:24. CREDITORS OF GRANTOR. The transfer of title under a deed may be defeated in some instances by creditors of the grantor.

(a) Fraudulent conveyances. Following an English statute, it is held in most states that a conveyance for the purpose of hindering, delaying, or defrauding creditors is voidable as against such creditors. The rule is applicable in the case of subsequent creditors, as well as those existing at the time of the conveyance. For example, when one, just before entering into debt, makes a conveyance that he knows is likely to render him unable to pay his obligations, subsequent creditors may avoid the conveyance. When the transfer is made to a bona fide purchaser without notice, the title passes under a deed free from the demands or claims of either existing or subsequent creditors. In any case the person who claims that a transfer of title has been made in fraud of creditors has the burden of proving that fact.

Under the Uniform Fraudulent Conveyance Act [7] conveyances in certain situations are classified as being in fraud of creditors. If the claim of a defrauded creditor of the grantor is due, he ordinarily may have the fraudulent conveyance set aside or he may disregard the conveyance and attach or levy execution upon the property conveyed.

(b) Federal Bankruptcy Act. Another situation in which the claims of creditors may defeat the passing of title is that in which the conveyance violates a provision of the Federal Bankruptcy Act. Under the provisions of that statute a conveyance that operates to give a preference to one creditor

---

[7] This Act has been adopted in Arizona, California, Delaware, Idaho, Maryland, Massachusetts, Michigan, Minnesota, Montana, Nevada, New Hampshire, New Jersey, New Mexico, New York, North Dakota, Ohio, Oklahoma, Pennsylvania, South Dakota, Tennessee, Utah, Washington, Wisconsin, Wyoming, and the Virgin Islands.

as against another may be set aside if the conveyance was made within four months prior to the time when the grantor was adjudged a bankrupt. The trustee in bankruptcy is also authorized to avoid any conveyance that is a fraud upon creditors.

§ 53:25. GRANTOR'S WARRANTIES.

(a) **Warranties of title.** In the common-law deed the grantor may expressly warrant or make certain covenants as to the title conveyed. The statutes authorizing a short form of deed provide that unless otherwise stated in the deed, the grantor shall be presumed to have made certain warranties of title.

The more important of the covenants or warranties of title which the grantor may make are: (a) *covenant of seizin*, or guarantee that the grantor owns the exact estate which he has purported to convey; (b) *covenant of right to convey*, or guarantee that the grantor, if he is not the owner, as in the case of an agent, has the right or authority to make the conveyance; (c) *covenant against encumbrances*, or guarantee that the land is not subject to any right or interest of a third person, such as a lien or easement; (d) *covenant for quiet enjoyment*, or covenant by the grantor that the grantee's possession of the land shall not be disturbed either by the grantor, in the case of a limited covenant, or by the grantor or any person claiming title under him, in the case of a general covenant; and (e) *covenant for further assurances*, or promise by the grantor that he will execute any additional documents that may be required to perfect the title of the grantee.

(b) **Nontitle warranties.** Distinct from the warranties of title, a grantor may make any warranty or guaranty he chooses, although such other obligations are more likely to be found in the sales contract, such as an undertaking to deliver the house in "new house condition." A buyer acts at his peril when the warranty or guaranty in the contract is not repeated in the deed, for in many instances the deed will supersede or take the place of the prior written sales contract. Thus, if the warranty or guaranty is only in the prior contract, the silence of the deed will bar proof of that prior sales contract provision.

(c) **Fitness for use.** In the absence of an express warranty in the deed, no warranty as to fitness arises under the common law in the sale or conveyance of real estate. Thus, by the common law there is no implied warranty that a house is reasonably fit for habitation, even though it is a new house sold by the builder.[8]

When a home is purchased directly from the builder, many courts imply a warranty that it was constructed in good workmanlike manner but do not go so far as to impose a warranty that the house is fit to use or free from

---

[8] Mitchem v Johnson, 7 Ohio2d 66, 218 NE2d 594. No warranty arises under the Sales Article of the UCC since its provisions apply only to sales of "goods." Vernali v Centrella, 28 ConnSupp 476, 266 A2d 200. The provision of the UCC requiring that a buyer give his seller notice of a defect is not applicable to the case of a defect in a house. Pollard v Saxe & Yolles Development Co. 32 CalApp3d 390, 108 CalRptr 174.

defects. Similarly, a buyer may have some protection against defects due to poor design of the building when he purchases his home from the contractor who prepared the building plans and specifications. In such a case the contractor may be held liable if, because of a defect in the plans and specifications, the building when constructed is not fit for the purpose for which it was constructed. And a builder is liable for fraud when he intentionally conceals defects in the construction which a buyer could not discover by inspection.

A growing number of courts, in approximately half of the states, hold that when a builder or real estate developer sells a new house to a home buyer, he makes an implied warranty that the house and foundation are fit for occupancy or use, without regard to whether the house was purchased before, during, or after completion of construction.

FACTS: Humber purchased a new house from Morton who was in the business of building and selling new houses. The first time that Humber lit a fire in the fireplace, the house caught on fire because of a defect in the fireplace and the house was partially damaged. She sued Morton who defended in part on the theory that the rule of caveat emptor, or "Let the buyer beware," barred the suit.

DECISION: The rule of caveat emptor did not bar suit because such a rule is based on the assumption that a buyer is able to protect himself by the exercise of diligence. "The . . . rule as applied to new houses is an anachronism patently out of harmony with modern buying practices" and encourages poor construction work. The court therefore rejected the rule of caveat emptor and implied a warranty of fitness for use in order to keep the law "abreast of the times." "Ancient distinctions which make no sense in today's society and tend to discredit the law should be readily rejected." [Humber v Morton (Tex) 426 SW2d 554]

There is likewise authority that strict tort liability may be applied to the developer or vendor of the new home for personal injuries sustained by the buyer or a member of his family. There is also a trend of authority by which a seller is required to inform the buyer of any respect in which government approval has not been obtained and to hold a seller liable for fraud when, knowing the truth, he remains silent. No warranty of fitness arises when the seller is a casual seller as when an owner sells his house to a buyer.

The warranty of habitability is not a guarantee with respect to neighboring property. Thus, a builder is not liable for breach of warranty when the improving of neighboring land, coupled with heavy rains, causes water to stand on the property improved and sold by him.

Akin to widening the seller's warranty liability is a widening of fraud liability to include unverified false statements made in selling. Thus, a real estate broker and his surety were held liable for fraud when the broker assured the purchaser that there was no water seepage problem and the statement proved false. It was immaterial whether or not the broker at the time he made the statement had knowledge that it was false. When a seller in good faith represented the building as sound, when in fact it was infested by termites, the seller was liable for damages to the buyer although no express statement had been made as to termites and even though the buyer had examined the house but did not know what to look for and did not detect the presence of termites.

There appears to be developing a concept of contractor's liability similar to a warranty or enterprise liability concept.

(d) Damages for breach of grantor's warranty. When the grantor has broken a warranty, he is liable for damages caused the grantee but he is not liable for damages greater than the loss actually sustained. For example, when a a grantor broke his warranty of title in that the true boundary line did not run up to the fences on the land but the grantee was able to acquire the "missing" strips between the boundary line and the fences from the neighbors for a nominal cost, the grantor was liable to the grantee only for such nominal damages.

§ 53:26. GRANTEE'S COVENANTS. In a deed the grantee may undertake to do or to refrain from doing certain acts. Such an agreement becomes a binding contract between the grantor and the grantee. The grantor may sue the grantee for its breach. When the covenant of the grantee relates directly to the property conveyed, such as an agreement to maintain fences on the property or that the property shall be used only for residential purposes, it is said not only that the covenant is binding between the grantor and the grantee but also that it *runs with the land.* This means that anyone acquiring the grantee's land from the grantee is also bound by the covenant of the grantee, even though this subsequent owner had not made any such agreement with anyone.

The right to enforce the covenant also runs with the land owned by the grantor to whom the promise was made. Thus, if A owns adjoining tracts of land and conveys one of them to B and B covenants to maintain the surface drainage on the land so that it will not flood A's land, the benefit of this covenant will run with the land retained by A. If A sells his remaining tract of land to C, B is bound to perform his covenant so as to benefit the neighboring tract even though it is now owned by C.

A covenant which provides that the grantee shall refrain from certain conduct is termed a *restrictive* (or negative) *covenant.* It runs with the land in the same manner as a covenant that calls for the performance of an act, that is, an *affirmative covenant.*

§ 53:27. SCOPE OF GRANTEE'S RESTRICTIVE COVENANTS. A restrictive covenant may impose both a limitation on the kind of structure that can be erected on the land and the use which may be made.

A covenant restricting the owner to one single-family private dwelling bars the owner from building a duplex apartment.

(a) General building scheme. When a tract of land is developed and individual lots or homes are sold to separate purchasers, it is common to use the same restrictive covenants in all deeds in order to impose uniform restrictions and patterns on the property. Any person acquiring a lot within the tract is bound by the restrictions if they are in his deed or a prior recorded deed, or if he has notice or knowledge of such restrictions. Any person owning one of the lots in the tract may bring suit against another lot owner to enforce the restrictive covenant. The effect is to create a zoning code based upon the agreement of the parties in their deeds, as distinguished from one based upon government regulation.

(b) **Restraints on alienation.** The covenants of the grantee may restrict him when he seeks to sell his property. It is lawful to provide that the grantor shall have the option to purchase the property, or that if the grantee offers to sell it to anyone, the grantor will be given an opportunity to match the price that a third person is willing to pay. Restrictions on the grantee's right to sell the property are not enforceable when the restriction discriminates against potential buyers because of race, color, creed, or national origin. Thus, a covenant that the grantee will only resell to a member of the Caucasian race cannot be enforced. A restraint on alienation that specifies that the grantee will not sell the property to anyone or that he will not sell to anyone other than the grantor or his heirs or representatives is contrary to public policy.

§ 53:28. INTERPRETATION OF RESTRICTIVE COVENANTS. Restrictive covenants of a grantee are generally interpreted strictly so as to impose the least restraint upon the grantee consistent with the letter of the covenant.

(a) **Parol evidence.** A covenant must be expressed in a deed; it cannot be established by parol evidence. Consequently, when the deed did not so specify, it could not be shown by parol evidence that the grantor and the grantee had agreed that the land conveyed would be used only as a baseball park.

(b) **Enforcement of grantee's covenants.** A grantee's covenant may be enforced by the grantor or by a neighboring property owner intended to be benefited by the covenant. The grantee's covenant may be enforced in an action at law for damages. In the case of restrictive or negative covenants, the complaining person may also obtain the aid of a court with equity jurisdiction to grant an injunction compelling the owner of the land to comply with the terms of the covenant. Equitable relief is generally denied, however, in the case of affirmative covenants. A declaratory judgment can often be obtained to determine the validity or meaning of both negative and affirmative covenants.

Relief, whether at law or in equity, will not be afforded when enforcement of the restriction would amount to a discrimination prohibited by the Fourteenth Amendment of the Constitution of the United States, or when the circumstances and neighborhood have so changed that it would be absurd to continue to enforce the restriction.

F. OTHER METHODS OF TRANSFERRING REAL PROPERTY

§ 53:29. PUBLIC GRANT OR PATENT. Real property may be acquired directly from the government. The method of transfer in such a case may be

by legislative grant or by patent, which has been commonly used by the federal government under the homestead laws.

§ **53:30. DEDICATION.** Any person possessing a legal or equitable interest in land may appropriate it to the use of the public. This is known as a *dedication.* The real property must be set apart with the intention to surrender it to the use of the public. An acceptance is usually necessary on the part of the municipality or the state.

§ **53:31. EMINENT DOMAIN.** Two important questions are involved in the transfer of property by this method; namely, whether there is a taking of property and whether the property is intended for public use. In respect to the first, it is not necessary that one be physically deprived of his land. It is sufficient if he is denied the normal use of his property. It is not necessary that the public actually use the land. It is sufficient that it is appropriated for the public benefit.

> FACTS: The Commonwealth of Pennsylvania proposed to take land by eminent domain in order to widen a highway. The effect of this would be to give better automobile access to the South Gate Shopping Center. The taking by eminent domain was objected to by Washington Park, which was a competing shopping center. Its objection was that the taking by eminent domain was improper because it would benefit private persons, the other shopping center, and not the public.

> DECISION: Judgment against Washington Park. The fact that there may be an individual or private benefit resulting from eminent domain does not impair the propriety of its exercise. The widening of the road would benefit travel by the public, and eminent domain is not concerned with the reason why the public would want to travel on the road. [In re Legislative Route 62214, 425 Pa 349, 229 A2d 1]

§ **53:32. ACCRETION.** The owner of land acquires or loses title to land that is added or taken away by the imperceptible action of water upon his property. An increase of land caused by the action of water upon its borders is known as *accretion.* This gain or increase may result from alluvion or dereliction. *Alluvion* occurs when soil or sand is washed up by the water and becomes attached to the land. *Dereliction* occurs when the water recedes, leaving bare a strip of land which was formerly a part of its bed. Thus, when the boundary line between two farms is the middle of a stream, gradual changes in the course of the stream add to the land on one side and take away from the land on the other.

There is no change of title in the case of *avulsion,* which occurs when a boundary river shifts suddenly or violently, as in the case of a storm or a channel breakthrough, resulting in land being on the other side of the river from the side where it had been.

§ **53:33. ADVERSE POSSESSION.** Title to land may be acquired by holding it adversely to the true owner for a certain period of time. In such a case one gains title by *adverse possession.* If such possession is maintained, the possessor automatically becomes the owner of the property even though he admittedly had no lawful claim to the land before.

In order to acquire title in this manner, possession must be (a) actual, (b) visible and notorious, (c) exclusive, (d) hostile, and (e) continuous for a required period of time.

The period during which land must be held adversely in order to gain title varies in the different states. In many states the statute prescribes 20 or 21 years, whereas in others the period is shorter.

Occupation of land in the mistaken belief that one is the owner is a "hostile" possession.

FACTS: Bradt believed his back yard ran all the way to a fence. Actually there was a strip on Bradt's side of the fence which belonged to his neighbor, Giovannone. Bradt never intended to take land away from anyone. Bradt later brought an action against Giovannone to determine who owned the strip on Bradt's side of the fence.

DECISION: The strip was owned by Bradt by adverse possession, even though such possession was based on a mistake and he had not intended to deprive anyone of his land. Bradt in fact possessed the strip of land to the exclusion of the rest of the world and did so in the belief that he was its owner, which was therefore a possession adverse to everyone else. [Bradt v Giovannone, 35 AppDiv2d 322, 315 NYS2d 961]

QUESTIONS AND CASE PROBLEMS

1. The land for the Mira Loma Subdivision had been conveyed by the Enfield Realty Co. to Hallie Houston by a deed which stated, "No mercantile business of any kind shall ever be carried on, on the premises hereby conveyed; . . . it being understood that all improvements to be created on said premises shall be built and used for residence purposes only, excepting such improvements as may be proper for use in connection with a residence." By subsequent conveyances MacDonald and Merritt acquired three lots in the subdivision, and title to 27 other lots was conveyed to other owners. MacDonald and Merritt brought an action against the other lot owners to obtain a decree declaring that they could subdivide their three lots and erect duplex homes. Were they entitled to such a decree? [MacDonald v Painter (Tex) 441 SW2d 179]

2. Miller executed a deed to real estate, naming Mary Zieg as grantee. He placed the deed in an envelope on which was written, "To be filed at my death," and put the envelope and deed in a safe deposit box in the National Bank. The box had been rented in the names of Miller and Mary Zieg. After his death Mary removed the deed from the safe deposit box. Moseley, as executor under Miller's will, brought an action against Mary to declare the deed void. Decide. [Moseley v Zieg, 180 Neb 810, 146 NW2d 72]

3. Price sued Whisnant, as guardian for McRary, who had cut and removed trees from certain land. Price claimed title on the basis that he owned the land by adverse possession. He proved that for a period of more than 20 years he had

from time to time entered on the land and cut and removed logs. Was Price the owner of the land? [Price v Whisnant, 236 NC 381, 72 SE2d 851]

4. Wyatt owned Crow Island in the White River. By the government land surveys of 1826 and 1854, the river separated the island from land to the east owned by Wycough. The river abruptly changed its course and cut a new channel to the east, with the result that part of the Wycough land was no longer separated by water from Crow Island. Wyatt brought a suit against Wycough, claiming that he now owned that portion of land which had been joined to his as a result of the movement of the river channel. Was he correct? [Wyatt v Wycough, 232 Ark 760, 341 SW2d 18]

5. Digirolamo owned a tract of land near the Philadelphia Gun Club. During shooting contests held by the club, buckshot from the contestants' guns sometimes fell on his land. He sued the club to compel it to stop. The club claimed that as it had held these contests for over 21 years, it had acquired an easement to do so. Decide. [Digirolamo v Philadelphia Gun Club, 371 Pa 40, 89 A2d 357]

6. Castlewood Terrace is a residential district which by the original deed of 1896 could only be used for single-family residences. Pashkow wanted to build a high-rise apartment in the area. Paschen bought an action for a declaratory judgment that Pashkow could not do so. Pashkow claimed that the restrictive covenant was no longer binding because a school had been built in the area and that the value of his land would be more than doubled if used for a high-rise apartment than if used for a single-family dwelling. Was the covenant binding? [Paschen v Pashkow, 63 IllApp2d 56, 211 NE2d 576]

7. Smikahl sold to Hansen a tract of land on which there were two houses and four trailer lots equipped with concrete patios and necessary connections for utility lines. The tract purchased by Hansen was completely surrounded by the land owned by Smikahl and third persons. In order to get onto the highway, it was necessary to cross the Smikahl tract. Several years later, Smikahl put a barbed wire fence around his land. Hansen sued to prevent obstruction to travel between his land and the highway over the Smikahl land. Smikahl defended on the ground that no such right of travel had been given to Hansen. Was he correct? [Hansen v Smikahl, 173 Neb 309, 113 NW2d 210]

8. Henry Lile owned a house. When the land on which it was situated was condemned for a highway, he removed the house to the land of his daughter, Sarah Crick. In the course of construction work, blasting damaged the house and Sarah Crick sued contractors, Terry & Wright. They claimed that Henry should be joined in the action as a plaintiff and that Sarah could not sue by herself because it was Henry's house. Were the defendants correct? [Terry & Wright v Crick (Ky) 418 SW2d 217]

9. Davis Store Fixtures sold certain equipment on credit to Head, who installed it in a building which was later used by the Cadillac Club. When payment was not made, Davis sought to repossess the equipment. If the equipment constituted fixtures, this could not be done. The equipment consisted of a bar for serving drinks, a bench, and a drainboard. The first two were attached to the floor or wall with screws, and the drainboard was connected to water and drainage pipes. Did the equipment constitute fixtures? [Davis Store Fixtures v Cadillac Club, 60 IllApp2d 106, 207 NE2d 711]

10. By a sealed writing, called a "lease," A declared that his neighbor B had the right to drive over a driveway in the rear of A's house. B later claimed that he had an easement. A denied this and contended that B had a "lease." Was A correct? [See Rice v Reich, 51 Wis2d 205, 186 NW2d 269]

54 LEASES

A. CREATION AND TERMINATION

§ **54:1 DEFINITION.** A lease exists whenever one person holds possession of the real property of another under an express or implied agreement.

The person who owns the real property and permits the occupation of the premises is known as the *lessor* or *landlord*. The *lessee* or *tenant* is the one who occupies the property. A *lease* establishes the relationship of landlord and tenant. It is in effect a conveyance of a leasehold estate in land. The term "lease" is also used to designate the paper that is evidence of this transfer of interest.

§ **54:2. ESSENTIAL ELEMENTS.** The following elements are necessary in the establishment of the relation of landlord and tenant:

(1) The occupying of the land must be with the express or implied consent of the landlord.

(2) The tenant must occupy the premises in subordination to the rights of the landlord.

(3) A reversionary interest in the land must remain in the landlord. That is, the landlord must be entitled to retake the possession of the land upon the expiration of the lease.

(4) The tenant must have an estate of present possession in the land. This means that he must have a right that entitles him to be in possession of the land now.

A lease may be a lease and nothing more. In contrast, a lease may be a part of a broader relationship or course of dealings, in which case the legal rights and duties of the parties are to be determined by the entire pattern of relationships and not merely the particular segment which is called a lease. Consequently, when a franchisor oil company leases a gas station to a franchisee, the relationship is not the traditional landlord-tenant relationship but "is essentially a form of commercial venture."[1]

---

[1] Shell Oil Co. v Marinello, 120 NJSuper 357, 294 A2d 253.

§ 54:3. CLASSIFICATION OF TENANCIES.

(a) Tenancy for years. A *tenancy for years* is one under which the tenant has an estate of definite duration. The term "for years" is used to describe such a tenancy even though the duration of the tenancy is for only one year or for less than a year.

(b) Tenancy from year to year. A *tenancy from year to year* is one under which a tenant, holding an estate in land for an indefinite period of duration, pays an annual, monthly, or weekly rent. A distinguishing feature of this tenancy is the fact that it does not terminate at the end of a year, month, or week except upon proper notice.

In almost all states a tenancy from year to year is implied if the tenant holds over after a tenancy for years with the consent of the landlord, as shown by his express statement or by conduct such as continuing to accept rent.[2] The lease will frequently state that a holding over shall give rise to a tenancy from year to year unless written notice to the contrary be given, or will expressly provide for an extension or renewal of the lease.

(c) Tenancy at will. When land is held for an indefinite period, which may be terminated at any time by the landlord, or by the landlord and the tenant acting together, a *tenancy at will* exists. A person who enters into possession of land for an indefinite period with the owner's permission but without any reservation of rent is a tenant at will. An agreement that a person can move into an empty house and live there until he finds a home to buy creates a tenancy at will.

Statutes in some states and decisions in others require advance notice of termination of this type of tenancy.

(d) Tenancy by sufferance. When a tenant holds over without permission of the landlord, the latter may treat him as a trespasser or as a tenant. Until the landlord elects to do one or the other, a *tenancy by sufferance* exists.

§ 54:4. ANTIDISCRIMINATION. Statutes in many states prohibit an owner who rents his property for profit from discriminating against prospective tenants on the basis of race, color, religion, or national origin. Enforcement of such statutes is generally entrusted to an administrative agency.

§ 54:5. CREATION OF THE LEASE RELATIONSHIP. The relationship of landlord and tenant is created by an express or implied contract. An oral lease is valid at common law, but statutes in most states require written

---

[2] In some jurisdictions, when rent is accepted from a tenant holding over after the expiration of the term of the lease and there is no agreement to the contrary, there results only a periodic tenancy from month to month rather than a tenancy from year to year. Bay West Realty Co. v Christy (NY CivCt) 61 Misc2d 891, 310 NYS2d 348.

leases for certain tenancies. Many statutes follow the English Statute of Frauds, by providing that a lease for a term exceeding three years must be in writing. Statutes in other states require written leases when the term exceeds one year.

§ 54:6. COVENANTS AND CONDITIONS.

Some obligations of the parties in the lease are described as covenants. Thus, a promise by the tenant to make repairs is called a *covenant to repair.* Sometimes it is provided that the lease shall be forfeited or terminated upon a breach of a promise, and that provision is then called a *condition* rather than a covenant.

§ 54:7. TERMINATION OF LEASE.

A lease is generally not terminated by the death, insanity, or bankruptcy of either party, except in the case of a tenancy at will. Provisions in a lease giving the landlord the right to terminate the lease under certain conditions are generally strictly construed against him.

When the landlord has the right to terminate the lease upon giving notice to the tenant, it is ordinarily immaterial what his motive is for so doing.

In an ordinary lease between private persons, each party has unlimited freedom to terminate the lease in accordance with its terms and to refuse to renew the lease. In the case of government-controlled housing, the tenant has a right to a hearing on the question of whether his lease should be renewed. Laws adopted to regulate housing, to impose rent controls, or to prevent discrimination may restrict the landlord in exercising his power to terminate leases.

Leases may be terminated in the following ways:

(a) **Expiration of term in a tenancy for years.** When a tenancy for years exists, the relation of landlord and tenant ceases upon the expiration of the agreed term, without any requirement that one party give the other any notice of termination. Express notice to end the term may be required of either or both parties by provisions in the lease, except when a statute prohibits imposing such a requirement.

(b) **Notice in a tenancy from year to year.** In the absence of an agreement of the parties, notice is now usually governed by statutes. Thirty or sixty days' notice is generally required to end a tenancy from year to year. As to tenancies for periods of less than a year, the provisions of the statute may require only one week.

(c) **Release.** The relation of landlord and tenant is terminated if the landlord makes a release or conveyance of his interest in the land to the tenant. A tenant may at any time purchase the rented property if the landlord and the tenant agree. In addition, the lease may give the tenant the option of purchasing at a stated time or at a stated price.

An option clause that gives the tenant the right to require the landlord to sell the property to him is to be distinguished from a preemption or "first offering" clause, under which the tenant cannot require the landlord to sell, but the landlord, should he decide to sell the property, must give the tenant the first chance to buy it.

(d) Merger. If the tenant acquires the landlord's interest in any manner, as by inheritance or purchase, the leasehold interest is said to disappear by merger into the title to the land now held by the former tenant. The result is the same if the tenant has an estate for years and inherits a life estate in the same premises.

(e) Surrender. A surrender or giving up by the tenant of his estate to the landlord terminates the tenancy if the surrender is accepted by the latter. A surrender may be made expressly or impliedly.

An express surrender must, under the statute of frauds, be in writing and signed by the person making the surrender or by his authorized agent.

A surrender by operation of law occurs only when the acts of the parties clearly show that both consider that the premises have been surrendered, as when the premises have been abandoned by the tenant and their return has been accepted by the landlord. An acceptance may be inferred from the conduct of the landlord, but such conduct must clearly indicate an intention to accept.

(f) Forfeiture. The landlord may terminate the tenancy by forfeiting the relation because of the tenant's misconduct or breach of a condition, if a term of the lease or a statute so provides. In the absence of such a provision the landlord may only make a claim for damages. Terminating the relationship by forfeiture is not favored by courts.

(g) Destruction of property. If a lot and the building on it are leased, either an express provision in the lease or a statute generally releases the tenant from his liability when the building is destroyed, or reduces the amount of rent in proportion to the loss sustained. Such statutes do not impose upon the landlord any duty to repair or restore the property to its former condition.

When the lease covers rooms or an apartment in a building, a destruction of the leased premises terminates the lease.

(h) Fraud. Since a lease is based on a contract, a lease may be avoided when circumstances are such that a contract may be avoided for fraud.

(i) Transfer of the tenant. Residential leases commonly contain a provision for termination upon the tenant's being transferred by his employer to another city or the tenant's being called into military service. Since such provisions are often strictly construed against the tenant, he should exercise care to see that the provision is sufficiently broad to cover the situations that may arise.

When the parties specify a particular condition subsequent which will terminate the lease, the occurrence of a different event has no effect.

FACTS: A tenant executed a lease which recited: "It is further agreed that the Lessee is a member of the Peace Corps and is subject to transfer; in the event of such transfer from the city, Lessee shall be released from the agreement by delivering to Lessor written orders of said transfer along with a 30-day notice to vacate. . . ." Some time later, the tenant was assigned to the A.I.D., a government agency distinct from the Peace Corps, and was transferred to India. Was the tenant released from the lease?

DECISION: No. The tenant was not transferred as a member of the Peace Corps but took employment with a different government agency. The tenant's going to India therefore did not come within the termination clause of the lease. [Satin v Buckley (DistColApp) 246 A2d 778]

§ 54:8. NOTICE OF TERMINATION.

When notice of termination is required, no particular words are necessary to constitute a sufficient notice, provided the words used clearly indicate the intention of the party. The notice, whether given by the landlord or the tenant, must be definite. For example, when the tenant merely stated that he "guessed he would have to give up the house," there was insufficient notice. Statutes sometimes require that the notice be in writing. In the absence of such a provision, however, oral notice is generally held to be sufficient.

FACTS: The Bhar Realty Corp. rented an apartment to Becker on a month-to-month lease. Later the corporation gave Becker written notice that the "monthly tenancy is hereby terminated" as of a certain date and that the tenant could renew the tenancy by paying a specified increased rental from that date on. Becker claimed that the notice did not terminate the lease because there was no demand for possession of the property.

DECISION: Judgment for Realty Corp. A notice to terminate a lease need only state that it is terminated as of a specific date. It need not demand possession of the premises but may offer the making of a new lease on different terms, as was done. [Bhar Realty Corp. v Becker, 49 NJSuper 585, 140 A2d 756]

The parties may agree to a specific method of giving notice.Thus, they may agree that the sending of a notice by registered or certified mail shall constitute sufficient notice. In such a case a notice mailed within the proper time is sufficient even though the notice is not received until after the period for giving notice has expired.[3]

Tenants in government housing projects who pay the required rental may generally remain in possession indefinitely. When a notice to terminate is necessary, the mere fact that the tenant knows that the landlord wants him to leave does not take the place of a notice. Under some statutes it is held that the notice by which the landlord seeks to terminate a lease must expressly declare that he terminates the lease and that it is not sufficient to direct the tenant to "remove from the apartment you occupy."

When the landlord had the right to terminate the lease by giving notice to the tenant, it was immaterial at common law what his motive was for so doing. Consequently, when the landlord had the right to terminate upon

---

[3] Trust Co. v Shea, 3 IllApp2d 368, 122 NE2d 292.

notice, it was immaterial that he may have been motivated by the desire to retaliate against the tenant for having made justified complaints as to the condition of the premises to the appropriate housing authority.

By modern cases such "retaliatory eviction" is prohibited. There is likewise authority that a franchisor cannot exercise a power to terminate a lease without cause when this would evade a franchisee-protection statute which prohibits the termination of franchises except upon cause.

§ 54:9. **RENEWAL OF LEASE.** When a lease terminates for any reason, it is ordinarily a matter for the landlord and the tenant to enter into a new agreement if they wish to extend or renew the lease. The power to renew the lease may be stated negatively by declaring that the lease runs indefinitely, as from year to year, subject to being terminated by either party by his giving written notice a specified number of days or months before the proposed date. If it is not clear whether a renewal provision gives the tenant only the right to renew for one term of the lease or whether it gives him the right to renew indefinitely for an unlimited number of times, the law will interpret the lease strictly as permitting only one additional term.

> **FACTS:** In June, 1966, Forester leased an apartment to Kilbourne for one year. The lease stated "The lease is renewable at the end of the year period." Kilbourne renewed the lease for the year 1967-1968. She again gave notice of renewal for the year 1968-1969 but Forester refused to recognize such renewal and brought an action to recover possession of the premises.

> **DECISION:** Judgment for Forester. The statement that the lease was renewable at the end of the year period meant exactly that. Hence, it could only be renewed once at the termination of the original term and could not be renewed a second or subsequent time. [Kilbourne v Forester (MoApp) 464 SW2d 770]

When the landlord is a state or local government, as in the case of the low-cost housing project, the landlord cannot refuse to renew the lease for a reason that would constitute a discrimination prohibited by the federal Constitution. This concept also applies when the landlord obtains financing from government funds. Likewise, a private landlord could not refuse to renew a lease in retaliation for a tenant's exercise of rights guaranteed by the First Amendment of the federal Constitution, when the landlord had acquired the property by purchase from a municipal housing authority and had entered into a detailed agreement with the authority as to the standards to be observed by the landlord.

In some instances the option will expressly state that the rental to be paid under the renewal term is to be negotiated. By the common law this destroyed the option because it was not definite. By the modern view the option is binding, obligating the tenant to pay and obligating the lessor to accept what would be a reasonable rental value of the premises when used for the purpose for which the tenant has leased them.

§ 54:10. **PURCHASE BY TENANT.** A lease of an entire building frequently gives the tenant the option to purchase the building either at a price specified in the lease or at the appraised value of the property at the time of the exercise of the option.

B. RIGHTS AND DUTIES OF THE PARTIES

§ 54:11. **POSSESSION.** Possession involves both the right to acquire possession at the beginning of the lease and the right to retain possession until the lease is ended. The modern lease commonly provides that if the lessor is late in making the premises available to the tenant, the commencement of the lease shall be postponed until the lessor notifies the tenant that occupancy is ready and the lease then runs for its original term. Such a provision is particularly attractive to the lessor when the rented premises is an apartment in a new building which is under construction at the time the lease is executed. In this way the lessor protects himself from losing his tenants when there is a construction delay.

Such a provision may be held not binding because it is unconscionable where its effect is not explained to the tenant and the provision is lost in a maze of fine print and technical terms.

(a) **Tenant's right to acquire possession.** By making a lease, the lessor impliedly covenants that he will give possession of the premises to the tenant at the agreed time. If the landlord rents a building which is being constructed, there is an implied covenant that it will be ready for occupancy at the commencement of the term of the lease.

(b) **Tenant's right to retain possession.** After the tenant has entered into possession, he has exclusive possession and control of the premises as long as the lease continues and so long as he is not in default under the lease, unless the lease otherwise provides. Thus, the tenant can refuse to allow the lessor to enter the property for the purpose of showing it to prospective customers, although today many leases expressly give this right to the landlord.

If the landlord interferes with this possession by evicting the tenant, he commits a wrong for which the tenant is afforded legal redress. An *eviction* exists when the tenant is deprived of the possession, use, and enjoyment of the premises by the interference of the lessor or one acting under him. If the landlord wrongfully deprives the tenant of the use of one room when he is entitled to the use of the whole building, there is a *partial eviction*.

(c) **Covenant for quiet enjoyment.** Most written leases today contain an express promise by the landlord to respect the possession of the tenant, called a *covenant for quiet enjoyment*. Such a provision protects the tenant from interference with his possession by the landlord, but it does not impose liability upon the landlord for the unlawful acts of third persons. Thus, such a covenant does not require the landlord to protect a tenant from damage by a rioting mob.

(d) **Constructive eviction.** An eviction may be actual or constructive. It is a *constructive eviction* when some act or omission of the landlord substantially deprives the tenant of the use and enjoyment of the premises.

It is essential in a constructive eviction that the landlord intended to deprive the tenant of the use and enjoyment of the premises. This intent may, however, be inferred from the results of his conduct. A tenant cannot claim that he has been constructively evicted by a particular condition unless he in fact has abandoned the occupancy of the premises because of that condition. If he continues to occupy the premises for more than a reasonable time after the acts claimed to constitute a constructive eviction, he is deemed to waive the eviction. He cannot thereafter abandon the premises and claim that he has been evicted.

> **FACTS:** Barash rented an office in a building owned by the Pennsylvania Terminal Real Estate Corporation. The building was completely sealed and depended upon air conditioning for ventilation. Barash claimed that the corporation failed to supply proper ventilation of his office after regular working hours. The corporation denied that it had undertaken to supply such ventilation. Barash did not move out of the office but brought an action against the corporation to establish that he was not required to pay the rent because of the failure to supply ventilation.

> **DECISION:** Judgment for Pennsylvania Terminal Real Estate Corporation. Barash was obligated to pay the rent because a tenant who stays in possession of the premises must pay the rent. Barash had not been evicted by the landlord. Even assuming that the failure to supply ventilation constituted a breach by the landlord, Barash could not claim that he was "constructively evicted" since he did not leave but remained in possession. [Barash v Pennsylvania Terminal Real Estate Corporation, 26 NY2d 77, 308 NYS2d 649, 256 NE2d 707]

A landlord commits a constructive eviction when he intentionally drives the tenant out of the property by shutting off the heat, gas, or water supply, or keeps him from entering the property by refusing to operate the elevators.

(e) Retaliatory eviction. A landlord may not evict a tenant or refuse to renew a lease in order to retaliate against the tenant because the tenant has exercised his statutory or constitutional rights.

§ **54:12. USE OF PREMISES.** The lease generally specifies the use to which the tenant may put the property and authorizes the landlord to adopt regulations with respect to the use of the premises that are binding upon the tenant as long as they are reasonable, lawful, and not in conflict with the terms of the lease. In the absence of express or implied restrictions, a tenant is entitled to use the premises for any purpose for which they are adapted or for which they are ordinarily employed, or in a manner contemplated by the parties in executing the lease. He is under an implied duty to use the premises properly even when the lease is silent as to the matter. What constitutes proper use of the premises depends, in the first place, upon the wording of the lease and, secondly, upon the nature of the property.

The tenant is under an implied duty to refrain from willful or permissive waste. At common law the tenant of farm land is entitled to cut sufficient timber for fuel and for repairs to fences, buildings, and farm implements. This rule is extended in many jurisdictions to allow the tenant to clear timber to a reasonable degree so that he may put the land under cultivation. If this would involve any substantial area, it is likely that the lease would define the rights of the parties in this respect.

Ordinarily a landlord is not responsible for the nature of the use to which the tenants put the property. However, if the landlord knows that the tenant will use the premises unlawfully, as for the purpose of running a gambling operation, the landlord may be subject to criminal prosecution.

(a) Change of use. The modern lease will in substance make a change of use a condition subsequent so that if the tenant uses the property for any purpose other than the one specified, the landlord has the option of declaring the lease terminated.

Other clauses of the lease frequently restrict the tenant in making a change of use. For example, if alterations to the building would be required for the new use, the tenant would ordinarily find that a clause of the lease required permission of the landlord to make alterations, with the consequence that the tenant might be unable to make the alterations necessary for a different use.

In general, courts are inclined to permit the tenant to make any use of the premises that is otherwise lawful and not prohibited by the lease and which can be made without any damage to or alteration of the premises.

(b) Continued use of property. With the increased danger of damage to the premises by vandalism or fire when the building is vacant and because of the common insurance provision making a fire insurance policy void when a vacancy continues for a specified time, the modern lease will ordinarily require the tenant to give the landlord notice of nonuse or vacancy of the premises. Likewise, in many situations, it is important to the landlord that the tenant operate a particular business. For example, when the landlord operated a truck stop station and rented an adjacent diner to a tenant, the operation of the diner during reasonable hours was an essential part of the transaction. Hence, there may be a duty on the tenant to make use of the premises as a counterpart of his right to possession.

(c) Rules. The modern lease generally contains a blanket agreement by the tenant to abide by the provisions of rules and regulations adopted by the landlord. These rules are generally binding on the tenant whether they exist at the time the lease was made or were thereafter adopted. As an exception, a rule adopted by the landlord is void when it restrains trade, as when it prohibits delivery of milk to the tenants by any truck unless the landlord gives permission to make deliveries. Moreover, a provision in a lease relating to rules will generally be strictly construed so as to favor the tenant.

(d) Restriction of animals. A restriction in a lease prohibiting the keeping of animals for pets is valid.

§ **54:13. RENT.** The tenant is under a duty to pay rent as compensation to the landlord. In times of emergency, war, and recovery from war, however, government may impose maximum limitations on rents that are charged.

When a business is conducted on the leased premises, it is quite common to provide for both a basc rent and an additional rent that is computed as a percentage of the sales made by the tenant. The lease may provide for the payment of additional rent when the tenant's profits exceed a specified minimum, in which case there is no liability for additional rent until the minimum is exceeded.

The time of payment of rent is ordinarily fixed by the lease. When the lease does not control, rent generally is not due until the end of the term. Statutes or custom, however, may require rent to be paid in advance when the agreement of the parties does not regulate the point. Rent that is payable in crops is generally payable at the end of the term.

If the lease is assigned, the assignee is liable to the landlord for the rent. The assignment, however, does not in itself discharge the tenant from his obligations under the lease. The landlord may bring an action for the rent against either the tenant or the assignee, or both, but he is entitled to only one satisfaction. A sublessee ordinarily is not liable to the original lessor for rent, unless he assumes such liability or unless the liability is imposed by statute.

§ 54:14. REPAIRS AND CONDITION OF PREMISES.
In the absence of an agreement to the contrary, the tenant has the duty to make those repairs that are necessary to prevent waste and decay of the premises, and he is liable for *permissive waste* if he fails to do so. When the landlord leases only a portion of the premises, or leases the premises to different tenants, he is under a duty to make repairs in connecting parts, such as halls, basements, elevators, and stairways, which are under his control. Some statutes require that a landlord who leases a building for dwelling purposes must keep it in condition fit for habitation. In some states, a warranty is implied as to the fitness of residential premises whether furnished or unfurnished.

When an apartment in a multiple unit apartment complex is rented, there is an implied warranty of habitability.

By the modern view that there is an implied warranty of habitability, a tenant can claim damages for the breach of this warranty and offset them against the landlord's claim for rent, with the result that if the damages exceed the rent, no rent is due and therefore the landlord cannot obtain repossession of the premises for nonpayment of rent. By the modern view, the obligations of landlord and residential tenant are regarded as mutually dependent, with the result that the tenant may deduct from the rent due an amount equal to the loss in value of the rented premises caused by a defect.[4]

It may be noted that the above rule, in effect, puts the tenant in the same position as the buyer from a merchant-seller under the Uniform Commercial Code. While the modern rule is stated in terms of residential leases, it can be expected that this is merely an opening wedge and that eventually the modern rule will be applied to all leases.

Some courts have given such recognition to the implied warranty of habitability as to permit the tenant to set off against the landlord's claim for

---

[4] Boston Housing Authority v Hemingway (Mass) 293 NE2d 831 (a Massachusetts statute authorized the tenant to pay the rent into court so that it could be used for repairs).

rent the damages of the tenant for nonhabitability even though the lease expressly declares that the tenant will not assert any setoff or counterclaim in any action brought against him by the lessor.

Most states deny the landlord the right to enter the leased premises to inspect them for waste and need of repairs except when the right is expressly reserved in the lease. It is customary for leases of apartments and commercial property to reserve to the landlord the right to enter to inspect the premises and to make repairs. When the landlord makes repairs by special permission of the tenant or under such a reserved power, he must exercise the care which a reasonable person would exercise to make the repairs in a proper manner but he is not automatically liable as an insurer if the tenant is injured after the landlord has made the repairs.

Various laws protect tenants, as by requiring landlords to observe specified safety, health, and fire prevention standards.

In order to protect tenants from unsound living conditions, it is constitutional for a statute to provide that the tenant is not required to pay the rent as long as the premises are not fit to live in.

FACTS: A New York statute provided that the rent owed by any tenant receiving welfare funds should "abate" if there was a "violation of law . . . dangerous, hazardous, or detrimental to life or health." Drew and two others, who were tenants of Farrell, received welfare funds. When Farrell brought an action to evict them for nonpayment of rent, they claimed that they were not required to pay rent because there was a dangerous and hazardous condition in the building rendering it unsafe for occupants. Farrell claimed the statute was unconstitutional.

DECISION: The statute was constitutional. A rent abatement plan is a valid means of protecting tenants from unsound housing conditions. The fact that the statute only applied to tenants who received welfare funds did not make the statute unconstitutional. The legislature could well conclude that that class of tenants were in particular need of protection from exploitation. [Farrell v Drew, 19 NY2d 486, 281 NYS2d 1, 227 NE2d 824]

As a compromise, some states require that the tenant continue to pay the rent but authorize him to pay it into an escrow or agency account from which it is paid to the landlord on proof that he has made necessary repairs to the premises.

Leases commonly require the tenant to obey local ordinances and laws relating to the care and use of the premises. If compliance with a law requires the making of repairs, such a provision imposes upon the tenant the duty to make the repairs necessary to comply with the law.

§ 54:15. IMPROVEMENTS. In the absence of special agreement, neither the tenant nor the landlord is under a duty to make improvements, as contrasted with repairs. Either party may, however, make a covenant for improvements, in which case a failure to perform will render him liable in an action for damages for breach of contract brought by the other party. In the absence of an agreement to the contrary, improvements that are attached to the land become part of the realty and belong to the landlord.

When the tenant has the right to remove trade fixtures, he must usually exercise the right of removal within the term of the lease, in the absence of a contrary provision in the lease. Some courts allow the tenant a reasonable time after the expiration of the lease in which to make such removal or allow the tenant to make the removal after the expiration of the lease but before the premises have been surrendered to the landlord.

§ **54:16. TAXES AND ASSESSMENTS.** In the absence of an agreement to the contrary, the landlord and not the tenant is usually under a duty to pay taxes or assessments. If the tax or assessment, however, is chargeable to improvements made by the tenant that do not become a part of the property, the tenant is liable.

If the tenant pays taxes or assessments to protect his interest, he may recover the amount, including damages, from the landlord, or withhold the amount from the rent.

When the premises are assigned by the tenant, the assignee is bound by any covenants of the tenant to pay taxes and assessments. Such covenants are said to "run with the land." The fact that the assignee is bound by the covenants does not, however, discharge the tenant from liability.

A sublessee is not bound by the covenants of the tenant, but he may expressly assume them. In the latter case, however, the tenant is not discharged from his covenants.

§ **54:17. TENANT'S DEPOSIT.**

(a) Custody. In some states protection is given the tenant who is required to make a payment to the landlord as a "deposit" to insure compliance by the tenant with the terms of the lease. It is sometimes provided that the landlord hold such a payment as a trust fund, that he must inform the tenant of any bank in which the money is deposited, and that he is subject to a penalty if he uses the money as his own before the tenant has breached the lease.

(b) Refund. A landlord may require a tenant to make a deposit to protect the landlord from any default on the part of the tenant. Once paid by the tenant, it frequently happens that the landlord will keep the entire deposit, even though it is in excess of any claim against the tenant, and tenants will not bring suit because the amount involved is too small to justify an action. Tenant protection statutes sometimes remedy this situation by requiring the landlord to refund any part of the deposit in excess of the amount actually needed to compensate him. Under such a statute, it is immaterial that the tenant had agreed that the deposit was nonrefundable.

When such a provision is combined with authorization to bring a class action on behalf of a group of tenants, it becomes economically feasible to bring a lawsuit against the landlord provided there is a significant number of tenants of the same landlord who have the same complaint of deposit withholding. If there are not a sufficient number of tenants involved, the practical aspects of litigation will generally bar any action by the tenants.

§ 54:18. REMEDIES OF LANDLORD.

(a) Landlord's lien. In the absence of an agreement or statute so providing, the landlord does not have a lien upon the personal property or crops of the tenant for money due him for rent. The parties may create by express or implied contract, however, a lien in favor of the landlord for rent, and also for advances, taxes, or damages for failure to make repairs.

In the absence of a statutory provision, the lien of the landlord is superior to the claims of all other persons, except prior lienors and bona fide purchasers without notice.

(b) Suit for rent. Whether or not the landlord has a lien for unpaid rent, he may sue the tenant on the latter's contract to pay rent as specified in the lease or, if payment of rent is not specified, he may enforce a quasi-contractual obligation to pay the reasonable value of the occupation and use of the property. In some jurisdictions the landlord is permitted to bring a combined action in which he recovers the possession of the land and the overdue rent at the same time.

(c) Distress. The common law devised a speedy remedy to aid the landlord in collecting his rent. It permitted him to seize personal property found on the premises and to hold it until the arrears were paid. The right was known as *distress*. It was not an action against the tenant for rent but merely a right to retain the property as security until the rent was paid. Statutes have generally either abolished or greatly modified the right of distress.[5]

(d) Recovery of possession. The lease commonly provides that upon the breach of any of its provisions by the tenant, such as the failure to pay rent, the lease shall terminate or the landlord may, at his option, declare it terminated. When the lease is terminated for any reason, the landlord then has the right to evict the tenant and retake possession of the property.

At common law the landlord, when entitled to possession, may regain it without resorting to legal proceedings. This *right of reentry* is available in many states even when the employment of force is necessary. Other states deny the right to use force.

Modern cases hold that a landlord cannot lock out a tenant for overdue rent and must employ legal process to regain possession even though the lease expressly gives the landlord the right to self-help.

A state statute permitting a landlord to lock out a tenant and hold his property for nonpayment of rent is unconstitutional as a denial of due process when the landlord may so act without any prior notice to the tenant nor judicial hearing, and the statute is not cured by the fact that the tenant

---

[5] There is authority that the due process clause of the United States Constitution requires that a hearing be held to determine whether the tenant is in default even though a state statute authorizes the sale of distrained property without a hearing. Santiago v McElroy (DC ED Pa) 319 FSupp 284; Dielen v Levine (DC Neb) 344 FSupp 823.

A Uniform Residential Landlord and Tenant Act has been adopted in Alaska, Arizona, Florida, Hawaii, Kentucky, Nebraska, Oregon, and Virginia.

can obtain his property by filing a bond for double the amount of the landlord's claim.

The landlord may resort to legal process to evict the tenant in order to enforce his right to possession of the premises. The action of ejectment is ordinarily used. In addition to common-law remedies, statutes in many states provide a summary remedy to recover possession that is much more efficient than the slow common-law remedies. Unless expressly stated, a statutory remedy does not replace those of the common law, but is merely cumulative. In many states today the landlord brings an action of trespass or a civil action to recover possession.

C. LIABILITY FOR INJURY ON PREMISES

§ 54:19. LANDLORD'S LIABILITY TO TENANT. When the tenant, a member of his family, or a third person is injured by a condition of the premises, the question arises as to who is liable for the damages sustained by the injured person. In the absence of a covenant to keep the premises in repair, the landlord is ordinarily not liable to the tenant for the latter's personal injuries caused by the defective condition of the premises that are placed under the control of the tenant by the lease. Likewise, the landlord is not liable for the harm caused by an obvious condition that was known to the tenant at the time the lease was made. For example, he is not liable for the fatal burning of a tenant whose clothing was set on fire by an open-faced radiant gas heater.

FACTS: The Golf Club Co. owned an apartment house and leased one of the apartments to Rothstein. In back of the apartment house was a grassy area which dropped off into a ravine. There was no protecting fence or other barrier to prevent someone from falling into the ravine. While playing on the grassy area, Rothstein's child fell down the ravine and was injured. Rothstein sued the Golf Club Co.

DECISION: Judgment for Golf Club Co. The condition of the grassy plot and the unguarded ravine were obvious to everyone when Rothstein rented his apartment, and the landlord was not liable for harm resulting from an obvious condition. [Golf Club Co. v H. I. Rothstein, 97 GaApp128, 102 SE2d 654]

The landlord is liable to the tenant for injuries caused by latent or nonapparent defects of which the landlord had knowledge.

When the landlord retains control of part of his building or land that is rented to others, he is liable to a tenant who is injured because of the defective condition of such retained portion if the condition was the result of the landlord's failure to exercise the proper degree of care.

In a number of states, by decision or statute, a landlord is liable to a tenant or a child or guest of the tenant where there is a defect which makes the premises dangerously defective, even though the landlord did not have any knowledge of the defect. By this view, a tenant's guest who sat on a railing which collapsed may recover for strict tort liability. Other states refuse to apply the strict tort liability concept and the landlord is then not liable for harm caused by a latent defect which could not have been reasonably discovered by him.

(a) Crimes of third persons. Ordinarily the landlord is not liable to the tenant for crimes committed on the premises by third persons, as when a third person enters the premises and commits larceny or murder. The landlord is not required to establish any security system to protect the tenant from crimes of third persons. Housing regulations apply only to the physical characteristics and use of the premises. They do not impose any duty on the landlord to maintain a security system to protect tenants from unlawful acts of third persons. When a landlord does not maintain the security system that existed when the lease was entered into, however, he may be liable for the harm sustained by the tenant by the illegal acts of third persons whose misconduct was foreseeable.

Thus, the landlord of a large apartment complex had the duty of taking reasonable steps to protect against the entry of third persons onto the premises and the commission of crimes by them when such crimes were being repeatedly committed and the landlord had eliminated a doorman and a garage attendant who had performed security duties when the tenant first moved into the apartment building.

(b) Limitation of liability. A provision in a lease excusing or exonerating the landlord from liability is generally valid, regardless of the cause of the tenant's loss. A number of courts, however, have restricted the landlord's power to limit his liability in the case of residential, as distinguished from commercial, leasing; so that a provision in a residential lease that the landlord shall not be liable for damage caused by water, snow, or ice is void. A modern trend holds that clauses limiting liability of the landlord are void with respect to harm caused by the negligence of the landlord when the tenant is a residential tenant generally or is a tenant in a government low-cost housing project.

FACTS: Crowell rented an apartment from the Housing Authority of the City of Dallas. The gas heater in the apartment was defective and carbon monoxide from the heater killed Crowell. His son, Lewis, sued the Housing Authority under the Texas Survival Statute to recover medical expenses and damages for the pain and suffering of his father. The Housing Authority raised the defense that the lease expressly declared that the Authority would not be liable for any damages. The lease expressly stated that the landlord shall not "be liable for any damage to person or property of the tenant, his family, or his visitors which might result from the condition of these or other premises of the landlord, from theft or from any cause whatsoever."

DECISION: The exculpation clause was not binding because it was contrary to public policy to permit one party to a contract to compel a party who was his bargaining inferior to agree to such a provision. The clause therefore did not bar the action for the father's death. [Crowell v Housing Authority (Tex) 495 SW2d 887]

Third persons on the premises, even though with the consent of the tenant, are generally not bound by such a clause and may therefore sue the landlord when they sustain injuries. Thus, it has been held that members of the tenant's family, employees, and guests, are not bound where they do not sign the lease, although there is authority to the contrary.

(c) Indemnification of landlord. The modern lease commonly contains a provision declaring that the tenant will indemnify the landlord for any liability of the landlord to a third person which arises in connection with the rented premises. These provisions will generally be worded so broadly that the tenant must indemnify the landlord even when the harm to the third person was caused by the negligence or fault of the landlord. Such indemnity clauses are valid although some states have adopted statutes declaring them invalid with respect to harm caused by the landlord's fault.

§ 54:20. LANDLORD'S LIABILITY TO THIRD PERSONS. The landlord is ordinarily not liable to third persons injured because of the condition of the premises when the landlord is not in possession of the premises. If the landlord retains control over a portion of the premises, such as hallways or stairways, however, he is liable for injuries to third persons caused by his failure to exercise proper care in connection with that part of the premises. The modern trend of cases imposes liability on the landlord when a third person is harmed by a condition that the landlord had contracted with the tenant to correct.

§ 54:21. TENANT'S LIABILITY TO THIRD PERSONS. A tenant in complete possession has control of the property and is therefore liable when his failure to use due care under the circumstances causes harm to (a) licensees, such as a person allowed to use his telephone, and (b) invitees, such as a customers entering his store. With respect to both classes, the liability of the tenant is the same as an owner in possession of his property. It is likewise immaterial whether the property is used for residential or business purposes, provided the tenant has control of the area where the injury occurs.

The liability of the tenant to third persons is not affected by the fact that the landlord may have contracted in the lease to make repairs which, if made, would have avoided the injury. The tenant can protect himself, however, in the same manner that the landlord can, by procuring public liability insurance to indemnify him for loss from claims of third persons.

Both the landlord and the tenant may be liable to third persons for harm caused by the condition of the leased premises. For example, if the landlord maintains unhealthy or dangerous conditions amounting to a nuisance and then leases the property to a tenant who continues the nuisance, both parties may be liable, the one for creating and the other for maintaining the nuisance. In some states no liability is imposed upon a tenant in such circumstances unless the person injured by the nuisance first requests the tenant to stop or abate the nuisance and the tenant refuses to do so.

D. TRANSFER OF RIGHTS

§ 54:22. TRANSFER OF LANDLORD'S REVERSIONARY INTEREST.
The reversionary interest of the landlord may be transferred voluntarily by
his act, or involuntarily by a judicial or execution sale. The tenant then
becomes the tenant of the new owner of the reversionary interest, and the
new owner is bound by the terms of the lease.

When the landlord assigns his reversion, the assignee is, in the absence
of an agreement to the contrary, entitled to subsequent accruals of rent. The
rent may, however, be reserved in an assignment of a reversion. The
landlord also has the right to assign the lease independent of the reversion,
or to assign the rent independent of the lease.

When the lessor transfers his reversionary interests, his transferee, the
new landlord, becomes bound by the obligations specified in the lease, such
as a covenant to repair. He is not liable, however, for damages for the prior
breach of any such covenants committed by the former landlord unless he
has expressly assumed liability for them.

§ 54:23. TENANT'S ASSIGNMENT OF LEASE AND SUBLEASE. An
assignment of a lease is a transfer by the tenant of his entire interest in the
premises to a third person. A tenancy for years may be assigned by the
tenant unless he is restricted from doing so by the terms of the lease or by
statute. A *sublease* is a transfer of any part of the premises by the tenant to a
third person, the *sublessee*, for a period less than the term of the lease.

Whether the transaction between the tenant and a third person is a
sublease or an assignment is determined by the effect of the transaction. If
the entire interest of the tenant is transferred to the third person, the
transaction is an assignment of the lease, without regard to whether the
parties have described the transaction as a sublease or an assignment. In
contrast, it there is some interest left over after the interest of the third
person expires, the relationship is a sublease.

(a) Limitations on rights. The lease may contain provisions denying the
right to assign or sublet or imposing specified restrictions on the privilege of
assigning or subletting. Such restrictions are enforceable in order to enable
the landlord to protect himself from tenants who would damage the
property or be financially irresponsible.

Restrictions in the lease are construed liberally in favor of the tenant. An
ineffectual attempt to assign or sublet does not violate a provision
prohibiting such acts. This is equally true when the tenant merely permits
someone else to use the land.

As a provision restricting the right of the tenant to assign the lease or
requiring the landlord's written consent thereto is for the benefit of the
landlord, it may be waived by him.

FACTS: Scheinfeld, doing business as Greenleaf Investors, leased a warehouse to Muntz TV, Inc. Thereafter, with Greenleaf's written consent, Muntz sublet the warehouse to Breuer Electric Manufacturing Co. Breuer later decided to sublet to Calument Manufacturing Co., but Greenleaf refused to consent thereto. Breuer vacated the premises. Scheinfeld then proceeded against Muntz TV for the full rent. Muntz TV claimed that it was only liable for the difference between the full rent and the rent that Calument would have paid. Was Muntz liable for the full rent?

DECISION: No. Muntz was only liable for the difference between its rent and the amount that Calument would have paid. The lease was a commercial lease. Therefore the difference between tenants related primarily to financial standing rather than to the way in which the property would be used. Consequently, when a financially sound subtenant was tendered to the landlord, he was under the duty to waive the no-assignment clause and to accept such subtenant. Having failed to do so, he cannot recover from the original tenant the rentals which the subtenant would have paid. [Scheinfeld v Muntz TV, Inc. 67 IllApp2d 8, 214 NE2d 506]

(b) Effect of assignment or sublease. An express covenant or promise by the sublessee is necessary to impose liability upon him. In contrast with the sublease, when the lease is assigned and the assignee takes possession of the property, he becomes bound by the terms of the lease.

Neither the act of subletting nor the landlord's agreement to it releases the original tenant from liability under the terms of the original lease.

When a lease is assigned, the original tenant remains liable for the rent which becomes due thereafter. If the assignee renews or extends the lease by virtue of an option contained therein, the original tenant is likewise liable for the rent for such extended period in the absence of a contrary agreement or novation by which the landlord agreed that the assignee shall be deemed substituted as tenant and the original tenant shall be released from further liability.

It is customary and desirable for the tenant to require the sublesse to covenant or promise that he will perform all obligations under the original lease and that he will indemnify the tenant for any loss caused by default of the sublessee. An express covenant or promise by the sublessee is necessary to impose liability upon him. The fact that the sublease is made "subject" to the terms of the original lease merely recognizes the superiority of the original lease, but does not impose any duty upon the sublessee to perform the tenant's obligations under the original lease. If the sublessee promises the tenant that he will assume the obligation of the original lease, the landlord, as a third-party beneficiary, may sue the sublessee for breach of the provisions of the original lease.

QUESTIONS
AND CASE
PROBLEMS

1. Dawson Enterprises was developing a shopping center. It rented one of the stores to Acme Markets by a lease which gave Acme the right to terminate the lease if Dawson did not make certain improvements by a specified date. The shopping center was a commercial failure, apparently because of the competition of a nearby center, and Dawson could not obtain any other tenants. Because the lease to Acme was outstanding, Dawson was not able to sell the land. Dawson brought an action against Acme to have the lease declared void on the theory that (a) it was not binding because of Acme's option to terminate, and (b) the lease could be avoided because of economic frustration in that it was impossible to develop the shopping center as had been contemplated. Could the lease to Acme be set aside? [Acme Markets v Dawson Enterprises, 253 Md 76, 251 A2d 920]

2. A landlord sued a tenant for possession of the rented premises when the tenant stopped paying rent. The tenant showed that the premises rented to him violated housing regulations and that a penalty had been assessed against the landlord because of such violations. The tenant contended that he was therefore excused from paying the rent. Was this contention correct? [See Saunders v First National Realty Corp. (CA DistCol) 245 A2d 836]

3. Clay, who owned a tract of land, permitted Hartney to occupy a cabin on the land. There was no agreement as to the length of time that it could be occupied, and either could terminate the relationship when he chose. There was no provision for rent. Hartney died. The next day Clay closed up the cabin and put Hartney's possessions outside the door. Paddock, who was appointed the executor under Hartney's will, claimed the right to occupy the cabin. Was he entitled to do so? [Paddock v Clay, 138 Mont 541, 357 P2d 1]

4. Joy White rented an apartment in an apartment house operated by Ridgleawood, Inc. After some discussion, she gave her apartment over to Allan and took a more expensive apartment in the same apartment house. Ridgleawood accepted rent from both White and Allan for the respective apartments. When Allan damaged his apartment, Ridgleawood sued White on the ground she was liable for the conduct of her assignee. Decide. [Ridgleawood, Inc. v White (TexCivApp) 380 SW2d 766]

5. Thompson rented property to Fletcher. Thompson sold the property to Bryan in February. Thereafter Thompson refused to accept Fletcher's offer of rent payments for March and April, but Fletcher did not know that the property had been sold. In April, Bryan declared the lease forfeited for nonpayment of rent. Decide. [Fletcher v Bryan, 76 NMex 221, 413 P2d 885]

6. Spears owned a building. On the first floor he rented space to a dry cleaner and a barber shop. The center door, which was at the top of an open stairway leading down into the basement, gave the appearance of a part of a double door leading into the dry cleaner's. There was no warning sign over the center door, and the door was unlocked. Trimble wanted to enter the dry cleaner's as a customer and by mistake opened the center door. Before she could realize her mistake, she fell down the stairs and was injured. When she sued Spears, he denied liability and further claimed that Trimble was guilty of contributory negligence. Decide. [Trimble v Spears, 182 Kan 406, 320 P2d 1029]

7. Martin leased a building for a 5-year period to a new tenant after making repairs to the building to fit it for the tenant and after having paid approximately $1,000 as commissions to a real estate agent to obtain the tenant. Under the lease the tenant was required to pay the last five months' rent in advance, or approximately $3,000. During the term of the lease the tenant defaulted in the payment of rent and Martin, acting within the terms of the lease, terminated it. Lochner, the receiver who was thereafter appointed for the tenant, sued for the return of the advance rent on the ground that there could be no "rent" due for an unexpired portion of a lease which had been terminated by the landlord and the landlord would be unjustly enriched if he were allowed to retain the advance payment. Decide. [Lochmer v Martin, 218 Md 519, 147 A2d 749]

8. Stockham owned certain real estate. For a consideration, he gave to the Borough Bill Posting Co. the exclusive privilege of erecting and using a signboard to be located on the land for bill posting purposes. He reserved the right, in case the property was sold or required for building purposes, to cancel all privileges upon returning to the company a pro rata amount of the consideration. In an action brought by Stockham against the company, it was contended that a landlord-tenant relationship had been created. Do you agree? [Stockham v Borough Bill Posting Co. 144 AppDiv 642, 129 NYS 745]

9. Catanese leased premises for use as a drug store from Saputa. Catanese moved his store to another location but continued to pay the rent to Saputa. Saputa entered the premises without the permission of Catanese and made extensive alterations to the premises to suit two physicans who had agreed to rent the premises from Saputa. Catanese informed Saputa that he regarded the making of the unauthorized repairs as ground for canceling the lease. Saputa then sued Catanese for the difference between the rent Catanese agreed to pay and the rent the doctors agreed to pay for the remainder of the term of the Catanese lease. Was Catanese liable for such rent? [Saputa v Catanese (La App) 182 So2d 826]

UNIFORM COMMERCIAL CODE

TITLE

AN ACT

To be known as the Uniform Commercial Code, Relating to Certain Commercial Transactions in or regarding Personal Property and Contracts and other Documents concerning them, including Sales, Commercial Paper, Bank Deposits and Collections, Letters of Credit, Bulk Transfers, Warehouse Receipts, Bills of Lading, other Documents of Title, Investment Securities, and Secured Transactions, including certain Sales of Accounts, Chattel Paper, and Contract Rights; Providing for Public Notice to Third Parties in Certain Circumstances; Regulating Procedure, Evidence and Damages in Certain Court Actions Involving such Transactions, Contracts or Documents; to Make Uniform the Law with Respect Thereto; and Repealing Inconsistent Legislation.

ARTICLE 1 / GENERAL PROVISIONS

PART 1 / SHORT TITLE, CONSTRUCTION, APPLICATION AND SUBJECT MATTER OF THE ACT

Section 1—101. Short Title.

This Act shall be known and may be cited as Uniform Commercial Code.

Section 1—102. Purposes; Rules of Construction; Variation by Agreement.

(1) This Act shall be liberally construed and applied to promote its underlying purposes and policies.

(2) Underlying purposes and policies of this act are

    (a) to simplify, clarify and modernize the law governing commercial transactions;

    (b) to permit the continued expansion of commercial practices through custom, usage and agreement of the parties;

    (c) To make uniform the law among the various jurisdictions.

(3) The effect of provisions of this Act may be varied by agreement, except as otherwise provided in this Act and except that the obligations of good faith, diligence, reasonableness and care prescribed by this Act may not be disclaimed by agreement but the parties may by agreement determine the standards by which the performance of such obligations is to be measured if such standards are not manifestly unreasonable.

(4) The presence in certain provisions of this Act of the words "unless otherwise agreed" or words of similar import does not imply that the effect of other provisions may not be varied by agreement under subsection (3).

(5) In this Act unless the context otherwise requires

    (a) words in the singular number include the plural, and in the plural include the singular;

(b) words of the masculine gender include the feminine and the neuter, and when the sense so indicates words of the neuter gender may refer to any gender.

Section 1—103. Supplementary General Principles of Law Applicable.

Unless displaced by the particular provisions of this Act, the principles of law and equity, including the law merchant and the law relative to capacity to contract, principal and agent, estoppel, fraud, misrepresentation, duress, coercion, mistake, bankruptcy, or other validating or invalidating cause shall supplement its provisions.

Section 1—104. Construction Against Implicit Repeal.

This Act being a general act intended as a unified coverage of its subject matter, no part of it shall be deemed to be impliedly repealed by subsequent legislation if such construction can reasonably be avoided.

Section 1—105. Territorial Application of the Act; Parties' Power to Choose Applicable Law.

(1) Except as provided hereafter in this section, when a transaction bears a reasonable relation to this state and also to another state or nation, the parties may agree that the law either of this state or of such other state or nation shall govern their rights and duties. Failing such agreement this Act applies to transactions bearing an appropriate relation to this state.

(2) Where one of the following provisions of this Act specifies the applicable law, that provision governs and a contrary agreement is effective only to the extent permitted by the law (including the conflict of laws rules) so specified:

Rights of creditors against sold goods. Section 2—402.

Applicability of the Article on Bank Deposits and Collections. Section 4—102.

Bulk transfers subject to the Article on Bulk Transfers. Section 6—102.

Applicability of the Article on Investment Securties. Section 8—106.

Policy and scope of the Article on Secured Transactions. Sections 9—102 and 9—103.

Section 1—106. Remedies to Be Liberally Administered.

(1) The remedies provided by this Act shall be liberally administered to the end that the aggrieved party may be put in as good a position as if the other party had fully performed, but neither consequential or special nor penal damages may be had except as specifically provided in this Act or by other rule of law.

(2) Any right or obligation declared by this Act is enforceable by action unless the provision declaring it specifies a different and limited effect.

Section 1—107. Waiver or Renunciation of Claim or Right After Breach.

Any claim or right arising out of an alleged breach can be discharged in whole or in part without consideration by a written waiver or renunciation signed and delivered by the aggrieved party.

Section 1—108. Severability.

If any provision or clause of this Act or application thereof to any person or circumstances is held invalid, such invalidity shall not affect other provisions or applications of the Act which can be given effect without the invalid provision or application, and to this end the provisions of this Act are declared to be severable.

Section 1—109. Section Captions.

Section captions are parts of this Act.

PART 2 / GENERAL DEFINITIONS AND PRINCIPLES OF INTERPRETATION

Section 1—201. General Definitions.

Subject to additional definitions contained in the subsequent Articles of this Act which are applicable to specific Articles or Parts thereof, and unless the context otherwise requires, in this Act:

(1) "Action" in the sense of a judicial proceeding includes recoupment, counterclaim, setoff, suit in equity and any other proceedings in which rights are determined.

(2) "Aggrieved party" means a party entitled to resort to a remedy.

(3) "Agreement" means the bargain of the parties in fact as found in their language or by implication from other circumstances including course of dealing or usage of trade or course of

performance as provided in this Act (Sections 1—205 and 2—208). Whether an agreement has legal consequences is determined by the provisions of this Act, if applicable; otherwise by the law of contracts (Section 1—103). (Compare "Contract".)

(4) "Bank" means any person engaged in the business of banking.

(5) "Bearer" means the person in possession of an instrument, document of title, or security payable to bearer or indorsed in blank.

(6) "Bill of lading" means a document evidencing the receipt of goods for shipment issued by a person engaged in the business of transporting or forwarding goods, and includes an airbill. "Airbill" means a document serving for air transportation as a bill of lading does for marine or rail transportation, and includes an air consignment note or air waybill.

(7) "Branch" includes a separately incorporated foreign branch of a bank.

(8) "Burden of establishing" a fact means the burden of persuading the triers of fact that the existence of the fact is more probable than its nonexistence.

(9) "Buyer in ordinary course of business" means a person who in good faith and without knowledge that the sale to him is in violation of the ownership rights or security interest of a third party in the goods buys in ordinary course from a person in the business of selling goods of that kind but does not include a pawnbroker. "Buying" may be for cash or by exchange of other property or on secured or unsecured credit and includes receiving goods or documents of title under a preexisting contract for sale but does not include a transfer in bulk or as security for or in total or partial satisfaction of a money debt.

(10) "Conspicuous": A term or clause is conspicuous when it is so written that a reasonable person against whom it is to operate ought to have noticed it. A printed heading in capitals (as: NON-NEGOTIABLE BILL OF LADING) is conspicuous. Language in the body of a form is "conspicuous" if it is in larger or other contrasting type or color. But in a telegram any stated term is "conspicuous." Whether a term or clause is "conspicuous" or not is for decision by the court.

(11) "Contract" means the total legal obligation which results from the parties' agreement as affected by this Act and any other applicable rules of law. (Compare "Agreement".)

(12) "Creditor" includes a general creditor, a secured creditor, a lien creditor and any representative of creditors, including an assignee for the benefit of creditors, a trustee in bankruptcy, a receiver in equity and an executor or administrator of an insolvent debtor's or assignor's estate.

(13) "Defendant" includes a person in the position of defendant in a crossaction or counterclaim.

(14) "Delivery" with respect to instruments, documents of title, chattel paper or securities means voluntary transfer of possession.

(15) "Document of title" includes bill of lading, dock warrant, dock receipt, warehouse receipt or order for the delivery of goods, and also any other document which in the regular course of business or financing is treated as adequately evidencing that the person in possession of it is entitled to receive, hold and dispose of the document and the goods it covers. To be a document of title a document must purport to be issued by or addressed to a bailee and purport to cover goods in the bailee's possession which are either identified or are fungible portions of an identified mass.

(16) "Fault" means wrongful act, omission or breach.

(17) "Fungible" with respect to goods or securities means goods or securities of which any unit is, by nature or usage of trade, the equivalent of any other like unit. Goods which are not fungible shall be deemed fungible for the purposes of this Act to the extent that under a particular agreement or document unlike units are treated as equivalents.

(18) "Genuine" means free of forgery or counterfeiting.

(19) "Good faith" means honesty in fact in the conduct or transaction concerned.

(20) "Holder" means a person who is in possession of a document of title or an instrument or an investment security drawn, issued or indorsed to him or to his order to bearer or in blank.

(21) To "honor" is to pay or to accept and pay, or where a credit so engages to purchase or discount a draft complying with the terms of the credit.

(22) "Insolvency proceedings" includes any assignment for the benefit of creditors or other proceedings intended to liquidate or rehabilitate the estate of the person involved.

(23) A person is "insolvent" who either has ceased to pay his debts in the ordinary course of business or cannot pay his debts as they become due or is insolvent within the meaning of the federal bankruptcy law.

(24) "Money means a medium of exchange authorized or adopted by a domestic or foreign government as a part of its currency.

(25) A person has "notice" of a fact when

(a) he has actual knowledge of it; or

(b) he has received a notice or notification of it; or

(c) from all the facts and circumstances known to him at the time in question he has reason to know that it exists.

A person "knows" or has "knowledge" of a fact when he has actual knowledge of it. "Discover" or "learn" or a word or phrase of similar import refers to knowledge rather than to reason to know. The time and circumstances under which a notice or notification may cease to be effective are not determined by this Act.

(26) A person "notifies" or "gives" a notice or notification to another by taking such steps as may be reasonably required to inform the other in ordinary course whether or not such other actually comes to know of it. A person "receives" a notice or notification when

(a) it comes to his attention; or

(b) it is duly delivered at the place of business through which the contract was made or at any other place held out by him as the place for receipt of such communications.

(27) Notice, knowledge or a notice or notification received by an organization is effective for a particular transaction from the time when it is brought to the attention of the individual conducting that transaction, and in any event from the time when it would have been brought to his attention if the organization had exercised due diligence. An organization exercises due diligence if it maintains reasonable routines for communicating significant information to the person conducting the transaction and there is reasonable compliance with the routines. Due diligence does not require an individual acting for the organization to communicate information unless such communication is part of his regular duties or unless he has reason to know of the transaction and that the transaction would be materially affected by the information.

(28) "Organization" includes a corporation, government or governmental subdivision or agency, business trust, estate, trust, partnership or association, two or more persons having a joint or common interest, or any other legal or commercial entity.

(29) "Party," as distinct from "third party," means a person who has engaged in a transaction or made an agreement within this Act.

(30) "Person" includes an individual or an organization (See Section 1—102).

(31) "Presumption" or "presumed" means that the trier of fact must find the existence of the fact presumed unless and until evidence is introduced which would support a finding of its nonexistence.

(32) "Purchase" includes taking by sale, discount, negotiation, mortgage, pledge, lien, issue or re-issue, gift or any other voluntary transaction creating an interest in property.

(33) "Purchaser" means a person who takes by purchase.

(34) "Remedy" means any remedial right to which an aggrieved party is entitled with or without resort to a tribunal.

(35) "Representative" includes an agent, an officer of a corporation or association, and a trustee, executor or administrator of an estate, or any other person empowered to act for another.

(36) "Rights" includes remedies.

(37) "Security interest" means an interest in personal property or fixtures which secures payment or performance of an obligation. The retention or reservation of title by a seller of goods notwithstanding shipment or delivery to buyer (Section 2—401) is limited in effect to a reservation of a "security interest." The term also includes any interest of a buyer of accounts, chattel paper, or contract rights which is subject to Article 9. The special property interest of a buyer of goods on identification of such goods to a contract for sale under Section 2—401 is not a "security interest," but a buyer may also acquire a "security interest" by complying with Article 9. Unless a lease or consignment is intended as security, reservation of title thereunder is not a "security interest" but a consignment is in any event subject to the provisions on consignment sales (Section 2—326). Whether a lease is intended as security is to be determined by the facts of each case; however, (a) the inclusion of an option to purchase does not of itself make the lease one intended for security, and (b) an agreement that upon compliance with the terms of the lease the lessee shall become or has the option to become the owner of the property for no additional consideration or for a nominal consideration does make the lease one intended for security.

(38) "Send" in connection with any writing or notice means to deposit in the mail or deliver for transmission by any other usual means of communication with postage or cost of transmission provided for and properly addressed and in the case of an instrument to an address specified thereon or otherwise agreed, or if there be none to any address reasonable under the circumstances. The receipt of any writing or notice within the time at which it would have arrived if properly sent has the effect of a proper sending.

(39) "Signed" includes any symbol executed or adopted by a party with present intention to authenticate a writing.

(40) "Surety" includes guarantor.

(41) "Telegram" includes a message transmitted by radio, teletype, cable, any mechanical method of transmission, or the like.

(42) "Term" means that portion of an agreement which relates to a particular matter.

(43) "Unauthorized" signature or indorsement means one made without actual, implied or apparent authority and includes a forgery.

(44) "Value." Except as otherwise provided with respect to negotiable instruments and bank collections (Sections 3—303, 4—208 and 4—209) a person gives "value" for rights if he acquires them

(a) in return for a binding commitment to extend credit or for the extension of immediately available credit whether or not drawn upon and whether or not a charge-back is provided for in the event of difficulties in collection; or

(b) as security for or in total or partial satisfaction of a pre-existing claim; or

(c) by accepting delivery pursuant to a pre-existing contract for purchase; or

(d) generally, in return for any consideration sufficient to support a simple contract.

(45) "Warehouse receipt" means a receipt issued by a person engaged in the business of storing goods for hire.

(46) "Written" or "writing" includes printing, typewriting or any other intentional reduction to tangible form.

Section 1—202. Prima Facie Evidence by Third Party Documents.

A document in due form purporting to be a bill of lading, policy or certificate of insurance, official weigher's or inspector's certificate, consular invoice, or any other document authorized or required by the contract to be issued by a third party shall be prima facie evidence of its own authenticity and genuineness and of the facts stated in the document by the third party.

Section 1—203. Obligation of Good Faith.

Every contract or duty within this Act imposes an obligation of good faith in its performance or enforcement.

Section 1—204. Time; Reasonable Time; "Seasonably."

(1) Whenever this Act requires any action to be taken within a reasonable time, any time which is not manifestly unreasonable may be fixed by agreement.

(2) What is a reasonable time for taking any action depends on the nature, purpose and circumstances of such action.

(3) An action is taken "seasonably" when it is taken at or within the time agreed or if no time is agreed at or within a reasonable time.

Section 1—205. Course of Dealing and Usage of Trade.

(1) A course of dealing is a sequence of previous conduct between the parties to a particular transaction which is fairly to be regarded as establishing a common basis of understanding for interpreting their expressions and other conduct.

(2) A usage of trade is any practice or method of dealing having such regularity of observance in a place, vocation or trade as to justify an expectation that it will be observed with respect to the transaction in question. The existence and scope of such a usage are to be proved as facts. If it is established that such a usage is embodied in a written trade code or similar writing, the interpretation of the writing is for the court.

(3) A course of dealing between parties and any usage of trade in the vocation or trade in which they are engaged or of which they are or should be aware give particular meaning to and supplement or qualify terms of an agreement.

(4) The express terms of an agreement and an applicable course of dealing or usage of trade shall be construed wherever reasonable as consistent with each other; but when such construction is unreasonable, express terms control both course of dealing and usage of trade and course of dealing controls usage of trade.

(5) An applicable usage of trade in the place where any part of performance is to occur shall be used in interpreting the agreement as to that part of the performance.

(6) Evidence of a relevant usage of trade offered by one party is not admissible unless and until he has given the other party such notice as the court finds sufficient to prevent unfair surprise to the latter.

Section 1—206. Statute of Frauds for Kinds of Personal Property Not Otherwise Covered.

(1) Except in the cases described in subsection (2) of this section, a contract for the sale of personal property is not enforceable by way of action or defense beyond five thousand dollars in amount or value of remedy unless there is some writing which indicates that a contract for sale has been made between the parties at a defined

or stated price, reasonably identifies the subject matter, and is signed by the party against whom enforcement is sought or by his authorized agent.

(2) Subsection (1) of this section does not apply to contracts for the sale of goods (Section 2—201) nor of securities (Section 8—319) nor to security agreements (Section 9—203).

Section 1—207. Performance or Acceptance Under Reservation of Rights.

A party who with explicit reservation of rights performs or promises performance or assents to performance in a manner demanded or offered by the other party does not thereby prejudice the rights reserved. Such words as "without prejudice", "under protest" or the like are sufficient.

Section 1—208. Option to Accelerate at Will.

A term providing that one party or his successor in interest may accelerate payment or performance or require collateral or additional collateral "at will" or "when he deems himself insecure" or in words of similar import shall be construed to mean that he shall have power to do so only if he in good faith believes that the prospect of payment or performance is impaired. The burden of establishing lack of good faith is on the party against whom the power has been exercised.

ARTICLE 2 / SALES

PART 1 / SHORT TITLE, GENERAL CONSTRUCTION AND SUBJECT MATTER

Section 2—101. Short Title.

This Article shall be known and may be cited as Uniform Commercial Code—Sales.

Section 2—102. Scope; Certain Security and Other Transactions Excluded from This Article.

Unless the context otherwise requires, this Article applies to transactions in goods; it does not apply to any transaction which although in the form of an unconditional contract to sell or present sale is intended to operate only as a security transaction nor does this Article impair or repeal any statute regulating sales to consumers, farmers or other specified classes of buyers.

Section 2—103. Definitions and Index of Definitions.

(1) In this Article unless the context otherwise requires

    (a) "Buyer" means a person who buys or contracts to buy goods.

    (b) "Good faith" in the case of a merchant means honesty in fact and the observance of reasonable commercial standards of fair dealing in the trade.

    (c) "Receipt" of goods means taking physical possession of them.

    (d) "Seller" means a person who sells or contracts to sell goods.

(2) Other definitions applying to this Article or to specified Parts thereof, and the sections in which they appear are:

    "Acceptance". Section 2—606.
    "Banker's credit". Section 2—325.
    "Between merchants". Section 2-104.
    "Cancellation". Section 2—106(4).
    "Commercial unit". Section 2—105.
    "Confirmed credit". Section 2—325.
    "Conforming to contract". Section 2—106.
    "Contract for sale". Section 2—106.
    "Cover". Section 2—712.
    "Entrusting". Section 2—403.
    "Financing agency". Section 2—104.
    "Future goods". Section 2—105.
    "Goods". Section 2—105.
    "Identification". Section 2—501.
    "Installment contract". Section 2—612.
    "Letter of Credit". Section 2—325.
    "Lot". Section 2—105.
    "Merchant". Section 2—104.
    "Overseas". Section 2—323.
    "Person in position of seller". Section 2—707.
    "Present sale". Section 2—106.
    "Sale". Section 2—106.
    "Sale on approval". Section 2—326.
    "Sale or return". Section 2—326.
    "Termination". Section 2—106.

(3) The following definitions in other Articles apply to this Article:

    "Check". Section 3—104.
    "Consignee". Section 7—102.

"Consignor". Section 7—102.

"Consumer goods". Section 9—109.

"Dishonor". Section 3—507.

"Draft". Section 3—104.

(4) In addition Article 1 contains general definitions and principles of construction and interpretation applicable throughout this Article.

Section 2—104. Definitions: "Merchant"; "Between Merchants"; "Financing Agency".

(1) "Merchant" means a person who deals in goods of the kind or otherwise by his occupation holds himself out as having knowledge or skill peculiar to the practices or goods involved in the transaction or to whom such knowledge or skill may be attributed by his employment of an agent or broker or other intermediary who by his occupation holds himself out as having such knowledge or skill.

(2) "Financing agency" means a bank, finance company or other person who in the ordinary course of business makes advances against goods or documents of title or who by arrangement with either the seller or the buyer intervenes in ordinary course to make or collect payment due or claimed under the contract for sale, as by purchasing or paying the seller's draft or making advances against it or by merely taking it for collection whether or not documents of title accompany the draft. "Financing agency" includes also a bank or other person who similarly intervenes between persons who are in the position of seller and buyer in respect to the goods (Section 2—707).

(3) "Between merchants" means in any transaction with respect to which both parties are chargeable with the knowledge or skill of merchants.

Section 2—105. Definitions: Transferability; "Goods"; "Future" Goods; "Lot"; "Commercial Unit".

(1) "Goods" means all things (including specially manufactured goods) which are movable at the time of identification to the contract for sale other than the money in which the price is to be paid, investment securities (Article 8) and things in action. "Goods" also includes the unborn young of animals and growing crops and other identified things attached to realty as described in the section on goods to be severed from realty (Section 2—107).

(2) Goods must be both existing and identified before any interest in them can pass. Goods which are not both existing and identified are "future" goods. A purported present sale of future goods or of any interest therein operates as a contract to sell.

(3) There may be a sale of a part interest in existing identified goods.

(4) An undivided share in an identified bulk of fungible goods is sufficiently identified to be sold although the quantity of the bulk is not determined. Any agreed proportion of such a bulk or any quantity thereof agreed upon by number, weight or other measure may to the extent of the seller's interest in the bulk be sold to the buyer who then becomes an owner in common.

(5) "Lot" means a parcel or a single article which is the subject matter of a separate sale or delivery, whether or not it is sufficient to perform the contract.

(6) "Commercial unit" means such a unit of goods as by commercial usage is a single whole for purposes of sales and division of which materially impairs its character or value on the market or in use. A commercial unit may be a single article (as a machine) or a set of articles (as a suite of furniture or an assortment of sizes) or a quantity (as a bale, gross, or carload) or any other unit treated in use or in the relevant market as a single whole.

Section 2—106. Definitions: "Contract"; "Agreement"; "Contract for Sale"; "Sale"; "Present Sale"; "Conforming to Contract"; "Termination"; "Cancellation".

(1) In this Article unless the context otherwise requires, "contract" and "agreement" are limited to those relating to the present or future sale of goods. "Contract for sale" includes both a present sale of goods and a contract to sell goods at a future time. A "sale" consists in the passing of title from the seller to the buyer for a price (Section 2—401). A "present sale" means a sale which is accomplished by the making of the contract.

(2) Goods or conduct including any part of a performance are "conforming" or conform to the contract when they are in accordance with the obligations under the contract.

(3) "Termination" occurs when either party pursuant to a power created by agreement or law puts an end to the contract otherwise than for its breach. On "termination" all obligations which are still executory on both sides are discharged but any right based on prior breach or performance survives.

(4) "Cancellation" occurs when either party puts an end to the contract for breach by the other and its effect is the same as that of "termination" except that the cancelling party also re-

tains any remedy for breach of the whole contract or any unperformed balance.

Section 2—107. Goods to Be Severed from Realty: Recording.

(1) A contract for the sale of timber, minerals or the like or a structure or its materials to be removed from realty is a contract for the sale of goods within this Article if they are to be severed by the seller, but until severance a purported present sale thereof which is not effective as a transfer of an interest in land is effective only as a contract to sell.

(2) A contract for the sale apart from the land of growing crops or other things attached to realty and capable of severance without material harm thereto but not described in subsection (1) is a contract for the sale of goods within this Article whether the subject matter is to be severed by the buyer or by the seller even though it forms part of the realty at the time of contracting, and the parties can by identification effect a present sale before severance.

(3) The provisions of this section are subject to any third party rights provided by the law relating to realty records, and the contract for sale may be executed and recorded as a document transferring an interest in land and shall then constitute notice to third parties of the buyer's rights under the contract for sale.

PART 2 / FORM, FORMATION AND READJUSTMENT OF CONTRACT

Section 2—201. Formal Requirements; Statute of Frauds.

(1) Except as otherwise provided in this section, a contract for the sale of goods for the price of $500 or more is not enforceable by way of action or defense unless there is some writing sufficient to indicate that a contract for sale has been made between the parties and signed by the party against whom enforcement is sought or by his authorized agent or broker. A writing is not insufficient because it omits or incorrectly states a term agreed upon but the contract is not enforceable under this paragraph beyond the quantity of goods shown in such writing.

(2) Between merchants if within a reasonable time a writing in confirmation of the contract and sufficient against the sender is received and the party receiving it has reason to know its contents, it satisfies the requirements of subsection (1) against such party unless written notice of objection to its contents is given within ten days after it is received.

(3) A contract which does not satisfy the requirements of subsection (1) but which is valid in other respects is enforceable

    (a) if the goods are to be specially manufactured for the buyer and are not suitable for sale to others in the ordinary course of the seller's business and the seller, before notice of repudiation is received and under circumstances which reasonably indicate that the goods are for the buyer, has made either a substantial beginning of their manufacture or commitments for their procurement; or

    (b) if the party against whom enforcement is sought admits in his pleading, testimony or otherwise in court that a contract for sale was made, but the contract is not enforceable under this provision beyond the quantity of goods admitted; or

    (c) with respect to goods for which payment has been made and accepted or which have been received and accepted (Section 2—606).

Section 2—202. Final Written Expression: Parol or Extrinsic Evidence.

Terms with respect to which the confirmatory memoranda of the parties agree or which are otherwise set forth in a writing intended by the parties as a final expression of their agreement with respect to such terms as are included therein may not be contradicted by evidence of any prior agreement or of a contemporaneous oral agreement but may be explained or supplemented.

    (a) by course of dealing or usage of trade (Section 1—205) or by course of performance (Section 2—208); and

    (b) by evidence of consistent additional terms unless the court finds the writing to have been intended also as a complete and exclusive statement of the terms of the agreement.

Section 2—203. Seals Inoperative.

The affixing of a seal to a writing evidencing a contract for sale or an offer to buy or sell goods does not constitute the writing a sealed instrument, and the law with respect to sealed instruments does not apply to such a contract or offer.

Section 2—204. Formation in General.

(1) A contract for sale of goods may be made in any manner sufficient to show agreement, including conduct by both parties which recognizes the existence of such a contract.

(2) An agreement sufficient to constitute a contract for sale may be found even though the moment of its making is undetermined.

(3) Even though one or more terms are left open, a contract for sale does not fail for indefiniteness if the parties have intended to make a contract and there is a reasonably certain basis for giving an appropriate remedy.

Section 2—205. Firm Offers.

An offer by a merchant to buy or sell goods in a signed writing which by its terms gives assurance that it will be held open is not revocable for lack of consideration during the time stated or if no time is stated for a reasonable time, but in no event may such period of irrevocability exceed three months; but any such term of assurance on a form supplied by the offeree must be separately signed by the offeror.

Section 2—206. Offer and Acceptance in Formation of Contract.

(1) Unless otherwise unambiguously indicated by the language or circumstances
  (a) an offer to make a contract shall be construed as inviting acceptance in any manner and by any medium reasonable in the circumstances;
  (b) an order or other offer to buy goods for prompt or current shipment shall be construed as inviting acceptance either by a prompt promise to ship or by the prompt or current shipment of conforming or nonconforming goods, but such a shipment of nonconforming goods does not substitute an acceptance if the seller seasonably notifies the buyer that the shipment is offered only as an accommodation to the buyer.

(2) Where the beginning of a requested performance is a reasonable mode of acceptance, an offeror who is not notified of acceptance within a reasonable time may treat the offer as having lapsed before acceptance.

Section 2—207. Additional Terms in Acceptance or Confirmation.

(1) A definite and seasonable expression of acceptance or a written confirmation which is sent within a reasonable time operates as an acceptance even though it states terms additional to or different from those offered or agreed upon, unless acceptance is expressly made conditional on assent to the additional or different terms.

(2) The additional terms are to be construed as proposals for addition to the contract. Between merchants such terms become part of the contract unless
  (a) the offer expressly limits acceptance to the terms of the offer;
  (b) they materially alter it; or
  (c) notification of objection to them has already been given or is given within a reasonable time after notice of them is received.

(3) Conduct by both parties which recognizes the existence of a contract is sufficient to establish a contract for sale although the writings of the parties do not otherwise establish a contract. In such case the terms of the particular contract consist of those terms on which the writings of the parties agree, together with any supplementary terms incorporated under any other provisions of this Act.

Section 2—208. Course of Performance or Practical Construction.

(1) Where the contract for sale involves repeated occasions for performance by either party with knowledge of the nature of the performance and opportunity for objection to it by the other, any course of performance accepted or acquiesced in without objection shall be relevant to determine the meaning of the agreement.

(2) The express terms of the agreement and any such course of performance, as well as any course of dealing and usage of trade, shall be construed whenever reasonable as consistent with each other; but when such construction is unreasonable, express terms shall control course of performance and course of performance shall control both course of dealing and usage of trade (Section 1—205).

(3) Subject to the provisions of the next section on modification and waiver, such course of performance shall be relevant to show a waiver or modification of any term inconsistent with such course of performance.

Section 2—209. Modification, Rescission and Waiver.

(1) An agreement modifying a contract within this Article needs no consideration to be binding.

(2) A signed agreement which excludes modification or rescission except by a signed writing cannot be otherwise modified or rescinded, but except as between merchants such a requirement on a form supplied by the merchant must be separately signed by the other party.

(3) The requirements of the statute of frauds section of this Article (Section 2—201) must be satisfied if the contract as modified is within its provisions.

(4) Although an attempt at modification or rescission does not satisfy the requirements of subsection (2) or (3) it can operate as a waiver.

(5) A party who has made a waiver affecting an executory portion of the contract may retract the waiver by reasonable notification received by the other party that strict performance will be required of any term waived, unless the retraction would be unjust in view of a material change of position in reliance on the waiver.

Section 2—210. Delegation of Performance; Assignment of Rights.

(1) A party may perform his duty through a delegate unless otherwise agreed or unless the other party has a substantial interest in having his original promisor perform or control the acts required by the contract. No delegation of performance relieves the party delegating of any duty to perform or any liability for breach.

(2) Unless otherwise agreed all rights of either seller or buyer can be assigned except where the assignment would materially change the duty of the other party, or increase materially the burden or risk imposed on him by his contract, or impair materially his chance of obtaining return performance. A right to damages for breach of the whole contract or a right arising out of the assignor's due performance of his entire obligation can be assigned despite agreement otherwise.

(3) Unless the circumstances indicate the contrary, a prohibition or assignment of "the contract" is to be construed as barring only the delegation to the assignee of the assignor's performance.

(4) An assignment of "the contract" or of "all my rights under the contract" or an assignment in similar general terms is an assignment of rights and unless the language or the circumstances (as in an assignment for security) indicate the contrary, it is a delegation of performance of the duties of the assignor and its acceptance by the assignee constitutes a promise by him to perform those duties. The promise is enforceable by either the assignor or the other party to the original contract.

(5) The other party may treat any assignment which delegates performance as creating reasonable grounds for insecurity and may without prejudice to his rights against the assignor demand assurances from the assignee (Section 2—609).

PART 3 / GENERAL OBLIGATION AND CONSTRUCTION OF CONTRACT

Section 2—301. General Obligations of Parties.

The obligation of the seller is to transfer and deliver and that of the buyer is to accept and pay in accordance with the contract.

Section 2—302. Unconscionable Contract or Clause.

(1) If the court as a matter of law finds the contract or any clause of the contract to have been unconscionable at the time it was made, the court may refuse to enforce the contract, or it may enforce the remainder of the contract without the unconscionable clause, or it may so limit the application of any unconscionable clause as to avoid any unconscionable result.

(2) When it is claimed or appears to the court that the contract or any clause thereof may be unconscionable, the parties shall be afforded a reasonable opportunity to present evidence as to its commercial setting, purpose and effect to aid the court in making the determination.

Section 2—303. Allocation or Division of Risks.

Where this Article allocates a risk or a burden as between the parties "unless otherwise agreed", the agreement may not only shift the allocation but may also divide the risk or burden.

Section 2—304. Price Payable in Money, Goods, Realty, or Otherwise.

(1) The price can be made payable in money or otherwise. If it is payable in whole or in part in goods, each party is a seller of the goods which he is to transfer.

(2) Even though all or part of the price is payable in an interest in realty, the transfer of the goods and the seller's obligations with reference to them are subject to this Article, but not the transfer of the interest in realty or the transferor's obligations in connection therewith.

Section 2—305. Open Price Term.

(1) The parties if they so intend can conclude a contract for sale even though the price is not settled. In such a case the price is a reasonable price at the time for delivery if
  (a) nothing is said as to price; or
  (b) the price is left to be agreed by the parties and they fail to agree; or
  (c) the price is to be fixed in terms of some agreed market or other standard as set or recorded by a third person or agency and it is not so set or recorded.

(2) A price to be fixed by the seller or by the buyer means a price for him to fix in good faith.

(3) When a price left to be fixed otherwise than by agreement of parties fails to be fixed through fault of one party, the other may at his option treat the contract as cancelled or himself fix a reasonable price.

(4) Where, however, the parties intend not to be bound unless the price be fixed or agreed and it is not fixed or agreed, there is no contract. In such a case the buyer must return any goods already received or if unable so to do must pay their reasonable value at the time of delivery and the seller must return any portion of the price paid on account.

Section 2—306. Output, Requirements and Exclusive Dealings.

(1) A term which measures the quantity by the output of the seller or the requirements of the buyer means such actual output or requirements as may occur in good faith, except that no quantity unreasonably disproportionate to any stated estimate or in the absence of a stated estimate to any normal or otherwise comparable prior output or requirements may be tendered or demanded.

(2) A lawful agreement by either the seller or the buyer for exclusive dealing in the kind of goods concerned imposes unless otherwise agreed an obligation by the seller to use best efforts to supply the goods and by the buyer to use best efforts to promote their sale.

Section 2—307. Delivery in Single Lot or Several Lots.

Unless otherwise agreed all goods called for by a contract for sale must be tendered in a single delivery and payment is due only on such tender, but where the circumstances give either party the right to make or demand delivery in lots the price if it can be apportioned may be demanded for each lot.

Section 2—308. Absence of Specified Place for Delivery.

Unless otherwise agreed
  (a) the place for delivery of goods is the seller's place of business or if he has none his residence; but
  (b) in a contract for sale of identified goods which to the knowledge of the parties at the time of contracting are in some other place, that place is the place for their delivery; and
  (c) documents of title may be delivered through customary banking channels.

Section 2—309. Absence of Specific Time Provisions; Notice of Termination.

(1) The time for shipment or delivery or any other action under a contract if not provided in this Article or agreed upon shall be a reasonable time.

(2) Where the contract provides for successive performances but is indefinite in duration it is valid for a reasonable time but unless otherwise agreed may be terminated at any time by either party.

(3) Termination of a contract by one party except on the happening of an agreed event requires that reasonable notification be received by the other party and an agreement dispensing with notification is invalid if its operation would be unconscionable.

Section 2—310. Open Time for Payment or Running of Credit; Authority to Ship Under Reservation.

Unless otherwise agreed
  (a) payment is due at the time and place at which the buyer is to receive the goods even though the place of shipment is the place of delivery; and
  (b) if the seller is authorized to send the goods he may ship them under reservation, and may tender the documents of

title, but the buyer may inspect the goods after their arrival before payment is due unless such inspection is inconsistent with the terms of the contract (Section 2—513); and

(c) if delivery is authorized and made by way of documents of title otherwise than by subsection (b) then payment is due at the time and place at which the buyer is to receive the documents regardless of where the goods are to be received; and

(d) where the seller is required or authorized to ship the goods on credit the credit period runs from the time of shipment but post-dating the invoice or delaying its dispatch will correspondingly delay the starting of the credit period.

Section 2—311. Options and Cooperation Respecting Performance.

(1) An agreement for sale which is otherwise sufficiently definite (subsection (3) of Section 2—204) to be a contract is not made invalid by the fact that it leaves particulars of performance to be specified by one of the parties. Any such specification must be made in good faith and within limits set by commercial reasonableness.

(2) Unless otherwise agreed specifications relating to assortment of the goods are at the buyer's option and except as otherwise provided in subsections (1) (c) and (3) of Section 2—319 specifications or arrangements relating to shipment are at the seller's option.

(3) Where such specification would materially affect the other party's performance but is not seasonably made or where one party's cooperation is necessary to the agreed performance of the other but is not seasonably forthcoming, the other party in addition to all other remedies

(a) is excused for any resulting delay in his own performance; and

(b) may also either proceed to perform in any reasonable manner or after the time for a material part of his own performance treat the failure to specify or to cooperate as a breach by failure to deliver or accept the goods.

Section 2—312. Warranty of Title and Against Infringement; Buyer's Obligation Against Infringement.

(1) Subject to subsection (2) there is in a contract for sale a warranty by the seller that

(a) the title conveyed shall be good, and its transfer rightful; and

(b) the goods shall be delivered free from any security interest or other lien or encumbrance of which the buyer at the time of contracting has no knowledge.

(2) A warranty under subsection (1) will be excluded or modified only by specific language or by circumstances which give the buyer reason to know that the person selling does not claim title in himself or that he is purporting to sell only such right or title as he or a third person may have.

(3) Unless otherwise agreed a seller who is a merchant regularly dealing in goods of the kind warrants that the goods shall be delivered free of the rightful claim of any third person by way of infringement or the like, but a buyer who furnishes specifications to the seller must hold the seller harmless against any such claim which arises out of compliance with the specifications.

Section 2—313. Express Warranties by Affirmation, Promise, Description, Sample.

(1) Express warranties by the seller are created as follows:

(a) Any affirmation of fact or promise made by the seller to the buyer which relates to the goods and becomes part of the basis of the bargain creates an express warranty that the goods shall conform to the affirmation or promise.

(b) Any description of the goods which is made part of the basis of the bargain creates an express warranty that the goods shall conform to the description.

(c) Any sample or model which is made part of the basis of the bargain creates an express warranty that the whole of the goods shall conform to the sample or model.

(2) It is not necessary to the creation of an express warranty that the seller use formal words such as "warranty" or "guarantee" or that he have a specific intention to make a warranty, but an affirmation merely of the value of the goods or a statement purporting to be merely the seller's opinion or commendation of the goods does not create a warranty.

Section 2—314. Implied Warranty: Merchantability; Usage of Trade.

(1) Unless excluded or modified (Section 2—316), a warranty that the goods shall be merchantable is implied in a comtract for their sale if the seller is a merchant with respect to goods of that kind. Under this section the serving for value of food or drink to be consumed either on the premises or elsewhere is a sale.

(2) Goods to be merchantable must be at least such as

    (a) pass without objection in the trade under the contract description; and

    (b) in the case of fungible goods, are of fair average quality within the description; and

    (c) are fit for the ordinary purposes for which such goods are used; and

    (d) run, within the variations permitted by the agreement, of even kind, quality and quantity within each unit and among all units involved; and

    (e) are adequately contained, packaged, and labeled as the agreement may require; and

    (f) conform to the promises of affirmations of fact made on the container or label if any.

(3) Unless excluded or modified (Section 2—316) other implied warranties may arise from course of dealing or usage of trade.

Section 2—315. Implied Warranty: Fitness for Particular Purpose.

Where the seller at the time of contracting has reason to know any particular purpose for which the goods are required and that the buyer is relying on the seller's skill or judgment to select or furnish suitable goods, there is unless excluded or modified under the next section an implied warranty that the goods shall be fit for such purpose.

Section 2—316. Exclusion or Modification of Warranties.

(1) Words or conduct relevant to the creation of an express warranty and words or conduct tending to negate or limit warranty shall be construed wherever reasonable as consistent with each other; but subject to the provisions of this Article on parol or extrinsic evidence (Section 2—202) negation or limitation is inoperative to the extent that such construction is unreasonable.

(2) Subject to subsection (3), to exclude or modify the implied warranty of merchantability or any part of it the language must mention merchantability and in case of a writing must be conspicuous, and to exclude or modify any implied warranty of fitness the exclusion must be by a writing and conspicuous. Language to exclude all implied warranties of fitness is sufficient if it states, for example, that "There are no warranties which extend beyond the description on the face hereof."

(3) Notwithstanding subsection (2)

    (a) unless the circumstances indicate otherwise, all implied warranties are excluded by expressions like "as is", "with all faults" or other language which in common understanding calls the buyer's attention to the exclusion of warranties and makes plain that there is no implied warranty; and

    (b) when the buyer before entering into the contract has examined the goods or the sample or model as fully as he desired or has refused to examine the goods, there is no implied warranty with regard to defects which an examination ought in the circumstances to have revealed to him; and

    (c) an implied warranty can also be excluded or modified by course of dealing or course of performance or usage of trade.

(4) Remedies for breach of warranty can be limited in accordance with the provisions of this Article on liquidation or limitation of damages and on contractual modification of remedy (Sections 2—718 and 2—719).

Section 2—317. Cumulation and Conflict of Warranties Express or Implied.

Warranties whether express or implied shall be construed as consistent with each other and as cumulative, but if such construction is unreasonable the intention of the parties shall determine which warranty is dominant. In ascertaining that intention the following rules apply:

    (a) Exact or technical specifications displace an inconsistent sample or model or general language of description.

    (b) A sample from an existing bulk displaces inconsistent general language of description.

    (c) Express warranties displace inconsistent implied warranties other than an implied warranty of fitness for a particular purpose.

Section 2—318. Third Party Beneficiaries of Warranties Express or Implied.

A seller's warranty whether express or implied extends to any natural person who is in the family or household of his buyer or who is a guest in his home if it is reasonable to expect that such person may use, consume or be affected by the goods and who is injured in person by breach of the warranty. A seller may not exclude or limit the operation of this section.

Section 2—319. F.O.B. and F.A.S. Terms.

(1) Unless otherwise agreed the term F.O.B. (which means "free on board") at a named place, even though used only in connection with the stated price, is a delivery term under which

    (a) when the term is F.O.B. the place of shipment, the seller must at that place ship the goods in the manner provided in this Article (Section 2—504) and bear the expense and risk of putting them into the possession of the carrier; or

    (b) when the term is F.O.B. the place of destination, the seller must at his own expense and risk transport the goods to that place and there tender delivery of them in the manner provided in this Article (Section 2—503);

    (c) When under either (a) or (b) the term is also F.O.B. vessel, car or other vehicle, the seller must in addition at his own expense and risk load the goods on board. If the term is F.O.B. vessel, the buyer must name the vessel and in an appropriate case the seller must comply with the provisions of this Article on the form of bill of lading (Section 2—323).

(2) Unless otherwise agreed the term F.A.S. vessel (which means "free alongside") at a named port, even though used only in connection with the stated price, is a delivery term under which the seller must

    (a) at his own expense and risk deliver the goods alongside the vessel in the manner usual in that port or on a dock designated and provided by the buyer; and

    (b) obtain and tender a receipt for the goods in exchange for which the carrier is under a duty to issue a bill of lading.

(3) Unless otherwise agreed in any case falling within subsection (1) (a) or (c) or subsection (2) the buyer must seasonably give any needed instructions for making delivery, including when the term is F.A.S. or F.O.B. the loading berth of the vessel and in an appropriate case its name and sailing date. The seller may treat the failure of needed instructions as a failure of cooperation under this Article (Section 2—311). He may also at his option move the goods in any reasonable manner preparatory to delivery or shipment.

(4) Under the term F.O.B. vessel or F.A.S. unless otherwise agreed the buyer must make payment against tender of the required documents and the seller may not tender nor the buyer demand delivery of the goods in substitution for the documents.

Section 2—320. C.I.F. and C. & F. Terms.

(1) The term C.I.F. means that the price includes in a lump sum the cost of the goods and the insurance and freight to the named destination. The term C. & F. or C.F. means that the price so includes cost and freight to the named destination.

(2) Unless otherwise agreed and even though used only in connection with the stated price and destination, the term C.I.F. destination or its equivalent requires the seller at his own expense and risk to

    (a) put the goods into the possession of a carrier at the port for shipment and obtain a negotiable bill or bills of lading covering the entire transportation to the named destination; and

    (b) load the goods and obtain a receipt from the carrier (which may be contained in the bill of lading) showing that the freight has been paid or provided for; and

    (c) obtain a policy or certificate of insurance, including any war risk insurance, of a kind and on terms then current at the port of shipment in the usual amount, in the currency of the contract, shown to cover the same goods covered by the bill of lading and providing for payment of loss to the order of the buyer or for the account of whom it may concern; but the seller may add to the price the amount of the premium for any such war risk insurance; and

    (d) prepare an invoice of the goods and procure any other documents required to effect shipment or to comply with the contract; and

    (e) forward and tender with commercial promptness all the documents in due form and with any indorsement necessary to perfect the buyer's rights.

(3) Unless otherwise agreed the term C. & F. or its equivalent has the same effect and imposes upon the seller the same obligations and risks as a C.I.F. term except the obligation as to insurance.

(4) Under the term C.I.F. or C. & F. unless otherwise agreed the buyer must make payment against tender of the required documents and the seller may not tender nor the buyer demand delivery of the goods in substitution for the documents.

Section 2—321. C.I.F. or C. & F.: "Net Landed Weights"; "Payment on Arrival"; Warranty of Condition on Arrival.

Under a contract containing a term C.I.F. or C. & F.

(1) Where the price is based on or is to be adjusted according to "net landed weights", "delivered weights", "out turn" quantity or quality or the like, unless otherwise agreed the seller must reasonably estimate the price. The payment due on tender of the documents called for by the contract is the amount so estimated, but after final adjustment of the price a settlement must be made with commercial promptness.

(2) An agreement described in subsection (1) or any warranty of quality or condition of the goods on arrival places upon the seller the risk of ordinary deterioration, shrinkage and the like in transportation but has no effect on the place or time of identification to the contract for sale or delivery or on the passing of the risk of loss.

(3) Unless otherwise agreed, where the contract provides for payment on or after arrival of the goods, the seller must before payment allow such preliminary inspection as is feasible; but if the goods are lost, delivery of the documents and payment are due when the goods should have arrived.

Section 2—322. Delivery "Ex-Ship".

(2) Under such a term unless otherwise agreed

(a) the seller must discharge all liens arising out of the carriage and furnish the buyer with a direction which puts the carrier under a duty to deliver the goods; and

(b) the risk of loss does not pass to the buyer until the goods leave the ship's tackle or are otherwise properly unloaded.

Section 2—323. Form of Bill of Lading Required in Overseas Shipment; "Overseas".

(1) Where the contract contemplates overseas shipment and contains a term C.I.F. or C. & F. or F.O.B. vessel, the seller unless otherwise agreed must obtain a negotiable bill of lading stating that the goods have been loaded on board or, in the case of a term C.I.F. or C. & F., received for shipment.

(2) Where in a case within subsection (1) a bill of lading has been issued in a set of parts, unless otherwise agreed if the documents are not to be sent from abroad the buyer may demand tender of the full set; otherwise only one part of the bill of lading need be tendered. Even if the agreement expressly requires a full set

(a) due tender of a single part is acceptable within the provisions of this Article on cure of improper delivery (subsection (1) of Section 2—508); and

(b) even though the full set is demanded, if the documents are sent from abroad the person tendering an incomplete set may nevertheless require payment upon furnishing an indemnity which the buyer in good faith deems adequate.

(3) A shipment by water or by air or a contract contemplating such shipment is "overseas" insofar as by usage of trade or agreement it is subject to the commercial, financing or shipping practices characteristic of international deep water commerce.

Section 2—324. "No Arrival, No Sale" Term.

Under a term "no arrival, no sale" or terms of like meaning, unless otherwise agreed,

(a) the seller must properly ship conforming goods and if they arrive by any means he must tender them on arrival, but he assumes no obligation that the goods will arrive unless he has caused the nonarrival; and

(b) where without fault of the seller the goods are in part lost or have so deteriorated as no longer to conform to the contract or arrive after the contract time, the buyer may proceed as if there had been casualty to identified goods (Section 2—613).

Section 2—325. "Letter of Credit" Term; "Confirmed Credit".

(1) Failure of the buyer seasonably to furnish an agreed letter of credit is a breach of the contract for sale.

(2) The delivery to seller of a proper letter of credit suspends the buyer's obligation to pay. If the letter of credit is dishonored, the seller may on seasonable notification to the buyer require payment directly from him.

(3) Unless otherwise agreed the term "letter of credit" or "banker's credit" in a contract for sale means an irrevocable credit issued by a financing agency of good repute and, where the shipment is overseas, of good international repute. The term "confirmed credit" means that the credit must also carry the direct obligation of

such an agency which does business in the seller's financial market.

Section 2—326. Sale on Approval and Sale or Return; Consignment Sales and Rights of Creditors.

(1) Unless otherwise agreed, if delivered goods may be returned by the buyer even though they conform to the contract, the transaction is

    (a) a "sale on approval" if the goods are delivered primarily for use, and

    (b) a "sale or return" if the goods are delivered primarily for resale.

(2) Except as provided in subsection (3), goods held on approval are not subject to the claims of the buyer's creditors until acceptance; goods held on sale or return are subject to such claims while in the buyer's possession.

(3) Where goods are delivered to a person for sale and such person maintains a place of business at which he deals in goods of the kind involved, under a name other than the name of the person making delivery, then with respect to claims of creditors of the person conducting the business the goods are deemed to be on sale or return. The provisions of this subsection are applicable even though an agreement purports to reserve title to the person making delivery until payment or resale or uses such words as "on consignment" or "on memorandum". However, this subsection is not applicable if the person making delivery

    (a) complies with an applicable law providing for a consignor's interest or the like to be evidenced by a sign, or

    (b) establishes that the person conducting the business is generally known by his creditors to be substantially engaged in selling the goods of others, or

    (c) complies with the filing provisions of the Article on Secured Transactions (Article 9).

(4) Any "or return" term of a contract for sale is to be treated as a separate contract for sale within the statute of frauds section of this Article (Section 2—201) and as contradicting the sale aspect of the contract within the provisons of this Article on parol or extrinsic evidence (Section 2—202).

Section 2—327. Special Incidents of Sale on Approval and Sale or Return.

(1) Under a sale on approval unless otherwise agreed

    (a) although the goods are identified to the contract, the risk of loss and the title do not pass to the buyer until acceptance; and

    (b) use of the goods consistent with the purpose of trial is not acceptance but failure seasonably to notify the seller of election to return the goods is acceptance, and if the goods conform to the contract acceptance of any part is acceptance of the whole; and

    (c) after due notification of election to return, the return is at the seller's risk and expense but a merchant buyer must follow any reasonable instructions.

(2) Under a sale or return unless otherwise agreed

    (a) the option to return extends to the whole or any commercial unit of the goods while in substantially their original condition, but must be exercised seasonably; and

    (b) the return is at the buyer's risk and expense.

Section 2—328. Sale by Auction.

(1) In a sale by auction if goods are put up in lots each lot is the subject of a separate sale.

(2) A sale by auction is complete when the auctioneer so announces by the fall of the hammer or in other customary manner. Where a bid is made while the hammer is falling in acceptance of a prior bid, the auctioneer may in his discretion reopen the bidding or declare the goods sold under the bid on which the hammer was falling'

(3) Such a sale is with reserve unless the goods are in explicit terms put up without reserve. In an auction with reserve the auctioneer may withdraw the goods at any time until he announces completion of the sale. In an auction without reserve, after the auctioneer calls for bids on an article or lot, that article or lot cannot be withdrawn unless no bid is made within a reasonable time. In either case a bidder may retract his bid until the auctioneer's announcement of completion of the sale, but a bidder's retraction does not revive any previous bid.

(4) If the auctioneer knowingly receives a bid on the seller's behalf or the seller makes or procures such a bid, and notice has not been given that liberty for such bidding is reserved, the buyer may at his option avoid the sale or take the goods at the price of the last good faith bid prior to the completion of the sale. This subsection shall not apply to any bid at a forced sale.

PART 4 / TITLE, CREDITORS AND GOOD FAITH PURCHASERS

Section 2—401. Passing of Title; Reservation for Security; Limited Application of This Section.

Each provision of this Article with regard to the rights, obligations and remedies of the seller, the buyer, purchasers or other third parties applies irrespective of title to the goods except where the provision refers to such title. Insofar as situations are not covered by the other provisions of this Article and matters concerning title become material the following rules apply:

(1) Title to goods cannot pass under a contract for sale prior to their identification to the contract (Section 2—501), and unless otherwise explicitly agreed the buyer acquires by their identification a special property as limited by this Act. Any retention or reservation by the seller of the title (property) in goods shipped or delivered to the buyer is limited in effect to the reservation of a security interest. Subject to these provisions and to the provisions of the Article on Secured Transactions (Article 9), title to goods passes from the seller to the buyer in any manner and on any conditions explicitly agreed on by the parties.

(2) Unless otherwise explicitly agreed, title passes to the buyer at the time and place at which the seller completes his performance with reference to the physical delivery of the goods, despite any reservation of a security interest and even though a document of title is to be delivered at a different time or place; and in particular and despite any reservation of a security interest by the bill of lading

  (a) if the contract requires or authorizes the seller to send the goods to the buyer but does not require him to deliver them at destination, title passes to the buyer at the time and place of shipment; but

  (b) if the contract requires delivery at destination, title passes on tender there.

(3) Unless otherwise explicitly agreed where delivery is to be made without moving the goods,

  (a) if the seller is to deliver a document of title, titles passes at the time when and the place where he delivers such documents; or

  (b) if the goods are at the time of contracting already identified and no documents are to be delivered, title passes at the time and place of contracting.

(4) A rejection or other refusal by the buyer to receive or retain the goods, whether or not justified, or a justified revocation of acceptance re-vests title to the goods in the seller. Such revesting occurs by operation of law and is not a "sale".

Section 2—402. Rights of Seller's Creditors Against Sold Goods.

(1) Except as provided in subsections (2) and (3), rights of unsecured creditors of the seller with respect to goods which have been identified to a contract for sale are subject to the buyer's rights to recover the goods under this Article (Sections 2—502 and 2—716).

(2) A creditor of the seller may treat a sale or an identification of goods to a contract for sale as void if as against him a retention of possession by the seller is fradulent under any rule of law of the state where the goods are situated, except that retention of possession in good faith and current course of trade by a merchant-seller for a commercially reasonable time after a sale or identification is not fraudulent.

(3) Nothing in this Article shall be deemed to impair the rights of creditors of the seller

  (a) under the provisions of the Article on Secured Transactions (Article 9); or

  (b) where identification to the contract or delivery is made not in current course of trade but in satisfaction of or as security for a pre-existing claim for money, security or the like and is made under circumstances which under any rule of law of the state where the goods are situated would apart from this Article constitute the transaction a fraudulent transfer or voidable preference.

Section 2—403. Power to Transfer; Good Faith Purchase of Goods; "Entrusting".

(1) A purchaser of goods acquires all title which his transferor had or had power to transfer except that a purchaser of a limited interest acquires rights only to the extent of the interest purchased. A person with voidable title has power to transfer a good title to a good faith purchaser for value. When goods have been delivered under a transaction of purchase, the purchaser has such power even though

  (a) the transferor was deceived as to the identity of the purchaser, or

  (b) the delivery was in exchange for a check which is later dishonored, or

  (c) it was agreed that the transaction was to be a "cash sale", or

(d) the delivery was procured through fraud punishable as larcenous under the criminal law.

(2) Any entrusting of possession of goods to a merchant who deals in goods of that kind gives him power to transfer all rights of the entruster to a buyer in ordinary course of business.

(3) "Entrusting" includes any delivery and any acquiescence in retention of possession regard-less of any condition expressed between the parties to the delivery or acquiescence and regardless of whether the procurement of the entrusting or the possessor's disposition of the goods have been such as to be larcenous under the criminal law.

(4) The rights of other purchasers of goods and of lien creditors are governed by the Articles on Secured Transactions (Article 9), Bulk Transfers (Article 6) and Documents of Title (Article 7).

PART 5 / PERFORMANCE

Section 2—501. Insurable Interest in Goods; Manner of Identification of Goods.

(1) The buyer obtains a special property and an insurable interest in goods by identification of existing goods as goods to which the contract refers even though the goods so identified are nonconforming and he has an option to return or reject them. Such identification can be made at any time and in any manner explicitly agreed to by the parties. In the absence of explicit agreement identification occurs

(a) when the contract is made if it is for the sale of goods already existing and identified;

(b) if the contract is for the sale of future goods other than those described in paragraph (c), when goods are shipped, marked or otherwise designated by the seller as goods to which the contract refers;

(c) when the crops are planted or otherwise become growing crops or the young are conceived if the contract is for the sale of unborn young to be born within twelve months after contracting or for the sale of crops to be harvested within twelve months or the next normal harvest season after contracting whichever is longer.

(2) The seller retains an insurable interest in goods so long as title to or any security interest in the goods remains in him, and where the identification is by the seller alone he may, until default or insolvency or notification to the buyer that the identification is final, substitute other goods for those identified.

(3) Nothing in this section impairs any insurable interest recognized under any other statute or rule of law.

Section 2—502. Buyer's Right to Goods on Seller's Insolvency.

(1) Subject to subsection (2) and even though the goods have not been shipped, a buyer who has paid a part or all of the price of goods in which he has a special property under the provisions of the immediately preceding section may on making and keeping good a tender of any unpaid portion of their price recover them from the seller if the seller becomes insolvent within ten days after receipt of the first installment on their price.

(2) If the identification creating his special property has been made by the buyer, he acquires the right to recover the goods only if they conform to the contract for sale.

Section 2—503. Manner of Seller's Tender of Delivery.

(1) Tender of delivery requires that the seller put and hold conforming goods at the buyer's disposition and give the buyer any notification reasonably necessary to enable him to take delivery. The manner, time and place for tender are determined by the agreement and this Article, and in particular

(a) tender must be at a reasonable hour, and if it is of goods they must be kept available for the period reasonably necessary to enable the buyer to take possession; but

(b) unless otherwise agreed the buyer must furnish facilities reasonably suited to the receipt of the goods.

(2) Where the case is within the next section respecting shipment, tender requires that the seller comply with its provisions.

(3) Where the seller is required to deliver at a particular destination, tender requires that he comply with subsection (1) and also in any appropriate case tender documents as described in subsections (4) and (5) of this section.

(4) Where goods are in the possession of a bailee and are to be delivered without being moved

(a) tender requires that the seller either tender a negotiable document of title covering such goods or procure acknowledgment by the bailee of the buyer's right to possession of the goods; but

(b) tender to the buyer of a nonnegotiable document of title or of a written direction to the bailee to deliver is sufficient tender unless the buyer seasonably objects, and receipt by the bailee of notification of the buyer's rights fixes those rights as against the bailee and all third persons; but risk of loss of the goods and of any failure by the bailee to honor the nonnegotiable document of title or to obey the direction remains on the seller until the buyer has had a reasonable time to present the document or direction, and a refusal by the bailee to honor the document or to obey the direction defeats the tender.

(5) Where the contract requires the seller to deliver documents

(a) he must tender all such documents in correct form, except as provided in this Article with respect to bills of lading in a set (subsection (2) of Section 2—323); and

(b) tender through customary banking channels is sufficient and dishonor of a draft accompanying the documents constitutes nonacceptance or rejection.

Section 2—504. Shipment by Seller.

Where the seller is required or authorized to send the goods to the buyer and the contract does not require him to deliver them at a particular destination, then unless otherwise agreed he must

(a) put the goods in the possession of such a carrier and make such a contract for their transportation as may be reasonable having regard to the nature of the goods and other circumstances of the case; and

(b) obtain and promptly deliver or tender in due form any document necessary to enable the buyer to obtain possession of the goods or otherwise required by the agreement or by usage of trade; and

(c) promptly notify the buyer of the shipment.

Failure to notify the buyer under paragraph (c) or to make a proper contract under paragraph (a) is a ground for rejection only if material delay or loss ensues.

Section 2—505. Seller's Shipment Under Reservation.

(1) Where the seller has identified goods to the contract by or before shipment:

(a) his procurement of a negotiable bill of lading to his own order or otherwise reserves in him a security interest in the goods. His procurement of the bill to the order of a financing agency or of the buyer indicates in addition only the seller's expectation of transferring that interest to the person named.

(b) a nonnegotiable bill of lading to himself or his nominee reserves possession of the goods as security but except in a case of conditional delivery (subsection (2) of Section 2—507) a nonnegotiable bill of lading naming the buyer as consignee reserves no security interest even though the seller retains possession of the bill of lading.

(2) When shipment by the seller with reservation of a security interest is in violation of the contract for sale, it constitutes an improper contract for transportation within the preceding section but impairs neither the rights given to the buyer by shipment and identification of the goods to the contract nor the seller's powers as a holder of a negotiable document.

Section 2—506. Rights of Financing Agency.

(1) A financing agency by paying or purchasing for value a draft which relates to a shipment of goods acquires to the extent of the payment or purchase and in addition to its own rights under the draft and any document of title securing it any rights of the shipper in the goods including the right to stop delivery and the shipper's right to have the draft honored by the buyer.

(2) The right to reimbursement of a financing agency which has in good faith honored or purchased the draft under commitment to or authority from the buyer is not impaired by subsequent discovery of defects with reference to any relevant document which was apparently regular on its face.

Section 2—507. Effect of Seller's Tender; Delivery on Condition.

(1) Tender of delivery is a condition to the buyer's duty to accept the goods and, unless otherwise agreed, to his duty to pay for them. Tender entitles the seller to acceptance of the goods and to payment according to the contract.

(2) Where payment is due and demanded on the delivery to the buyer of goods or documents of title, his right as against the seller to retain or dispose of them is conditional upon his making the payment due.

Section 2—508. Cure by Seller of Improper Tender or Delivery; Replacement.

(1) Where any tender or delivery by the seller is rejected because nonconforming and the time for performance has not yet expired, the seller may seasonably notify the buyer of his intention to cure and may then within the contract time make a conforming delivery.

(2) Where the buyer rejects a nonconforming tender which the seller had reasonable grounds to believe would be acceptable with or without money allowance, the seller may if he seasonably notifies the buyer have a further reasonable time to substitute a conforming tender.

Section 2—509. Risk of Loss in the Absence of Breach.

(1) Where the contract requires or authorizes the seller to ship the goods by carrier
  (a) if it does not require him to deliver them at a particular destination, the risk of loss passes to the buyer when the goods are duly delivered to the carrier even though the shipment is under reservation (Section 2—505); but
  (b) if it does require him to deliver them at a particular destination and the goods are there duly tendered while in the possession of the carrier, the risk of loss passes to the buyer when the goods are there duly so tendered as to enable the buyer to take delivery.

(2) Where the goods are held by a bailee to be delivered without being moved, the risk of loss passes to the buyer
  (a) on his receipt of a negotiable document of title covering the goods; or
  (b) on acknowledgment by the bailee of the buyer's right to possession of the goods; or
  (c) after his receipt of a nonnegotiable document of title or other written direction to deliver, as provided in subsection (4) (b) of Section 2—503.

(3) In any case not within subsection (1) or (2), the risk of loss passes to the buyer on his receipt of the goods if the seller is a merchant; otherwise the risk passes to the buyer on tender of delivery.

(4) The provisions of this section are subject to contrary agreement of the parties and to the provisions of this Article on sale on approval (Section 2—327) and on effect of breach on risk of loss (Section 2—510).

Section 2—510. Effect of Breach on Risk of Loss.

(1) Where a tender or delivery of goods so fails to conform to the contract as to give a right of rejection, the risk of their loss remains on the seller until cure or acceptance.

(2) Where the buyer rightfully revokes acceptance, he may to the extent of any deficiency in his effective insurance coverage treat the risk of loss as having rested on the seller from the beginning.

(3) Where the buyer as to conforming goods already identified to the contract for sale repudiates or is otherwise in breach before risk of their loss has passed to him, the seller may to the extent of any deficiency in his effective insurance coverage treat the risk of loss as resting on the buyer for a commercially reasonable time.

Section 2—511. Tender of Payment by Buyer; Payment by Check.

(1) Unless otherwise agreed tender of payment is a condition to the seller's duty to tender and complete any delivery.

(2) Tender of payment is sufficient when made by any means or in any manner current in the ordinary course of business unless the seller demands payment in legal tender and gives any extension of time reasonably necessary to procure it.

(3) Subject to the provisions of this Act on the effect of an instrument on an obligation (Section 3—802), payment by check is conditional and is defeated as between the parties by dishonor of the check on due presentment.

Section 2—512. Payment by Buyer Before Inspection.

(1) Where the contract requires payment before inspection, nonconformity of the goods does not excuse the buyer from so making payment unless
  (a) the nonconformity appears without inspection; or
  (b) despite tender of the required documents the circumstances would justify injunction against honor under the provisions of this Act (Section 5—114).

(2) Payment pursuant to subsection (1) does not constitute an acceptance of goods or impair the buyer's right to inspect or any of his remedies.

Section 2—513. Buyer's Right to Inspection of Goods.

(1) Unless otherwise agreed and subject to subsection (3), where goods are tendered or delivered or identified to the contract for sale, the buyer has a right before payment or acceptance to inspect them at any reasonable place and time and in any reasonable manner. When the seller is required or authorized to send the goods to the buyer, the inspection may be after their arrival.

(2) Expenses of inspection must be borne by the buyer but may be recovered from the seller if the goods do not conform and are rejected.

(3) Unless otherwise agreed and subject to the provisions of this Article on C.I.F. contracts (subsection (3) of Section 2—321), the buyer is not entitled to inspect the goods before payment of the price when the contract provides

(a) for delivery "C.O.D." or on other like terms; or

(b) for payment against documents of title, except where such payment is due only after the goods are to become available for inspection.

(4) A place or method of inspection fixed by the parties is presumed to be exclusive, but unless otherwise expressly agreed it does not postpone identification or shift the place for delivery or for passing the risk of loss. If compliance becomes impossible, inspection shall be as provided in this section unless the place or method fixed was clearly intended as an indispensable condition failure of which avoids the contract.

Section 2—514. When Documents Deliverable on Acceptance; When on Payment.

Unless otherwise agreed documents against which a draft is drawn are to be delivered to the drawee on acceptance of the draft if it is payable more than three days after presentment; otherwise, only on payment.

Section 2—515. Preserving Evidence of Goods in Dispute.

In furtherance of the adjustment of any claim or dispute

(a) either party on reasonable notification to the other and for the purpose of ascertaining the facts and preserving evidence has the right to inspect, test and sample the goods including such of them as may be in the possession or control of the other; and

(b) the parties may agree to a third party inspection or survey to determine the conformity or condition of the goods and may agree that the findings shall be binding upon them in any subsequent litigation or adjustment.

PART 6 / BREACH, REPUDIATION AND EXCUSE

Section 2—601. Buyer's Rights on Improper Delivery.

Subject to the provisions of this Article on breach in installment contract (Section 2—612) and unless otherwise agreed under the sections on contractual limitations of remedy (Sections 2—718 and 2—719), if the goods or the tender of delivery fail in any respect to conform to the contract, the buyer may

(a) reject the whole; or

(b) accept the whole; or

(c) accept any commercial unit or units and reject the rest.

Section 2—602. Manner and Effect of Rightful Rejection.

(1) Rejection of goods must be within a reasonable time after their delivery or tender. It is ineffective unless the buyer seasonably notifies the seller.

(2) Subject to the provisions of the two following sections on rejected goods (Section 2—603 and 2—604),

(a) after rejection any exercise of ownership by the buyer with respect to any commercial unit is wrongful as against the seller; and

(b) if the buyer has before rejection taken physical possession of goods in which he does not have a security interest under the provisions of this Article (subsection (3) of Section 2—711), he is under a duty after rejection to hold them with reasonable care at the seller's disposition for a time sufficient to permit the seller to remove them; but

(c) the buyer has no further obligations with regard to goods rightfully rejected.

(3) The seller's rights with respect to goods wrongfully rejected are governed by the provi-

sions of this Article on Seller's remedies in general (Section 2—703).

Section 2—603. Merchant Buyer's Duties as to Rightfully Rejected Goods.

(1) Subject to any security interest in the buyer (subsection (3) of Section 2—711), when the seller has no agent or place of business at the market of rejection, a merchant buyer is under a duty after rejection of goods in his possession or control to follow any reasonable instructions received from the seller with respect to the goods and in the absence of such instructions to make reasonable efforts to sell them for the seller's account if they are perishable or threaten to decline in value speedily. Instructions are not reasonable if on demand indemnity for expenses is not forthcoming.

(2) When the buyer sells goods under subsection (1), he is entitled to reimbursement from the seller or out of the proceeds for reasonable expenses of caring for and selling them, and if the expenses include no selling commission then to such commission as is usual in the trade or if there is none to a reasonable sum not exceeding ten percent on the gross proceeds.

(3) In complying with this section the buyer is held only to good faith, and good faith conduct hereunder is neither acceptance nor conversion nor the basis of an action for damages.

Section 2—604. Buyer's Options as to Salvage of Rightfully Rejected Goods.

Subject to the provisions of the immediately preceding section on perishables, if the seller gives no instructions within a reasonable time after notification of rejection, the buyer may store the rejected goods for the seller's account or reship them to him or resell them for the seller's account with reimbursement as provided in the preceding section. Such action is not acceptance or conversion.

Section 2—605. Waiver of Buyer's Objections by Failure to Particularize.

(1) The buyer's failure to state in connection with rejection a particular defect which is ascertainable by reasonable inspection precludes him from relying on the unstated defect to justify rejection or to establish breach
    (a) where the seller could have cured it if stated seasonably; or
    (b) between merchants when the seller has after rejection made request in writing for a full and final written statement of all defects on which the buyer proposes to rely.

(2) Payment against documents made without reservation of rights precludes recovery of the payment for defects apparent on the face of the documents.

Section 2—606. What Constitutes Acceptance of Goods.

(1) Acceptance of goods occurs when the buyer
    (a) after a reasonable opportunity to inspect the goods signifies to the seller that the goods are conforming or that he will take or retain them in spite of their nonconformity; or
    (b) fails to make an effective rejection (subsection (1) of Section 2—602), but such acceptance does not occur until the buyer has had a reasonable opportunity to inspect them; or
    (c) does any act inconsistent with the seller's ownership; but if such act is wrongful as against the seller it is an acceptance only if ratified by him.

(2) Acceptance of a part of any commercial unit is acceptance of that entire unit.

Section 2—607. Effect of Acceptance; Notice of Breach; Burden of Establishing Breach After Acceptance; Notice of Claim or Litigation to Person Answerable Over.

(1) The buyer must pay at the contract rate for any goods accepted.

(2) Acceptance of goods by the buyer precludes rejection of the goods accepted and, if made with knowledge of a nonconformity, cannot be revoked because of it unless the acceptance was on the reasonable assumption that the nonconformity would be seasonably cured, but acceptance does not of itself impair any other remedy provided by this Article for nonconformity.

(3) Where a tender has been accepted
    (a) the buyer must within a reasonable time after he discovers or should have discovered any breach notify the seller of breach or be barred from any remedy; and
    (b) if the claim is one for infringement or the like (subsection (3) of Section 2—312) and the buyer is sued as a result of such a breach, he must so notify the seller within a reasonable time after he receives notice of the litigation or be barred from any remedy over for liability established by the litigation.

(4) The burden is on the buyer to establish any breach with respect to the goods accepted.

(5) Where the buyer is sued for breach of a warranty or other obligation for which his seller is answerable over

    (a) he may give his seller written notice of the litigation. If the notice states that the seller may come in and defend and that if the seller does not do so he will be bound in any action against him by his buyer by any determination of fact common to the two litigations, then unless the seller after seasonable receipt of the notice does come in and defend he is so bound.

    (b) if the claim is one of infringement or the like (subsection (3) of Section 2—312) the original seller may demand in writing that his buyer turn over to him control of the litigation including settlement or else be barred from any remedy over and if he also agrees to bear all expense and to satisfy any adverse judgment, then unless the buyer after seasonable receipt of the demand does turn over control the buyer is so barred.

(6) The provisions of subsections (3), (4) and (5) apply to any obligation of a buyer to hold the seller harmless against infringement or the like (subsection (3) of Section 2—312).

Section 2—608. Revocation of Acceptance in Whole or in Part.

(1) The buyer may revoke his acceptance of a lot or commercial unit whose nonconformity substantially impairs its value to him if he has accepted it

    (a) on the reasonable assumption that its nonconformity would be cured and it has not been reasonably cured; or

    (b) without discovery of such nonconformity if his acceptance was reasonably induced either by the difficulty of discovery before acceptance or by the seller's assurances.

(2) Revocation of acceptance must occur within a reasonable time after the buyer discovers or should have discovered the ground for it and before any substantial change in condition of the goods which is not caused by their own defects. It is not effective until the buyer notifies the seller of it.

(3) A buyer who so revokes has the same rights and duties with regard to the goods involved as if he had rejected them.

Section 2—609. Right to Adequate Assurance of Performance.

(1) A contract for sale imposes an obligation on each party that the other's expectation of receiving due performance will not be impaired. When reasonable grounds for insecurity arise with respect to the performance of either party, the other may in writing demand adequate assurance of due performance and until he receives such assurance may if commercially reasonable suspend any performance for which he has not already received the agreed return.

(2) Between merchants the reasonableness of grounds for insecurity and the adequacy of any assurance offered shall be determined according to commercial standards.

(3) Acceptance of any improper delivery or payment does not prejudice the aggrieved party's right to demand adequate assurance of future performance.

(4) After receipt of a justified demand failure to provide within a reasonable time not exceeding thirty days such assurance of due performance as is adequate under the circumstances of the particular case is a repudiation of the contract.

Section 2—610. Anticipatory Repudiation.

When either party repudiates the contract with respect to a performance not yet due the loss of which will substantially impair the value of the contract to the other, the aggrieved party may

    (a) for a commercially reasonable time await performance by the repudiating party; or

    (b) resort to any remedy for breach (Section 2—703 or Section 2—711), even though he has notified the repudiating party that he would await the latter's performance and urged retraction; and

    (c) in either case suspend his own performance or proceed in accordance with the provisions of this Article on the seller's right to identify goods to the contract notwithstanding breach or to salvage unfinished goods (Section 2—704).

Section 2—611. Retraction of Anticipatory Repudiation.

(1) Until the repudiating party's next performance is due he can retract his repudiation unless the aggrieved party has since the repudiation cancelled or materially changed his position or otherwise indicated that he considers the repudiation final.

(2) Retraction may be by any method which clearly indicates to the aggrieved party that the repudiating party intends to perform, but must include any assurance justifiably demanded under the provisions of this Article (Section 2—609).

(3) Retraction reinstates the repudiating party's rights under the contract with due excuse and allowance to the aggrieved party for any delay occasioned by the repudiation.

Section 2—612. "Installment Contract"; Breach.

(1) An "installment contract" is one which requires or authorizes the delivery of goods in separate lots to be separately accepted, even though the contract contains a clause "each delivery is a separate contract" or its equivalent.

(2) The buyer may reject any installment which is nonconforming if the nonconformity substantially impairs the value of that installment and cannot be cured or if the nonconformity is a defect in the required documents; but if the nonconformity does not fall within subsection (3) and the seller gives adequate assurance of its cure the buyer must accept that installment.

(3) Whenever nonconformity or default with respect to one or more installments substantially impairs the value of the whole contract there is a breach of the whole. But the aggrieved party reinstates the contract if he accepts a nonconforming installment without seasonably notifying of cancellation or if he brings an action with respect only to past installments or demands performance as to future installments.

Section 2—613. Casualty to Identified Goods.

Where the contract requires for its performance goods identified when the contract is made, and the goods suffer casualty without fault of either party before the risk of loss passes to the buyer, or in a proper case under a "no arrival, no sale" term (Section 2—324) then

    (a) if the loss is total the contract is avoided; and

    (b) if the loss is partial or the goods have so deteriorated as no longer to conform to the contract, the buyer may nevertheless demand inspection and at his option either treat the contract as avoided or accept the goods with due allowance from the contract price for the deterioration or the deficiency in quantity but without further right against the seller.

Section 2—614. Substituted Performance.

(1) Where without fault of either party the agreed berthing, loading, or unloading facilities

fail or an agreed type of carrier becomes unavailable or the agreed manner of delivery otherwise becomes commercially impracticable but a commercially reasonable substitute is available, such substitute performance must be tendered and accepted.

(2) If the agreed means or manner of payment fails because of domestic or foreign governmental regulation, the seller may withhold or stop delivery unless the buyer provides a means or manner of payment which is commercially a substantial equivalent. If delivery has already been taken, payment by the means or in the manner provided by the regulation discharges the buyer's obligation unless the regulation is discriminatory, oppressive or predatory.

Section 2—615. Excuse by Failure of Presupposed Conditions.

Except so far as a seller may have assumed a greater obligation and subject to the preceding section on substituted performance:

    (a) Delay in delivery or nondelivery in whole or in part by a seller who complies with paragraphs (b) and (c) is not a breach of his duty under a contract for sale if performance as agreed has been made impracticable by the occurrence of a contingency the nonoccurrence of which was a basic assumption on which the contract was made or by compliance in good faith with any applicable foreign or domestic governmental regulation or order whether or not it later proves to be invalid.

    (b) Where the causes mentioned in paragraph (a) affect only a part of the seller's capacity to perform, he must allocate production and deliveries among his customers but may at his option include regular customers not then under contract as well as his own requirements for further manufacture. He may so allocate in any manner which is fair and reasonable.

    (c) The seller must notify the buyer seasonably that there will be delay or nondelivery and, when allocation is required under paragraph (b), of the estimated quota thus made available for the buyer.

Section 2—616. Procedure on Notice Claiming Excuse.

(1) Where the buyer receives notification of a material or indefinite delay or an allocation justified under the preceding section he may by

written notification to the seller as to any delivery concerned, and where the prospective deficiency substantially impairs the value of the whole contract under the provisions of this Article relating to breach of installment contracts (Section 2—612), then also as to the whole,

    (a) terminate and thereby discharge any unexecuted portion of the contract; or

    (b) modify the contract by agreeing to take his available quota in substitution.

(2) If after receipt of such notification from the seller the buyer fails so to modify the contract within a reasonable time not exceeding thirty days, the contract lapses with respect to any deliveries affected.

(3) The provisions of this section may not be negated by agreement except in so far as the seller has assumed a greater obligation under the preceding section.

PART 7 / REMEDIES

Section 2—701. Remedies for Breach of Collateral Contracts Not Impaired.

Remedies for breach of any obligation or promise collateral or ancillary to a contract for sale are not impaired by the provisions of this Article.

Section 2—702. Seller's Remedies on Discovery of Buyer's Insolvency.

(1) Where the seller discovers the buyer to be insolvent he may refuse delivery except for cash including payment for all goods theretofore delivered under the contract, and stop delivery under this Article (Section 2—705).

(2) Where the seller discovers that the buyer has received goods on credit while insolvent he may reclaim the goods upon demand made within ten days after the receipt, but if misrepresentation of solvency has been made to the particular seller in writing within three months before delivery the ten day limitation does not apply. Except as provided in this subsection, the seller may not base a right to reclaim goods on the buyer's fraudulent or innocent misrepresentation of solvency or of intent to pay.

(3) The seller's right to reclaim under subsection (2) is subject to the rights of a buyer in ordinary course or other good faith purchaser or lien creditor under this Article (Section 2—403). Successful reclamation of goods excludes all other remedies with respect to them.

Section 2—703. Seller's Remedies in General.

Where the buyer wrongfully rejects or revokes acceptance of goods or fails to make a payment due on or before delivery or repudiates with respect to a part or the whole, then with respect to any goods directly affected and, if the breach is of the whole contract (Section 2—612), then also with respect to the whole undelivered balance, the aggrieved seller may

    (a) withhold delivery of such goods;

    (b) stop delivery by any bailee as hereafter provided (Section 2—705);

    (c) proceed under the next section respecting goods still unidentified to the contract;

    (d) resell and recover damages as hereafter provided (Section 2—706);

    (e) recover damages for nonacceptance (Section 2—708) or in a proper case the price (section 2—709);

    (f) cancel.

Section 2—704. Seller's Right to Identify Goods to the Contract Notwithstanding Breach or to Salvage Unfinished Goods.

(1) An aggrieved seller under the preceding section may

    (a) identify to the contract conforming goods not already identified if at the time he learned of the breach they are in his possession or control;

    (b) treat as the subject of resale goods which have demonstrably been intended for the particular contract even though those goods are unfinished.

(2) Where the goods are unfinished an aggrieved seller may in the exercise of reasonable commercial judgment for the purposes of avoiding loss and of effective realization either complete the manufacture and wholly identify the goods to the contract or cease manufacture and resell for scrap or salvage value or proceed in any other reasonable manner.

Section 2—705. Seller's Stoppage of Delivery in Transit or Otherwise.

(1) The seller may stop delivery of goods in the possession of a carrier or other bailee when he discovers the buyer to be insolvent (Section 2—702) and may stop delivery of carload, truckload, planeload or larger shipments of express or freight when the buyer repudiates or fails to make a payment due before delivery or if for any

other reason the seller has a right to withhold or reclaim the goods.

(2) As against such buyer the seller may stop delivery until

    (a) receipt of the goods by the buyer; or

    (b) acknowledgment to the buyer by any bailee of the goods except a carrier that the bailee holds the goods for the buyer; or

    (c) such acknowledgment to the buyer by a carrier by reshipment or as warehouseman; or

    (d) negotiation to the buyer of any negotiable document of title covering the goods.

(3)(a) To stop delivery the seller must so notify as to enable the bailee by reasonable diligence to prevent delivery of the goods.

    (b) After such notification the bailee must hold and deliver the goods according to the directions of the seller, but the seller is liable to the bailee for any ensuing charges or damages.

    (c) If a negotiable document of title has been issued for goods, the bailee is not obliged to obey a notification to stop until surrender of the document.

    (d) A carrier who has issued a nonnegotiable bill of lading is not obliged to obey a notification to stop received from a person other than the consignor.

Section 2—706. Seller's Resale Including Contract for Resale.

(1) Under the conditions stated in Section 2—703 on seller's remedies, the seller may resell the goods concerned or the undelivered balance thereof. Where the resale is made in good faith and in a commercially reasonable manner the seller may recover the difference between the resale price and the contract price together with any incidental damages allowed under the provisions of this Article (Section 2-710), but less expenses saved in consequence of the buyer's breach.

(2) Except as otherwise provided in subsection (3) or unless otherwise agreed, resale may be at public or private sale including sale by way of one or more contracts to sell or of identification to an existing contract of the seller. Sale may be as a unit or in parcels and at any time and place and on any terms but every aspect of the sale including the method, manner, time, place and terms must be commercially reasonable. The resale must be reasonably identified as referring to the broken contract, but it is not necessary that

the goods be in existence or that any or all of them have been identified to the contract before the breach.

(3) Where the resale is at private sale the seller must give the buyer reasonable notification of his intention to resell.

(4) Where the resale is at public sale

    (a) only identified goods can be sold except where there is a recognized market for a public sale of futures in goods of the kind; and

    (b) it must be made at a usual place or market for public sale if one is reasonably available and except in the case of goods which are perishable or threaten to decline in value speedily the seller must give the buyer reasonable notice of the time and place of the resale; and

    (c) if the goods are not to be within the view of those attending the sale, the notification of sale must state the place where the goods are located and provide for their reasonable inspection by prospective bidders; and

    (d) the seller may buy.

(5) A purchaser who buys in good faith at a resale takes the goods free of any rights of the original buyer even though the seller fails to comply with one or more of the requirements of this section.

(6) The seller is not accountable to the buyer for any profit made on any resale. A person in the position of a seller (Section 2—707) or a buyer who has rightfully rejected or justifiably revoked acceptance must account for any excess over the amount of his security interest, as hereinafter defined (subsection (3) of Section 2—711).

Section 2—707. "Person in the Position of a Seller".

(1) A "person in the position of a seller" includes as against a principal an agent who has paid or become responsible for the price of goods on behalf of his principal or anyone who otherwise holds a security interest or other right in goods similar to that of a seller.

(2) A person in the position of a seller may as provided in this Article withhold or stop delivery (Section 2—705) and resell (Section 2—706) and recover incidental damages (Section 2—710).

Section 2—708. Seller's Damages for Non-acceptance or Repudation.

(1) Subject to subsection (2) and to the provisions of this Article with respect to proof of market price (Section 2—723), the measure of damages for nonacceptance or repudiation by the

buyer is the difference between the market price at the time and place for tender and the unpaid contract price together with any incidental damages provided in this Article (Section 2—710), but less expenses saved in consequence of the buyer's breach.

(2) If the measure of damages provided in subsection (1) is inadequate to put the seller in as good a position as performance would have done, then the measure of damages is the profit (including reasonable overhead) which the seller would have made from full performance by the buyer, together with any incidental damages provided in this Article (Section 2—710), due allowance for costs reasonably incurred and due credit for payments or proceeds of resale.

Section 2—709. Action for the Price.

(1) When the buyer fails to pay the price as it becomes due the seller may recover, together with any incidental damages under the next section, the price

  (a) of goods accepted or of conforming goods lost or damaged within a commercially reasonable time after risk of their loss has passed to the buyer; and

  (b) of goods identified to the contract if the seller is unable after reasonable effort to resell them at a reasonable price or the circumstances reasonably indicate that such effort will be unavailing.

(2) Where the seller sues for the price he must hold for the buyer any goods which have been identified to the contract and are still in his control except that if resale becomes possible he may resell them at any time prior to the collection of the judgment. The net proceeds of any such resale must be credited to the buyer and payment of the judgment entitles him to any goods not resold.

(3) After the buyer has wrongfully rejected or revoked acceptance of the goods or has failed to make a payment due or has repudiated (Section 2—610), a seller who is held not entitled to the price under this section shall nevertheless be awarded for damages for nonacceptance under the preceding section.

Section 2—710. Seller's Incidental Damages.

Incidental damages to an aggrieved seller include any commercially reasonable charges, expenses or commissions incurred in stopping delivery, in the transportation, care and custody of goods after the buyer's breach, in connection with return or resale of the goods or otherwise resulting from the breach.

Section 2—711. Buyer's Remedies in General; Buyer's Security Interest in Rejected Goods.

(1) Where the seller fails to make delivery or repudiates or the buyer rightfully rejects or justifiably revokes acceptance then with respect to any goods involved, and with respect to the whole if the breach goes to the whole contract (Section 2—612), the buyer may cancel and whether or not he has done so may in addition to recovering so much of the price as has been paid.

  (a) "cover" and have damages under the next section as to all the goods affected whether or not they have been identified to the contract; or

  (b) recover damages for nondelivery as provided in this Article (Section 2—713).

(2) Where the seller fails to deliver or repudiates the buyer may also

  (a) if the goods have been identified recover them as provided in this Article (Section 2—502); or

  (b) in a proper case obtain specific performance or replevy the goods as provided in this Article (Section 2—716).

(3) On rightful rejection or justifiable revocation of acceptance a buyer has a security interest in goods in his possession or control for any payments made on their price and any expenses reasonably incurred in their inspection, receipt, transportation, care and custody and may hold such goods and resell them in like manner as an aggrieved seller (Section 2—706).

Section 2—712. "Cover"; Buyer's Procurement of Substitute Goods.

(1) After a breach within the preceding section the buyer may "cover" by making in good faith and without unreasonable delay any reasonable purchase of or contract to purchase goods in substitution for those due from the seller.

(2) The buyer may recover from the seller as damages the difference between the cost of cover and the contract price together with any incidental or consequential damages as hereinafter defined (Section 2—715), but less expenses saved in consequence of the seller's breach.

(3) Failure of the buyer to effect cover within this section does not bar him from any other remedy.

Section 2—713. Buyer's Damages for Non-Delivery or Repudiation.

(1) Subject to the provisions of this Article with respect to proof of market price (Section

2—723), the measure of damages for non-delivery or repudiation by the seller is the difference between the market price at the time when the buyer learned of the breach and the contract price together with any incidental and consequential damages provided in this Article (Section 2—715), but less expenses saved in consequence of the seller's breach.

(2) Market price is to be determined as of the place for tender or, in cases of rejection after arrival or revocation of acceptance, as of the place of arrival.

Section 2—714. Buyer's Damages for Breach in Regard to Accepted Goods.

(1) Where the buyer has accepted goods and given notification (subsection (3) of Section 2—607) he may recover as damages for any nonconformity of tender the loss resulting in the ordinary course of events from the seller's breach as determined in any manner which is reasonable.

(2) The measure of damages for breach of warranty is the difference at the time and place of acceptance between the value of the goods accepted and the value they would have had if they had been as warranted, unless special circumstances show proximate damages of a different amount.

(3) In a proper case any incidental and consequential damages under the next section may also be recovered.

Section 2—715. Buyer's Incidental and Consequential Damages.

(1) Incidental damages resulting from the seller's breach include expenses reasonably incurred in inspection, receipt, transportation and care and custody of goods rightfully rejected, any commercially reasonable charges, expenses or commissions in connection with effecting cover and any other reasonable expense incident to the delay or other breach.

(2) Consequential damages resulting from the seller's breach include
  (a) any loss resulting from general or particular requirements and needs of which the seller at the time of contracting had reason to know and which could not reasonably be prevented by cover or otherwise; and
  (b) injury to person or property proximately resulting from any breach of warranty.

Section 2—716. Buyer's Right to Specific Performance or Replevin.

(1) Specific performance may be decreed where the goods are unique or in other proper circumstances.

(2) The decree for specific performance may include such terms and conditions as to payment of the price, damages, or other relief as the court may deem just.

(3) The buyer has a right of replevin for goods identified to the contract if after reasonable effort he is unable to effect cover for such goods or the circumstances reasonably indicate that such effort will be unavailing or if the goods have been shipped under reservation and satisfaction of the security interest in them has been made or tendered.

Section 2—717. Deduction of Damages From the Price.

The buyer on notifying the seller of his intention to do so may deduct all or any part of the damages resulting from any breach of the contract from any part of the price still due under the same contract.

Section 2—718. Liquidation or Limitation of Damages; Deposits.

(1) Damages for breach by either party may be liquidated in the agreement but only at an amount which is reasonable in the light of the anticipated or actual harm caused by the breach, the difficulties of proof of loss, and the inconvenience or nonfeasibility of otherwise obtaining an adequate remedy. A term fixing unreasonably large liquidated damages is void as a penalty.

(2) Where the seller justifiably withholds delivery of goods because of the buyer's breach, the buyer is entitled to restitution of any amount by which the sum of his payments exceeds
  (a) the amount to which the seller is entitled by virtue of terms liquidating the seller's damages in accordance with subsection (1), or
  (b) in the absence of such terms, twenty percent of the value of the total performance for which the buyer is obligated under the contract or $500, whichever is smaller.

(3) The buyer's right to restitution under subsection (2) is subject to offset to the extent that the seller establishes

(a) a right to recover damages under the provisions of this Article other than subsection (1), and

(b) the amount or value of any benefits received by the buyer directly or indirectly by reason of the contract.

(4) Where a seller has received payment in goods their reasonable value or the proceeds of their resale shall be treated as payments for the purposes of subsection (2); but if the seller has notice of the buyer's breach before reselling goods received in part performance, his resale is subject to the conditions laid down in the Article on resale by an aggrieved seller (Section 2—706).

Section 2—719. Contractual Modification or Limitation of Remedy.

(1) Subject to the provisions of subsections (2) and (3) of this section and of the preceding section on liquidation and limitation of damages,

(a) the agreement may provide for remedies in addition to or in substitution for those provided in this Article and may limit or alter the measure of damages recoverable under this Article, as by limiting the buyer's remedies to return of the goods and repayment of the price or to repair and replacement of nonconforming goods or parts; and

(b) resort to a remedy as provided is optional unless the remedy is expressly agreed to be exclusive, in which case it is the sole remedy.

(2) Where circumstances cause an exclusive or limited remedy to fail of its essential purpose, remedy may be had as provided in this Act.

(3) Consequential damages may be limited or excluded unless the limitation or exclusion is unconscionable. Limitation of consequential damages for injury to the person in the case of consumer goods is prima facie unconscionable, but limitation of damages where the loss is commercial is not.

Section 2—720. Effect of "Cancellation" or "Rescission" on Claims for Antecedent Breach.

Unless the contrary intention clearly appears, expressions of "cancellation" or "rescission" of the contract or the like shall not be construed as a renunciation or discharge of any claim in damages for an antecedent breach.

Section 2—721. Remedies for Fraud.

Remedies for material misrepresentation or fraud include all remedies available under this Article for nonfraudulent breach. Neither rescission of the contract for sale nor rejection or return of the goods shall bar or be deemed inconsistent with a claim for damages or other remedy.

Section 2—722. Who Can Sue Third Parties for Injury to Goods.

Where a third party so deals with goods which have been identified to a contract for sale as to cause actionable injury to a party to that contract

(a) a right of action against the third party is in either party to the contract for sale who has title to or a security interest or a special property or an insurable interest in the goods; and if the goods have been destroyed or converted, a right of action is also in the party who either bore the risk of loss under the contract for sale or has since the injury assumed that risk as against the other;

(b) if at the time of the injury the party plaintiff did not bear the risk of loss as against the other party to the contract for sale and there is no arrangement between them for disposition of the recovery, his suit or settlement is, subject to his own interest, as a fiduciary for the other party to the contract;

(c) either party may with the consent of the other sue for the benefit of whom it may concern.

Section 2—723. Proof of Market Price; Time and Place.

(1) If an action based on anticipatory repudiation comes to trial before the time for performance with respect to some or all of the goods, any damages based on market price (Section 2—708 or Section 2—713) shall be determined according to the price of such goods prevailing at the time when the aggrieved party learned of the repudiation.

(2) If evidence of a price prevailing at the times or places described in this Article is not readily available, the price prevailing within any reasonable time before or after the time described or at any other place which in commercial judgment or under usage of trade would serve as a reasonable substitute for the one described may be used, making any proper allowance for the cost of transporting the goods to or from such other place.

(3) Evidence of a relevant price prevailing at a time or place other than the one described in this Article offered by one party is not admissible unless and until he has given the other party such

notice as the court finds sufficient to prevent unfair surprise.

Section 2—724. Admissibility of Market Quotations.

Whenever the prevailing price or value of any goods regularly bought and sold in any established commodity market is in issue, reports in official publications or trade journals or in newspapers or periodicals of general circulation published as the reports of such market shall be admissible in evidence. The circumstances of the preparation of such a report may be shown to affect its weight but not its admissibility.

Section 2—725. Statute of Limitations in Contracts for Sale.

(1) An action for breach of any contract for sale must be commenced within four years after the cause of action has accrued. By the original agreement the parties may reduce the period of limitation to not less than one year but may not extend it.

(2) A cause of action accrues when the breach occurs regardless of the aggrieved party's lack of knowledge of the breach. A breach of warranty occurs when tender of delivery is made, except that where a warranty explicitly extends to future performance of the goods and discovery of the breach must await the time of such performance the cause of action accrues when the breach is or should have been discovered.

(3) Where an action commenced within the time limited by subsection (1) is so terminated as to leave available a remedy by another action for the same breach, such other action may be commenced after the expiration of the time limit and within six months after the termination of the first action unless the termination resulted from voluntary discontinuance or from dismissal for failure or neglect to prosecute.

(4) This section does not alter the law on tolling of the statute of limitations nor does it apply to causes of action which have accrued before this Act becomes effective.

ARTICLE 3 / COMMERCIAL PAPER

PART 1 / SHORT TITLE, FORM AND INTERPRETATION

Section 3—101. Short Title.

This Article shall be known and may be cited as Uniform Commercial Code—Commercial Paper.

Section 3—102. Definitions and Index of Definitions.

(1) In this Article unless the context otherwise requires
- (a) "Issue" means the first delivery of of an instrument to a holder or a remitter.
- (b) An "order" is a direction to pay and must be more than an authorization or request. It must identify the person to pay with reasonable certainty. It may be addressed to one or more such persons jointly or in the alternative but not in succession.
- (c) A "promise" is an undertaking to pay and must be more than an acknowledgment of an obligation.
- (d) "Secondary party" means a drawer or indorser.
- (e) "Instrument" means a negotiable instrument.

(2) Other definitions applying to this Article and the sections in which they appear are:

"Acceptance". Section 3—410.
"Accommodation party". Section 3—415.
"Alteration". Section 3—407.
"Certificate of deposit". Section 3—104.
"Certification". Section 3—411.
"Check". Section 3—104.
"Definite time". Section 3—109.
"Dishonor". Section 3—507.
"Draft". Section 3—104.
"Holder in due course". Section 3—302.
"Negotiation". Section 3—202.
"Note". Section 3—104.
"Notice of dishonor". Section 3—508.
"On demand". Section 3—108.
"Presentment". Section 3—504.
"Protest". Section 3—509.
"Restrictive Indorsement". Section 3—205.
"Signature". Section 3—401.

(3) The following definitions in other Articles apply to this Article:

"Account". Section 4—104.
"Banking Day". Section 4—104.
"Clearing house". Section 4—104.
"Collecting bank". Section 4—105.
"Customer". Section 4—104.
"Depositary Bank". Section 4—105.

"Documentary Draft". Section 4—104.
"Intermediary Bank". Section 4—105.
"Item". Section 4—104.
"Midnight deadline". Section 4—104.
"Payor bank". Section 4—105.

(4) In addition Article 1 contains general definitions and principles of construction and interpretation applicable throughout this Article.

Section 3—103. Limitations on Scope of Article.

(1) This Article does not apply to money, documents of title or investment securities.

(2) The provisions of this Article are subject to the provisions of the Article on Bank Deposits and Collections (Article 4) and Secured Transactions (Article 9).

Section 3—104. Form of Negotiable Instruments; "Draft"; "Check"; "Certificate of Deposit"; "Note".

(1) Any writing to be a negotiable instrument within this Article must
(a) be signed by the maker or drawer; and
(b) contain an unconditional promise or order to pay a sum certain in money and no other promise, order, obligation or power given by the maker or drawer except as authorized by this Article; and
(c) be payable on demand or at a definite time; and
(d) be payable to order or bearer.

(2) A writing which complies with the requirements of this section is
(a) a "draft" ("bill of exchange") if it is an order;
(b) a "check" if it is a draft drawn on a bank and payable on demand;
(c) a "certificate of deposit" if it is an acknowledgment by a bank of receipt of money with an engagement to repay it;
(d) a "note" if it is a promise other than a certificate of deposit.

(3) As used in other Articles of this Act, and as the context may require, the terms "draft", "check", "certificate of deposit" and "note" may refer to instruments which are not negotiable within this Article as well as to instruments which are so negotiable.

Section 3—105. When Promise or Order Unconditional.

(1) A promise or order otherwise unconditional is not made conditional by the fact that the instrument

(a) is subject to implied or constructive conditions; or
(b) states its consideration, whether performed or promised, or the transaction which gave rise to the instrument, or that the promise or order is made or the instrument matures in accordance with or "as per" such transaction; or
(c) refers to or states that it arises out of a separate agreement or refers to a separate agreement for rights as to prepayment of acceleration; or
(d) states that it is drawn under a letter of credit; or
(e) states that it is secured, whether by mortgage, reservation of title or otherwise; or
(f) indicates a particular account to be debited or any other fund or source from which reimbursement is expected; or
(g) is limited to payment out of a particular fund or the proceeds of a particular source, if the instrument is issued by a government or governmental agency or unit; or
(h) is limited to payment out of the entire assets of a partnership, unincorporated association, trust or estate by or on behalf of which the instrument is issued.

(2) A promise or order is not unconditional if the instrument
(a) states that it is subject to or governed by any other agreement, or
(b) states that it is to be paid only out of a particular fund or source except as provided in this section.

Section 3—106. Sum Certain.

(1) The sum payable is a sum certain even though it is to be paid
(a) with stated interest or by stated installments; or
(b) with stated different rates of interest before and after default or a specified date; or
(c) with a stated discount or addition if paid before or after the date fixed for payment; or
(d) with exchange or less exchange, whether at a fixed rate or at the current rate; or
(e) with costs of collection or an attorney's fee or both upon default.

(2) Nothing in this section shall validate any term which is otherwise illegal.

Section 3—107. Money.

(1) An instrument is payable in money if the medium of exchange in which it is payable is money at the time the instrument is made. An instrument payable in "currency" or "current funds" is payable in money.

(2) A promise or order to pay a sum stated in a foreign currency is for a sum certain in money and, unless a different medium of payment is specified in the instrument, may be satisfied by payment of that number of dollars which the stated foreign currency will purchase at the buying sight rate for that currency on the day on which the instrument is payable or, if payable on demand, on the day of demand. If such an instrument specifies a foreign currency as the medium of payment, the instrument is payable in that currency.

Section 3—108. Payable on Demand.

Instruments payable on demand include those payable at sight or on presentation and those in which no time for payment is stated.

Section 3—109. Definite Time.

(1) An instrument is payable at a definite time if by its terms it is payable
   (a) on or before a stated debt or at a fixed period after a stated date; or
   (b) at a fixed period after sight; or
   (c) at a definite time subject to any acceleration; or
   (d) at a definite time subject to extension at the option of the holder, or to extension to a further definite time at the option of the maker or acceptor or automatically upon or after a specified act or event.

(2) An instrument which by its terms is otherwise payable only upon an act or event uncertain as to time of occurrence is not payable at a definite time even though the act or event has occurred.

Section 3—110. Payable to Order.

(1) An instrument is payable to order when by its terms it is payable to the order or assigns of any person therein specified with reasonable certainty, or to him or his order, or when it is conspicuously designated on its face as "exchange" or the like and names a payee. It may be payable to the order of
   (a) the maker or drawer; or
   (b) the drawee; or
   (c) a payee who is not maker, drawer or drawee; or
   (d) two or more payees together or in the alternative; or
   (e) an estate, trust or fund, in which case it is payable to the order of the representative of such estate, trust or fund or his successors; or
   (f) an office, or an officer by his title as such in which case it is payable to the principal, but the incumbent of the office or his successors may act as if he or they were the holder; or
   (g) a partnership or unincorporated association, in which case it is payable to the partnership or association and may be indorsed or transferred by any person thereto authorized.

(2) An instrument not payable to order is not made so payable by such words as "payable upon return of this instrument properly indorsed."

(3) An instrument made payable both to order and to bearer is payable to order unless the bearer words are handwritten or typewritten.

Section 3—111. Payable to Bearer.

An instrument is payable to bearer when by its terms it is payable to
   (a) bearer or the order of bearer; or
   (b) a specified person or bearer; or
   (c) "cash" or the order of "cash", or any other indication which does not purport to designate a specific payee.

Section 3—112. Terms and Omissions Not Affecting Negotiability.

(1) The negotiability of an instrument is not affected by
   (a) the omission of a statement of any consideration or of the place where the instrument is drawn or payable; or
   (b) a statement that collateral has been given to secure obligations either on the instrument or otherwise of an obligor on the instrument or that in case of default on those obligations the holder may realize on or dispose of the collateral; or
   (c) a promise or power to maintain or protect collateral or to give additional collateral; or
   (d) a term authorizing a confession of judgment on the instrument if it is not paid when due; or
   (e) a term purporting to waive the benefit of any law intended for the advantage or protection of any obligor; or

(f) a term in a draft providing that tne payee by indorsing or cashing it acknowledges full satisfaction of an obligation of the drawer; or

(g) a statement in a draft drawn in a set of parts (Section 3—801) to the effect that the order is effective only ir no other part has been honored.

(2) Nothing in this section shall validate any term which is otherwise illegal.

Section 3—113. Seal.

An instrument otherwise negotiable is within this Article even though it is under a seal.

Section 3—114. Date, Antedating, Postdating.

(1) The negotiability of an instrument is not affected by the fact that it is undated, antedated or postdated.

(2) Where an instrument is antedated or post-dated the time when it is payable is determined by the stated date if the instrument is payable on demand or at a fixed period after date.

(3) Where the instrument or any signature thereon is dated, the date is presumed to be correct.

Section 3—115. Incomplete Instruments.

(1) When a paper whose contents at the time of signing show that it is intended to become an instrument is signed while still incomplete in any necessary respect, it cannot be enforced until completed, but when it is completed in accordance with authority given it is effective as completed.

(2) If the completion is unauthorized, the rules as to material alteration apply (Section 3—407), even though the paper was not delivered by the maker or drawer; but the burden of establishing that any completion is unauthorized is on the party so asserting.

Section 3—116. Instruments Payable to Two or More Persons.

An instrument payable to the order of two or more persons

(a) if in the alternative is payable to any one of them and may be negotiated, discharged or enforced by any of them who has possession of it;

(b) if not in the alternative is payable to all of them and may be negotiated, discharged or enforced only by all of them.

Section 3—117. Instruments Payable With Words of Description.

An instrument made payable to a named person with the addition of words describing him

(a) as agent or officer of a specified person is payable to his principal, but the agent or officer may act as if he were the holder;

(b) as any other fiduciary for a specified person or purpose is payable to the payee and may be negotiated, discharged or enforced by him;

(c) in any other manner is payable to the payee unconditionally and the additional words are without effect on subsequent parties.

Section 3—118. Ambiguous Terms and Rules of Construction.

The following rules apply to every instrument:

(a) Where there is doubt whether the instrument is a draft or a note the holder may treat it as either. A draft drawn on the drawer is effective as a note.

(b) Handwritten terms control typewritten and printed terms, and typewritten control printed.

(c) Words control figures except that if the words are ambiguous, figures control.

(d) Unless otherwise specified, a provision for interest means interest at the judgment rate at the place of payment from the date of the instrument, or if it is undated from the date of issue.

(e) Unless the instrument otherwise specifies, two or more persons who sign as maker, acceptor or drawer or indorser and as a part of the same transaction are jointly and severally liable even though the instrument contains such words as "I promise to pay."

(f) Unless otherwise specified, consent to extension authorizes a single extension for not longer than the original period. A consent to extension, expressed in the instrument, is binding on secondary parties and accommodation makers. A holder may not exercise his option to extend an instrument over the objection of a maker or acceptor or other party who in accordance with Section 3—604 tenders full payment when the instrument is due.

Section 3—119. Other Writings Affecting Instrument.

(1) As between the obligor and his immediate obligee or any transferee the terms of an instrument may be modified or affected by any other written agreement executed as a part of the same transaction, except that a holder in due course is not affected by any limitation of his rights arising out of the separate written agreement if he had no notice of the limitation when he took the instrument.

(2) A separate agreement does not affect the negotiability of an instrument.

Section 3—120. Instruments "Payable Through" Bank.

An instrument which states that it is "payable through" a bank or the like designates that bank as a collecting bank to make presentment but does not of itself authorize the bank to pay the instrument.

Section 3—121. Instruments Payable at Bank.

> **Note:** *If this Act is introduced in the Congress of the United States, this section should be omitted.*
> *(States to select either alternative)*

Alternative A—

A note or acceptance which states that it is payable at a bank is the equivalent of a draft drawn on the bank payable when it falls due out of any funds of the maker or acceptor for such payment.

Alternative B—

A note or acceptance which states that it is payable at a bank is not of itself an order or authorization to the bank to pay it.

Section 3—122. Accrual of Cause of Action.

(1) A cause of action against a maker or an acceptor accrues
  (a) in the case of a time instrument on the day after maturity;
  (b) in the case of a demand instrument upon its date or, if no date is stated, on the date of issue.

(2) A cause of action against the obligor of a demand or time certificate of deposit accrues upon demand, but demand on a time certificate may not be made until on or after the date of maturity.

(3) A cause of action against a drawer of a draft or an indorser of any instrument accrues upon demand following dishonor of the instrument. Notice of dishonor is a demand.

(4) Unless an instrument provides otherwise, interest runs at the rate provided by law for a judgment
  (a) in the case of a maker, acceptor or other primary obligor of a demand instrument, from the date of demand;
  (b) in all other cases from the date of accrual of the cause of action.

PART 2 / TRANSFER AND NEGOTIATION

Section 3—201. Transfer: Right to Indorsement.

(1) Transfer of an instrument vests in the transferee such rights as the transferor has therein, except that a transferee who has himself been a party to any fraud or illegality affecting the instrument or who as a prior holder had notice of a defense or claim against it cannot improve his position by taking from a later holder in due course.

(2) A transfer of a security interest in an instrument vests the foregoing rights in the transferee to the extent of the interest transferred.

(3) Unless otherwise agreed, any transfer for value of an instrument not then payable to bearer gives the transferee the specifically enforceable right to have the unqualified indorsement of the transferor. Negotiation takes effect only when the indorsement is made and until that time there is no presumption that the transferee is the owner.

Section 3—202. Negotiation.

(1) Negotiation is the transfer of an instrument in such form that the transferee becomes a holder. If the instrument is payable to order, it is negotiated by delivery with any necessary indorsement; if payable to bearer, it is negotiated by delivery.

(2) An indorsement must be written by or on behalf of the holder and on the instrument or on a paper so firmly affixed thereto as to become a part thereof.

(3) An indorsement is effective for negotiation only when it conveys the entire instrument or any unpaid residue. If it purports to be of less, it operates only as a partial assignment.

(4) Words of assignment, condition, waiver, guaranty, limitation or disclaimer of liability and the like accompanying an indorsement do not affect its character as an indorsement.

Section 3—203. Wrong or Misspelled Name.

Where an instrument is made payable to a person under a misspelled name or one other than his own he may indorse in that name or his own or both; but signature in both names may be required by a person paying or giving value for the instrument.

Section 3—204. Special Indorsement; Blank Indorsement.

(1) A special indorsement specifies the person to whom or to whose order it makes the instrument payable. Any instrument specially indorsed becomes payable to the order of the special indorsee and may be further negotiated only by his indorsement.

(2) An indorsement in blank specifies no particular indorsee and may consist of a mere signature. An instrument payable to order and indorsed in blank becomes payable to bearer and may be negotiated by delivery alone until specially indorsed.

(3) The holder may convert a blank indorsement into a special indorsement by writing over the signature of the indorser in blank any contract consistent with the character of the indorsement.

Section 3—205. Restrictive Indorsements.

An indorsement is restrictive which either
- (a) is conditional; or
- (b) purports to prohibit further transfer of the instrument; or
- (c) includes the words "for collection", "for deposit", "pay any bank", or like terms signifying a purpose of deposit or collection; or
- (d) otherwise states that it is for the benefit or use of the indorser or of another person.

Section 3—206. Effect of Restrictive Indorsement.

(1) No restrictive indorsement prevents further transfer or negotiation of the instrument.

(2) An intermediary bank, or a payor bank which is not the depositary bank, is neither given notice nor otherwise affected by a restrictive indorsement of any person except the bank's immediate transferor or the person presenting for payment.

(3) Except for an intermediary bank, any transferee under an indorsement which is conditional or includes the words "for collection", "for deposit", "pay any bank", or like terms (subparagraphs (a) and (c) of Section 3—205) must pay or apply any value given by him for or on the security of the instrument consistently with the indorsement, and to the extent that he does so he becomes a holder for value. In addition such transferee is a holder in due course if he otherwise complies with the requirements of Section 3—302 on what constitutes a holder in due course.

(4) The first taker under an indorsement for the benefit of the indorser or another person (subparagraph (d) of Section 3—205) must pay or apply any value given by him for or on the security of the instrument consistently with the indorsement, and to the extent that he does so he becomes a holder for value. In addition such taker is a holder in due course if he otherwise complies with the requirements of Section 3—302 on what constitutes a holder in due course. A later holder for value is neither given notice nor otherwise affected by such restrictive indorsement unless he has knowledge that a fiduciary or other person has negotiated the instrument in any transaction for his own benefit or otherwise in breach of duty (subsection (2) of Section 3—304).

Section 3—207. Negotiation Effective Although It May Be Rescinded.

(1) Negotiation is effective to transfer the instrument although the negotiation is
- (a) made by an infant, a corporation exceeding its powers, or any other person without capacity; or
- (b) obtained by fraud, duress or mistake of any kind; or
- (c) part of an illegal transaction; or
- (d) made in breach of duty.

(2) Except as against a subsequent holder in due course such negotiation is in an appropriate case subject to rescission, the declaration of the constructive trust or any other remedy permitted by law.

Section 3—208. Reacquisition.

Where an instrument is returned to or reacquired by a prior party he may cancel any indorsement which is not necessary to his title and reissue or further negotiate the instrument, but any intervening party is discharged as against the reacquiring party and subsequent holders not in due course and if his indorsement has been canceled is discharged as against subsequent holders in due course as well.

PART 3 / RIGHTS OF A HOLDER

Section 3—301. Rights of a Holder.

The holder of an instrument whether or not he is the owner may transfer or negotiate it and, except as otherwise provided in Section 3—603 on payment or satisfaction, discharge it or enforce payment in his own name.

Section 3—302. Holder in Due Course.

(1) A holder in due course is a holder who takes the instrument
- (a) for value; and
- (b) in good faith; and
- (c) without notice that it is overdue or has been dishonored or of any defense against or claim to it on the part of any person.

(2) A payee may be a holder in due course.

(3) A holder does not become a holder in due course of an instrument:
- (a) by purchase of it at judicial sale or by taking it under legal process; or
- (b) by acquiring it in taking over an estate; or
- (c) by purchasing it as part of a bulk transaction not in regular course of business of the transferor.

(4) A purchaser of a limited interest can be a holder in due course only to the extent of the interest purchased.

Section 3—303. Taking for Value.

A holder takes the instrument for value
- (a) to the extent that the agreed consideration has been performed or that he acquires a security interest in or a lien on the instrument otherwise than by legal process; or
- (b) when he takes the instrument in payment of or as security for an antecedent claim against any person whether or not the claim is due; or
- (c) when he gives a negotiable instrument for it or makes an irrevocable commitment to a third person.

Section 3—304. Notice to Purchaser.

(1) The purchaser has notice of a claim or defense if
- (a) the instrument is so incomplete, bears such visible evidence of forgery or alteration, or is otherwise so irregular as to call into question its validity, terms or ownership or to create an ambiguity as to the party to pay; or
- (b) the purchaser has notice that the obligation of any party is voidable in whole or in part, or that all parties have been discharged.

(2) The purchaser has notice of a claim against the instrument when he has knowledge that a fiduciary has negotiated the instrument in payment of or as security for his own debt or in any transaction for his own benefit or otherwise in breach of duty.

(3) The purchaser has notice that an instrument is overdue if he has reason to know
- (a) that any part of the principal amount is overdue or that there is an uncured default in payment of another instrument of the same series; or
- (b) that acceleration of the instrument has been made; or
- (c) that he is taking a demand instrument after demand has been made or more than a reasonable length of time after its issue. A reasonable time for a check drawn and payable within the states and territories of the United States and the District of Columbia is presumed to be thirty days.

(4) Knowledge of the following facts does not of itself give the purchaser notice of a defense or claim
- (a) that the instrument is antedated or postdated;
- (b) that it was issued or negotiated in return for an executory promise or accompanied by a separate agreement, unless the purchaser has notice that a defense or claim has arisen from the terms thereof;
- (c) that any party has signed for accommodation;
- (d) that an incomplete instrument has been completed, unless the purchaser has notice of any improper completion;
- (e) that any person negotiating the instrument is or was a fiduciary;
- (f) that there has been default in payment of interest on the instrument or in payment of any other instrument, except one of the same series.

(5) The filing or recording of a document does not of itself constitute notice within the provisions of this Article to a person who would otherwise be a holder in due course.

(6) To be effective notice must be received at such time and in such manner as to give a reasonable opportunity to act on it.

Section 3—305. Rights of a Holder In Due Course.

To the extent that a holder is a holder in due course he takes the instrument free from

(1) all claims to it on the part of any person; and

(2) all defenses of any party to the instrument with whom the holder has not dealt except

    (a) infancy, to the extent that it is a defense to a simple contract; and

    (b) such other incapacity, or duress, or illegallty of the transaction, as renders the obligation of the party a nullity; and

    (c) such misrepresentation as has induced the party to sign the instrument with neither knowledge nor reasonable opportunity to obtain knowledge of its character or its essential terms; and

    (d) discharge in insolvency proceedings; and

    (e) any other discharge of which the holder has notice when he takes the instrument.

Section 3—306. Rights of One Not Holder in Due Course.

Unless he has the rights of a holder in due course, any person takes the instrument subject to

    (a) all valid claims to it on the part of any person; and

    (b) all defenses of any party which would be available in an action on a simple contract; and

    (c) the defenses of want or failure of consideration, nonperformance of any condition precedent, nondelivery, or

delivery for a special purpose (Section 3—408); and

    (d) the defense that he or a person through whom he holds the instrument acquired it by theft, or that payment or satisfaction to such holder would be inconsistent with the terms of a restrictive indorsement. The claim of any third person to the instrument is not otherwise available as a defense to any party liable thereon unless the third person himself defends the action for such party.

Section 3—307. Burden of Establishing Signatures, Defenses and Due Course.

(1) Unless specifically denied in the pleadings each signature on an instrument is admitted. When the effectiveness of a signature is put in issue

    (a) the burden of establishing it is on the party claiming under the signature; but

    (b) the signature is presumed to be genuine or authorized except where the action is to enforce the obligation of a purported signer who has died or become incompetent before proof is required.

(2) When signatures are admitted or established, production of the instrument entitles a holder to recover on it unless the defendant establishes a defense.

(3) After it is shown that a defense exists a person claiming the rights of a holder in due course has the burden of establishing that he or some person under whom he claims is in all respects a holder in due course.

PART 4 / LIABILITY OF PARTIES

Section 3—401. Signature.

(1) No person is liable on an instrument unless his signature appears thereon.

(2) A signature is made by use of any name, including any trade or assumed name, upon an instrument, or by any word or mark used in lieu of a written signature.

Section 3—402. Signature in Ambiguous Capacity.

Unless the instrument clearly indicates that a signature is made in some other capacity, it is an indorsement.

Section 3—403. Signature by Authorized Representative.

(1) A signature may be made by an agent or other representative, and his authority to make it may be established as in other cases of representation. No particular form of appointment is necessary to establish such authority.

(2) An authorized representative who signs his own name to an instrument

    (a) is personally obligated if the instrument neither names the person represented nor shows that the representative signed in a representative capacity;

(b) except as otherwise established between the immediate parties, is personally obligated if the instrument names the person represented but does not show that the representative signed in a representative capacity, or if the instrument does not name the person represented but does show that the representative signed in a representative capacity.

(3) Except as otherwise established, the name of an organization preceded or followed by the name and office of an authorized individual is a signature made in a representative capacity.

Section 3—404. Unauthorized Signatures.

(1) Any unauthorized signature is wholly inoperative as that of the person whose name is signed unless he ratifies it or is precluded from denying it; but it operates as the signature of the unauthorized signer in favor of any person who in good faith pays the instrument or takes it for value.

(2) Any unauthorized signature may be ratified for all purposes of this Article. Such ratification does not of itself affect any rights of the person ratifying against the actual signer.

Section 3—405. Impostors; Signature in Name of Payee.

(1) An indorsement by any person in the name of a named payee is effective if
(a) an impostor by use of the mails or otherwise has induced the maker or drawer to issue the instrument to him or his confederate in the name of the payee; or
(b) a person signing as or on behalf of a maker or drawer intends the payee to have no interest in the instrument; or
(c) an agent or employee of the maker or drawer has supplied him with the name of the payee intending the latter to have no such interest.

(2) Nothing in this section shall affect the criminal or civil liability of the person so indorsing.

Section 3—406. Negligence Contributing to Alteration or Unauthorized Signature.

Any person who by his negligence substantially contributes to a material alteration of the instrument or to the making of an unauthorized signature is precluded from asserting the alteration or lack of authority against a holder in due course or against a drawee or other payor who pays the instrument in good faith and in accordance with the reasonable commercial standards of the drawee's or payor's business.

Section 3—407. Alteration.

(1) Any alteration of an instrument is material which changes the contract of any party thereto in any respect, including any such change in
(a) the number or relations of the parties; or
(b) an incomplete instrument, by completing it otherwise than as authorized; or
(c) the writing as signed, by adding to it or by removing any part of it.

(2) As against any person other than a subsequent holder in due course
(a) alteration by the holder which is both fraudulent and material discharges any party whose contract is thereby changed unless that party assents or is precluded from asserting the defense;
(b) no other alteration discharges any party and the instrument may be enforced according to its original tenor, or as to incomplete instruments according to the authority given.

(3) A subsequent holder in due course may in all cases enforce the instrument according to its original tenor, and when an incomplete instrument has been completed, he may enforce it as completed.

Section 3—408. Consideration.

Want or failure of consideration is a defense as against any person not having the rights of a holder in due course (Section 3—305), except that no consideration is necessary for an instrument or obligation thereon given in payment of or as security for an antecedent obligation of any kind. Nothing in this section shall be taken to displace any statute outside this Act under which a promise is enforceable notwithstanding lack or failure of consideration. Partial failure of consideration is a defense pro tanto whether or not the failure is in an ascertained or liquidated amount.

Section 3—409. Draft Not an Assignment.

(1) A check or other draft does not of itself operate as an assignment of any funds in the hands of the drawee available for its payment, and the drawee is not liable on the instrument until he accepts it.

(2) Nothing in this section shall affect any liability in contract, tort or otherwise arising from any letter of credit or other obligation or representation which is not an acceptance.

Section 3—410. Definition and Operation of Acceptance.

(1) Acceptance is the drawee's signed engagement to honor the draft as presented. It must be written on the draft and may consist of his signature alone. It becomes operative when completed by delivery or notification.

(2) A draft may be accepted although it has not been signed by the drawer or is otherwise incomplete or is overdue or has been dishonored.

(3) Where the draft is payable at a fixed period after sight and the acceptor fails to date his acceptance, the holder may complete it by supplying a date in good faith.

Section 3—411. Certification of a Check.

(1) Certification of a check is acceptance. Where a holder procures certification the drawer and all prior indorsers are discharged.

(2) Unless otherwise agreed a bank has no obligation to certify a check.

(3) A bank may certify a check before returning it for lack of proper indorsement. If it does so, the drawer is discharged.

Section 3—412. Acceptance Varying Draft.

(1) Where the drawee's proffered acceptance in any manner varies the draft as presented, the holder may refuse the acceptance and treat the draft as dishonored in which case the drawee is entitled to have his acceptance canceled.

(2) The terms of the draft are not varied by an acceptance to pay at any particular bank or place in the United States, unless the acceptance states that the draft is to be paid only at such bank or place.

(3) Where the holder assents to an acceptance varying the terms of the draft, each drawer and indorser who does not affirmatively assent is discharged.

Section 3—413. Contract of Maker, Drawer and Acceptor.

(1) The maker or acceptor engages that he will pay the instrument according to its tenor at the time of his engagement or as completed pursuant to Section 3—115 on incomplete instruments.

(2) The drawer engages that upon dishonor of the draft and any necessary notice of dishonor or protest he will pay the amount of the draft to the holder or to any indorser who takes it up. The drawer may disclaim this liability by drawing without recourse.

(3) By making, drawing or accepting the party admits as against all subsequent parties including the drawee the existence of the payee and his then capacity to indorse.

Section 3—414. Contract of Indorser; Order of Liability.

(1) Unless the indorsement otherwise specifies (as by such words as "without recourse") every indorser engages that upon dishonor and any necessary notice of dishonor and protest he will pay the instrument according to its tenor at the time of his indorsement to the holder or to any subsequent indorser who takes it up, even though the indorser who takes it up was not obligated to do so.

(2) Unless they otherwise agree, indorsers are liable to one another in the order in which they indorse, which is presumed to be the order in which their signatures appear on the instrument.

Section 3—415. Contract of Accommodation Party.

(1) An accommodation party is one who signs the instrument in any capacity for the purpose of lending his name to another party to it.

(2) When the instrument has been taken for value before it is due, the accommodation party is liable in the capacity in which he has signed even though the taker knows of the accommodation.

(3) As against a holder in due course and without notice of the accommodation, oral proof of the accommodation is not admissible to give the accommodation party the benefit of discharges dependent on his character as such. In other cases the accommodation character may be shown by oral proof.

(4) An indorsement which shows that it is not in the chain of title is notice of its accommodation character.

(5) An accommodation party is not liable to the party accommodated, and if he pays the instrument has a right of recourse on the instrument against such party.

Section 3—416. Contract of Guarantor.

(1) "Payment guaranteed" or equivalent words added to a signature mean that the signer engages that if the instrument is not paid when due he will pay it according to its tenor without resort by the holder to any other party.

(2) "Collection guaranteed" or equivalent words added to a signature mean that the signer engages that if the instrument is not paid when

due he will pay it according to its tenor, but only after the holder has reduced his claim against the maker or acceptor to judgment and execution has been returned unsatisfied, or after the maker or acceptor has become insolvent or it is otherwise apparent that it is useless to proceed against him.

(3) Words of guaranty which do not otherwise specify guarantee payment.

(4) No words of guaranty added to the signature of a sole maker or acceptor affect his liability on the instrument. Such words added to the signature of one or two or more makers or acceptors create a presumption that the signature is for the accommodation of the others.

(5) When words of guaranty are used, presentment, notice of dishonor and protest are not necessary to charge the user.

(6) Any guaranty written on the instrument is enforcible notwithstanding any statute of frauds.

Section 3—417. Warranties on Presentment and Transfer.

(1) Any person who obtains payment or acceptance and any prior transferor warrants to a person who in good faith pays or accepts that

    (a) he has a good title to the instrument or is authorized to obtain payment or acceptance on behalf of one who has a good title; and

    (b) he has no knowledge that the signature of the maker or drawer is unauthorized, except that this warranty is not given by a holder in due course acting in good faith

        (i) to the maker of a note; or

        (ii) to a drawer with respect to the drawer's own signature, whether or not the drawer is also the drawee; or

        (iii) to an acceptor of a draft if the holder in due course took the draft after the acceptance or obtained the acceptance without knowledge that the drawer's signature was unauthorized; and

    (c) the instrument has not been materially altered, except that this warranty is not given by a holder in due course acting in good faith

        (i) to the maker of a note; or

        (ii) to the drawer of a draft whether or not the drawer is also the drawee; or

        (iii) to the acceptor of a draft with respect to an alteration made prior to the acceptance if the holder in due course took the draft after the acceptance, even though the acceptance provided "payable as originally drawn" or equivalent terms; or

        (iv) to the acceptor of a draft with respect to an alteration made after the acceptance.

(2) Any person who transfers an instrument and receives consideration warrants to his transferee and, if the transfer is by indorsement, to any subsequent holder who takes the instrument in good faith that

    (a) he has a good title to the instrument or is authorized to obtain payment or acceptance on behalf of one who has a good title and the transfer is otherwise rightful; and

    (b) all signatures are genuine or authorized; and

    (c) the instrument has not been materially altered; and

    (d) no defense of any party is good against him; and

    (e) he has no knowledge of any insolvency proceeding instituted with respect to the maker or acceptor or the drawer of an unaccepted instrument.

(3) By transferring "without recourse" the transferor limits the obligation stated in subsection (2) (d) to a warranty that he has no knowledge of such a defense.

(4) A selling agent or broker who does not disclose the fact that he is acting only as such gives the warranties provided in this section, but if he makes such disclosure warrants only his good faith and authority.

Section 3—418. Finality of Payment or Acceptance.

Except for recovery of bank payments as provided in the Article on Bank Deposits and Collections (Article 4) and except for liability for breach of warranty on presentment under the preceding section, payment or acceptance of any instrument is final in favor of a holder in due course, or a person who has in good faith changed his position in reliance on the payment.

Section 3—419. Conversion of Instrument; Innocent Representative.

(1) An instrument is converted when

    (a) a drawee to whom it is delivered for acceptance refuses to return it on demand; or

(b) any person to whom it is delivered for payment refuses on demand either to pay or to return it; or

(c) it is paid on a forged Indorsement.

(2) In an action against a drawee under subsection (1) the measure of the drawee's liability is the face amount of the instrument. In any other action under subsection (1) the measure of liability is presumed to be the face amount of the instrument.

(3) Subject to the provisions of this Act concerning restrictive indorsements a representative, including a depositary or collecting bank, who has in good faith and in accordance with the reasonable standards applicable to the business of such representative dealt with an instrument or its proceeds on behalf of one who was not the true owner is not liable in conversion or otherwise to the true owner beyond the amount of any proceeds remaining in his hands.

(4) An intermediary bank or payor bank which is not a depositary bank is not liable in conversion solely by reason of the fact that proceeds of an item indorsed restrictively (Sections 3—205 and 3—206) are not paid or applied consistently with the restrictive indorsement of an indorser other than its immediate transferor.

PART 5 / PRESENTMENT, NOTICE OF DISHONOR AND PROTEST

Section 3—501. When Presentment, Notice of Dishonor, and Protest Necessary or Permissible.

(1) Unless excused (Section 3—511) presentment is necessary to charge secondary parties as follows:

(a) presentment for acceptance is necessary to charge the drawer and indorsers of a draft where the draft so provides, or is payable elsewhere than at the residence or place of business of the drawee, or its date of payment depends upon such presentment. The holder may at his option present for acceptance any other draft payable at a stated date;

(b) presentment for payment is necessary to charge any indorser;

(c) in the case of any drawer, the acceptor of a draft payable at a bank or the maker of a note payable at a bank, presentment for payment is necessary, but failure to make presentment discharges such drawer, acceptor or maker only as stated in Section 3—502(1)(b).

(2) Unless excused (Section 3—511)

(a) notice of any dishonor is necessary to charge any indorser;

(b) in the case of any drawer, the acceptor of a draft payable at a bank or the maker of a note payable at a bank, notice of any dishonor is necessary, but failure to give such notice discharges such drawer, acceptor or maker only as stated in Section 3—502(1)(b).

(3) Unless excused (Section 3—511), protest of any dishonor is necessary to charge the drawer and indorsers of any draft which on its face appears to be drawn or payable outside of the states and territories of the United States and the District of Columbia. The holder may at his option make protest of any dishonor of any other instrument and in the case of a foreign draft may on insolvency of the acceptor before maturity make protest for better security.

(4) Notwithstanding any provision of this section, neither presentment nor notice of dishonor nor protest is necessary to charge an indorser who has indorsed an instrument after maturity.

Section 3—502. Unexcused Delay; Discharge.

(1) Where without excuse any necessary presentment or notice of dishonor is delayed beyond the time when it is due

(a) any indorser is discharged; and

(b) any drawer or the acceptor of a draft payable at a bank or the maker of a note payable at a bank who, because the drawee or payor bank becomes insolvent during the delay, is deprived of funds maintained with the drawee or payor bank to cover the instrument may discharge his liability by written assignment to the holder of his rights against the drawee or payor bank in respect of such funds, but such drawer, acceptor or maker is not otherwise discharged.

(2) Where without excuse a necessary protest is delayed beyond the time when it is due, any drawer or indorser is discharged.

Section 3—503. Time of Presentment.

(1) Unless a different time is expressed in the instrument, the time for any presentment is determined as follows:

(a) where an instrument is payable at or a fixed period after a stated date, any presentment for acceptance must be made on or before the date it is payable;

(b) where an instrument is payable after sight, it must either be presented for acceptance or negotiated within a reasonable time after date or issue whichever is later;

(c) where an instrument shows the date on which it is payable, presentment for payment is due on that date;

(d) where an instrument is accelerated, presentment for payment is due within a reasonable time after the acceleration;

(e) with respect to the liability of any secondary party presentment for acceptance or payment of any other instrument is due within a reasonable time after such party becomes liable thereon.

(2) A reasonable time for presentment is determined by the nature of the instrument, any usage of banking or trade and the facts of the particular case. In the case of an uncertified check which is drawn and payable within the United States and which is not a draft drawn by a bank the following are presumed to be reasonable periods within which to present for payment or to initiate bank collection:

(a) with respect to the liability of the drawer, thirty days after date or issue whichever is later; and

(b) with respect to the liability of an indorser, seven days after his indorsement.

(3) Where any presentment is due on a day which is not a full business day for either the person making presentment or the party to pay or accept, presentment is due on the next following day which is a full business day for both parties.

(4) Presentment to be sufficient must be made at a reasonable hour, and if at a bank during its banking day.

Section 3—504. How Presentment Made.

(1) Presentment is a demand for acceptance or payment made upon the maker, acceptor, drawee or other payor by or on behalf of the holder.

(2) Presentment may be made

(a) by mail, in which event the time of presentment is determined by the time of receipt of the mail, or

(b) through a clearing house; or

(c) at the place of acceptance of payment specified in the instrument or if there be none at the place of business or residence of the party to accept or pay. If neither the party to accept or pay nor anyone authorized to act for him is present or accessible at such place, presentment is excused.

(3) It may be made

(a) to any one of two or more makers, acceptors, drawees or other payors; or

(b) to any person who has authority to make or refuse the acceptance or payment.

(4) A draft accepted or a note made payable at a bank in the United States must be presented at such bank.

(5) In the cases described in Section 4—210 presentment may be made in the manner and with the result stated in that section.

Section 3—505. Rights of Party to Whom Presentment Is Made.

(1) The party to whom presentment is made may without dishonor require

(a) exhibition of the instrument; and

(b) reasonable identification of the person making presentment and evidence of his authority to make it if made for another; and

(c) that the instrument be produced for acceptance or payment at a place specified in it, or if there be none at any place reasonable in the circumstances; and

(d) a signed receipt on the instrument for any partial or full payment and its surrender upon full payment.

(2) Failure to comply with any such requirement invalidates the presentment, but the person presenting has a reasonable time in which to comply and the time for acceptance or payment runs from the time of compliance.

Section 3—506. Time Allowed for Acceptance or Payment.

(1) Acceptance may be deferred without dishonor until the close of the next business day following presentment. The holder may also in a good faith effort to obtain acceptance and without either dishonor of the instrument or discharge of secondary parties allow postponement of acceptance for an additional business day.

(2) Except as a longer time is allowed in the case of documentary drafts drawn under a letter of credit, and unless an earlier time is agreed to

by the party to pay, payment of an instrument may be deferred without dishonor pending reasonable examination to determine whether it is properly payable, but payment must be made in any event before the close of business on the day of presentment.

Section 3—507. Dishonor; Holder's Right of Recourse; Term Allowing Representment.

(1) An instrument is dishonored when

    (a) a necessary or optional presentment is duly made and due acceptance or payment is refused or cannot be obtained within the prescribed time or in case of bank collections the instrument is seasonably returned by the midnight deadline (Section 4—301); or

    (b) presentment is excused and the instrument is not duly accepted or paid.

(2) Subject to any necessary notice of dishonor and protest, the holder has upon dishonor an immediate right of recourse against the drawers and indorsers.

(3) Return of an instrument for lack of proper indorsement is not dishonor.

(4) A term in a draft or an indorsement thereof allowing a stated time for representment in the event of any dishonor of the draft by nonacceptance if a time draft or by nonpayment if a sight draft gives the holder as against any secondary party bound by the term an option to waive the dishonor without affecting the liability of the secondary party, and he may present again up to the end of the stated time.

Section 3—508. Notice of Dishonor.

(1) Notice of dishonor may be given to any person who may be liable on the instrument by or on behalf of the holder or any party who has himself received notice, or any other party who can be compelled to pay the instrument. In addition an agent or bank in whose hands the instrument is dishonored may give notice to his principal or customer or to another agent or bank from which the instrument was received.

(2) Any necessary notice must be given by a bank before midnight of the third business day after dishonor or receipt of notice of dishonor.

(3) Notice may be given in any reasonable manner. It may be oral or written, and in any terms which identify the instrument and state that it has been dishonored. A misdescription which does not mislead the party notified does not vitiate the notice. Sending the instrument bearing a stamp, ticket or writing stating that acceptance or payment has been refused or sending a notice of debit with respect to the instrument is sufficient.

(4) Written notice is given when sent although it is not received.

(5) Notice to one partner is notice to each although the firm has been dissolved.

(6) When any party is in insolvency proceedings instituted after the issue of the instrument, notice may be given either to the party or to the representative of his estate.

(7) When any party is dead or incompetent, notice may be sent to his last known address or given to his personal representative.

(8) Notice operates for the benefit of all parties who have rights on the instrument against the party notified.

Section 3—509. Protest; Noting for Protest.

(1) A protest is a certificate of dishonor made under the hand and seal of a United States consul or vice consul or a notary public or other person authorized to certify dishonor by the law of the place where dishonor occurs. It may be made upon information satisfactory to such person.

(2) The protest must identify the instrument and certify either that due presentment has been made or the reason why it is excused and that the instrument has been dishonored by nonacceptance or nonpayment.

(3) The protest may also certify that notice of dishonor has been given to all parties or to specified parties.

(4) Subject to subsection (5) any necessary protest is due by the time that notice of dishonor is due.

(5) If, before protest is due, an instrument has been noted for protest by the officer to make protest, the protest may be made at any time thereafter as of the date of the noting.

Section 3—510. Evidence of Dishonor and Notice of Dishonor.

The following are admissible as evidence and create a presumption of dishonor and of any notice of dishonor therein shown:

    (a) a document regular in form as provided in the preceding section which purports to be a protest;

    (b) the purported stamp or writing of the drawee, payor bank or presenting bank on the instrument or accompanying it stating that acceptance or payment has been refused for reasons consistent with dishonor;

    (c) any book or record of the drawee, payor bank, or any collecting bank kept in the usual course of business which shows dishonor, even though there is no evidence of who made the entry.

Section 3—511. Waived or Excused Presentment, Protest or Notice of Dishonor or Delay Therein.

(1) Delay in presentment, protest or notice of dishonor is excused when the party is without notice that it is due or when the delay is caused by circumstances beyond his control and he exercises reasonable diligence after the cause of the delay ceases to operate.

(2) Presentment or notice or protest as the case may be is entirely excused when
  (a) the party to be charged has waived it expressly or by implication either before or after it is due; or
  (b) such party has himself dishonored the instrument or has countermanded payment or otherwise has no reason to expect or right to require that the instrument be accepted or paid; or

  (c) by reasonable diligence the presentment or protest cannot be made or the notice given.
(3) Presentment is also entirely excused when
  (a) the maker, acceptor or drawee of any instrument except a documentary draft is dead or in insolvency proceedings instituted after the issue of the instrument; or
  (b) acceptance or payment is refused but not for want of proper presentment.
(4) Where a draft has been dishonored by nonacceptance, a later presentment for payment and any notice of dishonor and protest for non-payment are excused unless in the meantime the instrument has been accepted.
(5) A waiver of protest is also a waiver of presentment and of notice of dishonor even though protest is not required.
(6) Where a waiver of presentment or notice or protest is embodied in the instrument itself, it is binding upon all parties; but where it is written above the signature of an indorser it binds him only.

PART 6 / DISCHARGE

Section 3—601. Discharge of Parties.

(1) The extent of the discharge of any party from liability on an instrument is governed by the sections on
  (a) payment or satisfaction (Section 3—603); or
  (b) tender of payment (Section 3—604); or
  (c) cancellation or renunciation (Section 3—605); or
  (d) impairment of right of recourse or of collateral (Section 3—606); or
  (e) reacquisition of the instrument by a prior party (section 3—208); or
  (f) fraudulent and material alteration (Section 3—407); or
  (g) certification of a check (Section 3—411); or
  (h) acceptance varying a draft (Section 3—412); or
  (i) unexcused delay in presentment or notice of dishonor or protest (Section 3—502).
(2) Any party is also discharged from his liability on an instrument to another party by any other act or agreement with such party which would discharge his simple contract for the payment of money.
(3) The liability of all parties is discharged when any party who has himself no right of action or recourse on the instrument

  (a) reacquires the instrument in his own right; or
  (b) is discharged under any provision of this Article, except as otherwise provided with respect to discharge for impairment of recourse or of collateral (Section 3—606).

Section 3—602. Effect of Discharge Against Holder in Due Course.

No discharge of any party provided by this Article is effective against a subsequent holder in due course unless he has notice thereof when he takes the instrument.

Section 3—603. Payment or Satisfaction.

(1) The liability of any party is discharged to the extent of his payment or satisfaction to the holder even though it is made with knowledge of a claim of another person to the instrument unless prior to such payment or satisfaction the person making the claim either supplies indemnity deemed adequate by the party seeking the discharge or enjoins payment or satisfaction by order of a court of competent jurisdiction in an action in which the adverse claimant and the holder are parties. This subsection does not, however, result in the discharge of the liability
  (a) of a party who in bad faith pays or satisfies a holder who acquired the instru-

ment by theft or who (unless having the rights of a holder in due course) holds through one who so acquired it; or

(b) of a party (other than an intermediary bank or a payor bank which is not a depositary bank) who pays or satisfies the holder of an instrument which has been restrictively indorsed in a manner not consistent with the terms of such restrictive indorsement.

(2) Payment or satisfaction may be made with the consent of the holder by any person including a stranger to the instrument. Surrender of the instrument to such a person gives him the rights of a transferee (Section 3—201).

Section 3—604. Tender of Payment.

(1) Any party making tender of full payment to a holder when or after it is due is discharged to the extent of all subsequent liability for interest, costs and attorney's fees.

(2) The holder's refusal of such tender wholly discharges any party who has a right of recourse against the party making the tender.

(3) Where the maker or acceptor of an instrument payable otherwise than on demand is able and ready to pay at every place of payment specified in the instrument when it is due, it is equivalent to tender.

Section 3—605. Cancellation and Renunciation.

(1) The holder of an instrument may even without consideration discharge any party

(a) in any manner apparent on the face of the instrument or the indorsement, as by intentionally cancelling the instrument or the party's signature by destruction or mutilation, or by striking out the party's signature; or

(b) by renouncing his rights by a writing signed and delivered or by surrender of the instrument to the party to be discharged.

(2) Neither cancellation nor renunciation without surrender of the instrument affects the title thereto.

Section 3—606. Impairment of Recourse or of Collateral.

(1) The holder discharges any party to the instrument to the extent that without such party's consent the holder

(a) without express reservation of rights releases or agrees not to sue any person against whom the party has to the knowledge of the holder a right of recourse or agrees to suspend the right to enforce against such person the instrument or collateral or otherwise discharges such person, except that failure or delay in effecting any required presentment, protest or notice of dishonor with respect to any such person does not discharge any party as to whom presentment, protest or notice of dishonor is effective or unnecessary; or

(b) unjustifiably impairs any collateral for the instrument given by or on behalf of the party or any person against whom he has a right of recourse.

(2) By express reservation of rights against a party with a right of recourse the holder preserves

(a) all his rights against such party as of the time when the instrument was originally due; and

(b) the right of the party to pay the instrument as of that time; and

(c) all rights of such party to recourse against others.

PART 7 / ADVICE OF INTERNATIONAL SIGHT DRAFT

Section 3—701. Letter of Advice of International Sight Draft.

(1) A "letter of advice" is a drawer's communication to the drawee that a described draft has been drawn.

(2) Unless otherwise agreed, when a bank receives from another bank a letter of advice of an international sight draft, the drawee bank may immediately debit the drawer's account and stop the running of interest pro tanto. Such a debit

and any resulting credit to any account covering outstanding drafts leaves in the drawer full power to stop payment or otherwise dispose of the amount and creates no trust or interest in favor of the holder.

(3) Unless otherwise agreed and except where a draft is drawn under a credit issued by the drawee, the drawee of an international sight draft owes the drawer no duty to pay an unadvised draft but if it does so and the draft is genuine, may appropriately debit the drawer's account.

PART 8 / MISCELLANEOUS

Section 3—801. Drafts in a Set.

(1) Where a draft is drawn in a set of parts, each of which is numbered and expressed to be an order only if no other part has been honored, the whole of the parts constitutes one draft, but a taker of any part may become a holder in due course of the draft.

(2) Any person who negotiates, indorses or accepts a single part of a draft drawn in a set thereby becomes liable to any holder in due course of that part as if it were the whole set, but as between different holders in due course to whom different parts have been negotiated the holder whose title first accrues has all rights to the draft and its proceeds.

(3) As against the drawee the first presented part of a draft drawn in a set is the part entitled to payment, or if a time draft to acceptance and payment. Acceptance of any subsequently presented part renders the drawee liable thereon under subsection (2). With respect both to a holder and to the drawer payment of a subsequently presented part of a draft payable at sight has the same effect as payment of a check notwithstanding an effective stop order (Section 4—407).

(4) Except as otherwise provided in the section, where any part of a draft in a set is discharged by payment or otherwise the whole draft is discharged.

Section 3—802. Effect of Instrument on Obligation for Which It Is Given.

(1) Unless otherwise agreed, where an instrument is taken for an underlying obligation
   (a) the obligation is pro tanto discharged if a bank is drawer, maker or acceptor of the instrument and there is no recourse on the instrument against the underlying obligor; and
   (b) in any other case the obligation is suspended pro tanto until the instrument is due or if it is payable on demand until its presentment. If the instrument is dishonored, action may be maintained on either the instrument or the obligation; discharge of the underlying obligor on the instrument also discharges him on the obligation.

(2) The taking in good faith of a check which is not postdated does not of itself so extend the time on the original obligation as to discharge a surety.

Section 3—803. Notice to Third Party.

Where a defendant is sued for breach of an obligation for which a third person is answerable over under this Article, he may give the third person written notice of the litigation, and the person notified may then give similar notice to any other person who is answerable over to him under this Article. If the notice states that the person notified may come in and defend and that if the person notified does not do so he will in any action against him by the person giving the notice be bound by any determination of fact common to the two litigations, then unless after seasonable receipt of the notice the person notified does come in and defend he is so bound.

Section 3—804. Lost, Destroyed or Stolen Instruments.

The owner of an instrument which is lost, whether by destruction, theft or otherwise, may maintain an action in his own name and recover from any party liable thereon upon due proof of his ownership, the facts which prevent his production of the instrument and its terms. The court may require security indemnifying the defendant against loss by reason of further claims on the instrument.

Section 3—805. Instruments Not Payable to Order or to Bearer.

This Article applies to any instrument whose terms do not preclude transfer and which is otherwise negotiable within this Article but which is not payable to order or to bearer, except that there can be no holder in due course of such an instrument.

ARTICLE 4 / BANK DEPOSITS AND COLLECTIONS

PART 1 / GENERAL PROVISIONS AND DEFINITIONS

Section 4—101. Short Title.

This Article shall be known and may be cited as Uniform Commercial Code—Bank Deposits and Collections.

Section 4—102. Applicability.

(1) To the extent that items within this Article are also within the scope of Articles 3 and 8, they are subject to the provisions of those Articles. In

the event of conflict the provisions of this Article govern those of Article 3, but the provisions of Article 8 govern those of this Article.

(2) The liability of a bank for action or non-action with respect to any item handled by it for purposes of presentment, payment or collection is governed by the law of the place where the bank is located. In the case of action or non-action by or at a branch or separate office of a bank, its liability is governed by the law of the place where the branch or separate office is located.

Section 4—103. Variation by Agreement; Measure of Damages; Certain Action Constituting Ordinary Care.

(1) The effect of the provisions of this Article may be varied by agreement except that no agreement can disclaim a bank's responsibility for its own lack of good faith or failure to exercise ordinary care or can limit the measure of damages for such lack or failure; but the parties may by agreement determine the standards by which such responsibility is to be measured if such standards are not manifestly unreasonable.

(2) Federal Reserve regulations and operating letters, clearing house rules, and the like, have the effect of agreements under subsection (1), whether or not specifically assented to by all parties interested in items handled.

(3) Action or nonaction approved by this Article or pursuant to Federal Reserve regulations or operating letters constitutes the exercise of ordinary care and, in the absence of special instructions, action or nonaction consistent with clearing house rules and the like or with a general banking usage not disapproved by this Article, prima facie constitutes the exercise of ordinary care.

(4) The specification or approval of certain procedures by this Article does not constitute disapproval of other procedures which may be reasonable under the circumstances.

(5) The measure of damages for failure to exercise ordinary care in handling an item is the amount of the item reduced by an amount which could not have been realized by the use of ordinary care, and where there is bad faith it includes other damages, if any, suffered by the party as a proximate consequence.

Section 4—104. Definitions and Index of Definitions.

(1) In this Article unless the context otherwise requires

    (a) "Account" means any account with a bank and includes a checking, time, interest or savings account;

    (b) "Afternoon" means the period of a day between noon and midnight;

    (c) "Banking day" means that part of any day on which a bank is open to the public for carrying on substantially all of its banking functions;

    (d) "Clearing house" means any association of banks or other payors regularly clearing items;

    (e) "Customer" means any person having an account with a bank or for whom a bank has agreed to collect items and includes a bank carrying an account with another bank;

    (f) "Documentary draft" means any negotiable or nonnegotiable draft with accompanying documents, securities or other papers to be delivered against honor of the draft;

    (g) "Item" means any instrument for the payment of money even though it is not negotiable but does not include money;

    (h) "Midnight deadline" with respect to a bank is midnight on its next banking day following the banking day on which it receives the relevant item or notice or from which the time for taking action commences to run, whichever is later;

    (i) "Properly payable" includes the availability of funds for payment at the time of decision to pay or dishonor;

    (j) "Settle" means to pay in cash, by clearing house settlement, in a charge or credit or by remittance, or otherwise as instructed. A settlement may be either provisional or final;

    (k) "Suspends payments" with respect to a bank means that it has been closed by order of the supervisory authorities, that a public officer has been appointed to take it over or that it ceases or refuses to make payments in the ordinary course of business.

(2) Other definitions applying to this Article and the sections in which they appear are:

(3) The following definitions in other Articles apply to this Article:

"Check" Section 3—104.

"Draft" Section 3—104.

"Holder in due course" Section 3—302.

"Notice of dishonor" Section 3—508.

"Presentment" Section 3—504.

"Protest" Section 3—509.

"Secondary party" Section 3—102.

(4) In addition Article 1 contains general definitions and principles of construction and interpretation applicable throughout this Article.

Section 4—105. "Depository Bank"; "Intermediary Bank"; "Collecting Bank"; "Payor Bank"; "Presenting Bank"; "Remitting Bank".

In this Article unless the context otherwise requires:

(a) "Depository bank" means the first bank to which an item is transferred for collection even though it is also the payor bank;

(b) "Payor bank" means a bank by which an item is payable as drawn or accepted;

(c) "Intermediary bank" means any bank to which an item is transferred in course of collection except the depositary or payor bank;

(d) "Collecting bank" means any bank handling the item for collection except the payor bank;

(e) "Presenting bank" means any bank presenting an item except a payor bank;

(f) "Remitting bank" means any payor or intermediary bank remitting for an item.

Section 4—106. Separate Office of a Bank.

A branch or separate office of a bank [maintaining its own deposit ledgers] is a separate bank for the purpose of computing the time within which and determining the place at or to which action may be taken or notices or orders shall be given under this Article and under Article 3.

Section 4—107. Time of Receipt of Items.

(1) For the purpose of allowing time to process items, prove balances and make the necessary entries on its books to determine its position for the day, a bank may fix an afternoon hour of two P.M. or later as a cut-off hour for the handling of money and items and the making of entries on its books.

(2) Any item or deposit of money received on any day after a cut-off hour so fixed or after the close of the banking day may be treated as being received at the opening of the next banking day.

Section 4—108. Delays.

(1) Unless otherwise instructed, a collecting bank in a good faith effort to secure payment may, in the case of specific items and with or without the approval of any person involved, waive, modify or extend time limits imposed or permitted by this Act for a period not in excess of an additional banking day without discharge of secondary parties and without liability to its transferor or any prior party.

(2) Delay by a collecting bank or payor bank beyond time limits prescribed or permitted by this Act or by instructions is excused if caused by interruption of communication facilities, suspension of payments by another bank, war, emergency conditions or other circumstances beyond the control of the bank provided it exercises such diligence as the circumstances require.

Section 4—109. Process of Posting.

The "process of posting" means the usual procedure followed by a payor bank in determining to pay an item and in recording the payment including one or more of the following or other steps as determined by the bank:

(a) verification of any signature;

(b) ascertaining that sufficient funds are available;

(c) affixing a "paid" or other stamp;

(d) entering a charge or entry to a customer's account;

(e) correcting or reversing an entry or erroneous action with respect to the item.

PART 2 / COLLECTION OF ITEMS: DEPOSITARY AND COLLECTING BANKS

Section 4—201. Presumption and Duration of Agency Status of Collecting Banks and Provisional Status of Credits; Applicability of Article; Item Indorsed "Pay Any Bank".

(1) Unless a contrary intent clearly appears and prior to the time that a settlement given by a collecting bank for an item is or becomes final (subsection (3) of Section 4—211 and Sections

4—212 and 4—213) the bank is an agent or sub-agent of the owner of the item and any settlement given for the item is provisional. This provision applies regardless of the form of indorsement or lack of indorsement and even though credit given for the item is subject to immediate withdrawal as of right or is in fact withdrawn; but the continuance of ownership of an item by its owner and any rights of the owner to proceeds of the item are subject to rights of a collecting bank such as those resulting from outstanding advances on the item and valid rights of setoff. When an item is handled by banks for purposes of presentment, payment and collection, the relevant provisions of this Article apply even though action of parties clearly establishes that a particular bank has purchased the item and is the owner of it.

(2) After an item has been indorsed with the words "pay any bank" or the like, only a bank may acquire the rights of a holder

    (a) until the item has been returned to the customer initiating collection; or

    (b) until the item has been specially indorsed by a bank to a person who is not a bank.

Section 4—202. Responsibility for Collection; When Action Seasonable.

(1) A collecting bank must use ordinary care in

    (a) presenting an item or sending it for presentment; and

    (b) sending notice of dishonor or non-payment or returning an item other than a documentary draft to the bank's transferor [or directly to the depositary bank under subsection (2) of Section 4—212](see note to Section 4-212) after learning that the item has not been paid or accepted, as the case may be; and

    (c) settling for an item when the bank receives final settlement; and

    (d) making or providing for any necessary protest; and

    (e) notifying its transferor of any loss or delay in transit within a reasonable time after discovery thereof.

(2) A collecting bank taking proper action before its midnight deadline following receipt of an item, notice or payment acts seasonably; taking proper action within a reasonably longer time may be seasonable but the bank has the burden of so establishing.

(3) Subject to subsection (1) (a), a bank is not liable for the insolvency, neglect, misconduct, mistake or default of another bank or person or

for loss or destruction of an item in transit or in the possession of others.

Section 4—203. Effect of Instructions.

Subject to the provisions of Article 3 concerning conversion of instruments (Section 3—419) and the provisions of both Article 3 and this Article concerning restrictive indorsements, only a collecting bank's transferor can give instructions which affect the bank or constitute notice to it and a collecting bank is not liable to prior parties for any action taken pursuant to such instructions or in accordance with any agreement with its transferor.

Section 4—204. Methods of Sending and Presenting; Sending Direct to Payor Bank.

(1) A collecting bank must send items by reasonably prompt method taking into consideration any relevant instructions, the nature of the item, the number of such items on hand, and the cost of collection involved and the method generally used by it or others to present such items.

(2) A collecting bank may send

    (a) any item direct to the payor bank;

    (b) any item to any nonbank payor if authorized by its transferor; and

    (c) any item other than documentary drafts to any nonbank payor, if authorized by Federal Reserve regulation or operating letter, clearing house rule or the like.

(3) Presentment may be made by a presenting bank at a place where the payor bank has requested that presentment be made.

Section 4—205. Supplying Missing Indorsement; No Notice from Prior Indorsement.

(1) A depositary bank which has taken an item for collection may supply any indorsement of the customer which is necessary to title unless the item contains the words "payee's indorsement required" or the like. In the absence of such a requirement a statement placed on the item by the depositary bank to the effect that the item was deposited by a customer or credited to his account if effective as the customer's indorsement.

(2) An intermediary bank, or payor bank which is not a depositary bank, is neither given notice nor otherwise affected by a restrictive indorsement of any person except the bank's immediate transferor.

Section 4—206. Transfer Between Banks.

Any agreed method which identifies the transferor bank is sufficient for the item's further transfer to another bank.

Section 4—207. Warranties of Customer and Collecting Bank on Transfer or Presentment of Items; Time for Claims.

(1) Each customer or collecting bank who obtains payment or acceptance of an item and each prior customer and collecting bank warrants to the payor bank or other payor who in good faith pays or accepts the item that

(a) he has a good title to the item or is authorized to obtain payment or acceptance on behalf of one who has a good title; and

(b) he has no knowledge that the signature of the maker or drawer is unauthorized, except that this warranty is not given by any customer or collecting bank that is a holder in due course and acts in good faith

(i) to a maker with respect to the maker's own signature; or

(ii) to a drawer with respect to the drawer's own signature, whether or not the drawer is also the drawee; or

(iii) to an acceptor of an item if the holder in due course took the item after the acceptance or obtained the acceptance without knowledge that the drawer's signature was unauthorized; and

(c) the item has not been materially altered, except that this warranty is not given by any customer or collecting bank that is a holder in due course and acts in good faith

(i) to the maker of a note; or

(ii) to the drawer of a draft whether or not the drawer is also the drawee; or

(iii) to the acceptor of an item with respect to an alteration made prior to the acceptance if the holder in due course took the item after the acceptance, even though the acceptance provided "payable as originally drawn" or equivalent terms; or

(iv) to the acceptor of an item with respect to an alteration made after the acceptance.

(2) Each customer and collecting bank who transfers an item and receives a settlement or other consideration for it warrants to his transferee and to any subsequent collecting bank who takes the item in good faith that

(a) he has a good title to the item or is authorized to obtain payment or acceptance on behalf of one who has a good title and the transfer is otherwise rightful; and

(b) all signatures are genuine or authorized; and

(c) the item has not been materially altered; and

(d) no defense of any party is good against him; and

(e) he has no knowledge of any insolvency proceeding instituted with respect to the maker or acceptor or the drawer of an unaccepted item.

In addition each customer and collecting bank so transferring an item and receiving a settlement or other consideration engages that upon dishonor and any necessary notice of dishonor and protest he will take up the item.

(3) The warranties and the engagement to honor set forth in the two preceding subsections arise notwithstanding the absence of indorsement or words of guaranty or warranty in the transfer or presentment and a collecting bank remains liable for their breach despite remittance to its transferor. Damages for breach of such warranties or engagement to honor shall not exceed the consideration received by the customer or collecting bank responsible plus finance charges and expenses related to the item, if any.

(4) Unless a claim for breach of warranty under this section is made within a reasonable time after the person claiming learns of the breach, the person liable is discharged to the extent of any loss caused by the delay in making claim.

Section 4—208. Security Interest of Collecting Bank in Items, Accompanying Documents and Proceeds.

(1) A bank has a security interest in an item and any accompanying documents or the proceeds of either

(a) in case of an item deposited in an account to the extent to which credit given for the item has been withdrawn or applied;

(b) in case of an item for which it has given credit available for withdrawal as of right, to the extent of the credit given whether or not the credit is drawn upon and whether or not there is a right of charge-back; or

(c) if it makes an advance on or against the item.

(2) When credit which has been given for several items received at one time or pursuant to a single agreement is withdrawn or applied in part, the security interest remains upon all the items, any accompanying documents or the proceeds of either. For the purpose of this section, credits first given are first withdrawn.

(3) Receipt by a collecting bank of a final settlement for an item is a realization on its security interest in the item, accompanying documents and proceeds. To the extent and so long as the bank does not receive final settlement for the item or give up possession of the item or accompanying documents for purposes other than collection, the security interest continues and is subject to the provisions of Article 9 except that

(a) no security agreement is necessary to make the security interest enforceable (subsection (1) (b) of Section 9—203); and

(b) no filing is required to perfect the security interest; and

(c) the security interest has priority over conflicting perfected security interests in the item, accompanying documents or proceeds.

Section 4—209. When Bank Gives Value for Purposes of Holder in Due Course.

For purposes of determining its status as a holder in due course, the bank has given value to the extent that it has a security interest in an item provided that the bank otherwise complies with the requirements of Section 3—302 on what constitutes a holder in due course.

Section 4—210. Presentment by Notice of Item Not Payable by, Through or at a Bank; Liability of Secondary Parties.

(1) Unless otherwise instructed, a collecting bank may present an item not payable by, through or at a bank by sending to the party to accept or pay a written notice that the bank holds the item for acceptance or payment. The notice must be sent in time to be received on or before the day when presentment is due and the bank must meet any requirement of the party to accept or pay under Section 3—505 by the close of the bank's next banking day after it knows of the requirement.

(2) Where presentment is made by notice and neither honor nor request for compliance with a requirement under Section 3—505 is received by the close of business on the day after maturity or in the case of demand items by the close of business on the third banking day after notice was sent, the presenting bank may treat the item as dishonored and charge any secondary party by sending him notice of the facts.

Section 4—211. Media of Remittance; Provisional and Final Settlement in Remittance Cases.

(1) A collecting bank may take in settlement of an item

(a) a check of the remitting bank or of another bank on any bank except the remitting bank; or

(b) a cashier's check or similar primary obligation of a remitting bank which is a member of or clears through a member of the same clearing house or group as the collecting bank; or

(c) appropriate authority to charge an account of the remitting bank or of another bank with the collecting bank; or

(d) if the item is drawn upon or payable by a person other than a bank, a cashier's check, certified check or other bank check or obligation.

(2) If before its midnight deadline the collecting bank properly dishonors a remittance check or authorization to charge on itself or presents or forwards for collection a remittance instrument of or on another bank which is of a kind approved by subsection (1) or has not been authorized by it, the collecting bank is not liable to prior parties in the event of the dishonor of such check, instrument or authorization.

(3) A settlement for an item by means of a remittance instrument or authorization to charge is or becomes a final settlement as to both the person making and the person receiving the settlement

(a) if the remittance instrument or authorization to charge is of a kind approved by subsection (1) or has not been authorized by the person receiving the settlement and in either case the person receiving the settlement acts seasonably before its midnight deadline in presenting, forwarding for collection or paying the instrument or authorization,—at the time the remittance instrument or authorization is finally paid by the payor by which it is payable;

(b) if the person receiving the settlement has authorized remittance by a nonbank check or obligation or by a cashier's check or similar primary obligation of or a check upon the payor or other remitting bank which is not of a kind approved by subsection (1) (b),—at the time of the receipt of such remittance check or obligation; or

(c) if in a case not covered by subparagraphs (a) or (b) the person receiving the settlement fails to seasonably present, forward for collection, pay or return a remittance instrument or authorization to it to charge before its midnight deadline,—at such midnight deadline.

Section 4—212. Right of Charge-Back or Refund.

(1) If a collecting bank has made provisional settlement with its customer for an item and itself fails by reason of dishonor, suspension of payments by a bank or otherwise to receive a settlement for the item which is or becomes final, the bank may revoke the settlement given by it, charge back the amount of any credit given for the item to its customer whether or not it is able to return the items if by its midnight deadline or within a longer reasonable time after it learns the facts it returns the item or sends notification of the facts. These rights to revoke, charge-back and obtain refund terminate if and when a settlement for the item received by the bank is or becomes final (subsection (3) of Section 4—211 and subsections (2) and (3) of Section 4—213).

[(2) Within the time and manner prescribed by this section and Section 4—301, an intermediary or payor bank, as the case may be, may return an unpaid item directly to the depositary bank and may send for collection a draft on the depositary bank and obtain reimbursement. In such case, if the depositary bank has received provisional settlement for the item, it must reimburse the bank drawing the draft and any provisional credits for the item between banks shall become and remain final.]

Note: *Direct returns is recognized as an innovation that is not yet established bank practice, and therefore, Paragraph 2 has been bracketed. Some lawyers have doubts whether it should be included in legislation or left to development by agreement.*

(3) A depositary bank which is also the payor may charge-back the amount of an item to its customer's account or obtain refund in accordance with the section governing return of an item received by a payor bank for credit on its books (Section 4—301).

(4) The right to charge back is not affected by
  (a) prior use of the credit given for the item; or
  (b) failure by any bank to exercise ordinary care with respect to the item, but any bank so failing remains liable.

(5) A failure to charge-back or claim refund does not affect other rights of the bank against the customer or any other party.

(6) If credit is given in dollars as the equivalent of the value of an item payable in a foreign currency, the dollar amount of any charge-back or refund shall be calculated on the basis of the buying sight rate for the foreign currency prevailing on the day when the person entitled to the charge-back or refund learns that it will not receive payment in ordinary course.

Section 4—213. Final Payment of Item by Payor Bank; When Provisional Debits and Credits Become Final; When Certain Credits Become Available for Withdrawal.

(1) An item is finally paid by a payor bank when the bank has done any of the following, whichever happens first:

  (a) paid the item in cash; or
  (b) settled for the item without reserving a right to revoke the settlement and without having such right under statute, clearing house rule or agreement; or
  (c) completed the process of posting the item to the indicated account of the drawer, maker or other person to be charged therewith; or
  (d) made a provisional settlement for the item and failed to revoke the settlement in the time and manner permitted by statute, clearing house rule or agreement.

Upon a final payment under subparagraphs (b) (c) or (d) the payor bank shall be accountable for the amount of the item.

(2) If provisional settlement for an item between the presenting and payor banks is made through a clearing house or by debits or credits in an account between them, then to the extent that provisional debits or credits for the item are entered in accounts between the presenting and payor banks or between the presenting and successive prior collecting banks seriatim, they become final upon final payment of the item by the payor bank.

(3) If a collecting bank receives a settlement for an item which is or becomes final (subsection

(3) of Section 4—211, subsection (2) of Section 4—213) the bank is accountable to its customer for the amount of the item and any provisional credit given for the item in an account with its customer becomes final.

(4) Subject to any right of the bank to apply the credit to an obligation of the customer, credit given by a bank for an item in an account with its customer becomes available for withdrawal as of right

- (a) in any case where the bank has received a provisional settlement for the item,—when such settlement becomes final and the bank has had a reasonable time to learn that the settlement is final;
- (b) in any case where the bank is both a depositary bank and a payor bank and the item is finally paid,—at the opening of the bank's second banking day following receipt of the item.

(5) A deposit of money in a bank is final when made but, subject to any right of the bank to apply the deposit to an obligation of the customer, the deposit becomes available for withdrawal as of right at the opening of the bank's next banking day following receipt of the deposit.

Section 4—214. Insolvency and Preference.

(1) Any item in or coming into the possession of a payor or collecting bank which suspends payment and which item is not finally paid shall be returned by the receiver, trustee or agent in charge of the closed bank to the presenting bank or the closed bank's customer.

(2) If a payor bank finally pays an item and suspends payments without making a settlement for the item with its customer or the presenting bank which settlement is or becomes final, the owner of the item has a preferred claim against the payor bank.

(3) If a payor bank gives or a collecting bank gives or receives a provisional settlement for an item and thereafter suspends payments, the suspension does not prevent or interfere with the settlement becoming final if such finality occurs automatically upon the lapse of certain time or the happening of certain events (subsection (3) of Section 4—211, subsections (1) (d), (2) and (3) of Section 4—213).

(4) If a collecting bank receives from subsequent parties settlement for an item which settlement is or becomes final and suspends payments without making a settlement for the item with its customer which is or becomes final, the owner of the item has a preferred claim against such collecting bank.

PART 3 / COLLECTION OF ITEMS: PAYOR BANKS

Section 4—301. Deferred Posting; Recovery of Payment by Return of Items; Time of Dishonor.

(1) Where an authorized settlement for a demand item (other than a documentary draft) received by a payor bank otherwise than for immediate payment over the counter has been made before midnight of the banking day of receipt, the payor bank may revoke the settlement and recover any payment if before it has made final payment (subsection (1) of Section 4—213) and before its midnight deadline it

- (a) returns the item; or
- (b) sends written notice of dishonor or nonpayment if the item is held for protest or is otherwise unavailable for return.

(2) If a demand is received by a payor bank for credit on its books, it may return such item or send notice of dishonor and may revoke any credit given or recover the amount thereof withdrawn by its customer, if it acts within the time limit and in the manner specified in the preceding subsection.

(3) Unless previous notice of dishonor has been sent, an item is dishonored at the time when for purposes of dishonor it is returned or notice sent in accordance with this section.

(4) An item is returned:

- (a) as to an item received through a clearing house, when it is delivered to the presenting or last collecting bank or to the clearing house or is sent or delivered in accordance with its rules; or
- (b) in all other cases, when it is sent or delivered to the bank's customer or transferor or pursuant to his instructions.

Section 4—302. Payor Bank's Responsibility for Late Return of Item.

In the absence of a valid defense such as breach of a presentment warranty (subsection (1) of Section 4—207), settlement effected or the like, if an item is presented on and received by a payor bank the bank is accountable for the amount of

(a) a demand item other than a documentary draft whether properly payable or not if the bank, in any case where it is not also the depositary bank, retains the item beyond midnight of the banking day of receipt without settling for it or, regardless of whether it is also the depositary bank, does not pay or return the item or send notice of dishonor until after its midnight deadline; or

(b) any other properly payable item unless within the time allowed for acceptance or payment of that item the bank either accepts or pays the item or returns it and accompanying documents.

Section 4—303. When Items Subject to Notice, Stop-Order, Legal Process or Setoff; Order in Which Items May Be Charged or Certified.

(1) Any knowledge, notice or stop-order received by, legal process served upon or setoff exercised by a payor bank, whether or not effective under other rules of law to terminate, suspend or modify the bank's right or duty to pay an item or to charge its customer's account for the item, comes too late to so terminate, suspend or modify such right or duty if the knowledge, notice, stop-order or legal process is received or served and a reasonable time for the bank to act thereon expires or the setoff is exercised after the bank has done any of the following:

(a) accepted or certified the item;

(b) paid the item in cash;

(c) settled for the item without reserving a right to revoke the settlement and without having such right under statute, clearing house rule or agreement;

(d) completed the process of posting the item to the indicated account of the drawer, maker or other person to be charged therewith or otherwise has evidenced by examination of such indicated account and by action its decision to pay the item; or

(e) become accountable for the amount of the item under subsection (1) (d) of Section 4—213 and Section 4—302 dealing with the payor bank's responsibility for late return of items.

(2) Subject to the provisions of subsection (1) items may be accepted, paid, certified or charged to the indicated account of its customer in any order convenient to the bank.

PART 4 / RELATIONSHIP BETWEEN PAYOR BANK AND ITS CUSTOMER

Section 4—401. When Bank May Charge Customer's Account.

(1) As against its customer, a bank may charge against his account any item which is otherwise properly payable from that account even though the charge creates an overdraft.

(2) A bank which in good faith makes payment to a holder may charge the indicated account of its customer according to

(a) the original tenor of his altered item; or

(b) the tenor of his completed item, even though the bank knows the item has been completed unless the bank has notice that the completion was improper.

Section 4—402. Bank's Liability to Customer for Wrongful Dishonor.

A payor bank is liable to its customer for damages proximately caused by the wrongful dishonor of an item. When the dishonor occurs through mistake, liability is limited to actual damages proved. If so proximately caused and proved, damages may include damages for an arrest or prosecution of the customer or other consequential damages. Whether any consequential damages are proximately caused by the wrongful dishonor is a question of fact to be determined in each case.

Section 4—403. Customer's Right to Stop Payment; Burden of Proof of Loss.

(1) A customer may by order to his bank stop payment of any item payable for his account but the order must be received at such time and in such manner as to afford the bank a reasonable opportunity to act on it prior to any action by the bank with respect to the item described in Section 4—303.

(2) An oral order is binding upon the bank only for fourteen calendar days unless confirmed in writing within that period. A written order is effective for only six months unless renewed in writing.

(3) The burden of establishing the fact and amount of loss resulting from the payment of an item contrary to a binding stop payment order is on the customer.

Section 4—404. Bank Not Obligated to Pay Check More Than Six Months Old.

A bank is under no obligation to a customer having a checking account to pay a check, other than a certified check, which is presented more than six months after its date, but it may charge its customer's account for a payment made thereafter in good faith.

Section 4—405. Death or Incompetence of Customer.

(1) A payor or collecting bank's authority to accept, pay or collect an item or to account for proceeds of its collection if otherwise effective is not rendered ineffective by incompetence of a customer of either bank existing at the time the item is issued or its collection is undertaken if the bank does not know of an adjudication of incompetence. Neither death nor incompetence of a customer revokes such authority to accept, pay, collect or account until the bank knows of the fact of death or of an adjudication of incompetence and has reasonable opportunity to act on it.

(2) Even with knowledge a bank may for ten days after the date of death pay or certify checks drawn on or prior to that date unless ordered to stop payment by a person claiming an interest In the account.

Section 4—406. Customer's Duty to Discover and Report Unauthorized Signature or Alteration.

(1) When a bank sends to Its customer a statement of account accompanied by items paid in good faith in support of the debit entries or holds the statement and items pursuant to a request or instructions of its customer or otherwise in a reasonable manner makes the statement and items available to the customer, the customer must exercise reasonable care and promptness to examine the statement and items to discover his unauthorized signature or any alteration on an item and must notify the bank promptly after discovery thereof.

(2) If the bank establishes that the customer failed with respect to an item to comply with the duties imposed on the customer by subsection (1) the customer is precluded from asserting against the bank

    (a) his unauthorized signature or any alteration on the item if the bank also establishes that it suffered a loss by reason of such failure; and

    (b) an unauthorized signature or alteration by the same wrongdoer on any other

item paid in good faith by the bank after the first item and statement was available to the customer for a reasonable period not exceeding fourteen calendar days and before the bank receives notification from the customer of any such unauthorized signature or alteration.

(3) The preclusion under subsection (2) does not apply if the customer establishes lack or ordinary care on the part of the bank in paying the item(s).

(4) Without regard to care or lack of care of either the customer or the bank, a customer who does not within one year from the time the statement and items are made available to the customer (subsection (1)) discover and report his unauthorized signature or any alteration on the face or back of the item or does not within three years from that time discover and report any unauthorized indorsement is precluded from asserting against the bank such unauthorized signature or indorsement or such alteration.

(5) If under this section a payor bank has a valid defense against a claim of a customer upon or resulting from payment of an item and waives or fails upon request to assert the defense, the bank may not assert against any collecting bank or other prior party presenting or transferring the item a claim based upon the unauthorized signature or alteration giving rise to the customer's claim.

Section 4—407. Payor Bank's Right to Subrogation on Improper Payment.

If a payor bank has paid an item over the stop payment order of the drawer or maker or otherwise under circumstances giving a basis for objection by the drawer or maker, to prevent unjust enrichment and only to the extent necessary to prevent loss to the bank by reason of its payment of the item, the payor bank shall be subrogated to the rights

    (a) of any holder in due course on the item against the drawer or maker; and

    (b) of the payee or any other holder of the item against the drawer or maker either on the item or under the transaction out of which the item arose; and

    (c) of the drawer or maker against the payee or any other holder of the item with respect to the transaction out of which the item arose.

PART 5 / COLLECTION OF DOCUMENTARY DRAFTS

Section 4—501. Handling of Documentary Drafts; Duty to Send for Presentment and to Notify Customer of Dishonor.

A bank which takes a documentary draft for collection must present or send the draft and accompanying documents for presentment and upon learning that the draft has not been paid or accepted in due course, must seasonably notify its customer of such fact even though it may have discounted or bought the draft or extended credit available for withdrawal as of right.

Section 4—502. Presentment of "On Arrival" Drafts.

When a draft or the relevant instructions require presentment "on arrival", "when goods arrive" or the like, the collecting bank need not present until in its judgment a reasonable time for arrival of the goods has expired. Refusal to pay or accept because the goods have not arrived is not dishonor; the bank must notify its transferor of such refusal but need not present the draft again until it is instructed to do so or learns of the arrival of the goods.

Section 4—503. Responsibility of Presenting Bank for Documents and Goods; Report of Reasons for Dishonor; Referee in Case of Need.

Unless otherwise instructed and except as provided in Article 5 a bank presenting a documentary draft

(a) must deliver the documents to the drawee on acceptance of the draft if it is payable more than three days after presentment; otherwise, only on payment; and

(b) upon dishonor, either in the case of presentment for acceptance or presentment for payment, may seek and follow instructions from any referee in case of need designated in the draft or, if the presenting bank does not choose to utilize his services, it must use diligence and good faith to ascertain the reason for dishonor, must notify its transferor of the dishonor and of the results of its effort to ascertain the reasons therefor and must request instructions.

But the presenting bank is under no obligation with respect to goods represented by the documents except to follow any reasonable instructions seasonably received; it has a right to reimbursement for any expense incurred in following instructions and to prepayment of or indemnity for such expenses.

Section 4—504. Privilege of Presenting Bank to Deal With Goods; Security Interest for Expenses.

(1) A presenting bank which, following the dishonor of a documentary draft, has seasonably requested instructions but does not receive them within a reasonable time may store, sell, or otherwise deal with the goods in any reasonable manner.

(2) For its reasonable expenses incurred by action under subsection (1) the presenting bank has a lien upon the goods or their proceeds, which may be foreclosed in the same manner as an unpaid seller's lien.

ARTICLE 5 / LETTERS OF CREDIT

Section 5—101. Short Title.

This Article shall be known and may be cited as Uniform Commercial Code—Letters of Credit.

Section 5—102. Scope.

(1) This Article applies

(a) to a credit issued by a bank if the credit requires a documentary draft or a documentary demand for payment; and

(b) to a credit issued by a person other than a bank if the credit requires that the draft or demand for payment be accompanied by a document of title; and

(c) to a credit issued by a bank or other person if the credit is not within subparagraphs (a) or (b) but conspicuously states that it is a letter of credit or is conspicuously so entitled.

(2) Unless the engagement meets the requirements of subsection (1), this Article does not apply to engagements to make advances or to honor drafts or demands for payment, to authorities to pay or purchase, to guarantees or to general agreements.

(3) This Article deals with some but not all of the rules and concepts of letters of credit as such rules or concepts have developed prior to this act or may hereafter develop. The fact that this Article states a rule does not by itself require, imply or negate application of the same or a converse rule to a situation not provided for or to a person not specified by this Article.

Section 5—103. Definitions.

(1) In this Article unless the context otherwise requires

- (a) "Credit" or "letter of credit" means an engagement by a bank or other person made at the request of a customer and of a kind within the scope of this Article (Section 5—102) that the issuer will honor drafts or other demands for payment upon compliance with the conditions specified in the credit. A credit may be either revocable or irrevocable. The engagement may be either an agreement to honor or a statement that the bank or other person is authorized to honor.
- (b) A "documentary draft" or a "documentary demand for payment" is one honor of which is conditioned upon the presentation of a document or documents. "Document" means any paper including document of title, security, invoice, certificate, notice of default and the like.
- (c) An "issuer" is a bank or other person issuing a credit.
- (d) A "beneficiary" of a credit is a person who is entitled under its terms to draw or demand payment.
- (e) "An "advising bank" is a bank which gives notification of the issuance of a credit by another bank.
- (f) A "confirming bank" is a bank which engages either that it will itself honor a credit already issued by another bank or that such a credit will be honored by the issuer or a third bank.
- (g) A "customer" is a buyer or other person who causes an issuer to issue a credit. The term also includes a bank which procures issuance or confirmation on behalf of that bank's customer.

(2) Other definitions applying to this Article and the sections in which they appear are:

"Notation of Credit". Section 5—108.
"Presenter". Section 5—112(3).

(3) Definitions in other Articles applying to this Article and the sections in which they appear are:

"Accepted" or "Acceptance". Section 3—410.
"Contract for sale". Section 2—106.
"Draft". Section 3—104.
"Holder in due course". Section 3—302.
"Midnight deadline". Section 4—104.
"Security". Section 8—102.

(4) In addition, Article 1 contains general definitions and principles of construction and interpretation applicable throughout this Article.

Section 5—104. Formal Requirements; Signing.

(1) Except as otherwise required in subsection (1) (c) of Section 5—102 on scope, no particular form of phrasing is required for a credit. A credit must be in writing and signed by the issuer and a confirmation must be in writing and signed by the confirming bank. A modification of the terms of a credit or confirmation must be signed by the issuer or confirming bank.

(2) A telegram may be a sufficient signed writing if it identifies its sender by an authorized authentication. The authentication may be in code and the authorized naming of the issuer in an advice of credit is a sufficient signing.

Section 5—105. Consideration.

No consideration is necessary to establish a credit or to enlarge or otherwise modify its terms.

Section 5—106. Time and Effect of Establishment of Credit.

(1) Unless otherwise agreed a credit is established

- (a) as regards the customer as soon as a letter of credit is sent to him or the letter of credit or an authorized written advice of its issuance is sent to the beneficiary; and
- (b) as regards the beneficiary when he receives a letter of credit or an authorized written advice of its issuance.

(2) Unless otherwise agreed, once an irrevocable credit is established as regards the customer, it can be modified or revoked only with the consent of the customer, and once it is established as regards the beneficiary it can be modified or revoked only with his consent.

(3) Unless otherwise agreed, after a revocable credit is established it may be modified or revoked by the issuer without notice to or consent from the customer or beneficiary.

(4) Notwithstanding any modification or revocation of a revocable credit, any person authorized to honor or negotiate under the terms of

the original credit is entitled to reimbursement for or honor of any draft or demand for payment duly honored or negotiated before receipt of notice of the modification or revocation and the issuer in turn is entitled to reimbursement from its customer.

Section 5—107. Advice of Credit; Confirmation; Error in Statement of Terms.

(1) Unless otherwise specified an advising bank by advising a credit issued by another bank does not assume any obligation to honor drafts drawn or demands for payment made under the credit, but it does assume obligation for the accuracy of its own statement.

(2) A confirming bank by confirming a credit becomes directly obligated on the credit to the extent of its confirmation as though it were its issuer and acquires the rights of an issuer.

(3) Even though an advising bank incorrectly advises the terms of a credit it has been authorized to advise, the credit is established as against the issuer to the extent of its original terms.

(4) Unless otherwise specified the customer bears as against the issuer all risks of transmission and reasonable translation or interpretation of any message relating to a credit.

Section 5—108. "Notation Credit"; Exhaustion of Credit.

(1) A credit which specifies that any person purchasing or paying drafts drawn or demands for payment made under it must note the amount of the draft or demand on the letter or advice of credit is a "notation credit".

(2) Under a notation credit
   (a) a person paying the beneficiary or purchasing a draft or demand for payment from him acquires a right to honor only if the appropriate notation is made and, by transferring or forwarding for honor the documents under the credit, such a person warrants to the issuer that the notation has been made; and
   (b) unless the credit or a signed statement that an appropriate notation has been made accompanies the draft or demand for payment, the issuer may delay honor until evidence of notation has been procured which is satisfactory to it, but its obligation and that of its customer continue for a reasonable time not exceeding thirty days to obtain such evidence.

(3) If the credit is not a notation credit
   (a) the issuer may honor complying drafts or demands for payment presented to it in the order in which they are presented and is discharged pro tanto by honor of any such draft or demand;
   (b) as between competing good faith purchasers of complying drafts or demands the person first purchasing has priority over a subsequent purchaser even though the later purchased draft or demand has been first honored.

Section 5—109. Issuer's Obligation to Its Customer.

(1) An issuer's obligation to its customer includes good faith and observance of any general banking usage but unless otherwise agreed does not include liability or responsibility
   (a) for performance of the underlying contract for sale or other transaction between the customer and the beneficiary; or
   (b) for any act or omission of any person other than itself or its own branch or for loss or destruction of a draft, demand or document in transit or in the possession of others; or
   (c) based on knowledge or lack of knowledge of any usage of any particular trade.

(2) An issuer must examine documents with care so as to ascertain that on their face they appear to comply with the terms of the credit but unless otherwise agreed assumes no liability or responsibility for the genuineness, falsification or effect of any document which appears on such examination to be regular on its face.

(3) A nonbank issuer is not bound by any banking usage of which it has no knowledge.

Section 5—110. Availability of Credit in Portions; Presenter's Reservation of Lien or Claim.

(1) Unless otherwise specified a person by presenting a documentary draft or demand for payment under a credit relinquishes upon its honor all claims to the documents, and a person by transferring such draft or demand or causing such presentment authorizes such relinquishment. An explicit reservation of claim makes the draft or demand noncomplying.

Section 5—111. Warranties on Transfer and Presentment.

(1) Unless otherwise agreed the beneficiary by transferring or presenting a documentary draft

or demand for payment warrants to all interested parties that the necessary conditions of the credit have been complied with. This is in addition to any warranties arising under Articles 3, 4, 7 and 8.

(2) Unless otherwise agreed a negotiating, advising, confirming, collecting or issuing bank presenting or transferring a draft or demand for payment under a credit warrants only the matters warranted by a collecting bank under Article 4, and any such bank transferring a document warrants only the matters warranted by an intermediary under Articles 7 and 8.

Section 5—112. Time allowed for Honor or Rejection; Withholding Honor or Rejection by Consent; "Presenter".

(1) A bank to which a documentary draft or demand for payment is presented under a credit may without dishonor of the draft, demand or credit

(a) defer honor until the close of the third banking day following receipt of the documents; and

(b) further defer honor if the presenter has expressly or impliedly consented thereto.

Failure to honor within the time here specified constitutes dishonor of the draft or demand and of the credit [except as otherwise provided in subsection (4) of Section 5—114 on conditional payment].

> **Note:** *The bracketed language in the last sentence of subsection (1) should be included only if the optional provisions of Section 5-114(4) and (5) are included.*

(2) Upon dishonor the bank may unless otherwise instructed fulfill its duty to return the draft or demand and the documents by holding them at the disposal of the presenter and sending him an advice to that effect.

(3) "Presenter" means any person presenting a draft or demand for payment for honor under a credit even though that person is a confirming bank or other correspondent which is acting under an issuer's authorization.

Section 5—113. Indemnities.

(1) A bank seeking to obtain (whether for itself or another) honor, negotiation or reimbursement under a credit may give an indemnity to induce such honor, negotiation or reimbursement.

(2) An indemnity agreement inducing honor, negotiation or reimbursement

(a) unless otherwise explicitly agreed applies to defects in the documents but not in the goods; and

(b) unless a longer time is explicitly agreed, expires at the end of ten business days following receipt of the documents by the ultimate customer unless notice of objection is sent before such expiration date. The ultimate customer may send notice of objection to the person from whom he received the documents, and any bank receiving such notice is under a duty to send notice to its transferor before its midnight deadline.

Section 5—114. Issuer's Duty and Privilege to Honor; Right or Reimbursement.

(1) An issuer must honor a draft or demand for payment which complies with the terms of the relevant credit regardless of whether the goods or documents conform to the underlying contract for sale or other contract between the customer and the beneficiary. The issuer is not excused from honor of such a draft or demand by reason of an additional general term that all documents must be satisfactory to the issuer, but an issuer may require that specified documents must be satisfactory to it.

(2) Unless otherwise agreed, when documents appear on their face to comply with the terms of a credit but a required document does not in fact conform to the warranties made on negotiation or transfer of a document of title (Section 7—507) or of a security (Section 8—306) or is forged or fraudulent or there is a fraud in the transaction

(a) the issuer must honor the draft or demand for payment if honor is demanded by a negotiating bank or other holder of the draft or demand which has taken the draft or demand under the credit and under circumstances which would make it a holder in due course (Section 3—302) and in an appropriate case would make it a person to whom a document of title has been duly negotiated (Section 7—502) or a bona fide purchaser of a security (Section 8—302); and

(b) in all other cases as against its customer, an issuer acting in good faith may honor the draft or demand for payment despite notification from the customer of fraud, forgery or other defect not apparent on the face of the documents, but a court of appropriate jurisdiction may enjoin such honor.

(3) Unless otherwise agreed an issuer which has duly honored a draft or demand for payment

is entitled to immediate reimbursement of any payment made under the credit and to be put in effectively available funds not later than the day before maturity of any acceptance made under the credit.

[(4) When a credit provides for payment by the issuer on receipt of notice that the required documents are in the possession of a correspondent or other agent of the issuer

(a) any payment made on receipt of such notice is conditional; and

(b) the issuer may reject documents which do not comply with the credit if it does so within three banking days following its receipt of the documents; and

(c) in the event of such rejection, the issuer is entitled by charge back or otherwise to return of the payment made.]

[(5) In the case covered by subsection (4) failure to reject documents within the time specified in subparagraph (b) constitutes acceptance of the documents and makes the payment final in favor of the beneficiary.]

> **Note:** *Subsection (4) and (5) are bracketed as optional. If they are included, the bracketed language in the last sentence of Section 5–112(1) should also be included.*

Section 5—115. Remedy for Improper Dishonor or Anticipatory Repudiation.

(1) When an issuer wrongfully dishonors a draft or demand for payment presented under a credit, the person entitled to honor has with respect to any documents the rights of a person in the position of a seller (Section 2—707) and may recover from the issuer the face amount of the draft or demand together with incidental damages under Section 2—710 on seller's incidental damages and interest but less any amount realized by resale or other use or disposition of the subject matter of the transaction. In the event no resale or other utilization is made the documents, goods or other subject matter involved in the transaction must be turned over to the issuer on payment of judgment.

(2) When an issuer wrongfully cancels or otherwise repudiates a credit before presentment of a draft or demand for payment drawn under it, the beneficiary has the rights of a seller after anticipatory repudation by the buyer under Section 2—610 if he learns of the repudiation in time reasonably to avoid procurement of the required documents. Otherwise the beneficiary has an immediate right of action for wrongful dishonor.

Section 5—116. Transfer and Assignment.

(1) The right to draw under a credit can be transferred or assigned only when the credit is expressly designated as transferable or assignable.

(2) Even though the credit specifically states that it is nontransferable or nonassignable, the beneficiary may before performance of the conditions of the credit assign his right to proceeds. Such as assignment is an assignment of a contract right under Article 9 on Secured Transactions and is governed by that Article except that

(a) the assignment is ineffective until the letter of credit or advice of credit is delivered to the assignee which delivery constitutes perfection of the security interest under Article 9; and

(b) the issuer may honor drafts or demands for payment drawn under the credit until it receives a notification of the assignment signed by the beneficiary which reasonably identifies the credit involved in the assignment and contains a request to pay the assignee; and

(c) after what reasonably appears to be such a notification has been received the issuer may without dishonor refuse to accept or pay even to a person otherwise entitled to honor until the letter of credit or advice of credit is exhibited to the issuer.

(3) Except where the beneficiary has effectively assigned his right to draw or his right to proceeds, nothing in this section limits his right to transfer or negotiate drafts or demands drawn under the credit.

Section 5—117. Insolvency of Bank Holding Funds for Documentary Credit.

(1) Where an issuer or an advising or confirming bank or a bank which has for a customer procured issuance of a credit by another bank becomes insolvent before final payment under the credit and the credit is one to which this Article is made applicable by paragraphs (a) or (b) of Section 5—102(1) on scope, the receipt or allocation of funds or collateral to secure or meet obligations under the credit shall have the following results:

(a) to the extent of any funds or collateral turned over after or before the insolvency as indemnity against or specifically for the purpose of payment of drafts or demands for payment drawn under the designated credit, the drafts or demands are entitled to payment in preference over depositors or other general creditors of the issuer or bank; and

(b) on expiration of the credit or surrender of the beneficiary's rights under it unused, any person who has given such funds or collateral is similarly entitled to return thereof; and

(c) a change to a general or current account with a bank if specifically consented to for the purpose of indemnity against or payment drawn under the designated credit falls under the same rules as if the funds had been drawn out in cash and then turned over with specific instructions.

(2) After honor or reimbursement under this section the customer or other person for whose account the insolvent bank has acted is entitled to receive the documents involved.

ARTICLE 6 / BULK TRANSFERS

Section 6—101. Short Title.

This Article shall be known and may be cited as Uniform Commercial Code—Bulk Transfers.

Section 6—102. "Bulk Transfers"; Transfers of Equipment, Enterprises Subject to This Article; Bulk Transfers Subject to This Article.

(1) A "bulk transfer" is any transfer in bulk and not in the ordinary course of the transferor's business of a major part of the materials, supplies, merchandise or other inventory (Section 9—109) of an enterprise subject to this Article.

(2) A transfer of a substantial part of the equipment (Section 9—109) of such an enterprise is a bulk transfer if it is made in connection with a bulk transfer of inventory, but not otherwise.

(3) The enterprises subject to this Article are all those whose principal business is the sale of merchandise from stock, including those who manufacture what they sell.

(4) Except as limited by the following section all bulk transfers of goods located within this state are subject to this Article.

Section 6—103. Transfers Excepted from This Article.

The following transfers are not subject to this Article:

(1) Those made to give security for the performance of an obligation;

(2) General assignments for the benefit of all the creditors of the transferor, and subsequent transfers by the assignee thereunder;

(3) Transfers in settlement or realization of a lien or other security interest;

(4) Sales by executors, administrators, receivers, trustees in bankruptcy, or any public officer under judicial process;

(5) Sales made in the course of judicial or administrative proceedings for the dissolution or reorganization of a corporation and of which notice is sent to the creditors of the corporation pursuant to order of the court or administrative agency;

(6) Transfers to a person maintaining a known place of business in this State who becomes bound to pay the debts of the transferor in full and gives public notice of that fact, and who is solvent after becoming so bound;

(7) A transfer to a new business enterprise organized to take over and continue the business, if public notice of the transaction is given and the new enterprise assumes the debts of the transferor and he receives nothing from the transaction except an interest in the new enterprise junior to the claims of creditors;

(8) Transfers of property which is exempt from execution.

Public notice under subsection (6) or subsection (7) may be given by publishing once a week for two consecutive weeks in a newspaper of general circulation where the transferor has its principal place of business in this state an advertisement including the names and addresses of the transferor and transferee and the effective date of the transfer.

Section 6—104. Schedule of Property, List of Creditors.

(1) Except as provided with respect to auction sales (Section 6—108), a bulk transfer subject to this Article is ineffective against any creditor of the transferor unless:

(a) The transferee requires the transferor to furnish a list of his existing creditors prepared as stated in this section; and

(b) The parties prepare a schedule of the property transferred sufficient to identify it; and

(c) The transferee preserves the list and schedule for six months next following the transfer and permits inspection of either or both and copying therefrom at all reasonable hours by any creditor of the transferor, or files the list and schedule in (a public office to be here identified).

(2) The list of creditors must be signed and sworn to or affirmed by the transferor or his agent. It must contain the names and business addresses of all creditors of the transferor, with the amounts when known, and also the names of all persons who are known to the transferor to assert claims against him even though such claims are disputed. If the transferor is the obligor of an outstanding issue of bonds, debentures or the like as to which there is an indenture trustee, the list of creditors need include only the name and address of the indenture trustee and the aggregate outstanding principal amount of the issue

(3) Responsibility for the completeness and accuracy of the list of creditors rests on the transferor, and the transfer is not rendered ineffective by errors or omissions therein unless the transferee is shown to have had knowledge.

Section 6—105. Notice to Creditors.

In addition to the requirements of the preceding section, any bulk transfer subject to this Article except one made by auction sale (Section 6—108) is ineffective against any creditor of the transferor unless at least ten days before he takes possession of the goods or pays for them, whichever happens first, the transferee gives notice of the transfer in the manner and to the persons hereafter provided (Section 6—107).

[Section 6—106. Application of the Proceeds.

In addition to the requirements of the two preceding sections:

(1) Upon every bulk transfer subject to this Article for which new consideration becomes payable, except those made by sale at auction, it is the duty of the transferee to assure that such consideration is applied so far as necessary to pay those debts of the transferor which are either shown on the list furnished by the transferor (Section 6—104) or filed in writing in the place stated in the notice (Section 6—107) within thirty days after the mailing of such notice. This duty of the transferee runs to all the holders of such debts, and may be enforced by any of them for the benefit of all.

(2) If any of said debts are in dispute, the necessary sum may be withheld from distribution until the dispute is settled or adjudicated.

(3) If the consideration payable is not enough to pay all of the said debts in full, distribution shall be made pro rata.]

Note: *This section is bracketed to indicate division of opinion as to whether or not it is a wise provision, and to suggest that this is a point on which State enactments may differ without serious damage to the principle of uniformity.*

In any State where this section is omitted, the following parts of sections, also bracketed in the text, should also be omitted, namely:

Section 6–107(2)(3).
6–108(3)(c).
6–109(2).

In any State where this section is enacted, these other provisions shall be also.

Optional Subsection (4)

[(4) The transferee may within ten days after he takes possession of the goods pay the consideration into the (specify court) in the county where the transferor had its principal place of business in this state and thereafter may discharge his duty under this section by giving notice by registered or certified mail to all the persons to whom the duty runs that the consideration has been paid into that court and that they should file their claims there. On motion of any interested party, the court may order the distribution of the consideration to the persons entitled to it.]

Note: *Optional subsection (4) is recommended for those states which do not have a general statute providing for payment of money into court.*

Section 6—107. The Notice.

(1) The notice to creditors (Section 6—105) shall state:

(a) that a bulk transfer is about to be made; and

(b) the names and business addresses of the transferor and transferee, and all other business names and addresses used by the transferor within three years last past so far as known to the transferee; and

(c) whether or not all the debts of the transferor are to be paid in full as they fall due as a result of the transaction, and if so, the address to which creditors should send their bills.

(2) If the debts of the transferor are not to be paid in full as they fall due or if the transferee is in doubt on that point, then the notice shall state further:

(a) the location and general description of the property to be transferred and the estimated total of the transferor's debts;

(b) the address where the schedule of property and list of creditors (Section 6—104) may be inspected;

(c) whether the transfer is to pay existing debts and if so the amount of such debts and to whom owing;

(d) whether the transfer is for new consideration and if so the amount of such consideration and the time and place of payment; [and]

[(e) if for new consideration the time and place where crediors of the transferor are to file their claims.]

(3) The notice in any case shall be delivered personally or sent by registered or certified mail to all the persons shown on the list of creditors furnished by the transferor (Section 6—104) and to all other persons who are known to the transferee to hold or assert claims against the transferor.

Note: *The words in brackets are optional.*

Section 6—108. Auction Sales; "Auctioneer".

(1) A bulk transfer is subject to this Article even though it is by sale at auction, but only in the manner and with the results stated in this section.

(2) The transferor shall furnish a list of his creditors and assist in the preparation of a schedule of the property to be sold, both prepared as before stated (Section 6—104).

(3) The person or persons other than the transferor who direct, control or are responsible for the auction are collectively called the "auctioneer". The auctioneer shall:

(a) receive and retain the list of creditors and prepare and retain the schedule of property for the period stated in this Article (Section 6—104);

(b) give notice of the auction personally or by registered or certified mail at least ten days before it occurs to all persons shown on the list of creditors and to all other persons who are known to him to hold or assert claims against the transferor; [and]

[(c) assure that the net proceeds of the auction are applied as provided in this Article (Section 6—106).]

(4) Failure of the auctioneer to perform any of these duties does not affect the validity of the sale or the title of the purchasers, but if the auctioneer knows that the auction constitutes a bulk transfer such failure renders the auctioneer liable to the creditors of the transferor as a class for the sums owing to them from the transferor up to but not exceeding the net proceeds of the auction. If the auctioneer consists of several persons, their liability is joint and several.

Note: *The words in brackets are optional.*

Section 6—109. What Creditors Protected; [Credit for Payment to Particular Creditors].

(1) The creditors of the transferor mentioned in this Article are those holding claims based on transactions or events occuring before the bulk transfer, but creditors who become such after notice to creditors is given (Sections 6—105 and 6—107) are not entitled to notice.

[(2) Against the aggregate obligation imposed by the application of the proceeds (Section 6—106 and subsection (3) (c) of 6—108) the transferee or auctioneer is entitled to credit for sums paid to particular creditors of the transferor, not exceeding the sums believed in good faith at the time of the payment to be properly payable to such creditors.]

Section 6—110. Subsequent Transfers.

When the title of a transferee to property is subject to a defect by reason of his noncompliance with the requirements of this Article, then:

(1) a purchaser of any of such property from such transferee who pays no value or who takes with notice of such noncompliance takes subject to such defect, but

(2) a purchaser for value in good faith and without such notice takes free of such defect.

Section 6—111. Limitation of Actions and Levies.

No action under this Article shall be brought nor levy made more than six months after the date on which the transferee took possession of the goods unless the transfer has been concealed. If the transfer has been concealed, actions may be brought or levies made within six months after its discovery.

Note to Article 6: *Section 6–106 is bracketed to indicate division of opinion as to whether or not it is a wise provision, and to suggest that this is a point on which State enactments may differ without serious damage to the principle of uniformity.*

In any State where Section 6–106 is not enacted, the following parts of sections, also bracketed in the text, should also be omitted, namely:

Section 6–107(2)(e).
6–108(3)(c).
6–109(2).

In any State where Section 6–106 is enacted, these other provisions should be also.

ARTICLE 7 / WAREHOUSE RECEIPTS, BILLS OF LADING AND OTHER DOCUMENTS OF TITLE

PART 1 / GENERAL

Section 7—101. Short Title.

This Article shall be known and may be cited as Uniform Commercial Code—Documents of Title.

Section 7—102. Definitions and Index of Definitions.

(1) In this Article, unless the context otherwise requires:

(a) "Bailee" means the person who by a warehouse receipt, bill of lading or other document of title acknowledges possession of goods and contracts to deliver them.

(b) "Consignee" means the person named in a bill to whom or to whose order the bill promises delivery.

(c) "Consignor" means the person named in a bill as the person from whom the goods have been received for shipment.

(d) "Delivery order" means a written order to deliver goods directed to a warehouseman, carrier or other person who in the ordinary course of business issues warehouse receipts or bills of lading.

(e) "Document" means document of title as defined in the general definitions in Article 1 (Section 1—201).

(f) "Goods" means all things which are treated as movable for the purposes of a contract of storage or transportation.

(g) "Issuer" means a bailee who issues a document except that in relation to an unaccepted delivery order it means the person who orders the possessor of goods to deliver. Issuer includes any person for whom an agent or employee purports to act in issuing a document if the agent or employee has real or apparent authority to issue documents, notwithstanding that the issuer received no goods or that the goods were misdescribed or that in any other respect the agent or employee violated his instructions.

(h) "Warehouseman" is a person engaged in the business of storing goods for hire.

(2) Other definitions applying to this Article or to specified Parts thereof, and the sections in which they appear are:

"Duly negotiate". Section 7—501.

"Person entitled under the document". Section 7—403(4).

(3) Definitions in other Articles applying to this Article and the sections in which they appear are:

"Contract for sale". Section 2—106.

"Overseas". Section 2—323.

"Receipt" of goods. Section 2—103.

(4) In addition Article 1 contains general definitions and principles of construction and interpretation applicable throughout this article.

Section 7—103. Relation of Article to Treaty Statute, Tariff, Classification or Regulation.

To the extent that any treaty or statute of the United States, regulatory statute of this State or tariff, classification or regulation filed or issued pursuant thereto is applicable, the provisions of this Article are subject thereto.

Section 7—104. Negotiable and Nonnegotiable Warehouse Receipt, Bill of Lading or Other Document of Title.

(1) A warehouse receipt, bill of lading or other document of title is negotiable

(a) if by its terms the goods are to be delivered to bearer or to the order of a named person; or

(b) where recognized in overseas trade, if it runs to a named person or assigns.

(2) Any other document is nonnegotiable. A bill of lading in which it is stated that the goods are consigned to a named person is not made negotiable by a provision that the goods are to be delivered only against a written order signed by the same or another named person.

Section 7—105. Construction Against Negative Implication.

The omission from either Part 2 or Part 3 of this Article of a provision corresponding to a provision made in the other Part does not imply that a corresponding rule of law is not applicable.

PART 2 / WAREHOUSE RECEIPTS: SPECIAL PROVISIONS

Section 7—201. Who May Issue a Warehouse Receipt; Storage Under Government Bond.

(1) A warehouse receipt may be issued by any warehouseman.

(2) Where goods including distilled spirits and agricultural commodities are stored under a statute requiring a bond against withdrawal or a license for the issuance of receipts in the nature of warehouse receipts, a receipt issued for the goods has like effect as a warehouse receipt even though issued by a person who is the owner of the goods and is not a warehouseman.

Section 7—202. Form of Warehouse Receipt; Essential Terms; Optional Terms.

(1) A warehouse receipt need not be in any particular form.

(2) Unless a warehouse receipt embodies within its written or printed terms each of the following, the warehouseman is liable for damages caused by the omission to a person injured thereby:

(a) the location of the warehouse where the goods are stored;

(b) the date of issue of the receipt;

(c) the consecutive number of the receipt;

(d) a statement whether the goods received will be delivered to the bearer, to a specified person, or to a specified person or his order;

(e) the rate of storage and handling charges, except that where goods are stored under a field warehouseing arrangement a statement of that fact is sufficient on a nonnegotiable receipt;

(f) a description of the goods or of the packages containing them;

(g) the signature of the warehouseman, which may be made by his authorized agent;

(h) if the receipt is issued for goods of which the warehouseman is owner, either solely or jointly or in common with others, the fact of such ownership; and

(i) a statement of the amount of advances made and of liabilities incurred for which the warehouseman claims a lien or security interest (Section 7—209). If the precise amount of such advances made or of such liabilities incurred is, at the time of the issue of the receipt, unknown to the warehouseman or to his agent who issues it, a statement of the fact that advances have been made

or liabilities incurred and the purpose thereof is sufficient.

(3) A warehouseman may insert in his receipt any other terms which are not contrary to the provisions of this Act and do not impair his obligation of delivery (Section 7—403) or his duty of care (Section 7—204). Any contrary provisions shall be ineffective.

Section 7—203. Liability for Nonreceipt or Misdescription.

A party to or purchaser for value in good faith of a document of title other than a bill of lading relying in either case upon the description therein of the goods may recover from the issuer damages caused by the nonreceipt or misdescription of the goods, except to the extent that the document conspicuously indicates that the issuer does not know whether any part or all of the goods in fact were received or conform to the description, as where the description is in terms of marks or labels or kind, quantity or condition, or the receipt or description is qualified by "contents, condition and quality unknown", "said to contain" or the like, if such indication be true, or the party or purchaser otherwise has notice.

Section 7—204. Duty of Care; Contractual Limitation of Warehouseman's Liability.

(1) A warehouseman is liable for damages for loss of or injury to the goods caused by his failure to exercise such care in regard to them as a reasonably careful man would exercise under like circumstances but, unless otherwise agreed, he is not liable for damages which could not have been avoided by the exercise of such care.

(2) Damages may be limited by a term in the warehouse receipt or storage agreement limiting the amount of liability in case of loss or damage, and setting forth a specific liability per article or item, or value per unit of weight, beyond which the warehouseman shall not be liable; provided, however, that such liability may on written request of the bailor at the time of signing such storage agreement or within a reasonable time after receipt of the warehouse receipt be increased on part or all of the goods thereunder, in which event increased rates may be charged based on such increased valuation, but that no such increase shall be permitted contrary to a lawful limitation of liability contained in the warehouseman's tariff, if any. No such limitation is effective with respect to the warehouseman's liability for conversion to his own use.

(3) Reasonable provisions as to the time and manner of presenting claims and instituting actions based on the bailment may be included in the warehouse receipt or tariff.

(4) This section does not impair or repeal . . .

Note: *Insert in subsection (4) a reference to any statute which imposes a higher responsibility upon the warehouseman or invalidates contractual limitations which would be permissible under this Article.*

Section 7—205. Title Under Warehouse Receipt Defeated in Certain Cases.

A buyer in the ordinary course of business of fungible goods sold and delivered by a warehouseman who is also in the business of buying and selling such goods takes free of any claim under a warehouse receipt even though it has been duly negotiated.

Section 7—206. Termination of Storage at Warehouseman's Option.

(1) A warehouseman may on notifying the person on whose account the goods are held and any other person known to claim an interest in the goods require payment of any charges and removal of the goods from the warehouse at the termination of the period of storage fixed by the document, or, if no period is fixed, within a stated period not less than thirty days after the notification. If the goods are not removed before the date specified in the notification, the warehouseman may sell them in accordance with the provisions of the section on enforcement of a warehouseman's lien (Section 7—210).

(2) If a warehouseman in good faith believes that the goods are about to deteriorate or decline in value to less than the amount of his lien within the time prescribed in subsection (1) for notification, advertisement and sale, the warehouseman may specify in the notification any reasonable shorter time for removal of the goods and in case the goods are not removed, may sell them at public sale held not less than one week after a single advertisement or posting.

(3) If as a result of a quality or condition of the goods of which the warehouseman had no notice at the time of deposit the goods are a hazard to other property or to the warehouse or to persons, the warehouseman may sell the goods at public or private sale without advertisement on reasonable notification to all persons known to claim an interest in the goods. If the warehouseman after a reasonable effort is unable to sell the goods, he may dispose of them in any lawful manner and shall incur no liability by reason of such disposition.

(4) The warehouseman must deliver the goods to any person entitled to them under this Article upon due demand made at any time prior to sale or other disposition under this section.

(5) The warehouseman may satisfy his lien from the proceeds of any sale or disposition under this section but must hold the balance for delivery on the demand of any person to whom he would have been bound to deliver the goods.

Section 7—207. Goods Must Be Kept Separate; Fungible Goods.

(1) Unless the warehouse receipt otherwise provides, a warehouseman must keep separate the goods covered by each receipt so as to permit at all times identification and delivery of those goods except that different lots of fungible goods may be commingled.

(2) Fungible goods so commingled are owned in common by the persons entitled thereto and the warehouseman is severally liable to each owner for that owner's share. Where because of overissue a mass of fungible goods is insufficient to meet all the receipts which the warehouseman has issued against it, the persons entitled include all holders to whom overissued receipts have been duly negotiated.

Section 7—208. Altered Warehouse Receipts.

Where a blank in a negotiable warehouse receipt has been filled in without authority, a purchaser for value and without notice of the want of authority may treat the insertion as authorized. Any other unauthorized alteration leaves any receipt enforceable against the issuer according to its original tenor.

Section 7—209. Lien of Warehouseman.

(1) A warehouseman has a lien against the bailor on the goods covered by a warehouse receipt or on the proceeds thereof in his possession for charges for storage or transportation (including demurrage and terminal charges), insurance, labor, or charges present or future in relation to the goods, and for expenses necessary for preservation of the goods or reasonably incurred in their sale pursuant to law. If the person on whose account the goods are held is liable for like charges or expenses in relation to other goods whenever deposited and it is stated in the receipt that a lien is claimed for charges and expenses in relation to other goods, the warehouseman also has a lien against him for such charges and expenses whether or not the

other goods have been delivered by the warehouseman. But against a person to whom a negotiable warehouse receipt is duly negotiated, a warehouseman's lien is limited to charges in an amount or at a rate specified on the receipt or if no charges are so specified then to a reasonable charge for storage of the goods covered by the receipt subsequent to the date of the receipt.

(2) The warehousman may also reserve a security interest against the bailor for a maximum amount specified on the receipt for charges other than those specified in subsection (1), such as for money advanced and interest. Such a security interest is governed by the Article on Secured Transactions (Article 9).

(3) A warehouseman's lien for charges and expenses under subsection (1) or a security interest under subsection (2) is also effective against any person who so entrusted the bailor with possession of the goods that a pledge of them by him to a good faith purchaser for value would have been valid but is not effective against a person as to whom the document confers no right in the goods covered by it under Section 7—503.

(4) A warehouseman loses his lien on any goods which he voluntarily delivers or which he unjustifiably refuses to deliver.

Section 7—210. Enforcement of Warehouseman's Lien.

(1) Except as provided in subsection (2), a warehouseman's lien may be enforced by public or private sale of the goods in block or in parcels, at any time or place and on any terms which are commercially reasonable, after notifying all persons known to claim an interest in the goods. Such notification must include a statement of the amount due, the nature of the proposed sale and the time and place of any public sale. The fact that a better price could have been obtained by a sale at a different time or in a different method from that selected by the warehouseman is not of itself sufficient to establish that the sale was not made in a commercially reasonable manner. If the warehouseman either sells the goods in the usual manner in any recognized market therefor, or if he sells at the price current in such market at the time of his sale, or if he has otherwise sold in conformity with commercially reasonable practices among dealers in the type of goods sold, he has sold in a commercially reasonable manner. A sale of more goods than apparently necessary to be offered to insure satisfaction of the obligation is not commercially reasonable except in cases covered by the preceding sentence.

(2) A warehouseman's lien on goods other than goods stored by a merchant in the course of his business may be enforced only as follows:

   (a) All persons known to claim an interest in the goods must be notified.
   (b) The notification must be delivered in person or sent by registered or certified letter to the last known address of any person to be notified.
   (c) The notification must include an itemized statement of the claim, a description of the goods subject to the lien, a demand for payment within a specified time not less than ten days after receipt of the notification, and a conspicuous statement that unless the claim is paid within that time the goods will be advertised for sale and sold by auction at a specified time and place.
   (d) The sale must conform to the terms of the notification.
   (e) The sale must be held at the nearest suitable place to that where the goods are held or stored.
   (f) After the expiration of the time given in the notification, an advertisement of the sale must be published once a week for two weeks consecutively in a newspaper of general circulation where the sale is to be held. The advertisement must include a description of the goods, the name of the person on whose account they are being held, and the time and place of the sale. The sale must take place at least fifteen days after the first publication. If there is no newspaper of general circulation where the sale is to be held, the advertisement must be posted at least ten days before the sale in not less than six conspicuous places in the neighborhood of the proposed sale.

(3) Before any sale pursuant to this section any person claiming a right in the goods may pay the amount necessary to satisfy the lien and the reasonable expenses incurred under this section. In that event the goods must not be sold, but must be retained by the warehouseman subject to the terms of the receipt and this Article.

(4) The warehouseman may buy at any public sale pursuant to this section.

(5) A purchaser in good faith of goods sold to enforce a warehouseman's lien takes the goods free of any rights of persons against whom the lien was valid, despite noncompliance by the warehouseman with the requirements of this section.

(6) The warehouseman may satisfy his lien from the proceeds of any sale pursuant to this section but must hold the balance, if any, for delivery on demand to any person to whom he would have been bound to deliver the goods.

(7) The rights provided by this section shall be in addition to all other rights allowed by law to a creditor against his debtor.

(8) Where a lien is on goods stored by a merchant in the course of his business, the lien may be enforced in accordance with either subsection (1) or (2) .

(9) The warehouseman is liable for damages caused by failure to comply with the requirements for sale under this section and in case of willful violation is liable for conversion.

PART 3 / BILLS OF LADING: SPECIAL PROVISIONS

Section 7—301. Liability for Nonreceipt or Misdescription; "Said to Contain"; Shipper's Load and Count"; Improper Handling.

(1) A consignee of a nonnegotiable bill who has given value in good faith or a holder to whom a negotiable bill has been duly negotiated relying in either case upon the description therein of the goods, or upon the date therein shown, may recover from the issuer damages caused by the misdating of the bill or the nonreceipt or misdescription of the goods, except to the extent that the document indicates that the issuer does not know whether any part or all of the goods in fact were received or conform to the description, as where the description is in terms of marks or labels or kind, quantity, or condition or the receipt or description is qualified by "contents or conditions of contents of packages unknown", "said to contain", "shipper's weight, load and count" or the like, if such indication be true.

(2) When goods are loaded by an issuer who is a common carrier, the issuer must count the packages of goods if package freight and ascertain the kind and quantity if bulk freight. In such cases "shipper's weight, load and count" or other words indicating that the description was made by the shipper are ineffective except as to freight concealed by packages.

(3) When bulk freight is loaded by a shipper who makes available to the issuer adequate facilities for weighing such freight, an issuer who is a common carrier must ascertain the kind and quantity within a reasonable time after receiving the written request of the shipper to do so. In such cases "shipper's weight" or other words of like purport are ineffective.

(4) The issuer may by inserting in the bill the words "shipper's weight, load and count" or other words of like purport indicate that the goods were loaded by the shipper; and if such statement be true, the issuer shall not be liable for damages caused by the improper loading. But their omission does not imply liability for such damages.

(5) The shipper shall be deemed to have guaranteed to the issuer the accuracy at the time of shipment of the description, marks, labels, number, kind, quantity, condition and weight, as furnished by him; and the shipper shall indemnify the issuer against damage caused by inaccuracies in such particulars. The right of the issuer to such indemnity shall in no way limit his responsibility and liability under the contract of carriage to any person other than the shipper.

Section 7—302. Through Bills of Lading and Similar Documents.

(1) The issuer of a through bill of lading or other document embodying an undertaking to be performed in part by persons acting as its agents or by connecting carriers is liable to anyone entitled to recover on the document for any breach by such other persons or by a connecting carrier of its obligation under the document, but to the extent that the bill covers an undertaking to be performed overseas or in territory not contiguous to the continental United States or an undertaking including matters other than transportation this liability may be varied by agreement of the parties.

(2) Where goods covered by a through bill of lading or other document embodying an undertaking to be performed in part by persons other than the issuer are received by any such person, he is subject with respect to his own performance while the goods are in his possession to the obligation of the issuer. His obligation is discharged by delivery of the goods to another such person pursuant to the document, and does not include liability for breach by any other such persons or by the issuer.

(3) The issuer of such through bill of lading or other document shall be entitled to recover from the connecting carrier, or such other person in possession of the goods when the breach of the obligation under the document occurred, the amount it may be required to pay to anyone entitled to recover on the document therefor. as

may be evidenced by any receipt, judgment, or transcript thereof, and the amount of any expense reasonably incurred by it in defending any action brought by anyone entitled to recover on the document therefor.

Section 7—303. Division; Reconsignment; Change of Instructions.

(1) Unless the bill of lading otherwise provides, the carrier may deliver the goods to a person or destination other than that stated in the bill or may otherwise dispose of the goods on instructions from

(a) the holder of a negotiable bill; or

(b) the consignor on a nonnegotiable bill notwithstanding contrary instructions from the consignee; or

(c) the consignee on a nonnegotiable bill in the absence of contrary instructions from the consignor, if the goods have arrived at the billed destination or if the consignee is in possession of the bill; or

(d) the consignee on a nonnegotiable bill if he is entitled as against the consignor to dispose of them.

(2) Unless such instructions are noted on a negotiable bill of lading, a person to whom the bill is duly negotiated can hold the bailee according to the original terms.

Section 7—304. Bills of Lading in a Set.

(1) Except where customary in overseas transportation, a bill of lading must not be issued in a set of parts. The issuer is liable for damages caused by violation of this subsection.

(2) Where a bill of lading is lawfully drawn in a set of parts, each of which is numbered and expressed to be valid only if the goods have not been delivered against any other part, the whole of the parts constitute one bill.

(3) Where a bill of lading is lawfully issued in a set of parts and different parts are negotiated to different persons, the title of the holder to whom the first due negotiation is made prevails as to both the document and the goods even though any later holder may have received the goods from the carrier in good faith and discharged the carrier's obligation by surrender of his part.

(4) Any person who negotiates or transfers a single part of a bill of lading drawn in a set is liable to holders of that part as if it were the whole set.

(5) The bailee is obliged to deliver in accordance with Part 4 of this Article against the first presented part of a bill of lading lawfully drawn in a set. Such delivery discharges the bailee's obligation on the whole bill.

Section 7—305. Destination Bills.

(1) Instead of issuing a bill of lading to the consignor at the place of shipment a carrier may at the request of the consignor procure the bill to be issued at destination or at any other place designated in the request.

(2) Upon request of anyone entitled as against the carrier to control the goods while in transit and on surrender of any outstanding bill of lading or other receipt covering such goods, the issuer may procure a substitute bill to be issued at any place designated in the request.

Section 7—306. Altered Bills of Lading.

An unauthorized alteration or filling in of a blank in a bill of lading leaves the bill enforceable according to its original tenor.

Section 7—307. Lien of Carrier.

(1) A carrier has a lien on the goods covered by a bill of lading for charges subsequent to the date of the receipt of the goods for storage or transportation (including demurrage and terminal charges) and for expenses necessary for preservation of the goods incident to their transportation or reasonably incurred in their sale pursuant to law. But against a purchaser for value of a negotiable bill of lading, a carrier's lien is limited to charges stated in the bill or the applicable tariffs, or if no charges are stated then to a reasonable charge.

(2) A lien for charges and expenses under subsection (1) on goods which the carrier was required by law to receive for transportation is effective, against the consignor or any person entitled to the goods unless the carrier had notice that the consignor lacked authority to subject the goods to such charges and expenses. Any other lien under subsection (1) is effective against the consignor and any person who permitted the bailor to have control or possession of the goods unless the carrier had notice that the bailor lacked such authority.

(3) A carrier loses his lien on any goods which he voluntarily delivers or which he unjustifiably refuses to deliver.

Section 7—308. Enforcement of Carrier's Lien.

(1) A carrier's lien may be enforced by public or private sale of the goods, in bloc or in parcels, at any time or place and on any terms which are commercially reasonable, after notifying all per-

sons known to claim an interest in the goods. Such notification must include a statement of the amount due, the nature of the proposed sale and the time and place of any public sale. The fact that a better price could have been obtained by a sale at a different time or in a different method from that selected by the carrier is not of itself sufficient to establish that the sale was not made in a commercially reasonable manner. If the carrier either sells the goods in the usual manner in any recognized market therefor or if he sells at the price current in such market at the time of his sale or if he has otherwise sold in conformity with commercially reasonable practices among dealers in the type of goods sold, he has sold in a commercially reasonable manner. A sale of more goods than apparently necessary to be offered to ensure satisfaction of the obligation is not commercially reasonable except in cases covered by the preceding sentence.

(2) Before any sale pursuant to this section any person claiming a right in the goods may pay the amount necessary to satisfy the lien and the reasonable expenses incurred under this section. In that event the goods must not be sold, but must be retained by the carrier subject to the terms of the bill and this Article.

(3) The carrier may buy at any public sale pursuant to this section.

(4) A purchaser in good faith of goods sold to enforce a carrier's lien takes the goods free of any rights of persons against whom the lien was valid, despite noncompliance by the carrier with the requirements of this section.

(5) The carrier may satisfy his lien from the proceeds of any sale pursuant to this section but must hold the balance, if any, for delivery on demand to any person to whom he would have been bound to deliver the goods.

(6) The rights provided by this section shall be in addition to all other rights allowed by law to a creditor against his debtor.

(7) A carrier's lien may be enforced in accordance with either subsection (1) or the procedure set forth in subsection (2) of Section 7—210.

(8) The carrier is liable for damages caused by failure to comply with the requirements for sale under this section and in case of willful violation is liable for conversion.

Section 7—309. Duty of Care; Contractual Limitation of Carrier's Liability.

(1) A carrier who issues a bill of lading whether negotiable or nonnegotiable must exercise the degree of care in relation to the goods which a reasonably careful man would exercise under like circumstances. This subsection does not repeal or change any law or rule of law which imposes liability upon a common carrier for damages not caused by its negligence.

(2) Damages may be limited by a provision that the carrier's liability shall not exceed a value stated in the document if the carrier's rates are dependent upon value and the consignor by the carrier's tariff is afforded an opportunity to declare a higher value or a value as lawfully provided in the tariff, or where no tariff is filed he is otherwise advised of such opportunity; but no such limitation is effective with respect to the carrier's liability for conversion to its own use.

(3) Reasonable provisions as to the time and manner of presenting claims and instituting actions based on the shipment may be included in a bill of lading or tariff.

PART 4 / WAREHOUSE RECEIPTS AND BILLS OF LADING: GENERAL OBLIGATIONS

Section 7—401. Irregularities in Issue of Receipt or Bill or Conduct of Issuer.

The obligations imposed by this Article on an issuer apply to a document of title regardless of the fact that

(a) the document may not comply with the requirements of this Article or of any other law or regulation regarding its issue, form or content; or

(b) the issuer may have violated laws regulating the conduct of his business; or

(c) the goods covered by the document were owned by the bailee at the time the document was issued; or

(d) the person issuing the document does not come within the definition of warehouseman if it purports to be a warehouse receipt.

Section 7—402. Duplicate Receipt or Bill; Overissue.

Neither a duplicate nor any other document of title purporting to cover goods already represented by an outstanding document of the same issuer confers any right in the goods, except as provided in the case of bills in a set, overissue of documents for fungible goods and substitutes for lost, stolen or destroyed documents. But the issuer is liable for damages caused by his overissue or failure to identify a duplicate document as such by conspicuous notation on its face.

Section 7—403. Obligations of Warehouseman or Carrier to Deliver; Excuse.

(1) The bailee must deliver the goods to a person entitled under the document who complies with subsections (2) and (3), unless and to the extent that bailee establishes any of the following:

(a) delivery of the goods to a person whose receipt was rightful as against the claimant;

(b) damage to or delay, loss or destruction of the goods for which the bailee is not liable [but the burden of establishing negligence in such cases is on the person entitled under the document];
Note: *The brackets in (1)(b) indicate that State enactments may differ on this point without serious damage to the principle of uniformity.*

(c) previous sale or other disposition of the goods in lawful enforcement of a lien or on warehousemen's lawful termination of storage;

(d) the exercise by a seller of his right to stop delivery pursuant to the provisions of the Article on Sales (Section 2—705);

(e) a diversion, reconsignment or other disposition pursuant to the provisions of this Article (Section 7—303) or tariff regulating such right;

(f) release, satisfaction or any other fact affording a personal defense against the claimant;

(g) any other lawful excuse.

(2) A person claiming goods covered by a document of title must satisfy the bailee's lien where the bailee so requires or where the bailee is prohibited by law from delivering the goods until the charges are paid.

(3) Unless the person claiming is one against whom the document confers no right under Section 7—503(1), he must surrender for cancellation or notation of partial deliveries any outstanding negotiable document covering the goods, and the bailee must cancel the document or conspicuously note partial delivery thereon or be liable to any person to whom the document is duly negotiated.

(4) "Person entitled under the document" means holder in the case of negotiable document, or the person to whom delivery is to be made by the terms of or pursuant to written instructions under a nonnegotiable document.

Section 7—404. No Liability for Good Faith Delivery Pursuant to Receipt or Bill.

A bailee who in good faith including observance of reasonable commercial standards has received goods and delivered or otherwise disposed of them according to the terms of the document of title or pursuant to this Article is not liable therefor. This rule applies even though the person from whom he received the goods had no authority to procure the document or to dispose of the goods and even though the person to whom he delivered the goods had no authority to receive them.

PART 5 /WAREHOUSE RECEIPTS AND BILLS OF LADING: NEGOTIATION AND TRANSFER

Section 7—501. Form of Negotiation and Requirements of "Due Negotiation".

(1) A negotiable document of title running to the order of a named person is negotiated by his indorsement and delivery. After his indorsement in blank or to bearer any person can negotiate it by delivery alone.

(2)(a) A negotiable document of title is also negotiated by delivery alone when by its original terms it runs to bearer.

(b) When a document running to the order of a named person is delivered to him, the effect is the same as if the document had been negotiated.

(3) Negotiation of a negotiable document of title after it has been indorsed to a specified person requires indorsement by the special indorsee as well as delivery.

(4) A negotiable document of title is "duly negotiated" when it is negotiated in the manner stated in this section to a holder who purchases it in good faith without notice of any defense against or claim to it on the part of any person and for value, unless it is established that the negotiation is not in the regular course of business or financing or involves receiving the document in settlement or payment of a money obligation.

(5) Indorsement of a nonnegotiable document neither makes it negotiable nor adds to the transferee's rights.

(6) The naming in a negotiable bill of a person to be notified of the arrival of the goods does not limit the negotiability of the bill nor constitute notice to a purchaser thereof of any interest of such person in the goods.

Section 7—502. Rights Acquired by Due Negotiation.

(1) Subject to the following section and to the provisions of Section 7—205 on fungible goods, a holder to whom a negotiable document of title has been duly negotiated acquires thereby:

    (a) title to the document;

    (b) title to the goods;

    (c) all rights accruing under the law of agency or estoppel, including rights to goods delivered to the bailee after the document was issued; and

    (d) the direct obligation of the issuer to hold or deliver the goods according to the terms of the document free of any defense or claim by him except those arising under the terms of the document or under this Article. In the case of a delivery order the bailee's obligation accrues only upon acceptance, and the obligation acquired by the holder is that the issuer and any indorser will procure the acceptance of the bailee.

(2) Subject to the following section, title and rights so acquired are not defeated by any stoppage of the goods represented by the document or by surrender of such goods by the bailee, and are not impaired even though the negotiation or any prior negotiation constituted a breach of duty or even though any person has been deprived of possession of the document by misrepresentation, fraud, accident, mistake, duress, loss, theft or conversion, or even though a previous sale or other transfer of the goods or document has been made to a third person.

Section 7—503. Document of Title to Goods Defeated in Certain Cases.

(1) A document of title confers no right in goods against a person who before issuance of the document had a legal interest or a perfected security interest in them and who neither

    (a) delivered or entrusted them or any document of title covering them to the bailor or his nominee with actual or apparent authority to ship, store or sell or with power to obtain delivery under this Article (Section 7—403) or with

power of disposition under this Act (Sections 2—403 and 9—307) or other statute or rule of law; nor

    (b) acquiesced in the procurement by the bailor or his nominee of any document of title.

(2) Title to goods based upon an unaccepted delivery order is subject to the rights of anyone to whom a negotiable warehouse receipt or bill of lading covering the goods has been duly negotiated. Such a title may be defeated under the next section to the same extent as the rights of the issuer or a transferee from the issuer.

(3) Title to goods based upon a bill of lading issued to a freight forwarder is subject to the rights of anyone to whom a bill issued by the freight forwarder is duly negotiated; but delivery by the carrier in accordance with Part 4 of this Article pursuant to its own bill of lading discharges the carrier's obligation to deliver.

Section 7—504. Rights Acquired in the Absence of Due Negotiation; Effect of Diversion; Seller's Stoppage of Delivery.

(1) A transferee of a document, whether negotiable or nonnegotiable, to whom the document has been delivered but not duly negotiated, acquires the title and rights which his transferor had or had actual authority to convey.

(2) In the case of a nonnegotiable document, until but not after the bailee receives notification of the transfer, the rights of the transferee may be defeated

    (a) by those creditors of the transferor who could treat the sale as void under Section 2—402; or

    (b) by a buyer from the transferor in ordinary course of business if the bailee has delivered the goods to the buyer or received notification of his rights; or

    (c) as against the bailee by good faith dealings of the bailee with the transferor.

(3) A diversion or other change of shipping instructions by the consignor in a nonnegotiable bill of lading which causes the bailee not to deliver to the consignee defeats the consignee's title to the goods if they have been delivered to a buyer in ordinary course of business and in any event defeats the consignee's rights against the bailee.

(4) Delivery pursuant to a nonnegotiable document may be stopped by a seller under Section 2—705, and subject to the requirement of due notification, there provided. A bailee honoring the seller's instructions is entitled to be indemnified by the seller against any resulting loss or expense.

Section 7—505. Indorser Not a Guarantor for Other Parties.

The indorsement of a document of title issued by a bailee does not make the Indorser liable for any default by the bailee or by previous indorsers.

Section 7—506. Delivery Without Indorsement; Right to Compel Indorsement.

The transferee of a negotiable document of title has a specifically enforceable right to have his transferor supply any necessary indorsement, but the transfer becomes a negotiation only as of the time the indorsement is supplied.

Section 7—507. Warranties on Negotiation or Transfer of Receipt or Bill.

Where a person negotiates or transfers a document of title for value otherwise than as a mere intermediary under the next following section, then unless otherwise agreed he warrants to his immediate purchaser only in addition to any warranty made in selling the goods

    (a) that the document is genuine; and

    (b) that he has no knowledge of any fact which would impair its validity or worth; and

    (c) that his negotiation or transfer is rightful and fully effective with respect to the title to the document and the goods it represents.

Section 7—508. Warranties of Collecting Bank as to Documents.

A collecting bank or other intermediary known to be entrusted with documents on behalf of another or with collection of a draft or other claim against delivery of documents warrants by such delivery of the documents only its own good faith and authority. This rule applies even though the intermediary has purchased or made advances against the claim or draft to be collected.

Section 7—509. Receipt or Bill: When Adequate Compliance With Commercial Contract.

The question whether a document is adequate to fulfill the obligations of a contract for sale or the conditions of a credit is governed by the Articles on Sales (Article 2) and on Letters of Credit (Article 5).

PART 6 / WAREHOUSE RECEIPTS AND BILLS OF LADING: MISCELLANEOUS PROVISIONS

Section 7—501. Lost and Missing Documents.

(1) If a document has been lost, stolen or destroyed, a court may order delivery of the goods or issuance of a substitute document and the bailee may without liability to any person comply with such order. If the document was negotiable, the claimant must post security approved by the court to indemnify any person who may suffer loss as a result of nonsurrender of the document. If the document was not negotiable, such security may be required at the discretion of the court. The court may also in its discretion order payment of the bailee's reasonable costs and counsel fees.

(2) A bailee who without court order delivers goods to a person claiming under a missing negotiable document is liable to any person injured thereby, and if the delivery is not in good faith becomes liable for conversion. Delivery in good faith is not conversion if made in accordance with a filed classification or tariff or, where no classification or tariff is filed, if the claimant posts security with the bailee in an amount at least double the value of the goods at the time of posting to indemnify any person injured by the delivery who files a notice of claim within one year after the delivery.

Section 7—602. Attachment of Goods Covered by a Negotiable Document.

Except where the document was originally issued upon delivery of the goods by a person who had no power to dispose of them, no lien attaches by virtue of any judicial process to goods in the possession of a bailee for which a negotiable document of title is outstanding unless the document be first surrendered to the bailee or its negotiation enjoined, and the bailee shall not be compelled to deliver the goods pursuant to process until the document is surrendered to him or impounded by the court. One who purchases the document for value without notice of the process or injunction takes free of the lien imposed by judicial process.

Section 7—603. Conflicting Claims; Interpleader.

If more than one person claims title or possession of the goods, the bailee is excused from delivery until he has had a reasonable time to ascertain the validity of the adverse claims or to bring an action to compel all claimants to interplead and may compel such interpleader, either in defending an action for nondelivery of the goods, or by original action, whichever is appropriate.

ARTICLE 8 / INVESTMENT SECURITIES

PART 1 / SHORT TITLE AND GENERAL MATTERS

Section 8—101. Short Title.

This Article shall be known and may be cited as Uniform Commercial Code—Investment Securities.

Section 8—102. Definitions and Index of Definitions.

(1) In this Article unless the context otherwise requires

  (a) A "security" is an instrument which
    (i) is issued in bearer or registered form; and
    (ii) is of a type commonly dealt in upon securities exchanges or markets or commonly recognized in any area in which it is issued or dealt in as a medium for investment; and
    (iii) is either one of a class or series or by its terms is divisible into a class or series of instruments; and
    (iv) evidences a share, participation or other interest in property or in an enterprise or evidences an obligation of the issuer.

  (b) A writing which is a security is governed by this Article and not by Uniform Commercial Code-Commercial Paper even though it also meets the requirements of that Article. This Article does not apply to money.

  (c) A security is in "registered form" when it specifies a person entitled to the security or to the rights it evidences and when its transfer may be registered upon books maintained for that purpose by or on behalf of an issuer or the security so states.

  (d) A security is in "bearer form" when it runs to bearer according to its terms and not by reason of any indorsement.

(2) A "subsequent purchaser" is a person who takes other than by original issue.

(3) A "clearing corporation" is a corporation all of the capital stock of which is held by or for a national securities exchange or association registered under a statute of the United States such as the Securities Exchange Act of 1934.

(4) A "custodian bank" is any bank or trust company which is supervised and examined by state or federal authority having supervision over banks and which is acting as custodian for a clearing corporation.

(5) Other definitions applying to this Article or to specified Parts thereof and the sections in which they appear are:

"Adverse claim".	Section 8—301.
"Bona fide purchaser".	Section 8—302.
"Broker".	Section 8—303.
"Guarantee of the signature".	Section 8—402.
"Intermediary bank".	Section 4—105.
"Issuer".	Section 8—201.
"Overissue".	Section 8—104.

(6) In addition Article 1 contains general definitions and principles of construction and interpretation applicable throughout this Article.

Section 8—103. Issuer's Lien.

A lien upon a security in favor of an issuer thereof is valid against a purchaser only if the right of the issuer to such lien is noted conspicuously on the security.

Section 8—104. Effect of Overissue; "Overissue."

(1) The provisions of this Article which validate a security or compel its issue or reissue do not apply to the extent that validation, issue or reissue would result in overissue; but

  (a) if an identical security which does not constitute an overissue is reasonably available for purchase, the person entitled to issue or validation may compel the issuer to purchase and deliver such a security to him against surrender of the security, if any, which he holds; or

  (b) if a security is not so available for purchase, the person entitled to issue or validation may recover from the issuer the price he or the last purchaser for value paid for it with interest from the date of his demand.

(2) "Overissue" means the issue of securities in excess of the amount which the issuer has corporate power to issue.

Section 8—105. Securities Negotiable; Presumptions.

(1) Securities governed by this Article are negotiable instruments.

(2) In any action on a security

  (a) unless specifically denied in the pleadings, each signature on the security or in a necessary indorsement is admitted;

(b) when the effectiveness of a signature is put in issue, the burden of establishing it is on the party claiming under the signature but the signature is presumed to be genuine or authorized;

(c) when signatures are admitted or established, production of the instrument entitles a holder to recover on it unless the defendant establishes a defense or a defect going to the validity of the security; and

(d) after it is shown that a defense or defect exists, the plaintiff has the burden of establishing that he or some person under whom he claims is a person against whom the defense or defect is ineffective (Section 8—202).

Section 8—106. Applicability.

The validity of a security and the rights and duties of the issuer with respect to registration of transfer are governed by the law (including the conflict of laws rules) of the jurisdiction of organization of the issuer.

Section 8—107. Securities Deliverable; Action for Price.

(1) Unless otherwise agreed and subject to any applicable law or regulation respecting short sales, a person obligated to deliver securities may deliver any security of the specified issue in bearer form or registered in the name of the transferee or indorsed to him or in blank.

(2) When the buyer fails to pay the price as it comes due under a contract of sale, the seller may recover the price

(a) of securities accepted by the buyer; and

(b) of other securities if efforts at their resale would be unduly burdensome or if there is no readily available market for their resale.

PART 2 / ISSUE—ISSUER

Section 8—201. "Issuer."

(1) With respect to obligations on or defenses to a security, "issuer" includes a person who

(a) places or authorizes the placing of his name on a security (otherwise than as authenticating trustee, registrar, transfer agent or the like) to evidence that it represents a share, participation or other interest in his property or in an enterprise or to evidence his duty to perform an obligation evidenced by the security; or

(b) directly or indirectly creates fractional interests in his rights or property which fractional interests are evidenced by securities; or

(c) becomes responsible for or in place of any other person described as an issuer in this section.

(2) With respect to obligations on or defenses to a security, a guarantor is an issuer to the extent of his guaranty whether or not his obligation is noted on the security.

(3) With respect to registration or transfer (Part 4 of this Article) "issuer" means a person on whose behalf transfer books are maintained.

Section 8—202. Issuer's Responsibility and Defenses; Notice of Defect or Defense.

(1) Even against a purchaser for value and without notice, the terms of a security include those stated on the security and those made part of the security by reference to another instrument, indenture or document or to a constitution, statute, ordinance, rule, regulation, order or the like to the extent that the terms so referred to do not conflict with the stated terms. Such a reference does not of itself charge a purchaser for value with notice of a defect going to the validity of the security even though the security expressly states that a person accepting it admits such notice.

(2) (a) A security other than one issued by a government or governmental agency or unit, even though issued with a defect going to its validity, is valid in the hands of a purchaser for value and without notice of the particular defect unless the defect involves a violation of constitutional provisons in which case the security is valid in the hands of a subsequent purchaser for value and without notice of the defect.

(b) The rule of subparagraph (a) applies to an issuer which is a government agency or unit only if either there has been substantial compliance with legal requirements governing the issue or the issuer has received a substantial consideration for the issue as a whole or for the particular security and a stated purpose of the issue is one for which the issuer has power to borrow money or issue the security.

(3) Except as otherwise provided in the case of certain unauthorized signatures on issue (Section 8—205), lack of genuineness of a security is a complete defense even against a purchaser for value and without notice.

(4) All other defenses of the issuer including nondelivery and conditional delivery of the security are ineffective against a purchaser for value who has taken without notice of the particular defense.

(5) Nothing in this section shall be construed to affect the right of a party to a "when, as and if issued" or a "when distributed" contract to cancel the contract in the event of a material change in the character of the security which is the subject of the contract or in the plan or arrangement pursuant to which such security is to be issued or distributed.

Section 8—203. Staleness as Notice of Defects or Defenses.

(1) After an act or event which creates a right to immediate performance of the principal obligation evidenced by the security or which sets a date on or after which the security is to be presented or surrendered for redemption or exchange, a purchaser is charged with notice of any defect in its issue or defense of the issuer

   (a) if the act or event is one requiring the payment of money or the delivery of securities or both on presentation or surrender of security and such funds or securities are available on the date set for payment or exchange and he takes the security more than one year after that date; and

   (b) if the act or event is not covered by paragraph (a) and he takes the security more than two years after the date set for surrender or presentation or the date on which such performance became due.

(2) A call which has been revoked is not within subsection (1).

Section 8—204. Effect of Issuer's Restrictions on Transfer.

Unless noted conspicuously on the security a restriction on transfer imposed by the issuer,

even though otherwise lawful, is ineffective except against a person with actual knowledge of it.

Section 8—205. Effect of Unauthorized Signature on Issue.

An unauthorized signature placed on a security prior to or in the course of issue is ineffective except that the signature is effective in favor of a purchaser for value and without notice of the lack of authority if the signing has been done by

   (a) an authenticating trustee, registrar, transfer agent or other person entrusted by the issuer with the signing of the security or of similar securities or their immediate preparation for signing; or

   (b) an employee of the issuer or of any of the foregoing entrusted with responsible handling of the security.

Section 8—206. Completion or Alteration of Instrument.

(1) Where a security contains the signatures necessary to its issue or transfer but is incomplete in any other respect

   (a) any person may complete it by filling in the blanks as authorized; and

   (b) even though the blanks are incorrectly filled in, the security as completed is enforceable by a purchaser who took it for value and without notice of such incorrectness.

(2) A complete security which has been improperly altered even though fraudulently remains enforceable but only according to its original terms.

Section 8—207. Rights of Issuer With Respect to Registered Owners.

(1) Prior to the presentment for registration of transfer of a security in registered form, the issuer or indenture trustee may treat the registered owner as the person exclusively entitled to vote, to receive notifications and otherwise to exercise all the rights and powers of an owner.

(2) Nothing in this Article shall be construed to affect the liability of the registered owner of a security for calls, assessments or the like.

Section 8—208. Effect of Signature of Authenticating Trustee, Registrar or Transfer Agent.

(1) A person placing his signature upon a security as authenticating trustee, registrar, transfer agent or the like warrants to a purchaser for value without notice of the particular defect that

   (a) the security is genuine; and

(b) his own participation in the issue of the security is within his capacity and within the scope of the authorization received by him from the issuer; and

(c) he has reasonable grounds to believe that the security is in the form and

within the amount the issuer is authorized to issue.

(2) Unless otherwise agreed, a person by so placing his signature does not assume responsibility for the validity of the security in other respects.

PART 3 / PURCHASE

Section 8—301. Rights Acquired by Purchaser; "Adverse Claim"; Title Acquired by Bona Fide Purchaser.

(1) Upon delivery of a security the purchaser acquires the rights in the security which his transferor had or had actual authority to convey except that a purchaser who has himself been a party to any fraud or illegality affecting the security or who as a prior holder had notice of an adverse claim cannot improve his position by taking from a later bona fide purchaser. "Adverse claim" includes a claim that a transfer was or would be wrongful or that a particular adverse person is the owner of or has an interest in the security.

(2) A bona fide purchaser in addition to acquiring the rights of a purchaser also acquires the security free of any adverse claim.

(3) A purchaser of a limited interest acquires rights only to the extent of the interest purchased.

Section 8—302. "Bona Fide Purchaser."

A "bona fide purchaser" is a purchaser for value in good faith and without notice of any adverse claim who takes delivery of a security in bearer form or of one in registered form issued to him or indorsed to him or in blank.

Section 8—303. "Broker."

"Broker" means a person engaged for all or part of his time in the business of buying and selling securities, who in the transaction concerned acts for, or buys a security from or sells a security to a customer. Nothing in this Article determines the capacity in which a person acts for purposes of any other statute or rule to which such person is subject.

Section 8—304. Notice to Purchaser of Adverse Claims.

(1) A purchaser (including a broker for the seller or, buyer but excluding an intermediary bank) of a security is charged with notice of adverse claims if

(a) the security whether in bearer or registered form has been indorsed "for collection" or "for surrender" or for some other purpose not involving transfer; or

(b) the security is in bearer form and has on it an unambiguous statement that it is the property of a person other than the transferor. The mere writing of a name on a security is not such a statement.

(2) The fact that the purchaser (including a broker for the seller or buyer) has notice that the security is held for a third person or is registered in the name of or indorsed by a fiduciary does not create a duty of inquiry into the rightfulness of the transfer or constitute notice of adverse claims. If, however, the purchaser (excluding an intermediary bank) has knowledge that the proceeds are being used or that the transaction is for the individual benefit of the fiduciary or otherwise in breach of duty, the purchaser is charged with notice of adverse claims.

Section 8—305. Staleness as Notice of Adverse Claims.

An act or event which creates a right to immediate performance of the principal obligation evidenced by the security or which sets a date on or after which the security is to be presented or surrendered for redemption or exchange does not of itself constitute any notice of adverse claims except in the case of a purchase

(a) after one year from any date set for such presentment or surrender for redemption or exchange; or

(b) after six months from any date set for payment of money against presentation or surrender of the security if funds are available for payment on that date.

Section 8—306. Warranties on Presentment and Transfer.

(1) A person who presents a security for registration of transfer or for payment or exchange warrants to the issuer that he is entitled to the registration, payment or exchange. But a

purchaser for value without notice of adverse claims who receives a new, reissued or reregistered security on registration of transfer warrants only that he has no knowledge of any unauthorized signature (Section 8—311) in a necessary indorsement.

(2) A person by transferring a security to a purchaser for value warrants only that

    (a) his transfer is effective and rightful; and

    (b) the security is genuine and has not been materially altered; and

    (c) he knows no fact which might impair the validity of the security.

(3) Where a security is delivered by an intermediary known to be entrusted with delivery of the security on behalf of another or with collection of a draft or other claim against such delivery, the intermediary by such delivery warrants only his own good faith and authority even though he has purchased or made advances against the claim to be collected against the delivery.

(4) A pledgee or other holder for security who redelivers the security received, or after payment and on order of the debtor delivers that security to a third person, makes only the warranties of an intermediary under subsection (3).

(5) A broker gives to his customer and to the issuer and a purchaser the warranties provided in this section and has the rights and privileges of a purchaser under this section. The warranties of and in favor of the broker acting as an agent are in addition to applicable warranties given by and in favor of his customer.

Section 8—307. Effect of Delivery Without Indorsement; Right to Compel Indorsement.

Where a security in registered form has been delivered to a purchaser without a necessary indorsement, he may become a bona fide purchaser only as of the time the indorsement is supplied, but against the transferor the transfer is complete upon delivery and the purchaser has a specifically enforceable right to have any necessary indorsement supplied.

Section 8—308. Indorsement, How Made; Special Indorsement; Indorser Not a Guarantor; Partial Assignment.

(1) An indorsement of a security in registered form is made when an appropriate person signs on it or on a separate document an assignment or transfer of the security or a power to assign or transfer it or when the signature of such person is written without more upon the back of the security.

(2) An indorsement may be in blank or special. An indorsement in blank includes an indorsement to bearer. A special indorsement specifies the person to whom the security is to be transferred, or who has power to transfer it. A holder may convert a blank indorsement into a special indorsement.

(3) "An appropriate person" in subsection (1) means

    (a) the person specified by the security or by special indorsement to be entitled to the security; or

    (b) where the person so specified is described as a fiduciary but is no longer serving in the described capacity,—either that person or his successor; or

    (c) where the security or indorsement so specifies more than one person as fiduciaries and one or more are no longer serving in the described capacity,—the remaining fiduciary or fiduciaries, whether or not a successor has been appointed or qualified; or

    (d) where the person specified is an individual and is without capacity to act by virtue of death, incompetence, infancy or otherwise,—his executor, administrator, guardian or like fiduciary; or

    (e) where the security or indorsement so specifies more than one person as tenants by the entirety or with rights of survivorship and by reason of death all cannot sign,—the survivor or survivors; or

    (f) a person having power to sign under applicable law or controlling instrument; or

    (g) to the extent that any of the foregoing persons may act through an agent,—his authorized agent.

(4) Unless otherwise agreed the indorser by his indorsement assumes no obligation that the security will be honored by the issuer.

(5) An indorsement purporting to be only of part of a security representing units intended by the issuer to be separately transferable is effective to the extent of the indorsement.

(6) Whether the person signing is appropriate is determined as of the date of signing and an indorsement by such a person does not become unauthorized for the purposes of this Article by virtue of any subsequent change of circumstances.

(7) Failure of a fiduciary to comply with a controlling instrument or with the law of the state having jurisdiction of the fiduciary relationship,

including any law requiring the fiduciary to obtain court approval of the transfer, does not render his indorsement unauthorized for the purpose of this Article.

Section 8—309. Effect of Indorsement Without Delivery.

An indorsement of a security whether special or in blank does not constitute a transfer until delivery of the security on which it appears or, if the indorsement is on a separate document, until delivery of both the document and the security.

Section 8—310. Indorsement of Security in Bearer Form.

An indorsement of a security in bearer form may give notice of adverse claims (Section 8—304) but does not otherwise affect any right to registration the holder may possess.

Section 8—311. Effect of Unauthorized Indorsement.

Unless the owner has ratified an unauthorized indorsement or is otherwise precluded from asserting its ineffectiveness

  (a) he may assert its ineffectiveness against the issuer or any purchaser other than a purchaser for value and without notice of adverse claims who has in good faith received a new, reissued or reregistered security on registration of transfer; and

  (b) an issuer who registers the transfer of a security upon the unauthorized indorsement is subject to liability for improper registration (Section 8—404).

Section 8—312. Effect of Guaranteeing Signature or Indorsement.

(1) Any person guaranteeing a signature of an indorser of a security warrants that at the time of signing

  (a) the signature was genuine; and

  (b) the signer was an appropriate person to indorse (Section 8—308); and

  (c) the signer had legal capacity to sign.

But the guarantor does not otherwise warrant the rightfulness of the particular transfer.

(2) Any person may guarantee an indorsement of a security and by so doing warrants not only the signature (subsection 1) but also the rightfulness of the particular transfer in all respects. But no issuer may require a guarantee of indorsement as a condition to registration of transfer.

(3) The foregoing warranties are made to any person taking or dealing with the security in reliance on the guarantee and the guarantor is liable to such person for any loss resulting from breach of the warranties.

Section 8—313. When Delivery to the Purchaser Occurs; Purchaser's Broker as Holder.

(1) Delivery to a purchaser occurs when

  (a) he or a person designated by him acquires possession of a security; or

  (b) his broker acquires possession of a security specially indorsed to or issued in the name of the purchaser; or

  (c) his broker sends him confirmation of the purchase and also by book entry or otherwise identifies a specific security in the broker's possession as belonging to the purchaser; or

  (d) with respect to an identified security to be delivered while still in the possession of a third person when that person acknowledges that he holds for the purchaser; or

  (e) appropriate entries on the books of a clearing corporation are made under Section 8—320.

(2) The purchaser is the owner of a security held for him by his broker but is not the holder except as specified in subparagraphs (b), (c) and (e) of subsection (1). Where a security is part of a fungible bulk, the purchaser is the owner of a proportionate property interest in the fungible bulk.

(3) Notice of an adverse claim received by the broker or by the purchaser after the broker takes delivery as a holder for value is not effective either as to the broker or as to the purchaser. However, as between the broker and the purchaser the purchaser may demand delivery of an equivalent security as to which no notice of an adverse claim has been received.

Section 8—314. Duty to Deliver, When Completed.

(1) Unless otherwise agreed, where a sale of a security is made on an exchange or otherwise through brokers

  (a) the selling customer fulfills his duty to deliver when he places such a security in the possession of the selling broker or of a person designated by the broker or if requested causes an acknowledgment to be made to the selling broker that it is held for him; and

  (b) the selling broker including a correspondent broker acting for a selling customer fulfills his duty to deliver by placing the security or a like security in the possession of the buying broker or a person designated by him or by effecting clearance of the sale in accordance with the rules of the exchange on which the transaction took place.

(2) Except as otherwise provided in this section and unless otherwise agreed, a transferor's duty to deliver a security under a contract of purchase is not fulfilled until he places the security in form to be negotiated by the purchaser in the possession of the purchaser or of a person designated by him or at the purchaser's request causes an acknowledgment to be made to the purchaser that it is held for him. Unless made on an exchange a sale to a broker purchasing for his own account is within this subsection and not within subsection (1).

Section 8—315. Action Against Purchaser Based Upon Wrongful Transfer.

(1) Any person against whom the transfer of a security is wrongful for any reason, including his incapacity, may against anyone except a bona fide purchaser reclaim possession of the security or obtain possession of any new security evidencing all or part of the same rights or have damages.

(2) If the transfer is wrongful because of an unauthorized indorsement, the owner may also reclaim or obtain possession of the security or new security even from a bona fide purchaser if the ineffectiveness of the purported indorsement can be asserted against him under the provisions of this Article on unauthorized indorsements (Section 8—311).

(3) The right to obtain or reclaim possession of a security may be specifically enforced and its transfer enjoined and the security impounded pending the litigation.

Section 8—316. Purchaser's Right to Requisites for Registration of Transfer on Books.

Unless otherwise agreed the transferor must on due demand supply his purchaser with any proof of his authority to transfer or with any other requisite which may be necessary to obtain registration of the transfer of the security, but if the transfer is not for value, a transferor need not do so unless the purchaser furnishes the necessary expenses. Failure to comply with a demand made within a reasonable time gives the purchaser the right to reject or rescind the transfer.

Section 8—317. Attachment or Levy Upon Security.

(1) No attachment or levy upon a security or any share or other interest evidenced thereby which is outstanding shall be valid until the security is actually seized by the officer making the attachment or levy, but a security which has been surrendered to the issuer may be attached or levied upon at the source.

(2) A creditor whose debtor is the owner of a security shall be entitled to such aid from courts of appropriate jurisdiction, by injunction or otherwise, in reaching such security or in satisfying the claim by means thereof as is allowed at law or in equity in regard to property which cannot readily be attached or levied upon by ordinary legal process.

Section 8—318. No Conversion by Good Faith Delivery.

An agent or bailee who in good faith (including observance of reasonable commercial standards if he is in the business of buying, selling or otherwise dealing with securities) has received securities and sold, pledged or delivered them according to the instructions of his principal is not liable for conversion or for participation in breach of fiduciary duty although the principal had no right to dispose of them.

Section 8—319. Statute of Frauds.

A contract for the sale of securities is not enforceable by way of action or defense unless

(a) there is some writing signed by the party against whom enforcement is sought or by his authorized agent or broker sufficient to indicate that a contract has been made, for sale of a stated quantity of described securities at a defined or stated price; or

(b) delivery of the security has been accepted or payment has been made but the contract is enforceable under this provision only to the extent of such delivery or payment; or

(c) within a reasonable time a writing in confirmation of the sale or purchase and sufficient against the sender under paragraph (a) has been received by the party against whom enforcement is sought and he has failed to send written objection to its contents within ten days after its receipt; or

(d) the party against whom enforcement is sought admits in his pleading, testimony or otherwise in court that a contract was made for sale of a stated quantity of described securities at a defined or stated price.

Section 8—320. Transfer or Pledge within a Central Depository System.

(1) If a security

    (a) is in the custody of a clearing corporation or of a custodian bank or a nominee of either subject to the instructions of the clearing corporation; and

    (b) is in bearer form or indorsed in blank by an appropriate person or registered in the name of the clearing corporation or custodian bank or a nominee of either; and

    (c) is shown on the account of a transferor or pledgor on the books of the clearing corporation;

then, in addition to other methods, a transfer or pledge of the security or any interest therein may be effected by the making of appropriate entries on the books of the clearing corporation reducing the account of the transferor or pledgor and increasing the account of the transferee or pledgee by the amount of the obligation or the number of shares or rights transferred or pledged.

(2) Under this section entries may be with respect to like securities or interests therein as a part of a fungible bulk and may refer merely to a quantity of a particular security without reference to the name of the registered owner, certificate or bond number or the like and, in appropriate cases, may be on a net basis taking into account other transfers or pledges of the same security.

(3) A transfer or pledge under this section has the effect of a delivery of a security in bearer form or duly indorsed in blank (Section 8—301) representing the amount of the obligation or the number of shares or rights transferred or pledged. If a pledge or the creation of a security interest is intended, the making of entries has the effect of taking of delivery by the pledgee or a secured party (Sections 9—304 and 9—305). A transferee or pledgee under this section is a holder.

(4) A transfer or pledge under this section does not constitute a registration of transfer under Part 4 of this Article.

(5) That entries made on the books of the clearing corporation as provided in subsection (1) are not appropriate does not affect the validity or effect of the entries nor the liabilities or obligations of the clearing corporation to any person adversely affected thereby.

PART 4 / REGISTRATION

Section 8—401. Duty of Issuer to Register Transfer.

(1) Where a security in registered form is presented to the issuer with a request to register transfer, the issuer is under a duty to register the transfer as requested if

    (a) the security is indorsed by the appropriate person or persons (Section 8—308); and

    (b) reasonable assurance is given that those indorsements are genuine and effective (Section 8—402); and

    (c) the issuer has no duty to inquire into adverse claims or has discharged any such duty (Section 8—403); and

    (d) any applicable law relating to the collection of taxes has been complied with; and

    (e) the transfer is in fact rightful or is to a bona fide purchaser.

(2) Where an issuer is under a duty to register a transfer of a security, the issuer is also liable to the person presenting it for registration or his principal for loss resulting from any unreasonable delay in registration or from failure or refusal to register the transfer.

Section 8—402. Assurance That Indorsements Are Effective.

(1) The issuer may require the following assurance that each necessary indorsement (Section 8—308) is genuine and effective

    (a) in all cases, a guarantee of the signature (subsection (1) of Section 8—312) of the person indorsing; and

    (b) where the indorsement is by an agent, appropriate assurance of authority to sign;

    (c) where the indorsement is by a fiduciary, appropriate evidence of appointment or incumbency;

    (d) where there is more than one fiduciary, reasonable assurance that all who are required to sign have done so;

    (e) where the indorsement is by a person not covered by any of the foregoing, assurance appropriate to the case corresponding as nearly as may be to the foregoing.

(2) A "guarantee of the signature" in subsection (1) means a guarantee signed by or on behalf of a person reasonably believed by the issuer to be responsible. The issuer may adopt standards with respect to responsibility provided such standards are not manifestly unreasonable.

(3) "Appropriate evidence of appointment of incumbency" in subsection (1) means

   (a) in the case of a fiduciary appointed or qualified by a court, a certificate issued by or under the direction or supervision of that court or an officer thereof and dated within sixty days before the date of presentation for transfer; or

   (b) in any other case, a copy of a document showing the appointment or a certificate issued by or on behalf of a person reasonably believed by the issuer to be responsible or, in the absence of such a document or certificate, other evidence reasonably deemed by the issuer to be appropriate. The issuer may adopt standards with respect to such evidence provided such standards are not manifestly unreasonable. The issuer is not charged with notice of the contents of any document obtained pursuant to this paragraph (b) except to the extent that the contents relate directly to the appointment or incumbency.

(4) The issuer may elect to require reasonable assurance beyond that specified in this section but if it does so and for a purpose other than that specified in subsection 3(b) both requires and obtains a copy of a will, trust, indenture, articles of co-partnership, by-laws or other controlling instrument, it is charged with notice of all matters contained therein affecting the transfer.

Section 8—403. Limited Duty of Inquiry.

(1) An issuer to whom a security is presented for registration is under a duty to inquire into adverse claims if

   (a) a written notification of an adverse claim is received at a time and in a manner, which affords the issuer a reasonable opportunity to act on it prior to the issuance of a new, reissued or reregistered security and the notification identifies the claimant, the registered owner and the issue of which the security is a part and provides an address for communications directed to the claimant; or

   (b) the issuer is charged with notice of an adverse claim from a controlling instrument which it has elected to require under subsection (4) of Section 8—402.

(2) The issuer may discharge any duty of inquiry by any reasonable means, including notifying an adverse claimant by registered or certified mail at the address furnished by him or if there be no such address at his residence or regular place of business that the security has been presented for registration or transfer by a named person, and that the transfer will be registered unless within thirty days from the date of mailing the notification, either

   (a) an appropriate restraining order, injunction or other process issues from a court of competent jurisdiction; or

   (b) an indemnity bond sufficient in the issuer's judgment to protect the issuer and any transfer agent, registrar or other agent of the issuer involved, from any loss which it or they may suffer by complying with the adverse claim is filed with the issuer.

(3) Unless an issuer is charged with notice of an adverse claim from a controlling instrument which it has elected to require under subsection (4) of Section 8—402 or receives notification of an adverse claim under subsection (1) of this section, where a security presented for registration is indorsed by the appropriate person or persons the issuer is under no duty to inquire into adverse claims. In particular

   (a) an issuer registering a security in the name of a person who is a fiduciary or who is described as a fiduciary is not bound to inquire into the existence, extent, or correct description of the fiduciary relationship; and thereafter the issuer may assume without inquiry that the newly registered owner continues to be the fiduciary until the issuer receives written notice that the fiduciary is no longer acting as such with respect to the particular security;

   (b) an issuer registering transfer on an indorsement by a fiduciary is not bound to inquire whether the transfer is made in compliance with a controlling instrument or with the law of the state having jurisdiction of the fiduciary relationship, including any law requiring the fiduciary to obtain court approval of the transfer; and

   (c) the issuer is not charged with notice of the contents of any court record or file or other recorded or unrecorded document even though the transfer is made on the indorsement of the fiduciary to the fiduciary himself or to his nominee.

Section 8—404. Liability and Nonliability for Registration.

(1) Except as otherwise provided in any law relating to the collection of taxes, the issuer is not liable to the owner or any other person suffering loss as a result of the registration of a transfer of a security if

    (a) there were on or with the security the necessary indorsements (Section 8—308); and

    (b) the issuer had no duty to inquire into adverse claims or has discharged any such duty (Section 8—403).

(2) Where an issuer has registered a transfer of a security to a person not entitled to it, the issuer on demand must deliver a like security to the true owner unless

    (a) the registration was pursuant to subsection (1); or

    (b) the owner is precluded from asserting any claim for registering the transfer under subsection (1) of the following section; or

    (c) such delivery would result in overissue, in which case the issuer's liability is governed by Section 8—104.

Section 8—405. Lost, Destroyed and Stolen Securities.

(1) Where a security has been lost, apparently destroyed or wrongfully taken and the owner fails to notify the issuer of that fact within a reasonable time after he has notice of it and the issuer registers a transfer of the security before receiving such a notification, the owner is precluded from asserting against the issuer any claim for registering the transfer under the preceding section or any claim to a new security under this section.

(2) Where the owner of a security claims that the security has been lost, destroyed or wrongfully taken, the issuer must issue a new security in place of the original security if the owner

    (a) so requests before the issuer has notice that the security has been acquired by a bona fide purchaser; and

    (b) files with the issuer a sufficient indemnity bond; and

    (c) satisifies any other reasonable requirements imposed by the issuer.

(3) If, after the issue of the new security, a bona fide purchaser of the original security presents it for registration of transfer, the issuer must register the transfer unless registration would result in overissue, in which event the issuer's liability is governed by Section 8—104. In addition to any rights on the indemnity bond, the issuer may recover the new security from the person to whom it was issued or any person taking under him except a bona fide purchaser.

Section 8—406. Duty of Authenticating Trustee, Transfer Agent or Registrar.

(1) Where a person acts as authenticating trustee, transfer agent, registrar, or other agent for an issuer in the registration of transfers of its securities or in the issue of new securities or in the cancellation of surrendered securities

    (a) he is under a duty to the issuer to exercise good faith and due diligence in performing his functions; and

    (b) he has with regard to the particular functions he performs the same obligation to the holder or owner of the security and has the same rights and privileges as the issuer has in regard to those functions.

(2) Notice to an authenticating trustee, transfer agent, registrar or other such agent is notice to the issuer with respect to the functions performed by the agent.

ARTICLE 9 / SECURED TRANSACTIONS: SALES OF ACCOUNTS, CONTRACT RIGHTS AND CHATTEL PAPER

PART 1 / SHORT TITLE, APPLICABILITY AND DEFINITIONS

Section 9—101. Short Title.

This Article shall be known and may be cited as Uniform Commercial Code—Secured Transactions.

Section 9—102. Policy and Scope of Article.

(1) Except as otherwise provided in Section 9—103 on multiple state transactions and in Section 9—104 on excluded transactions, this Article

applies so far as concerns any personal property and fixtures within the jurisdiction of this state

(a) to any transaction (regardless of its form) which is intended to create a security interest in personal property or fixtures including goods, documents, instruments, general intangibles, chattel papers, accounts or contract rights; and also

(b) to any sale of accounts, contract rights or chattel paper.

(2) This Article applies to security interests created by contract including pledge, assignment, chattel mortgage, chattel trust, trust deed, factor's lien, equipment trust, conditional sale, trust receipt, other lien or title retention contract and lease or consignment intended as security. This Article does not apply to statutory liens except as provided in Section 9—310.

(3) The application of this Article to a security interest in a secured obligation is not affected by the fact that the obligation is itself secured by a transaction or interest to which this Article does not apply.

Note: *The adoption of this Article should be accompanied by the repeal of existing statutes dealing with conditional sales, trust receipts, factor's liens where the factor is given a non-possessory lien, chattel mortgages, crop mortgages, mortgages on railroad equipment, assignment of accounts and generally statutes regulating security interests in personal property.*

Where the state has a retail installment selling act or small loan act, that legislation should be carefully examined to determine what changes in those acts are needed to conform them to this Article. This Article primarily sets out rules defining rights of a secured party against persons dealing with the debtor; it does not prescribe regulations and controls which may be necessary to curb abuses arising in the small loan business or in the financing of consumer purchases on credit. Accordingly there is no intention to repeal existing regulatory acts in those fields. See Section 9–203(2) and the Note thereto.

Section 9—103. Accounts, Contract Rights, General Intangibles and Equipment Relating to Another Jurisdiction; and Incoming Goods Already Subject to a Security Interest.

(1) If the office where the assignor of accounts or contract rights keeps his records concerning them is in this state, the validity and perfection of a security interest therein and the possibility and effect of proper filing is governed by this Article; otherwise by the law (including the conflict of laws rules) of the jurisdiction where such office is located.

(2) If the chief place of business of a debtor is in this state, this Article governs the validity and perfection of a security interest and the possibility and effect of proper filing with regard to general intangibles or with regard to goods of a type which are normally used in more than one jurisdiction (such as automotive equipment, rolling stock, airplanes, road building equipment, commercial harvesting equipment, construction machinery and the like) if such goods are classified as equipment or classified as inventory by reason of their being leased by the debtor and others. Otherwise, the law (including the conflict of laws rules) of the jurisdiction where such chief place of business is located shall govern. If the chief place of business is located in a jurisdiction which does not provide for perfection of the security interest by filing or recording in that jurisdiction, then the security interest may be perfected by filing in this state. [For the purpose of determining the validity and perfection of a security interest in an airplane, the chief place of business of a debtor who is a foreign air carrier under the Federal Aviation Act of 1958, as amended, is the designated office of the agent upon whom service of process may be made on behalf of the debtor.]

(3) If personal property other than that governed by subsections (1) and (2) is already subject to a security interest when it is brought into this state, the validity of the security interest in this state is to be determined by the law (including the conflict of laws rules) of the jurisdiction where the property was when the security interest attached. However, if the parties to the transaction understood at the time that the security interest attached that the property would be kept in this state and it was brought into this state within 30 days after the security interest attached for purposes other than transportation through this state, then the validity of the security interest in this state is to be determined by the law of this state. If the security interest was al-

ready perfected under the law of the jurisdiction where the property was when the security interest attached and before being brought into this state, the security interest continues perfected in this state for four months and also thereafter if within the four month period it is perfected in this state. The security interest may also be perfected in this state after the expiration of the four month period; in such case perfection dates from the time of perfection in this state. If the security interest was not perfected under the law of the jurisdiction where the property was when the security interest attached and before being brought into this state, it may be perfected in this state; in such case perfection dates from the time of perfection in this state.

(4) Notwithstanding subsections (2) and (3), if personal property is covered by a certificate of title issued under a statute of this state or any other jurisdiction which requires indication on a certificate of title of any security interest in the property as a condition of perfection, then the perfection is governed by the law of the jurisdiction which issued the certificate.

[(5) Notwithstanding subsection (1) and Section 9—302, if the office where the assignor of accounts or contract rights keeps his records concerning them is not located in a jurisdiction which is a part of the United States, its territories or possessions, and the accounts or contract rights are within the jurisdiction of this state or the transaction which creates the security interest otherwise bears an appropriate relation to this state, this Article governs the validity and perfection of the security interest and the security interest may only be perfected by notification to the account debtor.]

Note: *The last sentence of subsection (2) and subsection (5) are bracketed to indicate optional enactment. In states engaging in financing of airplanes of foreign carriers and of international open accounts receivable, bracketed language will be of value. In other states not engaging in financing of this type, the bracketed language may not be considered necessary.*

Section 9—104. Transactions Excluded from Article.

This Article does not apply

    (a) to a security interest subject to any statute of the United States such as the Ship Mortgage Act, 1920, to the extent that such statute governs the rights of parties to and third parties affected by

transactions in particular types of property; or

    (b) to a landlord's lien; or

    (c) to a lien given by statute or other rules of law for services or materials except as provided in Section 9—310 on priority of such liens; or

    (d) to a transfer of a claim for wages, salary or other compensation of an employee; or

    (e) to an equipment trust covering railway rolling stock; or

    (f) to a sale of accounts, contract rights or chattel paper as part of a sale of the business out of which they arose, or an assignment of accounts, contract rights or chattel paper which is for the purpose of collection only, or a transfer of a contract right to an assignee who is also to be the performance under the contract; or

    (g) to a transfer of an interest or claim in or under any policy of insurance; or

    (h) to a right represented by a judgment; or

    (i) to any right of set-off; or

    (j) except to the extent that provision is made for fixtures in Section 9—313, to the creation or transfer of an interest in or lien on real estate, including a lease or rents thereunder; or

    (k) to a transfer in whole or in part of any of the following: any claim arising out of tort; any deposit, savings, passbook or like account maintained with a bank, savings and loan association, credit union or like organization.

Section 9—105. Definitions and Index of Definitions.

(1) In this Article unless the context otherwise requires:

    (a) "Account debtor" means the person who is obligated on an account, chattel paper, contract right or general intangible;

    (b) "Chattel paper" means a writing or writings which evidence both a monetary obligation and a security interest in or a lease of specified goods. When a transaction is evidenced both by such a security agreement or a lease and by an instrument or series of instruments, the group of writings taken together constitutes chattel paper;

    (c) "Collateral" means the property subject to a security interest, and includes accounts, contract rights and chattel paper which have been sold;

(d) "Debtor" means the person who owes payment or other performance of the obligation secured, whether or not he owns or has rights in the collateral, and includes the seller of accounts, contract rights or chattel paper. Where the debtor and the owner of the collateral are not the same person, the term "debtor" means the owner of the collateral in any provision of the Article dealing with the collateral, the obligor in any provision dealing with the obligation, and may include both where the context so requires;

(e) "Document" means document of title as defined in the general definitions of Article 1 (Section 1—201);

(f) "Goods" includes all things which are movable at the time the security interest attaches or which are fixtures (Section 9—313), but does not include money, documents, instruments, accounts, chattel paper, general intangibles, contract rights and other things in action. "Goods" also include the unborn young of animals and growing crops;

(g) "Instrument" means a negotiable instrument (defined in Section 3—104), or a security (defined in Section 8—102) or any other writing which evidences a right to payment of money and is not itself a security agreement or lease and of a type which is in ordinary course of business transferred by delivery with any necessary indorsement or assignment;

(h) "Security agreement" means an agreement which creates or provides for a security interest;

(i) "Secured party" means a lender, seller or other person in whose favor there is a security interest, including a person to whom accounts, contract rights or chattel paper have been sold. When the holders of obligations issued under an indenture of trust, equipment trust agreement or the like are represented by a trustee or other person, the representative is the secured party.

(2) Other definitions applying to this Article and the sections in which they appear are:

"Account". Section 9—106.
"Consumer goods". Section 9—109(1).
"Contract right". Section 9—106.
"Equipment". Section 9—109(2).

"Farm products". Section 9—109(3).
"General intangibles". Section 9—106.
"Inventory". Section 9—109(4).
"Lien creditor". Section 9—301(3).
"Proceeds". Section 9—306(1).
"Purchase money security interest". Section 9—107.

(3) The following definitions in other Articles apply to this Article:

"Check". Section 3—104.
"Contract for sale". Section 2—106.
"Holder in due course". Section 3—302.
"Note". Section 3—104.
"Sale". Section 2—106.

(4) In addition Article 1 contains general definitions and principles of construction and interpretation applicable throughout this Article.

Section 9—106. Definitions: "Account"; "Contract Right"; "General Intangibles".

"Account" means any right to payment for goods sold or leased or for services rendered which is not evidenced by an instrument or chattel paper. "Contract right" means any right to payment under a contract not yet earned by performance and not evidenced by an instrument or chattel paper. "General intangibles" means any personal property (including things in action) other than goods, accounts, contract rights, chattel paper, documents and instruments.

Section 9—107. Definitions: "Purchase Money Security Interest".

A security interest is a "purchase money security interest" to the extent that it is

(a) taken or retained by the seller of the collateral to secure all or part of its price; or

(b) taken by a person who by making advances or incurring an obligation gives value to enable the debtor to acquire rights in or the use of collateral if such value is in fact so used.

Section 9—108. When After-Acquired Collateral Not Security for Antecedent Debt.

Where a secured party makes an advance, incurs an obligation, releases a perfected security interest, or otherwise gives new value which is to be secured in whole or in part by after-acquired property, his security interest in the after-acquired collateral shall be deemed to be taken for new value and not as security for an antecedent debt if the debtor acquires his rights in such collateral either in the ordinary course of his business or under a contract or purchase made pursuant to the security agreement within a reasonable time after new value is given.

Section 9—109. Classification of Goods; "Consumer Goods"; "Equipment"; "Farm Products"; "Inventory".

Goods are

(1) "consumer goods" if they are used or bought for use primarily for personal, family or household purposes;

(2) "equipment" if they are used or bought for use primarily in business (including farming or a profession) or by a debtor who is a non-profit organization or a governmental subdivision or agency or if the goods are not included in the definitions of inventory, farm products or consumer goods;

(3) "farm products" if they are crops or livestock or supplies used or produced in farming operations or if they are products of crops or livestock in their unmanufactured states (such as ginned cotton, wool-clip, maple syrup, milk and eggs), and if they are in the possession of a debtor engaged in raising, fattening, grazing or other farming operations. If goods are farm products, they are neither equipment nor inventory;

(4) "inventory" if they are held by a person who holds them for sale or lease or to be furnished under contracts for service or if he has so furnished them, or if they are raw materials, work in process or materials used or consumed in a business. Inventory of a person is not to be classified as his equipment.

Section 9—110. Sufficiency of Description.

For the purposes of this Article any description of personal property or real estate is sufficient whether or not it is specific if it reasonably identifies what is described.

Section 9—111. Applicability of Bulk Transfer Laws.

The creation of a security interest is not a bulk transfer under Article 6 (see Section 6—103).

Section 9—112. Where Collateral Is Not Owned by Debtor.

Unless otherwise agreed, when a secured party knows that collateral is owned by a person who is not the debtor, the owner of the collateral Is entitled to receive from the secured party any surplus under Section 9—502(2) or under Section 9—504(1), and is not liable for the debt or for any deficiency after resale, and he has the same right as the debtor

(a) to receive statements under Section 9—208;

(b) to receive notice of and to object to a secured party's proposal to retain the collateral in satisfaction of the indebtedness under Section 9—505;

(c) to redeem the collateral under Section 9—506;

(d) to obtain injunctive or other relief under Section 9—507(1); and

(e) to recover losses caused to him under Section 9—208(2).

Section 9—113. Security Interests Arising Under Article on Sales.

A security interest arising solely under the Article on Sales (Article 2) is subject to the provisions of this Article except that to the extent that and so long as the debtor does not have or does not lawfully obtain possession of the goods

(a) no security agreement is necessary to make the security interest enforceable; and

(b) no filing is required to perfect the security interest; and

(c) the rights of the secured party on default by the debtor are governed by the Article on Sales (Article 2).

PART 2 / VALIDITY OF SECURITY AGREEMENT AND RIGHTS OF PARTIES THERETO

Section 9—201. General Validity of Security Agreement.

Except as otherwise provided by this Act a security agreement is effective according to its terms between the parties, against purchasers of the collateral and against creditors. Nothing in this Article validates any charge or practice illegal under any statute or regulation thereunder

governing usury, small loans, retail installment sales, or the like, or extends the application of any such statute or regulation to any transaction not otherwise subject thereto.

Section 9—202. Title to Collateral Immaterial.

Each provision of this Article with regard to rights, obligations and remedies applies whether title to collateral is in the secured party or in the debtor.

Section 9—203. Enforceability of Security Interest; Proceeds, Formal Requisites.

(1) Subject to the provisions of Section 4—208 on the security interest of a collecting bank and Section 9—113 on a security interest arising under the Article on Sales, a security interest is not enforceable against the debtor or third parties unless

  (a) the collateral is in the possession of the secured party; or
  (b) the debtor has signed a security agreement which contains a description of the collateral and in addition, when the security interest covers crops or oil, gas or minerals to be extracted or timber to be cut, a description of the land concerned. In describing collateral, the word "proceeds" is sufficient without further description to cover proceeds of any character.

(2) A transaction, although subject to this Article, is also subject to . . . .-. . . .*, and in the case of conflict between the provisions of this Article and any such statute, the provisions of such statute control. Failure to comply with any applicable statute has only the effect which is specified therein.

> **Note:** At * in subsection (2) insert reference to any local statute regulating small loans, retail installment sales and the like.
>
> The foregoing subsection (2) is designed to make it clear that certain transactions, although subject to this Article, must also comply with other applicable legislation.
>
> This Article is designed to regulate all the "security" aspects of transactions within its scope. There is, however, much regulatory legislation, particularly in the consumer field, which supplements this Article and should not be repealed by its enactment. Examples are small loan acts, retail installment selling acts and the like. Such acts may provide for licensing and rate regulation and may prescribe particular forms of contract. Such provisions should remain in force despite the enactment of this Article. On the other hand if a Retail Installment Selling Act contains provisions on filing, rights on default, etc., such provisions should be repealed as inconsistent with this Article.

Section 9—204. When Security Interest Attaches; After-Acquired Property; Future Advances.

(1) A security interest cannot attach until there is agreement (subsection (3) of Section 1—201) that it attach and value is given and the debtor has rights in the collateral. It attaches as soon as all of the events in the preceding sentence have taken place unless explicit agreement postpones the time of attaching.

(2) For the purposes of this section the debtor has no rights

  (a) in crops until they are planted or otherwise become growing crops, in the young of livestock until they are conceived;
  (b) in fish until caught, in oil, gas or minerals until they are extracted, in timber until it is cut;
  (c) in a contract right until the contract has been made;
  (d) in an account until it comes into existence.

(3) Except as provided in subsection (4) a security agreement may provide that collateral, whenever acquired, shall secure all obligations covered by the security agreement.

(4) No security interest attaches under an after-acquired property clause

  (a) to crops which become such more than one year after the security agreement is executed, except that a security interest in crops which is given in conjunction with a lease or a land purchase or improvement transaction evidenced by a contract, mortgage or deed of trust may if so agreed attach to crops to be grown on the land concerned during the period of such real estate transaction;
  (b) to consumer goods other than accessions (Section 9—314) when given as additional security unless the debtor acquires rights in them within ten days after the secured party gives value.

(5) Obligations covered by a security agreement may include future advances or other value whether or not the advances or value are given pursuant to commitment.

Section 9—205. Use or Disposition of Collateral Without Accounting Permissible.

A security interest is not invalid or fraudulent against creditors by reason of liberty in the debtor to use, commingle or dispose of all or part of the collateral (including returned or repossessed goods) or to collect or compromise accounts, contract rights or chattel paper, or to accept the return of goods or make repossessions, or to use, commingle or dispose of proceeds, or by reason of the failure of the secured party to require the debtor to account for proceeds or replace collateral. This section does not relax the requirements of possession where perfection of a security interest depends upon possession of the collateral by the secured party or by a bailee.

Section 9—206. Agreement Not to Assert Defenses Against Assignee; Modification of Sales Warranties Where Security Agreement Exists.

(1) Subject to any statute or decision which establishes a different rule for buyers or lessees of consumer goods, an agreement by a buyer or lessee that he will not assert against an assignee any claim or defense which he may have against the seller or lessor is enforceable by an assignee who takes his assignment for value, in good faith and without notice of a claim or defense, except as to defenses of a type which may be asserted against a holder in due course of a negotiable instrument under the Article on Commercial Paper (Article 3). A buyer who as part of one transaction signs both a negotiable instrument and a security agreement makes such an agreement.

(2) When a seller retains a purchase money security interest in goods the Article on Sales (Article 2) governs the sale and any disclaimer, limitation or modification of the seller's warranties.

Section 9—207. Rights and Duties When Collateral Is in Secured Party's Possession.

(1) A secured party must use reasonable care in the custody and preservation of collateral in his possession. In the case of an instrument or chattel paper reasonable care includes taking necessary steps to preserve rights against prior parties unless otherwise agreed.

(2) Unless otherwise agreed, when collateral is in the secured party's possession

(a) reasonable expenses (including the cost of any insurance and payment of taxes or other charges) incurred in the custody, preservation, use or operation of the collateral are chargeable to the debtor and are secured by the collateral;

(b) the risk of accidental loss or damage is on the debtor to the extent of any deficiency in any effective insurance coverage;

(c) the secured party may hold as additional security any increase or profits (except money) received from the collateral, but money so received, unless remitted to the debtor, shall be applied in reduction of the secured obligation;

(d) the secured party must keep the collateral identifiable but fungible collateral may be commingled;

(e) the secured party may repledge the collateral upon terms which do not impair the debtor's right to redeem it.

(3) A secured party is liable for any loss caused by his failure to meet any obligation imposed by the preceding subsection but does not lose his security interest.

(4) A secured party may use or operate the collateral for the purpose of preserving the collateral or its value or pursuant to the order of the court of appropriate jurisdiction or, except in the case of consumer goods, in the manner and to the extent provided in the security agreement.

Section 9—208. Request for Statement of Account or List of Collateral.

(1) A debtor may sign a statement indicating what he believes to be the aggregate amount of unpaid indebtedness as of a specified date and may send it to the secured party with a request that the statement be approved or corrected and returned to the debtor. When the security agreement or any other record kept by the secured party identifies the collateral, a debtor may similarly request the secured party to approve or correct a list of the collateral.

(2) The secured party must comply with such a request within two weeks after receipt by sending a written correction or approval. If the secured party claims a security interest in all of a particular type of collateral owned by the debtor, he may indicate that fact in his reply and need not approve or correct an itemized list of such collateral. If the secured party without reasonable excuse fails to comply, he is liable for any loss caused to the debtor thereby; and if the debtor has properly included in his request a good faith statement of the obligation or a list of the collateral or both, the secured party may claim a security interest only as shown in the statement against persons misled by his failure to comply. If he no longer has an interest in the obligation or collateral at the time the request is received, he must disclose the name and address of any suc-

cessor in interest known to him and he is liable for any loss caused to the debtor as a result of failure to disclose. A successor in interest is not subject to this section until a request is received by him.

(3) A debtor is entitled to such a statement once every six months without charge. The secured party may require payment of a charge not exceeding $10 for each additional statement furnished.

PART 3 / RIGHTS OF THIRD PARTIES; PERFECTED AND UNPERFECTED SECURITY INTERESTS; RULES OF PRIORITY

Section 9—301. Persons Who Take Priority Over Unperfected Security Interests; "Lien Creditor".

(1) Except as otherwise provided in subsection (2), an unperfected security interest is subordinate to the rights of
  (a) persons entitled to priority under Section 9—312;
  (b) a person who becomes a lien creditor without knowledge of the security interest and before it is perfected; .
  (c) in the case of goods, instruments, documents, and chattel paper, a person who is not a secured party and who is a transferee in bulk or other buyer not in ordinary course of business to the extent that he gives value and receives delivery of the collateral without knowledge of the security interest and before it is perfected;
  (d) in the case of accounts, contract rights, and general intangibles, a person who is not a secured party and who is a transferee to the extent that he gives value without knowledge of the security interest and before it is perfected.

(2) If the secured party files with respect to a purchase money security interest before or within ten days after the collateral comes into possession of the debtor, he takes priority over the rights of a transferee in bulk or of a lien creditor which arises between the time the security interest attaches and the time of filing.

(3) A "lien creditor" means a creditor who has acquired a lien on the property involved by attachment, levy or the like and includes an assignee for benefit of creditors from the time of assignment, and a trustee in bankruptcy from the date of the filing of the petition or a receiver in equity from the time of appointment. Unless all the creditors represented had knowledge of the security interest, such a representative of creditors is a lien creditor without knowledge even though he personally has knowledge of the security interest.

Section 9—302. When Filing Is Required to Perfect Security Interest; Security Interests to Which Filing Provisions of This Article Do Not Apply.

(1) A financing statement must be filed to perfect all security interests except the following:
  (a) a security interest in collateral in possession of the secured party under Section 9—305;
  (b) a security interest temporarily perfected in instruments or documents without delivery under Section 9—304 or in proceeds for a 10 day period under Section 9—306;
  (c) a purchase money security interest in farm equipment having a purchase price not in excess of $2500; but filing is required for a fixture under Section 9—313 or for a motor vehicle required to be licensed;
  (d) a purchase money security interest in consumer goods; but filing is required for a fixture under section 9—313 or for a motor vehicle required to be licensed;
  (e) an assignment of accounts or contract rights which does not alone or in conjunction with other assignments to the same assignee transfer a significant part of the outstanding accounts or contract rights of the assignor;
  (f) a security interest of a collecting bank (Section 4—208) or arising under the Article on Sales (see Section 9—113) or covered in subsection (3) of this section.

(2) If a secured party assigns a perfected security interest, no filing under this Article is required in order to continue the perfected status of the security interest against creditors of and transferees from the original debtor.

(3) The filing provisions of this Article do not apply to a security interest in property subject to a statute

    (a) of the United States which provides for a national registration or filing of all security interests in such property; or

Note: *States to select either alternative A or Alternative B.*

Alternative A—

    (b) of this state which provides for central filing of, or which requires indication on a certificate of title of, such security interests in such property.

Alternative B—

    (b) of this state which provides for central filing of security interests in such property, or in a motor vehicle which is not inventory held for sale for which a certificate of title is required under the statutes of this state if a notation of such a security interest can be indicated by a public official on a certificate or a duplicate thereof.

(4) A security interest in property covered by a statute described in subsection (3) can be perfected only by registration or filing under that statute or by indication of the security interest on a certificate of title or a duplicate thereof by a public official.

Section 9—303. When Security Interest Is Perfected; Continuity of Perfection.

(1) A security interest is perfected when it has attached and when all of the applicable steps required for perfection have been taken. Such steps are specified in Sections 9—302, 9—304, 9—305 and 9—306. If such steps are taken before the security interest attaches, it is perfected at the time when it attaches.

(2) If a security interest is originally perfected in any way permitted under this Article and is subsequently perfected in some other way under this Article, without an intermediate period when it was unperfected, the security interest shall be deemed to be perfected continuously for the purposes of this Article.

Section 9—304. Perfection of Security Interest in Instruments, Documents, and Goods Covered by Documents; Perfection by Permissive Filing; Temporary Perfection Without Filing or Transfer of Possession.

(1) A security interest in chattel paper or negotiable documents may be perfected by fil-

ing. A security interest in instruments (other than instruments which constitute part of chattel paper) can be perfected only by the secured party's taking possession, except as provided in subsections (4) and (5).

(2) During the period that goods are in the possession of the issuer of a negotiable document therefor, a security interest in the goods is perfected by perfecting a security interest in the document, and any security interest in the goods otherwise perfected during such period is subject thereto.

(3) A security interest in goods in the possession of a bailee other than one who has issued a negotiable document therefor is perfected by issuance of a document in the name of the secured party or by the bailee's receipt of notification of the secured party's interest or by filing as to the goods.

(4) A security interest in instruments or negotiable documents is perfected without filing or the taking of possession for a period of 21 days from the time it attaches to the extent that it arises for new value given under a written security agreement.

(5) A security interest remains perfected for a period of 21 days without filing where a secured party having a perfected security interest in an instrument, a negotiable document or goods in possession of a bailee other than one who has issued a negotiable document therefor

    (a) makes available to the debtor the goods or documents representing the goods for the purpose of ultimate sale or exchange or for the purpose of loading, unloading, storing, shipping, manufacturing, processing or otherwise dealing with them in a manner preliminary to their sale or exchange; or

    (b) delivers the instrument to the debtor for the purpose of ultimate sale or exchange or of presentation, collection, renewal or registration of transfer.

(6) After the 21 day period in subsections (4) and (5) perfection depends upon compliance with applicable provisions of this Article.

Section 9—305. When Possession by Secured Party Perfects Security Interest Without Filing.

A security interest in letters of credit and advices of credit (subsection (2)(a) of Section 5—116), goods, instruments, negotiable documents or chattel paper may be perfected by the secured party's taking possession of the collateral. If such collateral other than goods covered by a negotiable document is held by a bailee, the secured party is deemed to have possession from the time the bailee receives notification of the secured party's interest. A security interest is perfected by possession from the time possession is taken without relation back and continues only so long as possession is retained, unless otherwise specified in this Article. The security interest may be otherwise perfected as provided in this Article before or after the period of possession by the secured party.

Section 9—306. "Proceeds"; Secured Party's Rights on Disposition of Collateral.

(1) "Proceeds" includes whatever is received when collateral or proceeds is sold, exchanged, collected or otherwise disposed of. The term also includes the account arising when the right to payment is earned under a contract right. Money, checks and the like are "cash proceeds". All other proceeds are "non-cash proceeds".

(2) Except where this Article otherwise provides, a security interest continues in collateral notwithstanding sale, exchange or other disposition thereof by the debtor unless his action was authorized by the secured party in the security agreement or otherwise, and also continues in any identifiable proceeds including collections received by the debtor.

(3) The security interest in proceeds is a continuously perfected security interest if the interest in the original collateral was perfected, but it ceases to be a perfected security interest and becomes unperfected ten days after receipt of the proceeds by the debtor unless

    (a) a filed financing statement covering the original collateral also covers proceeds; or

    (b) the security interest in the proceeds is perfected before the expiration of the ten day period.

(4) In the event of insolvency proceedings instituted by or against a debtor, a secured party with a perfected security interest in proceeds has a perfected security interest

    (a) in identifiable non-cash proceeds;

    (b) in identifiable cash proceeds in the form of money which is not commingled with other money or deposited in a bank account prior to the insolvency proceedings;

    (c) in identifiable cash proceeds in the form of checks and the like which are not deposited in a bank account prior to the insolvency proceedings; and

    (d) in all cash and bank accounts of the debtor, if other cash proceeds have been commingled or deposited in a bank account, but the perfected

security interest under this paragraph (d) is

    (i) subject to any right of setoff; and

    (ii) limited to an amount not greater than the amount of any cash proceeds received by the debtor within ten days before the institution of the insolvency proceedings and commingled or deposited in a bank account prior to the insolvency proceedings less the amount of cash proceeds received by the debtor and paid over to the secured party during the ten day period.

(5) If a sale of goods results in an account or chattel paper which is transferred by the seller to a secured party, and if the goods are returned to or are repossessed by the seller or the secured party, the following rules determine priorities:

    (a) If the goods were collateral at the time of sale for an indebtedness of the seller which is still unpaid, the original security interest attaches again to the goods and continues as a perfected security interest if it was perfected at the time when the goods were sold. If the security interest was originally perfected by a filing which is still effective, nothing further is required to continue the perfected status; in any other case, the secured party must take possession of the returned or repossessed goods or must file.

    (b) An unpaid transferee of the chattel paper has a security interest in the goods against the transferor. Such security interest is prior to a security interest asserted under paragraph (a) to the extent that the transferee of the chattel paper was entitled to priority under Section 9—308.

    (c) An unpaid transferee of the account has a security interest in the goods against the transferor. Such security interest is subordinate to a security interest asserted under paragraph (a).

    (d) A security interest of an unpaid transferee asserted under paragraph (b) or (c) must be perfected for protection against creditors of the transferor and purchasers of the returned or repossessed goods.

Section 9—307. Protection of Buyers of Goods.

(1) A buyer in ordinary course of business (subsection (9) of Section 1—201) other than a

person buying farm products from a person engaged in farming operations takes free of a security interest created by his seller even though the security interest is perfected and even though the buyer knows of its existence.

(2) In the case of consumer goods and in the case of farm equipment having an original purchase price not in excess of $2500 (other than fixtures, see Section 9—313), a buyer takes free of a security interest even though perfected if he buys without knowledge of the security interest, for value and for his own personal, family or household purposes or his own farming operations, unless prior to the purchase the secured party has filed a financing statement covering such goods.

Section 9—308. Purchase of Chattel Paper and Nonnegotiable Instruments.

A purchaser of chattel paper or a non-negotiable instrument who gives new value and takes possession of it in the ordinary course of his business and without knowledge that the specific paper or instrument is subject to a security interest has priority over a security interest which is perfected under Section 9—304 (permissive filing and temporary perfection). A purchaser of chattel paper who gives new value and takes possession of it in the ordinary course of his business has priority over a security interest in chattel paper which is claimed merely as proceeds of inventory subject to a security interest (Section 9—306), even though he knows that the specific paper is subject to the security interest.

Section 9—309. Protection of Purchasers of Instruments and Documents.

Nothing in this Article limits the rights of a holder in due course of a negotiable instrument (Section 3—302) or a holder to whom a negotiable document of title has been duly negotiated (Section 7—501) or a bona fide purchaser of a security (Section 8—301) and such holders or purchasers take priority over an earlier security interest even though perfected. Filing under this Article does not constitute notice of the security interest to such holders or purchasers.

Section 9—310. Priority of Certain Liens Arising by Operation of Law.

When a person in the ordinary course of his business furnishes services or materals with respect to goods subject to a security interest, a lien upon goods in the possession of such person given by statute or rule of law for such materials or services takes priority over a perfected security interest unless the lien is statutory and the statute expressly provides otherwise.

Section 9—311. Alienability of Debtor's Rights; Judicial Process.

The debtor's rights in collateral may be voluntarily or involuntarily transferred (by way of sale, creation of a security interest, attachment, levy, garnishment or other judicial process) notwithstanding a provision in the security agreement prohibiting any transfer or making the transfer constitute a default.

Section 9—312. Priorities Among Conflicting Security Interests in the Same Collateral.

(1) The rules of priority stated in the following sections shall govern where applicable: Section 4—208 with respect to the security interest of collecting banks in items being collected, accompanying documents and proceeds; Section 9—301 on certain priorities; Section 9—304 on goods covered by documents; Section 9—306 on proceeds and repossessions; section 9—307 on buyers of goods; Section 9—308 on possessory against nonpossessory interests in chattel paper or nonnegotiable instruments; Section 9—309 on security interests in negotiable instruments, documents or securities; Section 9—310 on priorities between perfected security interests and liens by operation of law; Section 9—313 on security interests in fixtures as against interests in real estate; Section 9—314 on security interests in accessions as against interest in goods; Section 9—315 on conflicting security interests where goods lose their identity or become part of a product; and Section 9—316 on contractual subordination.

(2) A perfected security interest in crops for new value given to enable the debtor to produce the crops during the production season and given not more than three months before the crops become growing crops by planting or otherwise takes priority over an earlier perfected security interest to the extent that such earlier interest secures obligations due more than six months before the crops become growing crops by planting or otherwise, even though the person giving new value had knowledge of the earlier security interest.

(3) A purchase money security interest in inventory collateral has priority over a conflicting security interest in the same collateral if

    (a) the purchase money security interest is perfected at the time the debtor receives possession of the collateral; and

(b) any secured party whose security interest is known to the holder of the purchase money security interest or who, prior to the date of the filing made by the holder of the purchase money security interest, had filed a financing statement covering the same items or type of inventory, has received notification of the purchase money security interest before the debtor receives possession of the collateral covered by the purchase money security interest; and

(c) such notification states that the person giving the notice has or expects to acquire a purchase money security interest in inventory of the debtor, describing such inventory by item or type.

(4) A purchase money security interest in collateral other than inventory has priority over a conflicting security interest in the same collateral if the purchase money security interest is perfected at the time the debtor receives possession of the collateral or within ten days thereafter.

(5) In all cases not governed by other rules stated in this section (including cases of purchase money security interests which do not qualify for the special priorities set forth in subsections (3) and (4) of this section), priority between conflicting security interests in the same collateral shall be determined as follows:

(a) in the order of filing if both are perfected by filing, regardless of which security interest attached first under Section 9—204(1) and whether it attached before or after filing;

(b) in the order of perfection unless both are perfected by filing, regardless of which security interest attached first under Section 9—204(1) and, in the case of a filed security interest, whether it attached before or after filing; and

(c) in the order of attachment under Section 9—204(1) so long as neither is perfected.

(6) For the purpose of the priority rules of the immediately preceding subsection, a continuously perfected security interest shall be treated at all times as if perfected by filing if it was originally so perfected and it shall be treated at all times as if perfected otherwise than by filing if it was originally perfected otherwise than by filing.

Section 9—313. Priority of Security Interests in Fixtures.

(1) The rules of this section do not apply to goods incorporated into a structure in the manner of lumber, bricks, tile, cement, glass, metal work and the like and no security interest in them exists under this Article unless the structure remains personal property under applicable law. The law of this state other than this Act determines whether and when other goods become fixtures. This Act does not prevent creation of an encumbrance upon fixtures or real estate pursuant to the law applicable to real estate.

(2) A security interest which attaches to goods before they become fixtures takes priority as to the goods over the claims of all persons who have an interest in the real estate except as stated in subsection (4).

(3) A security interest which attaches to goods after they become fixtures is valid against all persons subsequently acquiring interests in the real estate except as stated in subsection (4) but is invalid against any person with an interest in the real estate at the time the security interest attaches to the goods who has not in writing consented to the security interest or disclaimed an interest in the goods as fixtures.

(4) The security interests described in subsections (2) and (3) do not take priority over

(a) a subsequent purchaser for value of any interest in the real estate; or

(b) a creditor with a lien on the real estate subsequently obtained by judicial proceedings; or

(c) a creditor with a prior encumbrance of record on the real estate to the extent that he makes subsequent advances

if the subsequent purchase is made, the lien by judicial proceedings is obtained, or the subsequent advance under the prior encumbrance is made or contracted for without knowledge of the security interest and before it is perfected. A purchaser of the real estate at a foreclosure sale other than an encumbrancer purchasing at his own foreclosure sale is a subsequent purchaser within this section.

(5) When under subsections (2) or (3) and (4) a secured party has priority over the claims of all persons who have interests in the real estate, he may, on default, subject to the provisions of Part 5, remove his collateral from the real estate; but he must reimburse any encumbrancer or owner of the real estate who is not the debtor and who has not otherwise agreed for the cost of repair of any physical injury, but not for any diminution in value of the real estate caused by the absence of

the goods removed or by any necessity for replacing them. A person entitled to reimbursement may refuse permission to remove until the secured party gives adequate security for the performance of this obligation.

Section 9—314. Accessions.

(1) A security interest in goods which attaches before they are installed in or affixed to other goods takes priority as to the goods installed or affixed (called in this section "accessions") over the claims of all persons to the whole except as stated in subsection (3) and subject to Section 9—315(1).

(2) A security interest which attaches to goods after they become part of a whole is valid against all persons subsequently acquiring interests in the whole except as stated in subsection (3) but is invalid against any person with an interest in the whole at the time the security interest attaches to the goods who has not in writing consented to the security interest or disclaimed an interest in the goods as part of the whole.

(3) The security interests described in subsections (1) and (2) do not take priority over

(a) a subsequent purchaser for value of any interest in the whole; or

(b) a creditor with a lien on the whole subsequently obtained by judicial proceedings; or

(c) a creditor with a prior perfected security interest in the whole to the extent that he makes subsequent advances

if the subsequent purchase is made, the lien by judicial proceedings obtained or the subsequent advance under the prior perfected security interest is made or contracted for without knowledge of the security interest and before it is perfected. A purchaser of the whole at a foreclosure sale other than the holder of a perfected security interest purchasing at his own foreclosure sale is a subsequent purchaser within this section.

(4) When under subsections (1) or (2) and (3) a secured party has an interest in accessions which has priority over the claims of all persons who have interests in the whole, he may, on default, subject to the provisions of Part 5, remove his collateral from the whole; but he must reimburse any encumbrancer or owner of the whole who is not the debtor and who has not otherwise agreed for the cost of repair of any physical injury but not for any diminution in value of the whole caused by the absence of the goods removed or by any necessity for replacing them. A person entitled to reimbursement may refuse permis-

sion to remove until the secured party gives adequate security for the performance of this obligation.

Section 9—315. Priority When Goods Are Commingled or Processed.

(1) If a security interest in goods was perfected and subsequently the goods or a part thereof have become part of a product or mass, the security interest continues in the product or mass if

(a) the goods are so manufactured, processed, assembled or commingled that their identity is lost in the product or mass; or

(b) a financing statement covering the original goods also covers the product into which the goods have been manufactured, processed or assembled.

In a case to which paragraph (b) applies, no separate security interest in that part of the original goods which has been manufactured, processed or assembled into the product may be claimed under Section 9—314.

(2) When under subsection (1) more than one security interest attaches to the product or mass, they rank equally according to the ratio that the cost of the goods to which each interest originally attached bears to the cost of the total product or mass.

Section 9—316. Priority Subject to Subordination.

Nothing in this Article prevents subordination by agreement by any person entitled to priority.

Section 9—317. Security Party Not Obligated on Contract of Debtor.

The mere existence of a security interest or authority given to the debtor to dispose of or use collateral does not impose contract or tort liability upon the secured party for the debtor's acts or omissions.

Section 9—318. Defenses Against Assignee; Modification of Contract After Notification of Assignment; Term Prohibiting Assignment Ineffective; Identification and Proof of Assignment.

(1) Unless an account debtor has made an enforceable agreement not to assert defenses or claims arising out of a sale as provided in Section 9—206 the rights of an assignee are subject to

(a) all the terms of the contract between the account debtor and assignor and any defense or claim arising therefrom; and

(b) any other defense or claim of the account debtor against the assignor which accrues before the account debtor receives notification of the assignment.

(2) So far as the right to payment under an assigned contract right has not already become an account, and notwithstanding notification of the assignment, any modification of or substitution for the contract made in good faith and in accordance with reasonable commercial standards is effective against an assignee unless the account debtor has otherwise agreed, but the assignee acquires corresponding rights under the modified or substituted contract. The assignment may provide that such modification or substitution is a breach by the assignor.

(3) The account debtor is authorized to pay the assignor until the account debtor receives notification that the account has been assigned and that payment is to be made to the assignee. A notification which does not reasonably identify the rights assigned is ineffective. If requested by the account debtor, the assignee must seasonably furnish reasonable proof that the assignment has been made and unless he does so the account debtor may pay the assignor.

(4) A term in any contract between an account debtor and an assignor which prohibits assignment of an account or contract right to which they are parties is ineffective.

PART 4 / FILING

Section 9—401. Place of Filing; Erroneous Filing; Removal of Collateral.

First Alternative Subsection (1)

(1) The proper place to file in order to perfect a security interest is as follows:

(a) when the collateral is goods which at the time the security interest attaches are or are to become fixtures, then in the office where a mortgage on the real estate concerned would be filed or recorded;

(b) in all other cases, in the office of the [Secretary of State].

Second Alternative Subsection (1)

(1) The proper place to file in order to perfect a security interest is as follows:

(a) when the collateral is equipment used in farming operations, or farm products, or accounts, contract rights or general intangibles arising from or relating to the sale of farm products by a farmer, or consumer goods, then in the office of the . . . in the county of the debtor's residence or if the debtor is not a resident of this state then in the office of the . . . in the county where the goods are kept, and in addition when the collateral is crops in the office of the . . . in the county where the land on which the crops are growing or to be grown is located;

(b) when the collateral is goods which at the time the security interest attaches are or are to become fixtures, then in the office where a mortgage on the real estate concerned would be filed or recorded;

(c) in all other cases, in the office of the [Secretary of State].

Third Alternative Subsection (1)

(1) The proper place to file in order to perfect a security interest is as follows:

(a) when the collateral is equipment used in farming operations, or farm products, or accounts, contract rights or general intangibles arising from or relating to the sale of farm products by a farmer, or consumer goods, then in the office of the . . . in the county of the debtor's residence or if the debtor is not a resident of this state then in the office of the . . . in the county where the goods are kept, and in addition when the collateral is crops in the office of the . . . in the county where the land on which the crops are growing or to be grown is located;

(b) when the collateral is goods which at the time the security interest attaches are or are to become fixtures, then in the office where a mortgage on the real estate concerned would be filed or recorded;

(c) in all other cases, in the office of the [Secretary of State] and in addition, if the debtor has a place of business in only one county of this state, also in the office of . . . of such county, or if the debtor has no place of business in this state, but resides in the state, also in the office of . . . of the county in which he resides.

Note: *One of the three alternatives should be selected as subsection (1).*

(2) A filing which is made in good faith in an improper place or not in all of the places required by this section is nevertheless effective with regard to any collateral as to which the filing complied with the requirements of this Article and is also effective with regard to collateral covered by the financing statement against any person who has knowledge of the contents of such financing statement.

(3) A filing which is made in the proper place in this state continues effective even though the debtor's residence or place of business or the location of the collateral or its use, whichever controlled the original filing, is thereafter changed.

Alternative Subsection (3)

[(3) A filing which is made in the proper county continues effective for four months after a change to another county of the debtor's residence or place of business or the location of the collateral, whichever controlled the original filing. It becomes ineffective thereafter unless a copy of the financing statement signed by the secured party is filed in the new county within said period. The security interest may also be perfected in the new county after the expiration of the four-month period; in such case perfection dates from the time of perfection in the new county. A change in the use of the collateral does not impair the effectiveness of the original filing.]

(4) If collateral is brought into this state from another jurisdiction, the rules stated in Section 9—103 determine whether filing is necessary in this state.

Section 9—402. Formal Requisites of Financing Statement; Amendments.

(1) A financing statement is sufficient if it is signed by the debtor and the secured party, gives an address of the secured party from which information concerning the security interest may be obtained, gives a mailing address of the debtor and contains a statement indicating the types, or describing the items, of collateral. A financing statement may be filed before a security agreement is made or a security interest otherwise attaches. When the financing state-

ment covers crops growing or to be grown or goods which are or are to become fixtures, the statement must also contain a description of the real estate concerned. A copy of the security agreement is sufficient as a financing statement if it contains the above information and is signed by both parties.

(2) A financing statement which otherwise complies with subsection (1) is sufficient although it is signed only by the secured party when it is filed to perfect a security interest in

(a) collateral already subject to a security interest in another jurisdiction when it is brought into this state. Such a financing statement must state that the collateral was brought into this state under such circumstances.

(b) proceeds under Section 9—306 if the security interest in the original collateral was perfected. Such a financing statement must describe the original collateral.

(3) A form substantially as follows is sufficient to comply with subsection (1):

Name of debtor (or assignor) . . . .
. . . .
Address . . . .
. . . .
Name of secured party (or assignee)
. . . .
Address . . . .
. . . .

1. This financing statement covers the following types (or items) of property:
    (Describe) . . . .
. . . .

2. (If collateral is crops) The above described crops are growing or are to be grown on:
    (Describe Real Estate) . . . .
. . . .

3. (If collateral is goods which are or are to become fixtures) The above described goods are affixed or to be affixed to:
    (Describe Real Estate) . . . .
. . . .

4. (If proceeds or products of collateral are claimed) Proceeds—Products of the collateral are also covered.
    Signature of Debtor (or Assignor)
. . . .
                Signature of Secured Party
    (or Assignee) . . . .

(4) The term "financing statement" as used in this Article means the original financing statment

and any amendments but if any amendment adds collateral, it is effective as to the added collateral only from the filing date of the amendment.

(5) A financing statement substantially complying with the requirements of this Section is effective even though it contains minor errors which are not seriously misleading.

Section 9—403. What Constitutes Filing; Duration of Filing; Effect of Lapsed Filing; Duties of Filing Officer.

(1) Presentation for filing of a financing statement and tender of the filing fee or acceptance of the statement by the filing officer constitutes filing under this Article.

(2) A filed financing statement which states a maturity date of the obligation secured of five years or less is effective until such maturity date and thereafter for a period of sixty days. Any other filed financing statement is effective for a period of five years from the date of filing. The effectiveness of a filed financing statement lapses on the expiration of such sixty day period after a stated maturity date or on the expiration of such five year period, as the case may be, unless a continuation statement is filed prior to the lapse. Upon such lapse the security interest becomes unperfected. A filed financing statement which states that the obligation secured is payable on demand is effective for five years from the date of filing.

(3) A continuation statement may be filed by the secured party (i) within six months before and sixty days after a stated maturity date of five years or less, and (ii) otherwise within six months prior to the expiration of the five year period specified in subsection (2). Any such continuation statement must be signed by the secured party, identify the original statement by file number and state that the original statement is still effective. Upon timely filing of the continuation statement, the effectiveness of the original statement is continued for five years after the last date to which the filing was effective whereupon it lapses in the same manner as provided in subsection (2) unless another continuation statement is filed prior to such lapse. Succeeding continuation statements may be filed in the same manner to continue the effectiveness of the original statement. Unless a statute on disposition of public records provides otherwise, the filing officer may remove a lapsed statement from the files and destroy it.

(4) A filing officer shall mark each statement with a consecutive file number and with the date and hour of filing and shall hold the statement for public inspection. In addition the filing officer shall index the statements according to the name of the debtors and shall note in the index the file number and the address of the debtor given in the statement.

(5) The uniform fee for filing, indexing and furnishing filing data for an original or a continuation statement shall be $ . . . .

Section 9—404. Termination Statement.

(1) Whenever there is no outstanding secured obligation and no commitment to make advances, incur obligations or otherwise give value, the secured party must on written demand by the debtor send the debtor a statement that he no longer claims a security interest under the financing statement, which shall be identified by file number. A termination statement signed by a person other than the secured party of record must include or be accompanied by the assignment or a statement by the secured party of record that he has assigned the security interest to the signer of the termination statement. The uniform fee for filing and indexing such an assignment or statement thereof shall be $ . . . . . . If the affected secured party fails to send such a termination statement within ten days after proper demand therefor, he shall be liable to the debtor for one hundred dollars, and in addition for any loss caused to the debtor by such failure.

. (2) On presentation to the filing officer of such a termination statement he must note it in the index. The filing officer shall remove from the files, mark "terminated" and send or deliver to the secured party the financing statement and any continuation statement, statement of assignment or statement of release pertaining thereto.

(3) The uniform fee for filing and indexing a termination statement including sending or delivering the financing statement shall be $ . . . .

Section 9—405. Assignment of Security Interest; Duties of Filing Officer; Fees.

(1) A financing statement may disclose an assignment of a security interest in the collateral described in the statement by indication in the statement of the name and address of the assignee or by an assignment itself or a copy thereof on the face or back of the statement. Either the original secured party or the assignee may sign this statement as the secured party. On presentation to the filing officer of such a financing statement the filing officer shall mark the same as provided in Section 9—403(4). The uniform fee for filing, indexing and furnishing filing data for a financing statement so indicating an assignment shall be $ . . . .

(2) A secured party may assign of record all or a part of his rights under a financing statement by the filing of a separate written statement of assignment signed by the secured party of record and setting forth the name of the secured party of record and the debtor, the file number and the date of filing of the financing statement and the name and address of the assignee and containing a description of the collateral assigned. A copy of the assignment is sufficient as a separate statement if it complies with the preceding sentence. On presentation to the filing officer of such a separate statement, the filing officer shall mark such separate statement with the date and hour of the filing. He shall note the assignment on the index of the financing statement. The uniform fee for filing, indexing and furnishing filing data about such a separate statement of assignment shall be $ . . . .

(3) After the disclosure of filing of an assignment under this section, the assignee is the secured party of record.

Section 9—406. Release of Collateral; Duties of Filing Officer; Fees.

A secured party of record may by his signed statement release all or a part of any collateral described in a filed financing statement. The statement or release is sufficient if it contains a description of the collateral being released, the name and address of the debtor, the name and address of the secured party, and the file number of the financing statement. Upon presentation of such a statement to the filing officer, he shall mark the statement with the hour and date of filing and shall note the same upon the margin of the index of the filing of the financing statement. The uniform fee for filing and noting such a statement of release shall be $ . .

Section 9—407. Information from Filing Officer.

(1) If the person filing any financing statement, termination statement, statement of assignment, or statement of release, furnishes the filing officer a copy thereof, the filing officer shall upon request note upon the copy the file number and date and hour of the filing of the original and deliver or send the copy to such person.

(2) Upon request of any person, the filing officer shall issue his certificate showing whether there is on file on the date and hour stated therein, any presently effective financing statement naming a particular debtor and any statement of assignment thereof and if there is, giving the date and hour of filing of each such statement and the names and addresses of each secured party therein. The uniform fee for such a certificate shall be $ . . . . . . plus $ . . . . . . for each financing statement and for each statement of assignment reported therein. Upon request the filing officer shall furnish a copy of any filed financing statement or statement of assignment for a uniform fee of $ . . . . . . per page.

Note: *This new section is proposed as an optional provision to require filing officers to furnish certificates. Local law and practices should be consulted with regard to the advisability of adoption.*

PART 5 / DEFAULT

Section 9—501. Default; Procedure When Security Agreement Covers Both Real and Personal Property.

(1) When a debtor is in default under a security agreement, a secured party has the rights and remedies provided in this Part and, except as limited by subsection (3), those provided in the security agreement. He may reduce his claim to judgment, foreclose or otherwise enforce the security interest by any available judicial procedure. If the collateral is documents, the secured party may proceed either as to the documents or as to the goods covered thereby. A secured party in possession has the rights, remedies and duties provided in Section 9—207. The rights and remedies referred to in this subsection are cumulative.

(2) After default, the debtor has the rights and remedies provided in this Part, those provided in the security agreement and those provided in Section 9—207.

(3) To the extent that they give rights to the debtor and impose duties on the secured party, the rules stated in the subsections referred to below may not be waived or varied except as provided with respect to compulsory disposition of collateral (subsection (1) of Section 9—505) and with respect to redemption of collateral (Section 9—506) but the parties may by agreement determine the standards by which the fulfillment of these rights and duties is to be measured if such standards are not manifestly unreasonable:

    (a) subsection (2) of Section 9—502 and subsection (2) of Section 9—504 insofar as they require accounting for surplus proceeds of collateral;

(b) subsection (3) of Section 9—504 and subsection (1) of Section 9—505 which deal with disposition of collateral;

(c) subsection (2) of Section 9—505 which deals with acceptance of collateral as discharge of obligation;

(d) Section 9—506 which deals with redemption of collateral; and

(e) subsection (1) of Section 9—507 which deals with the secured party's liability for failure to comply with this Part.

(4) If the security agreement covers both real and personal property, the secured party may proceed under this Part as to the personal property or he may proceed as to both the real and the personal property in accordance with his rights and remedies in respect of the real property in which case the provisions of this Part do not apply.

(5) When a secured party has reduced his claim to judgment, the lien of any levy which may be made upon his collateral by virtue of any execution based upon the judgment shall relate back to the date of the perfection of the security interest in such collateral. A judicial sale, pursuant to such execution, is a foreclosure of the security interest by judicial procedure within the meaning of this section, and the secured party may purchase at the sale and thereafter hold the collateral free of any other requirements of this Article.

Section 9—502. Collection Rights of Secured Party.

(1) When so agreed and in any event on default, the secured party is entitled to notify an account debtor or the obligor on an instrument to make payment to him whether or not the assignor was theretofore making collections on the collateral, and also to take control of any proceeds to which he is entitled under Section 9—306.

(2) A secured party who by agreement is entitled to charge back uncollected collateral or otherwise to full or limited recourse against the debtor and who undertakes to collect from the account debtors or obligors must proceed in a commercially reasonable manner and may deduct his reasonable expenses of realization from the collections. If the security agreement secures an indebtedness, the secured party must account to the debtor for any surplus, and unless otherwise agreed, the debtor is liable for any deficiency. But, if the underlying transaction was a sale of accounts, contract rights, or chattel

paper, the debtor is entitled to any surplus or is liable for any deficiency only if the security agreement so provides.

Section 9—503. Secured Party's Right to Take Possession After Default.

Unless otherwise agreed a secured party has on default the right to take possession of the collateral. In taking possession a secured party may proceed without judicial process if this can be done without breach of the peace or may proceed by action. If the security agreement so provides, the secured party may require the debtor to assemble the collateral and make it available to the secured party at a place to be designated by the secured party which is reasonably convenient to both parties. Without removal a secured party may render equipment unusable, and may dispose of collateral on the debtor's premises under Section 9—504.

Section 9—504. Secured Party's Right to Dispose of Collateral After Default; Effect of Disposition.

(1) A secured party after default may sell, lease or otherwise dispose of any or all of the collateral in its then condition or following any commercially reasonable preparation or processing. Any sale of goods is subject to the Article on Sales (Article 2). The proceeds of disposition shall be applied in the order following to

(a) the reasonable expenses of retaking, holding, preparing for sale, selling and the like and, to the extent provided for in the agreement and not prohibited by law, the reasonable attorney's fees and legal expenses incurred by the secured party;

(b) the satisfaction of indebtedness secured by the security interest under which the disposition is made;

(c) the satisfaction of indebtedness secured by any subordinate security interest in the collateral if written notification of demand therefor is received before distribution of the proceeds is completed. If requested by the secured party, the holder of a subordinate security interest must seasonably furnish reasonable proof of his interest, and unless he does so, the secured party need not comply with his demand.

(2) If the security interest secures an indebtedness, the secured party must account to the debtor for any surplus, and, unless otherwise agreed, the debtor is liable for any deficiency. But if the underlying transaction was a sale of

accounts, contract rights, or chattel paper, the debtor is entitled to any surplus or is liable for any deficiency only if the security agreement so provides.

(3) Disposition of the collateral may be by public or private proceedings and may be made by way of one or more contracts. Sale or other disposition may be as a unit or in parcels and at any time and place and on any terms, but every aspect of the disposition including the method, manner, time, place and terms must be commercially reasonable. Unless collateral is perishable or threatens to decline speedily in value or is of a type customarily sold on a recognized market, reasonable notification of the time and place of any public sale or reasonable notification of the time after which any private sale or other intended disposition is to be made shall be sent by the secured party to the debtor, and except in the case of consumer goods to any other person who has a security interest in the collateral and who has duly filed a financing statement indexed in the name of the debtor in this state or who is known by the secured party to have a security interest in the collateral. The secured party may buy at any public sale and if the collateral is of a type customarily sold in a recognized market or is of a type which is the subject of widely distributed standard price quotations, he may buy at private sale.

(4) When collateral is disposed of by a secured party after default, the disposition transfers to a purchaser for value all of the debtor's rights therein, discharges the security interest under which it is made and any security interest or lien subordinate thereto. The purchaser takes free of all such rights and interests even though the secured party fails to comply with the requirements of this Part or of any judicial proceedings.

    (a) in the case of a public sale, if the purchaser has no knowledge of any defects in the sale and if he does not buy in collusion with the secured party, other bidders or the person conducting the sale; or

    (b) in any other case, if the purchaser acts in good faith.

(5) A person who is liable to a secured party under a guaranty, indorsement, repurchase agreement or the like and who receives a transfer of collateral from the secured party or is subrogated to his rights has thereafter the rights and duties of the secured party. Such a transfer of collateral is not a sale or disposition of the collateral under this Article.

Section 9—505. Compulsory Disposition of Collateral; Acceptance of the Collateral as Discharge of Obligation.

(1) If the debtor has paid sixty percent of the cash price in the case of a purchase money security interest in consumer goods or sixty percent of the loan in the case of another security interest in consumer goods, and has not signed after default a statement renouncing or modifying his rights under this Part, a secured party who has taken possession of collateral must dispose of it under Section 9—504 and if he fails to do so within ninety days after he takes possession, the debtor at his option may recover in conversion or under Section 9—507 (1) on secured party's liability.

(2) In any other case involving consumer goods or any other collateral a secured party in possession may, after default, propose to retain the collateral in satisfaction of the obligation. Written notice of such proposal shall be sent to the debtor and except in the case of consumer goods to any other secured party who has a security interest in the collateral and who has duly filed a financing statement indexed in the name of the debtor in this state or is known by the secured party in possession to have a security interest in it. If the debtor or other person entitled to receive notification objects in writing within thirty days from the receipt of the notification or if any other secured party objects in writing within thirty days after the secured party obtains possession, the secured party must dispose of the collateral under Section 9—504. In the absence of such written objection the secured party may retain the collateral in satisfaction of the debtor's obligation.

Section 9—506. Debtor's Right to Redeem Collateral.

At any time before the secured party has disposed of collateral or entered into a contract for its disposition under Section 9—504 or before the obligation has been discharged under Section 9—505(2) the debtor or any other secured party may unless otherwise agreed in writing after default redeem the collateral by tendering fulfillment of all obligations secured by the collateral as well as the expenses reasonably incurred by the secured party in retaking, holding and preparing the collateral for disposition, in arranging for the sale, and to the extent provided in the agreement and not prohibited by law, his reasonable attorney's fees and legal expenses.

Section 9—507. Secured Party's Liability for Failure to Comply with This Part.

(1) If it is established that the secured party is not proceeding in accordance with the provisions of this Part, disposition may be ordered or restrained on appropriate terms and conditions. If the disposition has occurred, the debtor or any person entitled to notification or whose security interest has been made known to the secured party prior to the disposition has a right to recover from the secured party any loss caused by a failure to comply with the provisions of this Part. If the collateral is consumer goods, the debtor has a right to recover in any event an amount not less than the credit service charge plus ten percent of the principal amount of the debt or the time price differential plus ten percent of the cash price.

(2) The fact that a better price could have been obtained by a sale at a different time or in a different method from that selected by the secured party is not of itself sufficient to establish that the sale was not made in a commercially reasonable manner. If the secured party either sells the collateral in the usual manner in any recognized market therefor or if he sells at the price current in such market at the time of his sale or if he has otherwise sold in conformity with reasonable commercial practices among dealers in the type of property sold, he has sold in a commercially reasonable manner. The principles stated in the two preceding sentences with respect to sales also apply as may be appropriate to other types of disposition. A disposition which has been approved in any judicial proceeding or by any bona fide creditors' committee or representative of creditors shall conclusively be deemed to be commercially reasonable, but this sentence does not indicate that any such approval must be obtained in any case nor does it indicate that any disposition not so approved is not commercially reasonable.

ARTICLE 10 / EFFECTIVE DATE AND REPEALER

Section 10—101. Effective Date.

This Act shall become effective at midnight on December 31st following its enactment. It applies to transactions entered into and events occurring after that date.

Section 10—102. Specific Repealer; Provision for Transition.

(1) The following acts and all other acts and parts of acts inconsistent herewith are hereby repealed:

(Here should follow the acts to be specifically repealed including the following:

    Uniform Negotiable Instruments Act
    Uniform Warehouse Receipts Act
    Uniform Sales Act
    Uniform Bills of Lading Act
    Uniform Stock Transfer Act
    Uniform Conditional Sales Act
    Uniform Trust Receipts Act
Also any acts regulating:
    Bank collections
    Bulk sales
    Chattel mortgages
    Conditional sales
    Factor's lien acts
    Farm storage of grain and similar acts
    Assignment of accounts receivable)

(2) Transactions validly entered into before the effective date specified in Section 10—101 and the rights, duties and interests flowing from them remain valid thereafter and may be terminated, completed, consummated or enforced as required or permitted by any statute or other law amended or repealed by this Act as though such repeal or amendment had not occurred.

Note
Subsection (1) should be separately prepared for each state. The foregoing is a list of statutes to be checked.

Section 10—103. General Repealer.

Except as provided in the following section, all acts and parts of acts inconsistent with this Act are hereby repealed.

Section 10—104. Laws Not Repealed.

[(1)] The Article on documents of Title (Article 7) does not repeal or modify any laws prescribing the form of contents of documents of title or the services or facilities to be afforded by bailees, or otherwise regulating bailees' businesses in respects not specifically dealt with herein; but the fact that such laws are violated does not affect the status of a document of title which otherwise complies with the definition of a document of title (Section 1—201).

   [(2) This Act does not repeal ....
....*, cited as the Uniform Act for the Simplification of Fiduciary Security Transfers, and if in any respect there is any inconsistency between that Act and the Article of this Act on investment securities (Article 8) the provisions of the former Act shall control.]

Note: *At * in subsection (2) insert the statutory references to the Uniform Act for the Simplification of Fiduciary Security Transfers if such Act has previously been enacted. If it has not been enacted, omit subsection (2).*

GLOSSARY

A

abandon: give up or leave employment; relinquish possession of personal property with intent to disclaim title.

abate: put a stop to a nuisance; reduce or cancel a legacy because the estate of the testator is insufficient to make payment in full.

ab initio: from the beginning.

abrogate: recall or repeal; make void or inoperative.

absolute liability: liability for an act that causes harm even though the actor was not at fault.

absolute privilege: protection from liability for slander or libel given under certain circumstances to statements regardless of the fact that they are false or maliciously made.

abstract of title: history of the transfers of title to a given piece of land, briefly stating the parties to and the effect of all deeds, wills, and judicial proceedings relating to the land.

acceleration clause: provision in a contract or any legal instrument that upon a certain event the time for the performance of specified obligations shall be advanced; for example, a provision making the balance due upon debtor's default.

acceptance: unqualified assent to the act or proposal of another; as the acceptance of a draft (bill of exchange), of an offer to make a contract, of goods delivered by the seller, or of a gift or a deed.

accession: acquisition of title to property by a person by virtue of the fact that it has been attached to property that he already owned or was the offspring of an animal he owned.

accessory after the fact: one who after the commission of a felony knowingly assists the felon.

accessory before the fact: one who is absent at the commission of the crime but who aided and abetted its commission.

accident: an event that occurs even though a reasonable person would not have foreseen its occurrence, because of which the law holds no one legally responsible for the harm caused.

accommodation party: a person who signs a commercial paper to lend credit to another party to the paper.

accord and satisfaction: an agreement to substitute a different performance for that called for in the contract and the performance of that substitute agreement.

accretion: the acquisition of title to additional land when the owner's land is built up by gradual deposits made by the natural action of water.

acknowledgment: an admission or confirmation, generally of an instrument and usually made before a person authorized to administer oaths, as a notary public; the purpose being to declare that the instrument was executed by the person making the instrument, or that it was his free act, or that he desires that it be recorded.

action: a proceeding to enforce any right.

action in personam: an action brought to impose liability upon a person, such as a money judgment.

action in rem: an action brought to declare the status of a thing, such as an action to declare the title to property to be forfeited because of its illegal use.

action of assumpsit: a common-law action brought to recover damages for breach of a contract.

action of ejectment: a common-law action brought to recover the possession of land.

action of mandamus: a common-law action brought to compel the performance of a ministerial or clerical act by an officer.

action of quo warranto: a common-law action brought to challenge the authority of an officer to act or to hold office.

action of replevin: a common-law action brought to recover the possession of personal property.

action of trespass: a common-law action brought to recover damages for a tort.

act of bankruptcy: any of the acts specified by the national bankruptcy law which, when committed by the debtor within the four months preceding the filing of the petition in bankruptcy, is proper ground for declaring the debtor a bankrupt.

act of God: a natural phenomenon that is not reasonably foreseeable.

administrative agency: a governmental commission or board given authority to regulate particular matters.

administrator—administratrix: the person (man—woman) appointed to wind up and settle the estate of a person who has died without a will.

adverse possession: the hostile possession of real estate, which when actual, visible, notorious, exclusive, and continued for the required time, will vest the title to the land in the person in such adverse possession.

advisory opinion: an opinion that may be rendered in a few states when there is no actual controversy before the court and the matter is submitted by private persons, or in some instances by the governor of the state, to obtain the court's opinion.

affidavit: a statement of facts set forth in written form and supported by the oath or affirmation of the person making the statement, setting forth that such facts are true to his knowledge or to his information and belief. The affidavit is executed before a notary public or other person authorized to administer oaths.

affinity: the relationship that exists by virtue of marriage.

affirmative covenant: an express undertaking or promise in a contract or deed to do an act.

agency: the relationship that exists between a person identified as a principal and another by virtue of which the latter may make contracts with third persons on behalf of the principal. (Parties—principal, agent, third person)

agency coupled with an interest in the authority: an agency in which the agent has given a consideration or has paid for the right to exercise the authority granted to him.

agency coupled with an interest in the subject matter: an agency in which for a consideration the agent is given an interest in the property with which he is dealing.

agency shop: a union contract provision requiring that non-union employees pay to the union the equivalent of union dues in order to retain their employment.

agent: one who is authorized by the principal or by operation of law to make contracts with third persons on behalf of the principal.

allonge: a paper securely fastened to a commercial paper in order to provide additional space for indorsements.

alluvion: the additions made to land by accretion.

alteration: any material change of the terms of a writing fraudulently made by a party thereto.

ambulatory: not effective and therefore may be changed, as in the case of a will that is not final until the testator has died.

amicable action: an action that all parties agree should be brought and which is begun by the filing of such an agreement, rather than by serving the adverse parties with process. Although the parties agree to litigate, the dispute is real, and the decision is not an advisory opinion.

amicus curiae: literally, a friend of the court; one who is appointed by the court to take part in litigation and to assist the court by furnishing an opinion in the matter.

annexation: attachment of personal property to realty in such a way as to make it become real property and part of the realty.

annuity: a contract by which the insured pays a lump sum to the insurer and later receives fixed annual payments.

anomalous indorser: a person who signs a commercial paper but is not otherwise a party to the instrument.

anticipatory breach: the repudiation by a promisor of the contract prior to the time he is required to perform when such repudiation is accepted by the promisee as a breach of the contract.

anti-injunction acts: statutes prohibiting the use of injunctions in labor disputes except under exceptional circumstances; notably the federal Norris-La Guardia Act of 1932.

Anti-Petrillo Act: a federal statute that makes it a crime to compel a radio broadcasting station to hire musicians not needed, to pay for services not performed, or to refrain from broadcasting music of school children or from foreign countries.

antitrust acts: statutes prohibiting combinations and contracts in restraint of trade, notably the federal Sherman Antitrust Act of 1890, now generally inapplicable to labor union activity.

appeal: taking the case to a reviewing court to determine whether the judgment of the lower court or administrative agency was correct. (Parties—appellant, appellee)

appellate jurisdiction: the power of a court to hear and decide a given class of cases on appeal from another court or administrative agency.

arbitration: the settlement of disputed questions, whether of law or fact, by one or more arbitrators by whose decision the parties agree to be bound. Increasingly used as a procedure for labor dispute settlement.

assignment: transfer of a right. Generally used in connection with personal property rights, as rights under a contract commercial paper, an insurance policy, a mortgage, or a lease. (Parties—assignor, assignee)

assumption of risk: the common-law rule that an employee could not sue the employer for injuries caused by the ordinary risks of employment on the theory that he had assumed such risks by undertaking the work. The rule has been abolished in those areas governed by workmen's compensation laws and most employers' liability statutes.

attachment: the seizure of property of, or a debt owed to, the debtor by the service of process upon a third person who is in possession of the property or who owes a debt to the debtor.

attractive nuisance doctrine: a rule imposing liability on a landowner for injuries sustained by small children playing on his land when the landowner permits a condition to exist or maintains equipment that he should realize would attract small children who could not realize the danger. The rule does not apply if an unreasonable burden would be imposed on the landowner in taking steps to protect the children.

authenticate: make or establish as genuine, official, or final, as by signing, countersigning, sealing, or any other act indicating approval.

B

bad check laws: laws making it a criminal offense to issue a bad check with intent to defraud.

baggage: such articles of necessity or personal convenience as are usually carried for personal use by passengers of common carriers.

bail: variously used in connection with the release of a person or property from the custody of the law, referring (a) to the act of releasing or bailing, (b) to the persons who assume liability in the event that the released person does not appear or it is held that the property should not be released, and (c) to

the bond or sum of money that is furnished the court or other official as indemnity for nonperformance of the obligation.

bailee's lien: a specific, possessory lien of the bailee on the goods for work done to them. Commonly extended by statute to any bailee's claim for compensation and eliminating the necessity of retention of possession.

bailment: the relation that exists when personal property is delivered into the possession of another under an agreement, express or implied, that the identical property will be returned or will be delivered in accordance with the agreement. (Parties—bailor, bailee)

bankruptcy: a procedure by which one unable to pay his debts may be declared a bankrupt, after which all his assets in excess of his exemption claim are surrendered to the court for administration and distribution to his creditors, and the debtor is given a discharge that releases him from the unpaid balance due on most debts.

bearer: the person in physical possession of commercial paper payable to bearer, a document of title directing delivery to bearer, or an investment security in bearer form.

beneficiary: the person to whom the proceeds of a life insurance policy are payable, a person for whose benefit property is held in trust, or a person given property by a will.

bequest: a gift of personal property by will.

bill of exchange (draft): an unconditional order in writing by one person upon another, signed by the person giving it, and ordering the person to whom it is directed to pay on demand or at a definite time a sum certain in money to order or to bearer.

bill of lading: a document issued by a carrier reciting the receipt of goods and the terms of the contract of transportation. Regulated by the federal Bills of Lading Act or the Uniform Commercial Code.

bill of sale: a writing signed by the seller reciting that he has sold to the buyer the personal property therein described.

binder: a memorandum delivered to the insured stating the essential terms of a policy to be executed in the future, when it is agreed that the contract of insurance is to be effective before the written policy is executed.

blank indorsement: an indorsement that does not name the person to whom the paper, document of title, or investment security is negotiated.

blue-sky laws: state statutes designed to protect the public from the sale of worthless stocks and bonds.

boardinghouse keeper: one regularly engaged in the business of offering living accommodations to permanent lodgers or boarders.

bona fide: in good faith; without any fraud or deceit.

bond: an obligation or promise in writing and sealed, generally of corporations, personal representatives, trustees; fidelity bonds.

boycott: a combination of two or more persons to cause harm to another by refraining from patronizing or dealing with such other person in any way or inducing others to so refrain; commonly an incident of labor disputes.

bulk sales acts: statutes to protect creditors of a bulk seller by preventing him from obtaining cash for his goods and then leaving the state. Notice must be given creditors, and the bulk sale buyer is liable to the seller's creditors if the statute is not satisfied. Expanded to "bulk transfers" under the UCC.

business trust: a form of business organization in which the owners of the property to be devoted to the business transfer the title of the property to trustees with full power to operate the business.

C

cancellation: a crossing out of a part of an instrument or a destruction of all legal effect of the instrument, whether by act of party, upon breach by the other party, or pursuant to agreement or decree of court.

capital: net assets of a corporation.

capital stock: the declared money value of the outstanding stock of the corporation.

cash surrender value: the sum that will be paid the insured if he surrenders his policy to the insurer.

cause of action: the right to damages or other judicial relief when a legally protected right of the plaintiff is violated by an unlawful act of the defendant.

caveat emptor: let the buyer beware. This maxim has been restricted by warranty and strict tort liability concepts.

certificate of protest: a written statement by a notary public setting forth the fact that the holder had presented the commercial paper to the primary party and that the latter had failed to make payment.

cestui que trust: the beneficiary or person for whose benefit the property is held in trust.

charter: the grant of authority from a government to exist as a corporation. Generally re-

placed today by a certificate of incorporation approving the articles of incorporation.

chattel mortgage: a security device by which the owner of personal property transfers the title to a creditor as security for the debt owed by the owner to the creditor. Replaced under the Uniform Commercial Code by a secured transaction. (Parties—chattel mortgagor, chattel mortgagee)

chattels personal: tangible personal property.

chattels real: leases of land and buildings.

check: an order by a depositor on his bank to pay a sum of money to a payee; a bill of exchange drawn on a bank and payable on demand.

chose in action: intangible personal property in the nature of claims against another, such as a claim for accounts receivable or wages.

chose in possession: tangible personal property.

circumstantial evidence: relates to circumstances surrounding the facts in dispute from which the trier of fact may deduce what had happened.

civil action: in many states a simplified form of action combining all or many of the former common-law actions.

civil court: a court with jurisdiction to hear and determine controversies relating to private rights and duties.

closed shop: a place of employment in which only union members may be employed. Now generally prohibited.

codicil: a writing by one who has made a will which is executed with all the formality of a will and is treated as an addition to or modification of the will.

coinsurance: a clause requiring the insured to maintain insurance on his property up to a stated amount and providing that to the extent that he fails to do so the insured is to be deemed a coinsurer with the insurer so that the latter is liable only for its proportionate share of the amount of insurance required to be carried.

collateral note: a note accompanied by collateral security.

collective bargaining: the process by which the terms of employment are agreed upon through negotiations between the employer or employers within a given industry or industrial area and the union or the bargaining representative of the employees.

collective bargaining unit: the employment area within which employees are by statute authorized to select a bargaining representative, who is then to represent all the employees in bargaining collectively with the employer.

collusion: an agreement between two or more persons to defraud the government or the courts, as by obtaining a divorce by collusion when no grounds for a divorce exist, or to defraud third persons of their rights.

color of title: circumstances that make a person appear to be the owner when he in fact is not the owner, as the existence of a deed appearing to convey the property to a given person gives him color of title although the deed is worthless because it is in fact a forgery.

commission merchant: a bailee to whom goods are consigned for sale.

common carrier: a carrier that holds out its facilities to serve the general public for compensation without discrimination.

common law: the body of unwritten principles originally based on the usages and customs of the community which were recognized and enforced by the courts.

common stock: stock that has no right or priority over any other stock of the corporation as to dividends or distribution of assets, upon dissolution.

common trust fund: a plan by which the assets of small trust estates are pooled into a common fund, each trust being given certificates representing its proportionate ownership of the fund, and the pooled fund is then invested in investments of large size.

community property: the contenancy held by husband and wife in property acquired during their marriage under the law of some of the states, principally in the southwestern United States.

complaint: the initial pleading filed by the plaintiff in many actions which in many states may be served as original process to acquire jurisdiction over the defendant.

composition of creditors: an agreement among creditors that each shall accept a part payment as full payment in consideration of the other creditors doing the same.

concealment: the failure to volunteer information not requested.

conditional estate: an estate that will come into being upon the satisfaction of a condition precedent or that will be terminated upon the satisfaction of a condition subsequent, provided in the latter case that the grantor or his heirs re-enter and retake possession of the land.

conditional sale: a credit transaction by which the buyer purchases on credit and promises to pay the purchase price in installments, while the seller retains the title to the goods, together with the right of repossession upon default, until the condition of payment in full has been satisfied. The conditional sale is replaced under the Uniform Commercial Code by a secured transaction.

confidential relationship: a relationship in which, because of the legal status of the parties or their respective physical or mental conditions or knowledge, one party places full confidence and trust in the other and relies upon him entirely for guidance.

conflict of laws: the body of law that determines the law of which state is to apply when two or more states are involved in the facts of a given case.

confusion of goods: the mixing of goods of different owners that under certain circumstances results in one of the owners becoming the owner of all the goods.

consanguinity: relationship by blood.

consideration: the promise or performance that the promisor demands as the price of his promise.

consignment: a bailment made for the purpose of sale by the bailee. (Parties—consignor, consignee)

consolidation of corporations: a combining of two or more corporations in which the corporate existence of each one ceases and a new corporation is created.

constructive: an adjective employed to indicate that the noun which is modified by it does not exist but the law disposes of the matter as though it did; as a constructive bailment or a constructive trust.

contingent beneficiary: the person to whom the proceeds of a life insurance policy are payable in the event that the primary beneficiary dies before the insured.

contract: a binding agreement based upon the genuine assent of the parties, made for a lawful object, between competent parties, in the form required by law, and generally supported by consideration.

contract carrier: a carrier who transports on the basis of individual contracts that it makes with each shipper.

contract to sell: a contract to make a transfer of title in the future as contrasted with a present transfer.

contribution: the right of a co-obligor who has paid more than his proportionate share to demand that the other obligor pay him the amount of the excess payment he has made.

contributory negligence: negligence of the plaintiff that contributes to his injury and at common law bars him from recovery from the defendant although the defendant may have been more negligent than the plaintiff.

conveyance: a transfer of an interest in land, ordinarily by the execution and delivery of a deed.

cooling-off period: a procedure designed to avoid strikes by requiring a specified period of delay before the strike may begin during which negotiations for a settlement must continue.

cooperative: a group of two or more persons or enterprises that act through a common agent with respect to a common objective, as buying or selling.

copyright: a grant to an author of an exclusive right to publish and sell his work for a period of 28 years, renewable for a second period of 28 years.

corporation: an artificial legal person or being created by government grant, which for many purposes is treated as a natural person.

cost plus: a method of determining the purchase price or contract price by providing for the payment of an amount equal to the costs of the seller or contractor to which is added a stated percentage as his profit.

costs: the expenses of suing or being sued, recoverable in some actions by the successful party, and in others, subject to allocation by the court. Ordinarily they do not include attorney's fees or compensation for loss of time.

counterclaim: a claim that the defendant in an action may make against the plaintiff.

covenants of title: covenants of the grantor in a deed that guarantee such matters as his right to make the conveyance, his ownership of the property, the freedom of the property from encumbrances, or that the grantee will not be disturbed in the quiet enjoyment of the land.

crime: a violation of the law that is punished as an offense against the state or government.

cross complaint: a claim that the defendant may make against the plaintiff.

cross-examination: the examination made of a witness by the attorney for the adverse party.

cumulative voting: a system of voting for directors in which each shareholder has as many votes as the number of voting shares he owns multiplied by the number of directors to be elected, which votes he can distribute for the various candidates as he desires.

cy-pres doctrine: the rule under which a charitable trust will be carried out as nearly as possible in the way the settlor desired, when for any reason it cannot be carried out exactly in the way or for the purposes he had expressed.

D

damages: a sum of money recovered to redress or make amends for the legal wrong or injury done.

damnum absque injuria: loss or damage without the violation of a legal right, or the mere fact that a person sustains a loss does not mean that his legal rights have been violated or that he is entitled to sue someone.

declaratory judgment: a procedure for obtaining the decision of a court on a question before any action has been taken or loss sustained. It differs from an advisory opinion in that there must be an actual, imminent controversy.

dedication: acquisition by the public or a government of title to land when it is given over by its owner to use by the public and such gift is accepted.

deed: an instrument by which the grantor (owner of land) conveys or transfers the title to a grantee.

de facto: existing in fact as distinguished from as of right, as in the case of an officer or a corporation purporting to act as such without being elected to the office or having been properly incorporated.

deficiency judgment: a personal judgment for the amount still remaining due the mortgagee after foreclosure, which is entered against any person liable on the mortgage debt. Statutes generally require the mortgagee to credit the fair value of the property against the balance due when the mortgagee has purchased the property. Also, a similar judgment entered by a creditor against a debtor in a secured transaction under Article 9 of the UCC.

del credere agent: an agent who sells goods for the principal and who guarantees to the principal that the buyer will pay for the goods.

delegation: the transfer to another of the right and power to do an act.

de minimis non curat lex: a maxim that the law is not concerned with trifles. Not always applied, as in the case of the encroachment of a building over the property line, in which case the law will protect the landowner regardless of the extent of the encroachment.

demonstrative evidence: evidence that consists of visible, physical objects, as a sample taken from the wheat in controversy or a photograph of the subject matter involved.

demonstrative legacy: a legacy to be paid or distributed from a specified fund or property.

demurrage: a charge made by the carrier for the unreasonable detention of cars by the cosignor or consignee.

demurrer: a pleading that may be filed to attack the sufficiency of the adverse party's pleading as not stating a cause of action or a defense.

dependent relative revocation: the doctrine recognized in some states that if a testator revokes or cancels a will in order to replace it with a later will, the earlier will is to be deemed revived if for any reason the later will does not take effect or no later will is executed.

deposition: the testimony of a witness taken out of court before a person authorized to administer oaths.

devise: a gift of real estate made by will.

directed verdict: a direction by the trial judge to the jury to return a verdict in favor of a specified party to the action.

directors: the persons vested with control of the corporation, subject to the elective power of the shareholders.

discharge in bankruptcy: an order of the bankruptcy court discharging the bankrupt debtor from the unpaid balance of most of the claims against him.

discharge of contract: termination of a contract by performance, agreement, impossibility, acceptance of breach, or operation of law.

discovery: procedures for ascertaining facts prior to the time of trial in order to eliminate the element of surprise in litigation.

dishonor by nonacceptance: the refusal of the drawee to accept a draft (bill of exchange).

dishonor by nonpayment: the refusal to pay a commercial paper when properly presented for payment.

dismiss: a procedure to terminate an action by moving to dismiss on the ground that the plaintiff has not pleaded a cause of action entitling him to relief.

disparagement of goods: the making of malicious, false statements as to the quality of the goods of another.

distress for rent: the common-law right of the lessor to enter the premises when he was not paid the rent and to seize all personal property found on the premises. Statutes have modified or abolished this right in many states.

distributive share: the proportionate part of the estate of the decedent that will be distributed to an heir or legatee, and also as devisee in those jurisdictions in which real estate is administered as part of the decedent's estate.

domestic bill of exchange: a draft drawn in one state and payable in the same or another state.

domestic corporation: a corporation that has been incorporated by the state as opposed to incorporation by another state.

domicile: the home of a person or the state of incorporation, to be distinguished from a place where a person lives but which he does not regard as his home, or a state in which a corporation does business but in which it was not incorporated.

double indemnity: a provision for payment of double the amount specified by the insurance contract if death is caused by an accident and occurs under specified circumstances.

double jeopardy: the principle that a person who has once been placed in jeopardy by being brought to trial at which the proceedings progressed at least as far as having the jury sworn cannot thereafter be tried a second time for the same offense.

draft: see bill of exchange.

draft-varying acceptance: one in which the acceptor's agreement to pay is not exactly in conformity with the order of the instrument.

due care: the degree of care that a reasonable man would exercise to prevent the realization of harm, which under all the circumstances was reasonably forseeable in the event that such care were not taken.

due process of law: the guarantee by the 5th and 14th amendments of the federal Constitution and of many state constitutions that no person shall be deprived of life, liberty, or property without due process of law. As presently interpreted, this prohibits any law, either state or federal, that sets up an unfair procedure or the substance of which is arbitrary or capricious.

duress: conduct that deprives the victim of his own free will and which generally gives the victim the right to set aside any transaction entered into under such circumstances.

E

easement: a permanent right that one has in the land of another, as the right to cross another's land or easement of way.

eleemosynary corporation: a corporation organized for a charitable or benevolent purpose.

embezzlement: a statutory offense consisting of the unlawful conversion of property entrusted to the wrongdoer with respect to which he owes the owner a fiduciary duty.

eminent domain: the power of a government and certain kinds of corporations to take private property against the objection of the owner, provided the taking is for a public purpose and just compensation is made therefor.

encumbrance: a right held by a third person in or a lien or charge against property, as a mortgage or judgment lien on land.

equity: the body of principles that originally developed because of the inadequacy of the rules then applied by the common-law courts of England.

erosion: the loss of land through a gradual washing away by tides or currents, with the owner losing title to the lost land.

escheat: the transfer to the state of the title to a decedent's property when he dies intestate not survived by anyone capable of taking the property as his heir.

escrow: a conditional delivery of property or of a deed to a custodian or escrow holder, who in turn makes final delivery to the grantee or transferee when a specified condition has been satisfied.

estate: the extent and nature of one's interest in land; the assets constituting a decedent's property at the time of his death, or the assets of a bankrupt.

estate in fee simple: the largest estate possible in which the owner has the absolute and entire property in the land.

estoppel: the principle by which a person is barred from pursuing a certain course of action or of disputing the truth of certain matters when his conduct has been such that it would be unjust to permit him to do so.

evidence: that which is presented to the trier of fact as the basis on which the trier is to determine what happened.

exception: an objection, as an exception to the admission of evidence on the ground that it was hearsay; a clause excluding particular property from the operation of a deed.

ex contractu: a claim or matter that is founded upon or arises out of a contract.

ex delicto: a claim or matter that is founded upon or arises out of a tort.

execution: the carrying out of a judgment of a court, generally directing that property owned by the defendant be sold and the proceeds first used to pay the execution or judgment creditor.

exemplary damages: damages in excess of the amount needed to compensate for the plaintiff's injury, which are awarded in order to punish the defendant for his malicious or wanton conduct so as to make an example of him; also punitive.

exoneration: an agreement or provision in an agreement that one party shall not be held liable for loss; the right of the surety to demand that those primarily liable pay the claim for which the surety is secondarily liable.

expert witness: one who has acquired special knowledge in a particular field through practical experience, or study, or both, which gives him a superior knowledge so that his opinion is admissible as an aid to the trier of fact.

ex post facto law: a law making criminal an act that was lawful when done or that increases the penalty for an act which was subject to a lesser penalty when done. Such laws are generally prohibited by constitutional provisions.

extraordinary bailment: a bailment in which the bailee is subject to unusual duties and liabilities, as a hotelkeeper or common carrier.

F

facility-of-payment clause: a provision commonly found in an industrial policy permitting the insurer to make payment to any member of a designated class or to any person the insurer believes equitably entitled thereto.

factor: a bailee to whom goods are consigned for sale.

factors' acts: statutes protecting persons who buy in good faith for value from a factor although the goods had not been delivered to the factor with the consent or authorization of their owner.

fair employment practice acts: statutes designed to eliminate discrimination in employment in terms of race, religion, natural origin, or sex.

fair labor standards acts: statutes, particularly the federal statute, designed to prevent excessive hours of employment and low pay, the employment of young children, and other unsound practices.

fair trade acts: statutes that authorize resale price maintenance agreements as to trademark and brand name articles, and generally provide that all persons in the industry are bound by such an agreement whether they have signed it or not although such provision is often invalid.

featherbedding: the exaction of money for services not performed, which is made an unfair labor practice generally and a criminal offense in connection with radio broadcasting.

Federal Securities Act: a statute designed to protect the public from fraudulent securities.

Federal Securities Exchange Act: a statute prohibiting improper practices at and regulating security exchanges.

Federal Trade Commission Act: a statute prohibiting unfair methods of competition in interstate commerce.

fellow-servant rule: a common-law defense of the employer that barred an employee from suing an employer for injuries caused by a fellow employee.

felony: a criminal offense that is punishable by confinement in prison or by death, or that is expressly stated by statute to be a felony.

financial responsibility laws: statutes that require a driver involved in an automobile accident to prove his financial responsibility in order to retain his license, which responsibility may be shown by procuring public liability insurance in a specified minimum amount.

financing factor: one who lends money to manufacturers on the security of goods to be manufactured thereafter.

firm offer: an offer stated to be held open for a specified time, which must be so held in some states even in the absence of an option contract, or under the Code, with respect to merchants.

fixture: personal property that has become so attached to or adapted to real estate that it has lost its character as personal property and is part of the real estate.

Food, Drug, and Cosmetic Act: a federal statute prohibiting the interstate shipment of misbranded or adulterated foods, drugs, cosmetics, and therapeutic devices.

forbearance: refraining from doing an act.

foreclosure: procedure for enforcing a mortgage resulting in the public sale of the mortgaged property and less commonly in merely barring the right of the mortgagor to redeem the property from the mortgage.

foreign (international) bill of exchange: a bill of exchange made in one nation and payable in another.

foreign corporation: a corporation incorporated under the laws of another state.

forgery: the fraudulent making or altering of an instrument that apparently creates or alters a legal liability of another.

franchise: (a) a privilege or authorization, generally exclusive, to engage in a particular activity within a particular geographic area, as a government franchise to operate a taxi company within a specified city, or a private franchise as the grant by a manufacturer of a right to sell his products within a particular territory or for a particular number of years; (b) the right to vote.

fraud: the making of a false statement of a past or existing fact with knowledge of its falsity or with reckless indifference as to its truth with the intent to cause another to rely thereon, and he does rely thereon to his injury.

freight forwarder: one who contracts to have goods transported and, in turn, contracts with carriers for such transportation.

fructus industriales: crops that are annually planted and raised.

fructus naturales: fruits from trees, bushes, and grasses growing from perennial roots.

fungible goods: goods of a homogenous nature of which any unit is the equivalent of any other unit or is treated as such by mercantile usage.

future advance mortgage: a mortgage given to secure additional loans to be made in the future as well as an original loan.

G

garnishment: the name given in some states to attachment proceedings.

general creditor: a creditor who has a claim against the debtor but does not have any lien on any of the debtor's property, whether as security for his debt or by way of a judgment or execution upon a judgment.

general damages: damages that in the ordinary course of events follow naturally and probably from the injury caused by the defendant.

general legacy: a legacy to be paid out of the assets generally of the testator without specifying any particular fund or source from which the payment is to be made.

general partnership: a partnership in which the partners conduct as co-owners a business for profit, and each partner has a right to take part in the management of the business and has unlimited liability.

gift causa mortis: a gift made by the donor because he believed he faced immediate and impending death, which gift is revoked or is revocable under certain circumstances.

grace period: a period generally of 30 or 31 days after the due date of a premium of life insurance in which the premium may be paid.

grand jury: a jury not exceeding 23 in number that considers evidence of the commission of crime and prepares indictments to bring offenders to trial before a petty jury.

grant: convey real property; an instrument by which such property has been conveyed, particularly in the case of a government.

gratuitous bailment: a bailment in which the bailee does not receive any compensation or advantage.

grievance settlement: the adjustment of disputes relating to the administration or application of existing contracts as compared with disputes over new terms of employment.

guarantor: one who undertakes the obligation of guaranty.

guaranty: an undertaking to pay the debt of another if the creditor first sues the debtor and is unable to recover the debt from the debtor or principal. (In some instances the liability is primary, in which case it is the same as suretyship.)

H

hearsay evidence: statements made out of court which are offered in court as proof of the information contained in the statements, which, subject to many exceptions, are not admissible in evidence.

hedging: the making of simultaneous contracts to purchase and to sell a particular commodity at a future date with the intention that the loss on one transaction will be offset by the gain on the other.

heirs: those persons specified by statute to receive the estate of a decedent not disposed of by will.

holder: the person in possession of a commercial paper payable to him as payee or indorsee, or the person in possession of a commercial paper payable to bearer.

holder in due course: the holder of a commercial paper under such circumstances that he is treated as favored and is given an immunity from certain defenses.

holder through a holder in due course: a person who is not himself a holder in due course but is a holder of the paper after it was held by some prior party who was a holder in due course, and who is given the same rights as a holder in due course.

holographic will: a will written by the testator in his own hand.

hotelkeeper: one regularly engaged in the business of offering living accommodations to all transient persons.

hung jury: a petty jury that has been unable to agree upon a verdict.

I

ignorantia legis non excusat: ignorance of the law is not an excuse.

implied contract: a contract expressed by conduct or implied or deduced from the facts. Also used to refer to a quasi-contract.

imputed: vicariously attributed to or charged to another, as the knowledge of an agent obtained while acting in the scope of his authority is imputed to his principal.

incidental authority: authority of an agent that is reasonably necessary to execute his express authority.

incontestable clause: a provision that after the lapse of a specified time the insurer cannot dispute the policy on the ground of misrepresentation or fraud of the insured or similar wrongful conduct.

in custodia legis: in the custody of the law.

indemnity: the right of a person secondarily liable to require that a person primarily liable pay him for his loss when the secondary party discharges the obligation which the primary party should have discharged; the right of an agent to be paid the amount of any loss or damage sustained by him without his fault because of his obedience to the principal's instructions; an undertaking by one person for a consideration to pay another person a sum of money to indemnify him when he incurs a specified loss.

independent contractor: a contractor who undertakes to perform a specified task according to the terms of a contract but over whom the other contracting party has no control except as provided for by the contract.

indictment: a formal accusation of crime made by a grand jury which accusation is then tried by a petty or trial jury.

inheritance: the interest which passes from the decedent to his heirs.

injunction: an order of a court of equity to refrain from doing (negative injunction) or to do (affirmative or mandatory injunction) a specified act. Its use in labor disputes has been greatly restricted by statute.

in pari delicto: equally guilty; used in reference to a transaction as to which relief will not be granted to either party because both are equally guilty of wrongdoing.

insolvency: an excess of debts and liabilities over assets or inability to pay debts as they mature.

insurable interest: an interest in the nonoccurrence of the risk insured against, generally because such occurrence would cause financial loss, although sometimes merely because of the close relationship between the insured and the beneficiary.

insurance: a plan of security against risks by charging the loss against a fund created by the payments made by policyholders.

intangible personal property: an interest in an enterprise, such as an interest in a partnership or stock of a corporation, and claims against other persons, whether based on contract or tort.

interlineation: a writing between the lines or adding to the provisions of a document, the effect thereof depending upon the nature of the document.

interlocutory: an intermediate step or proceeding that does not make a final disposition of the action and from which ordinarily no appeal may be taken.

international bill of exchange: a bill or draft made in one nation and payable in another.

interpleader: a form of action or proceeding by which a person against whom conflicting claims are made may bring the claimants into court to litigate their claims between themselves, as in the case of a bailor when two persons each claim to be the owner of the bailed property, or an insurer when two persons each claim to be the beneficiary.

inter se: among or between themselves, as the rights of partners inter se or as between themselves.

inter vivos: any transaction which takes place between living persons and creates rights prior to the death of any of them.

intestate: the condition of dying without a will as to any property.

intestate succession: the distribution made as directed by statute of property owned by the decedent of which he did not effectively dispose by will.

ipso facto: by the very act or fact in itself without any further action by any one.

irrebuttable presumption: a presumption which cannot be rebutted by proving that the facts are to the contrary; not a true presumption but merely a rule of law described in terms of a presumption.

irreparable injury to property: an injury that would be of such a nature or inflicted upon such an interest that it would not be reasonably possible to compensate the injured party by the payment of money damages because the property in question could not be purchased in the open market with the money damages which the defendant could be required to pay.

J

joint and several contract: a contract in which two or more persons are jointly and severally obligated or are jointly and severally entitled to recover.

joint contract: a contract in which two or more persons are jointly liable or jointly entitled to performance under the contract.

joint stock company: an association in which the shares of the members are transferable and control is delegated to a group or board.

joint tenancy: the estate held by two or more jointly with the right of survivorship as between them, unless modified by statute.

joint venture: a relationship in which two or more persons combine their labor or property for a single undertaking and share profits and losses equally unless otherwise agreed.

judgment: the final sentence, order, or decision entered into at the conclusion of the action.

judgment note: a promissory note containing a clause authorizing the holder of the note to enter judgment against the maker of the note if it is not paid when due. Also called cognovit note.

judgment n.o.v.: a judgment which may be entered after verdict upon the motion of the losing party on the ground that the verdict is so wrong that a judgment should be entered the opposite of the verdict, or non obstante veredicto (notwithstanding the verdict).

judgment on the pleadings: a judgment which may be entered after all the pleadings are filed when it is clear from the pleadings that a particular party is entitled to win the action without proceeding any further.

judicial sale: a sale made under order of court by an officer appointed to make the sale or by an officer having such authority as incident to his office. The sale may have the effect of divesting liens on the property.

jurisdiction: the power of a court to hear and determine a given class of cases; the power to act over a particular defendant.

jurisdictional dispute: a dispute between rival labor unions which may take the form of each claiming that particular work should be assigned to it.

justifiable abandonment by employee: the right of an employee to abandon his employment because of nonpayment of wages, wrongful assault, the demand for the performance of services not contemplated, or injurious working conditions.

justifiable discharge of employee: the right of an employer to discharge an employee for nonperformance of duties, fraud, disobedience, disloyalty, or incompetence.

L

laches. the rule that the enforcement of equitable rights will be denied when the party has delayed so long that rights of third persons have intervened or the death or disappearance of witnesses would prejudice any party through the loss of evidence.

land: earth, including all things imbedded in or attached thereto, whether naturally or by the act of man.

last clear chance: the rule that if the defendant had the last clear chance to have avoided injuring the plaintiff, he is liable even though the plaintiff had also been contributorily negligent. In some states also called the humanitarian doctrine.

law of the case: matters decided in the course of litigation which are binding on the parties in the subsequent phases of litigation.

leading questions: questions which suggest the desired answer to the witness, or assume the existence of a fact which is in dispute.

lease: an agreement between the owner of property and a tenant by which the former agrees to give possession of the property to the latter in consideration of the payment of rent. (Parties—landlord or lessor, tenant or lessee)

leasehold: the estate or interest which the tenant has in land rented to him.

legacy: a gift of personal property made by will.

legal tender: such form of money as the law recognizes as lawful and declares that a tender thereof in the proper amount is a proper tender which the creditor cannot refuse.

letters of administration: the written authorization given to an administrator as evidence of his appointment and authority.

letters testamentary: the written authorization given to an executor as evidence of his appointment and authority.

levy: a seizure of property by an officer of the court in execution of a judgment of the court, although in many states it is sufficient if the officer is physically in the presence of the property and announces the fact that he is "seizing" it, although he then allows the property to remain where he found it.

lex loci: the law of the place where the material facts occurred as governing the rights and liabilities of the parties.

lex loci contractus: the law of the place where the contract was made as governing the rights and liabilities of the parties to a contract with respect to certain matters.

lex loci fori: the law of the state in which the action is brought as determining the rules of procedure applicable to the action.

lex loci sitae rei: the law of the place where land is located as determining the validity of acts done relating thereto.

libel: written or visual defamation without legal justification.

license: a personal privilege to do some act or series of acts upon the land of another, as the placing of a sign thereon, not amounting to an easement or a right of possession.

lien: a claim or right against property existing by virtue of the entry of a judgment against its owner or by the entry of a judgment and a levy thereunder on the property, or because of the relationship of the claimant to the particular property, such as an unpaid seller.

life estate: an estate for the duration of a life.

limited jurisdiction: a court with power to hear and determine cases within certain restricted categories.

limited liability: loss of contributed capital or investment as maximum liability.

limited partnership: a partnership in which at least one partner has a liability limited to the loss of the capital contribution that he has made to the partnership, and such a partner neither takes part in the management of the partnership nor appears to the public to be a partner.

lineal consanguinity: the relationship that exists when one person is a direct descendant from the other.

liquidated damages: a provision stipulating the amount of damages to be paid in event of default or breach of contract.

liquidation: the process of converting property into money whether of particular items of property or all the assets of a business or an estate.

lis pendens: the doctrine that certain types of pending actions are notice to everyone so that if any right is acquired from a party to such action, the transferee takes that right subject to the outcome of the pending action.

lobbying contract (illegal): a contract by which one party agrees to attempt to influence the action of a legislature or Congress, or any members thereof, by improper means.

lottery: any plan by which a consideration is given for a chance to win a prize.

lucri causa: with the motive of obtaining gain or pecuniary advantage.

M

majority: of age, as contrasted with being a minor; more than half of any group, as a majority of stockholders.

malice in fact: an intention to injure or cause harm.

malice in law: a presumed intention to injure or cause harm when there is no privilege or right to do the act in question, which presumption cannot be contradicted or rebutted.

maliciously inducing breach of contract: the wrong of inducing an employee to break his contract with his employer or inducing the breach of any other kind of contract with knowledge of its existence and without justification.

malum in se: an offense that is criminal because contrary to the fundamental sense of a civilized community, as murder.

malum prohibitum: an offense that is criminal not because inherently wrong but is prohibited for the convenience of society, as overtime parking.

marshalling assets: the distribution of a debtor's assets in such a way as to give the greatest benefit to all of his creditors.

martial law: government exercised by a military commander over property and persons not in the armed forces, as contrasted with military law which governs the military personnel.

mechanics' lien: protection afforded by statute to various types of laborers and persons supplying materials, by giving them a lien on the building and land that has been improved or added to by them.

mens rea: the mental state that must accompany an act to make the act a crime. Sometimes described as the "guilty mind," although appreciation of guilt is not required.

merger by judgment: the discharge of a contract through being merged into a judgment which is entered in a suit on the contract.

merger of corporations: a combining of corporations by which one absorbs the other and continues to exist, preserving its original charter and identity while the other corporation ceases to exist.

mesne: intermediate or intervening, as mesne profits, which are the fruits or income from the land received in between the time that the true owner was wrongfully dispossessed and the time that he recovers the land.

misdemeanor: a criminal offense which is neither treason nor a felony.

misrepresentation: a false statement of fact although made innocently without any intent to deceive.

mobilia sequuntur personam: the maxim that personal property follows the owner and in the eyes of the law is located at the owner's domicile.

moratorium: a temporary suspension by statute of the enforcement of debts or the foreclosure of mortgages.

mortgage: an interest in land given by the owner to his creditor as security for the payment to the creditor of a debt, the nature of the interest depending upon the law of the state where the land is located. (Parties—mortgagor, mortgagee)

multiple insurers: insurers who agree to divide a risk so that each is only liable for a specified portion.

N

National Labor Management Relations Act: the federal statute, also known as the Taft-Hartley Act, designed to protect the organizational rights of labor and to prevent unfair labor practices by management or labor.

natural and probable consequences: those ordinary consequences of an act which a reasonable person would foresee.

negative covenant: an undertaking in a deed to refrain from doing an act.

negligence: the failure to exercise due care under the circumstances in consequence of which harm is proximately caused to one to whom the defendant owed a duty to exercise due care.

negligence per se: an action which is regarded as so improper that it is declared by law to be negligent in itself without regard to whether due care was otherwise exercised.

negotiable instruments: drafts, promissory notes, checks, and certificates of deposit in such form that greater rights may be acquired thereunder than by taking an assignment of a contract right; called negotiable commercial paper by the Code.

negotiation: the transfer of a commercial paper by indorsement and delivery by the person to whom then payable in the case of order paper, and by physical transfer in the case of bearer paper.

nominal damages: a nominal sum awarded the plaintiff in order to establish that his legal rights have been violated although he in fact has not sustained any actual loss or damages.

nominal partner: a person who in fact is not a partner but who holds himself out as a partner or permits others to do so.

Norris-LaGuardia Anti-Injunction Act: a federal statute prohibiting the use of the injunction in labor disputes, except in particular cases.

notice of dishonor: notice given to parties secondarily liable that the primary party to the instrument has refused to accept the instrument or to make payment when it was properly presented for that purpose.

novation: the discharge of a contract between two parties by their agreeing with a third person that such third person shall be substituted for one of the original parties to the contract, who shall thereupon be released.

nudum pactum: a mere promise for which there is no consideration given and which therefore is ordinarily not enforceable.

nuisance: any conduct that harms or prejudices another in the use of his land or which harms or prejudices the public.

nuisance per se: an activity which is in itself a nuisance regardless of the time and place involved.

nuncupative will: an oral will made and declared by the testator in the presence of witnesses to be his will and generally made during the testator's last illness.

O

obiter dictum: that which is said in the opinion of a court in passing or by the way, but which is not necessary to the determination of the case and is therefore not regarded as authoritative as though it were actually involved in the decision.

obliteration: any erasing, writing upon, or crossing out that makes all or part of a will impossible to read, and which has the effect of revoking such part when done by the testator with the intent of effecting a revocation.

occupation: taking and holding possession of property; a method of acquiring title to personal property after it has been abandoned.

open-end mortgage: a mortgage given to secure additional loans to be made in the future as well as the original loan.

operation of law: the attaching of certain consequences to certain facts because of legal principles that operate automatically, as contrasted with consequences which arise because of the voluntary action of a party designed to create those consequences.

opinion evidence: evidence not of what the witness himself observed but the conclusion which he draws from what he observed, or in the case of an expert witness, also from what he asked or what he has heard at the trial.

option contract: a contract to hold an offer to make a contract open for a fixed period of time.

P

paper title: the title of a person evidenced only by deeds or matter appearing of record under the recording statutes.

parol evidence rule: the rule that prohibits the introduction in evidence of oral or written statements made prior to or contemporaneously with the execution of a complete written contract, deed, or instrument, in the absence of clear proof of fraud, accident, or mistake causing the omission of the statement in question.

passive trust: a trust that is created without imposing any duty to be performed by the trustee and is therefore treated as an absolute transfer of the title to the trust beneficiary.

past consideration: something that has been performed in the past and which therefore cannot be consideration for a promise made in the present.

patent: the grant to an inventor of an exclusive right to make and sell his invention for a nonrenewable period of 17 years; a deed to land given by a government to a private person.

pawn: a pledge of tangible personal property rather than of documents representing property rights.

pecuniary legacy: a general legacy of a specified amount of money without indicating the source from which payment is to be made.

per autre vie: limitation of an estate. An estate held by *A* during the lifetime of *B* is an estate of *A* per autre vie.

per curiam opinion: an opinion written "by the court" rather than by a named judge when all the judges of the court are so agreed on the matter that it is not deemed to merit any discussion and may be simply disposed of.

perpetual succession: a phrase describing the continuing life of the corporation unaffected by the death of any stockholder or the transfer by stockholders of their stock.

perpetuities, rule against: a rule of law that prohibits the creation of an interest in property which will not become definite or vested until a date further away than 21 years after the death of persons alive at the time the owner of the property attempts to create the interest.

per se: in, through, or by itself.

person: a term that includes both natural persons, or living people, and artificial persons, as corporations which are created by act of government.

personal defenses: limited defenses that cannot be asserted by the defendant against a holder in due course. This term is not expressly used in Uniform Commercial Code.

per stirpes: according to the root or by way of representation. Distribution among heirs related to the decedent in different degrees, the property being divided into lines of descent from the decedent and the share of each line then divided within the line by way of representation.

petty jury: the trial jury of twelve. Also petit jury.

picketing: the placing of persons outside of places of employment or distribution so that by words or banners they may inform the public of the existence of a labor dispute.

pleadings: the papers filed by the parties in an action in order to set forth the facts and frame the issues to be tried, although under some systems, the pleadings merely give notice of a general indication of the nature of the issues.

pledge: a bailment given as security for the payment of a debt or the performance of an obligation owed to the pledgee. (Parties—pledgor, pledgee)

police power: the power to govern; the power to adopt laws for the protection of the public health, welfare, safety, and morals.

policy: the paper evidencing the contract of insurance.

polling the jury: the process of inquiring of each juror individually in open court as to whether the verdict announced by the foreman of the jury was agreed to by him.

possession: exclusive dominion and control of property.

possessory lien: a right to retain possession of property of another as security for some debt or obligation owed the lienor which right continues only as long as possession is retained.

possibility of reverter: the nature of the interest held by the grantor after conveying land outright but subject to a condition or provision that may cause the grantee's interest to become forfeited and the interest to revert to the grantor or his heirs.

postdate: to insert or place a later date on an instrument than the actual date on which it was executed.

power of appointment: a power given to another, commonly a beneficiary of a trust, to designate or appoint who shall be beneficiary or receive the fund upon his death.

power of attorney: a written authorization to an agent by the principal.

precatory words: words indicating merely a desire or a wish that another use property for a particular purpose but which in law will not be enforced in the absence of an express declaration that the property shall be used for the specified purpose.

pre-emptive offer of shares: the right, subject to many exceptions, that each shareholder has that whenever the capital stock of the corporation is increased he will be allowed to subscribe to such a percentage of the new shares as his old shares bore to the former total capital stock.

preferred creditor: a creditor who by some statute is given the right to be paid first or before other creditors.

preferred stock: stock that has a priority or preference as to payment of dividends or upon liquidation, or both.

preponderance of evidence: the degree or quantum of evidence in favor of the existence of a certain fact when from a review of all the evidence it appears more probable that the fact exists than that it does not. The actual number of witnesses involved is not material nor is the fact that the margin of probability is very slight.

prescription: the acquisition of a right to use the land of another, as an easement, through the making of hostile, visible, and notorious use of the land, continuing for the period specified by the local law.

presumption: a rule of proof which permits the existence of a fact to be assumed from the proof that another fact exists when there is a logical relationship between the two or when the means of disproving the assumed fact are more readily within the control or knowledge of the adverse party against whom the presumption operates.

presumption of death: the rebuttable presumption which arises that a person has died when he has been continuously absent and unheard of for a period of 7 years.

presumption of innocence: the presumption of fact that a person accused of crime is innocent until it is shown that he in fact is guilty of the offense charged.

presumption of payment: a rebuttable presumption that one performing continuing services which would normally be paid periodically, as weekly or monthly, has in fact been paid when a number of years have passed without any objection or demand for payment having been made.

presumptive heir: a person who would be the heir if the ancestor should die at that moment.

pretrial conference: a conference held prior to the trial at which the court and the attorneys seek to simplify the issues in controversy and eliminate matters not in dispute.

price: the consideration for a sale of goods.

prima facie: such evidence as by itself would establish the claim or defense of the party if the evidence were believed.

primary beneficiary: the person designated as the first one to receive the proceeds of a life insurance policy, as distinguished from a contingent beneficiary who will receive the proceeds only if the primary beneficiary dies before the insured.

primary liability: the liability of a person whose act or omission gave rise to the cause of action and who in all fairness should therefore be the one to pay the victim of his wrong, even though others may also be liable for his misconduct.

principal: one who employs an agent to act on his behalf; the person who as between himself and the surety is primarily liable to the third person or creditor.

principal in the first degree: one who actually engages in the commission or perpetration of a crime.

principal in the second degree: one who is actually or constructively present at the commission of the crime and who aids and abets in its commission.

private carrier: a carrier owned by the shipper, such as a company's own fleet of trucks.

privileged communication: information which the witness may refuse to testify to because of the relationship with the person furnishing the information, as husband-wife, attorney-client.

privilege from arrest: the immunity from arrest of parties, witnesses, and attorneys while present within the jurisdiction for the purpose of taking part in other litigation.

privity: a succession or chain of relationship to the same thing or right, as privity of contract, privity of estate, privity of possession.

probate: the procedure for formally establishing or proving that a given writing is the last will and testament of the person purporting to have signed it.

product liability: liability imposed upon the manufacturer or seller of goods for harm caused by a defect in the goods, embracing liability for (1) negligence, (2) fraud, (3) breach of warranty, and (4) strict tort.

profit à prendre: the right to take a part of the soil or produce of another's land, such as timber or water.

promissory estoppel: the doctrine that a promise will be enforced although it is not supported by consideration when the promisor should have reasonably expected that his promise would induce action or forbearance of a definite and substantial character on the part of the promisee, and injustice can only be avoided by enforcement of the promise.

promissory note: an unconditional promise in writing made by one person to another, signed by the maker engaging to pay on demand, or at a definite time, a sum certain in money to order or to bearer. (Parties—maker, payee)

promissory representation: a representation made by the applicant to the insurer as to what is to occur in the future.

promissory warranty: a representation made by the applicant to the insurer as to what is to occur in the future which the applicant warrants will occur.

promoters: the persons who plan the formation of the corporation and sell or promote the idea to others.

proof: the probative effect of the evidence; the conclusion drawn from the evidence as to the existence of particular facts.

property: the rights and interests one has in anything subject to ownership.

pro rata: proportionately, or divided according to a rate or standard.

protest: the formal certificate by a notary public or other authorized person that proper presentment of a commercial paper was made to the primary party and he defaulted, the certificate commonly also including a recital that notice was given to secondary parties.

proximate cause: the act which is the natural and reasonably foreseeable cause of the harm or event which occurs and injures the plaintiff.

proximate damages: damages which in the ordinary course of events are the natural and reasonably foreseeable result of the defendant's violation of the plaintiff's rights.

proxy: a written authorization by a shareholder to another person to vote the stock owned by the shareholder; the person who is the holder of such a written authorization.

public charge: a person who because of a personal disability or lack of means of support is dependent upon public charity or relief for sustenance.

public domain: public or government owned lands.

public easement: a right of way for use by members of the public at large.

public policy: certain objectives relating to health, morals, and integrity of government that the law seeks to advance by declaring invalid any contract which conflicts with those objectives even though there is no statute expressly declaring such contract illegal.

punitive damages: damages in excess of those required to compensate the plaintiff for the wrong done, which are imposed in order to punish the defendant because of the particularly wanton or willful character of his wrongdoing; also exemplary.

purchase-money mortgage: a mortgage given by the purchaser of land to the seller to secure the seller for the payment of the unpaid balance of the purchase price, which the seller purports to lend the purchaser.

purchaser in good faith: a person who purchases without any notice or knowledge of any defect of title, misconduct, or defense.

Q

qualified acceptance: an acceptance of a draft that varies the order of the bill in some way.

qualified indorsement: an indorsement that includes words such as "without recourse" evidencing the intent of the indorser that he

shall not be held liable for the failure of the primary party to pay the instrument.

quantum meruit: an action brought for the value of the services rendered the defendant when there was no express contract as to the payment to be made.

quantum valebant: an action brought for the value of goods sold the defendant when there was no express contract as to the purchase price.

quasi: as if, as though it were, having the characteristics of; a modifier employed to indicate that the subject is to be treated as though it were in fact the noun which follows the word "quasi:" as in quasi contract, quasi corporation, quasi public corporation.

quid pro quo: literally "what for what." An early form of the concept of consideration by which an action for debt could not be brought unless the defendant had obtained something in return for his obligation.

quitclaim deed: a deed by which the grantor purports only to give up whatever right or title he may have in the property without specifying or warranting that he is transferring any particular interest.

quorum: the minimum number of persons, shares represented, or directors who must be present at a meeting in order that business may be lawfully transacted.

R

ratification by minor: the approval of a contract given by a minor after attaining majority.

ratification of agency: the approval of the unauthorized act of an agent or of a person who is not an agent for any purpose after the act has been done, which has the same effect as though the act had been authorized before it was done.

ratio decidendi: the reason or basis for deciding the case in a particular way.

ratio legis: the reason for a principle or rule of law.

real defenses: certain defenses (universal) that are available against any holder of a commercial paper regardless of his character, although this term is not expressly used by the Uniform Commercial Code.

real evidence: tangible objects that are presented in the courtroom for the observation of the trier of fact as proof of the facts in dispute or in support of the theory of a party.

real property: land and all rights in land.

reasonable care: the degree of care that a reasonable man would take under all the circumstances then known.

rebate: a refund made by the seller or the carrier of part of the purchase price or freight bill. Generally illegal as an unfair method of competition.

rebuttable presumption: a presumption which may be overcome or rebutted by proof that the actual facts were different than those presumed.

receiver: an impartial person appointed by a court to take possession of and manage property for the protection of all concerned.

recognizance: an obligation entered into before a court to do some act, such as to appear at a later date for a hearing. Also called a contract of record.

redemption: the buying back of one's property, which has been sold because of a default, upon paying the amount which had been originally due together with interest and costs.

referee: an impartial person selected by the parties or appointed by a court to determine facts or decide matters in dispute.

referee in bankruptcy: a referee appointed by a bankruptcy court to hear and determine various matters relating to bankruptcy proceedings.

reformation: a remedy by which a written instrument is corrected when it fails to express the actual intent of both parties because of fraud, accident, or mistake.

registration of titles: a system generally known as the Torrens system of permanent registration of title to all land within the state.

reimbursement: the right of one paying money on behalf of another which such other person should have himself paid to recover the amount of the payment from him.

release of liens: an agreement or instrument by which the holder of a lien on property such as a mortgage lien, releases the property from the lien although the debt itself is not discharged.

remedy: the action or procedure that is followed in order to enforce a right or to obtain damages for injury to a right.

remote damages: damages which were in fact caused by the defendant's act but the possibility that such damages should occur seemed so improbable and unlikely to a reasonable person that the law does not impose liability for such damages.

renunciation of duty: the repudiation of one's contractual duty in advance of the time for performance, which repudiation may be accepted as an anticipatory breach by the other contracting party.

renunciation of right: the surrender of a right or privilege, as the right to act as administrator or the right to receive a legacy under the will of a decedent.

reorganization of corporation: procedure devised to restore insolvent corporations to financial stability through readjustment of debt and capital structure either under the supervision of a court of equity or of bankruptcy.

repossession: any taking again of possession although generally used in connection with the act of a secured seller in taking back the property upon the default of the credit buyer.

representations: statements, whether oral or written, made to give the insurer the information which it needs in writing the insurance, and which if false and relating to a material fact will entitle the insurer to avoid the contract.

representative capacity: action taken by one not on his own behalf but on behalf of another, as an executor's act on behalf of a decedent's estate, or action taken both on one's behalf and on behalf of others, as a shareholder bringing a representative action.

resale price maintenance agreement: an agreement that the buyer will not resell a trademark or brand name article below a stated minimum price which agreement, by virtue of fair trade laws, is valid not only as between the contracting parties but in some states may also bind other persons in the trade who know of the agreement although they did not sign it.

rescission upon agreement: the setting aside of a contract by the action of the parties as though the contract had never been made.

rescission upon breach: the action of one party to a contract to set the contract aside when the other party is guilty of a breach of the contract.

reservation: the creation by the grantor of a right that did not exist before, which he reserves or keeps for himself upon making a conveyance of property.

residuary estate: the balance of the testator's estate available for distribution after all administrative expenses, exemptions, debts, taxes, and specific, pecuniary, and demonstrative legacies have been paid.

res inter alios acta: the rule that transactions and declarations between strangers having no connection with the pending action are not admissible in evidence.

res ipsa loquitur: the permissible inference that the defendant was negligent in that the thing speaks for itself when the circumstances are such that ordinarily the plaintiff could not have been injured had the defendant not been at fault.

res judicata: the principle that once a final judgment is entered in an action between the parties, it is binding upon them and the matter cannot be litigated again by bringing a second action.

respondeat superior: the doctrine that the principal or employer is vicariously liable for the unauthorized torts committed by his agent or employee while acting within the scope of his agency or the course of his employment, respectively.

restraints on alienation: limitations on the ability of the owner to convey freely as he chooses. Such limitations are generally regarded as invalid.

restrictive covenants: covenants in a deed by which the grantee agrees to refrain from doing specified acts.

restrictive indorsement: an indorsement that prohibits the further transfer, constitutes the indorsee the agent of the indorser, vests the title in the indorsee in trust for or to the use of some other person, is unconditional, or is for collection or deposit.

resulting trust: a trust that is created by implication of law to carry out the presumed intent of the parties.

retaliatory statute: a statute that provides that when a corporation of another state enters the state it shall be subject to the same taxes and restrictions as would be imposed upon a corporation from the retaliating state if it had entered the other state. Also reciprocity statutes.

reversible error: an error or defect in court proceedings of so serious a nature that on appeal the appellate court will set aside the proceedings of the lower court.

reversionary interest: the interest that a lessor has in property which is subject to an outstanding lease.

revival of judgment: the taking of appropriate action to preserve a judgment, in most instances to continue the lien of the judgment that would otherwise expire after a specified number of years.

revival of will: the restoration by the testator of a will which he had previously revoked.

rider: a slip of paper executed by the insurer and intended to be attached to the insurance policy for the purpose of changing it in some respect.

riparian rights: the right of a person through whose land runs a natural watercourse to use the water free from unreasonable pollution or diversion by upper riparian owners and blocking by lower riparian owners.

risk: the peril or contingency against which the insured is protected by the contract of insurance.

Robinson-Patman Act: a federal statute designed to eliminate price discrimination in interstate commerce.

run with the land: the concept that certain covenants in a deed to land are deemed to "run" or pass with the land so that whoever owns the land is bound by or entitled to the benefit of the covenants.

S

sale or return: a sale in which the title to the property passes to the buyer at the time of the transaction but he is given the option of returning the property and restoring the title to the seller.

scienter: knowledge, referring to those wrongs or crimes which require a knowledge of wrong in order to constitute the offense.

scope of employment: the area within which the employee is authorized to act with the consequence that a tort committed while so acting imposes liability upon the employer.

seal: at common law an impression on wax or other tenacious material attached to the instrument. Under modern law, any mark not ordinarily part of the signature is a seal when so intended, including the letters "L. S." and the word "seal," or a pictorial representation of a seal, without regard to whether they had been printed or typed on the instrument before its signing.

sealed verdict: a verdict that is rendered when the jury returns to the courtroom during an adjournment of the court, the verdict then being written down and sealed and later affirmed before the court when the court is in session.

seaman's will: an oral or informal written will made by a seaman to dispose of his personal property.

secondary evidence: copies of original writings or testimony as to the contents of such writings which are admissible when the original cannot be produced and the inability to do so is reasonably explained.

secret partner: a partner who takes an active part in the management of the partnership but is not known to the public as a partner.

secured transaction: a credit sale of goods or a secured loan that provides special protection for the creditor.

settlor: one who settles property in trust or creates a trust estate.

severable contract: a contract the terms of which are such that one part may be separated or severed from the other, so that a default as to one part is not necessarily a default as to the entire contract.

several contracts: separate or independent contracts made by different persons undertaking to perform the same obligation.

severalty: sole ownership of property by one person.

severed realty: real property that has been cut off and made moveable, as by cutting down a tree, and which thereby loses its character as real property and becomes personal property.

shareholder's action: an action brought by one or more shareholders generally and of the corporation to enforce a cause of action of the corporation against third persons.

sheriff's deed: the deed executed and delivered by the sheriff to the purchaser at a sale conducted by the sheriff in his official capacity.

Sherman Antitrust Act: a federal statute prohibiting combinations and contracts in restraint of interstate trade, now generally inapplicable to labor union activity.

shop right: the right of an employer to use in business without charge an invention discovered by an employee during working hours and with the employer's material and equipment.

sight draft: a draft or bill of exchange payable on sight or when presented for payment.

silent partner: a partner who takes no active part in the business, without regard to whether he is known to the public as a partner.

sitdown strike: a strike in which the employees remain in the plant and refuse to allow the employer to operate it.

slander: defamation of character by spoken words or gestures.

slander of title: the malicious making of false statements as to a seller's title.

slander per se: certain words deemed slanderous without requiring proof of damages to the victim, as words charging a crime involving moral turpitude and an infamous punishment, a disease which would exclude from society, or words which tend to injure the victim in his business, profession, or occupation.

slowdown: a slowing down of production by employees without actual stopping work.

social security acts: statutes providing for assistance for the aged, blind, unemployed, and similar classes of persons in need.

soldier's will: an oral or informal written will made by a soldier to dispose of his personal estate.

special agent: an agent authorized to transact a specific transaction or to do a specific act.

special damages: damages that do not necessarily result from the injury to the plaintiff but at the same time are not so remote that the defendant should not be held liable therefor provided that the claim for special damages is properly made in the action.

special indorsement: an indorsement that specifies the person to whom the instrument is indorsed.

special jurisdiction: a court with power to hear and determine cases within certain restricted categories.

specific (identified) goods: goods which are so identified to the contract that no other goods may be delivered in performance of the contract.

specific lien: the right of a creditor to hold particular property or assert a lien on particular property of the debtor because of the creditor's having done work on or having some other association with the property; as distinguished from having a lien generally against the assets of the debtor merely because the debtor is indebted to him.

specific performance: an action brought to compel the adverse party to perform his contract on the theory that merely suing him for damages for its breach will not be an adequate remedy.

spendthrift trust: a trust, which to varying degrees, provides that creditors of the beneficiary shall not be able to reach the principal or income held by the trustee and that the beneficiary shall not be able to assign his interest in the trust.

spoliation: an alteration or change made to a written instrument by a person who has no relationship to or interest in the writing. It has no effect as long as the terms of the instrument can still be ascertained.

stare decisis: the principle that the decision of a court should serve as a guide or precedent and control the decision of a similar case in the future.

status quo ante: the original positions of the parties to a contract prior to the making of the contract or the doing of some other act.

Statute of Frauds: a statute, which in order to prevent fraud through the use of perjured testimony, requires that certain types of transactions be evidenced in writing in order to be binding or enforceable.

Statute of Limitations: a statute that restricts the period of time within which an action may be brought.

stop delivery: the right of an unpaid seller under certain conditions to prevent a carrier or a bailee from delivering goods to the buyer.

stop payment: an order by a depositor to his bank to refuse to make payment of his check when presented for payment.

strict tort liability: a product liability theory which imposes liability on the manufactuer, seller, or distributor of goods for harm caused by goods which are dangerously defective.

sublease: a transfer of the premises by the lessee to a third person, the sublessee or subtenant, for a period of less than the term of the original lease.

subpoena: a court order directing a person to appear as a witness. In some states also it is the original process that is to be served on the defendant in order to give the court jurisdiction over his person.

subrogation: the right of a party secondarily liable to stand in the place of the creditor after he has made payment to the creditor and to enforce the creditor's right against the party primarily liable in order to obtain indemnity from him.

subsidiary corporation: a corporation that is controlled by another corporation through the ownership by the latter of a controlling amount of the voting stock of the former.

subsidiary term: a provision of a contract that is not fundamental or does not go to the root of the contract.

substantial performance: the equitable doctrine that a contractor substantially performing a contract in good faith is entitled to recover the contract price less damages for noncompletion or defective work.

substantive law: the law that defines rights and liabilities.

substitution: discharge of contracts by substituting another in its place.

subtenant: one who rents the leased premises from the original tenant for a period of time less than the balance of the lease to the original tenant.

sui generis: in a class by itself, or its own kind.

sui juris: legally competent, possessing capacity.

summary judgment: a judgment entered by the court when no substantial dispute of fact is present, the court acting on the basis of affidavits or depositions which show that the claim or defense of a party is a sham.

summons: a writ by which an action was commenced under the common law.

superior servant rule: an exception to the fellow-servant rule that is made when the injured servant is under the control of the servant whose conduct caused him injury.

supersedeas: a stay of proceedings pending the taking of an appeal or an order entered for the purpose of effecting such a stay.

surcharge: a money judgment entered against a fiduciary for the amount of loss which his negligence or misconduct has caused the estate under his control.

suretyship: an undertaking to pay the debt or be liable for the default of another.

surrender: the yielding up of the tenant's leasehold estate to the lessor in consequence of which the lease terminates.

survival acts: statutes which provide that causes of action shall not terminate on death but shall survive and may be enforced by or against a decedent's estate.

survivorship: the right by which a surviving joint tenant or tenant by the entireties acquires the interest of the predeceasing tenant automatically upon his death.

symbolic delivery: the delivery of goods by delivery of the means of control, as a key or relevant document of title, as a negotiable bill of lading.

syndicate: an association of individuals formed to conduct a particular business transaction, generally of a financial nature.

T

tacking: adding together successive periods of adverse possession of persons in privity with each other in order to constitute a sufficient period of continuous adverse possession to vest title thereby.

Taft-Hartley Act: popular name for the National Labor Management Relations Act of 1947.

tenancy at sufferance: the holding over by a tenant after his lease has expired of the rented land without the permission of the landlord and prior to the time that the landlord has elected to treat him as a trespasser or a tenant.

tenancy at will: the holding of land for an indefinite period that may be terminated at any time by the landlord or by the landlord and tenant acting together.

tenancy for years: a tenancy for a fixed period of time, even though the time is less than a year.

tenancy from year to year: a tenancy which continues indefinitely from year to year until terminated.

tenancy in common: the relation that exists when two or more persons own undivided interests in property.

tenancy in partnership: the ownership relation that exists between partners under the Uniform Partnership Act.

tender of payment: an unconditional offer to pay the exact amount of money due at the time and place specified by the contract.

tender of performance: an unconditional offer to perform at the time and in the manner specified by the contract.

tentative trust: a trust which arises when money is deposited in a bank account in the name of the depositor "in trust for" a named person.

terminable fee: an estate that terminates upon the happening of a contingency without any entry by the grantor or his heirs, as a conveyance for "so long as" the land is used for a specified purpose.

testamentary: designed to take effect at death, as by disposing of property or appointing an executor.

testate: the condition of leaving a will upon death.

testate succession: the distribution of an estate in accordance with the will of the decedent.

testator—testatrix: a man—woman who makes a will.

testimonium clause: a concluding paragraph in a deed, contract, or other instrument, reciting that the instrument has been executed on a specified date by the parties.

testimony: the answers of witnesses under oath to questions given at the time of the trial in the presence of the trier of fact.

theory of the case: the rule that when a case is tried on the basis of one theory, the appellant in taking an appeal cannot argue a different theory to the appellate court.

third-party beneficiary: a third person whom the parties to a contract intend to benefit by the making of the contract and to confer upon him the right to sue for breach of the contract.

tie-in sale: the requirement imposed by the seller that the buyer of particular goods or equipment also purchase certain other goods from the seller in order to obtain the original property desired.

time draft: a bill of exchange payable at a stated time after sight or at a definite time.

title insurance: a form of insurance by which the insurer insures the buyer of real property against the risk of loss should the title acquired from the seller be defective in any way.

toll the statute: stop the running of the period of the Statute of Limitations by the doing of some act by the debtor.

Torrens System: see registration of titles.

tort: a private injury or wrong arising from a breach of a duty created by law.

trade acceptance: a draft or bill of exchange drawn by the seller of goods on the purchaser at the time of sale and accepted by the purchaser.

trade fixtures: articles of personal property which have been attached to the freehold by a tenant and which are used for or are necessary to the carrying on of the tenant's trade.

trademark: a name, device, or symbol used by a manufacturer or seller to distinguish his goods from those of other persons.

trade name: a name under which a business is carried on and, if fictitious, it must be registered.

trade secrets: secrets of any character peculiar and important to the business of the employer that have been communicated to the employee in the course of confidential employment.

treason: an attempt to overthrow or betray the government to which one owes allegiance.

treasury stock: stock of the corporation which the corporation has reacquired.

trier of fact: in most cases a jury, although it may be the judge alone in certain classes of cases, as in equity, or in any case when jury trial is waived, or an administrative agency or commission is involved.

trust: a transfer of property by one person to another with the understanding or declaration that such property be held for the benefit of another, or the holding of property by the owner in trust for another, upon his declaration of trust, without a transfer to another person. (Parties—settlor, trustee, beneficiary.)

trust corpus: the fund or property that is transferred to the trustee or held by the settlor as the body or subject matter of the trust.

trust deed: a form of deed which transfers the trust property to the trustee for the purposes therein stated, particularly used when the trustee is to hold the title to the mortgagor's land in trust for the benefit of the mortgage bondholders.

trustee de son tort: a person who is not a trustee but who has wrongly intermeddled with property of another and rather than proceed against him for the tort, the law will require him to account for the property as though he were such a trustee.

trustee in bankruptcy: an impartial person elected to administer the bankrupt's estate.

trust receipt: a credit security device under which the wholesale buyer executes a receipt stating that he holds the purchased goods in trust for the person financing the purchase by lending him money. The trust receipt is replaced by the secured transaction under the UCC.

U

uberrima fides: utmost good faith, a duty to exercise the utmost good faith which arises in certain relationships, as that between an insurer and the applicant for insurance.

ultra vires: an act or contract which the corporation does not have authority to do or make.

underwriter: an insurer.

undisclosed principal: a principal on whose behalf an agent acts without disclosing to the third person the fact that he is an agent nor the identity of the principal.

undue influence: the influence that is asserted upon another person by one who dominates that person.

unfair competition: the wrong of employing competitive methods that have been declared unfair by statute or an administrative agency.

unfair labor practice acts: statutes that prohibit certain labor practices and declare them to be unfair labor practices.

unincorporated association: a combination of two or more persons for the furtherance of a common nonprofit purpose.

union contract: a contract between a labor union and an employer or group of employers prescribing the general terms of employment of workers by the latter.

union shop: under present unfair labor practice statutes, a place of employment where nonunion men may be employed for a trial period of not more than 30 days after which the nonunion worker must join the union or be discharged.

universal agent: an agent authorized by the principal to do all facts that can lawfully be delegated to a representative.

usury: the lending of money at greater than the maximum rate allowed by law.

V

vacating of judgment: the setting aside of a judgment.

valid: legal.

verdict: the decision of the trial or petty jury.

vice-principal rule: the rule that persons performing supervisory functions or acting as vice employers are not to be regarded as fellow servants of those under their authority for the purpose of determining the liability of the employer for the injuries of the employee at common law.

void: of no legal effect and not binding on anyone.

voidable: a transaction that may be set aside by one party thereto because of fraud or similar reason but which is binding on the other party until the injured party elects to avoid.

voidable preference: a preference given by the bankrupt to one of his creditors, but which may be set aside by the trustee in bankruptcy.

voir dire examination: the preliminary examination of a juror or a witness to ascertain that he is qualified to act as such.

volenti non fit injuria: the maxim that the defendant's act cannot constitute a tort if the plaintiff had consented thereto.

voluntary nonsuit: a means of the plaintiff's stopping a trial at any time by moving for a voluntary nonsuit.

voting trust: the transfer by two or more persons of their shares of stock of a corporation to a trustee who is to vote the shares and act for such shareholders.

W

waiver: the release or relinquishment of a known right or objection.

warehouse receipt: a receipt issued by the warehouseman for goods stored with him. Regulated by the Uniform Commercial Code, which clothes the receipt with some degree of negotiability.

warehouseman: a person regularly engaged in the business of storing the goods of others for compensation. If he holds himself out to serve the public without discrimination, he is a public warehouseman.

warranties of indorser of commercial paper: the implied covenants made by an indorser of a commercial paper distinct from any undertaking to pay upon the default of the primary party.

warranties of insured: statements or promises made by the applicant for insurance which he guarantees to be as stated and which if false will entitle the insurer to avoid the contract of insurance in many jurisdictions.

warranties of seller of goods: warranties consisting of express warranties that relate to matters forming part of the basis of the bargain; warranties as to title and right to sell; and the implied warranties which the law adds to a sale depending upon the nature of the transaction.

warranty deed: a deed by which the grantor conveys a specific estate or interest to the grantee and covenants that he has transferred the estate or interest by making one or more of the covenants of title.

warranty of authority: an implied warranty of an agent that he has the authority which he purports to possess.

warranty of principal: an implied warranty of an agent that he is acting for an existing principal who has capacity to contract.

watered stock: stock issued by a corporation as fully paid when in fact it is not.

will: an instrument executed with the formality required by law, by which a person makes a disposition of his property to take effect upon his death or appoints an executor.

willful: intentional as distinguished from accidental or involuntary. In penal statutes, with evil intent or legal malice, or without reasonable ground for believing one's act to be lawful.

witness: a person who has observed the facts to which he testifies or an expert witness who may testify on the basis of observation, the testimony presented in the court, or hypothetical questions put to him by the attorneys in the case.

Wool Products Labeling Act: a federal statute prohibiting the misbranding of woolen fabrics.

workmen's compensation: a system providing for payments to workmen because they have been injured from a risk arising out of the course of their employment while they were employed at their employment or have contracted an occupational disease in that manner, payment being made without consideration of the negligence or lack of negligence of any party.

works of charity: in connection with Sunday laws, acts involved in religious worship or aiding persons in distress.

works of necessity: in connection with Sunday laws, acts that must be done at the particular time in order to be effective in saving life, health, or property.

Y

year and a day: the common-law requirement that death result within a year and a day in order to impose criminal liability for homicide.

Z

zoning restrictions: restrictions imposed by government on the use of property for the advancement of the general welfare.

INDEX *

---

* Page references for definitions are indicated in italic type.

1

W

Z